THE ROUTLEDGE COMPANION TO MINDFULNESS AT WORK

Given the ever-growing interest in the benefits of mindfulness to organizations and the individuals who work in them, this *Companion* is a comprehensive primary reference work for mindfulness (including creativity and flow) in the workplace, including business, healthcare, and educational settings.

Research shows that mindfulness boosts creativity through greater insight, receptivity, and balance, and increases energy and a sense of well-being. This *Companion* traces the genesis and growth of this burgeoning field, tracks its application to the workplace, and suggests trends and future directions.

With contributions from leading scholars and practitioners in business, leadership, psychology, healthcare, education, and other related fields, *The Routledge Companion to Mindfulness at Work* is an extensive reference work which will be a vital resource to the fields of management and organizational studies, human resource management, psychology, spirituality, cultural anthropology, and sociology. Each chapter will present a listing of key topics, a case or situation that illustrates the application of the themes, workplace lessons, and reflection questions.

Satinder K. Dhiman serves as the Associate Dean, Chair, and Director of the MBA Program and Professor of Management at Woodbury University, Burbank, California. A recognized leading thinker in the field of spirituality in the workplace and sustainability, he has also completed advanced executive leadership programs at Harvard, Stanford, and Wharton.

THE ROUTLEDGE COMPANION TO MINDFULNESS AT WORK

Edited by Satinder K. Dhiman

LONDON AND NEW YORK

First published 2021
by Routledge
2 Park Square, Milton Park, Abingdon, Oxon OX14 4RN

and by Routledge
52 Vanderbilt Avenue, New York, NY 10017

Routledge is an imprint of the Taylor & Francis Group, an informa business

British Library Cataloguing-in-Publication Data
A catalogue record for this book is available from the British Library

Library of Congress Cataloging-in-Publication Data
Names: Dhiman, Satinder, editor.
Title: The Routledge companion to mindfulness at work / edited by Satinder K. Dhiman.
Description: First Edition. | New York : Routledge, 2020. | Includes bibliographical references and index.
Identifiers: LCCN 2019054400 (print) | LCCN 2019054401 (ebook) | ISBN 9780367200046 (hardback) | ISBN 9780429244667 (ebook)
Subjects: LCSH: Job stress–Prevention. | Meditation–Therapeutic use. | Leadership–Psychological aspects. | Mindfulness (Psychology)
Classification: LCC HF5548.85 .R68 2020 (print) |LCC HF5548.85 (ebook) | DDC 158.7–dc23
LC record available at https://lccn.loc.gov/2019054400
LC ebook record available at https://lccn.loc.gov/2019054401

ISBN: 978-0-367-20004-6 (hbk)
ISBN: 978-0-429-24466-7 (ebk)

Typeset in Bembo
by Swales & Willis, Exeter, Devon, UK

This volume is humbly dedicated to
the first practitioner of Mindfulness,
Gautama Buddha,
who showed us the path to living attentively and compassionately;
and to all Seekers
who aspire to lead a life of Awareness and Presence
Rooted in the Eternal Now!

CONTENTS

NOTES ON CONTRIBUTORS

Francisco Eduardo Moreira Azeredo received an in-depth Catholic education from childhood in strict Jesuit schools. After giving up the idea of following a priestly life, he decided to engage in the Zen Buddhist and Macrobiotic philosophies. One of the founders of the Maha Muni Society, for almost ten years he was a devoted follower of Zen Master Tokuda Igarashi, from whom he received a Diamond Sutra crystal ball. After 42 years working in the engineering industry, influenced by his Master, he pursued a second career in Traditional Medical Shiatsu and Traditional Chinese Medicine. More recently, in the US, as a Devotional Teaching Committee Member of the Bahá'í Faith, he has been dedicated to an independent investigation on the teachings of the prophet Bahá'u'lláh.

Jason Beck is a doctoral student in Positive Organizational Psychology at Claremont Graduate University and hold a master's degree in the same field. His research focuses on mindfulness and leadership development. Overall, he is interested in helping leaders and organizations modernize the workplace for greater use of attention for increasing adaptation, engagement, and well-being. As an organizational development consultant and keynote speaker, Jason pulls from diverse experiences as an organizational psychologist, leadership development coach, improv comedy actor, and amateur athlete. He is also the Evaluation and Applied Research Manager for Potential Project, a global mindfulness training and development firm. Outside of work, Jason enjoys performing improv comedy, playing guitar, and playing sports.

Tracy F. H. Chang, PhD, is an Associate Professor of Organizational Behavior at the School of Management and Labor Relations at Rutgers University. She received her PhD in Sociology from the University of Iowa and MBA from New York University. She is also a qualified Mindfulness-Based Stress Reduction (MBSR) teacher trained at the Center for Mindfulness at the University of Massachusetts Medical School. She explores the intersection of the ancient yogic sciences and the modern science of positive organizational behavior. Her current research examines the impact of mindfulness-based pedagogical tools in higher education and the effect of classical yoga and meditation on flourishing for young adults and on psychological and work engagement in organizations.

Michael Chaskalson is the author of *Mindfulness in Eight Weeks* (Harper Thorson 2014) and *The Mindful Workplace* (Wiley 2011), and co-author of *Mindfulness for Coaches* (Routledge 2018) and *Mind Time* (Harper Thorson 2018). Professor of Practice at Hult Ashridge Executive Education in Hult International Business School and an associate at the Møller Institute at Churchill College in the University of Cambridge, Michael is founder and director at the UK consultancy Mindfulness Works Ltd. Listed on the Thinkers 50 Radar in 2017, Michael consults to organizations around the world focusing on teaching some of the ways in which our minds give rise to our experience and our behavior—and the practical ways in which we can all take greater responsibility for those processes in order to bring about the kinds of outcomes we value in our work and personal lives.

Andrea Cherman, PhD, was raised amidst a traditional Jewish background, where values given to study, work, and family predominated. After graduating in social communication, 24 years followed in related fields in the industry, partially in parallel to 14 years of an academic career, which broadened in her a holistic and profound organizational vision. Since her master's degree in 2002, she has deepened her Zen Buddhist philosophy, gaining attentiveness to the bridge that connects the organizational and spirituality universes and increasing her interests in studies that interrelate both sides of this bridge. Her research comprises *Integrative Knowledge in Organizations*, analyzing the dynamics of innovative knowledge creation in a scenario that science and spirituality can experience synergistic effects; *Spirituality in Knowledge Development*, examining the significant benefits of incorporating into organizational structures a more spiritual mindset; and *Ethics in Knowledge-Based Organizations*. Andrea works at the Polytechnic School, in the Ira A. Fulton Schools of Engineering at Arizona State University, teaching and researching.

Kerri Cissna, PhD, is an Adjunct Professor at Pepperdine where she teaches Leadership and Communication, Qualitative Research Methods, and Philanthropy for Social Change. She formerly served as the Assistant Vice-Chancellor at the Graduate School of Education and Psychology, Director of Housing and Residence Life, and the Leadership Development Coordinator. While at Pepperdine she founded Project LEAD, the graduate assistantship program in Student Affairs, and was a founding member of the sophomore experience task force, the Center for Women in Leadership, the Digital Women's Project at Pepperdine (research on women in leadership and work–family integration), and the Lifelong Learning Lecture Series for Women. In her free time, she is committed to nonprofits that empower children as a board member of Kiwanis of Santa Monica and Cause for Celebration.

Gabrielle Danna is currently a PhD student in the Industrial/Organizational Psychology program at the University at Albany, SUNY. Broadly, she is interested in the relationships between motivation, cognition, attention, and the self-regulation of learning behaviors. In the future, she looks forward to exploring the different ways in which organizations can design and deliver impactful training that will maximize learning and performance outcomes.

Debra J. Dean, PhD, is affiliated with Regent University as an adjunct professor. She is also President and CEO of Dean Business Consulting. Recent notable conference participation includes the Faith at Work Summit, Academy of Management MSR Consortium Planning, Academic Oasis, OPEX Week: Business Transformation World Summit, and the Regent University Roundtable. Latest research efforts include the following: (a) Integration of Christian Values in the Workplace: An examination of employee engagement, job satisfaction, and organizational commitment, (b) Religion and Spirituality in the Workplace: A quantitative evaluation of job satisfaction and organizational commitment, and (c) A Correlation Study of Employee Engagement and Servant Leadership. She received the Outstanding Reviewer award for the Management, Spirituality, and Religion (MSR) community, she was nominated as one of three top operational excellence leaders with OPEX, and was nominated as a top female leader within her previous global workplace.

Satinder K. Dhiman, PhD, EdD, serves as Associate Dean, Chair, and Director of the MBA Program and Professor of Management at Woodbury University's School of Business. He teaches courses pertaining to ethical leadership, sustainability, organizational behavior and strategy, and spirituality in the workplace in the MBA program. Professor Dhiman has completed advanced executive leadership programs at Harvard, Stanford, and Wharton. He has presented his work at various national and international conferences and venues, often serving as invited keynote speaker, and has published in multiple national and international academic journals. Author, translator, co-author, editor, and co-editor of more than 25 books, his most recent books include *Bhagavad Gītā and Leadership* (Palgrave, 2019); *Holistic Leadership* (Palgrave, 2017); *Gandhi and Leadership* (Palgrave, 2015); and *Seven Habits of Highly Fulfilled People* (Personhood, 2012/2014, USA/India). He is the Editor-in-Chief of three major reference works: *Springer Handbook of Engaged Sustainability* (Springer, 2018); *Palgrave Handbook of Workplace Spirituality and Fulfillment* (Palgrave, 2018); and *Palgrave Handbook of Workplace Well-being* (Palgrave, forthcoming, 2020).

Scott B. Dust, PhD, explores how awareness of self, others, and context affects workplace effectiveness and well-being in several areas: leadership, teams, work design, career management, and ethics. He earned his PhD in Management/Organizational Behavior at the LeBow College of Business, Drexel University, and his MBA and BS from the Kelley School of Business, Indiana University. His work has appeared in several academic journals including the *Journal of Applied Psychology*, *Journal of Organizational Behavior*, *Leadership Quarterly*, *Human Relations*, *Journal of Business and Psychology*, and *International Journal of Management Reviews*.

R. Ray Gehani, PhD, earned a Doctorate in Polymer Science and Engineering from Tokyo Institute of Technology on a Japanese Government Fellowship, and a PhD in Business from the City University of New York (and Columbia University). He was elected Chairperson of the College of Innovation and Entrepreneurship in TIMS/ORSA (1995–97), and Chairperson of Technology Management Section of INFORMS (1998). In addition to teaching graduate and undergraduate courses, he has more than a decade of consulting, R&D, and global leadership experience in the worldwide tire and high-performance polymer industries of Japan, India, and the USA. He has published his research in leading academic journals on integral and inclusive leadership and the role of spirituality and mindfulness in the management of innovation. In 1998, he authored *Management of Technology and Operations* (John Wiley & Sons, New York). Dr. Gehani enjoys writing poetry and giving public tours on art history.

Sunita Gehani, PhD, is a Headmistress of the award-winning Bal Bharati School in New Delhi, India, the first school established under the Child Education Society more than 75 years ago. For many years, she has been teaching their upper-level Sanskrit and Hindi language and literature classes. She earned her doctorate in Sanskrit from the University of Delhi, with a focus on Pali Buddhist scriptures. In August 2017, the Delhi Sanskrit Academy of Delhi Government felicitated her with the Sanskrit Promoter Honor Award. Bal Bharati School was recognized as one of the Top 20 Schools in National Capital Region, India, and a Microsoft Showcase School for demonstrating 'a commitment to embracing technology to transform education and improve learning outcomes for students.' Under her guidance Bal Bharati School also received the Education World Grand Jury Award in 2019.

Patricia Grant, PhD, is a member of the Management Team of Kenvale College of Hospitality and Events. She is responsible for a number of departments that relate directly to the student lifecycle, including Academic, Compliance and Quality, and Industry Liaison, as well as developing a research culture amongst staff. Her research interests include business ethics, sustainability, and spirituality in the workplace.

Sabine Grunwald, PhD, is the Director of the University of Florida (UF) Mindfulness Program and Professor. She earned a PhD in environmental sciences from the University in Giessen, Germany, a one-year Graduate Certificate in Integral Studies from Fielding Graduate University, Santa Barbara, CA, and an Authentic Leadership Certificate with Mindfulness training (Naropa University, Boulder, CO). She has undertaken graduate studies in Integral and Transpersonal Psychology at the California Institute of Integral Studies, San Francisco, CA. Dr. Grunwald is affiliate faculty member in the UF Center for Spirituality and Health. Since the 1980s, she has practiced qigong, tai chi, and various meditation styles. She trained extensively in mindfulness meditation, mind–body, and self-inquiry through retreats, workshops, and courses. She is a practicing *Tantrika* in Vajrayana Buddhism. Dr. Grunwald is interested in transpersonal psychology, mindfulness meditation, the hybridization of Buddhism in the West, American dharma, mind–body practices, and somatic meditation.

Matthew D. Hanson is currently a PhD student in the Industrial/Organizational Psychology program at the University at Albany, SUNY. Broadly, his research interests include training and development, the interaction between motivation, cognition, and affect, and diversity, inclusion, and equity. More specifically, he is researching the influence that a mindfulness practice and sham mindfulness practice have in a generic formal training setting, the influence that a mindfulness practice has in formal diversity training, the prevalence and effectiveness of informal learning, and the conceptualization of motivation as a force that acts as an accelerant on cognition. In the future, he looks forward to examining mindful workplace design, disfluency in a training environment, and regulating cognition, motivation, and affect during long-term, high-reliability environments.

Julia Hufnagel (Diplom-Wirtschaftschemikerin) studied Chemistry and Business Administration at Technische Universität Kaiserslautern (TUK). Since mid-2015, Julia has been a research and teaching assistant at the Chair of Business Administration, in particular Sustainability Management (TUK). In her dissertation she deals with the topics of mindfulness, spirituality, and their connection to sustainability management. Her teaching is meant to address the individual: what can we as individuals do (on different levels) to contribute to sustainable development? To address this, she uses innovative formats such as service learning, Aim2flourish, art, reflection, and digital tools. At the beginning of 2016 Julia co-founded—and coordinated until October 2017—the TUK Sustainability Office, a central institution for sustainability topics with student participation. She is a certified laughter yoga and mindfulness meditation teacher.

Ayça Kubra Hizarci-Payne is a PhD student and a research assistant at the Faculty of Business, Dokuz Eylul University, in Turkey. Her areas of interest are organizational behavior, international business, and strategic management. Her recent studies are published in the *European Journal of Innovation Management* and *International Journal of Innovation and Technology Management.*

Thushini S. Jayawardena-Willis, PhD, completed her doctoral degree at AUT University, Auckland, New Zealand in December 2017. She received the 2nd most promising dissertation proposal award by the AOM MSR group in August 2017. She has been an attorney-at-law of the Sri Lanka Supreme Court since August 2006. In the last two decades, she has worked in the banking, insurance, and telecommunication industries in Sri Lanka, a law firm in London, and in a market research company in Auckland, New Zealand. In February 2019, she co-founded the Buddhist Meditation Research Foundation (BMRF) in Auckland, New Zealand.

Stefan Karajovic is an avid researcher and educator from Toronto, Canada. He is currently a PhD candidate at York University's School of Human Resource Management, while also holding a Master of Industrial Relations and Human Resources degree from the University of Toronto and a Bachelor of Commerce (Honours) degree from Ryerson University. Stefan's research focuses on workplace diversity, positive organizational behavior, work–life balance, and industrial relations.

Alev Katrinli, PhD, is a full-time professor at the Faculty of Business, Dokuz Eylul University in Turkey. She earned her master's degree from Boğazici University and her PhD is from Dokuz Eylul University. She served as a visiting scholar at Rochester Institute of Technology (RIT) and West Georgia College. She has worked in different national and international universities. Currently, she is working as a full-time professor in Dokuz Eylul University, Faculty of Business. Her research areas are organizational behavior and strategic management.

Nidhi Kaushal, PhD, is a scholar of Management Studies at the Indian Institute of Technology Roorkee. She holds a master's degree in business administration and a bachelor's degree in computer science from Kurukshetra University, India. She has been interested in the research works related to entrepreneurship, leadership, literature, management, and indigenous studies. During her PhD, she has identified the indigenous studies of literature and folklore related to leadership and management and presented her work in various international conferences and research publications across the globe. She has also worked at many managerial and academic positions. Being a research fellow, she is also an event organizer and has organized conferences and other related events in the Institute. She is exploring leadership with the study of creative writings, and this is her contribution to her academic research. This area will not only enrich management studies but also become immensely useful for entrepreneurs.

Ravi S. Kudesia, PhD, is an Assistant Professor at the Fox School of Business at Temple University. He earned his PhD in Business Administration from Washington University in

St. Louis. In his research, he examines how cognition transfers across individuals as they assemble into collectives—and how these collectives solve problems and make sense of their environments—in systems including hospitals, protest crowds, darknet markets, sports teams, and explosive demolition firms. His research has appeared in *Academy of Management Review*, *Journal of Business Ethics*, *Mindfulness*, *Organizational Behavior and Human Decision Processes*, *Safety Science*, and other journals.

Liva LaMontagne, PhD, is currently a PhD student and graduate assistant in Youth Development and Family Sciences at the University of Florida. She holds a PhD in Social/Organizational Psychology from the University of Latvia and has facilitated mindfulness exercises as part of the SMART Couples Florida relationship skill workshops. Her research interests are related to the role of mindfulness in promoting positive outcomes for university employees, their families, and students. Her goal is to study the effectiveness of brief mindfulness-based interventions to reduce work–life conflict and physiological stress and increase well-being in working parents and students. She is also interested in the system-wide processes through which colleges and universities adopt or create mindfulness interventions to enhance health outcomes. Outside of work, Liva enjoys traveling and visiting family with her husband Derek and son David (8), watching superhero movies, and mindfully going to the beach.

Jenson Lau is a PhD student at the Fox School of Business at Temple University. He earned his BS in Electrical Engineering from the Georgia Institute of Technology. His research interests are mindfulness, humor, and artificial intelligence.

Huy Le is a second-year PhD student in the Industrial/Organizational program at the University at Albany. He finished his undergraduate degree at the University of Houston where he received a Bachelor of Science in Psychology. Huy's research aims to understand mind-wandering in the context of social interactions as well as mind-wandering's role on creativity and breaks at work.

Bena (Beth) Long, PhD, provides executive and performance coaching for being your best self and to establish business culture that places well-being on a par with business performance. She has taught at Wharton Executive Education, DeSales University, and Engineering Management at Temple University. Her unique advantage for her clients is her intuitive abilities and knowledge of building resilience, culture agility, and thriving in change. She was a NCAA Division One Competitor. She has taught Hatha Yoga and Meditation for more than 20 years and is a practitioner of the martial art Tai Chi. In addition, Dr. Long consults on organizational development and mindful leadership. Some of her past clients include: Bank of America, First Union Wachovia, Merck, Barclays Capital, Wyndham International, Citibank, Adelphi Research, GUNA, Inc., Merrill Lynch, and the United States Treasury.

Olga Louchakova-Schwartz, MD, PhD (neuroscience) is Clinical Professor at UC Davis, Professor of Philosophy of Religion, Spirituality, and Human Development at Hult International Business School, Visiting Scholar at the Graduate Theological Union, where she teaches at the Jesuit School of Theology, and Professor Emerita at the former Institute of Transpersonal Psychology in Palo Alto, California. Her interdisciplinary focus began when, while a senior scientist at the Pavlov Institute of Physiology, she became a student at the school of contemporary Hesychasm in Russia in the 1980s. She published more than 200 papers, guest-edited several topical issues in Open Theology (Dr. Gruyter), and is the editor and contributing author for *The Problem of Religious Experience*, volumes 1 and 2, Contributions to Phenomenology (Springer 2019). Her book *Husserl and Suhrawardi: Contemporary Reading of the Philosophy of Illumination* is forthcoming with Springer in 2021. She is the Founding President of the Society for the Phenomenology of Religious Experience.

Lasse Lychnell, PhD, is an affiliated researcher at the Stockholm School of Economics (SSE) and works in the borderland between leadership, organizational development, and inner development. His research is focused on how the interplay between spiritual development and work may contribute to more effective organizations and increased well-being. In 2017, he received the *Journal of Management, Spirituality, and Religion*'s best paper award for his paper 'When work becomes meditation.' At SSE, Lasse teaches in courses on global challenges, organizational change, and professional development. Lasse is also a member of the steering committee of the Center for Social Sustainability at the Karolinska Institute.

Petros G. Malakyan, PhD, is the Department Head of Organizational Leadership at Robert Morris University in Pittsburgh, Pennsylvania, USA. Petros holds terminal degrees from the Graduate School of Intercultural Studies at Fuller Theological Seminary in Pasadena, California in 1998. He served as Professor and Chair of Undergraduate Leadership Studies, Associate Professor and Program Director of Master of Arts in Organizational Leadership Program, Doctoral Advisor and Leadership Coach, Mentor and Educator in four universities in the United States and abroad. Petros has created and taught two dozen leadership courses, from undergraduate to doctoral levels, in 11 countries. Petros's research focuses on leadership, followership, and leader–follower relationships in organizations across cultures. He has published in the *Journal of Leadership Studies*, *Journal of Organizational Psychology*, *International Journal of Doctoral Studies*, *Journal of Leadership, Accountability, and Ethics*, *International Journal of Social Science Research*, *IntechOpen*, and others. His recent research interests are in the areas of doctoral education, leadership–followership in the digital age, and cybersecurity leadership.

Joan Marques, PhD, EdD, serves as Dean and Professor of Management at Woodbury University's School of Business. She holds a PhD from Tilburg University and an EdD from Pepperdine University's Graduate School of Education and Psychology. She teaches, presents, and writes on workplace spirituality, ethical leadership, Buddhist psychology in management, and leadership awareness. In 2015, Joan received the national decoration of *Commander in the Honorary Order of the Yellow Star*, by the President of the Republic of Suriname, her native country, while she also became the recipient of the *Dr. Nelle Becker-Slaton Pathfinder Award*, granted by the Association of Pan-African Doctoral Scholars to an academic female leader who has demonstrated groundbreaking leadership in her field. In 2016, Joan gave a TEDx Talk titled, 'An Ancient Path Towards a Better Future,' and in 2019, she received the Kankantrie Lifetime Achievement Award in Education from the Suriname-American Network Inc. She has been widely published in scholarly as well as practitioner-based journals, and has authored/co-authored and edited more than 20 books on management and leadership topics. Her most recent book is *Lead with Heart in Mind* (Springer, 2019).

Huda Masood is a doctoral candidate and a researcher at the School of Human Resource Management at York University, Toronto, ON. Huda researches and writes about the motivation and consequences of proactive behaviors at work, organizational justice, and the dark side of leadership. She is also passionate about research on the intersection of social media and human resource management functions. Huda has showcased her work at several North American platforms.

Claude-Hélène Mayer, PhD, is a Professor in Industrial and Organizational Psychology at the Department of Industrial Psychology and People Management at the University of Johannesburg, an Adjunct Professor at the European University Viadrina in Frankfurt (Oder), Germany, and a Senior Research Associate at Rhodes University, Grahamstown, South Africa. She holds a PhD in Psychology (University of Pretoria, South Africa), a PhD in Management (Rhodes University, South Africa), a doctorate in Political Sciences (Georg-August University, Germany), and a habilitation in Psychology with focus on Work, Organizational, and Cultural Psychology (European University Viadrina, Germany). She has published several monographs, text collections, accredited journal articles, and special issues on transcultural mental health, sense of coherence, shame, transcultural conflict management and mediation, women in leadership, creativity, and psychobiography.

Peter McGhee, PhD, is a senior lecturer in the Faculty of Business, Economics and Law at Auckland University of Technology, New Zealand. Prior to that he was an analyst and operations manager in the financial services industry. His research interests include the relationship between business and society, virtue ethics, spirituality in the workplace, and sustainability. He teaches undergraduates in sustainability leadership and business ethics, as well as postgraduates in responsible leadership. He is currently supervising PhD and master's students in the areas of spirituality, diversity, and ethical leadership.

Haziq Mehmood, PhD, specializes in the areas of industrial–organizational psychology, social psychology, human–computer interaction, and psychometrics. He received his PhD in Applied Psychology from Lingnan University. His PhD dissertation focused on the role of social network sites and their impact on employees' job performance and psychological well-being. As a tutor, he taught Psychology Applied to Occupational Safety and Health, Introduction to Psychology, Industrial and Organizational Psychology, and Stress Management, Health, and Life Balance courses. He currently serves as an Assistant Professor in the Department of Professional Psychology at Bahria University, Islamabad, Pakistan. He worked in the development sector and focused on the counseling and intervention plans for suicidal cases. He served as a testing and assessment associate and developed questionnaires for employees' screening. He is a member of the International Association of Applied Psychology (IAAP).

Katarina Katja Mihelič, PhD, is an Associate Professor of Management and Organization at the Faculty of Economics, the University of Ljubljana. Her research interests include (un) ethical behaviors, work–family dynamics, mindfulness, proactive employee behaviors, and psychological contracts of young talents. Her work has been published in scholarly outlets such as the *Journal of Business Ethics, Personnel Review, Business Ethics: A European Review*, and *Creativity Research Journal.*

Jutta Tobias Mortlock, PhD, is a social psychologist with over 20 years of work experience in organizational development and capacity-building in six countries on three continents. Jutta's research interest is focused on behavior change initiatives in workplaces geared at generating sustainable well-being and performance, using 'third wave' cognitive behavioral approaches such as acceptance and commitment therapy (ACT) and other evidence-based mindfulness frameworks. She teaches and advises on workplace mindfulness and leadership and is a popular keynote speaker on the link between well-being and performance. Jutta has published her work in a number of leading academic journals. She has also featured in the popular press, including in *The Times*, the *Sunday Times*, and *Newsweek*. In her life before academia, Jutta worked for nearly a decade as a consultant for several IT consultancies including Arthur Andersen, partnering with firms such as Goldman Sachs, Nomura, and McKinsey on IT and strategy projects.

Oi-ling Siu, PhD, is Chair Professor and Dean, Faculty of Social Sciences, Lingnan University. Her research interests are in occupational health psychology, specifically occupational stress, the psychology of safety, and work–life balance. Professor Siu also conducts research in environmental psychology and psychology of ageing. In the past few years, Professor Siu has been awarded many RGC's GRF (previously Earmarked Research Grants), National Natural Science Foundation (China), Australian Research Council, Quality Education Fund, and research grants by the Occupational Safety and Health Council.

Sharon Olivier is senior leadership faculty at Hult Ashridge International Business School where she teaches, researches, and consults in leadership and HR. Sharon specializes in 21st-century leadership intelligences, the future of HR, team and individual engagement, polarity management, and integrative thinking. She has established a record of accomplishment as an inspirational speaker, researcher, author, and facilitator of executive development programs.

Rudolf M. Oosthuizen received a BA degree (cum laude) from the University of Pretoria in 1992 and obtained a BA (Honours) in Psychology at the same university in 1993. In 1999, he received an MA degree in Industrial and Personnel Psychology from the Potchefstroom University for Christian Higher Education. In 1999, he registered as Industrial Psychologist with the Health Professions Council of South Africa. In 2005, he completed a DLitt et Phil in Industrial and Organizational Psychology at the University of South Africa (Unisa). Currently Rudolf is an associate professor in the Department of Industrial and Organizational Psychology at the University of South Africa. Rudolf's fields of interests are: career psychology, positive psychology, employment relations, and the 4th Industrial Revolution.

Rajnandini Pillai, PhD, is Professor of Management at the California State University San Marcos (CSUSM). She received her doctorate in 1994 from the State University of New York at Buffalo in Organizational Behavior. Her areas of teaching and research interests are leadership and cross-cultural management. She has published several articles on charismatic/transformational leadership and cross-cultural management in the leading journals in the field (e.g., *Leadership Quarterly*, *Journal of Management*, *Journal of International Business Studies*). She has also edited books on leadership and is a co-author (with Marty Gannon) of *Understanding Global Cultures*. She has been involved in a campus-wide initiative on mindfulness which attempts to bring mindfulness practices into the classroom. Throughout her career, she has received several awards for excellence in teaching and research, including CSUSM's highest faculty honor. She is also co-founder and Executive Director of the Center for Leadership Innovation and Mentorship Building (CLIMB) at CSUSM.

Edwina Pio, PhD, Fulbright Alumna, is New Zealand's first Professor of Diversity, and University Director of Diversity at the Auckland University of Technology, Aotearoa/New Zealand. Her research encompasses the intersections of work, ethnicity, indigenous studies, religion, and pedagogy. A thought leader, recipient of a Duke of Edinburgh Fellowship and widely published, her book *Sari: Indian women at work in New Zealand* was released by Sir John Key, former Prime Minister of New Zealand. Her work is published in journals such as the *British Journal of Management, Higher Education, Human Relations, Journal of Business Ethics, Gender Work & Organization, Asia Pacific Journal of Management, Academy of Management Learning & Education,* and *Journal of Management Inquiry*.

Jason G. Randall, PhD, is an Assistant Professor of Industrial/Organizational Psychology in the Psychology Department at the University at Albany, SUNY. He earned his PhD in I/O Psychology at Rice University in 2015. Jason's research interests and expertise include training, motivation, attention, and personnel selection. In particular, Dr. Randall's primary research addresses ways to help people stay focused during formal and informal learning and skilled performance episodes. He has also investigated why scores change due to retesting and what individual and methodological factors might lead to this phenomenon. His research has been published in outlets such as *Psychological Bulletin, Human Resource Management Review, Journal of Business and Psychology*, and *International Journal of Selection and Assessment*, among others, and has been funded by the US Army Research Institute.

Anne Randerson, PhD, currently teaches Global Studies courses at California State University San Marcos (CSUSM). She completed her master's and PhD degrees in Japan and her BA degree at UC Davis. She is an intercultural communication and global leadership trainer, consultant, and coach for Cross Cultural Horizons. A Mindfulness-Based Stress Reduction (MBSR) Teacher trained at the UCSD Center for Mindfulness, she teaches MBSR courses at her university and in the community. Her research interests focus on human sensitivity, contemplative pedagogy, social justice, cultural intelligence, intercultural communication, global diversity, LGBTQ inclusion, East–West differences in lifestyle, spirituality and religion, and palliative care. A member of the core leadership team of Mindful CSUSM, a campus-wide initiative to bring more contemplative pedagogy to her campus, she has been involved in Faculty Learning Communities for Compassion, Cultural Intelligence, Contemplative Pedagogy and Social Justice. She is also a former facilitator for the National Conflict Resolution Center.

Melita Balas Rant, PhD, is an Assistant Professor of Management and Organization at the Faculty of Economics, the University of Ljubljana. Her research interests include the study of orders of consciousness and stages of adult development, personality changes alongside the adult development process, leadership behaviors at different stages, and support mechanisms in stage transitions.

Christopher S. Reina, PhD, is an Assistant Professor in the Department of Management and Entrepreneurship at Virginia Commonwealth University, and the Founder and President of Leading Without Ego LLC. He consults and leads training on mindfulness and mindful leadership, and managing the emotional space within organizations. His research focuses on the intersection of leadership, mindfulness, and emotions in the workplace and how these constructs bring about employee and organizational well-being. Christopher received his

PhD in Business Administration from the W. P. Carey School of Business at Arizona State University, and he has extensive industry experience in leadership training and development as well as sales and marketing in the healthcare and food industries.

Megan Reitz, PhD, is Professor of Leadership and Dialogue at Hult Ashridge International Business School, where she speaks, researches, consults, and supervises on the intersection of leadership, change, dialogue, and mindfulness. She is on the Thinkers50 radar of global business thinkers and is ranked in *HR Magazine*'s Most Influential Thinkers listing. She has presented her research to audiences throughout the world and is the author of *Dialogue in Organizations* (Palgrave Macmillan, 2015) and co-author of *Mind Time* (Harper Thorsons, 2018) and *Speak Up* (FT Publishing). Her passion and curiosity centers around the quality of how we meet, see, hear, speak, learn with, and encounter one another in organizational systems. Her research and publications, featured in *Harvard Business Review* and *Forbes* magazine, explore the neuroscience of leadership, the links between mindfulness and leadership capacities for the 21st century, and the capacity to 'speak truth to power' and enable others to do the same.

Igor Ristić, PhD, earned his PhD degree from the University of Kansas in Lawrence, Kansas. His research focuses on intercultural and health communication. Igor has served as an editorial assistant for an edited collection, has been published in three books, including *Contemporary Case Studies in Health Communication: Theoretical and Applied Approaches* (Brann, M., 2011), and has been published in academic journals (*Journal of Communication, Culture, & Critique*).

H. Eric Schockman, PhD, is a Professor of Politics and International Relations and Coordinator of Humanities and the Center for Leadership at Woodbury University. He also teaches in the MPA program at CSU Northridge, and in the PhD program in Global Leadership and Change at Pepperdine University. A public policy expert, he previously served as Associate Adjunct Professor at the Sol Price School of Public Policy at the University of Southern California. He is President and founder of the Global Hunger Foundation, helping women in the developing world break the chains of poverty. He served in the Peace Corps in Sierra Leone.

Katharina Spraul (Univ.-Prof. Dr. habil.) is a full professor and holds the Chair of Business Administration, in particular Sustainability Management in the Department of Business Studies and Economics at Technische Universität Kaiserslautern (TUK), Germany. She initiated the Sustainability Office at the TUK in 2016 as a central institution for sustainability topics. She is responsible for the compulsory bachelor's and master's courses on sustainability management. Her research deals with sustainability management in and between the three sectors market, state and civil society, and has been published in scientific outlets such as *Business & Society*, *International Journal of Public Administration*, *Journal of Business Ethics*, and *Nonprofit & Voluntary Sector Quarterly*.

Dung Q. Tran, PhD, is an Assistant Professor of Organizational Leadership in the School of Leadership Studies at Gonzaga University. Working at the nexus of leadership and the humanities, Dr. Tran's research explores how storytelling and spirituality shapes leader identity development. He is co-editor of *Servant-Leadership and Forgiveness: How Leaders Help Heal the Heart of the World* (SUNY Press, 2020—with J. Song, S. R. Ferch, and L. C.

Spears). Dr. Tran's scholarship has also appeared in the *Humanistic Management Journal*; the *International Journal of Servant-Leadership; Communication Research Trends*; and (with M. R. Carey and/or L. C. Spears) in the following anthologies: *The Palgrave Handbook of Workplace Well-Being: Reimagining Human Flourishing* (Palgrave Macmillan, 2021); *Positive Leadership and Change: A Practical Guide for Workplace Transformation* (Springer, 2020); *Evolving Leadership for Collective Wellbeing: Lessons for Implementing the United Nations Sustainable Development Goals* (Emerald, 2019); *The Palgrave Handbook of Workplace Spirituality and Fulfillment* (Palgrave Macmillan, 2018); and *Breaking the Zero-Sum Game: Transforming Societies Through Inclusive Leadership* (Emerald, 2017).

Therese Walkinshaw, PhD, is the Head of Faculty Culture and Communication in the Faculty of Design and Creative Technologies at Auckland University of Technology in New Zealand. She completed her PhD in 2016 focusing on mindfulness and leaders. Her passion is in the well-being space of academic leaders and academic staff. She has developed and led several leadership programs focusing on self-leadership, mindfulness, and resilience. She is currently researching on emotion in leaders and mindfulness.

Lee Waller, PhD, is Leadership faculty at Hult Ashridge International Business School, where she works with leaders on developing their self-awareness, an authentic and compassionate leadership style, and inclusive leadership behaviors. A prolific researcher, her research specialisms focus on self, identity, and belonging in the workplace, workplace psychological well-being, the impact of psychological safety in organizational culture, and the neuroscience of leadership and learning. Lee publishes widely in academic and practitioner outlets and has presented her research to a range of audiences, including the Academy of Management, Health and Well-being Conference, the British Psychological Society, and the European Foundation of Management Development.

Wenli Wang, PhD, is a Professor of Computer and Information Systems at Robert Morris University. She obtained her PhD in Management Science and Information Systems from the University of Texas at Austin in 2000, and subsequently held academic posts at Emory University, University of Nevada at Las Vegas, and Trident University. Her research focuses on cybersecurity, health informatics, big data analytics, and artificial intelligence. She has published in the *Journal of Economic Theory, Decision Support Systems, IEEE Computer, International Journal of Electronic Commerce, Communications of the Association for Information Systems, Information Systems Education Journal, Journal of Information Technology Management, Technology in Society*, and so on. She has served on the editorial boards of the *Journal of Database Management* and the *International Journal of E-business Research*. Her other research interests are systems engineering, leadership, mindfulness, and ethics. She has a BS in Computer Engineering and Telecommunications. She is an avid meditator and a yoga teacher.

Jared Weintraub is the founder of The Flow Group, LLC., an organizational and business development firm that works with individuals and companies to create and maintain happy, healthy, and productive workplaces. He graduated from the University of Delaware with a BA in Psychology, holds a master's degree in I/O Psychology from the Chicago School of Professional Psychology (Washington, D.C. Campus), a Ph.D. from Hofstra University in Applied Organizational Psychology, is certified as a Senior Professional of Human Resources (SPHR), and is Hogan Certified. He has worked with start-ups and organizations across various industries, providing internal and external consulting, coaching, and managing marketing and sales teams. His research investigates how companies can leverage "nudge" technology and Positive Psychology (specifically Mindfulness and Flow Theory) in the workplace to help individuals, teams, and organizations flourish at work while maintaining a positive culture that encourages productivity and employee wellbeing.

Manoj Kumar Yadav, completed his Post Graduation in Psychology and is currently pursuing 'Fellow Programme in Management' (equivalent to a PhD) in Organizational Behavior and Human Resource Management from the Indian Institute of Management, Indore, India. He worked for ten years (four and half years' corporate experience and five and half years' academic experience) before joining the research program at IIM Indore. He has worked as research associate on two projects sponsored by the Ministry of Information and Broadcasting, New Delhi, India. He has also served as faculty for four and a half years. Manoj has presented papers in various international and national conferences of repute. He recently presented two papers in the *British Academy of Management* (2019). Manoj's research interests are around the domain of organizational behavior. Within organizational behavior he is particularly interested in subtle prejudice and discrimination, mindfulness at the workplace, organizational routines, and social network analysis.

ABOUT THE EDITOR

Recognized as a lead thinker for his pioneer contributions to the field of transformational leadership, workplace spirituality, workplace well-being, sustainability, and fulfillment in the personal and professional arena, Professor Satinder K. Dhiman is a sought-after keynote speaker at regional, national, and international conferences. In 2013, Dr. Dhiman was invited to be the opening speaker at the prestigious TEDx Conference @ College of the Canyons in Santa Clarita, California. Since then, he has led several major national and international conferences as co-organizer and/or as track chair.

With an instructional and research focus on leadership and organizational behavior—and with specific concentration on sustainability, workplace spirituality, and well-being—Professor Dhiman holds a PhD in Social Sciences from Tilburg University, Netherlands, an EdD in Organizational Leadership from Pepperdine University, Los Angeles, an MBA from West Coast University, Los Angeles, and a master's degree in Commerce from Panjab University, Chandigarh, India, having earned the Gold Medal. He has also completed advanced Executive Leadership Programs at Harvard, Stanford, and Wharton.

Recipient of several national and international academic and professional honors, Dr. Dhiman won the Woodbury University Ambassador of the Year Award in 2015 and 2017 and MBA Professor of the Year Award in 2015; Scholarly and Creative Writing Award, 2019; Most Valuable MBA Professor Award, 2018; Most Inspirational and Most Charismatic MBA Teacher Award 2012, 2013/2014/2018; the Steve Allen Excellence in Education Award in 2006; and the prestigious ACBSP International Teacher of the Year Award in 2004. Most recently, Professor Dhiman chaired a symposium at the Academy of Management that received 2019 Best Symposium Proposal Award.

Professor Dhiman has done over 50 conference presentations and more than 50 invited keynotes, plenary sessions, distinguished key guest lectures and creative workshops—nationally and internationally—and has published over 60 peer-reviewed journal articles and book chapters. He is the author, translator, editor, co-author, and co-editor of over 25 management, leadership, spirituality, and accounting-related books and research monographs. His recent books include: *Bhagavad Gītā and Leadership: A Catalyst for*

Organizational Transformation (Palgrave Macmillan, 2019); *Managing by the Bhagavad Gītā: Timeless Lessons for Today's Managers* (Springer, 2019; with Amar); *Holistic Leadership* (Palgrave, 2017); *Gandhi and Leadership* (Palgrave, 2015); *Seven Habits of Highly Fulfilled People* (2012); and co-editing and co-authoring, with Marques, *Spirituality and Sustainability* (Springer, 2016); *Leadership Today* (Springer, 2016); and *Engaged Leadership* (Springer, 2018). He has also translated several Indian spiritual classics into English, including the *Sahaja Gītā*.

He is the editor-in-chief of three multi-author major reference works: *Springer Handbook of Engaged Sustainability* (Springer International, Switzerland, 2018) and *Palgrave Handbook of Workplace Spirituality and Fulfillment* (Palgrave Macmillan, USA, 2018); *Routledge Companion to Mindfulness at Work* (2020); editor-in-chief of *Palgrave Studies in Workplace Spirituality and Fulfillment* and lead editor of *Springer Series in Management, Change, Strategy and Positive Leadership*. Some of his forthcoming titles include *Leading without Power: A Model of Highly Fulfilled Leaders* (Palgrave Macmillan, 2021); *Conscious Consumption: Healthy, Humane and Sustainable Living* (Routledge, UK, 2021); *Wise Leadership for Turbulent Times* (Routledge, UK, 2021); *Palgrave Handbook of Workplace Well-being*—a major reference work (Palgrave Macmillan; editor-in-chief, 2020); and *Positive Leadership and Change*, and *Social Entrepreneurship and Corporate Social Responsibility* (Springer; with Marques, 2020).

Currently, Professor Dhiman serves as the Associate Dean, Chair, and Director of the MBA Program, and as the Professor of Management at Woodbury University, Burbank, California. He has served as the Chair for a special MBA Program for the Mercedes-Benz executives, China. Dr. Dhiman also serves as Accreditation Consultant, Evaluator, and Site Visit Team Leader for the Accreditation Council for Business Schools and Programs (ACBSP) for various universities in the USA, Canada, Europe, and Asia.

Professor Dhiman is the Founder-Director of Forever Fulfilled, a Los Angeles-based well-being consultancy that focuses on workplace wellness, workplace spirituality, and self-leadership. He has served as the President of International Chamber for Service Industry (ICSI: 2016–2018) and now serves as a distinguished Patron, International Chamber for Service Industry (ICSI).

PROLEGOMENON

Satinder K. Dhiman

Mindfulness, I declare, is helpful everywhere.

– *The Buddha*

A modern Zen story talks about a novice approaching a Zen master, inquiring about the most important thing in life. "Attention," said the master. The student persisted: "What is the second most important thing?" "Attention," replied the master. "And the third thing?" asked the student. "Attention," the master added firmly. "Anything else?" continued the student. "You do not seem to be paying attention!" roared the master.

The faculty of self-awareness has been prized by various wisdom and spiritual traditions. While Hindu, Sufi, Hassidic, and Christian traditions employ some form of awareness to attune to current reality, it is the Buddhist meditative tradition in which mindfulness has really played a key role in developing a keen awareness of the present moment. Perhaps in no other tradition has mindfulness received such a comprehensive treatment as it has in Buddhist doctrine and discipline, both in the ancient manuals and in the modern Buddhist writings.

The term *mindfulness* has come to be used in a variety of ways and contexts in the modern times. Starting as a meditation technique more than 2,500 years ago, mindfulness has found its way in recent times into health clinics, prison houses, wellness centers, government offices, law firms, departments of navy and defense, and corporate boardrooms. In its original Buddhist form, the practice of mindfulness refers to the technique of developing natural awareness of the body and the mind in the present moment.

Underscoring the universal importance of mindfulness, Buddha observed, "Mindfulness, I declare, is helpful everywhere."[1] Various other wisdom traditions of the world also underscore the importance of garnering a heightened sense of awareness of present reality by focusing on a chosen object with intense absorption, meditation, contemplation, concentration, remembrance, and recollection. For example, Sufi masters use a special form of meditation called *Zikr* to develop "yearning for the divine" through constant remembrance and recollection.

Christian desert fathers likewise used the royal art of "the prayer of the heart" to garner the knowledge of the divine. The *Philokalia*, a collection of texts written between the fourth and fifteenth centuries by masters of the Greek Orthodox tradition, speaks of the virtue of developing mental silence and inner attention in the service of the divine. In modern times, Russian mystics Gurdjieff and Ouspenksy have placed special importance on "self-remembering" as a unique way to psychological self-evolvement. And J. Krishnamurti popularized the phrase "choiceless awareness" to denote a state of pure alertness where we are fully aware of the moment-to-moment reality "as it is," yet our awareness is not focused on any particular physical or mental object.

Research shows that mindfulness boosts creativity through greater insight, receptivity, balance, and clarity; ensures greater engagement at the workplace through increased energy and sense of well-being and expanding awareness and range of our responses, and less burnout.[2] Mindfulness and creativity are natural partners.[3] By its alert focus on the present state of mind, the practice of mindfulness contributes to the successful attainment of both flow and creativity. Intense focus on the task at hand is a hallmark of creativity, thus linking flow, creativity, and mindfulness as one single movement.

According to Csikszentmihalyi, whom this editor had the good fortune of interviewing twice, flow refers to a state of total immersion, effortless concentration, and rapt enjoyment in an activity in which one loses any sense of space, time, and self. First proposed by Csikszentmihalyi, flow is the mental state of operation in which the person is fully immersed in what he or she is doing, characterized by a feeling of energized focus, full involvement, and success in the process of the activity. It is marked by a certain delightful effortlessness borne of complete identification with the task at hand.[4] Recent research has underscored the vital link between happiness at work and workplace success: "Flow directly correlates to happiness at work and happiness at work directly correlates to success."[5]

We believe that the solution to the current leadership crisis lies in leaders' self-cultivation process—a life of attentive self-awareness, emanating from their deepest values and culminating in their contribution to the common good. Traditional approaches to leadership rarely provide any permeating or systematic framework to garner a sense of higher purpose or nurture deeper moral and spiritual dimensions of leaders. Now more than ever organizations must inspire a vision for fostering an environment of workplace engagement, encouragement, and commitment. Learning to be mindful leaders requires a deep understanding, awareness, and personal transformation on the part of its practitioners. Achieving insight into the art and science of mindful leadership is not as easy as it may seem. While some leaders may self-develop toward mindful awareness, many people need specific guidelines. This volume provides those guidelines.

There is nothing more exhilarating in life than celebrating the joy of cultivating presence in oneself and in others. This volume is a humble offering of 53 scholars and practitioners from around the world to the exciting adventure of living in the present moment, in life and leadership.

Bon Voyage and Godspeed!

INTRODUCTION

Satinder K. Dhiman

Just as deep down, the ocean remains calm, unperturbed by the waves at the surface, even so is the mind of the one who has cultivated mindfulness.

– *The Editor*

This companion aims to serve as an important reference work for understanding and practicing mindfulness at work. Truly global in scope and strength, it highlights the concerted efforts of 53 scholar-practitioners (from six continents) to understand and share their findings regarding living attentively and leading and managing mindfully. The humble goal is to operationalize in the workplace the final words of the Buddha to Ananda: "Live not inattentively."

In its secular form, mindfulness is the paying attention to our present experiences and accepting them without judgment. Studies to date suggest that mindfulness affects many aspects of our physical and psychological well-being—improving our mood, increasing positive emotions, and decreasing our anxiety, and distress, emotional reactivity, and job burnout.

We begin at the beginning by mapping the terrain of mindfulness and suggest its myriad applications at the individual, group, and organizational level. The work in this volume grew organically into five sections, each informing and integrating with the rest, to guide our journey to mindfulness in the workplace. The following pages provide a synoptic overview of the various sections and chapters in this volume.

Part I, comprising five chapters, maps the *conceptual framework of mindfulness in terms of its roots and development.*

- In Chapter 1, Dr. Satinder K. Dhiman explores the construct of mindfulness from multiple perspectives, especially from the standpoint of Theravada Buddhism. The Theravada represents, according to most Buddhist scholars (Bodhi, 2005, 2012, 2016, 2017; Carrithers, 1988; Gethin, 2001; Piyadassi, 1995, 2000; Nanamoli, 1992; Rahula, 1959, 1974), the "oldest" and, hence, the most "genuine" form of Buddhist teachings. The chapter will also briefly explore the existing mindfulness literature in health care and in cognitive and clinical psychology to create a pathway to the exploration of mindfulness in the workplace. Finally, it will chronicle applications of mindfulness in the workplace and leadership domain.

- In Chapter 2, Jared Weintraub and Dr. Scott B. Dust aver that scholars begin to consider mindfulness as one of many cognitive states, and that to fully understand its implications, we must evaluate how it relates to other cognitive states in an ongoing stream of consciousness. This chapter gently reminds scholars that different states can be either beneficial or harmful, depending on the context of the work situation. The authors call for additional research that investigates mindfulness, as well as related cognitive states, from a more holistic, temporal perspective. Finally, they discuss opportunities for temporal research grounded in the being versus doing framework, the contingency approach, and in mindfulness intervention processes.
- In Chapter 3, Dr. Ravi S. Kudesia and Jenson Lau present mindfulness as a metacognitive practice. They observe that scholars seeking to define mindfulness have typically attempted to turn definitions used by meditation practitioners into scientific constructs—ideally in a manner that honors their Buddhist roots and has relevance for organizations. This produces an abundance of components like present-centered attention, nonjudgment, self-acceptance, etc. that relate to each other only vaguely and point only abstractly to a common idea of mindfulness. Metacognitive practice is an alternative to this multicomponent approach. Such development of metacognition is not individual: it occurs within a community of practice that furnishes supportive technologies, social interactions, terminologies, and activities.
- In Chapter 4, Dr. Christopher S. Reina discusses a multidimensional conceptualization of mindfulness at work and presents a development and initial validation of the work mindfulness scale. This chapter reviews previous work on mindfulness, building the case for a multidimensional conceptualization of the construct in the context of the work domain. While six facets are initially proposed, empirical support emerged for a five-facet conceptualization. Future research directions are discussed to guide further scholarship in investigating the validity and usefulness of the WMS as mindfulness continues to gain traction within the organizational sciences.
- In Chapter 5, Manoj Kumar Yadav discusses antecedents and consequences of workplace mindfulness. Workplace mindfulness is a recent trend driving much academic focus in organizational research. However, systematic integration of the mindfulness literature highlighting the individual-, group-, and organizational-level antecedents and consequences is rare to find. This chapter presents a systematic representation of some of the established antecedents and consequences of mindfulness from the psychological and organizational science domain. Finally, the chapter highlights some conceptual and methodological limitations that exist within the current state of mindfulness research and throws light on the future research directions.

Part II, comprising six chapters, highlights various approaches to leading mindfully and how mindfulness impacts the way leaders connect and develop followers.

- In Chapter 6, Dr. Joan Marques portrays leadership as a practice that starts with personal responsibility. It explains that leadership is exerted through the choices leaders make. The chapter subsequently explains that many people fall prey to the subconscious habit of sleepwalking, a behavioral pattern based on a number of foundational aspects in our life. Sleepwalking is explained as having to do with focusing too much on the details and forgetting to zoom out in order to obtain a broader scope. Among the various mindfulness strategies presented are: engaging in constructive dialogues with creative thinkers, perceiving oneself from the other side, considering the big picture, and practicing Vipassana, or mindfulness meditation.

- In Chapter 7, Michael Chaskalson, Dr. Megan Reitz, Dr. Lee Waller, and Sharon Olivier survey how mindfulness training and practice impact three capacities that are seen as critical for leading in the 21st century: resilience, the ability to collaborate, and the ability to lead in complex contexts. They present the outcomes and procedures of a first-ever study with 57 senior leaders who undertook an eight-week "Mindful Leader" program. Their initial findings suggest that the program was effective in developing leaders' mindfulness, resilience, and key self-perceived leadership competencies such as collaboration and agility in complex situations. They conclude that mindfulness practice may be an effective method for leadership development. Their results suggest that mindfulness can be learned and developed by executive leaders, as long as they practice for at least ten minutes per day.
- In Chapter 8, Jason Beck examines how leaders who possess the ability to stay present, observe information, and correctly navigate the distractions of the workplace will be more likely to enact individualized consideration successfully. A multi-source, cross-sectional study with a sample of 155 leader–follower dyads from Amazon's Mechanical Turk examines how leader self-reported mindfulness relates to follower-reported individualized consideration. Implications suggest that emotional intelligence is instrumental to the mechanisms for leader mindfulness impacting individualized consideration with followers. Future directions are advised to explore more longitudinal relationships of mindfulness and leader–follower behaviors.
- In Chapter 9, Dr. Bena (Beth) Long explores how mindfulness at work has garnered empirical evidence that supports its positive impact. She shares her findings of a study that was designed to obtain new information from titled mid- to senior-level organizational leaders for their lived experience's impact of mindfulness upon their leadership. The qualitative phenomenological research study data was collected through in-depth interviews with 14 leaders of diverse industries, locations, and types of mindfulness practice that shared the common use of a minimum of ten years of continuous mindfulness practice. A qualitative seven-step analysis framework was utilized to determine all themes and findings. The results indicated that mindfulness is perceived to contribute to the development of awareness that is associated with improved leadership capabilities and growth.
- In Chapter 10, Dr. Therese Walkinshaw explores the experience of leaders practicing mindfulness in their leading. Using conversation as the research tool, the chapter follows the experience of four leaders in their daily lives. The chapter aims to show how mindfulness helped these leaders (and by extension, may help other leaders) lead *self* and others in their leadership practice. Part 1 of the chapter explains how the research conversations unfolded. Part 2 interprets the conversations using Heideggerian phenomenology as theoretical construct. The findings of this interpretive process indicate that moving beyond mere chatter into true conversation and a space of meaningfulness is deeply significant, not just because it develops better leaders and leading, but also because it assists individuals in their increasingly busy lives.
- In Chapter 11, Drs. Wenli Wang and Petros G. Malakyan integrate mindfulness, flow, and creativity in the context of leader–follower relationships at the 21st-century workplace. It builds upon the literature review on mindful leadership, flow, and creativity

and extends the discussions to mindful leadership–followership, co-flow, and co-creativity. It is suggested that mindfulness, flow, and creativity are interconnected in a symbiotic manner. As a result, mindful leadership–followership in the state of co-flow promotes resonant co-creativity. Therefore, it is suggested that both leaders and followers need to be mindful of the intricate systematic challenges for achieving and sustaining co-flow and co-creativity at the rapid-changing digital workplace, much like in dynamic jazz improvisations.

Part III, comprising five chapters, likewise explores various approaches to managing mindfully and how managers can successfully put the art of workplace mindfulness to work.

- In Chapter 12, Drs. Peter McGhee and Patricia Grant explore how workplace spirituality and mindfulness might interrelate, and their joint capacity to affect management behavior, and produce organizational transformation. The chapter opens with a concise literature review of spirituality and of mindfulness in organizations. This is followed by a discussion on how these might be combined as spiritual mindfulness to enhance management cognition, decision-making, and behavior. The chapter concludes with suggestions for organizations to develop managers' spiritual mindfulness.
- In Chapter 13, Drs. Melita Balas Rant and Katarina Katja Mihelič aver that the workplaces of today are characterized by working 24/7, anytime and anywhere, which has led to information overload, the impression of the "scarcity" of time, and a sense of working in a rush. As a result, we are witnessing an increased interest in mindfulness—a state of non-judgmental attentiveness and awareness of the moment—as a way to better cope with daily stressors. In this chapter, the authors adopt a multi-stakeholder perspective to explore the ways in which mindfulness can facilitate thriving and productive relationships with the self, co-workers, leaders, AI, clients, and family members. They offer specific recommendations and practical exercises on how mindfulness can be integrated in employees' daily lives through the mindful management of interactions.
- In Chapter 14, Dr. Jutta Tobias Mortlock maintains that currently most in-company mindfulness courses equate mindfulness with meditation. However, meditating is only one of numerous science-based ways to bring mindfulness into work contexts. Moreover, meditation is not always the most effective path towards workplace mindfulness. It can be counter-productive or even lead to adverse effects. This can occur especially in organizations where high dedication and self-sacrifice are prized commodities, while engaging in mindful self-care may be counter-cultural or, in extreme cases, might even bring up latent trauma. In this chapter, you will learn in a systematic manner what the management science of workplace mindfulness is, why it is not the same as mindfulness meditation, and how you can help embed mindfulness in your work culture sustainably.
- In Chapter 15, Huda Masood and Stefan Karajovic observe that the role of human resources (HR) in implementing and facilitating workplace mindfulness within organizations is understudied. Scholars suggest certain advantages of attaining and retaining the attention-focused attributes that often characterize mindfulness. Further, workplace mindfulness is positively associated with work engagement and job performance. Given the associated beneficial outcomes, fostering mindfulness among the employees is of interest to employers. Empirical evidence suggests that individual discrepancy in workplace mindfulness is contingent upon a variety of dispositional, experiential, and contextual factors. In that vein, the current chapter strives to evaluate the role of

organizational routines in effectively implementing workplace mindfulness through HR infrastructure.

- In Chapter 16, Drs. Thushini S. Jayawardena-Willis, Edwina Pio, and Peter McGhee aver that although in the West, mindfulness is understood as an individual's ability to be aware of what is happening at the present moment, in the Eastern tradition of Buddhism, mindfulness (*sati*) is not just awareness; it must be right (*samma*). Right mindfulness (*samma sati*) is practiced through two types of meditation: concentration (*samatha*) and insight (*vipassana*). Prior research on ethical decision-making (EDM) in the West has found that while mindfulness does not have an impact on individuals who choose to cheat, negative emotions such as anger, fear, and sadness have an adverse effect on their EDM. As such, in this chapter the authors contend how and why the concept of insight goes beyond the boundaries of mindfulness and how and why it could be used to extend our understanding of EDM and happiness in organizations.

Part IV, comprising eight chapters, presents various approaches to mindfulness-based learning, education, and intervention.

- In Chapter 17, Matthew D. Hanson, Dr. Jason G. Randall, Gabrielle C. Danna, and Huy Q. Le present five common challenges to modern workplace learning and draw on theoretical perspectives and empirical research to propose ways that mindfulness may help address these challenges. Challenges include: (1) creating sufficient infrastructure for learning, (2) creating a social climate for learning, (3) designing and delivering training in ways that promote attentional focus, (4) buffering against negative emotions that may accompany learning efforts, and (5) transferring or applying learning to the job. Each challenge is accompanied by recommendations to provide actionable steps that individuals and organizations may take to capitalize on the benefits of mindfulness as a tool to improve valuable learning outcomes.
- In Chapter 18, Drs. Anne Randerson and Rajnandini Pillai observe that in the turbulent, uncertain, and increasingly complex environments that managers face today, mindfulness practice may be an effective solution to helping business students and managers make better decisions. Drawing on over 30 years of combined teaching experience in the global management arena, the authors offer their own experiences introducing mindfulness practices in the global classroom. They propose alternatives to traditional teaching methods to expand perspectives on culturally sensitive issues by exploring human nature and mindfulness teachings from theoretical and philosophical perspectives. Through mindfulness practice, educators can open their students' minds to embrace cross-cultural diversity, deepening their desire to connect across borders during turbulent times.
- In Chapter 19, Drs. Sabine Grunwald and Liva LaMontagne review the state of mindfulness at top public US universities and identify the challenges to diffuse mindfulness into higher education institutions based on diffusion of innovation theory. Their research indicates that the diffusion process has been hampered by limited (1) perceived relative advantage of mindfulness compared with existing practices, (2) compatibility with existing lifestyles and academic culture, (3) trialability to test mindfulness practice, (4) observability of the effectiveness of mindfulness practices, and (5) the complexity of mindfulness practices that are perceived as confusing. A multifaceted approach is suggested to diffuse more mindfulness into academic culture that improves individuals' health and also transforms the organizational culture as a whole.

- In Chapter 20, Dr. Nidhi Kaushal advocates the notion of mindfulness practice through the conceptual framework of ancient literary writings, especially the *Upanishads*, the Śrīmad Bhagavad Gītā, and other literary texts to identify the new conceptions of mindfulness from a literary perspective. This chapter provides a new tactic of wisdom of mindfulness and gives an introduction to literature in the philosophy of modern management and organizational disciplines. It is an attempt to capsulize the texts and works of literature related to mindfulness at one place, with an outlook of enriching the notion of "mindfulness practice at the workplace," and presenting the universality of ancient texts.
- In Chapter 21, Drs. Haziq Mehmood and Oi-ling Siu maintain that employees face interruptions by using social network sites (SNSs) during office hours. This type of interruption affects the employee's job performance and well-being. In this scenario mindfulness plays an important role to mitigate the interruptions caused by social network use. They discuss an experiment to relate the role of mindfulness as an intervention to deal with these interruptions. "Mindfulness" was used as an intervention to mitigate the interruptions caused by SNSs. It was concluded that mindfulness meditation is helpful to reduce the distractions and interruption effects in employees. Employers and organizations need to consider this intervention plan to increase employees' job performance.
- In Chapter 22, Dr. Igor Ristić and Ayça Kübra Hizarci-Payne explore the interplay between mindfulness, emotional intelligence, and resilience through a quantitative study. This study seeks to contribute to the existing literature by uncovering the interplay of these three variables, specifically the enhancing role of mindfulness on emotional intelligence and resilience, in which emotional intelligence mediates the relationship between mindfulness and resilience. Four hypotheses predicted positive associations between the three major variables, in addition to a mediating role for emotional resilience. The results show that mindfulness increases individuals' adaptability to difficult situations by increasing their emotional intelligence and resilience, and that emotional intelligence mediated the relationship between mindfulness and resilience.
- In Chapter 23, Dr. Andrea Cherman and Francisco Eduardo Moreira Azeredo propose an integrative knowledge model that incorporates an innovative and valuable spiritual dimension of wisdom and awareness into current rational dimension of data and information, home of science. The model formulates an associated overpowering strength capable of boosting the development of an indissoluble integrative knowledge, which can lead an organization and their valuable individuals to a new vision, joining their mindsets closer together in a balanced implementation process that ultimately expands the current knowledge paradigm, acknowledging the most appreciated dimensions of human spirituality and rationality, its history and traditions, and its distinguishable contributions to the evolutionary progress of humankind.
- In Chapter 24, Lasse Lychnell offers a broader understanding of the opportunities and challenges of mindfulness-based interventions (MBIs) in the workplace by reporting on a longitudinal case study of a medium-sized Scandinavian company. The longitudinal study focuses on how specific participants experience the outcomes of an MBI over time and the role that the organizational environment plays in shaping these outcomes. The results of the case study suggest that several elements in the organizational context supported the implementation of the MBI: authentic top management support, alignment between the MBI and a larger organizational transformation, a stable

organizational environment, and the creation of a holding environment to support the managers' integration of what they have learned into their everyday working lives.

Part V, comprising eight chapters, explores some creative and novel approaches to mindfulness at work.

- In Chapter 25, Dr. Olga Louchakova-Schwartz introduces a distinction between religious and non-religious practice of mindfulness. It is noted that phenomenological philosophy provides the concepts and the research method necessary for the analysis of mindfulness. In the past, some researchers claimed similarities between mindfulness and phenomenology: the chapter delivers a brief description of the phenomenological approach, and argues against attempts to conflate it with Buddhist mindfulness. It is shown that the relationships between the two are quite specific: these are not two comparable systems of thought, but phenomenology should be used to understand the modifications of experience induced by mindfulness. The chapter further shows a major distinction between religious and non-religious mindfulness: religious mindfulness serves as means of reaching religious ends, i.e., enlightenment, while the non-religious mindfulness culminates in disclosing the phenomenological sphere of intersubjectivity.
- In Chapter 26, Dr. Tracy F. H. Chang introduces a novel "inner engineering" approach to the field of mindfulness and work engagement research. "Inner engineering" represents the process of using the yogic sciences and technologies to gain self-mastery over one's cognitive, emotional, physical, and energy systems in order to achieve optimal well-being and performance at work. This study evaluates the effect of an inner engineering online training program on energy, joy, mindfulness, and work engagement. The program was offered as a small pilot program by a Fortune 500 company to its employees at work. The results show that "inner engineering" training significantly increases energy, joy, mindfulness, and work engagement. These findings support the *broaden and build* theory of positive emotions.
- In Chapter 27, Dr. Dung Q. Tran explores a distinctive approach of practicing mindfulness in the workplace anchored in the spiritual philosophy of Ignatius of Loyola, often referred to as Ignatian spirituality. In particular, the chapter discusses how Ignatian spirituality, a nearly 500-year-old "vision of life, work, and of love," offers a model for discerning important decisions and becoming more mindfully present to the depth and significance of one's everyday experience. Following the development of a dialogical bridge between mindfulness in the workplace and Ignatian spirituality, this chapter concludes by proposing the Ignatian awareness "examen" as an adaptable and brief practice to reflectively review daily happenings and illuminate the currents and undercurrents of one's interior life.
- In Chapter 28, Dr. Debra J. Dean dives into the Christian aspect of mindfulness in the workplace to answer basic questions about how Christians use spirituality in workplaces to engage their whole self: body, heart, mind, and soul. In recent years, interest in this topic has grown rapidly, as scientific testing has shown positive workplace outcomes. Nevertheless, many concepts of spirituality and mindfulness seem to remain aloof as they are thought to be connected to Eastern religious activities, such as meditation and yoga. This chapter explores the relevance of mindfulness from a Christian perspective. It will articulate the separation and connection of religion and spirituality. Additionally, it offers Biblical reference for Christians to integrate their faith spiritually in their daily work.

- In Chapter 29, Ayça Kübra Hizarci-Payne and Dr. Alev Katrinli study the possibility of boosting creativity through the reduction power of mindfulness on emotional exhaustion. While mindfulness is addressed by clinical psychology scholars with a great deal of attention, the role of mindfulness still needs to be investigated from an organizational perspective. Motivated by this gap within the literature, this study attempts to shed some light on the interrelationships between mindfulness, emotional exhaustion, and creativity, where emotional exhaustion takes part as a mediator. The results of the study show that while emotional exhaustion can hinder employee creativity, mindfulness reduces the detrimental effect of emotional exhaustion through which it ignites individuals' creativity.
- In Chapter 30, Dr. Claude-Hélène Mayer and Rudolf Oosthuizen explore the topic of love, creativity, and mindfulness in international leaders: qualities for a successful future world of work by leaders. The authors maintain that leaders need certain qualities to successfully navigate future-related work spaces. "Mindfulness," "love," and "creativity" are concepts and qualities which strengthen and empower leaders to take on challenges created in future-related workplaces. The chapter therefore contributes to previous research opting for leadership qualities needed in times of rapid changes, technologization, and complex challenges. It further contributes to fill the void of exploring the concepts of mindfulness, love, and creativity in leadership from an in-depth perspective, giving international leaders a voice to speak out and define the worth of these qualities for their work.
- In Chapter 31, Drs. R. Ray Gehani and Sunita Gehani examine how the sociocultural context of a society influences the mindfulness practice and mindsets of that society's people in different cultural settings. This qualitative research study based chapter investigates the genesis and global diffusion and appropriation of mindfulness with a phenomenological qualitative research approach grounded in Ken Wilber's integral leadership theory. The chapter delves deep into the genesis of mindfulness in ancient Indian civilization and briefly examines how the West appropriated mindfulness in commercial organizations for actionable knowledge and decision-making that maximizes the profit potential of a workplace in the material outer world.
- In Chapter 32, Drs. Kerri Cissna and H. Eric Schockman observe that constant distraction has become the default setting for many humans, as access and connection to digital devices is now commonplace in most parts of the world. In response, a growing trend for mindfulness to enter the modern workplace is being explored by global leaders who want to thrive in the 21st century. The concept of "mindfulness" has traditionally been associated with religion(s), which may have created resistance for its integration into secular workplace settings. The authors provide an essential resource for those who want to better understand the role of mindfulness in leadership, followership, and organizational practices for the modern world. The authors introduce a new conceptual model for creating an organization's mindful meaningfulness ecosystem (adapted from Bailey & Madden, 2016).
- In Chapter 33, Julia Hufnagel and Dr. Katharina Spraul review the literature on the impact of mindfulness on employee pro-environmental behavior. In previously proposed research models, mindfulness served as the independent variable that leads to pro-environmental behavior, with other variables having a mediating effect. In this chapter, they address the intention–behavior gap in workplace behaviors and hypothesize that mindfulness moderates the intention–behavior relationship in employee pro-environmental behavior, relying on self-control and self-determination theory. They

conduct a pre-study with a student sample measuring intentions and behaviors in two points of time and find that, in that context, the hypothesis cannot be confirmed. The chapter finally discusses this finding and provides suggestions for a future study design.

- In Chapter 34, Dr. Satinder K. Dhiman presents an overview of the essential elements of Buddhist psychology as a mental discipline. Right mindfulness, right concentration, and right effort constitute the Buddhist mental discipline. The mind is trained, disciplined, and developed through these three practices, which aim at cleansing the mind of impurities and disturbances such as lustful desires, hatred, ill-will, indolence, worries and restlessness, and skeptical doubts. As a case in point, this overview is followed by a detailed description of the author's experience with a form of Buddhist meditation called Vipassana as taught by S. N. Goenka in the tradition of Sayagyi U Ba Khin.

This innovative survey of workplace mindfulness is humbly and respectfully offered as an important resource for current scholars, managers, and leaders who want to live and lead a life of attentive awareness of their inner and outer world. For only by living consciously and conscientiously in the ever-new and mysterious Eternal Now can we find our fulfillment and redeem our existence, practicing with skillfulness the twin virtues of wisdom and compassion.

May we all be so fortunate!

Notes

1 As cited in Bhikkhu Khantipalo, *Practical Advice for Meditators* (Kandy, Sri Lanka: Buddhist Publication Society, 2006), 8.

2 Mindfulness in the Age of Complexity: Spotlight Interview with Ellen Langer by Alison Beard. *Harvard Business Review*, March 14, 2014, 1–7.

3 See: Langer, *Mindfulness* (New York: Addison-Wesley, 1989). Ellen Langer, *On Becoming an Artist: Reinventing Yourself through Mindful Creativity* (New York: Ballantine Books, 2005), 16.

4 See: Mihaly Csikszentmihalyi, *Creativity: Flow and the Psychology of Discovery and Invention* (New York: Harper Perennial; Reprint edition, 2013), 79–83; Mihaly Csikszentmihalyi, *Flow: The Psychology of Optimal Experience* (New York, NY: Harper and Row, 1990).

5 Steven Kotler, *The Rise of Superman: Decoding the Science of Ultimate Human Performance* (New York: New Harvest, 2014), ix.

PART I

Mapping the terrain of mindfulness at work

1
ANATOMY OF MINDFULNESS AT WORK
Theoretical construct and practical applications

Satinder K. Dhiman

Mindfulness construct

> It is only when we've awakened that we realize how much of our lives we've actually slept through.
>
> – *Langer (2005, p. 16)*

Introduction

Many sages throughout the human history have pointed out that the normal state that we call 'waking' is a form of psychological slumber. Mindfulness represents a wake-up call to live more consciously and attentively. Only when we make a conscious effort to be more awake do we realize how mindlessly our life has been lived. As Langer has pointed out, 'It is only when we've awakened that we realize how much of our lives we've actually slept through' (2005, p. 16). Given our 'fast and fragmented lives'—both personally and professionally—few topics are more pertinent in the present times than the art of conscious living and working. Since awareness is considered a universal human capacity and the most fundamental quality of our being, mindfulness accords great application potential in myriad fields involving personal and collective well-being.

Mindfulness has come to be recognized as one of the most enduring catchwords in the recent times. Research has shown that mindfulness improves markers of health (Creswell et al., 2016), reduces physiological markers of stress (Pascoe et al., 2017), and can literally change our brain (Congleton et al., 2015). The research on mindfulness also suggests that meditation sharpens skills like attention, memory, resilience, and emotional intelligence, competencies critical to leadership effectiveness and productivity (Seppala, 2015). After reviewing the research on the myriad applications of mindfulness in the 'wider context' of psychological well-being (Brown & Ryan, 2003), this chapter will focus on the role and application of mindfulness in the workplace, both from the leadership and employees' perspective.

After defining the construct of mindfulness from multiple perspectives, the first part of this chapter will explore how Theravada Buddhism understands mindfulness. The Theravada tradition based on the Pali canon will be utilized to survey the Buddhist approach to mindfulness since it represents, according to most Buddhist scholars (Rahula, 1974; Carrithers, 1988; Nanamoli, 1992; Gethin, 1998; Bodhi, 2005, 2012, 2016, 2017; Piyadassi, 1991, 2005), the 'oldest' and, hence, the most 'genuine' form of Buddhist teachings. The second section will present a critical review of the existing mindfulness literature in cognitive and clinical psychology to create a pathway to the exploration of mindfulness in the workplace and leadership domain.

Mindfulness as a special form of self-awareness

Weick and Putnam (2006, p. 275) speak about a sign on the wall of a machine shop run by the New York Central railroad that reads: 'Be where you are with all your mind.' This essentially sums up the practice of mindfulness and suggests its potential application in myriad fields. Recently, we have seen mindfulness practice making its way to wellness and health clinics (Kabat-Zinn, 2005; Ludwig & Kabat-Zinn, 2008), prison houses, government offices (Parihar, 2004)[1], law firms (Keeva, 2004; Carroll, 2007), and business leadership (Jyoti, 2000; Nakai & Schultz, 2000; Carroll, 2004, 2007, 2012; Gaytso & Muyzenberg, 2008; Marturano, 2015).

Mindfulness is a complex and multi-dimensional concept, with exceedingly rich and evolving history. Historically a Buddhist practice, mindfulness is a universal human capacity (Ludwig & Kabat-Zinn, 2008) as well as a skill that can potentially be cultivated through many diverse paths (Bishop et al., 2004; Shapiro & Carlson, 2009). In its original Buddhist form, the practice of mindfulness refers to cultivating awareness of the body and the mind in the present moment.

The faculty of self-awareness, a facet of mindfulness, has always been prized by various wisdom and spiritual traditions (Wilber, 2000). Socrates believed that 'an unexamined life is not worth living' (Durant, 1962) and declared cultivating *gnothi seauton*—self-knowledge—to be the most important purpose of life. Various other wisdom traditions of the world also highlight the importance of garnering a heightened sense of awareness by keeping the attention focused on a chosen object through intense absorption, meditation, contemplation, concentration, remembrance, and recollection. For example, Sufi masters use a special form of meditation called a *Zikr* to develop 'yearning for the divine' through constant remembrance and recollection (Idries Shah, 2004).

Christian Desert Fathers likewise used the royal art of 'the prayer of the heart' according to which prayer is employed to garner the knowledge of the Divine (Merton, 2004). The ***Philokalia***, a collection of texts written between the fourth and fifteenth century by masters of the Greek Orthodox tradition (Kadloubovsky & Palmer, 1979), speaks of the virtue of developing mental silence and inner attention in the service of the Divine. In the modern times, Gurdjieff-Ouspenksy, two Russian mystics, have laid special importance on 'self-remembering' as a unique way to psychological self-evolvement (Ouspenksy, 1973; Burton, 2007). And Krishnamurti (2002), a modern Indian philosopher, popularized the phrase 'choiceless awareness' to denote a state of pure alertness where we are fully aware of the moment-to-moment reality 'as it is,' yet our awareness is not focused on any particular physical or mental object.

Although Hindu, Sufi, and Christian Orthodox traditions employ some form of mindfulness to attune to reality, yet, in no other spiritual tradition has mindfulness played such a key role in developing awareness of the present reality as it has in the Buddhist spiritual path. In no other tradition has mindfulness received such a comprehensive treatment as it has in the Buddhist doctrine and discipline, both in the ancient manuals and commentaries, and in the modern Buddhist writings.

Defining mindfulness

'Mindfulness,' as the traditional English word, has been around for over 300 years (Still, 2005; Dryden & Still, 2006, p. 3). In the early part of the twentieth century, the term 'mindfulness' was coined by the British scholar, T.H. Rhys-Davids, to translate the Pāli word *sati* (Thanissaro, 1996). During last 20 years, the word mindfulness has gained unprecedented popularity mainly due to Jon Kabat-Zinn's (1990) mindfulness-based stress reduction program that he pioneered at the University of Massachusetts Medical School during the 1980s. Other teachers who have contributed to bringing mindfulness to the mainstream consciousness in Western cultures include Nyanaponika Thera (Nyanaponika, 1962, 1996), Thich Nhat Hanh (1992), Ellen Langer (1989, 2005, 2014), Joseph Goldstein, and Jack Kornfield (2001).

Although the interest in application of mindfulness technique has grown exponentially over the last two decades, the term mindfulness has not been defined operationally (Bishop et al., 2004). The word has many connotations and various authors have described the term differently to suit their needs and purposes, mostly acknowledging—explicitly or implicitly–its Buddhist roots. Here is a sampling of a few of those definitions:

- 'a process of bringing a certain quality of attention to moment-to-moment experience' (Kabat-Zinn, 1990)
- 'moment to moment, non-judgmental awareness cultivated by paying attention' (Kabat-Zinn, 2015)
- 'Mindfulness is the awareness that emerges through paying attention on purpose, in the present moment, and non-judgmentally to things as they are' (Williams, Teasdale, Segal, and Jon Kabat-Zinn, 2007, p. 47)
- 'remembering to bring attention to present moment experience in an open and non-judgmental manner' (Huxter, 2008)
- 'keeping one's consciousness alive to the present reality' (Hanh,1975)
- 'awareness of what happens in your own mind and in the world around you' (Sangharakshita, 2000)
- 'process of drawing novel distinctions or noticing new things' (Langer, 1989; Langer & Moldoveanu, 2000)
- 'simply the knack of noticing without comment whatever is happening in your present experience. It involves just seeing from moment to moment what the mind is up to; the endless succession of ideas and feelings and perceptions and body sensations and memories and fantasies and moods and judgments arising and passing away' (Claxton, 1990)
- 'When you are mindful you are highly concentrated, focused on what you are doing, and you are collected—poised and calm with a composure that comes from being aware of yourself and the world around you as well as being aware of your purpose' (Kulananda & Houlder, 2002)
- 'Mindfulness is the capacity to be fully aware of all that one experiences *inside the self*—body, mind, heart, spirit—and to pay full attention to what is happening *around us*—people, the natural world, our surroundings, and events' (Boyatzis & McKee, 2005)

- 'a kind of nonelaborative, nonjudgmental, present-centered awareness in which each thought, feeling, or sensation that arises in the attentional filed is acknowledged and accepted as it is' (Bishop et al., 2004)

As is evident from the foregoing definitions, mindfulness refers to 'intentional awareness of what is unfolding in the present moment' (Williams, Teasdale & Segal, 2007). When used in the therapeutic sense, the definitions of mindfulness tend to incorporate an element of non-judgment to facilitate wider acceptance of its use (Gilpin, 2008). Within Buddhist context, mindfulness almost always denotes an awareness of moment-to-moment changes that are taking place in our body and mind.

Mindfulness in the earliest Pali canon

This section presents the fundamental teachings on *Satipatthana* as preserved in the Pali canon of Theravada Buddhism (the School of the Elders). The Buddha wrote no books or treatises. His earliest discourses are recorded in Pāli bhāshā—*the language of Buddhist texts*—which is closely related to Sanskrit. Meditation constitutes the essence of Buddhism, the very foundation of Buddhist practice. Meditation is to Buddhism what prayer is to Christianity (Conze, 1959, p. 11). The two main types of Buddhist meditation are: (1) *samatha meditation*, which deals with the development of serenity or calm, and (2) *vipassana*[2] *meditation*, which involves the development of insight.

Calm meditation aims to provide the mind essential clarity and makes the mind serene, stable, and strong. By preparing the mind to 'see the things as they really are,' it serves as a necessary foundation for Insight meditation. Together, Calm and Insight meditation form the Buddhist path leading to the realization of final awakening or enlightenment.

In an introduction to *Vissudhamagga—The Path of Purification*, Bhikkhu Nanamoli (2003, p. xliii; originally published 1972) has noted that

> concentration is training in intensity and focus and in single-mindedness. While Buddhism makes no exclusive claim to teach jhana concentration (samatha=samadhi), it does claim that the development of insight (vipassana) culminating in penetration of Four Noble Truths is peculiar to it. The two have to be coupled together to attain to the truths and the end of suffering. Insight is initially training to see experience as it occurs, without misperception, invalid assumptions or wrong inferences.

The foundations of mindfulness: Satipatthana Sutta

The most important and the most original discourse on the subject of meditation delivered by the Buddha is called *Satipatthana Sutta*. The 'Discourse on the Foundations of Mindfulness' (*Satipatthana Sutta*) occurs twice in Buddhist Scriptures: (1) as the 10th Discourse of Middle Collection of Discourses (*Majjhima Nikaya*), (2) as the 22nd Discourse of the Long Collections of Discourses (*Digha Nikaya*). In the second version, it is called *Maha-Satipatthana Sutta* ('Maha' means great) and differs from the first version only by a detailed treatment of the Four Noble Truths (Conze, 1959; Nyanaponika, 1962, 1996; Saddhatissa, 1971; Rahula, 1974; Soma, 1981; Narada, 1988; Sayadaw, 1990, 1999; Piyadassi, 1991; Nanamoli, 1998; Gunaratana, 2002; Thanissaro, 2004; Goenka, 2006; Analayo, 2007).

The elaboration of four foundations of mindfulness 'seem to be a direct outcome of Buddha's awakening.' In the opening and concluding sections of Satipatthana Sutta, Buddha himself has declared it to be the *direct path* to liberation (Analayo, 2007, pp. 16–17). Underscoring its universal importance, Buddha has observed, 'Mindfulness, I declare, is helpful everywhere' (cited in Khantipalo, 2006, 1986, p. 8).

The Buddha described *sati* as the *ability to remember,* to be aware of what one is doing in the movements of the body, in the movements of mind:

> And what is the faculty of sati? There is the case where a monk, a disciple of the noble ones, is mindful, highly meticulous, remembering & able to call to mind even things that were done & said long ago. He remains focused on the body in & of itself—ardent, alert, & mindful—putting aside greed & distress with reference to the world. He remains focused on feelings in & of themselves . . . the mind in & of itself . . . mental qualities in & of themselves—ardent, alert, & mindful—putting aside greed & distress with reference to the world.
>
> (SN 48:10, trans. *by Thanissaro Bhikkhu)*

Although the Pali word 'sati' originally meant 'memory' or 'remembrance,' in its general Buddhist usage, it has been mostly employed to denote a certain quality of 'attentiveness' or 'awareness' of the present that the Buddhist doctrine specifies as 'good,' 'wholesome,' 'skillful,' or 'right.' It is not just the 'bare attention' that is referred to here; rather, it is the 'appropriate' or 'wholesome' attention, denoted by the Pali word *yonisomaniskara.* Buddhist psychology identifies three 'unwholesome' roots of mind: greed, hatred, and ignorance. If our attention emanates from any of these three unwholesome roots, it is not 'appropriate' and will not give us the knowledge of reality as it truly is. Used in this sense, it is called *samma-sati* or Right Mindfulness and forms the seventh factor of the Noble Eightfold Path (Nyanaponika, 1962, 1996, pp. 9–10).

The *Satipatthana Sutta* (Sanskrit: Sutra) is divided into four sections that list 'four foundations of mindfulness'—the four spheres in which to develop mindfulness—as follows (Conze, 1959; Harvey, 1990; Piyadassi, 1991; Bodhi, 2000a; Nyanatiloka, 2000; Goenka, 2006; Analayo, 2007):

- Contemplation of the Body: *proceeds from mindfulness of*
    - Breathing, postures, and bodily activities to
    - Analysis of the body into its anatomical parts to develop disenchantment and concludes with
    - Series of 'Cemetery Meditations' to underscore 'impermanence'
- Contemplation of the Feelings: *through mindfulness*
    - Developing understanding and detachment regarding:
        - Pleasant, unpleasant, and neutral feelings
    - Developing insight into their 'fleeting' nature and
    - Overcoming three defilements of attachment, aversion, and delusion
- Contemplation of the States of Mind: mindfulness regarding different
    - Moods and Emotions as they arise and pass away

- Contemplation of the Mental Objects: such as
    - Five Hindrances: sensual desire, ill-will, dullness and drowsiness, restlessness and worry, and doubt
    - Five Aggregates: form, feelings, perceptions, mental states, and consciousness
    - Six Sense Spheres: eye and visible forms, ear and sounds, nose and odors, tongue and tastes, body and body impressions, mind and mind objects
    - Seven Factors of Enlightenment: mindfulness, investigation-of-dhammas, energy, joy, tranquility, concentration, and equanimity
    - Four Noble Truths: the truth regarding the reality of suffering, the cause of suffering, the cessation of suffering, and the path leading to the cessation of suffering

As is clear from the above classification, we start with the contemplation of the body—the first sphere of mindfulness—and move to the contemplation of the next three spheres—the spheres of the mind. We begin with the body because it is our most immediate experience and is most 'accessible to us.' From body, we proceed to the contemplation of feelings and note their emotive and ethical qualities. As Harvey (1990, p. 255) has noted:

> Once mindfulness of body is established, attention is turned to feelings. They are observed as they arise and pass away, noting simply whether they are pleasant, unpleasant, or neutral, born of the body or of the mind. No significance is attached to them; however, they are viewed simply as passing phenomenon.

Then we move to observe the fleeting phenomenon of mind and mind objects. To quote Harvey (1990, p. 255) again, 'Finally, mindfulness investigates *dhammas*, such as the five hindrances or seven factors of enlightenment, noting when they are present, when they are absent, how they come to arise, and how they come to cease.'

Speaking of the flexible and interrelation of the *Satipatthana* contemplations, Analayo (2007, p. 269) has observed:

> In actual practice, the different contemplations described in the discourse can be combined in a variety of ways and it would be a misunderstanding to take the progression in the discourse as prescribing the only possible sequence for the development of *satipatthana*.

Alchemy of mindfulness of breathing (Anapanasati)

The basic Buddhist practice here is the practice of being mindful of our breathing. It is said that proper breathing is more important than food. In the practice of yoga also, proper breathing holds a special place. In fact, breath provides the conscious connection between our body and our mind. It is a common knowledge that when we are agitated, we breathe differently than when we are calm and relaxed. Our breath has a wonderful capacity to help us awaken to complete awareness (Rosenberg, 2005).

Henepola Gunaratana, the author of a modern meditation classic, *Mindfulness in Plain English*, recommends to 'start with focusing your undivided attention on your breathing to gain some degree of basic concentration' (2002, p. 45). Accordingly, the following pages will describe the practice of mindfulness of breathing in greater detail. The 118 discourse of Majjhima Nikaya called *Anapanasati Sutta* is perhaps the 'most comprehensive single discourse on the subject' (Nanamoli, 1998, p. vi). The following excerpts present the basics of Anapanasati in the words of the Sutta (Nanamoli, 1998):

> Respiration-mindfulness, bhikkhus, developed and repeatedly practised, is of great fruit, of great benefit; respiration-mindfulness, bhikkhus, developed and repeatedly practised, perfects the four foundations of mindfulness; the four foundations of mindfulness, developed and repeatedly practised, perfect the seven enlightenment factors; the seven enlightenment factors, developed and repeatedly practised, perfect clear vision and deliverance.
>
> And how developed, bhikkhus, how repeatedly practised, is respiration-mindfulness of great fruit, of great benefit?
>
> Here, bhikkhus, a bhikkhu, gone to the forest, or to the root of a tree, or to an empty place, sits down; having folded his legs crosswise, set his body erect, established mindfulness in front of him, ever mindful he breathes in, mindful he breathes out.
>
> (i) Breathing in long, he knows, 'I breathe in long'; or breathing out long, he knows, 'I breathe out long.'
> (ii) Breathing in short, he knows, 'I breathe in short'; or breathing out short, he knows, 'I breathe out short.'
> (iii) 'Experiencing the whole body (of breath), I shall breathe in,' thus he trains himself; 'experiencing the whole body, I shall breathe out,' thus he trains himself.
> (iv) 'Calming the bodily formation, I shall breathe in,' thus he trains himself; 'calming the bodily formation,' I shall breathe out, thus he trains himself. (p. 5)

Regarding the simplicity of mindfulness of breathing, Bhikkhu Bodhi (2000a, p. 85) explains:

> The meditation requires no special intellectual sophistication, only awareness of the breath. One merely breathes naturally through the nostrils keeping the breath in mind at the contact point around the nostrils or upper lip, where the sensation of breath can be felt as the air moves in and out. There should be no attempt to control the breath or to force it into predetermined rhythms, only a mindful contemplation of the natural process of breathing in and out. The awareness of breath cuts through the complexities of discursive thinking, rescues us from pointless wandering in the labyrinth of vain imaginings, and grounds us solidly in the present. For whenever we become aware of breathing, really aware of it, we can be aware of it only in the present, never in the past or the future.

Here is the basic practice of mindfulness of breathing, in the words of Rahula (1974, p. 70):

> Breathe in and out as usual, without any effort or strain. Now, bring your mind on your breathing-in and breathing-out; let your mind be aware and observe your breathing in and breathing out ... Your mind should be so concentrated on your breathing that you are aware of its movements and changes. Forget all other

> things, your surroundings, your environment; do not raise your eyes or look at anything. Try to do this for five or ten minutes.

After some practice, we are assured, we develop a 'knack' for being mindful so that we can extend this awareness to all spheres of our life. Whatever we happen to be doing—eating, washing dishes, walking, etc.—at the moment, we should try to become fully aware and mindful of the act we are performing at the moment. This is called living in the present moment, in the present action. When informed about the English saying about *killing two birds with one stone*, Suzuki Roshi, a modern Soto Zen Master, is reported to have said: 'In Zen, our way is: One Bird, One Stone.'

Vipassana: insight meditation

As noted above, mindfulness of breathing occupies a prominent place in the practice of calm and insight meditation. Although each religious tradition has some form of serenity meditation as a part of its spiritual repertoire, the practice of insight meditation is the distinctive contribution of Buddhism to the spiritual heritage of the world. Mindfulness of breathing is employed in both Calm meditation and Insight meditation with different purpose and emphasis. In Calm meditation, the purpose of employing mindfulness is to gain a certain measure of clarity and serenity of mind through the power of concentration. However, in Insight meditation, concentration achieved through mindfulness of breathing is employed in a more analytical manner to gain an insight into the very nature of the phenomenon, i.e., seeing reality in the light of three signs of existence, namely: impermanence, unsatisfactoriness, and not-self.

Bhikkhu Bodhi (2000a) clarifies:

> Mindfulness facilitates the achievement of both serenity and insight. It can lead to either deep concentration or wisdom, depending on the mode in which it is applied. . . . To lead to the stages of serenity the primary chore of mindfulness is to keep the mind on the object, free from straying. . . . To lead to insight and the realizations of wisdom, mindfulness is exercised in a more differentiated manner. Its task, in this phase of practice, is to observe, to note, and to discern phenomena with utmost precision until their fundamental characteristics are brought to light.
>
> *(pp. 78–79)*

Insight meditation refers to analytical meditation that is practiced to gain direct insight into the very nature of ultimate reality. It means 'understanding things as they really are, that is seeing the impermanent, unsatisfactory, and non-substantial (non-self) nature of five aggregates of clinging' (Piyadassi, 1991, p. 229). In an important passage of *Samyutta-nikaya* iii 44 (Connected Discourses), the Buddha explains it thus:

> The five aggregates, monks, are impermanent (*anicca*); whatever is impermanent, that is *dukkha*, unsatisfactory; that is without self (*anatta*), that is not mine, that I am not, that is not myself. Thus should it be seen by perfect wisdom (sammappannaya) as it really is. He who sees by perfect wisdom as it really is, his mind not grasping, is detached from taints, he is liberated.
>
> *(Piyadassi, 1991, p. 231)*

So what is the purpose of gaining this insight into the real nature of things? How does a person benefit from this hard-won understanding? In the words of the recurring refrain of *Satipatthana Sutta*, the Buddha assures, thus: 'He lives independent, clinging to nothing in the world' (Analayo, 2007, pp. 3–13).

In the opening and concluding section of the *Satipatthana Sutta*, the Discourse on the Foundations of Mindfulness, the Buddha emphatically declares:

> This is the only way, monks, for the purification of beings, for the overcoming of sorrow and lamentation, for the destruction of pain and grief, for reaching the right path, for the attainment of Nibbana, namely the four foundations of mindfulness.
>
> *(Nynaponika, 1968, p. 7)*

The cultivation of mindfulness has been extolled as the key meditative practice—the 'heart of Buddhist meditation' or even the 'heart of the entire Doctrine' (Nyanaponika, 1962, 1996, p. 7)—leading to enlightenment and liberation. Buddha himself declared the four foundations—*satipatthanas*—of mindfulness as the *direct path to realization*. The ultimate aim of Satipatthana is nothing less than final liberation from samsara—the cyclic rounds of births and deaths perpetuated by our own desire-induced actions. Buddhists believe that 'for a proper understanding and implementation of mindfulness meditation, the original instructions by the Buddha on *Satipatthana* need to be taken into consideration' (Analayo, 2007, p. 1).

The anatomy of *right* mindfulness

Nyanaponika Thera, the German-born Buddhist scholar-monk, who along with Thich Nhat Hanh, is most responsible for raising awareness about mindfulness in the West, has explained right mindfulness as comprising two aspects: (1) bare attention and (2) clear comprehension. As bare attention, mindfulness refers to the 'clear and single-minded awareness of what actually happens to us and in us, at the successive moments of perception' (Nynaponika, 1968, p. 30). However, as the Theravada Buddhist scholar-monk Bhikkhu Bodhi (2006) has noted, the 'bare attention is never completely bare' and that the 'context and intention one brings to practice and how one practices are very important.' What bare attention really implies, according to Bodhi, is that we have removed our habitual 'emotional reactions, evaluations, judgments, and conceptual overlays.' Clear comprehension, according to Nyanaponika, is the right knowledge or wisdom, based on right attentiveness. Thus, 'Satipatthana, in the entirety of both of its aspects produces in human mind a perfect harmony or *receptivity* and *activity*' (Nyanaponika, 1962, 1996, pp. 55–56; italics in the original).

Thanissaro Bhikkhu (1987), a modern Theravada scholar-monk trained in the Thai Forest Tradition, has observed that the popular books on meditation assign so many meanings to the word mindfulness that 'the poor word gets totally stretched out of shape' and warns us 'not to load the word mindfulness with too many meanings or to assign it too many functions.' Thanissaro Bhikkhu (2008) further reminds us to always remember that mindfulness is a part of the larger path mapped by the Buddha leading up to the final goal of liberation from existential suffering. The fourfold foundations of mindfulness constitute only a part (7th factor) of this path called the Noble Eightfold Path. Buddhists believe that all eight factors of the path should be simultaneously cultivated to reach the goal of full enlightenment. The Buddhist path, according to Goleman (1988), begins with mindfulness, proceeds through insight, and culminates in Nirvana.

Is mindfulness a cognitive state of mind?

Ellen Langer (1989), a Harvard social psychologist, has adopted the term mindfulness in the cognitive sense to denote a state of alertness and lively awareness that is the opposite of 'mindlessness.' Langer (2000, pp. 1–2) describes mindfulness as a process of 'drawing novel distinctions' or 'noticing new things,' which can lead to a number of outcomes, including (1) a greater sensitivity to one's environment, (2) more openness to new information, (3) the creation of new categories for structuring perception, and (4) enhanced awareness of multiple perspectives in problem-solving. The hallmarks of this mindful condition, according to Carson and Langer (2006, p. 30) are: (1) ability to view both objects and situations from multiple perspectives, and (2) the ability to shift perspectives depending upon context. The first felt experience of mindfulness in essence is nothing short of awakening. Almost in the vein of Buddhist masters, Langer (2005, p. 16) observes insightfully: 'It's only after we've been awakened that we realize how much of our lives we've actually slept through.' Langer's research shows that when we are mindful, we are seen as charismatic, genuine, and authentic by those around us. *This observation points to the potential role of mindfulness in life and leadership.*

Langer (1989) likens the mindful state to

> living in a transparent house.... When in the living room, we can still see the object in the basement even if we chose not to think about it or use it at the moment. If we were taught mindfully, conditionally, we could be in this ever-ready state of mind.
>
> *(p. 201)*

Langer's description of the subjective 'feel' of mindfulness—as 'a heightened state of involvement and wakefulness or being in the present'—is very much in line with the Buddhist conception of mindfulness. Clearly, Langer's work is not based on a conscious link to Buddhism. As Carson and Langer (2006, p. 30) note: 'The cognitive state of mindfulness is distinct from the Buddhist tradition of mindfulness, although post-meditative states may indeed be mindful in the cognitive sense.' She agrees that the end result of both approaches —mindfulness as a cognitive state or mindfulness as a meditative practice—may very well be the same. In an interview conducted for this chapter, Langer (2009) opined: 'It is amazing that all you need to do is to notice new things and you get all the same effects that you will get from years and years of meditating.'

Langer's studies of mindfulness with relevance to social issues fall in three major categories: health, business, and education. Langer and her research associates conducted several investigations in elderly populations and found that mindful treatments had dramatic effects, such as decreased arthritis pain and alcoholism and increased life span (Langer, 1989). In the cognitive-behavior therapy realm, mindfulness fosters a state of self-acceptance since it encompasses an attitude of acceptance of and exploration of present experience rather than of self-evaluation and self-criticism (Carson & Langer, 2006, p. 31). Similarly, Langer's studies of mindfulness in the business context have shown that increases in mindfulness are associated with increased creativity and decreased burnout. For Langer, the capacity for mindfulness involves the development of a 'limber state of mind' (p. 70) and always remaining aware that the 'various possible perspectives will never be exhausted' (p. 69).

Langer believes that mindful, creative activities hold the key to living meaningful, fulfilled lives. In her book titled *On Becoming an Artist: Reinventing Yourself Through Mindful Creativity*, Langer (2005, p. xxi), backed by her landmark scientific work on mindfulness and artists' nature, shows us that 'leading a more mindful and rewarding life is readily available to anyone who can put evaluation aside and just engage in new, creative endeavors.' Langer defines creativity in terms of mindfulness—*the art of noticing new things* (2014); she approaches creativity in its most pragmatic sense; and she highlights the fact that creative activities hold the key to living meaningful, fulfilled lives.

Applications of mindfulness

The term 'mindfulness' has come to be used in a variety of ways and contexts in the modern times. Starting as a meditation technique more than 2,500 years ago, mindfulness has found its way in recent times into universities, schools, hospitals, health clinics, prison houses, wellness centers, police departments, government offices, law firms, corporate boardrooms, and other organizations.

Mindfulness-based stress reduction (MBSR)

MBSR is one of the original standardized programs for mindfulness meditation and remains 'the most frequently cited method of mindfulness training in clinical literature' (Baer, 2003, p. 123). The MBSR program, derived from Buddhist meditative practices but adapted to secular context, was originally developed as a stress reduction and pain management technique at the University of Massachusetts (UMass) Medical School during the early 1980s by Jon Kabat-Zinn and his colleagues. It is generally conducted as an eight-week course in which the participants meet for two to two and a half hours for instruction in mindfulness and various coping strategies. The participants are encouraged to practice these skills outside group meetings (first with the help of audio recordings) for about 45 minutes per day, six days per week. The practice (as summarized in Gilpin, 2008, p. 234) consists of two main categories:

I. Formal Practice: This comprises three distinct exercises: (a) the 'body scan', a gradual movement of attention/awareness through the body, feet up to the head, carried out while lying down; (b) 'sitting meditation', directing attention/awareness to the sensations of breathing while sitting; and (c) 'mindful movement', various slow, gentle stretches and postures designed to develop mindfulness when moving.
II. Informal Practice: This involves mindfully carrying out various everyday activities (e.g., walking, standing, and eating), the aim being to cultivate a continuity of awareness in all activities in daily life. It is this which is described as the 'heart of the practice' in MBSR, but which requires the continuing support of regular formal practice if it is to retain its ability to stabilize the mind (Kabat-Zinn, 1990, 2003)

In all the three formal practices mentioned above, mindfulness of breathing, suggests Kabat-Zinn (1990, p. 71) serves as 'a very powerful and effective anchor for all other aspects of meditative awareness.' Clearly, all of these formal practices are abstracted from the Vipassana system (as taught by S.N. Goenka based on U Ba Khin's method; particularly body scan and directing attention to body sensations in sitting meditation) and the informal practice takes its cue from Thich Nhat Hanh and his colleagues' work (1992, 2008) on mindfully carrying out daily activities with awareness of breath serving as an abiding anchor. There are, however, subtle differences (Gilpin, 2008): for example: there is 'little or no regard for the recollective aspect afforded it by the early Buddhist conception' (p. 233). Additionally, the need and the extent of the role for a preliminary degree of samadhi is unclear as well as the '[s] ubsequent development of samatha is not addressed and, therefore, seems not to be an important consideration of the [MBSR] training' (p. 235).

Kabat-Zinn (1990, pp. 33–40) describes the following seven attitudinal qualities that serve as a foundation of mindfulness practice:

1. Non-judging—Non-judging is described as a 'stance of an impartial witness to your experience' and involves 'suspending judgment and just watching *whatever* comes up, including your own judging thoughts, without pursuing them or acting on them in any way.'
2. Patience—The wisdom of patience involves an understanding and acceptance of the fact that things can only unfold in their own time.
3. Beginner's mind—Beginner's mind reminds us of the simple truth that each moment and experience is unique with unique possibilities. It involves a willingness to see everything as if for the first time. This perspective prevents us from getting stuck in the rut of our own expertise and brings freshness, clarity, and vitality to our experience in each moment rather than seeing things through a fog of preconceptions.
4. Trust—Developing a basic faith in one's intrinsic goodness and wisdom and in the validity of one's own thoughts, feelings, and intuition. The practice of mindfulness fosters trust in one's own being and thereby makes it easier for us to trust others.
5. Non-striving—Non-striving is 'having no goal other than for you to be yourself' as you currently are. In the meditative domain, says Kabat-Zinn, the best way to achieve your own goals is to back off from striving for results and instead start focusing carefully on seeing and accepting things as they are, moment by moment.
6. Acceptance—Acceptance here refers to an openness and willingness to see things as they actually are in the present moment, which sets the stage for acting appropriately in one's life under all circumstances. Acceptance, however, does not mean passive resignation to one's circumstances or conditions, nor does it mean to like everything or to abandon our values or principles.
7. Letting go—'Letting go is the way of letting things be, of accepting things as they are.' This attitude of non-attachment to both our pleasant and unpleasant feelings is the key to a successful mindfulness practice. Through mindfulness we can develop our ability to acknowledge the arising and passing of experience without becoming entangled in the content of it.

Mindfulness in the workplace

It has been said that the 'order or confusion of society corresponds to and follows the order or confusion of individual minds' (Nyanaponika, 1962, 1996, p. 22). The modern civilization which excels in 'manufacturing irrelevances'—to use a phrase coined by Aldous Huxley—has splendidly managed to shorten our attention span through myriad trivial pursuits geared toward instant satisfaction. In this age of 'continuous partial attention,' and in our 'TV-oriented and movie drenched carnival culture,' mindfulness has a great potential role to play in developing clarity through attentiveness and in sharpening the power of concentration by ensuring immunity from distraction, delusion, and discursive thoughts.

The practice of mindfulness accords greater value and presence to the activity at hand and thereby enhances our performance of the task and the resultant fulfillment.

Many business leaders and writers have acknowledged the benefits of meditative practice both in their personal as well as professional lives (Marturano, 2015; Chapman-Clarke, 2016; Steinhouse, 2017). 'Meditation has been integral in my career; it is the single best thing that happened to me in terms of my leadership,' says Bill George, the ex-CEO of Medtronics Inc., who also sits on the supervisory boards of Goldman Sachs Group Inc., Exxon Mobil Corp., and Novartis AG, and is a professor of management practices at Harvard Business School. The owner of the world's most popular Internet search engine, Google Inc., has had regular meditation sits for the past two years at its London, Pittsburgh, Mountain View, California, Sydney, and New York locations. In addition, the company in October 2007 initiated a 'search inside yourself' meditation and mindfulness course (Brandt, 2008).

In addition to Google, corporations such as Hughes Aircraft and Deutsche Bank have introduced meditation classes for their employees. Given the psychological pressures and the current financial state of the American economy, meditation, according to Brandt (2008, p. 2), in corporate America is more than an expression of an executive's goodwill or personal interest. Companies lose an estimated $300 billion annually to lowered productivity, absenteeism, health care, and related costs stemming from stress, according to a study by the American Institute of Stress. Stress-related ailments account for upwards of 60 percent of all doctor visits, according to the study.

In an informative brochure for annual retreats organized by the Center for Mindfulness in Medicine, Health Care, and Society, University of Massachusetts Medical School, aiming to bring awareness and insight to the business of life and life of business, Kabat-Zinn (2009) reminds us that

> in this era of mounting fluidity, uncertainty, and rapid change, against the backdrop of an increasing recognition of the interconnectedness and interdependence of the global marketplace and the global village, a deep grounding in mindfulness can help build more coherent, cohesive, and effective communities of purpose and value within the work environment. It can also lead to an improved climate for problem identification and problem solving, and wiser and more effective policy decisions, thus making work more satisfying, both for ourselves and for those with whom we work.

Mindfulness, for Kabat-Zinn (2009), is about 'being fully awake in our lives' to gain an 'immediate access to our own powerful inner resources for insight, transformation, and healing.' Mindfulness meditation is not for the faint-hearted, reminds Kabat-Zinn to his participants during a five-day intensive retreat for leaders and innovators: 'It is for individuals interested in the adventure and challenges of self-exploration and transformation, for those who wish to taste and explore new ways of knowing and new ways of being.' For individuals who are immersed in the warp and woof of the business of life as well as the life of business, mindfulness can give rise to greater insight and clarity, as well as greater empathy for oneself and others and can help us be more in touch with our own deepest and most trustworthy moral and ethical instincts, reminding us and grounding us in what is most important in our own lives.

Participants come away more focused, calmer, and inspired. Says one participant: 'My experience was profound. I came away more deeply committed to the practice of mindfulness because both intuitively and experientially I know it significantly enhances all aspects of my life.' Another participant describes its value in all walks of life:

> I find myself constantly going back to that place of comfort and tranquility I discovered through the Retreat. Wherever I am—during a stressful work day, waiting in a traffic jam, or any time I feel pulled in different directions—I know that I can go on 'retreat' and touch base with my being in a way that makes my life more healthy, happy, and productive.
>
> *(Power of Mindfulness Retreat with Jon Kabat-Zinn Brochure, 2009)*

More specifically, the following benefits accrue to the participants of these retreats, as a result of mindfulness training:

- greater integration of your *doing* life with your *being* life
- increased access to emotional intelligence for work and family
- enhanced clarity and creative thinking
- deeper insight into business and social situations and their connection to wise livelihood and meaningful work
- increased energy and sense of well-being
- heightened appreciation of what is really important
- a more refined sense of how you want to be as you pursue your life's calling.

As Marturano (2009), Director of Corporate Leadership Education, Center for Mindfulness, has noted:

> As leaders practicing mindfulness, we strengthen and hone the ability to see the big picture and selectively focus attention—to listen deeply and learn to respond rather than react. At the same time, mindfulness practice gives us the ability to relate in a disciplined and efficient manner to the steady stream of thoughts that can clutter the present moment and obscure the stillness from which true innovation and clear-seeing emerges.

In an explanatory study examining the effects of mindfulness on people's life, Hunter and McCormick (2009, p. 4) present their analysis of eight interviews with managers and professionals who had a meditative practice. Their initial analysis of the interviews tentatively suggests that practitioners of mindfulness

> are more accepting of their work situation; are more selfless; are less concerned with material acquisition and wealth; have a more internal locus of evaluation; are more likely to derive meaning in life from more sources than just work; are better able to cope and remain calm in difficult work situations; enjoy their work more; are more adaptable at work; and have more positive interpersonal relations at work.

These potential benefits of mindfulness are very similar to those shared by several participants of Jon Kabat-Zinn led annual retreats organized by the Center for Mindfulness in Medicine, Health Care, and Society, University of Massachusetts Medical School.

Application of mindfulness in leadership

In a video prepared by the Institute for Mindfulness in Management, Netherlands, Kabat-Zinn (2008) likens organizations to organisms and underscores the role of mindfulness in the survival of an organization:

> Mindfulness is incredibly important to organizations because organizations are like organisms; they are alive, they are made up of people and if you are not aware of the various ways in which people's mind expresses itself, then the organization can really get into some kind of mental space where no one is talking to anyone else and no one is really listening. People discount what other people are saying. So there are all sorts of examples in business as in every organization when at certain point the organization goes from being really successful to losing its way.... The kind of things people talk about when they are through this training translates into feeling in some sense more comfortable in their skin, more able to share, delegate responsibility, to trust in other people, to see the beauty in other people, to keep in mind the real purpose of the collective enterprise we call business.

Boyatzis and McKee (2005, pp. 2–4) view mindfulness as an essential element of resonant leadership and define it as the capacity to be fully aware of what is happening inside and around us. Cultivating mindfulness, according to these authors, 'is not just a nice-to-have or something to be done for private reasons: it is actually essential for sustaining good leadership.' By bringing together the fields of cognitive psychology and Buddhist philosophy, these authors are able to apply the abstract concept of mindfulness to the actual *practice* of leadership. They recommend a three-pronged regimen for cultivating mindfulness: reflection, meditative practice, and supportive relationship.

Mindfulness means being acutely awake, aware, and attentive. Boyatzis and McKee (2005, pp. 5,7) bring out the intrinsic ethical dimension of mindfulness, thus:

> When we attend to ourselves holistically, and become more fully engaged with people, our communities, and our environment, it becomes much less likely that we will do harm and more likely that we will do good.... Mindfulness, then, is both an antidote to shutting down (and creating dissonance) and also a necessary condition for creating resonance.

Much of leader's work consists of navigating the unknown and understanding the environment and people. Mindfulness plays a crucial role in both of these situations. When we are mindful, observe Boyatzis and McKee, we are more in control of ourselves and situations simply because we see reality more clearly. These authors equate developing mindfulness with developing emotional intelligence: 'When you are resonant within yourself, you can create resonance with others' (p. 28).

A new generation of business leaders is turning to mindfulness as a cutting-edge leadership tool. Consider some of the popular titles that have recently been published which suggest the application of mindfulness in the workplace and leadership arena: *Putting Buddhism to Work* (1997); *What would Buddha Do at Work* (2001); *Buddha 9 to 5* (2007); *The Art of Happiness at Work* (2003); and *Mindful Coach* (2004). And more specifically: *Mindfulness and Meaningful Work* (1994); *The Mindful Corporation* (2000); *The Mindful Leader* (2007); *The Leader's Way* (2008); and *Conscious Business* (2013). More recently: *Mindful*

Work: How Meditation Is Changing Business from the Inside Out (2015); *Leading Well from Within: A Neuroscience and Mindfulness-Based Framework for Conscious Leadership* (2016); *Mindful Management: The Neuroscience of Trust and Effective Workplace Leadership* (2016); *Leading Well: Becoming a Mindful Leader-Coach* (2017); *Mindful Business Leadership* (2017); *Mindfulness at Work: Turn your job into a gateway to joy, contentment and stress-free living (Mindful Living Series); Still Moving: How to Lead Mindful Change* (2017).

Michael Carroll, a Buddhist-trained HR executive with many years of experience in both the corporate and Zen worlds, states that 'mindfulness—learning to be fully present in the moment—can be a transformative leadership tool for gaining clarity, reducing stress, and optimizing job performance.' Carroll contends that a mindful leader demonstrates an inner authenticity that manifests itself in four marks: elegance, command, gentleness, and intelligence.

In his book *Mindful Leader: Ten Principles for Bringing out the Best in Ourselves and Others*, Carroll opines that the regular practice of mindfulness meditation can help develop ten innate leadership talents needed to revitalize our workplace: simplicity, poise, respect, courage, confidence, enthusiasm, patience, awareness, skillfulness, and humility. Developing these innate talents through mindfulness, the author believes, can lead to cultivating courage, establishing authenticity, building trust, eliminating toxicity, pursuing organizational goals mindfully, and leading with wisdom and gentleness (Carroll, 2007).

Carroll (2007, p. 2) provides the following examples of what is happening in the United States and across the world in terms of people taking the time to 'stop and sit still':

- Confronted with the distressing fact that over 60 percent of medical interns were exhibiting symptoms of severe burnout, Dr. Craig Hassad of Monash University Medical School in Melbourne, Australia, taught his doctors to meditate.
- Companies such as Raytheon, Procter & Gamble, Unilever, Nortel Networks, Comcast, and many law firms have offered their employees classes in mindfulness meditation.
- When Harvard Law School sponsored a conference of practicing attorneys to investigate why lawyers tend to get trapped in adversarial mindsets and suffer from remarkably high rates of depression, it began the conference by practicing mindfulness meditation.
- 'Protecting and Serving without Fear,' a seminar offered to law enforcement agents in Madison, Wisconsin, taught the attending police officers how to meditate.
- Executives such as Bill Ford Jr., the chairman of Ford Motor Company, Michael Stephen, the former chairman of Aetna International, Robert Shapiro, the ex-CEO of Monsanto, and Michael Rennie, the managing partner of McKinsey, meditate and consider such a practice beneficial to running a corporation.

Carroll (2007, pp. 7–8) sums up the essence of being a mindful leader:

> Learning to open up to our daily experience and discover a willingness to 'be' counterbalances our incessant drive to 'achieve'—and this ability to present in the moment is a natural wisdom that lies at the heart of being a mindful leader.

Concluding thoughts

Our modern civilization excels in 'manufacturing irrelevances' (to use Huxley's phrase). It has splendidly managed to shorten our attention span through myriad trivial pursuits geared toward instant gratification. In this age of 'continuous partial attention,' mindfulness has a great role to play in developing clarity through attentiveness and in sharpening the power of concentration by ensuring immunity from distraction and delusion. The practice of mindfulness accords greater value and presence to the activity at hand and thereby enhances our performance of the task and the resultant fulfillment.

When we carry out all activities in our usual daily life with mindfulness, with conscious presence, then every task becomes special, every act becomes a rite and a ceremony. And our whole life becomes a wondrous celebration! 'If we practice the art of mindful living,' says Thich Nhat Hanh, 'when things change, we won't have any regrets. We can smile because we have done our best to enjoy every moment of our life and to make others happy' (1998, p. 124). And in making others happy, moment to moment, we discover the true secret to our happiness!

Mindfulness has tremendous potential in enhancing workplace well-being through improved communications, efficient meetings, optimum performance, better decisions, and greater understanding. If 'change within is a prerequisite to a change without,' then mindfulness accords the best place to begin the journey of inner transformation, personally and professionally. In the ultimate analysis, one can only determine the efficacy of the practice of mindfulness by practicing it diligently. '*Ehipassiko*,' said the Buddha. 'Come and see for yourself.'

Chapter takeaways

1. Mindfulness has come to be recognized as one of the most enduring catch phrases in the recent times. Mindfulness is now being examined scientifically for stress reduction and overall happiness.
2. The research on mindfulness has shown that meditation sharpens skills like attention, memory, resilience, and emotional intelligence, competencies critical to leadership effectiveness.
3. The non-Buddhist definitions of mindfulness tend to incorporate an element of non-judgment to facilitate wider acceptance of its use. Within the Buddhist context, mindfulness almost always denotes an awareness of moment-to-moment changes that are taking place in our body and mind.
4. Calm meditation aims to provide the mind essential clarity and makes the mind serene, stable, and strong. By preparing the mind to 'see the things as they really are,' it serves as a necessary foundation for Insight meditation. Together, Calm and Insight meditation form the Buddhist path leading to the realization of final awakening or enlightenment.
5. The term 'mindfulness' has come to be used in a variety of ways and contexts in modern times. Starting as a meditation technique more than 2,500 years ago, mindfulness has found its way in recent times into universities, schools, hospitals, health clinics, prison houses, wellness centers, police departments, government offices, law firms, corporate boardrooms, and other organizations.

Reflection questions

1. What is the difference between mindfulness as defined in the early Buddhist literature and its modern secular adaptions?
2. How does mindfulness differ from ordinary forms of meditative and contemplative practices?

3. What are the most obvious applications of mindfulness for health and happiness?
4. How does mindfulness foster resilience and emotional intelligence, competencies critical to leadership effectiveness?
5. What are the challenges of implementing mindfulness in the workplace?

Notes

1 http://www.vipassana.co/research/The-Impact-of-Vipassana-in-Government

2 'Vipassana'= *vi* (accentuated) + *passana* (seeing or insight). It comes from the Sanskrit root, *pashyati*, to see. Vi-passana is right seeing or subtle seeing, a deep *insight into the essential nature of things.*

References

Analayo, V. (2007). *Satipatthana: Direct Path to Realization.* Birmingham: Windhorse Publications.

Baer, R. (2003). Mindfulness Training as A Clinical Intervention: A Conceptual and Empirical Review. *Clinical Psychology: Science and Practice, 10,* 125–143.

Bishop, S., Lau, M., Shapiro, S., Carlson, L., Anderson, N. D., Carmody, J., et al. (2004). Mindfulness: A Proposed Operational Definition.*Clinical Psychology: Science and Practice, 11,* 230–241.

Bodhi, B. (2000a). *The Noble Eightfold Path: Way to the End of Suffering.* Onalaska, WA: BPS Pariyatti First U.S. Edition.

Bodhi, B. (2000b). *The Vision of the Dhamma: Buddhist Writings of Nyanaponika Thera (Edited with Introduction).* Seattle, WA: BPS Pariyatti Editions.

Bodhi, B. (2005). *In the Buddha's Words: An Anthology of Discourses from the Pali Canon (Edited and Introduced).* Boston: Wisdom.

Bodhi B (2006). The nature of mindfulness and its role in Buddhist meditation: A correspondence between B. Alan Wallace and the Venerable Bhikkhu Bodhi: http://shamatha.org/sites/default/files/Bhikkhu_Bodhi_Correspondence.pdf

Bodhi, B. (2012). *The Numerical Discourses of the Buddha: A Complete Translation of the Anguttara Nikaya (The Teachings of the Buddha).* Boston: Wisdom.

Bodhi, B. (2016). *The Buddha's Teachings on Social and Communal Harmony: An Anthology of Discourses from the Pali Canon (The Teachings of the Buddha).* Boston: Wisdom.

Bodhi, B. (2017). *The Suttanipata: An Ancient Collection of the Buddha's Discourses Together with Its Commentaries (The Teachings of the Buddha).* Boston: Wisdom.

Boyatzis, R. & McKee, A. (2005). *Resonant Leadership: Renewing yourself and connecting with others mindfulness, hope, and compassion.* Boston: Harvard Business School Press.

Brandt, N. (2008, October 22). Wall Street Boses, Tiger Woods Meditate to Focus, Stay Calm. Bloom berg.com.

Brown, K. & Ryan, R. (2003). The Benefits of Being Present: Mindfulness and Its Role in Psychological Well-being.*Journal of Personality and Social Science, 84,* 822–848.

Burton, R. (2007). *Self-Remembering.* London: Red Wheel/Weiser.

Carrithers, M. (1988). *The Buddha.* Oxford: Oxford University Press.

Carroll, M. (2004). *Awake at Work: 35 Practical Buddhist Principles for Discovering Clarity and Balance in the midst of Work's Chaos.* Boston: Shambhala.

Carroll, M. (2007). *The Mindful Leader: Ten Principles for Bringing Out the Best in Ourselves and Others.* New York: Trumpeter.

Carroll, M. (2012). *Fearless at Work: Timeless Teachings for Awakening Confidence, Resilience, and Creativity in the Face of Life's Demands.* Shambhala.

Carson, S. & Langer, E. (2006). Mindfulness and Self-Acceptance. *Journal of Rational-Emotive & Cognitive-Behavior Therapy, 24*(1), 29–43.

Chapman-Clarke, M. (2016). *Mindfulness in the Workplace: An Evidence-based Approach to Improving Wellbeing and Maximizing Performance.* London, UK: Kogan Page.

Claxton, G. (1990). *The Heart of Buddhism: Practical Wisdom for an Agitated World.* London: HarerCollins.

Congleton, C., Britta, K., Hölzel, B. K. & Lazar, S. W. (January, 2015). Mindfulness Can Literally Change Your Brain. *Harvard Business Review.*

Conze, E. (1959). *Buddhist Meditation.* London: George Allen and Unwin Ltd.

Creswell, D. J., Taren, A. A., Lindsay, E. K., Greco, C. M., Gianaros, P. J., Fairgrieve, A., Marsland, A. L., Browne, K. W., Way, B. M., Rosen, R. K. & Ferris, J. L. (2016). Alterations in Resting-State Functional Connectivity Link Mindfulness Meditation with Reduced Interleukin-6: A Randomized Controlled Trial. *Biological Psychiatry*, *80*(1), 53–61.

Dalai Lama & Cutlter, H.C. (2003). *The Art of Happiness at Work*. New York: Riverside Books.

Dryden, W. & Still, A. (2006). Historical Aspects of Mindfulness and Self-acceptance in Psychotherapy. *Journal of Rational-Emotive & Cognitive-Behavior Therapy*, *24*(1), 3–28.

Doyle, O. (2017). *Mindfulness at Work: Turn your job into a gateway to joy, contentment and stress-free living* (Mindful Living Series).London: Orion Publishing Company.

Durant, W. (1962). *The Story of Philosophy: The Lives and Opinions of Great Philosophers*. New York: Time Incorporated.

Friedland, D. (2016). *Leading Well from Within: A Neuroscience and Mindfulness-Based Framework for Conscious Leadership*. San Diego, CA: SuperSmartHealth Publishing.

Gaytso, T. & Muyzenberg, L. (2008). *The Leader's Way*. Sydney, Australia: Nicholas Brealey Publishing Ltd.

Gethin, R. (1998). *The Foundations of Buddhism*. Oxford: Oxford University Press.

Gelles, D. (2015). *Mindful Work: How Meditation Is Changing Business from the Inside Out*. New York: Houghton Mifflin Harcourt Publishing.

Gilpin, R. (November 2008). The use of theravada buddhist practices and perspectives in mindfulness-based cognitive therapy. *Contemporary Buddhism*. *9*(2):227–251.

Gladis, S. (2017). *Leading Well: Becoming a Mindful Leader-Coach*. Annandale, VA: Steve Gladis Leadership Partners.

Goenka, S. (2006). *Mahasatipatthana Sutta*. Igatpuri: Vipassana Research Institute.

Goldstein, J. & Kornfield, J. (2001). *Seeking the Heart of Wisdom: The Path of Insight Meditation*. Boston: Shambhala.

Goleman, D. (1988). *The meditative mind: The Varieties of Meditative Experience*. New York: G.P. Putnam's Sons.

Gunaratana, H. (2002). *Mindfulness in Plain English* (Revised and Expanded ed.). Boston: Widom.

Harvey, P. (1990). *An Introduction to Buddhism* (Sixteenth Printing ed.). Cambridge: The Cambridge University Press.

Hunter, J. & McCormick (2009). Mindfulness in the Workplace: An Exploratory Study. Unpublished Manuscript.

Huxter, M. (2007). Mindfulness as Therapy from a Buddhist Perspective. In D. Einstein (Ed.), *Innovations and Advances in Cognitive Behavior Therapy* (pp. 43–55). Bowen Hills, Qld: Ausralia: Australian Academic Press.

Inoue, S. (1997). *Putting Buddhism to Work: A New Approach to Management and Business*. (D. R. Williams, Trans.). Tokyo: Kodansha International Ltd.

Jyoti, R. (2000). *Vipassana: An Art of Corporate Management*. Dhamma Giri, Igatpuri: Vipassana Research Institute.

Kabat-Zinn, J. (1990). *Full Catastrophic Living: Using the Wisdom of Your Body and Mind to Face Stress, Anxiety and Depression*. New York: Guildford Press.

Kabat-Zinn, J. (2003). Mindfulness Based Interventions in Context: Past, Present and Future. *Clinical Psychology: Scinece and Practice*, *10*, 144–156.

Kabat-Zinn, J. (2005). *Coming to Our Senses: Healing Ourselves and the World through Mindfulness*. New York: Hyperian.

Kabat-Zinn, J. (2009). *The Power of Mindfulness: A Transformative Retreat for Leaders and Innovators in Business and Non-Profit Organizations*. Boston: UMMS.

Kabat-Zinn, J. (2008). *Mindfulness and Leadership*. [DVD featuring Jon Kabat-Zinn]. Netherlands: Institute for Mindfulness in Management.

Kadloubovsky, E. & Palmer, G. E. (1979). *Writings from the Philokalia on Prayer of the Heart*. London: Faber and Faber.

Keeva, S. (2004). A Mindful Law Practice. *ABA Journal*, *90*, 78–79.

Kehoe, D. A. (2016). *Mindful Management: The Neuroscience of Trust and Effective Workplace Leadership*. Ontario, Canada: Communicate For Life Ltd.

Khantipalo, B. (2006, 1986). *Practical Advice for Meditators*. Kandy, Sri Lanka: Buddhist Publication Society.

Kofman, F. (2013). *Conscious Business: How to Build Value through Values*. MI: Sounds True Incorporated. Reprint edition.

Krishnamurti, J. (2002). *Meditations*. Boston: Shambhala.

Kulananda and Houlder, D. J.. (2002). *Mindfulness and Money: The Buddhist Path to Abundance*. New York: Broadway Books.

Langer, E. (1989). *Mindfulness*. New York: Addison-Wesley.

Langer, E. & Moldoveanu, M. (2000). The Construct of Mindfulness. *Journal of Social Issues*. 56. 1–9.10.1111/0022-4537.00148.

Langer, E. (2000b). The Construct of Mindfulness. *Journal of Social Issues*, *56*(1), 1–9.

Langer, E. (2005). *On Becoming an Artist: Reinventing Yourself Through Mindful Creativity*. New York: Ballantine Books.

Langer, E. (2009, April 5). Personal Interview with the Author. Unpublished Transcripts.

Langer, E. (2014 March). Mindfulness in the Age of Complexity: Spotlight Interview with Ellen Langer by Alison Beard. *Harvard Business Review*, 1–7.

Ludwig, D. & Kabat-Zinn, J. (2008). Mindfulness in Medicine. *JAMA*, *300*(11), 1350–1352.

Marturano, J. (2009). Personal Interview with the Author. Unpublished Transcripts.

Marturano, J. (2015). *Finding the Space to Lead: A Practical Guide to Mindful Leadership*. New York: Bloomsbury Press.

Merton, T. (2004). *The Wisdom of the Desert: Sayings from the Desert Fathers of the Fourth Century*. Boston: Shambhala.

Metcalf, F. & Hateley, B. G. (2001). *What Would Buddha Do at Work: 101 Answers to Workplace Dilemmas*. Berkeley, California: Seastone and Berrett-Koehler Publishers, Inc.

Nakai, P. & Schultz, R. (2000). *The Mindful Corporation: Liberating the Human Spirit at Work*. Long Beach, California: Leadership Press.

Nanamoli, B. (1992, 2001). *The Life of The Buddha: According to the Pali Canon*. Seattle, WA: BPS Pariyatti Editions.

Nanamoli, B. (1998). *Mindfulness of Breathing: Buddhist Texts from the Pali Canon and Commnentaries (Translated)*. Kandy, Sri Lanka: Buddhist Publication Society.

Nanamoli, B. (2003, Reprint ed.). *The Path of Purification: Visuddhimagga*. New York: Pariyatti Publishing; 1st BPE Pariyatti Ed edition).

Narada, T. (1988). *The Buddha and His Teachings*. Kuala Lumpur, Malaysia: Buddhist Missionary Society.

Nhat Hahn, T. & Vriezen, W. (2008). *Mindful Movements: Mindfulness Exercises Developed by Thich Nhat Hanh and the Plum Village Sangha*. Berkeley: Parallax Press.

Nhat Hanh, T. (1992). *The Miracle of Mindfulness: A Manual on Mindfulness*. Boston: Beacon Press.

Nhat Hanh, T. (1998). *The Heart of the Buddha's Teaching: Transforming Suffering into Peace, Joy & Liberation: The Four Noble Truths, the Noble Eightfold Path, & Other Basic Buddhist Teachings*. Berkeley: Parallax Press.

Nyanaponika, T. (1962, 1996). *The Heart of Buddhist Meditation: A Handbook of Mental Training Based on Buddha's Way of Mindfulness*. London: Ryder & Company.

Nyanatiloka, T. (2000). *The Buddha's Path to Deliverance: A Systematic Exposition in the Words of Sutta Pitaka* (Fifth ed.). Kandy, Sri Lanka: Buddhist Publication Society.

Nynaponika, T. (1968). *The Power of Mindfulness*. Kandy, Sri Lanka: Buddhist Publication Society.

Ouspenksy, P. (1973). *The Psychology of Man's Possible Evolution*. New York: Vintage.

Parihar, D. R. (2004). *Impact of Vipassana in Government: A Research Report*. Igatpuri, Maharashtra, India: Vipassana Research Institute.

Pascoe, M. C., Thompson, D. R., Jenkins, Z. M. & Ski, C. F. (2017). Mindfulness Mediates the Physiological Markers of Stress: Systematic Review and Meta-analysis. *Journal of Psychiatric Research*, *95*, 156–178.

Piyadassi, M. (1991). *The Spectrum of Buddhism: Writings of Piyadassi*. Taipei, Taiwan: The Corporate Body of the Buddha Educational Foundation.

Piyadassi, T. (2005). *Buddha's Ancient Path*. Bombay: Munshiram Manoharlal Publishers.

Rahula, W. (1974). *What the Buddha Taught* (Revised and Expanded ed.). New York: Grove Press.

Roland, D. (2017). *Still Moving: How to Lead Mindful Change*. Malden, MA: Wiley-Blackwell.

Rosenberg, L. (2005). *Breath by Breath: The Liberating Practice of Insight Meditation*. Boston: Shambhala.

Saddhatissa, H. (1971). *The Buddha's Way*. London: George Allen and Unwin Ltd.

Sangharakshita. (2000). *A Survey of Buddhism: Its Doctrines and Methods Through the Ages*. Birmingham: Windhorse Publications.

Sayadaw, L. (1999). *Manual of Mindfulness of Breathing.* (U. S. Tun, Trans.). Kandy, Sri Lanka: Buddhist Publication Society.

Sayadaw, M. (1990). *Satipatthana Vipassana: Insight through Mindfulness.* Kandy, Sri Lanka: Buddhist Publication Society.

Seppala, E. (December 2015). How Meditation Benefits CEOs. *Harvard Business Review.*

Shah, I. (2004). *The Way of the Sufi.* London: Octagon Press.

Shapiro, S. & Carlson, L. (2009). *The Art and Science of Mindfulness: Integrating Mindfulness into Psychology and the Helping Professions.* NE, Washington, DC: American Psychological Association (APA).

Silsbee, D. (2004) *Mindful Coach: Seven Roles for Helping People Grow.* New York: Ivy River Press.

Soma, T. (1981). *The Way of Mindfulness.* (T. Soma, Trans.). Kandy, Sri Lanka: Buddhist Publication Society.

Spears, N. (2007). *Buddha: 9 to 5: The Eightfold Path to Enlightening Your Workplace and Improving your Bottom Line.* Avon, Massachusegtts: Adams Media.

Steinhouse, R. (2017). *Mindful Business Leadership.* Abingdon, UK: Routledge.

Still, A. (2005). Introduction. *Journal of Rational-Emotive & Cognitive-Behavior Therapy, 23* (2)1–5.

Thanissaro, B. (1987). *Mindfulness Defined.* Available at www.Accesstoinsight.com.

Thanissaro, B. (1996). *The Wings to Awakening: An Anthology from the Pali Canon.* Barre, MA: Barre Center for Buddhist Studies.

Thanissaro, B. (2004). *Handful of Leaves: An Anthology from Dighya and Majjhima Nikayas.* Boston: The Sati Center for Buddhist Studies.

Thanissaro, B. (2008). Mindfulness defined. Available at: https://www.accesstoinsight.org/lib/authors/thanissaro/mindfulnessdefined.html

Van den Muyzenberg, L. (2009). *The Leader's Way: Business, Buddhism and Happiness in an Interconnected World.* London, UK: Nicholas Brealey Publishing.

Weick, K. E. & Putnam, T. (2006). Organizing for Mindfulness: Eastern Wisdom and Western Knowledge. *Journal of Management Inquiry, 15*(3), 275–288.

Whitmyer, C. (Ed.). (1994). *Mindfulness and Meaningful Work: Explorations in Right Livelihood.* Berkeley, California: Parallax Press.

Wilber, K. (2000). *Integral Psychology: Consciousness, Spirit, Psychology, Therapy.* Boston: Shambhala.

Williams, M., Teasdale, J. & Segal, Z. (2007). *The Mindful Way through Depression: Freeing Yourself from Chronic Unhappiness.* New York: The Guilford Press.

Williams, M., Teasdale, J., Segal, Z., & Kabat-Zinn, J. (2007). *The Mindful Way Through Depression: Freeing Yourself from Chronic Unhappiness.* New York: The Guilford Press.

2

WORKPLACE MINDFULNESS THEORY AND RESEARCH IN REVIEW

A call for temporal investigations

Jared Weintraub and Scott B. Dust

Stop. Take a deep breath in through your nose and slowly count to ten. Now, slowly exhale and count down from ten to one, allowing yourself to become more and more relaxed. Now, try this again with your eyes closed. Do you feel more relaxed? Research suggests that doing exercises like this for ten minutes or more a day could reduce stress, reduce turnover intentions, improve social relationships, performance, and other positive outcomes for work and at home (Baer, 2003; Glomb, Yang, Bono, & Duffy, 2011; Hafenbrack et al., 2019; Hyland, Lee, & Mills, 2015; Klatt, Buckworth, & Malarkey, 2009; Mesmer-Magnus, Manapragada, Viswesvaran, & Allen, 2017).

Mindfulness, or a state of "being attentive to and aware of what is taking place in the present" (Brown & Ryan, 2003, p. 822), has gained immense popularity since Kabat-Zinn's (1982) seminal work brought the construct into the public consciousness. While Hyland et al. (2015) and Glomb et al. (2011) note the millions of links and thousands of articles, books, etc., related to mindfulness, Hyland et al. (2015) mention that at the time of their article, the construct's popularity had been mostly overlooked by the industrial and organizational psychology literature. However, a Google Scholar (n.d.) search for "mindfulness" and "work" or "jobs" from 2015 to the present found 18,600 results. With the exponential growth in popularity of the construct in the work domain, it is essential to take a step back and evaluate the current state of the literature and discuss fruitful avenues for future research.

Along these lines, in this chapter we outline: (a) how it is measured; (b) its relationships with related constructs in its nomological network; (c) how it can be applied in the workplace; (d) its likely effects in the workplace; and (e) what researchers and practitioners alike should now be evaluating to move the conversation forward. As will soon be discussed, our primary recommendation is that scholars begin to consider mindfulness as one of many cognitive states, and that to fully understand its implications, we must evaluate how it relates to other cognitive states in an ongoing stream of consciousness. Said another way, it is important to evaluate mindfulness from a temporal perspective.

The roots and definitions of mindfulness

Mindfulness, as most Westerners know it, has its roots in Buddhism, a tradition which encourages followers to be intently aware and to live in the now (Glomb et al., 2011; Thera, 1998). Buddhism, however, does not hold exclusive rights to the concept. In fact, Christianity, Islam, and Hinduism all have contemplative practices which can be considered conceptually similar to mindfulness (Hyland et al., 2015). However, mindfulness itself is not inherently religious (Glomb et al., 2011).

As briefly mentioned, the popularization of mindfulness in a secular context can mostly be attributed to the work of Jon Kabat-Zinn (1982). Kabat-Zinn founded the Stress Reduction Clinic at the University of Massachusetts Medical Center (Ellis, 2006). There, he created a treatment regimen for his patients suffering from chronic pain or incurable disease called Mindfulness-Based Stress Reduction (MBSR). This initial work by Kabat-Zinn focuses on developing and practicing mindfulness using different forms of meditation and yoga (Kabat-Zinn, 1996).

MBSR has been completed by over 24,000 people and has been featured in countless popular media outlets such as CNN, NBC, CBS, etc. ("History of MBSR," 2016). Initially, it was developed as an eight-week, in-person course ("MBSR Courses," 2016). Currently, participants can take the original in-person course, an eight-week online course, a self-paced video program, or an in-person five-day residential retreat ("MBSR Courses," 2016). These programs range from $200 to $650, depending on the type of class ("MBSR Courses," 2016).

Kabat-Zinn's conceptualization of mindfulness has an emphasis on meditation. While meditation and mindfulness are often intertwined, Brown and Ryan (2003) suggest that meditation is not necessary for fostering a state of present-moment attention. Further, others conceptualize mindfulness as not only being present, but being attentive to and aware of the events happening around us (Dane, 2011; Giluk, 2009; Narayanan & Moynihan, 2006; Weick & Sutcliffe, 2006).

While many of the world's most prominent organizations such as Google, Aetna, General Mills, and the U.S. Military have implemented mindfulness programs (Hyland et al., 2015), these nuanced conceptualizations create confusion for scholars and practitioners alike. In fact, Dane (2011) documented 11 definitions of the construct by prominent authors. Such definitions include: "A receptive attention to and awareness of present-moment events and experience" (Brown, Ryan, & Creswell, 2007, p. 12), "Paying attention in a particular way: on purpose, in the present moment, and nonjudgmentally" (Jon Kabat-Zinn, 1994, p. 4), and "Keeping one's consciousness alive to the present reality" (Hạnh, 1976, p. 11). In consolidating these definitions, the author suggests that mindfulness is "a state of consciousness in which attention is focused on present-moment phenomena occurring both externally and internally" (Dane, 2011, p. 1000).

Each of the above definitions refers to mindfulness as a state. However, mindfulness can also be conceptualized as a dispositional trait (Baer, 2003; Hyland et al., 2015). This indicates that some people are more or less likely to be consistently present over time and throughout varying environmental circumstances. While understanding the nuances between definitions of mindfulness and agreeing upon its conceptualization is imperative to the ability of researchers to continue to further the research agenda surrounding the construct, it is also important to understand related, yet distinct, cognitive states. By understanding alternative cognitive states, researchers can begin to investigate mindfulness from a temporal perspective.

Differentiation of attention states

To help disentangle the differences between mindfulness and other constructs rooted in states of attention, Dane (2011) proposes a two-dimensional framework delineating high or low levels of present-moment orientation, and wide or narrow attentional breadth. In the quadrant indicating high present-moment orientation and wide attentional breadth, mindfulness lives alone. Meanwhile, flow, (Csikszentmihalyi, 1975), "an engrossing and enjoyable state of mind that occurs when people feel optimally challenged and are fully absorbed in their current activity" (Debus, Sonnentag, Deutsch, & Nussbeck, 2014, p. 713), is similar to mindfulness in that it requires high present-moment orientation, but is distinct in that it requires a relatively narrow attentional breadth.

Mind-wandering, defined as "thoughts or images that are not directed toward one's current activity" (Kane et al., 2007, p. 615), overlaps conceptually with mindfulness in that it entails wide attentional breadth, but entails low instead of high present-moment attention. Lastly, opposite to mindfulness, states with narrow attentional breadth and low present moment entail ruminating (past) or fantasizing (future) (Dane, 2011).

It is important to recognize that each of the cognitive states—mindfulness, flow, mind-wandering, ruminating/fantasizing—could be beneficial, but for different reasons (Dust, 2015). For example, Glomb et al. (2011) stipulate that mindfulness could be especially useful for activities and occupations that require a high degree of interacting with colleagues because of the need for a wide attentional breadth. On the other hand, Nolan, Weintraub, and Sachdev (2019) found evidence suggesting that jobs with high degrees of social interaction hinder the prevalence of flow at work. Instead, flow is more useful during individualized tasks that require concentration and high levels of skills and specialized knowledge (Dust, 2015; Nakamura & Csikszentmihalyi, 2002). Lastly, mind-wandering can be beneficial in that it serves as a natural break from the psychological demands of complex tasks and social interactions and allows the mind to make its own connections between previous and potential experiences (Smallwood & Schooler, 2006).

Integration of attention states

While the examples mentioned demonstrate that these concepts are distinct from one another and may be uniquely useful in different work situations, evidence also suggests that mindfulness may facilitate flow. For example, attentional control theory (Eysenck, Derakshan, Santos, & Calvo, 2007) proposes that if a person is feeling anxious about future events that they will be unable to control, they can't focus on the goals they need to accomplish. In line with this theory, anxiety has been shown to inhibit flow (Csikszentmihalyi, 1990; Fullagar, Knight, & Sovern, 2013; Jackson & Csikszentmihalyi, 1999), which requires deep concentration on the goal at hand, includes a feeling of control and reduced self-consciousness (Nakamura & Csikszentmihalyi, 2002).

One study by Scott-Hamilton and Schutte (2016) demonstrated that a mindfulness intervention given to cyclists reduced anxiety and facilitated flow experience. Additionally, yoga, a physical manifestation of mindfulness practice, has been shown to increase the prevalence of flow experience in young adult musicians (Butzer, Ahmed, & Khalsa, 2016). Furthermore, Jackson (2016, p. 150), suggests that "the inhibition of the thinking mind in mindfulness may facilitate a loss of self-consciousness and absorption in the task, which in turn can lead to flow experiences" (e.g., Cathcart, McGregor, & Groundwater, 2014; Kee & Wang, 2008; Salmon, Hanneman, & Harwood, 2010; Swann, Keegan, Piggott, & Crust, 2012).

There also appears to be a relationship between mind-wandering and mindfulness. Mrazek, Smallwood, and Schooler (2012) exposed undergraduate participants to a ten-minute mindfulness intervention and found that those in the mindfulness intervention were less likely to mind-wander following the intervention. Research by Arch and Craske (2006), Kiken and Shook (2011), and Long and Christian (2015) have each demonstrated a similar negative relationship between mindfulness and mind-wandering.

While research between mindfulness and flow, and mindfulness and mind-wandering, has been conducted as described, there seems to be very little research focusing on the temporal sequencing of each of these constructs in one model. Said another way, it is unclear how the cognitive states unfold over time and whether their pattern is representative of a higher-order phenomenon. To appropriately do so, however, it is important to understand how mindfulness (and its related constructs) have been measured and studied.

Measuring mindfulness

The measures typically employed in mindfulness studies include self-report and physiological tools. We will begin our review with the self-report methods. Several self-report surveys have been developed to measure mindfulness. The most popular seem to be the Freiburg Mindfulness Inventory (FMI; Walach, Buchheld, Buttenmüller, Kleinknecht, & Schmidt, 2006), the Mindful Attention Awareness Scale (MAAS; Brown & Ryan, 2003), the Kentucky Inventory of Mindfulness Scale (Baer, Smith, & Allen, 2004), and the Toronto Mindfulness Scale (Lau et al., 2006). However, in a review of the 11 most popular self-report measures, Qu, Dasborough, and Todorova (2015) remind readers that popularity does not equal quality and that many of these measures have inherent flaws. These authors suggest that mindfulness measures must have clear operational definitions, alignment between definition and measure, reliability, construct validity, and criterion-related validity. There is also a question as to whether these measures assess state or trait mindfulness.

According to Qu et al. (2015), many of the most popular measures suffer from major flaws. For example, two of the measures suffer from reliability issues, and several don't even provide operational definitions of the construct. Five of the 11 measures had low to no content validity, two had no discriminant validity, and four had no convergent validity. Meanwhile, nine of the 11 measures had no concurrent validity, and only four had predictive validity. Finally, an overwhelming number of the constructs measure mindfulness from a trait-based perspective, where only two measured mindfulness as a state.

Qu et al. (2015) suggest that future research should utilize either the MAAS (Brown & Ryan, 2003) or the Philadelphia Mindfulness Scale (Cardaciotto, Herbert, Forman, Moitra, & Farrow, 2008), with a preference for the MAAS. However, even the MAAS has been criticized for neglecting certain components of mindfulness such as the present focus and acceptance dimensions that others have focused on (Hyland et al., 2015; Walach et al., 2006). This highlights the idea that even the best measures of mindfulness have apparent flaws to be considered, and that there is still room for improvement in the development of such measures.

Other researchers have avoided the use of self-report measures as the sole source of mindfulness data. For example, researchers have utilized mindfulness interventions and then conducted physiological tests such as saliva cortisol as indicators of stress (Jensen, Vangkilde, Frokjaer, & Hasselbalch, 2012), others have used functional magnetic resonance imaging (fMRI) to examine how mindfulness affects the brain (Farb, Anderson, & Segal, 2012; Kilpatrick et al., 2011), while others have measured heart rate variability (Burg, Wolf, & Michalak, 2012).

Much about the construct has yet to be explored. Almost every article which reviews the literature recommends more work to be done surrounding the psychometric development and validation of mindfulness measures (Brown et al., 2007; Glomb et al., 2011; Good et al., 2016; Hyland et al., 2015; Lomas, Medina, Ivtzan, Rupprecht, & Eiroa-Orosa, 2018; Mesmer-Magnus et al., 2017). The range of definitions and tools currently being used in the literature and in practice make it very difficult to compare results across studies. Future research should work to consolidate or develop new operationalizations and measurements which the mindfulness community can agree upon and move forward with together. Additionally, researchers should continue to work to develop objective psychophysiological tools which can measure states of mindfulness without self-report data. The private sector is already selling such tools ("Muse—Meditation Made Easy," n.d.), and the industrial and organizational psychology community should partner with these companies to ensure their claims are valid, and to take advantage of the insights which could be gained from such valuable and objective tools.

Future scholarship should build upon this work in several ways. If researchers intend to investigate several cognitive states in one model, it is essential to select measures that are distinct from one another. For example, measures will need to be refined to ensure that mindfulness and flow are non-overlapping constructs. Further, to our knowledge, there is no measure available differentiating between each of the low present-moment states of mind-wandering and fantasizing/ruminating. To the degree that researchers are able to differentiate these constructs, future research will be more well equipped to investigate the antecedents and consequences associated with unique temporal sequences of attentional states.

Beneficial mindfulness outcomes

In a thorough review of mindfulness at work, Good et al. (2016) sort research outcomes of mindfulness into several categories. These categories include attention, cognition, emotion, behavior, physiology, performance, relationships, and well-being. This framework seems appropriate for the current chapter as well and thus will be utilized in the current section.

Attention

Work on mindfulness and attention can be categorized into subdomains, including attentional stability, attentional control, and attentional efficiency. In a seminal experience sampling method study, Killingsworth and Gilbert (2010) found that a surprisingly large portion of a typical person's day is spent with their mind wandering. In an experimental study conducted by Diaz (2013) in which students were placed into one of four groups (mindfulness induction paired with aesthetic response, mindfulness induction paired with flow response, aesthetic response, or flow response) and asked to listen to music, participants in the mindfulness conditions reported improved ability to pay attention.

As previously mentioned, in a two-part study by Mrazek et al. (2012), a short mindful breathing exercise was utilized before a Sustained Attention to Response Task (SART). Results showed that this simple breathing exercise reduced mind-wandering and improved sustained attention. Hasenkamp, Wilson-Mendenhall, Duncan, and Barsalou (2012) suggest that this improvement in attentional stability is a result of those who are mind-wandering taking notice of the change in their state, and thus are able to refocus as a function of mindfulness.

Having the ability to properly pay attention to the task at hand despite competing demands is known as attentional control (Ocasio, 2011). Wadlinger and Isaacowitz (2011) suggest that those who meditate are able to reduce their attention on distractions and focus more effectively on the true task at hand. Kee and Wang (2008) lend support to this assertion in a study with 182 university student-athletes in which they found that those high in mindfulness also had a higher degree of attentional control. Moreover, in one of the few studies investigating the relationship between flow and mindfulness, Aherne, Moran, and Lonsdale (2011) demonstrated that university athletes who had undergone mindfulness training felt more of a "sense of control" and "clear goals."

Good et al. (2016) suggest that as mindfulness helps people to keep their thoughts on task and away from distractions, the resulting increase in mental efficiency is known as attentional efficiency. A study by Bhayee et al. (2016), in which ten-minute daily mindfulness interventions were administered over six weeks, found improved attentional efficiency in the form of higher Stroop test performance. Additionally, brain scans indicate that meditators use fewer parts of their brain associated with executive attention (Kozasa et al., 2012).

Taken together, these results suggest that mindfulness and mindfulness interventions can improve multiple aspects of attention. In the work context, this has widespread implications. Paying attention in meetings, being able to focus on the necessary work tasks despite distractions, and the ability to use less energy to focus on what's important all clearly can benefit employees at all levels and in all types of organizations.

Cognition

Mindfulness has also been associated with cognitive capacity and cognitive flexibility (Good et al., 2016). Cognitive capacity refers to working memory and fluid intelligence (Good et al., 2016). After only four sessions of a brief meditation training in an experimental study, Zeidan, Johnson, Diamond, David, and Goolkasian (2010) found that those in the meditation group saw improved working memory and executive functioning.

Flexible cognition generates unique perspectives and responses to situations (Walsh, 1995). Colzato, Ozturk, and Hommel (2012) suggest that mindfulness improves creativity as well as convergent and divergent thinking. Likewise, Ostafin and Kassman (2012) suggest that mindfulness improves insight problem-solving. These findings support the assertion that mindfulness improves flexible cognition (Good et al., 2016).

Emotion

Mindfulness has also been associated with influencing emotions, especially in emotional reactivity. After a 15-minute recorded focused breathing induction in an experimental study, Arch and Craske (2006) found that the focused breathing group had significantly lower negative affect when reacting to neutral slides. In patients with mood disorders, Farb et al. (2012) found that mindfulness training directs attention towards monitoring experiencing the moment and reduces automatic self-evaluation, and increases the tolerance for negative affect, thereby helping patients to feel self-compassion and empathy. Sedlmeier et al. (2012) also found in their meta-analysis of the effects of meditation that improved emotional regulation was one of the most robust effect sizes in the literature with regards to outcomes of meditation.

Behavior

Mindfulness has also been shown to affect positive behavioral change (Good et al., 2016). Long and Christian (2015) found that mindfulness buffers retaliatory responses to injustice through its reduction of negative emotions and rumination. Likewise, Fix and Fix (2013) suggest that mindfulness can reduce aggression. Additionally, Westbrook et al. (2013) demonstrated that mindfulness can reduce cigarette cravings, thereby helping people to quit smoking. Good et al. (2016) suggest that mindfulness reduces automaticity and allows people to regulate their behaviors more deliberately. These results support this assertion.

Physiology

Physiology has also been shown to be affected by mindfulness. While the authors cite methodological concerns about publication bias, Fox et al. (2014) found in a meta-analytic review that eight different brain regions were consistently different for meditators than non-meditators. Good et al. (2016) also suggest that mindfulness has particularly important outcomes related to aging. In fact, Luders, Cherbuin, and Gaser (2016) found that meditators had brains which were estimated to be 7.5 years younger than those of controls of the same age.

Performance

Much has been written about the role of mindfulness and performance at work (Good et al., 2016). Dane and Brummel (2014) found in a sample of service industry workers that mindfulness did indeed have a positive effect on job performance. Likewise, Shonin et al. (2014) found that mindfulness positively affected work performance for middle managers. Despite these findings, the overall positive reviews of mindfulness at work by Hyland et al. (2015), Good et al. (2016), and others may be premature.

In fact, despite the findings by Dane and Brummel (2014), years later, Dane (2018) has suggested that mindfulness may only be promising for job performance in certain domains which require wider attentional breadth, and may not be helpful in others. Recent findings by Hafenbrack and Vohs (2018) suggest that mindfulness actually enables people to detach from stressors, improving task focus, but that task performance was unaffected. A follow-up meta-analyses which included file drawer findings supported these claims. However, Lomas et al. (2018) conducted a meta-analysis which showed that mindfulness interventions do improve job performance. Clearly, there are mixed findings on this mindfulness outcome which need to be further explored.

Relationships

Relationships at work is an area which has shown more straightforward results. Huston, Garland, and Farb (2011) found that mindfulness reduces negative reactivity in communication which could help to foster work relationships. Results from five studies conducted by Hafenbrack et al. (2019), in which they utilized diverse methodologies and sample populations, consistently found that mindfulness increased prosocial behavior at work. Two studies by Reb, Narayanan, and Chaturvedi (2014) found that leader mindfulness had a positive relationship with employee need satisfaction, which in turn had positive influences on employee job satisfaction, employee job performance, in-role performance, and employee OCBs. Furthermore, Lippincott (2018) conducted qualitative interviews with senior organizational leaders in ten countries. Leaders reported mindfulness resulted in personal transformations, improved self-awareness, self-management, social awareness, relationship management, development of new and existing leadership capabilities, and improved interpersonal competencies. These findings suggest that mindfulness can not only help improve interpersonal communication, but if leaders practice mindfulness, the benefits from the construct may also be spread to their employees as well.

Well-being

Well-being is the final outcome we will explore in relation to mindfulness. In a meta-analytic examination of the effects of mindfulness-based interventions, Lomas et al. (2018) found negative relationships with anxiety, burnout, distress, and stress. The authors also found positive relationships with compassion, health, and positive well-being. Mesmer-Magnus et al. (2017) found in their meta-analysis that employees high in trait mindfulness report less burnout, lower stress, and less work withdrawal. They also found that employees high in trait mindfulness had lower overall healthcare costs, rates of absenteeism, and more positive work attitudes.

Detrimental mindfulness outcomes

While the vast majority of these findings give glowing reviews for mindfulness at work, there are potential downsides which cannot be overlooked. Hyland et al. (2015) suggest that mindfulness may differentially impact people of different backgrounds or personality types. These differences may provide some employees with advantages over others. The authors also propose that mindfulness may be considered a religious belief by some, and that forcing employees to partake in such practices may be unethical and inappropriate. They also highlight arguments by Carrette and King (2004), which suggest that mindfulness can be used to manipulate unhappy employees into accepting their current situation and being pacified with their place in the organization.

Likewise Dane (2018) suggests that not only might mindfulness not be helpful for certain job tasks, the author says that "one might misallocate attention toward potentially trivial stimuli at the expense of attending to those stimuli that are most critical for performing a given task" (Dane, 2018, p. 1005). Specifically, the authors suggest that "although maintaining a wide external attentional breadth is likely to contribute favorably to task performance in a dynamic task environment, this wide external breadth of attention may prove detrimental in a static task environment" (Dane, 2018, p. 1007). Furthermore, some other aspects of the process linking mindfulness to self-regulation may not prove useful or helpful in all situations. For example, Glomb et al. (2011) suggest that mindfulness leads to a decoupling of the self from experiences and emotions and decreased automatic mental processes. While this may be beneficial in certain domains, the lack of feeling coupled with oneself and from experiencing emotions may make doing certain jobs more difficult. For example, a salesperson may need to speak passionately to potential customers about their products, and decoupling oneself from their emotions may cause the salesperson to fall flat and feel disingenuous.

Additionally, while decreased use of automatic mental processes (Glomb et al., 2011; Good et al., 2016) may also be useful for situations when someone needs to think critically and weigh many options at once, in other situations such automaticity may be especially helpful. For example, a factory worker who does repetitive tasks all day may not wish (or need) to be deliberate in every movement they make throughout the day, and such experience may make the day feel unbearably long. Instead, the expertise the employee has acquired over time may enable an automaticity which allows the worker to feel a sense of flow which mindfulness may otherwise not allow. Clearly, mindfulness is not a silver bullet for individual and organizational success. Future research should recognize that mindfulness is one cognitive state among many, and then consider how mindfulness fits within a broader sequencing of attentional states.

Future research

As outlined above, mindfulness is one of several attentional states. To more clearly understand how and why mindfulness is helpful in organizational settings, it is important to take a temporal perspective of mindfulness. More specifically, at any one point in time, one may find himself/herself in a state of mindfulness, flow, mind-wandering, or rumination/fascination. A limited, albeit growing, body of research is beginning to investigate two of these states in a single model. This is a promising direction, as our lives are not lived as a snapshot in time, but as an ongoing stream of attentional consciousness. We suggest three areas for future research that may help illuminate this broader, temporal perspective of mindfulness and alternative attentional states.

Being versus doing

The temporal perspective of mindfulness is aptly highlighted in Lyddy and Good's (2017) theory of "being while doing." "Being" is a state centered in the present, self-quieted, goalless, intentional, and focuses on direct experience, whereas "doing" is focused on the past and future, evaluation-based, self-centered, goal-directed, and automatic. The theory suggests that the cognitive mode of "being," which mindfulness entails, may be incompatible with the cognitive mode of "doing," which is required in many workplaces. This concept seems to have theoretical alignment with the model Dane (2011) proposes regarding different attentional states being useful for different types of work activities.

Lyddy and Good (2017) propose three scenarios in which different psychological states at work may be incompatible, contingent, or complementary. In qualitative interviews, the authors find that properties such as automatic and persistent thinking may be incompatible with a state of mental quiet, while others found that the two are reconcilable. This interesting and complex relationship of the boundary conditions of mindfulness at work may be crucial to understanding the efficacy of the construct in the future.

Questions remain, such as, can one be high in mindfulness and also be able to get into "the zone" when necessary? For example, while being in a mindful state may not be compatible with a state of flow, it seems that the positive outcomes associated with attentional control, reduction of anxiety, and other aspects of mindfulness may prove useful in promoting flow states during different periods than state mindfulness. In total, the being versus doing framework alludes to the fact that, depending on the conceptualization and theoretical framework adopted, attentional states may or may not be capable of being constructed into mutually exclusive categories. If there are perfectly distinct states, future scholars could begin investigating the degree to which being versus doing within a designated timeframe is helpful or harmful. Future scholars could also begin investigating the extent to which prolonged states of being facilitates more productive states of doing. Similarly, perhaps there is a naturally reoccurring cognitive cycle, such that an average individual moves from one attention state to another in a relatively uniform fashion. Building on this possibility, perhaps some individuals are more capable of engaging in productive attentional state cycles compared with others.

Situational approach

Prior mindfulness theory and research suggest that the utility of a certain attention state is dependent upon the context of the situation. For example, Dane's (2011) framework highlights that mindfulness is more or less useful in certain situations. Future research can build on this work in several ways. First, what are the contexts in which mind-wandering and fantasizing/ruminating may be beneficial? For example, perhaps the mental break from these low present-moment attention states sets up individuals to be more present or find flow in subsequent situations. Second, what are the personal characteristics that might facilitate individuals transitioning from a non-productive to a productive attentional state? For example, Dust (2015) argues that the self-regulatory capacities associated with trait-based mindfulness might facilitate such state–task alignment.

Mindfulness interventions

Researchers should think more broadly about the purpose of using, and the potential utility in using, mindfulness interventions at work. The private sector is leveraging several easy-to-use mindfulness interventions that are available at a moderate price point (Mani, Kavanagh, Hides, & Stoyanov, 2015) with varying degrees of validity and effectiveness. Perhaps mindfulness interventions do more than help employees become more present. If mindfulness is a precursor to flow, the broad-focused present-moment attention associated with a mindfulness intervention is freeing up psychological resources for narrow-focused present-moment attention. Alternatively, perhaps there is utility in sequencing interventions, going back and forth between mind-wandering and mindfulness. If we know that the mind is destined to mind-wander, it may be productive to help employees channel their attentional states in specific sequences.

Conclusion

Research on mindfulness at work has come a long way. The literature is beginning to settle on definitions and measures, and there is some relative consistency regarding its potential influence on workplace outcomes. However, there is still much to be uncovered about the construct and how it is measured. Furthermore, it is time to think more broadly about mindfulness as an attentional state. As discussed, mindfulness is one of several cognitive states which are likely to fluctuate from moment-to-moment, and we have very little understanding of when, how, or why these fluctuations occur. Additionally, we have little empirical evidence investigating when each of these states is more or less likely to be harmful or helpful in the context of the workplace, and what can be done to facilitate each state in their optimal contexts. We are hopeful that the review and recommendations presented here will encourage future researchers to take this broader, temporal perspective of mindfulness research.

Chapter takeaways/lessons

- Conceptualizing mindfulness as high presentmoment attention and broad attentional awareness facilitates a discussion about mindfulness as one of four primary attentional states.
- We need measures of mindfulness that align with alternative measures of related attentional states.
- We need to take a temporal perspective when evaluating mindfulness, evaluating the sequence of attention states (including mindfulness) across time.
- Future research should build upon findings evaluating the positive relationship between mindfulness and flow by including additional attentional states.
- Future research should build upon mindfulness intervention findings and begin evaluating interventions specific to alternative attentional states.

Reflection questions

- What are the situations in which mindfulness is unproductive?
- What are the situations in which alternative attentional states are productive?
- What is the typical and/or cyclical sequencing of our attentional states?
- Might certain types of attentional state sequences be more productive?
- Where does mindfulness fit within a larger model of attentional states?

References

Aherne, C., Moran, A. P., & Lonsdale, C. (2011). The effect of mindfulness training on athletes' flow: An initial investigation. *The Sport Psychologist, 25*(2), 177–189. doi:10.1123/tsp.25.2.177

Arch, J. J., & Craske, M. G. (2006). Mechanisms of mindfulness: Emotion regulation following a focused breathing induction. *Behaviour Research and Therapy, 44*(12), 1849–1858. doi:10.1016/j.brat.2005.12.007

Baer, R. A. (2003). Mindfulness training as a clinical intervention: A conceptual and empirical review. *Clinical Psychology: Science and Practice, 10*(2), 125–143. doi: 10.1093/clipsy.bpg015

Baer, R. A., Smith, G. T., & Allen, K. B. (2004). Assessment of mindfulness by self-report: The Kentucky inventory of mindfulness skills. *Assessment, 11*(3), 191–206. http://dx.doi.org.tcsedsystem.idm.oclc.org/10.1177/1073191104268029

Bhayee, S., Tomaszewski, P., Lee, D. H., Moffat, G., Pino, L., Moreno, S., & Farb, N. A. S. (2016). Attentional and affective consequences of technology supported mindfulness training: A randomised, active control, efficacy trial. *BMC Psychology, 4*(1), 60. doi: 10.1186/s40359-016-0168-6

Brown, K. W., & Ryan, R. M. (2003). The benefits of being present: Mindfulness and its role in psychological well-being. *Journal of Personality and Social Psychology, 84*(4), 822–848. doi: 10.1037/0022-3514.84.4.822

Brown, K. W., Ryan, R. M., & Creswell, J. D. (2007). Mindfulness: Theoretical foundations and evidence for its salutary effects. *Psychological Inquiry, 18*(4), 211–237. doi: 10.1080/10478400701598298

Burg, J. M., Wolf, O. T., & Michalak, J. (2012). Mindfulness as self-regulated attention: Associations with heart rate variability. *Swiss Journal of Psychology/Schweizerische Zeitschrift Für Psychologie/Revue Suisse de Psychologie, 71*(3), 135–139. http://dx.doi.org.tcsedsystem.idm.oclc.org/10.1024/1421-0185/a000080

Butzer, B., Ahmed, K., & Khalsa, S. B. S. (2016). Yoga enhances positive psychological states in young adult musicians. *Applied Psychophysiology and Biofeedback, 41*(2), 191–202. doi: 10.1007/s10484-015-9321-x

Cardaciotto, L., Herbert, J. D., Forman, E. M., Moitra, E., & Farrow, V. (2008). The assessment of present-moment awareness and acceptance: The Philadelphia mindfulness scale. *Assessment, 15*(2), 204–223. http://dx.doi.org.tcsedsystem.idm.oclc.org/10.1177/1073191107311467

Carrette, J., & King, R. (2004). *Selling spirituality: The silent takeover of religion* (1st ed.). London; New York: Routledge.

Cathcart, S., McGregor, M., & Groundwater, E. (2014). Mindfulness and flow in elite athletes. *Journal of Clinical Sport Psychology*, *8*(2), 119–141. doi: 10.1123/jcsp.2014-0018

Colzato, L. S., Ozturk, A., & Hommel, B. (2012). Meditate to create: The impact of focused-attention and open-monitoring training on convergent and divergent thinking. *Frontiers in Psychology*, *3*. http://dx.doi.org.tcsedsystem.idm.oclc.org/10.3389/fpsyg.2012.00116

Csikszentmihalyi, M. (1975). *Beyond boredom and anxiety: Experiencing flow in work and play* (25th Anniversary ed.). San Francisco: Jossey-Bass.

Csikszentmihalyi, M. (1990). *Flow: The psychology of optimal experience.* New York: Harper & Row.

Dane, E. (2011). Paying attention to mindfulness and its effects on task performance in the workplace. *Journal of Management*, *37*(4), 997–1018. doi: 10.1177/0149206310367948

Dane, E. (2018). Where is my mind? Theorizing mind wandering and its performance-related consequences in organizations. *Academy of Management Review*, *43*(2), 179–197. doi: 10.5465/amr.2015.0196

Dane, E., & Brummel, B. J. (2014). Examining workplace mindfulness and its relations to job performance and turnover intention. *Human Relations*, *67*(1), 105–128. doi: 10.1177/0018726713487753

Debus, M. E., Sonnentag, S., Deutsch, W., & Nussbeck, F. W. (2014). Making flow happen: The effects of being recovered on work-related flow between and within days. *Journal of Applied Psychology*, *99* (4), 713–722. doi: 10.1037/a0035881

Diaz, F. M. (2013). Mindfulness, attention, and flow during music listening: An empirical investigation. *Psychology of Music*, *41*(1), 42–58. doi: 10.1177/0305735611415144

Dust, S. B. (2015). Mindfulness, flow, and mind wandering: The role of trait-based mindfulness in state-task alignment. *Industrial and Organizational Psychology: Perspectives on Science and Practice*, *8*(4), 609–614. doi: 10.1017/iop.2015.87

Ellis, A. (2006). Rational emotive behavior therapy and the mindfulness based stress reduction training of Jon Kabat-Zinn. *Journal of Rational-Emotive and Cognitive-Behavior Therapy*, *24*(1), 63–78. doi: 10.1007/s10942-006-0024-3

Eysenck, M. W., Derakshan, N., Santos, R., & Calvo, M. G. (2007). Anxiety and cognitive performance: Attentional control theory. *Emotion*, 7(2), 336–353. doi: 10.1037/1528-3542.7.2.336

Farb, N. A. S., Anderson, A. K., & Segal, Z. V. (2012). The mindful brain and emotion regulation in mood disorders. *Canadian Journal of Psychiatry. Revue Canadienne De Psychiatrie*, *57*(2), 70–77.

Fix, R. L., & Fix, S. T. (2013). The effects of mindfulness-based treatments for aggression: A critical review. *Aggression and Violent Behavior*, *18*(2), 219–227. doi: 10.1016/j.avb.2012.11.009

Fox, K. C. R., Nijeboer, S., Dixon, M. L., Floman, J. L., Ellamil, M., Rumak, S. P., . . . Christoff, K. (2014). Is meditation associated with altered brain structure? A systematic review and meta-analysis of morphometric neuroimaging in meditation practitioners. *Neuroscience & Biobehavioral Reviews*, *43*, 48–73. doi: 10.1016/j.neubiorev.2014.03.016

Fullagar, C. J., Knight, P. A., & Sovern, H. S. (2013). Challenge/Skill Balance, Flow, and Performance Anxiety. *Applied Psychology: An International Review*, *62*(2), 236–259. doi: 10.1111/j.1464-0597.2012.00494.x

Giluk, T. L. (2009). Mindfulness, big five personality, and affect: A meta-analysis. *Personality and Individual Differences*, *47*(8), 805–811. doi: 10.1016/j.paid.2009.06.026

Glomb, T. M., Yang, T., Bono, J. E., & Duffy, M. K. (2011). Mindfulness at work. In *Research in personnel and human resources management: Vol. 30. Research in personnel and human resources management* (Vol. 30, pp. 115–157). doi: 10.1108/S0742-7301(2011)0000030005

Good, D. J., Lyddy, C. J., Glomb, T. M., Bono, J. E., Brown, K. W., Duffy, M. K., . . . Lazar, S. W. (2016). Contemplating mindfulness at work: An integrative review. *Journal of Management*, *42*(1), 114–142. doi: 10.1177/0149206315617003

Google Scholar. (n.d.). Retrieved May 20, 2019, from https://scholar.google.com/

Hafenbrack, A. C., Cameron, L. D., Spreitzer, G. M., Zhang, C., Noval, L. J., & Shaffakat, S. (2019). Helping people by being in the present: Mindfulness Increases Prosocial Behavior. *Organizational Behavior and Human Decision Processes.* doi: 10.1016/j.obhdp.2019.08.005

Hafenbrack, A. C., & Vohs, K. D. (2018). Mindfulness meditation impairs task motivation but not performance. *Organizational Behavior and Human Decision Processes*, *147*, 1–15. doi: 10.1016/j.obhdp.2018.05.001

Hạnh, T. N. (1976). *The miracle of mindfulness: A manual on meditation.* Boston: Beacon Press.

Hasenkamp, W., Wilson-Mendenhall, C. D., Duncan, E., & Barsalou, L. W. (2012). Mind wandering and attention during focused meditation: A fine-grained temporal analysis of fluctuating cognitive states. *NeuroImage, 59*(1), 750–760. doi: 10.1016/j.neuroimage.2011.07.008

History of MBSR. (2016, November 17). Retrieved May 20, 2019, from University of Massachusetts Medical School website: www.umassmed.edu/cfm/mindfulness-based-programs/mbsr-courses/about-mbsr/history-of-mbsr/

Huston, D. C., Garland, E. L., & Farb, N. A. S. (2011). Mechanisms of mindfulness in communication training. *Journal of Applied Communication Research, 39*(4), 406–421. http://dx.doi.org.tcsedsystem.idm.oclc.org/10.1080/00909882.2011.608696

Hyland, P. K., Lee, R. A., & Mills, M. J. (2015). Mindfulness at work: A new approach to improving individual and organizational performance. *Industrial and Organizational Psychology: Perspectives on Science and Practice, 8*(4), 576–602. 10.1017/iop.2015.41

Jackson, S. (2016). Flowing with mindfulness: Investigating the relationship between flow and mindfulness. In I. Ivtzan & T. Lomas (Eds.), (2016-07446-009) *Mindfulness in positive psychology: The science of meditation and wellbeing* (pp. 141–155). New York, NY: Routledge/Taylor & Francis Group.

Jackson, S., & Csikszentmihalyi, M. (1999). *Flow in sports: The keys to optimal experiences and performances* (1st ed.). Champaign, IL: Human Kinetics.

Jensen, C. G., Vangkilde, S., Frokjaer, V., & Hasselbalch, S. G. (2012). Mindfulness training affects attention—Or is it attentional effort? *Journal of Experimental Psychology. General, 141*(1), 106–123. doi: 10.1037/a0024931

Kabat-Zinn, J. (1982). An outpatient program in behavioral medicine for chronic pain patients based on the practice of mindfulness meditation: Theoretical considerations and preliminary results. *General Hospital Psychiatry, 4*(1), 33–47.

Kabat-Zinn, J. (1994). *Wherever You Go, There You Are: Mindfulness Meditation in Everyday Life* (1st ed.). Frankfurt/M; Berlin: Hyperion.

Kabat-Zinn, J. (1996). Mindfulness Meditation: What It Is, What It Isn't, And Its Role In Health Care and Medicine. In Y. Haruki, Y. Ishii, & M. Suzuki (Eds.), *Comparative and psychological study on meditation* (pp. 161–169). Netherlands: Eburon.

Kane, M. J., Brown, L. H., McVay, J. C., Silvia, P. J., Myin-Germeys, I., & Kwapil, T. R. (2007). For whom the mind wanders, and when: An experience-sampling study of working memory and executive control in daily life. *Psychological Science (0956–7976), 18*(7), 614–621. doi: 10.1111/j.1467-9280.2007.01948.x

Kee, Y. H., & Wang, C. K. J. (2008). Relationships between mindfulness, flow dispositions and mental skills adoption: A cluster analytic approach. *Psychology of Sport and Exercise, 9*(4), 393–411. doi: 10.1016/j.psychsport.2007.07.001

Kiken, L. G., & Shook, N. J. (2011). Looking up: Mindfulness increases positive judgments and reduces negativity bias. *Social Psychological and Personality Science, 2*(4), 425–431. doi: 10.1177/1948550610396585

Killingsworth, M. A., & Gilbert, D. T. (2010). A wandering mind is an unhappy mind. *Science, 330*(6006), 932. doi: 10.1126/science.1192439

Kilpatrick, L. A., Suyenobu, B. Y., Smith, S. R., Bueller, J. A., Goodman, T., Creswell, J. D., . . . Naliboff, B. D. (2011). Impact of mindfulness-based stress reduction training on intrinsic brain connectivity. *NeuroImage, 56*(1), 290–298. doi: 10.1016/j.neuroimage.2011.02.034

Klatt, M. D., Buckworth, J., & Malarkey, W. B. (2009). Effects of low-dose Mindfulness-Based Stress Reduction (MBSR-ld) on working adults. *Health Education & Behavior, 36*(3), 601–614. http://dx.doi.org.tcsedsystem.idm.oclc.org/10.1177/1090198108317627

Kozasa, E. H., Sato, J. R., Lacerda, S. S., Barreiros, M. A. M., Radvany, J., Russell, T. A., . . . Amaro, E. (2012). Meditation training increases brain efficiency in an attention task. *NeuroImage, 59*(1), 745–749. doi: 10.1016/j.neuroimage.2011.06.088

Lau, M. A., Bishop, S. R., Segal, Z. V., Buis, T., Anderson, N. D., Carlson, L., . . . Devins, G. (2006). The Toronto mindfulness scale: Development and validation. *Journal of Clinical Psychology, 62*(12), 1445–1467. http://dx.doi.org.tcsedsystem.idm.oclc.org/10.1002/jclp.20326

Lippincott, M. (2018). Deconstructing the relationship between mindfulness and leader effectiveness. *Leadership & Organization Development Journal, 39*(5), 650–664. doi: 10.1108/LODJ-11-2017-0340

Lomas, T., Medina, J. C., Ivtzan, I., Rupprecht, S., & Eiroa-Orosa, F. J. (2018). Mindfulness-based interventions in the workplace: An inclusive systematic review and meta-analysis of their impact upon wellbeing. *The Journal of Positive Psychology*. doi: 10.1080/17439760.2018.1519588

Long, E. C., & Christian, M. S. (2015). Mindfulness buffers retaliatory responses to injustice: A regulatory approach. *Journal of Applied Psychology, 100*(5), 1409–1422. http://dx.doi.org.tcsedsystem.idm.oclc.org/10.1037/apl0000019

Luders, E., Cherbuin, N., & Gaser, C. (2016). Estimating brain age using high-resolution pattern recognition: Younger brains in long-term meditation practitioners. *NeuroImage; Amsterdam, 134*, 508. http://dx.doi.org.tcsedsystem.idm.oclc.org/10.1016/j.neuroimage.2016.04.007

Lyddy, C. J., & Good, D. J. (2017). Being while doing: An inductive model of mindfulness at work. *Frontiers in Psychology*, 7. https://doi.org/10.3389/fpsyg.2016.02060

Mani, M., Kavanagh, D. J., Hides, L., & Stoyanov, S. R. (2015). Review and evaluation of mindfulness-based iphone apps. *JMIR MHealth and UHealth, 3*(3), e82. doi: 10.2196/mhealth.4328

MBSR Courses. (2016, November 16). Retrieved May 20, 2019, from University of Massachusetts Medical School website: www.umassmed.edu/cfm/mindfulness-based-programs/mbsr-courses/

Mesmer-Magnus, J., Manapragada, A., Viswesvaran, C., & Allen, J. W. (2017). Trait mindfulness at work: A meta-analysis of the personal and professional correlates of trait mindfulness. *Human Performance, 30*(2–3), 79–98. doi: 10.1080/08959285.2017.1307842

Mrazek, M. D., Smallwood, J., & Schooler, J. W. (2012). Mindfulness and mind-wandering: Finding convergence through opposing constructs. *Emotion, 12*(3), 442–448. http://dx.doi.org.tcsedsystem.idm.oclc.org/10.1037/a0026678

Muse—Meditation Made Easy. (n.d.). Retrieved May 22, 2019, from Muse website: https://choosemuse.com/

Nakamura, J., & Csikszentmihalyi, M. (2002). The concept of flow. In C. R. Snyder, S. J. Lopez, C. R. Snyder, & S. J. Lopez (Eds.), (2002-02382-007) *Handbook of positive psychology* (pp. 89–105). New York, NY, US: Oxford University Press.

Narayanan, J., & Moynihan, L. (2006). Mindfulness at work: The beneficial effects on job burnout in call centers. *Academy of Management Proceedings, 2006*(1), H1–H6. doi: 10.5465/ambpp.2006.22898626

Nolan, K., Weintraub, J., & Sachdev, A. (2019). Work-related flow: Factors influencing perceptions of utility and prevalence of experience. *34th Annual SIOP Conference*. Presented at the National Harbor, Maryland. National Harbor, Maryland.

Smallwood, J., & Schooler, J. W. (2006). The restless mind. *Psychological Bulletin, 132*(6), 946–958. https://doi.org/10.1037/0033-2909.132.6.946

Ocasio, W. (2011). Attention to attention. *Organization Science; Linthicum, 22*(5), 1286–1296.

Ostafin, B. D., & Kassman, K. T. (2012). Stepping out of history: Mindfulness improves insight problem solving. *Consciousness and Cognition; San Diego, 21*(2), 1031–1036. http://dx.doi.org.tcsedsystem.idm.oclc.org/10.1016/j.concog.2012.02.014

Qu, Y. (Elly), Dasborough, M. T., & Todorova, G. (2015). Which mindfulness measures to choose to use? *Industrial and Organizational Psychology; Bowling Green, 8*(4), 710–723. http://dx.doi.org.tcsedsystem.idm.oclc.org/10.1017/iop.2015.105

Reb, J., Narayanan, J., & Chaturvedi, S. (2014). Leading mindfully: Two studies on the influence of supervisor trait mindfulness on employee well-being and performance. *Mindfulness, 5*(1), 36–45. doi: 10.1007/s12671-012-0144-z

Salmon, P., Hanneman, S., & Harwood, B. (2010). Associative/dissociative cognitive strategies in sustained physical activity: Literature review and proposal for a mindfulness-based conceptual model. *The Sport Psychologist, 24*(2), 127–156. http://dx.doi.org.tcsedsystem.idm.oclc.org/10.1123/tsp.24.2.127

Scott-Hamilton, J., & Schutte, N. S. (2016). The role of adherence in the effects of a mindfulness intervention for competitive athletes: Changes in mindfulness, flow, pessimism, and anxiety. *Journal of Clinical Sport Psychology, 10*(2), 99–117. doi: 10.1123/jcsp.2015-0020

Sedlmeier, P., Eberth, J., Schwarz, M., Zimmermann, D., Haarig, F., Jaeger, S., & Kunze, S. (2012). The psychological effects of meditation: A meta-analysis. *Psychological Bulletin, 138*(6), 1139–1171. doi: 10.1037/a0028168

Shonin, E. (2014). Meditation Awareness Training (MAT) for work-related wellbeing and job performance: A randomised controlled trial. *International Journal of Mental Health and Addiction, 12*(6)

Link to external site, this link will open in a new window, Van Gordon, W., Dunn, T. J., Singh, N. N., Griffiths, M. D., & Link to external site, this link will open in a new window, 806–823. http://dx.doi.org.tcsedsystem.idm.oclc.org/10.1007/s11469-014-9513-2

Swann, C., Keegan, R. J., Piggott, D., & Crust, L. (2012). A systematic review of the experience, occurrence, and controllability of flow states in elite sport. *Psychology of Sport and Exercise, 13*(6), 807–819. doi: 10.1016/j.psychsport.2012.05.006

Thera, N. (1998). *Abhidhamma studies: Buddhist explorations of consciousness and time* (4th ed.). Boston: Wisdom Publications.

Wadlinger, H. A., & Isaacowitz, D. M. (2011). Fixing our focus: Training attention to regulate emotion. *Personality and Social Psychology Review; Thousand Oaks, 15*(1), 75–102. http://dx.doi.org.tcsedsystem.idm.oclc.org/10.1177/1088868310365565

Walach, H., Buchheld, N., Buttenmüller, V., Kleinknecht, N., & Schmidt, S. (2006). Measuring mindfulness—The Freiburg Mindfulness Inventory (FMI). *Personality and Individual Differences, 40*(8), 1543–1555. doi: 10.1016/j.paid.2005.11.025

Walsh, J. P. (1995). Managerial and organizational cognition: Notes from a trip down memory lane. *Organization Science, 6*(3), 280–321. http://dx.doi.org.tcsedsystem.idm.oclc.org/10.1287/orsc.6.3.280

Weick, K. E., & Sutcliffe, K. M. (2006). Mindfulness and the quality of organizational attention. *Organization Science, 17*(4), 514–524. doi: 10.1287/orsc.1060.0196

Westbrook, C., Creswell, J. D., Tabibnia, G., Julson, E., Kober, H., & Tindle, H. A. (2013). Mindful attention reduces neural and self-reported cue-induced craving in smokers. *Social Cognitive and Affective Neuroscience, 8*(1), 73–84. http://dx.doi.org.tcsedsystem.idm.oclc.org/10.1093/scan/nsr076

Zeidan, F., Johnson, S. K., Diamond, B. J., David, Z., & Goolkasian, P. (2010). Mindfulness meditation improves cognition: Evidence of brief mental training. *Consciousness and Cognition: An International Journal, 19*(2), 597–605. doi: 10.1016/j.concog.2010.03.014

3

METACOGNITIVE PRACTICE

Understanding mindfulness as repeated attempts to understand mindfulness

Ravi S. Kudesia and Jenson Lau

Introduction

Mindfulness is a topic of growing prevalence in organizational scholarship and practice alike. It faces a unique challenge, however, in that mindfulness refers to a set of practices (e.g., sustaining attention on the breath as a form of meditation) that were initially embedded within Buddhist teaching and have since been imported into Western contexts, including organizations. As a consequence, scholars have attempted to clarify various aspects of this realm of practice, by re-articulating mindfulness from within its "original" Buddhist teaching (Bodhi, 2011; Grabovac, Lau, & Willett, 2011; Kudesia & Nyima, 2015), documenting the translation of mindfulness from Buddhist into Western contexts (e.g., as part of the Buddhist modernism movement; Lopez, 2002; McMahan, 2008; Sharf, 1995) and into organizational contexts more specifically (Gelles, 2015; Kucinskas, 2019), as well as raising ethical concerns about how mindfulness is enacted in organizations (Islam, Holm, & Karjalainen, 2017; Purser & Milillo, 2015; Qiu & Rooney, 2017).

The challenge is to extract something coherent called "mindfulness" from this vast and variegated realm of practice—some psychological state or process that has roots in Buddhist teachings, relevance to organizations, and that meets scientific standards for construct clarity (cf. Suddaby, 2010). In so doing, scholars have discovered complications in each aspect of the realm of practice. First, Buddhism is not nearly monolithic enough to offer one "original" definition of the Sanskrit term *smṛti*, rendered into English as "mindfulness" (Anālayo, 2016; Bodhi, 2011; Gyatso, 1992). Second, in translating mindfulness from Buddhist to Western contexts, relatively minor concepts like "bare attention" took on a disproportionately important role (see G. Dreyfus, 2011; Sharf, 2014), while key translators such as Kabat-Zinn (2011) purposefully used the term "mindfulness" as a synecdoche: a small part of the Buddhist teaching stretched to symbolize the broader teaching. Thus, third, much of how we define and enact mindfulness, including within organizational scholarship and practice, bears little resemblance to its Buddhist roots (Grossman, 2011) and often excludes important ethical dimensions (Monteiro, Musten, & Compson, 2015).

In this chapter, we compare two approaches to dealing with this challenge: the common multicomponent approach (e.g., Bergomi, Tschacher, & Kupper, 2013; Nilsson & Kazemi, 2016) and the recent metacognitive practice approach (see Kudesia, 2019). After showing the relative benefits of the metacognitive practice approach, we review and extend this approach by offering key principles and elaborating its particular benefits for organizational theory and practice.

Key limitations in the multicomponent approach

To date, scholars have primarily tried to deal with the challenge of extracting a definition of mindfulness from the realm of practice by using a multicomponent approach, similar to work on personality traits (e.g., Nilsson & Kazemi, 2016). Unable to find one authentic or universal definition of mindfulness, the approach has been for scholars to identify "missing pieces" from the realm of practice they deem important, add them to the existing list of components in the literature, and then use psychometrics and factor analysis to justify putting all these components together under the banner of mindfulness. Mindfulness scholarship now explicitly measures at least nine such components: (1) broadly observing one's environment, (2) acting with present-centered attention, (3) accepting oneself, (4) having insight into the mind, and being (5) open to, (6) non-judgmental of, (7) non-reactive toward, (8) non-identifying with, and (9) capable of describing, one's internal experiences like their thoughts and feelings (Bergomi et al., 2013). To be sure, this multicomponent approach can certainly claim to cover the conceptual space of mindfulness practice more fully than selecting any one single component can (e.g., K. W. Brown, Ryan, & Creswell, 2007). But this approach also transforms mindfulness from something we can concretely observe into an abstract higher-order construct defined statistically as that latent factor which all nine of these components jointly point toward. In so doing, this multicomponent approach offers six important limitations.

First, in order to define mindfulness, one must now first define nine distinct components, specify their interrelations, and identify some overarching construct that unites all of them. The difficulty in defining mindfulness thus grows superlinearly with each new component added. By the time mindfulness starts to encompass more than five components, it becomes vanishingly impossible to consider their complete interactions (Halford, Baker, McCredden, & Bain, 2005).

Second, as the aforementioned list reveals, these components are often "controversial" among mindfulness scholars, "not themselves technical scientific terms," and may (therefore) even "have no agreed-upon meaning" (Greco & Hayes, 2008, p. 5). Oftentimes these components entail practitioner "jargon" from mindfulness-based interventions, including terms like "present-centered and nonjudgmental," that escape any clear scientific definition (Lutz, Jha, Dunne, & Saron, 2015, p. 634). For instance, what precisely is the "present moment" (see Purser, 2015)? Indeed, part of the reason some components are controversial is because components like "describing internal experience" appear to be interpolations from specific practitioner contexts, rather than being necessary parts of mindfulness (Grossman, 2008). Beyond interpolations, other components like "non-judgment" may even be inconsistent with the Buddhist context (G. Dreyfus, 2011). The imprecision in the definition of these components only complicates attempts to understand the abstract higher-order factor thought to emerge from across them all.

Third, these components cover a wide array of psychological abilities (e.g., to describe internal experiences), experiences (e.g., present-centered attention), techniques (e.g., not judging one's thoughts and feelings), and outcomes (e.g., insight into the mind). It is difficult to see theoretically why all these remarkably different components should be treated as equal and necessary aspects of mindfulness. They seem to be antecedents and consequences of each other, not different indicators of the same thing. Taking a multicomponent approach thus can take us further away from mindfulness. Instead of getting closer to what mindfulness actually looks like in practice, mindfulness becomes some abstract idea realized through statistics.

Fourth, even then, this multicomponent approach also creates measurement issues at the statistical level. Because this approach elevates the various terms that practitioners use (e.g., present-centered attention, non-judgment) to the status of scientific constructs, which are then operationalized in survey measures, it remains unclear whether these scientific constructs can be properly measured and examined outside the realm of practice. Psychometric work indeed reveals that practitioners and non-practitioners interpret the component measures differently (Van Dam, Earleywine, & Danoff-Burg, 2009), as exemplified by Grossman's (2008) story of binge drinkers reporting greater "mindfulness" than long-term meditators because their hangover symptoms led them to have greater awareness of internal experiences. Measures built on practitioner terms and jargon may therefore not be understandable by non-practitioners.

Fifth, these statistical and psychometric concerns become all the more important because of how the multicomponent approach situates mindfulness within a state-trait framework. The state-trait framework presumes that there are certain dimensions of thinking and behaving that apply meaningfully to all people within a population, and that people differ from each other along these dimensions in a relatively stable way. Dane (2011), for instance, discussed these three key points in describing mindfulness as "an inherent human capacity" that all people experience, even without any training in meditation, and as being "fundamentally a state-level construct that can also be assessed at the trait level," given that some people experience state mindfulness "more often than others" (p. 999). But if the components of mindfulness better reflect practitioner terms and jargon, rather than universal aspects of human psychology, it is inappropriate to situate mindfulness within a state-trait framework. People who have not received mindfulness training are not simply "low" on their trait levels of this multicomponent construct. Rather, the construct does not exist for them.

Sixth, and relatedly, this state-trait framework is best suited to explain consistency across situations. Its purpose is to explain how people who consistently differ in their mindfulness levels across their situations experience different outcomes, not the origin of why one person may differ in their mindfulness levels from situation to situation (Mischel & Shoda, 1998). It therefore leaves vastly underspecified the psychological processes by which people actually manifest these states because it does not consider within-person processes occurring at the level of situations. As a result, it offers a relatively limited sense of how the practice of mindfulness is learned in meditation training contexts and how it is enacted in organizational contexts. What is actually going on when people attempt to be mindful from one situation to the next? Mindfulness cannot simply be assumed as a universal capacity within a population whose appearance is unproblematic. Mindfulness is an effortful accomplishment whose appearance in any situation requires explanation.

In sum, there are good theoretical and empirical reasons to be wary of a multicomponent approach to mindfulness, despite its prevalence. But is there a plausible alternative approach?

Thought experiment comparing multicomponent and metacognitive practice approaches

In the present chapter, we review and extend a different approach to mindfulness, known as *metacognitive practice* (see Kudesia, 2019). Metacognitive practice departs markedly from the assumption that mindfulness means something universal and that scholars ought to simply adopt the language of practitioners (either Buddhist or Western) as multiple components in a definition. Instead, scholars ought to theorize about the processes by which practitioners come to understand mindfulness and how their understandings shape the variegated ways they try to "be mindful" in their everyday situations. A metacognitive practice approach does not take practitioner terms at face value or presume that these terms necessarily describe what practitioners actually do when trying to be mindful. It instead steps back and attempts to model this entire realm of practice.

As a thought experiment, consider how mindfulness is traditionally learned. Trainees enter into a meditation retreat, where a special room has been prepared to be most conducive to mindfulness (with all the appropriate technologies like dim lighting, comfortable and grounding seating, perhaps incense or images of gurus and enlightened masters). Once there, an expert with a calm, knowing demeanor introduces them to new terms like "monkey mind" or "beginner's mind," and does so with the appropriate nonverbals: minimal gestures, a tranquil vocal tone, and wise facial expressions. New activities—like sitting upright, attending to the sensations of breath at the tip of the nose, and noticing the odd and potentially unpleasant phenomena lurking just at the fringes of consciousness—are conveyed similarly. When interacting with the trainees, the expert embodies the meaning that underlies these terms and activities: he neither seeks to control their activities, nor is he uninterested in them, but is instead at once engaged, invested, and disinterested. As the many people learning mindfulness interact with each other, they do their best to embody this same meaning, not fully understanding it, but sensing its importance. Somehow this entire system, with its technologies, terms, activities, and interactions, all point toward some yet-unarticulated end. Even the expert may not fully understand the end, and to the extent that he does, may find it tacit, paradoxical, slippery, and fundamentally incapable of being articulated. And furthermore, part of how the expert comes to understand the meaning and end of his mindfulness practice may be the very process in which he shares the practice with trainees.

By situating ourselves in the realm of mindfulness practice through this brief thought experiment, we can now compare the two approaches to mindfulness. What a multicomponent approach takes from this mindfulness training thought experiment are the following. First, that the correct level at which to understand the process of mindfulness training is at the level of individual psychology. The effects manifested by this entire system somehow reduce down to psychological properties that are internalized and retained within the minds of each individual trainee. Second, that these psychological properties of trainees are adequately described by the terms they use. The complex of technologies, activities, and interactions that jointly help trainees attend to ongoing events in an engaged, invested, and disinterested manner can be summarized accurately by terms like paying attention "on purpose, in the present moment, and nonjudgmentally" (Kabat-Zinn, 1994, p. 4) and by survey measures that draw on these terms. Third, that once people have spent their time within this learning system, they then carry mindfulness with them seamlessly into other situations: in work meetings, interactions with spouses, and while waiting in heavy traffic. The meditation training simply turned up a pre-existing dial in their internalized psychology.

Metacognitive practice approaches this thought experiment in a rather different way. In particular, it does so by drawing on a set of theoretical perspectives known as practice theory (see Feldman & Orlikowski, 2011; Nicolini, 2012; Sandberg & Tsoukas, 2011; Schatzki, 2005). Practice theory offers three important insights that help us distinguish the metacognitive practice approach from the multicomponent approach.

First, that as people become experts in practices like mindfulness, their expertise is not retained primarily in their terms (see H. L. Dreyfus & Dreyfus, 2005). Rather, their expertise becomes something far more tacit and embodied, and likely incapable of being fully articulated. So, practitioner terms are certainly an important part of novice-level practice but are vanishingly important for expert-level practice. This creates a risk that if we derive our scientific language from practitioner terms, particularly those terms common to the Buddhist modernism movement (e.g., Lopez, 2002; McMahan, 2008; Sharf, 1995), we may miss out on deeper, and more expert, aspects of what mindfulness means and how it is practiced. On the other hand, the practitioner terms within traditional Buddhism typically relate to advanced levels of meditation practice, as is appropriate for monastics (e.g., the arūpajhānas or "formless dimensions" of the Pāli canon), rather than to the ways that mindfulness is applied in everyday situations outside of meditation. Far too often, scholars have conflated the terms used to describe meditation instructions for novices with prescriptions for how people who are experts in their organizational context should attempt to be mindful. Practice theory requires that we do not take the language of practitioners for granted, but focus on the ways that it is utilized in relation to the broader realm of practice.

Second, we must therefore include, but also go beneath, the language practitioners use. Doing so requires that we abandon the conventional individual psychological level of analysis and instead take the entire practice itself as our topic of study. If one is studying the practice of medicine, for instance, it is less important to study the psychology of the individuals who are also doctors. It is more important to study the ways they enact their role as a doctor in service of their ultimate end to "do no harm," the activities they undertake in doing so (like interviewing patients and performing procedures), along with the routines, tools, resources, and so on that they utilize along the way. Analogously, an analysis of the entire practice of mindfulness would entail studying: (1) the ends mindfulness practitioners are oriented toward (like productivity, well-being, enlightenment, etc.); (2) their standards of excellence for these ends (including historical and current exemplars of mindfulness as well as canonical and modern descriptions of mastery); (3) the concrete activities practitioners engage in (like daily meditation practice, reading books on mindfulness, choosing not to multitask, savoring each bite of their food, speaking in slow and measured tones); (4) the routine ways they interact with each other to pursue these ends (like colleagues "checking in" with each other daily to provide a space for them to mindfully process their thoughts and feelings); (5) the tools and resources they use in doing so (from mindfulness apps that cultivate skills to social support for meditating at work to job autonomy to schedule periods of deep attention); and (6) the underlying already-defined and often-tacit distinctions about what matters for a person trying to become mindful (see Sandberg & Tsoukas, 2011; Schatzki, 2005). These components, taken together, comprise the entire realm of practice.

Third, practice entails social interactions within a "community of practice," where many practitioners interactively deepen their understanding and enactment of mindfulness together, including by sharing and refining stories, resources, and experiences (see J. S. Brown & Duguid, 1991; Lave & Wenger, 1991). Rather than mindfulness training changing internal psychological properties of individuals, who are expected to then simply and singlehandedly bring mindfulness into new situations, metacognitive practice emphasizes both the system in which mindfulness is learned and the system in which it is enacted. Although there is some understanding of how the system of technologies, terms, activities, and interactions may function in mindfulness training contexts, we know little about how the ends, technologies, terms, activities, and interactions typical of organizations might influence mindfulness. Because the multicomponent psychology approach has been so prevalent, we have done little to ask, for instance, how technology related to automation (Bainbridge, 1983), terms like "busyness" (that we willingly adopt to show that our skills are in demand, even if doing so erodes our well-being; Gershuny, 2005), activities like performing "mindless work" (Elsbach & Hargadon, 2006), and social interactions like speaking up and "voicing" our concerns to others (Engemann & Scott, 2018) might influence mindfulness. Metacognitive practice shifts our attention from mindfulness as an internalized feature of individual psychology to consider the broader system as a no less important part of how mindfulness is actually practiced. If mindfulness requires an ecology to learn in a training context, why would it not require an ecology to enact in an organizational context? To truly understand how mindfulness is actually practiced, in a concrete manner, we would need to study the ways in which the ecologies typical of organizations are conducive to mindfulness or are not.

In sum, metacognitive practice does not presume that mindfulness is a universal property of human psychology that can be readily self-reported or that its meaning is exhausted by the terms practitioners use in making their self-reports. It therefore allows for a more interpretive approach to mindfulness, one that respects and examines the entire realm of practice, but that separates science from this realm of practice (see Gephart, 2018). The function of the scientist is to study the realm of practice and then build and test theory about this realm, including the ends, technologies, terms, activities, and interactions used by practitioners (Sandberg & Tsoukas, 2011; Schatzki, 2005). Scientists need not abstract away from practice with factor analysis, but rather must observe practice and identify the logic that underlies and animates it. When scientists do not attempt to enter the realm of practice and turn some of the many definitions there into constructs, they can instead start to theorize how practitioners try to make definitions work for their purposes. This insight lies behind the playful and purposefully odd title of this piece: to understand mindfulness (as scholars), we have to study repeated attempts (by practitioners) to understand what mindfulness means and how it can be enacted concretely in their situations.

Metacognitive practice and the paradox of understanding mindfulness

In theorizing about metacognitive practice, a paradox thus becomes evident. The paradox is that a critical part of mindfulness is attempting to understand what mindfulness means. Again, from a practice theory perspective, understanding does not imply having a purely theoretical definition that one can provide (e.g., "paying attention on purpose, in the present moment, non-judgmentally"). Understanding implies a practical sense of "how would I act right now if I was to act 'mindfully'?" In asking such a question, we see that reasonable people can disagree about whether the "mindful" way of responding to an interrupting colleague who frequently stops by the cubicle is to honor one's feelings of frustration and have an honest conversation with her or to detach from those feelings and engage with her small talk during interruptions. Or, more pointedly, when protestors interrupted the Google-sponsored panel on "3 Steps to Build Corporate Mindfulness the Google Way" during the Wisdom 2.0 conference in order to bring awareness to the negative consequences Silicon Valley firms have on local residents in terms of evictions and homelessness ("Wisdom means stop displacement! Wisdom means stop surveillance! San Francisco's not for sale!" they chanted), whether the mindful response was indeed to have them removed and ask audience members to "use this as a moment of practice. Check in with your body and see what's happening, what it's like to be around conflict and people with heartfelt ideas that may be different than what we're thinking" (Nisbet, 2019).

To be clear, scholars cannot hope to specify what mindfulness would look like in every situation. Doing so would, ironically, just end up being a set of rules that people could follow mindlessly. We must instead specify the logic that practitioners utilize as they try to instantiate their sense of what it means to be mindful from any situation to the next. Metacognitive practice provides a framework to help specify this logic. The initial statement of the theory of metacognitive practice focused especially on what mindfulness looks like across organizational situations where a person has varying levels of expertise: from gaining and retaining expertise at the novice stage in their career to refining and doubting expertise at the mastery stage (see Table 2 in Kudesia, 2019). Here, we offer a complementary view that describes not what mindfulness looks like at different levels of expertise in organizations, but what mindfulness looks like at different levels of expertise in mindfulness. Although this view is admittedly a rough sketch, it does help outline the relevant components of mindfulness practice that are worth considering.

Stage 1: Initial development of metacognition in the education systems

A key necessary but insufficient condition for mindfulness is *metacognition*: the processes by which people monitor and adjust their information processing—and the beliefs and strategies they rely upon in doing so (Fernandez-Duque, Baird, & Posner, 2000; Nelson, 1996). In educational and developmental psychology, scholars have noted that metacognition emerges as part of a natural process of development. Young children lack metacognition, which more fully develops into their adolescence, largely through the technologies, social interactions, and activities furnished by the education system (Flavell, 1979; Schraw & Moshman, 1995). For instance, students must not only be able to read textbooks and process the information contained within them, but they must also monitor the quality of their reading comprehension and make adjustments in strategy if their comprehension is low: taking a break, re-reading a paragraph, asking for help, etc. As people advance in their education, these basic metacognitive abilities are presumed, but are rarely developed any further. Some advanced degrees (like those in behavioral science or philosophy) may prompt students to think more systematically about the nature of their information processing. For instance, when graduate students in psychology learn about naïve scientist and cognitive miser theories of social information processing (Fiske & Taylor, 1991) or about cognitive biases and how they can be overcome (Larrick, 2004), they are also learning about how they process information, in ways that could develop their metacognition. But, for most, the process of developing metacognition ends as we progress in the education system.

Stage 2: Individual recognition of need for further development

Mindfulness entails a continuation of this process of metacognitive development that people undergo from childhood onward, but just taken further—and in a specific direction (see Shapiro, Carlson, Astin, & Freedman, 2006). Just as we must continue to grow in our knowledge of the world, we must also continue to grow in our knowledge about how to grow our knowledge of the world. But, without external education systems to encourage this metacognition, mindfulness may rely on our internal personal proactivity to seek out further metacognitive development. There is thus a starting point for the emergence of mindfulness, which builds on the mere capacity for metacognition and starts to motivate its use in practice. And that starting point is a recognition that escapes many of us. Most people recognize that there are more and less adaptive ways of *responding* to situations in terms of their *behavior*: not every action is equally effective in any given situation. But people less often recognize that there are also more and less adaptive ways of *processing* situations in terms of their *cognition*. Nor do people often realize how their cognition—namely, what information they pay attention to in a situation and how they interpret that information—is partly subject to their agency (Bandura, 2006). So how people act as agents to monitor and adjust their attention and interpretations will fundamentally shape their behavioral responses to situations. We more often think to change our actions than to change the quality of mind that generated those actions. Only when we realize the potential and the power of the latter does mindfulness become available to us. It signifies the possibility that, through metacognition, we can learn to systematically self-regulate our information processing—and that doing so can make us more likely to process incoming situations in adaptive ways. It turns our everyday situations into opportunities to improve the quality of our attention and interpretation processes. But fundamentally the recognition begins with a sense of dissatisfaction, that something about how we process information is limited. The ultimate end (and even the nature of the path through which we are to pursue it) remains yet unarticulated.

Stage 3: Cultivation of relevant metacognitive beliefs

Indeed, oftentimes our metacognitive beliefs remain mostly implicit, largely unarticulated, and, thus, almost entirely unquestioned (Schraw & Moshman, 1995). And, to the extent that our metacognitive beliefs remain unquestioned, they have the potential to limit us in ways that are not immediately obvious to us (e.g., Job, Dweck, & Walton, 2010). When people first enter into the practice of mindfulness, they can start to question these limiting metacognitive beliefs, and potentially replace them with more empowering beliefs. Mindfulness practice provides a sense that there is indeed a path to pursue, and that this path will lead to an end: traditionally, the profound alleviation of suffering, where suffering is not a negative emotion, but a condition of typical human psychology (Kudesia & Nyima, 2015; Purser, 2015). Indeed, numerous scholars have drawn our attention to these metacognitive processes and how they are uniquely enacted within the practice of mindfulness (e.g., Bernstein et al., 2015; Dunne, Thompson, & Schooler, 2019; Jankowski & Holas, 2014; Teasdale, 1999; Wells, 2005). A key takeaway from this research is that very often our unquestioned metacognitive beliefs limit our ability to regulate our attention and process our thoughts and feelings in an adaptive manner. In many cases, this work has been done in clinical psychology contexts, where patient metacognition may be especially lacking and in need of further development. But the insight transfers just as well to non-clinical contexts, as all of us could use further development of our metacognition.

Metacognitive practice identifies three metacognitive beliefs that supersede typical unquestioned and limiting beliefs and that are particularly emphasized within meditation training contexts: attentional sufficiency (the belief that attention is not depleted with use over time), virtue of monitoring (the belief that it is valuable to notice one's internal thoughts and feelings, even unpleasant ones, rather than avoiding them), and map-terrain differentiation (the belief that one's thoughts and feelings about a situation need not necessarily reflect any objective truth about it). These metacognitive beliefs essentially map onto the basic metacognitive processes of monitoring and adjusting and guide these processes to function in ways that they would not often function without training (see Kudesia, 2019). For instance, we far too often treat our attention as a scarce resource (even the term "pay attention" presumes scarcity, as if attention functioned like an economic good with limited supply). The attentional sufficiency belief directly overrides this belief. We also tend to treat our thoughts and feelings, particularly the unpleasant ones, as having an inherent meaning and therefore tend to avoid them. The virtue of monitoring belief guides us to continue observing our internal experience, because doing so is valuable—perhaps especially so for unpleasant internal experiences. And, finally, we also tend to presume that the world is as it appears to us: that "the map is the terrain." The map-terrain differentiation belief undoes this belief, leading to greater flexibility in how we interpret and thus act in everyday situations. In recent and ongoing research, these beliefs have started to be examined empirically. For instance, it was found that these three beliefs tend to co-occur. They also predict the use of metacognitive processes (e.g., regulating attention toward ongoing activities and monitoring thoughts and feelings from a detached perspective) above and beyond a host of other influential factors and over the temporal separation of a 12-hour work shift (Reina & Kudesia, 2020). To the extent that these metacognitive beliefs are cultivated in meditation training, they could point more concretely to one thing that people might actually internalize from training and then transfer to situations in organizational life. But these beliefs also point to ways in which organizations could be designed as systems, in order to encourage and further develop metacognition.

Stage 4: Repeated attempts to be mindful

Namely, simply holding metacognitive beliefs does not mean that one will be successful in enacting mindfulness. People need elaborated metacognitive strategies to translate these beliefs into action on a situation-to-situation basis (Schraw & Moshman, 1995). And these strategies are often developed through first-person experience: attempts to be mindful. Their success at these attempts to be mindful will be influenced by features of the organizational context. The strategies they develop must therefore be at least partly situation-specific, and their success in their attempts to be mindful will also depend on features of the situation. As noted previously, contextual factors like automation, busyness, mindless work tasks, opportunities for voice, and so forth could enhance or erode the likelihood of success in attempts to be mindful. Taken to a more general framework, organizational situations can help guide cognition toward tasks, which makes metacognition easier to enact, or can pose competing demands that make metacognition more challenging to enact (Beal, Weiss, Barros, & MacDermid, 2005; Reina & Kudesia, 2020). But even these features of situations are embedded within broader organizational structures that must be considered relative to mindfulness. Organizational structures provide people with institutionalized concepts for sensemaking, the resources that enable them to perform relevant work tasks and routines, and the information flows that guide which tasks and routines they perform, and which concepts they use when making sense of situations (see Kudesia, 2019). The broader organizational structures themselves can influence the relative success of people's attempts at mindfulness. In particular, organizational structures facilitate mindfulness to the extent that they: better appreciate the expertise among front-line employees embodied in their actions and improvisations, align actions across the organization by having top managers encode strategy into simple rules and heuristics rather than attempting to plan out all contingencies in advance, and utilize middle managers to ensure the improvisations of front-line employees are aligned with the strategy as well as to retain their adaptive improvisations and distribute them throughout the wider organization (see Kudesia & Reb, 2018). Without such organizational structures, attempts at being mindful become increasingly likely to backfire, and thereby "fragment" organizational routines (for a list of potential fragmentation risks and their remedies, see Table 3 in Kudesia, 2019). Such fragmentation discourages repeated attempts at being mindful.

The complex and dynamic nature of the situations within organizations therefore suggests that attempts at mindfulness will seldom be straightforward and unproblematic. Rich repertoires of metacognitive strategies are needed to bridge the more general metacognitive beliefs about how information processing functions with the specific actions required in any situation. People must draw on organizational concepts, resources, and information flows in their attempts at being mindful, but must also act to change this structure when necessary. These changes will affect the work of others in the organization, which will invariably trigger social negotiation and require ever-more refined strategies. But if more people in the organization are attempting to be mindful, they may better be able to make these changes and renegotiate the structure of their organization. Through their interactions, and the terms, technologies, activities, etc., they use in these interactions, they can guide each other to greater development of metacognition. This "amplifying effect" is an important promise of metacognitive practice: that when multiple people who are all attempting to develop their metacognition interact with each other, they "not only transform their situations but also strengthen the very metacognitive practice that enables them to transform situations" (Kudesia, 2019, p. 419). Indeed, such social interactions are one important way that we can develop our metacognition: through learning from others both directly and vicariously (Schraw & Moshman, 1995). Thus, although attempts at mindfulness must always be continued, this need not be an isolated individual experience. We become mindful with others.

Stage 5: Spontaneous accomplishment of mindfulness?

Mindfulness requires constant ongoing effort. It is never accomplished once and for all time. Organizations are constantly falling apart and need to be put back together (Weick, 1979), so our understanding of how to be mindful similarly must continually be enriched as situations change over time. It is possible, however, that this effort becomes easier with practice. As a person's repertoire of strategies is enriched, they become more spontaneous in enacting them (Pressley, Borkowski, & Schneider, 1987). Such spontaneity in enacting mindfulness requires both expertise in metacognition (i.e., having the appropriate beliefs and repertoire of strategies) and expertise in the organizational context (e.g., understanding the institutionalized concepts, accessing the relevant resources, and situating oneself in the appropriate information flows). In discussing the concept of enlightenment, Buddhist sources similarly talk about the "wisdom that accomplishes all" or kṛty-ānuṣṭhāna-jñāna in Sanskrit, which describes how enlightened people act spontaneously and without feelings of fatigue to improve the welfare of the broader system. This offers both good news and bad news. The bad news is that the path of mindfulness is unlikely to ever be completed. The good news is that the path becomes, with practice, easier and easier to walk. We gain insight into the ways in which our attention, thoughts, and feelings can work against us, or can be put to use in order to transform situations and systems to higher states. We learn to enroll the people with whom we interact—and involve the relevant terms, technologies, and activities in these interactions. And, in doing so, mindfulness can reverberate throughout the broader system, rather than being internalized merely into the psychology of the individuals in it.

Conclusion

In this chapter, we compared two approaches to mindfulness: the multicomponent and the metacognitive practice approach (see Table 3.1). The multicomponent approach turns the

Table 3.1 Two approaches to understanding mindfulness

	Multicomponent Approach	*Metacognitive Practice Approach*
Definition	Mindfulness as an abstract higher-order factor emerging from various psychological components (e.g., present-centered attention, non-judgment, self-acceptance)	Mindfulness as a concrete practice that involves specific activities aimed toward certain ends, accomplished using terms, technologies, and social interactions within a community
Level of Analysis	Individual psychology	Social practice
Framework	State-trait framework: emphasis on consistency across situations	Metacognition: emphasis on agency to flexibly adapt to situations
Ontology	Basic psychological state present in all people; involvement in relevant practices increases trait levels	Potential in all people, but requires unique metacognitive beliefs shaped by involvement in relevant practices
Training Mechanism	Meditation training changes internal psychological states and abilities, which people then readily transfer into all the other contexts they enter	Meditation training provides a context in which people learn and enter into a practice, transfer requires a conducive context to emerge
Central Questions	Is attention focused on the present moment? Is a person non-judgmental of her internal experiences? If so, she will experience benefits in her well-being or task performance	Is a person invoking strategies and beliefs to enact metacognition? If so, she will adjust her information processing to the situation at hand and grow in understanding from doing so

terms mindfulness practitioners use to describe psychological states (present-centered, non-judgmental, self-acceptance, etc.) into scientific constructs and treats mindfulness as an abstract higher-order factor that emerges from all these various components. The metacognitive practice approach attempts to model the broader realm of practice, beyond just the terms practitioners use to their concrete activities, with the relevant social interactions and technologies involved. Metacognitive practice is perhaps akin to Hutchins' (1995) argument that the airplane's cockpit remembers its speed, not its pilots. The speeds are remembered not merely in the minds of pilots, but in the social interactions between the pilots and with material technologies like gross weight readouts, speed cards, airspeed indicators, and so on. Similarly, when we see mindfulness being trained and enacted, we should not focus solely on individual psychology and ignore social interactions, terms, technologies, activities, and all the rest. These are all important aspects of mindfulness, and we cannot understand how mindfulness is actually practiced without considering them.

Metacognitive practice builds on prior work in the mindfulness literature that emphasizes metacognition (e.g., Bernstein et al., 2015; Dunne et al., 2019; Jankowski & Holas, 2014; Teasdale, 1999; Wells, 2005). In particular, it emphasizes the metacognitive beliefs and strategies people use to monitor and adjust their information processing from one situation to the next. Metacognitive practice further extends these insights in light of practice theory. The critical argument is that attempts at understanding and regulating our information processing are necessarily social in nature. As a result, mindfulness becomes a social practice. It is learned and enacted within communities of practice, in which people individually and interactively (re)shape their beliefs about how their mind works and what strategies best regulate it, given the situations they find themselves in on an ongoing basis. Being mindful requires both knowledge of these organizational situations as well as a developed repertoire of strategies that help people enact metacognitive beliefs in the situation. Given the dynamism and complexity of organizational situations—and the incomplete knowledge of strategies we can use to become mindful in these situations—mindfulness may never be finalized. Although people can most certainly improve their metacognition to dramatic outcomes, mindfulness is essentially an endless question, one that will never be resolved once and for all. As our situations continuously change (with new technologies, greater interdependence, less reliance on shared norms, etc.), so too must the ways in which mindfulness is actually practiced. Our role as scholars and scientists is to understand the repeated attempts that practitioners make at understanding mindfulness, as they act from one situation to the next. Perhaps if we succeed in our role, the understanding we develop can inform their practice and bring our systems closer to their ultimate, yet unarticulated end.

Chapter takeaways

1. Mindfulness is not a cognitive state of attention or non-judgment, per the common practitioner jargon, but is a metacognitive process of regulating one's information processing.
2. Regulation of information processing (e.g., attention, thoughts, feelings) in a mindful manner relies upon specific metacognitive beliefs that are cultivated in meditation training.
3. These metacognitive beliefs are attentional sufficiency (that attention does not get depleted by use), virtue of monitoring (that it is valuable to monitor one's ongoing information processing), and map-terrain differentiation (that one's experience of a situation need not necessarily reflect the truth).
4. To successfully enact metacognition in specific situations requires strategies that bridge expertise in mindfulness with expertise in organizational situations, such that one knows how to regulate their information processing (mindfulness expertise) and what type of information processing the situation requires (organizational expertise).
5. The practice of metacognition occurs within a broader community (which has its own ends, terms, technologies, activities, interactions, etc.) and is shaped by properties of the system in which it is enacted (including its concepts, resources, and information flows), such that attempts at being mindful can fragment the organization or amplify through interactions.

Reflection questions

1. What does "being mindful" actually look like in the situation I'm in? If I put away the jargon of "present-centered attention" and "non-judgment," what specific actions should I undertake?
2. What beliefs do I hold about my own information processing? Do I believe that attention is a scarce resource that gets used up, so I must conserve it? That it would be better to avoid unpleasant thoughts and feelings, rather than accept and observe them? That my experience of events must be accurate, so I shouldn't question it? Do these beliefs hold me back in any way?
3. What strategies do I use to enact mindfulness in specific situations? If I define mindfulness in terms of present-centered attention, what do I specifically do when I find that my attention is drifting away from the task at hand? Do I switch tasks? Reduce

situational distractions? Remind myself about the importance of the task? Which strategies are most effective in what types of situations?

4. How conducive to mindfulness are the situations in which I find myself? Do they draw my information processing toward my tasks, or do they pose additional demands? How can I redesign my work situations to better facilitate my attempts at mindfulness?
5. Am I optimally situated within the organizational structure? Is the expertise that I have being taken up and utilized by the organization? Am I integrating the information flows I receive with those of others who need this information? Might my attempts at mindfulness backfire if I'm operating with limited information at the system level?

References

Anālayo, B. (2016). Early Buddhist mindfulness and memory, the body, and pain. *Mindfulness*, 7(6), 1271–1280. doi: 10.1007/s12671-016-0573-1

Bainbridge, L. (1983). Ironies of automation. *Automatica*, *19*(6), 775–779. doi: 10.1016/0005-1098(83)90046-8

Bandura, A. (2006). Toward a psychology of human agency. *Perspectives on Psychological Science*, *1*(2), 164–180. doi: 10.1111/j.1745-6916.2006.00011.x

Beal, D. J., Weiss, H. M., Barros, E., & MacDermid, S. M. (2005). An episodic process model of affective influences on performance. *Journal of Applied Psychology*, *90*(6), 1054–1068. doi: 10.1037/0021-9010.90.6.1054

Bergomi, C., Tschacher, W., & Kupper, Z. (2013). The assessment of mindfulness with self-report measures: Existing scales and open issues. *Mindfulness*, *4*(3), 191–202. doi: 10.1007/s12671-012-0110-9

Bernstein, A., Hadash, Y., Lichtash, Y., Tanay, G., Shepherd, K., & Fresco, D. M. (2015). Decentering and related constructs: A critical review and meta-cognitive processes model. *Perspectives on Psychological Science*, *10*(5), 599–617. doi: 10.1177/1745691615594577

Bodhi, B. (2011). What does mindfulness really mean? A canonical perspective. *Contemporary Buddhism*, *12*(1), 19–39. doi: https://doi.org/10.1080/14639947.2011.564813

Brown, J. S., & Duguid, P. (1991). Organizational learning and communities-of-practice: Toward a unified view of working, learning, and innovation. *Organization Science*, *2*(1), 40–57. doi: 10.1287/orsc.2.1.40

Brown, K. W., Ryan, R. M., & Creswell, J. D. (2007). Mindfulness: Theoretical foundations and evidence for its salutary effects. *Psychological Inquiry*, *18*(4), 211–237. doi: 10.1080/10478400701598298

Dane, E. (2011). Paying attention to mindfulness and its effects on task performance in the workplace. *Journal of Management*, *37*(4), 997–1018. doi: 10.1177/0149206310367948

Dreyfus, G. (2011). Is mindfulness present-centred and non-judgmental? A discussion of the cognitive dimensions of mindfulness. *Contemporary Buddhism*, *12*(1), 41–54. doi: 10.1080/14639947.2011.564815

Dreyfus, H. L., & Dreyfus, S. E. (2005). Expertise in real world contexts. *Organization Studies*, *26*(5), 779–792. doi: 10.1177/0170840605053102

Dunne, J. D., Thompson, E., & Schooler, J. (2019). Mindful meta-awareness: Sustained and non-propositional. *Current Opinion in Psychology*, *28*, 307–311. doi: 10.1016/j.copsyc.2019.07.003

Elsbach, K. D., & Hargadon, A. B. (2006). Enhancing creativity through "mindless" work: A framework of workday design. *Organization Science*, *17*(4), 470–483. doi: 10.1287/orsc.1060.0193

Engemann, K. N., & Scott, C. W. (2018). Voice in safety-oriented organizations: Examining the intersection of hierarchical and mindful social contexts. *Human Resource Management Review*. doi: 10.1016/j.hrmr.2018.05.002

Feldman, M. S., & Orlikowski, W. J. (2011). Theorizing practice and practicing theory. *Organization Science*, *22*(5), 1240–1253. doi: 10.1287/orsc.1100.0612

Fernandez-Duque, D., Baird, J. A., & Posner, M. I. (2000). Executive attention and metacognitive regulation. *Consciousness and Cognition*, *9*(2), 288–307. doi: 10.1006/ccog.2000.0447

Fiske, S. T., & Taylor, S. E. (1991). *Social cognition (2nd Ed.)*. New York, NY: McGraw-Hill.

Flavell, J. H. (1979). Metacognition and cognitive monitoring: A new area of cognitive–developmental inquiry. *American Psychologist, 34*(10), 906–911. doi: 10.1037/0003-066X.34.10.906

Gelles, D. (2015). *Mindful work: How meditation is changing business from the inside out.* Boston, MA: Eamon Dolan.

Gephart, R. P. (2018). Qualitative research as interpretive science. In C. Cassell, A. L. Cunliffe, & G. Grandy (Eds.), *The SAGE handbook of qualitative business and management research methods* (pp. 33–53). Los Angeles, CA: SAGE Publications.

Gershuny, J. (2005). Busyness as the badge of honor for the new superordinate working class. *Social Research, 72*(2), 287–314.

Grabovac, A. D., Lau, M. A., & Willett, B. R. (2011). Mechanisms of mindfulness: A Buddhist psychological model. *Mindfulness, 2*(3), 154–166. doi: 10.1007/s12671-011-0054-5

Greco, L. A., & Hayes, S. C. (Eds.). (2008). *Acceptance and mindfulness treatments for children and adolescents: A practitioner's guide.* Oakland, CA: Context Press.

Grossman, P. (2008). On measuring mindfulness in psychosomatic and psychological research. *Journal of Psychosomatic Research, 64*(4), 405–408. doi: 10.1016/j.jpsychores.2008.02.001

Grossman, P. (2011). Defining mindfulness by how poorly I think I pay attention during everyday awareness and other intractable problems for psychology's (re)invention of mindfulness: Comment on Brown et al. (2011). *Psychological Assessment, 23*(4), 1034–1040. doi: 10.1037/a0022713

Gyatso, J. (Ed.). (1992). *In the mirror of memory: Reflections on mindfulness and remembrance in Indian and Tibetan Buddhism.* Albany, NY: State University of New York Press.

Halford, G. S., Baker, R., McCredden, J. E., & Bain, J. D. (2005). How many variables can humans process? *Psychological Science, 16*(1), 70–76. doi: 10.1111/j.0956-7976.2005.00782.x

Hutchins, E. (1995). How a cockpit remembers its speeds. *Cognitive Science, 19*(3), 265–288. doi:10.1207/s15516709cog1903_1

Islam, G., Holm, M., & Karjalainen, M. (2017). Sign of the times: Workplace mindfulness as an empty signifier. *Organization*, 135050841774064. doi: 10.1177/1350508417740643

Jankowski, T., & Holas, P. (2014). Metacognitive model of mindfulness. *Consciousness and Cognition, 28*, 64–80. doi: 10.1016/j.concog.2014.06.005

Job, V., Dweck, C. S., & Walton, G. M. (2010). Ego depletion—Is it all in your head? Implicit theories about willpower affect self-regulation. *Psychological Science, 21*(11), 1686–1693. doi: 10.1177/0956797610384745

Kabat-Zinn, J. (1994). *Wherever you go, there you are: Mindfulness meditation in everyday life.* New York, NY: Hyperion.

Kabat-Zinn, J. (2011). Some reflections on the origins of MBSR, skillful means, and the trouble with maps. *Contemporary Buddhism, 12*(1), 281–306. doi: 10.1080/14639947.2011.564844

Kucinskas, J. (2019). *The mindful elite: Mobilizing from the inside out.* New York: Oxford University Press.

Kudesia, R. S. (2019). Mindfulness as metacognitive practice. *Academy of Management Review, 44*(2), 405–423. doi: 10.5465/amr.2015.0333

Kudesia, R. S., & Nyima, V. T. (2015). Mindfulness contextualized: An integration of Buddhist and neuropsychological approaches to cognition. *Mindfulness, 6*(4), 910–925. doi: 10.1007/s12671-014-0337-8

Kudesia, R. S., & Reb, J. (2018). Mindfulness and the risk-resilience tradeoff in organizations. In B. D. Trump, M.-V. Florin, & I. Linkov (Eds.), *IRGC resource guide on resilience (Vol. 2): Domains of resilience for complex interconnected systems* (pp. 94–101). Lausanne, CH: EPFL International Risk Governance Center.

Larrick, R. P. (2004). Debiasing. In D. J. Koehler & N. Harvey (Eds.), *Blackwell handbook of judgment and decision making* (pp. 316–338). doi:10.1002/9780470752937.ch16

Lave, J., & Wenger, E. (1991). *Situated learning: Legitimate peripheral participation.* Cambridge, UK: Cambridge University Press.

Lopez, D. S. (2002). *A modern Buddhist bible: Essential readings from East and West.* Boston, MA: Beacon Press.

Lutz, A., Jha, A. P., Dunne, J. D., & Saron, C. D. (2015). Investigating the phenomenological matrix of mindfulness-related practices from a neurocognitive perspective. *American Psychologist, 70*(7), 632–658. doi:10.1037/a0039585

McMahan, D. L. (2008). *The making of Buddhist modernism.* New York, NY: Oxford University Press.

Mischel, W., & Shoda, Y. (1998). Reconciling processing dynamics and personality dispositions. *Annual Review of Psychology, 49*(1), 229–258. doi: 10.1146/annurev.psych.49.1.229

Monteiro, L. M., Musten, R. F., & Compson, J. (2015). Traditional and contemporary mindfulness: Finding the middle path in the tangle of concerns. *Mindfulness*, *6*(1), 1–13. doi: 10.1007/s12671-014-0301-7

Nelson, T. O. (1996). Consciousness and metacognition. *American Psychologist*, *51*(2), 102–116. doi: 10.1037/0003-066X.51.2.102

Nicolini, D. (2012). *Practice theory, work, and organization: An introduction*. Oxford, UK: Oxford University Press.

Nilsson, H., & Kazemi, A. (2016). Reconciling and thematizing definitions of mindfulness: The big five of mindfulness. *Review of General Psychology*, *20*(2), 183–193. doi:10.1037/gpr0000074

Nisbet, M. C. (2019). Sciences, publics, politics: Mindfulness Inc. *Issues in Science and Technology*, *36*(1), 33–35.

Pressley, M., Borkowski, J. G., & Schneider, W. (1987). Cognitive strategies: Good strategy users coordinate metacognition and knowledge. In R. Vasta & G. Whitehurst (Eds.), *Annals of child development* (Vol. *5*, pp. 89–129). Greenwich, CT: JAI Press.

Purser, R. E. (2015). The myth of the present moment. *Mindfulness*, *6*(3), 680–686. doi: 10.1007/s12671-014-0333-z

Purser, R. E., & Milillo, J. (2015). Mindfulness revisited: A Buddhist-based conceptualization. *Journal of Management Inquiry*, *24*(1), 3–24. doi: 10.1177/1056492614532315

Qiu, J. X. J., & Rooney, D. (2017). Addressing unintended ethical challenges of workplace mindfulness: A four-stage mindfulness development model. *Journal of Business Ethics*. doi: 10.1007/s10551-017-3693-1

Reina, C. S., & Kudesia, R. S. (2020). Wherever you go, there you become: How mindfulness arises in everyday situations. *Organizational Behavior and Human Decision Processes*. doi: 10.1016/j.obhdp.2019.11.008

Sandberg, J., & Tsoukas, H. (2011). Grasping the logic of practice: Theorizing through practical rationality. *Academy of Management Review*, *36*(2), 338–360. doi: 10.5465/amr.2009.0183

Schatzki, T. R. (2005). The sites of organizations. *Organization Studies*, *26*(3), 465–484. doi: 10.1177/0170840605050876

Schraw, G., & Moshman, D. (1995). Metacognitive theories. *Educational Psychology Review*, 7(4), 351–371.

Shapiro, S. L., Carlson, L. E., Astin, J. A., & Freedman, B. (2006). Mechanisms of mindfulness. *Journal of Clinical Psychology*, *62*(3), 373–386. doi: 10.1002/jclp.20237

Sharf, R. (1995). Buddhist modernism and the rhetoric of meditative experience. *Numen*, *42*(3), 228–283. doi: 10.1163/1568527952598549

Sharf, R. (2014). Mindfulness and mindlessness in early Chan. *Philosophy East and West*, *64*(4), 933–964.

Suddaby, R. (2010). Construct clarity in theories of management and organization. *Academy of Management Review*, *35*(3), 346–357. doi: 10.5465/AMR.2010.51141319

Teasdale, J. D. (1999). Metacognition, mindfulness and the modification of mood disorders. *Clinical Psychology & Psychotherapy*, *6*(2), 146–155. doi: 10.1002/(SICI)1099-0879(199905)6:2146::AID-CPP1953.0.CO;2-E

Van Dam, N. T., Earleywine, M., & Danoff-Burg, S. (2009). Differential item function across meditators and non-meditators on the Five Facet Mindfulness Questionnaire. *Personality and Individual Differences*, *47*(5), 516–521. doi: 10.1016/j.paid.2009.05.005

Weick, K. E. (1979). *The social psychology of organizing (2nd Ed.)*. Reading, MA: Addison-Wesley.

Wells, A. (2005). Detached mindfulness in cognitive therapy: A metacognitive analysis and ten techniques. *Journal of Rational-Emotive & Cognitive-Behavior Therapy*, *23*(4), 337–355. doi: 10.1007/s10942-005-0018-6

4

A MULTIDIMENSIONAL CONCEPTUALIZATION OF MINDFULNESS AT WORK

Development and initial validation of the work mindfulness scale

Christopher S. Reina

Introduction

Employee effectiveness has always been held at a premium in organizational work life. Yet, in today's 24/7 world, the demands on employees' time, energy, and skillsets are unprecedented as they are expected to simultaneously perform their job well, build relationships with co-workers, balance work and family commitments, and display positivity at work (Carmeli & Gittell, 2009; Peterson, Luthans, Avolio, Walumbwa, & Zhang, 2011; Shockley & Allen, 2014). The need to navigate these competing demands shows no sign of slowing down as the pace of work continues to increase and employees' well-being hangs in the balance.

In order to aid and support employees, organizations are increasingly embracing mindfulness in the workplace. Mindfulness is defined as intentional awareness of the present moment without judgment (Kabat-Zinn, 1994). Individuals who cultivate mindfulness are more aware in the current moment "without the overlay of discriminative, categorical, and habitual thought, [such that] consciousness takes on a clarity and freshness that permits more flexible, more objectively informed psychological and behavioral responses" (Brown, Ryan, & Creswell, 2007, p. 212). They do not fall into the trap of mindless, automatic processing which leads to mechanistic and rigid behavioral patterns (Langer, 1989). Instead, they engage in a process of emotional and cognitive self-regulation consisting of empathy, affective-regulation, and response flexibility, which, recent conceptualizations of mindfulness suggest, allows them to be more fully present, aware of, and in tune with their fellow employees (Glomb, Duffy, Bono, & Yang, 2011; Shapiro, Carlson, Astin, & Freedman, 2006).

In this chapter, I operationalize mindfulness at work by synthesizing past mindfulness research in order to make the mindfulness construct more relevant for the workplace. I adopt the simple definition of mindfulness articulated by Kabat-Zinn (1990) which refers to mindfulness as intentional, nonjudgmental awareness of the present moment and advance mindfulness theory by proposing that mindfulness consists of six components that reinforce each other and reflect the underlying construct of mindfulness. I use self-determination theory (Ryan & Deci, 2000) and self-regulation theory (Carver & Scheier, 1981; Ryan, Kuhl, & Deci, 1997) to guide my selection of mindfulness facets. Researchers have argued that mindfulness is a multifaceted construct (Bishop et al., 2004; Kudesia, 2019; Reina & Kudesia, 2020; Roemer & Orsillo, 2003), but mindfulness scales have tended to psychometrically measure the construct unidimensionally. Thus, there is a mismatch between mindfulness theory and measurement of the construct, and I seek to contribute to this ongoing conversation.

Advancing a multidimensional conceptualization of mindfulness

Mindfulness researchers have differentiated between two distinct approaches to mindfulness. The first arises from Eastern traditions that emphasize contemplation and nonjudgmental awareness of one's moment-to-moment experience and is derived from cultural and philosophical traditions such as Buddhism (Brown & Ryan, 2003; Kabat-Zinn, 1994). In this tradition, mindful individuals are able to clear their minds through meditation and through nonjudgmental attention of their inner experience, which ultimately allows them to see the world as it really is, a concept known as veridical perception (see Yeganeh, 2006). A second approach to mindfulness comes from a more Western perspective and emphasizes a mindset toward seeking out novelty and categorizing information in new and innovative ways (Beard, 2014; Langer, 1989; Weick & Sutcliffe, 2006). Individuals who are mindful exist within a heightened state of involvement in the present and experience increased environmental sensitivity, openness to new information, the ability to create new categories to structure perception, and increased awareness of multiple perspectives (Langer & Moldoveanu, 2000).

The current chapter and subsequent measure development focus on the Eastern tradition of mindfulness as a state of consciousness rather than the Western perspective which discusses mindfulness similar to a cognitive style (Sternberg, 2000). Both approaches are similar in their focus on the present moment and the importance placed on carefully attending to information in the environment (Dane, 2011), but the Western tradition heavily emphasizes the process of drawing novel distinctions (Langer, 2009; Langer & Moldoveanu, 2000), which is not a main focus within the Eastern tradition, nor in the current measure development process outlined in this chapter.

Mind*less* vs mindful processing

The concepts of awareness and attention figure prominently in defining mindfulness given their importance in facilitating the emergence of consciousness. Awareness refers to "conscious registration if stimuli, including the five physical senses, the kinesthetic senses, and the activities of the mind. Awareness is our most direct, most immediate contact with reality" (Brown, Ryan, & Creswell, 2007, p. 212). Awareness becomes attention when a stimulus is strong enough to cause an individual to take notice of a particular stimulus and turn toward it (Nyaniponika, 1973). In the case of *mindless* processing, individuals experience cognitive and emotional reactions to the stimuli which are characterized by three features. The first is a discriminative primary appraisal that assigns valence to the object. Second, these reactions are informed by prior experiences, and third, these reactions are fit into existing schema that inform future reactions (Brown et al., 2007). Together, these three features lead individuals to process information and experiences automatically in such a way that creates labels, automatically imposes judgments, and fits information into existing boxes (e.g., Bargh & Chartrand, 1999).

According to self-determination theory (Deci & Ryan, 2000), these automatic processes convey adaptive benefits through reinforcing stability but also necessarily ensure that individuals process information in a self-centered or egoic manner that bolsters further goal pursuit and attainment. The result is processing characterized by *mindlessness*, or processing that adds filters to the objective reality of the world and interprets events through the lens of prior conditioning rather than openness to new perspectives. On the other hand, *mindful* processing strips away the added layers of subjectivism to objective reality, leaving a stream of consciousness intact that has a "clarity and freshness that permits more flexible, more objectively informed psychological and behavioral responses" (Brown et al., 2007, p. 212). Mindful processing thus operates outside the automaticity that pervades mindless information processing by separating the three features described above such that they do not occur in rapid succession, but rather unfold via a more conscious and intentional experiencing of the present moment.

Foundations of mindfulness at work

Kabat-Zinn (1994, p. 4) discusses mindfulness as paying attention to the present moment, which suggests the important role of attention; "without judgment," which suggests the importance of operating with metacognitive awareness; and "on purpose," which suggests the importance of intention. I suggest that intention provides a motivational component for the attentional and metacognitive aspects of mindfulness to unfold. Over time, an individual may develop the capacity to demonstrate these aspects with less effort, but at a fundamental level, mindfulness requires *intentionality*. Thus, as defined in this chapter, mindfulness at work involves *intentional attention* with *metacognition*. Including a metacognitive component to the conceptualization of mindfulness is consistent with previous theoretical work (e.g., Bishop et al., 2004; Kudesia, 2019) and speaks to the importance of experiential processing rather than conceptual processing when operating with mindfulness (Brown et al., 2007; Good et al., 2016). I review each of the key foundations of mindfulness below, which span both attentional and metacognitive aspects.

First, individuals are aware of both their inner and outer worlds at any moment in time, which allows them to experience "bare" attention (Gunaratana, 2002; Nyaniponika, 1973). They are aware of what is going on inside them as well as what is going on around them (Dane, 2011). It is as if an individual is standing in front of a perfectly polished mirror that exactly reflects their appearance. This mirror is not fogged up with steam nor streaked with fingerprints and thus is free from all impurities that add bias to the reflected image.

Second, mindful individuals do not tightly intertwine attention and cognition together, as with cognitive processing, but rather allow themselves to become aware of inputs by simply noticing what is going on (Brown & Ryan, 2003). One does not interfere with the observance of events by comparing, labeling, judging, evaluating, or ruminating on events; instead, mindful individuals are able to see thoughts as objects of attention and awareness, just like other stimuli that an individual sees, hears, or touches. Individuals who are aware that their thoughts are simply thoughts and emotions are simply emotions in reaction to these thoughts, can break free from unenlightened processing that couples thoughts and emotions together into a tangled web of beliefs and prejudices that are not supported by objective experience (Niemiec, Ryan & Brown, 2008).

Third, mindfulness consists of a nonjudgmental openness and receptivity to new information (Brown et al., 2007). Mindful individuals fully participate in life by being open to information from all their senses and take on the role of objective scientists seeking to accurately collect information. They are engaged (Baer, Smith, Hopkins, Krietemeyer, & Toney, 2006) and alert (Gunaratana, 2002) and actively seek out information, while at the same time immerse themselves in their experiences. All told, this characteristic of mindfulness helps people make informed decisions more objectively (Nyaniponika, 1973).

Fourth, mindful individuals are fully present in the current moment and do not allow themselves to be taken away inside their head to the past or future. While such "time travel" or rumination can assist with goal pursuit by facilitating planning if done intentionally (Sheldon & Vansteenkiste, 2005), unintentionally dwelling on the past and thinking about the future means an individual misses out on the present moment. Colloquial sayings emphasize the importance of the current moment by calling it a gift (i.e., the "present"), but few say it as well as Eckart Tolle: "the past gives you an identity and the future holds the promise of salvation, of fulfillment in whatever form. Both are illusions" (1999, p. 36).

Fifth, mindfulness is based on flexibility in awareness and attention. Similar to a zoom lens on a camera, a mindful individual can zoom out completely to observe a clear picture of the larger perspective and then also zoom in very closely to expose the details of a specific object (Kornfield, 1993). An example of this would be an individual walking in a forest. A mindful individual is able to intentionally alternate their awareness and attention while on the walk such that they may focus on the overall experience comprising the beautiful mountain foliage and crisp air in one moment and then purposefully direct attention toward a specific tree in another moment by intentionally focusing attention on this tree. Awareness is the larger field of what is unfolding in front of an individual and attention represents the object that grabs an individual's focus. Mindful individuals can seamlessly alternate between selecting objects to focus attention on while not losing perspective on the larger whole (Brown et al., 2007).

Finally, mindful individuals are able to recognize that they have slipped out of present-moment awareness and into ruminations about past or future experiences. They are present in the current moment and also aware when they are not. Mindful individuals have control over their awareness and attention such that they reduce the opportunity for emotions and thoughts to hijack their present-moment awareness. They experience mindfulness with more continuity and thus are able to maintain their ability to seamlessly move from broad vision to narrow focus without becoming distracted (Brown et al., 2007).

Measuring mindfulness

With the surge in mindfulness research over the last decade, the number of measures that assess the construct have also expanded in response to researchers' calls to develop psychometrically sound measures of mindfulness (Dimidjian & Linehan, 2003). Both unidimensional and multifaceted operationalizations of the construct have emerged and below I review five of the most-often utilized measures of mindfulness.

The Mindful Attention Awareness Scale (MAAS; Brown & Ryan, 2003), which is the most frequently used assessment, measures an individual's proclivity to be present in the moment during their everyday life. The 15 items assess how much an individual runs on autopilot, is aware of their actions, and pays attention to the events that unfold in the present moment. It is not surprising that the MAAS yields a single-factor structure given its items primarily tap the present-moment awareness/attention aspects of mindfulness. The Freiburg Mindfulness Inventory (FMI; Buchheld, Grossman, & Walach, 2001) is a 30-item scale that measures present-moment awareness and whether individuals are open to negative experience in a nonjudgmental way. Researchers created this scale to measure mindfulness growth between pre and post intensive mindfulness retreats (3–14 days). Exploratory factor analysis suggested a four-factor solution, but given the scale exhibited some instances of instability across pre-treatment and post-treatment, the authors suggest that the scale be treated as a unidimensional measure.

The Kentucky Inventory of Mindfulness Skills (KIMS; Baer, Smith, & Allen, 2004) consists of 39 items that measure four facets of mindfulness: observing, describing, acting with awareness, and accepting without judgment. Authors created this scale using the dialectical behavior therapy (DBT; Linehan, 1993a, 1993b) conceptualization of mindfulness skills (Baer et al., 2004) and the scale reproduced the proposed four-factor structure using student and clinical samples. The Cognitive and Affective Mindfulness Scale (CAMS; Feldman, Hayes, Kumar, Greeson, & Laurenceau, 2007; Hayes & Feldman, 2004) measures an individual's attention, awareness, present focus, and nonjudgment throughout their daily experience. Although it captures multiple aspects of mindfulness, authors recommend summing the items and using a single total mindfulness score. Finally, the Mindfulness Questionnaire (MQ; Chadwick, Hember, Mead, Lilley, & Dagnan, 2005 as cited in Baer et al., 2006) measures the extent to which individuals mindfully approach stimuli that are distressing. The authors again measure multiple aspects of mindfulness including mindful observation, nonjudgment, non-reactivity, and withholding antipathy but suggest that a single-factor structure provides the best fit for the data and do not recommend interpretation of the four factors.

Baer et al. (2006) considered the factor structure of mindfulness by examining the psychometric properties of the five mindfulness questionnaires discussed above. They concluded that mindfulness consists of five interpretable facets, four of which loaded on a second-order mindfulness factor. These four factors are: nonreactivity to inner experience, acting with awareness/concentration, describing/labeling with words, and nonjudging of experience. A fifth component, *observing,* which encompasses being in tune with one's internal and external sensations, only emerged utilizing a sample of participants with mindfulness meditation experience.

A new instrument to measure mindfulness is justified for several reasons and would confer at least four benefits to organizational researchers and practitioners. First, researchers have argued that mindfulness is a multifaceted construct (Dimidjian & Linehan, 2003; Roemer & Orsillo, 2003), but yet psychometrically, mindfulness scales have measured the construct unidimensionally. Baer et al. (2006) empirically concluded that there are five facets of mindfulness after factor-analyzing the combination of five well-cited mindfulness measures. However, with the exception of the Kentucky Inventory of Mindfulness Skills (KIMS; Baer et al., 2004) and the combination of the five mindfulness scales, each of the individual mindfulness scales reproduced a one-factor solution rather than multiple dimensions (as opposed to a multidimensional solution that also had a higher-order factor structure). Thus, there is a mismatch between mindfulness theory and measurement of the construct.

Second, a new measure would capture the theoretical bandwidth of the mindfulness construct in one instrument rather than relying on the combined items of several instruments. Given that mindfulness may be a multifaceted construct according to mindfulness theory, it is important that researchers are able to identify and measure each facet reliably over time and that each facet correlates uniquely with other psychological constructs (Smith, Fischer, & Fister, 2003). For example, the most commonly used measure of mindfulness, the Mindful Attention Awareness Scale (MAAS; Brown & Ryan, 2003), largely taps only the attention/awareness aspects of mindfulness, so it is not surprising that the factor structure is unidimensional. Third, mindfulness research has only begun to accelerate recently within the field of management, and little attention has been given to defining mindfulness within this context. For example, the MAAS measures mindfulness during daily life activities, which may limit its relevance for measuring mindfulness within the workplace. Items such as "I drive places on autopilot and wonder why I went there" and "I snack without being aware that I'm eating" may be indicative that individuals are not aware of their actions, but the question remains whether these aspects of mindfulness translate to the work domain.

Finally, since organizational behavior scholars and practitioners seek to train employees to be more mindful, a measure of mindfulness for use in the workplace should be able to be easily understood by individuals with varying degrees of experience with mindfulness and meditation. It should also be able to differentiate individuals for whom mindfulness is new from those individuals who are experienced with mindfulness and accurately trace their growth over time.

Toward a new conceptualization of mindfulness at work

I seek to redefine mindfulness and to contextualize it in the work environment. I contribute to the mindfulness literature by using insights from self-determination theory (Ryan & Deci, 2000; Ryan et al., 1997) and self-regulation theory (Carver & Scheier, 1981) to theorize that mindfulness consists of six dimensions that capture the theoretical bandwidth of the mindfulness construct. I heavily draw on the work of Glomb et al. (2011), Shapiro et al. (2006), Brown et al. (2007), and Baer et al. (2006).

First, Baer et al. (2006) statistically derived five facets of mindfulness by combining five mindfulness scales together. Four of their derived facets (nonreactivity, observing, awareness, and nonjudgment) are highly in line with how I conceptualize mindfulness and thus I retain these four components (although I label the awareness dimension "present" as in present-moment awareness). The fifth derived component in Baer et al. (2006) is "describing/labeling with words," which may be more consistent with a practice utilized to help cultivate mindfulness (i.e., acknowledge the presence of something, give it a name, and then let it go), rather than being an integral component *of* mindfulness. This type of labeling behavior thus in some ways runs counter to nonjudgmental and open awareness, which is much more about noticing rather than categorizing. Additionally, most of the items from this labeling component were from the KIMS (Baer et al., 2004), which differed from the other four measures in its inclusion of a labeling dimension, and thus I thus do not include this dimension in the overall conceptualization of mindfulness at work.

Next, I add two components—decentering and awareness of interconnections—to account for two aspects of mindfulness which are discussed in the literature but are not represented in any of the measures of mindfulness. Decentering is frequently discussed within the mindfulness literature but is not included in measures of mindfulness because it is typically discussed as an outcome of mindfulness (Glomb et al., 2011; Shapiro et al., 2006). However, I offer a different view in line with self-regulation theory. I suggest that every thought an individual has is interpreted through the lens of satisfying their own needs and goals (Ryan et al., 1997). When individuals focus on themselves, they commit their energy and resources inward, which leads to information processing that reinforces efficiency and maintenance of the self-concept and identity (Brown & Ryan, 2007). As long as an individual is operating within this biased, automatic cognitive processing (Bargh, 1994; Kahneman & Treisman, 1984), other aspects of mindfulness such as nonjudgment, equanimity, and observing openly cannot take place. I thus include decentering as a vital element *within* mindfulness and suggest that it works in tandem with the other components to ensure that automatic processing does not take precedence.

The second component I add is awareness of interconnections. This component is discussed generally in the mindfulness literature as a "greater insight into self, others, and human nature" (Brown et al., 2007, p. 226). It refers to a greater awareness that one's own goal pursuit exists within the collective goal pursuit of everyone else with whom one interacts. This component does not suggest any specific feelings or cognitions that accompany this awareness, such as putting oneself in the shoes of another as one does when feeling empathy (Eisenberg, 2000). Instead, individuals are simply aware that they are part of a larger whole and are thus able to step away from the biased processing that occurs automatically inside their heads. This allows them to gain control of their thoughts, emotions, and behaviors. When individuals are mindful such that they are operating outside of ego control, they are fully aware of what is happening internally and externally, are processing information nonjudgmentally, and they are more in tune with others, which reinforces compassion and similarity (Shapiro & Carlson, 2009). I now consider in detail each of the underlying dimensions of mindfulness.

Mindfulness at work components

Below I discuss in more detail each of the components that I suggest comprise mindfulness at work.

Nonreactivity

The first component is nonreactivity, which refers to the ability to remain even-keeled and balanced despite one's initial reactions to think or behave in a way that creates suffering (Hanson, 2009). Individuals who experience nonreactivity are fully engaged in the world but do not get derailed when a negative event happens—rather, they remain centered. Similarly, positive events do not sweep them away—they are fully engaged and present in the positive event but do not grasp for such experiences or mourn when they are over. Over time, nonreactivity brings about an inner stillness that leads to contemplative absorption (Brahm, 2006). As the Dalai Lama says, "With Equanimity, you can deal with situations with calm and reason while keeping your inner happiness" (as cited by Hanson, 2009). Individuals high in equanimity do not have high reactivity with their own inner experience and are able to reflect on their own thoughts and emotions without getting wrapped up in these thoughts and emotions too intensely. Consistent with the tenets of self-regulation theory, individuals continually seek to balance proactive as well as reactive control over their environment (Bandura, 1991), and by maintaining nonreactivity, mindful individuals are able to ensure their thoughts and emotions do not upset their internal balance.

Decentering

The second component corresponds with the creation of a mental gap between a stimulus and one's behavior (Baumeister & Sommer, 1997), which other researchers have discussed using a variety of terms such as "decoupling" (Glomb et al., 2011), "decentering" (Fresco et al., 2007; Safran & Segal, 1990; Shapiro et al., 2006), and "silencing egoic thought" (Brown et al., 2007). While much of human behavior is influenced by processes that occur automatically and nonconsciously (Bargh, 1994; Kahneman & Treisman, 1984), self-regulation theory suggests that individuals must pay attention to their thoughts and behaviors in order to understand their motivations (Ryan et al., 1997). By paying attention to the content and the extent to which their thoughts impact emotions and behaviors, mindful individuals break free from automatic processing and "ego-invested preconceived notions" (Hodgins & Knee, 2002, p. 89). In other words, in order for individuals to be mindful, they must understand that the ego is constantly operating in the background of their own consciousness. When individuals have control over this ego, it does not affect their behavioral responses, emotions, or relationships with individuals or objects in their environment. Recognizing that we are not merely "the voice in [our] head" (Tolle, 2005, p. 59) is a key aspect of mindfulness that has been understudied in relation to the sheer power it has to unlock authentic functioning (Kernis & Goldman, 2006; Niemiec et al., 2008). Thus, we are not the voice *in* the head, but rather, the *awareness* of the voice in the head.

Present-moment attention

Attention represents the focal point toward which an individual directs their resources in a given moment. Awareness refers to "conscious registration of stimuli, including the five physical senses, the kinesthetic senses, and the activities of the mind. Awareness is our most direct, most immediate contact with reality" (Brown et al., 2007, p. 212). Awareness is thus broader than attention, as *attention* specifically occurs when a stimulus is sufficiently strong to be noticed and is selected to be the object of focus from a larger set of possible focal points. Mindful individuals thus are aware of a large set of internal and external experiences and can commit their attention on an ongoing basis to stimuli occurring in the present moment (Shapiro et al., 2006). Dane (2011) provides a useful matrix which distinguishes mindfulness from other constructs and emphasizes the wide attentional breadth and high present-moment attention that characterizes mindfulness. Mindfulness has often been called "bare attention," given this process occurs before any cognitive processing takes place (Gunaratana, 2002). This component of mindfulness fits squarely within the framework of self-determination theory in its focus on individual autonomy. Individuals who are mindful are fully aware of their internal and external environments and are thus able to effectively engage in self-regulation, which allows them to maintain autonomy rather than lose their autonomy to the automatic processes that take place within the mind (Deci & Ryan, 2000). I call this component "presence" throughout the chapter.

Nonjudgment

Nonjudgment represents a fourth dimension of mindfulness. Individuals process information in a way that separates attention and cognition so that they do not occur together (e.g., Marcel, 2003), which allows them to refrain from evaluating or categorizing incoming information (Brown & Ryan, 2003). Thus, mindful individuals simply notice what is going on around them and inside them but do not attach cognitions to these events. The result is a disentangling of consciousness from the content within consciousness, effectively allowing individuals to escape from the bias that necessarily becomes associated with bare awareness. Mindful individuals are aware that their thoughts and emotions are exactly that—thoughts and emotions. Thoughts are simply the cognitions that occur in the head, and emotions are the reactions to these cognitions. This enlightened consciousness allows individuals to separate these two from the actual sensory phenomena that enter consciousness, allowing mindful individuals to experience nonjudgmental, nondiscriminatory awareness without the prejudices and biases brought about by cognitions and emotions (Niemiec et al., 2008). This awareness extends to the thoughts and emotions individuals have about themselves, about others with whom they interact, and also the environment. Consistent with self-regulation and self-determination theories, removing judgment and bias reinforces authentic and integrated functioning through a reduction of self-esteem concerns (Niemiec et al., 2010) and an increase in autonomous self-regulation (Brown & Ryan, 2003).

Observing

Observing is the fifth component of mindfulness and it includes being able to see both the big and small picture. This component encompasses the ability to be flexible in one's attention and awareness (Brown et al., 2007) or, in other words, to be able to zoom out to have clear awareness of what is taking place in the larger perspective as well as be able to zoom in to focus attention in a more narrow way depending on the circumstance. Someone who has high flexibility of thought and awareness is mindful because they are able to seamlessly shift back and forth from understanding the larger connections between events, people, and actions to focusing attention more narrowly when necessary. This component has been described as an individual's ability to notice what is present internally or externally as well as notice what is *no longer* present by moving their attention from "narrow focus to broad vista without distraction or loss of collectedness" (Brown et al., 2007, p. 214). This is similar to Dane's (2011) conceptualization of mindfulness as a state of consciousness that has relatively wide attentional breadth and high present-moment orientation. Mindful individuals can adjust their focus from wide attentional breadth to a narrower attentional breadth seamlessly like a zoom lens, which has important implications for their ability to fully grasp the complexity of a situation and behave accordingly (Ryan & Deci, 2000).

Awareness of interconnections

The final component of mindfulness is an awareness of interconnections, and this component encompasses the idea of "expanding the category of us" (Hanson, 2009). It boils down to the idea that we are all part of one world and everyone and everything is connected to everything else. Mindful individuals can see the big picture and keep this in mind when making decisions and carrying out their day-to-day actions. Mindful individuals experience integrated functioning characterized by disassociation from an existence that continually reinforces self-preservation. In other words, mindful individuals step away from a self-serving day-to-day existence and step into an existence characterized by freedom *from* this "self" biasing lens, which supports feelings of belongingness and relatedness within the social determination theory framework (Ryan & Deci, 2000; Ryan et al., 1997). This allows individuals to see themselves as players *within* the larger whole rather than spectators that merely observe the larger whole. The journey from mindless to mindfulness is akin to an individual awakening to the idea that the sun is *not* the center of the universe, as heliocentrists once thought, but rather exists in a galaxy that itself exists within the universe. Similarly, individuals, like the sun or any star, do not exist such that all other objects revolve around them—rather, there is a delicate interplay between all individuals, and mindfulness brings about an awareness of these interconnections.

Together, I suggest that nonreactivity, decentering, present-moment awareness, observing, nonjudgment, and an awareness of interconnections comprise mindfulness at work. Similar to how Shapiro et al. (2006, p. 375) describe the three axioms of mindfulness (intention, attention, and attitude) not as separate stages but rather as "interwoven aspects of a single cyclical process" that occur simultaneously, I too posit that these six components of mindfulness previously discussed reinforce each other in a dynamic process. All six components fit within the theoretical framework of self-determination theory (Deci & Ryan, 1980, 2000) and, accordingly, share conceptual overlap in their core feature of reducing the bias and "static" that ultimately interferes with integrated and authentic human behavior in relation to others and the environment.

Method

As discussed above, my theoretical conceptualization of mindfulness consists of six dimensions: (1) nonreactivity, (2) decentering, (3) presence, (4) nonjudgment, (5) observing, and (6) awareness of interconnections. Below I detail the process I used to develop the new mindfulness scale according to suggestions of DeVellis (1991) and Hinkin (1998) to ensure the content validity, reliability, and stable factor structure of this new scale.

Work Mindfulness Scale (WMS) development and validation

I used the Baer et al. (2006) five-dimension and Brown and Ryan (2003) unidimensional mindfulness scales as a guide when adapting items for each of the dimensions of mindfulness. My goal was to expand the bandwidth of the mindfulness construct as conceptualized by Brown and Ryan (2003), and develop items that would explicitly capture mindfulness in the workplace.

Phase 1: Item generation and content validity assessment

Using a deductive approach, I created an initial pool of 58 items based on my understanding of the content domain of the six dimensions of mindfulness. I then asked for feedback on these items from two management professors familiar with the mindfulness construct and the definitions of each of the dimensions. I revised the 58 items based on this feedback to ensure item clarity. Next, according to the practices suggested by Hinkin (1998), I asked six PhD students to sort each item into the one category in which it fit best according to the definition of each of the six dimensions. I instructed participants to record whether there were multiple categories in which they thought an item could fit. Across the students, 27 items were categorized into multiple categories. Based on this feedback, I studied the items and categories in which participants were unclear and revised my definitions of the dimensions in order to more clearly distinguish between items. I deleted eight items that were put in three or more categories across raters, leaving a total of 50 items. I then sent the list of items and new definitions of the dimensions to five scholars very familiar with the construct of mindfulness, asking them to sort each item into the category in which it fit best. I also asked them to note if any items did not clearly fit into only one category. Across the five scholars, a total of four items were identified that did not fit clearly into one category. I deleted these items, leaving a total of 46 items. Of these 46 items, an additional four items were deleted based on wordiness, possible difficulty in understanding based on wording, and items that were double-barreled, leaving a total of 42 items.

Phase 2: Exploratory factor analysis and item reduction

In order to further reduce items and establish a stable factor structure, I conducted exploratory factor analysis (EFA). This step is necessary in order to suggest additional items for deletion (Ford, MacCallum, & Tait, 1986) and is consistent with the work of instrument development researchers who combine both EFA and confirmatory factor analysis (CFA) in order to develop theory (Gerbing & Hamilton, 1996).

Sample 1 participants and procedure

I administered the 42 items to a sample of 226 undergraduate students from a public university in the southwestern United States. Students were recruited to participate via an announcement on their course website and offered extra credit to take part in the survey. Fifty percent of these students were women, with 73% of participants being 18–22 years of age. Multiple suggestions exist in the literature regarding the appropriate number of participants per item. For example, Rummel (1970) suggests a minimum of 1:4 while Schwab (1980) suggests as many as 1:10. This student sample size met the requirements of Rummel (1970) at around 1:5. I asked participants to indicate their agreement with each of the statements according to how they usually feel or act while working using a seven-point Likert scale (1 = strongly disagree, 2 = disagree, 3 = slightly disagree, 4 = neither agree nor disagree, 5 = somewhat agree, 6 = agree, and 7 = strongly agree).

Analyses

I first ran a principal-axis factor analysis without constraining the number of factors to determine the number of factors with eigenvalues greater than one (Kaiser, 1958). I also examined the scree plot (Cattell, 1966). Second, I ran principal component analyses with varimax rotation. I considered items for possible deletion if they (1) did not load at least 0.4 on their theorized dimension, (2) had high cross-loadings on other factors besides the factor it was supposed to measure, or (3) did not load on the factor that it was theoretically supposed to load on (DeVellis, 1991; Hinkin, 1998). I deleted items that met any of the above criteria and repeated the process until a clean set of items emerged. I calculated Cronbach's alphas to ensure that each of the scales had a reliability of .70 or greater (Nunnally, 1978).

Results

The principal-axis factor analysis resulted in ten factors with eigenvalues greater than one but the scree plot suggested five factors. Because my theory predicted six factors rather than five factors, I decided to proceed with a six-factor model principal components EFA analysis (i.e., requesting six factors in the EFA command) to explore the factor structure at the item level to determine what might be occurring with the items. The principal components analysis revealed that only two items from the "interconnections" dimension met the criteria outlined above. Multiple items assessing "interconnections" loaded highly on both the "observing" and "awareness of interconnections" factor, suggesting that these dimensions might be candidates for collapsing into a single dimension. The way I theoretically conceptualized the "observing" dimension included being aware of both the details as well as the big picture. It thus makes sense that if an individual is taking in a broad set of information internally and externally, they would also be aware of the interconnections between individuals and events. Awareness of the big picture and the small details would likely reveal an awareness of how things are interconnected as well (Brown et al., 2007).

I thus collapsed the "observing" and the "awareness of interconnections" dimensions into one and proceeded again with a five-factor principal components analysis. From this point on, I will refer to this dimension as simply "observing." I used .55 as a loading cutoff to further cull the set of items. In all, I deleted a total of 19 items, leaving 23 total items for the five dimensions. A total of six items passed the criteria for the observing and awareness of interconnections combined dimension (alpha = .73), four for the "presence" dimension (alpha = .80), five for the "decentering" dimension (alpha = .78), four for "nonreactivity" (alpha = .77), and four for "nonjudgment" (alpha = .73), resulting in a total of 23 items for the five dimensions. These 23 items had no cross-loadings above .40, and each had a factor loading above .55 on its respective factor with an average loading of .66.

Phase 3: WMS refinement and validation

Based on the suggestions of DeVellis (1991) and Hinkin (1998), I obtained three more samples to further validate the mindfulness scale. Sample 2 was collected to conduct CFA analyses to reproduce the factor structure from the EFA analyses and to ensure appropriate model fit by further validating the factor structure if needed. Sample 3 was collected to assess the mindfulness scale's construct, convergent, discriminant, and criterion-related validity (Schwab, 1980). Sample 4 was collected to cross-validate the factor structure of the state mindfulness scale and to assess the incremental validity of the mindfulness scale.

Sample 2 participants and procedures

I administered the 23 items to a second sample of 177 undergraduate students from the same public university in the southwestern United States. Students were recruited to participate via the school's official subject pool. Thirty-three percent of these students were women, with 79% of participants being 18–22 years of age.

Analyses

I conducted the following analyses to validate the mindfulness measure. First, I conducted confirmatory factor analyses (CFA) on the 23 items using Bollen's (1989) model modification procedure in Mplus Version 6.12. I specified that each of the items load on it's *a priori* factor based on theory and then considered the fit indices. Using Hu and Bentler (1999), I selected root-mean-square error of approximation (RMSEA), Tucker-Lewis index (TLI), and comparative fit index (CFI) for fit indices. Acceptable fit values for each of these indices are less than .05 for RMSEA, and higher than .90 for TLI and CFI (Hu & Bentler, 1999). I checked the modification indices to identify items that may have been reducing the overall model fit. Modification indices correspond with the amount of decrease in chi square value that results when a given parameter is freed (allowed to correlate) or fixed to zero. Items that generated modification indices of more than 10 were candidates for deletion. I especially considered items in which MPlus identified that the fit of the model would significantly increase if error terms on individual items were allowed to correlate or if items were allowed to load on multiple factors. I deleted items that met these criteria and reran the model until there were no more items that generated modification indices greater than 10.

Results

The initial set of mindfulness items that underwent the measurement refinement process included 23 items for five dimensions. The baseline model generated the following goodness-of-fit indices: $\chi^2(220) = 490.82$, $p < 0.05$; CFI = 0.88, TLI = 0.86, and RMSEA = 0.083. RMSEA, CFI, and TLI did not pass the cutoff values. The items generating the highest modification indices were deleted. In all, four items total were deleted, leaving a total of 19 items (four decentering, four observing, four nonreactivity, four nonjudgment, and three presence). The final model generated the following goodness-of-fit indices: $\chi^2(142) = 222.45$ $p < 0.01$; CFI = 0.95, TLI = 0.94, and RMSEA = 0.057.

Because all five dimensions were expected to reflect mindfulness, a second-order CFA was conducted to determine whether a higher-order factor could better account for the item structure. I added a second-order factor to Model 2 such that each of the five mindfulness dimensions also was used as an indicator of a second-order work mindfulness factor. Because comparison between non-nested models is not appropriate using the fit indices previously discussed, I used Akaike's Information Criterion (AIC: Akaike, 1987) to compare Models 2 and 3. Model 3 generated a higher AIC than Model 2 ($AIC_{diff} = 10.1$). This suggests that the second-order measurement model fit the data less well when compared with the measurement model with five first-order factors.

Sample 3 participants and procedures

The purpose for Sample 3 was to assess the WMS's construct, convergent, discriminant, and criterion-related validity. Participants were recruited to participate via an organizational contact who sent out a request for participation to all business school staff employees at the same public university in the southwestern United States. A total of 168 usable surveys were completed out of a total possible 306 for a response rate of 55%. Sixty-two percent of the participants were female with 53% of the sample 31–50 years of age and 64% of the sample had over ten years of work experience.

Measures

All measures were obtained on a six-point Likert scale (1 = strongly disagree, 2 = disagree, 3 = somewhat disagree, 4 = somewhat agree, 5 = agree, 6 = strongly agree) unless otherwise noted.

Trait WMS

Mindfulness was measured with the 19 items that resulted from the Sample 2 CFA analyses using a six-point frequency scale (1 = almost always, 2 = very frequently, 3 = somewhat frequently, 4 = somewhat infrequently, 5 = very infrequently, 6 = almost never). The Cronbach's alpha of this scale was 0.87.

Brown and Ryan (2003) measure of trait mindfulness

A second measure of trait mindfulness was collected using 15 items from Brown and Ryan (2003). A sample item was "I break or spill things because I am careless, not paying attention, or thinking of something else." The Cronbach's alpha of this scale was 0.88.

Social desirability

Social desirability was measured with four items from Paulhus (1991). A sample item was "I never regret my decisions." The Cronbach's alpha of this scale was 0.59.

Emotional intelligence

Emotional intelligence was measured with two items from Wong and Law (2002). A sample item was "I have good control of my own emotions." The Cronbach's alpha of this scale was 0.74.

Openness to experience

Openness to experience was measured with two items form Gosling, Rentfrow, and Swann (2003). A sample item was "I see myself as someone who is open to new experiences, complex." The Cronbach's alpha of this scale was 0.71.

Neuroticism

Neuroticism was measured with two items from Gosling et al. (2003). A sample item was "I see myself as someone who is anxious and easily upset." The Cronbach's alpha of this scale was 0.85.

Anxiety

Anxiety was measured with four items from Bieling, Antony, and Swinson (1998). A sample item was "I worry too much over something that really doesn't matter." The Cronbach's alpha of this scale was 0.85.

Core self-evaluation

Core self-evaluation was measured with four items from Judge, Erez, Bono, and Thoresen (2003). A sample item was "I am confident I get the success I deserve in life." The Cronbach's alpha of this scale was 0.70.

Self-monitoring

Self-monitoring was measured with four items from Lennox and Wolfe (1984). A sample item was "I have found that I can adjust my behavior to meet the requirements of any situation I find myself in." The Cronbach's alpha of this scale was 0.79.

Analysis

Using this refined set of items, I ran several CFAs to evaluate the construct validity of the WMS. Using the procedures suggested by Podsakoff and MacKenzie (1994), construct validity of the mindfulness construct would be demonstrated if (1) the five-factor structure of the data would adequately explain the covariance between items, (2) each item loaded significantly on its respective factor, and (3) all five of the dimensions account for a substantial amount of variance for their respective indicators.

I evaluated the discriminant validity of the mindfulness measure as compared with other constructs including anxiety, neuroticism, core self-evaluation, self-monitoring, and openness to experience. I utilized the Anderson and Gerbing (1988) approach which utilizes CFA. I ran a six-factor baseline model with the WMS, anxiety, neuroticism, core self-evaluation, self-monitoring, and openness to experience each as their own factor. I then compared this baseline model with a series of five-factor models in which I combined the WMS and another one of the constructs. When all of the five-factor models generated worse fit indices when compared with the six-factor model, the results support the discriminant validity of the WMS.

Nomological validity of the WMSs was assessed by considering the correlations between mindfulness and other related constructs including emotional intelligence, neuroticism, openness to experience, anxiety, self-monitoring, social desirability, neuroticism, and the Brown and Ryan (2003) measure of mindfulness. Mindfulness was expected to relate positively to emotional intelligence, self-monitoring, openness to experience, the Brown and Ryan (2003) mindfulness measure, and negatively with neuroticism and anxiety.

Results

Construct validity of the WMS dimensions

I assessed the construct validity of the mindfulness measure by confirming the factor structure obtained from Sample 2, this time using an employee sample (Sample 3). The CFA generated good results $\chi^2(142) = 216.26$, $p < 0.01$; CFI = 0.95, TLI = 0.93, and RMSEA = 0.056. All items loaded on their specified factors significantly, and the standardized loadings were substantial in size (M = 0.74, SD = 0.05). The average composite reliability was .82, ranging from .79 for observing and .86 for presence. The five factors explained a moderate amount of variance in the items (M = 55%, SD = .07). Based on the overall model fit, the significant factor loadings, and amount of variance in items accounted for by the factor structure, the mindfulness scale demonstrated good construct validity. Table 4.1 demonstrates the factor structure and composite reliability for each dimension and lists the items for the final 19-item mindfulness scale. The standardized loading of each WMS dimension with the overall latent construct ranged from .40 to .80 (nonjudgment and decentering, respectively), with an average loading of .57.

Discriminant validity of the new mindfulness measure and other constructs

I used Omnibus CFA to evaluate the discriminant validity of the WMS. I fit a six-factor model in which I used the average score of each dimension as an indicator of mindfulness and each item as an indicator of its respective construct (i.e., anxiety, neuroticism, core self-evaluation, self-monitoring, and openness to experience). The baseline model generated

Table 4.1 Standardized factor loadings and composite reliability for each dimension of the WMS after refinement process using Sample 3 employee data[a].

Items	*CR*	*Loading*
Presence	.86	
1. When I'm working on something, part of my mind is occupied with other things, such as what I'll be doing later or things I'd rather be doing.		.61
2. My mind often wanders at work, which makes it difficult for me stay focused in the present moment.		.95
3. I find it difficult to stay focused on what's happening in the current moment at work due to being distracted.		.88
Observe	.79	
4. I am able to shift my focus from the big picture to the details at work.		.78
5. I understand how everyday tasks at work contribute to achieving the big picture.		.66
6. I recognize that my work impacts others both inside and outside my organization.		.71
7. I notice how people are interconnected at work.		.64
Nonreactivity	.82	
8. I don't allow my mood to be swayed when I experience negative or self-defeating thoughts at work.		.58
9. When something bad happens to me at work, I am able to quickly let it go.		.78
10. I experience thoughts and emotions at work but do not let them distract me.		.79
11. I am able to step back and be aware of my thoughts or emotions at work without getting taken over by them.		.74
Nonjudgment	.83	
12. I tend to form opinions about how worthwhile or worthless others' experiences are at work.		.75
13. I tend to make judgments about individuals quickly at work when meeting them for the first time.		.81
14. I am critical of others when they display irrational or inappropriate emotions at work.		.68
15. During a conversation at work, I often evaluate what an individual is saying and make judgments about their character.		.72
Decentering	.82	
16. I feel the need to reinforce my accomplishments at work to maintain my self-esteem.		.65
17. I get defensive at work in order to protect my feelings of self-worth.		.78
18. I feel personally attacked when my ideas are not validated at work.		.76
19. When I experience a setback at work, my ego takes a blow.		.74

a Final items for WMS. CR = composite reliability.

good fit indices: $\chi^2(209) = 356.14$ $p < 0.01$; CFI = 0.91, TLI = 0.89, and RMSEA = 0.065. I then compared this baseline model to six alternative models in which the mindfulness indicators were combined with the items from one of the other scales (i.e., I combined WMS with each of the other constructs). The sequential chi-square difference test (SCDT) tests were all significant, indicating that the baseline model with six dimensions for the six separate constructs was the best-fitting model, subsequently supporting the discriminant validity of the

Table 4.2 Results of Omnibus confirmatory factor analysis for WMS and discriminant validity with other constructs using Sample 3 employee data

Model	*χ2*	*df*	*SCDT*	*RMSEA*	*CFI*	*TLI*
Model 1 Baseline 7—Factor Model (WMS, anxiety, neuroticism, core self-evaluation, self-monitoring, openness to experience, and emotional intelligence)	356.14	209		.065	.91	.89
Model 2 WMS and anxiety	405.62	215	49.48**	.073	.88	.86
Model 3 WMS and neuroticism	405.26	215	49.12**	.073	.88	.86
Model 4 WMS and core self-evaluation	410.16	215	54.02**	.074	.88	.86
Model 5 WMS and self-monitoring	505.81	215	149.67**	.090	.82	.78
Model 6 WMS and openness to experience	434.62	215	78.48**	.078	.86	.84
Model 7 WMS and emotional intelligence	466.00	215	109.86**	.083	.84	.81

Note. SCDT = sequential chi-square difference test. ** p<.01.

WMS. Table 4.2 summarizes these omnibus CFA results when comparing the WMS to these related measures.

Nomological validity of the WMS

Table 4.3 shows the correlations between the WMS, the Brown and Ryan (2003) mindfulness measures, and other constructs. As expected, WMS exhibited small positive correlations with emotional intelligence, self-monitoring, and core self-evaluation, and it exhibited small to medium negative correlations with anxiety and neuroticism after controlling for social desirability.

Sample 4 participants and procedures

Sample 4 was collected to cross-validate the factor structure of the state WMS scale and to assess the incremental validity of the scale. Participants were recruited to participate via Amazon's Mechanical Turk (MTurk). A total of 237 usable surveys were completed out of a total of 310 for a response rate of 76%. Thirty-eight percent of the participants were female with 54% of the sample 25–34 years of age.

Table 4.3 Correlations between WMS and related measures using Sample 3 employee data

	WMS Mindfulness Scale	*Brown and Ryan (2003)*
Emotional intelligence	.34**	.21**
Self-monitoring	.26**	.15
Core self-evaluation	.32**	.29**
Anxiety	–.45**	–.45**
Openness to experience	.04	–.07
Neuroticism	–.32**	–.23*

Note. The standardized correlations between WMS and related measures partialling out the influence of social desirability to control for common method variance. * p<.05; ** p <.01

Measures

All measures were obtained on a five-point Likert scale (1 = strongly disagree, 2 = disagree, 3 = neither agree or nor disagree, 4 = agree, 5 = strongly agree).

State WMS

State mindfulness was measured with the 19 items from the previously validated trait mindfulness scale, with the items adjusted to be more in line with state measurement. For example, I adjusted the trait item "I am able to shift my focus from the big picture to the details" to "I was able to shift my focus from the big picture to the details" and adjusted the directions from "Please indicate the extent to which you agree/disagree with each of the following in general at work . . ." to "Thinking back on your day at work so far, please indicate the extent to which you agree/disagree with each of the following . . .". Table 4.4 lists the adjusted state mindfulness items. The

Table 4.4 State WMS items used to test nomological validity in Sample 4 Mturk data

Items
Presence
1. Part of my mind was occupied with other things, such as what I'll be doing later or things I'd rather be doing.
2. My mind wandered, which made it difficult for me stay focused in the present moment.
3. I found it difficult to stay focused on what was happening due to being distracted.
Observing
4. I was able to shift my focus from the big picture to the details.
5. I felt I understand how everyday tasks of my role contribute to achieving the big picture.
6. I recognized how my work impacts others both inside and outside my organization.
7. I noticed how people are interconnected at work.
Nonreactivity
8. I did not allow my mood to be swayed when I experienced negative or self-defeating thoughts.
9. When something bad happened to me, I was able to quickly let it go.
10. I experienced thoughts and emotions but did not let them distract me.
11. I found myself able to step back and be aware of my thoughts or emotions without getting taken over by them.
Nonjudgement
12. I tended to form opinions about how worthwhile or worthless others' experiences were at work.
13. I tended to make judgments about individuals quickly when seeing them for the first time in the morning.
14. I found myself being critical of others when they were irrational or displayed inappropriate emotions.
15. During conversations, I found myself evaluating what an individual was saying and making judgments about their character.
Decentering
16. I felt the need to reinforce my accomplishments at work to maintain my self-esteem.
17. I became defensive at work in order to protect my feelings of self-worth.
18. I felt personally attacked when my ideas were not validated at work.
19. When I experienced a setback at work, my ego took a blow.

standardized loading of each WMS dimension with the overall latent construct ranged from .37 to .81 (nonjudgment and nonreactivity, respectively), with an average loading of .65. The Cronbach's alpha of the overall scale was 0.89.

Brown and Ryan (2003) state mindfulness

State mindfulness was also measured by the five items from Brown and Ryan (2003) that have been used in previous research to assess state mindfulness. A sample item was "I rushed through activities without being really attentive to them." The Cronbach's alpha of this scale was 0.88.

Psychological well-being

Psychological well-being was measured with 18 items from Ryff and Keyes (1995). A sample item was "I have aims and objectives for living." The Cronbach's alpha of this scale was 0.90.

Job satisfaction

Job satisfaction was measured with three items from Hackman and Oldham (1974). A sample item was "I am generally satisfied with the kind of work I do in this job." The Cronbach's alpha of this scale was 0.89.

Life satisfaction

Life satisfaction was measured with five items from Diener, Emmons, Larsen, and Griffin (1985). A sample item was "In most ways, my life is close to ideal." The Cronbach's alpha of this scale was 0.91.

Social desirability

Social desirability was measured with four items from Paulhus (1991). A sample item was "I never regret my decisions." The Cronbach's alpha of this scale was 0.66.

Analysis

In order to investigate the incremental validity of the WMS, I conducted usefulness analysis (Darlington, 1990). I used hierarchical regression to test the contribution of the WMS over and above the predictive power of the Brown and Ryan (2003) Mindful Attention Awareness Scale (MAAS) consistent with the approach taken by Judge et al. (2003). I compared the results of the MAAS predicting job satisfaction in the first step and the WMS entered into the second step of the hierarchical regression analysis with the reverse-ordering of variables in which the WMS was entered first. I also conducted this analysis with psychological well-being and life satisfaction as dependent variables. All told, 12 separate hierarchical regressions were conducted, which attenuates multicollinearity that may be present between the independent measures (Cohen, Cohen, West, & Aiken, 2003). In order to control for the effects of social desirability given that all measures were self-report, I also included social desirability in the first step with the predictor.

Results

I assessed the convergent validity of the WMS by applying the factor structure previously validated. The CFA generated good results $\chi^2(142) = 226.02$, $p < 0.05$; CFI = 0.96, TLI = 0.96, and RMSEA = 0.050 providing support for the state WMS.

Finally, usefulness analysis results revealed that adding the WMS in the second step resulted in significant R^2 increases for job satisfaction ($\Delta R^2 = .14$, $p < .001$), psychological well-being ($\Delta R^2 = .18$, $p < .001$), and life satisfaction ($\Delta R^2 = .08$, $p < .001$). When the order was reversed, the WMS accounted for all of the variance in job satisfaction and psychological well-being with no significant R^2 increase when adding the Brown and Ryan (2003) mindfulness measure. For life satisfaction, the Brown and Ryan (2003) mindfulness measure predicted an additional 2% of variance ($\Delta R^2 = .02$, $p < .001$). Overall, these results provide strong evidence for the incremental validity of the WMS.

Discussion

In this chapter, I integrate mindfulness research and validate a measure of workplace mindfulness. This chapter seeks to makes two primary theoretical contributions to the mindfulness literature broadly and to the mindfulness at work literature more specifically. The first contribution is expanding the conceptual bandwidth of the mindfulness construct and creating a measure that differentiates between different aspects of mindfulness. The most often used scale to measure mindfulness by Brown and Ryan (2003) is unidimensional and primarily assesses an individual's attention and awareness in the present moment. This scale exhibits positive and moderate relationships with each of the five dimensions of mindfulness of the newly created and validated mindfulness scale, suggesting that the Brown and Ryan (2003) scale does a good job of getting at a "core" idea of mindfulness, but in doing so, is only gently tapping aspects of each of the underlying dimensions of mindfulness that are often referred to within mindfulness theory (cf. Brown & Ryan, 2003; Brown et al., 2007; Shapiro et al., 2006). The present work advances mindfulness theory by adding decentering as a fundamental component of mindfulness rather than an outcome of mindfulness. The current conceptualization of mindfulness suggests that recognizing the presence of one's ego being constantly activated in self-preservation mode, is a key component of enabling an individual to be present in the current moment. When individuals are less driven by their ego and the need to reinforce their self-value and worth, they exist more authentically within the here and now rather than being distracted by "head-talk" that pulls them away from the present moment and toward the future or the past.

A second theoretical contribution is to add to our understanding of how mindfulness manifests in the work domain. The new conceptualization of mindfulness created and validated in this chapter advances mindfulness theory at work by demonstrating that a broader conceptualization of mindfulness exhibits higher correlations with important outcomes than does the Brown and Ryan (2003) mindfulness measure. This makes sense theoretically given the more general nature of the items of the Brown and Ryan (2003) measure versus the more tightly worded items from the new conceptualization of workplace mindfulness that specifically taps into how mindfulness is demonstrated within the work domain. Thus, the expanded theoretical conceptualization of the mindfulness construct makes it more applicable to the work domain, and the new measure allows for a more nuanced understanding of mindfulness in the workplace rather than a general sense of paying attention to the present moment, which the Brown and Ryan (2003) scale provides.

There are also at least three practical contributions to the present work. The first is that the current conceptualization and measurement of workplace mindfulness introduces a new tool for managers and practitioners to track individuals' levels of mindfulness over time. Mindfulness interventions and workshops are increasingly being offered at multiple organizations across the world. For example, Google has offered its employees a mindfulness-based training program called "Search Inside Yourself" since 2007, in which employees focus on three main activities—attention training, self-knowledge and self-mastery, and creating useful mental habits (Tan, 2014). Employees have seen improvements in their ability to manage their emotions, their responses to stressors, their levels of compassion toward others, and their productivity levels in that they can accomplish more by giving themselves the mental and physical space to clear the head and calm their racing thoughts.

Aetna similarly offers employees free yoga and meditation classes, which has led to increased levels of employee productivity and reduced reports of stress and pain (Gelles, 2015). The WMS discussed in this chapter provides an additional tool for companies such as Google and Aetna who are leading the way among Fortune 100 companies in integrating mindfulness-based practices to help employees achieve higher levels of well-being. The new validated measure can help employees better understand their strengths and opportunities when it comes to integrating mindfulness more holistically into their work and personal lives given the multidimensional nature of the new instrument. For example, individuals can learn that they may be weak on the ability to decenter in the moment but strong on observing internal and external stimuli in the moment. This may lead to improved self-awareness and to the development of more effective interventions targeted toward improving specific aspects of mindfulness.

Second, the present work aids in further demystifying the mindfulness construct and normalizing its relevance and applicability to the workplace. Organizational scholars have been slow to integrate mindfulness: perhaps they lack understanding, dismiss it as simply the newest "fad" in management (see Fiol & O'Connor, 2003 for a discussion of mindfulness and bandwagons), or because they equate it with Eastern practices of spirituality. However, given its age-old practice and focus on how to truly connect with the world and the people in it, mindfulness has a vital place within our organizations given the importance of working in harmony with those around us in an organization to ensure its success. As people are increasingly seen as an organization's "most valuable asset" (Duncan, 2013), mindfulness will only continue to become more relevant as it makes genuine and compassionate interactions between organizational members more likely and frequent. Additionally, given that organizations are always trying to find ways to develop employees and that mindfulness is highly variable across days, human resource and training departments can utilize the WMS to help *develop* employees already working at a company, rather than solely relying on trait assessments of personality to aid in *selection* of employees.

Third, the current conceptualization of mindfulness is very accessible for organizational employees because it presents mindfulness more as a holistic set of behaviors rather than a philosophical way of viewing the world. While mindfulness is indeed a way of viewing the world, this conceptualization may not appeal to many organizational employees as it may seem foreign and too "touchy-feely" for wide adoption. However, the way I discuss mindfulness distills its underlying principles into more practical ways in which individuals can connect more authentically with others in the workplace or gain additional insight into their own biases and ways of processing information. Former CEO of Aetna Ron Williams challenged his employees to think about "how much better our workplaces would be if we all *assumed positive intent* on behalf of everyone with whom we interacted." When employees are mindful, I suggest that they *do* assume the best from others given that they are less likely to be driven by the need to reinforce their own egos. When individuals escape from this ego-based processing, they can more authentically connect with their coworkers.

Future research directions

Researchers have suggested that the effects of mindfulness on social relationships represent an area ripe for future research and theory development (Brown et al., 2007) and that an exploration of the mechanisms by which mindfulness impacts social relationships is especially warranted (Glomb et al., 2011). Previous research has supported positive relationships between mindfulness and intimate relationships (Saavedra, Chapman, & Rogge, 2010), social connectedness (Hutcherson, Seppala, & Gross, 2008), relatedness and interpersonal closeness (Brown & Kasser, 2005), and relationship satisfaction (Barnes, Brown, Krusemark, Campbell, & Rogge, 2007). Future research can utilize the WMS to better understand the effects of mindfulness on focal individuals (e.g., decreased rumination and increased working memory) as well as the effects of a focal individual's mindfulness on how they perceive and treat others (e.g., empathy, affective regulation, and response flexibility).

Future research should seek to understand how mindfulness at work relates to self-regulation, which may assist leaders in appreciating and reacting to follower needs. Mindfulness at work may be an important missing link when it comes to unlocking how leaders can more effectively come to understand what followers most require from them behaviorally in various situations and how they can adapt their behaviors to better meet these expectations. Mindful leaders may be better able to regulate their emotions so they do not become overtaken by negative emotions, feel more empathy toward others, and be able to respond more flexibly due to not being confined by automatic or routine ways of processing information (Glomb et al., 2011). Through these self-regulatory mechanisms, leaders may be able to remain attentive and focused on what their followers most require and the situation calls for without getting lost in their own heads. This tailored set of leadership behaviors allows leaders to best support their followers, which then translates to high levels of follower effectiveness. Future research should further seek to untangle this fascinating and elusive question regarding leaders' ultimate ability to "flex" their behaviors to meet the needs of dynamically changing environments.

As suggested in this chapter and in previous work, mindfulness may be best conceptualized as a state-like construct in the workplace given that individuals' thoughts and emotions come and go and largely are influenced by the events that occur on a given day. For example, a leader may come to work one day after having had an argument with their partner and may be replaying the conversation over and over in their head. If this individual filled out a measure of trait mindfulness on this particular morning, they would likely score lower on mindfulness than if they hasn't had that particular incident occur previously. Thus, it may be much more accurate and informative to measure individuals' levels of state mindfulness at multiple points in time to empirically derive an "average" level of mindfulness that is more indicative of their trait mindfulness than it is to collect a measure of trait mindfulness at one point in time. That being said, individuals will exhibit higher or lower average levels of mindfulness across a wide variety of situations, but it may be more instructive to consider state mindfulness aggregated over time to best understand how mindfulness operates within the work environment to affect important outcomes. Daily diary or experience sampling methodology (ESM) studies utilizing state measures of mindfulness would be especially well suited to understand how mindfulness fluctuates day-to-day and can account for variance in outcomes of interest throughout the work week.

Future work should continue to utilize the current mindfulness scale as well as the Brown and Ryan (2003) scale in order to investigate how mindfulness interventions lead to changes in state and trait mindfulness over time. Teasing out how each of the factors of the WMS may differentially predict outcomes at work represents an especially important area for future inquiry. Understanding the patterns of relationships which best *predict* facets of mindfulness and are best *predicted by* specific mindfulness at work facets will contribute to the usefulness and validity of the WMS.

Finally, future research should consider mindfulness of multiple individuals in tandem at work. For example, if followers are rating their leader's behaviors, the extent to which these followers are mindful may play an important role in determining whether their ratings are accurate and in tune with the leader's intentions rather than biased by the followers' own views of their leader or judgments they may make about them. Integrating a more follower-centric approach to leadership (Bligh, 2011; Shamir, 2007) by including both leader and follower mindfulness as well as studying the contagion effects of mindfulness across organizational members are two additional ways to advance the future study of mindfulness in the workplace.

Conclusion

The Work Mindfulness Scale (WMS) proposed and initially validated in this chapter provides a multidimensional approach to conceptualizing how mindfulness unfolds in the work context. Five factors tapping both attentional and metacognitive aspects of mindfulness were replicated across four distinct samples, providing initial evidence supporting the validity and usefulness of the new measure. Future research investigating the nomological network of each of the dimensions of the WMS represents an important next step in the validation process as scholarship and the practical interest in mindfulness at work continues to accelerate.

Key takeaways/lessons

1. Mindfulness has been previously discussed as a multidimensional construct yet measured unidimensionally.
2. Mindfulness at work can be conceptualized according to five facets—nonreactivity, observing, presence, decentering, and nonjudgment, which comprise aspects of both attention and metacognition.
3. The Work Mindfulness Scale (WMS) assesses mindfulness at work and has face validity for organizational employees.
4. Research distinguishing *intra*personal vs. *inter*personal outcomes of mindfulness is ripe for future inquiry.
5. Future research should consider how mindfulness can impact relationships at work by assessing mindfulness of multiple individuals at the same time.

Reflection questions

1. Why is it important to have a mindfulness measure specific to the work context?
2. Which of the WMS components might be most challenging for individuals to develop and why?

3. Are their particular patterns or configurations of mindfulness facets that individuals exhibit most frequently/infrequently?
4. Does mindfulness as a construct differ across cultures?
5. How might considering levels of mindfulness of multiple individuals simultaneously allow for a better understanding of the relationship they develop or the relationship trajectory?

References

Akaike, H. (1987). Factor analysis and AIC. *Psychometrika, 52*(3), 317–332.

Anderson, J. C., & Gerbing, D. W. (1988). Structural equation modeling in practice: A review and recommended two-step approach. *Psychological Bulletin, 103*(3), 411–423.

Baer, R. A., Smith, G. T., & Allen, K. B. (2004). Assessment of mindfulness by self-report the Kentucky inventory of mindfulness skills. *Assessment, 11*(3), 191–206.

Baer, R. A., Smith, G. T., Hopkins, J., Krietemeyer, J., & Toney, L. (2006). Using self-report assessment methods to explore facets of mindfulness. *Assessment, 13*(1), 27–45.

Bandura, A. (1991). Social cognitive theory of self-regulation. *Organizational Behavior and Human Decision Processes, 50*(2), 248–287.

Bargh, J. A. (1994). The four horsemen of automaticity: Intention, awareness, efficiency, and control as separate issues. In R. S. Wyer & T. K. Srull (Eds.), *Handbook of social cognition: Vol. 1, Basic processes* (2nd. ed., pp. 1–40). Hillsdale, NJ: Erlbaum.

Bargh, J. A., & Chartrand, T. L. (1999). The unbearable automaticity of being. *American Psychologist, 54*, 462–479.

Barnes, S., Brown, K. W., Krusemark, E., Campbell, W. K., & Rogge, R. D. (2007). The role of mindfulness in romantic relationship satisfaction and responses to relationship stress. *Journal of Marital and Family Therapy, 33*(4), 482–500.

Baumeister, R. E., & Sommer, K. L. (1997). Consciousness, free choice, and automaticity. In R. S. Wyer (Ed.), *Advances in social cognition* (Vol. 10, pp. 75–82). Mahwah, NJ: Lawrence Erlbaum.

Beard, A. (2014). Mindfulness in the age of complexity: An interview with Ellen Langer. *Harvard Business Review (Reprint R1403D), March, 1-7.*

Bieling, P. J., Antony, M. M., & Swinson, R. P. (1998). The state-trait anxiety inventory, Trait version: Structure and content re-examined. *Behavior Research and Therapy, 36*, 777–788.

Bishop, S. R., Lau, M., Shapiro, S., Carlson, L., Anderson, N. D., Carmody, J., . . . Devins, G. (2004). Mindfulness: A proposed operational definition. *Clinical Psychology: Science and Practice, 11*(3), 230–241.

Bligh, M. C. (2011). Followership and follower-centred approaches. In A. Bryman, D. Collinson, K. Grint, B. Jackson, & M. Ulh-Bien (Eds.), *The Sage handbook of leadership* (pp. 425–436). Los Angeles, CA: Sage.

Bollen, K. A. (1989). *Structural equations with latent variables*. New York: Wiley.

Brahm, A. (2006). *Mindfulness, bliss, and beyond: A meditator's handbook.* Boston: Wisdom Publications.

Brown, K. W., & Kasser, T. (2005). Are psychological and ecological wellbeing compatible? The role of values, mindfulness, and lifestyle. *Social Indicators Research, 74*, 349–368.

Brown, K. W. Richard M. Ryan & J. David Creswell (2007) Mindfulness: Theoretical Foundations and Evidence for its Salutary Effects, Psychological Inquiry, 18:4, 211–237, DOI: 10.1080/10478400701598298

Brown, K. W., & Ryan, R. M. (2003). The benefits of being present: Mindfulness and its role in psychological well-being. *Journal of Personality and Social Psychology, 84*(4), 822.

Brown, K. W., Ryan, R. M., & Creswell, J. D. (2007). Mindfulness: Theoretical foundations and evidence for its salutary effects. *Psychological Inquiry, 18*(4), 211–237.

Buchheld, N., Grossman, P., & Walach, H. (2001). Measuring mindfulness in insight meditation (Vipassana) and meditation-based psychotherapy: The development of the Freiburg Mindfulness Inventory (FMI). *Journal of Meditation and Meditation Research, 1*, 11–34.

Carmeli, A., & Gittell, J. H. (2009). High-quality relationships, psychological safety, and learning from failures in work organizations. *Journal of Organizational Behavior, 30*(6), 709–729.

Carver, C. S., & Scheier, M. F. (1981). *Attention and self-regulation: A control-theory approach to human behavior*. New York: Springer-Verlag.

Cattell, R. B. (1966). The scree test for the number of factors. *Multivariate Behavioral Research, 1*(2), 245–276.

Cohen, P., Cohen, J., West, S., & Aiken, L. (2003). *Applied Multiple Regression/Correlation for the Behavioral Sciences* (3rd ed.). NY: Routledge.

Dane, E. (2011). Paying attention to mindfulness and its effects on task performance in the workplace. *Journal of Management, 37*, 997–1018.

Darlington, R. B. (1990). *Regression and linear models*. New York, NY: McGraw-Hill.

Deci, E. L., & Ryan, R. M. (1980). The empirical exploration of intrinsic motivational processes. In L. Berkowitz (Ed.), *Advances in Experimental Social Psychology* (Vol. *13*, pp. 39–80). New York: Academic.

Deci, E. L., & Ryan, R. M. (2000). The" what" and" why" of goal pursuits: Human needs and the self-determination of behavior. *Psychological Inquiry, 11*(4), 227–268.

DeVellis, R. F. (1991). *Scale development: Theory and applications*. Newbury Park, CA: Sage.

Diener, E. D., Emmons, R. A., Larsen, R. J., & Griffin, S. (1985). The satisfaction with life scale. *Journal of Personality Assessment, 49*(1), 71–75.

Dimidjian, S., & Linehan, M. M. (2003). Defining an agenda for future research on the clinical application of mindfulness practice. *Clinical Psychology: Science and Practice, 10*, 166–171.

Duncan, R. D. (2013). *Nine Ways To Keep Your Company's Most Valuable Asset – Its Employees*. Forbes, 8/20/2013. Retrieved 3/ 15/15from www.forbes.com/sites/forbesleadershipforum/2013/08/20/nine-ways-to-keep-your-companys-most-valuable-asset-its-employees/

Eisenberg, N. (2000). Empathy and sympathy. In M. Lewis & J. M. Haviland-Jones (Eds.), *Handbook of emotions* (pp. 677–691). New York: Guilford Press.

Feldman, G., Hayes, A., Kumar, S., Greeson, J., & Laurenceau, J.-P. (2007). Mindfulness and emotion regulation: The development and initial validation of the Cognitive and Affective Mindfulness Scale–Revised (CAMS-R). *Journal of Psychopathology and Behavioral Assessment, 29*, 177–190.

Fiol, C. M., & O'Connor, E. J. (2003). Waking up! Mindfulness in the face of bandwagons. *Academy of Management Review, 28*(1), 54–70.

Ford, J. K., MacCallum, R. C., & Tait, M. (1986). The application of exploratory factor analysis in applied psychology: A critical review and analysis. *Personnel Psychology, 39*(2), 291–314.

Fresco, D. M., Moore, M. T., van Dulmen, M. H., Segal, Z. V., Ma, S. H., Teasdale, J. D., & Williams, J. M. G. (2007). Initial psychometric properties of the experiences questionnaire: Validation of a self-report measure of decentering. *Behavior Therapy, 38*(3), 234–246.

Gelles, D. (2015). At Aetna, a C.E.O.'s Management by Mantra. *New York Times*, February 27, 2015. Retrieved 3/15/2015 from www.nytimes.com/2015/03/01/business/at-aetna-a-ceos-management-by-mantra.html?_r=3

Gerbing, D. W., & Hamilton, J. G. (1996). Viability of exploratory factor analysis as a precursor to confirmatory factor analysis. *Structural Equation Modeling: A Multidisciplinary Journal, 3*(1), 62–72.

Glomb, T. M., Duffy, M. K., Bono, J. E., & Yang, T. (2011). Mindfulness at work. *Research in Personnel and Human Resources Management, 30*, 115–157.

Good, D. J., Lyddy, C. J., Glomb, T. M., Bono, J. E., Brown, K. W., Duffy, M. K., . . . Lazar, S. W. (2016). Contemplating mindfulness at work: An integrative review. *Journal of Management, 42*(1), 114–142.

Gosling, S. D., Rentfrow, P. J., & Swann, W. B. (2003). A very brief measure of the Big-Five personality domains. *Journal of Research in Personality, 37*(6), 504–528.

Gunaratana, B. H. (2002). *Mindfulness in Plain English*. Somerville, MA: Wisdom.

Hackman, J. R., & Oldham, G. R. (1974). The job diagnostic survey: An instrument for the diagnosis of jobs and the evaluation of job redesign projects. *Catalog of Selected Documents in Psychology*, 4: 148–149..

Hanson, R. (2009). *Buddha's brain: The practical neuroscience of happiness, love, and wisdom*. Oakland, CA: New Harbinger Publications.

Hayes, A. M., & Feldman, G. (2004). Clarifying the construct of mindfulness in the context of emotion regulation and the process of change in therapy. *Clinical Psychology: Science and Practice, 11*, 255–262.

Hinkin, T. R. (1998). A brief tutorial on the development of measures for use in survey questionnaires. *Organizational Research Methods, 1*(1), 104–121.

Hodgins, H. S., & Knee, C. R. (2002). The integrating self and conscious experience. In E. L. Deci & R. M. Ryan (Eds.), *Handbook of self- determination research* (pp. 87–100). Rochester, NY: University of Rochester Press.

Hu, L., & Bentler, P. M. (1999). Cutoff criteria for fit indexes in covariance structure analysis: Conventional criteria versus new alternatives. *Structural Equation Modeling, 6*(1), 1–55.

Hutcherson, C. A., Seppala, E. M., & Gross, J. J. (2008). Loving-kindness meditation increases social connectedness. *Emotion, 8*(5), 720.

Judge, T. A., Erez, A., Bono, J. E., & Thoresen, C. J. (2003). The core self-evaluations scale: Development of a measure. *Personnel Psychology, 56*(2), 303–331.

Kabat-Zinn, J. (1990). *Full catastrophe living: Using the wisdom of your body and mind to face stress, pain and illness.* NewYork: Delacourt.

Kabat-Zinn, J. (1994). *Wherever you go, there you are: Mindfulness meditation in everyday life.* New York: Hyperion.

Kahneman, D., & Treisman, A. (1984). Changing views of attention and automaticity. *Varieties of Attention, 1*, 29.

Kaiser, H. F. (1958). The varimax criterion for analytic rotation in factor analysis. *Psychometrika, 23*(3), 187–200.

Kernis, M. H., & Goldman, B. M. (2006). A multicomponent conceptualization of authenticity: Theory and research. *Advances in Experimental Social Psychology, 38*, 283–357.

Kornfield, J. (1993). *A Path with Heart.* New York: Bantam.

Kudesia, R. S. (2019). Mindfulness as metacognitive practice. *Academy of Management Review, 44*(2), 405–423.

Langer, E. J. (1989). *Mindfulness.* Reading, MA: Addison-Wesley.

Langer, E. J. (2009). Mindfulness versus positive evaluation. In C. R. Snyder & S. J. Lopez (Eds.), *Oxford handbook of positive psychology* (2nd ed., pp. 279–293). Oxford, UK: Oxford University Press.

Langer, E. J., & Moldoveanu, M. (2000). The construct of mindfulness. *Journal of Social Issues, 56*(1), 1–9.

Lennox, R. D., & Wolfe, R. N. (1984). Revision of the self-monitoring scale. *Journal of Personality and Social Psychology, 46*, 1349–1364.

Linehan, M. (1993a). *Cognitive-behavioral treatment of borderline personality disorder.* New York: Guilford.

Linehan, M. (1993b). *Skills training manual for treating borderline personality disorder.* New York: Guilford.

Marcel, A. J. (2003). Introspective report: Trust, self-knowledge and science. *Journal of Consciousness Studies, 10*, 167–186.

Niemiec, C. P., Brown, K. W., Kashdan, T. B., Cozzolino, P. J., Breen, W. E., Levesque-Bristol, C., & Ryan, R. M. (2010). Being present in the face of existential threat: The role of trait mindfulness in reducing defensive responses to mortality salience. *Journal of Personality and Social Psychology, 99*(2), 344.

Niemiec, C. P., Ryan, R. M., & Brown, K. W. (2008). The role of awareness and autonomy in quieting the ego: A self-determination theory perspective. In H. A. Wayment & J. J. Bauer (Eds.), *The quiet ego: Research and theory on the benefits of transcending egoistic self-interest* (pp. 107–115). Washington, DC: American.

Nunnally, J. C. (1978). *Psychometric theory.* New York, NY: McGraw-Hill.

Nyaniponika, T. (1973). *The heart of Buddhist meditation.* New York: Weiser Books.

Paulhus, D. L. (1991). Measurement and control of response bias. In J. P. Robinson, P. Shaver, & L. S. Wrightsman (Eds.), *Measures of personality and social psychological attitudes* (pp. 17–59). San Diego, CA: Academic Press.

Peterson, S. J., Luthans, F., Avolio, B. J., Walumbwa, F. O., & Zhang, Z. (2011). Psychological capital and employee performance: A latent growth modeling approach. *Personnel Psychology, 64*(2), 427–450.

Podsakoff, P. M., & MacKenzie, S. B. (1994). An examination of the psychometric properties and nomological validity of some revised and reduced substitutes for leadership scales. *Journal of Applied Psychology, 79*(5), 702–713.

Reina, C. S., & Kudesia, R. S. (2020). Wherever you go, there you become: How mindfulness arises in everyday situations. *Organizational Behavior and Human Decision Processes.* In press but available online https://doi.org/10.1016/j.obhdp.2019.11.008

Roemer, L., & Orsillo, S. M. (2003). Mindfulness: A promising intervention strategy in need of further study. *Clinical Psychology: Science and Practice, 10*(2), 172–178.

Rummel, R. J. (1970). *Applied factor analysis.* Evanston, IL: Northwestern University Press.

Ryan, R. M., & Deci, E. L. (2000). Self-determination theory and the facilitation of intrinsic motivation, social development, and well-being. *American Psychologist, 55*(1), 68.

Ryan, R. M., Kuhl, J., & Deci, E. L. (1997). Nature and autonomy: An organizational view of social and neurobiological aspects of self-regulation in behavior and development. *Development and Psychopathology, 9*, 701–728.

Ryff, C. D., & Keyes, C. L. M. (1995). The structure of psychological well-being revisited. *Journal of Personality and Social Psychology, 69*(4), 719–727.

Saavedra, M. C., Chapman, K. E., & Rogge, R. D. (2010). Clarifying links between attachment and relationship quality: Hostile conflict and mindfulness as moderators. *Journal of Family Psychology, 24*, 380–390.

Safran, J. D., & Segal, Z. V. (1990). *Interpersonal process in cognitive therapy*. New York: Basic Books.

Schwab, D. P. (1980). Construct validity in organizational behavior. In B. M. Staw & L. L. Cummings (Eds.), *Research in organizational behavior* (Vol. 2, pp. 3–43). Greenwich, CT: JAI Press Inc.

Shamir, B. (2007). From passive recipients to active co-producers: Followers' roles in the leadership process. In B. Shamir, R. Pilli, M. C. Bligh, & M. Uhl-Bien (Eds.), *Follower-centered perspectives on leadership a tribute to the memory of James R. Meindl* (pp. ix–xxx1x). Greenwich, CT: Information Age Publishing.

Shapiro, S. L., & Carlson, L. E. (2009). *The art and science of mindfulness: Integrating mindfulness into psychology and the helping professions*. Washington, DC: American Psychological Association.

Shapiro, S. L., Carlson, L. E., Astin, J. A., & Freedman, B. (2006). Mechanisms of mindfulness. *Journal of Clinical Psychology, 62*, 373–386.

Sheldon, K. M., & Vansteenkiste, M. (2005). Personal goals and time travel: How are future places visited, and is it worth it? In A. Strathman & J. Joreman (Eds.), *Understanding behavior in the context of time: Theory, research, and application* (pp. 143–163). Mahwah, NJ: Lawrence Erlbaum.

Shockley, K. M., & Allen, T. D. (2014). Deciding between work and family: An episodic approach. *Personnel Psychology*. doi:10.1111/peps.12077

Smith, G. T., Fischer, S., & Fister, S. M. (2003). Incremental validity principles in test construction. *Psychological Assessment, 15*, 467–477.

Sternberg, R. J. (2000). Images of mindfulness. *Journal of Social Issues, 56*, 11–26.

Tan, C.-M. (2014). *Search inside yourself: The unexpected path to achieving success, happiness (and world peace)*. New York: HarperCollins.

Tolle, E. (1999). *The power of now: A guide to spiritual enlightenment. Vancouver*. BC, Canada: Namaste Publishing.

Tolle, E. (2005). *A new earth: Awakening to your life's purpose*. NY: Penguin.

Weick, K. E., & Sutcliffe, K. M. (2006). Mindfulness and the quality of organizational attention. *Organization Science, 17*(4), 514–524.

Wong, C. S., & Law, K. S. (2002). The effects of leader and follower emotional intelligence on performance and attitude: An exploratory study. *The Leadership Quarterly, 13*(3), 243–274.

Yeganeh, B. (2006). *Mindful experiential learning* (Doctoral dissertation). Retrieved from https://etd.ohio link.edu/!etd.send_file?accession=case1163023095&disposition=inline.

5

WORKPLACE MINDFULNESS

Individual-, group-, and organizational-level antecedents and consequences

Manoj Kumar Yadav

Introduction

It is amazing to witness the level of progress that the concept of mindfulness, which started as Buddhist practice to attain higher levels of awareness and attention, has accomplished in both the academic (Glomb, Duffy, Bono, & Yang, 2011; Passmore, 2019; Sutcliffe, Vogus, & Dane, 2016) and practitioner world (Purser, 2018; Van Dam et al., 2018). Some of the researchers echoed the popularity of mindfulness by claiming its broad-reaching beneficial effects (Glomb et al., 2011), while some others dismiss it as another new fad (Carroll, 2006). Calling mindfulness research to have broad-reaching effects or simply a new fad can be attributed to the research output the concept has managed to produce in the last few decades. A search for mindfulness on EBSCO database for the last three decades draws 11,081 academic journals, 1,266 books (including e-books), and 103 dissertations/theses.[1] The comparative numbers for the same search in the last decade are 10,344 (academic journals), 1,169 (books and e-books), and 99 (dissertation/thesis).

The literature reviews so far conducted on the topic in itself is very wide.[1] The current body of literature reviews conducted on mindfulness when expressed in numbers is 95[2] across the disciplines of psychology, medical sciences, education, and, recently, organizational science. More so, these literature reviews have evolved from being very general to more specific, for example, from being a review based on general mindfulness to being more confined to dispositional mindfulness (Tomlinson, Yousaf, Vittersø, and Jones, 2018). The context of these literature reviews has also evolved from being more general to more specific, such as a literature review of mindfulness training used to alleviate math and science anxiety (Ahmed, Trager, Rodwell, Foinding, & Lopez, 2017). More so, even the literature review of the methodology used in mindfulness research was also conducted by researchers in the field, for example, the literature review of the mindfulness chapters using mixed-method methodology (Goldberg et al., 2017). Though the area of clinical/mental/medical health related issues shares the major portion of the entire literature (a total of 56[2] literature reviews), 14[2, 3] literature reviews had been conducted in the area of organization science/management. Besides this, the popularity of the concept of mindfulness can also be adjudged from the existence of a journal entitled *Mindfulness* dedicated explicitly to mindfulness research and practice since 2010.

The literature review so far conducted on the use of mindfulness since 2011 has also varied from being very general (Glomb et al., 2011; Passmore, 2019; Sutcliffe et al., 2016) to as specific as reviewing the literature only from the field of quality management (Bjurström, 2012), talent management (Gajda, 2017), or, more recently, mindfulness-based training interventions in the workplace (Bartlett et al., 2019; Eby et al., 2019). However, the only chapter which comes close to reviewing the antecedents and consequences of workplace mindfulness was conducted in 2016 (Sutcliffe et al., 2016). Even this review did not specifically feature the group-level antecedents and consequences of mindfulness in organizational research. Thus, there is a dearth of reviews conducted so far in mindfulness research in a workplace setting, which accounts for the antecedents and consequences of all the three levels of any organizational study (i.e., individual, group, and organizational levels). The importance of having such a review is recognized now (Sutcliffe et al., 2016). However, even Sutcliffe et al. (2016) did not accommodate the various types of individual mindfulness—trait, state, and process (Glomb et al., 2011)—in their review.

Past investigations have on the one hand glorified its usefulness for both individual and organizational benefits and, on the other hand, criticized it for its conceptual differences and methodological shortcomings. Therefore, a literature review to reconcile the path taken and clarify the way forward at this juncture can further strengthen the mindfulness literature and its practitioners. The current chapter aims to incorporate all forms of mindfulness known to literature and wide varieties of organizational- and group-level antecedents and consequences to mindfulness. Mindfulness practice explains various individual-level physical and psychological health-related outcomes in medical and psychological sciences. However, in organizational settings, it not only claims to list individual, but also various organizational-level outcomes (Glomb et al., 2011; Sutcliffe et al., 2016). It also aims to develop a conceptual model of workplace mindfulness based on past literature to understand its current status and clarity on future directions.

The current chapter identifies various individual-level antecedents—socio-demographic factors, cognitive capacity, personality, and job experience; and various consequences—individual well-being and performance, of mindfulness from psychology and organizational literature. Group-level antecedents—group membership, teamwork, and mindful infrastructure—and consequences—work engagement, relationships, performance, leadership, and negotiation—were identified from social psychology and organizational literature. The chapter also delves into the organizational-level antecedents—organizational environment, culture, practices, and leadership—and consequences—organizational performance, memory, routines, stability, change, climate, communication, and turnover intention. Lastly, it also identifies some limitations and future research directions for researchers interested in workplace mindfulness.

In the sections to follow, the chapter will first introduce the concept of mindfulness and workplace mindfulness. It will also elaborate on individual and collective/organizational mindfulness arising out of organizational literature and various scales available to measure them. Next, it will present the individual-, group-, and organizational-level antecedents of workplace mindfulness. Subsequently, it will also discuss the individual-, group-, and organizational-level consequences of workplace mindfulness. Finally, the chapter will delve into the limitations in the research conducted so far in the area of workplace mindfulness and the future research directions before concluding.

Mindfulness and workplace mindfulness

The term mindfulness has many meanings and connotations (Van Dam et al., 2018). The problem of having many meanings not only creates the issue of choosing the right one, but also creates ambiguity around the concept. In contrast, it even ends up reflecting the popularity and usefulness of the concept. It is this contrast that raises serious issues concerning misunderstandings and methodological shortcomings around the concept of mindfulness (Goldberg et al., 2017; Huynh, Hatton-Bowers, & Smith, 2018). Sternberg (2000) focused on the understanding of mindfulness from three lenses—mindfulness as cognitive capacity, mindfulness as a personality trait, and mindfulness as cognitive style. He elaborated each of these connotations of mindfulness and concluded that mindfulness as cognitive style comes closest to the definition of mindfulness. Assessing mindfulness as cognitive capacity means accepting individual differences in mindfulness. Similarly, treating mindfulness as a dispositional attribute means accepting low or no differences within the individual in a different context concerning their mindfulness capability. Lastly, examining mindfulness as a cognitive style means individuals' preferred way of thinking, i.e., the individual is free to choose 'when to use' and 'in what way to use' mindfulness in a given context.

Primarily, there are two leading schools of thought in mindfulness research that began in the 1970s—one initiated by E. J. Langer and the other by J. Kabat-Zinn (Hart, Ivtzan, & Hart, 2013). While Langer's conceptualization of mindfulness included attention and awareness as two components (Langer, 1989), Kabat-Zinn's conceptualization, which was considered closer to Buddhist preaching, included 'remembering' or 'memory' as the third component of mindfulness (Kabat-Zinn, 2003). There have been more than a dozen definitions for mindfulness present in different literature. Some of the definitions often used in organizational science and individual psychology are listed in Table 5.1. However, the leading schools of thought on mindfulness in Western psychology are considered to be the one initiated by J. E. Langer and her colleagues and the other started by J. Kabat-Zinn and his associates (Hart et al., 2013). The close analysis of the first two definitions in Table 5.1 also helps in summarizing the significant differences in the conceptualization of mindfulness by these two different, but leading, schools of mindfulness thought.

Langer (1989), in her definition, emphasizes being in the present, being open and non-judgmental, and keeping the mind flexible to experiences in the present. Being present-centered means being able to resist tendencies towards like/dislike and other sources of biases while receiving a particular stimulus. Being non-judgmental means awareness of external/internal stimuli without over-identification (Dreyfus, 2011). Being non-judgmental leads to resistance to like/dislike, reflection and not habitual reaction, and avoidance of over-identification, leading to the greater flexibility of easy acceptance of the stimulus. Thus, for Langer (1989), mindfulness is characterized by a heightened state of self-regulated attention and awareness to present external/internal stimuli while being non-judgmental about them. However, mindfulness in Kabat-Zinn's thought is conscious and moment-to-moment awareness. Being conscious not only means being aware of present moments, but also being able to relate every moment of external stimuli with the relevant past and anticipated future (Siegel, Germer, & Olendzki, 2009). It is not the present-centered non-judgment instead of the retentive capacity that allows an individual to hold with the current stimuli and also remember it later (Dreyfus, 2011). Kabat-Zinn's school of thought also stresses 'remembering' as one of the central tenets of mindfulness. Therefore, if one has to summarize the two schools of mindfulness thought, the central tenets of mindfulness include heightened levels of attention, awareness, and acceptance of the moment-to-moment present experience. One can be either non-judgmental or remembering the moment-to-moment lived experiences to derive meaning out of the event based on the way

Table 5.1 Definitions of mindfulness

Source	*Definition*
Langer (1989, p. 220)	'Mindfulness is a flexible state of mind in which we are actively engaged in the present, noticing new things and sensitive to context, with an open, nonjudgmental orientation to experience.'
Kabat-Zinn (1994) in Sutcliffe et al. (2016, p. 58)	'A state of conscious awareness resulting from living in the moment.'
Baer, Smith, Hopkins, Krietemeyer, and Toney (2006, p. 191)	'Mindfulness [. . .] is generally defined to include focusing one's attention in a nonjudgmental or accepting way on the experience occurring in the present moment.'
Brown and Ryan (2004, p. 245)	'Mindfulness is an open or receptive attention to and awareness of ongoing events and experience.'
Weick and Sutcliffe (2006, p. 518)	'Eastern mindfulness means having the ability to hang to current objects, to remember them, and not to lose sight of them through distraction, wandering attention, associative thinking, explaining away, or rejection.'
Dane (2011, p. 1000)	'Mindfulness may be defined as a state of consciousness in which attention is focused on present moment phenomena occurring both externally and internally.'
Roche, Haar, and Luthans (2014, p. 477)	'Mindfulness refers to an open state of mind where the leader's attention, informed by a sensitive awareness, merely observes what is taking place: worry about the future and negative ruminations or projections are brought back to the present moment where the situation is seen for what it is.'
Kudesia and Nyima, (2015, p. 923)	"Mindfulness is a state of heightened meta-awareness in which discursive cognition is diminished and attention is solely focused on and receptive to goal-relevant aspects of the present moment."
Long and Christian (2015, p. 1409)	"Mindfulness, a psychological construct associated with non-judgmental attention and awareness of present-moment experiences."

mindfulness is defined. Other definitions of mindfulness, as presented in Table 5.1, appear to be the derivative and extension of these two prominent and leading schools of thought.

Workplace mindfulness

The idea that mindfulness can be incorporated in the workplace, specifically in management literature, is in itself now more than two decades old. Weick and Roberts (1993) brought the concept of mindfulness to the domain of organizational science. They introduced the term collective mindfulness in an organizational setting to explain aircraft carrier operations. Collective mindfulness was defined by Weick and Roberts (1993) using the perspectives of heed—'dispositions to act with attentiveness, alertness and care' (p. 374); conduct—considering the 'expectations of others' (p. 374); and mind—'integration of feeling, thinking, and willing' (p. 374). Introduction of collective mindfulness led to the development of two forms of mindfulness, one from the tradition of psychology—the study of individuals, i.e., individual mindfulness comprising trait and state mindfulness—and the other collective mindfulness.

Individual mindfulness

Difference in opinion about individual-level mindfulness may exist across domains, but it is highly converged within the organization science domain (Sutcliffe et al., 2016). Therefore, the literature on individual mindfulness in the organization can be traced from both studies in psychology and health sciences (those that used the same connotation as used in most organization science domains) and those in organizational settings. One of the influential models of individual mindfulness, which regarded it as an intrapsychic process, is one presented by Langer (1989). It comprises 'active differentiation and refinement of existing categories and distinctions' (p. 138); 'creation of new discontinuous categories out of the continuous streams of events that flow through activities' (p. 157); and 'a more nuanced appreciation of context and of alternative ways to deal with it' (p. 159). Thus, Langer (1989) emphasized on shedding away the past habitual way of reaction, focusing on building a new way of reflecting in the present, and bringing in novelty and creative aspects of dealing with the new stimulus in the present. Later on, several studies mentioned dispositional attributes of mindfulness (Brown & Ryan, 2003; Sutcliffe et al., 2016). These studies generally held that individual-level differences exist in mindfulness across individuals. Thus, specific individuals may have more mindfulness capacity than others. Such dispositional attributes of mindfulness have been stated as trait mindfulness. However, often, researchers also believe that mindfulness is a state of being in a present moment (Brown & Ryan, 2003). This conceptualization of state mindfulness suggests that individuals can be more momentarily mindful rather than being mindful always.

Collective mindfulness

Collective mindfulness is the outcome of studies conducted in the area of high-reliability organizations (HROs). The review of HROs signifies a few essential characteristics of such organizations:

> they focus on failure rather than success, inertia as well as change, tactics rather than strategy, the present moment rather than the future, and resilience as well as anticipation.
>
> *(Weick, Sutcliffe, & Obstfeld, 1999, p. 84)*

Weick et al. (1999) extended the mindfulness model of Langer (as depicted above) and their review of HROs to develop the concept of collective mindfulness. They came up with five components of collective mindfulness (in an HRO setting)—preoccupation with failure, reluctance to simplify interpretations, sensitivity to operations, commitment to resilience, and underspecification of structures. Mu and Butler (2009) developed their scale for collective mindfulness—Organizational Mindfulness Process (OMP)—using the same model. Collective mindfulness, as developed within the organizational context, is also known as organizational mindfulness. Weick et al. (1999) based their idea of organizational mindfulness on Langer's Western perspective, and they regarded it as an enduring organizational attribute driven by top administrators and the structures and practice they implement. However, the outlook as inspired from Eastern mindfulness and later adapted by

Vogus and Sutcliffe (2012) argued for the existence of 'mindful organizing' within the same organization as a perspective. It considers mindfulness as relatively fragile, and is driven by employees enacting the context to think and act while working on the front line. Mindful organizing is regarded as a social process that becomes collective due to interactions among individuals within a particular organization (Vogus & Sutcliffe, 2012). For any organization to function reliably, it would want both its strategy to be driven by top administrators and its operations to be driven by front-line employees to intersect harmoniously. Thus, both organizational mindfulness and mindful organizing are essential for any organization.

The very reason from where the concept of collective mindfulness evolved was later criticized for being too context specific as a concept. As a result, the contextually loaded concept of collective mindfulness went into continuous refinement in various independent studies. Levinthal and Rerup (2006) criticized the heavy focus of collective mindfulness on attention and seeking novelty, as this focus undermined the importance of organizational routines and thereby the resultant organizational stability. Fiol and O'Connor (2003) criticized two of the five components of collective mindfulness—sensitivity to operations and preoccupation with failure—and suggested significant changes. They indicated that sensitivity to operations is in itself mindfulness and it is not distinctive in nature, while organizations, in general, can be preoccupied with failure as well as success. Lastly, like individual mindfulness, collective mindfulness was also presented out of context from Buddhist tradition (Sutcliffe et al., 2016).

The presence of various orientations to understand mindfulness and the criticisms thereof do not signify the prospective demise of the concept of mindfulness. Instead, they promise further refinement and development of the concept. To manage in today's world is to be aware of, to attend, and to sort priorities from the complexities of the chaotic business environment. Thus, management of the workplace is sure to benefit from trait/state/collective mindfulness. As arguably mindfulness had been predicted to improve those functions of employees, it in turn enhances the management process.

Measuring workplace mindfulness

Workplace mindfulness, as stated above, has been defined in various ways considering the two major perspectives. Some of these definitions and components of mindfulness can be operationalized, while others are difficult to boil down to a full scale to measure mindfulness. Most often, the Western psychological tradition and its way of understanding mindfulness were developed into a scale to measure the concept. Some of the measures constructed to measure mindfulness and often used in the management/organization context are presented in Table 5.2. These measures can be broadly classified into collective and individual mindfulness (Sutcliffe et al., 2016). Individual mindfulness is further classified into trait and state mindfulness. Each of these three categories of mindfulness—trait, state, and collective mindfulness—can be further categorized into single and multiple dimension scales. Further classification also identifies if these scales are based on meditation or non-meditation related scales. These elaborated classifications of mindfulness measure were presented by Sutcliffe et al. (2016).

Antecedents of workplace mindfulness

Psychological literature has cited a few sources of mindfulness; for example, Salomon and Globerson (1987) identified and categorized two sources of mindfulness—distal and proximal. For them, distal sources of mindfulness—'overall tendency to be mindful'

Table 5.2 Measures used for workplace mindfulness

Source	*Name of Measure*	*Type of Mindfulness Measure*	*Factors*
Individual Mindfulness Scale			
Brown & Ryan, 2003	Trait–Mindful Attention Awareness Scale (Trait–MAAS)	Single dimension; non-meditation related; Trait mindfulness	Attentiveness and Awareness
Buchheld, Grossman, & Walach, 2001	Freidberg Mindfulness Inventory (FMI)	Multiple dimensions; meditation related; Trait mindfulness	General
Cardaciotto, Herbert, Forman, Moitra, & Farrow, 2008	Philadelphia Mindfulness Scale (PHLMS)	Multiple dimensions; non-meditation related; Trait mindfulness	1. Acceptance 2. Awareness
Bodner & Langer, 2001	Mindfulness/Mindlessness Scale (MMS)	Multiple dimensions; non-meditation related; Trait mindfulness	1. Novelty seeking 2. Engagement 3. Flexibility 4. Novelty producing
Baer, Smith, Hopkins, Krietemeyer, & Toney, 2006	Five Facet Mindfulness Questionnaire (FFMQ)	Multiple dimensions; non-meditation related; Trait mindfulness	1. Nonreactivity 2. Observing 3. Awareness 4. Describing 5. Nonjudging
Brown & Ryan, 2003	State–Mindful Attention Awareness Scale (State–MAAS)	Single dimension; non-meditation related; State mindfulness	Attentiveness and Awareness
Bishop et al., 2003	Toronto Mindfulness Scale (TMS)	Multiple dimensions; meditation related; State mindfulness	1. Curiosity 2. Decentering
Tanay & Bernstein, 2013	State Mindfulness Scale (SMS)	Multiple dimensions; non-meditation related; State mindfulness	1. Body Mindfulness 2. Mind Mindfulness
Collective Mindfulness Scale			
Vogus & Sutcliffe, 2007	Safety Organizing Scale (SOS)	Single dimension; non-meditation related; Mindfulness	Safety Culture
Barrett, Novak, Venette, & Shumate, 2006	High-Reliability Organization Perceptions (HROP)	Multiple dimensions; non-meditation related; Mindfulness	1. Employee Self-efficacy 2. Organizational Risk
Mu & Butler, 2009	Organizational Mindfulness Process (OMP)	Multiple dimensions; non-meditation related; Mindfulness	1. Preoccupation with failure 2. Reluctance to simplify interpretations 3. Sensitivity to operations 4. Commitment to resilience and deference to expertise

Source: Adapted from (Sutcliffe et al., 2016).

(Salomon & Globerson, 1987, p. 627)—can only be indirectly inferred as it can be neither methodologically measured nor experimentally manipulated. Attributes like the general tendency to take a challenging task and socio-cultural factors like intellectual climate and shared habits are distal sources of mindfulness. Similarly, for them, proximal sources of mindfulness can be amenable to methodological and experimental manipulation and include perceived demands and value of the task and the instructional procedures.

The literature on mindfulness in organizations, on the other hand, is very scant and fragmented. One reason for the paucity of research in this field is attributed to the general understanding of building mindfulness among employees through mindfulness training and meditation at the workplace (Sutcliffe et al., 2016). Though the literature also suggests performance variation in post-mindfulness-based training (Good et al., 2016). Meditation practice sessions have been positively associated with improved mindfulness even at the workplace and thereby supporting the notion for meditation as one of the most important antecedents to both state and collective mindfulness. However, as the behavior in organizations is defined by the presence of its three levels—individual, group, and organizational—this review seeks to identify the scattered organizational literature on mindfulness, aided by higher inputs from the psychological research, to present the antecedents of the workplace at all three levels for all three forms of mindfulness.

Individual-level antecedents

All the individual-level antecedents identified in the review have been identified in extant literature to have a direct and indirect effect on both individual and collective mindfulness as depicted in Figure 5.1. Some of the individual-level antecedents to mindfulness as identified in the past literature include socio-demographic factors, personality, experience on the job, and individual cognitive capacity.

Socio-demographic factors

Socio-demographic variables like gender, race, and resourcefully vulnerable populations are the precursor to individual mindfulness. Association of gender with mindfulness was realized in a study conducted to know the interaction effect of gender and mindfulness on individual performance (Olano et al., 2015; Shao & Skarlicki, 2009). The study identified that females had a comparatively stronger association with mindfulness in predicting their academic performance. Similarly, Hispanics and non-Hispanic blacks were found to be less engaged in mindfulness practices in comparison with Whites and Asians in the US (Olano et al., 2015). Olano et al. (2015) concluded that because these groups were more vulnerable to worse health outcomes, they were less likely to engage in mindfulness practices. Kachan et al. (2017) and Olano et al. (2015) also found that lower educational level was associated with less engagement in mindfulness practices. Additionally, Kachan et al. (2017) also found comparatively lower association of blue-collar workers with mindfulness practices. Thus, gender, race, education level, health, and occupational group identities tend to be associated with the state and trait mindfulness, thereby playing a more significant role as its antecedents. However, research in the past has regularly underrepresented these groups in their sample, raising serious concerns over the sampling methodologies used in such studies (Waldron, Hong, Moskowitz, & Burnett-Zeigler, 2018).

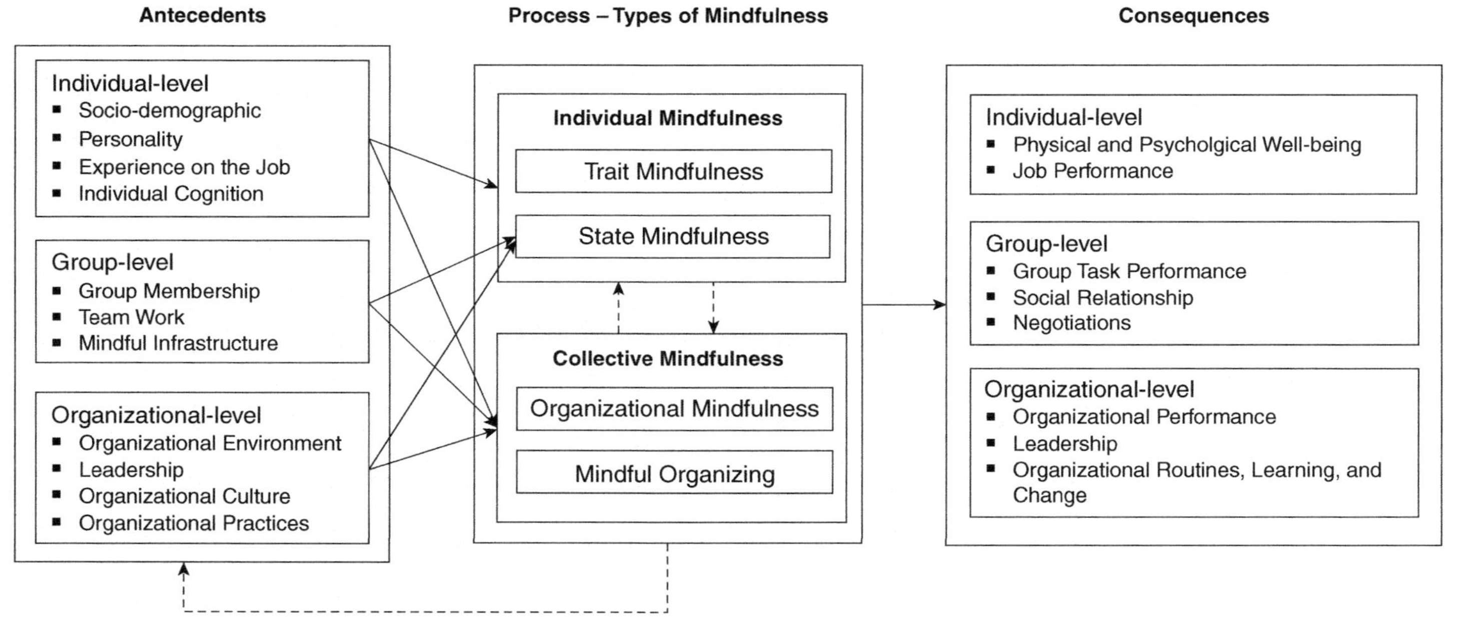

Figure 5.1 Antecedents and consequences of workplace mindfulness

Note.

Identification of variables like group membership, teamwork, team learning, and team psychological safety as group-level antecedents can also be accommodated as organizational level variables.

- - - - - - - - - - - - -➤ = Theoretical arguments not yet empirically tested.

Personality

Brown and Ryan (2003) correlated Big Five personality traits using the NEO-PI scale and found 'openness to experience' as positively related to mindfulness and 'neuroticism' as negatively associated with mindfulness. Big Five personality traits like 'agreeableness' and 'conscientiousness' were also found to be positively related to mindfulness by Thompson and Waltz (2007). Giluk (2009), in his meta-analysis of mindfulness and Big Five personality traits, also found 'conscientiousness' as one dimension of personality that correlated with mindfulness more than other factors. He further stated that though conscientiousness is one dimension that is found to be consistently associated with mindfulness, researchers in the field have regularly ignored giving it due credit.

Experience on the job

Dane (2013) observed that experienced lawyers in a courtroom context were found to be more mindful than inexperienced lawyers. However, research in this area has given diversified results. Mindfulness awareness was found to drop post initial rise (Mitmansgruber, Beck, & Schüßler, 2008), explaining that over learning or more considerable experience on the job may tend to develop a habitual instinct towards a job activity and thereby reducing the mindfulness while performing the same. Thus, the experience of the job may hinder or enhance mindfulness depending upon the different contexts. Other than experience on the job over the period and practice involved, the design of the job in terms of psychological demands it places and job control it facilitates may also work in favor of an employee to be mindful at the workplace (Lawrie, Tuckey, & Dollard, 2018).

Individual cognition

One could have a general tendency to take a mentally challenging job or task (Salomon & Globerson, 1987). These people enjoy effortful cognitive activity (Cacioppo & Petty, 1982). As a result, people with this tendency are expected to be high on trait and state mindfulness and would be more successful when trained for process mindfulness. Similarly, people with higher attention span can also be expected to show a higher level of mindfulness. There has also been evidence of people with higher *working memory capacity* exhibiting higher levels of mindfulness (Martin, 1997) and people whose cognitive capacity gets constrained were found to be low on mindfulness (Bargh & Chartrand, 1999). Hence, it can be argued that as being mindful requires one to attain a higher level of attention, awareness, and non-attachment with the present internal and external stimuli, a person with a higher degree of emotional and cognitive capacity will tend to have a higher level of mindfulness.

Group-level antecedents

There have been some indirect references to some variables that may be counted as group-level antecedents. However, work on group-level antecedents to workplace mindfulness has not found any prominence. Some studies from clinical psychology domains, though, have argued for group-level effects on mindfulness practices. *Group membership* was found to affect mindfulness practice and reported gains of mindfulness post mindfulness training—Mindfulness-based Stress Reduction (MBSR) Program (Imel, Baldwin, Bonus, & MacCoon,

2008). This study suggested having some effect on mindfulness-based group-level factors on state mindfulness. Similarly, *teamwork* is expected to ensure more mindfulness among team members. Salomon and Globerson (1987) argued that teamwork necessitates higher sharing of information and exploration of alternatives among group members, leading to higher levels of mindfulness. Lastly, Sutcliffe and Vogus proposed *mindful infrastructure*—'capacity to anticipate "unexpected" problems and the capacity to contain such problems' (c.f. Oeij, Dhondt, Gaspersz, & Vroome, 2016, p. 246)—and suggested that it depends upon the team members' feeling of being safe and upon the promotion of team learning in an organization. Thus, *team psychological safety* and *team learning* can work as a potential source of team mindfulness.

Organizational-level antecedents

Organizational-level antecedents, as identified in extant literature, were expected to exert effects on the efficiency of state and collective mindfulness as depicted in Figure 5.1. Four variables identified from the extant literature as organizational-level antecedents to mindfulness include the organizational environment, leadership, organizational culture, and organizational practices.

Organizational environment

Organizational environment has a role to play in facilitating or hindering workplace mindfulness (Reb, Narayanan, & Ho, 2015). In their study, Reb et al. (2015) found that *organizational support* facilitated and *organizational constraint* hindered workplace mindfulness. They argued that mindfulness at the workplace could grow when supported through resources needed to remain more aware and less absent-minded. Similarly, they further explained that when employees are constrained through routine and ambiguous tasks, they will be less conscious and more absent-minded. Thus, the organizational environment can affect the overall mindfulness in the organization by influencing the general awareness and absent-mindedness in the organization.

Leadership

The review conducted on mindfulness in the workplace by Sutcliffe et al. (2016) states that leadership can play a role of antecedents to mindfulness in a workplace setting, more specifically, collective mindfulness. Though there is no direct study reporting leadership as an antecedent, the review suggested that attributes related to leadership can be a key enabler of collective mindfulness. Leadership attributes like trust and support between leaders and followers may improve the collective mindfulness of the organization.

Organizational culture

Well-established cultural and social norms, shared habits, and common ways of perception may make individuals resist careful re-examination of those practices that otherwise necessarily demand to be assessed (Salomon & Globerson, 1987). Therefore, it is expected that the culture of the organization at large, which invokes certain types of regular habits and thinking, can affect mindfulness among employees of the organizations at large.

Organizational practices

Sutcliffe et al. (2016), in their review, identified organizational practices in 'high-reliability organizations' (HROs) as antecedents to the mindfulness of such organizations. They highlighted organizational practices like active socialization, extensive training, positive employee relations, and empowerment as key enablers of mindfulness in HROs. They also specified practices like IT-enabled routines and automation may inhibit mindfulness. Thus, any organizational practice that breaks manners in which works are habitually performed and also helps to enhance the ability to see and reflect upon works in a way it was never earlier perceived, can be expected to raise the mindfulness of the workplace.

Consequences of workplace mindfulness

Work on the consequences/outcomes of workplace mindfulness enjoys rich sources of research evidence. Consequently, psychology literature on mindfulness is full of individual-level outcomes of mindfulness—both positive and negative. However, organizational literature on mindfulness has concentrated mainly on positive outcomes of mindfulness. Additionally, all three levels of consequences, as identified in the present review, have been reported to be affected by both individual and collective mindfulness.

Individual-level consequences

The two broad categories in which individual-level consequences were thematized include physical and psychological well-being and job performance.

Physical and psychological well-being

One of the first scales developed to measure individual-level trait and state mindfulness was assessed not only for its reliability and validity but was also used to determine the effect of mindfulness on various aspects of physical and psychological well-being (Brown & Ryan, 2003). It was found that the scale successfully predicted multiple indicators of psychological well-being (Malinowski & Lim, 2015). Brown and Ryan (2003) also found that state mindfulness was more strongly related to the well-being of the individual in comparison with trait mindfulness. Though, they also argued that the result could have tilted in favor of state mindfulness due to the smaller time gap between the measure of mindfulness and well-being measure administered over participants. Some of the examples of physical and psychological well-being-related components that are directly affected from mindfulness or mindfulness-based training programs include stress reduction (Creswell & Lindsay, 2014), reverse age-related brain degeneration (Luders, Cherbuin, & Kurth, 2015), disease resistance (Davidson et al., 2003), work–family issues (Morganson, Rotch, & Christie, 2015), social anxiety, and self-esteem (Rasmussen & Pidgeon, 2011). A host of other work-related behaviors and capabilities that are improved either due to individual or collective mindfulness include self-regulation of attention (Moore, Gruber, Derose, & Malinowski, 2012), efficiency in allocating cognitive resources (Moore et al., 2012), and problem-solving (Ostafin & Kassman, 2012). These results may be related to research conducted in health-based settings, but they also have the benefits of contributing to the workplace settings (Passmore, 2019). Thus, psychological and health-setting-related studies that focused on improved attention, working memory, and focus may also be tested in workplace settings if not directly generalized. There had been few pieces of research which investigated negative effects of mindfulness-based meditation on psychological well-being, but most of these were conducted under the clinical psychology domain. There is a dearth of such adverse effect focus research in the field of organizational science.

Job performance

While improvement in physical and psychological well-being in itself can mediate or moderate the overall job performance of an individual, past research has also studied the direct effect of mindfulness on job performance. Previous research has acknowledged the direct positive effect of all forms of mindfulness—trait, state, and collective mindfulness—on the job performance of an individual. For example, the study conducted by Dane and Brummel (2014) established direct evidence of the positive relationship between mindfulness and job performance in a dynamic workplace context, namely, restaurant service work. Similarly, a few of the reviews conducted in the past also acknowledge this relationship (Donaldson-Feilder, Lewis, & Yarker, 2019; Eby et al., 2019; Good et al., 2016; Lomas et al., 2017; Passmore, 2019; Sutcliffe et al., 2016). Studies conducted within organizational settings have also delved upon a host of other benefits of mindfulness, such as *individual learning* (Cacioppe, 2017), *job satisfaction* (Hülsheger, Alberts, Feinholdt, & Lang, 2013), *work engagement* (Malinowski & Lim, 2015), and *scientific attitude of openness* (Martin, 1997), which may have a role to play in overall job performance. It was also found that mindfulness helps improve well-being and job performance of the employees directly by taming their attention and awareness and indirectly by improving employee performance and well-being (Reb, Narayanan, & Chaturvedi, 2014).

Group-level consequences

Most of the review conducted on workplace mindfulness has differentiated between individual- and organizational-level consequences. The consequences of mindfulness at a group level were never the part of any literature review undertaken so far. One reason could be that consequences at the organizational level can be generalized at group level and vice versa. The consequent theme identified for the purpose includes group task performance, social relationships, and negotiation. The category based on social relationships and negotiation can be generalized at the organizational-level consequences as well. However, it was assumed that building social relationships within the organization to perform a particular task will mean the coming-together of a group of a small number of organizational members. Similarly, it was also assumed that negotiation would also involve a small group of members, though they may negotiate for the entire organization. Therefore, these two categories were kept within the group-level consequences of workplace mindfulness.

Group task performance

Though the research in the area is minimal, there exists enough hints in the extant literature that group performance may improve after mindfulness-based interventions (Passmore, 2019). The mindfulness intervention of as brief as 10 minutes was found to significantly affect the performance of a group asked to complete a 40-minute group decision-making task (Cleirigh

& Greaney, 2015). Similarly, the performance of the treatment team in a health setting was significantly improved after mindfulness-based mentoring (Singh, Singh, Sabaawi, Myers, & Wahler, 2006). The treatment team performance was improved to the extent that both the staff and patients' satisfaction improved significantly after mindfulness intervention.

Social relationships

One of the reasons provided for better team performance is that mindfulness enhances relationships, social interactions (Brown, Ryan, & Creswell, 2007), and interpersonal behavior (Dekeyser, Raes, Leijssen, Leysen, & Dewulf, 2008). Improvement in social relationships is attributed to empathy and response flexibility that a mindful employee reflects upon when dealing with a fellow work colleague (Glomb et al., 2011). Beauchemin, Hutchins, and Patterson (2008), in their study of mindfulness meditation, revealed that the intervention helped students with learning disabilities to decrease their anxiety level and increase their self-focus. The improved attention and reduced anxiety, in turn, promoted social skills among these students. It can, therefore, be expected that careful intervention of mindfulness meditation in a group may foster their social skills, which, in turn, will help in building a positive social relationship among group members. Additionally, mindfulness-based brief interventions through audio recordings buffered employees' *response to injustice* (Long & Christian, 2015). The reduced retaliation instinct of the employees indicates a negative effect of mindfulness on conflicts and another reason for the improved social relationship among group members.

Negotiations

The effect of mindful negotiation on distributive bargaining was assessed using four experimental studies (Reb & Narayanan, 2014). The study concluded that a short mindfulness exercise before a negotiation task allowed participants to gain a larger share of the pie in comparison with participants who were randomly assigned to the control condition. Authors of the chapter argued that mindful attention intervention that participants underwent in an experimental condition allowed them to keep themselves away from any distractions and to have a complete focus on the task in hand. They theorized that improved attention would have allowed participants to keep a tap on the verbal and non-verbal cues of the less mindful negotiator.

Organizational-level consequences

Five broad categories in which the present review summarizes the consequences of mindfulness include organizational performance, leadership, organizational memory and learning, organizational stability and routines, and organizational change.

Organizational performance

Some of the benefits in the form of overall organizational performance due to mindfulness can be measured using parameters such as environmental performance, turnover intentions, organizational sustainability, and absenteeism. Mindful organizational activities like employment of third-party auditors, setting up of sustainability board, and linking the remuneration of management personnel was found to be linked to *environmental performance*

(Umar & Chunwe, 2019). Past research has also provided evidence for improved organizational reliability (HRO studies) and fewer errors in medical settings (Vogus & Sutcliffe, 2007) due to collective mindfulness. One of the health benefits of mindfulness is reduced stress, and social benefits such as reduced work–family issues, as mentioned in the previous section. Existing evidence in the extant literature states that reduction in stress and work–family issues is directly related to a reduction in employee *turnover intentions* and *absenteeism* (Passmore, 2019). This evidence further substantiates the possible role of mindfulness in the reduction of turnover and absenteeism in an organization. Moreover, Dane and Brummel (2014) found evidence for an indirect relationship between turnover intention and mindfulness. *Organizational and resource sustainability* was found to have a high relationship with organizational mindfulness mediated through mindful organizing (Ndubisi & Al-Shuridah, 2019). The study reported that the effects of organizational mindfulness on resource and organizational sustainability could be transmitted through mindful organizing.

Leadership

In the latest review of 19 papers aiming to examine the benefits of mindfulness interventions on leaders and managers, it was found that mindfulness may enhance leadership capabilities (Donaldson-Feilder et al., 2019; Sauer & Kohls, 2011) and leadership well-being (Donaldson-Feilder et al., 2019). Brendel and Bennett (2016) integrated the theory of mindfulness and leadership to present how mindfulness may enhance leadership capabilities. They argued that in a phase-wise process, mindfulness practices enhance awareness to receive mind–body insights, which in turn transforms behavior by improving the sense of clarity, wakefulness, and creativity, which finally culminates in more attuned and accepting ways of being. Similarly, it was found that trait mindfulness is indirectly related to transformational leadership as it is related to positive effect, which in turn is related to leadership self-efficacy leading to transformational leadership (Carleton, Barling, & Trivisonno, 2018). Singh, Sengupta, and Sharma (2016) argued that mindfulness could facilitate the development of authentic leadership by enhancing follower–leader relationships, self-awareness, and self-regulation. Though they did not find empirical evidence to support their argument, the potential of mindfulness as an antecedent to authentic leadership cannot be discarded entirely. The study used MAAS (a trait and state single-dimension mindfulness scale) to measure authentic leadership. It remains an open question if collective mindfulness may have a role to play in authentic leadership. We not only have the evidence about how mindfulness leads to various types of leadership—ethical, transformational, and authentic—but also about how mindfulness may lead to the well-being of leaders. Other than the direct effect of mindfulness on leadership, studies have also suggested the indirect effects of mindfulness on leadership. Eisenbeiss and van Knippenberg (2015) found empirical evidence on how higher follower mindfulness enhances the impact of ethical leadership on followers' discretionary work behavior. Similarly, Roche et al. (2014) demonstrated that leaders' mindfulness influences their mental well-being and that this relationship is further mediated by the psychological capital of leaders. They argued that leader mindfulness helps leaders combat various mental dysfunctional outcomes like anxiety, depression, emotional exhaustion, and cynicism.

Organizational routines, learning, and change

Rerup and Levinthal (2014) theoretically examined the relationship between organizational learning, organizational change, and mindfulness. They argued that mindfulness and mindlessness should not be viewed as two separate or parallel concepts, but instead as concepts on the same continuum. Formulating mindfulness in a continuum means that mindfulness and mindlessness are two polar concepts situated at the two ends of the continuum. It means an organization will have to identify from where on the continuum does the benefit of mindlessness end and the benefit of mindfulness begins. In doing so, Rerup and Levinthal (2014) argued that organizational learning and change could rarely occur, locally and inertly, when organizational routines are operated mindlessly. In contrast, organizational learning and change could occur more often at a global level and more reflectively when the same routines are operated mindfully. Levinthal and Rerup (2006) theoretically argued and hinted about the time when mindless and mindful dimensions of the organization meet. They suggest that organizations continue to perform less mindfully unless an obstacle or interruption occurs. Later, Cacioppe (2017) argued about how mindfulness-in-flow leads to individual and eventually to organizational learning. The chapter argues that organizational learning occurs when an individual is mindful of only the flow—an activity that they are fully immersed in. It is this integration of mindfulness and flow that involves loss of awareness of one's self and environment that leads to individual and finally organizational learning (Cacioppe, 2017). Empirical testing of the effect of mindfulness on organizational learning has rarely been conducted in the past. In one such study, Adams (2006) identified social capital as an antecedent to mindful use of IT systems and how this link leads to the development of organizational learning.

The diagrammatic representation of all the antecedents and consequences of workplace mindfulness is depicted in Figure 5.1. While utmost care was taken to describe only those relationships that have consistent research evidence, some of the moderators/mediators of these relationships were not accounted for, though found in the extant literature. The chapter also considers those relationships that are logically and theoretically argued but await thorough empirical investigations. These relationships are depicted in dotted lines in Figure 5.1. Reasonable care was also taken to include every antecedent and consequence of mindfulness in organizational settings.

Limitations in existing literature and directions for future research

Conceptual and methodological limitations and future research directions

Mindfulness research needs to balance the differences in the conceptualization of mindfulness before being implemented as one promising doctrine in organizations. Mindfulness is derived from Buddhist practice (Dreyfus, 2011; Kabat-Zinn, 2003; Weick & Putnam, 2006). The Pali word *'sati'*—the connection between memory and awareness (Bodhi, 2011)—is said to be the closest concept to mindfulness. The Sanskrit word that comes closest to the concept is *'smrti'*—to remember (Dreyfus, 2011). However, researchers in the Buddhism, mindfulness, and psychology domains have time and again contested that these translations do not fully capture the essence of mindfulness as explained in Buddhist doctrines (Brown et al., 2007; Dreyfus, 2011; Hart et al., 2013; Kudesia & Nyima, 2015). Furthermore, examining the differences in the Eastern and Western traditions of mindfulness and other conceptualizations of mindfulness will also help future researchers in choosing a mindfulness measure that suits their research contexts. For example, the notions of 'organizational mindfulness' and 'mindful organizing' are developed using Western and Eastern perspective, respectively (Ray, Baker, & Plowman, 2011). The current status of literature indicates the use of the same scale for both terms, and it is only the respondents which change from top administrator to front-line employees to measure organizational mindfulness and mindful organizing respectively. Future researchers may argue for separate scales for the two concepts, as being mindful of strategic decisions and being mindful of day-to-day operations are two different notions. Even the authors of the two concepts believe that top administrators need to be mindful of strategic decisions while the front-line employees take care of day-to-day operations continuously.

Additionally, quantitative empirical and conceptual chapters are common in mindfulness research within an organizational setting, but there has been an abysmal representation of empirical qualitative research in the field. I could only trace one qualitative study conducted by Islam, Holm, and Karjalainen (2017) in an organizational setting. This study was based on interviews conducted on 32 trainers and consultants of a mindfulness program to inquire about the divergent set of meaning-making, negotiations, and integration of the process of mindfulness that gets shaped in the organization. Van Maanen (1989) suggested having more descriptive organizational narratives as the very first ingredient for the development of any field. Though the mindfulness research is vast across various disciplines, carefully crafted qualitative illustrative stories about mindfulness within an organizational setting when analyzed using an interpretive approach could clarify the conceptual doubts around mindfulness research. Qualitative research also becomes relevant when the concept in question carries multiple meanings (Edmondson & McManus, 2007) as in the case of mindfulness. In the mindfulness context, one approach could be the use of the phenomenological approach for potential identification of what meaning is ascribed to mindfulness by employees. Future researchers can also use the hermeneutics approach to understand Buddhist literary and religious text. Lastly, future researchers may also use the ethnographic approach to understand the meaning of mindful activities in organizational settings as one of the various potential interpretive approaches. The use of such distinct qualitative approaches can reverberate the future path of mindfulness research. Thus, given the differences in the two conceptualizations, future researchers will have to account for it when they take up their studies on mindfulness rather than merely borrowing from popular domains of social science and implementing them as it is in an organization/management domain.

What more need to be known about antecedents?

Individual-level antecedents

First, future researchers may also need to assess the interactive effects of both individual and collective mindfulness on contextual factors in an organization. As noted in the current chapter, the organizational- and group-level antecedents to mindfulness have scarcely been studied in the past. Other than leadership (Eisenbeiss & van Knippenberg, 2015), organizational environment (Reb et al., 2015), and infrastructure (Oeij, Dhondt, Gaspersz, & Vroome, 2016), there is hardly any research that examined any other variables as a group- and organizational-level antecedents to mindfulness—more specifically, collective mindfulness. Second, mindfulness researchers will also have to accommodate all sections of the working population, especially those vulnerable to workplace-related physical and psychological well-being in terms of gender, race, occupational levels, and low-income and low-educational groups (Waldron et al., 2018). Lesser or complete non-representation of these groups may skew the results of mindfulness, reflecting only one side of the coin. Third, the researcher will also need to focus more on the cognition and emotional capacity required to perform mindfulness activity comfortably. The knowledge of emotional and cognitive capacity as an antecedent of mindfulness may have promising managerial implications. For example, it may not be wise to expect a certain level of mindfulness from a new recruit, but the interviewer can still be mindful of assessing the required level of emotional and cognitive capacity during the recruitment drive. Finally, the effect of various organization-specific capitals like psychological capital, human capital, and social capital may have a potential role to play in the development of trait, state, and collective mindfulness in an individual or an organization. Taking the cues from the past study where psychological capital was found to be partially mediating the effect of mindfulness on positive mental well-being (Malinowski & Lim, 2015; Roche et al., 2014), mindfulness researchers can look to assess the relationship between mindfulness and organization-relevant capitals, such as psychological capital, human capital, and social capital.

Group-level antecedents

Researchers have undermined studies on group-level antecedents of mindfulness in the workplace in the past. There are only a few studies that are suggestive of some effect of few identified precursors on only collective mindfulness. Thus, as this area of research remains relatively unexplored, future researchers may focus more on this domain. They will have to not only concentrate on group-level antecedents to mindfulness in general but also on various types of mindfulness—other than collective mindfulness.

Organizational-level antecedents

Considerable research is required to understand the organizational-level antecedents of state and collective mindfulness. Some of the antecedents that find occasional mention in the extant literature but remain missing from the rigorous examinations are leadership and organizational culture. Gajda (2017) argued that the top leadership of an organization signals prioritization given to mindfulness by paying attention to emerging operational issues and creating a culture that encourages mindful thinking, feeling, and acting. However, these arguments were again based on theoretical arguments and remain open to empirical testing. Within the domain of collective mindfulness, past researchers have so far touched upon some work on finding antecedents to organizational mindfulness. However, the work on antecedents to mindful organizing is yet to be explored.

Additionally, past literature has argued for the role of individual mindfulness in the development of collective mindfulness and vice versa (Sutcliffe et al., 2016). There have also been arguments found in extant literature that hint towards the possible existence of a reciprocal relationship between antecedents of mindfulness and mindfulness itself (Sutcliffe et al., 2016). These claims still await a rigorous empirical investigation to be pursued by mindfulness researchers. Therefore, it is presented in dotted lines in Figure 5.1.

What remains to be known about the consequences?

Individual-level consequences

The positive direct and indirect effects of all forms of mindfulness have been well researched and documented within organizational literature. However, organizational sciences will have to pick up from the mindfulness-based research of other domains to enlist the adverse effects of mindfulness, if any, in a workplace setting. Van Dam et al. (2018) warned against the possible adverse effects of mindfulness, which got sidelined in mainstream mindfulness research, often because of the exaggerated claims about the benefits of mindfulness. They cautioned against not only meditation-induced psychological health issues like psychosis, depersonalization, anxiety, mania, and panic, but also the possibility of being misled due to exaggerated claims made by mindfulness-based clinical practitioners. Organizations will have to meticulously investigate if mindfulness-based training can help resolve their issues at hand. Future researchers in this area can contribute to devising ways that allow practitioners in precisely deciding on investing to incorporate mindfulness-based training and build the right organizational culture and practices to promote mindfulness. Researchers also face challenges in terms of identifying potential mechanisms by which meditation-related adverse effects might occur. Identification of such mechanisms will help in devising precautionary measures before designing any mindfulness-based programs in any organization.

Group-level consequences

Group-level consequences are the least studied among all three levels and therefore require immediate attention. Moreover, when organizations can provide mindfulness training to their employees in a group rather than individually, the knowledge of group-level consequences becomes more critical. There are many other consequences like group/team learning, conflict management within the group, and group decision-making that could be other possible consequences of workplace mindfulness that need to be addressed by the future researchers.

Organizational-level consequences

The popular organizational-level outcomes like organizational performance using various parameters of organizational performance, leadership, and organizational learning (to a certain extent) are widely documented through empirical studies conducted in the past. However, the effect of mindfulness over other organizational-level variables (organizational routines, memory, climate, and communication) as an area remains neglected by mindfulness researchers.

Practical implications

Mindfulness-based training may be a double-edged sword. Hence, leaders and managers will have to resolve issues like the relevance of mindfulness-based training programs for a particular job/hierarchy in the organization, multiplicity of mindfulness-based interventions, and the possible outcomes that are targeted. Similarly, the assessment of this baseline information will equip them in a better way to engage with mindfulness consultants before getting the intervention implemented. Additionally, they will also have to explore how they can assess the benefits of the introduction of such programs. One way is to evaluate the benefit and comparing it with the target set before the implementation of the training. Long-term assessment of the benefits to confirm the sustainability of the improvement achieved through mindfulness training is another option that can be explored by managers. Lastly, the existence of trait mindfulness indicates that managers may look for alternatives to improve the mindfulness of the organization, e.g., recruiting individuals with a high inclination to mindfulness. Though, recruitment and selection may not be the only resort to improve the overall individual and collective mindfulness in the organization, but, so is the case with training interventions.

Conclusion

Management research in the area of mindfulness is neither nascent nor matured. However, given the maturity of mindfulness research in contemporary disciplines, it is a wake-up call to streamline mindfulness research within organizational science. The contemporary sciences such as clinical science have already started debating the potential opportunity cost and adverse effects of mindfulness research (Van Dam et al., 2018), whereas, the organization science fraternity is yet to explore the comprehensive list of antecedents and consequences. The current chapter is an attempt in this direction. Most of the research on mindfulness in organizational science is about reiterating the same individual-level antecedents and outcomes found in psychological studies. The repetition of psychological studies in organizational science undermines the unique context in which organizations work. Researchers will have to realize that mindfulness research in workplace settings needs to be contextually relevant. Hence, future studies will have to go beyond psychological variables and assess the relationship of mindfulness with organizationally relevant variables along with the mechanisms in which the relationship operates. Similarly, there have been occasional thought-provoking conceptual papers that highlight the intricacies of mindfulness in the workplace succinctly (Good et al., 2016; Rerup & Levinthal, 2014; Levinthal & Rerup, 2006; Weick, et al., 1999; Weick & Roberts, 1993). However, these papers still await an empirical investigation.

Five questions

Some of the interesting questions to ponder include:

1. What are the differences between Western and Eastern perspectives of workplace mindfulness? How do these different perspectives affect the choice of workplace mindfulness research in general and measure in particular?
2. Is workplace mindfulness more of trait or state? Do certain sections of society have a natural tendency to practice workplace mindfulness or practice matters more? And do organizational-level factors have a role to play in improving overall workplace mindfulness?
3. How are individual and collective mindfulness related to each other? Is there a basis for arguing a reciprocal relationship between them?
4. State which of the antecedents of workplace mindfulness may not only affect but also get affected by workplace mindfulness in turn.
5. How can a manager/practitioner evaluate the efficiency of the mindfulness program initiated in their respective organization?

Five takeaways

1. There are two leading schools of thought in mindfulness research. One of them was initiated by E. J. Langer in the 1970s and contained two primary components—attention and awareness. The other school of thought, initiated by J. Kabat-Zinn much later in the 2000s, had an additional component of 'remembering' or 'memory'. This school of thought is considered to be closer to Buddhist tradition.

2. Workplace mindfulness can be studied at two levels—individual and collective. *Individual-level workplace mindfulness* treats mindfulness as either trait or state. This adds to the debate between trait psychologists and behaviorism. The debate lies between considering mindfulness as trait and thereby inherent and enduring tendency of the individual to act in a particular way or considering mindfulness as state, which, in turn, contends that mindfulness can be trained and is enhanced with practice.
3. *Collective workplace mindfulness* can be further divided into organizational mindfulness and mindful organizing. Weick et al. (1999) extended the model of mindfulness as given by Langer and developed the concept of collective mindfulness. They came up with five components of collective mindfulness—preoccupation with failure, reluctance to simplify interpretations, sensitivity to operations, commitment to resilience, and underspecification of structures. Inspired from the Eastern perspective on mindfulness, Vogus and Sutcliffe (2012) argued for the existence of 'mindful organizing'. It considers mindfulness as relatively fragile and is driven by employees enacting the context to think and act while working on the front line. Thus, the current understanding of collective mindfulness suggests that mindfulness can be either driven from the top (organizational mindfulness) or from the employees at the bottom (mindful organizing).
4. Research in the workplace mindfulness context has established multiple individual-level (socio-demographic, personality, job experience, and cognition), group-level (group membership, teamwork, and mindful infrastructure), and organizational-level (organizational environment, leadership, culture, and practices) antecedents to mindfulness in organizational settings. Similarly, various individual-level (well-being and performance), group-level (performance, relationship, and negotiation), and organizational-level (performance, leadership, organizational learning, routines, and change) consequences of workplace mindfulness are also established in the extant literature.
5. While individual-level antecedents of workplace mindfulness may affect all forms of workplace mindfulness, group-level and organizational-level antecedents may not affect the trait mindfulness.

Annex

Table 5.3 Stages in the chapter-type specific (literature review chapters) mindfulness literature search

Stages	*Process*
Stage 1: Search (N = 459)	• ***Identified keywords:*** mindfulness, mindful, literature, and review • ***Identified phrases:*** 'mindfulness and literature review', and 'literature review'. • ***Identified database:*** EBSCO
Stage 2: Exclusion of irrelevant data (369 excluded from N = 459)	• Cleaning for duplicates • Articles published in the English language • Excluding dissertation/thesis and book reviews • Assessing the titles and abstracts (in some cases even the introduction) • Reviewing and coding articles in specific and related disciplines • The coded disciplines include:

(Continued)

Table 5.3 (Cont.)

Stages	*Process*
Stage 3: Coding (Total articles coded finally = 93)	1. Organization Science/Management (13) 2. Psychology/Social Psychology (10) 3. Clinical/Health/Mental Illness (56) 4. Education (9) 5. Information Technology (3) 6. Methodological Review (2) 7. Sustainability (2)

Table 5.4 List of literature reviews conducted for mindfulness in an organizational/management domain

Sr. No.	*Authors (Year of Publication)*	*Chapter Title*	*Name of Journal*
1	Theresa M. Glomb, Michelle K. Duffy, Joyce E. Bono, and Tao Yang (2011)	Mindfulness at work	Research in Personnel and Human Resource Management
2	Timothy J. Vogus, and Kathleen M. Sutcliffe (2012)	Organizational mindfulness and mindful organizing: A reconciliation and path forward	Academy of Management Learning and Education
3	Erik Bjurstrom (2012)	Minding the contexts of mindfulness in quality management	The International Journal of Quality and Reliability Management
4	Patrick K. Hyland, R. Andrew Lee, & Maura J. Mills (2015)	Mindfulness at work: A new approach to improving individual and organizational performance	Industrial and Organizational Psychology
5	Tammy D. Allen, Lillian T. Eby, Kate M. Conley, Rachel L. Williamson, Victor S. Mancini, & Melissa E. Mitchell (2015)	What do we really know about the effects of mindfulness-based training in the workplace?	Industrial and Organizational Psychology
6	Darren J. Good, Christopher J. Lyddy, Theresa M. Glomb, Joyce E. Bono, Kirk Warren Brown, Michelle K. Duffy, . . ., and Sara W. Lazar (2016)	Contemplating mindfulness at work: An integrative framework	Journal of Management
7	Kathleen M. Sutcliffe, Timothy J. Vogus, and Erik Dane (2016)	Mindfulness in organizations: A cross-level review	Annual Review of Organizational Psychology and Organizational Behaviour
8	Stephanie D. Jamieson, and Michelle R. Tuckey (2017)	Mindfulness interventions in the workplace: A critique of the current state of the literature	Journal of Occupational Health Psychology
9	Tim Lomas, Juan Carlos Medina, Itai Ivtzan, Silke Ruperecht,	The impact of mindfulness on well-being and performance in the workplace: A inclusive	European Journal of Work and Organizational Psychology

(Continued)

Table 5.4 (Cont.)

Sr. No.	*Authors (Year of Publication)*	*Chapter Title*	*Name of Journal*
	Rona Hart, and Jose Eiroa-Orosa (2017)	systematic review of the empirical literature	
10	Daniel Gajda (2017)	Talent management in the context of mindful organizing and organizational mindfulness	Journal of Positive Management
11	Larissa Bartlett, Angela Martin, Amanda L. Neil, Kate Memish, Petr Otahal, Michelle Kilpatrick, and Kristy Sanderson (2019)	A systematic review and meta-analysis of workplace mindfulness training randomized controlled trials	Journal of Occupational Health Psychology
12	Jonathan Passmore (2019)	Mindfulness in organizations (part 1): A critical literature review	Industrial and Commercial Training
13	Emma Donaldson-Feidler, Rachel Lewis, and Joanna Yarker (2019)	What outcomes have mindfulness and meditation interventions for managers and leaders achieved? A systematic review	European Journal of Work and Organizational Psychology
14	Lillian T. Ebby, Tammy D. Allen, Kate M. Conley, Rachel L. Williamson, Tyler G. Henderson, and Victor S. Mancini (2019)	Mindfulness-based training interventions for employees: A qualitative review of the literature	Human Resource Management Review

Notes

1 EBSCO database search for keyword 'mindfulness' on May 21, 2019.
2 Details of the search is presented in Table 5.3 in annexures section.
3 Detailed list of literature review conducted for mindfulness in organizational/management context is presented in Table 5.4 in annexures section.

References

Adams, H. L. (2006). Mindful use as a link between social capital and organizational learning: An empirical test of the antecedents and consequences of two new constructs. (Doctoral dissertation).

Ahmed, K., Trager, B., Rodwell, M., Foinding, L., & Lopez, C. (2017). A review of mindfulness research related to alleviating math and science anxiety. *Journal for Leadership and Instruction, 16*(2), 26–30.

Allen, T. D., Eby, L. T., Conley, K. M., Williamson, R. L., Mancini, V. S., & Mitchell, M. E. (2015). What do we really know about the effects of mindfulness-based training in the workplace? *Industrial and Organizational Psychology, 8*(4), 652–661.

Baer, R. A., Smith, G. T., Hopkins, J., Krietemeyer, J., & Toney, L. (2006). Using self-report assessment methods to explore facets of mindfulness. *Assessment, 13*(1), 27–45.

Bargh, J. A., & Chartrand, T. L. (1999). The unbearable automaticity of being. *American Psychologist, 54* (7), 462–479.

Barrett, M. S., Novak, J. M., Venette, S. J., & Shumate, M. (2006). Validating the high reliability organization perception scale. *Communication Research Reports, 23*(2), 111–118.

Bartlett, L., Martin, A., Neil, A. L., Memish, K., Otahal, P., Kilpatrick, M., & Sanderson, K. (2019). A systematic review and meta-analysis of workplace mindfulness training randomized controlled trials. *Journal of Occupational Health Psychology*, *24*(1), 108.

Beauchemin, J., Hutchins, T. L., & Patterson, F. (2008). Mindfulness meditation may lessen anxiety, promote social skills, and improve academic performance among adolescents with learning disabilities. *Complementary Health Practice Review*, *13*(1), 34–45.

Bishop, S. R., Lau, M., Segal, Z., Anderson, N., Abbey, S., Devins, G., & Carmody, J. (2003). Development and validation of the Toronto Mindfulness Scale. Unpublished Work.

Bjurström, E. (2012). Minding the contexts of mindfulness in quality management. *International Journal of Quality & Reliability Management*, *29*(6), 699–713.

Bodhi, B. (2011). What does mindfulness really mean? A canonical perspective. *Contemporary Buddhism*, *12*(01), 19–39.

Bodner, T. E., & Langer, E. J. (2001, June). Individual differences in mindfulness: The mindfulness/mindlessness scale. In *Poster presented at the 13th annual American Psychological Society Convention, Toronto, Ontario, Canada.*

Brendel, W., & Bennett, C. (2016). Learning to embody leadership through mindfulness and somatics practice. *Advances in Developing Human Resources*, *18*(3), 409–425.

Brown, K. W., & Ryan, R. M. (2003). The benefits of being present: Mindfulness and its role in psychological well-being. *Journal of Personality and Social Psychology*, *84*(4), 822–848.

Brown, K. W., & Ryan, R. M. (2004). Perils and promise in defining and measuring mindfulness: Observations from experience. *Clinical Psychology: Science and Practice*, *11*(3), 242–248.

Brown, K. W., Ryan, R. M., & Creswell, J. D. (2007). Mindfulness: Theoretical foundations and evidence for its salutary effects. *Psychological Inquiry*, *18*(4), 211–237.

Buchheld, N., Grossman, P., & Walach, H. (2001). Measuring mindfulness in insight meditation (vipassana) and meditation-based psychotherapy: The development of the Freiburg Mindfulness Inventory (FMI). *Journal for Meditation and Meditation Research*, *1*, 11–34.

Cacioppe, R. L. (2017). Integral mindflow: A process of mindfulness-in-flow to enhance individual and organization learning. *The Learning Organization*, *24*(6), 408–417.

Cacioppo, J. T., & Petty, R. E. (1982). The need for cognition. *Journal of Personality and Social Psychology*, *42*(1), 116–131.

Cardaciotto, L., Herbert, J. D., Forman, E. M., Moitra, E., & Farrow, V. (2008). The assessment of present-moment awareness and acceptance: The Philadelphia mindfulness scale. *Assessment*, *15*(2), 204–223.

Carleton, E. L., Barling, J., & Trivisonno, M. (2018). Leaders' trait mindfulness and transformational leadership: The mediating roles of leaders' positive affect and leadership self-efficacy. *Canadian Journal of Behavioural Science/Revue Canadienne Des Sciences Du Comportement*, *50*(3), 185.

Carroll, M. (2006). *Awake at work: 35 practical Buddhist principles for discovering clarity and balance in the midst of work's chaos* (2nd ed.). Boston: Shambhala.

Cleirigh, D. O., & Greaney, J. (2015). Mindfulness and group performance: An exploratory investigation into the effects of brief mindfulness intervention on group task performance. *Mindfulness*, *6*(3), 601–609.

Creswell, J. D., & Lindsay, E. K. (2014). How does mindfulness training affect health? A mindfulness stress buffering account. *Current Directions in Psychological Science*, *23*(6), 401–407.

Dane, E. (2011). Paying attention to mindfulness and its effects on task performance in the workplace. *Journal of Management*, *37*(4), 997–1018.

Dane, E. (2013). Things seen and unseen: Investigating experience-based qualities of attention in a dynamic work setting. *Organization Studies*, *34*(1), 45–78.

Dane, E., & Brummel, B. J. (2014). Examining workplace mindfulness and its relations to job performance and turnover intention. *Human Relations*, *67*(1), 105–128.

Davidson, R. J., Kabat-Zinn, J., Schumacher, J., Rosenkranz, M., Muller, D., Santorelli, S. F., . . . Sheridan, J. F. (2003). Alterations in brain and immune function produced by mindfulness meditation. *Psychosomatic Medicine*, *65*(4), 564–570.

Dekeyser, M., Raes, F., Leijssen, M., Leysen, S., & Dewulf, D. (2008). Mindfulness skills and interpersonal behaviour. *Personality and Individual Differences*, *44*(5), 1235–1245.

Donaldson-Feilder, E., Lewis, R., & Yarker, J. (2019). What outcomes have mindfulness and meditation interventions for managers and leaders achieved? A systematic review. *European Journal of Work and Organizational Psychology*, *28*(1), 11–29.

Dreyfus, G. (2011). Is mindfulness present-centred and non-judgmental? A discussion of the cognitive dimensions of mindfulness. *Contemporary Buddhism, 12*(01), 41–54.

Eby, L. T., Allen, T. D., Conley, K. M., Williamson, R. L., Henderson, T. G., & Mancini, V. S. (2019). Mindfulness-based training interventions for employees: A qualitative review of the literature. *Human Resource Management Review, 29*(2), 156–178.

Edmondson, A. C., & McManus, S. E. (2007). Methodological fit in management field research. *Academy of Management Review, 32*(4), 1246–1264.

Eisenbeiss, S. A., & van Knippenberg, D. (2015). On ethical leadership impact: The role of follower mindfulness and moral emotions. *Journal of Organizational Behavior, 36*(2), 182–195.

Fiol, C. M., & O'Connor, E. J. (2003). Waking up! Mindfulness in the face of bandwagons. *Academy of Management Review, 28*(1), 54–70.

Gajda, D. (2017). Talent management in the context of mindful organizing and organizational mindfulness. *Journal of Positive Management, 8*(3), 42–57.

Giluk, T. L. (2009). Mindfulness, Big Five personality, and affect: A meta-analysis. *Personality and Individual Differences, 47*(8), 805–811.

Glomb, T. M., Duffy, M. K., Bono, J. E., & Yang, T. (2011). Mindfulness at work. In A. Joshi, H. Liao, & J. J. Martocchio's (Eds.), *Research in personnel and human resources management, 30* (Vol. 30, pp. 115–157). Bingley, UK: Emerald Group Publishing Limited.

Goldberg, S. B., Tucker, R. P., Greene, P. A., Simpson, T. L., Kearney, D. J., & Davidson, R. J. (2017). Is mindfulness research methodology improving over time? A systematic review. *PloS One, 12*(10), 1–16.

Good, D. J., Lyddy, C. J., Glomb, T. M., Bono, J. E., Brown, K. W., Duffy, M. K., ... Lazar, S. W. (2016). Contemplating mindfulness at work: An integrative review. *Journal of Management, 42*(1), 114–142.

Hart, R., Ivtzan, I., & Hart, D. (2013). Mind the gap in mindfulness research: A comparative account of the leading schools of thought. *Review of General Psychology, 17*(4), 453–466.

Hülsheger, U. R., Alberts, H. J., Feinholdt, A., & Lang, J. W. (2013). Benefits of mindfulness at work: The role of mindfulness in emotion regulation, emotional exhaustion, and job satisfaction. *Journal of Applied Psychology, 98*(2), 310.

Huynh, T., Hatton-Bowers, H., & Smith, M. H. (2018). A critical methodological review of mixed methods designs used in mindfulness research. *Mindfulness, 10*, 786–798.

Hyland, P. K., Lee, R. A., & Mills, M. J. (2015). Mindfulness at work: A new approach to improving individual and organizational performance. *Industrial and Organizational Psychology, 8*(4), 576–602.

Imel, Z., Baldwin, S., Bonus, K., & MacCoon, D. (2008). Beyond the individual: Group effects in mindfulness-based stress reduction. *Psychotherapy Research, 18*(6), 735–742.

Islam, G., Holm, M., & Karjalainen, M. (2017). Sign of the times: Workplace mindfulness as an empty signifier. *Organization, 00*(0), 1–27.

Jamieson, S. D., & Tuckey, M. R. (2017). Mindfulness interventions in the workplace: A critique of the current state of the literature. *Journal of Occupational Health Psychology, 22*(2), 180.

Kabat-Zinn, J. (1994). *Wherever you go, there you are: mindfulness meditation in everyday life.* White Plains, NY: Hyperion.

Kabat-Zinn, J. (2003). Mindfulness-based interventions in context: Past, present, and future. *Clinical Psychology: Science and Practice, 10*(2), 144–156.

Kachan, D., Olano, H., Tannenbaum, S. L., Annane, D. W., Mehta, A., Arheart, K. L., ... Lee, D. J. (2017). Peer Reviewed: Prevalence of Mindfulness Practices in the US Workforce: National Health Interview Survey. Preventing chronic disease, 14.

Kudesia, R. S., & Nyima, V. T. (2015). Mindfulness contextualized: An integration of Buddhist and neuropsychological approaches to cognition. *Mindfulness, 6*(4), 910–925.

Langer, E. J. (1989). Minding matters: The consequences of mindlessness–mindfulness. In L. Berkowitz's (Ed.) *Advances in Experimental Social Psychology* (Vol. *22*, pp. 137–173). San Diego, CA: Academic Press.

Lawrie, E. J., Tuckey, M. R., & Dollard, M. F. (2018). Job design for mindful work: The boosting effect of psychosocial safety climate. *Journal of Occupational Health Psychology, 23*(4), 483–495.

Levinthal, D., & Rerup, C. (2006). Crossing an apparent chasm: Bridging mindful and less mindful perspectives on organizational learning. *Organization Science, 17*(4), 502–513.

Lomas, T., Medina, J. C., Ivtzan, I., Rupprecht, S., Hart, R., & Eiroa-Orosa, F. J. (2017). The impact of mindfulness on well-being and performance in the workplace: An inclusive systematic review of the empirical literature. *European Journal of Work and Organizational Psychology, 26*(4), 492–513.

Long, E. C., & Christian, M. S. (2015). Mindfulness buffers retaliatory responses to injustice: A regulatory approach. *Journal of Applied Psychology*, *100*(5), 1409.

Luders, E., Cherbuin, N., & Kurth, F. (2015). Forever Young (er): Potential age-defying effects of long-term meditation on gray matter atrophy. *Frontiers in Psychology*, *5*(1551), 1–7.

Malinowski, P., & Lim, H. J. (2015). Mindfulness at work: Positive affect, hope, and optimism mediate the relationship between dispositional mindfulness, work engagement, and well-being. *Mindfulness*, *6*(6), 1250–1262.

Martin, J. R. (1997). Mindfulness: A proposed common factor. *Journal of Psychotherapy Integration*, 7(4), 291–312.

Mitmansgruber, H., Beck, T. N., & Schüßler, G. (2008). "Mindful helpers": Experiential avoidance, meta-emotions, and emotion regulation in paramedics. *Journal of Research in Personality*, *42*(5), 1358–1363.

Moore, A. W., Gruber, T., Derose, J., & Malinowski, P. (2012). Regular, brief mindfulness meditation practice improves electrophysiological markers of attentional control. *Frontiers in Human Neuroscience*, *6*(18), 1–15.

Morganson, V. J., Rotch, M. A., & Christie, A. R. (2015). Being mindful of work–family issues: Intervention to a modern stressor. *Industrial and Organizational Psychology*, *8*(4), 682–689.

Mu, E., & Butler, B. S. (2009). The assessment of organizational mindfulness processes for the effective assimilation of IT innovations. *Journal of Decision Systems*, *18*(1), 27–51.

Ndubisi, N. O., & Al-Shuridah, O. (2019). Organizational mindfulness, mindful organizing, and environmental and resource sustainability. *Business Strategy and the Environment*, *28*(3), 436–446.

Oeij, P. R., Dhondt, S., Gaspersz, J. B., & Vroome, E. M. D. (2016). Can teams benefit from using a mindful infrastructure when defensive behaviour threatens complex innovation projects? *International Journal of Project Organisation and Management*, *8*(3), 241–258.

Olano, H. A., Kachan, D., Tannenbaum, S. L., Mehta, A., Annane, D., & Lee, D. J. (2015). Engagement in mindfulness practices by US adults: Sociodemographic barriers. *The Journal of Alternative and Complementary Medicine*, *21*(2), 100–102.

Ostafin, B. D., & Kassman, K. T. (2012). Stepping out of history: Mindfulness improves insight problem solving. *Consciousness and Cognition*, *21*(2), 1031–1036.

Passmore, J. (2019). Mindfulness in organizations (part 1): A critical literature review. *Industrial and Commercial Training*, *51*(2), 104–113.

Purser, R. E. (2018). Critical perspectives on corporate mindfulness. *Journal of Management, Spirituality & Religion*, *15*(2), 105–108.

Rasmussen, M. K., & Pidgeon, A. M. (2011). The direct and indirect benefits of dispositional mindfulness on self-esteem and social anxiety. *Anxiety, Stress, & Coping*, *24*(2), 227–233.

Ray, J. L., Baker, L. T., & Plowman, D. A. (2011). Organizational mindfulness in business schools. *Academy of Management Learning & Education*, *10*(2), 188–203.

Reb, J., & Narayanan, J. (2014). The influence of mindful attention on value claiming in distributive negotiations: Evidence from four laboratory experiments. *Mindfulness*, *5*(6), 756–766.

Reb, J., Narayanan, J., & Chaturvedi, S. (2014). Leading mindfully: Two studies on the influence of supervisor trait mindfulness on employee well-being and performance. *Mindfulness*, *5*(1), 36–45.

Reb, J., Narayanan, J., & Ho, Z. W. (2015). Mindfulness at work: Antecedents and consequences of employee awareness and absent-mindedness. *Mindfulness*, *6*(1), 111–122.

Rerup, C., & Levinthal, D. A. (2014). Situating the concept of organizational mindfulness: The multiple dimensions of organizational learning. In G. Becke (Ed.) *Mindful change in times of permanent reorganization* (pp. 33–48). Berlin, Heidelberg: Springer.

Roche, M., Haar, J. M., & Luthans, F. (2014). The role of mindfulness and psychological capital on the well-being of leaders. *Journal of Occupational Health Psychology*, *19*(4), 476–489.

Salomon, G., & Globerson, T. (1987). Skill may not be enough: The role of mindfulness in learning and transfer. *International Journal of Educational Research*, *11*(6), 623–637.

Sauer, S., & Kohls, N. (2011). Mindfulness in leadership: Does being mindful enhance leaders' business success? In S. Han & E. Poppel (Eds.), *Culture and neural frames of cognition and communication* (pp. 287–307). Berlin, Heidelberg: Springer.

Shao, R., & Skarlicki, D. P. (2009). The role of mindfulness in predicting individual performance. *Canadian Journal of Behavioural Science*, *41*(4), 195.

Siegel, R. D., Germer, C. K., & Olendzki, A. (2009). Mindfulness: What is it? Where did it come from? In F. Didonna (Ed.), *Clinical handbook of mindfulness* (pp. 17–36). New York, NY: Springer Science + Business Media LLC.

Singh, A., Sengupta, S., & Sharma, S. (2016). Empathy and Mindfulness: Potential antecedents to authentic leadership. *International Journal of Human Capital and Information Technology Professionals*, 7(4), 1–14.

Singh, N. N., Singh, S. D., Sabaawi, M., Myers, R. E., & Wahler, R. G. (2006). Enhancing treatment team process through mindfulness-based mentoring in an inpatient psychiatric hospital. *Behavior Modification*, *30*(4), 423–441.

Sternberg, R. J. (2000). Images of mindfulness. *Journal of Social Issues*, *56*(1), 11–26.

Sutcliffe, K. M., Vogus, T. J., & Dane, E. (2016). Mindfulness in organizations: A cross-level review. *Annual Review of Organizational Psychology and Organizational Behavior*, *3*, 55–81.

Tanay, G., & Bernstein, A. (2013). State Mindfulness Scale (SMS): Development and initial validation. *Psychological Assessment*, *25*(4), 1286–1299.

Thompson, B. L., & Waltz, J. (2007). Everyday mindfulness and mindfulness meditation: Overlapping constructs or not? *Personality and Individual Differences*, *43*(7), 1875–1885.

Tomlinson, E. R., Yousaf, O., Vittersø, A. D., & Jones, L. (2018). Dispositional mindfulness and psychological health: A systematic review. *Mindfulness*, *9*(1), 23–43.

Umar, S., & Chunwe, G. N. (2019). Advancing environmental productivity: Organizational mindfulness and strategies. *Business Strategy and the Environment*, *28*(3), 447–456.

Van Dam, N. T., van Vugt, M. K., Vago, D. R., Schmalzl, L., Saron, C. D., Olendzki, A., ... Meyer, D. E. (2018). Mind the hype: A critical evaluation and prescriptive agenda for research on mindfulness and meditation. *Perspectives on Psychological Science*, *13*(1), 36–61. doi:10.1177/1745691617709589

Van Maanen, J. (1989). Some notes on the importance of writing in organizational studies. In J. I. Cash & P. R. Lawrence (Eds.) *The information systems research challenge: Qualitative research methods – Methodology colloquium on qualitative research, Harvard Business School research colloquium* (Vol. 1, pp. 27–33). Boston, MA: Harvard Business School.

Vogus, T. J., & Sutcliffe, K. M. (2007). The safety organizing scale: Development and validation of a behavioral measure of safety culture in hospital nursing units. *Medical Care*, *45*(1), 46–54.

Vogus, T. J., & Sutcliffe, K. M. (2012). Organizational mindfulness and mindful organizing: A reconciliation and path forward. *Academy of Management Learning & Education*, *11*(4), 722–735.

Waldron, E. M., Hong, S., Moskowitz, J. T., & Burnett-Zeigler, I. (2018). A systematic review of the demographic characteristics of participants in US-based randomized controlled trials of mindfulness-based interventions. *Mindfulness*, *9*(6), 1671–1692.

Weick, K. E., & Putnam, T. (2006). Organizing for mindfulness: Eastern wisdom and Western knowledge. *Journal of Management Inquiry*, *15*(3), 275–287.

Weick, K. E., & Roberts, K. H. (1993). Collective mind in organizations: Heedful interrelating on flight decks. *Administrative Science Quarterly*, *38*(3), 357–381.

Weick, K. E., & Sutcliffe, K. M. (2006). Mindfulness and the quality of organizational attention. *Organization Science*, *17*(4), 514–524.

Weick, K. E., Sutcliffe, K. M., & Obstfeld, D. (1999). Organizing for high reliability: Processes of collective mindfulness. In B. M. Staw & L. L. Cummings, (Eds.), *Research in organizational behavior*, (Vol. 21, pp. 81–123). Greenwich, CT: JAI Press.

PART II

Leading mindfully

6

SLEEPWALKING VERSUS MINDFULNESS

A conscious leadership choice

Joan Marques

Leadership: a conscious choice

One of the reasons why leadership remains a fascinating topic is because it has so many dimensions and layers, and encompasses an immense range of perceptions. What one considers leadership, another may not agree with. What one considers a perfect leadership skill, another may disregard as unfitting in the leadership scope. Yet, there are some actions and skills that are generally agreed upon as being important in leadership. Some of these are vision, communication skills, understanding, knowledge, and determination.

An aspect that is as critical to leadership as the ones mentioned above is choice. Leaders make choices all the time, and they understand that every choice holds a degree of risk, because there are always factors that are not known or cannot be foreseen when making choices. And yet: choices are foundational in leading. In order to clarify this, we should consider the way leadership is defined here. Several theorists describe leadership as an act that involves a leader, followers, and a situation. In this chapter, however, leadership starts at an earlier stage, namely, even before followers or "others" are involved. Facing different situations, we have to make decisions, and whenever that happens, we are engaging in leadership, with or without others included. This necessary process in our lives could very well be described as self-leadership, and it should not be underestimated as leadership in the fullest sense of the word.

The subconscious habit of sleepwalking

When the term "sleepwalking" is used, many people may think of someone walking in their sleep, stereotypically with stretched arms and closed eyes. In this chapter we do not refer to that type of sleepwalking. Within the leadership perspective of this chapter, sleepwalking pertains to the many mindless acts we perform on a daily, weekly, monthly, or even yearly basis, without wondering about them. It's about implementing habitual patterns without questioning whether they still matter, and about staying in situations—personal or professional—that have long ago lost their luster to us. It's about walking, talking, acting, and deciding without critical or creative thinking.

Once the above is taken into consideration, we cannot escape the awareness that many people sleepwalk with their eyes wide open. They are everywhere: the colleague that has been complaining for ten years now about her job, but has not done anything to pursue a more rewarding career; the sister who's been dreading her marriage, but doesn't want to consider taking a leap toward her own happiness because she would be the first in the family to divorce; the brother who keeps feeling sorry for himself, because of all the chances he missed in the past; or the friend who remains stuck in his old routine, even though it stopped satisfying him years ago. When reflecting deeply, we will all be able to identify some sleepwalk patterns in our own behavior.

Sleepwalking is the opposite of being awake. People who sleepwalk, move through the motions of personal and professional life without questioning whether they still matter to them. Human beings have a tendency of becoming mindless and do things either because they have done them for a long time, or because they were done this way for a long time. Mindless continuation of traditions is an often occurring form of sleepwalking. Something was once done this way, and nobody wonders whether it still has a purpose today.

Some forms of sleepwalking are even brought within religious or cultural realms, making them even harder to challenge or change. Some people go to their church or temple two or three times a week, simply because the tradition has been set that way for decades. Unfortunately, they don't even pay attention to what their pastor or preacher says. Once out of their religious home, they live like savages with each other, mistrusting and insulting each other, unwilling to support any social cause, and filled with senses of discrimination, greed, and hatred. These are all serious forms of sleepwalking.

Some cultures prohibit their offspring from dating and marrying outside the racial or cultural boundaries. Youngsters who choose to oppose this rule get disowned and possibly even abandoned from their family or from the entire community. Protection of the ethnic purity is so important to them that it overbears any common or humane sense. And mindlessly, the tradition is observed year after year, decade after decade, without ever considering the bigger picture of human interconnectedness.

Sleepwalking has a lot to do with focusing too much on the details and forgetting to zoom out in order to obtain a broader scope. Discrimination of any kind is also a form of sleepwalking: it is an act that is based on superficial differences, mostly external or acquired, without considering the many overarching commonalities. Those who discriminate hold beliefs that they are somehow better than others, either because of their race, culture, education, age, status, or another parameter they erected and labeled as important. The mindset these discriminating folks nurture was most likely adopted from previous generations without any screening or critical reflection about its purpose, sense, or origins.

Racism and prejudice have been particular topics of interest in recent years, and the word is out that these forms of sleepwalking are to be attributed to a lower IQ (Pappas, 2012). Studies have revealed that there seems to be a vicious cycle at play here, where individuals with lower intelligence levels gravitate more to conservative trends, resist change, and are more prone to develop attitudes of prejudice. It is important to emphasize that the study findings pertain to large groups, and that there are definitely exceptions in every group (Pappas, 2012); in other words, not every person who holds conservative notions has a lower IQ, and not every liberal has a higher IQ. Yet, people who are more closed toward changes and "different ways of thinking" seem to suffer, on average, from lower intelligence levels, which disable them to place themselves in the place of those who are the subject of their prejudice.

Ending the sleepwalk habit begins with realizing that it is there: that we are a product of our environment, and that we have been shaped by the stimuli we were exposed to over the past decades: our upbringing, culture, religion, peers, teachers, perhaps even our ethnic group, neighborhood, generation, or workplace. Any source that impacted us over the years has contributed to the person we are today, thus, the perceptions we hold of "reality," and the decisions we make. It is important to consider, also, that it is easier to sleepwalk than to keep oneself awake! It is also easy to regress into the sleepwalking habit again after having been "awakened" and having made some bold decisions.

Effects of sleepwalking

As can be derived from the section above, sleepwalking can lead to a lot of trouble, not only for the person who sleepwalks, but also for those who are affected by this behavior. In the case of racism, for instance, the racist may not even suffer as much from their behavior as those who are subjected to the act. Oftentimes, however, sleepwalkers experience the disadvantages of their ways. Refusing to change is almost always equal to falling behind, especially in these times of continuous change.

It should be understood why sleepwalking is such a widespread phenomenon. It is because human beings, by default, are creatures of habit, hence, change-averse. We love to dwell in our comfort zones, and that is understandable to a great extent: once we have developed a pattern, it is just easier to follow the same trend repeatedly. It requires less mental energy to find our way through our routine. It is like performing on auto-pilot. But there are limits to everything: performing on auto-pilot for too long can derail our focus on new trends, and new trends keep emerging, whether we like it or not. Especially in professional circles, it will be self-destructive to behave like a sleepwalker.

Still, people fall prey to this mindless trend. They often make choices that feel good at one time, and then fail to keep track of the changes around them, and even those that happen within! Many people cannot understand their own change process. If they liked what they did once, how can they dislike it today? If they made such a deliberate decision to be where they currently are, how can it seem so unpleasant or unsuitable today? Of course, the answer is not too hard to retrieve: everything changes. Nothing is permanent. We live in a world where even our life is not infinite, let alone our relationships or professional circumstances. We are in constant flux, and regularly move up and down the ladder of progress. There is no guarantee that the trend will always be upward. Those who have experienced the economic downturn of 2008 can attest to that. Many people lost jobs that they thought would be theirs for the rest of their professional life. From one day to another, they had to give up their prestigious homes and some even became homeless. If there is one thing that doesn't change, it is the fact that life is unpredictable. Because of this unpredictability, we owe it to ourselves to remain mindful and refrain from sleepwalking.

Regardless of the measures we take to safeguard our life and circumstances, we don't have the ability to ensure that our life will be a smooth ride. And when we review challenges from this angle, we may be able to see their purpose: they shake us at our core and force us to refocus. If only for a short while, we snap out of the sleepwalking habit and understand the need to think creatively.

Thinking creatively is an immediate consequence of mindfulness, which will be discussed next in this chapter. As we become more alert of the shifting conditions of things around us, we realize that old solutions will not effectively solve new challenges. Our chance of success increases tremendously when we apply creativity and stop doing what everybody else does (Nissley, 2009). As an example, when we lose one job, we should be mindful in looking for another one in exactly the same field. This is what most people do. They try to recapture the same routine, even if they are forced to do it elsewhere. Instead of doing this, they could consider the disconnect from their prior work and habit pattern as an encouragement to explore a different path.

One Princeton University graduate who applied mindfulness in the midst of the 2008 economic downturn realized that his college degree was not going to help him in the dire circumstances he encountered upon returning home. He laid aside his previous intentions of becoming a major executive in a large corporation, scanned his hometown for local needs, and started a worm farm to make nutrient-rich compost for gardeners. Because so many businesses had closed, he could find cheap warehouse space for rent, and started collecting scraps from restaurants. "He surely didn't get a degree in worm farming, but he thought up an idea and made it work" (Nissley, 2009).

Individuals are not the only ones who sleepwalk. Organizations fall prey to this problematic behavior as well. This is understandable, because organizations are run by people, and if the people driving the organization are unaware or unwilling to apply necessary changes, the organization may land in an indolent situation that will harm its competitiveness and general performance and growth. There are numerous examples of businesses that once thrived but lost their edge due to sleepwalking (e.g., Blockbuster, Eastman Kodak, Motorola, Sony, Toys "R" Us). Within the organizational context, sleepwalking is usually equal to lack of innovation (Newman, 2010). Some major business corporations such as General Motors and Ford, once the biggest and most prestigious car companies on the globe, have been losing market share and profits due to their failure to keep up with younger generations of automakers.

Some of the most common reasons why individuals fall into the sleepwalking trap are the following:

1. They feel that thinking is a passive pursuit. They claim that they are too busy to make the time for sitting and thinking, while there's nothing lazy or passive about thinking.
2. They confine their thinking to their current field of action, or they have learned to think within the boundaries of their daily environment.
3. At work, they are not rewarded for creative thinking. There are still many work environments—and bosses—who can get very displeased with out-of-the-box thinkers or healthy risk-takers.
4. They may also be subject to peer pressure, sometimes even unconsciously. Especially those of us who are very close with our family or friends may want approval from them, but if they are traditionalists, they will not encourage anything out of the ordinary, or anything that may require you to move away.
5. They may face self-imposed blockades, which so many people maintain, such as self-esteem issues, or fear for what others may think of them, which prohibits them from wading into areas outside of their mental comfort zone (Lavine, 2009).
6. They are subjected to a highly routine-based (mechanistic) environment, which does not encourage critical thinking, because the actions to be applied are highly repetitive. This is why we often see telephone operators, checkout clerks, and airline personnel sleepwalk through their days, mechanically fulfilling the tasks that were outlined for them (Langer & Moldoveanu, 2000).
7. They may come from cultures or living environments where mindfulness was punished, or where mindless following was rewarded (King & Sawyer, 1998).

The effect of sleepwalking on business entities is decline, unless they manage to reinvent themselves and come up with a product or service that restores their position in their field. The effect of sleepwalking for human beings could be considered similar: we, too, can first fall off the bandwagon, but then wake up, and come up with a way to reinvent ourselves in order to return to the point of fulfillment or prestige we desire. That's the beauty of being alive and thinking: regardless of our mistakes, we can correct them and move on, sometimes even better than before.

However, when we are in sleepwalk mode, we may not think too deeply about it, but we usually feel depressed, and it is no secret what depression can do to us. Being unfulfilled and unhappy for long periods of time reduces our patience and can turn us into moody, grouchy people. Health-wise, it can cause us to acquire high blood pressure, push us toward destructive habits such as alcohol, drug abuse, or overeating, and possibly lead to a stroke, a heart attack, or other psychosomatically driven diseases.

On the other hand, mindful performance keeps us fulfilled, even though it would be foolish to think that every day will be at an equal high. Even wakeful people experience downs sometimes, because life is happening to them as well. They just don't allow these setbacks to get the best of them, and bounce back much more quickly than sleepwalkers do. Overall, the quality of their life is therefore at a much higher level.

The conscious practice of mindfulness

"Our consciousness can be transformed at its base through the practice of mindful consuming, mindfully guarding our senses, and looking deeply. The practice should aim at transforming both the individual and the collective aspects of our consciousness" (Nhat Hanh, 1998, p. 181).

Decision-making entails choices. In order to make a decision, we weigh alternatives, and select one option. That's a choice. Our life is filled with choices, and not only simple ones such as what clothes we will put on today, or whether we will take the bus, bike, or train to work. Who and what we are today is largely based on the choices we made in the past. Where we will be in the future is also largely dependent upon the choices we make today. Leaders are particularly aware of that. Choices are not always easy to make. They require skills that we often take for granted, but that can enhance the quality of the choices we make. Some of these skills are:

- *Mindfulness:* This refers to our ability to be aware of all the factors that matter in the choice process. Mindfulness is our basic human ability to be fully present and not reactive or distracted by external occurrences (Gero, 2019). In making choices, especially those with high impact, there is no room for neglecting factors that could be critical for the outcome. We will therefore have to be attentive to details, but also to the bigger picture.
- *Reflection:* Oftentimes, when we are facing choices, we have to tap from past experiences, but also use our imagination to envision possible outcomes. This reflective process can help us eliminate some choices that may seem appealing, but could carry consequences we may not want to deal with.
- *Courage:* No matter how much information we have at hand, there will always be unknown factors. Every choice is therefore a courageous act: a leap in the dark that may require smart adjustments when complications arise that we had not foreseen.

- *Intelligence:* Some choices require intellectual intelligence, such as knowledge, design thinking, and strategic insight, while others ask for emotional intelligence, including empathy and deep listening. This often depends on the nature of the choice and who or what is involved.
- *Consideration:* While reflection and intelligence do a decent job in getting to the choice to be made, it is consideration that can be seen as the final aspect. Consideration is the process of weighing all the options, just before making a decision.

In spite of its importance in the leadership process, choice is not often listed as a leadership skill. It is one of those qualities we take for granted, just like our breath, because we have all have made choices for the longest time in our lives. But choices can lead to wonderful or disastrous outcomes. It is therefore equally important for leaders to know that the choice is highly important, but the action implemented after a choice has been made underscores the ability of a leader to think creatively, show perseverance, and remain balanced.

Mindfulness at work

Mindfulness is considered a critical tool to enhance workplace spirituality that results in increasing work performance (Petchsawang & Duchon, 2012). The practice of mindfulness results in greater mental presence, which helps us connect better with others and engage more fully in our jobs (Federman, 2009). Hyland, Lee, and Mills (2015) confirm that mindfulness yields psychological, physiological, and performance benefits. This has therefore resulted in mindfulness training programs in major workplaces such as Google, the US Army, and Harvard Business School (Petchsawang & McLean, 2017). Reviewing the concerted implementation of mindfulness practices in two workplaces in New Jersey and Pennsylvania, Karlin (2018) states that participants praised the fact that mindfulness allowed them to be more present with their families and less stressed about work matters when they are home trying to relax, or trying to stay engaged during a significant time in their or their family's lives.

Metcalf and Hately (2001) reflect on nurturing a detached mindset in the workplace, and underscore the need for us to be mindful and understand that everything in life comes and goes, so there is no need to become attached. Morvay (1999) uses the term "healthy detachment," tying it into the practice of mindfulness, and explaining that being mindful can help us realize that we are open and receptive onlookers toward the ordinary stream of consciousness without preconception or judgment. Ghose (2004) also reminds us that Buddhist psychology strongly relies on the practice of mindfulness as the foundation of all actions and decisions. Thich Nhat Hanh (1976) underscores in that regard that all our feelings, whether positive or negative, strong or weak, should be considered with mindfulness, since this is what protects our psyche from harm.

Engaging in mindfulness practice could lead to positive changes in the lives of a practitioner and their stakeholders, as it may enhance insights into responsible and moral conduct toward all that exists. Foundational Buddhist implementation of mindfulness is inseparably linked to ethical conduct. It meticulously observes the Buddhist five precepts of non-killing, non-stealing, no sexual misconduct, no wrongful speech, and non-partaking in alcohol and drugs as part of mindfulness practice (Murphy, 2016). In several Western-developed mindfulness exercises, these concepts are disregarded, which may leave the door open to mindfulness without moral foundation. While therefore admitting to the enormous benefits in mindfulness training for non-Buddhist audiences, Murphy (2016) also warns for the possibility of a misinterpretation and malpractice of mindfulness, void of the Buddhist concepts of non-harming, morality, loving kindness, and compassion. She also raises the cautionary reasoning that mindfulness training can be presented in an overly positive light, thus downplaying abusive practices such as turning a blind eye to potential negative outcomes of this practice.

Van Gordon, Shonin, and Griffiths (2017) also advocate the Buddhist meditative practice of mindfulness as the one that will cultivate important foundational concepts of compassion, loving kindness, and moral responsibility. With that, they also support Nhat Hanh's (1999) notion that true aptitude in mindfulness requires not only awareness of the present moment, but also solid understanding of the true and absolute (self-less) mode in which the present moment exists. It is therefore prudent to underscore the necessity of including the moral aspect of mindfulness practice, which we could refer herewith as "mindful mindfulness."

The intersection of mindfulness and awareness

Awareness should not be confused with mindfulness. Awareness is a foundational quality of what was referred to above as "mindful mindfulness." Awareness should not be confused with attention either. Rapgay and Bystrisky (2009) clarify in that regard that attention denotes an ever-changing factor of consciousness, while awareness pertains to a stable and specific state of consciousness as well as a function. When considered a function, awareness is more an introspective or observational sensation that monitors experiences. When considered as a state, awareness refers to the nature of consciousness. The nature of consciousness is expansive, and is capable of containing a variety of experiences (Rapgay & Bystrisky, 2009). Also describing awareness as a function are Berkhin and Hartelius (2011), who assert that Buddhist practice is focused on meanings rather than events, and the meanings are instilled by moment-by-moment awareness of our condition. Sundararajan (2008) identifies reflexivity and second-order awareness, whereby reflexivity awareness pertains to the knowledge or insight in what we already know, while second-order awareness (as opposed to first-order experience) pertains to a higher-level consciousness, whereby we have an experience, and then an experience of that experience.

Nurturing mindfulness through Vipassana

Vipassana, or mindfulness meditation, is practiced to a continuously increasing degree in America. Business people, academicians, but also prison inmates, seem to experience significant transformations when engaging in this meditation practice. *Publishers Weekly* (Martinez, 2008) and the *Philadelphia Inquirer* (Rickey, 2009) write about the practice of Vipassana among prison inmates and how this practice helps them break their cycles of anger and revenge. In *McClatchy Tribune Business News*, Anderson (2009) describes a setting where she joined a group of six men and four women, all very busy people from the business and academic world, who deliberately created space in their hectic schedule for Vipassana meditation. The guidance during this meditation was downloaded from a website of the Insight Meditation Center, IMC, in Redwood, California. Several of these options are readily available: books, tapes, courses, Internet sites, and the like. They can be ordered at little or no cost, and increase tremendously in popularity. Anderson (2009) reports that some of the business people and academics explained to her after the session why they made such an effort in engaging in Vipassana in spite of their hectic lives: they felt that it helped them become less snappy and more restful, and they could think more clearly and creatively, thanks to the relaxation they allowed their mind to have during the meditation. Many of them were now meditating at least 20 minutes a day, and detected changes in their overall attitude and outlook on life, which they experienced as positive. Verbalizing the essence of this dissertation and the growing trend of today, the leader in Anderson's meditation circle, Chris, stated, "People are figuring out that the people who came up with this some 3,000 odd years ago might have been on to something" (par. 9).

Vipassana is praised by scholars on both Eastern and Western sides. Geshey Ngawang Dhargey (1974), for instance, explains that the teaching of Vipasyana is divided into three sections: (1) establishment of the concept of non-self-existence of personality; (2) establishment of the non-self-existence of all phenomena; and (3) the method of developing Vipasyana (p. 163). Michalon (2001) recommends this form of meditation to all who deal with life's major problems, and explains that Vipassana meditation works best when full and simultaneous attention is given to its two essential components, concentration (samatha) and mindfulness (a mental eye or a "sixth sense"). Gero (2019) adds that research has revealed several benefits for adults who practice Vipassana meditation, such as better sleep, progress toward weight loss goals, lowering stress levels and anxiety, decreasing loneliness in seniors, improving attention, decreasing negative thoughts, reducing pain, acquiring higher brain functioning, increasing immune function, lowering blood pressure, and increasing awareness. Goenka (2001), who initiated a widespread Vipassana movement from Burma to India, and subsequently to the rest of the world in recent decades, clarifies that Vipassana enables meditators to attain mastery over the mind on the basis of morality, and develop wisdom to eradicate all the blemishes of craving and aversion. Goenka adds that it is a practical technique, which provides useful results here and now, just as it did in the past. Pelled (2007) echoes Goenka's assertions regarding the discontinuation from suffering through Vipassana by stating that the relief from suffering (here fermentation) through meditation is connected to factors for awakening that should be cultivated. Pelled (2007) continues, "It can be understood that those factors represent components of mental activity: concentration, attention (here Mindfulness), and a state of mind called 'equanimity.' These are central factors in the practice of Vipassana meditation" (p. 1513).

The influence of Vipassana has frequently been linked to consciousness and general well-being. Goenka (2006), for instance, asserts that Vipassana is not merely a theory or philosophy but rather a down-to-earth, practical, rational, scientific, non-sectarian, and result-oriented practice. Goenka stresses that the practice of Vipassana contributes to becoming a better human being, and generating a peaceful and harmonious atmosphere around oneself and others. This was underscored by the findings of Anderson, Martinez, and Ricky earlier, in their reviews of Vipassana's great success among die-hard American managers, academics, and even prisoners. Goenka (2006) makes a strong statement for Vipassana as a useful instrument toward expanded and purified consciousness of people from all religions, cultures, and backgrounds. To that regard he affirms that nothing is objectionable in practicing the technique of concentration of the mind by observing one's natural, normal respiration, without adding any sectarian verbalization or any visualization, and imagination. He wonders which religion could possibly object to observing one's natural respiration. In extension, he also feels that nobody could possibly object to purifying the mind at the deepest level, by objectively observing the interaction of mind and matter within oneself, at the level of body sensations, because that, too, is universal. Goenka, who has established a large number of Vipassana institutes around the world, underscores an important value of Vipassana, which is the emerging awareness of craving for pleasant sensations and aversion to unpleasant ones.

Converting sleepwalking into mindfulness

Before we can do something about sleepwalking, we have to be aware that we do it, and that is often the biggest challenge. It's almost as challenging as trying to discover that you sleep while you are asleep. As indicated earlier in this chapter, the tendency to sleepwalk is so widespread, so common, that many people will choose to remain in denial and claim that they are not sleepwalking, but very wakeful instead. Yet, multiple psychology researchers are now sharing the conclusion that most human performance is mindless, hence, based on sleepwalking. "Without deliberative and reflective conscious activity, humans are simply mindless automatons" (Bandura, 2006).

In regards to sleepwalking, this chapter has thus far explained that, (1) there is such a phenomenon as sleepwalking or enduring mindlessness; (2) it leads to undesirable effects for the person who sleepwalks as well as those who are closely affiliated with this person; (3) it can be turned around through mindful behavior and creative thinking.

Before presenting a series of reminders toward staying mindful, here are, first and foremost, six suggestions on refraining from regressing into the sleepwalk habit:

1. Expose yourself to new environments. You don't necessarily have to travel to another country. Just visit places where you have not been before, and allow yourself to soak up some new impressions. This is a great way for ideas to sprout.
2. Expose yourself to people outside of your comfort zone. Talking to different people, and listening intensely to their conversations, can help you discover new opportunities and create new relationships that may be useful in the future.
3. Engage in critical self-reflection. There are many ways to do that: meditation is a proven strategy to realize a number of important things in your life, but a long, mindful walk, or just sitting and thinking in silence, may also be insightful. Think of the things you do that you don't enjoy, and ask yourself why you actually do them: what keeps you from ceasing them or working toward that?
4. Engage in a constructive learning process. In these exponential times we can do so from the comfort of our home or office: the internet offers numerous options to learn, many of them at no charge. Learning always brings insights: it can point us in new directions and make us aware of avenues we didn't realize were there.
5. Maintain a responsible work–life balance. Allow yourself time to enjoy different areas of your being, as they all contribute uniquely to the wholesome picture that is your life.
6. There are more ways to help you end the sleepwalk habit than the five listed above. These five are merely presented to give you an idea. However, it is first and foremost important to remember that you constantly change. Literally! Old cells die, and new ones are made. After a number of years, none of the cells you harbor today will still be part of you, so you will be an entirely different person. How can you expect, then, to have the same perspectives and needs in the future as you have today? What I am alluding to is that the things you were passionate about ten years ago may not do it for you anymore today, and there's nothing wrong with that! You have changed, and it would be a serious injustice if you kept holding on to people, situations, places, or processes that make you unhappy, because when you are unhappy, others around you feel it, and they also become unhappy.

It is also critical to emphasize that becoming and remaining mindful is not easy. It might help, therefore, to be mindful of the following:

1. Being mindful is not a one-time project. It requires ongoing effort, because it can evaporate so easily when we settle into our activities, work-, or lifestyles. Fortunately, mindfulness can be polished regularly, for instance through meditation, or through regular scanning of your thoughts (Junttila, n.d.), and asking yourself whether you are being mindful or are being mindless. The more you ask yourself that question, the more deliberate your actions will become, and the fewer mindless moments you will have.
2. Life is a continuous sequence of mindfulness disruptions, which may come in many forms: problems at home or work, relationship issues, loss or illness, which can give rise to old bad habits, distract you from your mindfulness efforts (Junttila, n.d.), thus propelling you back into sleepwalking mode.
3. The many distractions and setbacks in your work and private life may cause your mindfulness efforts to stall regularly or progress so slowly that you get discouraged (Junttila, n.d.). Of course, setbacks are the best opportunities to prove your determination and test your mindfulness. But that is easier said than done.
4. Your goals may infringe on your mindfulness efforts (Junttila, n.d.). You may get so geared up about reaching a goal that you suddenly realize that you have placed your mindfulness efforts on hold, and have fallen into many of your old sleepwalking habits. Goals are great, but they can also be powerful distractions to remaining mindful.
5. Achieving your goals may cause another major infringement on your mindfulness (Junttila, n.d.). If you reach a goal and don't set a new one, you run the chance of becoming languid, and losing the zest to move on. Lethargy is one of the major drivers of mindlessness. Lack of activity equals lack of purpose, and that equals lack of a reason to nourish mindfulness.
6. Dreading your current circumstances can also become an obstacle toward mindfulness. It may lead to depression, and rob you from the will to focus. However, dreadful situations are also a great opportunity for sharpening your mindfulness efforts and understanding the purpose of the current moment in the wholeness of your life (Junttila, n.d.).

Aside from the above described mindfulness meditation practice, Vipassana, here are three activities that can help you to practice mindfulness regularly:

1. Engage in constructive dialogues with people who have proven to be creative thinkers. If you know them well and feel comfortable to do so, ask them what qualities they see in you. What skills and talents do they think you have? What areas can they envision you in? Keep in mind that any idea is worth considering (Marques, Dhiman, & King, 2009).
2. Look at yourself from the other side: what are employers looking for today? Do you represent that? How? Try to put yourself in the shoes of various people you meet. Perhaps their job, their activity, their direction, may spark an idea within you that is useful toward your next career (Marques et al., 2009).
3. Consider the big picture. Take some distance. Step out of the daily routine, and go, if only for one day, to a place that inspires you. It does not have to be abroad, out of state, or even outside the city. Just a place you enjoy being. Places that break the daily rhythm also help open your mind and expand your horizons (Marques et al., 2009).

Five chapter takeaways

1. Sleepwalking is what we do when we go through the motions, day after day, year after year, without really questioning ourselves or our circumstances. Many people sleepwalk, because they don't realize that there is an alternative to the way they go

through life. Sleepwalking is the opposite of being awake. People who sleepwalk, move through the motions of personal and professional life without questioning whether they still matter to them.

2. Sleepwalking can lead to a lot of trouble, not only for the person who sleepwalks, but also for those who are affected by this behavior. Sleepwalkers frequently experience the disadvantages of their ways. Refusing to change is almost always equal to falling behind, especially in these times of continuous change.
3. Thinking creatively is an immediate consequence of mindfulness. As we become more alert of the shifting conditions of things around us, we realize that old solutions will not effectively solve new challenges. Our chance of success increases when we apply creativity and stop doing what everybody else does.
4. Becoming and remaining mindful is not easy. It is imperative to realize that, (1) being mindful is not a one-time project, but requires ongoing effort; (2) life is a continuous sequence of mindfulness disruptions, which come in many forms; (3) the many distractions and setbacks in work and private life may cause your mindfulness efforts to stall regularly or progress so slowly that you get discouraged; (4) your goals may infringe on your mindfulness efforts; (5) achieving your goals may also cause major infringement on your mindfulness; and (6) dreading your current circumstances can become an obstacle toward mindfulness as well.
5. Activities that can help you to practice mindfulness regularly: (1) engage in constructive dialogues with people who have proven to be creative thinkers; (2) look at yourself from the other side: what are employers looking for today? Do you represent that? How?; (3) consider the big picture. Take some distance. Step out of the daily routine, and expand your horizons.

Reflection questions

1. Based on the explanation of sleepwalking in this chapter, consider a situation, private or professional, where you were sleepwalking. Describe this situation, and explain how you have dealt with it so far.
2. The chapter provides seven reasons why human beings can fall into sleepwalking mode. On basis of your personal reflections, select two or three of these reasons, and explain how they pertain to you, and why.
3. Explain, in your own words, the difference as well as the common elements of awareness and mindfulness.
4. Becoming and remaining mindful is not easy. Six attention points are offered in the chapter, which we should be mindful about in our efforts to becoming mindful. Which of these attention points (select two) do you see as potential hurdles on your path to mindfulness? Please explain.
5. Review the six reminders brought forward near the end of the chapter to help maintain mindfulness. Which of these six reminders poses the biggest challenge to you, and why?

References

Anderson, S. (2009, February 8). Ah-ummmm ... : Meditation group offers calm in a stressful world. *McClatchy - Tribune Business News*. Retrieved from ABI/INFORM Dateline database.

Bandura, A. (2006). Toward a psychology of human agency. *Perspectives on Psychological Science*, *1*(2), 164–180.

Berkhin, I., & Hartelius, G. (2011). What altered states are not enough: A perspective from Buddhism. *International Journal of Transpersonal Studies, 30*(1–2), 63–68.

Dhargey, G. N. (1974). *Tibetan tradition of mental development.* Dharamsala, India: Library of Tibetan Works and Archives.

Federman, B. (2009). *Employee engagement: A roadmap for creating profits, optimizing performance, and increasing loyalty.* San Francisco, CA: Jossey-Bass.

Gero, J. (2019, 05). Mindfulness: Training the mind to be present. Workforce management (time and attendance). *Excellence Essentials.*

Ghose, L. (2004). A study in Buddhist psychology: Is Buddhism truly pro-detachment and anti-attachment? *Contemporary Buddhism, 5*(2), 105–120.

Goenka, S. N. (2001). *Was the Buddha a Pessimist?* Dhammagiri, Igatpuri: Vipassana Research Institute.

Goenka, S. N. (2006). *Peace within oneself for peace in the world.* Dhammagiri, Igatpuri: Vipassana Research Institute.

Hanh, T. (1998). *The heart of the Buddha's teaching: Transforming suffering into peace, joy, and liberation.* New York, NY: Broadway Books.

Hanh, T. N. (1976). *The miracle of mindfulness.* Boston, MA: Beacon Press.

Hyland, P. K., Lee, R. A., & Mills, M. J. (2015). Mindfulness at work: A new approach to improving individual and organisational performance. *Industrial and Organisational Psychology: Perspectives on Science and Practice, 8*(4), 576–602.

Junttila, H. (n.d.). 7 obstacles to mindfulness and how to overcome them. *TinyBuddha.com.* Retrieved from http://tinybuddha.com/blog/7-obstacles-to-mindfulness-and-how-to-overcome-them/

Karlin, D. S. (2018). Mindfulness in the workplace. *Strategic HR Review, 17*(2), 76–80.

King, P. E., & Sawyer, C. R. (1998). Mindfulness, mindlessness and communication instruction. *Communication Education, 47*(4), 326–336.

Langer, E., & Moldoveanu, M. (2000). The construct of mindfulness. *Journal of Social Issues, 56*(1), 1–9.

Lavine, D. S. (2009). Creative thinking. *National Law Journal, 31*(28), March 16, 13.

Marques, J., Dhiman, S., & King, R. (2009). What really matters at work in turbulent times. *Business Renaissance Quarterly, 4*(1), 13–29.

Martinez, J. (2008, September). New age pragmatism. *Publishers Weekly, 255*(38), 27. Retrieved from ABI/INFORM Global database).

Metcalf, F., & Hately, B. G. (2001). *What would Buddha do at work?.* San Francisco, CA: Seastone and Berrett-Koehler Publishers, Inc.

Michalon, M. (2001). "Selflessness" in the service of the ego: Contributions, limitations and dangers of Buddhist psychology for western psychotherapy. *American Journal of Psychotherapy, 55*(2), 202–218.

Morvay, Z. (1999). Horney, Zen, and the real self: Theoretical and historical connections. *American Journal of Psychoanalysis, 59*(1), 25–35.

Murphy, A. (2016). Mindfulness-based therapy in modern psychology: Convergence and divergence from early Buddhist thought. *Contemporary Buddhism, 17*(2), 275–325.

Newman, R. (2010, August 19). 10 great companies that lost their edge. *US News: Money.* Retrieved from http://money.usnews.com/money/blogs/flowchart/2010/08/19/10-great-companies-that-lost-their-edge

Nhat Hanh, T. (1999). *The Miracle of Mindfulness: An Introduction to the Practice of Meditation.* Boston, MA: Beacon Press.

Nissley, E. L. (2009, 29 March). Creative thinking goes long way. *McClatchy - Tribune Business News* originally posted by The Times-Tribune, Scranton, PA.

Pappas, S. (2012, January 26). Low IQ & conservative beliefs linked to prejudice. *LiveScience.* Retrieved from www.livescience.com/18132-intelligence-social-conservatism-racism.html

Pelled, E. (2007). Learning from experience: Bion's concept of reverie and Buddhist meditation: A comparative study. *International Journal of Psychoanalysis, 88*(6), 1507–1526.

Petchsawang, P., & Duchon, D. (2012). Workplace spirituality, meditation, and work performance. *Journal of Management, Spirituality & Religion, 9*(2), 189–208.

Petchsawang, P., & McLean, G. N. (2017). Workplace spirituality, mindfulness meditation, and work engagement. *Journal of Management, Spirituality & Religion, 14*(3), 216–244.

Rapgay, L., & Bystrisky, A. (2009). Classical mindfulness. *Annals of the New York Academy of Sciences, 1172,* 148–162.

Rickey, C. (2009, March 5). The Philadelphia inquirer Carrie Rickey column: The meditating prisoners: Transformative silence? *McClatchy - Tribune Business News*. Retrieved from ABI/INFORM Dateline database.

Sundararajan, L. (2008). Toward a reflexive positive psychology: Insights from the Chinese Buddhist notion of emptiness. *Theory & Psychology*, *18*(5), 655–674.

Van Gordon, W., Shonin, E., & Griffiths, M. D. (2017). Buddhist emptiness theory: Implications for psychology. *Psychology of Religion and Spirituality*, *9*(4), 309–318.

7
MINDFUL LEADERSHIP

Michael Chaskalson, Megan Reitz, Lee Waller, and Sharon Olivier

Introduction

The last 20 years have borne witness to significant changes to the context in which today's leaders operate. Navigating challenges such as increasing globalization, proliferation of social media, digital transformation, and climate change, to name but a few, means that leaders in the 21st century are required to lead in conditions that are complex rather than simply complicated (Uhl-Bien and Arena, 2017) and increasingly paradoxical (Lavine, 2014; Zhang, Waldman, Han and Li, 2015). To thrive in such conditions they must develop capacities that enable them to respond effectively to challenges whose outcomes are outside of their control (Lavine, 2014).

Training and development programs which set out to improve leadership capacities should therefore focus on the intrapersonal, interpersonal, and cognitive mindsets required to be effective in these complex conditions, and work to enhance leaders' and potential leaders' capacities for self-awareness and self-efficacy (Day and Dragoni, 2015); their resilience and cognitive flexibility (Abbatiello, Knight, Philpot and Roy, 2017); and their capacities for self-reflection and self-regulation (Nesbit, 2012). King and Nesbit (2015), however, question the ability of current leadership development interventions to develop such capacities and Nesbit (2012) argues that the development of meta-skills which enable leaders to continuously develop themselves is especially important.

In this chapter we suggest that mindfulness is one such meta-skill for leadership in that it has the potential to alter a range of crucial functions such as focus, adaptability, perspective-taking, empathy, and emotion regulation—and that it might usefully be considered a part of leadership training programs.

"Mindfulness" is a state, a trait, and a method of training the mind (Baer and Lykins, 2011). State mindfulness is spoken of as a way of paying attention—on purpose, in the present moment and non-judgmentally (Kabat-Zinn, 2003). Mindfulness training interventions such as Mindfulness-based Stress Reduction (MBSR) (Kabat-Zinn, 2003) and Mindfulness-Based Cognitive Therapy (MBCT) (Segal, Williams and Teasdale, 2002) set out to improve both state and trait mindfulness.

In such interventions, mindfulness training is delivered along with psychoeducational content about stress or chronic pain (MBSR) or relapsing depression (MBCT). The mindfulness meditation practices taught on these interventions derive from the Theravadin Buddhist tradition (Thera, 1975) and are secularized for the contexts in which they are used. Participants learn how to mindfully attend to thoughts, feelings, sensations, and impulses through the use of different meditations, gentle stretching, and yoga exercises, along with discussions and practices geared toward applying mindful awareness to daily life.

There are a number of studies that link mindfulness with *aspects* of leadership. Hyland, Lee and Mills (2015), for example, suggest that "flexible, objective and mindful employees may be more open to new ways of doing things and may be more observant and attentive whilst learning new behaviors" (p. 591). However, their argument is inferred from what is known about the various benefits of mindfulness practice rather than from empirical evidence of its impact on helping people deal with change and complexity. Studies such as Jha, Stanley, Kiyonaga, Wong and Gelfand (2010), which show an enhanced working memory capacity following eight weeks of mindfulness training, lead one to consider that this might boost leaders' capacities for processing multiple and dynamic sources of information, as could the improved flexibility response to mental inputs in dynamic circumstances that was found by Heydenfeldt, Herkenhoff and Coe (2011).

As regards the ability to collaborate, Hunter and McCormick (2008) found that mindfulness practitioners reported greater external awareness as well as an increased responsiveness that improved their interactions with their teams, allowing them to be more adaptive and flexible with individuals. They reported improved openness with others at work, were more inclusive of others' ideas, and better at conflict management. Singh, Singh, Sabaawi, Myers and Wahler (2006) found active listening, collaboration, and greater respect among team members after a mindfulness-based mentoring program.

Finally, mindfulness has been associated with workforce resilience (Shapiro, Wang and Peltason, 2015; Walach et al., 2007) as well as with resilience across a broad range of occupations—including managers and entrepreneurs (Roche, Haar and Luthans, 2014). It has been shown to improve coping mechanisms and cultivate faster recovery from negative events (Keng, Smoski and Robins, 2011). Glomb, Duffy, Bono and Yang (2011) found that mindfulness-based practices improved self-regulation and so enhanced employees' resilience in the face of challenges and improved their task performance.

Hunter and Chaskalson (2013) suggest that evidence from diverse sources suggests that increased mindfulness might be expected to improve a range of leadership capacities such as decreased reactivity, increased attention, enhanced objectivity, increased empathy, better decision-making capacity, and increased capacity for innovation.

To date, however, there is a relative scarcity of research that much more directly links mindfulness to leadership (King and Badham, 2018), and few studies have investigated the impact of mindfulness training for leadership development (Brendel, Hankerson, Byun and Cunningham, 2016; Good et al., 2016).

Given the considerable gap in the literature, we set out to discover whether mindfulness training for leaders (The Mindful Leader Training, MLT) could improve three key leadership capabilities: a leader's resilience; their capacity to lead in complexity; and their ability to collaborate with others.

A leader's resilience

Resilience has been defined in the context of organizational behavior as the "capacity to rebound, to 'bounce back' from adversity, uncertainty, conflict, failure or even positive change, progress and increased responsibility" (Luthans, 2002, p. 702).

A lack of resilience in the workplace comes with high costs—both to the person and to the organization (Hassard, Teoh, Visockaite, Dewe and Cox, 2018). Low resilience has been linked to burnout, stress, depression, and anxiety (Mealer et al., 2012), and as such has significant implications for individuals and for organizations in terms of, for example, their employees' performance, motivation, attitudes towards change, and ability to learn from failure.

Previous research has shown that mindfulness training can have a positive impact on various indicators of resilience. There is strong evidence, for example, that it improves the ability to cope with stress in healthy adults (Chiesa and Serretti, 2009) and it has a beneficial impact on a variety of psychological problems such as depression, anxiety, and substance abuse (Goldberg et al., 2018). In workplace settings, mindfulness training has been shown to help participants become more resilient in the face of occupational stress, with resilience being found to mediate the impact of mindfulness on engagement and well-being of full-time employees (Malinowski and Lim, 2015). Because emotion management is a factor in the development of resilience (Davda, 2011), emotion regulation skills might also mediate the relationship between mindfulness and resilience. Workplace mindfulness training decreases emotional exhaustion (Hülsheger et al., 2013) and it contributes to an improved ability to recover from work stress (Hülsheger, Feinholdt and Nübold, 2015).

Apart from our own, however, the only other leadership study to date investigating the specific link between mindfulness training and resilience failed to find significant changes in leaders' resilience or tolerance for ambiguity following a mindfulness training when compared with an active control condition (Brendel, Hankerson, Byun and Cunningham, 2016).

Leading in complex conditions

Rodriguez and Rodriguez (2015) suggest that a core leadership capacity today is the ability to adapt to and act flexibly in volatile, uncertain, complex, and ambiguous (VUCA) contexts. Complexity leadership theories emphasize this skill (Uhl-Bien and Arena, 2017), as do theories of leadership performance in conditions of change and ambiguity (Boyatzis, 2006). Leading in complexity calls for enhanced agility on the part of leaders in order to adapt to changing environments (Uhl-Bien and Arena, 2017).

Hyland, Lee and Mills (2015) suggest that "flexible, objective and mindful employees may be more open to new ways of doing things and may be more observant and attentive" (p. 591). As such, mindfulness training may help leaders to navigate complex conditions by enabling improved choicefulness, particularly in situations of high emotion which often prime automaticity (Brown and Ryan, 2004). Leaders with higher trait mindfulness show greater leadership flexibility, being better able to adapt their leadership style according to the demands of a situation (Baron, Rouleau, Grégoire and Baron, 2018). One mechanism that may increase the capability to lead in complexity is the ability to more skillfully filter, process, and manage the streams of information that are used in decision-making (Uhl-Bien and Arena, 2017). Mindfulness training may enhance that by training attention, awareness, and the increased responsiveness that comes with lower reactivity (Segal, Williams and Teasdale, 2002).

There is also a growing evidence base for improved cognitive functioning, such as working memory capacity, as a result of mindfulness training (Chiesa, Calati, and Serretti, 2011; Jha, Krompinger and Baime, 2007). Through mindfulness training participants achieved greater attentional control, as shown by a greater ability to redirect and maintain their attention on an object of their choice (Hasenkamp, Wilson-Mendenhall, Duncan and Barsalou, 2012), and a four-week training was effective in improving the working memory capacity in soldiers (Zanesco, Denkova, Rogers, MacNulty and Jha, 2019).

Collaboration

Abbatiello, Knight, Philpot and Roy (2017) report that 90 percent of companies are redesigning to become more dynamic and team-centered. That being the case, a leader's capacity to both collaborate and to enable collaboration in increasingly complex organizations should be a crucial domain of leadership development (Uhl-Bien and Arena, 2017).

Boyatzis and McKee (2005) advise leaders to create resonance rather than give orders. Cunliffe and Eriksen (2011) call on them to engage and relate with followers. Other theorists call on them to adopt a humble attitude of serving others (Greenleaf and Spears, 1998; van Dierendonck, Stam, Boersma, de Windt and Alkema, 2014) with the aim of establishing collaborative and friendlier working environments.

Mindfulness training may enhance a leader's capacity to collaborate and to foster collaboration. Mindfulness training has been found to be associated with greater other-orientation, such as a greater pro-sociality (Donald et al., 2018) and with more compassionate behavior (Condon, Desbordes, Miller and DeSteno, 2013). Leaders who discover through mindfulness training how to better regulate their own emotions may also prevent their own negative emotions from spilling over and affecting their teams. Ashkanasy and Dorris (2017) show how such spillage may inadvertently reduce the team's capacity to collaborate.

Mindfulness training may enable leaders to become more aware of their followers' needs (Reb, Narayanan and Chaturvedi, 2014); their emotional states (Quaglia, Goodman and Brown, 2015); and their motivations (Reb, Chaturvedi, Narayanan and Kudesia, 2018). Mindfulness has been found to be related to greater presence in interactions (Beckman et al., 2012); to less hostile communication (Krishnakumar and Robinson, 2015); and to a more positive emotional tone (Beach et al., 2013).

All of that might enhance collaboration.

Finally, Yu and Zellmer-Bruhn (2018) showed that the level of trait mindfulness within a team was negatively related to relationship conflict within that team. Mindfulness training might therefore equip leaders to cope with relationship conflicts more effectively and so enhance their team's capacity to collaborate.

It would seem that there are good grounds for presuming that mindfulness training is beneficial for the development of leaders' resilience, their effectiveness in enabling collaboration, and their capacity to lead in complexity. Yet, as noted above, few studies to date have investigated the impact of mindfulness training on leadership-specific outcomes, and more objective measures of leadership behavior, such as 360-degree instruments, have rarely been employed alongside measures that detail self-report outcomes.

The mindful leader study

Objectives

The purpose of our study was to test the feasibility and effectiveness of a Mindful Leadership Training (MLT) to improve mindfulness and leadership skills in a leadership sample. Specifically, our research set out to answer the following research questions:

1) Is an eight-week MLT feasible? Can busy leaders complete the program and sustain the home practices? Do they come to feel that the training delivers professional benefit in developing their capacities?

2) Do MLT participants show improvements in mindfulness, resilience, interpersonal reactivity, and cognitive functioning post-program than those in a waitlist control group?
3) Do MLT participants, their peers, colleagues, and direct reports notice improvements in leadership capacities compared with those in the control group?
4) Is home practice associated with the outcomes of the training?

Methods

Study design

This was a mixed-methods, non-randomized, waitlist-controlled trial with a sample of senior leaders. We advertised the course to alumni of Hult Ashridge Executive Education in England, through business connections, personal networks, and by way of social media.

The intervention took place at Hult Ashridge Executive Education from 2015 to 2016. Inclusion criteria were:

1) No previous participation in a mindfulness or meditation training.
2) Participants should currently hold a leadership position with management or supervisory responsibility for at least two people.
3) Participants should be able to attend all of the program workshops.

Although full randomization of participants was not possible, participants signed up blindly for either condition based on their availability.

We used a mix of qualitative and quantitative data to assess outcomes.

Participants completed baseline assessments before the beginning of the program (t1), within two weeks following the intervention (t2), and they completed qualitative questionnaires at three months' follow-up (t3).

In completing a 360-degree instrument, participants nominated two line managers, defined as people they reported to; between two and ten peers; and two to ten direct reports.

Participants paid £250 to participate in the program and all gave informed consent to participate in the research. The contribution is the average cost of a commercial mindfulness course, our rationale being that payment might be related to motivation to complete the course and home practices.

Sample

A total of 57 leaders were recruited for this study: 27 were assigned to the intervention group and the remaining 30 took part in the control group. Females were overrepresented being 81 percent of the combined sample. There were no significant differences in the gender distribution between the two groups. The age of participants ranged from 30 to 63 with a mean age of 46.8 years (SD=8.2). Compared with the control group, participants in the MLT were significantly younger ($F(1,53)=5.7$, $p=.02$)). The majority (N=42) worked in the private sector across a wide range of industries including consulting (N=7), food (N=6), finance (N=4), manufacturing (N=3), and insurance (N=3). Those working in the public sector predominantly worked in education (N=9) or government (N=6). There were no significant differences in the sector distribution between groups.

Intervention

The MLT is an eight-week intervention consisting of three half-day workshops delivered every two weeks, one full-day workshop delivered at week 6, and one small group conference call at week 8. The program builds on the broad format of both MBSR and MBCT, as described by Chaskalson (2014), and was adapted for a leadership context. The psychoeducational material around depression that is typically found in MBCT, for example, was omitted—as was some of the material concerning chronic pain in MBSR. Instead, we added teaching around leadership complexity, based on the work of Stacey and Griffin (2005), and much of the discussion in each workshop encouraged participants to relate what they were learning to their own experience of leading.

Participants were encouraged to apply what they were learning in their professional environment and they were given a variety of resources and practices aimed at training the core mindfulness capacities of observing, awareness, and non-judgment, both within their meditation practice and applied to their work lives.

Participants learned a variety of mindfulness meditation practices and were asked to practice them for 20 minutes each day. These included mindfulness of breathing meditations, a body-scan meditation, mindfulness of sounds and thoughts meditation, walking meditation, and mindful movement, as well as a meditation focused on mindfully sitting with difficulty. All of these practices are described in Chaskalson (2014).

Other key components of each workshop included: small group inquiry about home practice, presentation of leadership models and frameworks, and reflection on leadership challenges in small groups or pairs. To support their home practice, participants were given a mindfulness and course book, downloadable audio recordings, and were sent regular emails from the course tutors.

The course was led by Michael Chaskalson, a mindfulness teacher with over 40 years' personal experience of mindfulness approaches and a significant experience of teaching in organizational and leadership contexts; and Megan Reitz, a business school professor with extensive experience of facilitating leadership development programs and a personal daily mindfulness practice.

Quantitative data collection

The instruments used were selected with the three key capacities under investigation in mind. The Interpersonal Reactivity Index (IRI; Davis, 1980), a psychometric designed to assess empathic tendencies, was chosen to give insight into an aspect of collaboration; the Ashridge Resilience Questionnaire (ARQ; Davda, 2011) was used to investigate key aspects of resilience. The Automated Operation Span Task (OSPAN; Conway et al., 2005; Turner and Engle, 1989) was used to assess working memory capacity, a measure of cognitive functioning. Finally, we used the Five Facet Mindfulness Questionnaire—a widely used and validated measure of mindfulness (FFMQ; Baer, Smith, Hopkins, Krietemeyer and Toney, 2006)—to give us a measure of mindfulness that includes observing, describing, acting with awareness, non-judging of inner experience, and non-reactivity to inner experience.

Participants nominated managers, peers, and direct reports to complete a 360-degree questionnaire before and after the program, enabling us to gather multi-source information regarding the development of the specific leadership competences under investigation. The learning questionnaire was composed of 65 questions. Participants were asked to indicate their agreement with statements on a five-point Likert scale, ranging from "strongly disagree" to "strongly agree." The first factor was "collaboration" and this consisted of statements such as: "develops a culture of open communication within their team." The second factor, "resilience," consisted of statements such as "appears open-minded when faced with challenges or problems." The third factor, "care and concern for self and others," included statements such as "builds trust by showing care to others." The fourth factor, "perspective-taking," consisted of statements such as: "shows team members how they can re-frame difficult situations." The final factor, "agility in complexity," contained statements such as: "able to make decisions by working with contradictory ideas."

The waitlist control group conducted the same tests at t1 and t2 before themselves going on to attend the program.

Participants recorded the number of minutes of formal meditation practice they undertook every day. Participants and their data were divided into three groups: no practice, low practice, and high practice, according to the median level of practice in a similar method to that conducted in the work by Jha, Stanley, Kiyonaga, Wong and Gelfand (2010).

Program feasibility was measured by the participants' ability to complete the program and the assigned home practices. Participants were considered to have completed the program if they attended at minimum of three out of four workshops. They were asked to practice 20 minutes of formal mindfulness practices every day during the course and to log the amount of practice minutes during the MLT. From the logs received, a total number of practice minutes for each person was calculated.

Program satisfaction was assessed qualitatively at three months' follow-up. Participants were asked to rate the program's effect on the development of key leadership capacities: resilience, collaboration, and leading in complexity. Questions were asked in this style: To what extent do you think the program developed your collaboration skills? Answer choices ranged from 1 = not at all, to 5 = to a very great extent.

Qualitative data collection

Qualitative data were gathered throughout the eight-week period by voice recordings and transcription of the following:

- 32 fortnightly, un-facilitated, participant small group discussions during the program sessions relating to their experiences of home practice
- 12 small group conference call discussions at the end of the programs with one of the trainers
- 7 interviews with participants specifically on their experiences of applying mindfulness practice to their leadership challenges
- a post-program survey that asked open questions relating to the impact and sustainability of participants' mindfulness practice on the three areas this study explored.

In total, approximately 27 hours of transcribed data were collected. Starting with the hypothesis that mindfulness practice may impact the leadership capacities of collaboration, resilience, and leading in complexity, we undertook deductive thematic analysis. Codes, or conceptual labels, were developed collaboratively based on our hypotheses and the constructs we anticipated to find in our data. Throughout the process additional codes were created where unanticipated constructs were found. These codes were then clustered into themes that allowed us to identify patterns in the data and present a coherent analysis of our qualitative data. Data were then entered into NVivo in order for all the text against each code to be retrieved and considered in one place, facilitating the analysis.

Results

Quantitative findings

Without accounting for the level of home practice undertaken, simply taking part in the program appeared significantly to enhance self-report assessments of participants' resilience as measured by both the 360-degree questionnaire and the ARQ, and the "describing" element and total score on the FFMQ. Again, without accounting for the amount of mindfulness practice undertaken, the MLT alone did not impact self-report measures of care and concern for others, or perspective-taking, or others' perspectives of any of the factors assessed through the 360-degree questionnaire. Similarly, the MLT alone, without accounting for home practice, impacted none of the empathic tendencies measured by the IRI.

The importance of home practice

The benefits of the MLT appear to be dependent upon the amount of formal mindfulness practice undertaken during the training. The more formal mindfulness home practice a participant reported, the greater the improvement in their scores on many of the measures. That included resilience, as measured by both the 360-degree questionnaire and the ARQ as well as collaboration and agility in complexity. Higher home practice levels also correlated with increases in all the characteristics of mindfulness as measured by the FFMQ. Similarly, home practice times appeared to impact the empathic tendencies of fantasy and perspective-taking; and they predicted a reduction in personal distress as measured by IRI. Participants who practiced for ten minutes or more on average per day were significantly more likely to show improvements as measured by the FFMQ and the ARQ.

Mindfulness practice predicted changes to four of the five resilience scales measured on the ARQ but it did not predict changes in empathic concern. Nor did it seem to have any significant impact on others' perceptions in the 360-degree feedback. Unusually, neither mindfulness training nor practice appeared to impact working memory, as measured by the OSPAN, or anxiety, as measured by the BAI.

In the post-program survey, carried out approximately 12 weeks after the end of the program, participants reported how they felt the program had impacted their capacities for resilience, collaboration, and leading in complexity. Sixty-three percent of participants reported their capacity for resilience had been developed to a great or very great extent. Thirty-five percent reported increases in their capacity to collaborate and 24 percent reported increases in their ability to lead in complexity. When including the number of participants who acknowledged the program had improved these skills "to some extent," 93 percent, 85 percent, and 85 percent of participants recognized they had experienced a positive impact in relation to each of the three capacities: resilience, collaboration, and complexity.

When asked which part of their lives as leaders had been most impacted as a result of the program, a third of respondents gave answers relating to lower stress or increased calm. Together these two factors were reported in 40 percent of responses. The second most popular answer, related to perceived increase in emotional regulation, was their ability to respond rather than react (14 percent). The third most popular response (11 percent) was increased focus. Seventy-two percent reported that there was a was great or very great likelihood that their top-rated impact would be sustained, while 100 percent felt that it would be sustained to at least some extent.

Participants reported that the clearest impact the program had on them was an increase in their resilience and all of them felt that the impact of the program would be sustained to some degree.

Qualitative findings

The qualitative data, in line with the quantitative analysis, suggest that mindfulness training and practice can lead to improvements in resilience, collaboration, and leading in complexity as perceived by the participants.

The most widely reported impact found in the qualitative data was on personal resilience. This is reinforced by the findings of the 12-week post-program survey where nearly two-thirds of participants reported that the mindfulness program developed their resilience to a very great or great extent and it accords with the 360-degree self-report of resilience as well as findings from the ARQ.

Although the significant impacts shown by the 360-degree feedback were all for the self-reported categories and not for others' reports, the qualitative reports from participants offer many examples of perceived impacts on family members, which was not measured quantitatively, as well as on colleagues and leaders at work, for example:

> At home, my husband has told me that I am much more "chilled." Because I am much less judgmental these days, I feel there is a greater level of openness in our relationship and a willingness to share things sooner, before they become an issue. It feels more emotionally intimate.

And:

> My direct boss has noticed the difference—she thinks I have handled difficult situations better and I am more collaborative.

Resilience

Participants frequently spoke of an increased capacity to manage stressful situations and to regulate their emotions in the moment. They reported an increased capacity for self-awareness and self-management; an increased ability to regulate their emotions; for perspective-taking; and an increased ability to reframe difficult or stressful situations at home and at work. They also reported enhanced sleep quality and duration, reduced levels of stress, and improvements to work–life balance.

> That kind of conscious decision of, rather than it all crashing around you, it's like—well everything can wait, get it back into perspective.

This supports the findings of the IRI, which showed significant impacts on perspective-taking and a negative correlation to personal distress. They also accord with the FFMQ findings of significant impacts on non-reacting and acting with awareness.

Two aspects of resilience included in the definition in the ARQ—self-belief and purpose—did not show a significant result quantitatively and were not commonly reported in the qualitative data, although there was some reference to increased confidence in the face of difficulty:

> I have grown a bit more confidence in my own authority and ability.

Leading in complexity

Regarding this theme, participants most often spoke of an increased ability to focus; to remain calm under pressure; and an enhanced adaptability and agility which came from being less attached to fixed positions or particular points of view. All of that enabled better decision-making:

> Previously I would have shied away from complexity. Now I approach problems—after taking a deep breath or 3!—with openness and curiosity. I approach problems/issues, rather than running away from them or ignoring them.

The significant impact of practice on "balancing alternatives" in the ARQ, as well as the significant impact of practice on the "agility in complexity" dimension of the 360-degree feedback, was backed up by qualitative data:

> I have greater clarity about what the issue is and what needs doing.

Collaboration

Most commonly, regarding collaboration, were themes that emerged in relation to increased empathy coming from a heightened understanding of and appreciation for others' states and positions:

> I tend to talk at a thousand miles an hour, I have an agenda that is thirty points long, and I have been (laughing) exhausting to be around when we've got a lot to do. And I've really made a conscious effort to slow down, and take the time to, not so much just focus on the task, but recognize there's a person in front of me, and they're having their own experience of this stuff.

Participants sometimes summarized this in suggesting that their interactions felt more "human." That helped collaboration:

> Being more fully present: bringing all of myself to any interaction with anybody. So, I think that people at work have noticed that we have had richer conversations that have felt more human. I feel there's been more connection, that's what it is: more connection with the people.

Key cognitive and emotional skills

Five key cognitive and emotional skills, developed through the course, stood out: emotional regulation, perspective-taking, empathy, focus, and adaptability. In different ways, participants linked these to enabling increased resilience, leading in complexity, and collaboration.

Emotional regulation

Emotional regulation is an important aspect of emotional intelligence. Participants referred to an ability to make more conscious choices in responding to situations—rather than allowing their emotions to provoke automatic reactions. They spoke of how the training and practices enabled them better to notice their feelings and allow these simply to be what they are. That created a space for choice. Most commonly under this theme, they spoke of how that choice enabled greater focus in the face of anger or heightened emotion:

> I'm really liking the fact that I can put myself into quite a detached and objective place, almost at will…that includes when other people are unhappy…. Not taking on that emotion myself, but being able to acknowledge it in others, and not feel impacted and hijacked by it.

Perspective-taking

Emotion regulation was frequently linked to perspective-taking. Participants spoke of how calm increased created a "space" for them to see a situation from different angles. It allowed them to try out or take in a variety of viewpoints. That in turn enhanced the quality of decision-making:

> I find it easier to evaluate the different options more rationally and calmly, and probably base fewer decisions on prejudice and prior experience.

Empathy

Participants referred to an improvement in their ability to consider the experience of others and a wish to focus more on other people:

> I feel better able to tune into other people (because I am able to give them my focused attention in that moment), so I feel I serve them and our relationship better. My confidence with people has soared and I have had some wonderful, enjoyable interactions with individuals I never thought possible.

Focus

Mindfulness practice was commonly spoken of as enabling an increased capacity to focus. Participants reported greater clarity of thought and an increased ability to hold one thing at a time in their minds when faced with complex or stressful situations. This impacted on their ability to make better decisions. They spoke of being more fully "present," less distracted when called upon to take action:

> I feel like I've decluttered my head and I allow myself time and space to think on a problem and I allow myself: "this is the only thing I'm going to think about; let's see what comes up." Maybe this is leading to an ideal of problem-solving.

Adaptability

Adaptability is the ability to move between positions. Participants reported an increased capacity to adapt to different or difficult circumstances. They spoke of how they were able to change automatic responses to situations by being more focused on what matters. In this way, adaptability seems to intertwine with focus, emotion regulation, and perspective-taking:

> My partner notes I am calmer and more able to cope with unexpected events.

Meta-capacities

By meta-capacities we refer to the deepest, most fundamental enabling cognitive strategies that individuals apply to the processing of new information in a novel situation (Clark, 2008). When analyzing the qualitative data, three specific meta-capacities became evident. These appear fundamentally to underpin resilience, collaboration, and leading in complexity, as well as all the other skills referred to above. These meta-capacities are "allowing," "inquiry," and "meta-awareness." We refer to these under the acronym AIM.

AIM

Participants talked about how what we will now call AIM enabled them to experience a moment of time (or sometimes a space) for a different choice to be made. They discussed this in terms of being better able to consciously respond, less liable to mindlessly and habitually react:

> My ability to respond rather than react is very much improved. This makes me calmer at work, more able to free my mind to the solution rather than the event that has irritated me. Applies equally to conversations with the kids!

Allowing

Participants reported that as a result of developing an attitude of allowing—of letting what is the case be the case, rather than resisting or fighting the things—they discovered an enhanced ability to deal with complex or difficult situations. They referred frequently to how they had come to adopt an attitude of "it is what it is" when dealing with potentially stressful situations, discussing this in terms of their being better able to consciously respond, less liable to mindlessly and habitually react. Along with that, they spoke of an increase in the levels of compassion they had towards themselves:

> That ability to let a few things go more easily, and not worry about them overly. Take it as what it is. And also, the recognition, maybe the deeper recognition, is that there are things you just can't change, and then the best option is to go towards them and be with them.

And:

> So [I think], "Ooh, this is all a bit uncertain, and I'm quite unsure;" that's actually an okay place to be, and from there you can explore.

Inquiry

As they came to better notice their thoughts, feelings, and sensations, it seems that participants benefited from an attitude of curiosity towards their experience:

> I think that bit of stepping back and just saying, "What actually is the problem here? What is it that's getting at me?" I find really helpful, actually.

Meta-awareness

Meta-awareness is the capacity to step back from one's experience and notice it for what it is—a flow of thoughts, feelings, sensations, and impulses. Shapiro, Carlson, Astin and Freedman (2006), drawing on Peters (2004), refer to this as a state of "intimate detachment." It allows one to connect more intimately with moment-to-moment experience, letting it rise and fall naturally without being attached to it. One experiences what *is* instead of a commentary or story about what is. But this does not create apathy or indifference. Instead it allows one to experience greater richness, texture, and depth, moment by moment: the "intimate" aspect of "intimate detachment." As one participant put it:

> I think it gave me a way to take back, to own some of that control if you like, over my own thinking. So, recognizing that I'm choosing my thoughts, and they're not me, they're just the noise of what's going on.

And:

> [The program has] allowed me to just be able to see these things—thoughts, feelings, sensations—separately from me, view them, explore them.

Implications for leadership development

The importance of regular mindfulness meditation practice

Our data show significantly greater impact when the training is linked with mindfulness meditation practice than when it is not. The data also suggest that mindfulness can be learned and developed by executive leaders: so long as they formally practice it. Our participants formally practiced at a median level of ten minutes per day. Above this level, they were more likely to achieve significantly improved results in terms of their mindfulness (measured by FFMQ) and their resilience (measured by ARQ and 360-degree self-report) than if they practiced below this level.

This implies that one cannot expect a mindfulness training program or a standalone workshop that does not have regular home practice of meditation associated with it to deliver significant changes in leadership capacity, apart from an improvement in self-reported resilience.

Those delivering mindfulness interventions should therefore give careful thought as to how best to encourage and enable regular mindfulness practice. This could include helping participants to think through how to plan their mindfulness practice into their daily routine. Organizations might consider how they could encourage practice by providing spaces and times for those wishing to practice at work.

The difference between self- and other-assessed impact

The impact of mindfulness training on our participants as reported by others was lower than their own positive self-report perceptions.

This might be because it takes time for individual behavioral changes to become apparent to and observable by others. Eight weeks may be too short a period of time to allow for the kind of interactions between participant and manager or peers and reports in which differences in behavior might be signaled and noticed to emerge.

There is some evidence in the qualitative data that point to this:

> For me resilience is built up over time and needs sustained mindfulness practice and change in behaviors in many areas to gain balance—I don't believe this happens overnight. However, the learning from the program absolutely sets you up for success to build up that resilience should practice be sustained.

And:

> I'm not sure that others have noticed a difference at this point but believe that they will over a period of time.

Our participants spoke of positive feedback that they had received from colleagues, but they spoke more of feedback that they had received from close family members. It may be that participants naturally tend to manage the impression they give to their colleagues, presenting a façade that might be acceptable in a workplace environment (see Reitz 2015), whereas family members are permitted to see the more "authentic" self.

One participant spoke graphically to this theme:

> People [at work] have often described me as being quite serene and relaxed, but the little swan's feet would be flapping quite hard below the surface of the water. But [after the program] I felt as if the whole bird was gliding in a more serene way.

Conclusion

This study suggests that mindfulness practice is a promising method for leadership development. Our results indicate that mindfulness can be learned and developed by executive leaders, as long as they practice for at least ten minutes per day.

The overall impact of the program was well-summarized by one participant:

> Mindfulness is not a "silver bullet" solution as many books and courses would have one believe. Seen in context as a gradual increase in awareness of these aspects in ones' life, it is essential and a great help in interacting with collaborators, managing a team, decision-making and putting things in perspective.

Chapter takeaways

- Leadership in the 21st century requires different capacities including resilience, collaboration, and leading in complex circumstances.
- While considerable further research is needed, this study suggests that mindfulness practice shows some promise in developing these capacities through building "AIM": allowing, inquiry, and meta-awareness.
- Practice is critical—a minimum of ten minutes is indicated in this study (which is less than 1 percent of most executives' waking hours).
- However, practice can be difficult for leaders to commit to; developing a habit is critical and further studies which explore alternative ways of developing AIM would be beneficial

Reflection questions

- What capacities do you think are required of leaders today, given our volatile, uncertain, complex, and ambiguous world?
- If you practice meditation, how might it affect the way you lead?
- When might "allowing"—the capacity for non-judgmental acceptance of present-moment experience and circumstances—help you to lead more effectively?
- When is "inquiry" a useful skill for leaders and what balance of advocacy and inquiry do you typically demonstrate at work?
- What enables you to thrive in complex, pressured situations? In what ways can you develop those capacities through meditation and other means?

References

Abbatiello, A., Knight, M., Philpot, S. and Roy, I. (2017). "Leadership disrupted," in Walsh, B. (eds.), (2017). *Rewriting the Rules for the Digital Age 2017: Deloitte Global Human Capital Trends*, Deloitte University Press, London, pp. 76–85.

Ashkanasy, N. M. and Dorris, A. D. (2017). "Emotions in the workplace," *Annual Review of Organizational Psychology and Organizational Behavior*, Vol. 4, pp. 67–90.

Baer, R. A. and Lykins, E. L. M. (2011). "Mindfulness and positive psychological functioning," in Sheldon, K.M., Kashdan, T.B. and Steger, M.F., (eds.), *Designing Positive Psychology: Taking Stock and Moving Forward*, Oxford University Press, New York, NY, US, pp. 335–348.

Baer, R. A., Smith, G. T., Hopkins, J., Krietemeyer, J. and Toney, L. (2006). "Using self-report assessment methods to explore facets of mindfulness," *Assessment*, Vol. 13 No. 1, pp. 27–45.

Baron, L., Rouleau, V., Grégoire, S. and Baron, C. (2018). "Mindfulness and leadership flexibility," edited by Sheard, G. *Journal of Management Development*, Vol. 37 No. 2, pp. 165–177.

Beach, M. C., Roter, D., Korthuis, P. T., Epstein, R. M., Sharp, V., Ratanawongsa, N., Cohn, J., et al. (2013). "A multicenter study of physician mindfulness and health care quality," *The Annals of Family Medicine*, Vol. 11 No. 5, pp. 421–428.

Beckman, H. B., Wendland, M., Mooney, C., Krasner, M. S., Quill, T. E., Suchman, A. L. and Epstein, R. M. (2012). "The impact of a program in mindful communication on primary care physicians," *Academic Medicine*, Vol. 87 No. 6, pp. 815–819.

Boyatzis, R. E. (2006). "An overview of intentional change from a complexity perspective," *Journal of Management Development*, Vol. 25 No. 7, pp. 607–623.

Boyatzis, R. E. and McKee, A. (2005). *Resonant Leadership: Renewing Yourself and Connecting with Others through Mindfulness, Hope, and Compassion*, Harvard Business School Press, Boston.

Brendel, W., Hankerson, S., Byun, S. and Cunningham, B. (2016). "Cultivating leadership Dharma: Measuring the impact of regular mindfulness practice on creativity, resilience, tolerance for ambiguity, anxiety and stress," *Journal of Management Development*, Vol. 35 No. 8, pp. 1056–1078.

Brown, K. W. and Ryan, R. M. (2004). "Perils and promise in defining and measuring mindfulness: Observations from experience," *Clinical Psychology: Science and Practice*, Vol. 11 No. 3, pp. 242–248.

Chaskalson, M. (2014). *Mindfulness in Eight Weeks: The Revolutionary Eight-Week Plan to Clear Your Mind and Calm Your Life*, HarperThorsons, London.

Chiesa, A., Calati, R. and Serretti, A. (2011). "Does mindfulness training improve cognitive abilities? A systematic review of neuropsychological findings," *Clinical Psychology Review*, Vol. 31 No. 3, pp. 449–464.

Chiesa, A. and Serretti, A. (2009). "Mindfulness-Based Stress Reduction for stress management in healthy people: A review and meta-analysis," *Journal of Alternative and Complementary Medicine*, Vol. 15 No. 5, pp. 593–600.

Clark, D. (2008). Socialsciencedictionary.com [accessed on 29th June 2016].

Condon, P., Desbordes, G., Miller, W. B. and DeSteno, D. (2013). "Meditation increases compassionate responses to suffering," *Psychological Science*, Vol. 24 No. 10, pp. 2125–2127.

Conway, A. R. A., Kane, M. J., Bunting, M. F., Hambrick, D. Z., Wilhelm, O. and Engle, R. W. (2005). "Working memory span tasks: A methodological review and user's guide," *Psychonomic Bulletin & Review*, Vol. 12 No. 5, pp. 769–786.

Cunliffe, A. L. and Eriksen, M. (2011). "Relational leadership," *Human Relations*, Vol. 64 No. 11, pp. 1425–1449.

Davda, A. (2011). "Measuring resilience: A pilot study", Assessment & Development Matters, Autumn, pp. 11–14.

Davis, M. H. (1980). "A multidimensional approach to individual differences in empathy," *JSAS Catalogue of Selected Documents in Psychology*, Vol. 10, pp. 1–19.

Day, D. V. and Dragoni, L. (2015). "Leadership development: An outcome-oriented review based on time and levels of analyses," *Annual Review of Organizational Psychology and Organizational Behavior*, Vol. 2 No. 1, pp. 133–156.

Donald, J. N., Sahdra, B. K., Van Zanden, B., Duineveld, J. J., Atkins, P. W. B., Marshall, S. L. and Ciarrochi, J. (2018). "Does your mindfulness benefit others? A systematic review and meta-analysis of the link between mindfulness and prosocial behaviour," *British Journal of Psychology*, available at 10.1111/bjop.12338.

Hülsheger, U.R., Alberts, H.J.E.M., Feinholdt, A. and Lang, J.W.B. (2013). "Benefits of mindfulness at work: the role of mindfulness in emotion regulation, emotional exhaustion, and job satisfaction", *Journal of Applied Psychology*, Vol. 98 No. 2, pp. 310–325.

Glomb, T., Duffy, M., Bono, J. and Yang, T. (2011). "Mindfulness at work," *Research in Personnel and Human Resources Management, 30*(1), pp. 115–157.

Goldberg, S. B., Tucker, R. P., Greene, P. A., Davidson, R. J., Wampold, B. E., Kearney, D. J. and Simpson, T. L. (2018). "Mindfulness-based interventions for psychiatric disorders: A systematic review and meta-analysis," *Clinical Psychology Review*, Vol. 59, pp. 52–60.

Good, D. J., Lyddy, C. J., Glomb, T. M., Bono, J. E., Brown, K. W., Duffy, M. K., Baer, R. A., et al. (2016). "Contemplating mindfulness at work: An integrative review," *Journal of Management*, Vol. 42 No. 1, pp. 114–142.

Greenleaf, R. K. and Spears, L. C. (1998). *Servant Leadership: A Journey into the Nature of Legitimate Power and Greatness*, Paulist Press, New York.

Hasenkamp, W., Wilson-Mendenhall, C. D., Duncan, E. and Barsalou, L. W. (2012). "Mind wandering and attention during focused meditation: A fine-grained temporal analysis of fluctuating cognitive states," *NeuroImage*, Vol. 59 No. 1, pp. 750–760.

Hassard, J., Teoh, K. R. H., Visockaite, G., Dewe, P. and Cox, T. (2018). "The cost of work-related stress to society: A systematic review.," *Journal of Occupational Health Psychology*, Vol. 23 No. 1, pp. 1–17.

Heydenfeldt, J. A., Herkenhoff, L. and Coe, M. (2011). "Cultivating mind fitness through mindfulness training: Applied neuroscience," *Performance Improvement*, Vol. 50 No. 10, pp. 21–27.

Hülsheger, U. R., Feinholdt, A. and Nübold, A. (2015). "A low-dose mindfulness intervention and recovery from work: Effects on psychological detachment, sleep quality, and sleep duration," *Journal of Occupational and Organizational Psychology*, Vol. 88 No. 3, pp. 464–489.

Hunter, J. and Chaskalson, M. (2013). "Making the mindful leader: Cultivating skills for facing adaptive challenges," in Leonard, H. S., Lewis, R., Freedman, A. M., and Passmore, J. (eds.), *The Wiley-Blackwell*

Handbook of the Psychology of Leadership, Change and Organizational Development, Wiley-Blackwell, Chichester, pp. 195–220.

Hunter, J. and McCormick, D. W. (2008). "Mindfulness in the workplace: An exploratory study," in *Memorandum of the Annual Meeting of the Academy of Management, Anaheim, CA.*

Hyland, P. K., Lee, R. A. and Mills, M. J. (2015). "Mindfulness at work: A new approach to improving individual and organizational performance," *Industrial & Organizational Psychology*, Vol. 8 No. 4, pp. 576–602.

Jha, A. P., Krompinger, J. and Baime, M. J. (2007). "Mindfulness training modifies subsystems of attention," *Cognitive, Affective, & Behavioral Neuroscience*, Vol. 7 No. 2, pp. 109–119.

Jha, A. P., Stanley, E. A., Kiyonaga, A., Wong, L. and Gelfand, L. (2010). "Examining the protective effects of mindfulness training on working memory capacity and affective experience," *Emotion*, Vol. 10 No. 1, pp. 54–64.

Kabat-Zinn, J. (2003). "Mindfulness-based interventions in context: past, present, and future," *Clinical Psychology: Science and Practice*, Vol. 10 No. 2, pp. 144–156.

Keng, S. L., Smoski, M. J. and Robins, C. J. (2011). "Effects of mindfulness on psychological health: A review of empirical studies," *Clinical Psychology Review*, Vol. 31 No. 6, pp. 1041–1056.

King, E. and Badham, R. (2018). "The wheel of mindfulness: A generative framework for second-generation mindful leadership," *Mindfulness*, available at: 10.1007/s12671-018-0890-7.

King, E. and Nesbit, P. (2015). "Collusion with denial: Leadership development and its evaluation," *Journal of Management Development*, Vol. 34 No. 2, pp. 134–152.

Krishnakumar, S. and Robinson, M. D. (2015). "Maintaining an even keel: An affect-mediated model of mindfulness and hostile work behavior.," *Emotion*, Vol. 15 No. 5, pp. 579–589.

Lavine, M. (2014). "Paradoxical Leadership and the Competing Values Framework," *The Journal of Applied Behavioral Science*, Vol. 50 No. 2, pp. 189–205.

Luthans, F. (2002). "The need for and meaning of positive organizational behavior," *Journal of Organizational Behavior*, Vol. 23 No. 6, pp. 695–706.

Malinowski, P. and Lim, H. J. (2015). "Mindfulness at work: Positive affect, hope, and optimism mediate the relationship between dispositional mindfulness, work engagement, and well-being," *Mindfulness*, Vol. 6 No. 6, pp. 1250–1262.

Mealer, M., Jones, J., Newman, J., McFann, K. K., Rothbaum, B. and Moss, M. (2012). "The presence of resilience is associated with a healthier psychological profile in intensive care unit (ICU) nurses: Results of a national study," *International Journal of Nursing Studies*, Vol. 49, pp. 292–299.

Nesbit, P. L. (2012). "The role of self-reflection, emotional management of feedback, and self-regulation processes in self-directed leadership development," *Human Resource Development Review*, Vol. 11 No. 2, pp. 203–226.

Peters, C. (2004). Personal communication cited in Shapiro et al (2006).

Quaglia, J. T., Goodman, R. J. and Brown, K. W. (2015). "From mindful attention to social connection: The key role of emotion regulation," *Cognition and Emotion*, Vol. 29 No. 8, pp. 1466–1474.

Reb, J., Chaturvedi, S., Narayanan, J. and Kudesia, R. S. (2018). "Leader mindfulness and employee performance: A sequential mediation model of LMX quality, interpersonal justice, and employee stress," *Journal of Business Ethics*, available at: 10.1007/s10551-018-3927-x.

Reb, J., Narayanan, J. and Chaturvedi, S. (2014). "Leading mindfully: Two studies on the influence of supervisor trait mindfulness on employee well-being and performance," *Mindfulness*, Vol. 5 No. 1, pp. 36–45.

Reitz, M. (2015). *Dialogue in organizations: Developing relational leadership*. Springer.

Roche, M., Haar, J. and Luthans, F. (2014). "The role of mindfulness and psychological capital on the well-being of leaders," *Journal of Occupational Health Psychology*, Vol. 19 No. 4, pp. 476–489.

Rodriguez, A. and Rodriguez, Y. (2015). "Metaphors for today's leadership: VUCA world, millennial and 'Cloud Leaders'," *Journal of Management Development*, Vol. 34 No. 7, pp. 854–866.

Segal, Z. V., Williams, J. M. G. and Teasdale, J. D. (2002). *Mindfulness-Based Cognitive Therapy for Depression: A New Approach to Preventing Relapse*, The Guilford Press, London.

Shapiro, S. L., Carlson, L. E., Astin, J. A. and Freedman, B. (2006). "Mechanisms of mindfulness," *Journal of Clinical Psychology*, Vol. 62 No. 3, pp. 373–386.

Shapiro, Wang, M. C. and Peltason, E. H. (2015). "What is mindfulness, and why should organizations care about it?" in Reb, J., and Atkins, P. (eds.), *Mindfulness in Organizations*, Cambridge University Press, Cambridge, pp. 17–41.

Singh, N., Singh, S., Sabaawi, M., Myers, R. and Wahler, R. (2006). "Enhancing treatment team process through mindfulness-based mentoring in an inpatient psychiatric hospital," *Behavior Modification*, Vol. 30, pp. 423–441.

Stacey, R. D. and Griffin, D. (2005). "Introduction: Leading in a complex world," in Griffin, D., and Stacey, R. D. (eds.), *Complexity and the Experience of Leading Organizations*, Routledge, Taylor & Francis Group, London; New York, pp. 1–16.

Thera, S. (1975). *The way of mindfulness*, Buddhist Publication Society, Kandy, Sri Lanka.

Turner, M. L. and Engle, R. W. (1989). "Is working memory capacity task dependent?" *Journal of Memory and Language*, Vol. 28 No. 2, pp. 127–154.

Uhl-Bien, M. and Arena, M. (2017). "Complexity leadership," *Organizational Dynamics*, Vol. 46 No. 1, pp. 9–20.

van Dierendonck, D., Stam, D., Boersma, P., de Windt, N. and Alkema, J. (2014). "Same difference? Exploring the differential mechanisms linking servant leadership and transformational leadership to follower outcomes," *The Leadership Quarterly*, Vol. 25 No. 3, pp. 544–562.

Walach, H., Nord, E., Zier, C., Dietz-Waschkowski, B., Kersig, S. and Schüpbach, H. (2007). "Mindfulness-based stress reduction as a method for personnel development: A pilot evaluation," *International Journal of Stress Management*, Vol. 14 No. 2, pp. 188–198.

Yu, L. and Zellmer-Bruhn, M. (2018). "Introducing team mindfulness and considering its safeguard role against conflict transformation and social undermining," *Academy of Management Journal*, Vol. 61 No. 1, pp. 324–347.

Zanesco, A. P., Denkova, E., Rogers, S. L., MacNulty, W. K. and Jha, A. P. (2019). "Mindfulness training as cognitive training in high-demand cohorts: An initial study in elite military servicemembers," *Progress in Brain Research*, Vol. 244, pp. 323–354.

Zhang, Y., Waldman, D. A., Han, Y.-L. and Li, X.-B. (2015). "Paradoxical leader behaviors in people management: Antecedents and consequences," *Academy of Management Journal*, Vol. 58 No. 2, pp. 538–566.

8

HOW MINDFULNESS IMPACTS THE WAY LEADERS CONNECT WITH AND DEVELOP FOLLOWERS

Jason Beck

Effective leaders engage in individualized consideration, or the leadership behavior of connecting with and developing the unique needs of followers. Every follower has different needs in the workplace. Providing individualized leadership interaction with followers can transform follower job performance and follower well-being (Bass, 1999; Jiang, Zhao, & Ni, 2017). A skillful leader adapts leadership behaviors to the unique circumstance of the follower. If the follower needs coaching, the leader can adapt behaviors to provide the benefits of coaching (Theeboom, Beersma, & van Vianen, 2014). If the follower needs to voice opinions, the leader can adapt behaviors to provide the benefits of actively listening (Cooper, 1997). This leadership process of individualized consideration is related to followers' task performance and helping behavior (Jiang et al., 2017). Thus, individualized consideration is crucial to a high-functioning modern workplace (Bass, 1985). Despite the importance of these leadership behaviors, leaders do not always prioritize individualized consideration.

The endless amount of distracting information that pulls leaders in many directions limits the ability for them to spend quality time performing individualized consideration. Workplaces have diverse types of distractions that divert leaders' attention away from connecting with and developing followers (Jett & George, 2003). As knowledge work consumes 21st-century organizations in the information age, the ability not only to focus attention but also to efficiently use attention is purported to be a leader's biggest commodity (Newport, 2016). Efficiently using attention is especially necessary for leaders, who have intensified distractions and responsibilities. Ideally, leaders give full attention to understanding the needs of followers and provide individualized support to connect with followers. When distracted workplace elements absorb leaders, the lack of individualized consideration negatively impacts the follower interactions that could have helped meet follower developmental needs for better performance at work. Leaders who have a mental capacity to sift through distracting information can better perform individualized consideration.

Mindfulness, the awareness and nonjudgmental acceptance of the present experience (Bishop et al., 2004; Brown & Ryan, 2003; Kabat-Zinn, 1994), can be a mental effectiveness tool for course-correcting attention to what is most important for individualized consideration. Many leaders may know that showing personalized concern for each follower is important but are too busy caught up in rumination of past issues to be aware of how the followers are feeling in the present experience. Likewise, leaders may wish to take in information to aid followers, but those leaders with low mindfulness may have their attention hijacked by the myriad of other responsibilities. Mindful leaders can place adequate, sustained attention on followers and can invest in being aware of the personalized needs of followers.

Research has demonstrated that there is a positive relationship between mindfulness and leadership. Such research includes leaders' impact on employees' well-being (Reb, Narayanan, Chaturvedi, 2014) and leaders' well-being (Roche, Haar, & Luthans, 2014). But research is lacking on how mindfulness may contribute to leaders' individualized consideration. To bridge the two research disciplines of leadership and mindfulness, I seek to establish the intervening mediating mechanisms—emotional intelligence and attention control. Leaders who are aware of the present experience will better notice emotional cues (i.e., emotional intelligence; Mayer, Salovey, Caruso, & Sitarenios, 2001), allowing them to demonstrate effective individualized consideration. Furthermore, because mindfulness is essentially a variable within the quality of the mind, the ability to control one's attention (i.e., attention control) is relevant to the relationship between mindfulness and leadership.

In this study, I seek to understand how mindfulness relates to individualized consideration. I examine the role of mindfulness in the workplace by uncovering the mediating mechanisms that impact individualized consideration. I suggest that emotional intelligence and attention control explain the positive relationship between mindfulness and individualized consideration (see Figure 8.1 for the theoretical model).

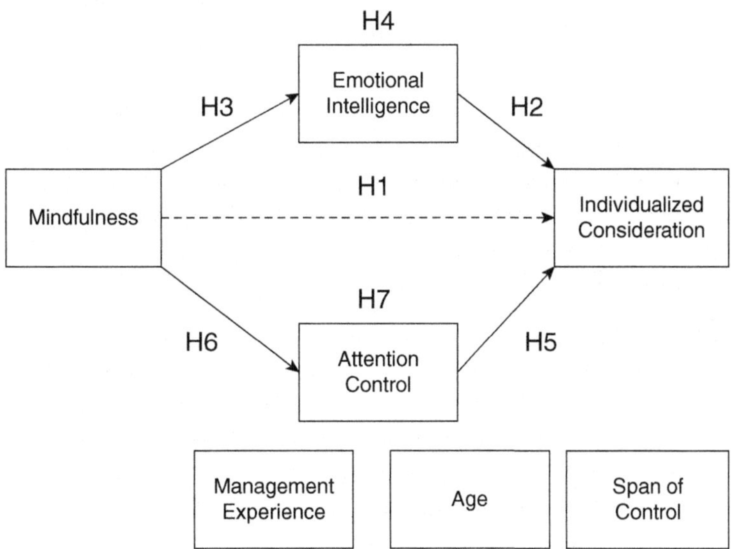

Figure 8.1 The theoretical model for the proposed study

This study contributes to the scientific understanding of mindfulness and leadership in at least two major ways. First, research on mindfulness and leadership is a relatively new area of study, and most understandings are only theoretically inferred rather than based on empirical evidence. Empirically examining these relationships will allow theory to be adjusted if necessary. Second, from a practical perspective, this study will contribute a clearer understanding regarding how practitioners can target antecedents to individualized consideration within leadership development programs. Leadership development is a $14 billion industry that often fails (O'Leonard & Loew, 2012). Understanding the mechanisms behind types of effective leadership behaviors like individualized consideration will not only create better criteria for successful leadership but will also help improve costly developmental programs. Practitioners can better formulate the theory of change in training programs, which can help with evaluating and improving effectiveness.

I will first discuss literature on leadership and relevant evidence and theory on individualized consideration. Then, I will review the research on mindfulness and how it relates to leadership effectiveness. Mediating variables of emotional intelligence and attention control will be discussed theoretically with a review of experimental studies to support the rationale for the five hypotheses presented. I then detail the methods for collecting leader and follower data, data analysis, results, and discussion of the results with implications for practitioners and researchers.

Leader effectiveness

Leadership is the process of enacting influence over others and organizations (Northouse, 2015). Influence necessitates communication and interaction. Generally speaking, the way leaders interact with followers can determine the success of their influence on leadership goals (Bass, 1985; Northouse, 2015). Therefore, an effective leadership style is one that can leverage the leader's interaction with the follower to impact the follower's motivation for attaining mutually beneficial goals.

Transformational leadership is one of the dominant paradigms for understanding leadership effectiveness. Introduced within the political leadership sphere, Burns (1978) described transformational leadership as a mutually supportive relationship between leader and follower that ultimately motivates the follower to join a shared vision of the future through the connection of deep, personal values. Alternatively, transactional leadership is a mutually dependent schema that depends on the contingent exchange of value. Although transactional leadership can be effective in some cases, transformational leadership elevates follower commitment (Avolio, Zhu, Koh, & Bhatia, 2004), follower satisfaction (Hater & Bass, 1988), and financial performance (Barling, Weber, & Kelloway, 1996). The transactional view of leadership has a limited conception of the leader–follower relationship, which involves extrinsically motivating followers in exchange for work productivity. Instead, the new genre, the transformational view of leadership, goes beyond exchange-based rewards. Transformational leadership utilizes the value system of followers to enhance beneficial outcomes. Transformational leadership is one of the most researched leadership frameworks at the onset of the new millennium (Dinh et al., 2014) and consists of four components—idealized influence, inspirational motivation, intellectual stimulation, and individualized consideration (Bass, 1985).

Individualized consideration

In this chapter, I focus on one important dimension of leader effectiveness—the individualized consideration dimension from transformational leadership. "Individualized consideration is displayed when leaders pay attention to the developmental needs of followers and support and coach the development of their followers" (Bass, 1999, p. 11). Leaders that perform individualized consideration pay acute attention to the concerns, developmental needs, and status of their followers (Bass, 1985).

Individualized consideration has two components: considerate intentions and individualized approach (Bass, 1985). First, *considerate intentions* mean acting in a developmental orientation for followers. The goal of a developmental orientation is to impact the abilities and motivations of followers. For example, a leader possessing a developmental orientation will delegate stretch assignment to followers, which will help followers learn from experiences of pushing capabilities to the test (McCauley, Eastman, & Ohlott, 1995). Additionally, a developmental orientation can involve mentoring, which facilitates many beneficial workplace behaviors and motivational outcomes (Eby, Allen, Evans, Ng, & DuBois, 2008). Providing consideration to followers can be amplified through the second dimension of individualized consideration—individualized approach.

Second, *individualized approach* means that leaders treat every follower according to the follower's unique characteristics. An individualized approach to leadership behaviors is relevant given that not all followers are the same. In other words, followers have different strengths, weaknesses, career aspirations, and developmental needs. Leaders will not be able to optimally connect with and develop their followers if they group followers into one unvarying category and disregard the individualized needs. Furthermore, acting with an individualized approach means leaders see differences in their followers based on the context. Leaders can easily fall into the trap of defining their followers based on their experience alone. Leaders high in individualized consideration recognize each follower's unique developmental trajectory. In summary, as one dimension of transformational leadership, individualized consideration refers to leadership behaviors of understanding and developing the unique needs of each follower (Bass, 1999).

Although scarce research has isolated the benefits of each specific dimension of transformational leadership, individualized consideration such as coaching, mentoring, and feedback have tremendous benefits for employees. Specifically, coaching has a beneficial impact on performance/skills, well-being, and work attitudes (Theeboom et al., 2014). Mentoring has a range of beneficial outcomes for organizations such that mentored protégées have higher job satisfaction, greater organizational commitment, and lower work stress than those not mentored (Underhill, 2006). Lastly, supportive feedback environments relate to higher performance ratings (Whitaker, Dahling, & Levy, 2007). Given its importance to effective leadership, I seek to investigate the specific antecedents to individualized consideration, beginning with mindfulness.

Mindfulness

Individualized consideration necessitates familiarity with followers. The beneficial leadership behaviors that assist in connecting with followers requires acute observation skills to notice what the follower needs in the present moment and how to adjust behavior correctly. Mindful leaders have the resources to perform quality individualized consideration. Thus, enacting individualized consideration requires mindfulness. To explain how mindfulness facilitates individualized consideration, I first review its origins, definitions, and benefits.

Defining mindfulness

Historically, mindfulness originates from Buddhist philosophy as a capacity to deepen awareness of the present moment (Hanh, 1976). Mindfulness has no religious undertone and is a practice adopted by both secular and nonsecular individuals alike (Grossman, 2010). What started as an Eastern philosophical concept is now a Western scientific construction with a variety of conceptualizations. One popular definition of mindfulness supposes a state of noticing novelty and has been applied collectively to failure-preventative workplaces (Langer, 1989; Weick & Sutcliffe, 2001). However, this definition is devoid of the Eastern perspective and relates more to cognitive differentiation of objects. Thus, I will focus more on the developments of mindfulness as it promotes awareness and attention to the present without judgment (Brown & Ryan, 2003). Although there are varied and disparate definitions, Kabat-Zinn (1994) provides a unifying definition of mindfulness as "paying attention in a particular way: on purpose, in the present moment, and nonjudgmentally" (p. 4).

Researchers conceptualize mindfulness as both a within-person state experience (Lau et al., 2006) and a between-person trait (Baer, Smith, Hopkins, Krietemeyer, & Toney, 2006). An individual can intentionally activate a mindfulness state experience (e.g., through a systematic cognitive process called meditation; Thera, 1962), whereas trait mindfulness is an individual's baseline level of mindfulness (Siegling & Petrides, 2014). Although trait and state concepts are independent, momentary mindfulness states are more frequent among individuals with greater trait mindfulness (Brown & Ryan, 2003). For this chapter, I will focus on trait mindfulness for two reasons. First, state mindfulness necessitates measuring state experiences, which is highly intrusive in the organizational context (especially for the population of leaders). Second, because this is early research on the topic of mindfulness and leadership, it is important to first understand the effects of trait mindfulness before delving into the complex nature of the effects of state mindfulness. Before examining its predicted relationship with individualized consideration, I discuss the general benefits of trait mindfulness and how it relates to organizational concepts.

Benefits of mindfulness

Researchers from diverse disciplines have begun to examine the physiological and psychological health benefits of mindfulness. Despite its recent introduction into clinical research, extensive research has supported benefits of mindfulness in relation to, but not limited to, lower depressive symptoms (Brown-Iannuzzi, Adair, Payne, Richman, & Fredrickson, 2014), stress reduction (Carmody & Baer, 2008), and healthy eating behaviors (Jordan, Wang, Donatoni, & Meier, 2014).

Furthermore, extant workplace research examines mindfulness in relation to stress-reduction and increasing positive affect at work. For example, one of the earliest findings demonstrated mindfulness as a moderating effect between psychological capital and positive emotions (Avey, Wernsing, & Luthans, 2008). Avey and colleagues suggest that mindfulness allows workers to step outside of harmful emotional patterns to replace negative thinking with more productive thinking habits. Other researchers found that when mindful employees create mental flexibility in responding to stressful work events, high job satisfaction emerges because of proactive appraisal of the stressful situations (Hülsheger, Alberts, Feinholdt, & Lang, 2013).

Mindfulness is not just beneficial for increasing well-being and positive affect at work (Malinowski & Lim, 2015; Reb, Narayanan, & Ho, 2015); researchers have also connected it to other indicators of employee and organizational success. Specifically, recent research strengthens the proposition that mindfulness is beneficial for the workplace with direct links to increased task performance (Reb et al., 2015), reduced turnover intention (Reb,

Narayanan, Chaturvedi, & Ekkirala, 2017), and greater work engagement (Leroy, Anseel, Dimitrova, & Sels, 2013).

Many of the issues that leaders encounter in the modern workforce limit their ability to listen and connect with their followers. Leaders can leverage mindfulness to surpass the obstacles that inhibit leadership effectiveness. More specifically, mindfulness can facilitate individualized consideration on behalf of leaders.

Mindfulness and individually considerate leadership

Organizations need leaders who have the greater ability to spend more time in the present moment with others. Managers tend to promote employees to a leadership role because of past success, which does not necessarily translate to the leadership requirements of formal leader positions (Peter & Hull, 1969). Leaders lose sight of important human capital development (e.g., failing to capitalize on formal mentoring relationships or getting bored with routine responsibilities).

Mindfulness does not only have an impact on the leader's well-being, positive affect, and organizational success, but it can have an impact on others in the workplace. The leader's internal psyche has a great impact on their followers. Theoretically, a mindful leader can better support self-regulatory processes in followers (Glomb, Duffy, Bono, & Yang, 2011). One empirical study supports this notion by showing that a supervisor's trait mindfulness positively relates to employee well-being and job performance (Reb et al., 2014). But how does mindfulness impact a leader's capacity to understand the unique needs of each follower and formulate personalized developmental support for followers? This question remains unanswered in extant theory and research.

Mindfulness relates to leaders' individualized consideration in two ways. First, mindfulness reduces the automaticity of thought, which can help leaders assimilate more information about followers before forming a judgment (Glomb et al., 2011). Mindfulness is the ability to observe and accept thoughts as they come into conscious awareness. Leaders can be aware of their thought without acting on it. For example, mindfulness is observing stress happening in the body as compared with being immersed in experiencing stress. When leaders are aware of their thoughts and emotions, they can prevent distracting thoughts. If a leader is quick to judge a follower over a past troubling incident, the leader could ignore present-moment vital information that would help positively impact individualized consideration. New information is required so that leaders can adapt their interactions to address unique needs. Thus, leaders can shift their approaches that best fit the current needs of followers, such as giving unique types of rewards, appreciation/recognition techniques, and setting unique structures for goal achievement.

Second, mindful leaders are more likely to acknowledge and adapt to the specific needs of each follower. Mindfulness is being able to observe both internal and external stimuli objectively. Leaders can then observe how self-serving internal desires get in the way of effective leadership. Leaders can simultaneously hold their situation in mind while also imagining the life of another (Glomb et al., 2011). Leaders who can decouple their selfish thoughts will better be able to imagine the situation faced by each follower. Leaders can thus understand that their followers have different types of needs similar to when the leaders were lower-level employees themselves. Research indicates that people who scored higher in the attention and acceptance facets of mindfulness were more likely to display helping behaviors towards others (Cameron & Fredrickson, 2015). Similarly, mindful leaders should be able to accept the present experiences, which then aids in understanding the individual needs of followers. In summary, mindful leaders create accurate assessments of the individualized needs of followers while also adapting behaviors to fit those needs. When these two facets are in place, leaders enact individualized consideration toward followers.

H1. *Leader mindfulness will be positively associated with leader individualized consideration.*

Emotional intelligence

Emotional intelligence is likely to mediate the relationship between mindfulness and individualized consideration. Fundamentally, emotional intelligence (EI) refers to the "ability to recognize the meanings of emotions and their relationships and to use them as a basis in reasoning and problem-solving" (Mayer et al., 2001, p. 234). The consensus of an ability-based perspective of EI states that it involves individuals understanding and managing others' emotions and one's own emotions (Jordan, Ashkanasy, & Härtel, & Hooper, 2002). Individuals with high emotional intelligence are characterized by the ability to have strong emotional clarity and the ability to use this information to direct emotions.

EI and individualized consideration

EI has been found to predict several leadership outcomes. A longitudinal study demonstrated that EI explained organizational advancements of managers better than cognitive measurements (Dulewicz & Higgs, 1999). EI was positively associated with a multi-rater performance management measure of a leader's ability to build effective work relationships (Rosete & Ciarrochi, 2005). Lastly, EI demonstrated a positive link with leadership emergence, such that, after a small group project, peers rated those students with high EI as demonstrating stronger leadership emergence (Côté, Lopes, Salovey, & Miners, 2010).

Research also supports the positive relationships between EI and transformational leadership styles, including the dimension of individualized consideration (Barling, Slater, & Kevin Kelloway, 2000; Palmer, Walls, Burgess, & Stough, 2001). EI helps leaders become sensitive to recognizing the individualized needs of followers (i.e., when employees are bored, frustrated, or energized). Needs change from situation to situation and depend on the person. By being better able to recognize the individual's affective state, leaders can then adapt behaviors to connect with and transform followers optimally.

Furthermore, understanding one's own emotions may promote individualized consideration. Being able to monitor one's own emotions will help leaders adapt behavior based on their emotional state. For instance, perhaps a leader cannot connect with a follower because of the leader's stress. Leaders taking care of themselves first will better enable individualized consideration for followers in the long term by providing followers with the right kind of interaction. In conclusion, leaders with high EI are better able to recognize the emotional needs of followers, while at the same time, manage personal emotions to perform individualized consideration best.

H2. *Leaders' emotional intelligence will be positively related to follower-rated leader individualized consideration.*

Mindfulness and EI

Mindful leaders will better be able to take in information for understanding emotions and thus have EI. Research indicates a moderate correlation between mindfulness and clarity of emotions (Brown & Ryan, 2003). Emotional clarity is the ability to quickly and vividly experience emotions. Mindfulness helps create a wide attentional breadth which helps mindful individuals notice emotional cues in the environment (Dane, 2011). Thus, mindful leaders would be able to notice their own and other emotions more easily. In turn, these leaders have greater access to emotional information that can be managed properly.

Additionally, managing emotions also explains the connection between mindfulness and EI through decreasing automatic thinking patterns, accepting negative emotions, and reappraising stressful events. Decreased automaticity of mental processes through mindfulness should help leaders have greater affective regulation (Glomb et al., 2011). The acceptance facet of mindfulness helps leaders come to terms with negative emotions that would otherwise restrict behavior (Brown, Ryan, & Creswell, 2007). Lastly, mindfulness creates a broadened state of awareness that enables reappraising of stressful events as empowering, a hallmark characteristic of being able to manage emotions in EI (Garland et al., 2010). Overall, mindfulness draws on the ability to recognize emotions clearly and increase the capability to regulate emotions.

H3. *Leader mindfulness will positively relate to leader emotional intelligence.*

EI mediates mindfulness and individualized consideration

The understanding and managing components of emotional intelligence explain the relationship between mindfulness and individualized consideration.

EI may exist as a mediating relationship between mindfulness and individualized consideration. Specifically, the clarity of emotions from mindfulness increases the ability to identify emotions accurately. Once properly identifying emotions, a leader can appropriately address the needs of a follower. For example, if Diane the leader can see that Jack the follower is frustrated with a challenging task at work, Diane knows to help coach Jack through his frustration and show genuine compassion while helping him problem-solve.

The EI component of managing emotions explains how mindfulness impacts individualized consideration. The reduction of automaticity of thought helps to reduce impulsiveness of ineffective emotions (Glomb et al., 2011). For instance, when emotions go un-regulated, leaders can have sudden bursts of emotional rage, creating negative workplaces. Separating oneself from a negative experience allows leaders to choose how to respond to stressful situations intentionally. Additionally, regulating one's emotions may allow leaders to decrease their recovery time from stressful experiences. When leaders are quick to manage their emotions and be resilient in stressful events, they are more frequently available to enact leadership behaviors to help their followers. Similarly, past research indicates that mindful supervisors were more likely to inspire higher job satisfaction among their followers (Hülsheger et al., 2014). One possible interpretation of this is that mindful leaders can better manage their followers' emotional workplace, which would aid in promoting individualized consideration.

Mindful leaders are hypersensitive to the emotional changes of employees, which would aid leaders to give accurate individualized care to followers (Dane, 2011; Glomb et al., 2011). Simultaneously, mindful individuals can pause and be aware of present experiences. During this pause, individuals are more aware of the present emotions of the follower because of the high emotional intelligence. Leaders can use this information to optimally and timely adapt their helping behavior for a targeted follower. Thus, EI, by allowing leaders to be more understanding of the emotions of followers, will mediate the relationship between mindfulness and individualized consideration.

H4. *Leader emotional intelligence will positively mediate the relationship between leader mindfulness and follower-rated leader individualized consideration.*

Attention control

In addition to EI, a second mediating mechanism between mindfulness and individualized consideration is attention control. Leaders can attempt to understand and manage emotions, but leaders will not achieve much if they don't have the necessary ability to control their attention. The relationship between mindfulness and individualized consideration should also incorporate the impact of the leader's quality of attention control. Exerting control over attention can be one of the biggest determinants of success. As psychology pioneer William James (1890) wrote:

> Everyone knows what attention is. It is taking possession of the mind, in clear and vivid form, of one out of what seems several simultaneously possible objects or trains of thought. Focalization, concentration of consciousness are of its essence. It implies a withdrawal from some things in order to deal effectively with others.
>
> *(p. 403)*

Individuals differ in their capacity to control and direct attention. The involuntary and voluntary attentional system model describes how individuals vary in their ability to direct voluntary attention to control in such a way to disengage from one stimulus, move to a new one, and engage in the new stimulus (Posner & Petersen, 1990). Thus, attention control means having the ability to shift attention as well as sustain attention despite rival demands (Derryberry & Reed, 2002; Ocasio, 2011). Those leaders who have better control of their attention have many advantages, such as protecting themselves from emotional disorders (Fajkowska & Derryberry, 2010). Additionally, attention control is a significant predictor of being more willing to invest effort in accomplishing the goals (Diehl, Semegon, & Schwarzer, 2006). Attention control is important for leaders who have goals to enact individualized consideration.

Attention control and individualized consideration

Individualized consideration requires sufficient attention control. Leaders need enough attention skills to shift away from previous work to perform a new task fully. Working memory capacity, or one's ability to maintain, manipulate, and select information over time without distraction (Redick & Engle, 2006), is especially important for leaders in chaotic environments making complex interpersonal decisions. Having the ability to sustain attention is extremely useful for the workplace, an area where leaders constantly struggle to find more time to engage in productive activities. With increased attention control, leaders have more opportunities to understand the unique needs of each follower for optimal interactions.

H5. *Leaders' attention control will be positively related to follower-rated leader individualized consideration.*

Mindfulness and attention control

Mindfulness positively relates to a leader's attention control. Mindfulness mainly impacts human functioning through the improvement of three qualities of attention: stability, control, and efficiency (Good et al., 2015). Amidst competing demands, mindful individuals can separate themselves from the environment to set their focus where they want it (Glomb et al., 2011). Whereas other situations may steal attention, utilizing mindfulness reduces the automaticity of being pulled in a different direction. Mindfulness is about observing without getting involved in, thus preventing unintentional rumination. The mindfulness ability to direct attention to the present experience is akin to sustaining attention deliberately. Research indicates that higher mindfulness individuals who participated in mindfulness training demonstrated a significantly greater working memory capacity and sustained attention control than a control group (Chambers, Lo, & Allen, 2008). Because mindfulness helps leaders to guide attention to the present experience intentionally, leader mindfulness should positively relate to leader attention control.

H6. *Leader mindfulness will positively relate to leader attention control.*

Attention control mediates mindfulness and individualized consideration

Mindful leaders will have a refined focus that creates wider options and better control over their attention to direct thinking for valuable information for individualized consideration. Mindful leaders have greater attention skills to move away from previous work and shift attention to engage sufficient time in understanding the individualized situation and needs of each follower.

Having greater attention control from high mindfulness means having the freedom to direct attention towards the information that is congruent with current motivations and free up brain space from the competing information that is incongruent with these motivations. Dane's (2011) contingency theory explains how attention explains the theoretically positive impact of mindfulness on work performance. Mindfulness benefits work performance by increasing attentional breadth, the degree to which individuals scan for environmental cues. Attentional breadth reduces the rate of errors by capturing critical environmental cues that otherwise would have gone unnoticed (Dane, 2011; Herndon, 2008; Stanton, Chambers, & Piggott, 2001). Individualized consideration enables leaders to notice key details. Leaders with mindfulness have greater cognitive space to notice details about individual follower needs. Attention control is the mechanism for this process. The space to take in new information plus the ability to control attention effectively creates the advantage for leaders to have time to connect with followers based on greater amounts of pertinent information about their followers. In summary, attention control explains the relationship between mindfulness and individualized consideration, such that mindful leaders have greater attention control to navigate new information that helps to create proactivity for the individualized needs of followers.

H7. *Attention control will positively mediate the relationship between leader mindfulness and follower-rated leader individualized consideration.*

Method

This study is a cross-sectional, multi-source survey design at the dyadic level of analysis. Often, cross-sectional research utilizes data from a single source, causing overlapping variances, creating difficulty in distinguishing the variances (Podsakoff, MacKenzie, Lee, & Podsakoff, 2003). As a result, I include two sources of data (i.e., leader and follower) for this research to minimize common source bias (Podsakoff et al., 2003).

Recruitment and study procedures

I collected data through Qualtrics online survey software. There were two surveys, one for the leader and one for the follower. Leaders filled out a survey containing demographics, mindfulness, EI, and attention control measures. Followers completed a survey containing demographics and perceived individualized consideration of the leader.

I recruited the leader participants on Mechanical Turk (MTurk). Based on recommendations, MTurk participant inclusion criteria was limited to workers with an approval rating of at least 95% for higher-quality responses (Peer, Vosgerau, & Acquisti, 2014). I set the country inclusion criteria to only receive responses from individuals from the United States. I used a monetary incentive for leaders. Even a low level of compensation for MTurk participants does not affect the quality of data (Buhrmester et al., 2011). The survey contained two questions about leader position in order to recruit participants within my inclusion criteria. First, the beginning of the survey included a prompt stating the research requires participants that have an active leadership role for at least one other person. I then defined what I mean by leader and detail examples. Participants indicated whether they fit the description. If a participant responded no, the participant exited the survey. The next question prompted the leader participants to write the number of current followers. If a participant indicated zero, the participant exited the survey.

At the beginning of the survey, the leader participants completed an informed consent document approved by the institutional review board. I informed the leader participants that the survey was voluntary, and they could discontinue at any time. At the end of the survey, participants were prompted to indicate their first name and initial of the last name. The abbreviated name helped to protect the leader's identity and secure a level of anonymity. The abbreviated leader name was then used in the follower survey to prompt the follower to think about this person's leadership capability. The survey instructions again repeated that the data was kept confidential. Then, the leader participant was instructed to nominate up to three followers' email addresses to complete the study. I ensured that the leader survey data would be confidential as I would not report scores to the followers. For leader participants to receive compensation, they would need to provide a valid email. A valid email is one that successfully sends an email (e.g., does not get bounced).

I randomly selected a follower from the leader's nomination. I then distributed an email to the follower via Qualtrics. The email explicitly stated that their leader has nominated the follower for a research survey. The follower email contained a short introduction message explaining the purpose of the research, the confidentiality of the data collection, and the incentive for completing the survey. I ensured that the survey was confidential, and I would not report scores to the leader. Additionally, information regarding response confidentiality was in the mandatory informed consent at the beginning of the survey. For the followers, a monetary incentive for completing the survey was a lottery of a $200 Amazon gift card. Although experts do not traditionally recommend lottery incentives for traditional mail surveys (Dillman, 2011), new research indicates that web survey responses benefit from a lottery incentive (Laguilles, Williams, & Saunders, 2011). By California law, followers had the option to enter the lottery without requiring survey participation. Lastly, the follower email explicitly stated that the leader was not made aware of the follower's responses. I automated a reminder email to be sent to the followers that had not responded after five business days, after seven business days, and a final reminder email stating that the follower had one day to complete the survey. If the follower did not respond, I randomly selected another follower and started the process over again. If none of the leaders' nominated followers completed the survey, I excluded the leader's data from the data analysis.

The leader's name was linked to the follower email in the Qualtrics interface to link the leader–follower responses for data analysis.

Participants

The inclusion criteria for recruiting leaders was an employee with at least six months currently serving in a formal supervisory or managerial role with at least one subordinate (i.e., formal leader position).

As noted, the sample consists of individuals on Amazon's Mechanical Turk (MTurk). Research supports that data collected via the internet are consistent with other traditional methods of data collection, given setting appropriate inclusion criteria (Buhrmester, Kwang, & Gosling, 2011). Furthermore, data collected from MTurk sufficiently met the psychometric standards of published research (Buhrmester et al., 2011). Landers and Behrend (2015) discuss in depth the satisfactory qualities of MTurk samples for organizational psychology research.

To determine the needed sample size to ensure power, I ran a Monte Carlo simulation for a two-mediator model using Mplus version 5.1 (Muthén & Muthén, 2008; Thoemmes, MacKinnon, & Reiser, 2010). Based on theoretical reasoning discussed earlier, the relationships of the model are expected to have medium strength. Thus, I am willing to detect a medium effect size. In the Monte Carlo simulation, I set all pathways to medium effect sizes, estimated additional parameters, requested 10,000 replications, and set the sample size to 150 (Thoemmes et al., 2010). According to the results of the Monte Carlo simulation, observed power was .98 in both indirect effects, suggesting an exceptional level of power given medium effect sizes among variables. Additionally, observed power was .394 in the direct effect, suggesting an acceptable level of power given medium effect size among the variables. The final sample size of 155 was adequate to detect an effect.

I collected a total of 751 leader participants. In the first set of nominated followers, I sent email invitations to 751 nominated followers' email addresses. One hundred and fifty followers (20%) responded in the first round of invitations. In the second set of nominated followers, I sent email invitations to 174 nominated leaders' email addresses. Eleven (6%) followers responded in the second round of invitations. Six (4%) of the 161 follower responses did not appropriately indicate a leader's name in the follower survey. Thus, I deleted the mismatched cases. The final sample size contained 155 total cases (155 leaders matched with 155 followers).

The leader participants' average age was 38.89 (SD = 9.87). They were majority female (52.3% were female, 47.1% were male, .6% reported as 'other') and white (75.5% white, 11.0% Black or African American, 5.8% Hispanic or Latino, 5.8% Asian, 1.3% Other, and .6% Native American or American Indian). The average span of control was 8.51 followers (SD = 9.85). The average number of years of management experience was 9.30 years (SD = 5.99).

The follower participants' average age was 36.6194 years (SD = 9.45). They were majority male (44.5% were male, 34.2% were female, 21.3% reported as 'other') and white (76% white, 9.7% Black or African American, 6.5% Hispanic or Latino, 6.5% Asian, .6% Other, and .6% Native American or American Indian). Follower participants' average tenure with the current company was 5.34 years (SD =4.72). Follower participants' average time under the specified leader was 3.53 years (ISD = 2.84).

Measures

Demographics

I collected basic demographic information including age, gender, and ethnicity in the survey for both leaders and followers. Additionally, the leader survey included a question regarding years of managerial experience and current span of control, and the follower survey included questions regarding the amount of time the follower has worked (a) for the company and (b) as a direct report of the leader.

Leader mindfulness

I measured leader mindfulness using the 15-item Mindful Attention Awareness Scale (MAAS; Brown & Ryan, 2003). The MAAS is a single-dimension self-reported measure of trait mindfulness that has been replicated to demonstrate consistent single-dimension qualities (MacKillop & Anderson, 2007). I used the MAAS because it is a measure of trait mindfulness and because the MAAS has been used in prior leadership and mindfulness research (Reb et al., 2014; Roche et al., 2014). A sample item includes, "It seems I am running on automatic without much awareness of what I'm doing." All items were reverse-scored and then summed up to indicate greater trait mindfulness. All items are on a six-point Likert scale, ranging from (1) *almost always* to (6) *almost never*. The leader completed this measure.

In previous research, the MAAS demonstrated strong reliability across four different levels of leadership (junior managers, middle managers, senior managers/CEOs, entrepreneurs; α = .81, .81, .72, and .84; Roche et al., 2014). The original psychometric development study of the scale assessed both convergent and divergent validity. Convergent validity was supported by positive associations with openness to experience ($r = .18$, $p < .01$) and Trait Meta-Mood Scale ($r = .37–.46$, $p < .0001$). Divergent validity was supported by negative associations with rumination ($r = -.29–.39$, $p < .0001$) and social anxiety ($r = -.19–.36$, $p < .01$). A replicated validation study examined the psychometric properties of the MAAS and found similar strong measures of reliability ($\alpha = .89$; MacKillop & Anderson, 2007). The reliability of this scale in the current study was acceptable ($\alpha = .942$).

Individualized consideration

I measured individualized consideration using the nine-item individualized consideration subscale of the Multifactor Leadership Questionnaire (MLQ) (Bass & Avolio, 1995). An example item is "Spends time to find out what I need." Items are on a five-point Likert scale ranging from (1) *not at all* to (5) *frequently, if not always*. The follower completed this measure by rating the leader on the characteristics.

A recent validation study indicates that the individualized consideration subscale showed strong reliability across four different samples (α = .91, .86, .93, and .92; Tejada, Scandura, & Pillai, 2001). Convergent validity is supported by positive associations with other transformation leadership dimensions of idealized influence behavior ($r = .70$, $p < .01$), inspirational motivation ($r = .74$, $p < .01$), and intellectual stimulation ($r = .33$, $p < .05$; Palmer et al., 2001). Divergent validity is supported by a negative association with the laissez-faire leadership style (Judge & Bono, 2000). The reliability of this scale in the current study was acceptable ($\alpha = .899$).

Attention control

Attention control was measured by the Attentional Control Scale (ACS), a 20-item measure of one's ability to focus perceptual attention, switch attention between tasks, and flexibly control thought (Derryberry & Reed, 2002; Fajkowska & Derryberry, 2010). A validation study supported the one-factor makeup of the scale (Fajkowska and Derryberry (2010). An example item is, "When trying to focus my attention on something, I have difficulty blocking out distracting thoughts." Items are on a four-point Likert scale ranging from (1) *almost never* to (4) *always*. The leader completed this measure.

Fajkowska and Derryberry (2010) demonstrated strong measures of reliability (α = .88). Convergent validity was demonstrated with positive associations with a working memory capacity test, the Letter-Number Sequencing Subtest (Wechsler, 1997; r = .x, $p < .005$). Divergent validity was supported by negative associations with cognitive failures (r = -.68, $p < .01$). The initial Cronbach's alpha was satisfactory (α = .866). However, upon further observation, numerous items had a corrected item-total correlation below the threshold of .4, indicating poor fit and should be removed (Gliem & Gliem, 2003). I subsequently removed nine items that were below the .4 threshold of the item-total correlation. Even though I did not include any subscales in my analysis, I checked the ratios of subscale items after item deletion to ensure the meaning of the scale was not changed. The subscales were proportionally represented in the scale after item deletion similar to the original scale. The final reliability of the adjusted 11-item scale in the current study was acceptable (α = .900).

Emotional intelligence

Emotional intelligence was measured by a short version of the Workgroup Emotional Intelligence Profile (WEIP-S), a 16-item measure designed to assess the emotional intelligence of individuals in work teams (Jordan & Lawrence, 2009). For this construct, emotional intelligence is operationalized as understanding and managing emotions for oneself and others. The average score across all items generate a general emotional intelligence score. Originally intended for a team setting, I adapted the scale to fit the context of a leader and follower relationship. Sample items include, "I can explain the emotions I feel to my followers" and "I am able to describe accurately the way my followers are feeling." All items are on a seven-point Likert scale, ranging from (1) *strongly disagree* to (7) *strongly agree*, with higher scores indicating higher ratings. The leader completed this measure.

In the construction of the short scale, Jordan and Lawrence (2009) critically examined the reliability of WEIP-S. The authors demonstrated strong measures of reliability ranging from .73 to .88 with an average reliability of .82. Furthermore, the authors performed a scale replication study and a test-retest reliability study to provide ample support for the construct and discriminant validity of the WEIP-S.

To ensure the adapted WEIP-S scale has satisfactory scale reliability, I piloted the scale on 50 MTurk participants. I utilized Cronbach's alpha for the measurement of scale reliability. Results indicated that the WEIP-S scale has acceptable internal consistency reliability (α = .962). In other words, this demonstrates that the set of items are related as a group in measuring the same construct (Crano, Brewer, & Lac, 2014). On the main study sample, the reliability of this scale within this research study analysis was acceptable (α = .909).

Control variables

Data was collected on the following control variables: managerial experience, age, and number of followers.

Managerial experience

Prior research suggested that a leader's formal position may relate to their mindfulness levels (Roche et al., 2014). This finding may be because as a leader increases their managerial experience with higher formal positions, their ability to be present becomes more impactful because of other skills they've learned along the way (Dane, 2011). To isolate the relationships in this study, I controlled for past managerial experience. Leaders respond to the following question, "How many years of management experience do you have (include outside of your current organization)?" The average number of years of management experience was 9.30 years (*SD* = 5.99). The leader participants are managerially experienced.

Age

Age has been used as control variables in recent mindfulness research to stabilize any differences across generations of leaders (Reb et al., 2017). Leaders and followers responded to the following question: "In what year were you born?"

Span of control

Leaders who have more followers may be spread thin with time and cannot devote individualized consideration evenly. Thus, I controlled for the number of followers in case this makes a statistical difference in leadership behaviors. Leaders responded to the following question, "How many direct reports do you currently have?" The average span of control was 8.51 followers (*SD* = 9.85). The leader participants generally have many followers; however, the spread of amount of followers is quite large. Controlling for span of control will be especially important.

Results

I conducted Structural Equation Modeling (SEM) analyses to test my hypotheses using the AMOS software package in SPSS (Arbuckle, 2006). SEM is appropriate in this case because it allows multiple paths to be tested simultaneously and evaluate the overall model fit (Kline, 2015).

The dataset initially contained responses from 155 cases (a case requires data from both the leader and one follower from each leader). Within the 155 cases, I identified 11 missing data values. To maximize the statistical power, I decided not to delete the missing data. I treated missing data using expectation-maximization (EM), which is a computational technique of getting maximum likelihood estimates to replace the missing data values, in SPSS v.22 (Allison, 2003).

Before running the model fit, I assessed that statistical assumptions were met. The values of skewness and kurtosis for all variables were below the absolute value of two, indicating satisfactory statistical assumption (Howell, 2012). I identified eight univariate outliers of

Table 8.1 Means, standard deviations, Cronbach's alphas, and zero-order correlations for all variables (N = 155)

Variable	M	SD	*A*	*1*	*2*	*3*	*4*	*5*	*6*	7
1. Leader Age	38.89	9.87	—	—						
2. Mgmt Exp	9.30	5.98	—	.66*	—					
3. Span of Control	8.51	9.85	—	-.04	.05	—				
4. Mindfulness	4.21	1.04	.942	.14	.26*	.10	—			
5. Emo. Intel.	5.46	0.79	.909	.09	.22*	.16*	.34*	—		
6. Att. Control	3.53	0.72	.900	.17*	.28*	.06	.72*	.25*	—	
7. Ind. Cons.	4.06	0.83	.899	-.05	.11	.09	.21*	.36*	.18*	—

Note. Correlation coefficients that are significant at $p < .05$ are marked with an asterisk. Ind. Cons. = Individualized Consideration; Emo. Intel. = Emotional Intelligence; Mgmt Exp. = Management Experience; Att. Control = Attentional Control.

scores that exceeded three standard deviations away from the mean (Howell, 2012). I used the Winsorize technique to adjust univariate outliers by setting the outlier values to the most extreme observed value within the three standard deviation cutoff (Howell, 2012). Using Mahalonobis distance to identify multivariate outliers, I found no evidence of multivariate normality violation by using chi-square equal to .001 as the cutoff (Tabachnick & Fidell, 2007).

Table 8.1 details the descriptive statistics and interclass correlation coefficients of key variables. As expected, all of the variables of interest significantly related to one another. In regards to demographics, as expected, management experience positively relates to both a leader's age as well as mindfulness. Surprisingly, management experience relates to all variables of interest except for individualized consideration. Additionally, span of control positively relates to emotional intelligence. Lastly, a leader's age positively relates to the leader's attention control.

Model estimation

I first evaluated the model fit of the hypothesized relationships by using the AMOS software package in SPSS (Arbuckle, 2006). I assessed the goodness-of-fit for the model by using chi-square testing, comparative fit indices (CFI), root mean square of approximation (RMSEA), and standardized root mean squared residual (SRMR). A good model fit is determined by χ^2/df ratio < 2, CFI = .95, RMSEA < .05, and SRMR < .05 and an acceptable model fit is determined by χ^2/df ratio < 5, CFI = .90, RMSEA < .08, and SRMR < .08 (Hu & Bentler, 1999; Kline, 2015). The model estimation for the hypothesized model demonstrated good fit with the data (χ^2 (1) = .035 p =.851, χ^2/df = .035, CFI = 1.000, RMSEA = .000, SRMR = .0019; Hu & Bentler, 1999; Kline, 2015). The initial model for path analysis testing with standardized coefficients is in Figure 8.2.

Hypothesis testing

Hypothesis 1, mindfulness would positively relate to individualized consideration, was supported by assessing the direct path of mindfulness to individualized consideration.

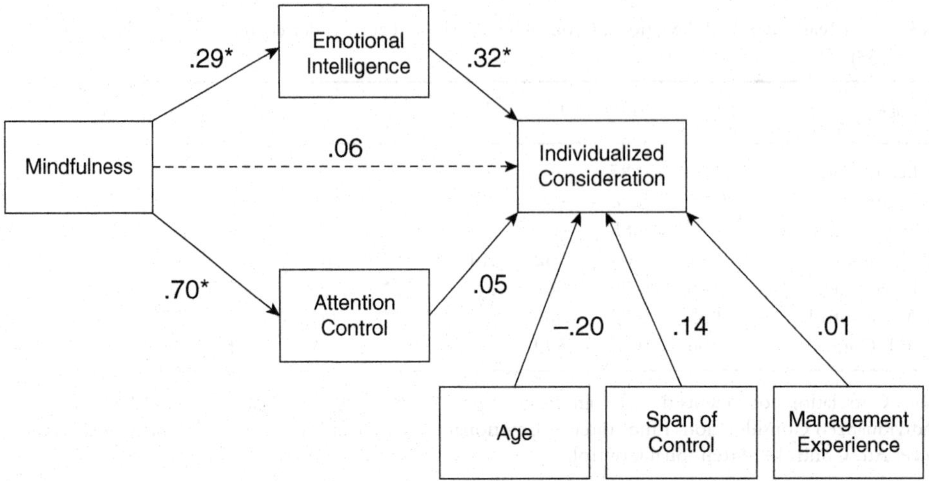

Figure 8.2 The hypothesized model for path analysis testing. Significant relationships at $p < .05$ are marked with an asterisk.

Table 8.2 Confirmatory factor analysis results of all variables (N = 424)

Model[a]	χ^2	df	χ^2/df[b]	*CFI*	*SRMR*	*RMSEA*
A	.035	1	.035	1.00	.0019	.000
B	1.74	3	.579	1.00	.0216	.000

Note. CFI = comparative fit index; SRMR = standardized root mean square residual; RMSEA = root mean square error of approximation. [a]Model A = hypothesized model; Model B = alternative model. [b]Each chi-square difference test is significant at $p < .00$"

Increased individualized consideration was positively associated with mindfulness ($\beta = .190$, $p = .018$). The more mindfulness the leader self-reported, the more individualized consideration the follower rated the leader.

Hypothesis 2, mindfulness would positively predict emotional intelligence, was supported through the significant positive path between emotional intelligence and mindfulness (ß = .292, $p < .001$). The more mindfulness the leader self-reported, the more emotional intelligence the leader self-reported.

Hypothesis 3, emotional intelligence would positively relate to individualized consideration, was supported. The path from individualized consideration was positive and significant to emotional intelligence (ß = .318, $p < .001$). The more emotional intelligence the leader self-reported, the higher on individualized consideration the follower rated the leader.

Hypothesis 4, the relationship of mindfulness to individualized consideration would be mediated by emotional intelligence, was supported. The indirect effect of mindfulness associated with emotional intelligence associated with individualized consideration was significant (ß = .092, $p = .005$, 95% CI [.031, .128]). In other words, emotional intelligence explains the direct effect of mindfulness positively predicting individualized consideration.

When both mediating variables were added, the direct effect of mindfulness on individualized consideration was not significant (ß = .061, p = .580).

Hypothesis 5, mindfulness would positively relate to attention control, was supported by a significant, positive path from attention control to mindfulness (ß = .698, $p < .001$). The more mindfulness the leader self-reported, the more attention control the leader self-reported.

Hypothesis 6, attention control would positively relate to individualized consideration, was not supported. The direct effect of attention control associated with individualized consideration was not significant (ß = .052, p = .629).

Hypothesis 7, the relationship of mindfulness to individualized consideration would be mediated by attention control, was also not supported. The indirect effect of mindfulness associated with attention control associated with individualized consideration was not significant (ß = .025 p = .739, 95% CI [-.078, .139]). Although mindfulness was associated with attention control, the mediating relationship was not apparent. As such, post-hoc analyses were conducted to reveal a better-fitting model to understand the relationship.

The control variables revealed significant relationships. Age is significantly associated with individualized consideration (ß = -.198, p = .046) and significantly covaried with mindfulness (ß = .146, p <.001). Management experience significantly covaried with mindfulness (ß = .260, p = .002).

Post-hoc analyses

No modification indices suggested alternative paths for a better-fitting model. Despite this, I removed paths on the current model that did not provide support for the hypothesized relationships. Specifically, I removed the path from mindfulness to individualized consideration, because evidence indicates that the relationship is explained through the mediation of emotional intelligence. Furthermore, I removed the path from attention control to individualized consideration because the analysis did not support that relationship.

Although not statistically significant, I kept in the control variable relationships for the analysis of the model because of the substantive importance in considering control variables that have both theoretical and empirical inclusion support (Bernerth & Aguinis, 2016; Bollen & Bauldry, 2011). All control variable relationships I included have empirical basis supported by significant relationships from the correlation matrix. Moreover, control variables require a theoretical support that justifies that the inclusion denotes an incremental advance in the study results. Management experience should be included because of the need to control for the interaction of different attention and emotional skills gained with more experience (Dane, 2011). Age should be included to stabilize quality of attention across different generations (Reb et al., 2017). Lastly, span of control should be included because greater amounts of followers alters the impact of emotional intelligence on followers (Lucas, Spence Laschinger, & Wong, 2008).

The model estimation for the new model (Model B) demonstrated acceptable fit with the data (χ^2 (8) = 6.664 p = .573, χ^2/df = .833, CFI = 1.000, RMSEA = .000, SRMR = .0331). Chi-square difference tests indicate the new model (Model B) is not significantly different than the default model initially used in this research study (model A); χ^2 (7) = 6.628, p = .469. See Table 8.2 for comparing the two models. This final SEM model with standardized coefficients is illustrated in Figure 8.3. The results of this model suggest that emotional intelligence mediated the relationship between mindfulness and individualized

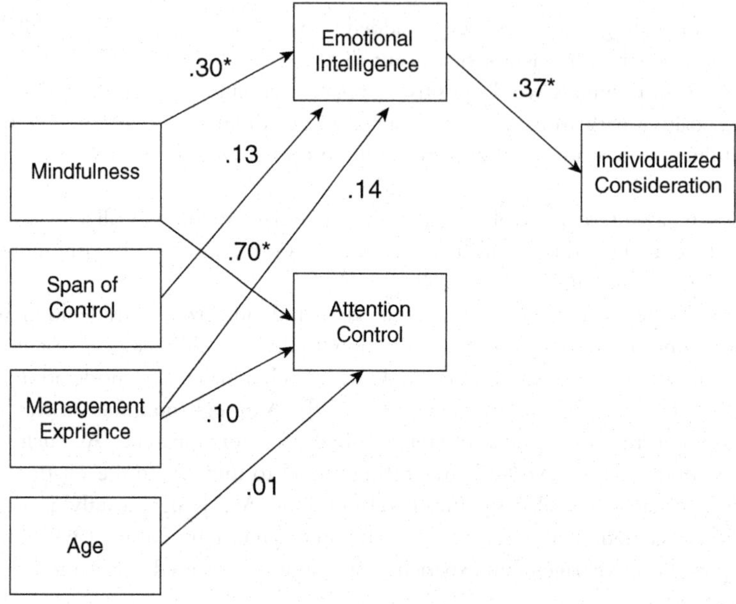

Figure 8.3 The final model. Significant relationships at $p < .05$ are marked with an asterisk.

consideration. Additionally, whereas mindfulness positively predicts attention control, attention control does not relate to individualized consideration.

Discussion

The modern workplace has intensifying forms of distraction that limit the degree to which leaders can connect with their followers (Theeboom et al., 2014; Underhill, 2006; Whitaker et al., 2007). Individualized consideration, the leadership behavior of connecting with and developing the distinct needs of followers, is especially difficult when the leader must ignore the competing demands to spend time understanding followers' needs (Bass, 1999; Jiang et al., 2017). The present study aimed to examine the mechanisms of individualized consideration.

Mindfulness matters for individualized considerate relationships

A main finding in this study is that mindfulness, already shown to have many intrapersonal well-being benefits in prior research (Brown & Ryan, 2003; Chiesa & Serretti, 2010), has interpersonal benefits. Past research demonstrates a link between mindfulness and intimate relationship quality (Wachs & Cordova, 2007). I examined a form of relationship quality within the workplace to build upon interpersonal mindfulness research. In essence, having higher mindfulness can have a positive impact on the way people interact with each other.

The interpersonal benefits found in this chapter are specifically within a scarce area of organizational research for mindfulness: leadership. This study demonstrates that mindfulness is related to a relational aspect of leadership capabilities in the individualized consideration dimension of transformational leadership, a major leadership theory in organizational psychology.

Mindfulness provides the necessary resources for leaders to perform such individualized considerate leadership behaviors in the modern workplace environment. The results of this study show that leaders with high mindfulness are more likely to demonstrate individualized consideration. The findings support theoretical suggestions that mindfulness helps to reduce automatic thoughts, which helps leaders integrate more information about their followers' needs before making judgments (Glomb et al., 2011). Additionally, past research demonstrates a link between the acceptance feature of mindfulness and helping behaviors (Cameron & Fredrickson, 2015). Possibly, leaders with higher mindfulness accept the emotions of their followers, which aids leader–follower interactions.

Emotional intelligence explains the individualized consideration benefits of mindfulness

Emotional intelligence explains the interpersonal benefit of mindfulness in this study. Specifically, findings from this study demonstrate unique empirical support that mindfulness impacts individualized consideration through the mechanism of emotional intelligence. This finding is consistent with past research indicating that emotional intelligence mediates the relationship between mindfulness and beneficial outcomes such as well-being (Schutte & Malouff, 2011).

The theoretical underpinnings for the discovered mediation are twofold. First, the mindfulness aspect of being aware of the present experience allows leaders to be more attentive to the emotional cues from their followers. Recognizing emotional cues is imperative for meeting the emotional needs of the follower for transformational leadership behaviors (Rubin, Munz, & Bommer, 2005). Second, the mindfulness aspect of accepting the present experience non-judgmentally helps leaders to proactively work with a follower's existing emotions for providing beneficial support. Alternatively, without accepting emotions, a leader may exhaust valuable cognitive resources expending self-regulatory faculties to solely change a follower's emotions (Baumeister, Muraven, & Tice, 2000). Emotional intelligence is one of the most valuable skills to combat the massive technological workplace disruptions because the pure human ability to think laterally across domains within creative teams is potentially only delegated to humans.

The mediating mechanism of emotional intelligence supports the idea that individualized consideration involves an emotional skill. Conventionally, inspiring values and providing confidence is utilized to generate general transformational leadership (Dvir, Eden, Avolio, & Shamir, 2002). Whereas past research has examined some positive relationship between emotional intelligence and general transformational leadership (Barling et al., 2000; Mandell & Pherwani, 2003), this research has specifically uncovered the mechanisms for one dimension of transformational leadership: individualized consideration. Emotional understanding and management should be considered as at least part of a sufficient antecedent of individualized consideration.

Only socially motivated attention may enhance individualized consideration

Interestingly enough, attention control did not explain the relationship between mindfulness and individualized consideration. Because emotional intelligence and attention control share a common denominator of attention quality, one might think that attention control would also mediate the relationship in the study as hypothesized. Yet, emotional intelligence has a social component aiding the relationship to individualized consideration that attention control does not contain.

One possible explanation is that attention control in and of itself does not drive individualized consideration. But rather, attention control in service of social connection does drive individualized consideration. Pure attention control is a tool for sustaining focus on one task and being able to shift focus between tasks (Derryberry & Reed, 2002). Leaders with high attention control could be using their strong attention faculties for any number of reasons other than social connection. Even during a leader–follower interaction, leaders could be highly focused on a previous task-oriented problem in their mind, while ignoring the follower. On the other hand, emotional intelligence is a tool for driving attention to use emotional information for social betterment (Keltner & Haidt, 1999; Lopes et al., 2004). Thus, the intention behind the attention matters for effective individualized consideration.

Intentionally focusing on present emotional experiences may be accounting for the relationship with individualized consideration. Attention control is supposed to benefit behavior by widening the extent of information a leader can absorb from the environment (Dane, 2011) and limit cognitively costly anxiety-provoking thoughts (Eysenck, Derakshan, Santos, & Calvo, 2007). Emotional cues may be the most important information to absorb from the environment for leader–follower interactions (Rubin et al., 2005). Thus, emotional intelligence contributes more variance because it applies attention to understanding/managing emotional cues (Glomb et al., 2011; Rubin et al., 2005). In other words, skillfully controlling one's general attention alone may not be the sole feature for individualized consideration. But rather, the ability to apply attention to the regulation of present emotions is the important feature for individualized consideration.

Despite the findings, attention control may still play a role in the relationship between mindfulness and individualization under the guise of a more nuanced operationalization of attention control. Emotional intelligence may subsume all relevant emotional utility of attention control for leader–follower rapport. However, individualized consideration involves aspects other than emotions. To properly perform individualized consideration, leaders may need to time-manage individual work properly. Although not found in this study, a non-social form of attention control would possibly benefit a leader's time management ability in favor of enacting certain types of leadership.

Lastly, the results uncovered two interesting, significant relationships with control variables. First, leaders with higher age may spend less time providing individualized consideration because they are more devoted to higher-level strategic decisions. Perhaps older leaders devote less time working with followers who benefit from individualized consideration. Second, age positively related to mindfulness possibly because older leaders may have wider experiences to draw on to understand how to accept the present-moment experiences.

Practical implications

The findings from this chapter can be implemented in organizations in three different ways: formal training, coaching, and during meetings. First, if an organization has the budget, a formal mindfulness training program will be beneficial to create the conditions for individualized consideration. Initial reports from a mindfulness training firm indicate self-reported increase in job performance and emotional intelligence

(Potential Project, 2019). Formats for the training vary, but one such program, Potential Project's Corporate-based Mindfulness Training, contains one session per week for five or ten weeks. Although both financially heavy and time-intensive, training programs can be beneficial to create mindfulness practices with the help of a long-form intervention.

Second, mindfulness can be integrated into executive coaching to facilitate a leader's development. A one-on-one coaching engagement could be used to facilitate necessary habit change for a leader to adopt a mindfulness practice. Furthermore, coaches could benefit from using mindfulness as a preparation tool for the coaching session (Passmore & Marianetti, 2007).

Lastly, mindfulness can be implemented at the start of meetings in order to optimize the time together. Specially, a mindfulness practice at the start of a performance review meeting will facilitate the driving mechanisms of emotional intelligence to then best enact a leader's individualized consideration.

Limitations and future directions

The limitations of this chapter are discussed within four pertinent areas: data collection, cross-sectional design, self-reported attention control measure, and lastly contextual consideration.

The nature of this study's data collection process has limitations in two ways. First, MTurk data collection, outside of the organizational context, prevented data analysis from considering the variation between multiple organizational contexts. Individualized consideration may vary depending upon the organization and team level of analysis. Future research should collect numerous leaders from the same organization to conduct multi-level modeling for understanding interactions between levels of analysis.

Second, follower recruitment in this study is a limitation because the leader participants nominated any follower of their choosing. Although other-reported data collection helps limit common source bias (Podsakoff et al., 2003), leaders may have only nominated their closest followers. The followers with the most (and perhaps only) received individualized considerate interactions might have been in the study. Leaders could have only been enacting individualized consideration to just one follower and disregarding other followers. Thus, follower ratings may not represent the entire picture of a leader's individualized consideration. Future research should include closeness of the follower or frequency of interaction with the follower as a moderator of individualized consideration.

The cross-sectional design in this study is limited because all variables are simultaneously reported and no temporal predictive ability is possible (Podsakoff et al., 2003). The conceptual and theoretical understanding of mindfulness, emotional intelligence, and individualized consideration will benefit from future longitudinal designed research. If a future study examines multiple collection time points, the relationships between mindfulness, emotional intelligence, and leadership behaviors will be better comprehended. Specifically, researchers should examine interventions aimed at heightening mindfulness and emotional intelligence to determine if leadership behavior changes occur over time.

Self-reported attention control is only one representation for understanding attention (Reinholdt-Dunne, Mogg, & Bradley, 2013). Future research should use multiple types of attention measures, such as objective behavioral measures, to deepen the understanding of the nuanced relationship between mindfulness, attention control, and leadership behaviors.

Lastly, this study did not consider specific industry contexts (healthcare, education, military, corporate, etc.) of leadership behavior. The results are aimed to understand the general interactions between leaders and followers. Future research should seek to understand specific contexts that moderate successful individualized consideration interactions. Perhaps environments with a culture of suppressed emotions may inhibit individualized consideration because leaders would have difficulty understanding and managing others' emotions. For example, the military would be a unique population to extend the research of mindfulness, emotional intelligence, and individualized consideration. Cadets are trained to regulate emotions to such a high degree that it might be difficult for commanding leaders to identify useful emotional cues in their followers.

Conclusion

Leaders need to understand the unique needs of followers and enact considerate behaviors based on those needs. However, leaders have difficulty finding the time amidst the volatile workplace to understand the unique needs of each follower. The expected results detailed one mechanism, emotional intelligence, by which leaders with high mindfulness enact individualized consideration to their followers. This study supports the notion that leaders with high mindfulness will be more likely to have high emotional intelligence to notice the emotional cues of their followers to best contribute to their followers' development.

Chapter takeaways

1. Leaders have trouble providing adequate development to their followers: Effective leaders engage in individualized consideration, or the leadership behavior of connecting with and developing the unique needs of followers. However, the plethora of distractions in the workplace prevent leaders from giving full attention to understand the needs of followers and provide support.
2. Mindfulness matters for individualized considerate relationships: Results indicate that leaders who have higher self-report mindfulness provide their followers with more individualized considerate behaviors (as measured by follower-rated individualized consideration).
3. Emotional intelligence explains the individualized consideration benefits of mindfulness: Leaders who have high mindfulness have greater ability to be aware and manage one's own emotions and others' emotions (emotional intelligence), which enables greater helping behaviors for developing followers.
4. Only socially motivated attention may enhance individualized consideration: Although hypothesized, attention control did not explain the relationship of a leader's mindfulness impacting their individualized considerate behaviors towards followers. One possible explanation is that high attention control can be used by leaders for any number of tasks. Attention control in service of understanding present emotional experiences may be accounting for the relationship with individualized consideration
5. Inspired by these preliminary results, future research should examine new areas of mindfulness in the workplace, such as how mindfulness and leadership changes over time in a mindfulness intervention, how follower closeness may affect the benefits of mindfulness to a leader, and how behavioral measures of attention may deepen the understanding of the relationships.

Five reflection questions (academic and applied)

1. What are the ways that the quality of one's attention may impact their performance as a leader?
2. Think about one to three people who you closely work with. How do you make time to be aware and acknowledge their emotions while interacting with them? How do you be aware and acknowledge your own emotional state?
3. How may a follower's mindfulness affect the leader's ability to perform individualized considerate behaviors?
4. In contexts where emotions are trained to be self-regulated at such a high degree (e.g., military), what are other ways that leaders can become aware of the emotional cues required for proper individualized consideration?
5. The CEO of a Fortune 500 company has requested from you a debrief of benefits of mindfulness for a leader. Write two to four sentences, in non-academic language, on how mindfulness may benefit a leader in the workplace.

References

Allison, P. D. (2003). Missing data techniques for structural equation modeling. *Journal of Abnormal Psychology*, *112*(4), 545. doi:10.1037/0021-843X.112.4.545

Arbuckle, J. L. (2006). Amos (Version 7.0) [Data analysis software]. Chicago: SPSS.

Avey, J. B., Wernsing, T. S., & Luthans, F. (2008). Can positive employees help positive organizational change? Impact of psychological capital and emotions on relevant attitudes and behaviors. *The Journal of Applied Behavioral Science*, *44*(1), 48–70. doi:10.1177/0021886307311470

Avolio, B. J., Zhu, W., Koh, W., & Bhatia, P. (2004). Transformational leadership and organizational commitment: Mediating role of psychological empowerment and moderating role of structural distance. *Journal of Organizational Behavior*, *25*(8), 951–968. doi:10.1002/job.283

Baer, R. A., Smith, G. T., Hopkins, J., Krietemeyer, J., & Toney, L. (2006). Using self-report assessment methods to explore facets of mindfulness. *Assessment*, *13*(1), 27–45. doi:10.1177/1073191105283504

Barling, J., Slater, F., & Kevin Kelloway, E. (2000). Transformational leadership and emotional intelligence: An exploratory study. *Leadership & Organization Development Journal*, *21*(3), 157–161. doi:10.1108/01437730010325040

Barling, J., Weber, T., & Kelloway, E. K. (1996). Effects of transformational leadership training on attitudinal and financial outcomes: A field experiment. *Journal of Applied Psychology*, *81*(6), 827–832. doi:10.1037/0021-9010.81.6.827

Bass, B. M. (1985). *Leadership and performance beyond expectations*. New York, NY: Academic Press.

Bass, B. M. (1999). Two decades of research and development in transformational leadership. *European Journal of Work and Organizational Psychology*, *8*(1), 9–32. doi:10.1080/135943299398410

Bass, B. M., & Avolio, B. J. (1995). *MLQ: Multifactor leadership questionnaire for research: Permission set*. Menlo Park, CA: Mind Garden.

Baumeister, R. F., Muraven, M., & Tice, D. M. (2000). Ego depletion: A resource model of volition, self-regulation, and controlled processing. *Social Cognition*, *18*(2), 130–150. doi:10.1521/soco.2000.18.2.130

Bernerth, J. B., & Aguinis, H. (2016). A critical review and best-practice recommendations for control variable usage. *Personnel Psychology*, *69*(1), 229–283. doi:10.1111/peps.12103

Bishop, S. R., Lau, M., Shapiro, S., Carlson, L., Anderson, N. D., Carmody, J., . . . Devins, G. (2004). Mindfulness: A proposed operational definition. *Clinical Psychology: Science and Practice*, *11*(3), 230–241. doi:10.1093/clipsy/bph077

Bollen, K. A., & Bauldry, S. (2011). Three Cs in measurement models: Causal indicators, composite indicators, and covariates. *Psychological Methods*, *16*(3), 265. doi:10.1037/a0024448

Brown, K. W., & Ryan, R. M. (2003). The benefits of being present: Mindfulness and its role in psychological well-being. *Journal of Personality and Social Psychology*, *84*(4), 822–848. doi:10.1037/0022-3514.84.4.822

Brown, K. W., Ryan, R. M., & Creswell, J. D. (2007). Mindfulness: Theoretical foundations and evidence for its salutary effects. *Psychological Inquiry, 18*(4), 211–237. doi:10.1080/10478400701598298

Brown-Iannuzzi, J. L., Adair, K. C., Payne, B. K., Richman, L. S., & Fredrickson, B. L. (2014). Discrimination hurts, but mindfulness may help: Trait mindfulness moderates the relationship between perceived discrimination and depressive symptoms. *Personality and Individual Differences, 56*, 201–205. doi:10.1016/j.paid.2013.09.015

Burns, J. M. (1978). *Leadership*. New York, NY: Harper & Row.

Buhrmester, M., Kwang, T., & Gosling, S. D. (2011). Amazon's Mechanical Turk: A new source of inexpensive, yet high-quality data? *Perspectives on Psychological Science*, 6, 3–5. doi:10.1177/1745691610393980

Cameron, C. D., & Fredrickson, B. L. (2015). Mindfulness facets predict helping behavior and distinct helping-related emotions. *Mindfulness, 6*(5), 1211–1218. doi:10.1007/s12671-014-0383-2

Carmody, J., & Baer, R. A. (2008). Relationships between mindfulness practice and levels of mindfulness, medical and psychological symptoms and well-being in a mindfulness-based stress reduction program. *Journal of Behavioral Medicine, 31*(1), 23–33. doi:10.1016/S0022-3999(03)00573-7

Chambers, R., Lo, B. C. Y., & Allen, N. B. (2008). The impact of intensive mindfulness training on attentional control, cognitive style, and affect. *Cognitive Therapy and Research, 32*(3), 303–322. doi:10.1007/s10608-007-9119-0

Chiesa, A., & Serretti, A. (2010). A systematic review of neurobiological and clinical features of mindfulness meditations. *Psychological Medicine, 40*(8), 1239–1252.

Cooper, L. O. (1997). Listening competency in the workplace: A model for training. *Business Communication Quarterly, 60*(4), 75–84. doi:10.1177/108056999706000405

Côté, S., Lopes, P. N., Salovey, P., & Miners, C. T. (2010). Emotional intelligence and leadership emergence in small groups. *The Leadership Quarterly, 21*(3), 496–508. doi:10.1016/j.leaqua.2010.03.012

Crano, W. D., Brewer, M. B., & Lac, A. (2014). *Principles and Methods of Social Research*. New York, NY: Routledge.

Dane, E. (2011). Paying attention to mindfulness and its effects on task performance in the workplace. *Journal of Management, 37*(4), 997–1018. doi:10.1177/0149206310367948

Derryberry, D., & Reed, M. A. (2002). Anxiety-related attentional biases and their regulation by attentional control. *Journal of Abnormal Psychology, 111*(2), 225–236. doi:10.1037//0021-843X.111.2.225

Diehl, M., Semegon, A. B., & Schwarzer, R. (2006). Assessing attention control in goal pursuit: A component of dispositional self-regulation. *Journal of Personality Assessment, 86*(3), 306–317. doi:10.1207/s15327752jpa8603_06

Dillman, D. A. (2011). *Mail and Internet surveys: The tailored design method–2007 Update with new Internet, visual, and mixed-mode guide*. New York: John Wiley & Sons.

Dinh, J. E., Lord, R. G., Gardner, W. L., Meuser, J. D., Liden, R. C., & Hu, J. (2014). Leadership theory and research in the new millennium: Current theoretical trends and changing perspectives. *The Leadership Quarterly, 25*(1), 36–62. doi:10.1016/j.leaqua.2013.11.005

Dulewicz, V., & Higgs, M. (1999). Can emotional intelligence be measured and developed? *Leadership & Organization Development Journal, 20*(5), 242–253. doi:10.1108/01437739910287117

Dvir, T., Eden, D., Avolio, B. J., & Shamir, B. (2002). Impact of transformational leadership on follower development and performance: A field experiment. *Academy of Management Journal, 45*(4), 735–744. doi:10.2307/3069307

Eby, L. T., Allen, T. D., Evans, S. C., Ng, T., & DuBois, D. L. (2008). Does mentoring matter? A multidisciplinary meta-analysis comparing mentored and non-mentored Individuals. *Journal of Vocational Behavior, 72*, 254–267. doi:10.1016/j.jvb.2007.04.005

Eysenck, M. W., Derakshan, N., Santos, R., & Calvo, M. G. (2007). Anxiety and cognitive performance: Attentional control theory. *Emotion*, 7(2), 336.

Fajkowska, M., & Derryberry, D. (2010). Psychometric properties of attentional control scale: The preliminary study on a polish sample. *Polish Psychological Bulletin, 41*(1), 1–7. doi:10.2478/s10059-010-0001-7

Garland, E. L., Fredrickson, B., Kring, A. M., Johnson, D. P., Meyer, P. S., & Penn, D. L. (2010). Upward spirals of positive emotions counter downward spirals of negativity: Insights from the broaden-and-build theory and affective neuroscience on the treatment of emotion dysfunctions and deficits in psychopathology. *Clinical Psychology Review, 30*(7), 849–864. doi:10.1016/j.cpr.2010.03.002

Gliem, J. A., & Gliem, R. R. (2003). Calculating, interpreting, and reporting Cronbach's alpha reliability coefficient for Likert-type scales. Midwest Research-to-Practice Conference in Adult, Continuing, and Community Education.

Glomb, T. M., Duffy, M. K., Bono, J. E., & Yang, T. (2011). Mindfulness at work. In A. Joshi, H. Liao, & J. J. Martocchio (Eds.), *Research in personnel and human resources management* (Vol. *30*, pp. 115–157). Bingley, UK: Emerald Group Publishing Limited.

Good, D. J., Lyddy, C. J., Glomb, T. M., Bono, J. E., Brown, K. W., Duffy, M. K., ... Lazar, S. W. (2015). Contemplating mindfulness at work: An integrative review. *Journal of Management,42*, (1), 114–142. doi:10.1177/0149206315617003

Grossman, P. (2010). Mindfulness for psychologists: Paying kind attention to the perceptible. *Mindfulness*, *1*(2), 87–97. doi:10.1007/s12671-010-0012-7

Hanh, T. N. (1976). *The miracle of mindfulness: A manual of meditation*. Boston, MA: Beacon Press.

Hater, J. J., & Bass, B. M. (1988). Superiors' evaluations and subordinates' perceptions of transformational and transactional leadership. *Journal of Applied Psychology, 73*(4), 695–702. doi:10.1037/0021-9010.73.4.695

Herndon, F. (2008). Testing mindfulness with perceptual and cognitive factors: External vs. internal encoding, and the cognitive failures questionnaire. *Personality and Individual Differences, 44*(1), 32–41. doi:10.1016/j.paid.2007.07.002

Howell, D. C. (2012). *Statistical methods for psychology* (8th ed.). Belmont, CA: Wadsworth.

Hu, L. T., & Bentler, P. M. (1999). Cutoff criteria for fit indexes in covariance structure analysis: Conventional criteria versus new alternatives. *Structural Equation Modeling: A Multidisciplinary Journal, 6* (1), 1–55. doi:10.1080/10705519909540118

Hülsheger, U. R., Alberts, H. J. E. M., Feinholdt, A., & Lang, J. W. B. (2013). Benefits of mindfulness at work: The role of mindfulness in emotion regulation, emotional exhaustion, and job satisfaction. *Journal of Applied Psychology*, 98, 310–325. doi:10.1037/a0031313

Hülsheger, U. R., Lang, J. W., Depenbrock, F., Fehrmann, C., Zijlstra, F. R., & Alberts, H. J. (2014). The power of presence: The role of mindfulness at work for daily levels and change trajectories of psychological detachment and sleep quality. *Journal of Applied Psychology, 99*(6), 1113–1128. doi:10.1037/a0037702

James, W. (1890). *Principles of psychology*. New York, NY: Henry Holt and Company.

Jett, Q. R., & George, J. M. (2003). Work interrupted: A closer look at the role of interruptions in organizational life. *Academy of Management Review, 28*(3), 494–507. doi:10.5465/AMR.2003.10196791

Jiang, W., Zhao, X., & Ni, J. (2017). The impact of transformational leadership on employee sustainable performance: The mediating role of organizational citizenship behavior. *Sustainability, 9*(9), 1567. doi:10.3390/su9091567

Jordan, C. H., Wang, W., Donatoni, L., & Meier, B. P. (2014). Mindful eating: Trait and state mindfulness predict healthier eating behavior. *Personality and Individual Differences, 68*, 107–111. doi:10.1016/j.paid.2014.04.013

Jordan, P. J., Ashkanasy, N. M., Härtel, C. E. J., & Hooper, G. S. (2002). Workgroup emotional intelligence: Scale development and relationship to team process effectiveness and goal focus. *Human Resource Management Review, 12*(2), 195–214. doi:10.1016S1053-4822(2)00046-3

Jordan, P. J., & Lawrence, S. A. (2009). Emotional intelligence in teams: Development and initial validation of the short version of the Workgroup Emotional Intelligence Profile (WEIP-S). *Journal of Management & Organization, 15*(4), 452–469. doi:10.1017/S1833367200002546

Judge, T. A., & Bono, J. E. (2000). Five-factor model of personality and transformational leadership. *Journal of Applied Psychology, 85*(5), 751. doi:10.1037/0021-9010.85.5.751

Kabat-Zinn, J. (1994). *Wherever you go, there you are: Mindfulness meditation in everyday life*. New York, NY: Hyperion.

Keltner, D., & Haidt, J. (1999). Social functions of emotions at four levels of analysis. *Cognition & Emotion, 13*(5), 505–521. doi:10.1080/026999399379168

Kline, R. B. (2015). *Principles and practice of structural equation modeling*. New York: Guilford Press.

Laguilles, J. S., Williams, E. A., & Saunders, D. B. (2011). Can lottery incentives boost web survey response rates? Findings from four experiments. *Research in Higher Education, 52*(5), 537–553. doi:10.1007/s11162-010-9203-2

Landers, R. N., & Behrend, T. S. (2015). An inconvenient truth: Arbitrary distinctions between organizational, Mechanical Turk, and other convenience samples. *Industrial and Organizational Psychology, 8*(2), 142–164. doi:10.1017/iop.2015.13

Langer, E. J. (1989). *Mindfulness*. Boston, MA: Addison-Wesley.

Lau, M. A., Bishop, S. R., Segal, Z. V., Buis, T., Anderson, N. D., Carlson, L., . . . Devins, G. (2006). The Toronto mindfulness scale: Development and validation. *Journal of Clinical Psychology*, *62*(12), 1445–1467. doi:10.1002/jclp.20326

Leroy, H., Anseel, F., Dimitrova, N. G., & Sels, L. (2013). Mindfulness, authentic functioning, and work engagement: A growth modeling approach. *Journal of Vocational Behavior*, *82*(3), 238–247. doi:10.1016/j.jvb.2013.01.012

Lopes, P. N., Brackett, M. A., Nezlek, J. B., Schütz, A., Sellin, I., & Salovey, P. (2004). Emotional intelligence and social interaction. *Personality and Social Psychology Bulletin*, *30*(8), 1018–1034. doi:10.1177/0146167204264762

Lucas, V., Spence Laschinger, H. K., & Wong, C. A. (2008). The impact of emotional intelligent leadership on staff nurse empowerment: The moderating effect of span of control. *Journal of Nursing Management*, *16*(8), 964–973. doi:10.1111/peps.12103

MacKillop, J., & Anderson, E. J. (2007). Further psychometric validation of the Mindful Attention Awareness Scale (MAAS). *Journal of Psychopathology and Behavioral Assessment*, *29*(4), 289–293. doi:10.1007/s10862-007-9045-1

Malinowski, P., & Lim, H. J. (2015). Mindfulness at work: Positive affect, hope, and optimism mediate the relationship between dispositional mindfulness, work engagement, and well-being. *Mindfulness*, *6* (6), 1250–1262. doi:10.1007/s12671-015-0388-5

Mandell, B., & Pherwani, S. (2003). Relationship between emotional intelligence and transformational leadership style: A gender comparison. *Journal of Business and Psychology*, *17*(3), 387–404. doi:10.1023/A:1022816409059

Mayer, J. D., Salovey, P., Caruso, D. R., & Sitarenios, G. (2001). Emotional intelligence as a standard intelligence. *Emotion*, *1*(3), 232–242. doi:10.1037///1528-3542.1.3.232

McCauley, C. D., Eastman, L. J., & Ohlott, P. J. (1995). Linking management selection and development through stretch assignments. *Human Resource Management*, *34*(1), 93–115. doi:10.1002/hrm.3930340107

Muthén, L. K., & Muthén, B. O. (2008). Mplus (Version 5.1). Los Angeles, CA: Muthén & Muthén.

Newport, C. (2016). *Deep work: Rules for focused success in a distracted world.* New York, NY: Grand Central Publishing.

Northouse, P. G. (2015). *Leadership: Theory and practice* (7th ed.). Thousand Oaks, CA: Sage.

O'Leonard, K., & Loew, L. (2012). *Leadership development factbook 2012: Benchmarks and trends in U.S. leadership development.* Oakland, CA: Bersin & Associates.

Ocasio, W. (2011). Attention to attention. *Organization Science*, *22*(5), 1286–1296. doi:10.1287/orsc.1100.0602

Palmer, B., Walls, M., Burgess, Z., & Stough, C. (2001). Emotional intelligence and effective leadership. *Leadership & Organization Development Journal*, *22*(1), 5–10. doi:10.1108/01437730110380174

Passmore, J., & Marianetti, O. (2007). The role of mindfulness in coaching. *The Coaching Psychologist*, *3*(3), 131–137.

Peer, E., Vosgerau, J., & Acquisti, A. (2014). Reputation as a sufficient condition for data quality on Amazon Mechanical Turk. *Behavior research methods*, *46*(4), 1023–1031. doi:10.3758/s13428-013-0434-y

Peter, L. J., & Hull, R. (1969). *The peter principle* (No. 04; RMD, PN6231. M2 P4). London: Souvenir Press.

Podsakoff, P. M., MacKenzie, S. B., Lee, J. Y., & Podsakoff, N. P. (2003). Common method biases in behavioral research: A critical review of the literature and recommended remedies. *Journal of Applied Psychology*, *88*(5), 879–903. doi:10.1037/0021-9010.88.5.879

Posner, M. I., & Petersen, S. E. (1990). The attention system of the human brain. *Annual Review of Neuroscience*, *13*(1), 25–42. doi:10.1146/annurev.ne.13.030190.000325

Potential Project. (2019). *Mindfulness training for leaders: Evaluation and technical report.* United States: Jason Beck.

Reb, J., Narayanan, J., & Chaturvedi, S. (2014). Leading mindfully: Two studies of the influence of supervisor trait mindfulness on employee well-being and performance. *Mindfulness*, *5*(1), 36–45. doi:10.1007/s12671-012-0144-z

Reb, J., Narayanan, J., Chaturvedi, S., & Ekkirala, S. (2017). The mediating role of emotional exhaustion in the relationship of mindfulness with turnover intentions and job performance. *Mindfulness*, *8*(3), 707–716. doi:10.1007/s12671-016-0648-z

Reb, J., Narayanan, J., & Ho, Z. W. (2015). Mindfulness at work: Antecedents and consequences of employee awareness and absent-mindedness. *Mindfulness*, *6*(1), 111–122. doi:10.1007/s12671-013-0236-4

Redick, T. S., & Engle, R. W. (2006). Working memory capacity and attention network test performance. *Applied Cognitive Psychology*, *20*(5), 713–721. doi:10.1002/acp.1224

Reinholdt-Dunne, M. L., Mogg, K., & Bradley, B. P. (2013). Attention control: Relationships between self-report and behavioural measures, and symptoms of anxiety and depression. *Cognition & Emotion*, *27*(3), 430–440. doi:10.1080/02699931.2012.715081

Roche, M., Haar, J. M., & Luthans, F. (2014). The role of mindfulness and psychological capital on the well-being of leaders. *Journal of Occupational Health Psychology*, *19*(4), 476–489. doi:10.1037/a0037183

Rosete, D., & Ciarrochi, J. (2005). Emotional intelligence and its relationship to workplace performance outcomes of leadership effectiveness. *Leadership & Organization Development Journal*, *26*(5), 388–399. doi:10.1108/01437730510607871

Rubin, R. S., Munz, D. C., & Bommer, W. H. (2005). Leading from within: The effects of emotion recognition and personality on transformational leadership behavior. *Academy of Management Journal*, *48*(5), 845–858.

Schutte, N. S., & Malouff, J. M. (2011). Emotional intelligence mediates the relationship between mindfulness and subjective well-being. *Personality and Individual Differences*, *50*(7), 1116–1119. doi:10.1016/j.paid.2011.01.037

Siegling, A. B., & Petrides, K. V. (2014). Measures of trait mindfulness: Convergent validity, shared dimensionality, and linkages to the five-factor model. *Frontiers in Psychology*, *5*, 1164. doi:10.3389/fpsyg.2014.01164

Stanton, N. A., Chambers, P. R. G., & Piggott, J. (2001). Situational awareness and safety. *Safety Science*, *39*(3), 189–204. doi:10.1016/S0925-7535(01)00010-8

Tabachnick, B. G., & Fidell, L. S. (2007). *Using multivariate statistics* (5th ed.). Boston: Allyn & Bacon/ Pearson Education.

Tejada, M., Scandura, T., & Pillai, R. (2001). The MLQ revisited. *Psychometric Properties and Recommendations.*, *12*(1), 31–52. doi:10.1016/S1048-9843(01)00063-7

Theeboom, T., Beersma, B., & van Vianen, A. E. (2014). Does coaching work? A meta-analysis on the effects of coaching on individual level outcomes in an organizational context. *The Journal of Positive Psychology*, *9*(1), 1–18. https://doi-org.ccl.idm.oclc.org/10.1080/17439760.2013.837499

Thera, N. (1962). *Satipatthana: The heart of Buddhist meditation: A handbook of mental training based on the Buddha's way of mindfulness*. New York, NY: Weiser.

Thoemmes, F., MacKinnon, D. P., & Reiser, M. R. (2010). Power analysis for complex mediational designs using Monte Carlo methods. *Structural Equation Modeling*, *17*(3), 510–534. doi:10.1080/10705511.2010.489379

Underhill, C. M. (2006). The effectiveness of mentoring programs in corporate settings: A meta-analytical review of the literature. *Journal of Vocational Behavior*, *68*(2), 292–307. doi:10.1016/j.jvb.2005.05.003

Wachs, K., & Cordova, J. V. (2007). Mindful relating: Exploring mindfulness and emotion repertoires in intimate relationships. *Journal of Marital and Family Therapy*, *33*(4), 464–481.

Wechsler, D. (1997) *Wechsler Adult Intelligence Scale* (3rd ed). [Measurement instrument]. San Antonio, TX: Pearson.

Weick, K. E., & Sutcliffe, K. M. (2001). *Managing the unexpected: Assuring high performance in an age of complexity*. San Francisco, CA: Jossey-Bass.

Whitaker, B. G., Dahling, J. J., & Levy, P. (2007). The development of a feedback environment and role clarity model of job performance. *Journal of Management*, *33*(4), 570–591. https://doi-org.ccl.idm.oclc.org/10.1177/0149206306297581

9

THE UNIVERSE'S DOORWAY

Long-term mindfulness as a way to leadership

Bena (Beth) Long

Introduction

> I would attribute to the practice [mindfulness] the ability to recognize when the universe wants something and you're the door.
>
> (*Organizational leader and long-term mindfulness practitioner*)

Thriving in continuous change, uncertainty, and the challenges of our time places demands upon effective human functioning as leaders. It also takes a great deal of skill to do the right thing, at the right time, for the right reasons. Mindfulness is playing a role in enabling leaders to access this ability of discernment along with many other benefits from the practice (Long, 2019). It has also become a recommended method for use by leaders and their organizations (Boyatzis & McKee, 2005; Gelles, 2015; Goleman, Boyatzis, & McKee, 2013). While mindfulness may be newly appearing in the mainstream work world, there are organizational leaders with 10 to 40 years' experience in mindfulness practice (George, 2010; Goleman & Davidson, 2017; Mackey & Sisodia, 2013; Tan, 2012). The leader-practitioners' voices of experience are brought forward with newly shared insights, meaningful applications, and the private revelations of their lived experiences in this research.

Leaders with long-term mindfulness—the literature

There are leaders who have been long-term practitioners of mindfulness and the information of their experiences can add a rich knowledge base to the field of organizational science and specifically leadership (Dane, 2011; Hyland, Lee, & Mills, 2015; Weick & Sutcliffe, 2006).

Mindfulness—attention and awareness

To gain a better sense of the concept of mindfulness, it is important to define the terms attention and awareness. Attention is the normal capability of functioning to focus in a one-pointed concentrative way or in an open and broad manner (Frizzell, Hoon,

Banner, 2016; Goleman, 1988; Hyland et al., 2015). When attention is focused and includes a meta-awareness, also known as witnessing awareness, that apprehends the current state of mind that is monitoring that focus, it becomes mindfulness. The integration of attention and awareness is how mindfulness is differentiated from other related states (Brown & Ryan, 2003; Dreyfus, 2011; Hyland et al., 2015). Mindfulness can occur whether an individual's focus is directed internally (e.g., thoughts, sensations, images) or externally (e.g., stimuli) (Brown & Ryan, 2003; Dane, 2011; Glomb, Duffy, Bono, & Yang, 2011; Goleman, 1988).

It is theorized that mindfulness's unique way of using attention is the primary cause of its impact on human functioning. It is further theorized that the impact on the human domains of cognition, emotion, behavior, and physiology then cascade into the workplace in the areas of performance, relationships, and well-being (Good et al., 2016).

Mindfulness's effects on human functioning occur primarily through attention and are researched in the areas of attentional stability, control, and efficiency. The studies on mindfulness demonstrated that it minimized mind-wandering and stabilized attention to the present (Brewer et al., 2011; Smallwood & Schooler, 2015). The minimization of mind-wandering and stabilization of attention to the present also has been shown as people's increased length of vigilance (Lykins & Baer, 2009; MacLean et al., 2010). The theory around why mindfulness is effective in this way is based on training in practices that purposefully attend to noticing of mind-wandering and then actively bringing the mind back to the present-moment focus (Good et al., 2016).

The control of attention is the ability to choose where attention is directed while experiencing competing demands. Research shows that meditators do not get lost in distractions and spend fewer attentional resources on distractions (Tang et al., 2007), and this is supported by neurological evidence of long-term meditators (Cahn, Delorme, & Polich, 2012).

In the literature, mindfulness is referred to in two prominent and frequent ways: (1) the use of attention and awareness to experience a quality of mind, or state of being; and (2) forms of practice that enable one to cultivate the quality and state (Hülsheger, Alberts, Feinholdt, & Lang, 2013; Kabat-Zinn, 2013; Purser & Milillo, 2015). To experience this state with greater regularity and reliability, most people need to perform some mindfulness practice for further cultivation (Kabat-Zinn, 2013; Weick & Putnam, 2006).

Definition of mindfulness

The most widely accepted and cited definition of mindfulness used by researchers is associated with the quality of consciousness as a state of being attentive and aware in the present moment (Brown & Ryan, 2003; Dane, 2011; Roche, Haar, & Luthans, 2014; Walsh & Shapiro, 2006). Mindfulness is also prominently referred to as a practice; in this way, mindfulness is considered a skill that can be developed (Bishop et al., 2004; Hülsheger et al., 2013; Kabat-Zinn, 2013; Purser & Milillo, 2015; Weick & Putnam, 2006). There can be formal practices in such forms as official organizational trainings, retreats, or personal practice (e.g., time spent and numbered repetitions). Along with informal situational mindfulness techniques (Miller, Fletcher, & Kabat-Zinn, 1995; Stanley & Jha, 2009; Stanley, Schaldach, Kiyonaga, & Jha, 2011), these practices cultivate the continuity of awareness into everyday life and work (Stanley & Jha, 2009; Stanley et al., 2011). Practitioners of mindfulness can come to practices that bring about being mindful from many possible cultural contexts, meditative traditions, or workplace interventions (Kabat-Zinn, 2013; Weick & Putnam, 2006).

Mindfulness and meditation

Some of the practices from the empirically tested Mindfulness-Based Stress Reduction (MBSR) program include body awareness, sitting meditation, and gentle yoga (Hyland et al., 2015; Lau et al., 2006). It is common for different practices to be available and beneficial as individuals may prefer some practices but not all (Christopher et al., 2011). The most common form of practice associated with the cultivation of mindfulness is the use of meditation (Gelles, 2015; Lau et al., 2006; Lomas, Ivtzan, & Fu, 2001; Roche et al., 2014). Mindfulness meditation and meditation in the broadest sense are ways of engaging the mind and share a common focus on the development of the skillful use of attention and awareness (Brown & Ryan, 2003; Dreyfus, 2011; Lomas et al., 2001) to improved voluntary control of mental processes (Dane & Brummel, 2014; Walsh & Shapiro, 2006). The state of being and quality of mind when continuously practiced can lead to attainment of skill at being mindful.

Some leaders are practitioners of mindfulness as meditation or forms of meditation (Gelles, 2015; Lomas et al., 2001; Roche et al., 2014). Meditation is traditionally relegated into two categories. It is concentrative, with a focused attention, or receptive, as in open monitoring (Lutz, Slagter, Dunne, & Davidson, 2008). Mindfulness meditation would be considered receptive (Frizzell et al., 2016) if it is unbiased attention and awareness to the moment without any focal point to return one's attention to. Meditation that is concentrative may make use of the breath, internal image, or internal sound (Nuernberger, 2003), and is also a common component of mindfulness programs such as MBSR. While mindfulness practices may contain concentrative meditations, it is important to note that in the literature, programs that train in practices such as focusing attention (e.g., on breath, image or sound, active everyday events like eating), open monitoring, and moving with attention (e.g., tai chi, chi gung, hatha yoga; Lutz et al., 2008) all involve daily practices that purposefully develop awareness of the flow of thought, emotion, sensation, and physiological reactions. An individual's cumulative experiences with the practices, such as lifetime meditation hours, are used synonymously for mindfulness (Good et al., 2016).

People come to practices that cultivate mindfulness for many reasons. Individuals who are long-term practitioners can be utilizing Western, secular, and/or Eastern forms of mindfulness. General motivations for practicing included self-regulation, self-exploration, and self-liberation (Lykins & Baer, 2009); improved task functioning (Weick & Sutcliffe, 2006); stress management, mental peace, improved concentration, and/or greater emotional discipline (Kabat-Zinn, 2013); deepening empathy and compassion in hopes of ending suffering (Goleman, 1988; Shapiro, 2009); and even seeking the spiritual, enlightenment, and beyond (Lykins & Baer, 2009). These paths to practicing mindfulness are unique even if practitioners may share one similar intended or unintended outcome of being mindful.

Neuroscience and long-term mindfulness practitioners

Neuroscientific studies utilizing technology, such as fMRI in brain science, provided viable examples to specifically reference expert meditators or long-term practice. Some findings have shown that expert meditators have increased brain activity patterns that are consistent for sustained attention (Good et al., 2016) and a reduction in neural network activity indicated for mind-wandering (Brewer et al., 2011). These expert meditators require less effort to direct their attention (Tang, Holzel, & Posner, 2015). Brain scans show that fewer resources are used in the areas linked to executive attention (Kozasa et al., 2012; Lutz et al.,

2008). Long-term meditators are less distractible (Cahn et al., 2012) and experience with meditation has links to convergent, divergent thinking, and creativity (Colzato, Szapora, & Hommel, 2012). Mindfulness dampens emotional reactivity (Brown, Goodman, & Inzlicht, 2012; Desbordes et al., 2012; Taylor et al., 2011) and slower declines in fluid intelligence (Gard, Hölzel, & Lazar, 2014). They have also shown brain changes associated with neuroplasticity, including the shrinking of the amygdala (Holzel et al., 2011). Based on the research, it appears that the benefits of long-term practice in mindfulness are substantial. This is important to consider as mindfulness is utilized within the workplace and over the long term.

Long-term mindfulness in the workplace

For greater clarity on how mindfulness is related to the workplace, several theories are considered. Within the context of managerial and organizational cognition (MOC), it is assumed an individual is goal-directed and using the aforementioned conceptual thinking to be fully in a mode of doing (Walsh, 1995) in the workplace. Conceptual processing (thinking) is a theory (Langer, 1989; Walsh, 1999) that is at the core of organizational life. Conceptual processing dominates daily work-life as a person evaluates, interprets, and judges their perceptions. But when the thinking turns upon itself with personal importance, it can turn into bias (Watkins, 2008) and forms of rumination and worry. These are negative aspects of conceptual processing. The psychological conceptual process associated with MOC is goal-oriented doing and is most often contrasted with the state of being aware and attentive in the moment without conceptualizing, also known as being (Brown, Ryan, & Creswell, 2007). Being is neither actively doing in a physical sense nor doing as the act of thinking. The concept of experiential processing is considered a state of being and being is the state that mindfulness is known for (Brown et al., 2007; Good et al., 2016).

Mindfulness allows for attention to be internal or external and also allows for attention to stimulus without making meaning of it because one is not actively conceptualizing. Mindfulness instead is viewing thoughts as thoughts within a wider context of awareness. As presented in the new research of Lyddy and Good (2017), these two cognitive modes of being and doing present a new possibility for differences in how mindfulness practitioners are functioning in the workplace. Specifically, because they are both being and doing as in a continuity, not separate modes (Good et al., 2016). If there is compatibility between being and doing modes, there may be benefits seen in the range of organizational activities that require doing mode (Lyddy & Good, 2017). Individuals with long-term mindfulness practices have the potential to cultivate being mindful while doing, a continuity of being mindful during their work. As a long-term mindfulness practitioner explains:

> I don't see how I would…be mindful and have it separate [from my work]. It's part of my life, part of who I am…I don't know how you could…not bring it to work. When I started meditating, it was a separate experience…I would…focus my mind. The rest of the time…I just went back to everyday life…So now when I sit in meditation, it's no different than when I'm not sitting in meditation…There's a continuity…it's not a separate thing…No matter what…that presence is still there.
>
> *(Lyddy & Good, 2017, p. 11)*

The research has shown that there can be fluctuation between the cognitive states of being and doing as well as the continuity of functioning with these two modes active at the same time (Lyddy & Good, 2017). With long-term practice, mindfulness may be experienced with regularity and may be present in continuity for leaders.

Leadership models and mindfulness

Although a clear and concise definition of leaders that are applying mindfulness is elusive, it has surfaced within frameworks such as authentic leadership (George, 2010), resonant leadership (Boyatzis & McKee, 2005; Goleman et al., 2013), servant leadership (Verdorfer, 2016), and contemplative management (Lyddy & Good, 2017). For the purpose of the study, the term "leader-practitioners" is used because it implies these are leaders who actively engage in practices to cultivate attention and awareness. The implications of purposeful cultivation hold even more promise in the benefits of mindfulness.

The resonant leadership, authentic leadership (George, 2010), and servant leadership (Verdorfer, 2016) models suggested that mindfulness is one way to make a major difference in performance and asserts that mindfulness is a means to developing emotional intelligence (Boyatzis & McKee, 2005; Goleman et al., 2013). Articulated as a possible mechanism to emotional intelligence through the neurological effects of such practice (Lippincott, 2016), emotional intelligence is the ability for the individual to monitor feelings and emotions that are their own and discriminate between their own emotions and others' while using the information to guide thinking and actions (Goleman et al., 2013; Lippincott, 2016). Pragmatically, leaders are integrating these practices for themselves and their organizations. Taking these theories into practice, organizations such as Aetna Insurance, Google, Mayo Clinic, and even the US Army are implementing aspects of mindfulness (Lutz, Jha, Dunne, & Saron, 2015; West et al., 2014; Wolever et al., 2012).

Practitioners of mindfulness who are in or have been in organizational leadership roles are at the forefront of leader-practitioner application of these theories. They are living mindfulness in their everyday lives and are a valuable resource into their impact within the context of everyday workplace, life, and organizational leadership. These leader-practitioners have long-term practice experience. We are only recently learning about their use of these practices. Some who have spoken about practicing include: Goldman Sachs Group Inc. supervisory board member William George, who was also the past CEO of Medtronic (George, 2010); Green Mountain Coffee Roasters Inc.'s founder Robert Stiller; Ramani Ayers, former Chairman and CEO of Hartford Financial Services Group, has engaged in practices for more than 25 years; along with Ray Dalio, CEO of the hedge fund Bridgewater Associates, who has practiced for more than 40 years (George, 2010). These are just some well-known examples of leader-practitioners that have direct experience with mindfulness.

Methods

Data collection

Participants interviewed were working, titled mid- to senior-level organizational leaders. The sample included participants with a minimum of ten continuous years with at least three times a week of mindfulness practice. Participants completed semi-structured interviews of 60–90 minutes. Interviews were conducted virtually via online audio and video services. This utilized a purposive and snowball recruiting process via LinkedIn and mindfulness online groups. There were 21 respondents to the initial recruitment letters. Four individuals were disqualified based on research criteria. Three individuals that did qualify dropped out after the initial phone meeting before the research interviewing took place. Of the 14 participants that were interviewed, the snowball process brought 5 of the 14 people to the study through other people. Of the 14 analyzed interviews, 6 participants were male, 8 were female. Participants had varying mindfulness backgrounds, number of years spent meditating, and types of meditative practices conducted. They also filled diverse industries, such as technology, manufacturing, hospitality, food manufacturing, healthcare, consulting, financial services, pharmaceuticals, management consulting, education, and media. Two of the 14 participants were outside the United States and the remaining 12 were from across the country.

Data analysis

Interviews in this phenomenological study illuminated the lived experience of a shared phenomenon (Husserl, 1962; Moustakas, 1994): the experience of leaders with a long-term mindfulness practice and its impact upon their leadership.

The first analysis began with a complete and thorough reading of each interview's verbatim transcript. Approaches to uncovering and isolating core aspects of the phenomenon include: (1) holistic, (2) selective, or (3) detailed line-by-line readings (van Manen, 1990). The second analysis was conducted using the holistic method. Then analysis continued with reading through each transcript to identify the significant statements followed by line-by-line coding, in which the coding was arranged to expose patterns that emerged as themes. Data saturation occurred by this level of analysis. The use of quantity of references per parent node determined the order of importance of the overall themes. The next stage combined and reduced the data to non-overlapping patterns through rereading all of the verbatim quotes per theme. Further analysis revealed that all parent nodes qualify as final themes because they are represented within all participant interview data, as shown by having relevance through direct quotes attributable to all 14 of the participants. These all became the final themes.

Findings

The findings of the study consisted of five themes found in the data of all 14 participants. The themes were: (1) constructive outcomes, (2) amplified awareness, (3) leadership development, (4) enhanced relationships, and (5) conscious decision-making.

Finding 1: constructive outcomes

The first finding showed that for all participants, mindfulness produced both positive and negative aspects that were all considered constructive for their leadership. These leaders were in positions that needed to influence, delegate, make decisions, develop people and relationships, and perform effectively, and the data showed beneficial influence of mindfulness on these leadership needs. Results revealed that due to increased present-centered attention, participants became less self-centered. Participants improved their ability to think more broadly, reflect, listen, and collaborate with others; some described the change as becoming an instrument through which leadership flows. With over 30 years of mindfulness practice, this executive explained a mature stage of mindfulness and leadership:

> I know that the work that I'm doing as a leader. . .it's not about me anyway, I'm simply an instrument. So, if I can find that place, which I can do fairly well with practice, I'm simply—sometimes it's called a hollow reed, I think of myself as a straw. . .through which the work flows. . .simply from practice. . . and practice being consciousness, meditation, breathing. . . for me, practice and leadership are aligned one hundred percent.

As expressed by participants, their professional roles affected a lot of people. So, they made sure they paid attention and took action from a state as present-centered, balanced, and unbiased as possible. The shared outcomes participants exhibited were potentially attributable to their development of the present-centered attention, indicative of being mindful (Bishop et al., 2004; Brown & Ryan, 2003; Kabat-Zinn, 2003).

For the field of organizational development in particular, leaders' use of mindfulness practice aligns well as a potential means to develop one's use of self, also known as self as instrument. The developing construct, as Jaimeson, Auron, and Schectman (2017) described, is self-awareness and the ability to "interpret what's going on as clearly as possible [and] take action appropriate to the situation [where] every Use-of-Self is instrumental in executing our role" (p. 9). Mindfulness practice, as in the findings of the study, impact leadership through a resultant increase in self-regulation and self-observation, which can improve clarity and objectivity (Shapiro, Carlson, Astin, & Freedman, 2006; Tsui & Ashford, 1994). Participants' specific stories illustrated the beneficial outcomes of the integration of mindfulness into their leadership. For instance, many participants elaborated on the way mindfulness enabled them to go from: distracted impatience and irritability in a high-pressure work environment to more patience, and from light-heartedness and better listening skills, while still achieving their goals. They linked the shift to situations that improved their leadership effectiveness in client development, developing positive long-term business relationships, leading through modeling behaviors, mentoring, and coaching; developing trust with others within the company at all levels, and conscious decision-making. Findings supported the range of benefits in human functioning (Good et al., 2016), improved quality and outcomes of work life (Glomb et al., 2011; Reb, Sim, Chintakananda, Bhave, 2015), and improved workplace functioning (Lutz et al., 2015; West et al., 2014; Wolever et al., 2012).

Finding 2: amplified awareness

The increased and improved self-awareness contributed to greater authentic leadership. With deepened development of witnessing awareness, the results showed minimization in thoughtless reactivity. Participants became better at handling difficult conversations and trained themselves to think in new ways, gaining fresh perspectives. The enhancement of awareness using intention was also indicated for directing focus to achieve goals. Awareness ultimately afforded participants the improved ability to respond from a state of calm objectivity.

The data was consistent across all participants for amplification of awareness, both internally and externally. The ability of deliberate action was shown in the data. For example, one participant expressed the importance of being aware and self-managing to not lead from a place of fear: "Fear is a huge issue in business and to the extent that you can get on top of your daily fears. . .life is just so much easier to lead and to manage to different ideas." The study findings exemplified the benefits of mindfulness as the quality of consciousness as a state of being attentive and aware in the present moment (Brown & Ryan, 2003; Dane, 2011; Roche et al., 2014; Walsh & Shapiro, 2006).

Determined by its emphasis on awareness specific to the development of self-awareness, Avolio and Gardner (2005) suggested authentic leaders are self-aware and utilize unbiased processing, have clarity in behaviors, and relational authenticity that strengthens the exchange relationship between leader and followers. Participants were self-aware and spoke of recognizing their own thoughts and feelings in a moment, as well as awareness of the situation they were in. Often the stakes are high for leaders and, as these participants showed, if they are aware of the present moment and act consciously, as one participant stated, "I'm giving 100% in that moment. . .I know that if I'm showing up that has an effect on other people. . .It's just contagious. . .in a meeting or decision process."

The study's findings, as they related to connecting mindfulness and authentic leadership, started with the shared component of awareness. Mindfulness is a means to achieving such awareness (Brown & Ryan, 2003; Kabat-Zinn, 1994; Roche et al., 2014). Whereas authentic leadership is the effect that mindfulness can cultivate through the development of awareness, awareness is the way authentic leadership is enabled. The participants experienced present-moment attention and witnessing awareness, and it is through this experience that self-awareness is facilitated. Self-awareness becomes the means for greater clarity and self-disclosure, qualities sought in authentic relationships (George, 2010; Reb et al., 2015). The relationships are then grounded in unbiased processing on behalf of the authentic leader, as the leader influences follower outcomes through developmental feedback and supports the self-determination of followers (Ilies, Morgeson, & Nahrgang, 2005).

Finding 3: leadership development

The overarching importance of the finding was in the participants' abilities to be the change they wanted, to maintain calm clarity and objectivity amidst complexity and the unknowns. Participants did for themselves, and consequently influenced others with their calm presence. These results also showed a loosening of the grip on control and reduction or elimination micro-management as a result. Ultimately the participants, to varying degrees, freed themselves from identifying with all of their thoughts. The freedom allowed them to playfully explore many perspectives and do things differently.

Leading change and being flexible may share similar enhancements because of mindfulness practice. Teasdale and Chaskalson (2011) suggested that there are mechanisms by which mindfulness practice helps leaders to be less caught in their patterned behavioral responses. The distancing from reactivity helped participants to filter their emotions and thoughts before acting on them. As one participant acknowledged, he used to get "angry" and "swear" at clients figuratively in his mind for days or weeks when things did not go his way. Through practice he was no longer as reactive and was able to act differently than he would in the past. His personal growth affected his leadership as he effectively became the change he was leading.

Shapiro et al. (2006) presented a theory of how mindfulness enables change. It is thought to occur through psychological distance from thoughts, feelings, and sensations. Many of the challenges that leaders face exceed their ability to perceive, understand, and adapt within their current contexts (Kegan & Lahey, 2010). Mindfulness practice enables leaders to disidentify themselves and shift perspectives, resulting in enhanced clarity in the present moment. As one executive acknowledged the positive role that engaging in long-term practice played in his leadership development:

> I had some of those moments, if not hours in the middle of momentous decisions for that corporation, huge global corporation. . .I think what allowed me to get to the point of [staying] on my own terms and not being cowed, I think I got there because of the yoga journey.

The personal shift in perspective, as the literature showed, goes by many names: witnessing awareness, reperceiving, decentering, de-automatization (Shapiro et al., 2006). The shift in perspective benefits leaders for its ability to not get caught in automatic perception or cognition. With a shift in perspective, such as psychological distancing, the subject of the mind becomes the object of witnessing awareness (Kegan, 1982). Developing awareness of thoughts and emotions within oneself is a maturity of development as expressed in the theory of self (Kegan, 1982). This maturing of self seems to be accelerated through the increasing capacity for personal objectivity through the use of mindfulness practice. As an individual observes the contents of their mind through witnessing awareness with greater capacity, the very act of observing of the contents loosens the grip of identification with it. As one participant explained, witnessing awareness enabled her to engage in "new performance" and "new relationships with your co-workers and entire organization." She could witness thoughts enough to play with them without the grip of identity. The participant's previous control over everything led to micro-managing, and she suffered the consequences of needing to "know everything about everything." Her practice changed the behavior and she was able to act differently.

When thoughts, emotions, and sensations can be witnessed, the observer recognizes that there is separation between the three; as a result, thoughts become less muddied by who they belong to. Another participant had a shift in his perspective because of his experience with mindfulness practice: "There's a place where you go where you don't have any more thoughts and it's sound and breath. And I think that's Nirvana." The ability to detach led to the notion that one must be more than the content of what one witnesses (Shapiro et al., 2006). Their new openness enabled participants to develop self-trust and trust in others, even under difficult changing situations. As one participant stated, "that essential person is really just my nature," and all mental constructs of role, title, pressure, or judgment "just washed away and what was left was not just my own essential nature, but just the essence of the moment." As presented by Kegan (1982), the enhanced ability of disidentification with the contents of the mind also commonly promotes a corresponding shift in the sense of self. The conception of a homogenous, stable self is eventually reconceived as a collection of ever-changing concepts, images, sensations, and beliefs (Kegan, 1982). The present awareness develops into witnessing awareness. As a mindfulness practitioner stands back from his inner commentary about life and the related experiences, he also strengthens his ability to witness his own story: who and what he is. The findings showed participants transformed themselves in a positive way through self-development. They increased internal capacities, such as expanded perceptual capacity, self-management, and self-direction (Csikszentmihalyi & Rathunde, 1993). The ability to change perspective of oneself and self-identity enabled the participants to lead and grow as leaders in new ways.

Finding 4: enhanced relationships

Overall, the results showed relationships improved by the development of greater empathy and emotional intelligence. Results showed the influence of mindfulness practice on the importance of their business relationships: "I learned how important it is to have so many good relationships. Relationships are key to business." The data showed that there was 100% significance in the enhancement of relationships. Participants spoke of their relationships being "much more pleasant," "trusting," and "authentic" as a result of their mindfulness practice (Goleman, Boyatzis & McKee, 2001). These relationships involved clients, bosses and colleagues, direct reports, project team members, and others within the workplace, creating a better-quality work environment (Glomb et al., 2011; Reb, Narayanan, & Ho, 2015).

The results in the findings showed that due to mindfulness practice, all the participants experienced improvement in the quality of their business relationships. However, the data showed that all participants began mindfulness practice for personal, as opposed to company-minded, reasons. According to Reichard and Johnson (2011), self-development may begin with the self-initiated action of the leader, whose primary goal is often to develop their personal leadership skills; participants initially came to mindfulness practice because they were thinking of themselves and their performance. After they gained mindfulness proficiency, they turned their improved attention to understanding, helping, and guiding others at work. As a participant stated, "Well as you get deeper and deeper into the journey, I think it just impacts you emotionally and behaviorally and certainly physically more and more."

It is significant that a positive, unintended consequence of self-development is that it raises the collective potential of the organization to which the leader belongs (Reichard & Johnson, 2011; Bohm, 2013). A participant's story exemplified the enhancements to relationships. He began his leadership in relationship to his executive team strictly as a transactional relationship. He would receive assignments and get results. He also felt like a "tool" of the organization that pushed projects through. Then he shifted his perspective. He described how if he approached a project in the old way it would get done, but that with his new approach, he was less likely to create other problems to solve because of improved relationships. This way of thinking reflects the shift in leadership style from transactional to transformational Avolio and Gardner (2005). His personal objectives were not so bound in personal identity and became more like objects that were distinct from his self-identity (Kuhnert & Lewis, 1987). The objective distancing opened the possibility of having empathy for and coordinating with others, which enabled him to make accommodations in his relationships.

Another aspect of relationship that saw improvement was around the participants' empathy. One participant stated, "I believe that I have a very special relationship with my clients because I have a lot of empathy. And I think that that is something that has been developed over the years because of my practice." In her case, the very success of her business was tested as business conditions changed and clients could have opted out of her services. In the end, "Because of my good relationships [with clients]" they chose to continue to give her their business (Boyatzis & McKee, 2005; Goleman, 1998; Lippincott, 2016).

Finding 5: conscious decision-making

Conscious decision-making was the beneficial improvement in doing the right thing at the right time for the right reasons. Decision-making was imbued with awareness that fostered objectivity, clarity within the complexity, holding the paradoxes of great diversity of perspectives, and maximizing benefit for the greater good.

Decision-making is an integral component of leadership and it appeared within all of the interview participants' data. The range expressed by the participants included decision-making that both minimized self-interest and considered the farthest-reaching consequences of their decision. Leaders aimed to be consistently reliable in their decision-making so they would retain the trust and professional relations with all involved.

With mindfulness practice, leaders acquired a much broader sense of identity and responsibility that included something much larger than themselves. They considered the environment and humanity. They made decisions with the intention of consciously being in harmony with the decision, moment, and life. For some, the results of this intention yielded a literal experience of doing the right thing, at the right time, for the right reasons, and was very difficult to put into words. Some called it a non-dual experience, harmony, being supported by angels and/or sages, and the undeniable. As one participant stated, "I think those miracles happen because of the harmony that you are with life and nature and so, for me, that is one of the most important things about meditation."

It transformed the experience of decision-making into one that held great certainty and no doubt. Being able to make complex decisions with such conviction while experiencing a deep state of being and objectivity was greatly prized by participants (Brown et al., 2007; Good et al., 2016; Weick & Putnam, 2006). Going beyond the limitations of conceptual ideas about people and act from knowledge of what the right action was (Purser & Milillo, 2015) is described as a result of such objectivity by this participant, "when you're dealing with people genuinely and in a present way. You know what the right thing to do is and you do it." The description encompassed more than the thinking before deciding; it included non-thinking instinctual and intuitive capacities (Nuernberger, 2003). The description is also being while doing (Lyddy & Good, 2017).

These experiences led participants, as the findings mentioned, to a preferred way to make decisions: from a state of being as calm, relaxed, centered, and as unbiased as possible. In these states of being, participants' decision-making was perceived to be clearer and more likely to result in the best decision possible. Also, in making the decision, the findings showed the importance participants placed on getting stakeholders' input and multiple perspectives. Divorcing the decision from personal interests also allowed leaders to better defend their decision. The capacity was intentionally developed, as one participant stated:

> As long as what I was arguing for was in the best interest of the company and presuming, we're in concert with the best interest of society...and that it wasn't about me, or my group, or anything that was mine...They could disagree with my position but, they couldn't disagree with my motives.

The objectivity went so far as to warrant statements such as acknowledging that the work goes beyond oneself as the decision-maker, "I know that the work that I'm doing as a leader. It's not about me anyway...I'm simply an instrument." Some had a keen ability to differentiate when something was limited to self-centeredness, to minimizing bias or if it was beyond the self. As another participant explained:

> I would attribute to the practice is the ability to recognize when the universe wants something and you're the door and it's supporting you completely versus something where it's yourself trying to make it happen because of some ego... something you really want to get done. [When it's self-centered] ...I call it...glitching out.

As the previous example illustrated, the participant does not specifically label the experience as spiritual. It is important to note that most of the participants did not specifically state they had a practice of spiritual mindfulness. However, participants' observations were in most agreement with research on spiritual leadership. The literature defined spiritual mindfulness as "mindful inner consciousness" (Petchsawang & Duchon, 2012, p. 191) that transcends an individual's ordinary life (Dhiman, 2009). Conscious decision-making is also the expressed experience deemed "undeniable" and a "visceral reality" by a participant. Other participants have stated that the skill provided resources for their leadership. This is the acknowledgement of resources as a leader that are the energy of the wisdom of "sages," "being part of something bigger," and having the experience, which as several participants described as a "universal access point," "universal connection," and a "universal mind." Another term for the experience as stated is a spirituality that has no religious context (Marques, Dhiman, & Biberman, 2011). One participant described how being in harmony both brings opportunities and possibly manifests them: "I think those miracles happen because of the harmony that you are with life and nature and so, for me, that is one of the most important things of meditation." For others, their leadership is an experience of a quality of energy that is like being a vessel for what actions need to take place in the moment. This is an experience of "the universe calls." Or, as another shared, the view of being a leader reacting to external, immovable factors, and commented:

> One of the things that I love with the ocean and the mountains is there is that same magic of "go with the flow" that is the same dynamic that shows letting a pair of skis slide, riding a wave, or sailing on a boat. There is that same dynamism. . .my practice as a leader. . .it's 100% real and undeniable in terms of "go."

Conscious decision-making is also the ability to enter a state of being where one can do things differently and create what did not exist before. The ability builds an awareness of the resources in being part of something much larger than one person as an experience. It also manifests environments and opportunities with the clarity to recognize and act upon them. As articulated by a participant on the aspect of conscious decision-making who stated that:

> mindfulness can allow you to do things that you never thought that you could. So, we talked about moving mountains. We were the first. We never published it. . .we could not talk about it, but it was the right thing to do and we paid it forward.

To consider these well-supported findings further, the literature presented a connection between mindfulness, leadership, and adult development theory (Kegan, 1982). Mindfulness practice improved the participants' ability to change perspective through witnessing awareness in their observation of inner experiences. Participants' resulting distanced sense of self may have cultivated their ability to consider all stakeholders and promoted a deeper concern for a decision's broader impact. The ability, as shown in the results, may correlate most to the highest level of adult maturity. At this level, it is said that the person does not need to enforce their values upon others. Those at this level have enough personal observational capacity that they can let go of their preferred, ego-driven choice for the benefit of putting others and the organization first (Phipps, 2010). These results are further supported by the research of Jim Collins (2001), where the highest level attainable in his leadership style system (levels 1–5) is the leader who is able to hold paradox. The holding of all the contradictory and diverse positions of stakeholders, society, and the world makes for a leader who functions with great humility. The findings supported the research and indicated that through the mindfulness-enhanced maturation, long-term mindfulness practitioners may have a purposeful process advantage in their leadership development and decision-making.

Conclusion

Leaders with a long-term mindfulness practice from the study exhibited a developmental trajectory that both integrated and expanded the use of attention and awareness. The interview participants were leaders with long-term mindfulness practice, and they had both a strong sense of self and the ability to suspend their personal needs. They developed a mature ability of witnessing awareness that was involved in the development and change in their self-awareness, relationships, and decision-making. In the context of leadership styles, they exhibited higher levels of attainment in authentic leadership, transformational leadership, servant leadership, and level 5 leadership. The link between mindfulness practice and leadership is attributed to the component of mindfulness known as witnessing awareness. Mindfulness practice can present a consistent means of leadership change and development that matures an individual over time, on purpose, and with consistency thanks to long-term practice.

With deeper and consistent practice, awareness can be amplified to a degree that opens the leader to a fresh perspective. From that perspective, the leader witnesses and observes in a manner that enables the contents of the mind to become data for leadership's needs. Areas important to leaders' decision-making, presence, and relationships all are benefited by practice. Of greatest potential for real-world application, exemplified in the study, is the capacity for leaders to consciously make decisions and develop relationships which benefit the organization along with many others involved. Mindfulness benefits the individual who practices and those they lead. A mindful leader becomes a better leader because of the constructive outcomes cultivated. This is especially evident in long-term practitioners who purposefully and consistently cultivate being mindful. These leader-practitioners with long-term mindfulness practice are worthy of continued study.

Five chapter takeaways

1. Mindfulness at work has garnered empirical evidence that supports its positive impact and the state of mindfulness can be cultivated through practice.
2. Long-term mindfulness practice yields significant constructive outcomes for leaders.
3. Leadership development is enhanced through psychological distance supported by long-term mindfulness.
4. Mindfulness supports maturing into higher levels of leadership styles such as authentic leadership, transformational leadership, servant leadership, and level 5 leadership.
5. Decision-making is enhanced by long-term mindfulness practice.

Five reflection questions

1. Based on the research, participants' long-term mindfulness had constructive outcomes for their leadership. In what ways can the workplace support the use of mindfulness for the long term? Should it?
2. Leaders in the study chose to practice mindfulness personally. Should mindfulness be utilized specifically inside work for leadership development? If so, what should be done for people who are not interested and do not want to do it?
3. There is ample room for continued research of mindfulness and leadership and especially of long-term leader-practitioners in the workplace. What in the culture of work can support these leaders to share more of their knowledge and experience?
4. Mindfulness is an enhancing factor in leadership style development, maturing sense of self, relationship development, and decision-making, yet it is not known if there are particular practices that place advantage on bringing this about. What research could help differentiate the impact of practices that bring about the state of being mindful?
5. If all leaders were practitioners of mindfulness, how could the world of work be different?

References

Avolio, B. J., & Gardner, W. L. (2005). Authentic leadership development: Getting to the root of positive forms of leadership. *The Leadership Quarterly*, *16*, 315–338. doi:10.1016/j/leaqua.2005.03.001

Bishop, S. R., Lau, M., Shapiro, S., Carlson, L., Anderson, N. D., Carmody, J., . . . Devins, G. (2004). Mindfulness: A proposed operational definition. *Clinical Psychology: Science and Practice*, *11*(3), 230–241. Retrieved from https://s3.amazonaws.com/academia.edu.documents/38930481/mindfulness- _a_proposed_operational_definition.pdf?AWSAccessKeyId=AKIAIWOWYYGZ 2Y53UL3A&Expires=1523458871&Signature=j%2F9yHV50zliSuUkKG2K8LSZqt0g%3D&response-content-osition=inline%3B%20filename%3DMindfulness- _a_proposed_operational_defi.pdf

Bohm, D. (2013). *On dialogue*. London, United Kingdom: Routledge.

Boyatzis, R., & McKee, A. (2005). *Resonant leadership: Renewing yourself and connecting with others through mindfulness, hope and compassion*. Boston, MA: Harvard Business Press.

Brewer, J. A., Worhunsky, P. D., Gray, J. R., Tang, Y. Y., Weber, J., & Kober, H. (2011). Meditation experience is associated with differences in default mode network activity and connectivity. *Proceedings of the National Academy of Sciences*, *108*(50), 20254–20259. Retrieved from www.researchgate.net/profile/Judson_Brewer/publication/51825876_Medi tation_Experience_Is_Associated_with_Differences_in_Default_Mode_Network_ Activity_and_Connectivity/links/0fcfd4fb52b48517e1000000/Meditation- Experience-Is-Associated-with-Differences-in-Default-Mode-Network-Activity- and-Connectivity.pdf

Brown, K. W., Goodman, R. J., & Inzlicht, M. (2012). Dispositional mindfulness and the attenuation of neural responses to emotional stimuli. *Social Cognitive and Affective Neuroscience*, *8*(1), 93–99.

Brown, K. W., & Ryan, R. M. (2003). The benefits of being present: Mindfulness and its role in psychological well-being. *Journal of Personality & Social Psychology*, *84*(4), 822–848. doi:10.1037/0022-3514.84.4.822

Brown, K. W., Ryan, R. M., & Creswell, J. D. (2007). Mindfulness: Theoretical foundations and evidence for its salutary effects. *Psychological Inquiry*, *18*(4), 211–237. Retrieved from www.jstor.org/stable/20447389?casa_token=SYc9IPI7JqEAAAAA:esrhu9s 5MKZIg64fjObGmEU493wbbCnlt_iBekevONqHQpph_gw40vxecZw1NKog875 qxy3GXSydhnIDEy8dBVk_HHFUgA3LcSiXRa-jk7jHt60_ECs&seq=1#page_scan_tab_contents

Cahn, B. R., Delorme, A., & Polich, J. (2012). Event-related delta, theta, alpha and gamma correlates to auditory oddball processing during Vipassana meditation. *Social Cognitive and Affective Neuroscience*, *8* (1), 100–111. doi:10.1093/scan/nss060

Christopher, J. C., Chrisman, J. A., Trotter-Mathison, M. J., Schure, M. B., Dahlen, P., & Christopher, S. B. (2011). Perceptions of the long-term influence of mindfulness training on counselors and psychotherapists: A qualitative inquiry. *Journal of Humanistic Psychology*, *51*(3), 318–349. Retrieved from 49.pdfx?AWSAccessKeyId=AKIAIWOWYYGZ2Y53UL3A&Expires=15233893 75&Si gnature=6 ryxY4%2BVZTpoxV123yWDkc4Up4k%3D&response-content- disposition=inline%3B%20filename% 3DPerceptions_of_the_long-t erm_influence_o.pdf

Collins, J. (2001). *Good to Great.* New York, NY: Harper, Collins.

Colzato, L. S., Szapora, A., & Hommel, B. (2012). Meditate to create: The impact of focused- attention and open-monitoring training on convergent and divergent thinking. *Frontiers in Psychology*, *3*, 116. doi:10.3389/fpsyg.2012.00116

Csikszentmihalyi, M., & Rathunde, K. (1993). The measurement of flow in everyday life: Toward a theory of emergent motivation. In J. E. Jacobs (Ed.), *Current theory and research in motivation, Vol. 40. Nebraska symposium on motivation, 1992: Developmental perspectives on motivation* (pp. 57–97). Lincoln, NE, US: University of Nebraska Press. https://psycnet.apa.org/record/1993-98639-002

Dane, E. (2011). Paying attention to mindfulness and its effects on task performance in the workplace. *Journal of Management*, *37*(4), 997–1018. doi:10.1177/0149206310367948

Dane, E., & Brummel, B. J. (2014). Examining workplace mindfulness and its relations to job performance and turnover intention. *Human Relations*, *67*(1), 105–128. Retrieved from www.research gate.net/profile/Bradley_Brummel/publication/280292518_Exami ning_workplace_mindfulness_an d_its_relations_to_job_performance_and_turnover_i ntention/links/563276f108aefa44c368519d.pdf

Desbordes, G., Negi, L. T., Pace, T. W., Wallace, B. A., Raison, C. L., & Schwartz, E. L. (2012). Effects of mindful-attention and compassion meditation training on amygdala response to emotional stimuli in an ordinary, non-meditative state. *Frontiers in Human Neuroscience*, *6*, 292. doi:10.3389/ fnhum.2012.00292

Dhiman, S. (2009). Mindfulness in life and leadership: An explanatory survey. *Interbeing*, *3*(1), 55–80. Retrieved from https://search.proquest.com/openview/767ec7b38943db8a59a90660949daba7/1?p q- origsite=gscholar&cbl=52509

Dreyfus, G. (2011). Is mindfulness present-centred and non-judgmental? A discussion of the cognitive dimensions of mindfulness. *Contemporary Buddhism*, *12*(01), 41–54. Retrieved from http://avani-yoga.co.uk/wp-content/uploads/2016/09/Mindfulness_-Diverse-Perspectives-on-Its-M-J.-Mark-G.-Williams.pdf#page=45

Farb, N. A., Segal, Z. V., Mayberg, H., Bean, J., McKeon, D., Fatima, Z., et al (2007). Attending to the present: Mindfulness meditation reveals distinct neural modes of self-reference. *Social Cognitive Affective Neuroscience*, *2*(4), 313–322. doi:10.1093/scan/nsm030

Frizzell, D. A., Hoon, S., & Banner, D. K. (2016). A phenomenological investigation of leader development and mindfulness meditation. *Journal of Social Change*, *8*(1). Retrieved from http://scholar works.waldenu.edu/cgi/viewcontent.cgi?article=1118&context=jsc

Gard, T., Hölzel, B. K., & Lazar, S. W. (2014). The potential effects of meditation on age- related cognitive decline: A systematic review. *Annals of the New York Academy of Sciences*, *1307*(1), 89–103. doi:10.1111/nyas.12348

Gelles, D. (2015). *Mindful work: How meditation is changing business from the inside out.* New York, NY: Houghton Mifflin Harcourt Publishing Company.

George, B. (2010). *True north: Discover your authentic leadership.* San Francisco, CA: John Wiley & Sons.

Glomb, T. M., Duffy, M. K., Bono, J. E., & Yang, T. (2011). Mindfulness at work. In *Research in personnel and human resources management* (pp. 115–157). Emerald Group Publishing Limited. Retrieved from http://institut-mindfulness.be/wp- content/uploads/2015/01/Mindfulness-at-work.-Research-in-Personnel-and- Human-Resources-Management.pdf

Goleman, D. (1988). *The meditative mind: The varieties of meditative experience.* New York, NY: G. P. Putnam's Sons.

Goleman, D. (1998). *Working with emotional intelligence.* New York, NY: Bantam.

Goleman, D., Boyatzis, R., & McKee, A. (2001). Primal leadership: The hidden driver of great performance. *Harvard business review*, *79*(11), 42–53.

Goleman, D., Boyatzis, R. E., & McKee, A. (2013). *Primal leadership: Unleashing the power of emotional intelligence.* Boston, MA: Harvard Business Press.

Goleman, D., & Davidson, R. J. (2017). *Altered traits: Science reveals how meditation changes your mind, brain, and body.* Penguin.

Good, D. J., Lyddy, C. J., Glomb, T. M., Bono, J. E., Brown, K. W., Duffy, M. K., & Lazar, S. W. (2016). Contemplating mindfulness at work: An integrative review. *Journal of Management*, *42*(1), 114–142. Retrieved from http://journals.sagepub.com/doi/abs/10.1177/0149206315617003

Hölzel, B. K., Carmody, J., Vangel, M., Congleton, C., Yerramsetti, S. M., Gard, T., & Lazar, S. W. (2011). Mindfulness practice leads to increases in regional brain gray matter density. *Psychiatry Research: Neuroimaging, 191*(1), 36–43. doi:10.1016/j.pscychresns.2010.08.006

Hülsheger, U. R., Alberts, H. J. E. M., Feinholdt, A., & Lang, J. W. B. (2013). Benefits of mindfulness at work: The role of mindfulness in emotion regulation, emotional exhaustion, and job satisfaction. *Journal of Applied Psychology, 98*(2), 310–325. doi:10.1037/a0031313

Husserl, E. (1962). *The crisis of European sciences and transcendental phenomenology*. (D. trans by Carr, Ed.). Evanston, IL: Northwestern University Press.

Hyland, P. K., Lee, R. A., & Mills, M. J. (2015). Mindfulness at work: A new approach to improving individual and organizational performance. *Industrial and Organizational Psychology, 8*(4), 576–602. doi:10.1017/iop.2015.41

Ilies, R., Morgeson, F. P., & Nahrgang, J. D. (2005). Authentic leadership and eudaemonic well- being: Understanding leader–follower outcomes. *The Leadership Quarterly, 16*(3), 373–394.

Jaimeson, D., Auron, M., & Schectman, D. (2017). *Managing use of self*. Retrieved from www.researchgate.net/publication/320556806_Jamieson_Managing_Use_of_Self_ 2

Kabat-Zinn, J. (1994). *Wherever you go, there you are*. London: Piatkus.

Kabat-Zinn, J. (2003). Mindfulness-based interventions in context: Past, present, and future. *Clinical Psychology: Science and Practice, 10*(2), 144–156. http://institutpsychoneuro.com/wp-content/uploads/2015/09/Kabat-Zinn-2003.pdf

Kabat-Zinn, J. (2013). *Full catastrophe living, revised edition: How to cope with stress, pain and illness using mindfulness meditation*. New York, NY: Bantam Books.

Kegan, R. (1982). *The evolving self: Problem and process in human development*. Boston, MA: Harvard College.

Kegan, R., & Lahey, L. L. (2010). From subject to object: A constructive-developmental approach to reflective practice. In *Handbook of reflection and reflective inquiry: Mapping a way of knowing for professional reflective inquiry* (pp. 433–449). Boston, MA: Springer.

Kozasa, E. H., Sato, J. R., Lacerda, S. S., Barreiros, M. A., Radvany, J., Russell, T. A., & Amaro, J. E. (2012). Meditation training increases brain efficiency in an attention task. *Neuroimage, 59*(1), 745–749. doi:10.1016/j.neuroimage.2011.06.088

Kuhnert, K. W., & Lewis, P. (1987). Transactional and transformational leadership: A constructive/developmental analysis. *Academy of Management Review, 12*(4), 648–657.

Langer, E. J. (1989). *Mindfulness*. Boston, MA: Addison-Wesley/Addison Wesley Longman.

Lau, M. A., Bishop, S. R., Segal, Z. V., Buis, T., Anderson, N. D., Carlson, L., & Devins, G. (2006). The Toronto mindfulness scale: Development and validation. *Journal of Clinical Psychology, 62*(12), 1445–1467. Retrieved from https://s3.amazonaws.com/academia.edu.documents/43602125/The_Toronto_Mindfulness_Scale_developmen20160310-26912- wcwcmq5.pdf?AWSAccessKeyId=AKIAIWOW YYGZ2Y53UL3A&Expires=1523459950&Signature=i%2FVwccpgX5Jvscu7Uj3fH2useq8%3D&response-content- disposition=inline%3B%20filename%3DThe_toronto _mindfulness_scale_Developmen.pdf

Lippincott, M. K. (2016). *A study of the perception of the impact of mindfulness on leadership effectiveness*. (Doctoral Dissertation), University of Pennsylvania. Retrieved from http://ezproxy.library.cabrini.edu/login?url=https://search.proquest.com/docview/18928 63666?accountid=40240

Lomas, T., Ivtzan, I., & Fu, C. H. (2001). A systematic review of the neurophysiology of mindfulness on EEG oscillations. *Rinsho Shinkeigaku (Clinical Neurology), 52*(11), 1279–1280. Retrieved from https://s3.amazonaws.com/academia.edu.documents/39223410/Lomas_et_al._2015_Ne urophysiology_of_mindfulness_uploadable.pdf?AWSAccessKeyId=AKIAIWOWYYG Z2Y53UL3A&Expires=1523472906&Signature=SYHa1Cu4Pt31iK6j5CcnmIdn0Hk% 3D&response-content dispositio n=inline%3B%20filename%3DA_systematic_review_of_the_neurophysiol o.pdf

Long, B. B. (2019). Mindfulness and leadership: The lived experience of long-term mindfulness practitioners (Doctoral Dissertation) Cabrini University. Retrieved from https://search.pro-quest.com/docview/2226062326?accoun tid=40240

Lutz, A., Jha, A. P., Dunne, J. D., & Saron, C. D. (2015). Investigating the phenomenological matrix of mindfulness-related practices from a neurocognitive perspective. *American Psychologist, 70*(7), 632. doi:10.1037/a0039585

Lutz, A., Slagter, H. A., Dunne, J. D., & Davidson, R. J. (2008). Attention regulation and monitoring in meditation. *Trends in Cognitive Sciences, 12*(4), 163–169. Retrieved from www.ncbi.nlm.nih.gov/pmc/articles/PMC2693206/?_escaped_fragment_=po=3. 57143/

Lyddy, C. J., & Good, D. J. (2017). Being while doing: An inductive model of mindfulness at work. *Frontiers in Psychology*, 7, 2060. Retrieved from www.frontiersin.org/articles/10.3389/fpsyg.2016.02060/full

Lykins, E. L., & Baer, R. A. (2009). Psychological functioning in a sample of long-term practitioners of mindfulness meditation. *Journal of Cognitive Psychotherapy*, *23*(3), 226. Retrieved from http://self-compassion.org/wp- content/uploads/publications /baermeditators.pdf

Mackey, J., & Sisodia, R. (2013). *Conscious capitalism: Liberating the heroic spirit of business.* Boston, MA: The Harvard Business Review.

MacLean, K. A., Ferrer, E., Aichele, S. R., Bridwell, D. A., Zanesco, A. P., Jacobs, T. L., ... Wallace, B. A. (2010). Intensive meditation training improves perceptual discrimination and sustained attention. *Psychological Science*, *21*(6), 829–839. Retrieved from www.ncbi.nlm.nih.gov/pmc/articles/PMC3132583/

Marques, J., Dhiman, S., & Biberman, J. (2011). Workplace Spirituality. In *Managing in the Twenty-first Century* (pp. 79–118). New York: Palgrave Macmillan.

Miller, J. J., Fletcher, K., & Kabat-Zinn, J. (1995). Three-year follow-up and clinical implications of a mindfulness meditation-based stress reduction intervention in the treatment of anxiety disorders. *General Hospital Psychiatry*, *17*(3), 192–200. Retrieved from www.psicoterapiabilbao.es/wp-content/uploads/2015/12/three-year_followup_and_clinical_implications_of_a_mindfulness_meditation-based_.pdf

Moustakas, C. (1994). *Phenomenological research methods.* Thousand Oaks, CA: Sage Publications, Inc.

Nuernberger, P. (2003). *Strong and fearless: The quest for personal power.* St. Paul, MN: Yes International Publishers.

Petchsawang, P., & Duchon, D. (2012). Workplace spirituality, meditation, and work performance. *Journal of Management, Spirituality & Religion*, *9*(2), 189–208. Retrieved from https://digitalcommons.unl.edu/cgi/viewcontent.cgi?referer=https://scholar.google.com/scholar?hl=en≈sdt=0%2C31&q=petchsawanga&btnG=&httpsredir=1&article=1095&context=managementfacpub

Phipps, K. A. (2010). Servant leadership and constructive development theory. *Journal of Leadership Education*, *9*(2), 151–170.

Purser, R. E., & Milillo, J. (2015). Mindfulness revisited: A Buddhist-based conceptualization. *Journal of Management Inquiry*, *24*(1), 3–24. https://s3.amazonaws.com/academia.edu.documents/34551742/Journal_of_Managemen t_Inquiry-2014-Purser-1056492614532315.pdf?AWSAccessKeyIdAKIAIWOWYYGZ2 Y53UL3A&Expires=1523493491&Signature=BcOV1OI6Ns9vlc9A1%2BUMpWuy6H %3D&responsecontent- disposition=inline%3B%20filename%3DMindfulness _Revisited_A_Buddhist-Based_C.pdf

Reb, J., Narayanan, J., & Ho, Z. W. (2015). Mindfulness at work: Antecedents and consequences of employee awareness and absent-mindedness. *Mindfulness*, *6*(1), 111–122. http://ink.library.smu.edu.sg/cgi/viewcontent.cgi?article=4539&=&context=lkcsb_r esearch&=&sei-redir=1&referer=https%253A%252F%252Fscholar.google.com %252Fscholar%253Fhl%253Den%2526as_sdt%253D0%25252C31%2526q%253D Reb%25252C%252BNarayanan%25252C%252B%252526%252BHo%25252C%252 B2015%2526btnG%253D#search=%22Reb%2C%20Narayanan%2C%20%26%20Ho %2C%202015%22

Reb, J., Sim, S., Chintakananda, K., & Bhave, D. P. (2015). Leading with mindfulness: Exploring the relation of mindfulness with leadership behaviors, styles, and development. *Mindfulness in organizations: Foundations, research, and applications* (pp. 256–284). Research Collection Lee Kong Chian School of Business. Available at: https://ink.library.smu.edu.sg/lkcsb_research/4409

Reichard, R. J., & Johnson, S. K. (2011). Leader self-development as organizational strategy. *The Leadership Quarterly*, *22*(1), 33–42.

Roche, M., Haar, J. M., & Luthans, F. (2014). The role of mindfulness and psychological capital on the well-being of leaders. *Journal of Occupational Health Psychology*, *19*(4), 476–489. Retrieved from http://psycnet.apa.org/buy/2014-24214-001

Shapiro, S. L. (2009). The integration of mindfulness and psychology. *Journal of Clinical Psychology*, *65*(6), 555–560. Retrieved from https://pdfs.semanticscholar.org/0a2b/d98d4b9f4bd6f469749725684f1f76499eb1.pdf

Shapiro, S. L., & Carlson, L. E. (2009). The art and science of mindfulness: Integrating mindfulness into psychology and the helping professions. *American Psychological Association.* 1 edition.

Shapiro, S. L., Carlson, L. E., Astin, J. A., & Freedman, B. (2006). Mechanisms of mindfulness. *Journal of Clinical Psychology*, *62*(3), 373–386. Retrieved from http://m.recoveryonpurpose.com/upload/Mechanisms%20of%20Mindfulness.pdf

Smallwood, J., & Schooler, J. W. (2015). The science of mind wandering: Empirically navigating the stream of consciousness. *Annual Review of Psychology*, *66*, 487–518. Retrieved from https://labs.psych.ucsb.edu/schooler/jonathan/sites/labs.psych.ucsb.edu.schooler.jonatha n/files/pubs/the_science_of_mind_wandering.pdf

Southern, N. L. (2005). Creating cultures of collaboration that thrive on diversity: A transformational perspective on building collaborative capital. In Beyerlein, M. M., Beyerlein, S. T. and Kennedy, F. A. (Ed.) *Collaborative Capital: Creating Intangible Value (Advances in Interdisciplinary Studies of Work Teams,* Vol. 11, pp. 33–72). Emerald Group Publishing Limited, Bingley. doi: 10.1016/S1572-0977(05)11002-4

Stanley, E. A., & Jha, A. P. (2009). Mind fitness. Improving operational effectiveness and building warrior resilience. *Joint Force Quarterly*, *55*, 144–151. Retrieved from http://intelros.ru/pdf/jfq_55/23.pdf

Stanley, E. A., Schaldach, J. M., Kiyonaga, A., & Jha, A. P. (2011). Mindfulness-based mind fitness training: A case study of a high-stress predeployment military cohort. *Cognitive and Behavioral Practice*, *18*(4), 566–576. Retrieved from http://vizenllc.com/research/mindfulness/MindfulnessBasedMindFitnessTraining. pdf

Tan, C. M. (2012). *Search inside yourself.* New York, NY: Harper Collins Publishers.

Tang, Y., Holzel, B., & Posner, M. (2015). The neuroscience of mindfulness meditation. *Nature Reviews Neuroscience*, *16*. doi:10.1038/nrn3916

Tang, Y., Ma, Y., Wang, J., Fan, Y., Feng, S., Lu, Q., . . . Posner, M. I. (2007). Short-term meditation training improves attention and self-regulation. *Proceedings of the National Academy of Sciences*, *104*(43), 17152–17156. Retrieved from www.pnas.org/content/104/43/17152.full?utm_source=buffer&utm_campaign=B uffer&utm_content=buffer67dff&utm_medium=google

Taylor, V. A., Grant, J., Daneault, V., Scavone, G., Breton, E., Roffe-Vidal, S., & Beauregard, M. (2011). Impact of mindfulness on the neural responses to emotional pictures in experienced and beginner meditators. *Neuroimage*, *57*(4), 1524–1533. Retrieved from http://pubman.mpdl.mpg.de/pubman/item/escidoc:1073601/component/escidoc:107360 0/Taylor%2520et%2520al.%25202011.pdf

Teasdale, J. D., & Chaskalson, M. (2011). How does mindfulness transform suffering? I: The nature and origins of dukkha. *Contemporary Buddhism*, *12*(01), 89–102.

Tsui, A. S., & Ashford, S. J. (1994). Adaptive self-regulation: A process view of managerial effectiveness. *Journal of Management*, *20*(1), 93–121.

van Manen, M. (1990). *Researching lived experience: Human science for an action sensitive pedagogy.* Albany: State University of New York Press.

Verdorfer, A. P. (2016). Examining mindfulness and its relations to humility, motivation to lead, and actual servant leadership behaviors. *Mindfulness*, 7(4), 950–961. doi:10.1007/s12671-016-0534-8

Walsh, J. P. (1995). Managerial and organizational cognition: Notes from a trip down memory lane. *Organization Science*, *6*(3), 280–321. Retrieved from www.jstor.org/stable/2635252?casa_token=P3XhUpL03fwAAAAA:qiyU0E5Rw 4WJ7vcX6OfPLYw5pllImWcwXpOFopyzAlJgTrezmyhujN1hOKnYb0mDvMse4PdW dAopYO4eBuo9Kr_9zEQ3eQ2OTMVN7t7Asflc9S7msTQ&seq=1#page_scan_tab_co ntents

Walsh, R. (1999). Asian contemplative disciplines: Common practices, clinical applications, and research findings. *The Journal of Transpersonal Psychology*, *31*(2), 83. Retrieved from www.atpweb.org/jtparchive/trps-31-99-01-083.pdf

Walsh, R., & Shapiro, S. L. (2006). The meeting of meditative disciplines and Western psychology: A mutually enriching dialogue. *American Psychologist*, *61*(3), 227. Retrieved from https://cloudfront.escholarship.org/dist/prd/content/qt7885t0n6/qt7885t0n6.pdf

Watkins, E. R. (2008). Constructive and unconstructive repetitive thought. *Psychological Bulletin*, *134*(2), 163. Retrieved from http://psycnet.apa.org/fulltext/2008-01984-001.html

Weick, K. E., & Putnam, T. (2006). Organizing for mindfulness: Eastern wisdom and Western knowledge. *Journal of Management Inquiry*, *15*(3), 275–287. doi:10.1177/1056492606291202

Weick, K. E., & Sutcliffe, K. M. (2006). Mindfulness and the quality of organizational attention. *Organization Science*, *17*(4), 514–524. doi:10.1287/orsc.1060.0196

Welcome to your qualitative research made easier. (n.d.). *NVivo for Mac.* Retrieved from www.qsrinternational.com/nvivo/nvivo-12-tutorial-mac/00-let-s-get-started

West, C. P., Dyrbye, L. N., Rabatin, J. T., Call, T. G., Davidson, J. H., Multari, A., & Shanafelt, T. D. (2014). Intervention to promote physician well-being, job satisfaction, and professionalism: A randomized clinical trial. *JAMA Internal Medicine*, *174*(4), 527–533. doi:10.1001/jamainternmed.2013.14387

Wolever, R. Q., Bobinet, K. J., McCabe, K., Mackenzie, E. R., Fekete, E., Kusnick, C. A., & Baime, M. (2012). Effective and viable mind-body stress reduction in the workplace: A randomized controlled trial. *Journal of Occupational Health Psychology*, *17*(2), 246. doi:10.1037/a0027278

10

CONVERSATION IN MINDFULNESS

Leading *self* to lead others

Therese Walkinshaw

Introduction

The foundation of the conversations in this research was based on the question, "What is the experience of a mindful leader leading *self* in a professional environment?" The question was formulated to direct my conversations towards the everyday life of leaders as they grapple with the pressures and difficulties of their jobs. My own experience as both as a mindfulness practitioner and as a senior organizational development professional engendered my fascination with this research topic. I was curious to see if there were parallels between the experiences of the four leaders and my own my personal and professional worlds. I was interested in how conversations naturally unfold in mindfulness and how conversations can open up not only a better awareness of the impact mindfulness has on others, but also an understanding of what the conversation is doing to bring this awareness to the surface. Doing research from a Heideggerian phenomenological perspective means that my involvement as a researcher had a significant impact on how the conversations proceeded and, later, were interpreted. Being in a deep reflective and mindful state during the conversations meant I could go deeper into the leaders' experiences to discover how mindful practice can help bring clarity to daily life.

This chapter is structured so that in the first part, readers will obtain an insight into the conversations and how they developed in the three-month period over which they took place. In the second part, the chapter offers a reflective summary of the conversations, and relates the themes of the conversations to current literature on the mindfulness.

The conversations

Part 1: The experience in conversations

I met with each participant three times each over a period of three months, and I allowed the semi-structured conversations to just happen, letting ideas and thinking flow. The conversations were recorded and later transcribed, but I also, with the participants' permission, unobtrusively took notes of changes in body language and other non-verbal signals. All the forms of data later fed into my analysis.

Conversation 1: Introduction

The purpose of the first conversation was getting to know the leaders so that they would be comfortable about sharing their experiences of leading with mindfulness and what the practice meant for them, and more than that, how they practiced it. This phase of the data-gathering was really a rewarding conversational exploration, and knowing that I would meet with them again meant there was no feeling of pressure to get as much information as possible in a short time. In fact, the lack of time pressure allowed a flowing conversation that was in every case led by the participants. I encountered a real openness in all four mindful leaders to participate in conversations. They willingly shared their stories of what mindfulness meant to them and how they moved into the space of mindfulness.

Conversation 2: The experience

The second session focused on the participants' life stories and particular experiences they had had in leading mindfully. I found their honesty and frankness humbling, and was grateful for the deep, rich reflections they shared with me, and for the opportunity to delve into points of particular significance.

Conversation 3: A symbolic focus

In the third and last conversation, we focused on insights into the symbolic aspects of their practice of mindfulness. This session started with some confusion but finished with deep understanding both for the participants and myself. The session also gave the leaders the opportunity to think about what they gained from being part of the project. Again, I was moved and humbled to find that they all felt that they had been rewarded by taking part in the conversations in which they considered and shared how mindfulness had been integrated into their lives.

I asked each participant to think about the symbol they would use to represent mindfulness, and each could articulate it by the end of our conversation. Sometimes they knew it before we talked, but some also found it during our talk.

Ruth *was not sure of her symbolic representation of mindfulness. We explored and discussed, and she came up with an example of the importance of movement, which for her represents realigning* self *into the space of mindfulness when she feels stuck in a less resourceful experience. I sensed her excitement in recognizing the importance of movement in whatever she does, and that this really allows her to enter a place of calm. She recognized that she is in a mindful space while walking in nature, by walking around on stage while presenting, moving important meetings to the right spot in her schedule, removing clients who do not connect with the services that she provides through her business, and so forth. For Ruth, movement means a release of energy that allows for creativity and interpretation of her intuitive activities.*

Fraser *was not sure if he had a symbolic representation of mindfulness, and therefore felt confused and hesitant at first. However, later he realized that he did use the symbol of elevation, of being on a balcony. This is a borrowed symbol that is used through a coaching approach. The balcony symbol allows him to elevate himself so as to see the full picture of what is happening in the moment, to get him back to what is important right here, right now. He elevates from his current experience, sometimes of chaos, to gain an overview of what is going on around him. This includes his own involvement in the event and his involvement with others. It has been evident in the conversations that I have had* *with him that moving on to the balcony has been repeated over and over again as a symbol to help him gain a full picture of the situation.*

Steve *was very clear about what symbolic representation of mindfulness is for him: calmness either in the desert or on the sea. For Steve, both are places of complete silence, containing a sense of "nothing, anywhere," which is transferred into the way he interacts with others and deals with chaos around him. This symbol helps him find a space of peace, clarity of being, and calm in moments that he needs it. In the conversation that we had about the symbols that represent mindfulness, it was evident that Steve has a clear concept of mindfulness and could readily articulate how he has integrated it into his life.*

Tony *experiences mindfulness through light and universal coherence, something that was repeated over and over throughout our conversations. For Tony, light represents his understanding of* self *and the understanding that light has its own personal experience and cannot be thought by anyone else. It needs to be part of an individual's personal experience; it cannot be the same for two people. Tony can sense it in his relationship with others, his intuitive living and his engagement with the world. Light and universal coherence gives him the space to be fully present in the moment. It is his purpose in what he does through his very creative thinking and innovative practices.*

The three conversations developed my understanding of these mindful leaders leading *self. A* significant realization during this journey was the deepening of my connection with the participants and the intensity of being in the space of their attentive present. I found that each participant was fully attentive, authentic, and passionate about the conversations, resulting in exchanges that were holistic and powerful and produced a high volume of material. The conversations worked on the principle of the hermeneutical spiral, which encourages conversations to grasp a point, inspect detail, and dig into a deep understanding (Van Manen, 1990). One of the outcomes was the chance to contemplate the flow of moods during the data-gathering process.

Moods

Each participant showed different aspects of mood during the conversations, revealed in their responses and how they communicated, connected, and shared during the conversations. The different moods set the tone of the conversations, and there was an unbroken sense of ease, seeking, openness, newness, and flow—even humor!—in the conversations, combined with a deep sense of knowing and understanding mindfulness in the conversations. The different moods were neither static nor hidden, but rather, were fluid and evident throughout the different conversations.

The different levels of mood indicated the level of connectedness each participant was experiencing within the mindful space. I found that it was rich and powerful to share the energy that emerged, and that being fully present in the conversations meant I could be part of their journeys. I took the opportunity to go on a "mood journey" with the leaders. For instance, the moment that Ruth discovered her symbol for mindfulness stands out in particular: her excitement was contagious, and I felt that something profound had been discovered. Also, because of the participants' willingness to share, some of the conversations had an immense flow of passion that gave the impression that the room had disappeared and the only thing left was the intense sharing and discovery between two individuals. I felt that I was experiencing the richness of mindfulness and meaningfulness, and as a researcher I am now even keener to take part in dialogue about life.

Body language

The body language of the participants was fascinatingly similar, and supported the impressions of openness and willingness that I gleaned from the words of the conversations. We sat at a table across from each other so that we each had our personal space, but could also connect physically. We situated ourselves in the room without formality or awkwardness. The arrangement felt natural and unplanned, and permitted intimate discussion. The table between us was not in any way a barrier, but simply a convenient place for the recording devices and for taking notes.

The sense of calm was evident in the participants' gestures. I noted that they looked up when they were visualizing their experiences and down when they were reliving their experiences. There was lots of laughter and welcoming smiles that made me feel that I was accepted into their personal space, and they were relaxed enough to emphasize certain points by clapping on the table. Some instances of hesitation or confusion were marked by fidgeting, but we had both the space and the time to move the confusion into a space of understanding. The energy that flowed gave a holistic sense of "give and take" in all the conversations.

Being in mindfulness

Connecting in the mindful moment with the participants during the conversations was personally enriching, but more importantly, mindfulness built an important platform for the research. When two mindful individuals come together to talk, neither is likely to try to impress the other, or use power to make a statement. I believe this is the truth of mindfulness in action, and I found that the conversation matched Heidegger's (1927/62) notion of moving beyond mere chatter into a real exchange of meaningful ideas. The conversations were powerful, not only because of the content of the sharing, but also because of the active, acute listening that took place that brought both parties to the sense of being "awake to and aware of what is." All in all, the process of data-gathering was an intense experience that derived from the sharing that took place, and I think the vividness of the encounters was because two people were feeling the space of mindfulness simultaneously, linking with a certain purity of existence rather than with suffering and pain.

Follow-up conversations

The first three conversations were the principal occasions of data-gathering, but I also organized an additional meeting to offer my analysis and interpretation back to the participants for their comment and critique. Obviously, I hoped that the fourth meeting would confirm and validate my interpretations, especially of the key insight that they all felt that the process of the research had developed a new appreciation of being mindful in leading *self*. In fact, the fourth conversation did prove useful for just that purpose: all participants mentioned that the conversations had provided an opportunity to verbalize their convictions, and they particularly valued the chance to think about the symbol they used to move into the mindful state. In this final conversation, the participants reviewed their stories, and gave me feedback on whether I had represented them and their stories authentically.

At this point, it is fair to say that my participants felt the research had changed them. Ruth, for instance, said that recognizing movement as her key had allowed her the full acceptance that mindfulness means different things for different people. Tony reported that he felt that his story reflected someone that he was not aware of, that although he was aware that mindfulness helped him, he had not previously been able to perceive it clearly. Overall, they were all appreciative of the chance to share their insights about themselves and the events that brought them to the practice of mindfulness. They all mentioned in the follow-up conversation that they were still caught in negative participation sometimes, but they were now more conscious of moving into mindfulness when problems occurred. It seems to be a strong commonality that mindfulness lends meaning to leading *self* as leaders and that continuing discussions with others is important to keep the learning going. I also noticed a sense of ease and fluidity in the follow-up conversations, and that there was a mutual recognition of the deep connections that were forged during the research process.

The emerging themes

Listening to the conversations and re-reading the transcripts allowed me to revisit the conversations holistically, and during the interpretation phase of the research, permitted me to reflect on the participants' stories over and over again in writing, reflection, reading, and rewriting (van Manen, 1984). The conversations revealed that there are commonalities among the mindful leaders in their experience and understanding of mindfulness in leading *self*.

Three themes emerged from the individual stories: *taking hold of self*, *opening up to self in being a leader*, and *moving forward authentically as a leader*. These themes synthesize the participants' experience. I have tried to write the themes up so that they holistically represent truths about the participants' lives as mindful leaders, but the naming and grouping of the content in the themes—the validity of the themes, in fact—is based on my own thoughtful interpretation of the stories, feedback, and agreement of the participants. The themes are presented in the table below.

Theme 1: Taking hold of *self*
Courage of being
Knowing-awareness
Authentic journey

Theme 2: Opening up to *self* in being a leader
Clarity and focus
Flow in experience
Being-with-one-another
Falling back to *theyness*

Theme 3: Moving forward authentically as a leader
Mood awareness
Emerging world of possibilities
Opening up to a creative existence
Meaningful existence

I found that the themes and sub-themes emerged readily from reflection on the conversations. Interpretation was not forced but seemed to flow from the data. I found that what the mindful leaders had in common was a sense that is important for individuals to find their own authentic journeys. Indeed, the commentaries offered by the mindful leaders seemed to chime with Heidegger's (1927/62) insistence on recognizing conformity, inauthenticity, and lostness, emerging from a cocoon state, and taking responsibility for living a life of personal ownership. The mindful leaders had discovered how to take their own journeys by using mindfulness to *take hold of self.* By this I mean that they had instinctively calibrated their mindfulness practice to their personal values and what felt right to them, which placed a buffer between them and the stress and pressure of their jobs. This struck me as both brave and powerful, as the majority of people tend to accept what they are taught and not only never find their authentic journeys, but sometimes never look for them (Passmore, 2009).

Heidegger (1927/62) explained how people often live in the *they*, which means they depend on others' opinions and ideas instead of facing actuality as an individual. In *opening up to self in being a leader*, the mindful leaders recognized that being mindful is a way of engaging with the world truthfully, and they found then that mindfulness helped them *move forward authentically as a leader.* Mindfulness helped the participants find clarity, focus and flow in their engagement with their individual worlds, and enabled them to operate with *care.* Without doubt, they sometimes fell back into *theyness*, but their awareness of leaving the mindful state often triggered them back into it.

The conversations with the participants allowed me deep insight into their experiences of leading mindfully, and in my view, those insights are profoundly important to forming a sound understanding of the world of leaders. I will now unfold the commonalities that emerged from the conversations, and relate them to current literature and my own thinking around the proposition that to lead others, it is important to first lead *self.*

The themes

Part 2: Summary of the findings explored as part of the conversations

The conversations confirmed my intuition that mindful leaders are profoundly involved in the processes and outcomes of leading. Here, "profound" is not a word that I am using lightly: it is a considered lexical choice which I want to unpack. The leaders in my research had found ways to connect to *self* (the awareness of self) in a way that imparts meaning to their lives. In a Heideggerian sense the leaders have let go of "theyness," the following of others (Heidegger, 1927/62, p. 177), and allowed themselves to interact with the world and their followers with no artificial barriers of ego or status needs. I think that the profound place from which my participants lead is defined by courage, which I have come to see as a necessary antecedent to entering and operating from a mindful space. In all contexts, but in leading in particular, becoming mindful requires courage: first, because it requires openness to the unfamiliar, and second, because also it may attract criticism, lying as it does outside the accepted norms and received wisdom of management behavior. The findings show how deeply the leaders embraced mindfulness, and how this integration permitted clarity of thought, openness to possibilities, and creative flow (Gadamer, 1975). Mindfulness seemed to diminish any drive for recognition and status, building instead a sense that the leaders lived true to themselves and to others, a finding that resonates with Heidegger's (1927/62) explication of authenticity towards the *self.*

The experience of my participants revealed that mindfulness does not remove unhappiness, problems, and stress, but rather, that it points a way towards comprehending and accepting the events that created adverse reactions. This finding supports Manz's (1986) notion that leading *self* mindfully prompts fewer reactive assessments of challenging situations. In the light of this finding about the advantageous outcomes of mindfulness, it would be wonderful to be able to report that mindfulness is easy to embrace, but unfortunately, it takes courage to be mindful, and courage is hardly ever easy or straightforward. I maintain that it is an act of courage to face and release the mistakes and disappointments of the past, and then review the present for possibilities and solutions. This is especially so for leaders, who are trained to understand problems by tracing their origins through organizational history, habits, and established practices. For a leader to adopt mindfulness is not just "doing some meditation": it is more about being open to personal change on multiple levels, Mindfulness seemed to make the leaders aware of procedures that had become unsatisfactory, of unproductive personal or organizational behaviors, of habits, ideas, values, and beliefs that no longer served them or the organization. Awareness then became a catalyst to release the past, and this process, clearly, could be painful. However, it appeared to allow the leaders to enter a place of possibilities and authenticity as part of the play of life.

Two other clear findings in this study are that becoming mindful is an experience that individuals open up to with purpose and intention, and further, that there is no one formula for how to be mindful. These ideas are closely intertwined: for instance, my participants related that (for different reasons) they all needed to find meaning in their lives, that in opening up to mindfulness, they changed, and in the change, they realized an openness to being real and authentic to themselves and others. At the same time, the four participants each experienced the change differently, though perhaps it might be more true to say that they each experienced a different change: Ruth, for instance, loosened her tight focus on her own affairs and realized the value and meaning of listening to others in their worlds. Tony found that mindfulness stimulated his creativity, while Steve experienced mindfulness as openness to new and different ways of understanding everyday life. Fraser's connection with mindfulness reduced his inner turbulence and had a positive effect on his work with projects and clients. Each participant, therefore, has reaped different benefits from mindfulness, because each took a different need to the mindful space. Similarly, each participant entered the mindful space in a different way: the metaphors of place or movement that signaled entry into the mindful state were as individual as the need and the experience. One interesting observation about my participants is that although they all come from a Western background, in the totality of their mindfulness practice, they exhibit strong elements of the Eastern perspective (Djikic, 2014; Weick & Putnam, 2006). In other words, they seem to have moved beyond merely "doing mindfulness" to the point that mindfulness has become a way of life.

The implication of these findings is that leaders and organizations should not envisage that the introduction of mindfulness programs is the "next big thing" as a form of professional development or (more cynically) as a cheap way of reducing stress and burnout among senior staff. There is no single teachable formula of mindfulness that that can be successfully delivered: mindfulness is not a vaccine against stress and unhappiness. In fact, it may even be counterproductive to push the concept of mindfulness to people who are not willing or ready to reach inside themselves to that place of profoundness accessed by the four mindful leaders in this study: unwilling, compulsory participation might well create anger and increase stress and suspicion.

Research shows that there has been a gradual but significant move in the conceptualization of leaders and leading, away from a dated model of command and control (Drucker, 1988) towards a greater self-reflection and self-awareness among leaders of their impact on the world around them (Argyris, 1994), towards understanding the management of meaning (Schein, 1985) and towards transformational leading and visionary thinking (Bass, 1985; Holladay & Coombs, 1993). Leaders are envisaged becoming more authentic in their interactions (Goleman, 1998; Mayfield, Mayfield, & Kopf, 1998; Terry, 1998) and as leading them*selves* in truth and happiness (Avolio & Gardner, 2005). Furthermore, the literature is clear that the practice of mindfulness can give leaders a beneficial awareness of followers' reactions and needs (Dhiman, 2008; Gehrke, 2008; Passmore, 2009).

Mindfulness moves thinking away from prescriptive models of leadership to the actual experience of leaders, digging into the core of the existence of leaders and the essence of leading *self.* Ancona, Malone, Orlikowski, and Senge (2007) argue that leaders carry a significant burden of expectations which can cause distress and affect their personal lives to the point of burnout and illness. My study shows that mindfulness in leading *self* develops positive awareness of the meaning of leading, which includes care of followers, the greater good, and importantly, one's own being. In this respect, my work supports Chakraborty (1995) in conceptualizing leaders moving into a place of wisdom and gentleness towards the *self* and their individual worlds.

The leaders in my study understood that leading *self* mindfully had potential for working good in the world. It meant they took responsibility for both their actions and their reactions, and that they were so conscious of the world in which they operated that they could adjust to the moment, not overemphasizing the matter at hand, but seeing each moment and trusting the outcome. For my participants, leading *self* developed self-trust by allowing space for their intuition. This deep self-trust developed "flow" (Chakraborty, 1995, p. 211) for the leaders, the people around them and the organization as a whole. In this sense and application, leading *self* created possibilities for movement and exploration where previously there was a feeling of being stuck and bound by certain ideas and procedures.

People who lead *self* are likely to recognize mindfulness as more than simply a tool for problem-solving or facilitating meetings, seeing it instead as a complete way of living that emanates from a deepened understanding of the essence of being. As more leaders realize the benefits that accrue from mindfully leading *self,* it will be increasingly important that they come to understand mindfulness not simply as learned knowledge but as an ontological awareness of the nature of being and becoming. Therefore, mindfulness must be introduced in ways that allow for individual development, and programs must emphasize an authentic journey, flexibility, and openness. *Self* is not easy to explain or define: people need to understand it as part of being and awareness of being: as the dimension of being that allows changes of viewpoint about the meaning of existence. Leaders who are willing to open up to mindful living will need to find their own ways into the space and their own meaning once they are there. The benefit of this, however, is that other leaders may, like the participants in my research, find open-mindedness, flow, clarity, and creativity, leading to useful new ideas, improved procedures, and trusting, meaningful relationships with colleagues and other leaders. Being mindful shows a high level of trust in *self* as well as in others (Gehani, 2011), which is evident in the conversations with the mindful leaders in this research. The lived experience of the mindful leaders resonate with the concept of being *in tune* with what is and their everyday experience, with the "realness" of individuals' existence (Avolio & Gardner, 2005). In this study, "to lead" is synonymous with awareness of the *self* in all aspects of leading behavior, and mindfulness has been shown to help the leaders move into space that is attuned to the true *self.*

The conversations indicated that for the leaders I conversed with, mindfulness is not simply a form of knowledge, it is a way of being, and the "way of being" therefore needs to be questioned (Heidegger, 1927/62). Carson and Langer (2006) argue that one of the positive effects of mindfulness is that it increases awareness of everyday situations because it tends to lead people into dialogue, and that these conversations create calm and clarity because people connect on a deep and authentic level. I would like to see such conversations occur more frequently between and among leaders, to help them release their practice from any limitations in their mindsets. I have witnessed the power of such conversations with leaders, and have observed that although they often cannot name what they gained, they are nevertheless cognizant that they did gain something of significance. My research has confirmed for me how important it is to let meaningful conversations happen so that leaders find the authentic self.

The leaders who participated in my conversations opened up to the possibilities of their lives by seeing *self* as it is, which resonates with the Heideggerian view of authenticity. My study shows examples of authentic existence: the participants see themselves for what they are and accept that insight into the essence of their being. Shamir and Eilam's (2005) definition of authenticity is borne out by my research. They nominate the following four characteristics of authentic leading: (1) "authentic leaders do not fake their leadership" (p. 396); (2) "authentic leaders do not take on a leadership role or engage in leadership activities for status, honour or other personal rewards" (p. 397); (3) "authentic leaders are originals, not copies" (p. 397); (4) "authentic leaders are leaders whose actions are based on their values and convictions" (p. 397). This study shows that the style of authenticity delineated by Shamir and Eilam (2005) occurs naturally when leaders move into mindfulness. I assert that by allowing their authenticity to come to fruition, the leaders will lead a simpler life because they will relinquish the complexity of the mind, often produced by fear and high expectations of themselves based on others' ideas. A different approach to the world may lead to a place of less strain, openness to others' views, and optimism about the benefits that might emerge from real conversations and a less judgmental attitude. Ultimately, organizations are likely to be served by such a change, because if pressure is less, productivity may well be more.

Previous research has revealed certain factors that can help people towards more mindful living: self-leadership (Brown & Fields, 2011; Chakraborty, 1995), emotional intelligence (Goleman, 2004; Landy, 2005; Scott-Hall, Shumate, & Blum, 2007), and an understanding of neuroscience (McDonald, 2009; Schmidt, 2011; Sousa, 2012), all of which provide leaders with a basis for developing self-awareness about how they interact with their worlds. Concepts such as self-leadership or emotional intelligence may be influential factors in the early stages of mindful understanding of *self*, but Heidegger (1927/62) maintains that the further individuals move into beingness, the less conceptual and the more experiential they become. Nevertheless, these are good starting points for becoming familiar with *self* and for entering mindfulness. When I began my journey into mindfulness, I used many concepts developed by others to try to understand the idea better. The ensuing confusion then encouraged me to simply let things be as they are, and I now find myself able to be the being that I am by being awake to and aware of my ongoing experience. I share with the participants in this research the benefits that mindfulness brings to my role as a leader: like them, I can take part in what is going on around me, but I am not held down by it.

Although it may seem counterintuitive, this study has shown that in developing awareness of *self*, mindfulness also fosters connection to the world beyond *self*. Leading *self* shows the mindful leaders investigating experience and becoming authentic in dealing with both the experience and the people around them. The mindful leaders have recognized the importance of bringing meaning into their everyday life and using it in their engagement with the world.

This finding bears out Langer's (1989, 2000) exploration of mindlessness, which in her work meant to be separated from authentic experience. The leaders in my research, however, were not mindless, and showed, in fact, that opening up to *self* has brought them richness in a world filled with suffering and pain. Mindfully leading *self* has not made them immune to pain, but for them, its effect is different: they are able to move from mindlessness to meaningfulness through the formal meditation or reflection of their mindfulness practice.

Gadamer (1975) speaks of "being of play" (p. 107), by which he primarily means both the interactions of people with one another and with phenomena, and also the intra-actions of individuals with *self*. The concept of play as action, whether inter- or intra-, however, is not fully realized unless it is understood in relation to the wide scope of meaning the word has in English. For instance, "play" can refer to "playfulness," passing the time and having fun, or it might bring to mind organized games, with rules and referees. It raises the idea of something being "in play": that is, going forward, taking place, under action. The same notion underpins "playing out": waiting for the result of an action (or inaction), seeing what will happen. It can also mean "performance," bringing something into being. My point here is not to give an exhaustive list of the different ways in which "play" can be used, but rather, to deepen the idea that leading *self* mindfully opens people up to the play in existence, which is interaction and intra-action interpreted through all the subtle variations of meaning possible in "play."

I maintain that the participants in my research function in, as I will call it, the *play in existence* in the richest way the word can be understood, and that this is the outcome of the *self* engaging with mindfulness. In this sense, the *self* is open to possibilities and limitless creativity as children are when they play. However, in another and very real way, the "play in existence" is also the performing of *self*: the bringing into being of the essence of an authentic person. This can be explored in opening up to the idea of ontology by being curious and passionate about the meaning of life.

An ontological questioning of the meaning of life is pivotal to this study, and the vehicle of this questioning is the experience of being a mindful leader leading *self*. Previous research talks about self-leadership from the point of view of self-motivation and following personal values and beliefs (Neck & Manz, 1996): moving forward, in other words, by self-regulation (Manz & Sims, 1987). My study shows that mindful leaders find a stronger sense of freedom in their existence and that this opens possibilities and creativity in leading. Current research (Baron, 2016; Sethi, 2009; Tuleja, 2014) shows how mindfulness can help in leader*ship*, but not much has been done to show how mindfulness affects *leaders*.

Gadamer (1975) asserted that play could be captured in the form of art, by the "true being in the fact that it becomes and experience that changes the person who experiences it" (p. 107). In relation to his idea, I will argue that the leaders themselves represent the art of being mindful, which is something that changes continuously, never setting into a firm shape. Gadamer (1975) refers to the idea of "being totally involved in and carried away by what one sees" (p. 125), which is not simply a search for knowledge, but a search for the truth in experience. The leaders in this study show their dedication to mindfulness and are, as Gadamer urges, "totally involved" in seeing the world from a perspective that allows life to be a play rather than a struggle. Leaders who can embrace "the play" (Gadamer, 1975, p. 107) will be creative and adaptable to failure and gain. This will lead to fewer arguments about what is right or wrong, and it encourages stronger relationships with less competition and fewer comparisons between and among people. Encouraging staff to be real about their participation in the play will bring more humor and lightness to organizations, and should encourage fruitful conversations, with less manipulation to gain favors or benefits. I personally believe being in the play of creativity will lead to a fruitful existence.

This chapter has summarized data captured in four "layered" conversations, and while it is true that the material is based on the experience of only four mindful leaders, nevertheless the depth of sharing that was achieved allows me to conclude that mindfulness allowed the leaders to live with a real and immediate sense of who they are and what they do. They do not lose themselves in the pressure of minutiae. The conversations in themselves were mindful exchanges that developed into true dialogue, and as the conversations deepened, I understood more of the way that leaders integrated mindfulness to their leading. The identified themes—*taking hold of self, opening up to self in being a leader, moving forward authentically as a leader*—express the concrete experience of moving into mindfulness, acting in mindfulness, and being in mindfulness.

Five lessons from this chapter

1. Mindfulness may help in deepening conversations to create true dialogue.
2. Mindfulness may help leaders experience more meaningfulness in their leading.
3. Leading mindfully may help others in becoming more reflective in their practice.
4. Mindfulness may help leaders taking hold of *self* to lead and open up to the *self.*
5. Mindfulness may help leaders lead more authentically.

Five reflective questions from this chapter

1. What would happen if leaders discovered the true power of mindfulness?
2. What would happen if leaders led their followers mindfully and reflectively?
3. What would happen if we allowed ourselves to be true and authentic in our conversations?
4. What would happen if mindfulness were seen as a key component for great leadership?
5. What would happen if world leaders took the time to practice mindfulness and truly reflect on their inner experience before they made any significant decisions?

References

Ancona, D., Malone, T. W., Orlikowski, W. J., & Senge, P. M. (2007). In praise of the incomplete leader. *Harvard Business Review, 85*(2), 92–100.

Argyris, C. (1994). Good communication that blocks learning. *Harvard Business Review, 72*(4), 77–85.

Avolio, B. J., & Gardner, W. L. (2005). Authentic leadership development: Getting to the root of positive forms of leadership. *The Leadership Quarterly, 16,* 315–338. doi:10.1016/j.leaqua.2005.03.001

Baron, L. (2016). Authentic leadership and mindfulness development through action learning. *Journal of Managerial Psychology, 31*(1), 296–311. doi:10.1108/JMP-04-2014-0135

Bass, B. M. (1985). *Leadership and performance beyond expectations.* New York, NY: The Free Press.

Brown, R. T., & Fields, D. (2011). Leaders engaged in self-leadership: Can followers tell the difference? *Leadership,* 7, 275–293. doi:10.1177/1742715011407383

Carson, S. H., & Langer, E. J. (2006). Mindfulness and self-acceptance. *Journal of Rational- Emotive & Cognitive-Behavior Therapy, 24*(1), 29–43. doi:10.1007/s10942-006-0022-5

Chakraborty, S. K. (1995). Wisdom leadership: Leading self by the SELF. *Journal of Human Values, 2*(1), 206–219. doi:10.1177/097168589500100205

Dhiman, S. (2008). Mindfulness in life and leadership: An exploratory survey. *Interbeing, 3*(1), 1–15.

Djikic, M. (2014). Art of mindfulness integrating eastern and western approaches. In A. Ie, C. T. Ngnoumen, & E. J. Langer (Eds.), *The Wiley Blackwell handbook on mindfulness* (pp. 140–148). New Jersey: John Wiley & Sons, Ltd.

Drucker, F. (1988). The coming of the new organization. *Harvard Business Review,* 45–53. Jan/Feb). Retrieved from. http://secure.tutorsglobe.com/Atten_files/1286_ENG.pdf

Gadamer, H.-G. (1975). *Truth and Method.* (J. Weinsheimer, & D. G. Marshall, Trans.). London: Bloomsbury.
Gehani, R. R. (2011). Individual creativity and the influence of mindful leaders on enterprise innovation. *Journal of Technology Management and Innovation, 6*(3), 83–91. doi:10.4067/S0718-27242011000300006
Gehrke, S. J. (2008). Leadership through meaning-making: An empirical exploration of spirituality and leadership in college students. *Journal of College Student Development, 49*(4), 351–359. doi:10.1353/csd.0.0014
Goleman, D. (1998). *Working with emotional intelligence.* New York, NY: Bantam Books.
Goleman, D. (2004). What makes a leader? *Harvard Business Review, 82*(1), 82–91.
Heidegger, M. (1927/62). *Being and Time.* (J. Macquarrie, & E. Robinson, Trans.). New York: HarperPerennial.
Holladay, S. J., & Coombs, T. W. (1993). Communicating visions: An exploration of the role of delivery in the creation of leader charisma. *Management Communication Quarterly, 6*(4), 405–427. doi:10.1177/0893318993006004003
Landy, F. J. (2005). Some historical and scientific issues related to research on emotional intelligence. *Journal of Organizational Behavior, 26*(4), 411–424. doi:10.1002/job.317
Langer, E. J. (1989). *Mindfulness.* New York: Addison Wesley Longman.
Langer, E. J. (2000). Mindful learning. *Current Directions in Psychologoical Sciences, 9*(6), 220–223. doi:10.1111/1467-8721.00099
Manz, C. C. (1986). Self-Leadership: Toward and expanded theory of self-influence processes in organization. *Academy of Management Review, 11*(3), 585–600. doi:10.5465/AMR.1986.4306232
Manz, C. C., & Sims, H. P. (1987). Leading workers to lead themselves: The external leadership of self-management work teams. *Administrative Science Quarterly, 32*(1), 106–129. doi:10.2307/2392745
Mayfield, J. R., Mayfield, M. R., & Kopf, J. (1998). The effects of leaders motivating language on subordinate performance and satisfaction. *Human Resources Management, 37*(3), 235–248.
McDonald, P. (2009). *Neurological Correlates to Authentic Leadership* (pp. 2–23). Wellington: Victoria Management School.
Neck, C. P., & Manz, C. C. (1996). Thought self-leadership: The impact of mental strategies training on employee cognition, behavior, and affect. *Journal of Organizational Behavior, 17*(5), 445–467. doi:10.1002/(SICI)1099-1379(199609)17:5<445::aid-job770=3.0.CO;2–N
Passmore, J. (2009). Mindfulness at work in coaching. *Danish Psychology Society Conference.* Copenhagen, Denmark: Danish Psychology Society. Retrieved from http://citeseerx.ist.psu.edu/viewdoc/download?doi=10.1.1.454.6504&rep=rep1&type
Schein, E. H. (1985). *Organisational culture and leadership: A dynamic view.* San Francisco: The Jossey-Bass.
Schmidt, S. (2011). Mindfulness in east and west - is it the same? In H. Walach (Ed.), *Neuroscience, consciousness and spirituality* (pp. 23–37). Consciousness and Spirituality 1. New York, NY: Springer.
Scott-Hall, S., Shumate, S. R., & Blum, S. (2007). Using model of emotional intelligence domains to indicate transformational leaders in hospitality industry. *Journal of Human Resources in Hospitality & Tourism,* 7(1), 99–113. doi:10.1300/J171v07n01_06
Sethi, D. (2009). Mindful leadership. *Leader to Leader, 51,* 7–11. doi:10.1002/ltl.311
Shamir, B., & Eilam, G. (2005). "What's your story"? A life-stories approach to authentic leadership development. *The Leadership Quarterly, 16,* 395–417. doi:10.1016/j.leaqua.2005.03.005
Sousa, D. (2012). *Brainwork.* Blommington, IN: Triple Nickel Press.
Terry, R. W. (1998). Authentic leadership: Courage in action. *Management Forum Series Speaker* (pp. 1–9). Executive Forum's Management Forum Series.
Tuleja, E. A. (2014). Developing cultural intelligence for global leadership through mindfulness. *Journal of Teaching in International Business, 25*(1), 5–25. doi:10.1080/08975930.2014.881275
Van Manen, M. (1984). Practicing Phenomenological Writing. *Phenomenology + Pedagogy,* University of Alberta *2*(1), 1984. pp. 36–72.
Van Manen, M. (1990). *Researching lived experience: Human science for an action sensitive pedagogy.* Ontario: Althouse Press.
Weick, K. E., & Putnam, T. (2006). Organizing for mindfulness eastern wisdom and western knowledge. *Journal of Management Inquiry, 15*(3), 275–287. doi:10.1177/1056492606291202

11

MINDFUL LEADERSHIP-FOLLOWERSHIP, CO-FLOW, AND CO-CREATIVITY

Wenli Wang and Petros G. Malakyan

1. Introduction

How is it possible to bring mindfulness, flow, and creativity into the workplace? Is it achievable? Creativity at the workplace could and should be as fun as improvisation in jazz. In order to avoid putting "creativity in a box," one ought to engage in mindful and co-creating activities with others.[1]

The seven lessons learned in jazz improvisation may shed light onto how to integrate *mindfulness*, *flow*, and *creativity* into the workplace:

1. provocative competence: deliberate efforts to interrupt habit patterns;
2. embracing errors as a source of learning;
3. shared orientation toward minimal structures that allow maximum flexibility;
4. distributed task: continual negotiation and dialogue towards dynamic synchronization;
5. reliance on retrospective sense-making;
6. "hanging out": membership in a community of practice;
7. taking turns soloing and supporting (Barrett, 1998).

The 21st-century workplace is changing rapidly. As a result, 80% of current work performances require team collaboration as opposed to the 20% team-based work of the 1980s (Hurwitz & Hurwitz, 2015). The digitalization of the workplace has interrupted traditional habitual patterns of work and work relationships. The followers' demand for authenticity forces leaders to admit their committed errors. Further, current employees share responsibilities that require minimal organizational structures with maximum flexibility. Work-related tasks are distributed not only among employees but also company leaders (Harris, Jones, & Baba, 2013) with ongoing dialogue and dynamic relationships.

Additionally, the rapidly changing workplace forces members of teams and organizations to adjust themselves to untested new realities by utilizing the only available tool—their "retrospective sense-making." It also makes members learn new skills and practice together to achieve group objectives. Lastly, as the line between leading and following roles becomes blurrier, the workforce is expected to develop multiple role identities by functioning as leaders in one and following in another situation. In other words, leadership and followership becomes a shared experience much like when the members of a jazz band "take turns soloing and supporting" (Barrett, 1998). Thus, today's organizations are challenged to not only play jazz well but also improvise (Alterhaug, 2004; Barrett, 1998; Gloor, Oster, & Fischbach, 2013; Weick, 1990).

Leading and following can be not only enjoyable for both parties but also creative. When leader and followers come together for a specific goal achievement, it often involves joyfully creating and co-creating something together "in the zone."

Let us "play jazz and improvise" in the workplace!

2. Mindful leaders and mindful leadership-followership

Literature on mindful leadership is nearly three decades old, while the use of the ancient Buddhist concept of mindfulness by various academic researchers and professionals date back to the second half of the 20th century. In leadership studies, mindful leadership takes both leader-focused and follower-focused theoretical approaches because the expectation is that leaders exercise mindfulness towards themselves as well as their followers. Thus, mindful leadership addresses not only personal but also interpersonal and social dimensions of mindfulness. How are mindfulness, mindful leaders, and mindful leadership–followership defined and applied in the workplace?

Mindfulness

Kabat-Zinn (1990), one of the early contributors, initially defined mindfulness as "a process of bringing a certain quality of attention to moment-by-moment experience." He later provided a more detailed definition of mindfulness as "the awareness that emerges through paying attention on purpose, in the present moment, and nonjudgmentally to the unfolding of experience moment by moment" (Kabat-Zinn, 2003, p. 145). Bishop and Associates (2004) proposed a similar operational definition of mindfulness as a meta-cognitive process of the self-regulation of attention "in order to bring a quality of nonelaborative awareness [self-knowledge] to current experience and a quality of relating to one's experience within an orientation of curiosity, experiential openness, and acceptance" (2004, p. 234). The origin of mindfulness stems from the Buddhist spiritual practices of meditation to end one's personal suffering (Hanh, 1976; Thera, 1962). The current understanding of mindfulness derives its meaning from Buddhist philosophy and cognitive psychology, which Dhiman (2009) defines as being awake to and aware of the external and internal environment, including "moment-to-moment changes that are taking place in our body and mind" (p. 58). Further, practicing mindfulness may foster physical, psychological, and emotional health due to its ability to cultivate conative, attentional, cognitive, and affective balance (Brown & Ryan, 2003; Wallace & Shapiro, 2006).

Why is mindfulness needed in the workplace? Malinowski and Lim (2015) observe mindfulness to have positive effects on work engagement by increasing positive affect, hope, and optimism. In other words, mindfulness at work has a direct impact on workplace wellbeing. The exploratory results of their research indicate that non-reactivity and non-judging mindfulness skills are important in the workplace.

Mindful leaders

The Institute for Mindful Leadership defines mindful leaders as

> Someone who embodies leadership presence by cultivating focus, clarity, creativity and compassion in the service of others. If we look more deeply into this

definition, we will notice that these four innate abilities are fundamentals of leadership excellence.[2]

Ellen Langer, who was the first pioneer to introduce mindfulness to organizational leadership, asserts, "In more than 30 years of research, we've found that increasing mindfulness increases charisma and productivity, decreases burnout and accidents, and increases creativity, memory, attention, positive affect, health, and even longevity" (2010. p. 60). Her research on leader mindfulness was based on three characteristics: "the continuous creation of new categories; openness to new information; and an implicit awareness of more than one perspective" (Langer, 1997, p. 4). As for *mindlessness*, Langer characterized it as a reliance on past categories; preventing attention to new information; and fixating on a single perspective. Leaders who operate from a mindlessness perspective seem to operate from confused understanding of stability of their assumptions with stability of their surroundings (Langer, 1989). In a more recent study, Carson and Langer (2006) argue that mindfulness is a path to achieving an unconditional self-acceptance. The more mindful people are, the more flexible they become, which leads to behavioral flexibility to adapt to the current changing environment. To achieve a full self-acceptance, the authors stress the importance of authenticity, the tyranny of evaluation, the mindfulness of mistakes, the mindfulness of social comparisons, the trap of rigid categories, and the acceptance of self as a mindful choice.

In today's digital era with "mounting fluidity, uncertainty, and rapid change," Kabat-Zinn (2009) asserts that mindfulness may help the members of the interconnected workplace to become more coherent, cohesive, and effective. The notion of unpredictability and uncertainty of today's personal and group experiences at work seem to require fluidity of leadership and mindfulness to cope with rapidly changing leading and following roles in the workplace. Thus, mindfulness is applicable to the leadership process and organizational life in order to navigate the unknown, understand the environment, and people (Dhiman, 2009). Such openness helps leaders to make new discoveries and find truth in the moment as opposed to seeking evidence or experience to validate their personal beliefs (Krishnamurti, 1982). This echoes with Sethi (2009), who sees mindful leadership as enabling leaders and organizations to live in the moment and enjoy what is "present and now" instead of spending most of their time and energy on reliving the past or fantasizing about the future. Mindfulness helps leaders to initiate balanced decision-making processes in organizations (Fiol & O'Connor, 2003) and enables them to embrace the present with nonjudgmental awareness (Hall-Renn, 2007).

Mindful leadership-followership

Eisenbeiss and Knippenberg (2015) studied the role of follower mindfulness and moral emotion on ethical leadership impact. After studying 135 leader–follower dyads, they found that followers' moral emotions (e.g., disgust, shame, anger, contempt, embarrassment, and guilt) and mindfulness "to stay attentive in the present and to precisely receive the external stimuli" or "attentive to what leadership and management influences are unfolding in their work surrounding" (p. 186). It is a discretionary work behavior due to its perception and response to ethical leadership. For managerial practices, Eisenbeiss and Knippenberg (2015) see a great promise in those employees who are prone to focus on the moral dimension of work and are more mindful than others. By relying on the clinical psychology research, they also recommend training on mindfulness (e.g., *mindfulness-based stress reduction*, or MBSR).

Additionally, the mindfulness training impacts "leadership stress, emotional reactivity, attention and working memory, perception and cognition, empathy, decision-making, and innovation" (Hunter & Chaskalson, 2013). McKee and Massimilian (2006) contend that senior executives who seem to be "always on" in today's digital age may renew themselves by using mindfulness, hope, and compassion in order to avoid burnouts and be able to cope with constantly mounting mental, physical, and psychological work-related pressure, perform at their best over a long period of time, and achieve a sustainable and long-term financial success for their organizations.

Mindful leadership boosts self-awareness, transforms oneself, and inspires others (Gonzalez, 2012). A number of scholars found compassion, contemplation and meditation, guided mindfulness, and engaged mindfulness as models for effective leadership development (Ashford & DeRue, 2012; George, 2010; Griffith, Sudduth, Flett, & Skiba, 2015; Lewis & Ebbeck, 2014). Further, an informed mindfulness is the foundation for leadership (Perlman, 2015).

Managers' spiritual mindfulness influences their work behavior and may result in ethical behaviors in organizations (McGhee & Grant, 2015). Equally, when managers fail in their spiritual mindfulness, it results in feeling frustrated, anxious, and defeated. The authors offer a model on spiritual mindfulness for producing ethical behaviors in organizations. The model proposes the following process: being intentionally attentive or authentic; holding intentionally other-oriented attitude; attention and attitude affect wellbeing, which may produce ethical behavior (p. 24). A similar study was conducted by Reb, Narayanan, and Chaturvedi (2014) on the impact of leaders' mindfulness on employee wellbeing and performance. They found that supervisors' trait of mindfulness is positively associated with different facets of employee well-being, such as job satisfaction and need satisfaction, and different dimensions of employee performance, such as in-role performance and organizational citizenship behaviors. They also found that the employee wellbeing and psychological need satisfaction play mediating roles between supervisor mindfulness and employee performance (p. 36).

In summary, the above studies indicate that mindfulness has a positive impact on both leaders' and followers' ethical behavior. Mindfulness reduces work-related stress and fosters physical, psychological, and emotional health. A mindful person easily adapts to change, initiates balanced decision-making processes, and embraces the present with nonjudgmental awareness. In addition, mindfulness improves leader–follower and manager–subordinate relationships; enables leaders to exercise presence at work through focus, clarity, creativity, and compassion in the service of others; enables leaders to be more follower-centered in the workplace and be sensitive toward the needs of their followers; and it fosters self, group, and environmental awareness. It helps to navigate the unknown, orient oneself to a rapidly changing work environment, and understand people; helps to create new categories, be open to new information, and have implicit awareness of multiple perspectives. Finally, supervisors' mindfulness is positively associated with employee job satisfaction and role performance and organizational citizenship behaviors. The literature also seems to implicitly indicate that leadership is a stressful role and that our minds and bodies are not designed to lead all the time and live under a constant stress. How should leadership responsibilities be handled? The next topic on flow in the workplace sheds some light on what can be done to minimize work-related stress and maximize personal and group satisfaction and wellbeing in the workplace.

3. Mindful leadership–followership in cultivating co-flow

Flow

Mihaly Csikszentmihalyi (2004), who studied human life to understand the sources of one's happiness, pleasure, joy, and lasting satisfaction that reaches to a state of "flow" has discovered that those who reach this optimal experience in what they do face great challenges matching with their high skills over a long period of time. To develop high skills to face matching challenges requires many years of practice (e.g., an athlete, a musician, a successful organizational leader).[3] Csikszentmihalyi (1990/2008) defines optimal experience or the concept of flow as "the state in which people are involved in an activity that nothing else seems to matter; the experience itself is so enjoyable that people will do it even at greater cost, for the sheer sake of doing it" (p. 4).

In the book on *Optimal Experience*, Csikszentmihalyi and Csikszentmihalyi (1992) argue that what makes a person experience genuine satisfaction in life is a state of controlled and sustainable order in consciousness referred to as *flow*. In this state, the person is fully involved with life and experiences deep pleasure and creativity with whatever activity or work they are involved. Thus, *optimal experience* is something that one makes happen. For instance, "the best moments usually occur when a person's body or mind is stretched to its limits in a voluntary effort to accomplish something difficult and worthwhile" (Csikszentmihalyi, 1990/2008, p. 3).

To further describe the state of *flow*, which was assessed through numerous interviews of famous and accomplished people, Csikszentmihalyi (1990/2008) also introduced the concept of *autotelic* ("intrinsically motivated") *activities*—those in which people are motivated by a drive within themselves, not just external forces such as family or wages.[4] "Autotelic" from Greek words *auto* (self) and *telos* (goal) means a self-contained activity that causes a self-fulfillment. For instance, people engage in various *autotelic activities* and enter a stage of *flow* through digital games that foster experiential learning (Romeo & Cantoia, 2011). Musical performances may also be viewed as *autotelic activities* leading to a state of *flow*. Walters (2016), a choral conductor, sought to know whether a conductor can intentionally create flow among singers. Through score study and analysis, he discovered fascinating evidence that suggests that musical students are inclined to "'catch' flow from their teacher," which indicates that "group flow may be an empirically observable phenomenon" (p. 18).

Co-flow in leadership-followership

Can *flow* apply to workplace contexts in leader–follower relationships? Hurwitz and Hurwitz (2015) answer this question from the perspective of a generational change from Csikszentmihalyi's "Me Generation" of the 1980s to the "We Generation" of the 21st century. The latter moved away from individual achievement to collective achievement. Hurwitz and Hurwitz (2015) write, "By 2010, 80% of work was team-based, up from only 20% in 1980 . . . . Because of the explosion in team-based work, flow has given way to co-flow as the target state. And that requires learning a new set of skills" (p. 4). Nevertheless, Csikszentmihalyi's (1990/2008) nine dimensions of *flow* can be adopted to Hurwitz and Hurwitz's (2015) modified concept of *co-flow*. Csikszentmihalyi and Csikszentmihalyi (1992) proposed nine dimensions of flow: (1) equilibrium of challenge and skills, (2) clear goals, (3) immediate feedback, (4) focused concentration, (5) merging of activity and awareness, (6) outcome under individual's control, (7) distorted time perception, (8) loss of self-awareness, and (9) autotelic or intrinsically rewarding. Hancock and Associates (2019) reiterate Csikszentmihalyi's nine dimensions by grouping them under three flow categories: (I) antecedents of flow (the first three dimensions), (II) experientials of flow, i.e., characteristics of the immediate momentary flow experience (the middle three dimensions), and (III) consequences of flow (the last three dimensions).

Applying nine dimensions of *flow* to leader–follower dynamic relationships:

1. *Equilibrium of challenge and skills.* Balancing the leadership challenge and skills continues to be a contemporary topic in the study and practice of leadership (Kouzes & Posner, 2012). The balancing act becomes even harder for the state of *co-flow*, where the equilibria need to expand from the match between leadership challenge and leadership skills to the matches between leadership challenge and followership skills, followership challenge and leadership skills, and followership challenge and followership skills. Therefore, a state of *co-flow* in leader–follower dynamic relationship is rare. Further, the digital age, unlike any other generation, brings new workplace challenges that require new sets of partnership skills between leaders and followers (Hurwitz & Hurwitz, 2015). To reach to a state of *co-flow*, one must develop both leading and following skills to face today's leadership and followership challenges. In other words, leaders must learn how to lead, and followers must learn how to follow. Conversely, leaders must acquire following skills, and followers must acquire leading skills. In addition, all need to mindfully be open to and understand the challenges on both sides. Most company or organizational leaders have no formal or professional education in leadership. Most employees, if not all, have not been educated on how to be courageous followers and to not only act ethically, but also hold unethical leaders accountable (Chaleff, 2009). In the era of entrepreneurship and information technology, where the distinction between following and leading roles are becoming more and more fuzzy, there is tension about who should truly take the role of the leader and how to balance the leadership and followership. In order to turn the tension into a *co-flow*, the following two options seem feasible:
   a. Leaders and followers become competent in working in teams as partners, together facing the challenges for both, much like in the tango (Chaleff, 2009).[5] This new relationship can also create new challenges that require new sets of skills for the "We Generation" (Hurwitz & Hurwitz, 2015). If individuals play both roles voluntarily and willingly, the "dance" of leading and following partnership may turn into a state of *co-flow*.
   b. Leaders become competent in leading and in following. Followers, in turn, are also competent in both following and leading. As a result, leaders and followers develop multiple role identities and have experiential understanding of challenges faced by multiple role identities. If they exchange their roles voluntarily and willingly, they may reach mutual optimal experiences or *co-flow*. Malakyan (2014) calls this exchange *leader–follower trade* based on one's competency and willingness to trade their leading or following role for collaboration, partnership, and workplace wellbeing.
2. *Clear goals.* In flow, people always know what to expect for "every step of the way" (Csikszentmihalyi, 1997, p. 111). The component of flow from a *clear goals* perspective can be experienced as a *co-flow* in leader–follower relationships if leaders communicate clear goals with their followers. Or, when followers share the same goals with the leader and they together engage in goal attainment activities, they may experience a *co-flow* of collaboration and partnership. It is important, however, that followers and leaders support goals set forth by both parties in order to experience a *co-flow*. If they run parallel, leaders and followers may pursue parallel goals that may never merge into shared goals. However, if separate and parallel goals pursued by leaders and followers arrive to a common network with shared hubs, it is possible to enable "the network to better optimize common communication patterns."[6]

3. *Immediate feedback*. A feedback loop (leaders providing feedback to followers and followers providing feedback to leaders) is essential in leader–follower relationships to guarantee a *co-flow* of positive emotions and highly effective team performances to achieve desired outcomes. Gigler and Bailur (2014) explore technology as an acceleration tool for closing the accountability gap between supply and demand. Their editorial volume reviews and assesses the links between empowerment, participation, transparency, and accountability. Further, Regine and Lewin (2000, p. 8) assert,

   > Feedback loops exist in complex adaptive systems, and through their dynamics the system evolves over time. When relationships and connections are weak in an organization, there is a poor flow of information, limiting feedback loops and thus adaptability. In order to have more positive outcomes, positive and constructive relationships need to feed into those loops, and a great deal of interconnection among people is needed to enrich the loops.

   Ongoing feedback from the leader to the follower and from the follower to the leader may secure a safe space for a *co-flow* in leader–follower relationships in the workplace.
4. *Focused concentration*. Csikszentmihalyi (1990/2008) discovered that "the best moments usually occur when a person's body or mind is stretched to its limits in a voluntary effort to accomplish something difficult and worthwhile. Optimal experience is thus something that we make happen" (p. 3). However, in leader–follower relationships the mind and body stretching to accomplish something difficult and worthwhile requires an equal focus and concentration by the leader as well as the followers. Thus, those best leader–follower moments can only occur when leader and followers agree to create them collaboratively. Once the components of focused concentration are present, such as intentionality, initiation, attention, absorption, and presence, leaders and followers may experience a *co-flow* (Agarwal & Karahanna, 2000).
5. *Merging of activity and awareness*. During intense emotional experiences when actions or events capture one's full attention to the extent that the person cares less about their safety or wellbeing, one may be carried away by a vision or a task ahead and be ready for everything. The merging of activities and awareness from the leader can initiate and inspire the *co-flow* from the followers. For instance, Martin Luther King Jr. was so absorbed by what was happening around him, he said the following in his speech on April 3, 1968, at Mason Temple (Church of God in Christ Headquarters), in Memphis, Tennessee:

   > And then I got into Memphis. And some began to say the threats, or talk about the threats that were out. What would happen to me from some of our sick white brothers? Well, I don't know what will happen now. We've got some difficult days ahead. But it really doesn't matter with me now, because I've been to the mountaintop.
   > And I don't mind.
   > Like anybody, I would like to live a long life. Longevity has its place. But I'm not concerned about that now. I just want to do God's will. And He's allowed me to go up to the mountain. And I've looked over. And I've seen the Promised Land. I may not get there with you. But I want you to know tonight, that we, as a people, will get to the Promised Land!
   > And so I'm happy, tonight.

I'm not worried about anything.
I'm not fearing any man!
Mine eyes have seen the glory of the coming of the Lord!!

The next day, Martin Luther King Jr. was assassinated. The people following his footsteps have forever carried on his spirit.

6. *Outcome under individual's control.* Leading and following behaviors are conscious and controlled activities, and the relationships between leaders and followers are always outcome-based. Both leading and following must have a purpose, goal, and anticipated outcome. Again, in leader–follower relationships, the outcome is not under the control of the leader or the follower, but both. As Hurwitz and Hurwitz (2015) rightly noted, in the "we generation" of the information and technology age outcomes are designed and shared collaboratively through leader–follower partnerships. Thus, outcomes controlled and achieved by leaders and followers have a potential to reach a state of *co-flow*.
7. *Distorted time perception.* When leaders and followers are engaged in meaningful and mutually enriching activities to accomplish common goals, the concept of time may cease to become a decisive factor to end that activity (Agarwal & Karahanna, 2000). In that state of *co-flow*, they may engage in those activities as long as it takes to reach their goals because both the process and the goals motivate them to carry on, regardless of time.
8. *Loss of self-awareness.* When leaders inspire and motivate followers for a cause and when followers affirm the leader's behavior and decisions, both the leader and followers become more altruistic, ready to sacrifice time, energy, and sometime their own personal lives. Transformational, charismatic, and servant leadership models fall within this category. For instance, Mahatma Gandhi, Martin Luther King Jr., and Nelson Mandela are prime examples for their selfless and self-denial postures and how their leadership activities shaped new identities in them. In return, they received loyalty and dedication from their followers that, in a sense, created a state of *co-flow* between them and their followers.
9. *Autotelic or intrinsically rewarding.* Leaders driven by their values or beliefs motivate and inspire followers to achieve extraordinary results for their organizations and communities. They do what they do voluntarily and not for money. They find their engagements with organizational or social issues intrinsically rewarding. Similarly, the autotelic efforts and contributions from the followers can also illicit the state of *co-flow* with the leader.

There is also caution for non-volunteered autotelic activity. Can work be considered an *autotelic activity*? Seemann and Seemann (2013) propose to balancing "the Big 4 factors challenge [C] vs. skill [S], and workload [WL] vs. capacity to work [CW]," as a new perspective for employee motivation, which may "help to increase satisfaction and achievements of employees and thus boost the effectiveness of organizations" (p. 1). If flow or optimal experience is promoted or initiated by the employer to motivate employees in order to achieve more productivity, this may lead to employee manipulations and exploitations. For instance, motivated by job security and group solidarity, Japanese companies encourage employees to socialize together after work hours, which causes employees to ignore time and personal needs and become addicted to long-hours harder work year around. As a result, the young Japanese work themselves to death; this is known as "karoshi."[7]

Hence, as discussed above, the nine dimensions of *flow* can be applied in the leader–follower dynamic relationship to create the state of *co-flow* at the group level. The categorizations of antecedence, experiential, and consequence dimensions still work.

However, complexity naturally increases with the application of an individual-level construct to that of the group level. For instance, for the dimension of "outcome under individual's control," there is no more individual, but instead, the group. The outcome should be under the group's control, of both the leader and the followers. It is much easier to get immediate feedback individually for one's own work, but it becomes difficult to allow group members to have immediate feedback at the group level for both peer-to-peer and leader-to-followers. Information transparency has been well studied as an enabler for the enhanced communications of feedback among group members. Hence, the state of *co-flow* calls for mindful leaders and mindful leadership–followership to create group-level informational flow and collaborations.

4. Mindful leadership–followership in cultivating co-creativity

Creativity

Prior to the Industrial Revolution, creativity has often referred to artistic activities such as music, painting, and writing (e.g., poetry and fiction). With the digital evolution in the late 20th century, creativity has become a source of competitive advantage for businesses and organizations. How to achieve and sustain creativity in any workforce at any workplace, way beyond the artistic domains, is a big challenge faced by organizational leaders.

Researchers in the artistic domains have historically examined creativity. Communication scholars Fulton and McIntyre (2013) ask: Where does creative writing come from? Is it from an external source (divine inspiration), from the author (romantic view), or from the audience (poststructuralist view)? The transmission model of communication refers to the first two sources of meaning-making, and the cultural context model refers to the audience who creates meanings. They argue that either the models address the process of creativity, as both focus only on individuals (producer or receiver). They concurred with the systems model of creativity, developed by Csikszentmihalyi (1988, 2015), where the individual (producer and receiver) is a crucial component of a creative system, together with the context providing creativity production.

Individual creativity is crucial because individuals produce novelty (at least at the time where artificial intelligence still has its vast limitations in comparison with that of human). How is it possible to create individual creativity? There are many approaches; flow and mindfulness are two exemplary pathways. The relationship between flow and creativity is bi-directional. Creative individuals tend to experience more state of flow. Individuals in the state of flow tend to be more creative. Csikszentmihalyi (1997) sees creativity as a flow, an opportunity for people to invent something for the sake of it and enjoy the process while creating it. Thus, "it is not *what* these people do that counts but *how* they do it" (p. 107).

Unfortunately, creativity is neither a subject that is well taught nor a skill that is well cultivated in education. Even worse, studies show that the typical western education system actually reduces creativity. George Land, who consulted NASA for selecting innovative engineers and scientists, developed a creativity test back in the 1960s. His team's longitudinal research (Land & Jarman, 1992) has shown that 98% of five-year-old children were creative, but that rate dropped to 30% when they were at the age of ten, and again to only 12% by the time they turned fifteen. More disheartening, merely 2% of adults are creative. Their conclusion of the education system's undermining of creativity is in alignment with that of Sir Ken Robinson, a creativity and education expert.[8] The de-emphasis of creativity in education is also reflected in the continuous under-appreciation of creativity at the workplace. Such under-appreciation is contradictory to the need and the wish of achieving more creativity in the workplace. However, managers dislike activities or attributes that are hard to measure or control. Creativity, definitely, is difficult to measure or control. Organizational leaders, especially mindful leaders with much broad vision seeing the potential high return on investment of creativity, are actually much more enthusiastic advocates for creativity.

Creativity is often sprung out of "autotelic or intrinsically rewarding" activities that are rooted in curiosity and delight. Creativity requires out-of-the-box thinking and such innovative thinking needs sufficient time to allow it to sprout and grow. The four dimensions of "focused concentration," "merging of activities and awareness," "loss of self-awareness," and "distorted time dimension" in the state of flow are reflections of mindfulness in the present moment without distractions, allowing the emergence and the development of innovative thinking into creative outcomes. Out-of-the-box thinking also implies the deviation from the typical routines. The other four dimensions of flow—"equilibrium of challenge and skills," "clear goals," "immediate feedback," and "outcome under controls"—imply the attachment to the past (e.g., existing skills) and the future (e.g., expectations, goals, the meeting/un-meeting with the intermediate expectations through the feedback, controllable outcome). The attachment to the past and the future is not mindfulness.

In contrast, mindfulness calls for actions without specifically aiming for the fruits of these actions. It implies total openness to actions without the pre-emptive planning of and the procedural attachment to the creative outcome pre- and during the actions. Whether or not the actions lead to creativity is not a concern, as concern implies a sense of fear, and any sense of fear could be an emotional obstacle for creativity. Being mindful means being open to and nonjudgmental of the actions and the actions' outcomes. There is also a caution that not all activities conducted in the state of flow can produce creative outcomes. It depends on the types of activities. The activities could be simple and repetitive tasks that call for no creativity. Many players of simple video games like card games can easily go into the state of flow. Their tasks are procedural, following a fixed set of simple rules. One can easily be cognitively and emotionally immersed in these games for the purpose of killing time and pure entertainment. They could play the games in a shorter time when in the state of flow; but that does not imply they achieve creativity because the games are designed with clear-cut predefined outcomes and prevent any circumvention of the rules of the games.

Although it is still inconclusive in neuroscience studies whether the brain chemicals of the flow state lead to creativity, there is strong neuroscience evidence of the benefits of mindfulness. Wallas's four-stage model of creative process (preparation, incubation, illumination, and verification) (Wallas, 1926, p. 10) and the later extended five-stage model (preparation, incubation, intimation, illumination, and verification) based on more detailed reading of the original work of Wallas have different proximity of consciousness (Sadler-Smith, 2015): preparation and verification are conscious work; incubation is close to nonconsciousness; intimation has proximity to fringe consciousness; and illumination is more related to focal consciousness. Similarly, more neuroscience studies of mindfulness and its relation to different levels of consciousness (consciousness, non-consciousness, fringe consciousness, focal consciousness) will further the connection between mindfulness and creativity as well.

Co-creativity in leadership-followership

Mindful leaders foster individual creativity and enterprise innovation (Gehani, 2011). Enterprise innovation is often a team effort in co-creativity. Individual creativity is a building block for

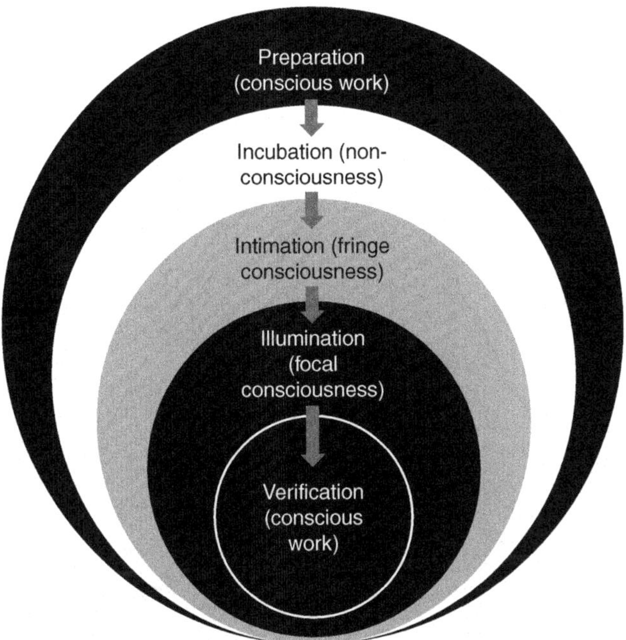

Figure 11.1 Five stages of creative process (adopted from Sadler-Smith, 2015)

team co-creativity. Creativity is hard; co-creativity is even harder. Mindful leadership–followership can play a stimulating role by providing the right context for co-creativity.

The right context refers to the society field and the cultural domain in the triangle systems model of creativity proposed by Csikszentmihalyi (2003), where the domain transmits information to the individual, the individual produces novelty, and the field may or may not select the novelty and pass it to the field. Applying this approach to the workplace creativity, it seems evident that co-creativity in the workplace requires a complex system of interactions between creative individuals, whose personalities and novelties play a pivotal point, groups within the organization, who co-create their own organizational culture, and the external influence of the broader field. Creative leadership

> is a philosophy and an act: it develops and realizes innovative ideas through the shared ambition of improving the world through enterprise formation. Those who employ creative leadership do so by forging an environment that promotes innovative thinking and mission-driven entrepreneurship[9]

Rill and Hämäläinen (2018) propose two conceptual models of co-creativity for various contexts, such as in design (co-design and human-centered design), in marketing (value co-creation between the producer and consumer during the use of the product), in organizations (tapping into the collective insight to generate breakthrough solutions by bringing diverse stakeholders together). According to Rill and Hämäläinen (2018), three components are essential for co-creativity: people, environment, and process. Creative design is a process through *intentional experience design* by which a mindful leader generates a creative "space between" people, environment, and process.

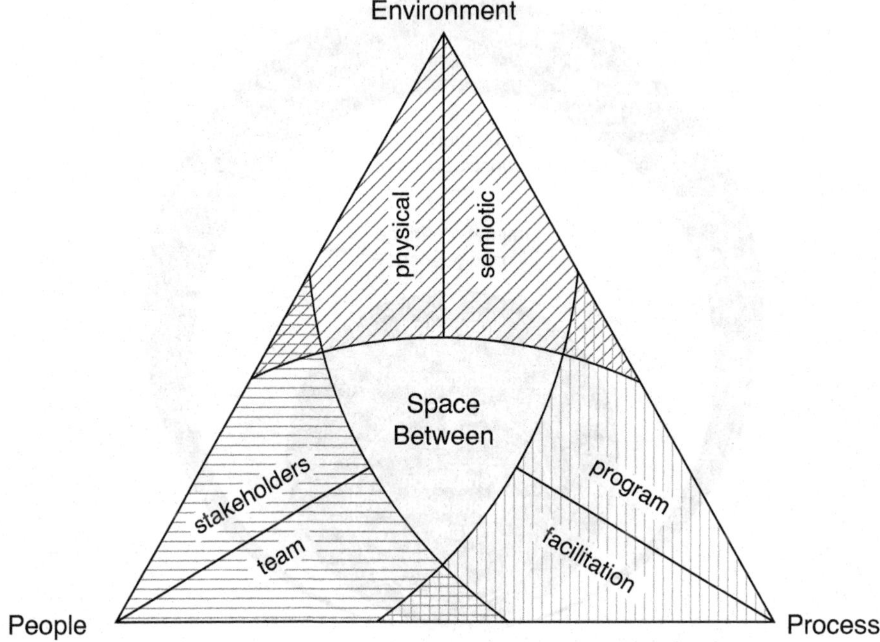

Figure 11.2 Intentional experience design of co-creativity (Rill & Hämäläinen, 2018)

Rill (2016) offers a co-creation model called "resonance." Resonance in physics is a vibration of objects when the natural frequency of one object is equalized with the natural frequency of another object by causing accelerated vibrations. In music, resonance may increase the intensity of a sound. Due to electrical resonance we are able to tune radios and television programs.

Rill's use of the theatrical performance is another metaphor for resonance to describe fluid and interdependent interactions between the performers, director, script, the audience, and the environment create a cohesive framework for co-creativity. He writes:

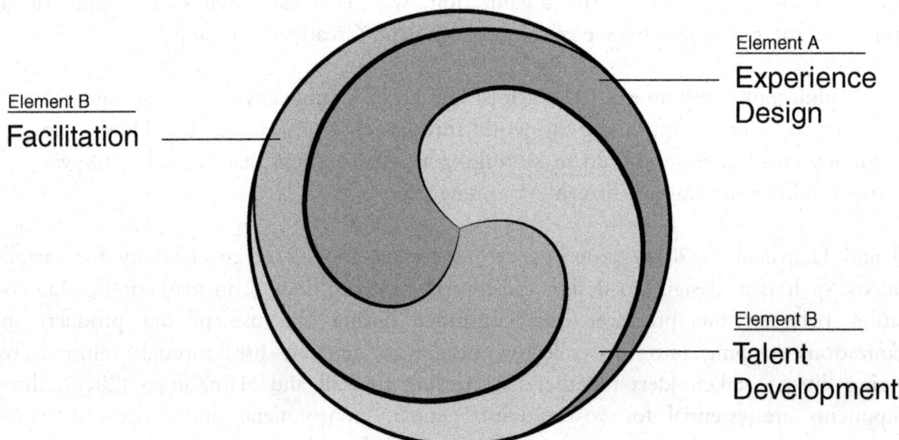

Figure 11.3 The resonant model of co-creativity (adopted from Rill, 2016)

> If we consider the metaphor of *performance theatre*, resonance is when a special synergy is felt in the space between. These are powerful moments when insights seem to just "pop out" from seemingly nowhere. They are the "*ah ha*" moments in creativity when everything shifts. What are occurring are moments of creativity that spontaneously emerge when a group is resonant (frequencies in harmony) with itself. In other terms, resonance is an amplification of creative output resulting from a harmony among elements.[10]

Rill's resonant co-creativity model consists of three elements: *experience design*, *talent development*, and *facilitation*, which require shared attention, trust, empathy, and synchrony as essential integrative skills for generating a co-creative mindset. Trust and empathy are attributes of mindfulness. Shared attention and synchrony are reflections of the state of co-flow.

6. Conclusion

From the leadership context, mindfulness implies an awareness of moment-to-moment changes that are taking place in leadership–followership. Leadership–followership involves leader, followers, leader–followers dyad, the role exchange dynamics, and their contextual environment.

Mindful leadership–followership has the high sensitivity of the contextual environment and all of the elements within. Mindful leaders are nonjudgmental to individuals involved to stimulate personal flow and creativity and are open-minded to introduce favorable interactive dynamics that promote group-level co-flow and co-creativity.

Mindful leaders have the trust that once the contextual environment is set to entice flow and co-flow, there would be individual creativity and team co-creativity sprung out of such natural flows. Mindful leaders have the patience to wait. It is often at the unknown time and at the most unexpected places that creativity strikes. Mindful leaders have the long-term vision and the endurance.

Mindful leaders are much more than managers. They have visions and have the entrepreneurial spirits to take risks within reasonable bounds. Unlike managers who favor routines and predictability, mindful leaders welcome non-routines and unexpected outcome. Unlike managers who assign workload, quotas, and assignments to subordinates, mindful leaders liberate followers from these extrinsic expectations/obligations and encourage their autotelic activities. Through mindful stress-reduction, they encourage flow and creativity.

Mindful leaders are systems thinkers. They understand the complexity of system dynamics—some dynamics are favorable, such as the synchrony among team members; some dynamics are unfavorable, such as disharmony with conflicts and offsets. Mindful leaders have the sensitivity and awareness to the subtleties and the intricacies. They can skillfully resolve conflicts, reduce offsets, and systematically encourage co-flow and co-creativity to induce synergy, moment-by-moment, even in the ever-changing workplace of the digital era.

Five chapter takeaways/lessons

1. It is possible to cultivate co-flow and co-creativity in organizations if leaders and followers practice mindfulness in the workplace. Mindfulness exercised in a team is a philosophical foundation/trait (antecedent) for achieving a state of co-flow (process) in order to achieve co-creativity (outcome) for collective wellbeing and productivity (purpose).
2. Mindful leadership–followership nurtures ethical relationships in the workplace and positively impacts leader and follower ethical behaviors. It reduces work-related stress, fosters physical and psychological health, and encourages balanced decision-making.

Mindfulness helps both leader and followers interdependently to exercise presence, develop nonjudgmental awareness, improve relationships, navigate the unknown, adapt to rapid change, and improve job satisfaction.

3. Csikszentmihalyi's (1990/2008) concept of *flow* may be expanded to *co-flow* to make it relevant to the "we generation" in the digital age. It is not mere individual *flow* that matters in today's team-based workplace but the *co-flow*, where members of the team create environments to experience *co-flow* in all nine dimensions of the flow theory. Hence, the state of *co-flow* calls for mindful leaders and mindful leadership–followership to create group-level informational flow and collaborations.
4. Mindfulness sets the stage for *flow* and *co-flow* experience, while the latter grants individuals and groups freedom to become creative. Thus, creativity is contingent upon the experience of high challenge and skills (flow; co-flow). However, it requires openness and presence, which is mindfulness.
5. Creativity is often sprung out of "autotelic or intrinsically rewarding" activities that are rooted in curiosity and delight. In order to turn the creativity into co-creativity in the workplace, leaders ought to mindfully design and cultivate the right system and culture to encourage and facilitate collaborative and synergistic new talent development.

Five reflection questions

1. Why is mindful leadership–followership needed in the digital workplace?
2. What are the challenges in achieving co-flow and co-creativity in the digital workplace?
3. What are the nine dimensions of co-flow in the context of leadership–followership?
4. How can creativity and co-creativity be systematically facilitated?
5. What roles do mindful leaders play in cultivating workplace co-flow and co-creativity?

Notes

1 See Miles Davis, *Blues by Five.* Retrieved from www.jazzadvice.com/10-brilliant-jazz-solos-and-what-you-can-learn-from-them/
2 Retrieved from www.huffpost.com/entry/welcome-institue-for-mindful-leadership_b_3698126
3 Retrieved from www.ted.com/talks/mihaly_csikszentmihalyi_on_flow?language=en#t-22203
4 Retrieved from www.cgu.edu/news/2000/09/mihaly-csikszentmihalyi-flow/
5 Watch "Leadership and Followership: What Tango Teaches Us about These Roles in Life," by Ira Chaleff. www.youtube.com/watch?v=Cswrnc1dggg
6 See https://web.eecs.umich.edu/~sugih/courses/eecs589/f16/34-Coflow.pdf
7 See www.bbc.com/news/business-39981997
8 For more information, visit www.ted.com/speakers/sir_ken_robinson
9 Retrieved from www.thnk.org/insights/what-is-creative-leadership/
10 Retrieved from http://cocreation.world/co-creation/

References

Agarwal, R., & Karahanna, E. (2000). Time flies when you're having fun: Cognitive absorption and beliefs about information technology usage. *MIS quarterly*, 665–694.

Alterhaug, B. (2004). Improvisation on a triple theme: Creativity, jazz improvisation and communication. *Studia Musicologica Norvegica, 30*(3), 97–117.

Ashford, S. J., & DeRue, S. D. (2012). Developing as a leader: The power of mindful engagement. *Organizational Dynamics, 41,* 146–154. doi:10.1016/j.orgdyn.2012.01.008

Barrett, F. J. (1998). Coda—creativity and improvisation in jazz and organizations: Implications for organizational learning. *Organization Science, 9*(5), 605–622.

Bishop, S. R., Lau, M., Shapiro, S., Carlson, L., Anderson, N. D., Carmody, J., & Devins, G. (2004). Mindfulness: A proposed operational definition. *Clinical Psychology: Science and Practice, 11*(3), 230–241. doi:10.1093/clipsy. bph077

Brown, K. W., & Ryan, R. M. (2003). The benefits of being present: Mindfulness and its role in psychological well-being. *Journal of Personality and Social Psychology, 84*(1), 822–848. doi:10.1037/0022-3514.84.4.822

Carson, S. H., & Langer, E. J. (2006). Mindfulness and self-acceptance. *Journal of Rational- Emotive & Cognitive-Behavior Therapy, 24*(1), 29–43. doi:10.1007/s10942-006-0022-5

Chaleff, I. (2009). *The courageous follower: Standing up to & for our leaders*. San Francisco, CA: Berrett-Koehler Publishers.

Csikszentmihalyi, M. (1988). The flow experience and its significance for human psychology. In M. Csikszentmihalyi & I. S. Csikszentmihalyi (Eds.), *Optimal experience: Psychological studies of flow in consciousness* (pp. 15–35). New York, NY, US: Cambridge University Press.

Csikszentmihalyi, M. (1990). *Flow: The psychology of optimal experience*. New York: Harper & Row.

Csikszentmihalyi, M. (1997). Flow and the psychology of discovery and invention. New York, 39: Harper Perennial.

Csikszentmihalyi, M. (2003). Implications of a systems perspective for the study of creativity. In R. Sternberg (Ed.), *Handbook of creativity* (pp. 313–335). Cambridge, UK: Cambridge University Press.

Csikszentmihalyi, M. (2004). *Good business: Leadership, flow, and the making of meaning*. New York: Penguin.

Csikszentmihalyi, M. (2008). *Flow: The psychology of optimal experience*. New York: Harper Collins Publishers.

Csikszentmihalyi, M. (2015). *The systems model of creativity: The collected works of Mihaly Csikszentmihalyi*. Dordrecht, The Netherlands: Springer.

Csikszentmihalyi, M., & Csikszentmihalyi, I. S. (Eds.). (1992). *Optimal experience: Psychological studies of flow in consciousness*. Cambridge, UK: Cambridge university press.

Dhiman, S. (2009). Mindfulness in life and leadership: An exploratory survey. *Interbeing, 3*(1), 1–15.

Eisenbeiss, S. A., & Knippenberg, D. (2015). On ethical leadership impact: The role of follower mindfulness and moral emotions. *Journal of Organizational Behavior, 36*(2), 182–195. doi:10.1002/job.1968

Fiol, C. M., & O'Connor, E. J. (2003). Waking up! Mindfulness in the face of bandwagons. *Academy of Management Review, 28*(1), 54–70.

Fulton, J., & McIntyre, P. (2013). Futures of communication: Communication studies creativity. *Review of Communication, 13*(4), 269–289.

Gehani, R. R. (2011). Individual creativity and the influence of mindful leaders on enterprise innovation. *Journal of Technology Management and Innovation, 6*(3), 83–91. doi:10.4067/S0718-27242011000300006

George, B. (2010). Mindful leadership: Compassion, contemplation and meditation develop effective leaders. *European Financial Review*.

Gigler, B. S., & Bailur, S. (Eds.). (2014). *Closing the feedback loop: Can technology bridge the accountability gap?* The World Bank.

Gloor, P. A., Oster, D., & Fischbach, K. (2013). JazzFlow—Analyzing "group flow" among jazz musicians through "honest signals". *KI-Künstliche Intelligenz, 27*(1), 37–43.

Gonzalez, M. (2012). *Mindful leadership: The 9 ways to self-awareness, transforming yourself, and inspiring others*. Mississauga, Ontario, Canada: John Wiley & Sons.

Griffith, R. L., Sudduth, M. M., Flett, A., & Skiba, T. S. (2015). Looking forward: Meeting the global need for leaders through guided mindfulness. In *Leading global teams* (pp. 325–342). New York, NY: Springer. doi:10.1007/978-1-4939-2050-1_14

Hall-Renn, K. E. (2007). Mindful journeys: Embracing the present with non-judgemental awareness. *Journal of Creativity in Mental Health, 2*(2), 3–16. doi:10.1300/J456v02n02_02

Hancock, P. A., Kaplan, A. D., Cruit, J. K., Hancock, G. M., MacArthur, K. R., & Szalma, J. L. (2019). A meta-analysis of flow effects and the perception of time. *Acta Psychologica, 198*, 102836.

Hanh, T. N. (1976). *The miracle of mindfulness: A manual for meditation*. Boston: Beacon.

Harris, A., Jones, M., & Baba, S. (2013). Distributed leadership and digital collaborative learning: A synergistic relationship? *British Journal of Educational Technology, 44*(6), 926–939.

Hunter, J., & Chaskalson, M. (2013). Making the mindful leader. In S. Leonard, R. Lewis, A. Freeman, & J. Passmore, *The Wiley-Blackwell handbook of the psychology of leadership, change and OD* (pp. 1–42). Chichester, England: Wiley-Blackwell.

Hurwitz, M., & Hurwitz, S. (2015). *Leadership is half the story: A fresh look at followership, leadership, and collaboration*. Toronto, Canada: University of Toronto Press.

Kabat-Zinn, J. (1990). *Full catastrophe living: Using the wisdom of your mind to face stress, pain and illness*. New York: Dell.

Kabat-Zinn, J. (2003). Mindfulness-based interventions in context: Past, present, and future. *Clinical Psychology: Science and Practice, 10*(2), 144–156. doi:10.1093/clipsy.bpg016

Kabat-Zinn, J. (2009). *Wherever you go, there you are: Mindfulness meditation in everyday life*. New York: Hachette Books.

Kouzes, J. M., & Posner, B. Z. (2012). *The leadership challenge: How to make extraordinary things happen in organizations*. San Francisco. CA: The Leadership Challenge.

Krishnamurti, J. (1982). *The network of thought*. London, England: Krishnamurti Foundation Trust.

Land, G., & Jarman, B. (1992). *Breakpoint and beyond: Mastering the future today*. New York: HarperCollins Publishers.

Langer, E. (2010). A call for mindful leadership. *Harvard Business Review, 28*, 60.

Langer, E. J. (1989). Minding matters: The consequences of mindlessness-mindfulness. In L. Berkowitz (Ed.), *Advances in experimental social psychology* (Vol. *22*, pp. 137–173). San Diego: Academic Press.

Langer, E. J. (1997). *The power of mindful learning*. Reading, MA: Addison-Wesley.

Lewis, A. B., & Ebbeck, V. (2014). Mindful and self-compassionate leadership development: Preliminary discussions with wildland fire managers. *Journal of Forestry, 112*(2), 230–236.

Malakyan, P. G. (2014). Followership in leadership studies: A case of leader–follower trade approach. *Journal of Leadership Studies*, 7(4), 6–22.

Malinowski, P., & Lim, H. J. (2015). Mindfulness at work: Positive affect, hope, and optimism mediate the relationship between dispositional mindfulness, work engagement, and well-being. *Mindfulness, 6* (6), 1250–1262. doi:10.1007/s12671-015-0388-5

McGhee, P., & Grant, P. (2015). The influence of managers' spiritual mindfulness on ethical behavirour in organisations. *Journal of Spirituality, Leadership and Management, 8*(1), 12–33. doi:10.15183/slm2015.08.1113

McKee, A., & Massimilian, D. (2006). Resonate leadership: A new kind of leadership for the digital age. *Journal of Business Strategy, 27*(5), 45–49. doi:10.1108/02756660610692707

Perlman, A. (2015). Informed mindfulness as the foundation for leadership. *Explore: The Journal of Science and Healing, 11*(4), 324–325. doi:10.1016/j.explore.2015.04.012

Reb, J., Narayanan, J., & Chaturvedi, S. (2014). Leading mindfully: Two studies on the influence of supervisor trait mindfulness on employee well-being and performance. *Mindfulness, 5*(1), 36–45. doi:10.1007/s12671-012-0144-z

Regine, B., & Lewin, R. (2000). Leading at the edge: How leaders influence complex systems. *Emergence, 2*(2), 5–23.

Rill, B. (2016). Resonant co-creation as an approach to strategic innovation. *Journal of Organizational Change Management, 29*(7), 1135–1152.

Rill, B. R., & Hämäläinen, M. M. (2018). *The art of co-creation: A guidebook for practitioners*. New York: Springer.

Romeo, L., & Cantoia, M. (2011). Reflective flow in digital games. In *European conference on games based learning* (pp. 510–517). Milan, Italy: Academic Conferences International Limited.

Sadler-Smith, E. (2015). Wallas' four-stage model of the creative process: More than meets the eye? *Creativity Research Journal, 27*(4), 342–352.

Seemann, M., & Seemann, T. (2013). New perspectives on employee motivation: Balancing the big four. *International Journal of Knowledge, Culture & Change in Organizations: Annual Review, 13*, 1–7.

Sethi, D. (2009). Mindful leadership. *Leader to Leader*, (51), 7–11. doi:10.1002/ltl.311

Thera, N. (1962). *The heart of Buddhist meditation: A handbook of mental training based on the Buddha's way of mindfulness*. London: Rider and Company.

Wallace, B. A., & Shapiro, S. L. (2006). Mental balance and well-being: Building bridges between Buddhism and Western psychology. *American Psychologist, 61*(7), 690–701.

Wallas, G. (1926). *The art of thought*. London: Jonathan Cape.

Walters, C. M. (2016). Choral singers "in the zone" toward flow through score study and analysis. *The Choral Journal, 57*(5), 8.

Weick, K. (1990). Managing as improvisation: Lessons from the world of jazz. Aubrey Fisher Memorial Lecture, Univ. of Utah, October 18.

PART III

Managing mindfully

12

SPIRITUAL MINDFULNESS FOR MANAGEMENT[1]

Peter McGhee and Patricia Grant

Be still, and know that I am God

Psalm 46:10

Introduction

The rise in interest in spirituality during the last three decades, both in society (Heelas, Woodhead, Seel, Szerszynski, & Tusting, 2005) and in business (Giacalone & Jurkiewicz, 2003), has become one of the more thought-provoking trends of this century. Interestingly, this attention appears to have come at the expense of institutional religion (Tracey, 2012; Zwissler, 2007). While early thinking on spirituality at work (SAW) came from seminal thinkers like Follet (Johnson, 2007) and Maslow (1970), in recent times it has developed in response to widespread sociocultural and sociodemographic changes in society (see, e.g., Biberman & Whitty, 1997; Kale, 2004; Nadesan, 1999; Sweet, 1999). Whatever the reason for this sudden focus on SAW, it appears that it is here to stay, as opposed to be being yet another management fad (Miller & Ewest, 2018).

Mindfulness has also gained increasing popularity in business over the last two decades (Atkins & Red, 2015; Glomb, Duffy, Bono, & Yang, 2011). Again, there are reasons for this sudden growth, including an increased awareness of Eastern contemplative traditions (Weick & Putnam, 2006) and a focus on employee health and wellbeing (Van Gordon, Shonina, Lomasc, & Griffiths, 2016). But right now, we are at the point where Congleton et al. (January 8, 2015), writing recently in the *Harvard Business Review*, can claim that:

> Mindfulness should no longer be considered a "nice-to-have" for executives. It's a "must-have": a way to keep our brains healthy, to support self-regulation and effective decision-making capabilities, and to protect ourselves from toxic stress. It can be integrated into one's religious or spiritual life, or practiced as a form of secular mental training. When we take a seat, take a breath, and commit to being mindful, particularly when we gather with others who are doing the same, we have the potential to be changed
>
> *(p. 5)*

This chapter explores how workplace spirituality and mindfulness might interrelate, and their joint capacity to affect management behavior, and produce organizational transformation. The chapter opens with a concise literature review of spirituality and of mindfulness in organizations. This is followed by a discussion on how these might be combined as spiritual mindfulness to enhance management cognition, decision-making, and behavior. The chapter concludes with suggestions for organizations to develop managers' spiritual mindfulness.

Spirituality at work (SAW)

A sizeable reasonable body of work exists discussing what SAW is, its antecedents, and its organizational outcomes. While some argue that SAW is difficult to conceptualize (Burack, 2000; Gibbons, 2000), others claim that a consensus-thin definition exists in the literature (Sheep, 2006). With such an account, as opposed to a single "thick" definition (see, e.g., Wigglesworth, 2013), scholars construe SAW as a multivariate construct incorporating three components: meaningfulness, inner life, and community (Benefiel, Fry, & Geigle, 2014; Karakas, 2010).

The first of these components, meaningfulness, involves spiritual people laboring for a greater purpose while seeking alignment between their spiritual and work values (Houghton, Neck, & Krishnakumar, 2016). If we take Christian SAW, for example, Christians want work that participates in God's new creation and that worships Him (McGhee & Habets, 2018). The second component, inner life, means that all spiritual persons have deep inner needs that come to work with them, which can be either enhanced or minimized (Houghton et al., 2016). Using another Christian illustration, a person's desire to do good and meaningful work that cooperates with God, and that anticipates the world to come, enhances a Christian's spiritual Self (Pio & McGhee, 2019). Work that counters God's plan for creation (e.g., dehumanizing toil such as sweatshop labor) diminishes that same Self. Finally, connectedness is an expression of spiritual nature that entails "people seeking to live in connection with others through processes of sharing, mutual obligation, and commitment" (Houghton et al., 2016, p. 180). As Duchon and Plowman (2005) note, true connectedness occurs when people view themselves, and their spirituality, as an integral part of their work community. From a Christian perspective, this posits that faith-based and/or faith-friendly organizations (Miller & Ewest, 2015) are best suited to achieve this.

Why is this relevant? Because the SAW literature is awash with research that establishes spirituality's benefits to organizations. In fact, Karakas (2010) helpfully provides a useful summary of these benefits based on the three components of SAW discussed above. Starting with meaningful work, Karakas claims that SAW "has potential to provide employees with a feeling of purpose, a sense of connection, and a sense of meaning at work" (p. 96). After reviewing authors in the field (see, e.g., Gull & Doh, 2004; Mitroff & Denton, 1999; Reave, 2005), Karakas claims that personnel who exercise their SAW find their efforts to be more fulfilling and, therefore, can achieve at a higher level. Similar positive findings occur with employees' inner lives when SAW is encouraged. Indeed, Karakas cites evidence (Bento, 1994; Burack, 2000; Fry & Cohen, 2009) that SAW enriches the overall welfare of workers by boosting morale, improving commitment to the organization, and by reducing the negative effects of stress and burnout. Finally, and again using several studies as evidence (see, e.g., Ashar & Lane-Mahar, 2004; Cash & Gray, 2000; Duchon & Plowman, 2005), Karakas claims that "spirituality provides employees a sense of community and connectedness; increasing their attachment, loyalty and belonging to the organization" (p. 96).

In addition to this, the SAW literature emphasizes the importance of spiritual leadership in contributing to these abovementioned positive organizational outcomes (Benefiel et al., 2014). It also notes that spiritual success and leadership success are not mutually exclusive (Reave, 2005). The work of Fry, and his many collaborators (Fry, 2003, 2005; Fry & Cohen, 2009; Fry, Hannah, Noel, & Walumbwa, 2011; Fry & Matherly, 2007), is probably the best-known approach in this area. Essentially, Fry argues that spiritual leaders empower followers' inner lives through visioning that provides meaning in their work. They also create an organizational culture of altruistic love that encourages caring for others, thus creating strong feelings of connectedness. Combined, these enhance commitment and improve performance, and they enable a greater focus on social responsibility by the organization.

Mindfulness

The common understanding of mindfulness has its roots in ancient Mahayana Buddhist spiritual practices, which "suggested means of enhancing attentional stability and clarity, and of then using these abilities in the introspective examination of conscious states to pursue the fundamental issues concerning consciousness itself" (Wallace, 2005, p. 5). It was considered an important construct because it counteracted an undisciplined mind which was "an unreliable instrument for examining mental objects, processes, and the nature of consciousness" (p. 176). The most common description of mindfulness comes from Kabat-Zinn (1994), who defines it as "paying attention in a particular way: on purpose, in the present moment, and nonjudgmentally" (p. 4). More recently, a blending of the psychology and management literature defined mindfulness "as a state of mind or mode of practice that permits the questioning of expectations, knowledge and adequacy of routines in complex and not fully predictable social, technological, and physical settings" (Jordan, Messner, & Becker, 2009, p. 466). As such, it is as an important construct for focusing on the "here and now," helping people better respond to their internal and external environment, and doing all this in a non-judgmental manner (Brown & Ryan, 2003; Dane, 2011; Valentine, Godkin, & Varca, 2010); and as with spirituality, everybody has the capability of being mindful in the workplace (Ruedy & Schweitzer, 2010). This is the conceptualization underlying the use of mindfulness in this chapter.

As a spiritual tradition, Buddhism is not alone in practicing a form of mindfulness. For instance, Tan (2011) argues that Christianity has used meditative practices for centuries. In general, these have focused on the sanctity of the present and/or subservience to the transcendent at all times, and in all areas of life, including the everyday. This is often expressed today in the phrase "letting go and letting God take control of the present" (p. 243). In agreement with this claim, Trammel (2017) notes salient parallels between Buddhist mindfulness and Christian meditation. Both, Trammel states, include practicing discernment of one's thinking, regulating emotion to attain enlightenment (Buddhism) or unity with God (Christianity), and listening to one's inner voice conceived as the Buddha nature within or the Spirit of God.

Research has found mindfulness improves individual psychological and physiological wellbeing (Brown & Ryan, 2003; Brown, Ryan, & Cresswell, 2007). Mindfulness also enhances creativity and novelty, especially when dealing with familiar tasks (Ruedy & Schweitzer, 2010). Interestingly, this corresponds with material in spirituality literature. Emmons (1999), for example, observes that spiritual individuals structure decision-making in line with their values and goals, which often take priority in their cognitive hierarchy. Such thinking approaches familiar problems with an unbounded rationality (Fernando & Jackson,

2006), which comes from "a consciousness experiencing oneness" (p. 32). Finally, several studies demonstrate that mindfulness is a learned skill, and that by cultivating this, individuals gain a better appreciation of their environment and deeper insights into their thought processes (Baer, 2003). Since both mindfulness and spirituality are inherent within human beings, and both can be learned, they are significant mental factors in our decisions and actions.

Like spirituality, mindfulness is related to positive organizational outcomes (Weick & Putnam, 2006). For example, Dane (2011) found that it improved task performance, while Glomb et al. (2011) established that mindfulness aided individuals to regulate their behavior in ways that improved work relations, wellbeing, and performance. For a deeper understanding of how such outcomes are realized, see Hyland, Lee, and Mills' (2015) excellent summary of performance-relevant and job-relevant effects of mindfulness. In terms of leadership and management, scholars claim that mindfulness improves leaders' ability to connect with followers and think through their affective needs (Reb, Narayanan, & Chaturvedi, 2014). Mindfulness also precludes people from thinking or acting in ways which are mechanical or mindless by disrupting automatic thought processes. Consequently, it is an important tool for management decision-making (Ruedy & Schweitzer, 2010). This is supported in earlier work by Fiol and O'Connor (2003), which established individuals practicing mindfulness are

> more likely to understand the value of information for current circumstances and interpret unexpected results as relevant rather than dismiss them, even when they do not fall in line with current or past (familiar) practices or findings.
>
> *(p. 588)*

As such, managers who practice mindfulness might be inclined to ignore the current situation or short-term gain for the bigger picture, which is an important aspect of highly spiritual people (P. K. McGhee & Grant, 2017), and a characteristic of enduring success and growth (Hyland et al., 2015).

Spiritual mindfulness

Traditionally, mindfulness was associated with spiritual growth. Consequently, when mindfulness and/or spirituality are applied instrumentally in organizations with the primary purpose of monetary gain, their use can be contentious (Carrette & King, 2005; Van Gordon et al., 2016). As Trammel (2017) notes, mindfulness is not just practicing self-awareness or emotional regulation, it has a spiritual connection that "transports the practitioners, whether Buddhist or Christian, to an experience with deeper religious meaning and implications" (p. 369). Deeper understanding of transcendent truths, rooted in these religious systems, is the ultimate goal of such experiences, not just enhanced job satisfaction, and/or improving the bottom line.

With this in mind, how might spirituality and mindfulness relate? Shapiro, Carlson, Astin, and Freedman (2006) postulate an approach that can be adapted for our purposes (see Figure 12.1). Grounded in Kabat- Zinn's (1994) earlier work, it consists of three axioms: "*On Purpose* or Intention, *Paying Attention* or Attention and *In a Particular Way* or Attitude" (p. 375). According to Shapiro et al., an axiom is a basic truth from which other things develop. Using these three axioms, we can determine what a spiritual mindfulness might look like, noting that all three axioms are an interconnected cyclical process that occurs at the same time. As Shapiro et al. notes, "mindfulness is this moment-to moment process" (*ibid.*).

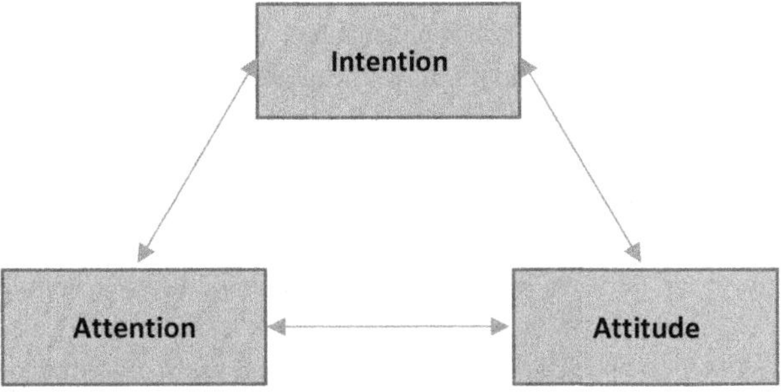

Figure 12.1 The interrelated axioms of mindfulness from Shapiro et al. (2006, p. 375)

Intention is about the goal or the *telos* of being mindful. As Shapiro et al. (2006) point out, this aspect has been lost in modern attempts to "extract the essence of mindfulness from its religious and cultural roots" (p. 375). From a Buddhist perspective a "right" mindfulness aims at spiritual enlightenment and a concern for all living things. For the Christian, such meditation aims at loving God and loving your neighbor. This spiritual *telos* is important because "your intentions set the stage for what is possible. They remind you from moment to moment of why you are practicing in the first place" (Kabat-Zinn, 1994, p. 32). Therefore, spiritual mindfulness/meditation is an ongoing process of understanding and regulating the self that ultimately frees a person to focus on others and one's Ultimate Other.

Attention involves "observing the operations of one's internal and external experience ... and the content of one's consciousness, moment by moment" (Shapiro et al., 2006, p. 376). We suspend judgment and pay attention to an experience as it is in the present, which leads to equanimity replacing reactivity; this "is the ability to recognize our world clearly without adulteration or manipulation, without pollution or exploitation" (Hyland et al., 2015, p. 578). From a Christian perspective, this is similar to the *via negativa*, which is when one suspends judgment and embraces the mystery and unknowability of God in everyday experience (Trammel, 2017), or contemplative prayer, whereby the stillness brings a present-moment awareness of oneself, expanding the experience so that God's presence is sensed and gained (Keating, 1999).

Attitude is how one focuses on their experiences. For instance, Shapiro et al. (2006) write one can be cold or critical, or they can be warm-hearted, compassionate, and open. They claim this attitude is possible even when one's experience is contrary to what they hoped for. What is important is that this is an explicit mindset that "practitioners must consciously commit to e.g. may I bring kindness, curiosity, and openness to my awareness" (p. 377). Teachers in the early Church also taught their followers to cultivate *nepsis*, that is, to be aware and focused on their inner thoughts and their external environment, and to enact this in ways that were pure, honest, and transparent (Vlachos, 1994). One must consciously commit to being mindful in ways that are amenable to enlightenment (Buddhist) or union with God (Christian), otherwise it "may well have consequences contrary to the intentions of the practice; for example cultivating the patterns of judgment and striving instead of equanimity and acceptance" (p. 377).

Shapiro et al. (2006) claim that a combination of these axioms results in a change of outlook called reperceiving. This "is a meta-mechanism of action, which overarches additional direct mechanisms that lead to change and positive outcomes" (p. 377). Essentially, reperceiving (another word for this might be reframing) enables one to step back and witness their experience without being immersed in it; it is the ability to detach or decenter oneself to fundamentally change how one sees the world. At the same time, reperceiving is also a developmental process. As time and practice go on, individuals get better at objectively perceiving their internal experience, and shifting consciousness away from the self and towards others (Petchsawang & McLean, 2017). This can lead to improved management and regulation of the self, clarification of personal values, and a change in one's thinking, emotions, and conduct (Shapiro et al., 2006)

As noted earlier, when mindfulness occurs in organizations outside of a spiritual system, it may have less value since it is often an attention-based psychological technique for improving the bottom line (2016). Such practices may actually feed the dominant schema of firms. Gull and Doh (cited in P. Mcghee & Grant, 2015) identify this schema as one of "rationalism, control, egocentrism and materialism which ensures work as it now exists provides little depth of meaning and limits understanding of how deeply connected we are" (p. 24). In such a schema, self-interest takes preference over the wider community, which ultimately fosters corrupt behavior. However, if we combine Shapiro et al.'s (2006) model with SAW, then together this may explain how managers with a spiritual mindfulness can transform the dominant schema of an organization for the better.

Spiritual mindfulness in management

Starting with the axiom of *intention*, spiritual managers consciously strive for an Ultimate Concern and/or an experience of transcendence through their work. They do this because spiritual values take precedence in their lives, and their cognitive goal hierarchy places spiritual goals higher than others (Emmons, 1999). Consequently, when such managers practice mindfulness/meditation in the workplace, they often do so with this overall purpose in mind. And since spiritual mindfulness aims at this transcendent end, it cultivates managers with a diminished ego, and an enhanced other-orientation that emphasizes care, respect, and justice. As Zsolnai (2011) confirms:

> Empirical evidence suggests that spiritual experiences help people transcend narrow self-conceptions and enable them to exercise genuine empathy with others and an all-encompassing perspective . . . the main ethical message is always the same: love and compassion, deep reverence for life and empathy with all sentient beings.
>
> *(pp. 45–46)*

The more managers practice spiritual mindfulness, the more self-regulation and self-management occur, thus motivating them to focus more on their spirituality, and act as a result. Consequently, spiritual mindfulness becomes a habitual part of who they are and what they do (i.e., it is dispositional), while they aim for a higher purpose (i.e., it is teleological). Ultimately, this produces what Jurkiewicz and Giacalone (2004) refer to as "a personal connection to the content and process of work, and to the stakeholders impacted by it, in a manner which extends beyond the limitations of self-interest" (p. 129).

Applying *attention* means spiritual managers possess "a spiritual awareness that is embodied and feelingful" (Stanley, 2012, p. 631) which they enact in their everyday work experiences. This has some resonance with the notion of authenticity prevalent in the SAW literature. As Kinjerski and Skrypnek (2004) note:

> authenticity is being who we are all of the time, even at work. It means speaking our truth and living with honesty and integrity. To be authentic, our actions are congruent with our inner [spiritual] values and beliefs ... it's about bringing your whole person to work.
>
> *(p. 32)*

In other words, it's about experiencing work without judgment and reactivity in a manner consistent with one's spiritual consciousness. A study by Fernando and Jackson (2006) supports this. They found that in difficult moments, management decision tools were supplemented by taking time to connect with their Ultimate Concern. Such decisions go beyond bounded rationality (Simon, 1998), and "come from a [spiritual] consciousness experiencing oneness" (Fernando & Jackson, 2006, p. 32). As Estanek (2006) notes, doing this repeatedly helps overcome one's self-locus and develop a greater connectedness to others.

Attitude means spiritual managers focus on their present experience in pure ways. From a Buddhist perspective this means "cleansing the mind of attachment, aversion, inertia, restlessness, and conflict, and securing it against their influx" (Nànàràma, 1993, p. 17). A similar notion applies in Christianity, where believers are requested to let go of things of this world, and to have a transcendent focus only (see e.g., Matt. 6:25–34; Col 3:1–3). When managers fail to bring a spiritual attitude to their experience, feelings of separateness and fear pervade (Fernando & Jackson, 2006). These feelings often result in negative organizational outcomes such as poor self-reflection, diminishing altruism, rejection of spiritual values, and the lessening of community (P. K. McGhee & Grant, 2017).

Taken together, these three axioms constitute a manager's spiritual mindfulness directed towards their external world. They occur simultaneously, and feed back into the manager's conscious identity (Mayer, 2000). Recently, a study by Mcghee and Grant (2015) found some support for this. They determined that managers were consciously aware of their spirituality, and they intentionally focused on being consistent with their spiritual beliefs and values in a manner that was affirming, open, and transparent in their daily experiences. When managers did this, they became less egocentric and more other-oriented. While such research might support the connection between spirituality and mindfulness, it does not answer the question as to how a manager's spiritual mindfulness might change an organization's dominant schema.

Recall that for Shapiro et al. (2006), "mindfulness leads to a significant shift in perspective, which we have termed reperceiving" (p. 377). Such reframing acts like a global mechanism to effect change in "*cognitive, emotional and behavioral flexibility*" (*ibid.*). However, reperceiving is no guarantee of better behavior. For instance, Duchon and Burns (2008) argue that Enron's narcissistic culture reframed management thinking, feelings, and action in terms of might is right, self-glorification, and denial, which resulted in "a toxic stew of shocking incompetence, unjustified arrogance, compromised ethics, and utter contempt for the market's judgment" (p. 358). If mindfulness in organizations is used as a psychometric device to enhance productivity and/or profitability, such an outcome is always possible, especially if the organization influences how and why a person is required to be mindful.

At least two reasons exist (there may be more) for why standard corporate approaches to mindfulness fail to generate real organizational transformation for the better. First, as Shapiro et al. (2012) note, "the core function of mindfulness involves being aware of what is arising without changing the experience, but rather changing the relationship to the experience" (p. 505). In other words, mindfulness is about changing one's perception of the context, rather than transcending that context. Second, and linked to the first limitation, is the divorcing of mindfulness in organizations from its spiritual roots. Used as a psychometric tool disconnected from any transcendent *telos*, mindfulness may be limited in its power to effect change (Emmons, 1986, 1999; Van Gordon et al., 2016). For example, from a Buddhist spiritual perspective, mindfulness involves practices that develop moral discernment, a caring spiritual attitude, and insight or wisdom (Nhat Hanh, 1999). A similar idea exists in Christian mindfulness, which encourages focusing on the above, and the renewing of our minds, to discern the will of God in order to lead lives that are pleasing to Him and morally transformative for the world (Rom. 12:2; Eph. 4:23–24). Therefore, properly applied, spiritual mindfulness, regardless of its religious roots, means individuals become wiser and more responsible world citizens.

Unlike standard corporate approaches, spiritual mindfulness intentionally focuses on spiritual goals and ends, which powers a manager's ability to be transcendent in the workplace. This ensures managers pay attention to their authentic spiritual consciousness, which acts as regulative ideal, adjusting thinking, will, and emotions in line with their beliefs and values, resulting in less self-locus and increasing alterity (i.e., increased respect, compassion, and fairness for others). Finally, spiritual mindfulness develops an enhanced attitude of wellbeing that reinforces this process and ensures its duplication in the future. While described in a linear manner, each of these occurs concurrently, each being necessary for spiritual mindfulness, and each feeding back into the others. Enacting this requires managers to reperceive (or reframe) organizational experiences in ways that enhance culture (Parboteeah & Cullen, 2003), structures (Pfeffer, 2003), role demands (Rozuel, 2011), and economic priorities (Lips-Wiersma & Nilakant, 2008). This process is shown in Figure 12.2.

The transformation that Gull and Doh (2004) advocate cannot be achieved by simply talking about it or by developing a mission statement and/or a code of ethics with a few choice lines pointing towards being more socially responsible. For Gull and Doh, real change comes when people reveal their SAW in their daily organizational lives. For instance, managers who reframe their work through a spiritually mindful lens are more likely to put ethical norms above self-interest, while taking a longer-term (as opposed to transitory) multiple stakeholders approach (Jurkiewicz & Giacalone, 2004; Lips-Wiersma & Nilakant, 2008; McKee, 2003). Such managers might also encourage others in the organization to have a vision and a purpose that goes beyond material ends alone (Fry, 2005). The direct link between being spiritually mindful and decision-making suggests such

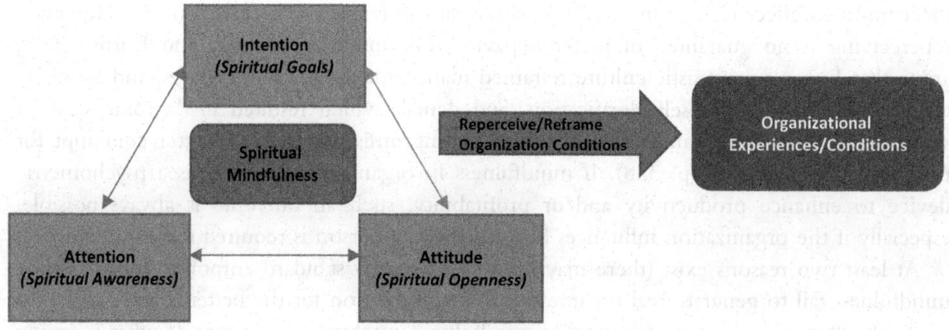

Figure 12.2 How spiritual mindfulness relates to organizational transformation, adapted from McGhee and Grant (2015, p. 24)

managers make better choices that move beyond a bounded rationality (Fernando & Jackson, 2006)—choices that re-interpret their context to create a reality that corresponds with their spiritual ideals. While spiritual mindfulness can be captured for monetary purposes (Lips-Wiersma, Dean, & Fornaciari, 2009), managers who consistently apply such a mindfulness will resist assimilation, while slowly transforming their organization's dominant schema to one that cares about people and the planet, as well as profit.

Developing managers' spiritual mindfulness

For Emmons (1999) spirituality is inherent within each of us, and it "strikes at the heart of who a person is; it is all-consuming and self-defining" (p. 96). Sheep (2006) concurs, noting that all persons are capable of being spiritual, and that all persons bring their spirituality to work. If this is the case, all managers are capable of developing and applying a spiritual mindfulness, as this is a learned skill. This section addresses what is required in organizations to encourage this.

As mentioned above, most corporate mindfulness programs are inevitably taught in the absence of spirituality. For example, Van Gordon et al. (2016) claim from a Buddhist perspective, "contemporary mindfulness is invariably taught in the absence of each of the seven Noble Eightfold Path elements, and it is generally not taught with the primary intention of fostering spiritual growth" (p. 78). They also note that most mindfulness instructors are usually not spiritual teachers. These are individuals who have "transcended the ego and cultivated a high level of spiritual awakening" and who "emanate spiritual awareness" (p. 77). Consequently, if an organization wants to effectively improve its managers' spiritual mindfulness, they need instruction from an authentic spiritual teacher, who bases their teaching on legitimate spiritual beliefs. This is the first and foremost requirement of developing this capacity. Otherwise, mindfulness is simply an "attention-based psychological technique that has demonstrable real-world applications" (p. 78), but that has minimal lasting psychological and/or behavioral effect (Shonin, Gordon, & Griffiths, 2015).

In addition to this, organizations could align values and goals with spiritual ends, such as right conduct and right speech, and/or loving your neighbor like you love yourself, since spirituality influences how individuals understand what a good life and a successful society should look like (Gotsis & Kortezi, 2008; Melé, 2016). Managers are more likely to embrace spiritual mindfulness if they feel that the organization also cherishes the ends that such practices ultimately aim for (Milliman, Gatling, & Bradley-Geist, 2017). This is important because any cultural change brought about in an organization is likely to be sourced in management spiritual preferences rather than by organizational design.

If spiritual mindfulness needs to be taught, and the teacher is authentic, organizations can do a number of things to enhance this. For instance, they could implement an individual development program for managers that could include meditation, spiritual lectures, yoga, prayer, and silent contemplation, among other things (Gupta, Kumar, & Singh, 2014; Marques, Dhiman, & Biberman, 2014). Any such program could be tied to aspects such as job characteristics (e.g., highly stressful or time-pressured roles are empowered to practice mindfulness more frequently) and evaluation (e.g., incorporate program completion and follow-ups into managers' key performance indicators). For Louis and Sutton (1991, cited in Jordan et al., 2009), mindfulness is often prompted by some element of surprise. Consequently, the procedures and processes in organizations that foster mindfulness paradoxically strive to destabilize structures. This means adopting a strategy whereby managers frequently adjust to novel conditions. For instance, rotating jobs and continual on-the-job training encourages adaptation to varying environments. However, such strategies should encourage managers to bring their spirituality to bear on their mindfulness. This means new job roles, tasks, and training should incorporate spiritual goals and inspire managers to exercise their spiritual values and strengthen their spiritual identity.

From a more abstract viewpoint, attention needs to be redirected away from the organization itself (i.e., its structure, procedures, and policies) toward organizing (Weick & Putnam, 2006). This is what managers are involved in, the ongoing daily experiences of work "infused with rising and falling, becoming and declining, emerging and disappearing" (p. 283). This shift in language, states Weick and Putnam, helps managers understand the three Buddhist characteristics of existence: (1) objects are impermanent; (2) the inevitability of suffering; and (3) they are not in control. Related ideas also exist within Christianity: (1) earthly things have no value (Matt. 6:19); (2) suffering is inherent to Christian life (Phil. 3:8); and (3) God is in control (Ps 103:19). Weick and Putnam suggest that if an organization can be designed around these realities, it will be:

> One where people pay more attention to failures than success, avoid simplicity rather than cultivate it, are just as sensitive to operations as they are to strategy, organize for resilience rather than anticipation, and allow decisions to migrate to experts wherever they are located.
>
> *(p. 284)*

When mindfulness is construed as a psychological tool to enhance the organization, it limits the process of knowledge construction because it is not linked to spiritual truths. Using spiritual mindfulness, and the more suited language of organizing, ensures management can detect, alter, suspend, or complement shortcomings in the organization with greater wisdom.

Conclusion

More than 20 years ago, Goodpaster (1994) claimed a disease was plaguing modern corporations. This disease ensured firms pursued short-term goals that rationalized immoral actions, and they practiced detachment from this through a "kind of callousness, what some observers have called a separation of head from heart" (p. 53), or for the purposes of this study, a separation of the mind from the spirit(ual). Has a lot changed since then? A quick scan of the media today will tell any reader that corruption, unethical practice, and social and environmental damage caused by business is an ongoing problem. Since the 1970s, the business ethics literature has offered suggestions for improvements to this problem (De George, 2005), and yet the question could be asked "has anything really changed?" In fact, some might say it has gotten worse (Ciulla, 2011; Freeman, 2000).

Perhaps it is time to return to the tried and true. An authentic spirituality governed by transcendent values that care for people and the planet may be our best hope. If this is the case, developing a spiritual mindset in today's managers may be the key to transforming business for the better. This chapter attempts to define spiritual mindfulness, it proposes a framework as to how such a mindset might change the dominant schema in modern firms, and it offers some suggestions as to how organizations might cultivate this practice.

Five chapter takeaways

1. Spirituality and mindfulness are historically and intimately connected.
2. Traditionally, mindfulness was associated with the transcendent and spiritual growth. Without such connections, mindfulness is at risk of simply becoming another management tool to enhance the bottom line.
3. Spiritual managers strive for the transcendent (intention), experience work without judgment or reactivity in a manner consistent with their spiritual consciousness (attention), and focus on the present through a transcendent lens (attitude).
4. A practiced spiritual mindfulness reframes cognition, affection, and behavior regarding organizational experiences and conditions, which ultimately enhances culture, structures, role demands, and economic priorities for the good.
5. All managers have the capacity for spiritual mindfulness, and organizational training programs can accommodate this as long as teachers are spiritual, and content is linked to legitimate spiritual beliefs.

Five reflection questions

1. What has caused the historical split between spirituality and mindfulness in modern organizations?
2. How valuable is mindfulness for enhancing organizational outcomes if it is divorced from the spiritual (and therefore the ethical)?
3. What happens when employees realize mindfulness (divorced from the transcendent) is just another management tool?
4. How might organizations incorporate spiritual (and therefore moral) ends into their long-term strategy, as well as their daily operations?
5. What is the difference between the organization itself (i.e., its structures, processes, and policies) and organizing, and why is this important for spiritual mindfulness?

Note

1 Some of the material in this chapter has been adapted from an earlier article by the authors published in the *Journal of Leadership, Management, & Spirituality* *8*(1), 12–33. doi:10.15183/slm2015.05.1113. Nonetheless, the majority of this chapter is new material.

References

Ashar, H., & Lane-Mahar, M. (2004). Success and spirituality in the new business paradigm. *Journal of Management Inquiry*, *13*(3), 249–260. doi:10.1177/1056492604268218

Atkins, P. W. B., & Red, J. (Eds.). (2015). *Mindfulness in organizations: Foundations, research, and applications*. Cambridge, UK: Cambridge University Press.

Baer, R. A. (2003). Mindfulness training as a clinical intervention. A conceptual and empirical review. *Clinical Psychology: Science & Practice*, *10*(2), 125–143.

Benefiel, M., Fry, L. W., & Geigle, D. (2014). Spirituality & religion in the workplace: History, theory, and research. *Psychology of Religion & Spirituality*, *6*(3), 175–187. doi:10.1037/a0036597

Bento, R. (1994). When the show must go on. *Journal of Managerial Psychology*, *9*(6), 35–44.

Biberman, J., & Whitty, M. (1997). A postmodern spiritual future for work. *Journal of Organizational Change Management*, *10*(2), 130–138. doi:10.1108/09534819710160790

Brown, K. W., & Ryan, R. M. (2003). The benefits of being present: Mindfulness and its role in psychological well-being. *Journal of Personality & Social Psychology*, *84*(4), 822–848.

Brown, K. W., Ryan, R. M., & Cresswell, J. D. (2007). Mindfulness: Theoretical foundations and evidence for its salutary effects. *Psychological Inquiry*, *18*(4), 211–237.

Burack, E. H. (2000). Spirituality in the workplace. In J. Biberman & M. D. Whitty (Eds.), *Work & Spirit* (pp. 95–110). Scranton: The University of Scranton Press.

Carrette, J., & King, R. (2005). *Selling spirituality: The Silent takeover of religion*. Abingdon, Oxfordshire: Routledge.

Cash, K. C., & Gray, G. R. (2000). A framework for accommodating religion and spirituality in the workplace. *Academy of Management Executive*, *14*(3), 124–134. doi:10.5465/AME.2000.4468072

Ciulla, J. (2011). Is business ethics getting better? A historical perspective. *Business Ethics Quarterly*, *21*(2), 335–343. doi:10.5840/beq201121219

Congleton, C., Hölzel, B. K., & Lazar, S. W. (January 8, 2015). Mindfulness can literally change your brain. *Harvard Business Review*. Retrieved from https://mindleader.org/wp-content/uploads/2017/08/HARVARD-BUSINESS-REVIEW_MIndfulness-can-change-your-brain.pdf

Dane, E. (2011). Paying attention to mindfulness and its effects on task performance in the workplace. *Journal of Management Inquiry*, *37*(4), 997–1018.

De George, R. T. (2005). A history of business ethics. *The Markkula Center for Applied Ethics*. Retrieved from www.scu.edu/ethics/practicing/focusareas/business/conference/presentations/business-ethics-history.html

Duchon, D., & Burns, M. (2008). Organizational narcissism. *Organizational Dynamics*, *37*(4), 354–363. doi:10.1016/j.orgdyn.2008.07.004

Duchon, D., & Plowman, D. A. (2005). Nurturing the spirit at work: Impact on work unit performance. *The Leadership Quarterly*, *16*(5), 807–833. doi:10.1016/j.leaqua.2005.07.008

Emmons, R. A. (1986). Personal strivings: An approach to personality and subjective well-being. *Journal of Personality & Social Psychology*, *51*(5), 1058–1068. doi:10.1037/0022-3514.51.5.1058

Emmons, R. A. (1999). *The psychology of ultimate concerns: Motivation & spirituality in personality*. New York: The Guilford Press.

Estanek, S. M. (2006). Redefining spirituality: A new discourse. *College Student Journal*, *40*(2), 270–281.

Fernando, M., & Jackson, B. (2006). The influence of religion-based workplace spirituality on business leaders decision-making: An inter-faith study. *Journal of Management and Organisation*, *12*, 23–39.

Fiol, C., & O'Connor, E. J. (2003). Waking up! Mindfulness in the face of bandwagons. *Academy of Management Review*, *28*, 54–70.

Freeman, R. (2000). Business ethics at the millennium. *Business Ethics Quarterly*, *10*(1), 169–180. doi:10.2307/3857703

Fry, L. W. (2003). Toward a theory of spiritual leadership. *The Leadership Quarterly*, *14*(6), 693–727. doi:10.1016/j.leaqua.2003.09.001

Fry, L. W. (2005). Toward a theory of ethical and spiritual well-being, and corporate social responsibility through spiritual leadership. In R. A. Giacalone (Ed.), *Positive Psychology in Business Ethics and Corporate Responsibility* (pp. 47–83). New York: Information Age Publishing.

Fry, L. W., & Cohen, M. P. (2009). Spiritual leadership as a paradigm for organizational transformation and recovery from extended work hours cultures. *Journal of Business Ethics*, *84*(2), 265–279. doi:10.1007/s10551-008-9695-2

Fry, L. W., Hannah, S. T., Noel, M., & Walumbwa, F. O. (2011). Impact of spiritual leadership on unit performance. *The Leadership Quarterly*, *22*(2), 259–270. doi:10.1016/j.leaqua.2011.02.002

Fry, L. W., & Matherly, L. L. (2007). Workplace spirituality, spiritual leadership and performance excellence. In S. G. Rogelberg (Ed.), *Encylopedia of industrial/organizational psychology* (Vol. 2, pp. 751–754). San Francisco: Sage Publications.

Giacalone, R. A., & Jurkiewicz, C. L. (2003). Toward a science of workplace spirituality. In R. A. Giacalone & C. L. Jurkiewicz (Eds.), *Handbook of workplace spirituality* (pp. 3–28). Armonk, NY: M.E. Sharpe.

Gibbons, P. (2000). Spirituality at work: Definitions, measures, assumptions and validity claims. In J. Biberman & M. Whitty (Eds.), *Work & spirit: A reader of new spiritual paradigms for organizations* (pp. 111–131). Scranton: The University of Scranton Press.

Glomb, T. M., Duffy, M. K., Bono, J. E., & Yang, T. (2011). Mindfulness at work. *Research in Personnel and Human Resources Management*, *30*, 115–157.

Goodpaster, K. E. (1994). Work, spirituality and the moral point of view. *International Journal of Value-Based Management*, 7(1), 49–62. doi:10.1007/BF00892148

Gotsis, G., & Kortezi, Z. (2008). Philosophical foundations of workplace spirituality. *Journal of Business Ethics*, *78*(4), 575–600. doi:10.1007/s10551-007-9369-5

Gull, G. A., & Doh, J. (2004). The "transmutation" of the organization: Towards a more spiritual workplace. *Journal of Management Inquiry*, *13*(2), 128–139. doi:10.1177/1056492604265218

Gupta, M., Kumar, V., & Singh, M. (2014). Creating satisfied employees through workplace spirituality: A study of the private insurance sector in Punjab (India). *Journal of Business Ethics*, *122*(1), 79–88.

Heelas, P., Woodhead, L., Seel, B., Szerszynski, B., & Tusting, K. (2005). *The spiritual revolution: Why religion is giving way to spirituality*. Oxford, UK: Blackwell.

Houghton, J. D., Neck, C. P., & Krishnakumar, S. (2016). The what, why, and how of spirituality in the workplace revisited: A 14-year update and extension. *Journal of Management, Spirituality & Religion*, *13* (3), 177–205. doi:10.1080/14766086.2016.1185292

Hyland, P. K., Lee, R. A., & Mills, M. J. (2015). Mindfulness at work: A new approach to improving individual and organizational performance. *Industrial and Organizational Psychology*, *8*(4), 576–602. doi:10.1017/iop.2015.41

Johnson, A. L. (2007). Mary Parker Follett: Laying the foundations for spirituality in the workplace. *International Journal of Public Administration*, *30*, 425439. doi:10.1080/01900690601156059

Jordan, S., Messner, M., & Becker, A. (2009). Reflection and mindfulness in organizations: Rationales and possibilities for integration. *Management Learning*, *40*, 465–473. doi:10.1177/1350507609339687

Jurkiewicz, C. L., & Giacalone, R. A. (2004). A values framework for measuring the impact of workplace spirituality on organizational performance. *Journal of Business Ethics*, *49*(2), 129–142. doi:10.1023/B:BUSI.0000015843.22195.b9

Kabat-Zinn, J. (1994). *Wherever you go, there you are: Mindfulness meditation in everyday life*. New York: Hyperion.

Kale, S. H. (2004). Spirituality, religion & globalization. *Journal of Macromarketing*, *24*(2), 92–107. doi:10.1177/0276146704269296

Karakas, F. (2010). Spirituality and performance in organizations: A literature review. *Journal of Business Ethics*, *94*(1), 89–106. doi:10.1007/s10551-009-0251-5

Keating, T. (1999). *Open mind, open heart: The contemplative dimension of the Gospel*. Warwick, NY: Amity House.

Kinjerski, V. M., & Skrypnek, B. J. (2004). Defining spirit at work: Finding common ground. *Journal of Organizational Change Management*, *17*(1), 26–42. doi:10.1108/09534810410511288

Lips-Wiersma, M., Dean, K. L., & Fornaciari, C. J. (2009). Theorizing the dark side of the workplace spirituality movement. *Journal of Management Inquiry*, *18*(4), 288–300. doi:10.1177/1056492609339017

Lips-Wiersma, M., & Nilakant, V. (2008). Practical compassion: Toward a critical spiritual foundation for corporate responsibility. In J. Biberman & L. Tischler (Eds.), *Spirituality in business: Theory, practice, and future directions* (pp. 51–72). New York: Palgrave Macmillan.

Marques, J., Dhiman, S. K., & Biberman, J. (2014). Teaching the un-teachable: Storytelling and meditation in workplace spirituality courses. *Journal of Management Development*, *33*(3), 196–217. doi: doi:10.1108/JMD-10-2011-0106

Maslow, A. H. (1970). *Religions, values and peak-experiences*. New York: The Viking Press.

Mayer, J. D. (2000). Spiritual intelligence or spiritual consciousness? *The International Journal for the Psychology of Religion*, *10*(1), 47–56. doi:10.1207/S15327582IJPR1001_5

Mcghee, P., & Grant, P. (2015). The influence of manangers' spritual mindfulness on ethical behaviour in organizations. *Journal of Spirituality, Leadership & Manangement*, *8*(1), 12–33. doi:10.15183/slm2015.05.1113

McGhee, P. K., & Grant, P. (2017). The transcendent influence of spirituality on ethical action in organizations. *Journal of Management, Spirituality & Religion*, *14*(2), 160–178. doi:10.1080/14766086.2016.1268539

McGhee, P. K., & Habets, M. (2018). Priests of creation, mediators of order: Taking god to work. In T. Ewest (Ed.), *Faith and work: Christian perspectives, research and insights into the movement* (pp. 77–96). Charlotte, NC: IAP.

McKee, D. (2003). Spirituality and marketing: An overview of the literature. In R. A. Giacalone & C. L. Jurkiewicz (Eds.), *Handbook of workplace spirituality and organizational performance* (pp. 57–75). Armonk, NY: M.E. Sharpe.

Miller, D. W., & Ewest, T. (2015). A new framework for analyzing organizational workplace religion and spirituality. *Journal of Management, Spirituality & Religion*, *12*(4), 305–328. doi:10.1080/14766086.2015.1054864

Miller, D. W., & Ewest, T. (2018). Spirituality at the workplace. In D. C. Poff & A. C. Michalos (Eds.), *Encyclopedia of business and professional ethics* (pp. 1–5). Cham: Springer International Publishing. doi:10.1007/978-3-319-23514-1_250-1

Milliman, J., Gatling, A., & Bradley-Geist, J. C. (2017). The implications of workplace spirituality for person-environment fit theory. *Psychology of Religion and Spirituality*, *9*(1), 1–12. doi:10.1037/rel0000068

Mitroff, I. I., & Denton, E. A. (1999). *A spiritual audit of corporate America: A hard look at spirituality, religion and values in the workplace*. San Francisco, CA: Jossey-Bass.

Nadesan, M. H. (1999). The discourses of corporate spiritualism and evangelical capitalism. *Management Communication*, *13*(1), 3–42. doi:10.1177/0893318999131001

Nànàràma, M. S. (1993). *The seven stages of purification and the insight knowledges*. Kandy: Buddhist Publication Society.

Nhat Hanh, T. (1999). *The heart of the Buddha's teaching: Transforming suffering into peace, joy and liberation*. New York: Broadway Books.

Parboteeah, K. P., & Cullen, J. B. (2003). Ethical climates and spirituality. In R. A. Giacalone & C. L. Jurkiewicz (Eds.), *Handbook of workplace spirituality* (pp. 137–151). Armonk, NY: M.E. Sharpe.

Petchsawang, P., & McLean, G. N. (2017). Workplace spirituality, mindfulness meditation, and work engagement. *Journal of Management, Spirituality & Religion*, *14*(3), 216–244. doi:10.1080/14766086.2017.1291360

Pfeffer, J. (2003). Business and the spirit: Management practices that sustain values. In R. A. Giacalone & C. L. Jurkiewicz (Eds.), *The handbook of workplace spirituality and organizational performance* (pp. 29–45). Armonk, NY: M.E. Sharpe.

Pio, E., & McGhee, P. K. (2019). Spirituality and religion at work: Christian traditions in action. In J. Marques (Ed.), *The Routledge companion to management & workplace spirituality* (pp. 88–100). New York: Routledge.

Reave, L. (2005). Spiritual values and practices related to leadership effectiveness. *The Leadership Quarterly*, *16*, 655–687.

Reb, J., Narayanan, J., & Chaturvedi, S. (2014). Leading mindfully: Two studies on the influence of supervisor trait mindfulness on employee well-being and performance. *Mindfulness*, *5*, 36–45. doi:10.1007/s12671-012-0144-z

Rozuel, C. (2011). The moral threat of compartmentalization: Self, roles and responsibility. *Journal of Business Ethics*, *102*(4), 685–697. doi:10.1007/s10551-011-0839-4

Ruedy, N., & Schweitzer, M. (2010). In the moment: The effect of mindfulness on ethical decision making. *Journal of Business Ethics*, *95*(1), 73–87. doi:10.1007/s10551-011-0796-y

Shapiro, S. L., Carlson, M. B., Astin, H. S., & Freedman, B. (2006). Mechanisms of mindfulness. *Journal of Clinical Psychology*, *62*(3), 373–386. doi:10.1002/jclp.20237

Shapiro, S. L., Jazaieri, H., & Goldin, P. R. (2012). Mindfulness-based stress reduction effects on moral reasoning and decision making. *The Journal of Positive Psychology*, 7(6), 504–515. doi:10.1080/17439760.2012.723732

Sheep, M. L. (2006). Nurturing the whole person: The ethics of workplace spirituality in a society of organizations. *Journal of Business Ethics*, *66*(4), 357–375. doi:10.1007/s10551-006-0014-5

Shonin, E., Gordon, W. V., & Griffiths, M. D. (2015). Does mindfulness work? *BMJ*, *351*, h6919. doi:10.1136/bmj.h6919

Simon, H. A. (1998). *The sciences of the artificial*. Cambridge: MIT Press.

Stanley, S. (2012). Mindfulness: Towards a critical relational perspective. *Social and Personality Psychology Compass*, *6*(9), 631–641.

Sweet, L. (1999). *Soultsunami: Sink or swim in new millennium culture*. Grand Rapids, MI: Zondervan.

Tan, S. (2011). Mindfulness and acceptance-based cognitive behavioral therapies: Empirical evidence and clinical applications from a Christian perspective. *Journal of Psychology and Christianity*, *30*(3), 243–249.

Tracey, P. (2012). Religion and organization: A critical review of current trends and future directions. *The Academy of Management Annals*, *6*(1), 87–134. doi:10.1080/19416520.2012.660761

Trammel, R. C. (2017). Tracing the roots of mindfulness: Transcendence in Buddhism and Christianity. *Journal of Religion & Spirituality in Social Work: Social Thought, 36*(3), 367–383. doi:10.1080/15426432.2017.1295822

Valentine, S. R., Godkin, L., & Varca, P. E. (2010). Role conflict, mindfulness, and organizational ethics in an education-based healthcare institution. *Journal of Business Ethics, 94*(3), 455–469. doi:10.1007/s10551-009-0276-9

Van Gordon, W., Shonina, E., Lomasc, T., & Griffiths, M. D. (2016). Corporate use of mindfulness and authentic spiritual transmission: Competing or compatible ideals? *Mindfulness & Compassion., 1*, 75–83. doi:10.1016/j.mincom.2016.10.005

Vlachos, H. (1994). *Orthodox psychotherapy: The science of the fathers*. Lavadia, Greece: Birth of the Theotokos Monastery.

Wallace, B. A. (2005). *Balancing the mind*. Ithaca, NY: Snow Lion.

Weick, K., & Putnam, T. (2006). Organizing for mindfulness: Eastern wisdom and western knowledge. *Journal of Management Inquiry, 15*(3), 275–287. doi:10.1177/1056492606291202

Wigglesworth, C. (2013). Spirtual intelligence. In J. Neal (Ed.), *Handbook of faith & spirituality in the workplace: Emerging research & practice* New York: Springer. doi:10.1007/978-1-4614-5233-1_27

Zsolnai, L. (2011). Moral agency and spiritual intelligence. In L. Bouckaert & L. Zsolnai (Eds.), *The Palgrave handbook of spirituality and business* (pp. 42–48). London: Palgrave Macmillan.

Zwissler, L. (2007). Spiritual, but religious. *Culture and Religion, 8*(1), 51–69. doi:10.1080/14755610601157120

13

BEING PRESENT IS A PRESENT

Mindfulness as a strategy to manage interactions in work and non-work life

Melita Balas Rant and Katarina Katja Mihelič

Introduction

The contemporary workplace is characterized by time pressure, the high speed of working, constant connectivity and the related expectation to respond quickly, and the blurring of boundaries between work and private lives (Kolb, Caza, & Collins, 2012). In addition, the fourth industrial revolution, commonly dubbed Industry 4.0, is changing the ways work is being performed. More specifically, digitalization, AI, and machine learning are transforming the traditional understanding of work lives, family lives, and societal well-being (Schwab, 2017). Consequently, people have increasingly started to turn to mindfulness—a state of non-judgmental attentiveness and awareness of the moment (Brown & Ryan, 2003)—in order to cope with their day-to-day challenges. The concept is also becoming more and more popular in scientific as well as practitioner circles (Greiser, 2018; Hyland, Lee, & Mills, 2015). A quick Google search using the keyword "mindfulness" yields about 116 million hits (as of September 2019), and according to Google Trends, interest among the general public in the topic of mindfulness has been increasing steadily over the last ten years.

Existing research has documented different physical and psychological benefits of mindfulness. The effects of mindfulness at work include lower emotional exhaustion, more job satisfaction (Hülsheger, Alberts, Feinholdt, & Lang, 2013), increased task performance (Dane & Brummel, 2014; Hyland et al., 2015), and decreased social loafing (Mihelič & Culiberg, 2019). Mindfulness also increases cognitive flexibility and attentional performance (Moore & Malinowski, 2009), elevates self-regulation (Atkins & Parker, 2012), decreases stress (Nezlek, Holas, Rusanowska, & Krejtz, 2016), and positively affects psychological and physical health (Glomb, Duffy, Bono, & Yang, 2011). In non-work domains, it contributes to feelings of happiness (Coo & Salanova, 2018) and increased psychological capital, which further increase an individual's well-being (Leroy, Anseel, Dimitrova, & Sels, 2013; Malinowski & Lim, 2015). Due to the recorded benefits of mindfulness and mindfulness meditation, we have observed a rise in the number of mindfulness-based practices and trainings offered in organizations, what is known as corporate mindfulness. Programs to increase mindful awareness were introduced in Google, Bosch, Aetna, Royal Dutch Shell, SAP, Goldman Sachs, and other enterprises (Greiser, 2018).

In this chapter, we adopt a multi-stakeholder perspective to outline the ways in which mindfulness can help us manage the relationships with various stakeholders, predominantly in the work domain, but also in the family domain. We aim to outline the mindful interactions with ourselves, co-workers, robots, our teams and supervisors, and our family members and friends by bringing together the latest research across disciplines, with an emphasis on industrial/organizational psychology. While organizations can design structures and systems that support healthy workplace relationships, individuals can play a pivotal role and be proactive in the fostering of mindful interactions.

The next section outlines the major trends shaping today's work environments, which are defining the properties of the contemporary and emerging workplace. This is followed by an overview of the inter-related concepts of mindfulness and consciousness, providing a multi-disciplinary understanding of the phenomenon. Then, we offer guidelines on how to create and nurture fruitful relationships with stakeholders in the organization and beyond. Here, we complement the findings of existing research with practical individual exercises that could lead to more mindful interactions in both work and non-work contexts.

Current trends shaping work and non-work lives

The world of work is undergoing significant changes underpinned by technological revolution. BCG reported that organizations are being faced with 12 forces that will radically change how they operate: automation, big data and advanced analytics, access to information and ideas, simplicity in complexity, agility and innovation, new customer strategies, a new demographic mix, skill imbalances, shifting geopolitical and economic power, diversity and inclusion, individualism and entrepreneurship, and well-being and purpose (Bhalla, Dyrchs, & Strack, 2017).

These forces are changing how work is performed. The increasing speed of work and resulting overwork can lead to stressful interactions with co-workers, supervisors, and clients. Next comes continuous connectivity and accessibility (Mazmanian, Orlikowski, & Yates, 2013), and the expectation that one is constantly available to respond to work-related demands, be it from clients, co-workers, or supervisors. Phones have become the norm in daily interactions in the workplace (Chotpitayasunondh & Douglas, 2016), and together with other electronic devices represent daily distractors in this context. First, there is the related noise that can trigger nervous reactions; second, there is the lost ability to concentrate and focus on the task at hand. Third, scrolling one's phone has now become an automatic behavior the minute one has a free couple of minutes, which may decrease the quality of interactions with colleagues. Existing research points to the fact that workplace "telepressure" has stress-related consequences in the form of physical and cognitive burnout and absenteeism (Barber & Santuzzi, 2015).

The norm of constant connectivity not only refers to being available during the workday, but includes checking one's email in the evenings and over the weekend, as well as sending emails on Sundays. The latter has altered the classical working week, and resulted in the saying, "Sunday night is a new Monday morning" (Gee, 2019). Moreover, with today's ease of connection, one can perform job duties in any location and at any time, which has increased working hours, making the boundaries between work and private lives increasingly blurred, while working in an "always-on culture" leads to more conflicts between work and family (Derks, van Duin, Tims, & Bakker, 2015). Aside from the increased complexity of the work and non-work domains, there are also high expectations that employees should be able to manage their performance in different life roles.

Some authors have argued that technology brings positive changes and offers more meaningful work (Brynjolfsson & McAfee, 2014), while others argue that digitalization is causing a further gap in equality, increasing the so-called precariat (Rubery, Grimshaw, Keizer, & Johnson, 2018) and the need for upskilling (WEF-BCG, 2018). For example, advances in digitalization, robotics, machine learning, and artificial intelligence are making certain jobs obsolete and require upskilling and learning of new procedures. These innovations are also causing a digital divide between older and younger generations. Due to the digital revolution employees are often required to learn new programs and systems, which can be stressful. Moreover, given the constant upgrades of existing programs and resulting information overload, employees may find it difficult to follow advances in the programs they work with on a daily basis (such as email managers), thus making performing tasks taking longer than originally planned.

In the near future, employees will be expected to work with humanoid robots on a daily basis and treat them as colleagues at work. Leaders will need to learn how to integrate robots in their work environments and teams, and how to manage tensions resulting from this change. Taken together, these changes carry substantial implications for people, societies, and economies, and are altering how individuals interact with people at work and beyond, in their families, friendship circles, and communities. Mindfulness is an individual practice that could serve as a strategy to manage these changes and renewed interactions. In the next section, we therefore explore mindfulness and consciousness.

Mindfulness and consciousness

Mindfulness is mostly defined as an awareness practice characterized by moment-to-moment, non-reactive, non-judgmental attention to the experience presented within the self (inner landscape) with the attitude of curiosity, kindness, acceptance, letting go, trust, patience, non-striving, gratitude, and generosity (Kabat-Zinn, 2003). The emphasis is thus on the attentive, non-judgmental, even appreciative observation of experience as played out within the self (in one's conscious awareness); it is a special form of attention that is seen as morally superior (Williams & Kabat-Zinn, 2013). A potent framework for the study of the different layers of awareness within the human consciousness was proposed by Rudolf Steiner in his books *Philosophy of Freedom* (1893/1999), *How to Know Higher Worlds* (1961/1994), and *Psychology of Body, Soul, and Spirit* (Steiner, 1909–1911/1999).

The foundational conceptual model was laid out in *Philosophy of Freedom* under the proposition that the world (existence) is essentially an indivisible unity, but our consciousness divides it into two worlds: (1) the outer world accessible through five-sense perceptions; and (2) the inner world accessible through thinking. Through thinking one perceives the world of concepts and ideas. Concepts are the carriers of meanings; a meaning is formed when a concept is matched with the percept; with this matching an inner mental picture is formed that is always arising within the inner landscape. The mental picture is a mixture of thoughts, feelings, emotions, and affects. This mental picture is a transporter of an experience of reality. The mental picture stays within when the perception disappears, and forms the basis of memory. The mental pictures that accumulate over time in a form of memory create a life story and biography through which a sense of self is defined. Memorized mental pictures and self-definitions present a base out of which the person attaches meaning to new experiences. This matching unfolds unconsciously; for Steiner (Steiner, R, 1893/1999) this is the essence of impulsive behavioral responses and the root of the non-freedom in one's life.

Human experiences of reality arise only with the formation of the sense of "I, the self," which allows for the conscious experience of the sense of self (Steiner, 1909–1911/1999) and for the development of a capacity to think. With the sense of self and capacity to think we lose a feeling of unity and interconnectedness with everything, and start feeling individuated. Thinking is what differentiates human beings from other living beings. In thinking, a person actively participates in the world. There resides the real creative power of human beings. Mindfulness can be considered the contemplative observation of own thinking and how one attaches the meaning to perceptions (Steiner, 1893/1999). In that sense mindfulness is a form of elevated thinking. Through mindfulness one shifts the perspective so that one can see oneself as an actor in one's own experience of reality and its creation.

More precisely, the creative power of human thinking (which is the real purpose of human existence) can be attained only through the kind of thinking that closely resembles the modern definition of mindfulness. The elevated thinking that resembles mindfulness is anchored in processes of emptying one's mind of all the pre-given concepts, and then observing all that is arising within the inner landscape, without exerting any need to attach pre-given concepts arising from the memory.

The result of the elevated thinking is the illumination (i.e., awakening) of the inner landscape in which the sense of the self resides. In the illuminated state one can liberate the self from impulsive, instinctual behaviors and unconscious drives; free the self from self-imposed limitations experienced as though they are imposed on the self from the external (outer) world; one can also gain access to the new insights, intuitions, and self-transformations through use of imagination.

For Steiner (1893/1999) imagination is a creative faculty of elevated thinking. This conclusion is derived logically from the proposition that the experience of life is actually an experience of a series of mental pictures in the inner landscape. We do not know reality per se, we only know the mental pictures (representations) of reality projected in the inner landscape. Through imagination one can mold the elements of this mental picture and make it different. However, Steiner on this note is very principled, arguing that imagination should be coupled with a proper attitude of appreciation, love, and forgiveness, which are the qualities of the contemporary definitions of mindfulness (Kabat-Zinn, 2003).

Mindfulness is currently practiced in a narrower way than that proposed by Steiner in his exposition on human freedom and creativity. In general, modern mindfulness programs can be classified into three subgroups (UK Mindfulness Initiative, 2019): (1) meditation in a form of contemplative non-judgmental attention to one's experience of the present moment; (2) breathing exercises; and (3) body scans. Within formal mindfulness-based programs there exist variations in terms of length, frequency, guidance, and group size. There is also a lack of methods for use in organizations that relate to the mindful use of the imagination as an adjusted use of mindfulness for creative purposes. Therefore, in what follows, we consider the holistic (Steiner's) view of contemplative observation, and offer practical exercises that facilitate the state of awakened consciousness and help nurture productive relationships with others.

Mindfulness to foster fruitful interactions: a multi-stakeholder perspective

In the center of mindfulness-based approaches is the protocol for the adjustment of human attention and formation of more positive mental pictures related to the stakeholder through the "inner landscape." We draw from the literature across different disciplines to document the effects of mindfulness in each of the relationships. Specifically, the following interactions with stakeholders are explored: mindful interactions with the self, with co-workers, with leaders/ superiors, with robots, with clients, and with family/friends. We outline specific recommendations in the form of exercises that can be used to increase conscious awareness in this context.

Mindful interactions with the self

The general tendency in connection with the self is to come across a limiting life experience that calls forth the transformation of the meaning-making mechanism and the system around which the sense of self is built. Kegan's (1982, 1994) research examined developmental regularities of the meaning-making mechanism and the system of the self in adults. A great majority of working adults are situated in a system of the self referred to as a "socialized mind;" during the working career (many, not all) tend to move towards a "self-authoring mind" (Kegan, 1994). When moving up in their career, a person takes in (breathes in) the definitions, expectations, and values of their surroundings and builds a sense of "self" around alignment and commitment to that (belief and value system) with which they have uncritically become identified. A limitation of such a "self-system" is revealed when the expectations of those with whom one identifies surpass the capacity of the self to handle them (Kegan, 1994). To resolve this challenge, a person needs to step back from the values and beliefs imposed by their surroundings and generate an internal "set of judgments." These constitute an ideology (belief system) through which one filters external expectations/demands, identifies and evaluates options, and makes choices.

When one fully adopts the self-authoring system of the self, the agency and behavioral capacity of a person to deal constructively with complex human interactions in the workplace are substantially increased (Kegan, 1994). This grand movement of the self-system requires a disassociation from many "unquestionable" beliefs and ideologies, a change that requires long-term contemplative observation of "limiting" experiences, thoughts, and emotions that accompany the inner perceptions of an experience, and the dismantling of some thoughts and beliefs. Regular mindfulness is recommended for the purpose to unpack one's own "immunity-to-change," unlock the behavioral system and start restructuring it. This can start unfolding by consistent awareness of behavioral slips and their conscious adjustment towards a less limiting response (Kegan & Lahey, 2009). This change should be consciously practiced in daily workplace situations. Furthermore, in order to create and nurture lasting fruitful relationships with others in the workplace, it is fundamental that individuals adopt a mindful approach to themselves and others.

Existing research finds that formal and long-term mindfulness meditation practices had the following effects: the improved immune systems of employees working in high-stress jobs; lower burnout, stress, and elevated well-being (Chiesa & Serretti, 2009; Jain et al., 2007); decreased stress during multi-tasking tests, longer attentive concentration on a task (Jha, Stanley, Kiyonaga, Wong, & Gelfand, 2010); a faster reaction response to cognitive challenges, better comprehension, and decision-making quality (Zeidan, Johnson, Diamond, David, & Goolkasian, 2010); more creative problem-solving skills (Ostafin & Kassman, 2012); a higher sensitivity to mistakes, and more fluid decision-making (Weick & Sutcliffe, 2006). An improvement in individuals' energy levels was also recorded (Davidson et al., 2003). What mindfulness training can also do is reduce the level of how emotionally exhausted employees feel in their jobs (Hülsheger et al., 2013). One way to be mindful is to intentionally make oneself aware of the tasks one performs at work a few times a day, with the aim to stop automatic behavior and bring awareness to the present. This can be done using an alarm clock. With energy-depleting work and during stressful situations, it is important for employees to recharge their emotional reserves. Gonzalez thus recommends micro-meditation, namely devoting one to three minutes to meditation over the course of the working day (Gonzalez, 2014) instead of automatically scrolling on the phone when one has a break.

Exercise 1

Purpose: Attaining a new meaning around the self

Method: Navigation of attention over different perspectives on the role of the self within a particular experience

Length: 5–10 minutes

Attention protocol:

- Close your eyes and take three deep breaths.
- Shift attention to the heart space.
- Select an event that has a significant role in your life story.
- Observe yourself as an actor in this scene.
- Allow feelings and emotions of joy, sorrow, worry, and thoughts about specific events, experiences, and memories to freely unfold in yourself, "an inner attention landscape;" do not put any resistance on the flow; do not judge; appreciate all that is shown to you.
- Bear in mind that we tend to perceive what other people have done or experienced completely differently than how we perceive what we have done and experienced; thus shift the perspective on the self and observe yourself as a stranger.
- Review your experiences, actions, and behaviors as though they belong to an unknown person, a stranger.
- Observe what new meaning is revealed to you from adopting the perspective of a "stranger": "What insights do you gain about yourself, about the experience, about the specific situation?"

Source: Steiner (1909–1911/1994)

Mindful interactions with co-workers

Mindfulness within the self also spills over into the transactions one has with co-workers. Mindfulness quietens the self talking to itself and reduces the story-telling power of the ego (Leary, Adams & Tate, 2006), dismantles automatisms related to ego-defensiveness and the tendency to respond reactively in a negative manner to co-workers when their actions do not comply with our expectations, desires, and wishes (Leary, Tate, Adams, Batts Allen, & Hancock, 2007). Mindfulness in relationships with co-workers can be beneficial in at least two ways. First, it can help bridge dysfunctional conflicts. Recent research has, for example, found that meditators showed more efficient cognitive control after conflicts (Jo, Malinowski, & Schmidt, 2017). This means that awareness of the present moment and conflict can help achieve faster conflict resolution, which leads to more effective team performance. Second, empathy is relevant when working in groups and teams, and there is some initial evidence that mindfulness-based interventions and loving-kindness meditation can elicit concern for others (Boellinghaus, Jones, & Hutton, 2014). Mindfulness has also successfully reduced aggressive behavioral tendencies (Borders, Earleywine, & Jajodia, 2010).

In a mindful state a person can better perceive other people's perspectives (the thoughts and emotions from which they are approaching the interaction). Other benefits include seeing things with greater clarity, an improvement in perspective-taking capacity (Block-Lerner, Adair, Plumb, Rhatigan, & Orsillo, 2007), pattern recognition (Karelaia & Reb, 2015), as well as creativity (Martin, 2012).

When employees encounter dysfunctional situations, it is useful for them to stop and become aware of what is going on, then analyze the situation before responding. It is recommended that in times of conflict, people feel more curiosity as to what is going on, as this raises their positive emotions (Laurent, Laurent, Lightcap, & Nelson, 2016).

Exercise 2

Purpose: Reducing the tension within a relationship

Method: Attentive scanning of different parts of the body to resolve the tension induced by conflict

Length: 10–15 minutes

Attention protocol:

- Close your eyes and take three deep breaths.
- Shift attention and bring it to your body; notice the edge where your body is touching the seat.
- Allow the formation of a picture in your mind of a recent stressful interaction with another person at work.
- Immerse yourself into the experience, remember the dialogue, identify what exactly the other person said or did, and the effect this had on you, the distress you experienced.
- Pay attention to your reaction in that moment of conflict; reconnect with yourself and become attentive: what do you sense in your body, what do you feel, and what are your thoughts?
- After observing your sensations, feelings, and thoughts in a remembered experience of conflict, assess the level of stress you are feeling. What grade would you give it on a scale from 1–10?
- Pay attention to the sense of (your)self in the conflict. Why was it defensive? What are your likely assumptions about the other person, about yourself, and about the world, working behind your conscious awareness?
- Ask yourself: are these assumptions true? How can you modify them to make the self less threatened? How can you modify your reaction to be more constructive and appreciative?
- Observe what comes into your mind.

Source: Adapted from Atkinson (2013)

Mindful interactions with clients

Interactions with clients are increasingly being shaped by customer-driven buying cycles, which creates substantial pressure on the personnel responsible for marketing and sales activities (Nirell, 2014). Activities related to client interactions are becoming highly "impermanent" and are characterized by erratic decision-making, isolation, and unnecessary stress. Nirell argues that mindful marketers and sales personnel are better at grasping the relevant information that is moving at record speed and crossing organizational hierarchies, can better select the marketing language, speed up the movement of clients in the marketing–sales pipeline, and increase the client conversion rates. Mindfulness marketing and sales activities can mediate the entrepreneurial (opportunity-scanning) behaviors by linking production with consumption (Ndubisi, Uslay, & Erdogan, 2014). Mindful marketing fosters mindful consumption and value co-creation (Malhotra, Lee, & Uslay, 2012).

In terms of fostering connections with clients, responding to feedback mindfully can contribute to a more favorable customer experience and their decision to engage again with the same employee. Particularly for the service industry, how employees respond to feedback, positively or negatively, can contribute to the quality of the relationships they develop. Research indicates that mindfulness can be useful here because it influences how people react to feedback. Specifically, mindful employees can be more accepting of criticism, both constructive and unconstructive, because they are less concerned and less inclined to start self-protective psychological mechanisms (Teper & Inzlicht, 2014). In turn, they are more open to accepting the recommendations for improvement.

Exercise 3

Purpose: Increase the value-creating potential within a business partnership

Method: Attentive observation of the success factors and assumptions related to the success of a client's business and the sensing of opportunities for value co-creation

Length: 60 minutes

Attention protocol:

- Invite your client to a business walk in nature; bear in mind that nature has a positive impact on a person's affective emotional state, making it less anxious, more peaceful; such a walk can increase sincerity, transparency, and trust in the communication.
- Conduct a conversation with the client with an attitude of non-judgment, appreciative listening, a sensing of the business opportunities signaled by the client, as well as the ideas and concepts arising within yourself, along with a greater willingness to trust.
- Present to the client a goal and the method; ask if it would be okay with them to try to rediscover the business relationship by going attentively through a set of questions.
- If the client does not agree, do not proceed; joint willingness to do the interview is critical with regard to raising the likelihood of discovering new business opportunities and recharging the business relationship with trust and positive affect.
- Facilitate the conversation with the following set of questions: What is the most important objective of your work and business? Related to that, what are your core challenges? Why do these challenges exist? How can we (I personally) help you realize these objectives and

resolve these challenges? What are your greatest sources of success? What criteria do you use to assess whether my/our contribution to your work (business, department) has been successful? In what aspects could we assist your business better? What initiatives do you suggest, recommend? If you were able to change two things in the way our business is run so that it would create the most value and benefit for you, what would that be? As the conversation unfolds, pay attention to and trust the questions that occur to you.

- Don't be afraid to ask simple questions or questions you think may reveal a lack of some basic knowledge. Leverage the power of presence and silence. Moments of silence can serve as important trigger points for deepening the relationship. Be courageous. Stay with the opening of the NOW.

Source: Adapted from Scharmer's theory U (2009) and the U-Lab toolkit

Mindful interactions with robots

With digital transformation people will be increasingly spending more time with robots (Kaivo-Oja, Roth, & Westerlund, 2017). A robot is any electromechanical construct designed to carry out a task, set of tasks, or engage in a function or behavior according to a set of rules defined by a computer program; these functions are carried out autonomously with little input from the user. Early research has shown that people experience anxiety and stress when working with robots. Anxiety levels increase with age, and are higher for females and the less educated, especially if the robots do not look human, the robot's behavior is too fast, or the interactions with the robots are not transparent and simple (Bagdasarov, Martin, & Buckley, in press). Humanoid robots, like MIT LEO, possess "artificial consciousness" that simulates human consciousness in many aspects: speech recognition and parsing, vision and attention, cognition and behavior, and motor control (Breazeal, Hoffman, & Lockerd, 2004). Though artificial consciousness is rooted in advanced learning algorithms, which may be more efficient in performing certain cognitive tasks than humans, this form of consciousness will never gain Steiner's quality of being "in-spirited." This can be viewed as an additional property, the lack of which may contribute to the anxiety experienced in interactions with robots.

Exercise 4

Purpose: Elevation of stress and discharge of negativity in the being state (from negative to positive)

Method: Mindful breathing with use of imagination

Length: 5–8 minutes

Attention protocol:

- Comfortably sit in a chair, back straight up.
- Soften your gaze on a point in the distance. Take a few slow, deep breaths.
- Bring your attention to the present moment by noticing how you're feeling physically. Scan your body from head to toe and consciously try to let any tension slip away.

- Take a moment to notice your environment—any sounds you might hear in the background, what the temperature feels like in the room.
- Then again refocus your attention on your breathing: notice the sensation of your breath in your nostrils or mouth; the rising and falling of your chest and belly as you breathe.
- Each time your mind wanders away from the breath, notice where it goes and then gently bring your attention back to the feeling of the breath going in and out.
- Then activate your imagination; imagine you are breathing shining white light into your legs, belly, chest, head, and whole body; and then imagine you are also breathing out stress and pain from your chest, belly, and whole body.
- Observe how the stressful feelings and sensations in the body get broken down and released.
- Smile when releasing them.
- Do this imaginative breathing practice for at least five minutes, and then open your eyes and return back to your tasks.

Source: Adapted from Steiner (1961/1996)

Mindful leadership

In the 21st century leaders need to acquire resilience with regard to feeling comfort in discomfort, master adaptability and authenticity (Morris et al., 2015), and build up their metacognition (Marshall-Mies et al., 2000). Metacognition is the ability to observe one's thoughts, feelings, sensations, and impulses as they are being experienced, and to see them as mental events rather than the "reality" or "truth" of the situation (Teasdale, 1999). Mindfulness thus closely correlates not only with resilience and collaboration, but also with metacognition. Furthermore, mindfulness also tends to reduce the tendency whereby decision-making gets biased by a leader's long-held beliefs, as shaped by past successes and failures (Good et al., 2015). It decreases the proclivity for the "sunk-cost bias" (Hafenbrack, Kinias, & Barsade, 2014). When it comes to leadership, mindfulness has been suggested to increase the capacity to lead as well as act as a role model (Sauer & Kohls, 2011). For example, leaders can become more aware of how their connections with digital devices can affect their teams. Recent research reveals that a supervisor who is using or is distracted by their phone while in the presence of co-workers is seen as less trustworthy by those they are supervising, which further leads to lower employee engagement (Roberts & David, 2017). Moreover, the recommendations about feedback also apply in the leader–employee relationship, specifically when it comes to giving and receiving performance feedback (Teper & Inzlicht, 2014). Here, leaders can bring attention to detecting how employees feel during the performance feedback. Leaders also need to act as role models when it comes to being mindful about employees' need for recovery, relaxation, and protecting time for their families. They should be demonstrating role-modelling behaviors in this regard. For example, just as supervisors can create expectations about responding to emails, they can also create expectations about being mindful and protecting non-work time, so employees can switch off and regain energy (Derks et al., 2015). One of the ways to nurture mindfulness during the enactment of leadership is through mindfulness-based strategic awareness training for leaders (Sauer & Kohls, 2011; Young, 2017). As written by George, the practice of mindful leadership forces the leader to focus on the present moment, recognize and control their own feelings, and notice the ways their behavior impacts on other people. He practices mediation on a daily basis and notes it has helped him be more focused in his leadership, let go of trivial worries, and better manage stressful situations (George, 2012).

Exercise 5

Purpose: Attainment of intuitive insight into the specific business challenge

Method: Imaginative connection with the flow of ideas behind nature and behind a business challenge

Length: 20–30 minutes

Attention protocol:

- Place a small seed from a plant in front of you on the table.
- Relax your posture and breathing.
- Focus your sight on the seed. Describe what you see: the form, color, other properties.
- Think of someone who you feel appreciation for. Sustain that appreciative feeling and refocus it on the seed. Feel appreciation and positive affect for the seed. (Note: it is very important before going on to the next steps that you shift your current state out of anxiety, worry, anger, fear, and other negative feelings. Stop here if you cannot move on from a negative affect and switch to the gratitude meditation presented in Exercise 6.)
- Soften your gaze on the seed and, while still gazing attentively, reflect on the idea that, "if this seed implanted in the ground, it will grow into a complex plant" (Steiner, 1909–1911/1999, p. 56).
- Then contemplate on the following thought: "Within the seed already lies concealed what —as the force of the whole plant—later grows out of it—as the force of the whole plant —later grows out of it." (Steiner, 1909–1911/1999, p. 56) This seed contains something invisible, a hidden force. Focus your feelings and thoughts on this invisible force behind the seed. Use imagination and visualize how the forces of earth, water, and light are transforming the seed into a plant; imagine that this invisible force is behind the reality of the seed.
- Try to sense this hidden force behind the seed; after connecting with this hidden force, refocus your attention and put under your attentive focus a specific business challenge/ situation; bring it into your "inner landscape," describe it as fully as possible.
- Open up your mind and allow thoughts, ideas, and associations to flow freely; do not judge them; accept each thought and say "thank you" to it, then let it go; observe the pattern in the flow of thoughts; this pattern presents the force working behind the challenge.
- After getting in touch with the pattern, try to describe it in words; put that description down on paper so the insight is not lost.

Source: Adapted from Steiner (1961/1996)

Mindful interactions in non-work life

A mindful approach can also be adopted when it comes to managing work and private obligations, and to relationships with significant others, children, other family members, friends, and the wider community. While previous research connecting mindfulness and work–family spillover is sparse, it is informative. For example, studies find that mindfulness at work helps develop personal resources, such as the perception of work–family balance (Zivnuska, Kacmar, Ferguson, & Carlson, 2016). Working parents who report being more mindful (as measured by trait mindfulness) were found to have a greater work–family balance (Allen & Kiburz, 2012). Moreover, there is also research on the impact of work–family conflict. More specifically, in an experimental study the authors investigated the effects of a brief mindfulness training intervention, which consisted of a one-hour workshop on mindfulness and then 13 days of self-monitoring one's own behavior, with the aim of reducing work–family conflict. The findings revealed that mindfulness practice decreased work–family conflict but did not decrease family–work conflict (Kiburz, Allen, & French, 2017). In another study, which included a three-week online self-training intervention, the participants reported less strain-based work–family conflict, more satisfaction with work–life balance, and were also more psychologically detached (Michel, Bosch, & Rexroth, 2014). When it comes to partner relationships, mindfulness diffuses the tensions surrounding interpersonal conflict. Specifically, curiosity during conflict (i.e., one feature of mindfulness) predicted the significant other's well-being through the increased positive affect felt during the conflict situation (Laurent et al., 2016).

It has also been proposed that employees can use mindfulness practice as a way to establish boundaries between their work and private lives (Michel et al., 2014), which, as noted above, have become increasingly blurred. Establishing boundaries helps reduce a person's psychological preoccupation with job demands. In addition, with the ease of "working anytime, anywhere," people can easily become drawn into working for a few hours despite promising their children they would play with them after answering just one email. Deliberate awareness of what is going on during non-work hours can help employees make alternative decisions about their time allocation.

Based on the above, mindfulness can therefore be utilized as another individual strategy for more fruitful relationships with family members and friends, as well as coping with work–family conflict and reducing it, be it in the form of journaling (i.e., recording feelings about daily events at work) or breathing exercises to disconnect from the world of work.

Exercise 6

Purpose: Develop an affective state of unconditional kindness towards an individual (a family member, a friend, etc.) and cultivate compassion and generosity

Method: Employs the imagining or actual experience of the emotional state as an object of attention and mindful awareness

Length: 8–15 minutes

Attention protocol:

- Comfortably sit in a chair, back straight up.
- Take a slow, deep breath.
- Check in with your body and notice how you're feeling right now; observe thoughts, emotions, and sensations with a non-judgmental attitude; and welcome relaxation and a sensation of comfort into the body; smile.
- Bring to mind someone whom you feel happy around, and appreciate (a child, significant other, family member . . .).
- Imagine them in front of you; try to feel them, sense them, see them.
- Notice how you are feeling inside; maybe you feel some warmth or there's some heat on your face like a smile, sense of expansiveness. This is loving kindness.
- Utter the following words in your mind: "May you be healthy. May you be happy. May you be loved. May you be abundant." Repeat this sentence four times in your mind and sense how you are sending the person you are thinking of health, happiness, love, and abundance.
- Then focus on a neutral person (i.e., a person who typically does not elicit either particularly positive or negative feelings, but who is commonly encountered during a normal day), and repeat the whole protocol.
- Then focus on a "difficult" person (i.e., a person who is typically associated with negative feelings and a difficult relationship), and repeat the whole protocol.

Source: Loving kindness meditation adopted from Hofmann, Grossman, and Hinton (2011)

Conclusion

Mindfulness not only benefits the inner experience of a person, but also raises the quality of their relationships with specific stakeholders, and in the long run has the potential to elicit positive effects with considerable transformational power. In this chapter we provided guidelines of how employees can foster fruitful relationships through a mindfulness-based approach to the management of stakeholder interactions in the work and non-work domain. When mindfulness is established with stakeholders, it could become a shared social practice in the family and in an organization, permeating across teams and departments and leading to resilience, sustainable performance in different roles, and well-being.

Chapter takeaways/lessons

1. Mindfulness is an approach to the management of one's inner state.
2. Mindfulness is one of the strategies for managing the demands of today's work and family contexts.
3. By effective management of one's own inner state, one can become more effective at establishing fruitful stakeholder relationships.
4. Fostering mindful interactions may contribute to well-being, improved decision-making, and greater creativity being manifested through the relationship.
5. The chapter offers adjusted mindfulness exercises for the more effective "navigation" of various stakeholder relationships.

Reflection questions

1. Consider your current work relationships. In what kind of situations do you see yourself behaving automatically and not paying attention to what is going on?
2. Consider your current non-work relationships. In what kind of situations do you see yourself behaving automatically and not paying attention to what is going on?
3. What can you commit to doing during the course of the next week in order to be more mindful? Provide details in terms of what you will do, which stakeholder you will take into consideration, when and how will you be more mindful, as well as why.
4. What practices recommended in this chapter make you feel the greatest resistance in the form of "I will not do it," "that's crazy," and similar judgmental thoughts? It is advisable to go back to this exact exercise and attempt to do it without judgment, but with a sense of curiosity and gratitude.

Acknowledgement

We gratefully acknowledge funding received from the European Union's Horizon 2020 Research and Innovation program under Marie Sklodowska-Curie grant agreement number 734824 that facilitated the writing of this chapter.

References

Allen, T. D., & Kiburz, K. M. (2012). Trait mindfulness and work–family balance among working parents: The mediating effects of vitality and sleep quality. *Journal of Vocational Behavior, 80*(2), 372–379.

Atkins, P. W., & Parker, S. K. (2012). Understanding individual compassion in organizations: The role of appraisals and psychological flexibility. *Academy of Management Review, 37*(4), 524–546.

Atkinson, B. J. (2013). Mindfulness training and the cultivation of secure, satisfying couple relationships. *Couple and Family Psychology: Research and Practice, 2*(2), 73–94.

Bagdasarov, Z., Martin, A. A., & Buckley, M. R. (in press). Working with robots: Organizational considerations. In *Organizational dynamics*. Available at: https://www.sciencedirect.com/science/article/abs/pii/S0090261618301475

Barber, L. K., & Santuzzi, A. M. (2015). Please respond ASAP: Workplace telepressure and employee recovery. *Journal of Occupational Health Psychology, 20*(2), 172–189.

Bhalla, V., Dyrchs, S., & Strack, R. (2017). Twelve forces that will radically change how organizations work. https://www.bcg.com/publications/2017/people-organization-strategy-twelve-forces-radically-change-organizations-work.aspx.

Block-Lerner, J., Adair, C., Plumb, J. C., Rhatigan, D. L., & Orsillo, S. M. (2007). The case for mindfulness-based approaches in the cultivation of empathy: Does nonjudgmental, present-moment awareness increase capacity for perspective-taking and empathic concern? *Journal of Marital and Family Therapy, 33*(4), 501–516.

Boellinghaus, I., Jones, F. W., & Hutton, J. (2014). The role of mindfulness and loving-kindness meditation in cultivating self-compassion and other-focused concern in health care professionals. *Mindfulness, 5*(2), 129–138.

Borders, A., Earleywine, M., & Jajodia, A. (2010). Could mindfulness decrease anger, hostility, and aggression by decreasing rumination? *Aggressive Behavior: Official Journal of the International Society for Research on Aggression, 36*(1), 28–44.

Breazeal, C., Hoffman, G., & Lockerd, A. (2004). Teaching and working with robots as a collaboration. In *Proceedings of the Third International Joint Conference on Autonomous Agents and Multiagent Systems—Volume 3* (pp. 1030–1037). IEEE Computer Society.

Brown, K. W., & Ryan, R. M. (2003). The benefits of being present: Mindfulness and its role in psychological well-being. *Journal of Personality and Social Psychology, 84*(4), 822–848.

Brynjolfsson, E., & McAfee, A. (2014). *The second machine age: Work, progress, and prosperity in a time of brilliant technologies*. New York, NY, US: WW Norton & Co.

Chiesa, A., & Serretti, A. (2009). Mindfulness-based stress reduction for stress management in healthy people: A review and meta-analysis. *The Journal of Alternative and Complementary Medicine, 15*(5), 593–600.

Chotpitayasunondh, V., & Douglas, K. M. (2016). How "phubbing" becomes the norm: The antecedents and consequences of snubbing via smartphone. *Computers in Human Behavior, 63*(1), 9–18.

Coo, C., & Salanova, M. (2018). Mindfulness can make you happy-and-productive: A mindfulness controlled trial and its effects on happiness, work engagement and performance. *Journal of Happiness Studies, 19*(6), 1691–1711.

Dane, E., & Brummel, B. J. (2014). Examining workplace mindfulness and its relations to job performance and turnover intention. *Human Relations, 67*(1), 105–128.

Davidson, R. J., Kabat-Zinn, J., Schumacher, J., Rosenkranz, M., Muller, D., Santorelli, S. F., ... Sheridan, J. F. (2003). Alterations in brain and immune function produced by mindfulness meditation. *Psychosomatic Medicine, 65*(4), 564–570.

Derks, D., van Duin, D., Tims, M., & Bakker, A. B. (2015). Smartphone use and work–home interference: The moderating role of social norms and employee work engagement. *Journal of Occupational and Organizational Psychology, 88*(1), 155–177.

Gee, K. (2019). Sunday night is the new Monday morning, and workers are miserable www.wsj.com/articles/sunday-night-is-the-new-monday-morning-and-workers-are-miserable-11562497212.

George, B. (2012). Mindfulness helps you become a better leader. *Harvard Business Review, 26*, 21–32.

Glomb, T. M., Duffy, M. K., Bono, J. E., & Yang, T. (2011). Mindfulness at work. In A. Joshi, H. Liao, & J. Martocchio (Eds.), *Research in personnel and human resources management* (Vol. 30, pp. 115–157). Bingley: Emerald Group Publishing Limited.

Gonzalez, M. (2014). Mindfulness for people who are too busy to meditate. *Harvard Business Review*, 1–3.

Good, D. J., Lyddy, C. J., Glomb, T. M., Bono, J. E., Brown, K. W., Duffy, M. K., ... Lazar, S. W. (2015). Contemplating mindfulness at work an integrative review. Contemplating mindfulness at work: an integrative review. *Journal of Management, 42*(1), 114–142.

Greiser, C. (2018). Unleashing the power of mindfulness in corporations. Retrieved from www.bcg.com/publications/2018/unleashing-power-of-mindfulness-in-corporations.aspx

Hafenbrack, A. C., Kinias, Z., & Barsade, S. G. (2014). Debiasing the mind through meditation mindfulness and the sunk-cost bias. *Psychological Science, 25*, 369–376.

Hofmann, S. G., Grossman, P., & Hinton, D. E. (2011). Loving-kindness and compassion meditation: Potential for psychological interventions. *Clinical Psychology Review, 31*(7), 1126–1132.

Hülsheger, U. R., Alberts, H. J., Feinholdt, A., & Lang, J. W. (2013). Benefits of mindfulness at work: The role of mindfulness in emotion regulation, emotional exhaustion, and job satisfaction. *Journal of Applied Psychology, 98*(2), 310–325.

Hyland, P. K., Lee, R. A., & Mills, M. J. (2015). Mindfulness at work: A new approach to improving individual and organizational performance. *Industrial and Organizational Psychology, 8*(4), 576–602.

Jain, S., Shapiro, S. L., Swanick, S., Roesch, S. C., Mills, P. J., Bell, I., & Schwartz, G. E. (2007). A randomized controlled trial of mindfulness meditation versus relaxation training: Effects on distress, positive states of mind, rumination, and distraction. *Annals of Behavioral Medicine, 33*(1), 11–21.

Jha, A. P., Stanley, E. A., Kiyonaga, A., Wong, L., & Gelfand, L. (2010). Examining the protective effects of mindfulness training on working memory capacity and affective experience. *Emotion, 10*(1), 54–64.

Jo, H.-G., Malinowski, P., & Schmidt, S. (2017). Frontal theta dynamics during response conflict in long-term mindfulness meditators. *Frontiers in Human Neuroscience, 11*, 299.

Kabat-Zinn, J. (2003). Mindfulness-based stress reduction (MBSR). *Constructivism in the Human Sciences, 8*(2), 73–107.

Kaivo-Oja, J., Roth, S., & Westerlund, L. (2017). Futures of robotics. Human work in digital transformation. *International Journal of Technology Management, 73*(4), 176–205.

Karelaia, N., & Reb, J. (2015) Improving decision making through mindfulness. (2015).Mindfulness in organizations: Foundations, research, and applications. 163-189. Research Collection Lee Kong Chian School Of Business. Retrieved from https://ink.library.smu.edu.sg/lkcsb_research/4809

Kegan, R. (1982). *The evolving self.* Cambridge, MA: Harvard University Press.

Kegan, R. (1994). *over our heads: The mental demands of modern life*. Cambridge, MA: Harvard University Press.

Kegan, R., & Lahey, L. L. (2009). *Immunity to change: How to overcome it and unlock potential in yourself and your organization*. Cambridge, MA: Harvard University Press.

Kiburz, K. M., Allen, T. D., & French, K. A. (2017). Work–family conflict and mindfulness: Investigating the effectiveness of a brief training intervention. *Journal of Organizational Behavior, 38*(7), 1016–1037.

Kolb, D. G., Caza, A., & Collins, P. D. (2012). States of connectivity: New questions and new directions. *Organization Studies, 33*(2), 267–273.

Laurent, H. K., Laurent, S. M., Lightcap, A., & Nelson, B. W. (2016). How situational mindfulness during conflict stress relates to well-being. *Mindfulness*, 7(4), 909–915.

Leary, M. R., Adams, C. E., & Tate, E. B. (2006). Hypo-egoic self-regulation: Exercising self-control by diminishing the influence of the self. *Journal of Personality*, *74*(6), 1803–1832.

Leary, M. R., Tate, E. B., Adams, C. E., Batts Allen, A., & Hancock, J. (2007). Self-compassion and reactions to unpleasant self-relevant events: The implications of treating oneself kindly. *Journal of Personality and Social Psychology*, *92*(5), 887–904.

Leroy, H., Anseel, F., Dimitrova, N. G., & Sels, L. (2013). Mindfulness, authentic functioning, and work engagement: A growth modeling approach. *Journal of Vocational Behavior, 82*(3), 238–247.

Malhotra, N. K., Lee, O. F., & Uslay, C. (2012). Mind the gap: The mediating role of mindful marketing between market and quality orientations, their interaction, and consequences. *International Journal of Quality & Reliability Management, 29*(6), 607–625.

Malinowski, P., & Lim, H. J. (2015). Mindfulness at work: Positive affect, hope, and optimism mediate the relationship between dispositional mindfulness, work engagement, and well-being. *Mindfulness, 6* (6), 1250–1262.

Marshall-Mies, J. C., Fleishman, E. A., Martin, J. A., Zaccaro, S. J., Baughman, W. A., & McGee, M. L. (2000). Development and evaluation of cognitive and metacognitive measures for predicting leadership potential. *The Leadership Quarterly*, *11*(1), 135–153.

Martin, J. (2012). Employee brain on stress can quash creativity and competitive edge. Retrieved from www.forbes.com/sites/work-in-progress/2012/09/05/employee-brain-on-stress-can-quash-creativi tycompetitive-edge/#2076d5031500

Mazmanian, M., Orlikowski, W. J., & Yates, J. (2013). The autonomy paradox: The implications of mobile email devices for knowledge professionals. *Organization Science*, *24*(5), 1337–1357.

Michel, A., Bosch, C., & Rexroth, M. (2014). Mindfulness as a cognitive–emotional segmentation strategy: An intervention promoting work–life balance. *Journal of Occupational and Organizational Psychology*, *87*(4), 733–754.

Mihelič, K. K., & Culiberg, B. (2019). Reaping the fruits of another's labor: The role of moral meaningfulness, mindfulness, and motivation in social loafing. *Journal of Business Ethics*, *160*, 713–727. doi:10.1007/s10551-018-3933-z

Mindfulness Initiative. Private Sector Working Group. Building the case for mindfulness in the workplace. Version 1.1 (October 2016). www.themindfulnessinitiative.org/building-the-case-for-mindfulness-in-the-workplace.

Moore, A., & Malinowski, P. (2009). Meditation, mindfulness and cognitive flexibility. *Consciousness and Cognition*, *18*(1), 176–186.

Morris, T., White, A., Smets, M., Moss Cowan, A., Athanasopoulou, A., Malloch, T., . . . McQuater, A. (2015). *The CEO report: Embracing the paradoxes of leadership and the power of doubt*. New York: Heidrick & Struggles.

Nelson Oly Ndubisi, Assoc. Prof. Can Uslay, P., Uslay, C. and Erdogan, E. (2014), The mediating role of mindful entrepreneurial marketing (MEM) between production and consumption, *Journal of Research in Marketing and Entrepreneurship*, *16* (1), 47–62.

Nezlek, J. B., Holas, P., Rusanowska, M., & Krejtz, I. (2016). Being present in the moment: Event-level relationships between mindfulness and stress, positivity, and importance. *Personality and Individual Differences*, *93*(1), 1–5.

Nirell, L. (2014). *The mindful marketer: How to stay present and profitable in a data-driven world*. New York: Palgrave Macmillan.

Ostafin, B. D., & Kassman, K. T. (2012). Stepping out of history: Mindfulness improves insight problem-solving. *Consciousness and Cognition*, *21*, 1031–1036.

Presencing Institute. U_lab. U-lab toolkit. Retrieved from www.presencing.org/resource/tools

Report by the Mindfulness All-Party Parliamentary Group (MAPPG). MINDFUL NATION UK. The Mindfulness Initiative. Accessed on 10.10.2019 www.themindfulnessinitiative.org.uk.

Roberts, J. A., & David, M. E. (2017). Put down your phone and listen to me: How boss phubbing undermines the psychological conditions necessary for employee engagement. *Computers in Human Behavior, 75*, 206–217.

Rubery, J., Grimshaw, D., Keizer, A., & Johnson, M. (2018). Challenges and contradictions in the 'normalising'of precarious work. *Work, Employment and Society, 32*(3), 509–527.

Sauer, S., & Kohls, N. (2011). Mindfulness in leadership: Does being mindful enhance leaders' business success? In E. P. ShihuiHan (Ed.), *Culture and neural frames of cognition and communication* (pp. 287–307). Springer.

Scharmer, C. O. (2009). *Theory U: Learning from the future as it emerges*. Oakland, CA: Berrett-Koehler Publishers.

Schwab, K. (2017). *The fourth industrial revolution*. New York, US: Currency.

Steiner, R. (1961/1994). *How to know higher worlds: A modern path of initiation*. Dornach, Switzerland: Anthroposophic Press.

Steiner, R. (1904-1905)/1994). *How to know higher worlds: A modern path of initiation*. Berlin: SteinerBooks.

Steiner, R. (1909-1911/1999). *Psychology of body, soul, and spirit*. Berlin: SteinerBooks.

Steiner, R.. (1893/1999). *The philosophy of freedom (the philosophy of spiritual activity): The basis for a modern world conception: Some results of introspective observation following the methods of natural science*. Berlin: Rudolf Steiner Press.

Teasdale, J. D. (1999). Metacognition, mindfulness and the modification of mood disorders. *Clinical Psychology & Psychotherapy: An International Journal of Theory & Practice, 6*(2), 146–155.

Teper, R., & Inzlicht, M. (2014). Mindful acceptance dampens neuroaffective reactions to external and rewarding performance feedback. *Emotion, 14*(1), 105–114.

Weick, K. E., & Sutcliffe, K. M. (2006). Mindfulness and the quality of attention. *Organization Science, 17* (4), 514–525.

Williams, J. M. G., & Kabat-Zinn, J. (2013). *Mindfulness: Diverse perspectives on its meaning, origins and applications*. London: Routledge.

Young, J. H. (2017). *Mindfulness-based strategic awareness training: A complete program for leaders and individuals*. Chichester, West Sussex, UK: John Wiley & Sons.

Zeidan, F., Johnson, S. K., Diamond, B. J., David, Z., & Goolkasian, P. (2010). Mindfulness meditation improves cognition: Evidence of brief mental training. *Consciousness and Cognition, 19*(2), 597–605.

Zivnuska, S., Kacmar, K. M., Ferguson, M., & Carlson, D. S. (2016). Mindfulness at work: Resource accumulation, well-being, and attitudes. *Career Development International, 21*(2), 106–124.

14

MORE THAN MEDITATION

How managers can effectively put the science of workplace mindfulness to work

Jutta Tobias Mortlock

1. What is this thing called mindfulness?

What mindfulness is can be explained quite simply by describing the opposite: when individuals or groups operate in "autopilot mode," essentially navigating through the challenges of the day with their minds absent and without really thinking about what is actually in front of them. Leaders all over the world immediately understand that it is a real problem for organizations when employees manage their daily work largely on autopilot, because organizations do not function when employees are physically present but mentally absent. If absent-mindedness or "being on autopilot" are the opposite of mindfulness, then mindfulness should be understood as a state of being conscious, awake, aware. Although these ideas sound rather complicated, everyone knows what it feels like to be fully present in the here and now, when you become aware of a situation with all of your five senses, open to receiving new information in the moment in real time, and perhaps also learning something new, grasping new perspectives. In a groundbreaking study in 2010, the American researchers Matthew Killingsworth and Daniel Gilbert found that over the course of a typical work day, we spend almost half of our time with our minds being elsewhere than where our bodies are, namely at our work desks (Killingsworth and Gilbert 2010). That this is bad for productivity was by far not as interesting to the researchers as the fact that this renders us less happy than if we were more able to consciously experience our work lives.

First mindfulness exercise for willing readers

If the last sentence in the paragraph above has made you pause, then that is appropriate. In fact, it really does sound at least somewhat naive or perhaps even paradoxical that we should be happier if we were to go through our everyday work lives more consciously. Often, work is not exactly "fun" and many a task at work has little to do with making employees happy. But the point here is that "being happy" means more than merely "having fun." Happiness researchers (they do indeed exist) such as Sonya Lyubomirsky define "happiness" as a construct that consists of two aspects: first, feeling good or pleasant, and second, having meaning in one's life (Lyubomirsky, Sheldon and Schkade 2005). Matthew Killingsworth and Daniel Gilbert have found that we often fail to recognize the (perhaps longer-term or more fundamental) meaning of our work when we are mentally absent or multi-tasking at work. The two researchers conclude that mental absence makes people unhappy at work.

Where has your mind been while reading this paragraph? Have you been able to concentrate exclusively on what you were reading? To what extent did your mind move in and out of being "on task," taking in the words in front of you? What might this mean for you right here and now, and for your ultimate satisfaction with reading this chapter?

Why has mindfulness become so interesting to business, politics, and even professional athletes like British racing cyclists Chris Froome and Bradley Wiggins, who invested considerable energy in applying the mindfulness techniques they had learned from sports psychologist Steve Peters before winning the Tour de France? Because a solid body of science links mindfulness with better physical and mental health and with better relationships at home and at work. And because mindfulness is not a quality that some have and others not. Instead, mindfulness is a state of mind or way of being that can be learned and that helps individuals face especially difficult situations in their (working) life. This latest insight is good news for companies interested in helping improve not only the wellbeing and working relationships of their employees, but also in promoting sustainable workplace performance. Mindfulness can be taught to any person who is open to learning and practicing this different way of being and acting in the present. Therefore, in principle, entire organizations may benefit from mindfulness, not just those individuals who are particularly interested in this topic.

So, then, what is mindfulness? Mindfulness is not easy to define. Although to date more than 33 definitions of mindfulness have been published in the scientific literature (Nilsson and Kazemi 2016), many mindfulness experts cite the definition of founder of the world's most well-known and extensively researched Mindfulness-Based Stress Reduction (MBSR) program, Jon Kabat-Zinn: paying attention to the present moment, on purpose, and non-judgmentally (Kabat-Zinn 1994).

That sounds complicated. And a little bit like Buddhism. This is because in the late 1970s, Jon Kabat-Zinn brought his knowledge of Buddhism to his research into stress-reduction at the Massachusetts Institute of Technology (MIT). Mindfulness is an important goal in Buddhism, and Buddhists learn mindfulness through meditation. The word "meditation" comes from the Latin *meditatum*, which means "contemplating" or "reflecting." Although meditating is often associated with religious practices, it is, in itself, an ideology-free mental act or brain exercise, during which one often sits still and does nothing but use the breath as an anchor, to become more aware of sensations, emotions, thoughts, physical impulses, and reactions.

Second mindfulness exercise for willing readers

[Please only do this exercise if you don't have any issues with controlling your breath (e.g., asthma or hyperventilation).]

Breathe slowly and deeply in and out three times. Where do you feel your breath in the body right now? Perhaps you can feel your breath in your nose or in your mouth or throat or maybe in your ribcage or stomach. As soon as you notice where you feel your breath, concentrate completely on this spot for a few moments. This is your breathing spot; you can use this spot in your body as an anchor to practice mindfulness meditation. How does it feel to concentrate on this breathing spot, your anchor for noticing your breath at will? What is it like to find this breathing spot after losing your concentration for a few moments?

Jon Kabat-Zinn, as well as hundreds of scientists following in his footsteps over the past 30 years, has explored the connection between mindfulness meditation, stress management, and mental health so extensively that there are literally thousands of scientific studies on the subject today. Researchers at Oxford University demonstrated a few years ago that mindfulness meditation can work just as effectively against chronic depression as antidepressants (Kuyken, Hayes, Barrett et al., 2015). This is a ground-breaking insight, as chronic depression is very often based on chemical alterations in the brain, assumed to be ameliorated most effectively by inducing external chemicals such as antidepressants. That mental exercise such as mindfulness meditation can achieve the same result (without any chemical or neurobiological side effects) speaks to the extensive link between mind and body (or rather between brain processes and bodily functions). And we can strengthen this connection if we proactively focus our attention in this way.

2. This is how mindfulness works: coming to our (five) senses

Mindfulness is not the same as meditation. As already mentioned, mindfulness is a state of mind or way of being that results from actions or (mental) practice. Some people are naturally mindful, live consciously, and avoid making premature judgments, but for many, mindfulness is the *outcome* of specific actions designed to increase it, e.g., through mindfulness meditation.

The important thing for managers is to know how to achieve such a mentally open and flexible state of mind and what can be done *concretely* to switch off the mental "autopilot" in order to become fully aware of the present moment.

To become mindful, we need to come to our senses. Literally and metaphorically.

We can come to our senses literally by focusing specifically on our five senses. This means focusing our attention on one of our five sensory perceptions, e.g., on seeing objects (such as a shape, color, or pattern), on feeling (e.g., sensing or noticing our breath), or on hearing stimuli (such as music, noise, or other sounds in the environment). The goal of such concentration exercises focused on our five senses is to develop an awareness of what is actually happening in and around us, as opposed to *imagining* that we know what is happening in the moment. Many of our thoughts come and go from moment to moment, and our inner "autopilot" constantly feeds us commentary about our situation and about our lives. Often this commentary is based on unconscious and sometimes outdated or rash judgments (such as "I'm too old for that" or "she will never be able to do this"). Thereby, coming to our senses means creating a certain degree of mental distance between our "self" and this inner "autopilot" and its never-ending flow of comments and judgments. This mental distance arises from consciously directing one's perception in the moment, particularly by focusing on one specific sensory perception alone, or on fewer ones than what we normally do, and in this way we are able to become more aware of all the information available to us in the situation, through our five senses. Mindfulness meditators are often encouraged to close their eyes because this restricts the sensory input through seeing and thus simplifies the act of concentrating on one of the other senses.

This conscious control over our perception of reality through our five senses can enable us to recognize new information available to us in the present moment, and in so doing, we may become aware of different perspectives of the present situation (e.g., "today my body/ the situation feels different than yesterday") and make decisions that are in line with the actual situation rather than based on subconscious impulses or automatic (pre-)judgments.

A few years ago, when I was researching the work of Daniel Kahneman, I realized why mindfulness has such great potential for helping improve decision-making for leaders in major projects. Kahneman is a Nobel Laureate in Economics and has systematically demonstrated in his work how many of our decisions are flawed, not only in private life, but especially in work situations. However, the one major advice that Kahneman gives to the readers of his book *Thinking Fast and Slow* (2011) to improve their decisions is that they should literally "experience" life as often as possible, and as often as possible suppress the urge "to anticipate remembering" (Kahneman 2011). By "anticipating remembering," Kahneman refers to the human tendency to, for example, imagine in the midst of a conversation how one will later look back on that conversation or tell others about it, all the while being involved in the conversation. Or the tendency that more and more of us have in today's interconnected world to take a picture of the dinner plate in front of us and send it to our social media contacts, instead of enjoying the sights and smells of the food, and *experiencing* these fully. Kahneman effectively advises people to come to their five senses. That essentially is the action of engaging in mindfulness practice.

Back to meditation. Meditation is definitely an effective method for increasing our attention on the present moment, but mindfulness training does not always have to contain meditation. Mindfulness is not just about taking a break from everyday life, sitting still, closing your eyes, and looking inward. On the contrary, Kahneman's advice suggests that we should be more consciously engaged in our lives rather than shut life out from our experience. In this way we can indeed perceive and process all the information available to us in the moment. This is how mindfulness helps us change our relationship with the data in front of us, and this is essential for making good decisions in important situations.

For example, researcher Esther Papies and her colleagues found that the participants in her research studies were consuming sweets less mindlessly after being instructed to look at images of food and not only to become aware of their reaction to these images and the impulses caused by them, but also to notice that such reactions spontaneously and constantly come and go (Papies, Barsalou and Custers 2012).

Ellen Langer, a professor at Harvard University who began studying mindfulness at the same time as Jon Kabat-Zinn, defines mindfulness as a flexible state of mind that enables us to become actively engaged in the present (Langer 1989), which resonates with Kahneman's advice above. This means that there are many more tools in the toolbox of a mindful manager than meditation exercises alone to help embed mindfulness into their projects and operations.

In 1979, when Ellen Langer began her research career on mindfulness, she conducted a groundbreaking study: she took a group of old, frail men into a location specially created for this experiment; a location that simulated the world of 1959, when all of these men were 20 years younger, more physically fit, and mobile. The only instruction that Langer gave to the participants in this study was that they should fully immerse themselves (with all five senses) in this environment and engage with each other *as if* they were in fact experiencing the world of 1959, rather than merely discussing this unfamiliar situation. Although these old men were all aware that this was an experiment, the researchers found that not only were their mental capacities improved when they returned to their normal lives at the end of the two-week immersion experiment, but also their physical condition had changed so positively that they were judged by strangers to be significantly younger than before the experiment, and much younger than another group of men of the same age who served as the control group, exclusively discussing the world of 1959 for two weeks. In other words, the experience of being in a "younger" environment had led to physiological "rejuvenation" of these men (Langer 2009).

You can do the next mindfulness exercise anytime, without sitting still or closing your eyes. The only requirement here is that you are mentally 100% present.

Third mindfulness exercise for willing readers

Come literally to your senses. Concentrate on two of your five senses over the next few moments: first concentrate on doing nothing but listen, and subsequently focus all your attention on seeing, looking around. Start by directing your attention exclusively to listening to all the sounds in your environment (without reading or doing anything else). Only when you have heard at least three sounds (voices, noise, etc.) that you had not noticed before, change your sensory focus and concentrate exclusively on what you see before your eyes: look around you, up and down, behind you. Look out for at least three colors, shapes, or patterns that you had not noticed before.

How are you feeling now?

For most people, such a mental exercise feels relaxing. We literally come to our senses when we consciously focus on our senses. Why is that? It is an automatic neurobiological process in the body. When we consciously perceive our experience of the present through our five senses, our body automatically mobilizes the parasympathetic nervous system, i.e., the "resting or recovery nerve" of the vegetative nervous system. The parasympathetic nervous system has a predominantly opposite function to its counterpart, the sympathetic. The sympathetic nervous system is mobilized when we feel we are under stress, challenge, or threat, and generates bodily processes designed to master this challenge. This is often called the fight/flight reflex. When the parasympathetic nervous system is mobilized, the sympathetic nerve is deactivated, and vice versa. Our body is designed to balance the parasympathetic and sympathetic; or, in other words, we are not designed to feel we are in fight/flight mode more often than feeling relaxed.

Mark Williams of Oxford University, the founder of Mindfulness-Based Cognitive Therapy (MBCT), explains that mindfulness meditation can help individuals switch from being in "doing mode" to "being mode," and this helps them feel more balanced (Williams 2010). In "doing mode" we act, or we think about acting. Quite often, we engage in several things at the same time, hence multi-tasking is a big part of "doing mode." We are also often engaged in "multi-thinking": thinking about two or three other things while doing something, e.g., reading a text while thinking of something else or making plans in our heads about what we want to do when we finish reading the text. While reading this text you are currently in "doing mode": processing information, analyzing facts, and, possibly, mentally preparing arguments for or against the reading material in front of your eyes.

Fourth mindfulness exercise for willing readers

Stop and think about what you have just thought about. In other words, what has just happened inside your mind? In addition to reading this reading, has your mind done anything else? Can you clarify for yourself what additional thoughts were on your mind while reading the previous paragraph, if any? How might this have impacted your concentration, perhaps even your current mood? What options or new choices might become possible for you with such awareness, for doing what is appropriate and right for you personally, right in this moment?

In contrast to the "doing mode," the "being mode" is not about acting, or thinking about (previous or future) actions, but about perceiving through our five senses, e.g., to consciously feel the wind or rain on your face when you are outdoors, or to hear the laughter of a child, or to fully appreciate the smell and taste of food. In "being mode" you are not goal-oriented. Words, thoughts, and often also actions are not in the foreground. Problem-solving and analyzing facts are pushed into the background. When we are operating in this mode, we simply exist, fully present in the moment, neither commenting nor judging it. It is probably because of this apparent lack of evaluating reality that, traditionally, organizations have not proactively encouraged their employees to dwell in this mode of being while being at work.

Nevertheless, this topic is becoming more and more relevant for managers interested in sustaining performance of their teams. This can be explained using a study conducted by Andrew Hafenbrack and his colleagues with numerous participants from all over the world. The research team instructed half of the study participants to practice mindfulness for 15 minutes (in similar ways to the exercises above); the other half was asked to simply relax for the same amount of time and thus served as control group. Subsequently, all participants were asked to make a decision regarding a short hypothetical case study concerned with "sunk costs." Investments become "sunk costs" when you have already invested a lot (money, time, work), but when—rationally speaking—they are no longer valuable and should be dropped to avoid further losses. Most people find it very difficult to make a rational "sunk cost" decision because nobody likes to make a loss. This is why many of us keep clothes in our wardrobes that we no longer fit into, and why many people find it hard to break long-standing relationships, no matter how unsatisfying they may be today.

In Hafenbrack's study, however, those participants who had practiced mindfulness before making the "sunk cost" decision consistently made the difficult but appropriate choice to shed these hypothetical "sunken costs," in stark contrast to the control group's decision pattern. More interesting, however, was how this mindful decision-making process came about. The researchers were able to see that two processes mediated the decision path towards a more rational choice: first, the mindfulness practitioners felt more relaxed and positive, and second, their attention was directly focused on the present, therefore they were able to fully concentrate on the data in the case study at hand (Hafenbrack, Kinias and Barsade 2014).

To summarize, mindfulness practice is neither unnatural nor esoteric. We need to "merely" come to our senses and, at least for a moment, switch gears: from the often fast-paced and sometimes impulsive "doing mode" to a "being mode." The precise way in which an individual can switch between these two modes, however, varies from person to person. Every person has their own natural tendencies and strategies to switch off the action impulse of the "doing mode;" and these tendencies change over the life span. Young people often have a lot of energy, and therefore feel most alive and present when they are physically active, feeling their body intensely through intense effort. Older people instead tend to seek out more calming, quieter ways to switch from "doing" to "being." In this context, Herbert Benson of Harvard Medical School has defined two critical success factors that must be in place so that any kind of mindfulness practice can invoke the relaxation response in the "being mode": first, *during* the mindfulness exercise we have to be able to focus our attention fully on the present (rather than continuing to think or worry about work or other things in our lives). And second, *afterwards*, we should feel more refreshed, relaxed, or re-energized. Only when both of these success factors are present can any mindfulness practice actually generate mindfulness. Only then can mindfulness become effective.

Fifth mindfulness exercise for willing readers

Think about how you came to your senses during the last week. What did you actually do to switch from "doing mode" to "being mode"? Do you need more or less sensory stimulation (sights, sounds, etc.) in order to be able to switch off? To what extent have you been able to stop worrying or thinking about problems when you were away from work? If you've switched to "being mode" at least once over the last week, did you also feel noticeably more relaxed or even just a little bit more energized afterwards? If not, what could you specifically do or change about your personal approach to relaxation to feel more balanced in your everyday life? What price would you be willing to pay to achieve this goal?

3. Why we should not conflate mindfulness with meditation

In my own research and teaching, I work with hundreds of senior leaders every year, primarily in government and in the military, to help embed mindfulness in their day-to-day work. Although many prominent mindfulness research projects and mindfulness training programs focus on meditation as their standard method to generate a state of mindfulness, meditation is only a small fraction of the interventions I work out in collaboration with my counterparts.

This approach is based on the insight that individuals in workplaces never act in isolation. Much of what influences us, both in life and in work, and what sometimes prevents us from coming to our senses and making the "right" decision (in other words consistent with our actual long-term goals, rather than momentary and perhaps even unconscious impulses), is based on complex factors that often operate outside of our conscious awareness, often competing with our personal motivations. Much of the work in the 21st century is interactive and decisions are negotiated in teams, depending on work routines (i.e., "the way we do things around here") or other internal policies or politics.

Embedding mindfulness in companies is much more about change management and modifying habitual behavior patterns—a more complex endeavor than a simplistic interpretation of the successes achieved by clinical and laboratory mindfulness studies might suggest.

In recent years, more scientific mindfulness studies have been published that somewhat curb the enthusiasm in the popular media for mindfulness and meditation. For example, Stephanie Coronado-Montoya and her colleagues demonstrated in 2016, through a thorough statistical analysis of all available published clinical mindfulness meditation studies, that the proportion of published studies with positive results is statistically higher than what would be likely under normal circumstances. The authors argue that these studies have been published proportionally more frequently than others documenting negative or zero effects of mindfulness initiatives because of the public's great interest in this type of research (Coronado-Montoya, Lewis, Kwakkenbos et al., 2016).

In addition, a group of 15 of the world's leading mindfulness mediation scholars and neurologists published an article in 2017 entitled "Mind the Hype." The authors explain how numerous methodologically flawed studies extoll the benefits of mindfulness meditation without verifying over a medium or longer term whether any initial enthusiasm about mindfulness is in fact sustained. This article also reports that there are at least 20 case studies in the scientific press documenting negative consequences of mindfulness meditation (Van Dam, van Vugt, Vago et al., 2017).

Leading management thinkers are even calling for an end to the "meditation madness" (Grant 2015). While this attitude may well judge mindfulness too prematurely, the scant peer-reviewed literature examining mindfulness meditation programs in companies over the medium term does not paint a more positive picture: the only article available in the scientific literature to date on this topic is the rigorously designed study by Jantien van Berkel and colleagues, who reported in 2014 that an intervention based on mindfulness meditation with 257 employees neither led to improved mental health nor reductions in stress or burnout after 6 and 12 months (Van Berkel, Boot, Proper, et al., 2014).

Most workplace mindfulness training programs are based on the eight-week MBSR course designed by Jon Kabat-Zinn and his colleagues (Kabat-Zinn 2011). MBSR is designed for individuals with chronic mental or physical health problems. As mentioned earlier, MBSR and related courses are highly effective with clinical populations. MBSR courses in companies are often shortened or modified in part and offered by human resources departments primarily to improve employees' mental health and wellbeing. Many mindfulness trainers introduce their mindfulness meditation courses to participants by telling stories of how meditation has helped them overcome traumatic life events and severe physical or mental health challenges. Andy Puddingcombe, co-founder of the meditation app Headspace, is a prominent example. He explained to a newspaper reporter that mindfulness meditation helps him cope with the physical and emotional effects of his cancer diagnosis (Jenkins 2014).

In my experience and observation, corporate mindfulness meditation programs are especially popular among people who are relatively open about being overwhelmed and suffering from a lack of physical or mental wellbeing, and for whom wellness is such a high priority that they welcome the opportunity to participate in a meditation program.

But most employees and leaders in the organizations I work with do not have such a profile. For numerous decision-makers in government projects, quick decisions need to be taken frequently and a strong culture of dedication and self-sacrifice drives the priorities of a fast-paced, mission-driven workplace, even though many of them value brief meditation training sessions with a mindfulness trainer and the perceived "holiday" these represent from the "true essence" of their work realities.

In many organizations that I observe and advise, quick thinking and acting is appreciated and celebrated. Employees who are extremely busy are at least informally celebrated as heroic problem-solvers. Achieving "more with less," quickly and promptly, seems to be in line with today's *zeitgeist*, even though many of these "heroic" overachievers complain in private that this is not sustainable in the long run. Mindfulness meditation is frequently mentioned as an antidote against the ever-increasing pace of today's work life, because it surely *makes sense* to *come to our senses* in the face of all this perpetual busyness. Many leaders tell me they know about the obvious benefits of mindfulness, saying that it is similar to the benefits of eating less meat or drinking less alcohol. But especially senior leaders in multi-stakeholder environments appear to find it difficult to translate this advice into real-life action. It seems that sitting still and meditating is somewhat analogous to a race car driver slamming on the brakes while speeding at full throttle.

Such a stark change from speeding at full throttle (metaphorically speaking) is, according to the latest findings in neurobiology, not always useful. Allow me to take a short detour into neurobiology to better explain the link between mindfulness and automatic stress response. This is because a more detailed understanding of how individuals deal with stress and perceived threats at a neurobiological (and thus largely unconscious, reflexive) level will help us unpack why meditation training can sometimes be less helpful in work contexts, even counterproductive.

Stephen Porges, behavioral neurobiologist at the Kinsey Institute of Indiana University, has been exploring our autonomic nervous system for the last 20 years. This somatic system determines our automatic (unconscious) reactive behavior when we are under stress. In addition to the sympathetic and parasympathetic mentioned before, our human nervous system has evolved to be hierarchical and adaptable, but it is important to note that our stress response is practically completely below our cognitive control (Porges 2004). Over the course of our development history, we have developed three behavioral strategies whenever our body senses a threat (which is synonymous with "feeling stressed"). The evolutionarily older strategies are less effective than those we have developed in our more recent evolutionary history. We share the evolutionarily oldest strategy with almost all vertebrates, especially reptiles: immobilization, i.e., *freeze* or dissociative behavior. The body thus signals to the brain that annihilation is imminent, and the best behavioral strategy is to anticipate this annihilation and pretend that it has already happened.

All mammals have additionally developed a mobilization system, which has proven to be more effective than immobilization: *fight or flight*. Fight or flight looks similar in all mammals: a raised voice, preparing the body for attack or escape if the source of the threat is judged (rapidly and unconsciously) to be more powerful. Finally, humans have developed another automatic stress response system in addition to mobilization: *social engagement*, i.e., seeking interpersonal contact in order to eliminate ambiguity and detect intentions through communication and nonverbal gestures, separating friend from foe by correctly identifying verbal tone and facial expressions, and overcoming conflict through negotiation and collaboration. From an evolutionary perspective, this has proven to be most effective in helping humans manage threats in their environments.

According to Porges (2004), every human being goes through the same three evolutionary stages of automatic stress response as they grow up. Young toddlers often freeze (or pretend to be invisible) when they realize they might be in danger. We often consider this amusing when this "danger" is nothing more than a reprimand from a parent.

Children practice dealing with conflict using fight or flight strategies: some children get into schoolyard brawls (*fight*) or avoid aggressive classmates (*flight*). As teenagers, most individuals learn how to recognize verbal and nonverbal communication signals during interpersonal interactions and start to manage and overcome difficulty through engaging with others: asking questions to clarify the intent behind behavior they find difficult to understand, offer emotional support through words and in the shape of hugs or sympathetic smiles when they notice others in distress, and other related actions that help individuals feel socially connected and supported.

Because our autonomic nervous system is not only hierarchical but also adaptable, we resort to older evolutionary strategies when we judge our more sophisticated strategies to be ineffective, e.g., we resort to *fight/flight* when communication is deemed futile, and we resort to *freeze* when *fight/flight* is deemed futile. And as our automatic stress response adapts over the course of our life span, we tend to resort more and more to those stress response strategies that were deemed most successful in the past. Even if more sophisticated (evolutionarily successful) strategies are theoretically available to us (such as *social engagement* or *fight/flight*), these may no longer be deemed appropriate. This can manifest itself in organizations when employees observe that *social engagement* is ineffective or not rewarded as a response to challenge and difficulty, and instead more and more frequently pick fights or work harder and longer hours. If over time these *fight/flight* strategies also come to be regarded as ineffective or futile, employees will effectively resort to *freeze*: they disconnect or dissociate from all organizational life.

What does all this have to do with mindfulness meditation and management or leadership in organizations? Porges' research suggests that especially in populations where individuals have consciously or unconsciously experienced trauma, such as personnel engaged in highly stressful work, e.g., in emergency services, healthcare, but also increasingly in fast-moving and highly competitive commercial and non-profit sectors, individuals' autonomic nervous systems adapt in a way to avoid immobilization at all cost. This is because during trauma, even the body's *freeze* stress response is experienced as futile and life-threatening. Therefore, any activities that simulate immobilization or *freeze*, such as a mindfulness meditation, may be perceived as threatening at an unconscious level. That's why an increasing number of highly dedicated and successful managers and leaders tend to practice extreme sports in their free time (e.g., triathlons or Ironman competitions). Essentially, these individuals' automatic bodily stress response pattern has adapted by perpetuating workplace behavior that simulates *fight/flight* in their leisure time.

Sixth mindfulness exercise for willing readers

Think about the behavioral strategies you have developed over the course of your life in response to stress and difficulty. To what extent can you discern a certain hierarchy or tendency in the stress response strategies you habitually resort to? What is your go-to strategy for dealing with challenging situations at work today? What advantages and disadvantages can you see here? What specific actions could you engage in to expand your behavioral repertoire in this regard?

4. Mindfulness as a collective phenomenon

As far as mindfulness for managers and for organizations as a whole is concerned, world-leading mindfulness researcher Katherine Sutcliffe and colleagues argue that mindfulness should be understood not merely as an individual phenomenon, but as a multidimensional concept that includes meditative as well as other non-meditative practices and individual as well as collective mindfulness processes applied to workplaces (Sutcliffe, Vogus and Dane 2016). In so doing, these researchers have linked the popular literature around individually focused mindfulness meditation with the lesser-known (but equally comprehensive) science on "collective mindfulness."

Since the early 1990s, University of Michigan psychologist Karl Weick and his colleagues have been investigating "collective mindfulness," studying teams and organizations who are *collectively* mindful. Weick and colleagues have published their findings in leading management journals and demonstrated that when mindfulness permeates the organization's daily routines as well as the micro and macro cultures that make up the organization, the entire organization is characterized by "collective mindfulness" (Weick and Roberts 1993; Weick, Sutcliffe and Obstfeld 2000; Weick and Sutcliffe 2007; Vogus and Sutcliffe 2012). It then becomes resilient at system-wide scale, and such an organization is then called a high-reliability organization (HRO; Weick and Sutcliffe 2006).

So what exactly is collective mindfulness about? Essentially, it is not all that different from the stated aims of many individually focused mindfulness training programs. Take the popular individual-focused MBSR course, for instance; its aim is to help individuals manage stress better. By the same token, collective mindfulness consists of five interpersonal or social processes designed to anticipate and successfully respond to difficulty and challenge, albeit at a higher level of analysis, i.e., concerning the whole team or organization. Essentially, this is mindfulness-based stress management at a larger scale.

Specifically, five processes are involved in collective mindfulness. In other words, teams organize mindfully when they have a collective culture characterized by:

1. noticing day-to-day operations; making sure the team is aware of dynamic changes that may occur from day to day in the organization's operations or its environment;
2. proactively anticipating errors and problems; specifically focusing on "negative" information so problems do not become disasters;
3. enabling real-time experts to make decisions; recognizing that the person with the most expertise and thus authority to decide on important issues may not always be the person with the highest rank or most long-standing experience;
4. valuing resource flexibility; investing time and effort in enabling team members to become sufficiently familiar with other roles' responsibilities so that individuals' tasks can be performed by anyone required in a particular situation;
5. refusing to simplify matters; by constantly questioning whether the current solutions are appropriate and striving to continuously improve.

That organizing mindfully at collective level is financially worthwhile has been well documented in science. For example, researchers found in a survey of US hospitals that collective mindfulness is associated with far fewer medication errors (Vogus and Sutcliffe 2007). A similar survey of a range of intensive care units and emergency clinics has concluded that employees who organize mindfully are 8.3% less likely to be emotionally exhausted and that there is 13.6% less work turnover in these mindful teams. The authors of this study speculate that these types of mindfulness-based workflows could, on average, save hospitals between $169,000 and $1,000,000 (Vogus, Cooil, Sitterding and Everett 2014).

However, empirical studies are rare that consider mindfulness as a multidimensional concept, focusing not only on individual-level outcomes but also on collective mindfulness. This is the focus of my current research with the UK government, aimed at increasing mindfulness at both individual and collective level reliably and sustainably.

The suggestions in the next section are based on this research.

5. How to embed mindfulness sustainably into organizations

Based on what I have outlined above, two conclusions for embedding mindfulness reliably and sustainably in organizations become apparent:

First, beware of mandating meditation mindlessly in a mindfulness training program. Not only might some participants consider sitting still and contemplating their inner landscape at some (often unconscious) level inappropriate, especially if they are highly dedicated performers in an organization characterized by high commitment and public service, and even if they intellectually connect with the motivation for engaging in meditative practice. In some cases, deep meditation practice can be extremely harmful, as Miguel Farias of Coventry University in the UK points out. According to Farias, two-thirds of all participants in meditation classes have experienced negative side effects, e.g., some degree of panic, depression, or confusion, and one in fourteen participants suffer severe side effects such as psychoses when participating in mindfulness meditation courses (Farias and Wikholm 2015). Many mindfulness trainers are not professionally trained psychotherapists; in these cases they may do more harm than good.

Second, through mindfulness exercises, one can learn to focus on other previously ignored impulses. Mindfulness meditation, which focuses on individuals, is primarily about becoming aware of inner impulses and about correctly identifying and consciously managing these according to the current situation and environment. The same principles apply to mindfulness at social or collective levels, but focusing collectively, i.e., on the (often unconscious) collective habits and routines that drive collective impulses. This is because our work environment and our decisions in work situations are less affected by the unconscious spontaneous impulses of individuals, but by the (often equally unconscious) behavioral tendencies, rituals, and *culture* of work communities.

Hence there is no point in introducing mindfulness into teams or organizations without a genuine understanding of the team's current work situation and their organizational environment. As mentioned above, being mindful means paying attention to the situation one finds oneself in. Management consultants sometimes quip that "culture eats strategy for breakfast," which essentially means that corporate culture is always more potent than any strategy set by a board of directors (based on a quote from a board member of an American hospital company who aptly expressed the great power of corporate culture; Davies 2002). It is this organizational culture that makes or breaks any mindfulness training strategy. For this reason, mindfulness interventions are more about change management than skills development.

What's the best way to do it? It starts with understanding the organization's culture. Only in this way can the context-specific behavioral structures be tackled systematically that cause employees to either integrate individual strategies such as mindfulness meditation in their behavioral repertoire or not. Only in this way can leaders learn to recognize relevant behavioral impulses and to steer the organization over the long term in the direction of mindfulness. Otherwise, all good intentions of a mindfulness training program that seeks solely to enhance the meditation skills of the employees are "eaten for breakfast" by the corporate culture.

In the previous section, I outlined the five work processes that, according to Weick and his colleagues, are crucial for ensuring that teams and organizations organize mindfully, and which in turn generate sustainable performance and resilience of the organization overall. In my mindfulness work, I use these five processes to take stock with managers and teams about how mindfully people at work interact with each other, and which aspects of collective mindfulness might most usefully be targeted through mindfulness intervention work.

Seventh mindfulness exercise for willing readers

Revisit the five collective mindfulness processes from section 4. Consider how you would rate your organization (or team) in each of these five characteristics, e.g., by assessing their performance against each point, e.g., "very good" for point 1, "sufficient" for point 2, "poor" for point 3, and so on. What insights might these assessments provide to you about how collectively mindful your organization (or team) operates currently? What strategies or actions might you take to help your organization (or team) become more collectively mindful?

In my experience, such an inventory of collective mindfulness at work is far more important than meditation training. Not because meditation is unimportant, but because the vast majority of participants in my mindfulness courses quickly learn relevant meditation skills. In addition, we are always much more concerned about the contrast between a mindful culture of action and specific behavioral routines and (sub-)cultures that work against individuals actually practicing mindfulness consistently and sustainably, especially when they are busy or when it seems that such acts of self-care are at risk of being relegated to the bottom of the list of corporate priorities. For my corporate collaborators, learning mindfulness meditation skills is the smallest challenge they face in terms of embedding mindfulness.

In addition, it is important to include multiple activity strands when defining a mindfulness strategy for an organization. This means that a mindfulness intervention would need to include training for individuals to engage in self-care and practice techniques to increase their personal wellbeing, such as setting boundaries around their work time and scope. But managers as well as visible organizational actors always need to be involved also. These actors can openly discuss their own self-care strategies with their team members and publicly endorse and support new behaviors as praiseworthy from others. This can signal a change from the status quo, and troubleshoot issues and concerns that will inevitably arise when a group of individuals are asked to change their behavioral repertoire. In this way, the organization's culture may have a chance of changing, slowly but sustainably.

Above all, however, all individual-oriented mindfulness strategies should be connected to the five characteristics of collective mindfulness. For example, it is essential to agree with an entire team or operation how any new self-care strategy, such as for example a daily meditation at work, individually or in a team, should be embedded flexibly and in recognition of upcoming dynamic changes in the team or in the organization's environment. How, for example, will the team make sure they keep their commitment to mindfulness practice intact despite changing priorities at work in future? What is the essence or underlying value that everyone can agree upon? Mindfulness is about being and *staying* present in *any* situation, especially a challenging one, hence focusing on challenging questions about uncertainty and situational change is key for successfully implementing a sustainable behavior change strategy towards mindfulness.

Chapter takeaways/lessons

1. Meditation is only one of many methods to increase mindfulness in workplaces.
2. We become mindful at work by coming to our (five) senses, literally and metaphorically.
3. In high-stress workplace populations, prolonged periods of silent meditation may bring up latent trauma.
4. Organizations should consider multiple levels of mindfulness interventions, at individual as well as at collective levels.
5. Understanding an organization's context and culture is more important for the success of a mindfulness intervention than training individuals in mindfulness skills.

Reflection questions

1. What is the difference between mindfulness and meditation?
2. What are some ways in which you can "come to your senses" at work, and how will this help you become more mindful?
3. How can you increase the level of social engagement in your workplace, and what effect will this have on performance under pressure in your organization?
4. What interpersonal qualities or characteristics enable the five collective mindfulness processes?
5. Why is it more effective to manage stress collectively than individually? How is this linked to the ultimate goal of mindfulness at work?

References

Coronado-Montoya S, Levis AW, Kwakkenbos L, et al. (2016) Reporting of positive results in randomized controlled trials of mindfulness-based mental health interventions. *Plos One* 11(4): 1–18.

Davies HTO (2002) Understanding organizational culture in reforming the national health service. *J R Soc Med* 95(3): 140–142.

Farias, M. & Wikholm, C. (2015). *The Buddha Pill: Can meditation change you?* London: Watkins Publishing. http://www.amazon.co.uk/The-Buddha-Pill-Meditation-Change/dp/1780287186

Grant A (2015) Can we end the meditation madness? In: New York Times 10 Oct 2015. www.nytimes.com/2015/10/10/opinion/can-we-end-the-meditation-madness.html?_r=1.

Hafenbrack AC, Kinias Z, Barsade SG (2014) Debiasing the mind through meditation: mindfulness and the sunk-cost bias. *Psychol Sci* 25: 369–376.

Jenkins M (2014) Mind over cancer: can meditation aid recovery? In: The Guardian 14 Feb 2014. www.theguardian.com/society/2014/feb/14/cancer-meditation-aid-recovery.

Kabat-Zinn J (1994) *Wherever You Go, There You are Mindfulness Meditation in Everyday Life.* New York: Hyperion.

Kabat-Zinn J (2011) Some reflections on the origins of MBSR, skilful means, and the trouble with maps. *Contemporary Buddhism* 12: 281–306.

Kahneman D (2011) *Thinking Fast and Slow.* London: Penguin.

Killingsworth MA, Gilbert DT (2010) A wandering mind is an unhappy mind. *Science* 330(6006): 932.

Kuyken W, Hayes R, Barrett B, et al. (2015) Effectiveness and cost-effectiveness of mindfulness-based cognitive therapy compared with maintenance antidepressant treatment in the prevention of depressive relapse or recurrence (PREVENT): a randomised controlled trial. *Lancet* 386(9988): 63–73.

Langer EJ (1989) *Mindfulness*. New York: Perseus Books.

Langer EJ (2009) *Counterclockwise: Mindful Health and the Power of Possibility*. New York: Ballantine Books.

Lyubomirsky S, Sheldon KM, Schkade D (2005) Pursuing happiness: the architecture of sustainable change. *Rev Gen Psychol* 9: 111–131.

Nilsson H, Kazemi A (2016) Reconciling and thematizing definitions of mindfulness: the big five of mindfulness. *Rev Gen Psychol* 20(2): 183–193.

Papies EK, Barsalou LW, Custers R (2012) Mindful attention prevents mindless impulses. *Soc Psych & Personality Science* 3(3): 291–299.

Porges SW (2004) Neuroception: A subconscious system for detecting threats and safety. *Zero To Three May* 2004: 19–24.

Sutcliffe KM, Vogus TJ, Dane E (2016) Mindfulness in organizations: a cross-level review. *Annu Rev Organ Psychol Organ Behav* 3: 55–81.

Van Berkel J, Boot CRL, Proper KI, et al. (2014) Effectiveness of a worksite mindfulness-related multi-component health promotion intervention on work engagement and mental health: results of a randomized controlled trial. *Plos One* 9(1): 1–10.

Van Dam NT, van Vugt MK, Vago DR, et al. (2017) Mind the hype: a critical evaluation and prescriptive agenda for research on mindfulness and meditation. *Perspectives on Psychol Sci* 13(1): 36–61.

Vogus TJ, Cooil B, Sitterding M, et al. (2014) Safety organizing, emotional exhaustion, and turnover in hospital nursing units. *Med Care* 52: 870–876.

Vogus TJ, Sutcliffe KM (2007) The impact of safety organizing, trusted leadership, and care pathways on reported medication errors in hospital nursing units. *Med Care* 45: 997–1002.

Vogus TJ, Sutcliffe KM (2012) Organizational mindfulness and mindful organizing: a reconciliation and path forward. *Acad Manag Learn Educ* 11: 722–735.

Weick KE, Roberts KH (1993) Collective mind in organizations: heedful interrelating on flight decks. *Adm Sci Q* 38: 357–381.

Weick KE, Sutcliffe KM (2006) Mindfulness and the quality of organizational attention. *Organ Sci* 16: 409–421.

Weick KE, Sutcliffe KM (2007) *Managing the Unexpected: Resilient Performance in an Age of Complexity*. Hoboken, New Jersey: John Wiley & Sons.

Weick KE, Sutcliffe KM, Obstfeld D (2000) High reliability: the power of mindfulness. *Lead. Lead.* 17: 33–38.

Williams JMG (2010) Mindfulness and psychological process. *Emotion* 10(1): 1–7.

15

WORKPLACE MINDFULNESS

The role of human resource management in engendering a mindful workplace

Huda Masood and Stefan Karajovic

Introduction

Despite the growth of scholarly interest in mindfulness, the scholarship on workplace mindfulness or one's undivided attention to the external and internal stimulants within work settings (Brown & Ryan, 2003; Dane, 2011) remains in its infancy (Badham & King, 2016; Hülsheger, Alberts, Feinholdt, & Lang, 2013). Consequently, scholars have urged the managerial research to outline the future of workplace mindfulness through recent calls for research (Qiu & Rooney, 2019). Addressing Qiu and Rooney's (2019) call for research, the current chapter investigates the role of human resource management in fostering workplace mindfulness.

Recent evidence suggests that workplace mindfulness is a multi-stage phenomenon, which may bring out challenging thought processes among individuals (Qiu & Rooney, 2019). This is based on a core assumption that workplace mindfulness cannot be used as a tool to sweep the problems and challenging realizations under the rug but to acknowledge and realize the existence of such issues with acceptance (Qiu & Rooney, 2019) so they can be ultimately conquered.

Mindfulness pivots around an individual's ability to focus on both internal (e.g., thoughts, affect, and sensations) and external (e.g., environment and interactions) triggers, in a non-judgmental manner (Glomb, Duffy, Bono, & Yang, 2011). Given it is a state of consciousness, mindfulness varies across individuals, suggesting that there are trait-like tendencies as well (Brown & Ryan, 2003; Brown, Ryan, & Creswell, 2007). Mindfulness has predominantly been studied as an intervention-based technique or employing a variety of key practices, suggesting it to be both teachable and learnable processes (Kabat-Zinn, 1990).

In a recent review of the literature, Good and colleagues (2016) proposed an integrative model of workplace mindfulness. Borrowing from the clinical psychology literature, mindfulness has been found to benefit human functioning in a number of key ways. Mindful employees benefit cognitively, emotionally, behaviorally, and physiologically, leading to positive organizational outcomes such as improved employee performance (including both task and citizenship behaviors), interpersonal performance, and well-being (both physical and psychological; Good et al., 2016). Given this backdrop, mindfulness purports to solve many of the human resource problems faced by organizations. As such, the human resource function has an important role to play in the dissemination of mindfulness throughout an organization.

The current chapter will explore the current state of the mindfulness literature, including workplace and HR mindfulness, followed by an overview of how the human resource infrastructure can help facilitate mindfulness in an organizational setting. The cornerstone argument of the current chapter highlights the function of HR as a tool in fostering workplace mindfulness at individual and organizational levels. Specifically, the role of mindful HR infrastructure is assessed as an instrument to (i) foster proactive work behaviors; (ii) maintain work–life balance; and (iii) leadership development. A brief discussion outlining the significance of HR in implementing workplace mindfulness as opposed to utilizing a traditional mindfulness training approach concludes the chapter.

Workplace mindfulness

Brown and Ryan (2003) argued mindfulness to be "an open undivided observation of what is occurring both internally and externally" (p. 823). Relatedly, Dane (2011) defined workplace mindfulness as "a state of consciousness in which attention is focused on present-moment phenomenon occurring both externally and internally" (p. 1000). Glomb and colleagues (2011) noted mindfulness to be a "process of paying attention to what is happening in the moment—both internal (thoughts, bodily sensations) and external stimuli (physical and social environment)" (p. 118). Both Dane (2011) and Glomb et al. (2011) outlined awareness, attention, and being present in the moment to be pivotal to mindfulness—all of which are crucial not only for employee learning but also for performance and well-being through self-regulation. Taken together, mindfulness can be understood in terms of an idiosyncratic state of consciousness based on its attentional bandwidth and primary focus on the present moment.

However, workplace mindfulness cannot be divorced from the core theoretical and experiential ideology of Buddhist mindfulness (Qiu & Rooney, 2019). The Buddhist approach to mindfulness entails a "no-gain" perspective (Magid & Poirier, 2016), to actualize an ego-less state of being that eschews self-centeredness and mitigates individual distress and discontent (e.g., Epstein, 1988). On the contrary, workplace mindfulness revolves around a "for-gain" perspective (Magid & Poirier, 2016), geared towards reinforcing a more productive self rather than demoting it (Qiu & Rooney, 2019). For instance, mindfulness allows individuals to interpret events in a more objective and impersonal manner (Shapiro, Carlson, Astin, & Freeman, 2006; Weinstein, Brown, & Ryan, 2009), while actively regulating their affect, emotions, and both physiological and psychological reactions (Lakey, Campbell, Brown, & Goodie, 2007; Masicampo & Baumeister, 2007; Papies, Barsalou, & Custers, 2012).

Mindfulness often rewires individual relationships with their affect, ideas, and self-concept and, therefore, cannot be studied as a trivial or predictable process (Qiu & Rooney, 2019). Although mindfulness has often been conceptualized and evaluated as a state, empirical evidence depicts disposition-based disparities in mindfulness among individuals (e.g., Baer, Smith, Hopkins, Krietemeyer, & Toney, 2006; Brown & Ryan, 2003; Lau et al., 2006). In that regard, mindfulness is comparable with both positive and negative affect, which can be conceptualized and studied as a state as well as a trait (Watson, Clark, & Tellegen, 1988).

Such individual difference argument is also applied to workplace settings, i.e., *ceteris paribus*, certain individuals tend to demonstrate more workplace mindfulness than others as a result of the unique set of experiences they have accrued (see Dane & Brummel, 2014). Further, research evidence highlights the significance of contextual attributes of one's workplace in shaping not only their work-related behaviors but also how they focus attention while at work (Elsbach & Pratt, 2007; George, 2009; Zhong & House, 2012). Henceforth, certain features of work settings may signal mindfulness to some workers and not others, allowing them to mindfully focus their attention at work owing to the contextual stimulation experienced within the work environment (Dane & Brummel, 2014). In a similar vein, research evidence demonstrates that through training and practice, individuals can hone their workplace mindfulness skills to optimize their performance (Fehr & Gelfand, 2012; Hülsheger et al., 2013; Lee, 2012).

Taken together, these assertions contend that individual variance in workplace mindfulness is often dependent on a combination of dispositional, experiential, and contextual factors experienced within work settings (Dane & Brummel, 2014). Given the complexity and malleability associated with workplace mindfulness, it is important to outline the role of the responsible party in insinuating it within employees along with understanding the associated outcomes. However, establishing mindfulness at an organizational level needs an adequate HR infrastructure entailing dialogue initiation and organizational routines (Levinthal & Rerup, 2006).

Previous research has outlined the role of HR in fostering workplace or organizational workforce through HR mindfulness (see, e.g., Becke, 2013). Studied as a sub-concept of workplace or organizational mindfulness (Weick & Sutcliffe, 2001), HR mindfulness refers to an enhanced realization of one's organizational surroundings outlining the pre-empted coping strategies for both external and internal ambiguities (Becke, 2013). However, the theorization of HR mindfulness is posited on three fundamental assumptions, as outlined by Becke (2013): first, a mindful infrastructure of HR routines and practices to enable a "flexible intervention system" for employee well-being; second, the development of sustainable work systems at organizational levels (see Busck, Knudsen, & Lind, 2010); and third, the design of intra-organizational power structure that promotes employee voice (Jordan, Messner, & Becker, 2009).

Organizational routines refer to the "repetitive, recognizable patterns of interdependent actions, carried out by multiple actors" (Feldman & Pentland, 2003, p. 95). As products of repeated interpersonal interactions, routines can be reciprocated, managed, and modified by human agency (Becke, 2013). Consequently, a mindful HR infrastructure would entail organizational routines that facilitate sustainable work systems or revitalized human and social resources "through the process of work while still maintaining productivity and competitive edge" (Docherty, Forslin, & Shani, 2002, p. 214). Notably, the mindful HR infrastructure incorporates two fundamental variants of organizational routines, namely interactive and reflective routines (Jordan et al., 2009, p. 468).

Interactive routines can be understood in terms of "scrum meetings" or collaborative project meetings (e.g., ad hoc or informal meetings of team members that allow individuals to exchange information, adjust coordination, or address unanticipated project-related concerns) (Becke, 2013). Given the interactive routines distinctly entail two fundamental elements, i.e., flexibility and proactivity, we have focused on its implications on (i) proactive work behaviors; and (ii) work–life balance (WLB).

Mindfulness as proactive work behaviors

Mindfulness is a state that may also be initiated as a form of proactive employee behavior. Although most research on mindfulness has delved into how organizations can encourage mindfulness via training (see, e.g., Hyland, Lee, & Mills, 2015), it is also something that an individual can self-teach and employ of their own accord. Mindfulness is a highly personal and introspective state, lending itself to self-initiation. However, despite the possibility of mindfulness being proactively implemented, organizational supports and constraints are, respectively, still able to encourage or discourage the development and practice of mindfulness (Reb, Narayanan, & Ho, 2015). According to Reb and colleagues (2015), awareness, a core component of mindfulness, and absent-mindedness, which detracts from mindfulness, are directly affected by the presence of specific organizational circumstances. Awareness is a conscious understanding of the contents of one's mind and is central to the concept of mindfulness (Mikulas, 2011). Absent-mindedness, on the other hand, is an inattentiveness to one's work and surroundings because the mind is distracted (Reb et al., 2015). Reb and colleagues (2015) identified autonomy and supervisor support as two forms of organizational support that encourage mental awareness at work. On the other hand, organizational constraints were identified as workplace scenarios which impede task completion (Spector & Jex, 1998). Examples of organizational constraints may include inadequate training, incomplete information, conflicting job demands, task routineness, and so on (Reb et al., 2015; Spector & Jex, 1998).

As the previously cited piece of research found, organizational constraints actively hinder the implementation of mindfulness by employees, while organizational supports are related to the facilitation of mindful work practices. One form of proactive behavior that might be able to help individuals develop and implement mindfulness at work is job crafting. Job crafting is defined as "the physical and cognitive changes individuals make in the task or relational boundaries of their work" (Wrzesniewski & Dutton, 2001, p. 179). Cognitive crafting is of particular interest in a mindfulness context as it engages a person's inner thoughts to change how they see themselves at work (Wrzesniewski & Dutton, 2001).

Furthermore, job crafting can be conceptualized through the lens of job demands-resources (JD-R) theory (Tims & Bakker, 2010). According to JD-R theory, which was initially developed by Bakker and Demerouti (2007), individuals engage in job crafting in response to hindering job demands. Hindering job demands are forces at work which impede one's completion of personal work goals. One way an individual can overcome such hindrances is to modify their job resources via job crafting (Tims & Bakker, 2010). This view of job crafting is particularly important to mindfulness research as it relates to our previous discussion on the effects of organizational constraints on mindfulness expression. Importantly, many organizational constraints (i.e., task repetitiveness, conflicting or confusing job demands, lack of information, and so on) can be viewed as hindering job demands in the JD-R model, as they are organizational phenomena that impede one's completion of tasks and attainment of goals—thus, cognitively crafting a sense of awareness of the present moment as a means of reducing the negative impact of hindering job demands (at least cognitively).

Autonomy and supervisor support were found by Reb and colleagues (2015) to promote mindfulness among employees in an organization. Job crafting is likewise associated with a sense of autonomy (given the self-directed nature of the behavior). Individuals are more likely to engage in job crafting when they perceive an opportunity to do so (Roczniewska & Puchalska, 2017; Wrzesniewski & Dutton, 2001). Although proactive behaviors like job crafting are typically self-initiated, organizations can still play a role in fostering them. Due to the proposed relationship with mindfulness, as well as a score of other benefits (i.e., increasing work engagement and satisfaction; Tims, Bakker, & Derks, 2013, 2015), it is in an organization's best interests to have a workforce engaged in job crafting. An organization can promote job crafting by explicitly greenlighting the behavior, letting employees know that it is both allowed and encouraged (this can be viewed as a form of supervisory support). Similarly, an organization may wish to encourage job crafting by granting more autonomy to its workers. And finally, although job crafting is a proactive behavior, organizations can still teach employees about the concept of job crafting, as well as providing training in it, with some measure of positive results (Kooij, van Woerkom, Wilkenloh, Dorenbosch, & Denissen, 2017).

Ultimately, job crafting is a potential proactive behavior which can be leveraged by workers to develop and engage in mindfulness at work. The catalyst for this proposed relationship is the pressure created by organizational constraints (hindering job demands), which job crafting, either task or cognitive, can attempt to resolve. One way in which an individual may choose to remove these constraints (or diminish their perceived effect on themselves) is through cognitive crafting of mindfulness.

Given the interactive routines often entail proactive initiatives outlining the "under-specification of structure" (Becke, 2013), we argue the significance of job crafting as a manifestation of employee-level mindfulness.

Mindful work–life balance

Ensuring work–life balance (WLB) among workers is an important goal of the human resources department in an organization. A number of negative task- and health-related outcomes can arise in employees experiencing work–life conflict (WLC), which occurs due to the lack of work–life balance. Work–life conflict occurs within the context of the stressor–strain relationship. That is to say, WLC occurs when stress in one role of someone's life strains another role and prevents performance in or enjoyment of that role (i.e., work versus non-work roles) (Goode, 1960; Greenhaus & Beutell, 1985). Some negative task-related outcomes of WLC are absenteeism, turnover intention, and reduced organizational commitment (Kossek & Ozeki, 1999; Podsakoff, LePine, & LePine, 2007). Additionally, WLC can negatively impact employee health and well-being, as well. Research has found that work–life conflict is positively associated with a myriad of mental health issues, including mood disorders, anxiety, and substance abuse (Frone, 2000). Employees suffering from mental illness arising from WLC are more likely to miss work and require ongoing treatment. This poses a significant financial burden on an organization. For these reasons, reducing experiences of WLC among workers poses both an important strategic as well as a health and safety function within organizations. A workforce that enjoys balance between their work and non-work roles will cost the organization less in terms of turnover and absenteeism, perform better, and suffer less from debilitating diseases. As such, organizations would be wise to mitigate the effects of work–life conflict as much as possible.

A number of studies have linked mindfulness to positive work–life balance outcomes (Allen & Kiburz, 2012; Michel, Bosch, & Rexroth, 2014; Zivnuska, Kacmar, Ferguson, & Carlson, 2016). Allen and Kiburz (2012) argued that mindfulness creates a sense of alertness across roles, allowing the individual to be more attentive and immersed in both work and non-work tasks. This attentiveness in all roles leads to an increase in perceived role balance.

Michel and colleagues (2014) argue that mindfulness allows an individual to segment their work and non-work roles, thus achieving work–life balance. This is because integration of work and non-work roles can lead to undesirable cognitive and emotional effects permeating between the different role boundaries. Work–life conflict occurs when strain from one role negatively affects one's performance in a different role (Goode, 1960; Greenhaus & Beutell, 1985), which can occur through the processes of spillover or crossover (Bakker & Demerouti, 2013). Mindfulness helps to alleviate this strain by allowing an individual to "shut off" when in a particular role, thereby preventing the mind from wandering and focusing on negative thoughts and emotions from a different role (Michel et al., 2014).

Zivnuska and colleagues (2016) theorized that mindfulness helps to build key energy resources at work. Specifically, work–life balance is seen as a resource in this model. When an individual's work and non-work roles are balanced, they experience higher energy at work (as well as in non-work settings). Mindfulness helps ensure healthy interpersonal relationships at work and at home, mitigating the effects of negative spillover of inter-role stress (Zivnuska et al., 2016).

The findings of these studies are consistent with more general findings linking mindfulness to positive organizational outcomes. A number of studies have linked mindfulness to workplace stress reduction (Chin, Slutsky, Raye, & Creswell, 2019; Klatt, Norre, Reader, Yodice, & White, 2017; Virgili, 2015). Given the nature of work–life conflict arising as a result of job stressors straining inter-role resources, the reduction of work stress via mindfulness will naturally help reduce role strain. Similarly, research has also found that mindfulness can help workers cope with emotional exhaustion at work, thereby reducing turnover intentions and improving performance (Reb, Narayanan, Chaturvedi, & Ekkirala, 2017). Emotional exhaustion and burnout arise from a depletion of personal resources caused by a variety of job stressors, which also ties into the stressor–strain model of work–life conflict.

Traditional work–life balance programs have endeavored to improve employee WLB by helping employees manage their non-work demands. This was done through the integration of the work and family roles in order to provide the employee more control and flexibility over their work (i.e., flexible scheduling, reduced work hours, telecommuting arrangements, etc.). The goal of these programs is to help employees manage their non-work demands so that they do not interfere with their work performance (Felstead, Jewson, Phizacklea, & Walters, 2002; Nord, Fox, Phoenix, & Viano, 2002). However, these programs are not always effective (Fleetwood, 2007), or are simply not possible due to the nature of the work. Thus, mindfulness training presents an alternative avenue for helping employees achieve work–life balance. Michel and colleagues (2014) designed a short, three-week-long intervention in their study, delivered electronically. Despite the low cost and time commitment of the intervention, it had a statistically significant impact on employees' perceptions of work–life balance. Mindfulness training programs were initially developed for clinical use (Kabat-Zinn, 2006), but have since been adapted by organizations due to the universal benefits of mindfulness.

From an HR infrastructure viewpoint, both organizational and employee representatives may focus on the collective reflection of a comprehensive interaction of job demands, the specification and interdependence of work roles and demands, and overarching levels of professional interdependence and coordination (Becke, 2013).

Leadership development

Brendel and Bennett (2016) argue that mindfulness helps leaders detect mismatches between their values and actions by possessing heightened self-awareness. Further, they conceptualize the idea of embodied leadership whereby an individual's personal identity and their leadership identity are a single whole (Brendel & Bennett, 2016). Baron (2016) found that action learning programs were an effective means of developing authentic leadership because they embodied aspects of mindfulness (awareness and unbiased processing). Action learning allows individuals to practice specific modeling behaviors, bringing awareness to their present state. It allows for reflection on the attitudes and behaviors one wants to change (Baron, 2016).

Reflection is understood in terms of a "practice of inquiry that is concerned with past, current or future phenomena ... means engaging in comparison, considering alternatives, seeing things from various perspectives, and drawing inferences" (Jordan et al., 2009, p. 466). Notably, the second variant of organizational routines, i.e., "reflective routine" (Jordan et al., 2009), encompasses practices such as training design project review or even steering committees including a wide range of decision-makers (Becke, 2013). Arguably, we pay attention to the implications of reflective routines as part of HR infrastructure in fostering leadership development.

Organizations worldwide are searching for a renewed focus on the kind of genuine leadership that can reinstate "confidence, hope and optimism; being able to rapidly bounce back from catastrophic events and display resiliency; helping people in their search for meaning and connection by fostering a new self-awareness; and genuinely relating to all stakeholders" (Avolio & Gardner, 2005, p. 316). Often referred to as authentic leadership (AL), such a style of leadership often entails "both greater self-awareness and self-regulated positive behaviors on the part of leaders and associates, fostering positive self-development" (Luthans & Avolio, 2003; p. 243).

Recent typology on AL is based on a set of four individual characteristics used in a burgeoning scholarship as specified by Walumbwa, Avolio, Gardner, Wernsing, and Peterson (2008, 2010). The specified characteristics include: self-awareness, interpersonal transparency, sense of balance, and morality (Walumbwa et al., 2008; Walumbwa, Wang, Wang, Schaeubroeck, & Avolio, 2010), as explained: first, self-awareness, or the state of being cognizant of one's own attributes (e.g., personal character, beliefs and values, strengths and weaknesses, etc.) and its influence on others; second, interpersonal transparency, or a tendency to share the available information, knowledge, and ideas to others; third, a sense of balance, or an impartial acceptance of contrasting opinions while evaluating one's own stance; and fourth, demonstrating morality through ethical decision-making.

Through a mixed-methods study, Baron (2016) noted that AL can, in fact, be successfully implemented through leadership development programs. The author argued that individuals' participation in leadership development may even facilitate mindfulness. These findings are of interest to both scholars and practitioners alike. Given the state of mindfulness is typically cultivated among individuals through interventions such as mindfulness-based stress reduction (MBSR; Kabat-Zinn, 1990), understanding its similarities and differences from work-based leadership development programs is crucial.

Further, leadership development programs in the workplace may be designed to foster mindfulness, to expand focus on present-moment experience, identify the relevant values and make a commitment towards the associated behaviors (Baron, 2016). Therefore, the design of mindfulness-cultivating leadership programs may allow individuals to reflect on their values, goals, and objectives before committing to taking any actions.

Consistent with general findings on the positive effects of the practice on employees, mindfulness was found to reduce a variety of negative outcomes (anxiety, depression, and burnout) in leaders across all levels of an organization (Roche, Haar, & Luthans, 2014). Roche and colleagues (2014) found that mindfulness builds psychological capital (PsyCap) in leaders, thereby helping them cope more successfully with negative psychological outcomes. Psychological capital (a type of positive organizational behavior) consists of the traits of resilience (coping with and recovering from adversity), optimism (maintaining a positive outlook), hope (persisting in goals), and efficacy (having confidence in self) (Luthans, Avey, Avolio, & Peterson, 2010).

Psychological capital consists of states, rather than traits, meaning that an individual can develop resilience, optimism, hope, and efficacy, and that these are not innate characteristics (Youssef & Luthans, 2007). Roche and colleagues (2014) argued that "mindfulness facilitates a separation between self and the event and this in turn facilitates the reflective choice of actions and reactions such as greater hope, efficacy, resiliency, and optimism" (Roche et al., 2014, p. 480). Given the nature of PsyCap as a developable series of states, organizations have engaged in funding training programs designed to build PsyCap (Luthans, Avey, Avolio, Norman, & Combs, 2006; Robertson, Cooper, Sarkar, & Curran, 2015). Resilience training in particular has been found to improve employees' mental health and well-being (Robertson et al., 2015). Given the success of mindfulness training programs, organizations may want to look at integrating mindfulness training into their broader PsyCap training programs as a means of enhancing their effectiveness. As Roche and colleagues (2014) found, psychological capital serves as a mediator between mindfulness and leadership well-being outcomes.

The presence of psychological capital has also been found to positively relate to authentic leadership behaviors (Jensen & Luthans, 2006; Luthans & Avolio, 2003). Authentic leaders can be defined as individuals who:

> act in accordance with deep personal values and convictions, to build credibility and win the respect and trust of followers by encouraging diverse viewpoints and building networks of collaborative relationships with followers, and thereby lead in a manner that followers recognize as authentic.
>
> *(Avolio, Gardner, Walumbwa, Luthans, & May, 2004, p. 806)*

Furthermore, authentic leadership requires a great deal of self-awareness and self-regulation (Luthans & Avolio, 2003). Thus, some scholars were led to hypothesize about a potential relationship between authentic leadership and mindfulness, given the ability of mindfulness to improve an individual's awareness of their present state. Ultimately, a positive association was found to exist (Baron, 2016). This may be due to the relationship between mindfulness and psychological capital, whereby mindfulness builds psychological capital, which leads to the improved psychological well-being of leaders (Roche et al., 2014). In Baron's (2016) model, psychological capital may likewise be mediating the relationship between mindfulness and authentic leadership.

Discussion and future directions

Research evidence suggests that mindfulness is directly related to vitality, satisfaction, and quality of interpersonal relationships while mitigating individuals' levels of stress, anxiety, and depression (see, for a summary, Brown et al., 2007; Glomb et al., 2011). Notably, contemporary workplaces operationalize mindfulness as a set of techniques to ameliorate stress and attain performance-related work outcomes (Qiu & Rooney, 2019).

Throughout this chapter, we argued the role of HR in implementing mindfulness within the members of an organization. In that vein, we discussed the implementation of three major applications of workplace mindfulness namely proactive work behaviors, work–life balance, and leadership development through HR infrastructure.

Notably, a number of different mindfulness training programs have been developed over the years (Chin et al., 2019; Krusche, Jack, Blunt, & Hsu, 2019; Napoli, 2004; Roeser et al., 2013; Roeser, Skinner, Beers, & Jennings, 2012; Slatyer, Craigie, Heritage, Davis, & Rees, 2018). These mindfulness training programs can be administered in a variety of ways, ranging from in-person coaching, to workshops, to the aforementioned electronic delivery (Roeser et al., 2012). Mindfulness training programs have been found to reduce stress (Roeser et al., 2012) and burnout (Roeser et al., 2013) as well improve focus (Mrazek, Franklin, Phillips, Baird, & Schooler, 2013) and build resilience (Roche et al., 2014; Roeser et al., 2012). Mindfulness training programs typically consist of formal teaching as well as meditation exercises (Walach et al., 2007). Due to the flexibility in delivery, and the ability of workers to practice mindfulness at home, the potential costs (both financial and time-based) can be limited by frugal organizations, while still achieving training targets. Studies have found that brief mindfulness training sessions can be very effective in achieving target outcomes (Krusche et al., 2019; Slatyer et al., 2018), which reiterates the idea that mindfulness training does not need to be a significant expense for an organization.

Hyland and colleagues (2015) highlighted the need to study workplace mindfulness training by depicting its role in fostering physical, emotional, and performance benefits to organizations and their members. Consequently, mindfulness training is often administered either in-house, within an organization, or externally through specialized firms (Saks & Gruman, 2015). Eby and colleagues (2019) identified several unsettled key questions and areas of concern in designing workplace mindfulness training, e.g., key practice features, duration, target audience, and occupations. Despite the effectiveness of workplace mindfulness training programs in stress reduction through building individual-level coping skills and resilience (Donald & Atkins, 2016), the implementation of workplace mindfulness training programs is heavily contingent upon organizational resources (Hyland et al., 2015). As part of a solution, Saks and Gruman (2015) offered integrating workplace mindfulness training to the existing training programs within an organization. This is because workplace mindfulness practices enhance self-regulation, which is further beneficial in facilitating individual learning and retention through increased attention span (Sitzmann & Ely, 2010).

The current chapter extends Saks and Gruman's (2015) argument by establishing the significance of HR infrastructure involving organizational routines in enabling workplace mindfulness. Future research can focus on one of the following research avenues.

How do the two organizational routines, i.e., reflective vs. interactive, intersect with the trait vs. state-like characteristics of workplace mindfulness? Given some employees may be more responsive and prone to benefit from workplace mindfulness than others (Eby et al., 2019), it would be interesting to dissect the kind of workplace mindfulness that surfaces as a result of the two kinds of routines.

Research indicates that certain contextual variables (e.g., self-efficacy, motivation to learn, and cognitive skills, etc.) may predict individuals' learning outcomes (Salas, Weaver, & Shuffler, 2012). In that regard, it would be interesting to investigate if a certain kind of organizational routine is more effective than the other in implementing workplace mindfulness through HR infrastructure.

Finally, given the linear relationship between mindfulness and coping skills (Donald & Atkins, 2016), there has been a debate on occupational variability in determining the effectiveness of implementing workplace mindfulness. Occupations requiring high emotional labor compared with physical or intellectual demands (e.g., physical and mental health professionals, social workers, etc.) tend to benefit from routine-induced workplace mindfulness.

Conclusion

The human resource function's duty is to enhance firm value by managing and developing the people who work there. Value can be added through both cost-cutting means as well as the proactive development of individuals. Health and safety costs associated with stress and overwork are becoming an increasingly noticeable burden on organizations. As employee work–life balance deteriorates, organizations must act to help re-establish balance or face the consequences of having an unhealthy workforce rife with high turnover and absenteeism. The benefits of HR solutions, like all other business solutions, must be weighed against their costs. This is where the value of mindfulness shines. We argued that implementing workplace mindfulness does not have to come at a significant expense and is attainable through HR infrastructures incorporating organizational routines.

In addition to helping reduce costs associated with work–life conflict, mindfulness can also be used proactively to enhance performance, particularly that of leaders, by building authenticity and psychological capital. Finally, by encouraging autonomy, organizations can indirectly help promote mindfulness development. Autonomy allows employees to pursue self-directed solutions, such as mindfulness, to dealing with work dissatisfaction and stress. Ultimately, by focusing on fostering mindfulness, human resources can build resilient and more productive workers.

Key takeaways

1. Mindfulness literature within the workplace context is rather scarce and requires further research.
2. Mindfulness at work can be implemented through HR infrastructure that incorporates organizational routines (i.e., interactive and reflective).
3. By effectively fostering workplace mindfulness, HR can promote proactive work behaviors and work–life balance through interactive routines.
4. Similarly, HR can significantly encourage mindful leadership development through reflective routines.
5. Workplace mindfulness implementation does not have to come at a significant expense but can easily be incorporated within organizational routines.

Reflective questions

1. Why is it relevant to study workplace mindfulness?
2. How is workplace mindfulness different from HR mindfulness?
3. Why should HR ensure an effective implementation of workplace mindfulness?
4. How can organizational routines promote workplace mindfulness?
5. How does workplace mindfulness prevail within different occupations?

References

Allen, T. D., & Kiburz, K. M. (2012). Trait mindfulness and work–family balance among working parents: The mediating effects of vitality and sleep quality. *Journal of Vocational Behavior, 80*(2), 372–379.

Avolio, B. J., & Gardner, W. L. (2005). Authentic leadership development: Getting to the root of positive forms of leadership. *The Leadership Quarterly, 16*, 315–338.

Avolio, B. J., Gardner, W. L., Walumbwa, F. O., Luthans, F., & May, D. R. (2004). Unlocking the mask: A look at the process by which authentic leaders impact follower attitudes and behaviors. *The Leadership Quarterly, 15*(6), 801–823.

Badham, R., & King, E. (2016). Mindfulness and organization: A literature re-view. Paper presented at European Group for Organizational Studies (EGOS 2016): *Organizing in the Shadow of Power*, Naples, Italy.

Baer, R. A., Smith, G. T., Hopkins, J., Krietemeyer, J., & Toney, L. (2006). Using self-report assessment methods to explore facets of mindfulness. *Assessment, 13*(1), 27–45.

Bakker, A. B., & Demerouti, E. (2007). The Job Demands-Resources model: State of the art. *Journal of Managerial Psychology, 22*(3), 309–328.

Bakker, A. B., & Demerouti, E. (2013). The spillover-crossover model. In Joseph G. Grzywacz *Current issues in work and organizational psychology. New frontiers in work and family research* (pp. 55–70). New York, NY, US: Psychology Press.

Baron, L. (2016). Authentic leadership and mindfulness development through action learning. *Journal of Managerial Psychology, 31*(1), 296–311.

Becke, G. (2013). Human resource mindfulness–promoting heath in knowledge-intensive SMEs. In I. Ehnert, W. Harry, & K. J. Zink (Eds.) *Sustainability and human resource management* (pp. 83–103). London: Springer.

Brendel, W., & Bennett, C. (2016). Learning to embody leadership through mindfulness and somatics practice. *Advances in Developing Human Resources, 18*(3), 409–425.

Brown, K. W., & Ryan, R. M. (2003). The benefits of being present: Mindfulness and its role in psychological wellbeing. *Journal of Personality and Social Psychology, 84*, 822–848.

Brown, K. W., Ryan, R. M., & Creswell, J. D. (2007). Mindfulness: Theoretical foundations and evidence for its salutary effects. *Psychological Inquiry, 18*, 211–237.

Busck, O., Knudsen, H., & Lind, J. (2010). The transformation of employee participation: Consequences for the work environment. *Economic and Industrial Democracy, 31*(3), 285–305.

Chin, B., Slutsky, J., Raye, J., & Creswell, J. D. (2019). Mindfulness training reduces stress at work: A randomized controlled trial. *Mindfulness, 10*(4), 627–638.

Dane, E. (2011). Paying attention to mindfulness and its effects on task performance in the workplace. *Journal of Management, 37*(4), 997–1018.

Dane, E., & Brummel, B. J. (2014). Examining workplace mindfulness and its relations to job performance and turnover intention. *Human Relations, 67*(1), 105–128.

Docherty, P., Forslin, J., & Shani, A. B. (2002). Sustainable work systems: Lessons and challenges. In P. Docherty, J. Forslin, & A. B. Shani (Eds.), *Creating sustainable work systems* (1st ed., pp. 213–225). London, New York: Routledge.

Donald, J. N., & Atkins, P. W. B. (2016). Mindfulness and coping with stress: Do levels of perceived stress matter? *Mindfulness*, 7, 1423–1436.

Eby, L. T., Allen, T. D., Conley, K. M., Williamson, R. L., Henderson, T. G., & Mancini, V. S. (2019). Mindfulness-based training interventions for employees: A qualitative review of the literature. *Human Resource Management Review, 29*(2), 156–178.

Epstein, M. (1988). The deconstruction of the self: Ego and "egolessness" in Buddhist insight meditation. *Journal of Transpersonal Psychology, 20*(1), 61–69.

Elsbach, K. D., & Pratt, M. G. (2007). The physical environment in organizations. *Academy of Management Annals, 1*(1), 181–224.

Fehr, R., & Gelfand, M. J. (2012). The forgiving organization: A multilevel model of forgiveness at work. *Academy of Management Review, 37*(4), 664–688.

Feldman, M. S., & Pentland, B. T. (2003). Reconceptualizing organizational routines as a source of flexibility and change. *Administrative Science Quarterly, 48*(1), 94–118.

Felstead, A., Jewson, N., Phizacklea, A., & Walters, S. (2002). Opportunities to work at home in the context of work–life balance. *Human Resource Management Journal, 12*(1), 54–76.

Fleetwood, S. (2007). Why work–life balance now? *The International Journal of Human Resource Management, 18*(3), 387–400.

Frone, M. (2000). Work-family conflict and employee psychiatric disorders: The national comorbidity survey. *The Journal of Applied Psychology, 85*, 888–895.

George, J. M. (2009). The illusion of will in organizational behavior research: Nonconscious processes and job design. *Journal of Management, 35*(6), 1318–1339.

Glomb, T. M., Duffy, M. K., Bono, J. E., & Yang, T. (2011). Mindfulness at work. *Research in Personnel and Human Resources Management, 30*, 115–157.

Good, D. J., Lyddy, C. J., Glomb, T. M., Bono, J. E., Brown, K. W., Duffy, M. K., … Lazar, S. W. (2016). Contemplating mindfulness at work: An integrative review. *Journal of Management, 42*(1), 114–142.

Goode, W. J. (1960). A theory of role strain. *American Sociological Review, 25*(4), 483.

Greenhaus, J. H., & Beutell, N. J. (1985). Sources of conflict between work and family roles. *Academy of Management Review, 10*(1), 76–88.

Hülsheger, U., Alberts, H., Feinholdt, A., & Lang, J. (2013). Benefits of mindfulness at work: The role of mindfulness in emotion regulation, emotional exhaustion, and job satisfaction. *Journal of Applied Psychology, 98*(2), 310.

Hyland, P. K., Lee, R. A., & Mills, M. J. (2015). Mindfulness at work: A new approach to improving individual and organizational performance. *Industrial and Organizational Psychology, 8*(4), 576–602.

Jensen, S. M., & Luthans, F. (2006). Entrepreneurs as authentic leaders: Impact on employees attitudes. *Leadership & Organization Development Journal, 27*(8), 646–666.

Jordan, S., Messner, M., & Becker, A. (2009). Reflection and mindfulness in organizations: Rationales and possibilities for integration. *Management Learning, 40*(4), 465–473.

Kabat-Zinn, J. (1990). *Full catastrophe living: Using the wisdom of your body and mind to face stress, pain and illness*. New York: Delacourt.

Kabat-Zinn, J. (2006). Mindfulness-based interventions in context: Past, present, and future. *Clinical Psychology: Science and Practice, 10*(2), 144–156.

Klatt, M., Norre, C., Reader, B., Yodice, L., & White, S. (2017). Mindfulness in motion: A mindfulness-based intervention to reduce stress and enhance quality of sleep in Scandinavian employees. *Mindfulness, 8*(2), 481–488.

Kooij, D. T. A. M., van Woerkom, M., Wilkenloh, J., Dorenbosch, L., & Denissen, J. J. A. (2017). Job crafting towards strengths and interests: The effects of a job crafting intervention on person–job fit and the role of age. *Journal of Applied Psychology, 102*(6), 971–981.

Kossek, E. E., & Ozeki, C. (1999). Bridging the work-family policy and productivity gap: A literature review. *Community, Work & Family, 2*(1), 7–32.

Krusche, A., Jack, C. D., Blunt, C., & Hsu, A. (2019). Mindfulness-based organisational education: An evaluation of a mindfulness course delivered to employees at the Royal Orthopaedic Hospital. *Mindfulness*.

Lakey, C. E., Campbell, W. K., Brown, K. W., & Goodie, A. S. (2007). Dispositional mindfulness as a predictor of the severity of gambling outcomes. *Personality and Individual Differences, 43*(7), 1698–1710.

Lau, M. A., Bishop, S. R., Segal, Z. V., Buis, T., Anderson, N. D., Carlson, L., . . . Carmody, J. (2006). The Toronto mindfulness scale: Development and validation. *Journal of Clinical Psychology, 62*(12), 1445–1467.

Lee, R. A. (2012). Accelerating the development and mitigating derailment of high potential through mindfulness training. *The Industrial-Organizational Psychologist, 49*(3), 23–34.

Levinthal, D., & Rerup, C. (2006). Crossing an apparent chasm: Bridging mindful and less-mindful perspectives on organizational learning. *Organization Science, 17*(4), 502–513.

Luthans, F., Avey, J. B., Avolio, B. J., Norman, S. M., & Combs, G. M. (2006). Psychological capital development: Toward a micro-intervention. *Journal of Organizational Behavior, 27*(3), 387–393.

Luthans, F., Avey, J. B., Avolio, B. J., & Peterson, S. J. (2010). The development and resulting performance impact of positive psychological capital. *Human Resource Development Quarterly, 21*(1), 41–67.

Luthans, F., & Avolio, B. J. (2003). Authentic leadership: A positive developmental approach. In K. S. Cameron, J. E. Dutton, & R. E. Quinn (Eds.), *Positive organizational scholarship* (pp. 241–261). San Francisco: Barrett-Koehler.

Magid, B., & Poirier, M. (2016). The three shaky pillars of Western Buddhism: Deracination, secularization, and instrumentalisation. In B. Magid & R. Resenbaun (Eds.), *What's wrong with mindfulness (and what isn't): Zen perspectives* (pp. 39–52). Somerville: Wisdom Publications.

Masicampo, E. J., & Baumeister, R. F. (2007). Relating mindfulness and self-regulatory processes. *Psychological Inquiry, 18*(4), 255–258.

Michel, A., Bosch, C., & Rexroth, M. (2014). Mindfulness as a cognitive–emotional segmentation strategy: An intervention promoting work–life balance. *Journal of Occupational and Organizational Psychology, 87*(4), 733–754.

Mikulas, W. L. (2011). Mindfulness: Significant common confusions. *Mindfulness, 2*(1), 1–7.

Mrazek, M. D., Franklin, M. S., Phillips, D. T., Baird, B., & Schooler, J. W. (2013). Mindfulness training improves working memory capacity and GRE performance while reducing mind wandering. *Psychological Science, 24*(5), 776–781.

Napoli, M. (2004). Mindfulness training for teachers: A pilot program. *Complementary Health Practice Review, 9*(1), 31–42.

Nord, W. R., Fox, S., Phoenix, A., & Viano, K. (2002). Real-world reactions to work–life balance programs: Lessons for effective implementation. *Organizational Dynamics, 30*(3), 223–238.

Papies, E. K., Barsalou, L. W., & Custers, R. (2012). Mindful attention prevents mindless impulses. *Social Psychological and Personality Science, 3*(3), 291–299.

Podsakoff, N. P., LePine, J. A., & LePine, M. A. (2007). Differential challenge stressor-hindrance stressor relationships with job attitudes, turnover intentions, turnover, and withdrawal behavior: A meta-analysis. *Journal of Applied Psychology, 92*(2), 438–454.

Qiu, J. X., & Rooney, D. (2019). Addressing unintended ethical challenges of workplace mindfulness: A four-stage mindfulness development model. *Journal of Business Ethics, 157*(3), 715–730.

Reb, J., Narayanan, J., Chaturvedi, S., & Ekkirala, S. (2017). The mediating role of emotional exhaustion in the relationship of mindfulness with turnover intentions and job performance. *Mindfulness, 8*(3), 707–716.

Reb, J., Narayanan, J., & Ho, Z. W. (2015). Mindfulness at work: Antecedents and consequences of employee awareness and absent-mindedness. *Mindfulness, 6*(1), 111–122.

Robertson, I. T., Cooper, C. L., Sarkar, M., & Curran, T. (2015). Resilience training in the workplace from 2003 to 2014: A systematic review. *Journal of Occupational and Organizational Psychology, 88*(3), 533–562.

Roche, M., Haar, J. M., & Luthans, F. (2014). The role of mindfulness and psychological capital on the well-being of leaders. *Journal of Occupational Health Psychology, 19*(4), 476–489.

Roczniewska, M., & Puchalska, M. (2017). Are managers also "crafting leaders"? The link between organizational rank, autonomy, and job crafting. *Polish Psychological Bulletin, 48*, 198–211.

Roeser, R. W., Schonert-Reichl, K. A., Jha, A., Cullen, M., Wallace, L., Wilensky, R., . . . Harrison, J. (2013). Mindfulness training and reductions in teacher stress and burnout: Results from two randomized, waitlist-control field trials. *Journal of Educational Psychology, 105*(3), 787–804.

Roeser, R. W., Skinner, E., Beers, J., & Jennings, P. A. (2012). Mindfulness training and teachers' professional development: An emerging area of research and practice. *Child Development Perspectives, 6* (2), 167–173.

Saks, A. M., & Gruman, J. A. (2015). Mindfulness and the Transfer of Training. *Industrial and Organizational Psychology, 8*(4), 689–694.

Salas, E., Weaver, S. J., & Shuffler, M. L. (2012). Learning, training, and development in organizations. In S. W. J. Kozlowski (Ed.), *The Oxford handbook of organizational psychology* (Vol. 1, pp. 330–372). New York: Oxford University Press.

Shapiro, S. L., Carlson, L. E., Astin, J. A., & Freeman, B. (2006). Mechanisms of mindfulness. *Journal of Clinical Psychology, 62*, 373–386.

Sitzmann, T., & Ely, K. (2010). Sometimes you need a reminder: The effects of prompting self-regulation on regulatory processes, learning, and attrition. *Journal of Applied Psychology, 95*, 132–144.

Slatyer, S., Craigie, M., Heritage, B., Davis, S., & Rees, C. (2018). Evaluating the effectiveness of a brief mindful self-care and resiliency (MSCR) intervention for nurses: A controlled trial. *Mindfulness, 9*(2), 534–546.

Spector, P. E., & Jex, S. M. (1998). Development of four self-report measures of job stressors and strain: interpersonal conflict at work scale, organizational constraints scale, quantitative workload inventory, and physical symptoms inventory. *Journal of Occupational Health Psychology, 3*(4), 356–367.

Tims, M., & Bakker, A. B. (2010). Job crafting: Towards a new model of individual job redesign. *SA Journal of Industrial Psychology, 36*(2), 1–9.

Tims, M., Bakker, A. B., & Derks, D. (2013). The impact of job crafting on job demands, job resources, and well-being. *Journal of Occupational Health Psychology, 18*(2), 230–240.

Tims, M., Bakker, A. B., & Derks, D. (2015). Job crafting and job performance: A longitudinal study. *European Journal of Work and Organizational Psychology, 24*(6), 914–928.

Virgili, M. (2015). Mindfulness-based interventions reduce psychological distress in working adults: A meta-analysis of intervention studies. *Mindfulness, 6*(2), 326–337.

Walach, H., Nord, E., Zier, C., Dietz-Waschkowski, B., Kersig, S., & Schüpbach, H. (2007). Mindfulness-based stress reduction as a method for personnel development: A pilot evaluation. *International Journal of Stress Management, 14*(2), 188–198.

Walumbwa, F. O., Avolio, B. J., Gardner, W. L., Wernsing, T. S., & Peterson, S. J. (2008). Authentic leadership: Development and validation of a theory-based measure. *Journal of Management, 34*(1), 89–126.

Walumbwa, F. O., Wang, P., Wang, H., Schaeubroeck, J., & Avolio, B. J. (2010). Psychological processes linking authentic leadership to follower behaviors. *The Leadership Quarterly, 21*(5), 901–914.

Watson, D., Clark, L. A., & Tellegen, A. (1988). Development and validation of brief measures of positive and negative affect: The PANAS scales. *Journal of Personality and Social Psychology, 54*(6), 1063–1070.

Weick, K. E., & Sutcliffe, K. M. (2001). *Managing the unexpected* (1st ed.). San Francisco: Jossey-Bass.

Weinstein, N., Brown, K. W., & Ryan, R. M. (2009). A multi-method examination of the effects of mindfulness on stress attribution, coping, and emotional well-being. *Journal of Research in Personality, 43*(3), 374–385.

Wrzesniewski, A., & Dutton, J. E. (2001). Crafting a job: Revisioning employees as active crafters of their work. *Academy of Management Review, 26*(2), 179–201.

Youssef, C. M., & Luthans, F. (2007). Positive organizational behavior in the workplace: The impact of hope, optimism, and resilience. *Journal of Management, 33*(5), 774–800.

Zhong, C. B., & House, J. (2012). Hawthorne revisited: Organizational implications of the physical work environment. *Research in Organizational Behavior, 32*, 3–22.

Zivnuska, S., Kacmar, K. M., Ferguson, M., & Carlson, D. S. (2016). Mindfulness at work: Resource accumulation, well-being, and attitudes. *Career Development International, 21*(2), 106–124.

16

WHY MANAGE WITH INSIGHT?

A Buddhist view that goes beyond mindfulness[1]

Thushini S. Jayawardena-Willis, Edwina Pio, and Peter McGhee

Introduction

Mindfulness in the workplace (Passmore, 2019) has gained momentum in the last few decades, as it has been identified as a management intervention tool (Donaldson-Feilder, Lewis, & Yarker, 2019; Khisty, 2010) that could be used to reduce unethical decision-making (Ruedy & Schweitzer, 2010), enhance employee wellbeing (Reb, Narayanan, & Chaturvedi, 2014; Schultz, Ryan, Niemiec, Legate, & Williams, 2015), develop emotional intelligence (Chapman-Clarke, 2017), increase work engagement (Petchsawang & McLean, 2017), and reduce stress in the workplace (Whitehead, Bates, Elphinstone, Yang, & Murray, 2018). However, Ruedy and Schweitzer's research revealed that mindfulness did not have an impact on the participants who chose to cheat. This raises a question as to whether there is a distinction between mere mindfulness (as taught in the West) and right mindfulness in Buddhism (which is founded on Buddhist ethics).

Mindfulness in the West is defined as "a state of being attentive to and aware of what is taking place in the present" (Brown & Ryan, 2003, p. 822). It enables an individual to be aware of the present moment (Bouckaert & Zsolnai, 2012; Kauanui, Thomas, Sherman, Waters, & Gilea, 2010) without reaction or judgment (Schuyler, Skjei, Sanzgiri, & Koskela, 2017). Moreover, while some define mindfulness as awareness of self, others, and life situations (Kauanui et al., 2010), others hold that mindfulness develops qualities that enhance work relationships, fine-tune individuals' perceptions, and increase the ethicality of decisions (Bouckaert & Zsolnai, 2012; Gould, 1995). Kabat-Zinn (1994), whose definition of mindfulness is influenced by Zen Buddhism, notes that mindfulness arises when an individual is aware that they are purposely paying attention to the present moment in a non-judgmental way (Donaldson-Feilder et al., 2019).

Nevertheless, according to Buddhism, mindfulness is not only just being aware attentively to the present moment in a non-judgmental way, but it also must be ethical (right). As such, it is this ethical component of Buddhist mindfulness that distinguishes it from the concept of mindfulness in the West (Purser & Milillo, 2015). Right mindfulness (*samma sati*) in Buddhism is cultivated through the practice of meditation and is a factor that prevents an individual from committing any act, through body, speech, or mind, which will harm themselves or others

(Marques, 2012a). Although most research acknowledges that Eastern mindfulness has its roots in Buddhism (Purser & Milillo, 2015; Ruedy & Schweitzer, 2010; Vogus, Rothman, Sutcliffe, & Weick, 2014; Vogus & Sutcliffe, 2012; Weick & Putnam, 2006), meditation techniques seem to have existed even before (and contemporary to) the Buddha. An example is the story that Gautama attained "trances" (*dhyana*) (Rahula, 1978, p. 48), under the guidance of two teachers, before he left them to seek liberation on his own.

In the management literature, mindfulness research is twofold: mindful organizing and organizational mindfulness. Whereas mindful organizing focuses on operations, organizational mindfulness is practiced at a strategic level by the organization's top administrators (i.e., strategic, stable, and top–down) (Vogus & Sutcliffe, 2012). Although prior research has shown that organizational mindfulness results in highly reliable organizations, little is known about the effects of an individual's mindfulness on organizational mindfulness and mindful organizing (Vogus et al., 2014; Vogus & Sutcliffe, 2012). Buddhism seems to provide a solution to this problem as it explains how to cultivate right mindfulness through the practice of meditation. For example, following the recommendation of Weick and Putnam (2006) to reconceptualize mindfulness through Eastern philosophies, Purser and Milillo (2015) have developed a Buddhist-based right mindfulness model for organizational theory. However, their work does not inquire in-depth the similarities and differences (if any) between the concepts of right mindfulness and insight in Buddhism and their significance to management. Consequently, this chapter seeks to address this. The conceptual model elaborated in this chapter is depicted in Figure 16.1.

Buddhist ethics (*sila*)

Buddhist ethics are essential in order for an individual to establish their practice of Buddhist meditation. They consist of the five precepts, ethical conduct of the Noble Eightfold Path (hereinafter referred to as the Path), and the code of discipline for

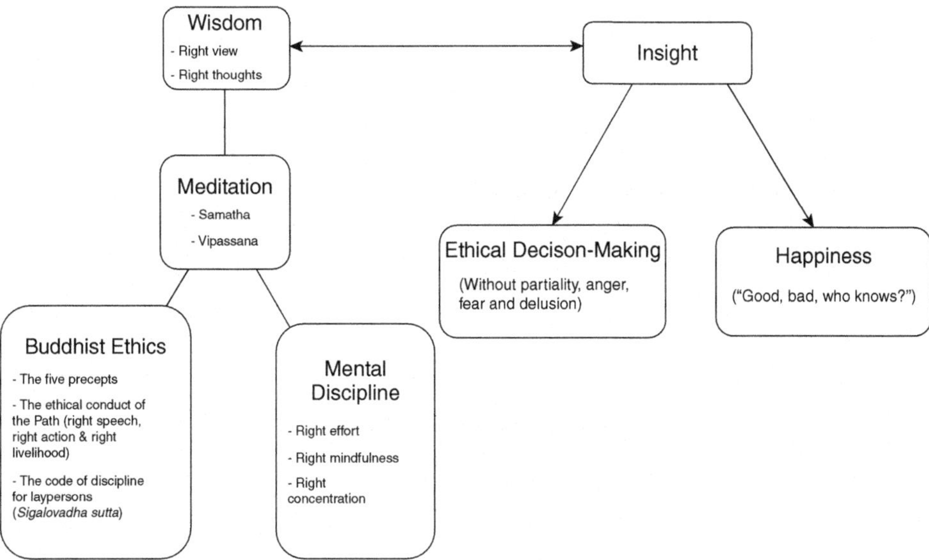

Figure 16.1 The influence of insight in Buddhism in management

laypersons (i.e., *Sigalovadha sutta*) (Hill, 2007; Saddhatissa, 2003). They provide the moral foundation for laypersons, before they proceed to the mental discipline and wisdom elements of the Path.

In Buddhism, the five precepts are the bare minimum discipline required for laypersons (Saddhatissa, 2003). The five precepts provide that individuals should abstain from killing, stealing, sexual misconduct, false speech, and intoxication. The adherence to these precepts assists individuals to cultivate qualities such as non-harm and honesty. Fernando and Jackson (2006), for instance, found that Buddhist entrepreneurs' perception of what a right decision means was influenced by their spirituality, which was in turn informed by their practice of the five precepts. Moreover, individuals are expected to uphold these precepts scrupulously when they embark on the Path.

Ethical conduct of the Path consists of right speech, right action, and right livelihood (Narada, 1998; Rahula, 1978; Saddhatissa, 2003). Right speech means refraining from four types of communication: false speech or lies, hateful speech, malicious or abusive speech, and idle speech or gossip. Right action provides that one should abstain from destroying life, stealing, dishonest dealings, sexual misconduct, and encourage others to lead an honorable and peaceful life in an ethical way. The third component of ethical conduct is right livelihood. It provides that individuals should not engage in an occupation which may bring harm to others. According to Buddhism, there are five such professions: "trading in arms and lethal weapons, intoxicating drinks, poisons, killing animals, and cheating" (Rahula, 1978, p. 47).

Furthermore, according to Buddhism, there are four groups that deserve to be respected and worshipped: parents and children, husbands and wives, teachers and students, and employers and employees (Hill, 2007; Narada, 1996; Rahula, 1978; Saddhatissa, 2003). The responsibilities and duties of these four groups are illustrated in the Buddhist discourse of the *Sigalovadha sutta*. It is also known as the code of discipline for laypersons, because of its lengthy discussions and emphasis on the dos and don'ts for laypersons. In this discourse, laypersons are advised to maintain discipline by avoiding the four vices in conduct, the four motives of evil action, and the six causes of wasting wealth (Rahula, 1978). The four vices of conduct are destruction of life, stealing, adultery, and lying. The four motives that lead to an evil action are "partiality, enmity, stupidity, and fear" (Rahula, 1978, p. 120). In the English translation of *Sigalovadha sutta* by Narada, these four motives are referred to as partiality, anger, fear, and delusion. Research on ethical decision-making (EDM) in organizations has shown an adverse impact of negative emotions (such as anger, fear, and sadness) on EDM (Kligyte, Connelly, Thiel, & Devenport, 2013; Krishnakumar & Rymph, 2012; Thiel, Connelly, & Griffith, 2011).

Interestingly, Buddhism also prescribes how to overcome these negative states of mind by cultivating loving-kindness, compassion, sympathetic-joy, and equanimity (Nyanaponika Thera, 1958). For instance, Fredrickson, Cohn, Coffey, Pek, and Finkel (2008) found that cultivation of loving-kindness meditation helps to overcome negative emotions, such as anger, fear, lust, and ill-will. As such, Buddhist meditation techniques seem to be the key to an individual developing positive emotions.

Meditation in Buddhism

In Buddhism, meditation assists one to foster self-awareness and consciousness prior to one's actions towards others (Gould, 1995). Some scholars claim that consciousness or sense cognition (i.e., *viññāṇa*) may be cultivated through the practices of loving-kindness, compassion, sympathetic-joy, and equanimity, which play a significant role in one's spiritual growth and experience of self and others (Marques, 2012a). Meditation has also been identified as a technique that may be used to teach workplace spirituality in business higher education (Marques, Dhiman, & Biberman, 2014) and business ethics (Forge, 1997). As a result, some argue that if Buddhism is approached as a way of life, it may inform a wider audience such as religious or secular organizations (Marques, 2012b).

Concentration (*samatha*) and insight (*vipassana*) are the two main categories of meditation in Buddhism (Dhiman, 2008, 2009; Marques & Dhiman, 2009). While *samatha* meditation enables individuals to cultivate mindfulness or concentration, insight meditation assists them to observe the truth or reality as it is, in a non-judgmental, compassionate way (Petchsawang & Duchon, 2012). Many Buddhist meditation teachers advise their students to practice *samatha* meditation prior to proceeding to *vipassana* meditation (Dhammaratana, 2011; Hart, 1987; Marques & Dhiman, 2009). Therefore, according to Buddhism, while concentration meditation techniques assist an individual to enhance right mindfulness, *vipassana* meditation helps them to progress to insight.

Insight is the highest spiritual faculty an individual can develop (Weick & Putnam, 2006). As per *Visuddhimaga* (path of purification), there are 40 concentration meditation techniques that an individual can use to enhance their calmness, tranquility, and concentration. Amongst these, loving-kindness (*metta*) and mindfulness of breath (*anapanasati*) are two meditation techniques that can be applied by anyone universally due to the nature of their practice. Research on mindfulness by incorporating a sample of past, current, and non-meditators has shown a significant distinction between their levels of awareness, non-judgment, and non-reaction (Pang & Ruch, 2019). Yet, little is known about the distinction between right mindfulness and insight in Buddhism and their significance in management. Hence, the following sections of this chapter will elaborate how this may occur.

Mental discipline (*samadhi*)

Mental discipline of the Path comprises right effort, right mindfulness, and right concentration (Purser & Milillo, 2015; Rahula, 1978). Right effort is the effort one makes to prevent unwholesome thoughts from arising and to generate wholesome thoughts. Thus, some refer to right effort as due diligence (Collins, 2010). There are four characteristics of right effort: intentionally preventing an evil or unwholesome state of mind from arising; eliminating an evil or unwholesome state of mind which has already arisen; generating good or wholesome states of mind that have not arisen; and developing further already perfected, good, or wholesome states of mind (Rahula, 1978).

According to Buddhist teachings, there are four types of right mindfulness: mind, body, sensations, and bodily objects/*dhammas* (Bhikkhu, 2010; Dhammaratana, 2011; Goenka, 1999; Purser & Milillo, 2015). These are cultivated by being aware of body, mind, sensations, and bodily objects as they are without reacting to them by maintaining an equanimous mind (Hart, 1987; Marques & Dhiman, 2009; Rahula, 1978). This process is linked to awakening or enlightenment. The Buddha, for example, is called the awakened one (Rhys Davids, 1900) because he realized the ultimate truth. In contrast, mindfulness in the West usually involves awareness of external situations and the contents of the mind (Schuyler et al., 2017; Weick & Putnam, 2006). The term waking up is defined as "the fleeting moments when people notice they are more aware and present to what is happening within or around them" (Schuyler et al., 2017, p. 87). Hence, it seems that while Buddhism concentrates on awareness of internal factors such as mind, sensations, body, and bodily objects, the Western perspective of mindfulness seems to be primarily focused on awareness of external factors.

The third element of mental discipline in the Path is right concentration. It is attained through the four "*dhyanas*". The first *dhyana* helps an individual to discard unwholesome thoughts such as lust, desire, passion, and worry. In the second *dhyana*, all cerebral actions are released, while the characteristics of happiness and equanimity remain. Thus, feelings of joy and happiness still exist at this stage. When a meditator reaches the third *dhyana*, the feeling of joy vanishes, and equanimity arises. Then once an individual attains the fourth *dhyana*, they will lose both positive and negative sensations, such as joy and sorrow. At this stage the meditator will experience only "pure equanimity and awareness" (Rahula, 1978, p. 49). Consequently, in Buddhism, equanimity (i.e., the ability to maintain a balanced mind, devoid of attachment) is the highest form of happiness.

Wisdom (*panna*)

Wisdom consists of right thoughts and right view. While right thoughts enable an individual to cultivate non-attachment (or renunciation), loving-kindness, and harmlessness, right view assists them to know, practice, cultivate, experience, and understand things just as they are (Anderson, 2001; Gethin, 2004). Right view is three-fold: received wisdom, intellectual wisdom, and experiential wisdom (Hart, 1987).

The literal meaning of received wisdom is wisdom that is acquired from others through reading or listening. For instance, one may learn about business ethics by perusing books, codes of ethics, journal articles, or by attending seminars, courses, or workshops. Second, when one examines what is right or wrong by analyzing or rationalizing the advantages or disadvantages of one's actions or behaviors at an intellectual level, such wisdom is called intellectual wisdom (Hart, 1987). An example of intellectual wisdom may be where one rationalizes whether the concepts of love or compassion are ethical or unethical. If one rationalizes how cultivation of love or compassion may result in reducing one's negative emotions (such as anger or fear) and thereby increasing one's resilience and wellbeing (Fredrickson, 2001), such wisdom is called intellectual wisdom. Finally, experiential wisdom is where one realizes the truth or reality through direct experience, that is, through the constant practice of meditation. Hence, some argue that Buddhist ethics, wisdom, and mental discipline of the Path are intertwined (Collins, 2010; Rahula, 1978).

Insight

Insight (also known as insight-wisdom) is an individual's ability to "seeing things as they truly are" (Purser & Milillo, 2015, p. 9). According to Bhikkhu (2010), insight into body, feelings, mind, and bodily objects/*dhammas* means contemplating absence of beauty, unsatisfactoriness, impermanence, and absence of self respectively. In Theravada Buddhism, these are broadly categorized under three themes: suffering, impermanence, and non-self (Pace, 2013; Pio, 1988).

Suffering (dukkha), impermanence (anicca), and non-self (anatta)

Suffering (*dukkha*) is the first noble truth. It contends that all suffer or experience unsatisfactoriness (Kalupahana, 1976; Pace, 2013). The meaning of *dukkha* includes "sorrow, misery, distress, agony, affliction, suffering, discomfort, pain, etc." (Pio, 1988, p. 21). As per the Buddhist teachings, unsatisfactoriness, discomfort, or suffering occurs because of the impermanent nature of conventional reality (Kalupahana, 1976). Some researchers argue that suffering is not an "expression of pessimism" (Pio, 1988, p. 21), since Buddhism does not negate satisfaction (Kalupahana, 1976). Rather, what Buddhism denies is the consequences of satisfaction. In other words, suffering occurs due to our attachment to things which are impermanent (Kalupahana, 1976). For instance, an individual may be attached to the way they look, their possessions, and the titles or positions they hold in an organization. However, the nature of reality is such that an individual's looks change with time as they age and their health deteriorates as they get closer to death. An individual may have to leave their titles and possessions behind upon retirement, dismissal, or death. Being attached to the self or things may cause suffering or sorrow to an individual. Thus, what Buddhism teaches is that attachment to self or things that are themselves impermanent brings unhappiness and suffering to individuals (Brahm, 2013).

The causes of suffering are desire, delusion, and anger (Pace, 2013). These three causes bind individuals to a cycle of continuous rebirth (Pace, 2013; Skilton, 2013), which can be ceased by attaining enlightenment. Enlightenment is achieved by the elimination of the cause of suffering, which brings an end to conditional arising/dependent origination or "the wheel of life" (Skilton, 2013, p. 76). Dependent origination consists of 12 links: ignorance, volition, consciousness, mental and physical phenomena, the six faculties (five sense organs and mind), contact, feeling/sensation, craving, clinging, the process of becoming, birth, ageing, and death (Rahula, 1978). In Buddhism, this process can be reversed by an individual by breaking the link of ignorance as they start to see things as they are through insight-wisdom.

Insight-wisdom prevents an individual from generating craving and clinging (Gowans, 2013) towards pleasant sensations and aversion towards unpleasant sensations. Prior research has shown that excessive materialistic consumption based on craving and attachment results in suffering (Pace, 2013) and that people who are less attached to money are less likely to commit unethical behavior (Tang & Chiu, 2003). Moreover, Ermongkonchai (2010) found that employee misconduct in Thai organizations was affected by greed and therefore recommended application of Buddhism to enhance organizations' ethical culture. However, others have highlighted the challenges of the application of Buddhism in modern profit-oriented capitalistic organizations (Marques, 2009, 2011, 2012b; Rees & Agocs, 2011), which are driven by greed (Wang & Murnighan, 2011). Therefore, an individual's ability to see greed and clinging as they are through insight-wisdom may impact on how they make ethical decisions in organizations.

According to Buddhism, an individual suffers because of the delusion of the existence of self (Gowans, 2013; Pace, 2013). Our perception of the existence of self is a result of our inability to see the impermanent or changing nature of all conventional realities (Pace, 2013; Pérez-Remón, 1980). In Buddhism, this perception of the existence of self is no more than an illusion or delusion (Brazier, 2003), because what we refer to as the self by convention is a constantly changing phenomenon (Hart, 1987). Thus, some scholars argue that what Buddha rejected in the *Aggi-Vachchagotta sutta* is the illusion or delusion of a fixed or unchanging self, rather than the notion of self itself (Pérez-Remón, 1980).

In Theravada Buddhist scriptures, all *dhamma* are made of the five aggregates (corporeality, sensation, perception, mental formations, and consciousness), the six elements (earth, water, heat, air, space, and consciousness), 18 elements (the six sense tools, their contact, and consciousness), and the 12 avenues of sense-perception and mental cognition (Galmangoda, 2008). Since these elements are constantly changing, there is no fixed self to be identified with. Our perception of self, therefore, is merely an imposition by society on an individual after their birth (e.g., name, religion, color, race, gender, sex, or sexuality). When an individual starts to practice meditation, they realize this ultimate truth through insight-wisdom. Pace (2013), for example, notes that the Buddhist concept of non-self is relevant to management research for two reasons: first, because Buddhism emphasizes the reality of the chain of cause and effect, which produces self, rather than denying an existence of a conventional self; second, the concept of non-self requires empathy rather than altruism.

Equanimity

Equanimity is the perfect, unshakeable, balanced mind rooted in insight that enables an individual to refrain from reacting to either positive or negative emotions (Pace, 2013). According to Buddhism, an individual's reaction to these positive and negative emotions is due to their delusion or ignorance (Hart, 1987; Rahula, 1978). So, when an individual generates insight-wisdom, they are able to see things as they are without reacting to positive or negative emotions with craving or aversion. Hence, equanimity is the highest form of happiness in Buddhism, which is devoid of attachment. For instance, when an individual practices equanimity, they learn to remain calm at both bad and good times without reacting with either joy or sadness (e.g., Brahm's (2013) "good? bad? who knows?"). As such, equanimity may have a significant impact on an individual's EDM as well as their happiness in organizations. The following quotation from an Indian business leader emphasizes the significance of developing awareness, insight-wisdom, and equanimity:

> Of course, I get angry. Of course, I get frustrations. But they will not be long lasting. You need to practice, you know. Some of these diehard negative habits, they will not go away just like that. We need wisdom: constant study, constant meditation, and constant awareness. In Buddhism, they call these afflictive emotions our sworn enemies: worse than the external enemies.
>
> *(Marques, 2010, p. 219)*

The business leader's words indicate that his awareness of the importance of eradicating negative habits through insight-wisdom may have influenced his willingness to act ethically without reacting with greed (Vadera & Pratt, 2013; Wang & Murnighan, 2011), anger, or fear (Thiel et al., 2011). The business leader also mentions that the negative emotions one feels within are far greater than the external enemies or factors. This view seems to question the Western notion of waking up, which is primarily focused on awareness of external factors (Schuyler et al., 2017).

Another quotation from the same research indicates the significance of an individual letting go of their negative emotions, once they are aware of them, in a competitive business environment, to maintain their team's wellbeing (Marques, 2010).

> It's not unusual for the business and I am speaking of the Wall Street business force to have competition and antagonism going between departments, specifically between sales and trading yelling, screaming, just a lot of emotional outbursts and that type of stuff there's very little of that here. I just won't allow it. And it doesn't have that much to do with being a Buddhist. I just don't think it's a good environment, so I just don't tolerate it. It's not as if we never have it, and sometimes the situation is such that you let it pass.
>
> *(p. 220)*

Orange Electric Ltd. in Sri Lanka is one such organization that encourages its employees to practice insight meditation, as a method of developing equanimous individuals (Daily FT, 2014; Gunarathne, Peiris, Edirisooriya, & Jayasinghe, 2014; Kulamannage, 2015; Orange Electric, 2012). According to Orange Electric Ltd.'s website, they use insight meditation to assist individuals to dissolve impurities in their minds, and thereby create inner peace by sustaining awareness, non-delusion, and self-control. Meditation and yoga programs were introduced to Orange Electric Ltd. after its managing director, Kushan Kodituwakku, attended a silent vipassana meditation retreat around 2009 (Daily FT, 2014). Since then, the company has been offering an annual monetary incentive and paid leave to any of its employees who attend a ten-day vipassana meditation retreat. According to its finance manager, these meditation programs have a direct impact on the company's production process by making its employees efficient and effective (Gunarathne et al., 2014). Moreover, the meditation and yoga programs were used to promote work–life balance in the organization (Daily FT, 2014).

Another organization in Sri Lanka that incorporates vipassana meditation as an organizational strategy to enhance employee wellbeing is the Sri Lankan Army (Daily News, 2014; Sri Lanka Army, 2014). After the civil war of 30 years ended in 2009, the Sri Lankan Army was challenged with enhancing employees' psychological wellbeing as they suffered from post-combat fatigue, combat neurosis, depression, and mental restlessness (Sri Lanka Army, 2014). According to the Sri Lankan Army website, as of 2014, 31 one-day meditation sessions were held for 2,253 officers, and 21 ten-day meditation retreats were held for 210 officers, including those from the Navy and the Sri Lankan Air Force (Sri Lanka Army, 2014). These meditation programs are still being conducted for their employees to date.

Implications for management

In behavioral ethics management scholarship, EDM is either non-cognitive (Aquino & Reed, 2002; Elfenbein, 2008; Gaudine & Thorne, 2001; Haidt, 2001; Reynolds, 2006; Soneshein, 2007; Weaver, Reynolds, & Brown, 2014; Weick, 1995), cognitive (Jones, 1991; Rest, 1986; Treviño, 1986), or an integration of both cognitive and non-cognitive (Schwartz, 2016). However, EDM in Buddhism consists of two elements. First, it must be free from anger, fear, ill-will, and partiality (Narada, 1996). Second, the consequences of such a decision must be beneficial to both self and others (Premasiri, 1990). For example, the divine states (i.e., loving-kindness, compassion, sympathetic-joy, and equanimity) in Buddhism prescribe how to overcome negative emotions such as anger, fear, and envy through cultivation of loving-kindness, compassion, sympathetic-joy, and equanimity (Nyanaponika Thera, 1958; Tevijja Sutta, DN 13; Wallis, 2011) through meditation. Since they are considered Buddhist virtues (Pace, 2013) that enable individuals to cultivate God-like qualities, they may have an influence on EDM in organizations (Jayawardena-Willis, et al., 2019).

Awakening in Buddhism arises as an individual realizes reality as it is through awareness and insight while maintaining perfect equilibrium in their mind. This helps an individual to see the interconnectedness of all, and realize their role is to protect and be responsible, not only for themselves, but also for others in an organization. For example, when an individual starts to cultivate love, compassion, sympathetic-joy, and equanimity towards themselves and others, they may develop altruism. This practice enables an individual to open their heart to the suffering of others by generating love and compassion and taking joy at another's success through sympathetic-joy and equanimity. Consequently, awakening through insight may lead to a reduction in narcissism (Rijsenbilt & Commandeur, 2013) and envy (Kwon, Han, & Nam, 2017) and thereby happiness in organizations.

Insight is a spiritual faculty (Weick & Putnam, 2006) that can be developed through Buddhist meditation. This spiritual faculty seems to go beyond Aristotle's practical wisdom (Zhu, 2015), which is an intellectual virtue that enables an individual to practically reason the ethicality of their decision. In contrast, Buddhist meditation is an experiential wisdom that is founded on Buddhist ethics and mental discipline. Hence, if an individual develops insight-wisdom, they may be less likely to engage in lying, cheating, or harassment in organizations.

Moreover, while research on loving-kindness meditation indicates how it may result in reduction of anxiety, anger, and depression (Garrison, Scheinost, Constable, & Brewer, 2014), research on the impact of insight meditation has indicated a link between workplace spirituality and work performance (Petchsawang & Duchon, 2012), personal and professional excellence (Marques, 2008), and happiness among health care workers in Sri Lanka (Gunathunga, 2016). In addition, research also suggests that when individuals consider "what could I do?" in an ethical dilemma, this leads them to develop moral insight (Zhang, Gino, & Margolis, 2018), which is a deviation from the traditional view of "what should I do?" in ethical leadership (Brown & Treviño, 2006). In Buddhism, when an individual sees reality as it is with an objective equanimous mind, they learn not to react to pleasant or unpleasant sensations with craving or aversion respectively. This insight may lead to an individual's happiness (Brahm, 2013; Rahula, 1978). However, little is known of to what extent right mindfulness and/or insight impact on employee wellbeing (Fernando & Chowdhury, 2010) and thereby economic performance (Kumarasinghe & Hoshino, 2010). Hence, future research may investigate this relationship using quantitative methods, such as surveys and/or experiments.

Conclusion

In this chapter we highlighted the distinction between mindfulness in the West and right mindfulness and insight in Buddhism. Right mindfulness in Buddhism is founded on Buddhist ethics and it lays the mental foundation to proceed to wisdom. Insight is the ability of an individual to see things as they truly are: absence of beauty, unsatisfactoriness, impermanence, and absence of self. Hence, in this chapter we argued that insight may enable an individual to make ethical decisions and be happy in organizations.

Five takeaways

1. Buddhist ethics (*sila*) are the foundation for meditation practice.
2. There are two types of Buddhist meditation: *samatha* (concentration) and *vipassana* (insight).
3. While concentration meditation enables mastery of one's mind, insight meditation helps one to see things as they truly are.
4. Insight is cultivated by observing suffering, impermanence, and non-self while maintaining a balanced or equanimous mind.
5. Managers' ability to see things as they are assists them to make ethical decisions in organizations and thereby contributes to happiness in the workplace.

Five reflection questions

1. How do Buddhist ethics enhance right mindfulness?
2. What is the distinction between concentration and insight meditation in Buddhism?
3. What does happiness mean in Buddhism?
4. How does managers' insight influence their ethical decision-making?
5. How does managers' ethical decision-making impact on happiness in the workplace?

Note

1 An earlier version of this chapter was presented at the meeting of the 10th Asia Pacific Symposium on Emotions in Work life, in Queenstown, New Zealand in December 2015, for which the primary author received a doctoral student travel scholarship.

References

Anderson, C. S. (2001). *Pain and its ending: The four noble truths in the Theravada Buddhist canon*. Delhi: Motilal Banarsidass Publishers Private Limited.

Aquino, K., & Reed, A. (2002). The self-importance of moral identity. *Journal of Personality and Social Psychology, 83*(6), 1423–1440. doi:10.1037//0022-3514.83.6.1423

Bhikkhu, A. (2010). *Satipaṭṭhāna: The direct path to realization*. Kandy: Buddhist Publication Society.

Bouckaert, L., & Zsolnai, L. (2012). Spirituality and business: An interdisciplinary overview. *Society and Economy, 34*(3), 489–514. doi:10.1556/SocEc.34.2012.3.8

Brahm, A. (2013). *Good? bad? who knows?* Sri Lanka: Ajahn Brahm Society.

Brazier, C. (2003). *Buddhist psychology: Liberate your mind, embrace life*. London, UK: Robinson.

Brown, K. W., & Ryan, R. M. (2003). The benefits of being present: Mindfulness and its role in psychological well-being. *Journal of Personality and Social Psychology, 84*(4), 822–848.

Brown, M. E., & Treviño, L. K. (2006). Ethical leadership: A review and future directions. *The Leadership Quarterly, 17*, 595–616.

Chapman-Clarke, M. (2017). Why mindfulness at work matters – The 'reboot' for emotional intelligence development. *Development and Learning in Organizations: An International Journal, 31*(2), 1–4. doi:10.1108/DLO-10-2016-0097

Collins, D. (2010). Designing ethical organizations for spiritual growth and superior performance: An organization systems approach. *Journal of Management, Spirituality & Religion*, 7(2), 95–117. doi:10.1080/14766081003746414

Daily, F. T. (2014, April 21). *Orange sheds new light on 'work life balance'*. Retrieved August 12, 2015, from www.ft.lk/article/282430/Orange-sheds-new-light-on-%E2%80%98Work-life-Balance%E2%80%99

Daily News. (2014). *Lankan armed forces personnel highly disciplined - Army chief*. Retrieved from www.dailynews.lk/?q=police-legal/lankan-armed-forces-personnel-highly-disciplined-army-chief

Dhammaratana, U. (2011). *Guide through the Visuddhimagga*. Kandy, Sri Lanka: Buddhist Publication Society.

Dhiman, S. (2008). Cultivating mindfulness: The Buddhist art of paying attention to attention. *Interbeing, 2*(2), 35–52.

Dhiman, S. (2009). Mindfulness in life and leadership: An exploratory survey. *Interbeing, 3*(1), 55–80.

Donaldson-Feilder, E., Lewis, R., & Yarker, J. (2019). What outcomes have mindfulness and meditation interventions for managers and leaders achieved? A systematic review. *European Journal of Work and Organizational Psychology, 28*(1), 11–29. doi:10.1080/1359432X.2018.1542379

Elfenbein, H. A. (2008). Emotions in organizations. *The Academy of Management Annals, 1*(1), 315–386. doi:10.1080/078559812

Ermongkonchai, P. (2010). Managerial perceptions on employee misconduct and ethics management strategies in Thai organizations. *International Journal of Business and Management, 5*(8), 124–137.

Fernando, M., & Chowdhury, R. M. (2010). The relationship between spiritual well-being and ethical orientations in decision making: An empirical study with business executives in Australia. *Journal of Business Ethics, 95*(2), 211–225. doi:10.1007/s10551-009-0355-y

Fernando, M., & Jackson, B. (2006). The influence of religion-based workplace spirituality on business leaders' decision-making: An inter-faith study. *Journal of Management and Organization, 12*(1), 23–39. doi:10.1017/S1833367200004144

Forge, P. G. L. (1997). Teaching business ethics through meditation. *Journal of Business Ethics, 16*, 1283–1295.

Fredrickson, B. L. (2001). The role of positive emotions in positive psychology: The broaden-and-build theory of positive emotions. *American Psychologist, 56*(3), 218–226. doi:10.1037%2F0003-066X.56.3.218

Fredrickson, B. L., Cohn, M. A., Coffey, K. A., Pek, J., & Finkel, S. M. (2008). Open hearts build lives: Positive emotions, induced through loving-kindness meditation, build consequential personal resources. *Journal of Personality and Social Psychology, 95*(5), 1045–1062. doi:10.1037/a0013262

Galmangoda, S. (2008). *Reality: The abhidhammic analysis*. Divulapitiya: Sri Lanka: Saraswathi Publications.

Garrison, K. A., Scheinost, D., Constable, R. T., & Brewer, J. A. (2014). BOLD signal and functional connectivity associated with loving-kindness meditation. *Brain and Behavior, 4*(3), 337–347. doi:10.1002/brb3.219

Gaudine, A., & Thorne, L. (2001). Emotion and ethical decision-making in organizations. *Journal of Business Ethics, 31*(2), 175–187. doi:10.1023/A:1010711413444

Gethin, R. (2004). Wrong view (miccha-di hi) and right view (samma-di hi) in the Theravada abhidhamma. *Contemporary Buddhism: An Interdisciplinary Journal, 5*(1), 15–28.

Goenka, S. N. (1999). *Discourses on Satipatthana sutta*. Dhamma Giri, Igatpuri: Vipassana Research Institute.

Gould, S. J. (1995). The Buddhist perspective on business ethics: Experiential exercises for exploration and practice. *Journal of Business Ethics, 14*, 63–70. doi:10.1007/BF00873737

Gowans, C. W. (2013). Ethical thought in Indian Buddhism. In S. M. Emmanuel (Ed.), *A companion to Buddhist philosophy* (pp. 429–451). Hoboken: John Wiley & Sons, Inc.

Gunathunga, M.W. (2016). Improving performance and happiness among healthcare workers through a body-mind approach in a healthcare setting in Sri Lanka. *Work*, 55, 305–309. doi:10.3233/WOR-162395

Gunarathne, A. D. N., Peiris, S., Edirisooriya, K., & Jayasinghe, R. (2014). *Environmental management accounting in Sri Lankan enterprises*. Sri Lanka: Department of Accounting, University of Sri Jayewardenepura. Retrieved from www.academia.edu/11548473/Environmental_Management_Accounting_in_Sri_Lankan_Enterprises

Haidt, J. (2001). The emotional dog and its rational tail: A social intuitionist approach to moral judgment. *Personal Review, 108*(4), 814–834. doi:10.1037%2F0033-295X.108.4.814

Hart, W. (1987). *The art of living: Vipassana meditation as taught by S.N. Goenka*. San Francisco: Harper & Row.

Hill, J. S. (2007). Religion and the shaping of East Asian management styles: A conceptual examination. *Journal of Asia-Pacific Business, 8*(2), 59–88.

Jayawardena-Willis, T. S., Pio, E., & McGhee, P. (2019). The divine states (brahmaviharas) in managerial ethical decision-making in organisations in Sri Lanka: An interpretative phenomenological analysis. *Journal of Business Ethics*. doi:10.1007/s10551-019-04240-6

Jones, T. M. (1991). Ethical decision making by individuals in organizations: An issue-contingent model. *Academy of Management Review, 16*(2), 366–395. doi:10.2307/258867

Kabat-Zinn, J. (1994). *Wherever you go, there you are*. New York: Hyperion.

Kalupahana, D. J. (1976). *Buddhist philosophy: A historical analysis*. Honolulu, Hawaii: The University Press of Hawaii.

Kauanui, S. K., Thomas, K. D., Sherman, C. L., Waters, G. R., & Gilea, M. (2010). An exploration of entrepreneurship and play. *Journal of Organizational Change Management & Marketing, 23*(1), 51–70.

Khisty, C. J. (2010). The practice of mindfulness for managers in the marketplace. *Systemic Practice and Action Research, 23*(2), 115–125. doi:10.1007/s11213-009-9151-y

Kligyte, V., Connelly, S., Thiel, C., & Devenport, L. (2013). The influence of anger, fear, and emotion regulation on ethical decision making. *Human Performance, 26*(4), 297–326. doi:10.1080/08959285.2013.814655

Krishnakumar, S., & Rymph, D. (2012). Uncomfortable ethical decisions: The role of negative emotions and emotional intelligence in ethical decision-making. *Journal of Managerial Issues, 24*(3), 321–344. doi:10.1108/JMD-02-2018-0045

Kulamannage, S. (2015). *How I did it Kushan Kodituwakku*. Retrieved August 12, 2015, from www.echelon.lk/ipg/how-i-did-it-kushan-kodituwakku/

Kumarasinghe, S., & Hoshino, Y. (2010). The role and perceptions of middle managers and their influence on business performance: The case of Sri Lanka. *International Business Research*, *3*(4), 3–16. doi:10.5539/ibr.v3n4p3

Kwon, M., Han, Y., & Nam, M. (2017). Envy takes you further: The influence of benign envy on risk taking. *Social Behavior and Personality*, *45*(1), 39–50. doi:10.2224/sbp.5977

Marques, J. (2008). Spirituality at work: Internal growth with potential external challenges. *The Journal for Quality and Participation*, *31*(3), 24–27.

Marques, J. (2009). Is there a place for Buddhism in the workplace? Experiential sharing from three Buddhist business leaders. *Journal of Global Business Issues*, *3*(1), 51–59.

Marques, J. (2010). Toward greater consciousness in the 21st century workplace: How Buddhist practices fit in. *Journal of Business Ethics*, *92*, 211–223. doi:10.1007/s10551-009-0150-9

Marques, J. (2011). Buddhism in the United States: Implications for managers of Buddhist values in the workplace. *International Journal of Management*, *28*(2), 564–572.

Marques, J. (2012a). Consciousness at work: A review of some important values, discussed from a Buddhist perspective. *Journal of Business Ethics*, *105*, 27–40. doi:10.1007/s10551-011-0932-8

Marques, J. (2012b). Making Buddhism work @ work: The transformation of a religion into a seasoned ethical system. *Journal of Management Development*, *31*(6), 537–549. doi:10.1108/02621711211230849

Marques, J., & Dhiman, S. (2009). Vipassana meditation as a path toward improved management practices. *Journal of Global Business Issues*, *3*(2), 77–84.

Marques, J., Dhiman, S. K., & Biberman, J. (2014). Teaching the un-teachable: Storytelling and meditation in workplace spirituality courses. *Journal of Management Development*, *33*(3), 196–217. doi:10.1108/JMD-10-2011-0106

Narada. (1996). Sigalovada sutta: The discourse to sigala (The layperson's code of discipline).

Narada. (1998). *The Buddha and his teachings*. Taipei, Taiwan: The Corporate Body of the Buddha Educational Foundation.

Orange Electric. (2012). *About us*. Retrieved September 19, 2014, from http://orelcorporation.com/index.php/about-us-2

Pace, S. (2013). Does religion affect the materialism of consumers? An empirical investigation of Buddhist ethics and the resistance of the self. *Journal of Business Ethics*, *112*(1), 25–46. doi:10.1007/s10551-012-1228-3

Pang, D., & Ruch, W. (2019). Scrutinizing the components of mindfulness: Insights from current, past, and non-meditators. *Mindfulness*, *10*, 492–505. doi:10.1007/s12671-018-0990-4

Passmore, J. (2019). Mindfulness in organizations (part 1): A critical literature review. *Industrial and Commercial Training*, *51*(2), 104–113. doi:10.1108/ICT-07-2018-0063

Pérez-Remón, J. (1980). *Self and non-self in early Buddhism*. Great Britain: Mouton Publishers.

Petchsawang, P., & Duchon, D. (2012). Workplace spirituality, meditation, and work performance. *Journal of Management, Spirituality & Religion*, *9*(2), 189–208. doi:10.1080/14766086.2012.688623

Petchsawang, P., & McLean, G. N. (2017). Workplace spirituality, mindfulness meditation, and work engagement. *Journal of Management, Spirituality*, *14*(3), 216–244. doi:10.1080/14766086.2017.1291360

Pio, E. (1988). *Buddhist psychology: A modern perspective*. New Delhi: India: Abhinav Publications.

Premasiri, P. D. (1990). Ethics. In G. P. Malalasekera & W. G. Weeraratne (Eds.), *Encyclopaedia of Buddhism* (Vol. *V*, pp. 144–165). Sri Lanka: State Printing Corporation.

Purser, R. E., & Milillo, J. (2015). Mindfulness revisited: A Buddhist-based conceptualization. *Journal of Management Inquiry*, *24*(1), 3–24. doi:10.1177/1056492614532315

Rahula, W. S. (1978). *What the Buddha taught*. (Reprinted from 2006). Colombo: Sri Lanka: Buddhist Cultural Centre.

Reb, J., Narayanan, J., & Chaturvedi, S. (2014). Leading mindfully: Two studies on the influence of supervisor trait mindfulness on employee well-being and performance. *Mindfulness*, *5*, 36–45. doi:10.1007/s12671-012-0144-z

Rees, B., & Agocs, T. (2011). The application of Buddhist theory and practice in modern organizations. In L. Zsolnai (Ed.), *Ethical principles and economic transformation - A Buddhist approach* (pp. 155–165). New York: Springer.

Rest, J. R. (1986). *Moral development advances in research and theory*. NY: Praeger Publishers.

Reynolds, S. J. (2006). A neurocognitive model of the ethical decision-making process: Implications for study and practice. *Journal of Applied Psychology*, *91*(4), 737–748. doi:10.1037/0021-9010.91.4.737

Rhys Davids, T. W. (1900). Buddhism. *The North American Review, 171*(527), 517–527.

Rijsenbilt, A., & Commandeur, H. (2013). Narcissus enters the courtroom: CEO narcissism and fraud. *Journal of Business Ethics, 117*, 413–429.

Ruedy, N. E., & Schweitzer, M. E. (2010). In the moment: The effect of mindfulness on ethical decision making. *Journal of Business Ethics, 95*, 73–87. doi:10.1007/s10551-011-0796-y

Saddhatissa, H. (2003). *Buddhist ethics* (3rd ed.). Boston: Wisdom Publications.

Schultz, P. P., Ryan, R. M., Niemiec, C. P., Legate, N., & Williams, G. C. (2015). Mindfulness, work climate, and psychological need satisfaction in employee well-being. *Mindfulness, 6*, 971–985. doi:10.1007/s12671-014-0338-7

Schuyler, K. G., Skjei, S., Sanzgiri, J., & Koskela, V. (2017). "Moments of waking up": A doorway to mindfulness and presence. *Journal of Management Inquiry, 26*(1), 86–100.

Schwartz, M. (2016). Ethical decision-making theory: An integrated approach. *Journal of Business Ethics, 139*(4), 755–776. doi:10.1007/s10551-015-2886-8

Skilton, A. (2013). Theravada. In S. M. Emmanuel (Ed.), *A companion to Buddhist philosophy* (1st ed., pp. 71–85). Hoboken: John Wiley & Sons, Inc.

Soneshein, S. (2007). The role of construction, intuition, and justification in responding to ethical issues at work: The sensemaking-intuition model. *The Academy of Management Review, 32*(4), 1022–1040. doi:10.2307/20159354

Sri Lanka Army. (2014). *Servicemen to undergo meditation for spiritual development in new complex*. Retrieved 12 August, 2015, from www.army.lk/detailed.php?NewsId=8076

Sutta, T. (DN 13). Tevijja sutta (on the knowledge of the vedas). Retrieved October 09, 2014, from www.metta.lk/tipitaka/2Sutta-Pitaka/1Digha-Nikaya/Digha1/13-tevijja-e.html

Tang, T. L. P., & Chiu, R. K. (2003). Income, money ethic, pay satisfaction, commitment, and unethical behavior: Is the love of money the root of evil for Hong Kong employees? *Journal of Business Ethics, 46*(1), 13–30.

Thera, N. (1958). *The four sublime states: Contemplations of love, compassion, sympathetic-joy, and equanimity*. (Reprinted from 2013). Kandy: Sri Lanka: Buddhist Publication Society.

Thiel, C. E., Connelly, S., & Griffith, J. A. (2011). The influence of anger on ethical decision making: Comparison of a primary and secondary appraisal. *Ethics & Behavior, 21*(5), 380–403. doi:10.1080/10508422.2011.604295

Treviño, L. K. (1986). Ethical decision making in organizations: A person-situation interactionist model. *The Academy of Management Review, 11*(3), 601–617. doi:10.2307/258313

Vadera, A. K., & Pratt, M. G. (2013). Love, hate, ambivalence, or indifference? A conceptual examination of workplace crimes and organizational identification. *Organization Science, 24*(1), 172–188.

Vogus, T. J., Rothman, N. B., Sutcliffe, K. M., & Weick, K. E. (2014). The affective foundations of high-reliability organizing. *Journal of Organizational Behavior, 35*, 592–596.

Vogus, T. J., & Sutcliffe, K. M. (2012). Organizational mindfulness and mindful organizing: A reconciliation and path forward. *Academy of Management Learning & Education, 11*(4), 722–735.

Wallis, G. (2011). The Buddha counsels a theist: A reading of the Tevijja sutta (Dighanikaya 13). *Religion, 38*(1), 54–67.

Wang, L., & Murnighan, J. K. (2011). On greed. *The Academy of Management Annals, 5*(1), 279–316.

Weaver, G. R., Reynolds, S. J., & Brown, M. E. (2014). Moral intuition: Connecting current knowledge to future organizational research and practice. *Journal of Management, 40*(1), 100–129. doi:10.1177/0149206313511272

Weick, K. E. (1995). *Sensemaking in organizations*. Thousand Oaks: Sage Publications.

Weick, K. E., & Putnam, T. (2006). Organizing for mindfulness: Eastern wisdom and Western knowledge. *Journal of Management Inquiry, 15*(3), 275–287. doi:10.1177/1056492606291202

Whitehead, R., Bates, G., Elphinstone, B., Yang, Y., & Murray, G. (2018). Non attachment mediates the relationship between mindfulness and psychological well-being, subjective well-being, and depression, anxiety and stress. *Journal of Happiness Studies*, 1–18. doi:10.1007/s10902-018-0041-9

Zhang, T., Gino, F., & Margolis, J. D. (2018). Does "could" lead to good? On the road to moral insight. *Academy of Management Journal, 61*(3), 857–895. doi:doi.org/10.5465/amj.2014.0839

Zhu, Y. (2015). The role of qing (positive emotions) and li (rationality) in Chinese entrepreneurial decision making: A Confucian ren-yi wisdom perspective. *Journal of Business Ethics, 126*(4), 613–630. doi:10.1007/s10551-013-1970-1

PART IV

Mindfulness-based learning and interventions

17

ENHANCING WORKPLACE LEARNING THROUGH MINDFULNESS

Matthew D. Hanson, Jason G. Randall, Gabrielle C. Danna, and Huy Q. Le

Learning on the job is a foundational cog in the organizational machine that directly contributes to the success of an organization (Arthur, Bennett, Edens, & Bell, 2003; Yang, 2007). Workplace learning can take many forms, including formal, guided instruction, as well as more informal learning opportunities, such as when ideas are shared between co-workers (Park & Choi, 2016). In order to properly develop and utilize a highly skilled workforce, it is important for organizations to invest time and resources to ensure that employees are learning as efficiently and effectively as possible in both formal and informal learning environments. However, organizations are likely to face several learning-related challenges in the workplace, which include difficulties in establishing the infrastructure and a social climate to promote a learning culture, getting and maintaining employees' attention, attenuating negative affect that arises during learning, and providing support and opportunities for employees to develop and transfer new learning on the job. In this chapter, we make the argument that mindfulness may be one key tool through which these challenges to workplace learning may be addressed.

The phenomenal manifestation of mindfulness in people involves the skill or ability to allocate more or less resource to internal and external stimuli and, as such, is directly related to self-regulation of attention (Burg, Wolf, & Michalak, 2012), motivation (Leyland, Rowse, & Emerson, 2019), and emotion (Friese & Hofmann, 2016). Mindfulness has traditionally been defined as "paying attention in the present moment with awareness and nonjudgment" (Bravo, Pearson, Wilson, & Witkiewitz, 2018, p. 199). Although metacognition—cognition about cognition (Veenman,Van Hout-Wolters, & Afflerbach, 2006)—is theoretically similar to mindfulness, metacognition is considered to be a constituent of mindfulness that captures its attentional and emotional control aspects but falls short of capturing its present-moment experience and acceptance aspects (Solem, Thunes, Hjemdal, Hagen, & Wells, 2015). When it comes to discussing the role that mindfulness plays in learning, two relatively divergent paths have evolved. Down the first path, mindful learning is conceptualized as a union between the traditional definitions of both mindfulness and learning. Therefore, mindful learning under this conceptualization is defined as "any effort toward learning that is characterized by present-moment awareness and nonjudgmental acceptance in support of cognitive, motivational, and emotional learning processes and outcomes" (Randall, Zajac, & Hanson, 2019, p. 8). This involves utilizing the core dimensions of mindfulness (e.g., awareness, nonjudgment) to support and direct the core cognitive, motivational, and emotional processes involved in learning. We will refer to this conceptualization of mindful learning as the additive approach.

Down the second path, mindful learning is conceptualized as a distinct form of learning that is categorically different from other, more traditional forms of learning. Specifically, mindful learning under this conceptualization is defined as "a flexible state of mind in which we are actively engaged in the present, noticing new things, and sensitive to context" (Langer, 2000, p. 220). Although there are aspects of this conceptualization of mindful learning that are similar to the traditional definition of mindfulness (e.g., a focus on the present), the overall theme of this conceptualization is a more open and deep consideration of learned information. For instance, while a traditional classroom full of students may be taught that water comprises two atoms of hydrogen and one atom of oxygen, a classroom that is practicing this conceptualization of mindful learning might be taught to consider instances where water could comprise different atoms and how that may be advantageous and disadvantageous. We will refer to this conceptualization of mindful learning as the derived approach.

Mindfulness as a construct can take on one of three different forms, including a state, a trait, or a practice (Jamieson & Tuckey, 2017). As a state, people's level of mindfulness is flexible and can change within person across time. As such, state mindfulness is defined as the extent to which one is currently "attentive to and aware of what is taking place in the present" (Brown & Ryan, 2003, p. 822). Although people's state level of mindfulness can fluctuate across time, their overall trait level of mindfulness tends to remain rather stable. Indeed, trait mindfulness is defined as "the tendency to be mindful" (Mesmer-Magnus, Manapragada, Viswesvaran, & Allen, 2017, p. 91). Finally, as a practice, mindfulness is a skill that can be trained and honed. A mindfulness practice is a "mechanism directed at enhancing one's state mindfulness and subsequently trait mindfulness, which can be cultivated through mindfulness-based interventions" (Jamieson & Tuckey, 2017, p. 180). It is important to note the difference between state mindfulness and practicing mindfulness, because increasing state mindfulness should not be conflated with actively practicing mindfulness. Instead, state mindfulness simply refers to the extent to which someone is currently paying attention to and is aware of the present moment. Although practicing mindfulness contributes to increased state mindfulness, and frequently increasing state mindfulness contributes to increased trait mindfulness, state mindfulness can be increased from external sources without an individual actually engaging in formal mindfulness practice (Kiken, Garland, Bluth, Palsson, & Gaylord, 2015). For instance, although mindfulness meditation is a mindfulness practice that increases state mindfulness, daily state mindfulness can also be increased by providing employees with more daily job control (Lawrie, Tuckey, & Dollard, 2018), which is not considered a practice. Therefore, state mindfulness may be fostered in different ways, with some requiring more cognitive resources, such as through mindfulness practices, and others not requiring any cognitive resources, such as through job design or organizational procedures that encourage present-moment awareness and nonjudgmental acceptance.

In this chapter, we will draw from both conceptualizations of mindfulness (i.e., the additive approach and the derived approach) and the three forms of mindfulness (i.e., as a state, trait, or practice) to demonstrate how mindfulness can help organizations address the modern-day challenges to workplace learning. Since our recommendations address workplace challenges, we will mostly focus on increasing state mindfulness through external means (e.g., work design, supervisor support, training delivery methods) to influence learning, although some recommendations will also involve the direct practice of mindfulness. We will first discuss how workplace learning can be structured, the process of learning, and important outcomes of learning. Next, we will cover five common learning-related challenges that organizations are likely to face, and then we will draw on theoretical perspectives and empirical research to recommend ways in which mindfulness can address each challenge. These challenges and recommendations involve (1) creating sufficient infrastructure for learning, (2) creating a social climate for learning, (3) designing and delivering training in ways that promote attentional focus, (4) using mindfulness to buffer negative emotions that may accompany learning efforts, and (5) relying on mindfulness as a tool to transfer or apply learning to the job. Furthermore, these recommendations will include actionable steps that organizations or individuals can take to capitalize on the benefits of mindfulness as a tool to improve valuable learning outcomes. Finally, we will cover future directions that organizations, individuals, and researchers can advance toward to continue exploring the benefits of mindful workplace learning.

Workplace learning

Learning—a relatively stable change in knowledge, skills, and attitudes—is an essential part of the workplace because it equips individuals, teams, and companies with an avenue to succeed (Kraiger, Ford, & Salas, 1993). This is part of the reason that organizations invest billions in training and development every year (ATD, 2017). Workplace training efforts aim to develop individuals, groups, and organizations and do so, in part, by creating an environment where learning is recognized as important for competition and growth (Salas, Tannenbaum, Kraiger, & Smith-Jentsch, 2012). This can occur top–down from organizational leaders who recognize errors or deficiencies and design training to remedy them, or bottom–up, where individuals or teams notice their own weaknesses and take steps to correct them.

These different routes to workplace learning (i.e., top–down and bottom–up) mirror a broad distinction between learning efforts as either formal or informal. Formal learning is structured, time-bound, and guided by an instructor or other source, and it has clearly defined objectives. By contrast, informal learning is predominantly self-directed, occurs in an unstructured environment, has no predetermined start and end time, and allows for some level of reflection and development (Cerasoli et al., 2017). Although the majority of research on workplace learning has focused on formal learning, the majority of workplace learning actually occurs in informal settings (Cerasoli et al., 2017). Thus, in this chapter we emphasize both formal and informal learning efforts, as both are important for individual and organizational success.

Foundationally, learning is a multidimensional process with multidimensional outcomes. As a multidimensional process, learning involves the self-regulation of cognitive, motivational, and emotional resources to obtain a learning goal (Sitzmann & Ely, 2011). The cognitive dimension of the learning process is well researched and psychologists have identified three steps to this process (Clark & Mayer, 2003). The first step involves the selection and attention to relevant material; the second step involves the coherent mental organization of material; and the third step involves the integration of new material with existing knowledge. Motivational and emotional dimensions of learning support this core cognitive process by influencing the degree to which learners *want* to engage in learning, feel confident in their ability to learn (i.e., self-efficacy), and the extent to which they are emotionally equipped to handle the challenges, such as boredom and frustration, that often accompany learning (Beier & Kanfer, 2010; Kanfer & Heggestad, 1997; Simons & de Jong,

1992). Thus, effective workplace learning will enlist cognitive, motivational, and emotional processing in pursuit of a learning goal.

There are also multidimensional outcomes of workplace learning because learning manifests in different ways. Some of the most well-recognized learning outcomes include the acquisition of knowledge (e.g., score on a multiple-choice test at the end of a class), a demonstration of behavior or skill (e.g., performance on a driving test), a change in attitude (e.g., attitudes toward diversity following diversity training), reactions to training (e.g., learners see training as enjoyable and/or useful), and self-efficacy (e.g., whether learners feel confident in their ability to use learning in the future; Alliger, Tannenbaum, Bennett, Traver, & Shotland, 1997; Kirkpatrick, 1967; Kraiger et al., 1993). Researchers and professionals also recognize the importance of training transfer, or the generalization of learning from one domain to another and the maintenance of learning over time (Blume, Ford, Baldwin, & Huang, 2010). Transfer represents the importance of flexibly applying learning to new tasks and domains in order to persistently influence job performance over time, as failing to do so means that learning is essentially squandered (Desse, 1958).

This brief synopsis of why workplace learning is important, what it looks like, and how it is evaluated provides several key points. First, individuals and organizations that continuously learn are best positioned for growth and success. Second, learning occurs in formal training environments and informal on-the-job settings as employees engage in unstructured, self-directed learning. Third, learning is a well-understood cognitive process that is supported by equally important motivational and emotional processes. Fourth, learning can be demonstrated in various ways—knowledge and skill acquisition, attitude change and reactions, and the important transfer of learning to the job. However, despite these key points about the importance and function of learning, there are also several common challenges that individuals and organizations face when trying to create a culture of continuous learning. In the sections below, we introduce five key challenges to workplace learning and demonstrate how mindfulness may be utilized to effectively address these challenges in order to capitalize on the benefits of workplace learning. Each section is structured so that we: (a) introduce the challenge to learning, (b) present relevant theoretical and empirical evidence concerning how mindfulness may be drawn on to address the particular challenge, and (c) recommend how to incorporate mindfulness into workplace learning efforts in order to address each challenge.

Challenge one: creating sufficient infrastructure for learning

What is the challenge?

Organizations that endeavor to remain competitive in the modern industry landscape face myriad challenges, including those brought on by climate change, income inequality, lack of education, and a burgeoning world market that is transforming from one focused on manufacturing into one in which the focus is largely on knowledge creation and management (Gould, 2009; Kirby, Knapper, Evans, Carty, & Gadula, 2003; Siebenhüner & Arnold, 2007). To address these challenges, organizations must implement sustainable development practices (Siebenhüner & Arnold, 2007), which requires that the conventional operations of organizations become flexible enough to adapt. Such adaptations necessitate incorporating learning mechanisms into the infrastructure of organizations to encourage a diffuse learning culture that fosters employees' capacity to continually learn and develop (Kirby et al., 2003; Siebenhüner & Arnold, 2007). Indeed, although learning is an everyday occurrence in the workplace (Döös, 2007), successful organizations should intentionally transform into learning organizations (Gould, 2009) by implementing formal systems and procedures that enable continuous learning and development (Kluge & Schilling, 2003). To better understand the challenges associated with enabling continuous learning and development, we must first delineate between the environmental factors that contribute to workplace learning.

Workplace learning is a process that occurs at the intersection between the technical-organizational learning environment, the social-cultural learning environment, and the employees' learning process (Illeris, 2004). It is in the dynamic interaction between the learner and these workplace environments (i.e., the organizational and social environments) where learning occurs. The technical-organizational learning environment refers to the infrastructure of the workplace, such as the physical design of the workplace and workplace policies, including the autonomy that the infrastructure may afford and the stress that the infrastructure may illicit (Goldman, Plack, Roche, Smith, & Turley, 2009; Illeris, 2004). The social-cultural learning environment refers to the communities, cultures, and politics of work (Illeris, 2004). In this section, we focus on the challenges inherent to the infrastructure of the workplace that prevent learning; we discuss the challenges inherent to the communities, cultures, and the politics of work in the next section.

Therefore, one challenge that organizations face is how to adapt the infrastructure of their organizations toward those of a learning organization by implementing formal systems and procedures that foster a diffuse learning culture. What constitutes a learning culture, though? How does an organization know that they have what may be considered a learning culture? The answers to these questions are relatively unclear. Indeed, a learning culture is a theoretical concept that is vague and hard to operationally define (Kluge & Schilling, 2003). However, we argue that one way for organizations to move toward a learning culture is through the implementation of infrastructure that promotes employees' mindfulness.

How can mindfulness help?

Formal systems of procedures that lead to greater mindfulness may (1) preserve employees' attentional resources in the present moment and encourage nonjudgment, and (2) promote a flexible state of mind, which may allow employees to allocate more attentional resources in the present moment and be able to more deeply and openly consider information. Indeed, using formal systems to foster mindfulness incorporates the additive and derived approaches to mindful learning. First, by preserving employees' attentional resources in the present moment and encouraging nonjudgment, they will be better able to engage in cognitive, motivational, and emotional learning processes (Lawrie et al., 2018). Second, by preserving employees' attentional resources in the present moment and promoting a flexible state of mind, they may be better able to consider and notice new information (Greenberg, Reiner, & Meiran, 2012; Langer, 2000). Furthermore, as changes in infrastructure and work design do not constitute a mindfulness practice nor influence levels of mindfulness outside of work, implementing formal systems to foster mindfulness is expected to influence only state mindfulness. Additionally, since workplace infrastructure refers to the physical design of the workplace and workplace policies, it is expected to be influential for informal and formal learning. The argument that work may be redesigned to promote mindfulness, and that this could benefit workplace learning, also builds on Parker's (2014) recommendations that work should be redesigned in order to promote employee well-being and ambidexterity, and that such efforts are key for learning and development.

Recommendation one

The first recommendation that we propose is for organizations to *move toward a learning culture through the implementation of infrastructure that promotes employees' mindfulness by taking steps to increase their perceived autonomy and to provide time for reflection.* This recommendation constitutes a top–down method of increasing employees' state levels of mindfulness that may subsequently lead to greater self-regulation of cognitive and motivational resources, which may lead to more informal and formal learning on the job. Specifically, employers may increase employees' perceived autonomy by elevating the level of control that is given to their employees. According to the job demands-resources model (Dollard & Bakker, 2010), "job demands and job resources are the core aspects of jobs that affect employee health and well-being" (Lawrie et al., 2018, p. 485). Job demands, such as a fast-paced work environment, act as psychological stressors, which can deplete employees' energy (Bakker & Demerouti, 2007). Job resources, such as job control, help drive employees' motivation by providing them with the ability to perform their skills and manage their time, which can protect them from job strain (Bakker & Demerouti, 2007). Job demands, although necessary for an organization to function, may also decrease mindfulness in the workplace. Specifically, greater strain makes it more difficult for employees to maintain their attention in the present moment, on the task at hand, and to maintain a flexible perspective. Job control acts as a buffer against these negative outcomes. By providing employees with more control over their time and effort, they are able to dedicate more attention to the task and maintain a more open awareness. One step that organizations can take to accomplish this is to begin encouraging their employees to manage and organize how their jobs are done, including the process and timing, and to consider ways in which it can be done more efficiently. Organizations may even allow employees to learn more about the positions that are lateral to their own to allow for an even deeper understanding of how and why their tasks are important, and how their tasks influence those further down the line.

Likewise, organizations can move toward a learning culture through the implementation of infrastructure that promotes employees' mindfulness by allowing time for and otherwise promoting reflection throughout the workday. Reflection may constitute a practice through which employees bring their attentional resources to their inner experience, but it is not considered a mindfulness practice, as reflecting on what occurred in the past is not mindfulness. It may still lead to increases in state mindfulness, however, as employees who reflect on their past experiences learn to regulate their own attentional resources toward a volitionally chosen experience. Furthermore, as employees continue to reflect on their experiences at work, greater mindfulness may lead to greater concurrent reflection, meaning that the employees may begin to reflect on their experiences as they happen (Blanke, Schmidt, Mirjam, Riediger, & Brose, 2019). This increase in state mindfulness as employees reflect may ultimately lead to greater informal learning. As mentioned, most of what is learned on the job occurs informally rather than formally (Baer et al., 2008). Although informal learning may occur through experimentation, seeking new experiences, or observing others, informal learning may also occur while employees are debriefing about experiences encountered at work (Wolfson, Mathieu, Tannenbaum, & Maynard, 2019). One step that organizations can take to promote reflection is through the use of diaries to codify what was experienced throughout the day. Indeed, just taking 15 minutes at the end of the day to reflect on what was learned throughout the day leads to greater learning (Di Stefano, Gino, Pisano, & Staats, 2016).

Challenge two: creating a social climate for learning

What is the challenge?

Echoing the first challenge, organizations that strive to remain competitive in the modern industry landscape must promote a continuous learning culture (Kirby et al., 2003), which is indicative of a learning organization and is achieved through the implementation of formal systems and procedures (Kluge & Schilling, 2003). In addition to the infrastructure of the organization—the point of the previous section—organizations may also promote a continuous learning culture through the social-cultural learning environment, which refers to the communities, cultures, and politics of work (Illeris, 2004). Inherent in communities, cultures, and politics of work are supervisors and co-workers. Therefore, another challenge that organizations face is how to adapt the social culture of work, such as the interactions between employees and their leaders, toward one of a learning organization by implementing formal systems and procedures that foster a continuous learning culture. Although this may seem simple enough, a learning culture, diffuse or otherwise, is difficult to achieve due to the ambiguity surrounding this concept (Kluge & Schilling, 2003). We argue that one way for organizations to move toward a learning culture is through the implementation of formal systems and procedures that target the social culture of the workplace to promote employees' mindfulness.

How can mindfulness help?

Organizations that implement formal systems that target the social culture of the workplace to promote mindfulness may find that their employees are more comfortable with considering new information, trying new things, and seeking out more knowledge, which may ultimately result in a greater learning environment. Specifically, the derived approach of mindful learning states that mindful learning involves a flexible state of mind where one's attentional resources are engaged in the present moment. The overall theme of the derived approach suggests that mindful learning comprises a more fluid view of the world, which leads one to be more open to considering new information and considering old information in new ways (Langer, 2000). In order for employees to feel comfortable enough to learn and try new ways to perform a task, they must feel safe enough to understand that they have the support of their co-workers and supervisors. This comfort will subsequently lead to more experimentation and ultimately more informal learning (Cerasoli et al., 2017; Wolfson et al., 2019).

Additionally, considering the additive approach, when employees feel less judgmental toward their own thoughts and feelings, they may also be more willing to consider new ways of performing their task and learning from experience. Rather than ruminating on any negative affect that may arise from failure, they may also be more willing to take what they can learn from their experience and leave the negative affect behind, especially in challenging situations (Ding et al., 2019; Eisenlohr-Moul, Peters, Pond, DeWall, 2016; Svendsen, Kvernenes, Wiker, & Dundas, 2017). Furthermore, if they believe that others will be less judgmental and also open to trying new things, especially team members and leaders, they may also be more willing to try new things. Indeed, similar to job control, social support is considered a type of job resource (Bakker & Demerouti, 2007), which may allow employees to dedicate more attention to their tasks and maintain a more open awareness (Lawrie et al., 2018). Together, this suggests that taking a more nonjudgmental stance toward oneself and others, which is indicative of the additive approach, may lead one to feel more comfortable engaging in informal learning behaviors: considering new information, trying new things, and seeking out more knowledge at work.

Recommendation two

The second recommendation that we propose is for organizations to *move toward a learning culture through the cultivation of a social culture that promotes employees' mindfulness by taking steps to increase employees' level of comfort with considering new information, trying new things, and seeking out additional knowledge.* This recommendation constitutes a top–down and bottom–up method of increasing employees' state levels of mindfulness that may subsequently lead to greater self-regulation of cognitive, motivational, and emotional resources, which may result in more informal and formal learning on the job. Specifically, leaders and teams have the capacity to facilitate psychological safety, which is the "perception of the consequences of taking interpersonal risks in a particular context such as a workplace" (Edmondson & Lei, 2014, p. 24). Psychological safety is associated with myriad phenomenon in the workplace, but of interest in this chapter is its influence on learning and innovation in modern organizations (Edmondson & Lei, 2014).

Obviously, errors can be costly, but they are also a natural occurrence during learning and can be very informative. One way in which an organization can signal to their employees that they encourage considering new information, trying new things, and seeking out additional knowledge—aspects of the derived approach to mindful learning—is through the implementation of an error management training method. Under an error management training method, errors are viewed as inevitable, positive, and informative; learners are encouraged to actively explore the environment and notice where their knowledge and skills need further improvement (Keith & Frese, 2008). Error management training may influence state mindfulness at work, and subsequently increase daily learning, in three ways. First, by utilizing an error management training method during formal trainings, especially during new employees' onboarding training, the organization is directly communicating that the workplace climate is one in which employees are safe to consider new information and try new things. Second, utilizing error management training communicates to employees that their team members and leaders are to nonjudgmentally accept errors in the workplace, which indirectly supports the workplace climate as one that promotes psychological safety. Together, these first two cement the organization's workplace climate as one in which employees are encouraged to be mindful while working and continuously learn. Finally, a formal error management training allows employees to utilize an error management method of learning in an informal setting. For instance, an employee who goes through a formal training that utilizes an error management training method may feel more aware of and comfortable seeking out and approaching other co-workers to learn about a task than employees who are taught that there is only one way to complete a task.

Likewise, organizations can move toward a learning culture through the cultivation of a social culture that promotes employees' mindfulness by taking steps to encourage leaders to provide employees with feedback regarding their performance and development. Feedback—"a dynamic communication process occurring between two individuals that convey[s] information regarding the receiver's performance in the accomplishment of work-related tasks" (Baker, Perreault, Reid, & Blanchard, 2013, p. 260)—allows employees to be aware of and monitor their performance (Di Bernardi, 2014) and propels trust within the organization (Baker et al., 2013). Indeed, even the expectation of feedback leads to deeper processing of information (Vollmeyer & Rheinberg, 2005). This may ultimately lead employees to be aware of and seek more feedback contemporaneously, which may lead to greater learning (van der Rijt, van de Wiel, Van den Bossche, Segers, & Gijselaers, 2012). It may also further signal to the employees that their leaders encourage learning from errors and that the climate is one in which leaders and co-workers generally nonjudgmentally accept others' work. Overall, this subsequent increase in mindfulness may accompany a greater feeling of psychological safety and ultimately lead to more informal learning on the job.

Challenge three: getting and keeping learners' attention

What is the challenge?

Formal and informal learning may be inhibited if employees are not fully attentive during both formal training delivery and their everyday work environment. Many organizations today use computer-based technologies to deliver formal training instruction, in which the learner has a large amount of control over their learning experience (Bell & Kozlowski, 2002). There are many potential opportunities for the learners' attention to be captured by distractors in such settings. These distractors may arise either in the environment or may stem from the fact that the training design or method of delivery may not be implemented in ways that adequately engage learners (Johnson & Randall, 2018). Relative to time spent in a formal learning environment, the majority of organizational learning takes place in an informal manner while on the job, since employees spend a significantly greater amount of time "working" (Cerasoli et al., 2017). It is critical that employees and teams are continuously able to identify areas for improvement and self-direct their learning in an informal manner so that informal learning behaviors may take place (Tannenbaum, Beard, McNall, & Salas, 2010). If employees are operating in an "autopilot" manner, they will not be fully present and intentional with their attention, meaning that areas for improvement may never be identified, preventing informal learning from occurring.

How can mindfulness help?

Incorporating mindfulness skills into learning initiatives may help create a mindful state both during and after training in order to better direct attention towards content to be learned during formal training, and to better identify opportunities to engage in informal learning. Since mindfulness is directly related to behavioral and attentional self-regulation (Burg et al., 2012), learners may benefit from utilizing self-regulatory skills while in a formal training environment and in the work environment. Furthermore, engaging in metacognitive activity throughout the duration of training may assist individuals in improving strategic performance, and developing strategic knowledge is a gradual and unfolding process (Sitzmann, Bell, Kraiger, & Kanar, 2009). During training, the accepting present-moment attentiveness aspect of mindfulness may enable learners to maintain their attention directed at relevant learning material without being preoccupied with negative thought processes. Outside of the training environment, employees may be able to identify areas of potential work performance improvement, which may give rise to informal learning behaviors. Mindful individuals may be able to objectively assess their current performance levels and where they have room for development in their work performance—a key component of self-regulated learning (Sitzmann & Ely, 2011). If employees perceive these performance-goal discrepancies in a mindful accepting manner, they may again be protected from the negative consequences of ruminative thoughts. If individuals are able to acceptingly recognize gaps or deficiencies in work performance, in addition to having the motivation to diminish these gaps (Lord, Diefendorff, Schmidt, & Hall, 2010), they may be better equipped to engage in informal learning behaviors by eliminating the identified deficiency in a self-directed manner.

It is especially important that the motivational pathway to learning is engaged during formal training for ongoing informal learning to actually take place while on the job. Individuals must be motivated to actually diminish or correct their observed performance-goal discrepancy, since the recognized opportunity for learning must be acted upon. Mindfulness is positively related to self-efficacy (Greason & Cashwell, 2009), which, in turn, is positively related to having the intention to participate in self-development activities (Maurer & Palmer, 1999). Additionally, motivation and self-efficacy predict both informal learning behaviors and individuals' motivation to engage in formal training programs (Beier & Kanfer, 2010; Choi & Jacobs, 2011). Therefore, mindful individuals may perceive themselves as more capable of approaching new problems or challenges on the job, which has positive consequences for informal learning behaviors, training engagement, and the maintenance of knowledge and skills learned during training. The way in which individuals approach challenging tasks will be further elaborated on in the fifth identified challenge and is important for discussion, since engagement in challenging tasks may increase maintenance of what was learned during training and serve as an opportunity for informal learning.

Although mindfulness itself may help learners learn, the way in which mindfulness is introduced to learners must be considered in order for learners to reap the full benefits. Since mindfulness itself must be learned, resources will need to be dedicated to practicing mindfulness (Creswell, Pacilio, Lindsay, & Brown, 2014). Therefore, if mindfulness techniques are introduced to learners during job-related training, this may result in a net neutral, or even a net negative, effect on the resources that employees can dedicate to the to-be-learned materials for job training. It is critical that the amount of available resources are maximized during the beginning of new knowledge and skill acquisition, since this is the time in which resource demands are highest (Kanfer & Ackerman, 1989). This is not to say that practicing mindfulness is always harmful to learning; rather, organizations should be judicious when implementing such practices and introduce mindfulness practice outside of novel job-related training contexts that could interfere with the learning process.

Recommendation three

We recommend that organizations *introduce employees to mindful learning strategies that may be utilized during training sessions and in the work environment to better focus their attention and motivation on self-regulated learning goals.* Organizations may offer a seminar in which mindfulness techniques to encourage present-moment focus and the practice of nonjudgmental acceptance are taught, and the utility of such skills as tools to support learning are emphasized to employees so that they are motivated to learn and practice mindfulness skills on their own. Following the introduction and development of mindfulness skills, organizations may strategically deliver self-regulatory prompts (Schmidt & Ford, 2003) in conjunction with a mindfulness check during and after job-related training initiatives to further encourage the use of mindfulness skills during learning (i.e., mindful learning; Randall et al., 2019). We use the term "mindfulness check" to represent self-regulatory prompts and statements reinforcing a nonjudgmental and accepting perspective on goal-performance discrepancies (e.g., "Are you making progress toward your learning goal? Remember to remain nonjudgmental as you evaluate your progress."). Such reminders may help keep learners' attention directed towards relevant to-be-learned material and allow learners to view their progress in an accepting way while preventing negative emotions from interfering with learning and performance. To help facilitate skill maintenance and informal learning back on the job, organizations may take actions such as periodically sending out check-in reminder emails containing mindful statements similar to the mindfulness checks delivered during formal training to prompt learners to recall mindful approaches to learning. By delivering reminders post training, employees will be reminded of skills they practiced during training and may be more motivated to engage in more informal learning behaviors in the work environment.

Challenge four: managing negative affect during learning

What is the challenge?

The learning process can stimulate a wide spectrum of emotions, ranging from positive affect when trainees feel confident in their abilities to negative affect when challenging material causes trainees to feel frustrated and anxious. Emotions can alter mental states such that intense arousal interferes with information processing. That is, the trainee's limited pool of cognitive resources becomes divided into processing new material and appraising internal states (Kanfer & Ackerman, 1996). Emotions such as frustration and anxiety often occur when employees face new and challenging material. Particularly, affect regulation is a source of off-task attentional demand that requires cognitive resources to regulate (Beal, Weiss, Barros, & MacDermid, 2005). From a resource allocation perspective, negative emotions compete for attentional resources and hinder learning and performance—especially during the initial stages of training when cognitive demands are high (Kanfer & Ackerman, 1989). For example, anxiety engenders worrisome thoughts that interfere with attention to learning, thus decreasing the amount of available resources to encode new information (Eysenck & Calvo, 1992; Eysenck, Derakshan, Santos, & Calvo, 2007). Likewise, feelings of frustration may decrease self-efficacy, which, in turn, has negative consequences on learning outcomes and motivation (Margolis & McCabe, 2004; Waterhouse & Child, 1953). Failure to effectively regulate these emotions has important consequences for learning. Indeed, feelings of frustration and anxiety can cause trainees to consume mental resources for rumination. Thus, trainees who are unable to regulate their emotions effectively may find it difficult to focus on the primary learning task. As a result, negative emotions have been found to attenuate learning (Linnenbrink & Pintrich, 2004). Moreover, frustrated trainees may give up or skip the challenging sections, consequently leaving training with incomplete knowledge of the material.

Although people tend to view stress as negative and inhibitory, research has found mixed results on the effects of stress on learning outcomes. On one hand, stress increases arousal, which increases learning performance (Smeets et al., 2009); however, over-arousal or extended periods of stress may actually harm learning (Yerkes & Dodson, 1908). Additionally, scholars have differentiated *hindrance stress*, stress that is appraised as hindering mastery, from *challenging stress*, stress that is appraised as promoting mastery. The extent to which trainees experience hindrance stress attenuates learning (LePine, LePine, & Jackson, 2004). If the training program presents challenging material that requires great mental effort and persistence to complete, extended feelings of negative affect may become a hindrance rather than a challenge. Thus, effective management of stress and negative emotions are key to addressing the challenges these introduce for learners in formal and informal settings.

How can mindfulness help?

When an emotion is felt, it is typically appraised in two steps. First, primary appraisal is a judgment of the emotion's valence and its association to one's well-being (Smith & Kirby, 2001). This is a relatively automatic process that requires few resources and is unlikely to affect learning outcomes. After primary appraisal, trainees may engage in secondary appraisal—a more cognitively demanding process whereby the emotion is identified and assessed for coping potential, self-accountability, and particular expectancies. When experiencing negative emotions, secondary appraisal may result in rumination (Martin & Tesser, 1996), which consumes cognitive resources that could be used to process new information. As such, mindfulness may be a potent solution to buffer the mental costs of secondary appraisal. A mindful learner will judge negative emotions with neutral valence during primary appraisal, which decreases the likelihood of further rumination (Baer, 2003; Teasdale, 1999). That is, mindfulness stops secondary appraisal from occurring by promoting an accepting and nonjudgmental attitude towards negative emotions. Furthermore, mindfulness may decrease negative affect and stress by facilitating positive emotions and enhancing resource recovery (Hülsheger, Alberts, Feinholdt, & Lang, 2013). Positive emotions broaden the scope of cognition (Fredrickson, 1998) and free up resources that can be devoted to the learning task. Similarly, being mindful during breaks and recovery time may help trainees psychologically detach from training to recover resources (Hülsheger, Feinholdt, and Nubold, 2015; Hülsheger, et. al. 2014), subsequently decreasing emotional exhaustion (Sonnentag, Kuttler, & Fritz, 2010) and decreasing the likelihood that the negative emotions and stress experienced during learning will be as detrimental and long-lasting.

Recommendation four

Therefore, we recommend that organizations *facilitate mindfulness to reduce the detrimental impact of negative emotions and stress during learning.* Three ways to do this would be by encouraging learners to adopt a mastery orientation, to encourage resource recovery, and to attempt to normalize the experience of negative affect during learning as part of the organizations' continuous learning culture. First, whereas a performance orientation reflects a desire to accomplish more than others, a mastery orientation reflects a desire to develop knowledge, skills, and task mastery (Elliot & McGregor, 2001). Performance-oriented trainees tend to make social comparisons, which can cause anxiety (Butzer & Kuiper, 2006; Taylor & Lobel, 1989). Adopting a mastery orientation promotes present-moment focus by encouraging trainees to learn the material without comparing themselves with others (Farr, Hofmann, & Ringenbach, 1993). This should reduce performance anxiety and other negative emotions that occur when trainees make upward comparisons with their peers. Second, we recommend that organizations implement "mindful breaks," which might involve mindful breathing, meditation, or yoga, as short breaks during formal and informal learning efforts. In general, breaks help recover resources needed to regulate attention (Beal, Weiss, Barros, & MacDermid, 2005). Mindful breaks can encourage a present-moment focus and nonjudgmental attitude, thereby helping trainees maintain a nonjudgmental attitude towards their emotions when they re-engage with the learning task (Calogero & Pedrotty, 2007; La Forge, 2005; Netz & Lidor, 2003). Finally, we also endorse Recommendation Two from this chapter as an effective way to manage negative emotions during learning. Organizations can cultivate a psychological work climate that normalizes negative affect. That is, if negative affect is accepted to be a typical outcome of learning difficult materials, trainees will be less likely to have an adverse reaction towards negative emotions (Keith & Frese, 2005).

Challenge five: transferring learning

What is the challenge?

Training transfer represents the application of learned skills, knowledge, or affect in a new time, place, or manner on the job (Baldwin & Ford, 1988). Maximizing positive training transfer is contingent upon individuals successfully learning and retaining information delivered during training; further, the depth of learning that occurred affects the degree to which an individual is able to generalize learned behaviors to the new job context and maintain these newly learned skills over time (Baldwin & Ford, 1988). Post training, individuals may have impaired transfer performance if they obtain only a shallow understanding of content learned during training, experience performance anxiety when applying newly learned skills back on the job, or do not have the opportunity to perform newly learned skills. Specifically, adaptive training transfer losses are most relevant to these issues, as this requires learners to more flexibly adapt new knowledge and skills to contexts and problems that differ from original learning (Baldwin & Ford, 1988). Transfer includes generalizing learning from formal training environments to on-the-job performance and also generalizing learning in one domain to another during the informal learning process. If organizations encounter transfer losses in either formal or informal settings, the resources invested in employee learning may have been wasted if the learned material is never actually utilized and performed to ultimately enhance job performance (Desse, 1958).

How can mindfulness help?

Cultivating state mindfulness at two different time points may help employees transfer new learning from one context or time to another: first, during the actual formal learning process of training; second, while applying what was learned back on the job post training. According to Craik and Lockhart's (1972) levels of processing framework, the depth at which an input is processed will determine the nature and durability of the memory trace. Cultivating present-moment awareness and nonjudgmental acceptance during training in order to facilitate deeper, more decay-resistant learning may result in better training transfer and improved job performance. For example, since metacognition is positively related to adaptive transfer (Keith & Frese, 2005) and deep learning (Biggs, 1988), this cognitive process, which is similar to the present-moment awareness component of mindfulness, must be stimulated during the learning process to facilitate effective retrieval for performance. Therefore, the first lever to target when striving to achieve positive training transfer is training design and delivery, since the way in which trainees engage with training content during learning will determine the depth of processing that occurs.

Factors in the training environment may be manipulated to encourage the opportunity for state mindfulness during training delivery; adopting a mindful learning orientation in the learning environment may be a key influencer for positive training transfer. The nonjudgmental dimension of mindfulness may be promoted in training by incorporating active learning interventions into the training design. Active learning strategies require the learner to engage in an inductive learning process, which means that the learner explores unfamiliar and potentially difficult tasks and material right at the onset of learning (Bell & Kozlowski, 2008). If learners are prompted to engage in experimentation with the task rather than being given step-by-step guidance, they may not have as critical a view about making errors or undesirable choices, which may facilitate deeper learning. Thus, active learning may foster state mindfulness in training, as mindfulness is positively related to enhanced emotional self-awareness (Creswell, Way, Eisenberger, & Lieberman, 2007) and better metacognitive skills. By mindfully approaching new and unfamiliar challenging tasks and material, learners may be better able to devote their attentional resources more fully to the actual learning material instead of being preoccupied with negative distracting thoughts. Additionally, if employees are encouraged to look at errors as part of the learning process during training, this may make employees more likely to approach challenging tasks or ask more questions while back on the job (i.e., adaptive transfer; Keith & Frese, 2005). Engaging in challenging tasks, asking constructive questions, and attempting to flexibly apply learning to new situations may spark additional informal learning behaviors. Thus, active learning strategies that are supported by the nonjudgmental acceptance dimension of mindfulness have positive implications for positive training transfer and informal learning.

The other major dimension of mindfulness, holding a sustained present-moment awareness to internal and external events, may also be promoted during active learning. Active exploration of information induces metacognitive activity, which enhances performance in tasks that require new solutions (Keith & Frese, 2005). Trainees' metacognitive activity, which is related to mindfulness, requires an individual to attend to the present-moment internal cognitive processes and allow the learner to recognize changes in the task demands, devise new solutions, and also evaluate the effectiveness of their solution (Ivancic & Hesketh, 2000). Trainees mindfully approaching a problem will hold a broadened and more attentive awareness of the true nature of the parameters of a task or problem in addition to the context in which the task exists. Mindfully aware employees may be better equipped to draw on learned material and generate more context-appropriate solutions for new problems (Langer, 2000). Context-appropriate responding and solution-generation is further enhanced by cognitive flexibility, which enables learners to generalize learned material to new tasks in new contexts, similar to the derived approach to mindful learning. Generalizing learned behaviors to new problems in new scenarios is critical to adaptive transfer. Cognitive flexibility is positively related to mindfulness (Moore & Malinowski, 2009), and individuals high on the non-reactivity trait of mindfulness are better able to regulate the cognitive control system in a manner likely to be context-adaptive. An adaptive transfer environment exists in a different time, place, or manner from which learning took place and demands employees to more flexibly apply learning since (Baldwin & Ford, 1988). The cognitive flexibility that mindful individuals have will help promote divergent thinking and creativity (Langer, 2000). This will allow them to successfully generalize learned skills to new contexts post training. Metacognition and cognitive flexibility may arguably allow trainees to engage with learning material on a conceptually deeper level during training, which therefore results in a better ability to generalize learned training content to different job contexts.

It should also be noted that self-efficacy, a malleable learner characteristic, is positively related to both mindfulness (Greason & Cashwell, 2009) and training transfer (Blume et al., 2010), and that trainee motivation has a direct effect on the generalization and maintenance of transfer (Baldwin & Ford, 1988). Mindful individuals may be more motivated to continually apply their learned knowledge in the post-training context if they perceive themselves as capable of responding to challenging demands. Practicing skills and behaviors helps trainees maintain what was learned, which is one of the conditions of successful training transfer. By completing challenging tasks in more self-directed active learning and informal learning environments, self-efficacy is enhanced and may equip learners to successfully and flexibly transfer learning for the benefit of the individual and the organization.

In addition to trainee motivation, emotions also influence training transfer. A mindful state may buffer the potential threat of performance anxiety that employees may experience when performing new skills for the first time by allowing individuals to direct attention away from the self, and keep attention directed toward the task to be completed (Kanfer & Ackerman, 1996; Keith & Frese, 2005). By drawing upon the positive perspective taken toward challenges when framing errors as positive opportunities for learning, individuals will apply what was learned more successfully and maintain a more positive affective state (Keith & Frese, 2005, 2008). Thus, in summary, the effects that mindfulness has on an individual's motivation and emotions allow them to more successfully engage with their post-training environment in an ongoing manner while performing and drawing upon newly learned skills and knowledge.

Recommendation five

We recommend that organizations *draw on active learning principles when structuring training design and delivery in a manner that promotes present-moment awareness and nonjudgmental acceptance in order to improve the likelihood of positive, adaptive training transfer.* The first target area for transfer performance should be the context in which learning took place, since this affects the depth of learning and encoding that occurs. Implementing active learning interventions, where learners engage in a constructive and inductive learning process, may diminish the gap between learning and potential job performance. In active learning strategies, the goal is indeed to improve training transfer rather than performance during actual training (Bell & Kozlowski, 2008). Cognitive flexibility, in addition to self-efficacy facilitated by a mindful state during training, will enable employees to maintain learned material and generalize it to new contexts post training. In addition to positive training transfer, more informal learning behaviors may occur if employees become more comfortable and confident with having a more proactive approach to unfamiliar tasks. Further, a more flexible approach to learning may also help individuals generalize the transfer of informal learning to new situations in the work environment.

Future directions

Although the recommendations that are laid out in this chapter are based on the extant literature, many of the propositions that we make need more solid and direct empirical support. For example, although it follows that error management training leads employees to be more willing to consider new information and old information in new ways, and this is in line with the derived approach to mindful learning, the proposition that error management training leads to greater mindfulness is an underexplored area of research. Indeed, the arguments that we make in this chapter are largely theoretical, with some exceptions, as research on mindfulness in the workplace is still relatively nascent, particularly as it applies to workplace learning. Therefore, future research should continue to examine the various ways in which mindfulness is manifested in the workplace and the subsequent outcomes that it may benefit.

Furthermore, some additional antecedents and outcomes of enhancing workplace learning through mindfulness that have yet to be considered include other individual differences that may influence (1) whether fostering mindfulness in the workplace is effective at influencing mindfulness, and (2) whether the beneficial effects of fostering mindfulness in the workplace on workplace learning is reduced or reversed. For instance, some individual differences that may play a role include cognitive ability, personality, and motivation. There is some evidence to suggest that cognitive ability and attentional resources may moderate the effectiveness of mindfulness as a tool to benefit workplace learning. Specifically, as we discussed previously, learning is an attentional resource-dependent task (Kanfer & Ackerman, 1989), which means that the maximum level of attentional resources that a learner can draw from would influence how well they learn new things and practice mindfulness at the same time. The benefits of mindful interventions targeting workplace design and climate is that they do not require that the learner practice mindfulness while also trying to learn. However, when a mindfulness practice is involved, a better understanding of how cognitive abilities moderate the beneficial relationship between mindfulness and daily workplace learning would be valuable.

Additionally, there is meta-analytic evidence to suggest that neuroticism is negatively associated with trait mindfulness, and conscientiousness is positively associated with trait mindfulness (Giluk, 2009). Although organizations are likely unable to manipulate trait levels of conscientiousness or neuroticism, these may also be important variables to consider when trying to foster mindfulness in order to improve workplace learning. For instance, it may be that the influence of mindfulness on daily workplace learning is considerably stronger with conscientious employees, or that conscientious employees' level of mindfulness is already near its ceiling. Furthermore, fostering mindfulness in those who are high in neuroticism may actually increase the occurrence and quality of daily workplace learning. More research is needed, however, so we can gain a better understanding of how these constructs all relate to each other.

Conclusions

In conclusion, organizations that strive to be successful in the modern-day industry landscape are sure to face several learning-related workplace challenges, and mindfulness may be one tool that organizations can add to their toolbox to overcome these challenges. In this chapter, we covered five such challenges, including (1) creating sufficient infrastructure for learning, (2) creating sufficient climate for learning, (3) getting and keeping learners' attention, (4) managing negative affect during learning, and (5) transferring learning. We make five recommendations, summarized in Table 17.1, for how organizations may attempt to overcome these learning-related challenges by facilitating mindful learning. We propose that, by following these recommendations, organizations can better prepare themselves to meet and surmount learning-related challenges today as well as into the future.

Table 17.1 Five common workplace learning challenges and mindfulness-related recommendations

Challenge	*Recommendation*
Creating Sufficient Infrastructure for Learning	Move toward a learning culture through the implementation of infrastructure that promotes employees' mindfulness by taking steps to increase their perceived autonomy and to provide time for reflection.
Creating a Social Climate for Learning	Move toward a learning culture through the cultivation of a social culture that promotes employees' mindfulness by taking steps to increase employees' level of comfort with considering new information, trying new things, and seeking out additional knowledge.
Getting and Keeping Learners' Attention	Introduce employees to mindful learning strategies that may be utilized during training sessions and in the work environment to better focus their attention and motivation on self-regulated learning goals.
Managing Negative Affect during Learning	Facilitate mindfulness to reduce the detrimental impact of negative emotions and stress during learning.
Transferring Learning	Draw on active learning principles when structuring training design and delivery in a manner that promotes present-moment awareness and nonjudgmental acceptance in order to improve the likelihood of positive, adaptive training transfer.

Five chapter takeaways/lessons

1. Promoting mindfulness in the workplace, either through an additive approach (learning coupled with a present-moment, nonjudgmental awareness) or a derived approach (adopting a more open and deep consideration of learned information), may help organizations develop a continuous learning culture.
2. Five learning-related challenges that organizations are likely to face include (1) creating sufficient infrastructure for learning, (2) creating a social climate for learning, (3) getting and keeping learners' attention, (4) managing negative affect during learning, and (5) transferring learning.
3. Mindfulness-based recommendations for organizations to overcome learning-related challenges include promoting mindfulness by creating a continuous learning culture. This includes: (1) increasing employees' perceived autonomy and providing time for reflection, and (2) increasing employees' level of comfort with considering new information, trying new things, and seeking out additional knowledge.
4. In order to address challenges related to getting and keeping attention and coping with negative emotions during learning efforts, organizations should use strategies that prompt present-moment focus and nonjudgment in order to better focus employees' attention and motivation and to reduce the detrimental impact of negative emotions and stress.
5. Mindfulness may be key to improving the likelihood of positive, adaptive transfer of learned knowledge and skills by supporting the active learning process in ways that prompt presence and acceptance.

Five reflection questions

1. Explain the difference between the additive approach to mindful learning and the derived approach to mindful learning.
2. What are the three pathways through which learning occurs and how is mindfulness theorized to be able to influence these pathways?
3. How can mindfulness be used to influence the technical-organizational learning environment and the social-cultural learning environment within an organization to foster a continuous learning culture?
4. As a construct that is closely related to self-regulation of attention and motivation, how can mindfulness help and harm learning in a formal environment?
5. Considering the many ways in which mindfulness may influence positive and negative affect, in what ways is mindfulness expected to benefit or harm the occurrence of and effectiveness of formal and informal learning?

References

Alliger, G. M., Tannenbaum, S. I., Bennett, W., Jr, Traver, H., & Shotland, A. (1997). A meta-analysis of the relations among training criteria. *Personnel Psychology, 50*, 341–358.

Arthur, W., Jr., Bennett, W., Jr., Edens, P. S., & Bell, S. T. (2003). Effectiveness of training in organizations: A meta-analysis of design and evaluation features. *Journal of Applied Psychology, 88*(2), 234–245.

Association for Talent Development. (2017). *2017 state of the industry report.* Alexandria, VA: ATD Research.

Baer, R. A. (2003). Mindfulness training as a clinical interventional: A conceptual and empirical review. *Clinical Psychology: Science and Practice, 10*(2), 125–143.

Baer, R. A., Smith, G. T., Lykins, E., Button, D., Krietemeyer, J., Sauer, S., . . . Williams, J. M. G. (2008). Construct validity of the five facet mindfulness questionnaire in meditating and nonmeditating samples. *Assessment, 15*(3), 329–342.

Baker, A., Perreault, D., Reid, A., & Blanchard, C. M. (2013). Feedback and organizations: Feedback is good, feedback-friendly culture is better. *Canadian Psychology, 54*(4), 260.

Bakker, A. B., & Demerouti, E. (2007). The job demands-resources model: State of the art. *Journal of Managerial Psychology, 22*(3), 309–328.

Baldwin, T. T., & Ford, J. K. (1988). Transfer of training: A review and directions for future research. *Personnel Psychology, 41*, 63–105.

Beal, D. J., Weiss, H. M., Barros, E., & MacDermid, S. M. (2005). An episodic process model of affective influences on performance. *Journal of Applied Psychology, 90*(6), 1054–1068.

Beier, M. E., & Kanfer, R. (2010). Motivation in training and development: A phase perspective. In S. W. J. Kozlowski & E. Salas (Eds.), *SIOP organizational frontiers series. Learning, training, and development in organizations* (pp. 65–97). New York, NY, US: Routledge/Taylor & Francis Group.

Bell, B. S., & Kozlowski, S. W. J. (2002). Adaptive guidance: Enhancing self-regulation, knowledge, and performance in technology-based training. *Personnel Psychology, 55*(2), 267–306.

Bell, B. S., & Kozlowski, S. W. J. (2008). Active learning: Effects of core training design elements on self-regulatory processes, learning, and adaptability. *Journal of Applied Psychology, 93*(2), 296–316.

Biggs, J. (1988). The role of metacognition in enhancing learning. *Australian Journal of Education, 32*(2), 127–138.

Blanke, E. S., Schmidt, M. J., Riediger, M., & Brose, A. (2019). Thinking mindfully: How mindfulness relates to rumination and reflection in daily life. *Emotion*. Advance online publication.

Blume, B. D., Ford, J. K., Baldwin, T. T., & Huang, J. L. (2010). Transfer of training: A meta-analytic review. *Journal of Management, 36*(4), 1065–1105.

Bravo, A. J., Pearson, M. R., Wilson, A. D., & Witkiewitz, K. (2018). When traits match states: Examining the associations between self-report trait and state mindfulness following a state mindfulness induction. *Mindfulness, 9*(1), 199–211.

Brown, K. W., & Ryan, R. M. (2003). The benefits of being present: Mindfulness and its role in psychological well-being. *Journal of Personality and Social Psychology, 84*(4), 822.

Burg, J. M., Wolf, O. T., & Michalak, J. (2012). Mindfulness as self-regulated attention. *Swiss Journal of Psychology, 71*(3), 135–139.

Butzer, B., & Kuiper, N. A. (2006). Relationships between the frequency of social comparisons and self-concept clarity, intolerance of uncertainty, anxiety, and depression. *Personality and Individual Differences, 41*(1), 167–176.

Calogero, R., & Pedrotty, K. (2007). Daily practices for mindful exercise. In L. L'Abate, D. Embry, & M. Baggett (Eds.), *Low-cost approaches to promote physical and mental health* (pp. 141–160). New York, NY: Springer-Verlag.

Cerasoli, C. P., Alliger, G. M., Donsbach, J. S., Mathieu, J. E., Tannenbaum, S. I., & Orvis, K. A. (2017). Antecedents and outcomes of informal learning behaviors: A meta-analysis. *Journal of Business and Psychology, 33*(2), 203–230.

Choi, W., & Jacobs, R. L. (2011). Influences of formal learning, personal learning orientation, and supportive learning environment on informal learning. *Human Resource Development Quarterly, 22*(3), 239–257.

Clark, R. C., & Mayer, R. E. (2003). *e-Learning and the science of instruction: Proven guidelines for consumers and designers of multimedia learning*. San Francisco: Pfeiffer.

Craik, F. I. M., & Lockhart, R. S. (1972). Levels of processing: A framework for memory research. *Journal of Verbal Learning and Verbal Behavior, 11*(6), 671–684.

Creswell, J. D., Pacilio, L. E., Lindsay, E. K., & Brown, K. W. (2014). Brief mindfulness meditation training alters psychological and neuroendocrine responses to social evaluative stress. *Psychoneuroendocrinology, 44*, 1–12.

Creswell, J. D., Way, B. M., Eisenberger, N. I., & Lieberman, M. D. (2007). Neural correlates of dispositional mindfulness during affect labelling. *Psychosomatic Medicine, 69*(6), 560–565.

Desse, J. (1958). *Transfer of training: The psychology of learning*. New York: McGraw-Hill.

Di Bernardi, L. C. (2014). Learning from feedback: The neural mechanisms of feedback processing facilitating better performance. *Behavioural Brain Research, 261*, 356–368.

Di Stefano, G., Gino, F., Pisano, G. P., & Staats, B. R. (2016). Making experience count: The role of reflection in individual learning. *Harvard Business School NOM Unit Working Paper*, (14-093), 14-093.

Ding, X., Du, J., Zhou, Y., An, Y., Xu, W., & Zhang, N. (2019). State mindfulness, rumination, and emotions in daily life: An ambulatory assessment study. *Asian Journal of Social Psychology*, *22*(4), 369–377.

Dollard, M. F., & Bakker, A. B. (2010). Psychosocial safety climate as a precursor to conducive work environments, psychological health problems, and employee engagement. *Journal of Occupational and Organizational Psychology*, *83*(3), 579–599.

Döös, M. (2007). Organizational learning: Competence-bearing relations and breakdowns of workplace relatonics. In L. Farrell, & T. Fenwick (Eds.), *World yearbook of education 2007: Educating the global workforce; Knowledge, knowledge work and knowledge workers* (pp. 141–153). London, UK: Routledge.

Edmondson, A. C., & Lei, Z. (2014). Psychological safety: The history, renaissance, and future of an interpersonal construct. *Annual Review of Organizational Psychology and Organizational Behavior*, *1*, 23–43.

Eisenlohr-Moul, T. A., Peters, J. R., Pond, R. S., Jr., & DeWall, C. N. (2016). Both trait and state mindfulness predict lower aggressiveness via anger rumination: A multilevel mediation analysis. *Mindfulness*, 7(3), 713–726.

Elliot, A., & McGregor, H. A. (2001). A 2 2 achievement goal framework. *Journal of Personality and Social Psychology*, *80*, 501–519.

Eysenck, M. W., & Calvo, M. G. (1992). Anxiety and performance: The processing efficiency theory. *Cognition & Emotion*, *6*(6), 409–434.

Eysenck, M. W., Derakshan, N., Santos, R., & Calvo, M. G. (2007). Anxiety and cognitive performance: Attentional control theory. *Emotion*, 7(2), 336.

Farr, J. L., Hofmann, D. A., & Ringenbach, K. L. (1993). Goal orientation and action control theory: Implications for industrial and organizational psychology. *International Review of Industrial and Organizational Psychology*, *8*(2), 193–232.

Fredrickson, B. L. (1998). What good are positive emotions? *Review of General Psychology*, *2*, 300–319.

Friese, M., & Hofmann, W. (2016). State mindfulness, self-regulation, and emotional experience in everyday life. *Motivation Science*, *2*(1), 1–14.

Giluk, T. L. (2009). Mindfulness, big five personality, and affect: A meta-analysis. *Personality and Individual Differences*, *47*(8), 805–811.

Goldman, E., Plack, M., Roche, C., Smith, J., & Turley, C. (2009). Learning in a chaotic environment. *Journal of Workplace Learning*, *21*(7), 555–574.

Gould, J. M. (2009). Understanding organizations as learning systems. *Strategic Learning in a Knowledge Economy*, *19*(6), 56–59.

Greason, P. B., & Cashwell, C. S. (2009). Mindfulness and counseling self-efficacy: The mediating role of attention and empathy. *Counselor Education and Supervision*, *49*, 2–19.

Greenberg, J., Reiner, K., & Meiran, N. (2012). "Mind the trap": Mindfulness practice reduces cognitive rigidity. *PloS One*, 7(5), e36206.

Hülsheger, U. R., Alberts, H. J., Feinholdt, A., & Lang, J. W. (2013). Benefits of mindfulness at work: The role of mindfulness in emotion regulation, emotional exhaustion, and job satisfaction. *Journal of Applied Psychology*, *98*(2), 310–325.

Hülsheger, U. R., Feinholdt, A., & Nübold, A. (2015). A low-dose mindfulness intervention and recovery from work: Effects on psychological detachment, sleep quality, and sleep duration. *Journal of Occupational and Organizational Psychology*, *88*(3), 464–489.

Hülsheger, U. R., Lang, J. W., Depenbrock, F., Fehrmann, C., Zijlstra, F. R., & Alberts, H. J. (2014). The power of presence: The role of mindfulness at work for daily levels and change trajectories of psychological detachment and sleep quality. *Journal of Applied Psychology*, *99*, 1113–1128.

Illeris, K. (2004). A model for learning in working life. *Journal of Workplace Learning*, *16*(8), 431–441.

Ivancic, K., & Hesketh, B. (2000). Learning from errors in a driving simulation: Effects on driving skill and self-confidence. *Ergonomics*, *43*(12), 1966–1984.

Jamieson, S. D., & Tuckey, M. R. (2017). Mindfulness interventions in the workplace: A critique of the current state of the literature. *Journal of Occupational Health Psychology*, *22*(2), 180.

Johnson, R. D., & Randall, J. G. (2018). A review of design considerations in e-learning. In D. L. Stone & J. H. Dulebohn (Eds.), *Research in human resource management* (pp. 141–188). Charlotte, NC: Information Age Publishing.

Kanfer, R., & Ackerman, P. L. (1989). Motivation and cognitive abilities: An integrative/aptitude-treatment interaction approach to skill acquisition. *Journal of Applied Psychology*, 74(4), 657–690.

Kanfer, R., & Ackerman, P. L. (1996). A self-regulatory skills perspective to reducing cognitive interference. In I. G. Sarason, B. R. Sarason, & G. R. Pierce (Eds.), *Cognitive interference: Theories, methods, and findings* (pp. 153–171). Mahwah, NJ: Erlbaum.

Kanfer, R., & Heggestad, E. D. (1997). Motivational traits and skills: A person-centered approach to work motivation. In L. L. Cummings & B. M. Staw (Eds.), *Research in organizational behavior* (Vol. *19*, pp. 1–56). Greenwich, CT: JAI Press, Inc.

Keith, N., & Frese, M. (2005). Self-regulation in error management training: Emotion control and metacognition as mediators of performance effects. *Journal of Applied Psychology, 90*(4), 677–691.

Keith, N., & Frese, M. (2008). Effectiveness of error management training: A meta-analysis. *Journal of Applied Psychology, 93*(1), 59–69.

Kiken, L. G., Garland, E. L., Bluth, K., Palsson, O. S., & Gaylord, S. A. (2015). From a state to a trait: Trajectories of state mindfulness in meditation during intervention predict changes in trait mindfulness. *Personality and Individual Differences, 81*, 41–46.

Kirby, J. R., Knapper, C. K., Evans, C. J., Carty, A. E., & Gadula, C. (2003). Approaches to learning at work and workplace climate. *International Journal of Training and Development*, 7(1), 31–52.

Kirkpatrick, D. L. (1967). Evaluation of training. In R. L. Craig & L. R. Bittel (Eds.), *Training and Development Handbook* (pp. 87–112). New York: McGraw Hill.

Kluge, A., & Schilling, J. (2003). Organizational learning and learning organizations: Theory and empirical findings. *The Psychologist-Manager Journal, 6*(1), 31–50.

Kraiger, K., Ford, J. K., & Salas, E. (1993). Application of cognitive, skill-based, and affective theories of learning outcomes to new methods of training evaluation. *Journal of Applied Psychology, 78*, 311–328.

La Forge, R. (2005). Aligning mind and body: Exploring the disciplines of mindful exercise. *ACSM's Health & Fitness Journal, 9*(5), 7–14.

Langer, E. J. (2000). Mindful learning. *Current Directions in Psychological Science, 9*(6), 220–223.

Lawrie, E. J., Tuckey, M. R., & Dollard, M. F. (2018). Job design for mindful work: The boosting effect of psychosocial safety climate. *Journal of Occupational Health Psychology, 23*(4), 483–495.

LePine, J. A., LePine, M. A., & Jackson, C. L. (2004). Challenge and hindrance stress: Relationships with exhaustion, motivation to learn, and learning performance. *Journal of Applied Psychology, 89*(5), 883.

Leyland, A., Rowse, G., & Emerson, L.-M. (2019). Experimental effects of mindfulness inductions on self-regulation: Systematic review and meta-analysis. *Emotion, 19*(1), 108–122.

Linnenbrink, E. A., & Pintrich, P. R. (2004). Role of affect in cognitive processing in academic contexts. In D. Y. Dai & R. J. Sternberg (Eds.), *Motivation, emotion, and cognition: Integrative perspectives on intellectual functioning and development* (pp. 57–87). Mahwah, NJ: Routledge.

Lord, R. G., Diefendorff, J. M., Schmidt, A. M., & Hall, R. J. (2010). Self-regulation at work. *Annual Review of Psychology, 61*, 543–568.

Margolis, H., & McCabe, P. P. (2004). Self-efficacy: A key to improving the motivation of struggling learners. *The Clearing House: A Journal of Educational Strategies, Issues and Ideas*, 77(6), 241–249.

Martin, L. L., & Tesser, A. (1996). Some ruminative thoughts. In R. S. Wyer, Jr. (Ed.), *Advances in social cognition* (Vol. *9*, pp. 1–47). Mahwah, NJ: Erlbaum.

Maurer, T. J., & Palmer, J. K. (1999). Management development intentions following feedback–Role of perceived outcomes, social pressures, and control. *Journal of Management Development, 18*(9), 733–751.

Mesmer-Magnus, J., Manapragada, A., Viswesvaran, C., & Allen, J. W. (2017). Trait mindfulness at work: A meta-analysis of the personal and professional correlates of trait mindfulness. *Human Performance, 30*(2–3), 79–98.

Moore, A., & Malinowski, P. (2009). Meditation, mindfulness and cognitive flexibility. *Consciousness and Cognition, 18*(1), 176–186.

Netz, Y., & Lidor, R. (2003). Mood alterations in mindful versus aerobic exercise modes. *The Journal of Psychology, 137*(5), 405–419.

Park, Y., & Choi, W. (2016). The effects of formal learning and informal learning on job performance: The mediating role of the value of learning at work. *Asia Pacific Education Review*, 17(2), 279–287.

Parker, S. K. (2014). Beyond motivation: Job and work design for development, health, ambidexterity, and more. *Annual Review of Psychology, 65*, 661–691.

Randall, J. G., Zajac, S. A., & Hanson, M. D. (2019). *Mindful training: Integrating mindfulness into workplace learning*. Manuscript submitted for publication.

Salas, E., Tannenbaum, S. I., Kraiger, K., & Smith-Jentsch, K. A. (2012). The science of training and development in organizations: What matters in practice. *Psychological Science in the Public Interest, 13*, 74–101.

Schmidt, A. M., & Ford, J. K. (2003). Learning within a learner control training environment: The interactive effects of goal orientation and metacognitive instruction on learning outcomes. *Personnel Psychology, 56*, 405–429.

Siebenhüner, B., & Arnold, M. (2007). Organizational learning to manage sustainable development. *Business Strategy and the Environment, 16*(5), 339–353.

Simons, P. R., & de Jong, F. P. (1992). Self-regulation and computer-aided instruction. *Applied Psychology, 41*, 333–346.

Sitzmann, T., Bell, B. S., Kraiger, K., & Kanar, A. M. (2009). A multilevel analysis of the effect of prompting self-regulation in technology-delivered instruction. *Personnel Psychology, 62*(4), 697–734.

Sitzmann, T., & Ely, K. (2011). A meta-analysis of self-regulated learning in work-related training and educational attainment: What we know and where we need to go. *Psychological Bulletin, 137*, 421–442.

Smeets, T., Wolf, O. T., Giesbrecht, T., Sijstermans, K., Telgen, S., & Joëls, M. (2009). Stress selectively and lastingly promotes learning of context-related high arousing information. *Psychoneuroendocrinology, 34*(8), 1152–1161.

Smith, C. A., & Kirby, L. D. (2001). Affect and cognitive appraisal processes. In J. P. Forgas (Ed.), *Handbook of social cognition* (pp. 75–92). Hillsdale, NJ: Erlbaum.

Solem, S., Thunes, S. S., Hjemdal, O., Hagen, R., & Wells, A. (2015). A metacognitive perspective on mindfulness: An empirical investigation. *BMC Psychology, 3*(1), 24.

Sonnentag, S., Kuttler, I., & Fritz, C. (2010). Job stressors, emotional exhaustion, and need for recovery: A multi-source study on the benefits of psychological detachment. *Journal of Vocational Behavior, 76*(3), 355–365.

Svendsen, J. L., Kvernenes, K. V., Wiker, A. S., & Dundas, I. (2017). Mechanisms of mindfulness: Rumination and self-compassion. *Nordic Psychology, 69*(2), 71–82.

Tannenbaum, S. I., Beard, R. L., McNall, L. A., & Salas, E. (2010). Informal learning and development in organizations. In S. W. J. Kozlowski & E. Salas (Eds.), *Learning, training, and development in organizations* (pp. 303–332). New York, NY: Taylor & Francis Group, LLC.

Taylor, S. E., & Lobel, M. (1989). Social comparison activity under threat: Downward evaluation and upward contacts. *Psychological Review, 96*(4), 569.

Teasdale, J. D. (1999). Metacognition, mindfulness and the modification of mood disorders. *Clinical Psychology and Psychotherapy, 6*(2), 146–155.

van der Rijt, J., van de Wiel, M. W. J., Van den Bossche, P., Segers, M. S. R., & Gijselaers, W. H. (2012). Contextual antecedents of informal feedback in the workplace. *Human Resource Development Quarterly, 23*(2), 233–257.

Veenman, M. V., Van Hout-Wolters, B. H., & Afflerbach, P. (2006). Metacognition and learning: Conceptual and methodological considerations. *Metacognition and Learning, 1*(1), 3–14.

Vollmeyer, R., & Rheinberg, F. (2005). A surprising effect of feedback on learning. *Learning and Instruction, 15*(6), 589–602.

Waterhouse, I. K., & Child, I. L. (1953). Frustration and the quality of performance. *Journal of Personality, 21*, 298–311.

Wolfson, M. A., Mathieu, J. E., Tannenbaum, S. I., & Maynard, M. T. (2019). Informal field-based learning and work design. *Journal of Applied Psychology, 104*(10), 1283–1295.

Yang, J. T. (2007). The impact of knowledge sharing on organizational learning and effectiveness. *Journal of Knowledge Management, 11*(2), 83–90.

Yerkes, R. M., & Dodson, J. D. (1908). The relation of strength of stimulus to rapidity of habit-formation. *Journal of Comparative Neurology and Psychology, 18*(5), 459–482.

18

MANAGEMENT EDUCATION IN TURBULENT TIMES

Mindfulness in the classroom

Anne Randerson and Rajnandini Pillai

In our present world of heightened financial uncertainty, mistrust of diverse beliefs, and constant threats of violence, it is vital that humans seek to become more culturally intelligent beings. The philosophical origin of management education shows a connection between how students are taught and how well they achieve (Campbell & Campbell, 2009; Carson, Shih, & Langer, 2001; Jouillé, 2016). We argue that developing our management students' ability to engage in mindfulness practices will help them better understand how to make more effective decisions in a multicultural, multipolar VUCA (post-Cold War acronym developed by the US military and now used in business—*volatility*, *uncertainty*, *complexity*, and *ambiguity*) world. In recent times, some of that turbulence has come from the surprise election of Donald Trump in 2016, Brexit in the United Kingdom and its implications for the British economy, the European Union and the world at large, anti-immigration sentiments and populism in different parts of the world, the ongoing wars in the Middle East, and the ever-present threat of terrorist attacks, both domestic and foreign. Mindfulness predicts positive emotional states and effective stress management (Brown & Ryan, 2003) and demonstrates great success in many clinical settings. Ruedy and Schweitzer (2010) showed that higher levels of mindfulness even curtailed unethical behavior. Perhaps developing mindfulness in managers will better equip them to manage during these challenging times.

Researchers define the term "mindfulness" in a variety of ways. Brown, Ryan, and Creswell (2007) define mindfulness as: "a receptive attention to and awareness of present events and experience" (p. 212). We argue that ultimately, this heightened cultural intelligence through mindfulness should have a direct effect on how our management students view the world, thereby influencing the future business decisions they will make with counterparts in other countries (Gehrke & Claes, 2014; Thomas & Inkson, 2009). The end result could even motivate them, as cohorts or teams, to unite and help foster peace in our world, rather than focusing on self-interest and greed (Bosse & Phillips, 2016; Harung,

Heato, & Alexander, 1995). For instance, Weare's (2014) research in the Mindfulness in Schools Project concludes:

> Mindfulness has been shown to impact on many of the complex and interrelated mental qualities which underlie wellbeing, such as the ability to accept experience, to manage difficult feelings, to be resilient, motivated, persistent and optimistic, to enjoy good relationships and experience a sense of meaning.
>
> *(p. 13)*

Research studies and philosophical texts show the multiple benefits of mindfulness in education, health care, and the corporate world (Borker, 2013a; Brown et al., 2007; Fredrickson, Cohn, Coffey, Pek, & Finkel, 2008; Good et al., 2016; Grauer, 2016; Kok et al., 2013). In addition to highlighting prior theoretical, philosophical, and empirical research, we include personal perspectives from our own experiences using mindfulness practices while teaching global business and leadership courses to management students.

For at least 50 years, applied research on human effectiveness has demonstrated that individuals are greatly influenced by their notion of time and their perceptions of reality (Brown et al., 2007; Honoré, 2004; Mullen & Suls, 1982; Raz & Buhle, 2006). Yoga, meditation, and the act of becoming more mindful, with the aim of remaining in the present as often as possible—despite modern society's expectations of always functioning in the "future mode"—can make significant differences in hard-working business professionals' lives (Kabat-Zinn, 2005b). Worries about the past or future constantly occupy the attention of most managers as they deal with the turbulent environments they face today. These preoccupations draw their attention away from the present moment (Kabat-Zinn, 2003). We believe that teaching managers how to practice mindfulness will better equip them to make thoughtful decisions based on undergoing a richer experience of events as they occur (Ruedy & Schweitzer, 2010).

When practiced regularly, mindful practices—such as mindful listening, mindful speaking, and mindful breathing—can make a person feel more whole, more compassionate, and more mentally accessible to one's self and others through heightened sensory perception and awareness (Davis, Lau, & Cairns, 2009; Hanna, 1988; Lau et al., 2006; Schmidt-Wilk, Alexander, & Swanson, 1996; Tolle, 2011). These beneficial results should be particularly inspiring to management instructors at business schools who are pressed for time due to the requirements of their demanding academic careers, where they are forced to constantly multitask (Honoré, 2004). Cognitive neuroscience literature shows an erosion of the quality of the tasks we perform when we engage in multitasking, including learning and instruction (Burgess, 2000; Pearsall, 1996).

Being more mindful makes us more efficient, yet rare is the awakened teacher who softens boundaries while maintaining curiosity about others (Grauer, 2016). This mindful, awakened teacher "embraces the occasional chaos of not knowing where the lesson will end, feels unburdened by stodgy old authority systems and ... remains confident in the capacity and depth of students" (Grauer, 2016, p. 37). If management instructors can grasp the benefits of mindfulness like this awakened teacher, we contend that they can make a difference in their students' lives and the world (Shrivastava, 2010). Through meditation and reflective exercises, the intuitive human mind, purged of extraneous thoughts, becomes more relaxed. This makes the body's physical and emotional state better prepared to perceive new situations with more clarity and insight (Brown et al., 2007; Ho, 2011; Hofmann, Grossman, & Hinton, 2011). The mind reacts to unexpected issues with more strength, inner courage, spontaneity, and gentleness. This, in turn, creates more joyful and productive individuals who, according to research, come across as more focused, genuine, and caring about others (Fredrickson et al., 2008; Kabat-Zinn, 2005a; Langer, 2000; Schmidt-Wilk et al., 1996). In addition, this inner reflection allows people to interpret problems in a more profound manner, lessening the need for rationalization about their own behavior (Loughran, 2002). As a consequence, not only does overall wellbeing improve, such as stronger immune systems, increased brain activity measured by EEG tests, reduced stress levels, lower heart rate, and lower blood pressure (Harung et al., 1995; Ho, 2011; Hofmann et al., 2011; Oschsner, Bunge, Gross, & Gabrieli, 2002), but others can sense a positive shift in the person's energy, optimism, and equilibrium. This greater resiliency and wellbeing is sorely needed as we teach our management students to navigate the turbulent times that we live in.

Psychological researchers, especially cognitive behavioral therapists, are increasingly realizing the multiple benefits of mindfulness (Carson et al., 2001; Fredrickson et al., 2008; Ho, 2011; Kok et al., 2013). As they research its effects on human physiological and cognitive processes, they have seen positive results treating symptoms such as extreme suffering through Mindfulness-Based Cognitive Therapy and culturally congruent health care (Baer, 2011; Harung et al., 1995; Hofmann et al., 2011; Segal, Williams, & Teasdale, 2002; Tonelli & Wachholtz, 2014).

Why is this important for management instructors to understand? Because it highlights the incredible potential of mindfulness to transform us into more grounded, more caring, and more thriving instructors and students (Hawk & Lyons, 2008; Langer, 2000; Nhat Hanh, 1987). Remaining in the present helps shield us from the pain of the past and the angst of the future. This affects how managers relate to their employees, just as it affects how management instructors relate to their students, and vice versa (Good et al., 2016).

Lessons from research in the Far East

Unfortunately, many business schools place lesser importance on how instructors care for their students and do not often realize the philosophy behind mainstream management thought, which comes largely from the West (Jouillé, 2016; Ray, Baker, & Plowman, 2011). Institutions that realize the many benefits of mindfulness, however, such as Maharishi University of Management (see Schmidt-Wilk et al., 1996), which offers management courses while students practice transcendental meditation, realize the value of prioritizing instructor–student interactions in a more humanistic and caring way (Baetz & Sharp, 2004; Burton & Dunn, 2005; Ghoshal, 2005; Mintzberg, 2004; Mitroff, 2004; Pfeffer, 2005; Ray et al., 2011). When we disregard the importance of meaningful relationships and the small things in life that really matter, we lose out on the quality of our experiences (Finley, 2007). This especially holds true in the context of cross-cultural business interactions, if we focus primarily on ourselves (Bosse & Phillips, 2016). This important wisdom reflects the traditional Buddhist notions of detachment, mindfulness, truthful living, and compassion. Some researchers feel it would be advantageous to combine these Far Eastern ancient practices into our modern way of living, especially in business organizations (Morgan & Lawton, 1996; Nhat Hanh, 1987; Randerson, 2015; Schmidt-Wilk et al., 1996). One way to fully appreciate life's experiences is to slow down (Honoré, 2004; Miller, 2004). Practitioners of Far Eastern martial arts such as tai chi chuan learn to feel what they are experiencing in each moment through a gentle flow of mindful movements, which helps them develop a deeper mind–body connection and heightened sensitivity to their environment. Slowing down in this way would be especially beneficial to management instructors and students. "Like the garden burned up from being watered at midday, when the water itself turns hot, we, too, can be burned up by forcing ourselves at an unnatural pace" (Cameron, 2004, p. 144).

Buddhist monks, such as Thich Nhat Hanh (1987), author of *The Miracle of Mindfulness*, have been practicing the art of slowing down for centuries. So have yogis, Native American healers, shamans, and many other spiritual leaders, such as Mahatma Gandhi.

Research on traditional wisdom from Far Eastern cultures maintains that if humans can become more mindful—experiencing each moment in our lives as if it were the last one we would ever have—we can open up new pathways to consciousness (Harung et al., 1995). This concept is in direct opposition to "mindlessness," according to Carson et al. (2001), which "leads to a relatively stable and rigid categorization of information" (p. 184). Many spiritual authors write that these new pathways to individual consciousness lead us to a greater collective consciousness, which can potentially impact the world (Cameron, 2004; Chopra, 2003; Dyer, 2003; Nepo, 2005; Nhat Hanh, 1987; Tolle, 2011). They extol the art of being—the art of living in the present moment—as one of the main paths to happiness. These individuals are spiritual masters, teachers, and healers. They teach people how to connect with their inner selves, and with others, through deeper levels of consciousness. They maintain that the key to this higher state of consciousness, or presence, is constantly being attentive and being aware of one's bodily sensations at all times. When the body feels more relaxed, the mind is able to deepen its wisdom and intuition (Hanna, 1988), giving us the reflex to step back and reflect before taking action. This means staying mindful, compassionate, grateful for life's blessings, and becoming more accepting of others.

When we are fully aware of our bodily sensations, our thought processes are transformed (Brown & Ryan, 2003; Hanna, 1988; Langer, 2000; Tolle, 2011), creating an effortless yet powerful experience. Not only can these processes help boost our individual and organizational productivity (Harung et al., 1995; Schmidt-Wilk et al., 1996), but they can greatly enhance how we communicate with people from diverse cultures. Being more mindful can give us a deeper perspective of others, by opening up a new path of consciousness (Harung et al., 1995). As explained by J. Schmidt-Wilk (2009), "developmental theory suggests that teaching to only the surface levels of the mind will not develop students' greatest potentials" (p. 657). Schmidt-Wilk (2009) refers to this as the "concrete thinking mind," which we believe we rely on in our Western world more than in Asia, which tends to use "the full range" of the mind as it reaches out to others before one's self.

This theory relates to the idea of viewing social reality in practice as "individual interests and social norms ... are always in relation to one another" (Feldman & Worline, 2016, p. 309). While the first author was living in Japan, she learned the true meaning of connecting with others—to not only think about others but to always place their needs before hers. This is how things are usually done in Asian countries, which tend to have more collectivistic attitudes (Tseng & Seidman, 2007). Social rules in Asian societies place a stronger importance on relationships than in the United States, one of the most individualistic nations in the world, with a score of 91 out of 100 on Geert Hofstede's cultural dimension for individualism (Hofstede, 2015). Cross-cultural researchers Walls and Triandis (2014) confirm this:

> In a collectivist culture, the self is viewed as part of a collective group. In such cultures, the needs of others are taken into account before one's own needs, and therefore collective goals, norms, and obligations regulate social behavior. By

> contrast, individualist cultures define the self as independent and autonomous. Personal goals are given priority over collective ones, in favor of individual freedom and enjoyment.
>
> (*p. 347*)

In Japan there is an underlying basis of mindful consideration for others, linking knowledge to behavior (Thomas, 2006), focusing on preserving a sense of *wa*, or harmony, in all interactions. In her fieldwork, the first author noticed a strong distinction between the Japanese and Western ways of interacting with others, showing respect, and viewing the world. Much of the mindful consideration evidenced in Japan showed up in nuanced ways; so nuanced, in fact, it was almost undetectable to foreign visitors, yet recognizable to those who had spent time living in the country and mastering the intricacies of the Japanese language.

Cultural nuances expressed through mindful consideration, such as what she experienced in Japan, are essential for instructors to transmit to cross-cultural management students (Tseng & Seidman, 2007). It is important to give them a more in-depth perception of culture, which we do not readily see in our Western world (Gehrke & Claes, 2014; Kaufman, 2013; McCollum, 1999). For example, in Japan, contrary to the USA, people rarely say what they truly think, or what they really want, to others. Not even to close, intimate friends. It is vital to not rock the boat or disrupt the *wa* (harmony) that should continually exist between individuals and the community. If one does disrupt the *wa*, everyone involved loses face. If it is a major offense, a person is likely to be excluded from the community; this is accompanied by a profound sense of shame felt by the offender—the worst punishment someone in Japan can ever have. In our Western, more individualistic society, however, being excluded does not bring the intense sense of shame that the Far-Easterner feels. This is because our Western society emerges from the "homo economicus" model of social order (Feldman & Worline, 2016). Exclusion might provoke fleeting sensations of guilt, which will most likely fade while we rush to achieve the next item in our increasingly full agendas.

The impact of mindfulness on information processing

How can we learn to use mindfulness to help us develop our students' cultural intelligence? How can we give our students the ability to calmly process information and make effective decisions through turbulent times? One aspect of mindfulness means being present for every action and non-action that we experience throughout the day. It signifies not only being present, but awake, observant, compassionate, and grateful. Vietnamese Buddhist monk and author Thich Nhat Hanh (1987) provides an explicit example of this by comparing two ways to wash dishes: "The first is to wash the dishes in order to have clean dishes and the second is to wash the dishes in order to wash the dishes" (p. 4). When we do actions mindfully, with full presence, we are aware, we are lucid, and we are in harmony with our soul—holistically present in mind, body, and spirit. Likewise, Mariechild and Goodman (1987) express the powerful sensation of opening ourselves through mindfulness:

> Opening the self is a process that begins in silence as we spend time observing and exploring our breathing, the sensations and feelings in our bodies, the thoughts and images in our minds. Our experiences in life may have been such that, without

> knowing it, we have chosen to shut down. We may not even be aware of our feelings or of the constant chatter that goes on in our minds. We may get flashes of insight and not trust them.
>
> *(p. 71)*

When humans practice this sense of extreme presence, their minds are free to think clearer thoughts. The state of heightened awareness that comes from practicing mindfulness creates a deeper space in our minds and bodies (Brown et al., 2007; Good et al., 2016; Nhat Hanh, 1987). Practicing mindfulness focuses our attention—yet broadens our perspectives—and ultimately transforms our perception of reality by creating more meaning in our lives (Schwandt, 2005). It also relies on our continual monitoring of both internal and external stimuli. This development of transcendental consciousness (Harung et al., 1995; Thomas, 2006) can lead to higher leadership potential. For when we create this deeper space in our minds—when we are living in the "gap" between thoughts—not only do we experience a heightened sense of freedom, we go through our day with a greater sense of clarity (Chopra, 2003; Dyer, 2003). This sense of clarity will allow us to process information calmly, weigh the pros and cons of a crisis situation, and take the appropriate actions without getting into panic mode and making rash decisions. This is an important skill for managers operating in these challenging times.

This is why it is recommended to start our days with meditation. "The morning meditation focuses your intention for the day, even when you are not even thinking about it" (Chopra, 2003, p. 178). If we explore the Asian way of appreciating human existence through traditional Far Eastern religions, such as Buddhism and Hinduism—and its connection to the ancient art of yoga—we might conclude that a greater connection between the human body, mind, and spirit can be reached through contemplative meditation. This form of meditation involves the practice of setting intentions to create our external realities by reflecting on our internal world. This practice relates to theories of quantum physics (Pavlovich & Krahnke, 2012; Pearsall, 1996), as well as relationships between cognition, computers, and mindfulness, which attracted the early attention of researchers around the world, especially in the West (Chopra, 2003; Harung et al., 1995; Langer & Moldoveanu, 2000; McCollum, 1999).

Similarly, Kornfield (1993) explores mindful concentration through meditation, which may take months to achieve. This concentration slowly settles like grains of sand in an old-fashioned timer. He explains, "Initially, we may have struggled to focus, trying to hold on to the subject of our meditation. Then gradually the mind and the heart become eased from distractions, and periodically we sense them as purer, more workable and malleable" (p. 61). Once our minds become clear, with a heightened sense of awareness and insight, we are in the "flow" and better ready to act, and react, to life's unexpected surprises and challenges (Carson et al., 2001; Czikszentmihalyi, 1990; Dyer, 2003). Likewise, Cameron (2004), an expert on tapping into human creativity, explains: "When we are 'in the flow'—even the word speaks of water—ideas come to us naturally" (p. 145). Through this process we unearth our passions, which helps us realize our unique transformational potential (Shrivastava, 2010).

From these perspectives, can we not see how the practice of mindfulness might give our management students a distinct advantage in our increasingly complex global world of business? Consider the creative abundance and clarity it can bring to their thoughts (Czikszentmihalyi, 2003; Gehrke & Claes, 2014; Good et al., 2016; Harung et al., 1995; Honoré, 2004; Schmidt-Wilk, 2009). Tapping into their unique, inner source of wisdom at deeper levels potentially awakens a powerful sense of curiosity, like a child's, to explore the world and strive to make it a better place. Opening up this way could replace the "trouble" we get into when we become adults, which Palmer (1998) describes in *The Courage to Teach*. According to Palmer, when we enter adulthood we establish "partitions between thinking and feeling, personal and professional, shadow and light" (p. 64). Mindfulness teaches us to relax these mental/emotional partitions and soften these divisions, created by our discriminatory adult minds.

Strengthened minds through greater awareness

Contrary to what one might imagine, the process of loosening our thoughts through mindful presence actually strengthens our minds (Cameron, 2004; Chopra, 2003; Dyer, 2003; Tolle, 2011). This comes about when we pay closer attention to our breathing. "Mindful breathing puts the mind and body in a state of calm presence in the moment with openness to perceptions, ideas or concepts without mental obstructions or distractions" (Borker, 2013b, p. 497). This may seem contrary to logic, yet the reasoning makes sense once we have experienced it. The act of meditation may appear daunting at first, as most adults are not used to sitting still and concentrating on nothing except for breathing or a short, repetitive mantra (a special word, or series of words).

When we begin meditating, we often become restless, our minds wander; our incessant thoughts—created by what is commonly referred to in Buddhist philosophy as our "monkey mind"—send our body signals that we would rather do something else, anything else, than sit immobile on a cushion, struggling to empty our brains (Carson et al., 2001). We are tired of playing still—we want action. Used to living for the future through present-moment sacrifice, our short-term, quick-fix, consumption-oriented mentalities cultivated in the West (Brodowsky, Granitz, & Anderson, 2008) demand to know what comes next (Sheldon & Vansteenkiste, 2005). If taken to an extreme, the energy we spend focusing outside ourselves can very well lead us to burnout or other mental or workplace-related illnesses.

Yet it is precisely when we believe that nothing is happening that powerful changes are occurring in our lives (Kabat-Zinn, 2005a; Nepo, 2005; Tolle, 2011). This is when we need most to concentrate on our breathing, as expressed by Borker (2013b), "Mindful breathing provides the student with a solid, stable base for dealing with what happens not only in our environment, but internally" (p. 44). And Kornfield (1993) explains:

> Breathing meditation can quiet the mind, open the body, and develop a great power of concentration. The breath is available to us at any time of day and in any circumstance. When we have learned to use it, the breath becomes a support for awareness throughout our life.
>
> *(p. 60)*

It is precisely this deeper sense of awareness that needs to be cultivated in our management students, especially those who will interact constantly—through advanced technological connectivity—with executives around the globe (Colbert, Yee, & George, 2016; Schmidt-Wilk, 2009; Schmidt-Wilk et al., 1996). By remaining in the present tense and training their minds to step back and reflect on sudden "crisis" situations, our managers can gain more profound and precise insight into the actual situation. This will help them better handle the multiple challenges that they have to face as they deal with rapid changes in the global context (e.g., impact of trade policies, immigration and labor issues, nationalism and anti-globalization).

In fact, the enlightened and compassionate former leader of India, Mahatma Gandhi, would declare that he needed to spend twice as much time meditating in anticipation of an extremely busy day. This impactful leader realized the direct relationship between higher states of human consciousness that he developed through meditation and his effective leadership performance. This relationship could be explained in part by Vedic philosophy, even before researchers found evidence of it in leadership studies. "Vedic psychology explains that the single intervention of developing consciousness exerts a positive influence on the complete psychology, physiology, behavior, and environment of the individual" (Harung et al., 1995, p. 45). This can also be explained by the Buddhist tradition of meditation and living mindfully, as "a person with a clouded mind will not be able to make wise decisions and will not have a firm grasp of the truth about the way things are, and the consequences of his or her actions" (Morgan & Lawton, 1996, p. 72).

In the Western business world, we tend to rely on our logical brains to analyze situations (Shanahan, 2000). Our priority is to make immediate judgments and take swift action. Otherwise, we may fear that our stakeholders' investments will be lost, future deals will fall through, or worse. Yet practicing mindfulness strengthens individuals from within, reducing a persistent sense of fear that often results from focusing on external situations alone. This is why teaching management students to look inside and cultivate their sense of awareness can produce more resilient managers, especially on an international level (Borker, 2013a; Earley, 2002; Good et al., 2016; Harung et al., 1995). Mindfulness might also make them more motivated to perform (Eisenberg et al., 2013; Hawk & Lyons, 2008).

Despite increasing evidence that our internal, cultural biases can be minimized by this reflective process through measurements in mindfulness (Schmidt-Wilk et al., 1996), it is truly unfortunate that training to foster deeper awareness is not systematically taught in our university business courses (Williams & Kabat-Zinn, 2013). Considering this, we may want to revisit the priorities of our education systems (Bensimon, Polkinghorne, Bauman, & Vallejo, 2004).

The role of mindful listening

A positive outcome of developing this deep state of awareness is that it has the potential to transform the human collective consciousness, which could generate more mutual understanding and willingness for diverse cultures to get along. After all, "nourishing the soul at work may be good for business" (Ashmos & Duchon, 2000, p. 136). We see this increased awareness making an impact on an even broader, globalized scale. Imagine a more enlightened and compassionate world where policymakers, politicians, and citizens from all countries prioritize peaceful international negotiations and conflict resolution (Bosse & Phillips, 2016). Creating situations of peace may largely be a matter of focusing on the other before one's self, with less bounded self-interest, and being mindful in all situations.

We could start this transformational process by introducing the concepts of mindful listening in our management classes (Fiumara, 1990; Hawk & Lyons, 2008). We regularly ask our business students to close their eyes, concentrate on their breathing, listen for a full minute to their surroundings, and tell the class how they felt during the exercise. A handful of students usually report feeling uncomfortable with silence and introspection (Langer, Blank, & Chanowitz, 1978), while others express feelings of peace and tranquility.

Even brief listening exercises such as this at the start of class can heighten management students' state of awareness, their perspective on their current life situation, and their view of the world (Borker, 2013a; Hawk & Lyons, 2008; Kaufman, 2013; Loughran, 2002). Mindful listening is *authentic* listening; it gives full attention to the speaker, as well as compassion, empathy, and respect (Fiumara, 1990; Hoffman, 2000). It can also be practiced when a speaker is addressing the class, inviting meaningful discourse and conversation (Borker, 2013b; Schwandt, 2005). It is beneficial at all times, especially in the present tense, when students remain actively alert to what is happening around them (Brown et al., 2007; Fiumara, 1990; Morgan & Lawton, 1996; Palmer, 1998; Slote, 2007).

How can these mindful practices help our management students succeed in the turbulent times that characterize our global workplace? As an example of a brief reflective exercise, we often ask our students: "Have you ever noticed when somebody is not listening to you? How does it make you feel?" After reflection, student responses may vary, but in our classes, they usually include feelings of anger, frustration, or loneliness—the opposite of connection, which we are trying to achieve. According to Borker (2013b), "Mindful listening can have a powerfully supportive effect on the person who is being listened to. There is a great satisfaction in feeling really heard" (p. 46). This is certainly true for our students in culturally diverse environments who need to be heard in a culturally intelligent context (Kaufman, 2013), especially during the turbulent times we are experiencing in the global arena.

Introducing meditation and mindful practices in the classroom

Once the first author had broken the ice through informal self-reflective activities—such as drawing stick figures to represent themselves and labeling essential aspects of their cultural identities—she introduced the concept of meditation to her students at the second class session. As soon as the students walked in the door, she gave them a piece of paper with a basic description of how to meditate. She brought a little metallic bell and asked them to sit down with their backs straight and feet firmly planted on the floor. She read from the paper, guiding the students how to breathe during meditation, how to close their eyes, how to focus on a mantra—a special word or unique series of words that they would choose for themselves. She told them the aim of the brief exercise was to empty their minds—but not to worry if thoughts came up in the process—and to ultimately relax, allowing their bodies and minds to become receptive and peaceful. After she explained the multiple benefits of meditation, as evidenced by numerous scientific research studies, she asked the students how many had already tried it. Only a few hands went up; those who had experienced it reported that they found it beneficial. She then conducted ten-minute meditation sessions at the start of each class session. Halfway through the semester she asked for class feedback on this meditative exercise. Most of the students who participated each week reported a heightened feeling of peace. It began at the start of class and lasted throughout their daily activities. Several wrote private emails to thank her for introducing meditation to them. Some said they were practicing it at home. Many were sleeping better and several reported being happier. Moreover, during informal group discussions, the students expressed that their thoughts were clearer, with more distinct priorities—not only in class, but at home and in the workplace. Many were able to accomplish more tasks each day; they suddenly had more energy. Moreover, it appeared that their notion of time seemed to stretch, whereas before, they were always rushing to get from one place or one task to another.

The second author participated in a year-long faculty development program on campus that was designed to introduce mindfulness practices in courses in different disciplines across the campus. She was teaching a leadership course in the college of business administration at a state university and decided to gradually introduce mindfulness in her class. Students were faced with a lot of stress because of the uncertainties and turbulence caused by a very difficult election year in the United States. The second author felt that introducing mindfulness practices might in some small way help the business students cope with all the stress. She set the stage by defining the concept of mindfulness, the growing research on its effectiveness, and its adoption by large business corporations, including Google, which even has a Search Inside Yourself Leadership Institute that has trained a number of mindfulness practitioners. She then gently introduced the students to a simple two-minute mindfulness breathing practice. In order to ensure that the class experimented with and experienced mindful activities on a regular basis, she listed a series of daily practices (e.g., mindful eating, walking, showering, and listening) that the students could try out each week. In class, she linked it to effective leadership behaviors such as active listening and explained how mindful listening practices could greatly improve the leader–follower relationship. She also required the students to maintain a reflective journal, which they submitted at the end of the semester. Reflective journaling fosters reflexivity (Dyer & Hurd, 2016) and teaches students to second-guess their own first instincts and how to show appreciation and respect towards others. It also opens their minds to their inner source of creativity, which they cannot always express freely in traditional business classroom environments. Here are some excerpts from the reflective journals:

> Learning how to breathe deeply and focus on the present helped me use my car for "me" time and I absolutely love it.
>
> Reading *Search Inside Yourself* by Google's Chade-Meng Tan solidified my understanding. I wake up ten minutes earlier every day to practice mindful meditation and find a positive way of starting the day.
>
> Instead of reacting negatively to an altercation at a non-profit that I work for, I used mindful breathing to tactfully resolve the situation and walk away without wronging anyone.
>
> Focusing on my breath has not only helped me be less distracted, but it does help me with my impatient nature. I realized that knowing how to calm one's mind and remain patient are practices that my CEO uses constantly.
>
> Instead of panicking at work during a crisis, I decided to stop what I was doing, close my eyes, and breathe. This allowed me to focus my attention on my breath and my physical sensations of actually breathing. It helped me calm down and realize that I can handle the situation. I will definitely be using this practice more often.

Other contemplative exercises and self-reflective activities

In addition to meditation, instructors can use other contemplative exercises and self-reflective activities, such as a "Self-Assessment Exercise on Interpersonal Communication in the Workplace" (Brislin, 1994), and journaling, to guide management students towards a more peaceful and meaningful classroom experience. These contemplative exercises can also greatly increase awareness (Borker, 2013b; Langer, 2000). For example, one student expressed that applying the course readings to a personal ethical issue and meditating contributed most to his learning. And when students journal about their emotions, they can become more self-aware of their tendencies to judge (Bradberry & Greaves, 2009). Fortunately, innovative ideas are starting to take root in management curricula across the globe, including courses introducing mindfulness and business/leadership practices, along with more in-depth cultural integration studies (Armstrong, 2011; Czikszentmihalyi, 2003; Eisenberg et al., 2013; Good et al., 2016; Ramsey & Lorenz, 2016).

Conclusion

In this chapter, we have offered a global perspective on the importance of using mindfulness in the business classroom. We believe that in these turbulent times, teaching managers some useful mindfulness practices that they can either adopt on a daily basis or deploy under stressful conditions will go a long way toward helping them cope effectively with the challenges of their environment. We offer our own experiences using these practices in our classrooms. Both authors are currently participating in a campus-wide initiative to bring contemplative pedagogy to classrooms in every discipline on campus and to benefit large groups of students and staff through mindfulness sits and programs. We have also just begun to gather some preliminary data on the impact of these practices on our business students (including managers). To expand on the beneficial effects of mindfulness presented in this chapter, more studies should be conducted on mindfulness and compassion and their connection to students' levels of cultural intelligence. Not only could researchers initiate long-term quantitative and qualitative studies in business classrooms across the nation, but they could extend these studies to small and medium-sized enterprises, governmental organizations, and non-governmental organizations (NGOs) around the world.

Despite our increased digital connectivity (Colbert et al., 2016), given the current state of international unrest in our world, developing and maintaining successful long-term relationships with global business counterparts is vital (Blasco, 2009; Ma, 2010). We strongly believe that introducing mindfulness to management courses by knowledgeable and caring instructors who already have a daily mindfulness practice of their own will bring important added value and meaning to our students' lives. Introducing contemplative practices such as mindfulness into professional learning environments appears not only timely, but essential, judging from the rising popularity of mindfulness training programs offered worldwide, in a wide variety of settings including hospitals, schools, large and small businesses, clinics, prisons, and universities (Kabat-Zinn, 2003).

Chapter takeaways

1. We live in a VUCA world (volatility, uncertainty, complexity, and ambiguity) and mindfulness can be one of the solutions to help us cope with current and future turbulence felt within ourselves and our environments.
2. Mindfulness has shown to benefit human physiological and cognitive processes and can help management students and instructors become more grounded, contemplative, and caring.
3. Mindfulness can help us integrate cross-cultural differences and bridge the cultural gaps between Eastern management thought and practices and Western management philosophy.

4. Managers can better understand how to handle crisis and rapid change by gaining a profound insight into particular situations through the process of cultivating a deep sense of awareness and by training their minds to step back and reflect before reacting.
5. Our experiences with mindfulness practices in the business classroom (e.g., mindful listening, mindful journaling) have shown us that we can help our students both inside and outside the classroom (e.g., reducing stress, developing empathy, fostering reflexivity, becoming better leaders).

Questions for reflection

1. Is mindfulness a potential solution to cope with the stresses of the rapidly changing world we live in or is it a fad that will eventually fade away?
2. Is it possible to teach management students and business people mindfulness in cross-cultural settings? How can we adapt what is essentially derived from Far Eastern wisdom practices to the Western cultural context in a secular way while still respecting its origin and deep meaning?
3. What can we do to overcome possible skepticism about mindfulness from students in the management classroom who will stop reading or listening as soon as they read or see "mindfulness" and "meditation"?
4. How can we design effective studies to measure the benefits of mindfulness across cultures and over time?
5. Which kinds of contemplative practices, such as mindfulness meditation, mindful listening, mindful eating, and mindful movement, for example, yoga, qi gong, or tai chi chaun, do you prefer and why?

References

Armstrong, S. J. (2011). From the editors: Continuing our quest for meaningful impact on management practice. *Academy of Management Learning & Education, 10*(2), 181–187.

Ashmos, D. P., & Duchon, D. (2000). Spirituality at work: A conceptualization and measure. *Journal of Management Inquiry, 9*(2), 134–145.

Baer, R. A. (2011). Measuring mindfulness. *Contemporary Buddhism, 12*(1), 241–261.

Baetz, M. C., & Sharp, D. J. (2004). Integrating ethics content into the core business curriculum: Do core teaching materials do the job? *Journal of Business Ethics, 51*(1), 53–63.

Bensimon, E. M., Polkinghorne, D. E., Bauman, G. L., & Vallejo, E. (2004). Doing research that makes a difference. *Journal of Higher Education, 75*(1), 104–126.

Blasco, M. (2009). Cultural pragmatists? Student perspectives on learning culture at a business school. *Academy of Management Learning & Education, 8*(2), 174–187.

Borker, D. R. (2013a). Mindfulness practices and learning economics. *American Journal of Business Education, 6*(5), 495–504.

Borker, D. R. (2013b). Mindfulness practices for accounting and business education: A new perspective. *American Journal of Business Education, 6*(1), 41–55.

Bosse, D. A., & Phillips, R. A. (2016). Agency theory and bounded self-interest. *Academy of Management Review, 41*(2), 276–297.

Bradberry, T., & Greaves, J. (2009). *Emotional intelligence 2.0.* San Diego, CA: TalentSmart.

Brislin, R. W. (1994). Working cooperatively with people from different cultures. In R. W. Brislin & T. Yoshida (Eds.), *Improving intercultural interactions: Modules for cross-cultural training programs* Multicultural aspects of counseling series 3 (pp. 17–33). Thousand Oaks, CA: Sage.

Brodowsky, G. H., Granitz, N., & Anderson, B. B. (2008). The best of times is now: A study of the gay subculture's attitudes toward time. *Time & Society, 17*(2/3), 233–260.

Brown, K. W., & Ryan, R. M. (2003). The benefits of being present: Mindfulness and its role in psychological well-being. *Journal of Personality and Social Psychology, 84*, 822–848.

Brown, K. W., Ryan, R. M., & Creswell, J. D. (2007). Mindfulness: Theoretical foundations and evidence for its salutary effects. *Psychological Inquiry, 18*(4), 211–237.

Burgess, P. K. (2000). Real-world multitasking from a cognitive neuroscience perspective. In S. Monsell & J. Driver (Eds.), *Control of cognitive processes: Attention and performance XVIII* (pp. 465–472). Cambridge, MA: MIT Press.

Burton, B. K., & Dunn, C. P. (2005). The caring approach and social issues in management education. *Journal of Management Education, 29*(3), 453–474.

Cameron, J. (2004). *The sound of paper: Starting from scratch*. New York, NY: Tarcher/Penguin.

Campbell, L., & Campbell, B. (2009). *Mindful learning*. Thousand Oaks, CA: Corwin Press.

Carson, S., Shih, M., & Langer, E. (2001). Sit still and pay attention? *Journal of Adult Development, 8*(3), 183–188.

Chopra, D. (2003). *The spontaneous fulfillment of desire: Harnessing the infinite power of coincidence*. New York, NY: Harmony Books.

Colbert, A., Yee, N., & George, G. (2016). From the editors—The digital workforce and the workplace of the future. *Academy of Management Journal, 59*(3), 731–739.

Czikszentmihalyi, M. (1990). *Flow: The psychology of optimal experience*. New York, NY: HarperCollins.

Czikszentmihalyi, M. (2003). *Good business: Leadership, flow, and the making of meaning*. New York, NY: Viking Penguin.

Davis, K., Lau, M., & Cairns, D. (2009). Development and preliminary validation of a trait version of the Toronto mindfulness scale. *Journal of Cognitive Psychotherapy, 23*, 185–197.

Dyer, S. L., & Hurd, F. (2016). "What's going on?" Developing reflexivity in the management classroom: From surface to deep learning and everything in between. *Academy of Management Learning & Education, 15*(2), 287–303.

Dyer, W. W. (2003). *Getting in the gap: Making conscious contact with god through meditation*. Carlsbad, CA: Hay House.

Earley, P. C. (2002). Redefining interactions across cultures and organizations: Moving forward with cultural intelligence. *Research in Organizational Behavior, 24*, 271–299.

Eisenberg, J., Lee, H. J., Brück, F., Brenner, B., Claes, M. T., Mironski, J., & Bell, R. (2013). Can business schools make students culturally competent? Effects of cross-cultural management courses on cultural intelligence. *Academy of Management Learning & Education, 12*(4), 603–621.

Feldman, M., & Worline, M. (2016). The practicality of practice theory. *Academy of Management Learning & Education, 15*(2), 304–324.

Finley, G. (2007). *The secret of letting go*. Woodbury, MN: Llewellyn Worldwide.

Fiumara, G. C. (1990). *The other side of language: A philosophy of listening*. New York, NY: Routledge.

Fredrickson, B. L., Cohn, M. A., Coffey, K. A., Pek, J., & Finkel, S. M. (2008). Open hearts build lives: Positive emotions, induced through loving-kindness meditation, build consequential personal resources. *Journal of Personality and Social Psychology, 95*(5), 1045–1062.

Gehrke, B., & Claes, M. T. (2014). *Global leadership practices: A cross-cultural management perspective*. Basingstoke, United Kingdom: Palgrave Macmillan.

Ghoshal, S. (2005). Bad management theories are destroying good management practices. *Academy of Management Learning & Education, 4*(1), 74–91.

Good, D. J., Lyddy, C. J., Glomb, T. M., Bono, J. E., Brown, K. W., Duffy, M. K., . . . Lazar, S. W. (2016). Contemplating mindfulness at work. *Journal of Management, 42*(1), 114–142.

Grauer, S. (2016). *Fearless teaching*. Roslyn Heights, NY: Alternative Education Resource Organization.

Hanna, T. (1988). *Somatics: Reawakening the mind's control of movement, flexibility, and health*. Cambridge, MA: Da Capo Press.

Harung, H. S., Heato, D. P., & Alexander, C. N. (1995). A unified theory of leadership: Experiences of higher states of consciousness in world-class leaders. *Leadership & Organization Development Journal, 16*(7), 44–59.

Hawk, T. F., & Lyons, P. R. (2008). Please don't give up on me: When faculty fail to care. *Journal of Management Education, 32*(3), 316–338.

Ho, L. A. (2011). Meditation, learning, organizational innovation and performance. *Industrial Management & Data Systems, 111*(1), 113–131.

Hoffman, M. L. (2000). *Empathy and moral development: Implications for caring and justice*. Cambridge, United Kingdom: Cambridge University Press.

Hofmann, S. G., Grossman, P., & Hinton, D. E. (2011). Loving-kindness and compassion meditation: Potential for psychological interventions. *Clinical Psychology Review, 31*(7), 1126–1132.

Hofstede, G. (2015). *What about the USA?* Retrieved from http://geert-hofstede.com/united-states.html

Honoré, C. (2004). *In praise of slowness: Challenging the cult of speed.* New York, NY: HarperCollins.

Jouillé, J. E. (2016). The philosophical foundations of management thought. *Academy of Management Learning & Education, 15*(1), 157–179.

Kabat-Zinn, J. (2003). Mindfulness-based interventions in context: Past, present, and future. *Clinical Psychology: Science and Practice, 10*(2), 144–156.

Kabat-Zinn, J. (2005a). *Coming to our senses: Healing ourselves and the world through mindfulness.* New York, NY: Hyperion.

Kabat-Zinn, J. (2005b). *Full catastrophe living: Using the wisdom of your body and mind to face stress, pain, and illness.* New York, NY: Delta Trade.

Kaufman, S. R. (2013). The role of mindfulness in cultural intelligence: Impact on culturally congruent patient care. *ETD Collection for Pace University.* Doctoral dissertation, Pace University. Retrieved from http://digitalcommons.pace.edu/dissertations/AAI3691841

Kok, B. E., Coffey, K. A., Cohn, M. A., Catalino, L. I., Vacharkulksemsuk, T., Algoe, S. B., ... Fredrickson, B. L. (2013). How positive emotions build physical health: Perceived positive social connections account for the upward spiral between positive emotions and vagal tone. *Psychological Science, 24*(7), 1123–1132.

Kornfield, J. (1993). *A path with heart: A guide through the perils and promises of spiritual life.* New York, NY: Bantam.

Langer, E. J. (2000). Mindful learning. *Current Directions in Psychological Science, 9*(6), 220–223.

Langer, E. J., Blank, A., & Chanowitz, B. (1978). The mindlessness of ostensibly thoughtful action: The role of "placebic" information in interpersonal interaction. *Journal of Personality and Social Psychology, 36*(6), 635–642.

Langer, E. J., & Moldoveanu, M. (2000). The construct of mindfulness. *Journal of Social Issues., 56*(1), 1–9.

Lau, M., Bishop, S., Segal, Z., Buis, T., Anderson, N., Carlson, L., ... Devins, G. (2006). The Toronto mindfulness scale: Development and validation. *Journal of Clinical Psychology, 62*, 1445–1467.

Loughran, J. J. (2002). Effective reflective practice: In search of meaning in learning about teaching. *Journal of Teacher Education, 53*(1), 33–43.

Ma, Z. (2010). The sins in business negotiations: Explore the cross-cultural differences in business ethics between Canada and China. *Journal of Business Ethics, 91*, 123–135.

Mariechild, D., & Goodman, S. (1987). *The inner dance: A guide to spiritual and psychological unfolding.* Freemont, CA: The Crossing Press.

McCollum, B. (1999). Leadership development and self-development: An empirical study. *Career Development International, 4*(3), 149–154.

Miller, J. (2004). *The slow down book: A pathway to the fullness of life.* Napa, CA: Jessel Gallery.

Mintzberg, H. (2004). *Developing managers not MBA's: A hard look at the soft practice of managing and management development.* New York, NY: FT Prentice Hall.

Mitroff, I. (2004). An open letter to the deans and the faculties of American business schools. *Journal of Business Ethics, 54*(2), 185–190.

Morgan, P., & Lawton, C. (Eds.). (1996). *Ethical issues in six religious traditions.* Edinburgh, Scotland: Edinburgh University Press.

Mullen, B., & Suls, J. (1982). The effectiveness of attention and rejection as coping styles: A meta-analysis of temporal differences. *Journal of Psychosomatic Research, 26*, 43–49.

Nepo, M. (2005). *The exquisite risk: Daring to live an authentic life.* New York, NY: Harmony.

Nhat Hanh, T. (1987). *The miracle of mindfulness: A manual on meditation.* Boston, MA: Beacon Press.

Oschsner, K. N., Bunge, S. A., Gross, J. J., & Gabrieli, J. D. E. (2002). Rethinking feelings: An fMRA study of the cognitive regulation of emotion. *Journal of Cognitive Neuroscience, 14*(8), 1215–1229.

Palmer, P. J. (1998). *The courage to teach: Exploring the inner landscape of a teacher's life.* San Francisco, CA: Jossey-Bass.

Pavlovich, K., & Krahnke, K. (2012). Empathy, connectedness and organisation. *Journal of Business Ethics, 105*, 131–137.

Pearsall, P. (1996). *The pleasure prescription: To love, to work, to play–life in the balance.* Alameda, CA: Hunter House.

Pfeffer, J. (2005). Why do bad management theories persist? A comment on Ghoshal. *Academy of Management Learning & Education, 4*(1), 96–101.
Ramsey, J. R., & Lorenz, M. P. (2016). Exploring the impact of cross-cultural management education on cultural intelligence, student satisfaction, and commitment. *Academy of Management Learning & Education, 15*(4), 79–99.
Randerson, A. (2015). Human sensitivity towards nature: Eastern and Western perspectives. *World Journal of Science, Technology and Sustainable Development, 12*(3), 172–182.
Ray, J. L., Baker, L. T., & Plowman, D. A. (2011). Organizational mindfulness in business schools. *Academy of Management Learning & Education, 10*(2), 188–203.
Raz, A., & Buhle, J. (2006). Typologies of attentional networks. *Nature Reviews Neuroscience*, 7, 367–379.
Ruedy, N. E., & Schweitzer, M. E. (2010). In the moment: The effect of mindfulness on ethical decision making. *Journal of Business Ethics, 95*, 73–87.
Schmidt-Wilk, J. (2009). Teaching to the levels of the mind. *Journal of Management Education, 33*(6), 655–658.
Schmidt-Wilk, J., Alexander, C. N., & Swanson, G. C. (1996). Developing consciousness in organizations: The transcendental meditation program in business. *Journal of Business and Psychology, 10*(4), 429–444.
Schwandt, D. R. (2005). When managers become philosophers: Integrating learning with sensemaking. *Academy of Management Learning & Education, 4*(2), 176–192.
Segal, Z. V., Williams, J. M., & Teasdale, J. D. (2002). *Mindfulness-based cognitive therapy for depression: A new approach to preventing relapse*. New York, NY: Guilford.
Shanahan, M. J. (2000). Pathways to adulthood in changing societies: Variability and mechanisms in life course perspective. *Annual Review of Sociology, 26*, 667–692.
Sheldon, K. M., & Vansteenkiste, M. (2005). Personal goals and time travel: How are future places visited, and it is worth it? In A. Strathman & J. Joireman (Eds.), *Understanding behavior in the context of time: Theory, research, and application* (pp. 143–163). Mahwah, NJ: Lawrence Erlbaum.
Shrivastava, P. (2010). Pedagogy of passion for sustainability. *Academy of Management Learning & Education, 9*(3), 443–455.
Slote, M. (2007). *The ethics of care and empathy*. New York, NY: Routledge.
Thomas, D. C. (2006). Domain and development of cultural intelligence: The importance of mindfulness. *Group & Organization Management, 31*(1), 78–99.
Thomas, D. C., & Inkson, K. (2009). *Cultural intelligence: Living and working globally* (2nd ed.). San Francisco, CA: Berrett-Koehler.
Tolle, E. (2011). *The power of now: A guide to spiritual enlightenment*. London, United Kingdom: Hodder & Stoughton.
Tonelli, M. E., & Wachholtz, A. B. (2014). Meditation-based treatment yielding immediate relief for meditation-naïve migraineurs. *Pain Management Nursing, 15*(1), 36–40.
Tseng, V., & Seidman, E. (2007). A systems framework for understanding social settings. *American Journal of Community Psychology, 39*(3–4), 217–228.
Walls, J. L., & Triandis, H. C. (2014). Universal truths: Can universally held cultural values inform the modern corporation? *Cross Cultural Management, 21*(3), 345–356.
Weare, K. (2014). *Evidence for mindfulness: Impacts on the wellbeing and performance of school staff*. Retrieved from http://mindfulnessinschools.org/wpcontent/uploads/2014/10/Evidence-for-Mindfulness-Impact-on-school-staff.pdf
Williams, J. M. G., & Kabat-Zinn, J. (Eds.). (2013). *Mindfulness: Diverse perspectives on its meaning, origins, and multiple applications at the intersection of science and dharma*. New York, NY: Routledge.

19

THE STATE OF MINDFULNESS AT TOP US PUBLIC UNIVERSITIES

A brief review and lessons learned

Sabine Grunwald and Liva LaMontagne

The state of mindfulness at top US public universities: a brief review and path forward

According to the National Center for Education Statistics, NCES (2019), about 19.9 million students will attend US colleges and universities in fall 2019. During the 2019–2020 academic year, about 184,000 doctoral degrees, 820,000 master degrees, and 1.975 million bachelor degrees will be awarded by US colleges and universities, producing human capital for the next generation. Universities have been a strong catalyst for US economic growth (Litan, Mitchell, & Reedy, 2007). However, there are growing costs associated with being in the highly competitive higher education work environment in the US for faculty and students alike.

For faculty, universities have created a two-tier labor system, with a declining pool of tenure positions at the top and an increasing amount of lower-paid or no-benefit jobs as adjuncts or temporary lecturers (Entin, 2005). Rankings of institutions of higher education have translated into costs for academic degrees that are indicative of the competitive hierarchical nature of corporate universities (Agasisti & Johnes, 2015). Standardized testing culture and meritocracy have amplified the stresses imposed on academics in the US (Stein, 2019). A synthesis of literature from various studies has shown that there is a current mental health crisis in academia with one of the highest incidences of mental illness when compared with other occupations (Lau & Pretorius, 2019). According to Lau and Pretorius, the factors that have contributed to this mental health crisis entail the increasing pressure to compete for research funding and publish in high-impact journals, lack of work–life balance, isolation, increasing work demands with fewer resources, career and financial insecurity, interpersonal conflicts, and lack of support systems.

In a recent study of college freshmen by the World Health Organization (Auerbach et al., 2018), 35% of participants had at least one of common lifetime disorders and 31% screened positive for at least one disorder in the last 12 months. Data from a survey with 621 respondents of counseling center directors from US universities paint a dire picture how stress has translated into mental health issues. Anxiety continues to be the most frequent concern among college students (48.2%), followed by stress (39.1%), depression (34.5%), suicidal ideation (25.2%), specific relationship concerns (22.9%), family concerns (21.2%), interpersonal functioning problems (18.8%), sleep problems (15.8%), and loneliness/social isolation (15.5%). A total of 25.5% of students seeking services were taking psychotropic medications (LeViness, Bershad, & Gorman, 2017). Xiao et al.'s (2017) empirical study undergirded these alarming numbers in regard to the mental health crisis that counseling centers at colleges have faced. The trends for mental health at universities are aligned with US-wide increasing trends in the prevalence of self-harm and suicide-related issues, anxiety, and depression. Mental health problems among PhD students are prevalent, impacting the higher education work organization. One in two PhD students have experienced psychological distress and one in three are at risk of a common psychiatric disorder (Levecque, Anseel, De Beuckelaer, Van der Heyden, & Gisle, 2017).

Mindfulness has been identified to counter these trends, reduce stress among faculty and students, and help address the mental health crisis. Mindfulness and contemplative practices have gained attention in large public institutions of higher education over the past decade concurrently with the unfolding mindfulness and yoga movement in the US (Barbezat, & Bush, 2014; Hedstrom, 2018; Pickert, 2014). In this chapter we explore three questions that are related to the issues that US higher education institutions face:

1. What kind of mindfulness is practiced at large public universities? How is mindfulness represented in teaching, research, community outreach, counseling, and therapy?
2. What are the challenges to diffuse mindfulness interventions into higher education institutions?
3. What are the lessons learned from the infusion of mindfulness into a large public university?

Mindfulness in the United States: secularization of Buddhist mindfulness or contemporary universal mindfulness

Jon Kabat-Zinn's mindfulness-based stress reduction (MBSR) program has been transformative for thousands of patients with chronic pain and anxiety and it has greatly contributed to reduce stress and post-traumatic stress disorder (PTSD; Grossman, Niemann, Schmidt, & Walach, 2004). Since 2014 the popularity of MBSR has spawned a mindfulness revolution in North America with a broad range of training opportunities as well as therapeutic and clinical applications (Pickert, 2014).

Evidence-based mindfulness research has exponentially increased since the 1980s (Brown, Creswell, & Ryan, 2015). A comprehensive review and meta-analysis of meditation programs for psychological stress and well-being was presented by Goyal et al. (2014). A meta-analysis of MBSR and health (Grossman et al., 2004), a meta-analysis for mindfulness-based therapy (Khoury et al., 2013), a comprehensive synthesis of evidence-based mindfulness research (Hempel, Shekelle, Taylor, Marshall, & Solloway, 2014), and review of various empirical mindfulness studies (MacDonald, Walsh, & Shapiro, 2013) have demonstrated its positive effects on health, well-being, cognitive, emotional, physiological functioning, and self-regulation. According to Greeson (2009), clinical trials and laboratory studies alike suggest that the mechanisms of mindfulness involve not only relaxation, but important shifts in cognition, emotion, biology, and behavior that work synergistically to improve health. Mindfulness practice can influence the neural structure, the autonomic nervous system, stress hormones, the immune system, and health behaviors. Research has shown what mindfulness practitioners have known for centuries—that greater attention, awareness, acceptance, and compassion can facilitate more flexible, adaptive responses to stress, which, in turn, can help free us from suffering and realize greater health and well-being (e.g., Garland, Farb, Goldin, & Fredrickson, 2015; Garland et al., 2010).

Kabat-Zinn (1994) defined mindfulness as paying attention in a particular way, on purpose, in the present moment, and non-judgmentally. Although this definition of mindfulness has been promulgated widely, it is not the only one. In a comprehensive literature review, MacDonald et al. (2013) identified more than 30 different mindfulness definitions that have been conceptualized in the Western psychological context. More recent definitions tend to emphasize mechanisms involved in the practice of mindfulness. A main distinction is found between concentration approaches (i.e., attention focused on an object, sense, image, or idea) versus mindfulness (i.e., attention but not attachment to the field of experience). Lutz, Slagter, Dunne, and Davidson (2008) identified another distinction between focused attention and open-monitoring techniques. Diverse perspectives on the meaning, origins, and applications of mindfulness suggest that mindfulness is not one, but has many different facets (Williams & Kabat-Zinn, 2013).

The plurality of definitions of the mindfulness construct has raised concerns about how mindfulness meditation is taught and practiced in the Western context (Compson, 2014). Questions have been raised whether mindfulness is a stress-reduction method, relaxation method, breathing protocol, treatment approach for mental pathologies, method to increase cognitive performance (e.g., performance of students on exams or in schools), or a spiritual practice?

Sharf (2015) pointed out that Buddhist mindfulness has been practiced for more than 2,500 years within the Buddhist cultural and ethical context centered in Asia. Mindfulness from the Buddhist perspective clearly differs from Jon Kabat Zinn's mindfulness. The practice of mindfulness, even within Buddhist traditions, has undergone profound changes influenced by beliefs, philosophical and metaphysical views, culture, and ethics. For example, mindfulness in the ancient Pali canon has been referred to as remembrance, reminiscence, and memory. In contrast, the later conceptualizations of mindfulness in the Tibetan Buddhist context have emphasized the four foundations of mindfulness: (1) mindfulness of body: a sense of being in the psychosomatic body, a sense of groundedness, (2) mindfulness of life: the fundamental tendency of the mind to cling, attach, and grasp, (3) mindfulness of effort: a deliberate effort to practice meditation, and (4) mindfulness of mind: being watchful, rather than watching some object which requires presence (Chögyam Trungpa Rinpoche, 2010). There have been notable misunderstandings while transferring Buddhist notions into Western psychology due to poor translations and attempts to merge or equate metaphysical notions and psychological constructs, not to mention other cross-cultural issues (Berkhin & Hartelius, 2011; van Gordon, Shonin, & Griffiths, 2016).

Kabat-Zinn (1990) asserted that mindfulness involves purposively bringing one's full attention to experiences in the present moment, in a non-judgmental way. Such non-judgment is viewed integral to mindfulness in numerous Western science-based definitions (Brown & Ryan, 2004). However, the notion of non-judgment in mindfulness practice represents a departure from canonical mindfulness (Bhikkhu, 2011). Buddhist scholars have emphasized that a non-judgmental attitude does not allow to discern wholesome (positive) from unwholesome (negative) states of mind, and thus, is not inherent to the description of mindfulness. Although, non-judgment may be useful as a practical instruction on the path enabling a disengagement from habitual mental discursiveness and reactivity that inhibits sustained attentiveness (Dreyfus, 2011).

Buddhist critique of the Western secular mindfulness movement has centered on the assertion that Buddhist philosophy has been reduced to a therapeutic technique, because mindfulness was decoupled from wisdom and ethics (Gleig, 2019). The claim is that mindfulness in the West as a secular health practice has been de-contextualized from the original Buddhist notions. This decoupling and commodification in modern culture has been denoted as McMindfulness (Purser, 2019)—a $4 billion industry branded as a secular spirituality. This mindfulness industry has offered a buffet of New Age spiritual mindfulness at centers (e.g., Omega or Garrison Institute) at which CDs, candles, big malas, incense, and books support a broad audience of interested millennials, GenX, GenY, and others (Gleig, 2019; Tisdale, 2015). Mindfulness as a buzzword—"Mindful Eating. Mindful Knitting. The Mindful Child. The Mindful Way through Anxiety. The Mindful Path through Shyness. Mindful Recovery. A Mindful Nation. The Joy of Mindful Sex"—has been used for commercialization (Hedstrom, 2018, p. 57). Mindfulness has been one of the emergent New Age spiritualities attuned to individualistic and achievement-oriented culture in Western society. In Purser's view, "mindfulness-based interventions fulfill the purpose by therapeutically optimizing individuals to make them mentally fit, attentive, and resilient so they may keep functioning within the system" (Purser, 2019, p. 19). According to Purser, in capitalist culture mindfulness serves to quiet the mind, and relieve the stress of individuals. However, without ethics that invites to look deeper and more broadly at societal issues, such as social inequity, polarized politics, economic disparities, injustice, environmental devastation (global climate change), and dispassion in corporate industry, McMindfulness is a tranquilizer that closes the mind. Literally, mindfulness has been instrumentalized by corporate industry and institutions as an expedient technique for assuaging stress without wisdom and insight, while it has served to improve productivity and focus to meet demands of 80-hour work weeks or work on two to three jobs to sustain livelihood. Such submissive "shutting-up the mind" is different from Buddhist quieting the mind to become spacious and open and bring forth non-attachment, wisdom, compassion, loving-kindness, and liberation from the "I" (no-self; Ray, 2002). Purser (2019) claimed that McMindfulness is consumed as "another thing you do," which sharply contrasts embodied mindfulness practices, mindful living, and being in the world to achieve one's full potential (Ray, 2016).

From the Zen Buddhist perspective, approaching mindfulness meditation practice as a goal-oriented technique has troubling consequences because quieting the mind for personal gains only reifies the self (Poirier, 2015). Poirier argued that the incorporation of mindfulness in institutional context, such as corporations or corporate universities, is very concerning.

How we understand mindfulness depends on whether it is considered a concept (e.g., psychological construct), process or mechanism grounded in neurobiology (e.g., neuroplasticity), activity, a goal (e.g., to achieve wellness, reduce stress, or enlightenment), intervention or therapy (e.g., mindfulness-based cognitive therapy (MBCT) or mindfulness-based intervention), spiritual practice, experience to explore the existence of life and the cosmos, cultivated as a way of life (e.g., to arouse compassion and love), or path to wisdom and liberation (e.g., Buddhist realization of the true nature; emptiness, Skt. *śūnyatā*; non-self, Skt. *anātman*).

The issue is not whether there is a "right" or "wrong" mindfulness or which one is the "best" mindfulness—Buddhist, Kabat-Zinn, or some other mindfulness. Eskimos have 50 different words for snow (Washington Post, 2013), but mindfulness has been construed as one and the same, which has led to confusion.

Lindahl (2015) pointed out that the polarization between Buddhist doctrines of mindfulness and contemporary secular mindfulness is less helpful. Instead, a reframing to the question "what kind of mindfulness practice may reduce the suffering or stress, emotional deregulation, depression, or other forms of pain" moves one toward less stress/pain/suffering. This view suggests that mindfulness is situational, and the positionality determines what kind of mindfulness is most effective to foster transformation. In a corporate setting, five minutes of mindful breathing for a student or faculty member that has literally no time to practice due to perceived stress level may provide temporary relief from stress and bears the possibility to sow the seed for a healthier work–life balance. In contrast, in a retreat setting among Buddhist practitioners who have acquired mindfulness as a trait, the purpose of mindfulness meditation practice is to enter into deeper spiritual inquiry or experiences that provide transformative transpersonal meaning.

Mindfulness at top public US universities

The expansion of mindfulness in US higher education has mirrored the trends in mainstream American culture, Fortune 500 companies, corporate industry, and military (Rechtschaffen, 2014). The prevalence, patterns, and predictors of meditation use among US adults was shown in a nationally representative health survey by Cramer et al. (2016). Among a large sample of US adults (N = 34,525), lifetime and 12-month prevalence of meditation use were 5.2% and 4.1%, respectively. Meditation was mainly used for general wellness (76.2%), improving energy (60.0%), and aiding memory or concentration (50.0%). Anxiety (29.2%), stress (21.6%), and depression (17.8%) were the top health problems for which people used meditation; 63.6% reported that meditation had helped a great deal with these conditions. These numbers may mirror the adoption of mindfulness meditation in academia.

Mindfulness in higher education involves different modalities including research, for example, studying the effectiveness of mindfulness through neuroscience, quantitative and qualitative research methods (Davidson, 2010; Davidson & Kaszniak, 2015), education and training through mindfulness courses (Bush, 2011), explicit incorporation of mindfulness practices, for example, contemplative practices viewed as powerful methods to transform teaching and learning as part of a curricula (Barbezat & Bush, 2014), and preventive intervention or therapy to address mental health issues (Block-Lerner & Cardaciotto, 2016). Roeser (2014) pointed out that the emergence of mindfulness-based interventions in educational settings is on the rise due to increased interest in secular mindfulness.

To identify how mindfulness-based practices and information is currently disseminated through teaching, research, community outreach, counseling, and therapy at US universities, publicly available information on university websites was screened. The Internet was searched to identify mindfulness-related practices and offerings at 25 top public universities. The universities were selected based on the current rankings list of *US News and World Report* (2019). The search terms included the name of each university and "mindfulness." Search results were summarized into the following categories (see Table 19.1):

1) center/department hosting the mindfulness-related offering;
2) mindfulness-related research;
3) teaching mindfulness to students and/or employees (internal);
4) outreach to the community (including student groups/organizations).

Table 19.1 Mindfulness research, teaching, and community outreach at the top 25 public US universities

University by Rank	*Center or Institute*	*Research Program or Research Lab (Focus Areas)*	*Teaching*	*Community Outreach (Programs, Practice Groups, Student Clubs & Groups)*
1. University of California—Los Angeles	MARC (Mindful Awareness Research Center) Partner with the Norman Cousins Center for Psychoneuroimmunology and with Jand and Terry Semel Institute for Neuroscience and Human Behavior at UCLA	• Psychoneuroimmunology—mind–body interactions in ageing, alcohol and substance abuse, cancer, infectious diseases, inflammatory diseases; evaluation of mindfulness interventions • As part of UCLA Healthy Campus Initiative—research and evaluation for funded student groups, identify campus-wide data sets that inform policies and programs, and explores internal and external partnerships/funding opportunities to conduct research	• Partners with UCLA Healthy Campus Initiative to prioritize the health and wellness of students, faculty and staff • Mindfulness Practice and Theory—open to UCLA students and the public • Free drop-in mindfulness practice in law school, counseling center, library, medical centers, museum	• Community events • Training in Mindfulness Facilitation (TMF) for general public
2. University of California—Berkeley	Greater Good Science Center	• Collaborations with UC Davis—science of gratitude • Collaborate with social interactions lab • Fellowships for researchers studying "meaningful life" • Summarize existing research and publish white papers, advise and consult institutions	• Free online course • Professional certificate in the science of happiness at work	• Serve educators (consult on social-emotional learning), parents & families, students & faculty • Several externally funded research and dissemination projects on gratitude
3. University of Michigan—Ann Arbor	Integrative Family Medicine Program	• Oncology and quality of life; mindfulness, health messages, and exercise motivation; nature-deficit disorder as a medical matter	• Two-day annual conference, some topics in the medical school curriculum, one-year on-site Integrative Medicine fellowship	• Serves community through primary care
	University Psychological Clinic at the Rackham Institute		• Educates mental health professionals in MBCT (mindfulness-based cognitive therapy) and MSC (mindful self-compassion)	• Serves university and community through MBCT group therapy

4. University of Virginia	UVA Mindfulness Center (School of Medicine)	• MBSR and burnout, well-being of healthcare practitioners • Mindfulness and pain management • Mindfulness practices and student well-being	• Classes for medicine students, staff, faculty	• Classes and programs for the general public
5. Georgia Institute of Technology, Atlanta	• Mindfulness offerings as "Signature Programs" under Health Initiatives (teaching mindfulness) • Center for Academic Success—mindfulness and stress management section, currently no info • Counseling Center—mindfulness and meditation workshop for students		• "Mindful Mondays"—drop-in practice for students • Student mindfulness book club + breakfast • 4-week course in mindfulness for graduate students only	
6. University of North Carolina–Chapel Hill	The Mindfulness Center, hosted by the program on integrative medicine, UNC School of Medicine	• Parent self-compassion, pre-teen well-being, and parent–child interaction • Mindful self-compassion intervention to decrease job stress and turnover for nursing assistants in long-term care • Mindfulness-based approaches to pain management • Mindfulness intervention for adolescents and emotional well-being in alternative high school	• Fellowship (post-doc) in complementary & alternative medicine • Mindfulness-based stress and pain management courses (foundations, self-compassion, stress reduction, mindful eating, mindful parenting) • Open to students, staff, and public	• Mindfulness-based stress and pain management; mindfulness for youth and teens; mindful eating • Mindfulness scholarship fund to help cover cost for community members for whom it would be a barrier
7. University of California—Santa Barbara	Center for Mindfulness and Human Potential, Psychological & Brain Sciences	• With support from US Dept. of Education, developed evidence-based, digital mindfulness courses for high school students, teachers, and staff • Plasticity Initiative—developed a cognitive, affective, and neural plasticity training program (growth mindset and self-regulation)		• Multimedia mindfulness training for high schools

(Continued)

Table 19.1 (Cont.)

University by Rank	*Center or Institute*	*Research Program or Research Lab (Focus Areas)*	*Teaching*	*Community Outreach (Programs, Practice Groups, Student Clubs & Groups)*
8. University of Florida	Interdisciplinary Mindfulness Program— Collaborates with Counseling and Wellness Center, Center for Spirituality and Health, Integrative Medicine, Human Resources Services/Wellness, and GatorWell		• Weekly mindfulness practice group—many facets of mindfulness • Open to students and employees • Graduate Certificate in Spirituality and Health (incl. mindfulness courses)	• Events, conferences, student clubs
9. University of California—Irvine	Center for student wellness & health promotion		• Intro to mindfulness & meditation (4 sessions)	
	Environmental Health & Safety in collaboration with Susan Samueli Center for Integrative Medicine The whole UC system (UCSF, UCR, UCI, UCLA, UCM)	• The impact of mindfulness on workplace health and safety • Sponsored by UC Office of the President Risk Services • Stress Free UC study, run by UCI Department of Psychological Sciences—assessing how stress affects health and well-being, and testing the effectiveness of the Headspace digital intervention to reduce workplace stress in employees		
	UCI Health Susan Samueli Integrative Health Institute		• 8-week MBSR training (discount for students and employees)	• MBSR training
10. University of California—San Diego	Center for Mindfulness, Department of Family Medicine and Public Health	• Efficacy of mindfulness therapies in clinical conditions • The effect of mindfulness and compassion training on well-being • Mechanisms of action in mindfulness and contemplative-based practices (physiological, neuroimaging methods, etc.)	• MBSR, self-compassion, mindful eating, mindful parenting, mPEAK for students, employees, general public	• Programs open to general public (MBSR, self-compassion, mindful eating, mindfulness for teens & kids, mindful parenting) • Workplace programs

11. University of California—Davis	Center for Mind and Brain	• Shamatha project—how contemplative training benefits mental and physical health	• Lunchtime meditation for staff, faculty (UCD Safety Services) • Student health and counseling services–mindfulness meditation 101 for stress (students) • Mindfulness and the Law course (School of Law)	
12. College of William and Mary	New (2017) Center for Mindfulness and Authentic Excellence, Health & Wellness Counseling Center		• Mindfulness for stress relief (4 sessions) • Authentic Excellence Initiative to promote flourishing and resilience • Relearn to relax guide to meditation (Human Resources)	• Introduction to mindfulness for parents & families
13. University of Wisconsin—Madison	Center for Healthy Minds	• Neuroscience of well-being • Mindfulness-based program for children—attention and emotion regulation in classrooms • Effectiveness of brief trainings (breath awareness, loving-kindness, gratitude practices) to buffer negative effects of acute stress on behavior and cognitive abilities • Experiences and perceptions of different practices of mindfulness		• The Loka Initiative-faith and ecology—supporting faith-led environmental and climate efforts
	Mindfulness program, Department of Psychiatry; Health-emotions Research Institute	• Emotion regulation, stress, and physical health	• Mindfulness program (8–10 weeks)	

(Continued)

Table 19.1 (Cont.)

University by Rank	*Center or Institute*	*Research Program or Research Lab (Focus Areas)*	*Teaching*	*Community Outreach (Programs, Practice Groups, Student Clubs & Groups)*
	School of Medicine and Public Health			• Mindfulness classes for adults and youth open to general public (MBSR, parenting, ageing, emotion, eating). • Financial assistance possible upon request
14. University of Illinois—Urbana-Champaign	McKinley Health Center	• Perceived mindfulness and depressive symptoms among people with chronic pain (Kinesiology and Community Health Department) • The impact of mindfulness and life stress on maternal well-being (Psychology Department)	• Workshops in stress management and mindfulness (Counseling Center) • Mindfulness Mondays (students, faculty & staff) • Relaxation exercises (guided meditation online, McKinley Center)	
15. University of Texas—Austin	Integrated Health Program, Counseling and Mental Health Center	• Applications of self-compassion (Kristin Neff, Educational Psychology)	• Mindfulness-based services under Counseling and Mental Health Center	• Mindfulness course for adults with IDDs
16. University of Georgia	Mindfulness-related events co-sponsored by Center for Teaching and Learning, Faculty Learning Community on Mindfulness in Education and Research and the Certificate Program in Marriage and Family Therapy		• Weekly morning mindfulness (in Art Museum) • Yoga in the Galleries	
17. Ohio State University—Columbus	Wexler Medical Center, integrative medicine, Dr. Maryanna Klatt at College	• Mindfulness and stress reduction, especially in health care workers. Developed and tested Mindfulness in Motion intervention	• Mindfulness-based treatments to reduce stress,	• Mindfulness Meditation Interest Group (student

	of Nursing, Clinical Neuroscience Lab does research on mindfulness	for adults, Move into Learning classroom intervention for children (Dr. Maryanna Klatt, Clinical Family Medicine) • Clinical Neuroscience Lab (multiple faculty)	chronic pain, anxiety, depression, etc.	organization, Clinical Psychology program)
18. Florida State University	No specific center	• Washing dishes—informal contemplative practice and well-being (Hanley et al., College of Education) • Mindfulness in romantic relationships (Kimmes et al., Child and Family Studies)	• Mindfulness in the classroom—seminar for teaching faculty	
19. Pennsylvania State University—University Park	Department of Human Development and Family Studies (Dr. Robert Roeser)—research in contemplative practices (e.g., mindfulness, compassion) in education for staff and students	• Developed MindUp, an early-learning program aimed at improving children's readiness for kindergarten and later grades to help children develop social-emotional and self-regulation skills, including learning how to manage their emotions, get along and cooperate with others, focus their attention, follow directions and be persistent at completing tasks		• Coached health educators as they implemented the Learning to Breathe mindfulness program for adolescents in school district (Edna Bennett Pierce Prevention Research Center)
20. Purdue University—West Lafayette	Recreation & Wellness		• Free mindfulness practice (3 days a week) • Mindfulness workshops (intro, mindful eating, etc.)	
21. University of Pittsburgh	Mindful Wellness, Human Resources		• Mindfulness coaching sessions—mindfulness on the go	
	Center for Mindfulness and Consciousness Studies, Graduate School of Public Health's Department of Infectious Diseases and Microbiology	• Monthly research meetings—an informal lab where the group gives feedback to students or faculty developing mindfulness studies.	• Free, drop-in weekly sessions (30 mins) for students, faculty, staff, open to public • Collective practice, "stress-free zone"	• Mindfulness fair—mindfulness informing compassionate activities in communities. Open to the public

(Continued)

Table 19.1 (Cont.)

University by Rank	*Center or Institute*	*Research Program or Research Lab (Focus Areas)*	*Teaching*	*Community Outreach (Programs, Practice Groups, Student Clubs & Groups)*
22. Rutgers University—New Brunswick	Student Affairs/Student Health	• Effectiveness of mindfulness training programs of different lengths for reducing stress and depression in medical students	• Several mindfulness-based groups and workshops • MBSR	• School of Social Work implementing mindfulness intervention in China in collaboration with professors from China and Hong Kong
23. University of Washington	UW Recreation		• Mindfulness, meditation, yoga classes, mindful eating	
	Counseling Center		• Mindfulness Mondays drop-in guided practice	
		• Mindfulness practice for parents improves child outcomes (Center for Child and Family Well-being)		• Student-organized UW Mindfulness Project—not active anymore
24. University of Connecticut	The Systematic Health Action Research Program (SHARP)	• Randomized controlled trial of different methods/tools for college students to learn how to meditate		• UConn Mindfulness Club (student organization)
	Student Support Services		• Resilience through mindfulness—pilot course for first-generation students	
25. University of Maryland—College Park	Positive Coping, Health, and Well-being Lab, College of Education	• Barriers to meditation in non-meditators • Mindfulness and healthy adaptation to major life events	• Mindful self-care for educators (College of Education) • Mindfulness skills for better living 4-week course (Counseling Centers)	

Note. Mindfulness is conceptualized broadly including mindfulness meditation, yoga, contemplative practices, and compassion practices. MBSR: Mindfulness-based stress reduction short course; MBCT: Mindfulness-based cognitive therapy; PTSD: post-traumatic stress disorder

In addition, two private US universities—University of Massachusetts and Harvard University—need to be mentioned since both have been influential to establish large and transformative mindfulness programs and centers. The University of Massachusetts' Medical School has long been home of the Center for Mindfulness in Medicine, Health Care, and Society, with Jon Kabat-Zinn as its founding executive director.

The University of Massachusetts has implemented mindfulness system-wide, through research, providing practice workshops for students and employees, and academic teaching. In 2018, the Division of Mindfulness was established at the medical school, with research focusing on mindfulness-based treatment programs for addiction, including mobile-based programs. The center is disseminating mindfulness-based interventions widely outside the university by teaching and certifying teachers in MBSR and MBCT. Within the university, mindfulness practices are diffused through coordinating weekly meditation groups, in person and online.

Harvard University also has implemented mindfulness system-wide, by being involved in research on contemplative practices and disseminating findings to other researchers, providing practice workshops for students and employees, and academic teaching. Harvard's Medical School and Brigham & Women's Hospital is part of the Mindfulness Research Collaborative, studying contemplative neuroscience and integrative medicine, functional neuroimaging, and translational research. Within the university, mindfulness-based practices, such as guided meditations, regular groups, and courses for students, are disseminated by university health services, while seminars on mindfulness at work and mindfulness training for employees are disseminated by human resources. Mindfulness is also diffused via academic teaching, as evidenced by mindfulness courses in the divinity school and law school.

Centers/departments hosting the mindfulness-related offerings

Results in Table 19.1 show that all 25 top public universities had posted at least one mindfulness-based intervention for stress management and wellness purposes, hosted by on-campus health/wellness/mental health counseling/student affairs/support service centers.

In 13 out of 25 universities, a center disseminating mindfulness-related activities was either hosted by, or working in a collaborative relationship with, the medical school, in line with the founding tradition of the Center for Mindfulness in Medicine, Health Care, and Society at University of Massachusetts' Medical School.

Nine schools had established separate mindfulness-related, interdisciplinary research centers, eight schools showed organized efforts in research on mindfulness-related topics housed in neuroscience/integrative medicine/well-being-related research institutes/ programs, and the remaining eight schools had only individual faculty members researching some aspect of the topic.

Mindfulness-related research

Overall, most of the universities (17 out of 25) displayed signs of coordinated research activity on mindfulness-related topics. Major themes involved (1) mind–body interactions in health outcomes (quality of life, addictions, inflammatory diseases, cancer, and pain management); (2) gratitude, compassion, and meaningful life; (3) well-being/burnout/stress reduction in healthcare workers/medical students/other employees; (4) parent and adolescent well-being and mindful parenting; (5) cognitive, affective, and neural plasticity;

(6) neurological mechanisms of action in mindfulness; (7) evaluation of the effectiveness of mindfulness interventions/different methods of teaching it.

Teaching mindfulness to students and/or employees (internal)

Face-to-face workshops and practice groups were the most popular method of disseminating mindfulness-based interventions on campuses, evidenced in all 25 universities. Most health/ wellness/counseling centers at universities also listed links to online resources/recordings on their websites for remote practice. Some schools had special places designated for collective mindfulness practice (e.g., the "stress free zone" at the University of Pittsburgh), while others infused mindfulness practice into existing spaces like art galleries, meeting spaces, libraries, and museums. Beyond practice workshops, students in specific fields of study, like the medical professions, law, and spirituality, were most likely to have mindfulness infused into their academic curricula.

Outreach to the community (including student groups/organizations)

Universities with established research centers for mindfulness-related practices were disseminating evidence-based information outside of the university via consulting and advising organizations, parents, and schools (e.g., the Greater Good Science Center at UC Berkeley), teaching and/or certifying teachers of mindfulness-based practices (e.g., UCLA, UC Berkeley, University of Michigan), and developing and/or evaluating mindfulness-based interventions (e.g., mindfulness-based stress and pain management interventions at UNC Chapel Hill's Mindfulness Center; digital mindfulness courses for high school students, teachers, and staff at UC Santa Barbara; testing the effectiveness of the Headspace app to reduce stress at the university system of California; effectiveness of brief trainings to buffer negative effects of stress at UW Madison; MindUp—an early learning program to improve children's readiness for kindergarten at PSU University Park).

Many universities also disseminated mindfulness-based practices by making their workshops open to the public and organizing community events/mindfulness fairs. Several universities provided scholarships for community members with financial barriers to attend workshops. The UW Madison stood out with its Loka Initiative, supporting faith-led environmental and climate efforts in the community. Some universities helped implement mindfulness-based practices overseas (e.g., Rutgers University with collaborators in China) and in their community school districts (e.g., Pennsylvania State University's Edna Bennett Pierce Prevention Center), while some delivered mindfulness courses to special groups in the community (e.g., University of Texas—Austin, extension workshop for adults with intellectual and developmental disabilities).

In a couple of universities, students were actively creating their own mindfulness-related experiences through clubs/student organizations. UCLA stood out as a vibrant example of community-based participatory research (Israel, Schulz, Parker, & Becker, 1998) with its Healthy Campus Initiative. Student groups were given funding to create, test, and evaluate their own interventions, with the results informing campus-wide policies and programs and potentially identifying other sources of funding and support.

To sum up, all top 25 US public universities employed at least one mindfulness-based intervention to reduce stress and increase well-being in their student and employee populations. On the other hand, with the caveat that we did not have full information beyond what was publicly available on university websites, not all schools treated their mindfulness-based interventions as applied research projects and measured the effectiveness and documented the feasibility and acceptability of these practices to their populations. Gathering and dissemination of research-based outcomes and process information might help other higher education institutions evaluate their options of mindfulness-based interventions when choosing what to implement but would also move the field forward by specifying what kind of mindfulness practices work for whom and under what conditions.

Challenges to diffuse mindfulness into higher education institutions

Mindfulness viewed as a practice to be present in the moment, stress-reduction technique, or approach to work and living contrasts in many ways the culture that undergirds contemporary corporate higher education in the US, which is profit- and achievement-oriented and fast-paced (Schrecker, 2010). The doing-orientation of higher education institutions contrasts the being-orientation that underlies mindfulness. Block-Lerner and Cardaciotto (2016) provided a vision for building acceptance and psychological flexibility in higher education through mindfulness-informed educators. Palmer and Zajonc (2010) proposed integrative education, a higher education that unites intellectual rigor with compassion and love. In this vision, mindfulness and contemplative practices are explicitly integrated into the living fabric of academia. As mainstream American culture is secularizing with more people being spiritual but not religious (Parsons, 2018), the higher education culture will also be transformed by these changes in memes (i.e., cultural patterns) and religiosity/spirituality. Stein (2019) calls this shift an education in a time between worlds in which traditional organizational corporate structures and academic culture transform, reflecting the emerging trends of re-humanizing higher education, in which people's well-being, fulfillment, and health are prime values that express the health of the whole organization.

How does mindfulness diffuse into a university and what are the potential challenges? Answers to this question can be found in theories of diffusion, such as the diffusion of innovation theory (Rogers, 2003). The diffusion of innovation theory explains how and at what rate a new idea or technology spreads in an organization or community. According to Rogers, there are five elements of a new or substitute practice that will each partly determine whether adoption or diffusion of a new practice will occur: relative advantage, compatibility, complexity, trialability, and observability.

Relative advantage refers to the degree to which the new practice improves valued outcomes in comparison with the practice that is being replaced. In case mindfulness interventions are offered as they currently are in the top 25 public universities, for example as wellness workshops on top of other scheduled activities in the already full calendars of students and faculty, the relative advantage of engaging in an optional wellness activity over engaging in a required work or family activity might not be evident to the audience universities are trying to reach.

Compatibility refers to the degree to which a new practice is perceived to be aligned with the values, existing practices, and needs of its potential users. While all top public universities might be aligned with the instrumental values mindfulness can provide in terms of health benefits, existing practices in health and wellness promotion may not always be compatible with delivering mindfulness interventions effectively. In many universities, existing practices for wellness promotion are run through the mental health/counseling and recreational sports centers, where mindfulness-based practices have currently been implemented most widely (e.g., mindfulness-based therapies and workshops in counseling centers, yoga in sports facilities). However, some universities have moved mindfulness out of the traditional health-promotion locations and into innovative spaces like galleries, libraries, and newly created spaces for collective use (e.g., centers). Compatibility with the needs of potential users who have increasingly busy schedules is also being addressed in some universities, e.g., the effectiveness of the Headspace app for employees is being considered and evaluated in the University of California system; different tools of teaching mindfulness are evaluated with students at the University of Connecticut.

Complexity refers to the degree to which a new practice is perceived as difficult to understand and use. Although there is considerable debate about the many definitions and components of mindfulness in the academic literature which could confuse potential users, some applied researchers (Wolever, Schwartz, & Schoenberg, 2018, p. 405) argued that this might not be a problem for practice: "When one really engages with the practices, one's world-view changes. It is not about understanding concepts or reviewing mindfulness research; transformation results from embodied experience that plays into one's social–ethical compass."

Trialability refers to how easy is it to test the new practice. How accessible is it? Many universities have posted online guided meditation resources on the websites of their counseling and wellness centers for the campus community to try remotely. Some universities also provide drop-in sessions that do not require a regular and advance time commitment. Beyond what universities offer, there is a plethora of mobile apps and websites available to the public, some with more research on their effectiveness than others (see Jayewardene, Lohrmann, Erbe, & Torabi (2017) for a meta-analysis of preventive online mindfulness interventions), offering free guided meditation tools to try at a convenient place and time.

Finally, *observability* refers to the degree to which effectiveness of the new practice is visible to observers within their social circles. Mindfulness practice has been proven to reduce stress and improve well-being; however, the cause of reduced stress, for example, in somebody who practices mindfulness at home might go unnoticed by colleagues or fellow students, unless they share their positive experiences about their practices with the people around them. Many universities currently provide places and times for collective mindfulness practice, which heightens the observability factor. Observability is also increased when participants can observe the teacher. A mindfulness teacher who is less stressed can serve as a role model. During live sessions, which can be delivered face-to-face or via communication technology, students can mirror the mindful states in their teachers.

In addition to the abovementioned characteristics of a new practice, two social factors are crucial for promoting innovation diffusion—communication and leadership (Rogers, 2003). In regard to communication, the new intervention needs to be communicated in a way that sparks action—two-way communication with peers who share values and issues, involvement of an opinion leader in the field, and a local champion are usually necessary. Two-way communication would be enhanced if practitioners (e.g., specialists at university wellness and counseling centers or other interested structures) worked with university leaders and researchers to create, adapt, and maintain the most effective mindfulness-based interventions for the intended audience, while contributing data to the scientific development of the field.

Leaders and opinion leaders at universities have the power to promote evidence-based mindfulness interventions in universities; however, that depends on their opinion of whether the benefits of these interventions outweigh the costs, both financially and in terms of other considerations. In the academy, cognitive appraisal, attention, and emotional resilience are saliently important to maximize academic performance, which translates into higher rankings of a university. Mindfulness studies have demonstrated that all of these factors improve through mindfulness interventions/practice (Desbordes et al., 2012; Mikulincer & Florian, 1998). There is also empirical evidence for improved health and productivity from mindfulness practices in organizations (e.g., Goyal et al., 2014; Luken & Sammons, 2016). In addition, the theory of organizational mindfulness (Vogus & Sutcliffe, 2012) posits that organizational mindfulness at the top management level (e.g., deans in business schools) improves strategic outcomes, but also enables middle managers and front-line employees to engage in "mindful organizing," which in turn improves operational outcomes.

On the cost side, one consideration for implementing mindfulness-based interventions is that these can be complex interventions that demand innovative ways to be delivered and to ensure access for everybody who needs them (Demarzo, Cebolla, & Garcia-Campayo, 2015). To manage the demand for mindfulness-based interventions with the limited resources of trained teachers who can deliver them, the "stepped-care" concept has been proposed in the literature on mental health services, namely making low-intensity, self-care-based interventions available to the clients with the lowest levels of problems, while highly trained therapists only see the patients with acute issues which require the highest level of competence.

In university settings, this could mean making preventive mobile apps or online mindfulness interventions available to everybody and utilizing specialized therapies like MBCT for treatment of more acute problems. Universities could also utilize structural interventions that would enhance mindfulness and be accessible to everyone as a preventative or health-promotion factor. These could be creating mindfulness-facilitating environments like natural spaces or cutting-edge designs intentionally made to facilitate mindfulness based on findings from neuroscience and architecture (e.g., Kawai, O'Connor Duffany, & Garrison, 2018). However, for structural interventions to succeed, universities would also need to establish routines that allow their employees to mindfully experience these environments (e.g., walking meetings in gardens instead of meetings in conference rooms without windows).

Case study: lessons learned from the infusion of mindfulness into a large public university

A brief case study from the University of Florida (UF) is presented honing into the positionality of mindfulness at a large public university. The UF ranked 7th in the list of public universities according to the *US News and World Report* (2019) Best College rankings and is one of the largest public Land Grant universities in the US. In 2019, there were about 52,500 students enrolled at UF, of which about 67% were undergraduate students and the rest graduate students (MS or PhD). The race/ethnicity of enrolled students comprised 57.5% White Caucasian, 14.6% Hispanic/Latino, 7.3% Asian, 7.2% Black or African, and others. The external research funding in 2019 amounted to $776.2 million in the fiscal year 2019, while the University Athletic Association had an operating budget of $128 million (2018–2019). The UF is situated in the southeastern US in Gainesville Florida, which is the conservative Bible Belt of America. In the community, 42.1% identify as religious, of which 10.0% are Baptist, 8.3% Catholic, 6.8% Methodist, 6.5% Other Christian, 1.5% Eastern religions, 1.1% Islam; and rest other (e.g., Jewish, Pentecostal).

In 2015 the UF Mindfulness Program (https://mindfulness.ufl.edu/) was launched with a small Creative Campus seed grant to form an interdisciplinary group of faculty members. The project aimed to connect the small silos of mindfulness on campus that existed in 2015 and develop a communication structure to raise awareness about mindfulness through training and teaching. The long-term vision of UF Mindfulness is to co-create a more mindful campus culture. Since 2017 the UF Mindfulness Program is self-funded through faculty volunteers without support from the institution.

At the time UF Mindfulness was launched, mindfulness was hardly visible at UF, with few scattered individual thesis and dissertation research projects and graduate courses. Before 2015, the mindfulness-related activities were relatively small compared with the size of UF, focused on athletic programs, and siloed within the 16 colleges, mainly the medical school. For example, the Center for Spirituality and Health has been situated within the UF Medical School to serve medical students and offers graduate courses focused on mindfulness (e.g., Mindful Living and Multicultural Mindfulness) under the certificate program in *Spirituality and Health.* Integrative Medicine, part of UF Health, developed a wellness orientation (one week) for medical graduate students that is offered once a year, which includes mindfulness training. The Department of Psychiatry offers the weekly Mindfulness Relaxation Minutes with guided meditations and mindfulness practices. The UF Counseling and Wellness Center (CWC) offers group therapy and counseling services with mindfulness components, however, participation is reserved for students with mental indications. Individual therapy and counseling services are available, though demands have exceeded offerings with long waiting lists; thus, a substantial number of students are referred to the greater Gainesville community to be serviced in timely fashion though at greater cost for patients. One workshop, *Taming the Anxious Mind*, has been regularly offered by the UF-CWC to students; almost all other workshops are group therapy-oriented in the form of closed groups. The UF Recreation and Sports Center provides service classes in yoga and tai chi, though the portfolio of the center is mainly gym and athletics focused. The GatorWell Health Promotion Services, which serves specifically students at UF, has started in 2019 four-week, four-hour mindfulness trainings based on the Koru Certified Mindfulness Approach, which trains participants in short practice segments (e.g., ten minutes' mindfulness breathing practice or body scans). Wellness and health-oriented offerings (e.g., ten minutes' mindfulness) were recently added to the portfolio among other health and fitness trainings by UF Human Resources that serve faculty and staff members. Various yoga classes that include mindfulness components have emerged across campus to serve students, staff, and faculty. Designated spaces to practice mindfulness meditation on campus are rare (e.g., one reflection room in the Student Union; and one room in the Cancer Center UF), while open green space is highly regulated for teaching of mindfulness (e.g., specific policies and acquisition of permits) or is noisy. Some green space is organically used by students for relaxation and as resting space.

Overall, the offerings of "mindfulness light" versions have increased over the past four years as part of increased awareness in regard to wellness and health at the workplace and the increasing needs to address the mental health crisis at UF. Still, athletics and recreational sports that are fitness-oriented dominate when compared with mindfulness training and practice opportunities. The few courses that are offered with limited seats speak for the shadow-existence of mindfulness at the large corporate UF.

To assess the receptivity of student, staff, and faculty members in regard to different mindfulness teachings, training, action awareness, and intervention events offered free-of-charge through the UF Mindfulness Program, the attendance scores were tracked (2015–2019). Receptivity served as an indicator for openness and preference to identify the best modalities to diffuse mindfulness into campus culture at UF. Results of the receptivity analysis are shown in Table 19.2.

The receptivity to different mindfulness activities coordinated by UF Mindfulness has varied widely. Overall, the enthusiasm for mindfulness is high with engagement in social media and online resources. Face-to-face activities have shown low attendance, though those who attend are genuinely engaged to benefit from the mindfulness practices. Possible reasons for low receptivity to mindfulness offerings are overloaded schedules and curricula ("no time to practice mindfulness"), distractedness ("I forgot"), mindlessness ("I cannot practice because I have too many thoughts"), confusion ("I did not know that mindfulness is offered"), devaluation ("other things are more important"), aloofness ("why would I need mindfulness, leave me alone"), ignorance ("I don't need mindfulness in my life"), or mental or emotional health limitations (erroneous belief "I am not able to be mindful"). For mindfulness activities that require pre-registration, only about a quarter of participants who sign up actually show up, which further underpins the busyness of people in the campus community. Mindfulness, even if a practice or training is short, is viewed as an add-on to the already overloaded work schedule.

Table 19.2 Activities of the UF Mindfulness Program (2015–2019) and level of participation

Type of activity	*Specific activities*	*Average count of participants*
Teaching	Mindfulness Wave, 1–2 hours introduction to mindfulness incl. mindfulness practice offered in 16 different colleges	5–10; some colleges < 5
	Guest teaching mindfulness; mindfulness seminars	20–25
Talks, presentations	Invited keynote speakers, UF Mindfulness Day (academic or spiritual teachers)	130–350
	Invited guest talks, mindfulness	20–30
Retreats	Mindfulness retreats, 1/2 day or 1 day off-campus (e.g., mindfulness meditation, compassion practices, trauma-informed mindfulness)	10–20
Practices	360° Embodied Mindfulness Practice Group (1 hour per week; teacher-facilitated guided mindfulness meditation and mind–body practices)	10–15
	UF Mindfulness Day; once per year (a whole day of 50 min. mindfulness practice sessions, talks, keynotes, and dialogue)	10–25
	Self-facilitated group meditation practice (indoors) [the room policy did not allow to provide mindfulness instructions]	0–4
	Self-facilitated meditation practice (outdoors), meditation mob on the lawn	0–4
	Meditation chain (1-day continuous mindfulness practice, pop-in style)	10–13
Online	Website 360° Mindfulness with recordings of guided meditations and mindfulness practices (only participants of the practice group have access)	N/A
	UF Mindfulness websites with resources including audio and video recordings (public)	N/A
	Social media (Facebook, Twitter, and Instagram)	Popular following

Final remarks and five reflection questions

Mindfulness in US public universities is still in its infancy, despite pressing needs to address the mental health crisis, stresses among students and faculty members due to a demanding achievement-oriented work environment, and its proven potential to buffer these stresses. To diffuse more mindfulness into the campuses of universities would require a multifaceted approach of infusion into the fabric of academic culture—mindful curricula, mindful teaching in the classroom, mindful research, mindful breaks, mindful spaces for practice, and mindful living and studying. The following five questions invite to reflect on the future of mindfulness in higher education in the US and elsewhere:

1. What kind of mindfulness practices would make the most difference in improving the everyday functioning of public higher education institutions? How would you implement them?
2. What are some barriers to implementing mindfulness-based interventions or practices in large organizations?
3. Should high-performing public universities be role models in their communities in terms of prioritizing health and well-being of their employees and students? Should business organizations look at universities for best practices in mindfulness, or should universities learn from best practices in business organizations?
4. What physical, emotional, and social benefits does mindfulness offer to academics and students when compared with mindlessness (e.g., running on "autopilot"; being in a chronic state of distress—fight, flight, or freeze responses)?
5. What could be the pros and cons of starting formal lectures in universities with a short mindfulness practice, like focusing on the breath?

References

Agasisti, T., & Johnes, G. (2015). Efficiency, costs, rankings and heterogeneity: The case of US higher education. *Studies in Higher Education*, *40*(1), 60–82. doi:10.1080/03075079.2013.818644

Auerbach, R. P., Mortier, P., Bruffaerts, R., Alonso, J., Benjet, C., Cuijpers, P., ... Kessler, R. C. (2018). WHO world mental health surveys international college student project: Prevalence and distribution of mental disorders. *Journal of Abnormal Psychology*, *127*(7), 623–638. doi:10.1037/abn0000362

Barbezat, D. P., & Bush, M. (2014). *Contemplative practices in higher education: Powerful methods to transform teaching and learning*. San Francisco, CA: Jossey-Bass Publ.

Berkhin, I., & Hartelius, G. (2011). Why altered states are not enough: A perspective from Buddhism. *International Journal of Transpersonal Studies*, *30*(1–2), 63–68. Retrieved from https://digitalcommons.ciis.edu/ijts-transpersonalstudies/vol30/iss1/7/

Bhikkhu, B. (2011). What does mindfulness really mean? A canonical perspective. *Contemporary Buddhism*, *12*(1), 19–39. doi:10.1080/14639947.2011.564813

Block-Lerner, J., & Cardaciotto, L. A. (Eds.). (2016). *The mindfulness-informed educator: Building acceptance and psychological flexibility in higher education*. New York, NY: Routledge.

Brown, K. W., & Ryan, R. M. (2004). Perils and promise in defining and measuring mindfulness: Observations from experience. *Clinical Psychology: Science and Practice*, *11*(3), 242–248. doi:10.1093/clipsy.bph078

Brown, K. W., Creswell, J. D., & Ryan, R. M. (2015). Introduction: The evolution of mindfulness science. In K. W. Brown, J. D. Creswell, & R. M. Ryan (Eds.), *Handbook of mindfulness: Theory, research, and practice* (pp. 1–8). New York, NY: Guildford Press.

Bush, M. (2011). Mindfulness in higher education. *Contemporary Buddhism*, *12*(1), 183–197. doi:10.1080/14639947.2011.564838

Compson, J. (2014). Meditation, trauma and suffering in silence: Raising questions about how meditation is taught and practiced in Western contexts in the light of a contemporary trauma resiliency model. *Contemporary Buddhism, 15*, 2. doi:10.1080/14639947.2014.935264

Cramer, H., Hall, H., Leach, M., Frawley, J., Zhang, Y., Leung, B., … Lauche, R. (2016). Prevalence, patterns, and predictors of meditation use among US adults: A nationally representative survey. *Scientific Reports, 6*, 1–9. doi:10.1038/srep36760

Davidson, R. J., & Kaszniak, A. W. (2015). Conceptual and methodological issues in research on mindfulness and meditation. *American Psychologist, 70*(7), 581–592. doi:10.1037/a0039512

Davidson, R. J. (2010). Empirical exploration of mindfulness: Conceptual and methodological conundrums. *Emotion, 10*(1), 8–11. doi:10.1037/a0018480

Demarzo, M. M. P., Cebolla, A., & Garcia-Campayo, J. (2015). The implementation of mindfulness in healthcare systems: A theoretical analysis. *General Hospital Psychiatry, 37*(2), 166–171. doi:10.1016/j.genhosppsych.2014.11.013

Desbordes, G., Negi, L. T., Pace, T. W. W., Wallace, B. A., Raison, C. L., & Schwartz, E. L. (2012). Effects of mindful-attention and compassion meditation training on amygdala response to emotional stimuli in an ordinary, non-meditative state. *Frontiers in Human Neuroscience, 6*. doi:10.3389/fnhum.2012.00292

Dreyfus, G. (2011). Is mindfulness present-centered and non-judgmental? A discussion of the cognitive dimensions of mindfulness. *Contemporary Buddhism, 12*(1), 41–54. doi:10.1080/14639947.2011.564815

Entin, J. (2005). Contingent teaching, corporate universities, and the academic labor movement. *The Radical Teacher*, (73), 26–32. Retrieved from www.jstor.org/stable/20710311?seq=1#page_scan_tab_contents

Garland, E. L., Farb, N. A., Goldin, R., & Fredrickson, B. L. (2015). Mindfulness broadens awareness and builds eudaimonic meaning: A process model of mindful positive emotion regulation. *Psychological Inquiry, 26*(4), 293–314. doi:10.1080/1047840X.2015.1064294

Garland, E. L., Fredrickson, B., Kring, A. M., Johnson, D. P., Meyer, P. S., & Penn, D. L. (2010). *Upward spirals of positive emotions counter downward spirals of negativity: Insights from the broaden-and-build theory and affective neuroscience on the treatment of emotion dysfunctions and deficits in psychopathology* (Vol. *30*). doi:10.1016/j.cpr.2010.03.002

Gleig, A. (2019). *American dharma: Buddhism beyond modernity*. New Haven, CT: Yale University Press.

Goyal, M., Singh, S., Sibinga, E. M. S., Gould, N. F., Rowland-Seymour, A., Sharma, R., … Haythornthwaite, J. A. (2014). Meditation programs for psychological stress and well-being: A systematic review and meta-analysis. *JAMA Internal Medicine, 174*(3), 357–368. doi:10.1001/jamainternmed.2013.13018

Greeson, J. M. (2009). Mindfulness research update: 2008. *Complementary Health Practice Review, 14*(1), 10–18. doi:10.1177/1533210108329862

Grossman, P., Niemann, L., Schmidt, S., & Walach, H. (2004). Mindfulness-based stress reduction and health benefits: A meta-analysis. *Journal of Psychosomatic Research, 57*(1), 35–43. doi:10.1016/S0022-3999(03)00573-7

Hedstrom, M. S. (2018). Buddhist fulfillment of a protestant dream: Mindfulness as scientific spirituality. In W. B. Parsons (Ed.), *Being spiritual but not religious: Past, present, future(s)* (pp. 57–71). New York, NY: Routledge.

Hempel, S., Shekelle, P. G., Taylor, S. L., Marshall, N. J., & Solloway, M. R. (2014). *Evidence map of mindfulness*. Washington, DC: Department of Veterans Affairs.

Israel, B. A., Schulz, A. J., Parker, E. A., & Becker, A. B. (1998). Review of community-based research: Assessing partnership approaches to improve public health. *Annual Review of Public Health, 19*(1), 173–202. doi:10.1146/annurev.publhealth.19.1.173

Jayewardene, W. P., Lohrmann, D. K., Erbe, R. G., & Torabi, M. R. (2017). *Effects of preventive online mindfulness interventions on stress and mindfulness: A meta-analysis of randomized controlled trials* (Vol. *5*). doi:10.1016/j.pmedr.2016.11.013

Kabat-Zinn, J. (1990). *Full catastrophe living: Using the wisdom of your body and mind to face stress, pain, and illness*. New York, NY: Bantam Dell.

Kabat-Zinn, J. (1994). *Wherever you go, there you are: Mindfulness meditation in everyday life*. New York, NY: Hyperion.

Kawai, Y., O'Connor Duffany, K., & Garrison, K. A. (2018). Blurring the self/space boundary to increase mindfulness: Perspectives from Japanese architectural philosophy, neuroscience and psychology. *Academy of Neuroscience for Architecture*, 84–85. doi:10.1017/CBO9781107415324.004

Khoury, B., Lecomte, T., Fortin, G., Masse, M., Therien, P., Bouchard, V., … Hofmann, S. G. (2013). Mindfulness-based therapy: A comprehensive meta-analysis. *Clinical Psychology Review*, *33*(6), 763–771. doi:10.1016/j.cpr.2013.05.005

Lau, R. W. K., & Pretorius, L. (2019). Intrapersonal wellbeing and the academic mental health crisis. In L. Pretorius, L. Macaulay, & B. Cahusac de Caux (Eds.), *Wellbeing in doctoral education* (pp. 37–45). Singapore: Springer.

Levecque, K., Anseel, F., De Beuckelaer, A., Van der Heyden, J., & Gisle, L. (2017). Work organization and mental health problems in PhD students. *Research Policy*, *46*(4), 868–879. doi:10.1016/j.respol.2017.02.008

LeViness, P., Bershad, C., & Gorman, K. (2017). *The Association for University and College Counseling Center Directors (AUCCCD) annual survey: Reporting period September 1, 2015 through August 31, 2016* (pp. 1–71). Retrieved from The Association for University and College Counseling Center Directors (AUCCCD) website: www.aucccd.org/assets/2017%20aucccd%20survey-public-apr17.pdf

Lindahl, J. R. (2015). Why right mindfulness might not be right for mindfulness. *Mindfulness*, *6*(1), 57–62. doi:10.1007/s12671-014-0380-5

Litan, R. E., Mitchell, L., & Reedy, E. J. (2007). Commercializing university innovations: Alternative approaches. *Innovation Policy and the Economy*, *8*, 31–57. doi:10.1086/ipe.8.25056198

Luken, M., & Sammons, A. (2016). *Systematic review of mindfulness practice for reducing job burnout* (Vol. *70*). doi:10.5014/ajot.2016.016956

Lutz, A., Slagter, H., Dunne, J. D., & Davidson, R. J. (2008). Attention regulation and monitoring in meditation. *Trends in Cognitive Sciences*, *12*(4), 163–169. doi:10.1016/j.tics.2008.01.005

MacDonald, D. A., Walsh, R., & Shapiro, S. L. (2013). Meditation - Empirical research and future directions. In H. L. Friedman & G. Hartelius (Eds.), *The Wiley-Blackwell handbook of transpersonal psychology* (1st ed., pp. 433–458). Malden, MA: Wiley & Sons.

Mikulincer, M., & Florian, V. (1998). The relationship between adult attachment styles and emotional and cognitive reactions to stressful events. In J. A. Simpson & W. S. Rholes (Eds.), *Attachment theory and close relationships* (pp. 143–165). New York, NY: Guilford Press.

National Center for Education Statistics (NCES). (2019). Back to school statistics. Retrieved from IES>NCES website: https://nces.ed.gov/fastfacts/display.asp?id=372

Palmer, P. J., & Zajonc, A. (2010). *The heart of higher education: A- a call for renewal and transforming the academy through collegial conversation*. San Francisco, CA: Jossey-Bass Publ.

Parsons, W. B. (2018). *Being spiritual but not religious: Past, present, future(s)*. New York, NY: Routledge.

Pickert, K. (2014). The mindful revolution. *Time Magazine*.

Poirier, M. R. (2015). Mischief in the marketplace for mindfulness. In R. M. Rosenbaum & B. Magid (Eds.), *What's wrong with mindfulness (and what isn't)* (pp. 13–28). London, United Kingdom: Watkins.

Purser, R. E. (2019). *McMindfulness: How mindfulness became the new capitalist spirituality*. London, United Kingdom: Repeater.

Ray, R. A. (2002). *Secret of the vajra world: The tantric Buddhism of Tibet*. Boston, MA: Shambhala.

Ray, R. A. (2016). *The awakening body: Somatic meditation for discovering our deepest life*. Boulder, CO: Shambhala.

Rechtschaffen, D. J. (2014). *The way of mindful education: Cultivating well-being in teachers and students*. New York, NY: Norton Books.

Rinpoche, C. T. (2010). *The heart of the Buddha: Entering the Tibetan Buddhist path*. Boston, MA: Shambhala.

Roeser, R. W. (2014). The emergence of mindfulness-based interventions in educational settings. In *Advances in motivation and achievement: Vol. 18. Motivational interventions* (Vol. *18*, pp. 379–419). doi:10.1108/S0749-742320140000018010

Rogers, E. (2003). *Diffusion of innovations* (5th ed. ed.). New York, NY: Free Press.

Schrecker, E. (2010). *The lost soul of higher education*. New York, NY: New York Press.

Sharf, R. H. (2015). Is mindfulness Buddhist? (and why it matters). *Transcultural Psychiatry*, *52*(4), 470–484. doi:10.1177/1363461514557561

Stein, Z. (2019). *Education in a time between worlds: Essays on the future of schools, technology, and society*. London, United Kingdom: Bright Alliance.

Tisdale, S. J. (2015). The buffet: Adventures in the new age. In R. M. Rosenbaum & B. Magid (Eds.), *What's wrong with mindfulness (and what isn't)* (pp. 81–92). London, United Kingdom: Watkins.

US News and World Report, L.P. (2019). *US News & World Report Best Colleges*. Retrieved from https://link.gale.com/apps/pub/00EV/PROF?u=gain40375&sid=PROF

van Gordon, W., Shonin, E., & Griffiths, M. D. (2016). Buddhist emptiness theory: Implications for psychology. *Psychology of Religion and Spirituality, Online*, 1–10. doi:https://doi.org/10.1037/rel0000079

Vogus, T. J., & Sutcliffe, K. M. (2012). Organizational mindfulness and mindful organizing: A reconciliation and path forward. *Academy of Management Learning & Education, 11*(4), 722–735. doi:10.5465/amle.2011.0002c

Washington Post. (2013). There really are 50 Eskimo words for 'snow'. Retrieved from www.washingtonpost.com/national/health-science/there-really-are-50-eskimo-words-for-snow/2013/01/14/e0e3f4e0-59a0-11e2-beee-6e38f5215402_story.html

Williams, J. M. G., & Kabat-Zinn, J. (Eds.). (2013). *Mindfulness: Diverse perspectives on its meaning, origins and applications*. London, UK: Routledge.

Wolever, R. Q., Schwartz, E. R., & Schoenberg, P. L. A. (2018). Mindfulness in corporate America: Is the Trojan horse ethical? *Journal of Alternative and Complementary Medicine, 24*(5), 403–406. doi:10.1089/acm.2018.0171

Xiao, H., Carney, D. M., Youn, S. J., Janis, R. A., Castonguay, L. G., Hayes, J. A., & Locke, B. D. (2017). Are we in crisis? National mental health and treatment trends in college counseling centers. *Psychological Services, 14*(4), 407. doi:10.1037/ser0000130

20

CONCEPTUALIZATION OF MINDFULNESS PRACTICE AND ITS PERMANENCE THROUGH PRIMEVAL WORKS

A holistic-literary outlook

Nidhi Kaushal

Introduction

Mindfulness is a fundamental part of a broad program of psycho-spiritual development, aiming to help people reach enlightenment within its original religious context (Ivtzan, 2016). It has a deep, wide, and rich history, as does the study of virtues and strengths and other positive qualities that reveal our humanness (Niemiec, 2013).

> Mindfulness is generally defined as a type of non-judgmental and accepting attention that is brought to bear on experiences occurring in the present moment, including internal phenomena such as sensations, cognitions, and emotions, and external stimuli such as sights, sounds, and smells.
>
> *(Baer, 2010, p. 142)*

The way of mindfulness may rightly be called 'the heart of Buddhist meditation' and it is called as Satipaṭṭhāna method, an ancient way of mindfulness which is 2,500 years old, given in Buddhist discourse (Thera, 2005). Smith (2015) writes that the Satipaṭṭhāna-sutta is known as Buddha's teachings and describes sensations of the body, impressions on self, mental attitude, and activities of the mind as the foundations for the practice of mindfulness. These four foundations of mindfulness are a set of practices through which we can develop a more refined set of skills for understanding the world of both internal and external landscapes. It is theorized and analyzed to have an emotional impact on human functioning, primarily through attention and awareness (Good et al., 2015). The phenomenon of mindfulness also has implications for how we view and represent the mind and its connection to the brain (Langer, 2000). Power of self-motivation, personal vision, lifelong commitment, and the right attitude is innate in all of us. All it takes is paying attention, and being kind to ourselves; and that 'this now' is always available to us (Kabat-Zinn, 2010). The application of mindfulness, if properly analyzed through ancient literature, may be a substantial methodology for improving the personality of present leaders, and is developed in five subsections: (1) the impression of mindfulness practice as an open monitoring, (2) the literary exploration of mindfulness through the *Śrīmad Bhagavad Gītā* (3) the perspective of the *Upanishads* and relevance of mantra in mindfulness practice, (4) erudition of mindfulness practice through the narrative approach of tales, (5) an overview of influential and embodied aspects of mindful leadership.

1. The impression of mindfulness practice as an open monitoring

Mindfulness encompasses both bare attention and concentrated attention to the body, feeling, etc., before gaining knowledge and insight. The body, being the agent of consciousness on the physical sphere, supports the mind in its operations regarding all feelings and various states (Crangle, 1994). The Sanskrit word *Smriti*, most often translated as mindfulness, literally means remembering. Mindfulness always arises in the context of relationship within ourselves and with other people or things (Boccio & Feuerstein, 2005). It can also be characterized as awareness and attention. Mindfulness has a rich texture and capacity to influence the unfolding of our lives and it has an equal capacity to influence the larger world within which we are seamlessly embedded. The foundation for mindfulness practice, for all meditative inquiry and exploration, lies in ethics and morality (Kabat-Zinn, 2005), while mindlessness can show up as the direct cause of human error in complex situations, of prejudice and stereotyping, and of the sensation of alternating between anxiety and boredom that characterizes many lives (Langer, 2000). By nurturing benevolent motivations and actively avoiding reacting reflexivity out of total unawareness, in a word, by committing to and living an inwardly and outwardly ethical and moral life, moment by moment, we can prepare the ground for transformation and healing (Kabat-Zinn, 2005). Mindfulness is also identical to the concept of 'Gestalt philosophy of being' given in the *Gestalt Therapy* (1951) by Frederick Perls, Ralph Hefferline, and Paul Goodman, which recognizes that people use the same philosophical and practical guidance wherever they go, and it contributes to who they are; it becomes part of their individuated character (Levine, 2012). It is not merely a concept; it has very real psychophysiological consequences that affect every aspect of our quality of life (Roberts, 2009).

From the Buddhist perspective, mindfulness is an ancient practice which has profound relevance for our present-day lives and has been called the heart of Buddhist meditation (Kabat-Zinn, 1994). Mindfulness is a way of being from the moment of the moment rather than an end in itself, and Buddhists envisage it as just one—albeit essential—element of a much broader program for promoting happiness and contentment (Kingsland, 2016). From its traditional emphasis on contemplation and meditation, the contemporary practice of mindfulness includes paying attention and being aware of one's everyday activities (Ragoonaden, 2015). The ancient contemplative practices are essential to mindful leadership and creating the type of supportive organizational culture that allows business and people to thrive. The Buddha's original discourse on the foundations of mindfulness (Satipaṭṭhāna-sutta) occurs twice in Buddhist scriptures: (1) as the 10th discourse of the middle collection of discourses (Majjima Nikaya), and (2) as the 22nd discourse of the long collection (Dīgha Nikāya) where it has the title Mahāsatipaṭṭhāna sutta, such that the great discourse, etc. (Thera, 2005). Another ancient practice of mindfulness is the Hawaiian healing system known as Huna Kane. The practice of Huna Kane, in short, is translated into English as 'the inner knowing of the higher self.' It's a way of coming into alignment with all parts of ourselves and of waking up to the present moment, experiencing the mind, body, and spirit of who we are. This system of healing shed a new perspective on mindfulness (Macpherson, 2018). In mindfulness practice the focus is on changing the relationship one has to one's thoughts, body, and feelings; it can be understood by mechanisms of mindfulness which involve cognitive diffusion (a term used in acceptance and commitment therapy) or decentering (a term used in mindfulness-based cognitive therapy), which refer to seeing thoughts as mental events passing through the mind rather than paying attention to the content of the thoughts (Niemiec, 2013). Meditation is about training in awareness and understanding how and why we think and feel the way we do and getting a healthy sense of perspective in the process (Puddicombe, 2011). It is also considered as a deeply contemplative discipline developed elaborately in the śramaṇa (pre-6th century BCE) tradition which includes Jainism (900 BCE) and Buddhism (4th century BCE) of ancient India (Pradhan, 2014).

The concept of mindfulness can be described as the human capacity for observation, participation, and acceptance of life's moments from a loving, compassionate stance (Ragoonaden, 2015). Organizational structures are changing dramatically, providing more opportunities for efficiency, effectiveness, challenging and rewarding work, and achievement of goals (Boyatzis & McKee, 2005). A mindful vision is about creating an organization with which people can connect emotionally, and in doing so enrich their lives, making them more meaningful and worthwhile (Bunting, 2016). Through understanding and remembering our connection to everything around us, we can engage with intentional living and find fulfillment, both within and around us (Macpherson, 2018). Mindfulness and goals go well together. Our mind operates simultaneously on conscious and subconscious levels and mindfulness allows us to better align conscious goals with subconscious processes, keeping goals at the core, and enhances chances of success. Positively framing goals also makes it easier for the subconscious mind to process them (Hougaard et al., 2016). It may support goal pursuit through improved attentional and motivational properties (Good et al., 2015). Mindfulness is the key ingredient of most meditation techniques and it means to be present, at the moment, undistracted. It implies resting the mind in its natural state of awareness, which is free of bias or judgment (Puddicombe, 2011). Hanh (2014) observes that mindfulness is the energy that helps the body and the mind come together and mindful breathing embrace the whole body. It's very important to come home to your body, to recognize it, take care of it, and make peace with it.

Literature review

The subjective 'feel' of mindfulness is that of a heightened state of involvement and wakefulness or being in the present (Langer, 2000). Mindfulness is about finding a way as we are, but with an underlying sense of fulfillment (Puddicombe, 2011). It has the power to make every moment of daily life peaceful, clear, and loving (Hanh, 2014). It has been implicated not only in emotional reactivity but also general emotional tone (Good et al., 2015). Spirituality helps transcend the analytical functioning and cognitive process of the mind and makes room for other experiences (Ivtzan, 2015). Gnaur (2018) finds that as spiritual practice, mindfulness, even without using the term, has been an essential element of all spirituality through the ages, including Yoga. The Śrīmad Bhagavad Gītā gives a clear intellectual understanding about life, soul as well as the dos and don'ts (Nithyananda, 2011). It emphasizes the individual, their capacity for work, their motivational levels, their commitment to society and the organization, in that order, and also visualizes the growth of the organization as being coterminous with that of its members (Mitchell, 2010). The verse [6.6] of the Śrīmad Bhagavad Gītā states that if we can not control our mind then we are the sole reason for our sorrow because the mind keeps on running before sensual and mental. We have to stop it and become calm (Saurabhnath, 2017). Emotional intelligence refers to the capacity for recognizing our feelings and those of others, for motivating ourselves, and for managing emotions well in ourselves and our relationships. The emotional focal points are lower in the brain, in the more ancient sub-cortex; emotional intelligence involves these emotional points at work, in concert with intellectual focuses (Goleman, 1998). Mindfulness is typically construed as a mental practice that requires self-discipline and a commitment to trying to maintain reflective awareness of each passing moment (Sheldon et al., 2015). Mantra practice stills turbulent emotions and thereby stills the turbulent mind. Chanting helps us to achieve this stillness by bringing the breath and the emotions under control (Sivananda, 1993).

The soul is pure consciousness, albeit in an extremely attenuated form, and the body is transformed consciousness, like the cosmos, perceptible to our senses (Krishna, 1990). Consciousness seems to fabricate a narrative of our actions that fits our self-concept as the controller of all actions (Blakeslee, 2004). Hanh (1996) observes that hopelessness often involves difficulty in controlling negative thoughts (Paulson, 2010), but individuals can choose the way they think (Seligman, 2011), and the practice of mindfulness helps develop a positive mind. Modern leaders should cultivate mindfulness as well as learn to engage the experiences of hope and compassion to face unprecedented challenges in the organization (Boyatzis & McKee, 2005). Meditation is an internal discipline to make the mind one-pointed, absolutely concentrated (Easwaran, 2007). Meditation helps us live with an appreciation of the power and preciousness of human life and mindfulness means fully present for life, opening to what is without being swept up by judgments and or getting lost in efforts to cling to or avoid experiences. Mindfulness practice itself originated within rich spiritual traditions that have developed and transformed over thousands of years. Besides, over the centuries mindfulness has been adapted and integrated to meet the most vibrant and pressing needs of society—not only influencing spiritual traditions but seeping into many facets of daily life and culture. Mindful leaders lead and face challenges with optimistic attitude and self-awareness, which is a key aspect of mindfulness practice—the intent is more than awareness of one's self (Lesser & Siegel, 2019). A realized meditator understands that situation can only impact the body, mind, and intellect, but this not the self, and remains peaceful in all situations. The individual's nature is complete and content with knowledge and wisdom, they do not need anything else and have full control over mind and senses (Marballi, 2013). Carroll (2008) writes that mindful leadership is tremendously practical because it rests on simple yet profound insight that expands the entire notion of leadership altogether. Psychology is the science of mental life, both of its phenomena (feelings, desires, cognitions, reasoning, and decisions) and their condition (James, 1890). Ethics is autonomous of psychology in the sense that it sets normative standards for human character and conduct but need not in any way reflect already realized, or even realizable, personalities (Flanagan, 1991). The mindful processes orienting towards the present, being open to novelty, noticing distinctions, attending to differences in contexts, and managing multiple perspectives all serve to test outdated assumptions against novel circumstances (Langer & Ngnoumen, 2017).

Sustained mindfulness practice requires that we maintain willingness for self-honesty and self-reflection that changes our self-mechanism (Smith, 2015). It is both an antidote to shutting down and creating dissonance, and also the necessary condition for resonance (Boyatzis & McKee, 2005). Tales are ancient guidance, containing a pearl of wisdom, distilled through millennia of telling, for our instinctual survival, growth, and integration in the face of inner and outer demons and dragons, dark woods, and wastelands (Kabat-Zinn, 1994). Stories are a central means by which we come to know ourselves and others, thereby enriching our conscious awareness (Fireman et al., 2003). The approach of learning from tales and becoming aligned to a particular paradigm can be a new concept in mindfulness practices (Alterio & McDrury, 2003). Interestingly, engaged interpretation of the tales is the primary pathway towards the competencies and expertise needed for achievement through gaining motivation and strategy development (Guthrie & Wigfield, 2004). Nithyananda (2011) observes that the mind is nothing but a bunch of conditioning. When past and future are available to be experienced here and now, one has attained a timeless state and thus has become an inseparable part of infinity; and infinite knowledge then remains at their disposal (Rama, 1985). Meditation or prayer is the technique by which we tune ourselves to the highest perfection and thereby come to invoke in ourselves a greater perfection of both the mind and the intellect (Chinmayananda, 2017). Mindfulness opens the doors to potential self-improvement and growth while character strength use is often the growth itself (Niemiec, 2013).

2. The literary exploration of mindfulness through the *Śrīmad Bhagavad Gītā*

Rama (1985) writes that *Buddhi* (intellect) has three main functions—judgment, discrimination, and decision—and these functions of intellect are distinct from ego in Eastern psychology. In this framework the path of Sadhana is perfect and profound, the focus is on self-training, and method leads one to become therapist for themselves, whereas in modern or Western psychology these qualities of *Buddhi* are considered to be aspects of ego and this psychological framework is still in an evolving stage because, in modern practices, counsellors are inconsistent and egotistical people who are not interacted in developing themselves but who are only interested in instructions. To the West, philosophy is one of the avenues for self-gratification and self-satisfaction, but in the East, philosophy is for self-adoration and self-satisfaction. With ever-changing vicissitudes of national life, war, revolutions, and through rearrangement of material values, there has been a change in the attitudes of mind and intellect of people towards life. But the Eastern ancient eternal writings of the *Vedas* and *Upanishads* are as true today as they were when taught in the flowery valleys of the sacred Ganga (Chinmayananda, 2017). The purpose of Eastern religion, philosophy, and psychology is to attain self-realization, while Western philosophy is intellectual and deals with man's relationship with the universe (Rama, 1985). Eastern and Eastern-derived approaches of mindfulness emphasize meditative practices geared toward controlling the mind by regulating and disciplining the body, whereas Western conceptions reinforce a more flexible process of attending to novelty and variability as an avenue for increasing control over one's internal and external environments (Langer & Ngnoumen, 2017).

Spirituality is the total understanding and enjoyment of life—materially, physically, emotionally, relationally, and in all senses—without discontent and with responsibility. This enjoyment and responsibility arises out of awareness of the present moment (Nithyananda, 2011). The *Śrīmad Bhagavad Gītā* in its written form, at any rate, is generally thought to date from the 2nd to 3rd century AD and is considered a later interpolation in the long epic, the Mahābhārata (Sargeant & Smith, 2010, p. 4). It is not theology or religion—it's poetry. And it is more than just a book, more than mere words or concepts (Hawley,

2011). The *Śrīmad Bhagavad Gītā* is also known as Gitopanished. It is the essence of Vedic knowledge and one of the most important *Upanishads* in Vedic literature (Prabhupada, 1993); it is included in Bhishma Parva, a part of epic Mahābhārata, by sage Vyasa. This also describes the essence of Indian philosophy (Saurabhnath, 2017). As a scripture, it is part of the ancient knowledge base of the Vedic tradition, which is the expression of the experiences of great sages and the manual for enlightenment (Nithyananda, 2011). It presents some of the most important truths of human existence in a language that is clear, memorable, and charged with emotion (Mitchell, 2010). It claims that the root of all suffering is the agitation of the mind, the consequence of selfish desire. The only means of extinguishing this desire are by simultaneously stilling the mind through Yoga and engaging oneself in higher forms of activity (Pradhan, 2014). Meditation is the culmination of the entire curriculum of the *Śrīmad Bhagavad Gītā*, which aims at removing the three main defects of our personality: mala, vikshepa, and aavarana. Mala (japa), or chanting of mantra, causes the mind to rush into the world of sense objects due to a sense of finitude; vikshepa is the tendency of the mind to get distracted; and aavarana prevents us from getting fully established in the knowledge of the eternal essence (Marballi, 2013). According to the *Śrīmad Bhagavad Gītā*, the meditator should be prashaantha (calm), vigatabheehi (fearless) and establish themselves with the vow of renunciation (Marballi, 2013). It offers knowledge that can help the modern therapist to know the unknown dimensions of life (Rama, 1985).

'The *Śrīmad Bhagavad Gītā* is officially *Smrti*, a part of the venerable tradition; it is not *Sruti*, Revelation, as are only the *Vedas*' (Bolle, 1979, p. 256). It leads the person to awareness of the core of consciousness, then to training that focuses on understanding and mastery of one's internal states, and lastly to the skillful and selfless performance of actions in the external world (Rama, 1985). In this scripture, the mind is comparable to a steady flame. Once it is at home in the depths of contemplation, the mind becomes steady, like an upright, flickering flame in a windless place. In the deep meditation, and only there, can a human being find true fulfillment; then the still mind touches Brahman (Supreme-self) and enjoys bliss (Easwaran, 2007). Rama (1985) writes that the *Śrīmad Bhagavad Gītā* aims to teach the aspirant how to establish equanimity, both in their personal life and their activities in the outside world. The wisdom of this holy book has universal implacability and we have identified some verses from this scripture related to the concept of mindfulness practice, meditation, and mindful leaders in this work.

The significance of mindfulness practice and to be mindful have been given in the [6.7], [6.8] and [6.9] verses of the *Śrīmad Bhagavad Gītā* as follows:

> *jitātmanaḥ praśhāntasya paramātmā samāhitaḥ*
> *śhītoṣhṇa-sukha-duḥkheṣhu tathā mānāpamānayoḥ [6.7]*

Explanation—one who is self-controlled and calm remains merged in Supreme Self while in cold and heat, happiness and sorrow, and also in honor and dishonor (Saurabhnath, 2017). The effect of controlling the mind is that one automatically follows the dictation of Paramatma or super soul. This transcendental position is at once achieved by one who is in Supreme Self-consciousness (Prabhupada, 1993). The preserving yogi succeeds in metamorphosing their physical ego into the true soul. By further spiritual advancement, they realize their soul as the reflection of the omnipresent spirit, and when this state of realization is reached, the soul permanently perceives the Supreme Self or God (Yogananda, 2007). Whenever we face an unpleasant situation, our mind is agitated. We should console the mind by telling it that everything is transient, so we should remain calm in favorable and unfavorable situations because everything passes soon (Saurabhnath, 2017). The Supreme Reality stands revealed in the consciousness of those who have conquered themselves. They live in peace like cold, heat, pleasure and pain, praise and blame (Easwaran, 2007).

jñāna-vijñāna-tṛiptātmā kūṭa-stho vijitendriyaḥ
yukta ityuchyate yogī sama-loṣhṭāśhma-kāñchanaḥ [6.8]

Explanation—A person is called as a devotee (Connected to God or Self) when they become content with knowledge and experience of that knowledge, who is situated within, who has control over senses, such as a yogi equally treats a lump of clay, stone, and gold (Saurabhnath, 2017). It is the realized soul who is self-controlled because it is surrendered to Supreme Self (Prabhupada, 1993). Always united with the Lord, they realize the phenomenal world and its various appearances as emanations from the one divine consciousness (Yogananda, 2007). They are completely fulfilled by spiritual wisdom and self-realization. Having conquered their senses, they have climbed to the summit of human consciousness. To such people a clod of dirt, a stone, and gold are the same (Easwaran, 2007).

suhṛin-mitrāryudāsīna-madhyastha-dveṣhya-bandhuṣhu
sādhuṣhvapi cha pāpeṣhu sama-buddhir viśhiṣhyate [6.9]

Explanation—The person who is impartial towards well-wishers, friends, enemies, neutrals, arbiters, haters, relatives, gentlemen and sinners, is superior (Saurabhnath, 2017). In order to concentrate the mind, one should always remain in seclusion and avoid disturbance by external objects. One should be very careful to accept favorable and reject unfavorable that affect their realization (Prabhupada, 1993). They endorse the activities of the virtuous who serve as harbingers of good to their fellow humans, and they denounce the activities of the evil who harm themselves and others (Yogananda, 2007). They are equally disposed to family, enemies, and friends, to those who support them and those who are hostile, to the good and the evil alike. Because they are impartial, they rise to great heights (Easwaran, 2007).

Mindfulness involves taking a compassionate, gentle, and accepting approach toward one's mind and body (Niemiec, 2013). The *Śrīmad Bhagavad Gītā* has emphasized remaining patient, calm, and unperturbed in the face of both internal impulses and external pressures (Gnaur, 2018), and proposed mindfulness as a way of being separated from the assault of senses, to attain the state of Stithapragna (a state of unperturbedness) (Srivastava, 2018).

The practice of meditation to attain mindfulness has been exemplified in the following verses of this scripture:

śhuchau deśhe pratiṣhṭhāpya sthiram āsanam ātmanaḥ
nātyuchchhritaṁ nāti-nīchaṁ chailājina-kuśhottaram [6.11]
tatraikāgraṁ manaḥ kṛitvā yata-chittendriya-kriyaḥ
upaviśhyāsane yuñjyād yogam ātma-viśhuddhaye [6.12]

Explanation—Select a clean spot, neither too high nor too low, and sit firmly on a cloth, deerskin, or *kusha* grass. Then, once seated, strive to still the thoughts. Make the mind one-pointed in meditation, and our heart will be purified with this practice. Hold your body, head, and neck firmly in a straight line, and keep your eyes from wandering. With all fears dissolved in the peace of the Self and all action dedicated to Brahman, controlling the mind and fixing it on me, sit in meditation with me as your only goal.

> *samaṁ kāya-śhiro-grīvaṁ dhārayann achalaṁ sthiraḥ*
> *samprekṣhya nāsikāgraṁ svaṁ diśhaśh chānavalokayan [6.13]*
> *praśhāntātmā vigata-bhīr brahmachāri-vrate sthitaḥ*
> *manaḥ sanyamya mach-chitto yukta āsīta mat-paraḥ [6.14]*
> *yuñjann evaṁ sadātmānaṁ yogī niyata-mānasaḥ*
> *śhantiṁ nirvāṇa-paramāṁ mat-sansthām adhigachchhati [6.15]*

Explanation—With senses and mind constantly controlled through meditation, united with the Self within, an aspirant attains nirvana, the state of abiding joy and peace in me (Easwaran, 2007). Yogananda (2007) writes that the devotee who sits in a good posture and meditates at the point between the eyebrows learns to practice yoga, the uniting of ego and soul; in deep concentration, they find their mind and heart (chitta, feeling) free from sensory distractions and emotional likes and dislikes. With the unification of the ego into the taintless soul, they engage in the ultimate 'self-purification.' Meditation involves the withdrawal, through the spine, of life current from the sensory nerve branches, and concentration of that accumulation of life force within the spherical spiritual eye. By the practice of eightfold yoga, the devotee first experiences ecstasy for a short time; by deeper practice, they can remain divinely entranced for a longer period.

3. The perspective of the *Upanishads* and relevance of mantra in mindfulness practice

There are two notions of mind. First, on the phenomenal concept, the mind is characterized by the way it feels; on the psychological concept, the mind is characterized by what it does. For instance, sensation, in its central sense, is best taken as a phenomenal concept: to have a sensation is to have a state with a certain sort of feel. On the other hand, the concepts of learning and memory might best be taken as psychological (Chalmers, 1996). Every great tradition teaches a way to remember the Supreme (the Lord), either by remembering a mantra, a word, a syllable, or a set of words, and the mantra is remembered consciously, it is recorded by the unconsciousness (Rama, 1985). The root 'man' in the word 'mantra' means in Sanskrit 'to think'; 'tra' comes from 'trai,' meaning 'to protect or free from the bondage of samsara or the phenomenal world.' Therefore mantra means 'the thought that liberates and protects' (Sivananda, 1993). Consciousness is an awareness that projects itself as the future to forecast the continuance of the universe on the experience of the past (Krishna, 1990). 'Consciousness is *Buddhi*, the power of discrimination and understanding that holds the key to the development of the consciousness' (Rama et al., 1976, p. 80). It yields to experience and prudence, and molds us every hour (Sathe, 1990). Consciousness is always accompanied by awareness (Chalmers, 1996), and it converts our mind into a mirror of our times (Sathe, 1990). It is marvelously creative and deceptive, constructing an orderly picture of the world imagined into a format that will be more useful for survival (Blakeslee, 2004), and awareness can be broadly analyzed as a state wherein we have access to some information and can use that information in the control of behavior (Chalmers, 1996).

The highest source of knowledge is human consciousness. Our perception, imagination, memory, judgment, understanding, and reasoning are all the result of our consciousness and intense reflective activity (Sathe, 1990). The chanting or recitation of mantras activates and accelerates the creative spiritual force, promoting harmony in all parts of the human being (Sivananda, 1993). The very nature of conscious experience in our culture has evolved significantly as the self-concept has evolved (Blakeslee, 2004). Conscious states don't inherit their consciousness from higher-order mental states; rather, a state's being conscious consists simply in one's being conscious of oneself as being in that state, and that happens by having a high-order thought that one is in that state (Rosenthal, 2005). Sivananda (1993) finds that the awareness is an essential factor in the practice of mantras. With the application, with the purifying of the emotions and the mind more single-pointed, stillness will ensue and a sense of the 'ever-present Presence' may be felt. Mantras have a strong implication in the practice of mindfulness and to reach the state of supreme consciousness, which has been identified and analyzed through the ancient Indian literary texts like the *Upanishads* and the *Śrīmad Bhagavad Gītā*. The *Upanishads* have made a clear distinction between knowledge and wisdom through their inspiring and instructive passages and verses because they are concerned with the process of thinking (Rama, 1978). The *Upanishads*' view of mindfulness practice includes *Sarvana*, *Manana*, and Nididhyasana. The *Sarvana* (literature, listening to, and hearing) implies that comprehension of *Upanishadic* sayings has its only purpose and goal in Brahman. *Manana* (thinking over) means the use of proper arguments to get rid of the apparent contradiction between *Sruti* sayings. *Nididhyasana* (deep meditation) is the removal from the adept's consciousness of everything superfluous and the concentration of the mind on Brahman (Isayeva, 1993). The purpose of 'repetition of the mantra' (japa) is to lead the mind to rungs of meditation, and when japa is carried on amid worldly activities, it is called meditation in action (Rama, 1978).

The *Māṇḍukya – Upanishad* derives its name after its seer Manduka (Chinmayananda, 2017) and belongs to the group of *Upanishads* attached to *Atharva Veda*, belonging most probably to the Shounakiya Shakha of the *Veda*, as the *Upanishad* was given out to Shounaka (Vedic Rishi, Sanskrit author, and grammarian) (Sharvanada, 1920). Gauḍapādācārya (c. 6th century CE), the great-preceptor of Sri Śaṅkarācārya (788 CE – 820 CE, 8th-century theologian of Advaita Vedanta), wrote a *Kārikā* (glossary) called as *Māṇḍukya Kārikā* (7th century CE) on this *Upanishad* in the Sanskrit language, providing an insight into a unique system of thought (Chinmayananda, 2017).

Saurabhnath (2017) writes that the *Māṇḍukya Upanishad* has described the four states of consciousness—waking state (jagruta avastha), dreaming state (svapna avastha), deep sleep (sushupti avastha), and a state of supreme consciousness (turiya)—and the following shlokas of the *Māṇḍukya Kārikā* represents the significance of Om (Brahman or God) and these states of consciousness respectively.

> *Hari Om. Om-ity-etad-aksharam-idam sarvam,*
> *tasyopavyākhyānam bhūtam bhavad bhavishyaditi sarvam-omkāra eva.*
> *Yaccānyat trikālātītam tadapy omkāra eva. [1]*

Explanation—Harih Om. Om, the word is all this. A clear explanation of it is (the following)—all that is past, present, and future, verily is Om. That which is beyond the three periods is also, indeed, Om (Chinmayananda, 2017).

Bahis-prajno vibhur-visvo hyantah-prajnastu taijasah,
ghana-prajnas-tatha prajna eka eva tridha smrtah [1.1]

Explanation—Visva, the first quarter (pāda) is He who is all-pervading and who experiences the external, the gross objects (the waker). The Taijasa, the second quarter (pāda), is He who cognizes the internal, the subtle bodies (the dreamer). Prājana is He who is a mass of Consciousness. He is one alone who is thus known as three in different planes of consciousness (Chinmayananda, 2017).

nivṛtteḥ sarvaduḥkhānāmīśānaḥ prabhuravyayaḥ,
advaitaḥ sarvabhāvānāṃ devasturyo vibhuḥ smṛtaḥ [1.10]

Explanation—In that which is indicated as the changeless and the supreme Lord, there is a total cessation of all miseries. It is the One without a second among the plurality; it is known as turiyā, the ever-effulgent, and all-pervading.

The *Māṇḍukya-Upanishad* analyzes the entire range of human consciousness and provides a symbol for meditation in the monosyllable AUM, comprising three sounds—A, U, M—detailing its philosophical implication (Chinmayananda, 2017). Om is that which enables all articulate words to come to existence and it is that which has remained inarticulate even after all the articulate sounds have been produced. Om is indeed Akshara Brahma—The Imperishable One. In the *Chandogya Upanishad*, Om has been indicated as Udgitha—the Sacred Word that is sung (Mehta, 1970). The word Om called Pranava (Brahman or God) is a compound of letters A, U, M. These three states stand for three states of consciousness. As the A, U, and M next merge into silence, then Om represents the fourth state that can be experienced. It is called Turiya (a state of pure awareness where all activity ceases) and is above feelings and thoughts (Rama, 1978).

Mehta (1970) finds the five function groups of mind from the *Upanishads* such as:

1. Conception or Sānkālpā, Thought or Māti, and Thoughtfulness or Mānshā. It constitutes the forming of concepts and building up of the logical structures of thought.
2. Consciousness or *Sānjnānā*, Perception or *Ajnānā*, and Discrimination or *Vijnānā*. It denotes a process of selectivity whereby the mind discriminates between good and bad.
3. Steadfastness or *Dhriti*, Impulse or *Jūti*, and memory or *Smriti*. It shows the mind's continuity through memory and impulse or the mind's instincts.
4. Purpose or *Krātu*, Life or *Āsu*, Desire or *Kāmā*, and Will or *Vāsā*. In this function, the mind generates through imagination, energy for the maintenance of a continuity of that which it has declared as good, true, or beautiful.
5. Intelligence or *Prājnānā*, Wisdom or *Medhā*, and Insight or *Drīshti*. It is the coordinating element of the mind's functioning.

Rama (1985) defines the link between the states of consciousness and mindfulness practice that the consciousness of Samadhi is as wide as infinite space; it is all-inclusive and is an unlimited and perennial source of knowledge. The other three states of waking, dreaming, and sleeping are experienced by all creatures, but the fourth state, the highest state of equilibrium, is attained by a true aspirant. Mindfulness involves cultivating an observer of consciousness, trying to maintain reflective awareness of each moment (Sheldon et al., 2015).

Nithyananda (2011) describes the four states of consciousness, which are similar to the states of mindfulness practice as well.

- The state with thoughts and with 'I' consciousness is the waking state, Jagrat, in which most of us are now. This is the conscious state.
- Another state is when we have thoughts, but 'I' consciousness is absent. This is the dream state—Svapna. This is a sub-conscious state.
- Neither 'I' consciousness nor the flow of thoughts exists. This is deep sleep or Susupti Avastha.
- There is the fourth state, where we have no flow of thoughts yet we have 'I' consciousness. This is Samadhi, thoughtless awareness or self-realization.

Kabat-Zinn (1994) writes that mindfulness means being awake and it can also help us to appreciate feelings such as joy, peacefulness, and happiness, which often go by fleetingly and unacknowledged. Bringing awareness to our breathing, we remind ourselves that we are here now, so we might as well be fully awake for whatever is already happening. The spirit of mindfulness is to practice for its own sake, and just to take each moment as it comes—pleasant or unpleasant, good, bad, or ugly—and then work with that because it is what is present now. It includes paying attention in a particular way: on purpose, in the present moment, and nonjudgmentally.

> There are four kinds of mindfulness, identical in function but different in focus. Mindfulness can focus on the body, on the feeling, on the mind, or the objects. In the mindfulness of the body, the mediator notes his body motion and position regardless of what he does. In mindfulness of feeling, the meditator focuses on his internal sensations, disregarding whether they are pleasant or unpleasant. In mindfulness of mental state, the meditator focuses on each state as it comes to awareness. Whatever mood, mode of thought, or psychological state presents itself, he simply registers it as such. The fourth technique, mindfulness of mind-objects, is virtually the same as the one just described save for the level at which the mind working is observed. As each thought arises, the mediator notes it in the term of a detailed schema for classifying mental content. From these observations emerge a series of realizations about the nature of the mind and with these realizations, mindfulness matures into insight.
>
> *(Goleman, 1979, p. 134)*

In Sadhana (spiritual practice) all the faculties of the mind are trained in a unified way. The spiritual practice of mindfulness (Sadhana) requires the discipline of mind, action, and speech. One who experiences turiya (samadhi) is called a person of equanimity (Rama, 1985).

The implication of the association amid chanting of mantra, meditation, and mindfulness can also be identified from the verses of the *Śrīmad Bhagavad Gītā*. In the following verse [8.8], the need for meditation has been described seamlessly, which can also be achieved by chanting of particular mantras, and the next shloka [2.53] has described the state of self-realization and mindfulness or turiya (a state of supreme consciousness).

Abhyāsa-yoga-yuktena chetasā nānya-gāminā
paramaṁ puruṣhaṁ divyaṁ yāti pārthānuchintayan [8.8]

Explanation—When the mind is not moving towards any other thing, made steadfast by the method of habitual meditation, and constantly meditating on the Supreme Self (Purusa) or God, the Resplendent, O Partha, he goes (to him) (Chinmayananda, 2014). One's memory of the Supreme Lord is revived by chanting the mantra. By this practice of chanting and hearing the sound vibration of the mantra, one's ear, tongue, and mind are engaged. This mystic meditation is very easy to practice, and it helps one attain the Supreme Self or Lord (Prabhupada, 1993).

> *śhruti-vipratipannā te yadā sthāsyati niśhchalā*
> *samādhāv-achalā buddhis tadā yogam avāpsyasi [2.53]*

Explanation—The highest perfection of self-realization is to understand that one is eternally the servitor of the Supreme Lord and that one's only business is to discharge one's duties in Supreme consciousness (Prabhupada, 1993). When your wisdom takes you beyond delusion, you shall be indifferent to what has been heard and what is yet to be heard (Nithyananda, 2011). When your intellect, though perplexed by what you have heard, shall stand immovable and steady in the 'Self,' then you shall attain self-realization (Chinmayananda, 2014). 'Holy indifference'—a very positive state in which we learn to make the mind undisturbed and equal under all circumstances. When the mind is calm, it is ready for Samadhi (Easwaran, 1979).

4. Erudition of mindfulness practice through the narrative approach of tales

Good fictional works affect us profoundly by arousing psychological reactions of emotion and motivation. These psychological reactions create a belief mechanism which is based on the principle that 'a necessary condition of feeling sympathy, sadness, awareness, etc. is that you believe that something good or bad has happened, or is or maybe going to happen, to some real person or thing' (New, 1999). These are based on the 'make-believe' theory and helpful in the development of mindfulness. The introduction of tales to enhance motivation and conceptual knowledge, building strategies and social interaction can also enrich the field of mindfulness practices. Tales create a link between motivation and mindfulness by creating awareness with a core integration of positive psychology (Guthrie & Wigfield, 2004). The relation of narrative and consciousness can be explained in the context of Flanagan's *Natural Method* (1992). The natural method was designed originally to corral consciousness by paying attention to its phenomenology, psychology, and neurobiology. Tales and narratives play a powerful role in the construction of self-awareness and self- knowledge to a significant degree. Narrative does not merely capture aspects of the self for description, communication, and examination; it constructs the self (Fireman et al., 2003). Motivational tales provide reflective learning processes and demonstrate how leaders use the ideas, strategies, and processes to better prepare the mindful workforce the for rigors and uncertainties inherent in the professional practice of the organization (Alterio & McDrury, 2003). Tales are ancient maps, offering their guidance for the development of full human beings. The wisdom of these tales comes down to our day from a time before writing, having been told in twilight and darkness around fires for thousands of years. While they are entertaining and engaging stories in their own right, they are so in large part because they are emblematical of the dramas we encounter as we seek wholeness, happiness, and peace (Kabat-Zinn, 1994).

Tales have a very novel approach in the practice of mindfulness through literature and they are helpful in developing mindfulness at the workplace in three ways. First, it helps in the emotional release, which is the dominant motivating factor and the outcome is likely to be primarily cathartic. It helps people in expressing an intense feeling, identifying recurring emotions, reliving past experiences, and gaining insight. The second key factor is learning through experience, which requires interaction and dialogue-sharing between a teller and listener. When stories are described and processed by using reflective dialogue, it creates a possibility of change in ourselves and others. The third way is to bring about change to practice, because the potential for change is always present in us. A changed perspective increases self- knowledge and insight into personal and professional relationships. It happens by engagement of employees through self-reviewing, a reflective capacity which develops through reflective discussion at the workplace (Alterio & McDrury, 2003). Chaille and Britain (1991) describe the reflection of tales and their positioning that is also applicable in the practice of learning mindfulness—learners do not acquire knowledge that is transmitted to them, rather they construct knowledge through their intellectual activity and make it their own. Tales have the cultural and traditional effect of their origin and require a framework to idealize and visualize the tales from the perspective of mindfulness (Alterio & McDrury, 2003). Just as there is a stream of thought, there is a parallel stream of feeling, because thought and feeling are inextricably woven together (Goleman, 1998).

Stories remind us that it is worth seeking the altar where our own fragmented and isolated being-strands can find each other and marry, bringing new levels of harmony and understanding to our lives, to the point where we might live happily ever after, which means in the timeless here and now. They are wise, ancient, surprisingly sophisticated blueprints for our full development as human beings. Tales from the fabulous Indian works of literature, like the *Panchatantra* (200 BCE), have contained significant lessons for every practice of modern life. The related morals from the tales—such as, 'if we are mindful then we can easily face any vulnerable situation bravely' from the tale *The Crafty Crane and the Craftier Crab*, and 'intellectuality, awareness and mindfulness are always won together' from *The Monkey and the Crocodile*, etc.—have been analyzed from the perspective of learning 'mindfulness practice' and been found to be very effective in this field. Alterio and McDrury (2003) find that the stories have educative and transformative possibilities and allow us to glimpse the worlds of others and come to know our world more fully. The significance of the narrative approach in mindfulness is to facilitate emotional release, to learn from the experience, and to bring about thoughtful change to practice. Tales not only provide motivation but also wisdom helpful for moral judgment. The implication of stories can be analyzed by the famous proverb that 'a picture is worth a thousand words' (an English adage) given by Arthur Brisbane (1864–1936) in the article 'Speakers Give Sound Advice' published in *The Post-Standard* (1911). The folk wisdom contained in the tales helps rationalize the theme, concepts, and situations, and the picture created in the heart and mind of a person by the story is worth ten thousand words, providing a better perspective (Covey, 1999).

The work of mindfulness demands honoring and heeding our dwarf energy, rather than rushing headlong into things with a mind that is sorely out of touch with large parts of our self, a mind driven by narrow ambition and ideas of personal gain. The story says we can only fare well if we proceed with an awareness of the way things are, including a willingness to admit not knowing where we are going (Kabat-Zinn, 1994). We are not consciously aware of the real motivation of much for our behavior and our consciousness is at front place which is, at best, the receiver of consensus by motivational factions in the inner mind or, at worst, a puppet of the factors under life preservation (includes defense/offense consumption, conflict/challenge, and procreation) (Ahmose, 2007). Our psychology must, therefore, take account not only of the conditions antecedent to mental states but of their resultant consequences as well (James, 1890). The significant factors for behavioral changes include motivation, ability, psychological capital, and the supporting environment (Kinley & Ben-Hur, 2015). The integration of mindfulness with strengths practice allows for an individual to become more aware of not only troubling thoughts and feelings but also to become more aware of positive thoughts, emotions, and behaviors (Niemiec, 2013). The job of epistemology is to set standards for reasoning, not simply to reflect our practices (Flanagan, 1991). The five-stage mirror of learning from tales includes noticing (purpose and perceptive of learning), making sense (integration of ideas), making meaning (meaningful learning and understanding), working with meaning (develops awareness and problem-solving strategies), and transformative learning (involves critical overview of own and others' knowledge) (Alterio & McDrury, 2003). Tales or stories enthrall and inspire us, with a sense of excitement and with recognition of our freedom, potential, and power (Covey, 1999).

5. An overview of influential and embodied aspects of mindful leadership

The role of mindfulness practice as a source of renewal in leadership can be identified through the scholarship of ancient literary texts because they provide a holistic conceptual framework for understanding the concept of mindfulness practice. This framework integrates influential impressions from mindfulness theory and literary writings and seeks to better explain the notion of mind, mindful leader, and states of mindfulness. Mindfulness needs to be maintained regularly (Smith, 2015). Awareness of our inherent connection is the foundation of mindfulness and the beginning of waking up to who we are, thus living an inspired life (Macpherson, 2018). Individuals engage in the meditation and mindfulness practices to become mindful because they include the intellectual amount of enlightened awareness, which enables employees to use the strategy liberally when it is advantageous and required (Guthrie & Wigfield, 2004). Rama (1985) writes that all persons can be divided into two categories of equanimity and disharmony. Great leaders are emotionally intelligent, mindful, and seek to live in full consciousness of self, others, nature, and society (Boyatzis & McKee, 2005). They seek to create a vision of business that is conscious of its impact on all people and the environment (Bunting, 2016). The primary act of mindful leadership is to open, to fully appreciate the circumstances. The Tibetan word for this vulnerable openness is *jinpa*, which means 'complete generosity,' and cultivating *jinpa* is a wisdom that is assured, skillful, and astute (Carroll, 2008). Internal distractions might also be managed with mindfulness (Good et al., 2015).

The need and significance of controlling the mind is given in verse [6.5] of the *Śrīmad Bhagavad Gītā* as follows:

uddhared ātmanātmānaṁ nātmānam avasādayet
ātmaiva hyātmano bandhur ātmaiva ripur ātmanaḥ [6.5]

One must deliver oneself with the help of one's mind, and not degrade oneself. The mind is the friend of the conditioned soul, and its enemy as well. The word Atma denotes body, mind, and soul—depending upon circumstances. Since the mind is the central point of Yoga practice, Atma refers here to the mind. The purpose of the Yoga system is to control the mind and to draw it away from the attachment of sense objects. The best way to disentangle oneself is to always engage the mind in the Supreme (Lord) consciousness (Prabhupada, 1993). We should ourselves raise our levels, not allowing our stature to recede and go down. No external agent can do this for us, for we are ourselves and our friends and our foes (Dhar, 2003).

The following verses of the Śrīmad Bhagavad Gītā have described the state of a mindful person:

bandhur ātmātmanas tasya yenātmaivātmanā jitaḥ
anātmanas tu śhatrutve vartetātmaiva śhatru-vat [6.6]

By whom one's own my is conquered by oneself, of that person one's mind is the friend of oneself, But of the person whose mind is not under control, one's very mind inimical, (and) behaves like an enemy (Saurabhnath, 2017). The mindful leader is the person of equanimity is the ideal person of the *Śrīmad Bhagavad Gītā.* The mindful leader remains unattached, undisturbed, happy, and joyous in all external circumstances. This verse is closely related to the *Mandukya Upanishad*, which explains the states of mind (Rama, 1985). The self-governed yogi can also be called a mindful leader. A mindful person is one who has realized the eternal essence through meditation, specifically through their outlook toward situations, objects, and people. No matter what situation one finds oneself in, the mind remains even, calm, and peaceful—called 'prashaantaha' (Marballi, 2013).

mat-karma-kṛin mat-paramo mad-bhaktaḥ saṅga-varjitaḥ
nirvairaḥ sarva-bhūteṣhu yaḥ sa mām eti pāṇḍava [11.55]

When one entirely abandons all the desires that come into the mind, O son of Pritha, satisfied within the Self by the Self, then one is called a stable of wisdom. Those who make me (Supreme Lord) the supreme goal of their work and act without selfish attachment, who devotes themselves to me completely and are free from ill will for any creature, enter into me (Easwaran, 2007).

dhṛityā yayā dhārayate manaḥ-prāṇendriya-kriyāḥ
yogenāvyabhichāriṇyā dhṛitiḥ sā pārtha sāttvikī [18.33]

The sattvic will, developed through meditation, keeps prana, mind, senses in vital harmony. (Easwaran, 2007). That fortitude which is accomplished through Yoga, which regulates the activities of the mind, life forces, and that senses, such unwavering fortitude is sattvic (Marballi, 2013).

The seminal concepts of optimism, trust, awareness, generosity, patience, openness, compassion, empathy, kindness, values, attention, spirituality, and intention are significant features as well as embodied states of mindfulness. Optimism has been associated with diverse aspects of human experience, including goal pursuit behavior, the developing of social networks and relationships, emotional well-being, and physical health (Bouchard et al., 2017). The optimists tend to believe defeat is just a temporary setback, that its causes are confined to one case, and defeat is not their fault (Seligman, 1991). Hanh (1996) writes that when we are mindful, we must be conscious of each breath, each movement, every thought and feeling, everything which has any relation to ourselves. Psychology represents the 'grounding' effect, in which the mind is used for thinking, rationalizing, and understanding life. Spirituality transcends rational thoughts and evolves intuitively over one's lifetime. Therefore psychology is crucial to the spiritual journey for transcendence (Ivtzan, 2015). Our outlook on the world, others, and ourselves can be changed if we spend a large part of our mental energy on nicer, more optimistic, and interesting things. Positive thinking helps to think beyond limitation and the world will emerge out of darkness (Paulson, 2010). 'People who have emerged as leaders in the world are those who took time to think through problems facing humanity until they could proffer the necessary solutions' (Akindele, 2016, p. 37). People who believe good events have permanent causes try even harder after they succeed (Seligman, 2011).

'Mindful optimism is about examining the way we think and avoiding negative, "knee-jerk", pessimistic reactions as well as aggrandized optimistic reactions' (Fields, 2008, p. 65). Mindfulness requires a whole range of applications that need to be maintained and balanced all at once. It allows us to apply critical thinking and discernment, logic, ethics, an openness to question old ideas and core beliefs (Smith, 2015). Empathy is based on development of external awareness, one of the key aspects of mindfulness. External awareness includes the ability to sense and read other people's state of mind, as well as be aware of how we can influence or help them (Hougaard et al., 2016). Being mindful entails an open awareness that creates a state of trust in which the brain's social engagement system is turned on and we connect with others, and even our own inner life, with more acceptance and clear thinking (Lesser & Siegel, 2019). Trust is a feeling of confidence or conviction that things can unfold within a dependable framework that embodies order and integrity. The feeling state of trust is important to cultivate in mindfulness practice. Generosity is another quality which, like patience, letting go, non-judging, and trust, provides a solid foundation for mindfulness practice. Patience is an ever-present alternative to the mind's endemic restlessness and impatience. In taking up meditation, we are cultivating the quality of patience every time we stop and sit and become aware of the flow of our breathing. Meditation is about letting the mind be as it is and knowing something about how it is in this moment. To let go means to give up coercing, resisting, or struggling, in exchange for something more powerful and wholesome which comes out of allowing things to be as they are without getting caught up in your attraction to or rejection of them, in the intrinsic stickiness of wanting, of liking and disliking (Kabat-Zinn, 1994).

Mindfulness, hope, and compassion enable us to be resilient and function effectively even in the face of challenges. Hope engages and raises our spirit and mobilizes energy. It is an emotional magnet and keeps people going even during challenges. Compassion is a combination of deep understanding, concern, and a willingness to act on that concern for the benefit of oneself and others (Boyatzis & McKee, 2005). The degree of selfless compassion is based on what Buddhists call 'right mindfulness' and 'right understanding' (Kabat-Zinn, 1994). A controlled mind can accomplish many beneficial endeavors, whereas an uncontrolled mind can degrade the consciousness with most ignoble thoughts (Srivastava, 2018). Mindfulness and character strength deepen one another (Niemiec, 2013. We have found abstract and absolute of 'unity and diversity' as the mixture of self or personality (James, 1890). Character strengths are viewed as 'who we are,' in other words, they are part of our core identity and can be considered positive personality characteristics (Niemiec, 2013). The ego may be described as the eye through which the mind perceives reality (Ivtzan, 2015). The ego acts as its own best friend when by meditation and the exercise of its innate soul qualities it spiritualizes itself and ultimately restores its true soul nature. Conversely, the physical ego serves as its own worst enemy when by delusive material behavior it eclipses its true nature as the ever-blessed soul (Yogananda, 2007). One of the aims of mindfulness is to bring about the presence of mind in each moment, truly experiencing it, rather than being carried away hither and dither by thoughts, emotions, and wishful thinking (Gnaur, 2018).

Mindfulness practice can cultivate an enlightened awareness and serenity by transforming the personality and behavior of individuals. Tranquility of the mind is the core of this aspect, in which the ancient meditative approaches have a pivotal role and the application of these traditional procedures of meditation as described in the *Śrīmad Bhagavad Gītā*, for attaining the states of steadfastness and equanimity, is significantly relevant and helpful to a mindful leader in mindfulness practice. The significance of mantras in achieving the state of supreme consciousness, and, on the other hand, the examination of the anecdotes and folklore to get wisdom on mindfulness, are two different noteworthy mechanisms to get insight and they have enriched the notion of mindfulness as well. Awareness and consciousness are synonymous and inherit features of mindfulness, and literary texts have been analyzed in this context because these are valuable requirements for people to be awake and mindful at the workplace, and work as influential and motivational factors of the people engaged in mindfulness practice.

Conclusion

Mindfulness practice is an evolving field of study which has its roots in primeval literature and can be learned through the study of scriptures. The narrative approach of getting wisdom and enlightened awareness from the literature has not only explored the dynamic areas of mindfulness but also enriched its practice. The significant use of mantras like Om to get the Supreme consciousness along with the meditation technique for controlling the mind provides two different but integrated traditions of being mindful. Knowledge has been seen both as a thing and a flow, requiring varied attitudes to get wisdom. Therefore, through mindfulness, one can use this reflection of literary texts as a link between knowledge and action. This intensive work on scrutinizing and developing mindfulness practice can indeed be useful for leaders and executives as it may enrich the procedures for regulating 'body and mind' in mindful leadership in the workplace.

Relevant lessons that can be drawn from the chapter

1. Mindfulness practice is a way of developing and controlling the stability of mind in which the applicability of meditation has a significant place. It enhances the performance and improves the behavior of people in the workplace.
2. The *Śrīmad Bhagavad Gītā* has the qualitative lessons on every aspect of life in the form of its verses, and in the notion of mindfulness practice. This scripture has profoundly defined the technique of meditation to attain supreme consciousness.
3. A sacred mantra like Om from the *Vedas* and *Upanishads* contains the positive psychological power which can be utilized by people for stabilizing their emotions; chanting Om is also helpful to gain consciousness. This conscious state is called mindfulness.
4. The wisdom contained in the morals of tales has valuable lessons on how 'to be mindful' in life and work. Therefore, learning mindfulness through tales can be an alternative source of the present scenario.
5. Mindfulness practice has a connection with the various aspects of mindful leadership, and it is immensely helpful in developing character strength and enlightened awareness in the leader.

Reflection questions

1. How is mindfulness practice beneficial in the development of people in the workplace?
2. What is the role of the *Śrīmad Bhagavad Gītā* in exploring mindfulness practice and identifying the features of a mindful person?
3. How can the significance of mindfulness be realized through the study of ancient Indian works of literature like the *Upanishads*?
4. How are tales useful and how do they act as a source of wisdom in the notion of mindfulness?
5. How can the states of consciousness be similar to the states of mindfulness practice?

References

Ahmose, R. M. (2007). *R. M. Ahmose Presents More Grim Tales to Enlighten*. Maryland, United States: America Star Books.

Akindele, B. (2016). Great Leaders are Great Thinkers. In T. Akinyemi (Ed.), *The Power of Meditative Thinking* (p. 37). North Carolina, United States: Lulu.com.

Alterio, M., & McDrury, J. (2003). *Learning through Storytelling in Higher Education: Using Reflection and Experience to Improve Learning*. Abingdon, United Kingdom: Routledge.

Baer, R. A. (2010). *Assessing Mindfulness and Acceptance Processes in Clients: Illuminating the Theory and Practice of Change*. California, United States: New Harbinger Publications.

Blakeslee, T. (2004). *Beyond the Conscious Mind: Unlocking the Secrets of the Self*. Indiana, United States: iUniverse.

Boccio, F. J., & Feuerstein, G. (2005). *Mindfulness Yoga: The Awakened Union of Breath, Body, and Mind*. New York, United States: Simon and Schuster.

Bolle, K. W. (1979). Meditation and Redundance. In K. W. Bolle (Ed.), *The Bhagavadgītā: A New Translation* (p. 256). California, United States: University of California Press.

Bouchard, L. C., Carver, C. S., Mens, M. G., & Scheier, M. F. (2017). Optimism, Health and Well-Being. In D. S. Dunn (Ed.), *Positive Psychology: Established and Emerging Issues* (pp. 112–130). Abingdon, United Kingdom: Routledge.

Boyatzis, R., & McKee, A. (2005). *Resonant Leadership: Renewing Yourself and Connecting with Others through Mindfulness, Hope and Compassion*. Massachusetts, United States: Harvard Business Press.

Bunting, M. (2016). *The Mindful Leader: 7 Practices for Transforming Your Leadership, Your Organisation and Your Life*. New Jersey, United States: John Wiley & Sons.

Carroll, M. (2008). *The Mindful Leader: Awakening Your Natural Management Skills through Mindfulness Meditation*. Massachusetts, United States: Shambhala Publications.

Chaille, C., & Britain, L. (1991). *The Young Child as Scientist: A Constructive Approach to Early Childhood Science Education*. New York, United States: HarperCollins.

Chalmers, D. J. (1996). *The Conscious Mind: In Search of a Fundamental Theory*. New York, United States: OUP.

Chinmayananda, S. (2014). *Srimad Bhagawad Geeta (Verses & Meaning)*. Mumbai, India: Central Chinmaya Mission Trust.

Chinmayananda, S. (2017). *Mandukya Upanishad with Gaudapada's Karika: Truth: Witness of Waking, Dream and Deep Sleep*. Mumbai, India: Central Chinmaya Mission Trust.

Covey, S. R. (1999). *Living the 7 Habits: Stories of Courage and Inspiration*. New York, United States: Simon and Schuster.

Crangle, E. F. (1994). *The Origin and Development of Early Indian Contemplative Practices*. Wiesbaden, Germany: Otto Harrassowitz Verlag.

Dhar, T. (2003). *Bhagavad Gita: The Elixir Of Life*. New Delhi, India: Mittal Publications.

Easwaran, E. (1979). *The End of Sorrow: The Bhagavad Gita for Daily Living*, Vol. ume I. Tomales, CA, United States: Nilgiri Press.

Easwaran, E. (2007). *The Bhagavad Gita: (Classics of Indian Spirituality)*. California, United States: Nilgiri Press.

Fields, R. (2008). *Section One: Foundation. Awakening to Mindfulness: 10 Steps for Positive Change* (p. 65). Florida, United States: Health Communications, Inc.

Fireman, G. D., McVay, T. E., & Flanagan, O. J. (2003). Introduction. In G. D. Fireman, T. E. McVay & O. J. Flanagan (Eds.), *Narrative and Consciousness: Literature, Psychology and the Brain* (pp. 3–13). Oxford, United Kingdom: Oxford University Press.
Flanagan, O. J. (1991). *Varieties of Moral Personality*. Cambridge, MA, United States: Harvard University Press.
Gnaur, J. (2018). *Being One: The Vision and Way of the Bhagavad Gita*. Norderstedt, Germany: BoD – Books on Demand.
Goleman, D. (1979). A Map of Inner Space. In D. Goleman & R. J. Davidson (Eds.), *Consciousness, the Brain, States of Awareness, and Alternate Realities* (p. 134). London, United Kingdom: Ardent Media.
Goleman, D. (1998). *Working with Emotional Intelligence*. New York, United States: Bantam Books.
Good, D. J., Lyddy, C. J., Glomb, T. M., Bono, J. E., Brown, K. W., Duffy, M. K., Baer, R. A., Brewer, J. A., & Lazar, S. W. (2015). Contemplating Mindfulness at Work: An Integrative Review. *Journal of Management*, Vol. XX, No. X, Month XXXX, 1–29.
Guthrie, J. T., & Wigfield, A. (2004). Classroom Context for Engaged Reading: An Overview. In A. Wigfield, K. C. Perencevich & J. T. Guthrie (Eds.), *Motivating Reading Comprehension: Concept-Oriented Reading Instruction* (pp. 1–24). Abingdon, United Kingdom: Routledge.
Hanh, T. N. (1996). *The Miracle of Mindfulness: An Introduction to the Practice of Meditation*. Massachusetts, United States: Beacon Press.
Hanh, T. N. (2014). *Peace of Mind: Becoming Fully Present*. New York, United States: Random House.
Hawley, J. (2011). *The Bhagavad Gita: A Walkthrough for Westerners*. California, United States: New World Library.
Hougaard, R., Carter, J., & Coutts, G. (2016). *One Second Ahead: Enhance Your Performance at Work with Mindfulness*. Berlin, Germany: Springer.
Isayeva, N. (1993). *Shankara and Indian Philosophy*. New York, United States: SUNY Press.
Ivtzan, I. (2015). *Awareness Is Freedom: The Adventure of Psychology and Spirituality*. London, United Kingdom: John Hunt Publishing.
Ivtzan, I. (2016). *Mindfulness in Positive Psychology: The Science of Meditation and Wellbeing*. Abingdon, United Kingdom: Routledge.
James, W. (1890). *The Principles of Psychology*, Volume 1. London, United Kingdom: Macmillan.
Kabat-Zinn, J. (1994). *Mindfulness Meditation for Everyday Life*. Loughton, United Kingdom: Judy Piatkus Publishers.
Kabat-Zinn, J. (2005). *Coming to Our Senses: Healing Ourselves and the World through Mindfulness*. London, United Kingdom: Hachette.
Kabat-Zinn, J. (2010). *Letting Everything Become Your Teacher: 100 Lessons in Mindfulness*. New York, United States: Random House Publishing Group.
Kingsland, J. (2016). *Siddhartha's Brain: Unlocking the Ancient Science of Enlightenment*. New York, United States: HarperCollins.
Kinley, N., & Ben-Hur, S. (2015). *Changing Employee Behavior: A Practical Guide for Managers*. Berlin, Germany: Springer.
Krishna, G. (1990). *The Odyssey of Science, Culture, and Consciousness*. New Delhi, India: Abhinav Publications.
Langer, E. J. (2000). The Construct of Mindfulness. *Journal of Social Issues*, Vol. 56, No. 1, 1–9.
Langer, E. J., & Ngnoumen, C. T. (2017). Mindfulness. In D. S. Dunn (Ed.), *Positive Psychology: Established and Emerging Issues* (pp. 97–111). Abingdon, United Kingdom: Routledge.
Lesser, M., & Siegel, D. J. (2019). *Seven Practices of a Mindful Leader: Lessons from Google and a Zen Monastery Kitchen*. California, United States: New World Library.
Levine, T. B. Y. (2012). *Gestalt Therapy: Advances in Theory and Practice*. Abingdon, United Kingdom: Routledge.
Macpherson, K. (2018). *Making Sense of Mindfulness: Five Principals to Integrate Mindfulness Practice into Your Daily Life*. New York, United States: Morgan James Publishing.
Marballi. (2013). *Journey through the Bhagavad Gita - A Modern Commentary*. North Carolina, United States: Lulu.com.
Mehta, R. (1970). *The Call of the Upanishads*. New Delhi, India: Motilal Banarsidass Publications.
Mitchell, S. (2010). *The Bhagavad Gita*. New York, United States: Random House.
New, C. (1999). *Philosophy of Literature: An Introduction*. Abingdon, United Kingdom: Psychology Press.
Niemiec, R. M. (2013). *Mindfulness and Character Strengths*. Göttingen, Germany: Hogrefe Publishing.
Nithyananda, P. (2011). *BhagavadGītā Demystified*. Ashburn, VA, United States: eNPublishers.

Paulson, T. L. (2010). *The Optimism Advantage: 50 Simple Truths to Transform Your Attitudes and Actions into Results*. New Jersey, United States: John Wiley & Sons.

Prabhupada, S. (1993). *Bhagavad-gita as It Is*. Los Angeles, United States: The Bhaktivedanta Book Trust.

Pradhan, B. (2014). *Yoga and Mindfulness Based Cognitive Therapy: A Clinical Guide*. Berlin, Germany: Springer.

Puddicombe, A. (2011). *The Headspace Guide to Mindfulness & Meditation: 10 Minutes Can Make All the Difference*. London, United Kingdom: Hachette.

Ragoonaden, K. (2015). *Mindful Teaching and Learning: Developing a Pedagogy of Well-Being*. New York, United States: Lexington Books.

Rama, S. (1978). *Book of Wisdom: Ishopanishad*. Pennsylvania, United States: Himalayan Institute Press.

Rama, S. (1985). *Perennial Psychology of the Bhagavad Gita*. Pennsylvania,United States: Himalayan Institute Press.

Rama, S., Ballentine, R., & Ajaya, S. (1976). *Buddhi: Guide through the Unknown. Yoga and Psychotherapy: The Evolution of Consciousness* (p. 80). Pennsylvania, United States: Himalayan Institute Press.

Roberts, T. (2009). *The Mindfulness Workbook: A Beginner's Guide to Overcoming Fear and Embracing Compassion*. California, United States: New Harbinger Publications.

Rosenthal, D. M. (2005). *Consciousness and Mind*. Oxford, United Kingdom: Oxford University Press.

Sargeant, W., & Smith, H. (2010). The Language of the Bhagavad Gita. In C. K. Chapple (Ed.), *The Bhagavad Gita: Twenty-fifth Anniversary Edition* (p. 4). New York, United States: SUNY Press.

Sathe, V. (1990). A New Step Towards Human Evolution. In K. Gandhi (Ed.), *The Odyssey of Science, Culture, and Consciousness* (pp. 13–15). New Delhi, India: Abhinav Publications.

Saurabhnath, S. (2017). *Bhagavad Gita - Pure - A Comprehensive Study without Sectarian Contamination: By Swami Saurabhnath*. Phaltan, India: Swami Saurabhnath.

Seligman, M. E. (1991). *Learned Optimism: How to Change Your Mind and Your Life*. New York, United States: Simon & Schuster Audio.

Seligman, M. E. (2011). *Learned Optimism: How to Change Your Mind and Your Life*. New York, United States: Knopf Doubleday Publishing Group.

Sharvanada, S. (1920). *Mundaka and Mandukya Upanishads*. Mylapore, Madras, India: Sri Ramakrishna Math.

Sheldon, K. M., Prentice, M., & Halusic, M. (2015). The Experiential Incompatibility of Mindfulness and Flow Absorption. *Social Psychological and Personality Science*, Vol. 6, no. 3, pp. 276–283.

Sivananda, S. (1993). *Mantras: Words of Power*. New Delhi, India: Motilal Banarsidass Publishers.

Smith, D. (2015). *Ethical Mindfulness*. Las Vegas, United States: Central Recovery Press, LLC.

Srivastava, O. P. (2018). *Bhagavad Gita: The Art and Science of Management for the 21st Century*. Gurgaon, India: Zorba Books.

Thera, N. (2005). *The Heart of Buddhist Meditation: Satipaṭṭhāna: A Handbook of Mental Training Based on the Buddha's Way of Mindfulness, with an Anthology of Relevant Texts Translated from the Pali and Sanskrit*. Kandy, Sri Lanka: Buddhist Publication Society.

Yogananda, P. (2007). *God Talks With Arjuna*. New Delhi, India: Diamond Pocket Books (P) Ltd.

21

REDUCING DISRUPTIONS CAUSED BY SOCIAL NETWORKING SITES THROUGH MINDFULNESS

A case in point

Haziq Mehmood and Oi-ling Siu

Interruptions and social networking sites

In the present era, everyone is connected with digital devices in their workplaces. No one can deny the importance of personal computers (PCs) and smartphones in our daily lives. Further, people's digital environments are becoming increasingly complex, as many people multitask with different applications across different devices. Every person from every facet of life, including employees, is connected with digital devices. Many people's work is influenced by digital technology. The use of new technology increases workers' efficiency and output, but at the same, technology can interrupt this productivity. Likewise, interruptions in work environments include emails, social media notifications, equipment malfunctions, and colleagues, and are reported as the most common daily work stressor among employees (Baethge, Rigotti, & Roe, 2015). Research evidence proved that knowledge workers faced an average 22 interruptions in everyday life, which is mainly due to the escalation of new technologies in workplaces (Wajcman & Rose, 2011).

Interruptions are defined as the suspension of one's primary task because of a new or secondary task. Interruptions can be stimulated by cellular phones, email, or the presence of others (e.g., boss, colleague). In this case, during the interruption, a person focuses on the secondary task initially with the possibility to focus back on the primary task. The time before the interruption in which a person disengages from the primary task is called the "interruption lag," and the time when a person makes a decision on the interruption task and goes back again toward the primary task is called the "resumption lag." Interruption is measured by the time required to resume the primary task. Cades, Boehm-Davis, Trafton, and Monk's (2011) study interrupted participants with frequent and infrequent conditions, and measured the resumption time on the primary task. It was found that people in the frequent interruption group exhibited lower lag times to resume the suspended task, in comparison with the infrequent condition. Frequent interruptions give opportunities for employees to adopt or rehearse their primary task. When interrupted infrequently, employees struggle to resume the suspended task because interruptions are not habitual. McFarlane and Latorella (2002) proposed that cognitive costs and resumption lags during interruption affects the productivity of employees. Interruptions can be internal (i.e., caused by oneself) or external (i.e., caused by factors present in surroundings). Czerwinski and colleagues (2004) found that 60% of task switching occurs due to external interruptions such as emails and phone calls, and around 40% occurs due to self-interruptions.

Self-interruption is defined as "discretionary interweaving tasks." Adler and Benbunan-Fich (2013) categorized self-interruption based on positive and negative triggers. Stimulation, reorganization, and exploration were mentioned as positive triggers while frustration, exhaustion, and obstruction as negative triggers. Similarly, Jin and Dabbish's (2009) grounded theory research suggested that adjustment, break, inquiry, recollection, routine, trigger, and wait are types of self-interruptions.

The situations in which employees are tempted to use social media include boredom or stress. Some employees actively engage in social media use, and sometimes can give the false impression that they are working hard and busy (Andreassen, Torsheim, & Pallesen, 2014). Some employees perceive that the use of SNSs during work is a guilty pleasure because they are using it for personal interest (i.e., communicating with friends and family). In addition, some employees hold that SNS use is not work-related, so one should not use them openly. Zywica and Danowski's (2008) study showed that users on social media amplify more productivity, success, and happiness, which may also give a negative image toward their honesty at work. It means an employee's excessive use of SNSs gives rise to misunderstandings in organizational life and affects the employee's image as well.

Kuss and Griffiths' (2011) study showed that people preoccupied with SNSs are likely to become habitual users and this habit leads toward addiction. Although social media addiction is not presently a medically recognized disorder, the cluster of behaviors associated with an extreme preoccupation with social media is thought to be a somewhat compulsive desire and is a subject of widespread scholarly discussion. For example, a week-long experiment in which participants' desire to engage in various behaviors (e.g., sleep, relaxing, exercise, shopping, smoking, and using social media) was collected in real time over cellphones. They also recorded the number of instances that the participant failed to resist these urges. The highest failure rates occurred with desires to participate in social media, suggesting that social media usage may be more addictive than activities typically associated with addiction such as smoking.

Individuals who are preoccupied with SNSs are likely to be driven by compulsions, which results in inconsistencies given one's purposes, and goal-oriented motivation to use online social media. Therefore, this type of user is engaged in more deviant behaviors such as personal and non-work in comparison with task-oriented social media use (e.g., relationship building, seeking help from professionals). This preoccupation with online social networks may be linked with boredom, loneliness, feelings of detachment from work, and declined life satisfaction (Kuss & Griffiths, 2011).

Previous studies explored the role of social media both as positive and negative effects on employees, and found that it depends on the person themselves. In some cases, employees use SNSs to relax from work burdens or to take a break from work. When employees are not aware of the consequences of SNS use, they lose interest and focus on the work. Literature suggested that people who are using social media without awareness and have low mindfulness can quickly become distracted and may develop social media addiction (Andreassen, Torsheim, Brunborg, & Pallesen, 2012; Kuss & Griffiths, 2011).

Employees who feel lonely and bored at work may turn to SNSs to socialize with others. In a study, researchers gave instructions to participants to use Facebook more because they were interested in the effects of SNSs over time on subjective wellbeing. The participants used more Facebook, and after that, they felt more regret, negative and had lower life satisfaction and psychological wellbeing. (Kross et al., 2013)

Another adverse effect of SNSs is the interruption caused by them. Interruptions caused by technology take place through external interruptions such as phone calls and notifications for SNSs, and sometimes it is because of the employee's internal interruption (e.g., having some tedious task to do, or complex tasks in which worker loses attention quickly). There are many negative impacts of interruptions, including increased time to complete primary tasks, errors, and quality of the work. Trafton, Altmann, Brock, and Mintz (2003) concluded in their experiment that interruptions increase the time to complete primary tasks.

Self-regulation

Primarily, regulation means to change in a particular way, according to some conditions and/or rules. Second, self-regulation means "regulation of the self by self" (Heatherton & Tice, 1994; Carver, Scheier, & Weintraub, 1989). Some authors distinguished between self-control and self-regulation, and prioritized the active and conscious effortful capacity of the self-regulation.

Self-regulation has three main elements. First, it is a standard in which the individual has some standard (e.g., law, rules, social norms) according to which they change their behavior or habit. In some cases when a standard is conflicting, it causes the breakdown of self-regulation such as moral dilemma situations. The second element is to monitor the task and activities to achieve the standard or goal. The third phase is the capacity to change, in which an individual must have to struggle. Self-regulation can be broken down in many ways. Lack of self-regulation occurs when individuals are not clear, unstable, and fail to meet their standards because they are unable to monitor their actions. In some situations, individuals try to control behaviors that cannot be directly controlled, or give importance to their emotions, and resultantly neglect the main problems. Besides, to control attention is another factor that comes under the framework of self-regulation. Conversely, a capable self-regulation state needs to consider long-term effects and consequences. It was assumed that self-regulation failure occurs because of irresistible impulses. Recent studies showed that it depends on people, and they freely choose to lose control. Culture also plays a vital role in teaching people to abandon self-control. Modern Western culture is a consequence of weakening self-control. In this case, our society remains in threat from the failure of self-control, which causes problems.

Miller, Galanter, and Pribram (1960) proposed a feedback loop model for better self-regulation. This model consists of four steps. First is to "test" (i.e., compare the individual's status with others). The next step is to operate, where changes are made to change the desired behavior. However, if the desired standard is already kept, there is no need to operate. The third phase is to retest, which will occur during or after the operate phase. If the standard is met, the feedback will be exited;,which is the last phase. The feedback loop will continue to operate if the standard is not met. It is suggested that self-regulation is the same as the feedback loop phenomenon.

When employees are using SNSs, they are losing their self-regulation while focusing on their emotions and need fulfillment. As a result, this impacts employees' job performance and work quality. To eradicate these negative effects and to enhance self-regulation, mindfulness is helpful for employees.

Mindfulness and employees

Mindfulness is defined as "bringing one's complete attention to the experiences occurring in the present moment, in a non-judgmental or accepting way" (Baer, Smith, Hopkins, Krietemeyer, & Toney, 2006). Mindfulness is an ability in which a person can entirely focus on the present task. Researchers found that mindfulness increases psychological wellbeing, increases focus, reduces stress and depression, and increases mental quality to increase work outcomes (Van Gordon, Shonin, Zangeneh, & Griffiths, 2014).

In general, mindfulness is an individual's capacity to be conscious of the present moment without being distracted by any stimulus or own judgment. This nonjudgment of the moment enables one to understand the nature, sensations, and emotions occurring in an individual. The main philosophy behind the concept of mindfulness is that attachment is not suitable, so when people acknowledge things in a nonjudgmental manner, good or bad, and let them come and go, it will not cause suffering by not developing any attachment. Mindfulness is not only responsible for increasing psychological wellbeing but also positively affects work-related outcomes (Weinstein, Brown, & Ryan, 2009).

Lang, Zettler, Ewen, and Hülsheger (2012) conducted an experiment in which they explored the effect of a mindfulness intervention on employees' emotional exhaustion and job satisfaction. Mindfulness self-training was used for ten days, and participants had to complete the diary every day. In this study, they recruited 203 participants from different sectors, but experienced high attrition rates. At the end of the study, half of the participants dropped out of the study and did not complete the diary task. The final sample consisted of 64 participants, with treatment (n = 22) and control (n = 42) groups. The results of the study showed that the mindfulness intervention was associated with a decrease in emotional exhaustion, and an increase in job satisfaction. Another study by Hülsheger, Alberts, Feinholdt, and Lang (2013) found that mindful employees have more strength to regulate their negative feelings and have effective coping strategies during stressful situations in comparison with less mindful employees.

Leroy, Anseel, Dimitrova, and Sels (2013) conducted a study on employee population to explore the role of mindfulness and authentic functioning with work engagement. They focused on the mindfulness-based stress reduction (MBSR) program developed by Kabat-Zinn (2003) and gave training to the employees for eight weeks. The findings of the study revealed that mindfulness is a significant factor in strengthening one's personal resources for work engagement, which is an antecedent of authentic functioning. Charoensukmongkol (2014) conducted a study to find the effect of mindfulness meditation on general perceived stress, emotional intelligence, and self-efficacy. Demographically, 49% of participants were full-time employees. The results of the study showed that practicing mindfulness meditation was strongly associated with higher emotional intelligence and higher general self-efficacy, and it lowers general perceived stress. It was found that those employees who are practicing mindfulness meditation have positive coping strategies, and they focused on quick solutions to problems to reduce the stress. These findings suggest that mindfulness improves individuals' ability to monitor their thoughts, and control negative emotions and behavior, while they are at work.

Mindful employees are more aware of the events happening around them; as a result, it is possible for them to get carried away from the use of SNSs. They enjoy more SNS experience, use it for a definite purpose to relax, and can be more productive at work (Brown & Ryan, 2003). The employees who use social media mindlessly can quickly get away from their work, and they have more chance to become addicted to social media use. Employees with this behavior are not only affecting their personal life and work performance, but also face consequences in their social life, as they depend more on virtual relationships. Researchers suggest that mindfulness is a useful intervention to buffer employees' behavior from negative consequences, and to reduce social media addiction (Shonin, Van Gordon, Dunn, Singh, & Griffiths, 2014).

It is difficult for employees to think clearly, rationally, and deal with problems without mindfulness skills (Christopher & Gilbert, 2010). Specifically, mindfulness has been shown to improve three qualities of attention: stability, control, and efficiency. The human mind is estimated to wander roughly half of its waking hours, but mindfulness can stabilize attention in the present moment. Studies in organizational setup showed that individuals who practice mindfulness training appear to remain vigilant longer on both visual and listening tasks (Brown & Ryan, 2003; Christopher & Gilbert, 2010).

Sriwilai and Charoensukmongkol (2016) conducted a study on the addiction of social media and mindfulness. They demonstrated that those employees who are addicted to social media have lower levels of mindfulness and they prefer emotion-focused coping strategies, which is linked with emotional exhaustion (Sriwilai & Charoensukmongkol, 2016). This work suggested that meditation training is helpful to train employees to understand problems and choose effective coping strategies.

Lutz, Slagter, Dunne, and Davidson (2008) suggested that some forms of meditation training are helpful for employees to enhance their attention and easily switch attention between objects more fluidly. Levy, Wobbrock, Kaszniak, and Ostergren (2012) used a focused meditation approach, which is a type of mindfulness meditation training. Their result showed that focused meditation strengthens the ability of participants to notice interruptions without turning down the current task. Participants reduced task switching and showed more considerable time on task. This suggests that mindfulness meditation is effective to build awareness, helps employees to understand the nature of interruptions, and facilitates decision-making according to the situation.

Parry and Ie Roux's (2018) study on interventions for media multitasking categorized the interventions into three categories: mindfulness, awareness, and restrictions. Shonin et al.'s (2014) study suggested that mindfulness meditation decreases the chances of behavioral addiction. In many studies, researchers use this as a reference and argue that mindfulness interventions help users cope with addiction, including social media addiction (i.e., while also arguing that social media is similar to other addictions)

Charoensukmongkol (2014) hypothesized that mindfulness will moderate the relationship between social media use intensity, emotional exhaustion depersonalization, and lack of personal accomplishment. He surveyed 211 participants from 13 different organizations. Mindfulness level was measured by a developed questionnaire. The results of the study concluded that mindfulness moderates this relationship and has a significant negative relationship with the use of social network intensity, exhaustion, and depersonalization. Mindfulness also moderates personal accomplishment positively but was not statistically significant in this study.

Hülsheger et al. (2013) used the self-training mindfulness intervention with 64 employees. In the experimental group, they had 22 participants and 42 in the control group. They used the diary method and extended the self-training over ten working days. Participants were given the diary book, and were instructed to practice pre-specified activities every day. In another study by Hülsheger, Feinholdt, and Nübold (2015), in which they used the same self-training mindfulness intervention, the researchers recruited a total of 140 participants using convenience sampling. They contacted the participants directly and mostly in person, using email and by distributing flyers to their colleagues and supervisors. Sixty-seven participants were in the training group, and the remaining 73 formed the control group. In this study, participants of the experimental group were asked if they were following the diary schedule every day to check treatment fidelity. Zeidan, Johnson, Diamond, David, and Goolkasian (2010) conducted a study to explore the role of mindfulness meditation on cognition among students. Sixty-three students volunteered to become part of the experiment, but 14 participants were not able to complete the protocol, so the total sample comprised 49 participants. The researchers assigned 24 participants to the experiment group and 25 were in the control group. The meditation intervention was divided into four sessions. Results of the study showed that four days of training had similar results as long-term training, and it enhanced the ability to sustain attention.

Hafenbrack, Kinias, and Barsade (2014) explored the relationships between the de-biasing effect of mindfulness. Fifty-four university participants were recruited, screened, and divided into mindfulness meditation and control groups. According to Hafenbrack et al. (2014), the treatment group received a 15-minute meditation intervention, and the researchers found that mindfulness had significant positive results on the students' decision-making. The same study was repeated by adding different decision-making tasks, in which researchers recruited the 109 participants and followed the same procedure but different tasks.

Previous literature guided software application users to reduce internal and external interruptions and improve self-regulation. Ko et al. (2015) found a way to help those individuals who had difficulty in choosing the appropriate management technique due to their lack of self-regulation. For this purpose, they developed the application NUGU (no use is good use). This application is based on social cognitive theory. The three key features of this application were self-monitoring, setting goals, and sharing practices for limiting smartphone use. Similarly, Kim, Cho, and Lee (2017) worked on the application to restrict users' behavior. They developed the application PomodoLock for self-interruption management. PomodoLock has three features (i.e., timer, application/website blocker, and multiple device synchronization). In the timer option, the user sets a time to work on a task (e.g., 25 minutes). During that timeframe, the application blocks notifications to allow work without any disturbance or interruption. When the user completes the session, a bell rings, and it is called one session of Pomodoro. The other feature is blocking websites that interrupt users. The user can choose the applications that they want to block. It is a daily life practice that some people opt to delete social applications, create physical distance from their phone during work or study, or use "PomodoLock" features to block non-work-related applications. The third function is to synchronize one's devices (e.g., laptop and mobile). If the user adds a timer on one device, it will automatically work on the other synchronized devices. Applications such as Facebook, Twitter, and YouTube are available on phone and computers, and the user can access them from anywhere. This feature of synchronization is helpful to manage interruptions from all of a user's devices. In most cases, employees use SNSs through their cellular phones during office hours, but may also access SNS on other devices.

Mindfulness at work: case study of Hong Kong

Previous literature clearly showed the relationship between social media use and mindfulness of employees. Most studies focused on the addiction to SNSs, with the objective to reduce the habitual use and addiction to these sites (e.g., Kuss & Griffiths, 2011). In some studies, researchers focused on trait mindfulness and explored the relationship between lower and higher level of mindfulness with respect to social media. Researchers have argued that self-regulation can reduce external and internal interruptions. This study focused on the self-regulation and the effect of a mindfulness intervention on reducing the negative consequences of SNSs.

The present study was conducted to mitigate employees' interruptions caused by the use of SNSs during office hours. To mitigate the effect of interruption, the study explored the effect of a mindfulness self-guided intervention on interruptions. The main objective of the study was to explore the impact of mindfulness training in mitigating the effects of self-interruptions caused by SNS usage. Mindfulness intervention facilitate successful unwinding from the demands of work and promoted recovery in terms of psychological detachment (Hülsheger, Alberts, Feinholdt, & Lang, 2013). This study is linked with the chapter to understand the relationship between interruption caused by SNSs and the role of mindfulness to mitigate its effect.

Mindfulness-Based Cognitive Therapy (MBCT; Segal, Teasdale, Williams, & Gemar, 2002) and Mindfulness-Based Stress Reduction (MBSR; Kabat-Zinn, 2003) are the two therapies. MBCT and MBSR consist of guided mindfulness meditation and simple daily exercises both aiming to cultivate an accepting, nonjudgmental attitude to what one experiences in every moment. Both of these interventions are used to improve stress management and psychological wellbeing. Clinical literature supports these interventions for use with chronic pain. After the effectiveness of this training, it was also used in non-patient samples. Both interventions are delivered in group settings, with weekly meetings and daily homework assignments.

Based on these two interventions, Hülsheger et al. (2013) developed a self-training intervention, which spanned for two weeks (ten working days). This intervention is relatively brief and mainly focused on employees' daily work lives. The main parts of the mindfulness self-training intervention are as follows.

The Body Scan, the Three-Minute Breathing Space, the Daily Routine Activities, and the Raisin Exercise were incorporated from the Mindfulness-Based Cognitive Therapy (MBCT) and Mindfulness-Based Stress Reduction (MBSR). In this training, they also added the "loving-kindness meditation" to cultivate a compassionate mindset. The Body Scan is a formal meditation practice, where bodily sensations are used as an anchor for attention. In this exercise, participants develop body awareness and awareness of distractions. Three-Minute Breathing Space is a cornerstone for many mindfulness interventions. It is an exercise that helps to reconnect with the present moment. It aims at creating through training awareness of thoughts, feelings, and bodily sensations by paying attention to them. It has specifically been designed to be applicable in everyday life. Loving-Kindness Meditation cultivates caring, kindness, and love for oneself and others. It starts with an initial focus on the breath and then directs warm, compassionate, and tender feelings to oneself and subsequently to others (i.e., loved ones, neutral persons, and difficult people). It teaches mindful attitudes of acceptance, compassion for oneself, and others, which is particularly important for employees working in helping professions.

In the second part comes "Daily Routine Activities;" the author had given knowledge about the multitasking, email, and phone-related routine work activities. In this step the researcher adapted some changes in this already developed self-training intervention by adding the following features in training; email practice, telephone practice, and multitasking. This self-training of mindfulness was administered in the present study as an intervention.

Previous literature clearly showed the relationships between social media use and employee mindfulness. Most studies focused on the addiction to SNSs, and focused on lowering the habit and addiction of SNS use. In some studies, researchers focused on trait mindfulness and explored the relationship between lower and higher levels of mindfulness with respect to social media. The present study explored the effect of mindfulness training on interruptions through SNS use. The researcher focused on self-regulation and implemented a mindfulness self-guided intervention to reduce the negative consequences of SNSs.

A quasi-experimental pre-test and post-test research design was used to measure the baseline of the participants in the start and at the end of the study. The participants were divided into treatment and control groups. In the experimental group, participants received the treatment in the form of a mindfulness intervention. The control group did not receive any intervention.

In the present study, 22 participants were recruited by using convenience sampling. Participants were recruited from the full-time staff members working at Lingnan University, Hong Kong. Participants were administrative staff who spend the majority of their time working on computer-related tasks. They were recruited through email, flyers posted on boards, and contacting them directly to ask them to participate in the study.

In the present study, workplace interruptions were measured by the Workplace Interruptions Measure (WIM), which is a 12-item self-report measure (Wilkes, Barber, & Rogers, 2018). The WIM has four subscales which measure interruption-related behaviors in workplace settings. Intrusion measures unanticipated interruptions that stop an employee's work; intrusions may be in the form of in-person interruptions or interruptions via email, phone, texting, or other modes of technology. Distraction measures irrelevant stimuli that employees must actively filter out to avoid breaking their concentration on a primary task. Discrepancy detection measures work stoppages that occur when employees perceive an inconsistency between their knowledge or expectations and information in their work environment. The fourth subscale measures breaks, which are described as temporary respites from tasks that are either scheduled or spontaneous.

The Mindful Attention Awareness Scale (MAAS) was developed by Brown and Ryan (2003). It measures the state in which attention is informed by a sensitive awareness of what is happening around in the present. Participants' activity on SNSs are measured by an application called "Focus Me." It was installed on the computers and cellphones of the participants after taking consent from them. There are many features of the application, but the fundamental purpose of this application is to record the disturbances from internet access. It counts SNS launches by the user, and reports this information on a daily, weekly, and monthly basis. It provided easy access to get records to measure the intensity of SNS use.

It was hypothesized that mindfulness would mitigate the effect of self-interruption by using SNSs. This hypothesis was accepted that in the pre-test after practicing mindfulness training participants showed a significant decrease in distraction by using SNSs through a cellphone.

Results indicated that there is a highly significant mean difference between scores of Intrusions in pre- ($M = 5.45$, $SD = 2.70$) and post-test ($M = 3.45$, $SD = 1.7$, $p < .05$). The Distraction at workplace is also reduced and indicated the significant mean differences in pre- ($M = 6.73$, $SD = 3.41$) and post-test ($M = 3.82$, $SD = 2.56$, $p < .05$).

Employees who are using SNSs mindlessly can easily get away from their work and they have more chances to become addicted to SNSs. Self-mindfulness training focused on the daily activities, in which participants were given the training on "letting go technology" in different situations. This part of the training was quite helpful for employees and the results showed significant decreases in the distraction by cellphone to use SNSs.

Individuals who use social media frequently have more chances to be easily distracted during work. It was found that those addicted to social media have a lower level of mindfulness in comparison with non-addicted social media users (Sriwilai & Charoensukmongkol, 2016). This study focused on the solution by increasing participants' mindfulness.

Attention and losing focus is also an important factor in interruption, and researchers suggested that some forms of meditation training are helpful for employees to improve attention. Mindfulness is a type of meditation that mainly focuses on awareness and attention. The present study also revealed that mindfulness training strengthens the employee's personal resources for work engagement and authentic functioning. Self-efficacy of the employees, in which they feel that they can accomplish the specific task, is also linked with mindfulness. Mindfulness increases self-efficacy, psychological wellbeing, and mental quality to increase the work outcomes (Charoensukmongkol, 2014).

Parry and le Roux (2019) suggested that mindfulness interventions can increase awareness and reduce restrictions to reduce the problems related to multitasking. Self-trained mindfulness interventions also increase awareness by adding daily activities to the training. In the present study, during mindfulness training, participants had reported information about multitasking, and the pros and cons of SNS use. The second study showed the role of SNS-related policies: an employee who has policies in the workplace had higher intensity to use SNSs per day as compared with employees of organizations with no policies. It suggests that organizations in which employers want to control employee usage of SNSs need to focus on other strategies, like meditation and awareness programs, in comparison with introducing new policies on SNS use. Mindfulness intervention effectively decreases interruptions by using SNSs on cellphones and the frequency of intrusions and disturbances in workplaces.

In the present study focus is on the internal interruptions which are caused by some known factors: work is boring and employees' mood swings. Internal interruptions were measured by using a scale in which the main focus was on the employees' distractions from using SNSs. The measure we used in the experiment mainly focused on distraction by using SNSs during office hours by cellphones. The use of cellphones causes distractions in daily life in different tasks and this affects employees' focus.

Results of the post-test showed the decrease in interruption caused by using SNSs through cellphones, distractions and intrusion during office hours. It was concluded that mindfulness meditation is helpful to reduce the interruption effects in employees. Employers and organizations need to consider these intervention plans to increase employees' job performance.

Conclusion

This chapter provides insight for mindfulness and to minimize social networking site usage among employees through self-regulation. Mindful interruptions of SNSs during work hours could be helpful in enhancing employees' performance and wellbeing. Based on self-regulation scores of employees, training modules could be developed for mindful usage of SNSs. Employees can improve their performance and learn how to manage SNS interruptions during office hours. It is helpful to understand self-regulation and adds practical implications to theories and literature in industrial and organizational psychology. This chapter also helps to understand the applications of mindfulness in employees' daily lives. In addition, organizations need to consider mindfulness strategies for their employees' wellbeing and performance in their workplaces. Self-regulation and mindfulness could be incorporated in organizations' policies on SNSs. Results obtained from the present case study are helpful for employers as well, because mindfulness interventions can positively affect employees' mental and physical health. Employers can increase work performance and productivity of their employees by mitigating the interruption effect. Some organizations developed policies for employees to use SNSs during office hours, but in most cases, it is not workable. This chapter is helpful in this context to manage this issue without implementing policies or restrictions. In some cases, employees perceive the restrictions on using SNSs as negative and they become involved in cyber-loafing. Many organizations provide training to their employees, and the present study demonstrates the potential benefits of mindfulness training that could increase productivity and wellbeing.

Five chapter takeaways/lessons

1. Social networking site use creates social media addiction and adversely affects job performance and psychological wellbeing of employees.
2. Employees' quality of work is also affected by the interruptions of social networking site usage.
3. Self-regulation fosters ability to reduce interruptions caused by social networking sites.
4. Mindfulness also paves the way for effectively controlling social networking site usage.
5. Organizations could benefit from the mindfulness implications in using social networking sites during office hours.

Five reflection questions

1. How does social networking site use impact employee performance through interruptions?
2. How can self-regulation help mitigate self-interruptions caused by social networking sites?
3. What is the association of self-regulation and mindfulness in the context of social networking site usage?
4. What is the role of mindfulness in reducing interruptions?
5. How does mindfulness empower employees to reduce interruptions caused by social networing sites during office hours?

References

Adler, R. F., & Benbunan-Fich, R. (2013). Self-interruptions in discretionary multitasking. *Computers in Human Behavior, 29*(4), 1441–1449.

Andreassen, C. S., Torsheim, T., Brunborg, G. S., & Pallesen, S. (2012). Development of a Facebook addiction scale. *Psychological Reports, 110*(2), 501–517.

Andreassen, C. S., Torsheim, T., & Pallesen, S. (2014). Predictors of use of social network sites at work-a specific type of cyberloafing. *Journal of Computer-Mediated Communication, 19*(4), 906–921.

Baer, R. A., Smith, G. T., Hopkins, J., Krietemeyer, J., & Toney, L. (2006). Using self-report assessment methods to explore facets of mindfulness. *Assessment, 13*(1), 27–45.

Baethge, A., Rigotti, T., & Roe, R. A. (2015). Just more of the same, or different? An integrative theoretical framework for the study of cumulative interruptions at work. *European Journal of Work and Organizational Psychology, 24*(2), 308–323.

Brown, K. W., & Ryan, R. M. (2003). The benefits of being present: Mindfulness and its role in psychological well-being. *Journal of Personality and Social Psychology, 84*(4), 822.

Cades, D. M., Boehm-Davis, D. A., Trafton, J. G., & Monk, C. A. (2011). Mitigating disruptive effects of interruptions through training: What needs to be practiced? *Journal of Experimental Psychology: Applied, 17*(2), 97.

Carver, C. S., Scheier, M. F., & Weintraub, J. K. (1989). Assessing coping strategies: A theoretically based approach. *Journal of Personality and Social Psychology, 56*(2), 267.

Charoensukmongkol, P. (2014). Benefits of mindfulness meditation on emotional intelligence, general self-efficacy, and perceived stress: Evidence from Thailand. *Journal of Spirituality in Mental Health, 16*(3), 171–192.

Christopher, M. S., & Gilbert, B. D. (2010). Incremental validity of components of mindfulness in the prediction of satisfaction with life and depression. *Current Psychology, 29*(1), 10–23.

Czerwinski, M., Horvitz, E., & Wilhite, S. (2004, April). A diary study of task switching and interruptions. In Proceedings of the SIGCHI conference on Human factors in computing systems (pp. 175–182). ACM.

Hafenbrack, A. C., Kinias, Z., & Barsade, S. G. (2014). Debiasing the mind through meditation: Mindfulness and the sunk-cost bias. *Psychological Science, 25*(2), 369–376.

Heatherton, T., & Tice, D. M. (1994). *Losing control: How and why people fail at self-regulation.* San Diego, CA: Academic Press, Inc.

Hülsheger, U. R., Alberts, H. J., Feinholdt, A., & Lang, J. W. (2013). Benefits of mindfulness at work: The role of mindfulness in emotion regulation, emotional exhaustion, and job satisfaction. *Journal of Applied Psychology, 98*(2), 310.

Hülsheger, U. R., Feinholdt, A., & Nübold, A. (2015). A low-dose mindfulness intervention and recovery from work: Effects on psychological detachment, sleep quality, and sleep duration. *Journal of Occupational and Organizational Psychology, 88*(3), 464–489.

Jin, J., & Dabbish, L. A. (2009, April). Self-interruption on the computer: A typology of discretionary task interleaving. In Proceedings of the SIGCHI conference on human factors in computing systems (pp. 1799–1808). ACM.

Kabat-Zinn, J. (2003). Mindfulness-based stress reduction (MBSR). *Constructivism in the Human Sciences, 8*(2), 73.

Kim, J., Cho, C., & Lee, U. (2017). Technology supported behavior restriction for mitigating self-interruptions in multi-device environments. *Proceedings of the ACM on Interactive, Mobile, Wearable and Ubiquitous Technologies, 1*(3), 64.

Ko, M., Yang, S., Lee, J., Heizmann, C., Jeong, J., Lee, U., ... Chung, K. M. (2015, February). NUGU: A group-based intervention app for improving self-regulation of limiting smartphone use. In *Proceedings of the 18th ACM conference on computer supported cooperative work & social computing* (pp. 1235–1245). ACM.

Kross, E., Verduyn, P., Demiralp, E., Park, J., Lee, D. S., Lin, N., ... Ybarra, O. (2013). Facebook use predicts declines in subjective well-being in young adults. *PloS One, 8*(8), e69841.

Kuss, D. J., & Griffiths, M. D. (2011). Online social networking and addiction—A review of the psychological literature. *International Journal of Environmental Research and Public Health, 8*(9), 3528–3552.

Lang, J. W., Zettler, I., Ewen, C., & Hülsheger, U. R. (2012). Implicit motives, explicit traits, and task and contextual performance at work. *Journal of Applied Psychology, 97*(6), 1201.

Leroy, H., Anseel, F., Dimitrova, N. G., & Sels, L. (2013). Mindfulness, authentic functioning, and work engagement: A growth modeling approach. *Journal of Vocational Behavior, 82*(3), 238–247.

Levy, D. M., Wobbrock, J. O., Kaszniak, A. W., & Ostergren, M. (2012, May). The effects of mindfulness meditation training on multitasking in a high-stress information environment. In Proceedings of Graphics Interface 2012 (pp. 45–52). Canadian Information Processing Society.

Lutz, A., Slagter, H. A., Dunne, J. D., & Davidson, R. J. (2008). Attention regulation and monitoring in meditation. *Trends in Cognitive Sciences, 12*(4), 163–169.

McFarlane, D. C., & Latorella, K. A. (2002). The scope and importance of human interruption in human-computer interaction design. *Human-Computer Interaction, 17*(1), 1–61.

Miller, G. A., Galanter, E., & Pribram, K. H. (1960). Plans and the structure of behavior.

Parry, D. A., & le Roux, D. B. (2019). Media multitasking and cognitive control: A systematic review of interventions. *Computers in Human Behavior, 92*, 316–327.

Segal, Z. V., Teasdale, J. D., Williams, J. M., & Gemar, M. C. (2002). The mindfulness-based cognitive therapy adherence scale: Inter-rater reliability, adherence to protocol and treatment distinctiveness. *Clinical Psychology & Psychotherapy, 9*(2), 131–138.

Shonin, E., Van Gordon, W., Dunn, T. J., Singh, N. N., & Griffiths, M. D. (2014). Meditation awareness training (MAT) for work-related wellbeing and job performance: A randomised controlled trial. *International Journal of Mental Health and Addiction, 12*(6), 806–823.

Sriwilai, K., & Charoensukmongkol, P. (2016). Face it, don't Facebook it: Impacts of social media addiction on mindfulness, coping strategies and the consequence on emotional exhaustion. *Stress and Health, 32*(4), 427–434.

Trafton, J. G., Altmann, E. M., Brock, D. P., & Mintz, F. (2003). Preparing to resume an interrupted task: Effects of prospective goal encoding and retrospective rehearsal. *International Journal of Human-Computer Studies, 58*, 583–603.

Van Gordon, W., Shonin, E., Zangeneh, M., & Griffiths, M. D. (2014). Work-related mental health and job performance: Can mindfulness help? *International Journal of Mental Health and Addiction, 12*(2), 129–137.

Wajcman, J., & Rose, E. (2011). Constant connectivity: Rethinking interruptions at work. *Organization Studies, 32*(7), 941–961.

Weinstein, N., Brown, K. W., & Ryan, R. M. (2009). A multi-method examination of the effects of mindfulness on stress attribution, coping, and emotional well-being. *Journal of Research in Personality, 43*(3), 374–385.

Wilkes, S. M., Barber, L. K., & Rogers, A. P. (2018). development and validation of the workplace interruptions measure. *Stress and Health, 34*(1), 102–114.

Zeidan, F., Johnson, S. K., Diamond, B. J., David, Z., & Goolkasian, P. (2010). Mindfulness meditation improves cognition: Evidence of brief mental training. *Consciousness and Cognition, 19*(2), 597–605.

Zywica, J., & Danowski, J. (2008). The faces of Facebookers: Investigating social enhancement and social compensation hypotheses; predicting Facebook™ and offline popularity from sociability and self-esteem, and mapping the meanings of popularity with semantic networks. *Journal of Computer-Mediated Communication, 14*(1), 1–34.

22

THE INTERPLAY BETWEEN MINDFULNESS, EMOTIONAL INTELLIGENCE, AND RESILIENCE

Igor Ristić and Ayça Kübra Hizarci-Payne

Introduction

The workplace can be a stressful environment that can cause "significant psychological, physiological, and financial costs on both the individual employee and the organization" (Colligan & Higgins, 2005, p. 96). Amongst the most important variables involved in successfully managing tension and stress at work and, crucially, in ensuring peak performance and other positive workplace outcomes, are mindfulness, emotional intelligence, and resilience. While mindfulness has been considered for centuries by Eastern philosophers, it has only recently become a focus of modern scientists too (Dane, 2011). The benefits of mindfulness in the workplace context are countless and elaborated upon below. Similarly, there has been a resurgence recently with research on the effect of emotions in the workplace (Zeidner, Matthews, & Roberts, 2004), with much support showing the importance and benefits of strong emotional health. Finally, it is important to be resilient when dealing with challenges, and individuals with higher resilience have been associated with many workplace benefits as well (e.g., Magnano, Craparo, & Paolillo, 2016). While there has been much written about these three variables in the last two decades, they are still a relatively recent addition to management literature and there is a need for more scientific research focusing on their mechanisms and potential benefits in workplace contexts. For instance, writing of mindfulness, Dane (2011) notes that "simply put, there is a dearth of theory on whether and how mindfulness fosters or inhibits task performance in the workplace" (p. 999). These three variables must continue to be studied so that best practices can be discovered and disseminated to other researchers and also appropriate industry practitioners. The current study proposes and tests a model which attempts to contribute to this objective.

In the current study, a mediation model, based on previous literature, is developed and tested. Specifically, the model predicts that mindfulness is associated with both emotional intelligence (EI) and resilience, where EI mediates the relationship between mindfulness and resilience. Following is a brief overview of the three variables in the current model (mindfulness, emotional intelligence, and resilience) and a description of the relationships between the aforementioned variables and associated four hypotheses predicted in the current model. The first variable to be elaborated upon is mindfulness.

Mindfulness

Mindfulness has only recently become a highly studied variable amongst social science scholars; however, the concept has been around for millennia. Mindfulness dates back thousands of years; it is mostly rooted in Buddhist psychology but also shares ideas from other traditions, such as some of the ancient Greek philosophers (Brown, Ryan, & Creswell, 2007; Dane, 2011). Dane (2011) carried out an overview of recent academic conceptualizations of mindfulness and argued that for a long time, it was associated primarily with Eastern traditions and dismissed by scientists as too "Zen-like," perhaps because it was incorrectly associated with meditation (p. 998).

However, more recently scholars have concluded mindfulness and related practices of Eastern traditions, such as meditation, are not necessarily interchangeable and that mindfulness can indeed be scientifically studied apart from its more "Zen" origins (Dane, 2011). Dane (2011) adds that there have recently been many different perspectives on, and conceptualizations of, the term, many of them focusing on three common features: mindfulness as a state of consciousness, mindfulness as a focus on present phenomena (e.g., Brown & Ryan, 2003), and third, mindfulness as a process involving both internal and external phenomena. Combining all three elements, Dane proposed the following definition: mindfulness is a "state of consciousness in which attention is focused on present-moment phenomena occurring both externally and internally" (2011, p. 1000).

Similarly, Long and Christian have (2015) defined mindfulness as a "psychological construct associated with nonjudgmental attention and awareness of present-moment experiences" (p. 1409). Mindfulness reflects the state when we become so aware of our thought processes that we become open to novel perspectives (Gudykunst, 1993; Langer, 1989). Being mindful is being able to focus only on specific chosen things or events in the present moment, and not consider the past, the future, or other distractions. Previous literature has also focused on the nature of mindfulness, such as how the variable can be operationalized.

Shapiro, Carlson, Astin, and Freedman (2006), for instance, posited three axioms/components of mindfulness—intention, attention, and attitude—and argued these are "interwoven aspects of single cyclic process and occur simultaneously" as mechanisms of the mindfulness process (p. 375). Baer, Smith, Hopkins, Krietemeyer, and Toney (2006) also argued for five multiple dimensions of mindfulness; Taylor and Millear (2016) describe these multiple dimensions, or attributes, as: (1) observing the immediate/present external environment, (2) describing said environment with words, (3) acting based on awareness of that environment, (4) not assessing/judging the environment in any way, and (5) not reacting before thinking in regards to that environment. Finally, mindfulness has been described as both a *state*, for example a state achieved during meditation, and a *trait*, or an individual predisposition towards being mindful every day (Kiken, Garland, Bluth, Palsson, & Gaylord, 2015). In fact, Kiken et al. (2015) have found that increasing state mindfulness (i.e., through meditation) over time can lead to greater trait mindfulness. These problematizations and operationalizations of the term ensure research about mindfulness is more precise. Mindfulness has also been shown to have numerous benefits, as elaborated upon below.

For instance, Dane and Brummel (2013) found mindfulness increased job performance and decreased turnover intention. Bao, Xue, and Kong (2015) found mindfulness was negatively related to perceived stress. Taylor and Millear (2016) discovered that facets of mindfulness were associated with lower levels of burnout in the workplace and suggested mindfulness "could be part of a broad intervention programme to buffer employees against burnout" (p. 127). Long and Christian (2015) indicated mindfulness might help with reducing retaliation in the workplace. Another investigation indicated mindfulness has allowed employees to concentrate more and procrastinate less (Karlin, 2018). Finally, greater mindfulness has also been positively associated with positive affect and life satisfaction, and negatively with negative affect (Schutte & Malouff, 2011). It is clear the benefits of mindfulness in the workplace are vast. One of the key areas of benefits relates to another variable the current study focused on, emotional intelligence (EI).

Emotional intelligence

Zeidner et al. (2004) argue that the resurging focus on emotions, which they indicate entered the mainstream of psychological research in the 1990s, "resonates with a current zeitgeist emphasizing the importance between intellect and emotion" in the West (p. 372). Emotional intelligence (EI) is "the ability to monitor one's own and others' emotions, to discriminate among them and to use the information to guide one's thinking and actions" (Salovey & Mayer, 1990, p. 189). Emotional intelligence has also been described as including "the abilities to accurately perceive emotions, to access and generate emotions so as to assist thought, to understand emotions and emotional knowledge, and to reflectively regulate emotions so as to promote emotional and intellectual growth" (Mayer & Salovey, 1997; as cited by Mayer, Salovey, & Caruso, 2004, p. 197). Emotional intelligence has been operationalized into two general categories: mental ability models based on aptitude for affective information processing, and mixed models based on more diverse constructs, such as perception (Zeidner et al., 2004, describing previous work). The concept has also been studied from the perspective of differentiating between EI as a dispositional ability/trait and EI as a learned competency/skill (Bao et al., 2015). *Ability EI* has been classified into four dimensions, which include the ability to perceive emotions accurately, to access feelings, to understand emotions, and to regulate emotions and grow from them (Bao et al., 2015), while *trait EI* has been described as more of a disposition and self-perception (Petrides, Pita, & Kokkinaki, 2007). Emotional intelligence, like mindfulness, has been shown to have many benefits.

Competencies associated with EI have been described by Goleman (1998) as "major qualities differentiating successful form unsuccessful executives" (as cited by Zeidner et al., 2004, p. 377). Zeidner et al. (2004) add that EI has been claimed to affect many different work behaviors, including "employee commitment, teamwork, development of talent, innovation, quality of service, and customer loyalty" (p. 386). Emotional intelligence has also been positively associated with more career success and more effective leadership, among other benefits (Cooper, 1997, as cited by Zeidner et al., 2004). Extremera, Durán, and Rey (2007) concluded that perceived EI served as a "significant predictor of perceived stress and life satisfaction" (p. 1076). Schutte and Malouff (2011) also found that "higher levels of emotional intelligence were associated with higher levels of positive affect, lower levels of negative affect, and greater life satisfaction" (p. 1118). Finally, EI has also been shown to help individuals to engage in coping behaviors to deal with stress at work (Bar-On, 1997, as cited by Zeidner et al., 2004). Another important variable to dealing with stress at work is resilience, the third variable used in the current model.

Resilience

Resilience is defined by Bajaj and Pande (2015) as a "personal trait that helps individuals cope with adversity and achieve good adjustment and development during trying circumstances" (p. 63). Along the same lines, Keye and Pidgeon (2013) define it as "the ability an individual has to recover from distressing and challenging life events with increased knowledge to adaptively cope with similar adverse situations in the future" (p. 1). Previous research on resilience, as with mindfulness and EI, has revealed many benefits.

Avey, Luthans, and Jensen (2009) stated resilience is "arguably the most important positive resource to navigating a turbulent and stressful workplace" (p. 682). Citing Tugade and Fredrickson (2004), Avey et al. (2009) add that resilient individuals have been shown to be better at dealing with workplace stressors, to be more open-minded to new experiences and flexible to change, and more emotionally stable in times of adversity. Magnano et al. (2016) add that resilience, along with other core positive psychological factors, "represents a core factor of motivation, perseverance, and success expectancies, increasing the probabilities of success and goal accomplishment" (p. 16). People who are resilient also maintain mental and physical health through better inoculation against negative effects of hard times (Bajaj & Pande, 2015; Connor & Davidson, 2003).

Now that all three major variables of the current model have been introduced, some examples of previously studied relationships between them and the current hypothesized model (i.e., mindfulness–EI; mindfulness–resilience; and resilience–EI) will be described. First, the relationship between mindfulness and EI is described.

Relationship between mindfulness and emotional intelligence

Schutte and Malouff (2011) found higher levels of mindfulness were associated with higher emotional intelligence and that EI also mediated the relationship between mindfulness and greater positive affect, lower negative affect, and higher life satisfaction. They further indicated that the "core aspects of mindfulness may make it more likely that individuals develop the competencies comprising emotional intelligence," insofar as the focus on the present necessary in mindfulness can also encourage people to be more accurately aware of their own and others' emotions (p. 1117). Higher levels of mindfulness have been positively associated with greater emotional intelligence (Baer, Smith, & Allen, 2004; Schutte & Malouff, 2011).

Similarly, in a study of Chinese adults, Bao et al. (2015) found that mindfulness and EI were positively related. Individuals who are more mindful will naturally also have higher associated EI because mindfulness involves, among other factors described earlier, being more aware of one's own dispositions and reactions to life events. Thus, the current model predicts a positive association between mindfulness and emotional intelligence:

H1: There is a positive association between mindfulness and emotional intelligence.

The second relationship predicted in the current model is between mindfulness and resilience.

The relationship between mindfulness and resilience

Bajaj and Pande (2016) found that resilience partially mediated the relationship between mindfulness and affect and life satisfaction elements. They proposed mindfulness has the "potential to foster resilience as mindful people are better able to respond to difficult situations without reacting in automatic and non-adaptive ways" (Bajaj & Pande, 2015, pp. 63–64). Furthermore, Thompson, Arnkoff, and Glass (2011) indicated that "trait mindfulness and acceptance may contribute to resilience to trauma" in a mental health context (p. 231). In a study of university students, Keye and Pidgeon (2013) also found mindfulness, along with academic self-efficacy, significantly predicted resilience. Further, their review of literature "revealed an association between mindfulness and resilience" (Keye & Pidgeon, 2013, p. 2). As with the relationship between mindfulness and EI, it follows logically that resilience (as described earlier) will be positively associated with mindfulness as well. As a result, the second prediction in the current model is:

H2: There is a positive association between mindfulness and resilience.

The current study predicts that EI and resilience will be related to each other as well, and that EI will mediate the relationship between mindfulness and resilience.

The relationship between emotional intelligence and resilience

Today's daily life is carried out by a host of complexities of emotions (Tugade & Fredrickson, 2007), which makes emotional intelligence a critical feature of individuals. As indicated earlier, emotional intelligence is a useful tool in coping with negative experiences that an individual can engage in everyday life. The current literature provides an overarching array of evidence of the relationship between EI and resilience (Sarrionandia, Ramos-Díaz, & Fernández-Lasarte, 2018). Previous studies showed that there is a positive association between emotional intelligence and resilience (Armstrong et al., 2011; Connor & Slear, 2009; Droppert et al., 2019; Magnano et al., 2016; Matthews, Zeidner, & Roberts, 2002). As summarized earlier in this chapter, resilience as a positive trait reflects the high level of adaptability and coping with stressful events, and changes or unpleasant situations with a fast recovery process (Campbell-Sills, Cohan, & Stein, 2006; Connor & Davidson, 2003). Individuals high in emotional intelligence can show understanding of what is happening around them and further understanding of what other people think and feel. In this vein, they can react to the events or other individuals in a manner with empathy. The ability to understand and monitor emotions reflects an individual's ability to react accordingly to a given situation that fosters an individual's adaptation and coping ability with stressful or unpleasant life experiences (Salovey, Mayer, Caruso, & Yoo, 2002a; Salovey, Stroud, Woolery, & Epel, 2002b). Therefore, emotional intelligence can foster an individual's adaptation. Scholars assert that individuals high in self-awareness and emotion regulation can easily adapt to emotional demands of hardships from stressful events, buffer the effects of adversities, and cultivate more positive emotions (Salovey, Bedell, Detweiler, & Mayer, 1999; Tugade & Fredrickson, 2007). Resilient individuals can maintain a positive mood by buffering the negative effects of difficult times (Magnano et al., 2016; Schneider, Lyons, & Khazon, 2013). Individuals high in self-awareness and emotion regulation can generate more positive and less negative emotions; therefore, in stressful moments or adversities, they can generate fewer negative emotions. Emotionally intelligent individuals can give adaptive reactions in stressful moments (Armstrong et al., 2011) as they can understand, assess what they feel, and know how and when to react in stressful times (Salovey et al., 1999). The ability of regulation of emotions can foster emotion repairment, which reflects the degree of adaptation and recovery (Cejudo, 2016). Moreover, emotional intelligence can facilitate emotional and intellectual growth (Mayer & Salovey, 1995; Salovey & Mayer, 1990), which can enhance individual adaptation and help in overcoming the negative effects of hardships (Block & Kremen, 1996; Bonanno, 2004; Droppert et al., 2019). Particularly, self-awareness and emotion regulation can facilitate positive mood maintenance and inhibit the impact of negative effects from stressful experiences on cognition that can foster resilience (Ciarrochi, Chan, & Caputi, 2000). In addition, it has been indicated that individuals high in emotional intelligence can induce more positive moods by managing their emotions and showing positive reactions in any circumstances (Ciarrochi et al., 2001). Monitoring emotions is related with adaptive behaviors (Salovey et al., 2002a, 2002b); therefore, emotional intelligence is considered as a necessary skill in order to improve resilience (Droppert et al., 2019). Furthermore, understanding and showing empathy to others can increase the resilience level of individuals (Armstrong et al., 2011). In the light of the literature, the third hypothesis developed herein is as follows:

H3: There is a positive association between emotional intelligence and resilience.

Finally, the relationship between all three variables in the current model, specifically the mediation model, will be expanded upon.

The interplay between mindfulness, emotional intelligence, and resilience

The mechanisms that underlie mindfulness involve the receptive attention of individuals to their psychological states; that is also one of the aspects of emotional intelligence (Brown & Ryan, 2003). Mindfulness can enhance emotion regulation functions of an individual (Koole, 2009). The core features of mindfulness can lead individuals to improve their emotional intelligence (Bao et al., 2015; Schutte & Malouff, 2011). The non-evaluative nature of mindful individuals results in a better understanding of one's own and others' emotions (Bao et al., 2015). The emotion regulation competencies of an individual can be rooted in mindfulness (Brown et al., 2007). Mindful individuals are characterized by awareness and acceptance of their current experiences (Sinclair & Feigenbaum, 2012), through which they can improve their EI and become more flexible and willing to adapt to conditions. Prior studies have indicated that the nonjudgmental and self-regulating aspects of mindful individuals can stimulate the further improvement of emotion regulation and awareness of one's own and others' emotions, which can affect the reactions of individuals to events through those competencies (Schutte & Malouff, 2011; Wang & Kong, 2014). In this vein, individuals high in mindfulness can show high levels of emotional intelligence and accordingly better adaptation and coping competencies. Consequently, mindfulness is associated with more adaptive behaviors that decrease psychological distress (Mesmer-Magnus, Manapragada, Viswesvaran, & Allen, 2017; Schutte & Malouff, 2011). The acceptance stance of mindfulness can enhance emotional competencies of individuals through which they can adapt and overcome unpleasant situations (Grabbe, Nguy, & Higgins, 2012). In particular, mindfulness enhances effective regulation of emotions that fosters emotional intelligence through which individuals become better able to handle negative experiences and cultivate more positive emotions. Hence, the core features of mindfulness are associated with emotional intelligence (Miao, Humphrey, & Qian, 2018) that can foster resilience in turn. The aforementioned statements lead to the fourth and final hypothesis:

H4: Emotional intelligence intervenes the relationship between mindfulness and resilience.

Research design

In order to test the hypotheses, participants with full-time jobs were recruited through Mechanical Turk (MTurk) by Amazon, which allows researchers and practitioners to collect data online. MTurk is useful and efficient in the data collection process, especially in the social sciences, as it can provide reliable data at low cost (Buhrmester, Kwang, & Gosling, 2011; Casler, Bickel, & Hackett, 2013; Shapiro, Chandler, & Mueller, 2013). In this study, each participant was paid \$0.50 for the completion of the survey. In total, 140 (81 female, 59 male) participants were recruited for this study. The age of participants ranged from 19 to 65 (SD=9.77; Mean=36.98).

Measurement model

The scales that were utilized in this study have an acceptable level of reliability and composite reliability since they were higher than 0.70 (Anderson & Gerbing, 1988; Fornell & Larcker, 1981; Nunnally, 1982). In addition, average extracted values (AVE) were higher than 0.50, which shows that this study did not suffer from validity or reliability issues. In addition, item loadings were higher than 0.50; however, two items from the resilience scale were excluded as the item loadings were lower than 0.50 and not significant. This exclusion increased the reliability of the scale (Hair, Hult, Ringle, & Sarstedt, 2016). In addition, there was no multicollinearity among the constructs, as the variance inflation factor (VIF) values were lower than the recommended value of 5 as measured through SPSS (Hair et al., 2016; Henseler, Ringle, & And Sinkovics, 2009). Through confirmatory factor analysis, the measurement model was evaluated by utilizing AMOS. The measurement model generated acceptable levels of goodness of fit values ($\chi 2/df$ = 1.770, NFI = 0.78, TLI = 0.803, CFI = 0.816, RMSEA = 0.077). The results showed that discriminant validity is not a concern for this study. The instruments used to measure the constructs were as follows.

Mindfulness: Mindfulness was measured by the unidimensional version of the 14-item Freiburg Mindfulness Inventory (FMI) (Walach, Buchheld, Buttenmüller, Kleinknecht, & Schmidt, 2006). The FMI is considered one of the most useful instruments to measure mindfulness. The four-point Likert-type scale is used with responses ranging from "1 (rarely)" to "4 (almost always)" (Cronbach α = 0.89).

Emotional intelligence: Emotional intelligence was measured using Wong and Law's (2002) scale, which includes 16 items with responses ranging from "1 (Completely Disagree)" to "5 (Completely Agree)" (Cronbach α = 0.93).

Resilience: In order to measure resilience of participants, the Connor-Davidson Resilience scale was used, which comprises ten items (Campbell-Sills and Stein, 2007; Connor & Davidson, 2003). The participants were asked the frequency of feelings that they have experienced in the last month. The four-point Likert scale is used for responses that range from "1 (Never)" to "5 Almost Always)" (Cronbach α = 0.90). As mentioned above, two items were excluded due to reliability and validity issues.

Results

In the current study, the method of analysis proposed by Preacher and Hayes (2008) was carried out. In addition, the bootstrapping method was used to evaluate the hypothesized mediation effect (Preacher & Hayes, 2008; Preacher et al. 2007); in this bootstrapping method, the indirect effects are measured through the confidence interval values by

Table 22.1 Descriptive statistics

Construct	*Mean*	*SD*	*1*	*2*	*3*
1. Mindfulness	2.81	0.554	1		
2. Emotional intelligence	3.98	0.645	0.648**	1	
3. Resilience	3.70	0.676	0.535**	0.588**	1

N=140 **Correlation is significant at 0.01 level.

Table 22.2 Direct and indirect effects

	Hypothesized Relationships	*β*	*P*	*LLCI*	*ULCI*
H1✓	Mindfulness → Emotional intelligence (Model 1)	0.748	p<0.001	0.6056	0.9041
H2✓	Mindfulness → Resilience (Model 2)	0.344	p<0.01	0.1121	0.5360
H3✓	Emotional intelligence → Resilience (Model 2)	0.435	P<0.001	0.2532	0.6172
Bootstrapping Results for Indirect Effect		0.308	——	**BootLLCI**	**BootULCI**
H4 ✓	Indirect effects of mindfulness on resilience through emotional intelligence			0.1451	0.5121

bootstrapping 5,000 samples (Preacher & Hayes, 2008). The descriptive values are shown in Table 22.1. The results show mindfulness was positively correlated with emotional intelligence and resilience, and there was a positive association between emotional intelligence and resilience. Based on the analysis, the developed hypotheses are supported as shown in Table 22.2. The results show that mindfulness was positively associated with emotional intelligence ($\beta = 0.748$, $t = 10.002$, $p<0.001$), which supports the first hypothesis. In addition, there were positive correlations between emotional intelligence and resilience ($\beta = 0.435$, $t = 4.72$, $p<0.001$), and mindfulness and resilience ($\beta = 0.324$, $t = 3.02$, $p<0.01$). Therefore, H2 and H3 were supported as well. In order to test for the hypothesized mediation in H4, the indirect effect of mindfulness on resilience was analyzed, which showed that there was a partial mediation, since both the direct effect and the confidence intervals of the indirect effect were significant and did not include zero (0.1451–0.5121).

Conclusion

To the authors' best knowledge, this is the first study that tackled the interrelationships between mindfulness, emotional intelligence, and resilience in these specific pathways, in which emotional intelligence mediated the relationship between mindfulness and resilience. The results are in line with the literature as they significantly show that mindfulness plays an important role in enhancing resilience (Chavers, 2013; Jha, Stanley, Kiyonaga, Wong, & Gelfand, 2010). As summarized in this chapter, the existing literature stresses the countless benefits of mindfulness on individuals' physical and psychological wellbeing. Among other benefits, mindfulness helps individuals to shield and isolate themselves from their memories of past events and generate more positive emotions during present/future stressful events. The current study points out that mindful individuals can improve their ability to understand their own and others' emotions, show empathy and sympathy towards others, and monitor their behaviors. Through these abilities, they can enhance their competences to easily adapt to difficult situations or get over the negative effects of hardships at work. Mindfulness can help individuals to avoid rumination; therefore, they can get over the effects of unpleasant events that happened in the past. As the results indicate, mindfulness can also foster individuals' resilience by improving emotional intelligence. Mindful employees can avoid negative interpretations of situations happening in the workplace and generate more positive emotions. In this sense, organizations with more mindful individuals also have individuals with high emotional intelligence and resilience. Therefore, mindfulness can help individuals to cope with hardships and to avoid experiencing any emotional frustrations that can affect their organizational performance.

Results herein suggest organizations' human resources and other relevant practitioners should consider encouraging their employees to engage in proven mindfulness trainings, as there is a high probability more mindful employees will also display more emotional intelligence and resilience, and will thus lead to positive outcomes in the workplaces for individual employees and organizations, too.

Chapter takeaways

1. In the last few decades, mindfulness has gained considerable credibility as a psychological cognitive process and has grown to become an important topic of study for social scientists.
2. Mindfulness has been shown to have numerous benefits in the workplace, including but not limited to increasing job performance and decreasing turnover intentions. Emotional intelligence (EI) and resilience have also been shown to have many benefits in the workplace.
3. Results of the current study showed mindfulness was positively correlated with emotional intelligence (EI) and with resilience, that EI was positively correlated with resilience, and that EI partially mediated the relationship between mindfulness and resilience. These results supported all four hypotheses that were proposed.
4. Results described above indicate that as mindfulness of individuals increases, so does their emotional intelligence and resilience. Further, emotional intelligence has a mediating influence on the relationship between mindfulness and resilience. These findings suggest mindful individuals improve their ability to understand their own and others' emotions, to show empathy and sympathy towards others, and to monitor their behaviors. Through these abilities, they also enhance their competencies to easily adapt to difficult situations and negative effects of hardships at work.
5. The current study gives further credence to the assertion that human resources and other relevant practitioners should create programming and initiatives designed to encourage and help employees to increase their mindfulness, emotional intelligence, and resilience levels at work. Programming and initiatives like these, in turn, can have positive outcomes for the whole organization by improving employee performance and decreasing turnover intentions, among other benefits.

Reflection questions

1. Dane (2011) described that for a long time, mindfulness was associated primarily with Eastern traditions and dismissed by scientists as too "Zen-like." What factors might have contributed to this oversimplistic interpretation of mindfulness?

2. What are the five dimensions of mindfulness as reviewed by Taylor and Millear (2016)? After listing them, think of a hypothetical workplace stressor and write down how each of the five dimensions of mindfulness might be used by a worker to help them deal with the stressor.
3. In the current study, mindfulness, emotional intelligence (EI), and resilience have all been shown to have benefits in the workplace and to relate to each other. Describe at least one potential benefit of each construct and then explain how all three constructs connect to each other.
4. Imagine you are a human resources (HR) practitioner who has been asked by your supervisor to read the study in this chapter and to come up with some practical suggestions for how to use the findings to increase workers' performance in your office. What are three specific suggestions you would share with your staff?
5. What are some other potential future directions that research on mindfulness, emotional intelligence (EI), and resilience in the workplace should focus on? In other words, what questions do the results of the current study inspire going forward?

References

Anderson, J. C., & Gerbing, D. W. (1988). Structural equation modeling in practice: A review and recommended two-step approach. *Psychological Bulletin, 103*(3), 411–423.

Armstrong, A. R., Galligan, R. F., & Critchley, C. R. (2011). Emotional intelligence and psychological resilience to negative life events. *Personality and Individual Differences, 51*(3), 331–336. doi:10.1016/j.paid.2011.03.025

Avey, J. B., Luthans, F., & Jensen, S. M. (2009). Psychological capital: A positive resource for combating employee stress and turnover. *Human Resource Management, 48*(5), 677–693. doi:10.1002/hrm.20294

Baer, R. A., Smith, G. T., & Allen, K. B. (2004). Assessment of mindfulness by self-report. the kentucky inventory of mindfulness skills. *Assessment, 11*, 191–206. doi:10.1177/1073191104268029

Baer, R. A., Smith, G., Hopkins, J., Krietemeyer, J., & Toney, L. (2006). Using Self-report Assessment Methods to Explore Facets of Mindfulness. *Assessment, 13* (1), 27–45. doi:10.1177/1073191105283504.

Bajaj, B., & Pande, N. (2016). Mediating role of Reliance in the impact of mindfulness on life satisfaction and affect as indices of subjective well-being. *Personality and Individual Differences, 93*, 63–67. doi:10.1016/j.paid.2015.09.005

Bao, X., Xue, S., & Kong, F. (2015). Dispositional mindfulness and perceived stress: The role of emotional intelligence. *Personality and Individual Differences, 78*, 48–52. doi:10.1016/j.paid.2015.01.007

Block, J., & Kremen, A. M. (1996). IQ and ego-resiliency: Conceptual and empirical connections and separateness. *Journal of Personality and Social Psychology, 70*(2), 349–361. doi:10.1037/0022-3514.70.2.349

Bonanno, G. A. (2004). Loss, trauma, and human resilience: Have we underestimated the human capacity to thrive after extremely aversive events? *American Psychologist, 59*(1), 20–28. doi:10.1037/0003-066X.59.1.20

Brown, K. W., & Ryan, R. M. (2003). The benefits of being present: Mindfulness and its role in psychological well-being. *Journal of Personality and Social Psychology, 84*(4), 822–848. doi:10.1037/0022-3514.84.4.822

Brown, K. W., Ryan, R. M., & Creswell, J. D. (2007). Mindfulness: Theoretical foundations and evidence for its salutary effects. *Psychological Inquiry, 18*, 211–237. doi:10.1080/10478400701598298

Buhrmester, M., Kwang, T., & Gosling, S. (2011). Amazon's mechanical turk: A new source of inexpensive, yet high quality, data? *Perspectives on Psychological Science, 6*(1), 3–5. doi:10.1177/1745691610393980

Campbell-Sills, L., Cohan, S. L., & Stein, M. B. (2006). Relationship of resilience to personality, coping, and psychiatric symptoms in young adults. *Behaviour Research and Therapy, 44*(4), 585–599. doi:10.1016/j.brat.2005.05.001

Campbell-Sills, L., & Stein, M. B. (2007). Psychometric analysis and refinement of the Connor–Davidson Resilience Scale (CD-RISC): Validation of a 10-item measure of resilience. *Journal of Traumatic Stress: Official Publication of the International Society for Traumatic Stress Studies, 20*(6), 1019–1028.

Casler, K., Bickel, L., & Hackett, E. (2013). Separate but equal? A comparison of participants and data gathered via Amazon's MTurk, social media, and face-to-face behavioral testing. *Computers in Human Behavior, 29*(6), 2156–2160. doi:10.1016/j.chb.2013.05.009

Cejudo, J. (2016). Relationship between emotional intelligence and mental health in school counselors. *Electronic Journal of Research in Educational Psychology, 14* (1), 131–154. doi: 10.14204/ejrep.38.15025

Chavers, D. J. (2013). *Relationships between spirituality, religiosity, mindfulness, personality, and resilience.* Doctoral Dissertation, Alabama: University of South Alabama.

Ciarrochi, J. V., Chan, A. Y., & Caputi, P. (2000). A critical evaluation of the emotional intelligence construct. *Personality and Individual Differences, 28*(3), 539–561. doi:10.1016/S0191-8869(99)00119-1

Ciarrochi, J., Chan, A. Y., & Bajgar, J. (2001). Measuring emotional intelligence in adolescents. *Personality and individual differences, 31*(7), 1105–1119.

Colligan, T. W., & Higgins, E. M. (2005). Workplace stress: Etiology and consequences. *Journal of Workplace Behavioral Health, 21*(2), 89–97. doi:10.1300/J490v21n02_07

Connor, B., & Slear, S. (2009). Emotional intelligence and anxiety; Emotional intelligence and resiliency. *International Journal Of Learning, 16*(1), 249–260. doi:10.18848/1447-9494/CGP/v16i01/46089

Connor, K. M., & Davidson, J. R. T. (2003). Development of a new resilience scale: The Connor–Davidson Resilience Scale (CD-RISC). *Depression and Anxiety, 18*(2), 76–82. doi:10.1002/da.10113

Dane, E. (2011). Paying attention to mindfulness and its effects on task performance in the workplace. *Journal of Management, 37*(4), 997–1018. doi:10.1177/0149206310367948

Dane, E., & Brummel, B. J. (2013). Examining workplace mindfulness and its relations to job performance and turnover intention. *Human Relations, 67*(1), 105–128. doi:10.1177/0018726713487753

Droppert, K., Downey, L., Lomas, J., Bunnett, E. R., Simmons, N., Wheaton, A., ... Stough, C. (2019). Differentiating the contributions of emotional intelligence and resilience on adolescent male scholastic performance. *Personality and Individual Differences, 145*, 75–81. doi:10.1016/j.paid.2019.03.023

Extremera, N., Durán, A., & Rey, L. (2007). Perceived emotional intelligence and dispositional optimism-pessimism: Analyzing their role in predicting psychological adjustment among adolescents. *Personality and Individual Differences, 42*, 1069–1079. doi:10.1016/j.paid.2006.09.014

Fornell, C., & Larcker, D. F. (1981). Structural equation models with unobservable variables and measurement error: Algebra and statistics. *Journal of Marketing Research, 18*(3), 382–388.

Grabbe, L., Nguy, S. T., & Higgins, M. K. (2012). Spirituality development for homeless youth: A mindfulness meditation feasibility pilot. *Journal Of Child And Family Studies, 21*(6), 925–937. doi:10.1007/s10826-011-9552-2

Gudykunst, W. B. (1993). Toward a theory of effective interpersonal and intergroup communication: An Anxiety/Uncertainty Management (AUM) perspective. In R. L. Wiseman & J. Koester (Eds.), *Intercultural communication competence* (pp. 33–71). Newbury Park, CA: Sage.

Hair, J. F., Jr, Hult, G. T. M., Ringle, C., & Sarstedt, M. (2016). *A Primer on Partial Least Squares Structural Equation Modeling (PLS-SEM)*. Thousand Oaks, CA: Sage Publications.

Henseler, J., Ringle, C. M., & And Sinkovics, R. R. (2009). The use of partial least squares path modeling in international marketing. In R. Sinkovics & P. Ghauri (Eds.), *New challenges to international marketing* (pp. 277–319). Bingley, UK: Emerald Group Publishing Limited.

Jha, A. P., Stanley, E. A., Kiyonaga, A., Wong, L., & Gelfand, L. (2010). Examining the protective effects of mindfulness training on working memory capacity and affective experience. *Emotion, 10*(1), 54–64. doi:10.1037/a0018438

Karlin, D. S. (2018). Mindfulness in the workplace. *Strategic HR Review, 17*(2), 76–80. doi:10.1108/SHR-11-2017-0077

Keye, M. D., & Pidgeon, A. M. (2013). An investigation of the relationship between resilience, mindfulness, and academic self-efficacy. *Open Journal of Social Sciences, 1*(6), 1–4. doi:10.4236/jss.2013.16001

Kiken, L. G., Garland, E. L., Bluth, K., Palsson, O. S., & Gaylord, S. A. (2015). From a state to a trait: Trajectories of state mindfulness in meditation during intervention predict changes in trait mindfulness. *Personality and Individual Differences, 81*, 41–46. doi:10.1016/j.paid.2014.12.044

Koole, S. L. (2009). The psychology of emotion regulation: An integrative review. *Cognition And Emotion, 23*(1), 4–41. doi:10.1080/02699930802619031

Langer, E. J. (1989). Minding matters: The consequences of mindlessness-mindfulness. *Advances in Experimental Social Psychology, 22*, 137–173. doi:10.1016/S0065-2601(08)60307-X

Long, E. C., & Christian, M. S. (2015). Mindfulness buffers retaliatory responses to injustice: A regulatory approach. *Journal of Applied Psychology, 100*(5), 1409–1422. doi:10.1037/apl0000019

Magnano, P., Craparo, G., & Paolillo, A. (2016). Resilience and emotional intelligence: Which role in achievement motivation. *International Journal of Psychological Research, 9*(1), 9–20. doi:10.21500/20112084.2096

Matthews, G., Zeidner, M., & Roberts, R. D. (2002). *Emotional intelligence: Science and myth*. Cambridge, MA: MIT Press.

Mayer, J. D., & Salovey, P. (1995). Emotional intelligence and the construction and regulation of feelings. *Applied and Preventive Psychology, 4*(3), 197–208. doi:10.1016/S0962-1849(05)80058-7

Mayer, J. D., Salovey, P., & Caruso, D. R. (2004). Emotional intelligence: Theory, findings, and implications. *Psychological Inquiry, 15*(3), 197–215. www.tandfonline.com/doi/abs/10.1207/s15327965pli1503_02

Mesmer-Magnus, J., Manapragada, A., Viswesvaran, C., & Allen, J. W. (2017). Trait mindfulness at work: A meta-analysis of the personal and professional correlates of trait mindfulness. *Human Performance, 30*(2–3), 79–98. doi:10.1080/08959285.2017.1307842

Miao, C., Humphrey, R. H., & Qian, S. (2018). The relationship between emotional intelligence and trait mindfulness: A meta-analytic review. *Personality And Individual Differences, 135*, 101–107. doi:10.1016/j.paid.2018.06.051

Nunnally, J. C. (1982). *Reliability of measurement. Encyclopedia of educational research* (Vol. 4). New York: Free Press.

Petrides, K. V., Pita, R., & Kokkinaki, F. (2007). The location of trait emotional intelligence in personality factor space. *British Journal of Psychology, 98*, 273–289. doi:10.1348/000712606X120618

Preacher, K. J., Rucker, D. D., & Hayes, A. F. (2007). Addressing moderated mediation hypotheses: Theory, methods, and prescriptions. *Multivariate behavioral research, 42*(1), 185–227.

Preacher, K. J., & Hayes, A. F. (2008). Asymptotic and resampling strategies for assessing and comparing indirect effects in multiple mediator models. *Behavior Research Methods, 40*(3), 879–891. doi:10.3758/BRM.40.3.879

Salovey, P., Bedell, B. T., Detweiler, J. B., & Mayer, J. D. (1999). Coping intelligently: Emotional intelligence and the coping process. In C. R. Snyder (Ed.). *Coping: The psychology of what works* (pp. 141–164). New York: Oxford University Press.

Salovey, P., & Mayer, J. D. (1990). Emotional intelligence. *Imagination, Cognition and Personality, 9*(3), 185–211. doi:10.2190/DUGG-P24E-52WK-6CDG

Salovey, P., Mayer, J. D., Caruso, D., & Yoo, S. H. (2002a). The positive psychology of emotional intelligence. In C. R. Snyder & S. J. Lopez (Eds.), *Handbook of positive psychology* (pp. 159–171). New York, NY: Oxford University Press.

Salovey, P., Stroud, L. R., Woolery, A., & Epel, E. S. (2002b). Perceived emotional intelligence, stress reactivity, and symptom reports: Further explorations using the trait meta- mood scale. *Psychology And Health, 17*(5), 611–627. doi:10.1080/08870440290025812

Sarrionandia, A., Ramos-Díaz, E., & Fernández-Lasarte, O. (2018). Resilience as a mediator of emotional intelligence and perceived stress: A cross-cultural study. *Frontiers In Psychology, 6*, 1–8. doi:10.3389/Fpsyg.2015.01895

Schneider, T. R., Lyons, J. B., & Khazon, S. (2013). Emotional intelligence and resilience. *Personality and Individual Differences, 55*(8), 909–914. doi:10.1016/j.paid.2013.07.460

Schutte, N. S., & Malouff, J. M. (2011). Emotional intelligence mediates the relationship between mindfulness and subjective well-being. *Personality and Individual Differences, 50*(7), 1116–1119. doi:10.1016/j.paid.2011.01.037

Shapiro, D. N., Chandler, J., & Mueller, P. A. (2013). Using mechanical turk to study clinical populations. *Clinical Psychological Science, 1*(2), 213–220. doi:10.1177/2167702612469015

Shapiro, S. L., Carlson, L. E., Astin, J. A., & Freedman, B. (2006). Mechanisms of mindfulness. *Journal of Clinical Psychology, 62*(3), 373–386. doi:10.1002/jclp.20237

Sinclair, H., & Feigenbaum, J. (2012). Trait emotional intelligence and borderline personality disorder. *Personality and Individual Differences, 52*(6), 674–679. doi:10.1016/j.paid.2011.12.022

Taylor, N. Z., & Millear, P. M. R. (2016). The contribution of mindfulness to predicting burnout in the workplace. *Personality and Individual Differences*, *89*, 123–128. doi:10.1016/j.paid.2015.10.005

Thompson, R. W., Arnkoff, D. B., & Glass, C. R. (2011). Conceptualizing mindfulness and acceptance as components of psychological resilience to trauma. *Trauma, Violence & Abuse*, *12*(4), 220–235. doi:10.1177/1524838011416375

Tugade, M. M., & Fredrickson, B. L. (2007). Regulation of positive emotions: Emotion regulation strategies that promote resilience. *Journal Of Happiness Studies*, *8*(3), 311–333. doi:10.1007/s10902-006-9015-4

Walach, H., Buchheld, N., Buttenmüller, V., Kleinknecht, N., & Schmidt, S. (2006). Measuring mindfulness—The Freiburg Mindfulness Inventory (FMI). *Personality and Individual Differences*, *40*(8), 1543–1555. doi:10.1016/j.paid.2005.11.025

Wang, Y., & Kong, F. (2014). The role of emotional intelligence in the impact ff mindfulness on life satisfaction and mental distress. *Social Indicators Research*, *116*(3), 843–852. doi:10.1007/s11205-013-0327-6

Wong, C. S., & Law, K. S. (2002). The effects of leader and follower emotional intelligence on performance and attitude: An exploratory study. *The Leadership Quarterly*, *13*(3), 243–274. doi:10.1016/S1048-9843(02)00099-1

Zeidner, M., Matthews, G., & Roberts, R. D. (2004). Emotional intelligence in the workplace: A critical review. *Applied Psychology: An International Review*, *53*(3), 371–399. doi:10.1111/j.1464-0597.2004.00176.x

23
INTEGRATIVE KNOWLEDGE
A mindful approach to science

Andrea Cherman and Francisco Eduardo Moreira Azeredo

Introduction

With the spread of the knowledge era, people witnessed great and rapid changes in society that brought about immense development in many areas. However, these changes cannot be dissociated from the new and stressful social and personal imbalances that have severely and negatively affected human lives and the environment. Individuals are experiencing a decrease in the quality of their attention due to overwhelming demands and limited response time (Weick and Sutcliffe 2008). Paradoxically, an unprecedented and increasing amount of natural resources have been swallowed up by this steady knowledge generation. Never has such severe personal and social disharmony been witnessed in the midst of so much available technology and knowledge. These issues include (i) global warming (United Nations 2014); (ii) the concentration of income and rising inequality (Piketty 2014); (iii) problems of ethnic and racial prejudice (Bauman 2007), from which Black Lives Matter emerged amidst the attendant separatist and terrorist movements; (iv) relentless discrimination and violence against women; (v) the dismantling of the family structure and fragmentation of families (Bauman 2000); (vi) the issue of personal health, expressed as epidemic rates of cancer, heart disease, and obesity (NHC 2016); (vii) adult anxiety and stress syndromes and attention deficit and hyperactivity disorders in children and young adults (CDC 2014); and (viii) the deterioration of the environment, biodiversity, the food chain, water and air, with tremendous consequences, many of which are yet to be experienced and scientifically understood and proven.

At the same time, organizations are facing equally serious challenges, many of which overlap with those listed above: (i) the mega-corporatization and empowerment of organizations over individuals and society as part of social movements toward an extremely effective (in an economic sense and not in a human sense) globalization and hyper-competitiveness; (ii) governance and transparency dilemma, as organizations are becoming more politicized and increasingly dependent on lobbying and endemic corruptive activities to achieve their strategic goals, which ends up in a negative feedback loop; (iii) ethical and value conflicts between organizations and individuals, resulting in the latter's breakdown at work amidst multiple identities and their exposure to the high stress of an increasingly fluid and superficial personal/family/professional life (Bauman 2000; Bauman 2005); (iv) the precariousness of the workplace in all organizational levels, reflected on the disappearance of the boundary between personal and professional life, the invasion of work into people's homes, and the imbalance between leisure/work time (Sennett 1998); and (v) the decline in mutual loyalty and commitment between workers and companies, leading to feelings of distress and unhappiness within organizations.

Thus, organizations' difficulties in relating to and connecting with important social, political, and economic demands—holding the individual as a central part of the issue and the solution—are palpable. Evidence shows that the pathological growth of individualism in people is analogous to the problem of the organization seeing itself as an individual that is dissociated from others and that seeks to survive decoupled from the problems of society and the very individuals that depend on it (Bauman 2004, 2005; Fromm 1995; Sennett 1998).

More broadly, studies have reiterated that the knowledge model that continues to be predominantly used in the structural design of organizations follows the traditional view that knowledge derives from the transformation of data into information (i.e., data accumulated over the course of time experienced by the organization) (Ackoff 1989; Bierly, Kessler and Christensen 2000; Rowley 2006a) and by the individual (Kessler 2006), for which the enabling process is learning. The ultimate goal is to consider organizations' short-term results and goals, in which the interests of board members and shareholders overlap those of individuals. Hence, studies have identified an introverted and self-referential vision in which the model fails to expand knowledge of value—or even the knowledge already held by the organization/individual. Moreover, the resulting knowledge frontiers are still untouched. They remain conservative and non-evolutionary, based on models that limit the synergy between process and result, learning and knowledge (Cherman and Rocha-Pinto 2016).

These findings suggest that the current paradigm related to organizational knowledge is showing its age and ineffectiveness for building organizations with greater awareness and wisdom regarding their role in the environment in which they operate. Thus, evidence shows that the current knowledge paradigm requires a disruption, an evolution that can accompany the insertion of a completely new Spiritual Dimension in the current rational one. These two dimensions are present in individuals' lives, in mindful minds; why are they not present in organizations' knowledge models? And why not in an integrative way? This conceptual chapter proposes to deepen the discussion of an Integrative Knowledge Model that encompasses the Spiritual Dimension of wisdom and awareness into the Rational Dimension of data and information and hence expands into the organizational context.

In an attempt to understand the growing contemporary significance of the "spirituality and organization" discourse and its evolving historical, social, cultural, and political positioning, Calás and Smircich (2003, p. 327) reported "concerns regarding the limits of science as a mode of understanding, laments about the lack of meaning in work and a sense of lack of purpose in the workplace, and an interest in connecting work with love and social justice." In conclusion, they remarked that "altogether, it appears that the 'spirituality and organization' discourse is conceived as a means to counteract self-interest at a time when all other messages seem to point in the opposite direction."

Wisdom in organizations

Wisdom in organizations is a field of study that emerged at the end of the 1990s together with—and perhaps because of—the learning organizations and knowledge management movements. The roots of these movements harken back to works in sociology and psychology by Bateson (1972), Sternberg (1990), and Srivastva and Cooperrider (1998). The seminal text by Ackoff (1989), *From Data to Wisdom*, addressed the paradigm propagated by the data–information–knowledge (DIK) hierarchy by adding the layer of wisdom (thus, DIKW). According to the author, whereas the DIK paradigm deals with increased efficiency and with growth that can be rationalized, planned, and automated, wisdom is related to the effectiveness of development in terms of values, the exercise of judgment and subjectivity, which are never independent of the actors involved (Ackoff 1989).

The concept of organizational wisdom spread in the 2000s, with academia seeking to instrumentalize and operationalize the concept and make it practicable for organizations. In 2004, the *Eastern Academy of Management* established organizational wisdom as its central theme, *Organizational Wisdom: Human, Managerial and Strategic Implications* (Kessler 2006), which was followed by the publication of the *Handbook of Organizational and Managerial Wisdom* (Kessler and Bailey 2007). Movements for social responsibility, ethics, and organizational citizenship endorsed the importance of wisdom in organizations (Hays 2007), so much so that Rowley (2006b) claims that wisdom is the sum of knowledge, ethics, and action.

One term—wisdom—in four conceptual streams

The term wisdom and, therefore, the area of interest related to the study of organizational wisdom can be classified into four conceptual streams based on its origin and mode of dealing with the phenomenon.

The first stream, which is rooted in psychology studies, conceptualizes wisdom as the "integration of the affective, conative, and cognitive aspects of human abilities in response to life's tasks and problems. Wisdom is a balance between the opposing valences of intense emotion and detachment, action and inaction, and knowledge and doubts" (Birren and Fisher 1990, p. 326). Analogously, wisdom comprises the integrative dynamics resulting from the synthesis of the dimensions of cognition (knowledge and understanding), reflection (perspective and introspection), and affection (compassion and empathy) (Ardelt 2004). This perspective is concerned with establishing instruments to measure individual and organizational wisdom without proposing to integrate these aspects of wisdom in the organizational environment.

The second stream, which is rooted in knowledge management (although it may seek bases in other conceptual streams), attempts to instrumentalize the concept of wisdom for practical applicability (Bierly, Kessler and Christensen 2000). Kessler (2006, p. 297), for example, defines wisdom as the "synthesis of knowledge-based potential with higher order visioning and practical implementation." Thus, organizational wisdom expresses the judgment, selection, and use of specific knowledge for a specific context; that is, it relates the ability to select and apply appropriate knowledge in a given situation, to establish and employ knowledge to achieve certain objectives (Bierly, Kessler and Christensen 2000), and to achieve greater strategic assertiveness (Hays 2007). As such, organizational wisdom involves the collection, transfer, and integration of the knowledge of individuals and the use of institutional and social processes (structure, culture, leadership) for strategic action (Kessler 2006).

This stream is based on the movements of organizational learning (Bierly, Kessler and Christensen 2000; Hays 2007), knowledge management, and information management (Ackoff 1989; Hays 2007; Rowley 2006b, 2007) by appropriating (i) their concepts and their data–information–knowledge (DIK) paradigm; (ii) the pyramidal or sequential/linear/hierarchical conception of increasing importance among the elements in an upward direction from data to knowledge and, at the top of the chain, wisdom (DIKW), as shown in Figure 23.1; and (iii) the learning process as the generative means that transforms each level of the hierarchy to the next.

According to these authors, data are raw facts learned from the accumulated evidence that, upon gaining form and functionality, become information—that is, data that are useful and provided with meaning based on understanding. A clear understanding of information through the process of analysis and synthesis produces knowledge. Wisdom is the ability to best use knowledge to establish and achieve desired goals through discerning judgments and action for better living and success (Bierly, Kessler and Christensen 2000). Figure 23.2 illustrates this model.

The third stream, rooted in philosophical studies, incorporates and rekindles Aristotle's ideas of phronesis presented in his treatise *The Nicomachean Ethics* (Küpers 2013; Nonaka et al. 2014; Shotter and Tsoukas 2014). Wisdom, based on phronesis, is the prudential judgment by which equivocal circumstances are negotiated with both the individual and the collective good in mind (Nonaka et al. 2014). Phronesis is a practice based on everyday

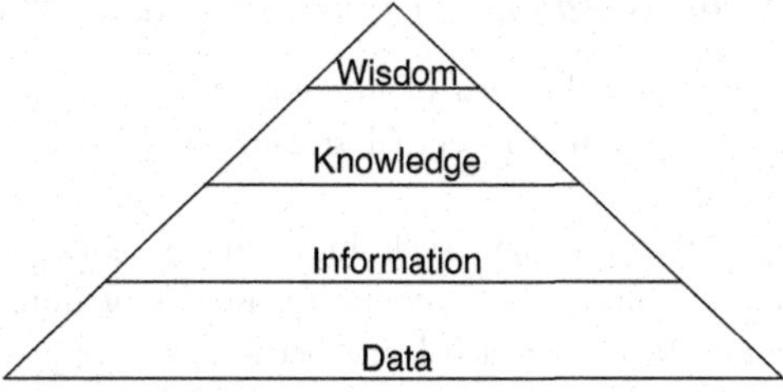

Figure 23.1 DIKW hierarchy model (Rowley, 2006b, 2007)

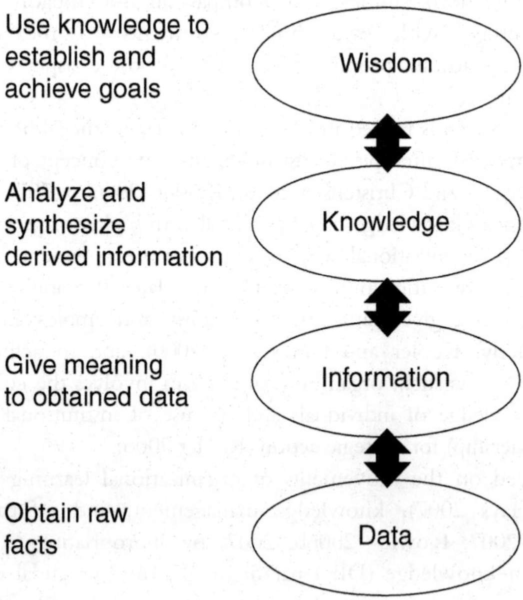

Figure 23.2 Data, information, knowledge, and wisdom framework (Bierly, Kessler, and Christensen 2000).

experiences and is concerned with a self-cultivating form of doing well at whatever it is that we do. It is inherent and tacit in humankind and cannot be contained by explicit standards or rules (Nonaka et al. 2014). Thus, it is a human skill that has a reflective, contemplative aspect of mindfulness (Shotter and Tsoukas 2014) that manifests in the aspect of the action. Thus, phronesis expresses the kind of person that someone is, a virtue, rather than the kind of knowledge a person has or may develop.

From this foundation, Shotter and Tsoukas (2014) propose that thought and intelligence give way to the perception and understanding of reality in all of its contours, nuances, conflicts, and subjectivity present at the moment of action. By acting in this way, from a practical situation, alternatives and solutions will emerge that the individual can adopt and that bypass the problem-solving intellect. Nonaka et al. (2014) incorporate this view of phronesis as an element that allows the spiral of knowledge creation to occur (Nonaka and Takeuchi 1995), particularly in processes involving tacit knowledge.

The fourth stream, rooted in a spiritual background, captures the contrasting meanings and visions of wisdom in the East and the West (Chia and Holt 2007; Weick and Putnam 2006) that seek to recover concepts rooted in Eastern religions such as Buddhism, Taoism, and Hinduism (Chia and Holt 2007; Goleman 2015; Marshall and Simpson 2014; Weick and Putnam 2006; Zaidman and Goldstein-Gidoni 2011). Such religions seek to explore the continuous unfolding of wise action in day-to-day practice (Marshall and Simpson 2014). Specifically, the influence of Buddhism ranges from the work of Bateson (1972) on the ecology of the human mind to recent developments that champion compassion and gratitude as relevant dimensions of companies' organizing actions (Dutton et al. 2006; Frost 1999), to workplaces that are friendly and meaningful for individuals (Hays 2007), to the increasing interest in mindfulness in organizations (Vogus and Sutcliffe 2012; Weick and Putnam 2006; Weick and Sutcliffe 2006), and to studies on faith and spirituality in organizations (Neal 2012) and in society (Goleman 2015).

Hays (2007) defines wisdom in terms of doing the right thing, appreciating the completeness of the context and breadth of vision for purposes of a greater common good. Therefore, wisdom, based on values, transcends typical problems and known contexts in which previous knowledge and experiences may bias and limit understanding (Hays 2007). Chia and Holt (2007) contrast true wisdom, based on the Eastern tradition, Zen Buddhist spirituality and the Tao, with Western knowledge. Thus, true wisdom manifests as a cultivated humility, a meekness of demeanor, and an openness of mind and spirit that is distinct and different from the aggressive and relentless pursuit, acquisition, and exploitation of Western knowledge. Wisdom, in this view, is not about having more information in a quantifiable sense or constructing irrefutable propositions; on the contrary, it is about obtaining signs of uncertainty, doubt, and ambiguity. Hence, one must necessarily unlearn what is known, empty the mind to understand subtleties and contemplate the whole context holistically. Individual and organizational wisdom are exemplified by the internalized ability to resist superficial appearances, quantification, and (false) knowledge representations to rediscover the true measure of things so that wise decisions can be made (Chia and Holt 2007).

Wisdom also goes beyond Western thought centered in the being (form, substance, coherence, completeness, and finality) to the absolute and undetermined nothingness (Chia and Holt 2007; Goleman 2015; Marshall and Simpson 2014). For Marshall and Simpson (2014), the application of a Buddhist perspective in learning networks points to new and specific modes of groups working together to develop the practice of wisdom.

Zaidman and Goldstein-Gidoni (2011), in turn, consider workplace spirituality a form of wisdom that is developed both at the individual and organizational levels. It promotes awareness at work, enhanced communication, and reduced stress—individual aspects that operate in the context of better organizational behaviors. However, spirituality remains an underutilized source for bringing new insights into the processes and practices of organizational learning, in which it is recognized that the wisdom arising from spirituality, such as Buddhism, can only be achieved through intensive training and concerted effort (Marshall and Simpson 2014). The stream of spirituality seeks to explore the deepening of Eastern wisdom by highlighting the conflict of logic and understanding with Western knowledge.

Considering all knowledge encompassed by the four streams, wisdom entirely transcends the logic/Rational Dimension where data, information, and, consequently, science and technology reside. Wisdom seems to fit better into a new Spiritual Dimension where ancient religious traditions, mindfulness, humanism, individuals' values, virtues, morals, and ethics reside.

On wisdom and its conceptual streams

The stream based on psychological studies addresses and establishes the relevance of wisdom as something intrinsic to an individual's mental and emotional faculties. These faculties should be exploited and used to their fullest degree (Ardelt 2004). Even if it were possible, this stream is weakened by the evidence brought to light by the fourth stream, which defines wisdom in a much broader context whereby spirituality is the basis of wisdom (Chia and Holt 2007; Goleman 2015; Zaidman and Goldstein-Gidoni 2011) and the spirit—the human soul—is something great, universal, and infinite in scope that transcends the mind, the body, and the very individual (Goleman 2015). Whereas the psychological stream of research focuses on the individual, the spirituality stream assumes that wisdom can only be fully experienced in the context of the collective, community, and society (Marshall and Simpson 2014) deeply embedded in Nature. Without this, there is no possible wisdom, there is no possible spirituality, there is no possible happiness—there is not even any reason for human existence (Goleman 2015). The admission, acceptance, and expansion of contemplative (Dutton et al. 2006; Frost 1999; Hays 2007), meditative, and mindfulness practices in organizations (Vogus and Sutcliffe 2012; Weick and Putnam 2006; Weick and Sutcliffe 2006) ultimately questions and weakens this psychological approach to human wisdom.

The stream based in knowledge management, by approaching and contextualizing human wisdom, admits—regardless of the definition and depth of knowledge proposed by other scholars—that it can only benefit individuals, organizations, and society if an analysis and a different and grounded proposal are presented based on the same available data/information/knowledge (Ackoff 1989; Bierly, Kessler and Christensen 2000; Kessler 2006; Rowley 2007). Even if the organizational wisdom resulting from the processing of these layers turns out to be more enlightened, this enlightenment is judged based on the same view as the prevailing wisdom; it is not reconstructed, not revalued, and devoid of intrinsic value. This stream is demonstrably the weakest of the four perspectives because it reduces and instrumentalizes wisdom to a mere accumulation of knowledge that is disconnected and lacking the deep wisdom that spirituality provides to the human soul and human nature.

The stream based on philosophical studies recognizes that wisdom exists and is relevant to individuals and the collective such that the individual must exploit and use this full tacit skill of the individual's being and self (Küpers 2013; Nonaka et al. 2014; Shotter and Tsoukas 2014). However, people only recognize its value if the wisdom applied brings practical gains to knowledge in the form of what is already known and practiced individually, organizationally, or socially (Küpers 2013; Nonaka et al. 2014). That is, wisdom results in a vision analogous to the previous stream (i.e., organizational wisdom). Although we find here a deeper philosophical foundation, the instrumentalization and simplification of practical wisdom weakens the stream.

The stream based on a spiritual background brings an ancient and profound approach to wisdom, consolidating the way it is perceived by many traditional Eastern religions. It is all but undisputed that the deepening of wisdom grounded in spirituality and a more integrated and ecumenical vision of human religiosity brings great value to the formation of knowledge (Goleman 2015; Neal 2012). Thus, we present some key, albeit more subtle, aspects: (i) spirituality and wisdom are similar, converging visions of the same nature; they can live together harmoniously (Chia and Holt 2007; Zaidman and Goldstein-Gidoni 2011) and at the same level, hereinafter referred to as "layer"; (ii) awareness is formed from spirituality/wisdom (through spiritually deepening practices such as meditation) and extrapolates the individual (Chia and Holt 2007; Goleman 2015; Neal 2012; Weick and Putnam 2006), which is part of the group, the Sangha, which coexists with the different origins, essences and karmas of the individual and of the community/society in which it is inserted (Marshall and Simpson 2014) (this will differ for Chinese, Japanese, European, and American society, for example); (iii) Integrative Knowledge does not form at the Wisdom Layer, in one specific dimension or in each individual's mind; rather, it forms from the community of individuals (Goleman 2015; Marshall and Simpson 2014).

The stream of spiritual background proves to be valuable as a builder of wisdom, despite its weakness in failing to recognize the distinct and relevant nature of a layer of awareness, a step forward from the individual's meditation practices. Moreover, it is all the more fragile because it does not refrain from admitting that rationality and all information (generated and yet to be generated) is fundamental and plays a very relevant role in the formation of an Integrative Knowledge that recognizes and brings together the corporeal, mental, and spiritual capabilities of individuals—and of individuals collectively.

Spirituality and rationality in two dimensions

The perception of an extremely important need for integration between spirituality and rationality is not a new discussion. In the last century, it was well noted and recorded by eminent thinkers, philosophers, and scientists concerned with the tortuous destinies of mankind. Eminent academics and humanists such as Einstein and Fromm expressed the misconception of the supremacy of scientific rationality above all other spheres of human life, especially affecting all domains that cannot thereby be explained through scientific rationality, such as spirituality and wisdom itself, the deep bonds of love and compassion, and virtues and values in human relationships, with others and with the environment. One of the causes of this split originated, according to Fromm (1994), at the end of Middle Ages, when "faith in God as a vital experience began to vanish because critical thought began to undermine the rational basis for the faiths" (p. 117). By undermining the spiritual foundations of millenary philosophies/religions, arguing the absence of scientific evidence that proves them and seeking to extinguish or devalue them, rational thought has finally ravaged and debilitated an entire dimension of human spirituality and its natural connection with the precepts and teachings handed down for millennia by the prophets and masters of the human soul. When deifying the intellect, giving an ephemeral life to a multitude of illusive gods enlivened in the mind of each individual, rationality questions the divine side of human nature, the spiritual side, as any other prejudiced thoughts and deeds would do, forcing all humanity to walk in endless, distinct, and conflicting directions without the compass of unison and unidirectional energy that guides and draws us through spirituality, the universal language of love, compassion, fraternity, and ethics.

Einstein (1978), in his writings on humanism, said, "By painful experience we have learnt that rational thinking does not suffice to solve the problems of our society" (p. 31).

> Our age is proud of the progress it has made in man's intellectual development. [. . .] And certainly, we should take care not to make intellect our god: it has, of course, powerful muscles, but no personality. [. . .] The intellect has a sharp eye for methods and tools, but is blind to ends and values.
>
> *(p. 139)*

Fromm (1995), in turn, explained this phenomenon as the intensive process of human alienation and the dissociation of individuals:

> I mean by intellectuals people who talk about things that they don't feel, people who are mainly cerebrally related to the world and to other people, mainly manipulating thought rather than experiencing the creative fusion of thought and feeling; [. . .] that the heart and the brain of intellectuals are not connected, or in philosophical terms, they are alienated.
>
> *(p. 30)*

Similarly, according to Jung (2006), the instinctual nature of humans embodies the collective unconscious and the natural capacity of human beings to relate to the more spiritual side, with their feelings, with their religiosity, and with an understanding of humanity's very existence that is unattainable by the rational deepening of knowledge or by the self-aggrandizement of their own consciousness. The unconscious is "the only accessible source of religious experience, [. . .] the medium from which the religious experience seems to flow" (Jung 2006, p. 89). The author also argues that the deification of the conscious to the detriment of the unconscious, of the intellect to the detriment of feelings, of reason to the detriment of spirituality (extramundane authority), generates a rupture between faith and knowledge, "a symptom of the *split consciousness*, which is so characteristic of the mental disorder of our day" (Jung 2006, p. 73), "a split that becomes pathological the moment his consciousness is no longer able to neglect or suppress his instinctual side" (Jung 2006, p. 79). In this context, the proposal of a model of Integrative Knowledge, formed and developed from individuals themselves, also seems to align with the proposition of a human being who is more integrated, complete, and harmonious with their psychic, rational, and spiritual forces, conscious and unconscious (Jung 2006).

In a more recent view, Goleman (2015) speaks of the partnership between spirituality and science whereby the two work together, particularly in the service of compassion. This partnership largely reconciles with the contemporary perspective of humanism that in its pillars harmonizes (i) the scientific method, which is commonly based on empirical or measurable evidence subject to specific principles of reasoning; (ii) empathy, which links science with what distinguishes humanism as a positive philosophy, a deep-seated compassion for mankind and the world at large; and (iii) the egalitarian-based sense of fairness, of justice for the rights of minorities (Speckhardt 2015). All three are strongly related to human spirituality since they lack the method and scientific proof. Fromm, declared Humanist of the Year in 1966 by the American Humanist Association, stated:

> Humanism, as a philosophy, is about 2,500 years old. There's nothing new in it except that is new for us ... I would have to talk about Chinese and Indian humanism expressed in Taoism and Buddhism, but ... I might as well begin with the idea of humanism in the Old Testament.
>
> *(Fromm 1994, p. 63)*

Therefore, when analyzing the various streams of studies in the spiritual and rational arena, there seems to be a lack of fundamental elements that might help to conceive a knowledge that is truly wise, mindful, and integrative of the distinct forms of human thinking, feeling, and understanding, capable of guiding the actions of individuals through more balanced and sustainable ways. A new knowledge must be grounded in all capabilities of human nature, material and immaterial, harmonically working together to bring to light alternative solutions to the multiple complex problems that the organizations (and their individuals) face today.

Then, from the deepening of the analysis of this rational and millenarian dispute through spaces of spirituality and rationality in the minds of individuals, arose the concepts of the Five Pillars of Integrative Knowledge: (i) spirituality is as relevant as rationality in the formation of Integrative Knowledge and shouldn't show prevalence one over the other, no matter their stages in the evolutionary cycle of humanity; (ii) creative and positive energy drives Integrative Knowledge development and shouldn't be exposed to prejudice and judgments, deriving either from spiritual or rational sides; (iii) spirituality and rationality are sisterly and complementary forces with a character of oneness and of indivisibility, and in isolation, shouldn't be considered conducive to Integrative Knowledge; (iv) Integrative Knowledge comes from two distinct and antagonistic dimensions, and their intrinsic and dualistic nature shouldn't be questioned nor merged previous to the Integrative Knowledge formation; (v) Integrative Knowledge is independent from individuals' religion options (even if these options are to be atheists or agnostics), but dependent on their pure spirituality, which will always be an essential and common part of all human beings.

In this regard, a proposal, the Integrative Knowledge Model, is presented in the next section.

An integrative proposal: Integrative Knowledge Model

The proposed model intends to be an evolution of the current dichotomous paradigm between rationality and spirituality, acknowledging their unquestionable value for knowledge development and for humanity evolution, and their inner nature of being unique, complementary, and indissociable, two powerful forces of human nature that, like religion and science, must work hand in hand to bring to light the best of knowledge, the brightest routes and actions for the continual progress of humankind. This fundamental change in knowledge formation and development is being called Integrative Knowledge.

The model is an integrated set consisting of two dimensions: (i) the Rational Dimension, formed by Data and Information Layers (abundant, excessive, available, and mostly contradictory in the knowledge era), which follows the current paradigm of its successive transformation of data into information and knowledge based on logical thinking and grounded in concrete facts by the instrumental-functionalist rationality (in which the learning assessment in its gamut of forms is the transforming element); and (ii) the Spiritual Dimension, composed of the layers of wisdom and awareness—harking back to traditional and profound spirituality and nature itself for the consciousness of individuals through attentive and concentrated reflection (mindful assessment) as a transforming element, based on the broadest possible purposes for individuals, organizations, and society in their complex relationships. Figure 23.3 illustrates the Integrative Knowledge Model, of which aspects are described below.

Each dimension contains a vector—the Rational Knowledge Vector and the Spiritual Knowledge Vector—such that each is derived from elements of different natures—data/information and wisdom/awareness, respectively—in terms of the mode of generation and conception of the knowledge resulting from them. The creation of the vectors entails a recognition of the importance and complexity of the Integrative Knowledge formation amidst the continuous changes, evolutions, and dynamic interrelations and movements between these layers.

Thus, a parameterization of the Rational Vector is proposed because it enables its measurement and, consequently, a tracking of its evolution for decision-making and the proposal of actions and solutions. Vis-à-vis the Spiritual Vector, it would be paradoxical to attempt to measure aspects arising from spiritual practices and from a broader understanding of life because in attempting to measure them, one runs the risk of simplifying, reducing, and eventually rendering them merely rational aspects. Moreover, feelings and beliefs understood and shared by the individual, such as love and compassion, are almost impossible to quantify or, even more, to measure because of their deep and subjective nature.

The two vectors converge to a central layer of Integrative Knowledge that merges and consolidates these different results arising from the disparate approaches. From the convergence of the rational and spiritual vectors in the Integrative Knowledge Layer, a direction follows, the Integrative Action Vector, a force to propagate organizations' actions that make sense to the whole society and that brings about relevant changes for

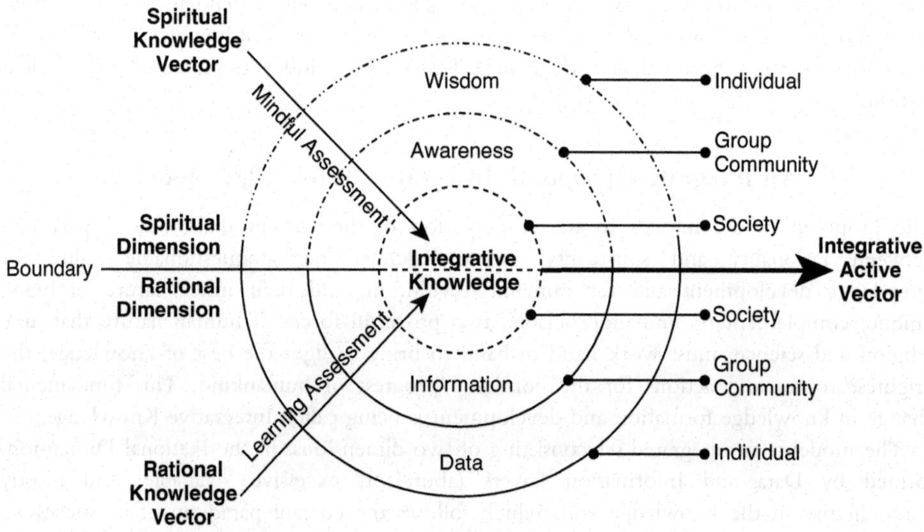

Figure 23.3 Integrative Knowledge Model (developed by the authors)

individuals—individuals who are whole, complete, integral; individuals who are of sound body, mind, and spirit in the Rational and Spiritual Dimensions.

Thus, in the model proposed here, knowledge is presented as a central integrating element, the result of the meeting and the desired balance between forces coming from two "vectors" of opposite natures arising from the component forces of the layers of data/information and wisdom/awareness. The layer is thus a set of structured actions of individuals placed in a defined medium with common goals. The vector, in contrast, is a concentrator of forces of the individuals and/or group that thrusts them through the layers in the direction of Integrative Knowledge and to transformative organizational and social changes, all the while respecting the integrity of the individual in body, mind, and spirit.

One must not overlook the boundary between the layers of data and wisdom and of information and awareness. This boundary is both tenuous and fluid, and it recognizes the migratory character of individuals between these layers. However, the central layer of Integrative Knowledge in the proposed model necessarily has no border. It must accommodate debate, transparency, and dialog vis-à-vis the antagonistic visions arising from the two different vectors of knowledge.

The Rational Dimension

This dimension originates from the second stream of organizational wisdom (Ackoff 1989; Bierly, Kessler and Christensen 2000; Hays 2007; Kessler 2006; Rowley 2006a, 2006b, 2007), whose transformation process is based on learning. One characteristic of this vector is its scientific, Cartesian, functionalist reality based on the accumulation of evidence and on objective knowledge targeted at a particular purpose in which the excess of data, information, and technology circulating through the postmodern world strongly contributes to its formation and adoption (Chia and Holt 2007; Goleman 2015).

This Rational Dimension is much more present, abundant, valued, and practiced in current society. It is the dimension that—although without disruptive proposals for transformative action on the current great contradictions and impasses—has an almost unquestionable force driven by the accumulation of scientific progress that ultimately determines human rationality and the way society thinks and acts. Three parameters are suggested to assess the force of the Rational Knowledge Vector: (i) comprehensiveness of the scope of available data; (ii) the maturity of the information generated; and (iii) the effectiveness of the proposals conveyed by the vector to the Integrative Knowledge Layer.

It is important to note that the Data Layer is individual-centered: the individual collects, researches, filters, and gathers data to incorporate and ascribe them meaning in the Information Layer. However, as the vectors transverse the layers, the pressure and effort required to advance increases, as does the interaction between individuals. Both pose a major obstacle to progress toward knowledge because they impose restrictions, comparisons, conflicts, and competition, which bolster individualism and materialism and therefore need to be overcome. Such behavior can be encountered in every situation of the Knowledge Layer, including the family, community, organization, or society.

The Spiritual Dimension

This dimension originates from the spiritual stream (Chia and Holt 2007; Goleman 2015; Marshall and Simpson 2014; Neal 2012; Weick and Putnam 2006), whose process of the transformation of wisdom into awareness and then into Integrative Knowledge is through attentive and concentrated reflection (i.e., mindful assessment) in aspects involving both the broader situational context and the unfolding of the actions taken. The respective vector is characterized by broader goals for organizations regarding their relationships with individuals, society, and other stakeholders. In it, the traditional wisdom spreads over the community of individuals and contributes to an improvement that is better at discerning objectives and better at aligning organizational actions. Admittedly, its vector is, in today's world, somewhat fragile; however, it has the power to positively question, discuss, and guide organizations and society for the long term (Goleman 2015).

In the Spiritual Dimension the Wisdom Layer is a unique, personal pathway that is achieved only through the practice of contemplation, meditation, and individual engagement in deeper spiritual activity (Chia and Holt 2007; Goleman 2015; Marshall and Simpson 2014). After individuals have incorporated wisdom arising out of spiritual practices, after the experiences of the subject with the search for the fullness of their being, it is still necessary for these individuals to externalize, commune with, and manifest in the collective environment the changes that they understand as necessary and capable of being proposed, analyzed, and, especially, of being feasible in the consensus of their collectivity, in the consensus of the wisdom attained and understood by each individual while respecting their disparities, their diverse views, and their different depths of understanding and enlightenment.

Along the path of wisdom, individuals must recognize the progress of all who, like themselves, strive for the absorption, the experience, the illumination of their lives, no matter how small the steps toward spirituality may be. This endeavor progresses in the Awareness Layer, a layer in which the individual recognizes the other, the collective. The individual recognizes the different pathways and the different understandings reached and perceived. Only enlightened masters have the same perception and understanding of reality, of what must change, of what suffering is, of what enlightenment is. All individuals must understand their limitations, the diversity of the understandings experienced, and the suffering still present in their spirits. They must learn to live, to understand one another, to forgive one another, and to practice self-compassion to allow the formation, in the Awareness Layer, of a new environment and a new collective that is understood as challenging, albeit possible and achievable.

Awareness is a layer that is complex and of high aggregated value for the subsequent formation of Integrative Knowledge, and it is as rich and diverse regarding objectives and activities as the Information Layer. Thus, just as information builds from data a more cohesive, comprehensive, and refined set of information in a creative environment already inserted in the collective organization, extrapolating the individual so that the information set can be worked to generate knowledge, so too does awareness develop a spiritual communal sense from the set of individual practices and understandings that come from wisdom.

Also, just as information is an evolution of data, awareness is an evolution of wisdom. It enables wisdom to form a realistic, concrete, and holistic view of the problems and difficulties of the organizational and social environment, prioritizing the issues and most relevant analyses for the formation of an Integrative Knowledge. Whereas the Wisdom Layer can assume an individual and quieter mindfulness, in the Awareness Layer, a global vision of individuals and the organization/community should be formed. However, the Awareness Layer is the most difficult and most arduous for individuals; it is the most avoided and the most opaque of the model's layers. Indeed, it is where individuals recognize their limits, admit their sufferings and ignorance, and yet still proceed to externalize them, to hear, to accept the most meaningful social changes, and to differentiate between what can and what cannot be modified—and to then set forth in the Integrative Knowledge propositions ideas and questions about which changes could or should be implemented.

The contribution of the Spiritual Dimension is exemplified in the strong adoption of the mindfulness movement in school education (Bakosh and Houlihan 2016), in work at organizations (GGSC 2016; Vogus and Sutcliffe 2012; Weick and Putnam 2006; Weick and Sutcliffe 2006), in law practice (Magee 2015), and in integrative medicine (Lazar 2016), consolidated under the rubric of contemplative science research (Vago 2016). Meditation is one of the most recognized Eastern practices for achieving spiritual development. Undoubtedly, its adoption in educational and corporate environments has greatly benefited the individuals so engaged. It has enhanced focus and concentration on the present moment and provided a more accurate view of the whole, vanquishing of anxiety, greater empathy for and forgiveness of others, and improved self-knowledge and self-compassion (Vogus and Sutcliffe 2012; Weick and Putnam 2006; Weick and Sutcliffe 2006).

However, one must be attentive so that these practices generate an action, a transformational change, and avoid making mindfulness an exercise disconnected from the reality of the group, the community, and the organization and remaining only in the Spiritual Dimension. One must also be careful that mindfulness does not become a simple practice based on the Rational Dimension where the purpose of its adoption is simply to (i) have individuals who are more focused, productive, and effective amid the high stress of these environments; (ii) have individuals who are more resigned, erasing their motivation to relate to and become involved in trying to transform the environment, a motivation inherent in an alive and indivisible body–mind–spirit individual; and (iii) create escapism—a tranquilizer to survive in stressful environments. Without the Awareness Layer, it is just a technique of molding dejá vu knowledge and mind control, far from its real purpose of enabling full attention, to broaden the understanding and connection with aspects essential for Life. Mindfulness should highly benefit individuals, institutions, and organizations, helping them to rethink Life and the context of Life in these social environments.

The Integrative Knowledge Layer and the Integrative Action Vector

This central layer of knowledge is called Integrative Knowledge; it is the result of consolidating forces from the two vectors. It provides uniqueness, wholeness, and completeness of knowledge composed of distinct natures. Therefore, Integrative Knowledge is a merger of two visions of knowledge into a third proposition/idea/solution, which encompasses the beneficial aspects and challenges of each force.

A concrete example relevant to the proposed model is integrative medicine in the United States (Horrigan et al. 2012) and its adoption at the Children's Hospital of Philadelphia (Wood 2016), where it was necessary to combine the power of science and technology built on rationality with an ancient wisdom only understood in the context of the connection with Nature. In the area of medicine, research in neuroscience and mindfulness seeks to reconcile these views (Lazar 2016). Other examples, no less relevant, are found in the mindfulness movement in law practice (Magee 2015); the local economy movement; the hybrid company and social business models; and even the decision of major retail chains to ban products from companies deemed not socially responsible in their goal of becoming large networks of fair-trade, organic, and sustainable products. These movements are in addition to the previously mentioned movements of integrative medicine and mindfulness in education and organizations. Note that none of these situations portrays a scenario with easy decisions; therefore, the Integrative Knowledge Model seeks to balance, weigh, and reconcile both vector forces for an unbiased, impartial, and long-term decision.

It is worth repeating that the Integrative Knowledge Layer is individual-centered and socially oriented. It occurs within individuals and then expands to society, consolidating the integrative actions. For the knowledge generated to be put into practice, it is necessary to consider, in its formation, all of the grandeur and perceptions of the individual (obtained in the Wisdom Layer) and of the collectivity, the community in which the individual is inserted (expanded in the Awareness Layer), thus hosting an array of individual and group capabilities in their most diverse expressions and intelligences. A complete group of individuals is sought who are socially present in body, mind, and spirit, with their various intelligences, whether rational, emotional, or spiritual. Therefore, the merger of knowledge—incorporated and made possible by these two vectors in the same layer of Integrative Knowledge—gives rise to recommendations for democratic (albeit initially quite antagonistic) solutions and actions by consensus.

Integrative knowledge should be the result of broad and deep discussions among groups of individuals that include in the debate both the Rational and Spiritual Dimensions, which are assumed to be components of one inseparable whole. A conflicting boundary between the layers, which appears between data–wisdom and information–awareness, should be avoided. Through the Awareness Layer, convictions should arise regarding what is wrong, what must be changed, and what changes should be made. Only after these ideas are formed are they negotiated, reviewed, and objectively defined in the Integrative Knowledge Layer. These solutions and the resulting actions will therefore be more effective as the ideas and visions of both sides are more respected, argued, and debated, starting from a comprehensive perception of the true nature and purpose of each of the original vectors. There is, therefore, no one vector that is better or more important; they are distinct merely among themselves, and the suspension of judgments is paramount for the actions to be formulated.

The characterization of a transition phase is recommended to obtain this stage of Integrative Knowledge. A slow but necessary transition is necessary for the adoption of this model in any social segment due to the disparate and conflicting forces that are predominant in the frontier of these two vectors. The Rational Knowledge Vector overlaps all aspects of society due to the massive and increasing efforts made in the layers of data and information since the dawn of the modern era with its notion of progress (synonymous with science and technology) and accelerated with the era of knowledge. If this transition stage is not well addressed by each institution of each social segment, numerous and stressful conflicts may ensue, leading to the breakdown of the oneness of the Integrative Knowledge Layer and the loss of any gain or effectiveness previously achieved and guaranteed. At this stage, for example, an increasing awareness of the participants of the organization develops through readings, discussions, and workshops following spiritual and/or meditative practices. A committee is established to embrace and nurture the Integrative Knowledge in the organization, thereby continuously maintaining the balance and equanimity of the rational and spiritual visions.

The Integrative Action Vector consolidates the integrative actions and all resulting actions in the direction of necessary organizational and social changes. When researching data and information and/or meditating and raising their consciousness, individuals become locked in an inner struggle. However, the greatest challenges and their inherent solutions will come from a more balanced force of movement, which emerges from transformation and from action. The powerful force concentrated in that vector thus becomes evident.

The predominance of any one of the vectors, whether rational or spiritual, over another will be harmful to the Integrative Knowledge Layer because it will proportionally divert the vector resulting from the integrative action, making it drop to the dimension possessing the vector of greatest force. Therefore, it must be admitted that different levels of effectiveness of integrative actions will depend on the intensity of the source vectors and their absorption of Integrative Knowledge. Hence, care must be taken so that Integrative Knowledge is devoid of criticism, prejudices, and preconceived ideas in both dimensions.

Furthermore, the Integrative Action Vector has the critical role of filtering and neutralizing disruptions occurring in the generation of knowledge, especially in the Rational Dimension. These distortions concern (i) the biased or distorted use of information; (ii) the deliberate omission of information; (iii) the absence of information or the lack of research to obtain it; and (iv) the excess of unidirectional information or excess of research in just a few areas of interest. These intrinsic biases do not seem to occur with this same intensity in the Spiritual Dimension given the character of the quest for a more transparent and deeper understanding of reality. Thus, the Integrative Action Vector mediates the actions to be taken during the course of discussion and debate for the formation of Integrative Knowledge.

In the context of building Integrative Knowledge in organizations, business ethics, a topic of paramount relevance, emerges as a very effective form of guidance and protection against biased actions from both dimensions. Business ethics is at the core of the most important debates and challenges defying our society. Thus, business ethics considerations are essentially a corollary of the model presented, both reinforcing it significantly and reducing its implementation risks enormously. Both the Rational and Spiritual Dimensions, where ethics is inserted, go far beyond the current organizational culture and environment. The Rational Dimension, for example, brings to the organization all market possibilities and opportunities out-of-the-box, not just the knowledge and interests already established and consolidated by the organization. In turn, when the individual meditates, their mind also expands to a world of values and virtues shared by the majority, the universal mind, which obviously goes beyond the boundaries of the organization as well, including its cultural boundaries.

For all these reasons, in the model proposed in this chapter, individuals have a prominent role in all layers. This role is represented by their full human potential for soundness of body, mind, and spirit in their personal, organizational, and social living. In sum, the aim is to redeem individuals so they can live to the fullness of their being, integrated into all forms of the environment around them, their own nature, and the surrounding Nature. The aim is to produce a whole individual, one who does not live parallel and distinct lives depending on which segment they are inserted in at a certain point in their life; a sensitive individual who understands the force of these vectors acting on their person, all along their transformative lives, and who feels a part of them at these same moments of their existence, thereby allowing them to seek out and experience happiness. This happiness can only be complete if also attained by those around them, whether family, co-workers, or members of the community where they live.

As such, the model underscores the relevance of the conscious essence of the individuals—neither individualistic nor individualized (disassociated from each other), neither fragmented nor in conflict from the various spheres of life. Though it may seem complex or romantic, it is merely a question of making sense of, and seeking, a deeper meaning in life. Thus, only individuals of integrity, in their full potential, will formulate Integrative Knowledge and be able to generate the maximum effectiveness of the proposed actions and solutions in the environments in which the necessary changes are implemented, in the voluminous and complex challenges and problems increasingly facing society in which are inserted families, communities, and organizations.

In this context, both the strengthening of the Spiritual Dimension and its integration into the Rational Dimension of individuals should be prioritized, together with the elevation of knowledge to the status of the strategic pillar of the organizational management model. Addressing these topics, which gain relevance and priority among organizational actions and initiatives, will contribute to reducing two deep gaps that are so prevalent in many of the incumbent models of the last decades.

Individuals and their organizations must seek, in this slow process of change, to walk in unison with each "integrative innovation" in management, each achievement, every step forward, inserted slowly in the context of each organizational action; individuals becoming more integrated, conscious, holistic, fulfilled, and happy; organizations becoming more knowledgeable, humanistic, socially responsible, ethical, and respected by individuals, communities, and society. Though the process of implementation is slow, it is robust and permanent, internalized in individuals and in the very culture of the organization. This process is a win–win move toward a more enlightened way of doing business, of engaging individuals in non-dualistic views, in non-dichotomous paths, in a deep common sense and humanistic way that will prove much more effective in dealing with and overcoming the very real threats and weaknesses and the resulting complex problems and challenges that, if not completely addressed and understood, may undermine the evolutionary progress of organizations and (why not?) the whole of humanity.

Conclusion

This study aimed to propose and deepen the discussion of an Integrative Knowledge Model that encompasses and incorporates a Spiritual Dimension with layers of Wisdom and Awareness into the Rational Dimension of data and information in the context of various social environments. Thus, the chapter explored the existing streams of wisdom, from psychological to spiritual approaches, passing through organizational wisdom and practical wisdom, including models that added new dimensions or layers to the current DIKW paradigm.

The proposed Integrative Knowledge Model represents a dynamic and disruptive process of knowledge generation, making it far off from those models commonly used not only by academia but also by organizations. These disruptive and dynamic properties result from two main factors. First, Spirituality is present, triggering and driving the entire process of integrative knowledge generation in harmony with all human capacities. Spirituality not only drives but also determines the prevailing direction and path of the entire process of integrative knowledge generation such that, once designed, it can be formatted and put into practice in absolute coherence and harmony with Rationality and therefore with human nature itself.

Second, the model assumes that the Spiritual Dimension and the Rational Dimension are equally balanced, assigning the same degree of relevance to each dimension throughout the integrative knowledge generation process. For this purpose, Spirituality must be fully present, with sufficient strength and consistency to not only counteract Rationality but also guide it throughout the process. In this context, the current fragility of the Spiritual Dimension of human knowledge must be acknowledged given the robustness reached by Rationality, mostly due to the excessive valorization of knowledge acquired through material resources and mental capacities, primarily focused on science and technology. In addition, its first layer of Wisdom (inward, to awaken and enlighten the human soul) precedes and prevails over the subsequent layer of Awareness (outward, to integrate the human soul with Nature), of Consciousness, which is only fully experienced if enlightened by Wisdom. Therefore, without Wisdom, there is neither Awareness nor Integrative Knowledge, nor the Integrative Action Vector to promote the necessary changes. Thus, the pivotal and critical success factor of the model is reached: how can one develop human wisdom to achieve equality of robustness and value between the Integrative Knowledge dimensions?

One of the possible answers can be found in the mindfulness movement, which has been gaining momentum in the Western world. This movement reflects a global perception—albeit not fully conscious—of an emptiness, of a "de-humanization" of knowledge, generated by a powerful negative vortex that has been, slowly but increasingly, draining all human spirituality and that derives precisely from the aforementioned excessive valorization of rationality, amid two equally human dimensions.

According to Cherman and Azeredo (2018, p. 216), when deeply rooted in millennial spiritual traditions, particularly Buddhist traditions, mindfulness can counter this perverse vortex, this spirituality fragility, and the widening gap between these two dimensions. In this case:

> Mindfulness must be seen as a state, an upright practice [...] of experiencing the buddhic Body, Mind and Soul, of the ceasing of doubts and attachments, [...] the realization of the wisdom that infinitely transcends the ego and its original karmas, [...] in the consciousness that comes from becoming One with one's own nature, with the Nature of all beings, with Buddha Nature.

According to the authors, only true mindfulness—the use of practices of contemplation, meditation, and engagement by an individual in a deeper spiritual activity—can awaken Wisdom, now so latent, and enable individuals to experience Right Understanding in their lives, regardless of the size and magnitude of changes and steps toward new and more enlightened paths to human knowledge. As Mindfulness effort progresses in the layer of awareness, the existence of the Other, of the collective, and of human beings' different views and perceptions will harmoniously build the paths ahead as the necessary changes are being revealed. Individuals become conscious of their limits, accepting their suffering and ignorance, understanding the cause–effect relationship between reality and the environment around them, and yet proposing to, at every moment, listen (to their spirit and mind), evolve, accept necessary and illumined changes, while wisely differentiating what can and cannot be changed, and then, following an unique and real evolutionary path.

Then, Rationality must be created and developed through successive, interlinked, and exhausting efforts of the human mind, whereas Spirituality only needs to be found and revealed, without any participation or effort of the human mind. Spirituality only requires an everlasting learning process of reception of a Light and immersion in communion with a Truth that already exists and that is One, Omnipresent and Omniscient. Thus, it seems more evident that these two dimensions are completely different and derive from opposite worlds. Therefore, this integration should be extremely complex indeed, and simultaneously, so crucial to a more enlightened knowledge generation. Human spirituality should not be destroyed just because we were endowed with the ability to be rational by Nature, a true gift that must not become, because of a sheer miscomprehension of the mind, an autophagic process of destruction of the very nature that created it, and of human existence itself. Respect and fraternity, as well as equality of rights, and efforts, must exist between Spirituality and Rationality, thereby avoiding antagonism, conflict, and even a secular or religious war, which will be more than innocuous, in fact, a war hopelessly lost since the beginning of times, simply because it aims to destroy what it seeks to save, the indivisible Human Nature. Undeniably, true mindfulness is the force able to broaden the enlightened Spiritual Dimension and curtail the random Rational Dimension. However, it is much more important to acknowledge the sleeping giant of Spirituality, which neither requires nor is capable of being created but is instead naturally revealed, comprehended, and enlightened.

The cause of the evolution of these models in the direction of greater depth suggests a move to address human exhaustion before a world of growing complexity, individualism, and materialism and with little connection and integration with Nature and Spirituality. It seems that humanity, thus far, has bet heavily on Rationality alone, in which social changes are evaluated according to the same rationale with little or no regard for Spirituality. However, the obvious social problems arising from this unilateral model require an urgent change of direction.

Some insights turned in precepts and then in guidelines, enabling the materialization of the model, which are: (i) the simplicity over complexity approach to design a model that just in two dimensions and five layers is able to synthesize how Rationality and Spirituality could come together to generate new and meaningful knowledge to the advancement of humanity; (ii) the vortex of energy formed by the central layer of Integrative Knowledge gravitationally attracting the outermost layers, generating a communal environment where collectivity, and not individuality, drives the knowledge development; (iii) the integrity and indivisibility of the individual—a unique and miraculous composition of body, mind, and spirit; (iv) the equality between the two dimensions of the model, where Rationality and Spirituality are presented in equilibrium, inseparable, and indissociable, in all human beings.

Then, the relevant contribution of the Integrative Knowledge Model for the advancement of knowledge in organizations can then be summarized as follows in the Ten Knowledge Enhancement Topics.

1. A reference for scholars, professionals, executives, and all other organizations' stakeholders committed to the necessary balance between spirituality and rationality in a quantitative and qualitative way along the development of a new knowledge, effectively put into action in the process of organizational change based in a consensus of these two dimensions rather than a prevalence of one over another.
2. Evidence that a new knowledge and, consequently, its precedented two dimensions know no boundaries and are relevant in all types of organizations regardless of their size, location, structure of capital and management, market insertion, and strategies.
3. An objective and effective simplification of the historical dimensions that have been and will ever be the source and the strength of human knowledge, allowing concentrated human efforts to be exerted on their formation, confluence, convergence, and synergy.
4. A devoted recognition that conflicting dimensions with stressed frontiers will not necessarily impede the development of a new knowledge, but bringing to light that this new knowledge will certainly have an equivalent imbalanced implementation that produces even more discomfort and stress to individuals with an obvious impact in their organizations.
5. A potential threshold in knowledge generation and development considering that other models differ significantly in dimensions and integrative concepts, making it almost impossible to establish a pattern of knowledge governance accepted by innumerous and diversified organizations, including academic institutions and faculties.
6. An opportunity to formulate future measurement tools to qualify and quantify new knowledge development adherence to the model presented and so to the expected

balance between spirituality and rationality in their support to make this development feasible and effective in individuals' integrative body, mind, and soul.

7. A milestone in establishing a definitive connection and integration between the vector rationality>spirituality>knowledge>action and all other efforts originated in individuals to make their lives worth living, their organizations worth working at, and their society worth being represented by them.
8. A clearer borderline for what may be considered true Knowledge for a steady advancement of humankind—its values, virtues, and creeds, its peace, happiness, and love sentiments, and its connection with Nature—to scientific and technological advancements deprived of meaning, wisdom, and spirituality, deprived of social justice, equality, ethics, and Oneness.
9. An expanding concept for Integrative Knowledge, embracing the integration of religion and science, spirituality and rationality, admitting as a resultant force knowledgeable actions that will move our organizations and, consequently, our society in a more sustainable and humanistic direction.
10. An Integrative Knowledge that reconciles Nature with human beings, their inner-self, and their inner-nature, able to ground relevant social transformations led by spirituality, in which the mindfulness movement is at its core, preserving the Oneness spirit transmitted through millennia by the Prophets.

The Integrative Knowledge Model recommends a balance of forces via the convergence of the Rational and Spiritual Vectors in the Integrative Knowledge Layer, thereby resulting in a vector for an integrative action; that is, a force for promoting social actions that make sense and leverage change for individuals—individuals who are whole, complete, integral, of sound body, mind, and spirit in both the Rational and Spiritual Dimensions.

On the one hand, ethics, understood as an extramural and global concept deeply and naturally embedded in individuals' wiser minds, will undoubtedly be inserted in this new organizational consciousness framework, helping to significantly expand the boundaries of knowledge and allowing it to form and consolidate in an integrative way, outwardly, making sense of an evolving and growing global consciousness.

On the other hand, the main fragility of the model relates to the difficulty inherent in spiritual practices in each layer of the Spiritual Dimension as well as the necessary openness to fair, transparent, and effective discussion of the proposals from both dimensions toward solutions for the organization's and society's main problems.

For future research, relevant aggregated value would come from the development of a broad, validated scale, capable of measuring how deeply integrative knowledge is embedded in individuals and, consequently, in the organization processes. Both the Spiritual and Rational Dimensions, considered separately, have had their validated scales applied in innumerous studies, notably those of Delaney (2005), Cacioppo and Petty (1982), and Cacioppo, Petty and Feng (1984). However, an Integrative Knowledge Scale is yet to be developed that could evaluate individuals' commitment to (then and now, in the present moment) gather, in a balanced way, the best of the two dimensions to make the right decisions and take the right actions in the most effective direction of the resultant Integrative Action Vector. This scale is indispensable for quantitative and mixed-method research.

In addition, it is essential to apply the model to practical reality through case studies with the purpose of (i) detailed characterization of the dimensions, the layers, and the behavior of the boundary and/or vectors, not only in existing projects (such as those exemplified), but also in innovative proposals; (ii) analysis of how the dimensions influence each other in the generation of the Integrative Knowledge and in the Integrative Action Vector; and (iii) evaluation and validation of the way in which the model can enhance the lives of individuals, communities, organizations, and society.

A number of interesting reflections regarding both the actual impact and the relevance of this Integrative Knowledge Model may arise from the propositions and strategic decisions made by organizations. The impact and relevance will be less significant as the Integrative Knowledge Model remains extraneous from the prevailing precepts leading the current model of knowledge generation and management in organizations. Conversely, they will be more significant as they promote a strategic change in this current model. That is, the Integrative Knowledge Model needs to be considered and tested in full so that changes can be implemented and evaluated considering new referential indicators that would reflect the efficacy of the design of new paths for individuals in their organizations. This will also avoid judging and evaluating these changes based on the precepts and indicators in force, which would make the change process highly conflicting, dissonant, and even ineffective. This is because human rationality overwhelmingly prevails over spirituality in the current model of knowledge, which is reinforced by a blind and obstinate "faith" in too rational and even not-so-purist scientific "discoveries" as well as in some of their pervasive ramifications in the field of applied technology.

In the current model, rationality judges and evaluates itself using self-generated parameters and indicators, which are taught in a tautological way through a mythology of reason unfathomable to human wisdom and spirituality. In this traditional model, spirituality, even when fading away, paradoxically, serves only to attenuate, catalyze, and cushion the negative and harmful impacts of its continuous and progressive implementation on human spirituality. Mysteriously, human beings are naturally holders of a divine soul that persistently distinguishes good from evil, happiness from anguish, love from hatred, hope from fear, and harmony from distress, that persistently attaches great importance to positive and inspiring feelings brought about by a greater comprehension and awareness of life—umbilically inserted into the placenta of human nature and into the nature of living beings. The simplest consumerism of spirituality for rationality, or a simpler submissiveness to rationality, will never be a solution to either the conflicts and sufferings experienced by individuals in organizations, to the utopian dichotomy between mind and spirit, between desiring and experiencing happiness, or to the obscure alienation and the indelible consequences of the dehumanization of individuals in their organizational and social functions. In a more emphatic and objective way, rationality simply does not know and will never guide individuals on the path toward the cessation of human suffering, while the simple attempt of rationality in instrumentalizing spirituality for their own benefit only masks the failure, fragility, and uselessness of the current model of human development.

In the proposed integrative model, everything happens in reverse. The supremacy of spirituality gives direction and energy to the generation of knowledge through a deeper and more universal language that is less inquisitive and more inspiring, less self-centered, and more insight-driven: the language of spirituality (Cherman and Azeredo, forthcoming). In the spirituality dimension—where dwell the most enlightened and virtuous sentiments of the human-divine soul, where dwell the nature of all sentient beings in perfect communion with all that is most sacred, with the sacred brilliance given to the mind and its rationality—predominates and prevails the energy and illumination emerging from the depths of wisdom and consciousness at all stages of knowledge generation, evenly integrated with the dimension of human rationality. In order to ensure the supremacy of spirituality, it is crucial to revive, reinforce, and develop an extensive and complex language of spirituality, which, ultimately, is the expression that gives life to everything and everyone, including the mind, with which it interacts through the language of rationality. With this integration, the language of rationality will lose its self-destructive component, the domination of subconscious forces of evil—which have been propagating genetically and mentally for uncountable generations—besides exposing to the light of spirituality the blind and malign deification of reason by reason itself. Humanity will gain direction and effectiveness in this search for an authentic knowledge aiming to advance the progress of humanity by distinctive and nobler parameters of evolution, distant from those unequal and unsustainable parameters of material growth and wealth accumulation, which dangerously flirt with the decay of the human soul and Nature itself.

Some questions can be raised in future research in order to promote deeper reflections regarding the dichotomy between the Spiritual and Rational Dimensions, as well as the necessary integration between them. These questions relate to:

1. Governability (of nations): Considering the predominance of the lay state and the humanist philosophy, which emerged from the growing absence or denial of God, would the presence of "integrative" spirituality make a difference? Furthermore, could it contribute in any way to the advancement of models of democracy that would bring to people of all nations greater equality, justice, peace, and happiness?
2. Sustainability (of the planet): The Rational Dimension fights with all its might to avoid its self-destruction, meanwhile trying, rationally, to defend the idea that the current model of progress is completely sustainable. Can paths taken by human beings toward truly sustainable progress, encompassing the balance of the human body and soul and the body and soul of all living beings, disregard "integrative" spirituality?
3. Integrity (of individuals): Human health seems to be increasingly dependent on both rationality and its creations, on science and its resulting technology. How can "integrative" spirituality act and contribute toward maintaining the health of the body and soul of human beings just as they are losing their ability to balance and preserve themselves, aggravated by the decay of the environment, natural resources, and their nutrients?
4. Spirituality (of humankind): Where does human spirituality go? Will humankind continue progressing amid this humanist eagerness, without prophets, spiritual leaders, Nature, and God, without any other dimension that can be comprehended beyond rationality? Will we continue to be guided by the false prophets of rationality, eminent—though suffered—scientists affected by the "Einstein Syndrome" (Cherman and Azeredo, forthcoming)? Are human beings condemned to live as slaves of rationality, being poorly nourished by it, while merely having their survival guaranteed?
5. Integrative education (of the world community): How can we promote a complete renewal of patterns of education towards new and more enlightened organizational and social paths? In a continuous but slow pace, the integration of spirituality with rationality can promote a new educational model, not only for students of all ages in future generations, but mainly for those who generate and teach knowledge (teachers, scholars, and professors). The language of spirituality not only needs to be developed much further but also needs to be taught and transmitted from the beginning of childhood, even from the moment a new human being is conceived. It is true that the (lay) State has been gradually assuming the task of educating our children, in an absolutely rational way, but would it not be up to the families, parents, grandparents, clerics, spiritual leaders, and even mindfulness teachers—all together—to educate them in spirituality, human divine nature, and Nature itself, which ultimately is the source of all virtues?

References

Ackoff RL (1989) From Data to Wisdom. In Ackoff RL (ed) *Ackoff's Best.* New York, NY: John Wiley & Sons, 170–172.

Ardelt M (2004) Wisdom as Expert Knowledge System: A Critical Review of A Contemporary Operationalization of an Ancient Concept. *Human Development* 47: 257–285.

Bakosh LS, Houlihan JL (2016) A Million Mindful Children. [Video File]. Wisdom 2.0 Conference. Available at: www.youtube.com/watch?v=yaQhfpaaddM.

Bateson G (1972) *Steps to an Ecology of Mind: Collected Essays in Anthropology, Psychiatry, Evolution, and Epistemology.* Chicago, IL: University of Chicago Press.

Bauman Z (2000) *Liquid Modernity.* London: John Wiley & Sons.

Bauman Z (2004) *Work, Consumerism and the New Poor.* Berkshire: McGraw-Hill Education.

Bauman Z (2005) *Liquid Life.* Cambridge, MA: Polity Press.

Bauman Z (2007) *Liquid Times: Living in an Age of Uncertainty.* Cambridge, MA: Polity Press.

Bierly PE, Kessler EH, Christensen EW (2000) Organizational Learning, Knowledge and Wisdom. *Journal of Organizational Change Management* 13: 595–618.

Birren JE, Fisher LM (1990) The Elements of Wisdom: Overview and Integration. In Sternberg RJ (ed) *Wisdom: Its Nature, Origins, and Development.* New York, NY: Cambridge University Press, 317–332.

Cacioppo JT, Petty RE (1982) The Need for Cognition. *Journal of Personality and Social Psychology* 42: 116–131.

Cacioppo JT, Petty RE, Feng KC (1984) The Efficient Assessment of Need for Cognition. *Journal of Personality Assessment* 48: 306–307.

Calás M, Smircich L (2003) Introduction: Spirituality, Management and Organization. *Organization* 10: 327–328.

CDC (Centers for Disease Control and Prevention) (2014) *Key Findings: Trends in the Parent-Report of Health Care Provider-Diagnosis and Medication Treatment for ADHD: United States, 2003—2011.* www.cdc.gov/ncbddd/adhd/features/key-findings-adhd72013.html. Accessed July, 29, 2016.

Cherman A, Azeredo FEM (2018) Mindfulness in the Context of Integrative Knowledge: Separating Science from the Hype. In Dihman S, Crossman J, Roberts G (eds) *The Palgrave Handbook of Workplace Spirituality and Fulfilment.* NY: Palgrave Macmillan, Cham, 211–235.

Cherman A, Azeredo FEM (2020) The Languages of Spirituality and Science: Two Fraternal Twins. In Dihman S (ed) *The Palgrave Handbook of Workplace Wellbeing.* NY: Palgrave Macmillan, Cham Online at .doi:10.1007/978-3-030-02470-3_17-1

Cherman A, Rocha-Pinto SR (2016) Valuing of Knowledge in Organizations: Conceptions of the Individuals at the Work Context. *Organizações & Sociedade* 23: 307–328.

Chia R, Holt R (2007) Wisdom as Learned Ignorance: Integrating East-West Perspectives. In Kessler EH, Bailey JR (eds) *Handbook of Organizational and Managerial Wisdom.* Los Angeles: Sage Publications, 505–526.

Delaney C (2005) The Spirituality Scale: Development and Psychometric Testing of a Holistic Instrument to Assess the Human Spiritual Dimension. *Journal of Holistic Nursing* 23: 145–167.

Dutton JE, Worline MC, Frost PJ, Lilius J (2006) Explaining Compassion Organizing. *Administrative Science Quarterly* 51: 59–96.

Einstein A (1978) *Essays in Humanism.* New York, NY: Philosophical Library.

Fromm E (1994) *On Being Human.* New York, NY: Continuum Publishing Company.

Fromm E (1995) *The Essential Fromm: Life between Having and Being.* New York, NY: Continuum.

Frost PJ (1999) Why Compassion Counts! *Journal of Management Inquiry* 8: 127–133.

GGSC (2016) *The Greater Good Science Center Studies the Psychology, Sociology, and Neuroscience of Well-Being, and Teaches Skills that Foster a Thriving, Resilient, and Compassionate Society.* Berkeley, CA: University of California.

Goleman D (2015) *A Force for Good: The Dalai Lama's Vision for Our World.* London: Bloomsbury Publishing.

Hays JM (2007) Dynamics of Organisational Wisdom. *Business Renaissance Quarterly* 2: 77–122.

Horrigan B, Lewis S, Abrams DI, Pechura C (2012) *Integrative Medicine in America: How Integrative Medicine Is Being Practiced in Clinical Centers across the United States.* Minneapolis, MN: The Bravewell Collaborative.

Jung CG (2006) *The Undiscovered Self: The Dilemma of the Individual in Modern Society.* New York, NY: Signet Psychology.

Kessler EH (2006) Organizational Wisdom: Human, Managerial, and Strategic Implications. *Group & Organization Management* 31: 296–299.

Kessler EH, Bailey JR (2007) *Handbook of Organizational and Managerial Wisdom*. Thousand Oaks, CA: Sage Publications.

Küpers W (2013) The Art of Practical Wisdom: Phenomenology of an Embodied, Wise Inter-Practice in Organisation and Leadership. In Küpers W, Pauleen DJ (eds) *A Handbook of Practical Wisdom: Leadership, Organization and Integral Business Practice*. London: Ashgate Gower, 19–45.

Lazar S (2016) The Lazar Lab of Neuroscience of Yoga and Meditation. Harvard University. http://scholar.harvard.edu/sara_lazar. Accessed July, 28, 2016.

Magee RV (2015) *The Way of ColorInsight: Understanding Race and Law Effectively through Mindfulness-Based Color Insight Practices*. Research Paper No. 2015-19, University of San Francisco Law.

Marshall N, Simpson B (2014) Learning Networks and the Practice of Wisdom. *Journal of Management Inquiry* 23: 421–432.

Neal J (2012) *Handbook of Faith and Spirituality in the Workplace: Emerging Research and Practice*. New York, NY: Springer Science & Business Media.

NHC (National Health Council) (2016) About Chronic Conditions. www.nationalhealthcouncil.org/newsroom/about-chronic-conditions. Accessed July, 28, 2016.

Nonaka I, Chia R, Holt R, Peltokorpi V (2014) Wisdom, Management and Organization. *Management Learning* 45: 640.

Nonaka I, Takeuchi H (1995) *The Knowledge-Creating Company: How Japanese Companies Create the Dynamics of Innovation*. New York, NY: Oxford University Press.

Piketty T (2014) *Capital in the Twenty-First Century*. Cambridge: Belknap Press.

Rowley J (2006a) What Do We Need to Know about Wisdom? *Management Decision* 44: 1246–1257.

Rowley J (2006b) Where Is the Wisdom that We Have Lost in Knowledge? *Journal of Documentation* 62: 251–270.

Rowley J (2007) The Wisdom Hierarchy: Representations of the DIKW Hierarchy. *Journal of Information Science* 33: 163–180.

Sennett R (1998) *The Corrosion of Character: The Personal Consequences of Work in the New Capitalism*. New York, NY: Norton.

Shotter J, Tsoukas H (2014) Performing Phronesis: On the Way to Engaged Judgment. *Management Learning* 45: 377–396.

Speckhardt R (2015) *Creating Change Through Humanism*. Washington, DC: Humanist Press.

Srivastva S, Cooperrider DL (1998) *Organizational Wisdom and Executive Courage*. San Francisco: Lexington Books.

Sternberg RJ (1990) *Wisdom: Its Nature, Origins, and Development*. Cambridge, MA: Cambridge University Press.

United Nations (2014) Climate Change 2014: Synthesis Report. www.ipcc.ch/report/ar5/syr/. Accessed July, 25, 2016.

Vago DR (2016) Contemplative Science Research Centers. http://davidvago.bwh.harvard.edu/mindfulness-resources/contemplative-science-research-centers/. Accessed July, 29, 2016.

Vogus TJ, Sutcliffe KM (2012) Organizational Mindfulness and Mindful Organizing: A Reconciliation and Path Forward. *Academy of Management Learning & Education* 11: 722–735.

Weick KE, Putnam T (2006) Organizing for Mindfulness: Eastern Wisdom and Western Knowledge. *Journal of Management Inquiry* 15: 275–287.

Weick KE, Sutcliffe KM (2006) Mindfulness and the Quality of Organizational Attention. *Organization Science* 17: 514–524.

Weick KE, Sutcliffe KM (2008) Information Overload Revisited. In Hodgkinson GP, Starbuck WH (eds) *The Oxford Handbook of Organizational Decision Making*. New York, NA: Oxford University Press, 56–75.

Wood S (2016) *After Rejecting Alternative Medicine, CHOP Gives Acupuncture a Shot*. Philly.com. June 29, Philadelphia Media Network, PBC.

Zaidman N, Goldstein-Gidoni O (2011) Spirituality as a Discarded Form of Organizational Wisdom: Field-Based Analysis. *Group & Organization Management* 36: 630–653.

24

MINDFULNESS-BASED INTERVENTIONS IN CONTEXT

A case study of managers' experiences and the role of the organizational environment

Lasse Lychnell

Introduction

A growing number of studies of mindfulness-based interventions (MBIs) at work show promising results related to both well-being and performance—for example, reduced work stress and anxiety and improved mood (Grover, Teo, Pick, & Roche, 2017; Manocha, Black, Sarris, & Stough, 2011); increased job satisfaction (Hülsheger, Alberts, Feinholdt, Lang, 2013); more positive relationships to opportunity recognition and proactive behavior (Ahlvik, 2019); and enhanced performance (Cleirigh & Greaney, 2015; Ostafin & Kassman, 2012; Reb, Narayanan, & Chaturvedi, 2014; Reb, Narayanan, & Ho, 2015). However, the development of mindfulness is a long and complex process, and studies on this topic usually focus solely on the early phase of preliminary concentration, in which outcomes are relatively superficial and primarily positive (Qiu & Rooney, 2017). As MBIs in organizations is a rapidly growing phenomenon (e.g., Hougaard, Carter, & Coutts, 2016; Tan, 2012), there is a need for longitudinal, qualitative studies from which we can learn more about how specific individuals experience the outcomes of an MBI over time and the role that the organizational environment plays in shaping these outcomes. In this chapter, I will explore these questions with a view to offering a broader understanding of the opportunities and challenges of MBIs in the workplace than traditional mindfulness research usually captures. I will do this by reporting on a case study of an MBI at a medium-sized Scandinavian company.

The structure of the chapter is as follows. While this section briefly addressed the possible outcomes of mindfulness in organizations, the next one will discuss how mindfulness is believed to work and some potential challenges in terms of its implementation in the workplace. I will then account for the method used, after which I will present the case study. The chapter will conclude with a discussion of the findings, avenues for future research, key takeaways, and questions for reflection.

How mindfulness works

While studies in the field of organizational behavior have contributed to our understanding of the possible work-related outcomes of MBIs, research in psychology and neuroscience has examined how mindfulness works at the individual level. Its core mechanism is believed to be *decentering*, which is a shift in experiential perspective that occurs when the individual steps back and examines the content of their own consciousness, rather than being absorbed by it. According to Bernstein et al. (2015), decentering entails three interrelated processes: *meta-awareness*, which is being aware of one's own experiences; *disidentification from internal experience*, which is the experience of internal states as separate from one's self; and *reduced reactivity to thought content*, which is a diminished propensity to react habitually to stimuli. As a result, mindfulness has the potential to restructure an individual's relationship with their thoughts, feelings, and sense of self (Qiu & Rooney, 2017). Consequently, the potential of MBIs in organizations appears to differ qualitatively from that of stress reduction and task performance and may facilitate *personal transformation*. A personal transformation typically entails moving from a self-centered view to having increased concern for the greater good, and this can occur because of a normal evolutionary process, unintentional consequences, or intentional interventions (Neal, 2018). Accordingly, individuals who move beyond the early phases of mindfulness may reach stages of self-transcendence and re-engagement, wherein they may experience greater assertiveness and a redefined life purpose (Qiu & Rooney, 2017).

Few empirical studies have investigated how MBIs in organizations contribute to rendering such shifts in individuals' experiential perspectives. However, a qualitative study by Shonin and Van Gordon (2015), using interpretative phenomenological analysis, reports that managers who participated in an MBI started to view work and life as parts of an inseparable whole and experienced improvements in job performance due to the development of a more present-moment-oriented working style and enhanced people management skills. Further, by developing an intuitive awareness and loosening their strong sense of "I," participants were able to broaden their perspectives, better align their work roles with corporate strategies, and respond to situations as they arise. Additionally, the participants experienced themselves as being involved in a continuous process of inner growth, rather than in a one-time intervention; consequently, the managers felt a strong sense of responsibility to also continue this open-ended journey themselves after the event.

Such developmental processes, by which one's sense of self may change, are, however, not without potential challenges. Qiu and Rooney (2017) suggested that mindfulness can cause a number of psychological problems, such as the unveiling of traumatic memories, depression caused by deceleration, existential meaninglessness, and anxiety caused by conflicts between mindfulness practice and corporate requirements. Glomb, Duffy, Bono, and Yang (2011) hypothesize that a more mindful employee may act contrary to the organization's interests, and Brendel (2015) noted that one of his coaching clients struggled with returning to task-oriented thinking after periods of meditating and that he used mindfulness to avoid confronting an underperforming worker. Additionally, Qiu and Rooney (2017) suggested that there are also risks at the organizational level; a shift in the organizational culture may be needed to support the change processes ignited by the MBI, and a misalignment of values may cause employees to leave the organization.

All in all, while reduced stress and increased job performance may be attributed to the early phases of mindfulness, deepened practice may provide a powerful tool for facilitating personal transformation over time. Such a journey may, however, put the individual in a situation in which they face challenges that are not only psychological but also related to the organizational environment.

Method

The purpose of this chapter is not to generalize from the unique case reported here but, rather, the opposite: to present a specific instance to highlight aspects that are typically overlooked in mainstream mindfulness research. A longitudinal single-case study provides a useful method for studying an MBI in an organization over time in greater depth than quantitative factor research typically allows (Van de Ven, 2007; Yin, 2009). The empirical material reported in this chapter was primarily generated using a clinical approach (Schein, 2001)—that is, a collaborative project with the dual aim of helping an organization and creating academic knowledge (Adler, Shani, & Styhre, 2004). I met the chief executive officer (CEO) of Theta, a medium-sized Scandinavian company, at a so-called "wisdom conference" and was later invited by the CEO for discussions regarding its journey to becoming a more conscious company. As a consequence, the CEO and I decided to conduct a collaborative research project in 2016 with the aim of better understanding the effects of a mandatory MBI on the partner group one and a half years prior. The collaborative project had two phases. In the first phase, I interviewed the company's seven partners and reported the results back in a focus group setting that included a joint discussion about avenues for continued development. In the second phase, I analyzed the project-generated material with the specific purpose of contributing to a broader understanding of MBIs in organizations than traditional mindfulness research usually captures. While the first phase was financed by the company, the second was not.

I conducted an in-depth, two-hour semi-structured interview with each of the seven partners, including the CEO, resulting in almost 300 pages of double-spaced transcripts. I also gathered material from preparatory meetings with the CEO, the two-hour concluding focus group, and a clinical group intervention in which two of the managers from Theta participated (c.f., Lychnell & Mårtensson, 2017).

The interviews centered on the experiential process that the partners underwent in relation to the MBI before, during, and after the event and concentrated on three focal points:

- How did the individual relate to the MBI?
- What outcomes did they experience for themselves and others?
- How did these outcomes manifest in situated action?

The interviews also addressed the content of the MBI in addition to the relevant organizational environment. Consequently, there was a significant overlap between the company's needs and my own research interest, although some questions were more focused on the assignment and others more targeted toward the research aims.

The empirical material was primarily coded and analyzed to identify the similarities and differences between participants' experiences. The analysis revealed close similarities related to the outcomes they experienced, but there were differences in the extent to which these outcomes were manifested in situated action. These differences possibly stemmed from how interviewees related to the MBI as a whole. Below, the accounts of three participants—Amy, Linda, and Chris—will be used to illustrate these similarities and differences. While these three individuals represent extreme cases, the other participants can be seen as lying somewhere in between, reflecting similarities and differences to a greater or lesser extent. Before presenting their journeys, I will introduce the case company, Theta, and offer background information on how the MBI came to be implemented. The section will end with an epilogue about how the organization continued to develop after the MBI.

The case study

Theta

Tom (CEO) and Hank (sales director) founded Theta in 1989 when they were in their twenties, and they are still the company's majority owners. While they initially focused on property and commercial premises-related financial and legal services, they began to grow the business in 2005 by including relocation and, more recently, change management projects in their operations. In 2016, Theta had 80 employees in two Scandinavian cities.

Theta is profitable and stable, and it is managed by the book with a clear mission, well-developed organizational routines, and information technology, all of which supports the business. For several consecutive years, the company has been ranked highly on "Great Places to Work," which is a European survey focused on employee satisfaction. Tom and Hank run the company with a team of five partners; however, Tom is the one who has started and sponsored many of the initiatives behind the company's development over the years.

Although Tom achieved almost all his materialistic goals around 2005, he was not happy. He consequently faced a so-called midlife crisis and started to search for a new meaning in his life. During this process, he learned about meditation and compassion, and he gradually began to change his life. He did not want to sell his share of the company to enable him to lead a contemplative life; rather, he was curious about integrating what he had learned about awareness and compassion into his active life as a businessman:

> There is something about doing business in a conscious way that excites me. Having the frame that the company should be profitable in both the short term and the long term. How can we maintain or increase our total output with less energy and greater harmony? This is probably all I'm longing for.

Beginning in 2011, Tom gradually incorporated a different set of exercises (e.g., Aikido and mindfulness) into company conferences. Influenced by the meditation courses he had attended, he started to become critical of the way in which the company was being run, and he became curious about how he could implement a new way of working. Subsequently, the company's vision, mission, and values were updated in a change initiative that engaged the whole organization.

The mindfulness-based intervention

In 2014, Tom suggested the introduction of a new company-wide course that was focused on mindfulness and emotional intelligence; it was being offered by a company that was certified by the Search Inside Yourself Institute. Soon thereafter, in August 2014, the MBI in question was presented at a company conference for all employees. A month later, the training for the partners and top managers began; it consisted of three mandatory two-day modules taken over five months, followed by voluntary and slightly shorter training for all employees in January and September 2015. While the first module centered on learning to observe oneself, the subsequent ones focused on observing oneself in relation to others and to the world.

After the MBI was completed, the company offered continued sessions with meditation and sharing every second week. The company-wide Monday morning meetings always started with a short meditation, and from time to time, different speakers were invited to give talks about mindfulness-related topics, such as self-leadership and vulnerability. Furthermore, the management team usually started its meetings with guided meditation or a moment of silence. While this resulted in an increased focus during the meetings, the main outcome was probably a more inclusive atmosphere that allowed the managers to show more of themselves at work. According to one participant:

> We are not there yet; we still use our phones, check our emails, and talk ... but we show more of who we really are. You can say that you are not feeling well, you may cry, and that's okay.

Amy's journey

Amy is a project manager who specializes in large and complex relocation projects. She enjoys focusing on delivering task results, explaining that she prefers to let other people handle the soft project-related issues. According to Amy, her interest in meditation and personal development was limited before the MBI, though she had practiced yoga for a few years. She added, "Not the last two years, though; I bought a dog instead of going to yoga." Nevertheless, she perceived herself as curious and open when the MBI was introduced, stating, "I was pretty open minded. I thought it was going to be interesting. I wouldn't have thought so 15 years ago." However, since the start of the MBI, she has been working on a demanding off-site project. She was, therefore, not able to participate in all the MBI sessions nor in the in-house activities implemented after the MBI. She nonetheless experienced positive outcomes from the process.

According to Amy, her major takeaways are an improved ability to step out of a situation and view it objectively, as well as an enhanced understanding of and respect for other people's motives. She explained this as follows:

> I think that I have become better at being objective [and] seeing things ... like "Yes, this is the way it is." It is probably because I am getting older and hopefully wiser ... not so categorical [and] subjective ... Even though you don't think the same, you respect each other. Well, I also thought so before, but much, much more [now] ... Practice makes me improve, and we did many good exercises in pairs and alone, including reflection, stepping out and viewing the situation, respecting that there are multiple ways, and understanding what drives people to choose different ways of [performing tasks].

Amy also emphasized that what she learned has had consequences for her well-being because she can now handle situations more constructively, even though it is difficult for her to find the right words:

> I have difficulties articulating it, but it's just this thing to take a step back and look—get some perspective on things—that calms this heated feeling in my belly and the stress that is always there, and then, when you do this, these situations rarely feel so serious.

Chris's journey

Chris was the vice president of Theta at the time of the MBI. He had the core responsibility of managing the operations, and all the team leaders reported directly to him. About five years earlier, he had faced serious life challenges when the stress of being the father of two small children was added to his responsibilities at Theta. He explained this:

> I was almost burned out due to anxiety about the kids and a lot at work. I remember that I was shoveling snow off the roof [and] I had to get down . . . I was shaking . . . I had spots all over my body . . . I called an ambulance. I was off work for three weeks. I got to see a psychologist and talked to him about my self-image. Since then, I have been searching [for meaning] . . . [I've] meditated, read a few books, [and practiced] mindfulness and yoga.

Chris's recovery was, to a large extent, supported by Tom, who connected him with the psychologist and later suggested that he take some personal development courses that he had taken himself. Consequently, when Theta decided to implement an MBI, this concept was not unfamiliar to Chris. He explained, "To me, the MBI was very welcomed. It was exactly what I was looking for, so I received it with open arms; I was very open to it." In effect, the MBI became an opportunity for him to continue down a path on which he had already embarked.

One of Chris's major learning points from the MBI was his increased understanding of himself and how his behavior affects other people. He stated:

> I have always been forward-thinking, organized, [and] perfect, but . . . kind of . . . impersonal [and] not open, [having] difficulties with intimate and trustful relationships [at work]. For me, the result has always been important . . . I have been very controlling, I think. I like control, follow-up, structure . . . like, "Fill in this sheet, and deliver numbers on the decimal." So, I would say that the difference lies in how I treat other people . . . I realize that I have a better understanding of the fact that other people need other things.

After the MBI, it became easier for Chris to perceive his colleagues' stress and empathize more with their situations, even though this remains difficult for him at times. He explained:

> I don't always succeed, of course. But I'm aware of this. I can see my new abilities, but I can't reach them. Then, I become irritated . . . grumpy. I'm losing energy, and everything becomes meaningless. It's interesting; I can see that it's only my own idea, but I can't break it.

Chris's journey began before the MBI started, and it continued after its completion with a search for meaning in his work. About two years after the MBI, he began to question his role as vice president, and he decided to step down while continuing to be a partner and a member of the management team. He explained, "Vice president on my card . . . it is not so important. What is problematic is that I do not know what is important." The need to be true to his emerging self had become greater than his need for intellectual certainty.

Linda's journey

Linda, the company's human resource manager, works primarily in the areas of recruitment, performance appraisals, and incentive structures, as well as the current organizational transformation. When she first heard about the MBI, she was both curious and excited. She thought, "Now, I will eventually learn to do a job task from the beginning to the end without losing my concentration or starting to do other things. Isn't this what mindfulness is all about? Staying focused?" However, since the implementation of the MBI, Linda has not really experienced any improvement in her focus in this regard. Rather, what she describes is a shift in attitude toward herself and her own behavior:

> I have understood that I actually don't want [that ability to focus]. It is not me. I like to be the way I am, and that has really boosted my self-esteem. I was judging myself for being mindless before.

In addition, she has started to acknowledge her intuition, which she previously downplayed.

While Linda experienced deep personal changes after the implementation of the MBI, she would not attribute them entirely to the intervention. Inspired by her husband, she later took an intensive course in personal development, which affected her deeply: "I remember that I was glad that we did the MBI, but the other course was overwhelming anyway . . . It started a lot of things in my head." This course delved much deeper in personal development and when she came back to work, she felt destabilized and experienced a period of crisis during which she questioned both her work and her marriage.

According to her, this change in attitude was facilitated by the realization of how much she had been influenced by events in her childhood—for example, when her math teacher made a dismissive comment about her intelligence, and Linda stopped believing in her ability to be good at math. This realization brought about a new understanding of not only herself but also of others. She explained that she was usually quick to judge others, thinking that there was something wrong with the people whom she did not like:

> It is some kind of change in my understanding of [other people] . . . it isn't that there's something wrong with them, but they trigger something in me. And when you understand that, you are freer to relate to what is. I guess all people do their best in all situations. Me too!

Epilogue

After the MBI, organizational transformation continued, and different consultants were invited to help transform the company into a more conscious organization. Tom has continued to pursue his goal of creating a more conscious company, and what started as short mindfulness exercises at conferences has evolved into value-based self-leadership and self-organization. Tom has often been far ahead of his management team in his thinking about the company's direction, and the change process has not been without friction and unwanted consequences.

Recently, a large change effort was initiated, whereby the managerial hierarchy and individually based incentive system were removed, and the company was organized according to self-management principles. While this development is outside the scope of the current chapter, it is important to note the continued path of development along lines that are consistent with the MBI.

Discussion

This chapter set out to explore how specific individuals experience the outcomes of an MBI over time and the role of the organizational environment in shaping these outcomes. In this section, I will discuss patterns identified in the case study. Taken together, these patterns contribute to a more practice-oriented and contextualized view of MBIs in organizations and help to shed light on the opportunities and challenges of MBIs in organizations.

MBIs as a way to develop new abilities

Mindfulness research is typically concerned with exploring the relationship between mindfulness and work-related factors. In this chapter, however, I present a perspective that is focused on how participants experienced the MBI and what they actually do in their everyday working lives. From this perspective, the central outcome of MBIs can be understood as the development of certain mindfulness-related abilities, such as perspective-taking, self-reflection, empathy, authentic functioning, and the meta-ability to be aware of how these are used. As these abilities manifest in situated action, work-related outcomes, such as improved communication, increased task performance, and reduced stress, may surface. While further research is needed to more thoroughly identify and systematize these abilities, I will expand on those that were revealed in the three accounts.

(1) Perspective-taking. The ability to take a step back and view people and situations from a different perspective may be one of the most commonly mentioned abilities among the participants. For example, Amy stated that she is able to see situations more objectively and create distance between a situation and herself. This aligns with previously reported outcomes, such as improved cognitive capacity (Kane et al., 2007) and cognitive flexibility (Moore & Malinowski, 2009). Amy explained that this ability helps her to reduce stress and remain strong in challenging situations. She also stated that it has affected her well-being positively.

(2) Self-reflection. Many of the participants displayed a considerable capacity to reflect on and learn about themselves, as well as a willingness to share more of who they are with their colleagues. When they learned more about themselves, the way in which they viewed others also changed. When Linda realized that events in her childhood had greatly affected her, she realized that this is true for all people. Further, she understood how quickly she had previously judged other people and that her judgments had essentially been about herself and not them. Chris, in turn, became aware of the extent to which he wanted to be in control, as well as how this negatively affected his work relationships. Linda's and Chris's accounts suggest that self-reflection is closely connected to empathy.

(3) Empathy. All three participants emphasized that they have become better at understanding other people and respecting that there are multiple ways to handle situations.

This echoes Taylor et al.'s (2016) finding that various aspects of emotion regulation and prosocial tendencies changed as a function of the mindfulness training and helped participants to reduce their stress levels. In this way, the abilities presented here reflect the three kinds of empathy suggested by Goleman (2013): cognitive empathy, emotional empathy, and empathic concern.

(4) Authentic functioning. Chris, who was already focused on inner growth from the beginning, started to question his career path, eventually vacating the role of vice president to find new ways of contributing to the organization that were more aligned with his intrinsic driving force—authentic functioning (Wood, Linley, Maltby, Baliousis, & Joseph, 2008). Similarly, Linda felt empowered when she stopped judging herself for relying extensively on her intuition and instead embraced the benefits of this quality. This observation is supported by research showing that authentic functioning is a mediator between mindfulness and other work-related outcomes (Ahlvik, 2019; Leroy, Anseel, Dimitrova, & Sels, 2013).

(5) The meta-ability. In addition to the three abilities mentioned above, the empirical material also provides examples of the meta-ability to become aware of situations in which one is failing to use one's abilities. This goes back to the mechanism of meta-awareness, which is foundational for developing mindfulness (Bernstein et al., 2015) but also seems necessary for allowing abilities developed through the MBI to manifest in situated practice.

The practical and spiritual aspects of MBIs

While the case study shows that similar abilities were developed among different individuals, the extent to which they were developed and applied in situated action varied. Here, I will discuss this in terms of how the participants relate to two different aspects of the MBI: the *practical* and the *spiritual.*

From the practical side, the MBI was viewed as a means to an end—for example, as a way to become better at focusing on one task at a time, reducing stress, and making better decisions. Examples of this were provided by all the participants. While the practical side is atomistic and outcome-oriented, the spiritual side is holistic and process-oriented. From the spiritual perspective, the MBI was seen as a stepping-stone on a continuous path of inner growth that extends beyond the intervention and the workplace. For example, based on their accounts, Chris and Linda were able to easily switch between the domains of their work and private lives. They openly shared the difficulties they have faced privately and how these related to their situations at work. For them, inner growth is about *finding more constructive ways of relating to life as a whole*, by viewing work and private life as two aspects of an inseparable whole. An individual who focuses primarily on the practical aspect of the MBI has probably not reached the latter stages of self-transcendence and re-engagement suggested by Qiu and Rooney (2017).

While it is easy to see the practical and spiritual aspects as two mutually exclusive elements, evidence from the case study suggests that they are not. Despite their commitment to inner growth, Chris and Linda also continue to be committed to the organization. They are taking their lived experiences seriously, looking at their own reactions from a distance, and seeking to respond according to the needs of the situation, rather than following unexamined impulses. Chris and Linda display an attitude that encompasses *both* the spiritual and the practical, but the practical is seen through a spiritual lens. From this perspective, Amy's account can be interpreted as evidence that she rather sees spirituality through a practical lens; the spiritual aspect of the MBI may be beneficial because it can help her to achieve concrete outcomes but not necessarily to grow as a person.

The case study results also suggest that the capacity to engage with the spiritual aspect of the MBI is closely connected to the individual's personal transformation. In accordance with Neal (2018), the case study substantiates that personal transformation can be triggered in different ways. Both Chris and Linda demonstrated a *disruptive* path, triggered by life-changing events that enhanced their spiritual development. Amy also referred to a process of personal transformation, but more so in terms of an *evolutionary* and much slower process, when speaking about "getting older and hopefully wiser."

These results represent an invitation to think about the spiritual and the practical as two fundamental aspects of life, because as human beings, we are always on a path to inner development, and there will always be practical situations to handle in our everyday working lives. While we can downplay the importance of either side, both will continue to exist. The accounts provided by Chris and Linda suggest that openness to the spiritual aspect of the MBI may enhance and deepen the outcomes of the intervention, because it bridges the inside with the outside. In this way, MBIs may provide openings for more humanistic values to sprout in a world that is typically dominated by mechanistic thought and short-term goals (e.g., Purser & Milillo, 2014). This may have implications for future research, as it may shed light on how and why different individuals develop different kinds of outcomes as a result of an MBI.

Ways in which the organizational environment may be supportive

So far, the analysis has been at the individual level. However, the reported findings suggest that it is difficult to make sense of how the outcomes of the MBI are manifested in situated action without reference to the organizational environment. The following section suggests four themes that were recognized as supporting the implementation of the MBI at Theta.

(1) Authentic top management support. The CEO, equally a founder and majority owner, had undergone a challenging life situation and a personal transformation. The interviews revealed that when the partners saw how he had changed—he had become more interested in people and kinder to himself—they became curious. Soon thereafter, some of the partners, including Hank, embarked on their own developmental journeys. Accordingly, the MBI did not begin with words on a PowerPoint presentation; rather, it was already anchored in the participants' own experiences of Tom's behavior. Consequently, the MBI had strong top management support in terms of agenda-setting, time allocation, and finances, but, above all, it was embodied by the CEO.

(2) Alignment between the MBI and the organization's development. The MBI was part of an emerging organizational transformation that could be seen in part as an extension of the CEO's personal journey. This linkage helped legitimize the MBI and connect it to changes in the company's vision, mission, and values, bringing them into closer alignment with mindfulness, compassion, and self-leadership. Such an initiative may mitigate the risk that, during MBIs, the participants will develop new values that do not align with those of the organization (Qiu & Rooney, 2017).

(3) Stable organizational environment. The fact that the company was small, healthy, and well managed meant that there was actually space for this relatively substantial and radical intervention. The CEO argued that the company could afford a year with lower profits as a consequence of the intervention, although this never occurred. To some extent this goes

against the common suggestion that sense of urgency is necessary to create readiness for change (c.f., Kotter, 1996) and points toward a radically different way of managing change: starting with the expansion of the individuals' consciousness and then transforming the organization based on a new mindset that is better adapted to the challenges at hand.

(4) Holding environment at work. A key to allowing the new abilities to manifest in situated action was the creation of a holding environment, that is, a support system in which the individuals' experiences may be recognized, critically examined, and reframed (c.f., Baron & Cayer, 2011). One example of this is the management team meetings in which the partners could be themselves in the midst of a workday. Furthermore, several middle-aged partners underwent personal transformations before, during, and after the MBI and received beneficial support from the organization—for example, seeing a psychologist, changing work tasks, and experiencing a deep understanding from their peers. Some of the partners attributed this to the personal transformation that the CEO underwent. The question of whether it is the job of organizations to start deep personal transformation processes and support individuals who are facing difficulties is an ethical one that has no easy answer (Qiu & Rooney, 2017). If, however, we accept that personal transformations happen in life, the organization can then be seen as a site that welcomes and supports them as they occur. Consequently, the MBI could be a way to create a space that encourages individuals to open up and show more of themselves at work (c.f., Kegan, Lahey, Fleming, Miller, 2014). As suggested above, this could help them to embrace the spiritual aspect of MBIs, which would, in turn, allow more humanistic values to spread throughout the organization.

In sum, incorporating the organizational environment contributes to a more contextualized understanding of the MBI, which traditional mindfulness research that is focused on measuring outcomes would miss. Such an understanding may be crucial to the creation of beneficial conditions that enable MBIs to develop desired outcomes and mitigate ethical risks (Qiu & Rooney, 2017). While it is impossible to generalize from this case study, it reveals the existence of a complex relationship between the abilities developed through the implementation of the MBI, the individual's personal transformation, and the organizational environment. This relationship should be more closely examined by researchers in the future. To gain a more in-depth understanding of the processes by which both intended and unintended consequences are shaped, future longitudinal studies might apply a process perspective (c.f., Langley & Tsoukas, 2010), focusing on the interplay between the MBI and the organizational environment and, from an organizational point of view, the interplay between the development of individuals and that of the organization.

Lessons learned for managers

What can a manager who wants to implement an MBI learn from this case? Here, I will briefly outline the main lessons learned.

- The major outcome of the MBI is seen here as the development of new mindfulness-related abilities, such as perspective-taking, self-reflection, empathy, authentic functioning, and the meta-ability to see how the other abilities are used.
- When these abilities manifest in situated action at work, results such as improved communication, reduced stress, and increased performance may occur. Thus, such results are not caused by mindfulness; rather, they occur when individuals apply what they have learned in their everyday working lives.

- For the new abilities to be applied to a significant extent, a favorable organizational environment, which includes authentic top management support, a strong link to the organization's development, a stable organizational environment, and a holding environment at work, is required.
- Individuals who embrace both the practical and spiritual aspects of the MBI are likely to experience more benefits from the intervention. This, in turn, makes it more likely for the humanistic values induced by the MBI to spread throughout the organization.

Reflective questions for managers

For managers who are considering implementing an MBI to achieve organizational outcomes, the following questions may be a helpful starting point for reflecting on some crucial characteristics of its implementation.

- What do I want to achieve by implementing the MBI?
- Does what I want to achieve align with the way in which the organization is developing?
- Is there strong and authentic top management support?
- In what ways can I help participants to embrace both the practical and the spiritual aspects of the MBI?
- Can I provide a holding environment that may help participants to integrate what they have learned into their everyday working lives?

References

Adler, N., Shani, A. B., & Styhre, A. (Eds.). (2004). *Collaborative research in organizations: Foundations for learning, change, and theoretical development.* Thousand Oaks, CA: Sage Publications Inc.

Ahlvik, C. (2019). *The power of awareness: Unlocking the potential of mindfulness in organizations.* Doctoral dissertation, Hanken School of Economics. Helsinki, Finland.

Baron, C., & Cayer, M. (2011). Fostering post-conventional consciousness in leaders: Why and how? *Journal of Management Development, 30*(4), 344–365.

Bernstein, A., Hadash, Y., Lichtash, Y., Tanay, G., Shepherd, K., & Fresco, D. M. (2015). Decentering and related constructs: A critical review and metacognitive processes model. *Perspectives on Psychological Science, 10*(5), 599–617.

Brendel, D. (2015). There are risks to mindfulness at work. *Harvard Business Review.* (February).

Cleirigh, D. O., & Greaney, J. (2015). Mindfulness and group performance: An exploratory investigation into the effects of brief mindfulness intervention on group task performance. *Mindfulness, 6*(3), 601–609.

Glomb, T. M., Duffy, M. K., Bono, J. E., & Yang, T. (2011). Mindfulness at work. In M. R. Buckely, J. R. B. Halbesleben, & A. R. Wheeler (Eds.), *Research in personnel and human resources management* (Vol. *30*, p. 115). Bingley, UK: Emerald.

Goleman, D. (2013). The focused leader. *Harvard Business Review, 91*(12), 51–60.

Grover, S. L., Teo, S. T. T., Pick, D., & Roche, M. (2017). Mindfulness as a personal resource to reduce work stress in the job demands–resources model. *Stress and Health, 33*(4), 426–436. doi:10.1002/smi.2726

Hougaard, R., Carter, J., & Coutts, G. (2016). *One second ahead: Enhance your performance at work with mindfulness.* New York: Palgrave Macmillan.

Hülsheger, U. R., Alberts, H. J. E. M., Feinholdt, A., & Lang, J. W. B. (2013). Benefits of mindfulness at work: The role of mindfulness in emotion regulation, emotional exhaustion, and job satisfaction. *Journal of Applied Psychology, 98*(2), 310.

Kane, M. J., Brown, L. H., McVay, J. C., Silvia, P. J., Myin-Germeys, I., & Kwapil, T. R. (2007). For whom the mind wanders, and when: An experience-sampling study of working memory and executive control in daily life. *Psychological Science, 18*(7), 614–621.

Kegan, R., Lahey, L., Fleming, A., & Miller, M. (2014). Making business personal. *Harvard Business Review* (April).

Kotter, J. P. (1996). *Leading change.* Boston, MA: Harvard Business School Press.

Langley, A., & Tsoukas, H. (2010). Introducing "perspectives on process organization studies.". In T. Hernes & S. Maitlis (Eds.), *Process, sensemaking & organizing* (Vol. 1, pp. 1–26). New York, NY: Oxford University Press.

Leroy, H., Anseel, F., Dimitrova, N. G., & Sels, L. (2013). Mindfulness, authentic functioning, and work engagement: A growth modeling approach. *Journal of Vocational Behavior, 82*(3), 238–247.

Lychnell, L., & Mårtensson, P. (2017). Straight from the heart: A clinical group intervention to research management spirituality. *Management Research Review, 40*(8), 870–889. doi:10.1108/MRR-05-2016-0128

Manocha, R., Black, D., Sarris, J., & Stough, C. (2011). A randomized, controlled trial of meditation for work stress, anxiety and depressed mood in full-time workers. *Evidence-Based Complementary and Alternative Medicine, 2011*, 8. doi:10.1155/2011/960583

Moore, A. W., & Malinowski, P. (2009). Meditation, mindfulness and cognitive flexibility. *Consciousness and Cognition, 18*(1), 176–186.

Neal, J. (2018). An overview of the field of transformation. In *Handbook of personal and organizational transformation* (pp. 3–46). New York: Springer.

Ostafin, B. D., & Kassman, K. T. (2012). Stepping out of history: Mindfulness improves insight problem solving. *Consciousness and Cognition, 21*(2), 1031–1036.

Purser, R. E., & Milillo, J. (2014). Mindfulness revisited: A Buddhist-based conceptualization. *Journal of Management Inquiry, 24*(1), 3–24.

Qiu, J. X., & Rooney, D. (2017). Addressing unintended ethical challenges of workplace mindfulness: A four-stage mindfulness development model. *Journal of Business Ethics, 157*, 1–16.

Reb, J., Narayanan, J., & Chaturvedi, S. (2014). Leading mindfully: Two studies on the influence of supervisor trait mindfulness on employee well-being and performance. *Mindfulness, 5*(1), 36–45.

Reb, J., Narayanan, J., & Ho, Z. W. (2015). Mindfulness at work: Antecedents and consequences of employee awareness and absent-mindedness. *Mindfulness, 6*(1), 111–122.

Schein, E. H. (2001). Clinical inquiry/research. In P. Reason & H. Bradbury (Eds.), *Handbook of action research: Participative inquiry and practice* (pp. 228–237). London: Sage Publishing.

Shonin, E., & Van Gordon, W. (2015). Managers' experiences of meditation awareness training. *Mindfulness, 6*(4), 899–909. doi:10.1007/s12671-014-0334-y

Tan, C.-M. (2012). *Search inside yourself: The unexpected path to achieving success, happiness (and world peace).* New York, NY: HarperCollins.

Taylor, C., Harrison, J., Haimovitz, K., Oberle, E., Thomson, K., Schonert-Reichl, K., & Roeser, R. W. (2016). Examining ways that a mindfulness-based intervention reduces stress in public school teachers: A mixed-methods study. *Mindfulness*, 7(1), 115–129. doi:10.1007/s12671-015-0425-4

Van de Ven, A. H. (2007). *Engaged scholarship: A guide for organizational and social research.* Oxford, NY: Oxford University Press.

Wood, A. M., Linley, P. A., Maltby, J., Baliousis, M., & Joseph, S. (2008). The authentic personality: A theoretical and empirical conceptualization and the development of the authenticity scale. *Journal of Counseling Psychology, 55*, 385–399.

Yin, R. K. (2009). *Case study research: Design and methods.* Beverly Hills, CA: Sage Publications.

PART V

Creative and novel approaches to mindfulness

25

NON-RELIGIOUS MINDFULNESS, PHENOMENOLOGY, AND INTERSUBJECTIVITY

Olga Louchakova-Schwartz

Introduction

In its origin, mindfulness is a religious practice. While mindfulness became best known by association with early Theravada Buddhism, it is not limited to Buddhism: various forms of mindfulness appear in Christian mysticism under the names of "sobriety," "watchfulness," "wakefulness," "guarding of the mind" (of the heart, of senses, etc.), and in Sufism, under the name "sobriety." Indian Vedanta uses differentiation between the seer and the seen, which is similar to the practice of mindfulness. Greek Stoics, shamans, Tantric yogis, and followers of G. Gurdjieff, to name a few, also used different forms of mindfulness. The key in such practices is switching the usual absorption in the flow of experience to witnessing this flow. Witnessing opens a gateway into deeper layers of consciousness (cf. Costello, 2015). Under consciousness, I mean neither the function of the brain, nor awareness per se, nor "subtle energy," nor some kind of subtle substance, but simply one's lived-through experience.

In religions, all practices of mindfulness ultimately have religious goals. Most often, the goal is this or that form of immortality, e.g., nirvana in Theravada Buddhism, *theosis* (God-Union) in Christian Hesychasm, etc. Of course, one cannot know whether one will be indeed immortal. The only way traditions can make a judgment is based on the quality of experience: they offer criteria to which experience must conform if one were to reach an enlightened state. It can be equanimity in Buddhism, or a loss of fear in Vedanta, etc. Of course, internal practice is not the only means to change experience: symbols, chants, philosophy, rituals, texts, community, art, ethical and behavioral observances, all shape the expected change. Stripped of religious contexts of practice, mindfulness changes experience as well, but as I show in this chapter, the change goes in a different direction. Understanding experience "helps to explain how people really think, feel, and behave—that is, what motivates them to act apart from concern for the easily forgettable parameter of 'efficiency'" (Walden, 2017, from the back cover). In this chapter, I investigate how exactly subjectively lived experience is modified by the practice of non-religious mindfulness, as distinct from the religious one. To do so, I will describe experience of mindfulness in terms of philosophical categories provided by phenomenology.

First, I explain why I use phenomenology (in Section 1, Why Phenomenology?). Then I show the difference in the regions of consciousness targeted by religious and non-religious mindfulness (Section 1 and Section 2, Mindfulness and the Spheres of Experience respectively). While religious mindfulness works predominantly with the psychological sphere, the practice of non-religious mindfulness over a long run accesses the sphere of intersubjectivity. I will then explain what intersubjectivity is, and how consciousness puts it together (Section 3, Constitution of Intersubjectivity). Having laid the ground for the analysis of intersubjectivity, I will then add another necessary set of concepts regarding the internal architectonics of consciousness. Then, I will use these concepts to explain how non-religious mindfulness reveals the deep layers of consciousness, including the input of other people (Section 4, The Internal Architectonics of Consciousness). In the final Section, 5, I will describe concrete modifications of experience in non-religious mindfulness.

1. Why phenomenology?

Phenomenology is a scientific approach by which one can research experience without losing its lived, first-person character (Davidsen, 2013; Neisser, 1959). While each experience is individual and unique, its individual character develops around generalizable structures of consciousness. These structures play in phenomenology the same role as anatomy or physiology play in medicine by providing a generalizable structural foundation of individual health or disease. Phenomenology discovered that elusive, messy, and always changing human experience has a generalizable structural foundation. If one knows this phenomenological foundation, one can describe and understand individual forms of experience, e.g., in non-religious mindfulness.

Philosophical concepts of phenomenology also serve as research tools (cf. O'Rourke, 2018). While natural science examines physical objects by means of physical objects, e.g., the brain by means of encephalography or distant stars by means of telescopes, phenomenology examines concrete meanings by means of theoretical meanings. For example, in his early work *Logical Investigations* (2001), the founder of phenomenology Edmund Husserl demonstrated that consciousness can be analyzed by the theory of wholes and parts. This allows me to approach consciousness of mindfulness as a whole which consists of different parts (spheres of experience); I also use other phenomenological tools, such as the theory of intentionality, ideas related to passive syntheses, etc.

Similarly to how different scientific methodologies serve different purposes, there are different kinds of phenomenology. The most abstract of them all, transcendental phenomenological philosophy, helps understand how it is possible for the human subject to adequately experience the external world and to have an ongoing flow of internal experience and reasoning.

A second set of concepts, the theory of intentionality, is less abstract: it describes the structural organization of consciousness (as mentioned above). Phenomenology suggests consciousness to be not a thing, but a special kind of relationship. These relationships are characterized by intentionality. Being conscious means being aware of something, in other words, intending on and grasping something other than the self. These relationships are not between something and something, e.g., a large vs. a small cup of tea, or a subject (source) of intention and an object of it. Rather, it is a characterization of relationships per se. Yet, despite seeming very abstract, this is a description of exactly what one means by saying "consciousness." This descriptive and generalizable concept of intentionality doesn't include the idea of its origin because its origin is impossible to locate. For example, the phenomenological philosopher Michel Henry (2008, 2016) argued that intentionality, consciousness, or reason arise in the alive human body. Nevertheless, he could not describe exactly how the body gives rise to intentionality. Intentionality seems to be directed from the body-self to the world; but it can also be reversed. If one examines actual self-awareness as a possible source of intentionality, self-awareness already intends on itself, i.e., already includes intentionality. Another "would be" possible source of intentionality, the pure subjectivity of awareness, is, first, similarly intending on itself, and second, takes different forms (as mental subjectivity, bodily subjectivity, etc.). Hence, Husserl (2001, pp. 91–93) concluded that the empirical ego-pole of intentionality is in itself a composite consisting of different intentionalities and can change dependent on the form of experience.

The only invariable feature of experience is that it is always *about* something, i.e., consists of meaning. Natorp (cited by Husserl, 1970, p. 103), a neo-Kantian philosopher close to phenomenology, famously stated: "if anyone can catch his consciousness in anything else than the existence of a content for him, I am unable to follow him." Having awareness of the content, i.e., intentionality, characterizes each and every experience; without intentionality, experience would not be possible.

The phenomenological theory of intentionality proved to be very useful for detailed describing and differentiating between various forms of experience. Intentionality implies not only awareness of the objects of knowledge (e.g., my awareness of this computer screen, of my thoughts at the moment, of the words I use to make this description, etc.), but also a particular quality in this awareness, such as judgment, expression, doubt, certainty, etc. Different classes of intentionality have different "lived through" characteristics. In every act of meaning-making, many intentionalities of different qualities and contents come together in a unity; and the unities of meaning come together in the empirical unity of one's consciousness.

To discern the internal scaffolding of experience, one uses the so-called phenomenological method. To analyze intentionality, one has to interrupt the usual attitude towards experience as something happening inside one's head in response to the real physical world. Then, experience becomes viewed as the contents of consciousness, i.e., the field of presentations: instead of working behind the scenes, consciousness now comes up front and can be examined. The contents of consciousness remain the same as before, i.e., includes awareness of the world and one's "internal" experience, but what is meant by "experience" has changed: it becomes visible that experience consists of different regions with distinct characteristics, such as, e.g., the region of the world, of internal life, etc.

After this initial phenomenological reduction, other reductions can be used. In our concern, which is the analysis of non-religious mindfulness, reductions towards the sphere of ownness and reduction towards the sphere of intersubjectivity help to recognize that experience has hidden structures which contain a massive input from others (Sections 3, 4, and 5). Another aspect of the method are imaginal variations: one determines which intentionalities can, and which cannot, be taken away without losing this concrete form of experience. In this chapter, the methodological part is just mentioned but not reported in detail; the focus is on the findings.

For the reader less familiar with phenomenology, it can be helpful to describe the phenomenological method as a series of mental experiments which clarify the contents of experience. To give an example: a recent report by Ratnayake (2019) suggests that Buddhist mindfulness causes a loss of interest in life, and confusion regarding one's feelings and thoughts. But the report doesn't make it clear whether the reason for these effects is Buddhist philosophy, or whether the reason if the mindfulness practice per se. Would a practice of non-religious mindfulness produce the same result? Since it can be meaning which causes the problem, it would be difficult to design a real physical experiment for testing this fact. But understanding the experience of the loss of interest in life by means of imaginal variations would help to determine if the latter is linked to Buddhist philosophy; and the further phenomenological analysis of feelings can show which are one's own, and which are internalized from others (cf. Sections 3–5 below).

As a philosophy of consciousness, phenomenology should not be confused with Buddhism or Vedanta. The purpose in phenomenology is not to make one enlightened or immortal, but to understand creation of meaning. Experience consists of meaning; in the first place, this meaning is pre-reflective, simply as our knowledge of the world. This pre-reflective meaning is correlated with how the world is in reality, and meaning is itself real. There is also the meaning of experience, i.e., the ways one interprets things. The purpose of phenomenology is to understand both pre-reflective and reflective meaning, both in general and in specific experience, e.g., in the practice of mindfulness. Mentioned above, different kinds of phenomenology created a phenomenological map of consciousness specifically for such purposes.

Buddhism also provides a map of consciousness, but this map cannot be used to understand the meaning which constitutes experience. According to Buddhism (and Advaita Vedanta), the world is an illusion. Thereby, experience is also an illusion, and it would make no sense to investigate creation of something which doesn't really exist. If one wants to know the truth, one should get rid of illusion and attain a content-free mind, i.e., attain nirvana. Hence, the maps of consciousness in Buddhism are simple inventories of deposited impressions. But for phenomenology, an idea of content-free mind makes no sense. The mind, i.e., consciousness, is a living system of real relationships, with complex internal architectonics which makes it into a vehicle of knowledge of the real world. This approach creates a completely different map. Unlike the Buddhist map, phenomenology doesn't help eliminating the content of consciousness: phenomenology aims at quite the opposite, which is revealing the hidden processes in the constitution of this content.

Mindfulness is one of the powerful practices of Buddhism, and Buddhism is a religion. Hence, religious mindfulness practice is tailored to a soteriological, salvatory religious goal. In a secular setting, it loses its metaphysical orientation. This means it stops functioning in the same way as it does within Buddhism. In fact, people who practice non-religious mindfulness for the benefit of self-regulation, when interviewed about their attitudes to Buddhism, distance themselves from Buddhism quite vigorously and insist on the secular, non-spiritual, and non-Buddhist character of their practice. Their experience doesn't progress along the lines of canonical Buddhist psychology. Quite differently, consistent mindfulness sans religious ideation is historically novel and is not at all a described or researched form of experience. One can expect that in such a practice, where attention goes and what it brings to the surface will be guided not by an eschatological intent but by the self-organizing living consciousness itself, in its ongoing coordination with the real world. Our purpose here is not to compare Buddhism and phenomenology, but to clarify a particular form of experience, of non-religious mindfulness, by means of phenomenology.

2. Mindfulness and the spheres of experience

The Buddhist concern with enlightenment took the practice in the direction of individual mastery. One goes to solitary retreats, minimizes the diversity and intensity of relationships with others, and increases the introspective focus. Mindfulness is personal: even if, out of compassion, one delays individual nirvana to be around until everybody catches up (e.g., follows the idea of Boddhisattva), the practice of mindfulness is still about one's internal life, individual responses, habits, memories, and fantasies. Other practices, such as, e.g., *metta*-loving kindness in Theravada, or *Tnoglen* in Vajrayana Buddhism, address relationships with others, but the focus of attention will nevertheless still be on the internal psychological aspects of these relationships.

By contrast, if direction of mindfulness is not predetermined by an individual metaphysical agenda, the practice reaches into one's consciousness more deeply and broadly than merely one's psychological province of meaning. What are "provinces"? Introduced by Edmund Husserl's follower, philosopher Alfred Schutz, the so-called finite province of meaning refers to an area of one's lifeworld (= the world of meaning, another phenomenological term) in which meaning is interconnected, and altogether different from the neighborhood province. Being personal doesn't necessarily mean psychologically personal: for example, one's knowledge of mathematics or skills of shoe-making are both personal but not psychological. Non-psychological provinces vastly exceed the dimension of one's internal life, and there is no reason why attentional training should not reach this expanse (cf. Kozhevnikov, Louchakova, Josipovic & Motes, 2009, for the effects of Buddhist meditation which are not just psychological). Phenomenology further differentiates between the sphere of one's ownness (everything "mine," or personal), the sphere of intersubjectivity which refers to other people (beings) and the world. Others show up in our consciousness not simply as images of things called people, but as fully fleshed, conscious, alive beings endowed with their own conscious subjectivity and internal life (see the sphere of intersubjectivity in Figure 25.1).

There is no reason why the sphere of intersubjectivity should not be affected by non-religious mindfulness. In turn, the sphere of intersubjectivity donates its content to the sphere of ownness, including the psychological province. Our subjectively lived experience

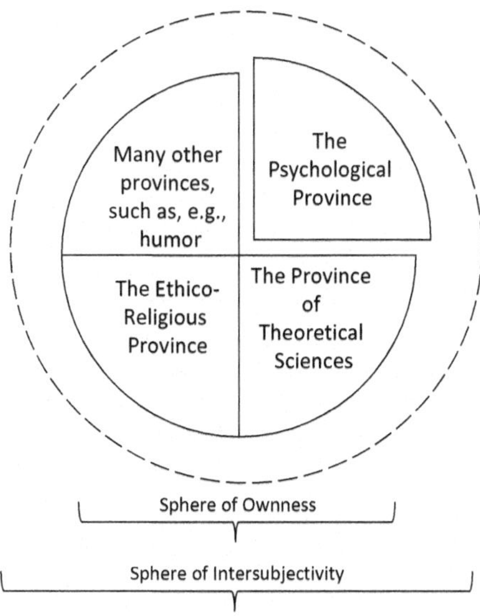

Figure 25.1 The sphere of intersubjectivity and the sphere of ownness with finite provinces of meaning (based on Barber, 2017; Husserl, 1993)

influences others, and the reverse is also true: people "light up" around a happy person, in contrast with feeling depleted around somebody who doesn't feel good. And isn't it that successful leadership consists exactly in a somewhat mysterious attunement to the other, others, and the world which we inhabit together? The sphere of ownership and the sphere of intersubjectivity are interrelated and interpenetrating, and the practice of non-religious mindfulness affects both of them.

3. Constitution of intersubjectivity

Ordinarily, consciousness seems to be "inside" one's head, whereas other people appear to be "outside." The change of attitude by means of phenomenological reduction causes one to recognize that both the "inside" and the "outside" are in the same unified field of consciousness. Not only is the "outside" in one's consciousness, but in major ways it shapes the "inside." One lives not just through individual relationships with the external physical universe, but in a shared human lifeworld, "the world for us all" (Husserl, 1970, p. 209). Similarly to constitution of the physical bodies, others are constituted by consciousness through many "snapshots," but differently from physical bodies, others are also constituted as conscious subjects:

> other egos ... are not a mere intending and intended *in me*, merely synthetic unities of possible verification *in me*, but, according to their sense, precisely *others* ... I experience them at the same time [as natural objects and] as subjects for this world, as experiencing I, and, in doing so, experiencing me too, even as I experience the world and others in it.
>
> *(Husserl, 1993, p. 89)*

The early self develops by constituting the intersubjectivity and mirroring the emotions of others (Johnson, 1987). Existing "in the world through the living body," our constituting egos are "interwoven with one another and extended into the infinite" (Husserl, 1970, p. 210). What on the surface appears to be "my responses" may, in reality, be the unnoticed absorbed habits of others.

Consciousness presents other persons by attributing to them the same sense of the body one experiences in oneself: the so-called "bodily transfer" (Husserl, 1993). One doesn't perceive other people's emotions just by recognizing their facial expressions, but also by the empathic feeling of their emotions as directed at her. Because one is the subject who is feeling, these "reversed" emotions are constituted out of the phenomenological materiality of one's own body, they can be built into the habits of one's ego, and then change the direction of their intentionality and become a part of the sphere of ownness as one's own emotions. In this aspect, individual experience works like a kaleidoscope which puts together infinite varieties of patterns by reusing the same pieces of colored glass reflected by rotating mirrors.

Ortega y Gasset famously stated: "I am me and my circumstances." The "I," myself, includes not only what I choose to own, but also what I am given. As one younger colleague quipped: "All my life, I was choosing my friends—so how am I now supposed to get along with all these different people?" These alien others are difficult to get out of one's head: "made" out of the phenomenological "material" of our own consciousness, they are us (Figure 25.2).

"Internalized" emotions are directed at us, i.e., have a reversed intentionality. However, they become included into the sphere of ownness and become a habit of the ego. If this happens, one would be likely to reuse such absorbed emotion in relationships (including to oneself). A conclusion must be made that in order for one's wellbeing to exist, the passive

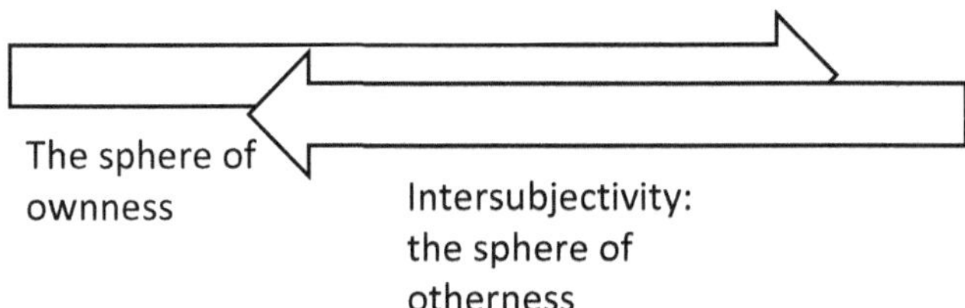

Figure 25.2 Directions of intentionality, and the overlap of the sphere of ownness and the sphere of intersubjectivity

processes in the constitution of intersubjectivity must be brought to awareness and somehow "edited" in line with one's conscious, adult choice.

Even though religions did not possess the analytic research apparatus of phenomenology, they did notice these deep dependencies. For example, a visionary metaphor of Hinduism presents cosmos as the Creator's net, in which each person is a jewel node connected with other jewel nodes. Buddhism refers to the wheel of *karma* which *ad infinitum* cycles the souls between the realms of heaven and hell. Sufism specifically indicates that seeing others is seeing oneself. The phenomenological actuality of this interconnectedness is not that of a blissful oneness (as it is often presented in New Age groups), but a very concrete, direct experience that every facet of one's individuality is shaped by a memory, and that every aspect of one's consciousness has its origin in the collective. In their quest for enlightenment, religions worked out the practical ways of escaping the dependence on intersubjectivity. However, these traditions are also filled with stories of how renunciation doesn't work: for example, a Buddhist sage Milarepa and a Christian saint St. Seraphim of Sarov, while in solitary retreats, were both assaulted by robbers. Another, more humorous, Hindu story is about an ascetic who keeps mice out of his beginning bowl by getting a cat, feeds the cat by getting a cow's milk, and then a cow, etc., losing his ascetic habits to the web of dependencies.

Perhaps the highest achievement of non-religious mindfulness is that it discloses a presence of sphere of intersubjectivity *within the sphere of ownness*. In other words, not only can mindfulness bring to awareness the layers of earlier, now inadequate, internalized responses, but it can also show what in these responses is ours, and what comes from others. This new awareness registers the direction of intentionalities and increases the adequacy of recognition of how others feel, think, and behave while they direct their activities at us. To gain awareness of reverse intentionalities, mindfulness has to uncover the internal architectonics of consciousness.

4. The internal architectonics of consciousness

Like software, meaning has internal architecture, but unlike software, meaning is alive. Aliveness of meaning comes from the body in the form of the so-called primary impressions. These impressions are called "primary" because consciousness uses them as a foundation for building its complex internal architectonics. The base of the structure is created by a passive synthesis of these impressions with basic proto-intentionalities of sense—"passive" because these "bottom" processes are not controlled by the ego, but submitted to it; and "synthesis" because in the process, various impressions are forming unities. This bottom–up synthesis, from sensations to the sense of time, to self-awareness, thinking by association, and feeling, meets with the top–down meaning-bestowal from the ego. In some forms of consciousness, e.g., emotion or a religious sense, passivity and participation of the body are more noticeable than in others, such as, e.g., abstract thinking in which constitutive acts of the ego dominate the scene.

Both kinds of mindfulness, religious and non-religious, begin with switching the usual absorption in the flow of experience to observations of this flow and thereby objectifying it. Then, the self both lives the experience, and observes it, i.e., becomes split. This weakens its habits, and eventually deconstructs and reconstructs it. Similarly to how removing the roof of a house would expose its internal organization, mindfulness brings awareness to previously hidden structures of consciousness. Different kinds of mindfulness end up in different locations of this structure, but because the whole of consciousness is a unity, and because acts of consciousness are often dependent on one another (Husserl, 2001), mindfulness in one area eventually reaches other areas as well. The mindfulness described below in this chapter is a body-oriented kind of mindfulness which rather quickly reaches into the bottom of the structures of consciousness (into the sphere of passive synthesis), and thereby opens a gateway into the sphere of intersubjectivity. By "rather quickly," I mean five and more years of practice; accessing the internalized otherness takes more time; in general, the maturation of mindfulness is slow.

In the absence of the practice of mindfulness, i.e., in ordinary consciousness, the processes in the sphere of passive synthesis remain unnamed, not explicitly expressed, or "anonymous" as phenomenology puts it: they work in the background of consciousness but are not explicit for the living, experiencing self. But when one becomes sufficiently mindful, one's meaning shows up in infinite entanglements with the meanings coming from others—donated, inherited, and borrowed. Some emotions, which appeared to be one's own, will be seen as induced by others, and so on. A discovery that an experience which I thought is mine has large chunks of feeling and thought which are not just co-constituted by the presence of others, but are simply not mine, is one of the main insights during the advanced stages of non-religious mindfulness: with the maturation of meditative experience, the whole content of awareness will be shown to depend on others.

5. Modifications of experience in the practice of non-religious mindfulness

Below I give an example of how experience develops in the body-focused non-religious mindfulness in the technique developed by S.N. Goenka. S.N. Goenka himself learned mindfulness from monks, but, being a lay person (not a Buddhist monk), he encouraged a non-religious use of the practice. Goenka-style mindfulness begins with training control over attention by focusing on breath sensations on the upper lip. These sensations are distinctly cooling on inhalation, warm on exhalation; the small size of the affected area requires attention to be stable and selectively "energize" intended areas. This beginning stage of the practice reveals an overwhelming amount of random thoughts, images, and associations, all being quite spontaneous and out of control. Accordingly, for the beginning stages of practice, one needs a comfortable, quiet room for at least an hour (this is not necessary at the later stages of practice).

One should not strive to quiet the mind, but rather, sustain the focus: because the origin of a busy mind is in the bottom layer of consciousness, in the sphere of passive synthesis, these disturbances are, in fact, disorganized memories. Not paying attention to them would prevent the ego from making sense out of these passing impressions, and the mind will eventually quiet down by itself. Another essential skill gained at this preliminary stage consists in inhibiting the ego's proclivities of attraction and repulsion (i.e., intentionalities of judgment and valuation) which are implicit in the constitution of consciousness. Thereby, the ego loses its main tools in the constitution of meaning, which is the attribution of ontological validities, and has to relax its drive to constantly interpret the world and bestow a new meaning on it. In the Buddhist frame of reference, inhibition of attraction and repulsion interrupts the "karmic" chain of events; and in the non-religious frame of reference, this inhibition opens an access to the spheres of passive synthesis and intersubjectivity.

In a single session of the practice, the first 15 minutes may be the most successful. Attention begins flickering at about the fifteenth minute, and it becomes more difficult to keep the focus tied to the skin sensations (on the upper lip, or later, while scanning the surface of the body). But this is exactly where the training really begins: when one notices that attention has slipped away, one should gently bring it back. With an hour of practice every other day or, alternatively, 30 minutes of practice every day, in approximately a week one has enough attentional skill to proceed to the main body of the practice.

The main practice consists in scanning the sensations of the skin in an orderly manner, covering the whole surface of the body, and repeating these scans again and again. It is usually possible to run two full body scans within the 30 minutes of practice. As in the preliminary training, one should sustain the focus, but this time the focus itself is moving like a scan. Also, again as in the preliminary training, one should inhibit the tendency of the *ego* to grasp at impressions. As Goenka says: "No attraction, no repulsion; just observe, just observe."

Anchoring attention to tactile impressions brings out of anonymity the unities of meaning in a manner which makes their composition visible all the way down to the primary impressions. Against objectification and ego-split provided by the practice, this review may not be pleasant, and not what one would normally choose to experience, e.g., a long-forgotten memory. The process is not predictable, but not random either: the surfacing meaning-complexes make sense in the context of one's life narrative. The perfection of the letting-go, aspect of the practice ("no attraction," etc.) changes the direction of witnessing: instead of having an orientation top–down, with the ego-pole associated with the region of the head, it becomes horizontal, not "on" impressions, but rather, "in" them. This appears to further enhance the change. But as long as experience remains to be seen as strictly "mine," i.e., within the sphere of ownness, such unworking of traces will have only a temporary effect.

As the practice matures, the scans become detached from the surface of the body, and attention dives into the body's perceived inner space. But a couple of months or even years down the road, experience transforms into an informational continuum which expands outwards. This is the most interesting and rewarding stage of the practice, because it is at this stage that one begins seeing the co-constitution of meaning between the self and others, and the weight of intersubjectivity in one's mental makeup. There is an immense sense of unfreedom that arises at this stage because one realizes how much space the other or others occupy within the sphere of consciousness which felt totally owned as "mine." There are distinctive, bounded emotions which one had considered as one's own but which show up as absorbed from other people. And there are memories of decision-making, and memories of behaviors which are founded on these emotions, and the other way around, emotions which are based on such acts—the whole complex of which might have been empathically produced by the bodily transfer and appropriated without noticing by the ego. There is a recognition of the real content of these reverse intentionalities and of the time of their origin in the past, e.g., in childhood. From this, a space formerly out of reach of understanding opens—towards groups and individuals, but much more adequate to how they really are in their living subjectivities, as opposed to the earlier, psychologically projected others.

The sense of unease may be immense but passing, because penetrating into the sphere of intersubjectivity opens the gate to a real change. Using the skills of focus, "no attraction, no repulsion," and emotional release, one can let go of strategies shaped in past relationships and radically change habits of behavior and thinking on a very foundational level. This not only leads to the surfacing of wholesome, pleasant feelings in the internal field of experience, but brings in new, more productive and real forms of interaction with others. These new behaviors will harmonize the interactions and lead to a new form of intersubjectivity, an intersubjectivity informed by wellbeing.

Takeaway lessons

1. Practicing mindfulness with and without religious ideation will produce different results.
2. The practice of non-religious mindfulness takes many years to mature, and the results can be quite interesting and unexpected.
3. During the advanced stages of non-religious mindfulness, one can sort out what emotions, habits, and thoughts, and altogether, in one's mental make-up belongs to her, and what was internalized from others. Then, one's insight about things grows; and one can radically improve and harmonize the ways of interaction with others, human community, and the world.
4. Opening of the above awareness is not a pleasant experience because one realizes how much of herself was, in fact, not herself—but this new awareness is a gateway into real freedom.
5. Phenomenological research is indispensable in sorting out the puzzles of human experience.

Reflection questions

1. What is a difference between religious and non-religious mindfulness?
2. What is phenomenology?
3. What is intersubjectivity, and how is it different from one's psychological inner life?
4. How does non-religious mindfulness develop?
5. What part do others occupy in one's consciousness?

References

Barber, M. (2017). *Religion and humor as emancipating provinces of meaning*. Dordrecht: Springer.

Costello, P. (2015). *Layers in Husserl's phenomenology*. Toronto: University of Toronto Press.

Davidsen, A. S. (2013). Phenomenological approaches in psychology and health sciences. *Qualitative Research in Psychology*, *10*(3), 318–339. doi:10.1080/14780887.2011.608466

Henry, M. (2008). *Material phenomenology*. New York: Fordham University Press.

———. (2016). Ontological destruction of the Kantian critique of the paralogism of rational psychology. *Analecta Hermeneutica*, *8*, 17–53. Retrieved from http://journals.library.mun.ca/ojs/index.php/analecta/article/view/1708. Accessed April 26, 2019.

Husserl, E. (1970). *The crisis of European sciences and transcendental phenomenology*. Evanston, IL: Northwestern University Press.

———. (1993). *Cartesian meditations*. Trans. Dorian Cairns. Dordrecht: Kluwer.
———. (2001). *Logical investigations* (Vol. 2). London: Routledge.
Johnson, S. (1987). *Humanizing the narcissistic style*. New York: Norton.
Kozhevnikov, M., Louchakova, O., Josipovic, Z., & Motes, M. A. (2009). The enhancement of visuospatial processing efficiency through Buddhist deity meditation. *Psychological Science, 20*(5), 645–653.
Neisser, H. (1959). The phenomenological approach in social science. *Philosophy and Phenomenological Research, 20*(2), 198–212. doi:10.2307/2104356
O'Rourke, J. (2018). Heidegger on expression: Formal indication and destruction in the early Freiburg lectures. *Journal of the British Society for Phenomenology*, 2332–2486. doi:10.1080/00071773.2018.1431133
Ratnayake, S. The problem of mindfulness. *Aeon*, 25 July, 2019. Retrieved November 2, 2019 from https://aeon.co/essays/mindfulness-is-loaded-with-troubling-metaphysical-assumptions
Walden, S. (2017). *Customer experience management rebooted*. London: Palgrave Macmillan.

26

ENERGY, JOY, MINDFULNESS, AND ENGAGEMENT AT WORK

A pilot study of an "Inner Engineering" approach

Tracy F. H. Chang

Introduction

Work engagement is a critical factor for success for both individuals and organizations (Whittington, Meskelis, Asare & Beldona, 2017). Engaged employees have a sense of energetic and affective connection with their work activities (Schaufeli, Martinez, Pinto, Salanova & Bakker, 2002). They are more committed to their organizations and willing to go extra miles in helping colleagues and employers in accomplishing goals (Bakker & Demerouti, 2008; Christian, Garza & Slaughter, 2011). Engaged employees also perform their work tasks better and contribute to positive social and psychological conditions in organizations (Christian et al., 2011; Rich, Lepine & Crawford, 2010). Yet, the level of employee engagement is not as high as desired in the US and globally. Only one-third of American employees are fully engaged; worldwide, only 13% of employees are "highly engaged" (Whittington et al., 2017). Thus, how to increase work engagement becomes a central interest to organizational leaders and researchers.

Fundamentally, there are two approaches to increasing work engagement—structural and agentic. The structural approach recognizes the impact of structure, such as work organizational strategy, human resource practices, transformational leadership, and job design, on employee engagement (Whittington et al., 2017). The agentic approach appreciates the far-reaching and rippling effect of human agency in shaping one's psychological experiences and social behavior and ultimately in designing social structure and systems. Bandura (2006) proposes that "social cognitive theory rejects a duality between human agency and social structure. People create social systems, and these systems, in turn, organize and influence people's lives" (p. 164). Howard (1991) argues that "social movements can be understood fully only by directing explicit attention to the experienced selves of individual actors ... self-change is an essential component of sustained social change" (p. 209). This agentic perspective is consistent with the eastern wisdom that "you can not transform the world with transforming the individual on self-transformation as the foundation for social change" (J. V. Sadhguru, 2016). Applying these western theories of the self and the eastern yogic sciences of self-transformation, the present study proposes that self-change is an essential component of sustained organizational change and the yogic sciences provide tools for this sustainable change in oneself.

With this agentic perspective, the study introduces a novel intervention approach, "Inner Engineering," to the study of mindfulness and work engagement. Sadhguru (2016a) considers wellbeing as "a deep sense of pleasantness" within oneself and that "human experience may be stimulated or catalyzed by external situations, but the source is within." Thus, "engineering" one's interiority is the key to inner wellbeing. Applying this approach to the study of work engagement, "Inner Engineering" represents the process of using the yogic sciences and technologies to gain self-mastery over one's cognitive, emotional, physical, and energy systems in order to achieve optimal wellbeing and performance at work.

Originated from the yogic traditions, mindfulness meditation has been found to have a positive effect on work engagement (Atkins, Hassed & Fogliati, 2015; Coo & Salanova, 2018; Silver, Caleshu, Casson-Parkin & Ormond, 2018; Zivnuska, Kacmar, Ferguson & Carlson, 2016). Aikens et al. (2014) find that an online mindfulness intervention (17.8 hours) increases employee mindfulness, resilience, and vigor at work. Additional studies have further examined the mediating mechanisms through which mindfulness affects work engagement. These studies find that mindfulness improves work engagement indirectly through positive affect, psychological capital (self-efficacy, hope, resilience, and optimism) (Kotzé, 2018; Malinowski & Lim, 2015), and "authentic functioning" (Leroy, Anseel, Dimitrova & Sels, 2013). As a result, employer-sponsored mindfulness-based programs, both in-person and online formats, have grown in recent years.

Interestingly, energy has not been a direct target outcome of mindfulness-based interventions. Yet, energy is the source of powering up human functioning and realizing human capacities—cognitively, emotionally, and physically. Kahn (1990) defines personal engagement work as "the harnessing of organization members' selves to their work roles; in engagement, people employ and express themselves physically, cognitively, and emotionally during role performance" (p. 694). He recognizes that "personal, internal energies" are required to drive physical, cognitive, and emotional labor and "presence" during role performance. Schaufeli, Bakker, and Salanova (2006) define engagement as "a positive, fulfilling, work-related state of mind that is characterized by vigor, dedication, and absorption" (p. 702). Vigor means high levels of energy, mental resilience, and willingness to invest effort in work even while facing challenges at work (Schaufeli et al., 2006). Energy is a core dimension that predicts work engagement (Costa, Passos & Bakker, 2016) and proactively managing energy leads to work engagement (Bakker, Petrou, Op Den Kamp & Tims, 2018). The present study proposes that energy is a crucial factor of work engagement. It evaluates the impact of "Inner Engineering" tools on activating energy and the impact of energy on work engagement.

Another gap in the mindfulness research toward engagement is positive emotions, particularly *joy*. Both the dedication and absorption dimensions of work engagement contain experiences and expressions of positive emotions. Dedication involves experiencing enthusiasm, inspiration, and pride, whereas absorption involves experiencing happiness while working intensively. Joy is one of the key emotions in the *broaden and build* theory of positive emotions (B. L. Fredrickson, 2001). The present study proposes that positive emotions, particularly joy, are essential for work engagement and evaluates the effect of Inner Engineering tools on generating joy from within and the impact of joy on work engagement.

The study contributes to the mindfulness and work engagement literature by (1) introducing classical yogic tools and processes that heighten energy and joy; (2) proposing a more encompassing model of work engagement that includes energy, joy, and mindfulness; and (3) examining the effectiveness of the Inner Engineering training on promoting wellbeing and enriching work experience and engagement. Next, the theoretical model will be presented and discussed further, followed by methodology and findings. The chapter will conclude with implications of the findings and suggestions for future research.

Theoretical model

Work engagement

Originally, Kahn (1990) observes that "people can use varying degrees of their selves, physically, cognitively, and emotionally in their work role performances, which has implications for both their work and experiences;" he is concerned with "the moments in which people bring themselves into or remove themselves from particular task behaviors" (p. 692). Work contexts, mediated by people's perceptions, create the conditions in which they personally engage or disengage (Kahn, 1990). The research question for the present study is: could the ancient yogic sciences and tools influence people's perception of their work contexts and psychological experiences of work from within?

In contrast to Kahn, Schaufeli et al. (2006) conceptualize work engagement as "a more persistent and pervasive affective-cognitive state that is not focused on any particular object, event, individual, or behavior" (p. 702) rather than a momentary and specific state. Schaufeli et al. (2006) identify vigor, dedication, and absorption as three key qualities of work engagement:

> Vigor is characterized by high levels of energy and mental resilience while working, the willingness to invest effort in one's work, and persistence even in the face of difficulties. Dedication refers to being strongly involved in one's work and experiencing a sense of significance, enthusiasm, inspiration, pride, and challenge. Absorption is characterized by being fully concentrated and happily engrossed in one's work, whereby time passes quickly, and one has difficulties with detaching oneself from work.
>
> *(p. 702)*

Based on the yogic sciences, the Inner Engineering approach consists of comprehensive yogic tools that enable one to manage one's cognition, emotion, action, and energy toward wellbeing and engagement at work. Mental perception and psychological experiences are self-generated from within, therefore "engineer" one's interiority is foundational toward wellbeing and engagement (Sadhguru, 2016b). This premise is consistent with the social cognitive theory of self-change and social change (Bandura, 2006, 2018; Howard, 1991). In contrast to the social modeling approach to self-efficacy proposed by social cognitive theory, the Inner Engineering approach enhances life energies, positive emotions, and perceptions by employing classical yogic sciences and technologies. Energy heightens awareness and enhances capacities for engaging in cognitive reappraisal and "uncoupling" sensory experience from affective and evaluative reaction (Kabat-Zinn, 1982). Energy builds up the necessary groundwork for mindfulness so that one could respond more consciously rather than react automatically to external stimuli and context. The study hypothesizes that Inner Engineering training increases work engagement by activating energy, joy, and mindfulness. Furthermore, vital energy leads to vigor, joy connects with dedication, and mindfulness contributes to absorption (see Figure 26.1).

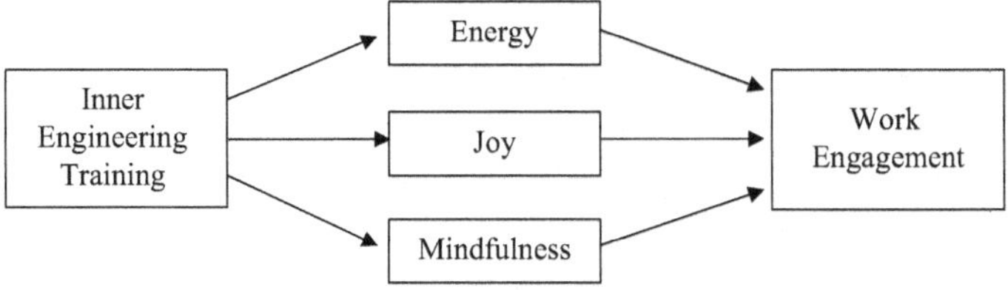

Figure 26.1 Inner Engineering increases work engagement through energy, joy, and mindfulness

What is significant about energy, joy, and mindfulness is that they are also among the seven factors of "awakening" in the Buddhist traditions—mindfulness, interest and investigation, energy, joy and rapture, relaxation and tranquility, unification and concentration of mind, and equanimity and equipoise (Analayo, 2003; Brewer, Davis & Goldstein, 2013; Goldstein, 2016). Mindfulness comes on the top of the list of seven factors, so the mindfulness-based interventions are developed. Without subscribing to any tradition or lineage, Sadhguru (2013), yogi, mystic, and the creator of the Inner Engineering approach, offers an alternative perspective with regard to the relationship between energy and awareness:

> If we have to use an analogy, let us say we turn down the voltage for the lights. Now let us say just one light is there. It just lights up only so much, and only that much we see. If you turn up the voltage, suddenly you are able to see much more because the light has spread. Awareness is just like this. Right now, your energies, your body, your emotion, your mind, everything is functioning with a certain limited voltage. You crank up the voltage, suddenly you start seeing so many things which were not in your experience until that moment.
>
> In a way, to put it very simply, to put it technically, you need to turn up your voltage. You can turn up your voltage simply with your enthusiasm, but that will not take you all the way. There are other kinds of technologies to turn up your voltage in a certain way where all the time you are high.
>
> *(pp. 175–176)*

Energy

In the yogic sciences, "*prana*" refers to vital energy (Sadhguru, 2016b), the energy that enables life. It is the cosmic energy, which includes all forms of energy (Brahmananda Sarasvati, 1987). "Pranayama is the science where, by consciously breathing in a particular way, the very way one thinks, feels, understands, and experiences life can be changed" (Sadhguru, 2016b). Recent neurophysiological studies show that the rhythm of breathing creates electrical activity in the brain that enhances emotional judgment and memory recall (Zelano et al., 2016) and "volition control and awareness of breath engage distinct but overlapping brain circuits" (Herrero, Khuvis, Yeagle, Cerf & Mehta, 2018). In the field of positive psychology, *vitality* is "the state of feeling alive and alert—to having energy available to the Self" (Ryan & Frederick, 1997). Ryan and Deci (2001) consider vitality as an aspect of eudaimonic wellbeing and suggest that "being vital and energetic is part of what it means to be fully functioning and psychologically well." Energy is gaining interests from positive organizational scholars who have begun to investigate the role of energy in organizations and the strategies employees use to manage their own energy (Fritz,

Lam & Spreitzer, 2011; Spreitzer, Lam & Quinn, 2012). Fritz et al. (2011) find that strategies related to learning, meaning, and positive relationships affect employees' energy the most.

Joy

Joy has received the most research attention among the seven positive emotion dispositions (joy, contentment, pride, love, compassion, amusement, and awe) with the most findings associated with facial expressions, appraisal patterns, neurological correlates, and cognitive effects (Shobitha & Agarwal, 2013). Fredrickson (1998) describes four positive emotions—joy, interest, contentment, and love—and adopted the "emotion families" approach toward these positive emotions. For example, *joy* represents more than a single affective state, encompassing a family of related affective states that share a common theme and variations on that theme (Fredrickson, 1998). According to the *broaden-and-build theory* (Fredrickson, 1998), joy and its "emotion families" broaden one's "momentary thought-action repertoire" as well as building the individual's enduring personal resources—physical, intellectual, and social. These resources promote both individual and collective wellbeing in organizations.

Mindfulness

The growing field of mindfulness research brings a growing number of definitions for mindfulness. The term *mindfulness* has been used to represent a trait, a state, a practice, a skill, or an intervention (Good et al., 2016; Kabat-Zinn, 2013). There are two traditions of mindfulness research. One is meditative practice oriented and research on this approach was originated by Kabat-Zinn (1982); the other is cognitive flexibility oriented and research on this approach originated by Langer (1989). Kabat-Zinn (2013) defined mindfulness simply as "the moment to moment non-judgmental awareness" (p. xlix) as well as an attentional skill—"pay attention on purpose, in the present moment, and non-judgmentally." Mindfulness meditation is rooted in what is known as the *sattipatana vipassana* in the Theravada Buddhism (Kabat-Zinn, 2013).

Langer (1989) portrayed the key qualities of a mindful state as creating new categories, being open to new experiences, and being aware of more than one perspective. Studies have found that mindfulness-based intervention enhances *flow* state in athletes (Jian-Hong, Tsai, Yin-Chou, Chen & Ching-Yen, 2019). *Flow* is the state in which "one is fully immersed in a feeling of energized focus, full involvement, and enjoyment in an activity" (Sinnott, Hilton, Wood & Douglas, 2018). Other non-interventional studies also found mindfulness is associated with *flow* state (Moore, 2013; Sinnott et al., 2018).

Methodology

Inner Engineering Online (IEO)

The Inner Engineering Online (IEO) program was offered as a pilot program to employees by a Fortune 500 company. Participating in the program is voluntary and free of cost to employees. The company capped the pilot program to a small number of employees.

The program consists of seven online sessions and an hour of Upa Yoga instruction and demonstration. The online sessions involve discourses, awareness activities, and guided meditations; each session is 90 minutes. Upa Yoga essentially means "sub-yoga" or "pre-yoga"

(Sadhguru, 2016b), which is suitable for beginners and can be taught through an online format. The protocol is to complete the seven online sessions within one month and review principles of Inner Engineering and practice the sequence of Upa Yoga and meditation daily for 40 to 48 days. The Upa Yoga practices take about 30 minutes. The pre-program survey was administered before the participants started the first online session and the post-program survey was administered 40 days following course completion (one month).

Sample

Forty-two employees participated in the pre-program survey and 18 participated in the post-program survey, with a retention rate of about 43%. Among pre-program survey participants, 15 (36%) were men and 27 (64%) were women; 30 (71%) were white and 12 (29%) were non-white. Among post-program survey participants, 7 (39%) were men and 11 (61%) were women; 14 (73%) were white and 4 (27%) were non-white. The average age for the pre-program subjects is 38.6 years old, ranging from 23 to 63. The average age for the post-program subjects is 38.2, ranging from 24 to 63. There are significant variations in terms of participant demographics pre- and post-programs.

Measures

Energy

Energy is measured by the Subjective Vitality Scale (six-item) (Bostic, Rubio & Hood, 2000; Ryan & Frederick, 1997). Bostic et al. (2000) find that the six-item is a better scale. The survey asked the participants to "indicate the degree to which the statement is generally true for you in your life." Here is a sample statement—"I feel alive and vital." The response is coded on a seven-point scale from 1 (not very true) to 7 (very true). The items of the entire scale are presented Appendix. The Cronbach's alpha score of the six-item scale is .87 (pre and post).

Joy

Joy is measured by the Joy Subscale of the Dispositional Positive Emotion Scales (six-item) (Shioata, Keltner & John, 2006). The scale contains six items. Here is a sample statement—"I often feel burst of joy." The other statements are listed in Appendix. The response is coded on a seven-point Likert scale from 1 (strongly disagree) to 7 (strongly agree). The Cronbach's alpha is .88 (pre) and .77 (post).

Mindfulness

Mindfulness is measured by the Mindful Attention Awareness Scale (MAAS) (five-item) (Brown & Ryan, 2003; Osman, Lamis, Bagge, Freedenthal & Barnes, 2016). Osman et al. (2016) find that the short scale with five items is as reliable as the original MAAS. The five-item scale asked the question, "In the last month, how often do you feel the following way?" Here is a sample statement—"It seems I am 'running on automatic,' without much awareness of what I'm doing." The response is coded on a six-point scale from 1 (almost always) to 6 (almost never). The Cronbach's alpha score of the five-item scale is .87 (pre) and .82 (post).

Work engagement

Work engagement is measured by the Utrecht Work Engagement (nine-item) (Schaufeli & Bakker, 2003). The survey asked participants, "How frequently do you feel the following ways?" The statements include three subscales—vigor, dedication, and absorption. Here is a sample statement for each subscale—"At my work, I feel bursting with energy" (vigor), "I am enthusiastic about my job" (dedication), and "I feel happy when I am working intensely" (absorption). The response is coded on a seven-point scale from 0 (never) to 7 (every day). The Cronbach's alpha for the nine-item scale is .94 (pre) and .90 (post).

Analysis

The study uses paired-sample t-test to determine the effect of the IEO program on energy, joy, mindfulness, and engagement. Cohen's *d* is calculated to estimate the effect size. In general, Cohen (1992) suggests a Cohen's *d* of .2 indicates a small effect, .5 a medium effect, and .8 a large effect. The sample size is too small to run multivariate regression analysis, and a simple mediation model, Pearson's r correlation and univariate regression, is calculated to estimate the effect of energy, joy, and mindfulness on work.

Results

Paired-samples t-test

A paired-samples t-test was conducted to compare energy between pre-program survey and post-program surveys. There is a significant increase in subjective vitality score from pre-program (M=24, SD=7.01) to post-program (M=28.25, SD=5.22); t(15)=2.69, p <.01, one-tailed); d=.67. These results suggest that the IEO program makes a difference to employees' energy. Specifically, after employees completed the IEO, their subjective vitality significantly increased. The effect size is between medium (.50) and large (.80) (see Figure 26.2).

Similarly, there is a significant increase in experience of joy from pre-program (M=26.38, SD=7.78) to post-program (M=28.69, SD=4.48); t (15) =2.00, p <.05); d=.50. These results suggest that the IEO program makes a difference to employees' level of joy. Specifically, after employees completed the IEO, they became more joyful in their daily lives. The effect size is medium.

With regard to mindfulness, there is also a significant increase in mindfulness from pre-program (M=16.06, SD=4.89) to post-program (M=18.63, SD=3.90); t (15) =2.34, p <.05). These results suggest that the IEO program makes a difference to employees' mindfulness. Specifically, after employees completed the IEO, they became more mindful in their daily activities. The effect size is medium.

Furthermore, there is also a significant increase in the work engagement scale from pre-program (M=37.06, SD=10.74) to post-program (M=47.15, SD=7.45); t (15) =2.37, p <.05); d=.59. These results indicate that the IEO program made a difference to employees' overall engagement work. Specifically, after employees completed the IEO, they become more engaged at work. The effect size is medium.

Among the three subscales of work engagement, there is a significant increase in the vigor subscale from pre- (M=10.75, SD=3.44) to post-program (M=12.67, SD=2.75); t (15) =2.337, p <.05); d=.59. The effect size is medium. There is also a significant increase in the dedication subscale from pre- (M=12.81, SD=3.73) to post-program (M=14.75, SD=3.04);

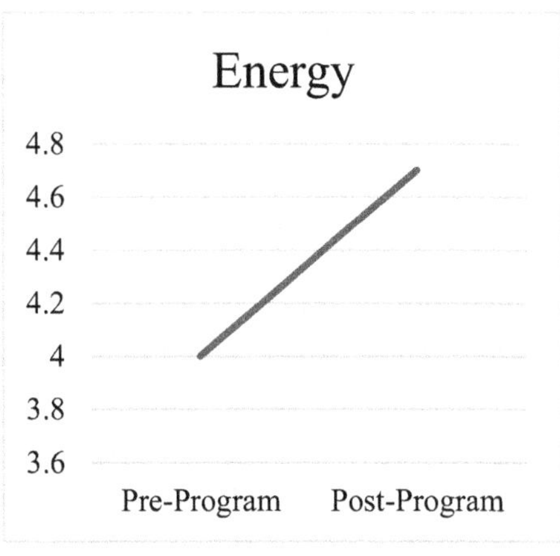

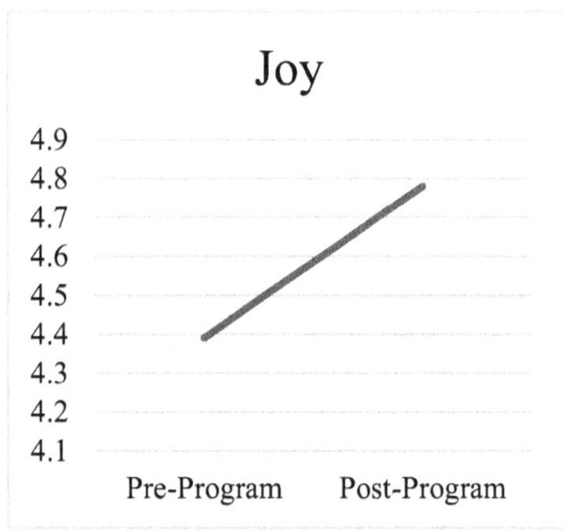

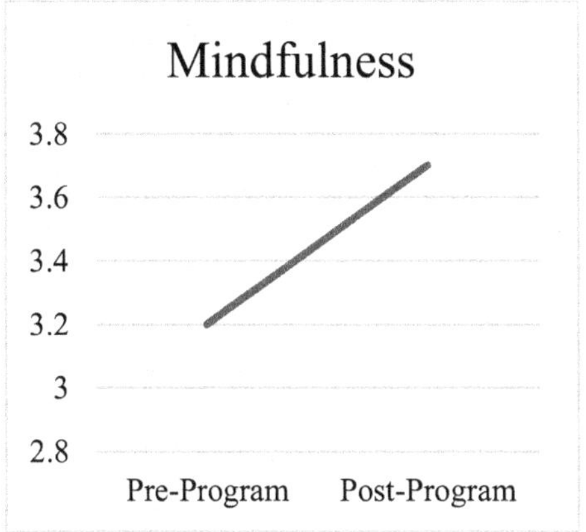

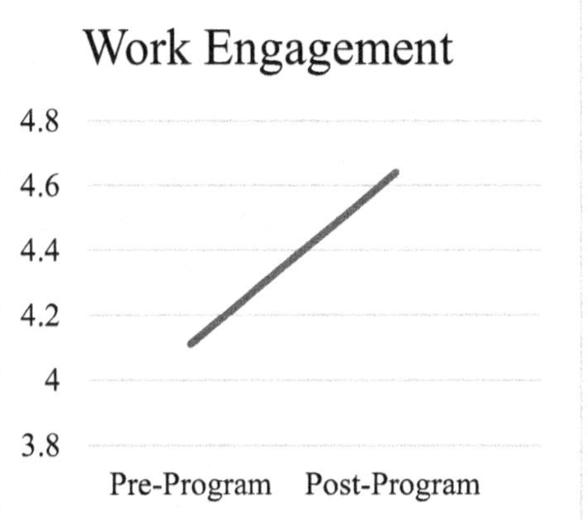

Figure 26.2 Energy, joy, mindfulness, and work engagement pre- and post-program scores

t (15) =2.800, p <.01); d= .70. The effect size is almost large. However, there is no significant difference in the absorption subscale from pre- (M=13.50, SD=4.37) to post-program (M=14.31, SD=2.89); t (15) =.99, p <.20).

Pearson r correlations

Table 26.1 reports the pair-wise Pearson *r* correlations among vitality, joy, mindfulness, the work engagement global scale and its subscale scores. The results show that vitality is significantly correlated with joy, mindfulness, work engagement, and its subscales of vigor and absorption. Joy is correlated with work engagement and its subscales of dedication and absorption. Mindfulness is not significantly related to work engagement and any of its subscales.

Univariate regressions

Univariate regressions are calculated to predict work engagement based on vitality, joy, and mindfulness independently. The results show that vitality is a significant predictor of work

Table 26.1 Pearson correlations between vitality, joy, mindfulness, and global work engagement scale and its subscale scores (n =17)

	1	*2*	*3*	*4*	*5*	*6*	*7*
1.Vitality							
2. Joy	.489*						
3. Mindfulness	.610*	.174					
4. Work Engagement	.521*	.522*	.351				
5. Vigor	.431*	.228	.314	.837*			
6. Dedication	.353	.568**	.297	.913*	.684		
7. Absorption	.572**	.536*	.298	.835	.497	.662**	

* p < .05
** p < 0.01

engagement (F (1,15) = 5.584, p < .05), with an R^2 of .271. Joy is also a significant predictor of work engagement (F (1,15) = 5.604, p < .05), with an R^2 of .272. However, mindfulness is not a significant predictor of work engagement. Table 26.2 reports the unstandardized and standardized beta coefficients. The standardized coefficients for vitality and joy show that both have a medium positive effect on work engagement.

Discussion

Work engagement is a critical factor for individual, team, and organizational performance (Costa et al., 2016).Yet, the level of employee engagement in the US and worldwide is not optimal and is declining (Whittington et al., 2017). How do we promote sustainable work engagement that draws on human agency?

The study introduces the novel "Inner Engineering" training program into the field of mindfulness and work engagement research. "Inner Engineering" is the process of using the yogic sciences and technologies to gain mastery over the functioning of one's cognitive, emotional, physical, and energetic systems in order to achieve optimal wellbeing and performance at work. The study hypothesizes that Inner Engineering training equips individuals with yogic knowledge and tools to raise levels of energy, joy, and mindfulness, all of which in turn uplift work engagement. These hypotheses are tested by conducting a study on the Inner Engineering Online program offered as a small pilot workplace program in a Fortune 500 company.

The data suggests that the Inner Engineering Online training increases participants' energy, joy, mindfulness, and work engagement. Furthermore, both energy and joy increase

Table 26.2 Univariate regressions of vitality, joy, and mindfulness on work engagement

Source	*B*	*SE B*	*β*	*t*	*p*
Vitality	.77	.32	.52	2.36	.032
Joy	.89	.38	.52	2.37	.032
Mindfulness	.67	.46	.45	0.58	.167

work engagement. Contrary to previous findings (Coo & Salanova, 2018), mindfulness does not seem to have a significant effect on work engagement. Mindfulness-based interventions usually do not involve tools that are designed to directly activate the energy system. Yet, energy is the power source for awareness and positive emotions; without energy, awareness is difficult (Sadhguru, 2016b). Engagement requires "personal or internal" energies that drive physical, emotional, and cognitive labor (Kahn, 1990). The finding that energy is a key contributor of work engagement supports previous findings (Costa et al., 2016).

According to the *broaden-and-build* theory of positive emotions, many positive emotions broaden a person's momentary thought–action repertoire. Experiences of certain positive emotions, such as joy, prompt individuals to reject automatic reactions and behavioral routines and to pursue novel, creative, and often more responsive (conscious) and new paths of thought and action (Fredrickson, 1998). Fredrickson (1998) explains the power of joy:

> Joy creates the urge to play and be playful in the broadest sense of the word, encompassing not only physical and social play, but also intellectual and artistic play. In addition to broadening an individual's momentary thought–action repertoire, joy can have the incidental effect of building an individual's physical, intellectual, and social skills. Importantly, these new resources are durable and can be drawn on later, long after the instigating experience of joy has subsided.
>
> (*p. 6*)

This power of joy emboldens individuals to perceive work as play. To a joyful employee, work is playful. The *broaden-and-build theory* may explain why joy has a rippling positive effect on work engagement and its multiple subdomains—dedication and absorption. Dedication refers to being intensely involved in one's work and experiencing positive affect (e.g., a sense of significance, enthusiasm, inspiration, pride, and challenge). Absorption entails being happily and fully immersed in work activities. In this study, participants experience a greater level of joy and work engagement without changing work contexts. If Inner Engineering training enables individuals to generate joy from within and if joy empowers engagement free of work context, Inner Engineering training has the potential of instigating context-free absolute and enduring joy and engagement.

More importantly, the findings suggest that similar to joy, energy may also have the *broaden-and-build* capacity. The results show that vitality also is positively related to multiple subdomains of work engagement, particularly vigor and absorption. Vitality in life in general (e.g., feeling alive, vital, alert, awake, and energized) can carry over to the workplace—look forward to going to work and feeling bursting with energy, and feeling strong and vigorous at work. Energy can manifest itself mentally, emotionally, and physically. Different kinds and levels of energy lead to different kinds and levels of emotion, mindfulness, and engagement. The results suggest that a higher level of "life energies" as conceived in the yogic traditions may give rise to joy, intention, attention, awareness, and attitudes that allow one to be fully immersed and experience a *flow*-like state while working.

Fredrickson et al. (2017) find that six weeks of mindfulness meditation and loving-kindness meditation training have a similar positive effect on one's day-to-day experiences of positive emotions (amusement, awe, gratitude, hope, inspiration, interest, joy, love, pride, and serenity) over time. The present study shows that Inner Engineering training, consisting of a repertoire of discourses, processes, and practices, covers multiple dimensions—energy, joy, and mindfulness. The findings raise questions about the relationship between energy, joy, and mindfulness and their effects on work engagement.

Brewer et al. (2013) point that the Theravada Buddhist texts outline seven psychological factors known as the seven factors of awakening—mindfulness, interest and investigation, energy, joy and rapture, relaxation and tranquility, unification and concentration of mind, and equanimity and equipoise. Based on these textual suggestions, Brewer et al. (2013) incorporate phrases that are intended to generate positive emotions into mindful breathing practice—"focusing on the breath and *in particular the feeling of interest, wonder, and joy* that arises in conjunction with subtle, mindful breathing" (p. 7). Based on the operant conditioning theory, Brewer et al. (2013) use joy as a "reward" for learning mindfulness in order to overcome the difficulties of paying attention for the novice. What about energy? What role does energy play in the training of mindfulness? Without the necessary energy, being aware is extremely difficult. The Inner Engineering approach incorporates "sadhana" (tools) to activate the energy first (Sadhguru, 2016a).

The study is limited in several ways. First the sample is small, which could lower statistical power and greater baseline imbalances. Second, the study lacks a randomized control group, resulting in sample selection bias. Third, the post-program response rate is not optimal. These aspects limit the option of data analysis, for example, multivariate regression models could be calculated to examine the independent effect of energy, joy, and mindfulness on work engagement with a larger sample. Additionally, future research also may inspect whether mindfulness serves as a mediating mechanism for energy and joy. Do energy and joy affect work engagement through mindfulness?

Conclusion

The study introduces the "Inner Engineering" approach to the study of mindfulness and work engagement. Inner Engineering is the process of using the yogic sciences and technologies to gain mastery over the functioning of one's cognitive, emotional, physical, and energetic systems in order to achieve optimal wellbeing and performance at work. The study hypothesizes that Inner Engineering training equips individuals with principles and tools to raise levels of energy, joy, and mindfulness, all of which in turn uplift work engagement. These hypotheses are tested by conducting a study on the Inner Engineering Online program offered as a small pilot workplace program in a Fortune 500 company.

The findings suggest that Inner Engineering training significantly enhances energy, joy, mindfulness, and work engagement. Both energy and joy increase work engagement. When employees feel more energetic, vital, alert, and awake in life, they carry this vitality with them to the workplace—look forward to going to work and feeling bursting with energy, feeling strong and vigorous at work. Similarly, when employees feel joyful, they carry this sense of joy into the workplace—feeling inspired and pride and happily immersed in their work activities. Both energy and joy have a spillover effect from feeling energetic and joyful in life in general to work in particular. The Inner Engineering approach gives rise to the possibility of context-free absolute joy and engagement at work. Future research may further evaluate the effectiveness of the Inner Engineering approach in enhancing work engagement with a large sample size and a randomized control group.

Chapter takeaways

1. "Inner Engineering" is the process of using yogic sciences and technologies to gain self-mastery over the functioning of one's cognitive, emotional, physical, and energy

systems so that these systems function at the optimal level for optimal wellbeing and work performance.
2. Inner Engineering training enhances energy, joy, mindfulness, and work engagement.
3. Joy has the *broaden-and-build* property, impacting work engagement and its subdomains of dedication and absorption.
4. Similar to positive emotions, energy also has the *broaden-and-build* function, enhancing work engagement and its subdomains of vigor and absorption.
5. Contrary to previous findings, mindfulness does not seem to affect work engagement.

Reflection questions

1. Modern mindfulness-based interventions are rooted in the Buddhism traditions, part of the ancient yogic sciences. These sciences offer a wealth of principles, tools, processes, and practices from different traditions. In addition to mindfulness meditation, what other yogic tools can be preserved in its authentic principles and yet be adopted for the modern lifestyles for optimal wellbeing and engagement at work?
2. As yoga, meditation, and mindfulness-based programs spread in the workplace, they facilitate the growth of spirituality in the workplace. Mindfulness meditation is rooted in spirituality, but the current mindfulness-based interventions are designed to be devoid of spiritual association. What would be the short-term and long-term impacts of mindfulness-based interventions vs spirituality-based yoga and meditations on wellbeing, work engagement, and other organizational outcomes?
3. Energy has not been a focus of mindfulness-based interventions but has attracted growing interest among positive organizational scholars. The conceptualization and measurement of "energy" in the organizational context await development. What can we learn from the concept of "life energies" conceived by the yogic sciences?
4. The list of positive emotions that have the *broaden-and-build* capacity is growing in the literature of positive psychology. What can we learn from the yogic sciences about the typology of emotions and what emotions are more foundational than others in the workplace?
5. The western theories of social cognition and positive psychology point to varying degrees of influences of interpersonal conditions and work contexts on inner experiences. What if inner experiences, such as joy, could be trained in such a way that one has the skills to experience absolute and context-free joy and inner wellbeing?

References

Aikens, K. A., Astin, J., Pelletier, K. R., Levanovich, K., Baase, C. M., Park, Y. Y., & Bodnar, C. M. (2014). Mindfulness goes to work: Impact of an online workplace intervention. *Journal of Occupational and Environmental Medicine, 56*(7), 721–731.

Analayo. (2003). *Satipatthaana: The direct path to realization.* Cambridge, UK: Windhorse.

Atkins, P., Hassed, C., & Fogliati, V. (2015). Mindfulness improves work engagement, wellbeing and performance in a university setting. 1–17.

Bakker, A. B. & Demerouti, E. (2008). Towards a model of work engagement. *Career Development International, 13*(3), 209–223. doi:10.1108/13620430810870476

Bakker, A. B., Petrou, P., Op Den Kamp, E. M., & Tims, M. (2018). Proactive vitality management, work engagement, and creativity: The role of goal orientation. *Applied Psychology*. doi:10.1111/apps.12173

Bandura, A. (2006). Toward a psychology of human agency. *Perspectives on Psychological Science, 1*(2), 164–180. doi:10.1111/j.1745-6916.2006.00011.x

Bandura, A. (2018). Toward a psychology of human agency: Pathways and reflections. *Perspectives on Psychological Science, 13*(2), 130–136. doi:10.1177/1745691617699280

Bostic, T. J., Rubio, D. M., & Hood, M. (2000). A validation of the subjective vitality scale using structural equation modeling. *Social Indicators Research, 52*, 313–324.

Brahmananda Sarasvati, S. (1987). *Fundamentals of yoga: A handbook of theory, practice, and application* (1987 ed.). New York, NY: Julian Press.

Brewer, J. A., Davis, J. H., & Goldstein, J. (2013). Why is it so hard to pay attention, or is it? Mindfulness, the factors of awakening and reward-based learning. *Mindfulness, 4*(1). doi:10.1007/s12671-12012-10164-12678; 10.1007/s12671-012-0164-8.

Brown, K. W. & Ryan, R. M. (2003). The benefits of being present: Mindfulness and its role in psychological well-being. *Journal of Personality and Social Psychology, 84*(4), 822–848.

Christian, M., Garza, A., & Slaughter, J. (2011). Work engagement: A quanttitative review and test of its relations wiht task and contextual performance. *Personnel Psychology, 64*(1), 89–136. doi:10.1111/j.1744-6570.2010.01203.x

Cohen, J. (1992). A power primer. *Psychological Bulletin, 112*(1), 155–159. doi:10.1037/0033-2909.112.1.155

Coo, C. & Salanova, M. (2018). Mindfulness can make you happy-and-productive: A mindfulness controlled trial and its effects on happiness, work engagement and performance. *Journal of Happiness Studies, 19*(6), 1691–1711. doi:10.1007/s10902-017-9892-8

Costa, P. L., Passos, A. M., & Bakker, A. B. (2016). The work engagement grid: Predicting engagement from two core dimensions. *Journal of Managerial Psychology, 31*(4), 774–789. doi:10.1108/JMP-11-2014-0336

Fredrickson, B., Boulton, A., Firestine, A., Van Cappellen, P., Algoe, S., Brantley, M., … Salzberg, S. (2017). Positive emotion correlates of meditation practice: A comparison of mindfulness meditation and loving-kindness meditation. *Mindfulness, 8*(6), 1623–1633. doi:10.1007/s12671-017-0735-9

Fredrickson, B. L. (1998). what good are positive emotions? *Review of General Psychology, 2*(3), 300–319. doi:10.1037/1089-2680.2.3.300

Fredrickson, B. L. (2001). The role of positive emotions in positive psychology. *American Psychologist, 56* (3), 218–226. doi:10.1037/0003-066X.56.3.218

Fritz, C., Lam, C. F., & Spreitzer, G. M. (2011). It's the little things that matter: An examination of knowledge workers' energy management. *The Academy of Management Perspectives, 25*(3), 28–39.

Goldstein, J. (2016). *Mindfulness*. Boulder, CO: Sounds True.

Good, D. J., Lyddy, C. J., Glomb, T. M., Bono, J. E., Brown, K. W., Duffy, M. K., … Lazar, S. W. (2016). Contemplating mindfulness at work: an integrative review. *Journal of Management, 42*(1), 114–142. doi:10.1177/0149206315617003

Herrero, J. L., Khuvis, S., Yeagle, E., Cerf, M., & Mehta, A. D. (2018). Breathing above the brain stem: Volitional control and attentional modulation in humans. *Journal of Neurophysiology, 119*(1), 145. doi:10.1152/jn.00551.2017

Howard, J. A. (1991). From changing selves toward changing society. In J. A. Howard & P. L. Callero (Eds.), *The self-soceity dynamic: Cognition, emotion, and action* (pp. 209–238). Cambridge: Cambridge University Press.

Jian-Hong, C., Tsai, P.-H., Yin-Chou, L., Chen, C.-K., & Ching-Yen, C. (2019). Mindfulness training enhances flow state and mental health among baseball players in Taiwan. *Psychology Research and Behavior Management, 12*, 15–21. doi:10.2147/PRBM.S188734

Kabat-Zinn, J. (1982). An outpatient program in behavioral medicine for chronic pain patients based on the practice of mindfulness meditation: Theoretical considerations and preliminary results. *General Hospital Psychiatry, 4*, 33–47.

Kabat-Zinn, J. (2013). *Full catastrophe living*. New York, NY: Bantam Books.

Kahn, W. (1990). Psychological conditions of personal engagement and disengagement at work. *Academy of Management Journal, 33*(4), 692. doi:10.2307/256287

Kotzé, M. (2018). The influence of psychological capital, self-leadership, and mindfulness on work engagement. *South African Journal of Psychology, 48*(2), 279–292. doi:10.1177/0081246317705812

Langer, E. J. (1989). *Mindfulness* (25th Anniversary ed.). Jackson, TN: Da Capo Lifelong Books.

Leroy, H., Anseel, F., Dimitrova, N. G., & Sels, L. (2013). mindfulness, authentic functioning, and work engagement: A grwoth modeling approach. *Journal of Vocational Behavior, (82)*, 238–247.

Malinowski, P. & Lim, H. J. (2015). Mindfulness at work: positive affect, hope, and optimism mediate the relationship between dispositional mindfulness, work engagement and well-being. *Mindfulness, 6* (6), 1250–1262.

Moore, B. A. (2013). Propensity for experiencing flow: The roles of cognitive flexibility and mindfulness. *The Humanistic Psychologist, 41*(4), 319–332. doi:10.1080/08873267.2013.820954

Osman, A., Lamis, D., Bagge, C. L., Freedenthal, S., & Barnes, S. M. (2016). The mindful attention awareness scale: Further examination of dimensionality, reliability, and concurrent validity estimates. *Journal of Personality Assessment, 98*(2), 189–199.

Rich, B. L., Lepine, J. A., & Crawford, E. R. (2010). Job engagement: Antecedents and effects on job performance. *Academy of Management Journal, 53*(3), 617–635.

Ryan, R. M. & Deci, E. L. (2001). To be happy or to be self-fullfilled: A review of research on hedonic and eudaimonic well-being. In S. Fiske (Ed.), *Annual review of psychology* (Vol. 52, pp. 141–166). Palo Alto, CA: Annual Reviews.

Ryan, R. M. & Frederick, C. (1997). On energy, personality, and health: Subjective vitality as a dynamic reflection of well-being. *Journal of Personality, 65*(3), 529–565. doi:10.1111/1467-6494.ep9710314567

Sadhguru. (2016a). *Inner engineering*. New York, NY: Pengiun Random House.

Sadhguru, J. V. (2013). *Life and death in one breath*: Jaico Publishing House.

Sadhguru, J. V. (2016b). *Inner engineering*. New York, NY: Penguin Random House.

Schaufeli, W. & Bakker, A. (2003). *Utrecht work engagement scale*. Retrieved from. https://www.wilmarschaufeli.nl/publications/Schaufeli/Test%20Manuals/Test_manual_UWES_English.pdf

Schaufeli, W. B., Bakker, A. B., & Salanova, M. (2006). The measurement of work engagement with a short questionnaire: A cross-national study. *Educational and Psychological Measurement, 66*(4), 701–716. doi:10.1177/0013164405282471

Schaufeli, W. B., Martinez, I. M., Pinto, A. M., Salanova, M., & Bakker, A. B. (2002). Burnout and engagement in university students: A cross-national study. *Journal of Cross-Cultural Psychology, 33*(5), 464–481.

Shioata, M. N., Keltner, D., & John, O. P. (2006). Positive emotion dispositions differntially associatd with big five personality and attachement style. *The Journal of Positive Psychology, 1*(2), 61–71.

Shobitha, M. & Agarwal, J. L. (2013). Electroencephalographic pattern and galvanic skin resistance levels during short duration of "aum" mantra chanting. *International Journal of Physiology, 1*(1), 68–72.

Silver, J., Caleshu, C., Casson-Parkin, S., & Ormond, K. (2018). Mindfulness among genetic counselors is associated with increased empathy and work engagement and decreased burnout and compassion fatigue. *Journal of Genetic Counseling, 27*(5), 1175–1186. doi:10.1007/s10897-018-0236-6

Sinnott, J., Hilton, S., Wood, M., & Douglas, D. (2018). Relating flow, mindfulness, cognitive flexibility, and postformal thought: Two studies. *Journal of Adult Development*. doi:10.1007/s10804-018-9320-2

Spreitzer, G. M., Lam, C. F. L., & Quinn, R. W. (2012). Human energy in organizations: Implications for POS from six interdisciplinary streams. In Cameron, Kim S. Spreitzer, Gretchen M. *The Oxford handbook of positive organizational scholarship* (pp. 155–167). New York, NY: Oxford University Press.

Whittington, J. L., Meskelis, S., Asare, E., & Beldona, S. (2017). *Enhancing employee engagement: An evidence-based apporach*. Switzerland: Palgrave Macmillan.

Zelano, C., Jiang, H., Zhou, G., Arora, N., Schuele, S., Rosenow, J., & Gottfried, J. A. (2016). Nasal respiration entrains human limbic oscillations and modulates cognitive function. *The Journal of Neuroscience: The Official Journal of the Society for Neuroscience, 36*(49), 12448. doi:10.1523/JNEUROSCI.2586-16.2016

Zivnuska, S., Kacmar, K. M., Ferguson, M., & Carlson, D. S. (2016). Mindfulness at work: Resource accumulation, well-being, and attitudes. *Career Development International, 21*(2), 106–124. doi:10.1108/CDI-06-2015-0086

Appendix

Measurement items of energy, joy, mindfulness, and work engagement

Survey Questions	*Coding*
Energy	
Please indicate the degree to which the statement is generally true for you in your life.	1= Not at all true, 7= Very true
1. I feel alive and vital.	
2. Sometimes I feel so alive I just want to burst.	
3. I have energy and spirit.	
4. I look forward to each new day.	
5. I nearly always feel alert and awake.	
6. I feel energized.	
Joy	
How strongly do you agree or disagree with the following statement?	1= Strongly disagree, 7= Strongly agree
1. I often feel a burst of joy.	
2. I am an intensely cheerful person.	
3. I am often completely overjoyed when something good happens.	
4. On a typical day, many events make me happy.	
5. Good things happen to me all the time.	
6. My life is always improving.	
Mindfulness	
In the last month, how often do you feel the following way?	1= Almost always, 6=Almost never
1. It seems I am "running on automatic," without much awareness of what I'm doing.	
2. I rush through activities without being really attentive to them.	
3. I get so focused on the goal I want to achieve that I lose touch with what I'm doing right now to get there.	
4. I do jobs or tasks automatically, without being aware of what I'm doing.	
5. I find myself doing things without paying attention.	
Work Engagement	
How frequently do you feel the following ways?	0= Never, 6= Every day
1. At my work, I feel bursting with energy. (vigor)	
2. At my job, I feel strong and vigorous. (vigor)	
3. When I get up in the morning, I feel like going to work. (vigor)	
4. I am enthusiastic about my job. (dedication)	
5. My job inspires me. (dedication)	
6. I am proud of the work that I do. (dedication)	
7. I feel happy when I am working intensely. (absorption)	
8. I am immersed in my work. (absorption)	
9. I get carried away when I'm working. (absorption)	

27

ATTENTION, REVERENCE, AND DEVOTION

An Ignatian method for fostering mindfulness at work

Dung Q. Tran

Introduction

Historically associated with the centuries-old Buddhist spiritual tradition (Brown, Creswell & Ryan, 2016), mindfulness is a universal, yet complex (Dhiman, 2009) human construct (Schultz & Ryan, 2015), capacity (Ludwig & Kabat-Zinn, 2008), and processual practice (Germer, 2013) that can be developed in a diversity of ways (Shapiro & Carlson, 2009). Regardless of application and/or etymological rendering by ancient Buddhists or contemporary scholar-practitioners—"Pali *sati*, Sanskrit *smṛti*, Chinese *nian*, and Tibetan *dran pa*" (Gethin, 2016, p. 9)—mindfulness, an intentional posture and process of nonjudgmental attentiveness "toward one's present moment experience that fosters conscious awareness of phenomenal experience" (Quaglia, Brown, Lindsay, Creswell & Goodman, 2016, p. 155), continues to capture the "popular imagination as a means of enhancing well-being, as reflected through the extensive coverage it currently receives within social media and mainstream news outlets [such as the *Washington Post* (Cortez, 2019) and the *New York Times* (Richtel, 2019)]" (Carleton, Barling & Trivisonno, 2018, p. 185). While the majority of mindfulness research "has been conducted in the field of health sciences" (Arendt, Pircher Verdorfer & Kugler, 2019, p. 1), organizational leadership practitioners and scholars have more recently entered the emerging mindfulness arena, "predicated on the assumption that more mindful employees will experience better health, lower health care costs, and higher levels of productivity" (Carleton et al., 2018, p. 185). Myriad institutions, across a range of sectors, such as hospitals, business schools, investment banks, the military, and corporations such as Google, General Mills, and IBM (Hyland, Lee & Mills, 2015; Rupprecht & Walach, 2016), have instituted mindfulness trainings into their human resource development offerings.

Mindfulness in the workplace programs are often connected with a wider workplace spirituality strategy aimed at reducing stress (Mayer & Geldenhuys, 2019). While the role of mindfulness as a spiritual activity in the workplace has received attention in the literature (Alberts & Hülsheger, 2015; Choi & Leroy, 2015; Reb & Atkins, 2015), and interest in examining the nexus of Ignatian spirituality with organizational leadership (Byron, 2010,

2011; Lowney, 2003; Lozano, 2017; Nullens, 2019; Rothausen, 2017; Tran & Carey, 2018) and Eastern wisdom traditions continues to abound (Cline, 2018; Habito, 2013; Haight, 2012; Newman, 1996; Tyler, 2018), as of the writing of this chapter, I am only aware of one standalone intersectional investigation of Buddhist mindfulness and Ignatian spirituality (Rehg, 2002). Though the article does a fine job of bridging the Buddhist notion of mindfulness with the Ignatian ideal of being a contemplative-in-action or "finding God in all things," it does not draw specifically upon the work of Jesuit Howard Gray, who played a pivotal role "in the rescue of Jesuit spirituality from the moralism into which it had largely fallen over the course of the centuries and in promoting Ignatian spirituality, whose blossoming we experience today" (O'Malley, 2018, para. 10). Additionally, given the nearly 20 years since its publication and a recent desire from a global Jesuit leader to share Ignatian spirituality with non-Christians (Nicolas, 2009), an updated inquiry is warranted.

Consequently, this chapter explores a distinctive approach of practicing mindfulness in the workplace anchored in the spiritual philosophy of Ignatius of Loyola, often referred to as Ignatian spirituality. In particular, I discuss how Ignatian spirituality, a nearly 500-year-old "vision of life, work, and of love" (Fleming, 2008, p. 2), offers a model for discerning important decisions and becoming more mindfully present to the depth and significance of one's everyday experience. This inquiry is guided by the insights of Jesuit Howard Gray (1999, 2000, 2001, 2008), an internationally regarded interpreter of Ignatian spirituality, who mined the writings of Ignatius and advanced a "model of what spiritual growth and development meant for the Jesuit leader" (Traub, 2008, p. 48). Following the development of a dialogical bridge between mindfulness as part of workplace spirituality initiatives, Ignatian spirituality, and Gray's (1999, 2000, 2001, 2008) synthesis of an Ignatian method of how to lead a more mindfully attuned life, this chapter concludes by proposing the Ignatian awareness examen as a mindful (and adaptable) practice for the workplace. The Ignatian examen invites practitioners to reflectively review daily happenings and illumine the currents and undercurrents of one's interior life.

The historical origins and contemporary appropriation of mindfulness in the workplace

Mindfulness is rooted within the 2,500-year-old spiritual philosophy and practice of Buddhism (Rupprecht & Walach, 2016). According to Thich Nhat Hanh (1999), an internationally regarded Vietnamese Buddhist monk, peace activist, and spiritual leader (McIntyre, 2019), "mindfulness is at the heart of the Buddha's teachings" (p. 64). In a historical review of Buddhist conceptualizations of mindfulness, Quaglia et al. (2016) concluded that mindfulness is "a state of sustained, receptive attentiveness, evaluations and judgements, memories, and other cognitive operations [that] can be closely attended to, and actively engaged, by a mind that is aware of what is happening moment to moment" (p. 154).

Since the 1980s, "the interest in the application of mindfulness technique has grown exponentially" as a variety of authors, across many sectors and disciplines, "have described the term differently to suit their needs and purposes" (Dhiman, 2009, p. 57). According to McIntyre (2019), "the introduction of a secular style of mindfulness to the West is most often attributed to, among other people, Jon Kabat-Zinn" (p. xvi). In 1979, Kabat-Zinn pioneered an eight-week mindfulness-based stress reduction program at the University of Massachusetts Medical School that combined "meditation, yoga, and mindfulness exercises that is now used worldwide in hospitals, corporations, prisons, and schools" (p. xvi). For Carmody (2016), "Recognition of the common goal that Buddhism, medicine, and psychology each have in reducing suffering has helped pave the way for the entry of mindfulness and Buddhist MT [mindfulness training] exercises into Western medicine and psychotherapeutic programs" (p. 63).

Although there is not a "universal definition of mindfulness in Western psychology" (Gaymer, 2017, p. 155), "The following are two frequently cited definitions in the modern mindfulness literature" (Gethin, 2016, p. 31):

1. "Mindfulness means paying attention in a particular way: on purpose, in the present moment, and nonjudgmentally" (Kabat-Zinn, 1994, p. 4).
2. "A kind of nonelaborative, nonjudgemental, present-centered awareness in which each thought, feeling, or sensation that arises in the attentional field is acknowledged and accepted as it is" (Bishop et al., 2004, p. 232).

Similar to the aforementioned and influential work of Kabat-Zinn (1994) and Bishop et al. (2004), most definitions of mindfulness in the scientific literature "suggest the possibility that both attention and awareness are needed for mindfulness to arise, and that attention is a necessary precondition for awareness" (Quaglia et al., 2016, p. 155). For Good et al. (2016), the integration of attention and awareness distinguishes mindfulness from other similar states of being. Along with the integration of attention and awareness, another important process of mindfulness "is the ability to mentally 'step back' from one's own experiences" (Arendt et al., 2019, p. 2), which can enhance an individual's "capacity to be fully aware of all that one experiences *inside the self*—body, mind, heart, spirit—and to pay full attention to what is happening *around us*—people, the natural world, our surroundings, and events" (Boyatzis & McKee, 2005, p. 112). As Raney (2014) noted, "This formulation resonates strongly with clinical social work's commitment to self-determination and recovery principles" (p. 313).

Overall, research inquiries from disciplines such as psychology, neuroscience, medicine, and other related fields have furnished "a wealth of evidence that mindfulness affects attention, cognition, emotions, behavior, and physiology in positive ways" (Good et al., 2016, p. 115). At the same time, efforts to empirically investigate mindfulness "exposed significant disagreements in approaches to the construct" (Carmody, 2016, p. 64). Some researchers (Grossman, 2011; Purser & Milillo, 2015; Quaglia et al., 2016), "object that current approaches in Western psychology and the conceptualization of mindfulness as a bare, non-judgmental awareness of the current experience do not fully live up to the true nature and complexity of the 'original' Buddhist concept of mindfulness" (Arendt et al., 2019, p. 2). While "this criticism is countered by a growing body of research that views mindfulness" (p. 2) as "an inherent human capacity" (Kabat-Zinn, 2003, p. 146) that can decouple mindfulness practice from Buddhism (Brown & Ryan, 2004; Brown, Ryan, Loverich, Biegel & West, 2011), this robust scholarly debate provides ample opportunity for further inquiry and interchange among scholars and practitioners from a variety of intellectual vistas.

According to Good et al. (2016), research in the various health sciences "laid the groundwork" (p. 127) for the investigation of mindfulness in the workplace. In the 1990s, Weick and Roberts (1993), influenced by Langer's (1989) scholarship, "introduced mindfulness into the management literature" (Good et al., 2016, p. 116). In their integrative review of the literature, Good and associates (2016) found that mindfulness positively influenced workplace outcomes related to performance, relationships, and well-being (p. 122). For instance, in their examination of 85,004 responses from US workers aged 18 or older, who participated in the 2002, 2007, and 2012 National Health Interview Survey (NHIS), Kachan et al. (2017) found that, "Approximately 1 in 7 workers report engagement in some form of mindfulness-based activity, and these individuals can bring awareness of the benefit of such practices into the workplace" (p. 4).

Incidentally, given the increasing interest among business leaders to reduce stress in the workplace in order to positively enhance employee well-being and, ultimately, organizational performance, the introduction of mindfulness in organizational contexts has occurred as part of the emerging trend of leveraging spirituality to cultivate a more life-affirming and wellness-oriented organizational culture (Mayer & Geldenhuys, 2019). At the same time, Khanna and Khanna (2019) expressed an understandable concern about mindfulness and workplace spirituality being used by some organizational leaders as another fashionable technique or tool to enhance the bottom line and "rob humanity of essential wisdom from ancient traditions" (Mishra & Varma, 2019, p. 5). To honor the essence of their historical roots, further enhance the benefits of mindfulness at work, and manage the frenetic pace and chaotic nature that can characterize contemporary workplaces, Good et al. (2016) suggested that "organizations might consider adapting design elements from contemplative contexts [such as retreat centers and monasteries] to support mindfulness" (p. 135).

Ignatian spirituality's resonance with corporate mindfulness and workplace spirituality

The spiritual philosophy of Ignatius of Loyola (1491–1556) is one "eminently adaptable" (Cline, 2018, p. 2) and enduring contemplative context that is uniquely positioned to advance both the humanistic and higher-performance aims of the corporate mindfulness and workplace spirituality movement. In addition to sharing "some mutually resonant themes" (Habito, 2013, p. xix) with the Buddhist origins of mindfulness (Rehg, 2002) and workplace spirituality (Tran & Carey, 2018), Ignatian spirituality, especially when considered alongside the Benedictine tradition of monasticism, "is oriented towards the world outside the walls of the cloister" (Nullens, 2019, p. 194). As Martin (2010) maintained, "Instead of seeing the spiritual life as one that can exist only if it is enclosed by the walls of a monastery, Ignatius asks you to see the world as your monastery" (p. 8). A spiritual innovator,

> Ignatius departed from a monastic or cloistered style of religious [and spiritual] life and introduced an active form that would enable Jesuits [and lay collaborators] to be fully engaged in worldly events and yet remain in touch with the pervasive presence and action of God throughout.
>
> *(Au, 2010, pp. 6–7)*

Given that innovation was central to the discovery of Ignatian spirituality and founding of the Jesuits, *and* continues to be a core concern of business leaders and politicians (Dodgson, 2018), it is no wonder why interest in Ignatian spirituality and leadership continues to abound (Byron, 2011; Darmanin, 2005; Dufresne, Botto & Steele, 2015; Lowney, 2003; Lozano, 2017; Moberg & Calkins, 2001; Nullens, 2019; Rothausen, 2017; San Juan, 2007; Tran & Carey, 2018).

However, as of this writing, only one standalone inquiry of Ignatian spirituality and mindfulness has been performed (Rehg, 2002). While an important scholarly integration,

Rehg's work did not leverage Howard Gray's (1999, 2000, 2001, 2008) method of cultivating contemplatives-in-action (finding God in all things in the normative Ignatian lexicon) as a tripartite process of attention, reverence, and devotion.

Before turning to Gray's (2001) accessible summary of Ignatius's method for awakening human persons "from a self-centered way of life to a life sustained and empowered by love" (Habito, 2013, p. xxii), this chapter provides a (very) brief overview of Ignatius of Loyola, his world-affirming spiritual vision, and how that spirituality led to the founding of the Society of Jesus or the Jesuits, and an international network of educational institutions committed to forming discerning human persons to lead lives of service and leadership. This historical context will set the stage for the building of a dialogical bridge between mindfulness and Ignatius of Loyola's *Spiritual Exercises*, which will be illumined by Howard Gray's (1999, 2000, 2001, 2008) practical method for fostering devotion, or in more accessible Ignatian language, a more contemplative sensibility.

Ignatius of Loyola: spiritual visionary, Jesuit founder, and educational entrepreneur

Steeped in the spiritual insights of a 16th-century Spanish would-be romantic and courtier-soldier, turned pilgrim, spiritual guide, and founder of the Society of Jesus or the Jesuits, Ignatius of Loyola's "way of life has helped millions of people discover joy, peace, and freedom and, not incidentally, experience God in their daily lives" (Martin, 2010, p. 1). During their own lifetime, Ignatius and the first Jesuits became a "worldwide missionary order, a major force in the sixteenth-century renewal of Catholicism, and created an educational system that transformed Europe and beyond" (Sparough, Manney & Hipskind, 2010, p. 29). With nearly 16,000 members serving in 112 countries, they are currently the largest order of priests and brothers in the Catholic Church (Giberti, 2015). Additionally, with 188 institutions of higher learning and 827 secondary schools in 70 countries (International Commission on the Apostolate of Jesuit Education, 2019), the Jesuits and their Ignatian-inspired lay colleagues have been, and continue to be, well situated to prepare people for positions of leadership and impact across many sectors and societies.

Regarded as a "towering figure in the history of spirituality" (Sparough et al., 2010, p. ix), Ignatius is also known for his spiritual classic on decision-making, *The Spiritual Exercises*—"the oldest handbook still applicable in real time" (Tetlow, 2008, p. x). Printed in 1548 (Ganss, 1991, p. 50), Ignatius's book is a manual of meditations and guidelines for discernment—"the process of becoming aware of, understanding, and responding to the spiritual stirrings of our hearts" (Gallagher, 2007, p. 3). Ignatius's insights into the spiritual dimension of discernment, his psychology of choosing, and method for transformation, also referred to as Ignatian discernment, discernment of spirits, or more broadly as Ignatian spirituality, have endured for nearly 500 years (Kracher, 2016). His handbook of meditations is arguably one of the most important spiritual classics ever written (Barry & Doherty, 2002) and continues to "influence human culture across historical and geographical boundaries" (Habito, 2013, p. 3).

Ignatius's manual of *Spiritual Exercises* was the fruit of a profound set of experiences during and after his six-month recovery from a life-threatening injury suffered during a battle against the French at the border fortress of Pamplona, Spain, in 1521. Bored and restless while recuperating at his family's castle, Ignatius, who, as a budding soldier at the time, "preferred stirring tales of chivalry, of knights doing gallant deeds to impress women" (Martin, 2010, p. 12), reluctantly read the only available literature his sister-in-law could find: Ludoph of Saxony's *Life of Christ* and selections from Jacopo da Voragine's *The Golden Legend*, "a medieval collection of lives of saints" (O'Malley, 2014, p. 6). As Ignatius read and pondered both books, he was surprised by his heartfelt reactions: daydreams about resuming his path as a Spanish soldier left him unsettled and unhappy, whereas the possibility of emulating servant-leaders such as Jesus of Nazareth and Francis of Assisi "brought him serenity and comfort" (O'Malley, 1993, p. 24). Ignatius started recording his reactions and reflecting on the,

> contrasting experiences of what he came to call desolation and consolation, and, as he considered the way the story of his life had unfolded, Ignatius gradually began to ground his life in the following central conviction of Ignatian spirituality: We can discern how God [or however we perceive God] is calling us to lives of freedom and wholeness and integrity if we pay attention to the feelings moving in our hearts as we reflect on our own life experiences.
>
> *(Kalscheur, 2007, p. 11)*

Simply put, Ignatius's "great discovery was that we can [learn to] listen to the language of our hearts when making decisions" (Sparough et al., 2010, p. 33) that enable one to live generously in service with and for others.

Over time and through trial and error, Ignatius would put his profound insights into practice and realize the two-fold purpose of his *Spiritual Exercises*:

1. "to assist people facing a major life choice to make a decision resonant with God's call and freed from personal attachments that obstruct listening to and embracing God's lead with confident trust," and
2. "to foster devotion" (Au, 2010, p. 7).

Since much has been written about Ignatian discernment (Byron, 2011; Gallagher, 2007; Healey, 2009; Gula, 1989, 2003, 2011; Lonsdale, 2000; Martin, 2010, O'Brien, 2011; Silf, 1999; Thibodeaux, 2010; Traub, 2008; Wolff, 2003), the primary purpose of the *Spiritual Exercises*, and, since the secondary purpose of the Exercises, fostering devotion or "an ease or facility to find God in all things" (Au, 2010, p. 6), can be summarized in more accessible language by Howard Gray, this chapter will now focus its attention on his threefold process of attention, reverence, and devotion.

Attention, reverence, and devotion: Howard Gray's method for becoming more mindful

Although Ignatius of Loyola is most known for his manual of *Spiritual Exercises*, he also composed the *Constitutions of the Society of Jesus*, an *Autobiography*, and at least 7,000 letters. According to Nullens (2019), a stronger grasp of the *Exercises* comes from reading them "against the background of Ignatius' wider corpus of texts" (p. 193). Accordingly, in a section of the *Constitutions* that addresses educational formation, Ignatius proposed a tripartite process for becoming more "attuned to God's presence" (Gray, 1999, p. 31) amidst the daily activities of life. For Gray (1999), an internationally known expert on Ignatian spirituality, this process unfolds across three movements or "attitudes of heart" (Kalscheur, 2007, p. 22)—attention, reverence, and devotion.

Attention: a long loving look at reality

In Gray's (1999) view, living a life attuned to God or divine mystery's presence involves the following:

> First, bring focus to your life by taking the time to listen to others and to see what lies before you. Bring yourself to a self-possession before reality. Then give your attention (maybe attentiveness is a better word) to what is really there. For example, let that person or that poem or that social injustice or that scientific experiment become as genuinely itself as it can be. Then reverence what you see before you. Reverence is giving acceptance to, cherishing the differences of, holding in awe the uniqueness of another reality. So, before you judge or assess or respond, give yourself time to esteem and accept what is there in the other. And if you learn to do this, Ignatius urged, then you will gradually discover devotion, the singularly moving way in which God works in that situation, revealing goodness and fragility, beauty and truth, pain and anguish, wisdom and ingenuity.
>
> *(as cited in Au, 2010, p. 11 & Kalscheur, 2007, p. 22)*

The first movement of attention is the,

> ability to be present in a relationship in its particularity. It stands for that presence in which one person allows another reality ... to enter [one's] awareness on [one's] own terms. It is acceptance of that reality, not an intrusion—through fear or bias or lack of concentration—on that reality.
>
> *(Gray, 2000, pp. 9–10)*

In more concrete terms, Walter Burghardt (2008), a Jesuit theologian, described devotion as a "long and loving look at the real" (p. 89). For Burghardt, "reality is living, pulsing people," as "fire and ice," as "the sun setting over the Swiss Alps," as a "gentle doe streaking through the forest," as a "ruddy glass of Burgundy," as a "child lapping a chocolate ice cream cone," and as "a striding [person] with wind-blown hair" (p. 91). Therefore, an Ignatian spiritual method of fostering attentive awareness involves a "long and loving look at such realities" (Au, 2010, p. 11).

Coupled with the distractions of handheld mobile devices and social media, the complex and chaotic nature of contemporary organizational and personal contexts makes the cultivation of such a contemplative and attentive mindset challenging. Hence, Ignatius's encouragement to stay with and savor one's experience, however pleasurable and painful it might be. Facing the uncomfortable dimensions of human experiencing may explain why daydreaming and fantasizing about alternative realities is more attractive. For Au (2010), staying with the fullness of one's reality is an invitation to accept one's immediate experience and "surrender to being just as we are" (p. 11).

Reverence: respecting the revealed reality

Rather than "seeing what one would like to be there, or what one hopes is there, or what has been told by others is there," reverence, the second movement for finding God in all things, is about "the gradually stripping away of the self so that one can see what is there" (Himes, 2008, p. 233). For Gray (2000), reverence "represents another level of acceptance, not only allowing the reality to be present to me but accepting that reality as different from, unique in … self-expression, worthy of [one's] own integrity" (p. 10). As Au (2010) asserted,

> Respect for the unique otherness of people means that we regard them as unprecedented selves. It requires that we see each person with fresh eyes, cleared of the prejudices and biases that can distort our perceptions. Calling for an undefended and unguarded openness, reverence entails a certain vulnerability that lets persons and events affect us with their full resonance. Reverence excludes any kind of attempt to manipulate, control, or categorize people, instead allowing them to speak for themselves, to express their meaning and truth in their own words.
>
> *(p. 13)*

Simply put, "reverence is the exclusion of exclusion, e.g., my biases and prejudices, my fears and hesitancies" (Gray, 2008, p. 65), and the "heart of contemplative listening" (Au, 2010, p. 13).

Devotion: a moment of personal clarity

If attention is reflectively allowing reality to be present, and reverence is embracing the authentic reality that has been allowed in, then devotion, the final movement, "represents a privileged moment of personal revelation" that "can be characterized as peace or as a strengthened sense of being called or of a renewed insight into the personality of Jesus" (Gray, 2008, p. 66). Devotion can be experienced as a heartfelt perception of reality with wonder and awe, an intuition of a wider sense of ultimate concerns beyond human understanding. At the same time, one's experience of devotion "may not be as gentle" and draw "a person to a harsh honesty where one experiences the discrepancy between [one's] operational values and God's revelation" (p. 66). Ultimately, the interplay of attention, reverence, and devotion is a tripartite processual method for "letting privileged moments speak more deeply, of dwelling on them, savouring them, entering into them," (Campbell-Johnson, 1992, p. 434), which can facilitate, should an individual desire, one's ability to find God in all things (Au, 2010) or be a contemplative-in-action.

Developing discerning contemplatives-in-action in the workplace

Although Habito (2013) and Haight (2012) have developed initial inclusive approaches, the "centrality of God" (Cline, 2018, p. 181) can be a stumbling block for some non-religious and non-Christian spiritual seekers. However, as Adolfo Nicolas (2009), former superior general of the Jesuits, asserted in a university lecture,

> the *Spiritual Exercises* can be shared by non-Christians. Even though Christ is at the heart of the full experience of the *Exercises,* it is also true that their structure involves a process of liberation—of opening to new horizons—that can benefit people who do not share our life of faith. This is something I would like to see explored more and more. We particularly experienced this challenge in Japan when non-Christians came to visit and asked if they could make the *Exercises*. This triggered a reflection, and it is one that we need to continue. What are the

> dynamics in the *Exercises* that non-believers might make their own to find wider horizons in life, a greater sense of spiritual freedom?
>
> *(p. 10)*

According to Nicolas, despite the "radically Christo-centric" nature of Ignatian spirituality, "important elements of the *Spiritual Exercises*, especially those concerned with spiritual freedom, equipoise and discernment, can be fruitfully appropriated even by non-Christians" (p. 9). In fact, as Newman (1996) noted, several of the general guidelines for those embarking on the *Spiritual Exercises* contain a semblance of mindfulness. For example, in the seventeenth annotation of the *Exercises*, the discerner is encouraged to share "various agitations and thoughts" with their spiritual guide, and that every dimension of the experience "together produce a cumulative watchfulness of what passes in mind and heart" (p. 52). Also, as evidenced by the breakthrough insights about feelings of consolation and desolation during his convalescence, Rehg (2002) concluded that Ignatius's insights "portray discernment as a practice in mindfulness" and "display a relation to affect and practical engagement" (p. 21). In other words,

> Ignatian discernment—in particular the Rules for the Discernment of Spirits—links mindfulness with explicit evaluation and judgment. That is, one pays attention to interior states and movements precisely in order to evaluate them in relation to possible choices and practical commitments. Like his Buddhist brothers and sisters, Ignatius insists that right choices and actions flow from a freedom from attachments or, as he puts it, "indifference." And like the Buddhists, Ignatius provides us with a set of "spiritual exercises" for arriving at such indifference. In contrast to many Buddhists, however, Ignatius also provides us with a method or set of instructions for making explicit judgments about which choices are appropriate, that is, in sync with God's action in the world.
>
> *(p. 21)*

As evidenced above, even though mindfulness is most associated with Buddhism, "its phenomenological nature is embedded in most religious and spiritual traditions" (Shapiro & Carlson, 2009, pp. 3–4), including Ignatius Loyola's nearly 500-year-old *Spiritual Exercises*. At the same time, Ignatian spirituality is "not bound up in technical terminology or confined to the arm chair reflections of theologians and religious leaders" (Cline, 2018, p. 3), making it a desirable option for secular spiritual seekers and/or organizational decision-makers to consider as they discern the return on investment of incorporating mindfulness as part of a workplace spirituality initiative.

The Ignatian examen: an adaptable mindfulness practice for the workplace

As organizations continue their quest of reducing work-related stress and absenteeism, and enhancing performance and competitive advantage, they are turning to mindfulness and workplace spirituality initiatives to enable workers to "express their spiritual selves which may help them find renewed purpose and meaning in their work" (Khanna & Khanna, 2019, p. 181). Both the Buddhist and Ignatian spiritual traditions—and their celebrated contemplative practices—are two paths of awakening and transformation that have much to offer the modern, and often secular, workplace. While many mindfulness trainings, influenced by the work of Kabat-Zinn (1994), continue to capture the imagination of scientists, social-media influencers, and organizational leadership scholar-practitioners alike (Carleton et al., 2018), "The Ignatian *Spiritual Exercises* are worthy of greater attention in contemplative studies and the wider culture" (Cline, 2018, p. 11). To that end, this chapter concludes by offering a process-driven and eminently adaptable mindfulness practice from Ignatius of Loyola's *Spiritual Exercises*.

One of the very few rules of Ignatian spirituality is to practice a daily self-inventory of one's spiritual life. Near the beginning of the *Spiritual Exercises*, Ignatius furnished a method of reflection that he termed, "a method for making the general examination of conscience" (Ganss, 1991, pp. 134–135), which is now more commonly known as the examen. For Ignatius, a periodic pause to review daily happenings in a spirit of reflection is a process of spiritual maintenance, i.e., paying closer attention to the subtle movements of one's inner life. The examen consists of five movements:

1. Gratitude: Recall anything from the day for which you are especially grateful, and give thanks.
2. Review: Recall the events of the day, from start to finish, noticing where you felt God's presence, and where you accepted or turned away from any invitations to grow in love.
3. Sorrow: Recall any actions for which you are sorry.
4. Forgiveness: Ask for God's forgiveness. Decide whether you want to reconcile with anyone you have hurt.
5. Grace: Ask God for the grace you need for the next day and an ability to see God's presence more clearly (Martin, 2010, p. 97).

In an adapted and more expansive manner, Lowney (2009) articulated the following six steps:

1. Compose yourself in a contemplative and mindful manner and step back from the daily flux of events.
2. Seek enlightenment and wisdom.
3. Be grateful! You have so much; don't take it for granted. Focus for a moment on what you already have rather than on what you want.
4. Mentally scroll through the past few hours to draw lessons learned from the day so far. You might think about your near- or long-term goals or about some characteristic weakness that hobbles your effectiveness. Pay attention to what you've been thinking and feeling, not just to what you've been doing.
5. Be honest with yourself. If you've not been executing your plan or living the values you aspire to, acknowledge that.
6. Finish with hopeful resolution for the future. Be thankful for the opportunity to have recollected yourself, taken stock, and reoriented your thoughts or actions as necessary. And as you have extracted lessons from the past, put the past behind you and look forward (pp. 174–175).

More recently, Lowney (2018) created an "oversimplified version" that he called a "mental pit stop" in order to "render it accessible to tech workers, teachers, and office managers [as well as] those of any (or no) religious tradition to tap its wisdom" (p. 86):

1. Remind yourself why you're grateful.
2. "Lift your horizon." That is, don't focus six inches ahead, at the next email to answer or the next errand to do. Instead, focus on the big picture. Call to mind what

ultimately matters to you, your sense of purpose, or your most important life goals this year. Then,

3. Relive the past few hours. What was going on inside you? What can you learn from these past hours that might benefit your next few hours? For example, if you were upset all morning, why? If you snapped at a colleague or your spouse and need to make amends, resolve to do so.

As Fleming (2008) noted,

> Over the years, Jesuits and others have developed many versions of the examen. They are like successive editions of a great textbook. They are based on the same insight and ideas, but they differ in order to emphasize certain things and adapt to diverse audiences.
>
> *(p. 21)*

Since it is often challenging to assess meaning and significance of events as they occur, the examen is a reflective tool that enables mindfulness practitioners to "stay in touch with the currents and undercurrents of our fast-paced lives" (Au, 2000, p. 138). At bottom, Ignatius of Loyola's examen and his *Spiritual Exercises* offer an invitation and broad framework for mastering three vital skills that can enhance corporate mindfulness and workplace spirituality:

1. Articulate a purpose worth the rest of your life.
2. Make wise career and relationship choices in this changing, uncertain world.
3. Make every day matter by paying mindful attention to your thoughts, actions, and results (Lowney, 2009, p. ix).

Conclusion

As evidenced by the preceding presentation, the purpose of this chapter was to explore a distinctive approach of practicing mindfulness in the workplace anchored in the spiritual philosophy of Ignatius of Loyola, often referred to as Ignatian spirituality. At its core, "Ignatian spirituality is missional: inner growth must lead to a [person's freely made decision to contribute to] change in society" (Nullens, 2019, p. 194). Over time and through trial and error, Ignatius put his profound insights into practice and realized the two-fold purpose of his *Spiritual Exercises*: "to facilitate discernment in a major life choice and form modern-day contemplatives in action ... in the midst of busy lives" (Au, 2010, p. 7).

Consequently, I examined how Ignatian spirituality, a nearly 500-year-old "vision of life, work, and of love" (Fleming, 2008, p. 2), offers a model for discerning important decisions and becoming more mindfully present to the depth and significance of everyday experience. This inquiry was guided by the insights of Jesuit Howard Gray (1999, 2000, 2001, 2008), an internationally regarded interpreter of Ignatian spirituality, who mined the writings of Ignatius and advanced a "model of what spiritual growth and development meant for the Jesuit leader" (Traub, 2008, p. 48). Following the development of a dialogical bridge between mindfulness in the workplace, Ignatian spirituality, and Gray's (1999, 2000, 2001, 2008) synthesis of an Ignatian method of how to lead a more mindfully attuned life, this chapter concluded by proposing the Ignatian awareness examen as an adaptable and brief practice to reflectively review daily happenings and illumine the currents and undercurrents of one's interior life.

Ultimately, the "eminently adaptable" (Cline, 2018, p. 2) nature of Ignatian spirituality is what makes the spiritual philosophy of Ignatius of Loyola a suitable candidate for organizational decision-makers interested in instituting and/or enhancing their corporate mindfulness and workplace spirituality initiatives.

Chapter takeaways

1. Historically associated with Buddhism, mindfulness is a universal, yet complex human construct, capacity, and processual practice that can be developed in a diversity of ways.
2. With "some mutually resonant themes" (Habito, 2013, p. xix) with the Buddhist origins of mindfulness (Rehg, 2002) and workplace spirituality (Tran & Carey, 2018), the spiritual philosophy of Ignatius of Loyola is an adaptable and enduring contemplative context that is uniquely positioned to advance both the humanistic and higher-performance aims of the corporate mindfulness and workplace spirituality movement.
3. Ignatius of Loyola's *Spiritual Exercises* have two purposes: "to facilitate discernment in a major life choice and form modern-day contemplatives in action ... in the midst of busy lives" (Au, 2010, p. 7).
4. Jesuit Howard Gray, an internationally known expert on Ignatian spirituality, summarized Ignatius's method of becoming a contemplative in action as a tripartite process of attention, reverence, and devotion.
5. The Ignatian awareness examen is a practical and adaptable daily mindfulness practice that can serve as an antidote to the increasingly hyper-fast pace of organizational life.

Reflection questions

1. What is mindfulness?
2. What ideas have historically influenced the development of mindfulness?
3. As one spiritual path to human wholeness, what can Ignatian spirituality contribute to the development of mindfulness theory and practice?
4. What is the Ignatian awareness examen? What aspects of the awareness examen appeal to you?
5. How might you appropriate and integrate the Ignatian examen into your own practice of mindfulness in professional and personal contexts?

References

Alberts, H. J. E. M. & Hülsheger, U. R. (2015). Applying mindfulness in the context of work. In J. Reb & P. W. B. Atkins (Eds.), *Mindfulness in organisations: Foundations, research, and applications* (pp. 100–132). Cambridge, UK: Cambridge University Press.

Arendt, J. F. W., Pircher Verdorfer, A., & Kugler, K. G. (2019). Mindfulness and leadership: Communication as a behavioral correlate of leader mindfulness and its effect on follower satisfaction. *Frontiers in Psychology, 10*. doi:10.3389/fpsyg.2019.00667

Au, W. (2000). *The enduring heart: Spirituality for the long haul*. Mahwah, NJ: Paulist Press.

Au, W. (2010). The Ignatian method: A way of proceeding. *Presence: An International Journal of Spiritual Direction, 16*(3), 6–17.

Barry, W. A. & Doherty, R. G. (2002). *Contemplatives in action: The Jesuit way*. Mahwah, NJ: Paulist Press.

Bishop, S. R., Lau, M., Shapiro, S. L., Carlson, L., Anderson, N. D., Carmody, J., Segal, Z. V., Abbey, S., Speca, M., Velting, D., & Devins, G. (2004). Mindfulness: A proposed operational definition. *Clinical Psychology, 11*, 230–241.

Boyatzis, R. & McKee, A. (2005). *Resonant leadership: Renewing yourself and connecting with others through mindfulness, hope, and compassion*. Boston, MA: Harvard Business School Press.
Brown, K. W., Creswell, J. D., & Ryan, R. M. (2016). Introduction: The evolution of mindfulness science. In K. W. Brown, J. D. Creswell, & R. M. Ryan (Eds.), *Handbook of mindfulness: Theory, research, and practice* (pp. 1–8). New York, NY: Guilford.
Brown, K. W. & Ryan, R. M. (2004). Perils and promise in defining and measuring mindfulness: Observations from experience. *Clinical Psychology, 11*, 242–248.
Brown, K. W., Ryan, R. M., Loverich, T. M., Biegel, G. M., & West, A. M. (2011). Out of the armchair and into the streets: Measuring mindfulness advances knowledge and improves interventions: Reply to Grossman (2011). *Psychological Assessment, 23*, 1041–1046.
Burghardt, W. J. (2008). Contemplation: A long loving look at the real. In G. W. Traub (Ed.), *An Ignatian spirituality reader* (pp. 89–98). Chicago, IL: Loyola Press.
Byron, W. J. (2010). *Next-generation leadership: A toolkit for those in their teens, twenties, & thirties, who want to be successful leaders*. Scranton, PA: University of Scranton Press.
Byron, W. J. (2011). Humility, magis, and discernment: A Jesuit perspective on education for business leadership. *Journal of Jesuit Business Education, 2*, 9–20.
Campbell-Johnson, M. (1992, August 4). Being and doing. *Tablet.*
Carleton, E. L., Barling, J., & Trivisonno, M. (2018). Leaders' trait mindfulness and transformational leadership: The mediating roles of leaders' positive affect and leadership self-efficacy. *Canadian Journal of Behavioral Science, 50*(3), 185–194.
Carmody, J. (2016). Reconceptualizing mindfulness: The psychological principles of attending in mindfulness practice and their role in well-being. In K. W. Brown, J. D. Creswell, & R. M. Ryan (Eds.), *Handbook of mindfulness: Theory, research, and practice* (pp. 62–80). New York, NY: Guilford.
Choi, E. & Leroy, H. (2015). Methods of mindfulness: How mindfulness is studied in organisations. In J. Reb & P. W. B. Atkins (Eds.), *Mindfulness in organisations: Foundations, research, and applications* (pp. 67–99). Cambridge, UK: Cambridge University Press.
Cline, E. M. (2018). *A world on fire: Sharing the Ignatian spiritual exercises with other religions*. Washington, DC: Catholic University Press.
Cortez, M. (2019, June 13). Mindfulness. *Washington Post.* Retrieved from www.washingtonpost.com/business/energy/mindfulness/2019/06/13/01647684-8de5-11e9-b6f4-033356502dce_story.html
Darmanin, A. (2005). Ignatian spirituality and leadership in organizations today. *Review of Ignatian Spirituality, 109*, 1–14.
Dhiman, S. (2009). Mindfulness in life and leadership: An exploratory survey. *Interbeing, 3*(1), 55–80.
Dodgson, M. (2018). *Innovation management: A research overview*. New York, NY: Routledge.
Dufresne, R. L., Botto, K., & Steele, E. S. (2015). Contributing to an Ignatian perspective on leadership. *Journal of Jesuit Business Education, 6*(1), 1–19.
Fleming, D. L. (2008). *What is Ignatian spirituality?* Chicago, IL: Loyola Press.
Gallagher, T. M. (2007). *Spiritual consolation: An Ignatian guide for the greater discernment of spirits*. New York, NY: Crossroad.
Ganss, G. E. (Ed.). (1991). *Ignatius of Loyola: Spiritual exercises and selected works*. Mahwah, NY: Paulist Press.
Gaymer, L. (2017). The relationship between mindfulness and burnout and the role of emotion regulation in university students. In T. Ditrich, R. Wiles, & B. Lovegrove (Eds.), *Mindfulness and education: Research and practice* (pp. 153–182). Newcastle upon Tyne, UK: Cambridge Scholars Publishing.
Germer, L. (2013). Mindfulness: What is it? What does it matter? In C. K. Germer, R. D. Siegel, & P. R. Fulton (Eds.), *Mindfulness and psychotherapy* (2nd ed., pp. 3–35). New York, NY: Guilford.
Gethin, R. (2016). Buddhist conceptualizations of mindfulness. In K. W. Brown, J. D. Creswell, & R. M. Ryan (Eds.), *Handbook of mindfulness: Theory, research, and practice* (pp. 9–41). New York, NY: Guilford.
Giberti, C. N. (2015). Jesuits. In M. Odekon (Ed.), *The SAGE encyclopedia of world poverty* (pp. 857–858). Thousand Oaks, CA: Sage.
Good, D. J., Lyddy, C. J., Glomb, T. M., Bono, J. E., Brown, K. W., Duffy, M. K., Baer, R. A., Brewer, J. A., & Lazar, S.W. (2016). Contemplating mindfulness at work: An integrative review. *Journal of Management, 42*(1), 114–142.
Gray, H. J. (1999). As I see it: Ignatius' method for letting God shine through life's realities. *Company, 16*, 30–31.

Gray, H. J. (2000). The experience of Ignatius of Loyola: Background to Jesuit education. In V. J. Duminuco (Ed.), *The Jesuit Ratio Studiorum: 400th anniversary perspectives* (pp. 1–21). New York, NY: Fordham University Press.

Gray, H. J. (2001). Ignatian spirituality. In T. M. Landy (Ed.), *As leaven in the world: Catholic perspectives on faith, vocation, and the intellectual life* (pp. 321–340). Franklin, WI: Sheed & Ward.

Gray, H. J. (2008). Ignatian spirituality. In G. W. Traub (Ed.), *An Ignatian spirituality reader* (pp. 59–84). Chicago, IL: Loyola Press.

Grossman, P. (2011). Defining mindfulness by how poorly I think I pay attention during everyday awareness and other intractable problems for psychology's (re)invention of mindfulness: Comment on Brown et al. (2011). *Psychological Assessment, 23*, 1034–1040.

Gula, R. M. (1989). *Reason informed by faith: Foundations of Catholic morality*. Mahwah, NJ: Paulist Press.

Gula, R. M. (2003). *The call to holiness: Embracing a fully Christian life*. Mahwah, NJ: Paulist Press.

Gula, R. M. (2011). *The way of goodness and holiness: A spirituality for pastoral ministers*. Collegeville, MN: Liturgical Press.

Habito, R. L. F. (2013). *Zen and the spiritual exercises*. Maryknoll, NY: Orbis.

Haight, R. (2012). *Christian spirituality for seekers: Reflections on the spiritual exercises of Ignatius of Loyola*. Maryknoll, NY: Orbis.

Hanh, T. N. (1999). *The heart of Buddha's teaching: Transforming suffering into peace, joy, and liberation*. New York, NY: Harmony.

Healey, C. J. (2009). *The Ignatian way: Key aspects of Jesuit spirituality*. Mahwah, NJ: Paulist Press.

Himes, M. (2008). Living conversation: Higher education in a Catholic context. In G. W. Traub (Ed.), *An Ignatian spirituality reader* (pp. 225–241). Chicago, IL: Loyola Press.

Hyland, P. K., Lee, R. A., & Mills, M. K. (2015). Mindfulness at work: A new approach to improving individual and organizational performance. *Industrial and Organizational Pyschology: Perspectives on Science and Practice, 8*, 576–602.

International Commission on the Apostolate of Jesuit Education. (2019, June 11). Society of Jesus education statistics. Retrieved from www.sjweb.info/documents/education/reports_ICAJE_2019-summary_20190611.pdf

Kabat-Zinn, J. (1994). *Wherever you go, there you are: Mindfulness for everyday life*. London: Piatkus.

Kabat-Zinn, J. (2003). Mindfulness-based interventions in context: Past, present, and future. *Clinical Psychology, 10*, 144–156.

Kachan, D., Olano, H., Tannenbaum, S. L., Annane, D. W., Mehta, A., Arheart, K. L., Fleming, L.E., Yang, X., McClure, L.A., & Lee, D. J. (2017). Prevalence of mindfulness practices in the U.S. workforce: National health interview survey. *Preventing Chronic Disease, 14*, 1–12. doi:10.5888/pcd14.160034

Kalscheur, G. A. (2007). Ignatian spirituality and the life of the lawyer: Finding God in all things—Even in the ordinary practice of law. *Journal of Catholic Legal Studies, 46*(1), 7–28.

Khanna, V. & Khanna, P. D. (2019). Critical perspectives on corporate mindfulness and workplace spirituality. In S. K. Mishra & A. Varma (Eds.), *Spirituality in management: Insights from India* (pp. 179–194). New York, NY: Palgrave Macmillan.

Kracher, A. (2016). Mr. Spock and the gift of prophecy: Emotion, reason, and the unity of the human person. In D. Evers, M. Fuller, A. Runehov, & K. W. Saether (Eds.), *Issues in science and theology: Do emotions shape the world?* (pp. 251–272). New York, NY: Springer.

Langer, E. J. (1989). *Mindfulness*. Reading, MA: Addison-Wesley.

Lonsdale, D. (2000). *Eyes to see, ears to hear: An introduction to Ignatian spirituality*. Orbis Books.

Lowney, C. (2003). *Heroic leadership: Best practices from a 450-year-old company that changed the world*. Chicago, IL: Loyola Press.

Lowney, C. (2009). *Heroic living: Discover your purpose and change the world*. Chicago, IL: Loyola Press.

Lowney, C. (2018). *Make today matter: 10 habits for a better life (and world)*. Chicago, IL: Loyola Press.

Lozano, J. M. (2017). Leadership: The being component. Can the *Spiritual Exercises* of Saint Ignatius contribute to the debate on business education? *Journal of Business Ethics, 145*(4), 795–809.

Ludwig, D. & Kabat-Zinn, J. (2008). Mindfulness in medicine. *JAMA, 300*(11), 1350–1352.

Martin, J. (2010). *The Jesuit guide to (almost) everything: A spirituality for real life*. New York, NY: HarperOne.

Mayer, C. H. & Geldenhuys, D. (2019). Workplace spirituality and wellness: An organizational neuroscientific perspective. In J. Marques (Ed.), *The Routledge companion to management and workplace spirituality* (pp. 140–153). New York, NY: Routledge.

McIntyre, A. (2019). *Elementary students practicing mindfulness: A meeting of the minds.* Lanham, MD: Lexington Books.
Mishra, S. K. & Varma, A. (2019). Introduction: Spirituality and organization. In S. K. Mishra & A. Varma (Eds.), *Spirituality in management: Insights from India* (pp. 1–6). New York, NY: Palgrave Macmillan.
Moberg, D. J. & Calkins, M. (2001). Reflection in business ethics: Insights from St. Ignatius' spiritual exercises. *Journal of Business Ethics, 33*(3), 257–270.
Newman, J. W. (1996). *Disciplines of attention: Buddhist insight meditation, the Ignatian Spiritual Exercises, and classical psychoanalysis.* New York, NY: Peter Lang.
Nicolas, A. (2009, February 2). Companions in mission: Pluralism in action. Retrieved from www.udmercy.edu/about/mission-vision/mission-identity/files/Nicolas_LMU.pdf
Nullens, P. (2019). From spirituality to responsible leadership: Ignatian discernment and theory-u. In J. Kok & S. C. van den Heuvel (Eds.), *Leading in a VUCA world: Integrating leadership, discernment, and spirituality* (pp. 185–207). New York, NY: Springer.
O'Brien, K. (2011). *The Ignatian adventure: Experiencing the Spiritual Exercises of St. Ignatius in daily life.* Loyola Press.
O'Malley, J. W. (1993). *The first Jesuits.* Cambridge, MA: Harvard University Press.
O'Malley, J. W. (2014). *The Jesuits: A history from Ignatius to the present.* New York, NY: Rowman & Littlefield.
O'Malley, J. W. (2018, May 14). 70 years of friendship: John O'Malley on Jesuit spiritual master Howard Gray. *America.* Retrieved from www.americamagazine.org/faith/2018/05/14/70-years-friendship-john-omalley-jesuit-spiritual-master-howard-gray
Purser, R. E. & Milillo, J. (2015). Mindfulness revisited: A Buddhist-based conceptualization. *Journal of Management Inquiry, 24*, 3–24.
Quaglia, J. T., Brown, K. W., Lindsay, E. K., Creswell, J. D., & Goodman, R. J. (2016). From conceptualization to operationalization of mindfulness. In K. W. Brown, J. D. Creswell, & R. M. Ryan (Eds.), *Handbook of mindfulness: Theory, research, and practice* (pp. 151–170). New York, NY: Guilford.
Raney, A. F. (2014). Agility in adversity: Integrating mindfulness and principles of adaptive leadership in the administration of a community health center. *Clinical Social Work Journal, 42*, 312–320.
Reb, J. & Atkins, P. W. B. (Eds.). (2015). *Mindfulness in organisations: Foundations, research, and applications.* Cambridge, UK: Cambridge University Press.
Rehg, W. (2002). Christian mindfulness: A path to finding God in all things. *Studies in the Spirituality of Jesuits, 34*(3), 1–32.
Richtel, M. (2019, April 5). The latest in military strategy: Mindfulness. *New York Times.* Retrieved from www.nytimes.com/2019/04/05/health/military-mindfulness-training.html
Rothausen, T. J. (2017). Integrating leadership development with Ignatian spirituality: A model for designing a spiritual leader development practice. *Journal of Business Ethics, 145*(4), 811–829.
Rupprecht, S. & Walach, H. (2016). Mindfulness at work: How mindfulness training may change the way we work. In M. Wiencke, M. Cacace, & S. Fischer (Eds.), *Healthy at work: Interdisciplinary perspectives* (pp. 311–328). New York, NY: Springer.
San Juan, K. (2007). *The spiritual formation of leaders based on the Ignatian tradition.* (Unpublished doctoral dissertation). Gonzaga University, Spokane, WA.
Schultz, P. P. & Ryan, R. M. (2015). The "why," "what," and "how" of healthy self-regulation: Mindfulness and well-being from a self-determination theory perspective. In B. D. Ostafin, M. D. Robinson, & B. P. Meier (Eds.), *Handbook of mindfulness and self-regulation* (pp. 81–94). New York, NY: Springer.
Shapiro, S. & Carlson, L. (2009). *The art and science of mindfulness: Integrating mindfulness into psychology and the helping professions.* Washington, DC: American Psychological Association.
Silf, M. (1999). *Inner compass: An invitation to Ignatian spirituality.* Chicago, IL: Loyola Press.
Sparough, J. M., Manney, J., & Hipskind, T. (2010). *What's your decision? How to make choices with confidence and clarity.* Chicago, IL: Loyola Press.
Tetlow, J. A. (2008). *Making choices in Christ: The foundations of Ignatian spirituality.* Chicago, IL: Loyola Press.
Thibodeaux, M. E. (2010). *God's voice within: The Ignatian way to discover God's will.* Loyola Press.
Tran, D. Q. & Carey, M. R. (2018). Toward a discerning mind and heart: An Ignatian approach to workplace spirituality and spiritual leadership. In S. Dhiman, G. E. Roberts, & J. E. Crossman (Eds.),

The Palgrave handbook of workplace spirituality and fulfillment (pp. 753–772). New York, NY: Palgrave Macmillan.

Traub, G. W. (2008). Introduction. In G. W. Traub (Ed.), *An Ignatian spirituality reader: Contemporary writings on St. Ignatius of Loyola, the Spiritual Exercises, Discernment, and more* (pp. 48–49). Loyola Press.

Tyler, P. (2018). *Christian mindfulness: Theology and practice.* London: SCM Press.

Weick, K. E. & Roberts, K. H. (1993). Collective mind in organizations: Heedful interrelating on flight decks. *Administrative Science Quarterly*, *38*, 357–381.

Wolff, P. (2003). *Discernment: The art of choosing well* (Rev. ed.). Liguori, MO: Triumph.

28

PRACTICAL STEPS FOR CHRISTIANS TO LIVE OUT THEIR FAITH AT WORK

Mindfulness in practice

Debra J. Dean

Introduction

When Dean (2017) sought to examine if religion and spirituality in the workplace had an impact on job satisfaction and organizational commitment, she found that spiritual leadership variables of altruistic love, faith/hope, inner life, meaningful work, sense of community, and vision were related to and some could predict the desired workplace outcomes. However, for the purpose of this chapter, her focus on religion and spirituality is of more importance. Dean's (2017) study included 177 participants from Iran, Ireland, the United Kingdom, and the United States of America. Their religious backgrounds were mostly Christian, but also included Hindu, Jewish, Neopagan, and Pagan. The different types of Christianity were self-reported as Baptist, Catholic, Christian, Christian Reformed Church (CRCNA), Christian Protestant Non-denomination, Christian/non-denominational, Episcopal, Evangelical, Evangelical Christian, Latter Day Saints, Lutheran, Methodist, Non-denominational, Progressive Christian, and Southern Baptist. When Dean (2017) asked the following questions, her revelation was that many people are confused as to the definition of meditation and prayer, or the relationship of the two, if any. The questions were: (a) do you meditate on a routine basis, (b) if applicable, how often per week do you meditate, and (c) if applicable, what type of meditation do you practice? The responses to the first question are detailed in Table 28.1. This first question points to the confusion of how prayer and meditation relate, or if they do at all. It also begins to demonstrate the guardedness that some Christians have pertaining to their practice of prayer and the exercise of meditation.

The responses to the second question varied. Of those that answered, they responded with "daily," as well as various responses from 1–7 days a week. Some were more specific with "7 days a week, 2 hours per day," "14 times per week," or "14+." Some stated they prayed once or twice per day. And others clarified that they "pray at least seven times per week" or they "pray twice a day." And, some questioned, "if it [prayer] counts, 7."

The types of meditation also differed from participant to participant. Table 28.2 provides a list of their answers verbatim (duplicates were removed). Again, these responses report the

Table 28.1 Do you meditate on a routine basis?

- Does reading the Bible count?
- If that includes prayer and scripture reading, yes
- No, but I do pray
- No, I do pray though
- No, I pray
- No, ruminate
- Nope, but I do pray
- Prayer

Table 28.2 If applicable, what type of meditation do you practice?

A filling of my mind with the Word of God seeking to know Him more and asking Him to conform me into the image of His Son, Christ Jesus.			
Bible readings, praying to the God of the Bible (Father Son & Holy Spirit).			
I ponder the Word of God. Christian mediatization is actively thinking about the Word of God.			
Breathing	Mindful	Prayer and Bible Study	Relaxation
Buddhist	Mindfulness	Prayer and meditation on scripture	Scripture study. Prayer
Considering scripture passages	Morning quiet mindfulness	Prayer and reading the Bible	Seated meditation and prayer (no titles)
Deep breathing	N/A not a defined meditation, self-guided	Prayer and reflection	Shabda
God's Word (Bible)	Not sure. I use an app for guided meditation	Prayer and reflection on Scripture	TM
Guided	Personal	Prayer and scripture reading	TM and TM-Sidhi program
Hitting the gym.	Personal—Prayer	Prayer to God the Father in the name of Christ my Savior	Transcendental
I don't meditate, there's a difference	Praise (Christian song worship)	Prayer, moments of silence, deep focused breathing	Typically, one chapter of the Bible per day
Image and hesychia	Prayer	Prayer, worship, Bible reading	Yoga
Meditation on the Bible through memorization	Prayer and Bible reading	Praying, studying	Zazen

opinions on what meditation is as well as the varying Christian spiritual practices experienced by the random sample of participants.

One of the takeaways from Dean's study was that people are confused as to the relationship between meditation and prayer, if there is one. Some also seem guarded as to their Christian spiritual practice as opposed to pagan meditation practices. This chapter will help to explain several of these practices in more detail as well as understanding why the guardedness is present and if it is warranted.

Scouring the literature for workplace spirituality and mindfulness brought about several articles specifically about Buddhism. Trammel (2015) explained that "most of the research literature on mindfulness has focused on Buddhist practices" (p. 171). Although, many forms of mindfulness meditation derive from a Buddhist tradition, "some Christian adults may prefer to turn to their own religious heritage, rather than the Buddhist tradition" (Knabb, 2012, p. 909).

Perhaps, then, the guardedness and confusion on this topic come from the amount of research on this topic conducted from a Buddhist perspective in comparison with the number of Christians in the world. Pew Research Center (2015) reports 70.6% of Americans as Christians, 5.9% as non-Christian faiths, 1.5% as other faiths (such as atheist, agnostic, or none), and 15.8% as nothing in particular. From a global perspective, Pew Research Center reports that "Christians remain the world's largest religious group" with 31.2% of the world's population Christian, 24.1% Muslim, 16% unaffiliated, 15.1% Hindu, and 6.9% Buddhist (Hackett & McClendon, 2017). From this perspective, it makes sense for more research to focus on Christian spiritual practices in the workplace and this chapter attempts to fill some of that large gap.

Defining the terms

Mindfulness

Glomb, Duffy, Bono and Yang (2011) "argues that ... mindfulness and mindfulness-based practices in the workplace should enhance employee outcomes" (p. 115). The scholars explained that mindfulness is rooted in Buddhist philosophy and the "literal translation of the Buddhist word *sati* means 'intentness of mind,' 'wakefulness of mind,' and 'lucidity of mind'" (p. 117). While some consider mindfulness to be a fad or remedy for an overwhelmed and stressed society, there is a growing body of literature from a practical and theoretical perspective that supports the use of mindfulness practices to help employees with their mental and physical well-being. Glomb et al. define mindfulness as "a state of consciousness characterized by receptive attention to and awareness of present events and experiences, without evaluation, judgment, and cognitive filters" (p. 119).

Burk (2014) wrote that mindfulness has always been important to Buddhism, yet it was not until the 1980s that mindfulness became known from a practical and theoretical viewpoint within the Western culture. He explained that the first step to mindfulness is "learning to pay attention to what's going on in the present moment" (Burk, 2014). The typical Eastern mindfulness methodology includes emptying the mind with the use of mantras, koans, chanting, breathing, or some other technique (Kopel & Habermas, 2019, p. 309). Such a practice of "emptying the mind" has caused concern for some Christians, who fear that an empty mind could provide a place for evil or demonic activity. Kopel and Habermas (2019) explained that Christian mindfulness focuses on the "spiritual reflection of biblical teachings and God's interactions" (p. 308). Specifically, Christians focus on biblical truth, an attribute or promise of God, the reality of heaven, or scripture passages.

Paganism

In short, paganism is the study of religious beliefs other than the main world religions. The term pagan is similar to the ancient word gentile or heathen. Pagan is not an ancient word but is thought to have emerged in the fourth century when early Christians made reference to those that practiced polytheism. According to Boin (2014), non-Christians were labeled with the word *paganus*, meaning a lack of culture, rustic, or civilian. He explains that "paganismus was a rhetorical word" summoning "one half of the two-headed beast that threatened 'Christianism' at its core." Essentially, the word pagan derived from the Latin Christian vocabulary during a debate of Christian "assimilation and accommodation to the Roman World" (Boin, p. 193). At which time, Christians feared they could be viewed as one extreme or another with the word *paganus* on one end of the spectrum and *Hellene* on the other end. Today, a search for pagan and neo-paganism brings mention of witchcraft and ritual magic (Britannica) as well as Roman pagan gods such as Zeus, Athena, Poseidon, and Aphrodite (Land, 2019).

Religion

In workplace spirituality literature, there have been many debates over religion and spirituality. The question is whether religion and spirituality are one and the same. Fry (2003), in pursuit of his spiritual leadership theory, includes a generic definition of God as a "higher power with a continuum upon which humanistic, theistic, and pantheistic definitions of God can be placed" (p. 693). Hicks (2003) contends that the separation of religion and spirituality is not sustainable. Giacalone, Jurkiewicz and Fry (2005) addressed the matter of religion and spirituality by stating that "spirituality is necessary for religion, but religion is not necessary for spirituality" (p. 517). Giacalone (2010) later wrote, "We no longer argue whether facets of religion and spirituality are assessable—they are" (p. 4). While many studies separate the two and recognize that a person can have a spiritual experience of nourishing their soul without religion, this chapter will focus on the religious aspects of Christian spiritual practices.

Secularism

According to Britannica, secularism is "any movement in society directed away from otherworldliness to life on earth." The encyclopedia notes that the "movement toward secularism has been in progress during the entire course of modern history and has often been viewed as being anti-Christian and antireligious." Bester and Muller (2017) explained that secularism dates back to the 1850s as a term used by Holyoake in denoting "a system which seeks to interpret and order life on principles taken solely from this world, without recourse to belief in God and a future life" (p. 6). The scholars believe that secularism is an attempt to move from "religion to other concepts such as mindfulness" (p. 6). In this regard, the emphasis is placed on removing religion from secular institutions.

Many studies have shown that removing religion from institutions has caused harm, and rebirth of religion in schools, prisons, and workplaces is under review. A study of 225 high school students in Austria found a positive correlation between healthy choices and religion (Gabler, et al., 2017). The Core Foundations program, developed by Dr. Sid Webb, is an example of a concept known as "released time religious education" where Georgia and South Carolina public school students are dismissed for off-campus, elective, for-credit Bible classes. Kentucky Governor Matt Bevin signed the Bible Literacy Bill into law in 2017, allowing Bible courses to be taught in public schools.

At a 2018 meeting in Virginia, Former Governor Bob McDonnell explained that the separation of church and state was never meant to remove religion from the government, but to keep the government out of religion. Stansfield, O'Connor and Duncan (2019) evaluated 571 people in an Oregon prison to compare reoffending behavior of people identified as (a) religious and spiritual, (b) spiritual but not religious, (c) religious but not spiritual, and (d) neither spiritual nor religious. They found that inmates who self-identified as religious and spiritual were less likely to reoffend than the others.

Spiritual warfare

Spiritual warfare looks differently to different people; some will see it more willingly than others. By definition, it is battle between secular and Christian worldviews (Stambach, 2009) and includes battles with "Satan, moral evil, and battles against ungodly cultures and environments" (Fernandez, 2015, p. iv). Spiritual warfare is the "term used to capture the breadths of battles common to all believers that include the classic formulation of temptation and attack coming from the world, the flesh, and the devil" (Fernandez, p. xi). Satan's attack on the family is depicted in Genesis 4:1–8. Satan's personal attack on believers of Christ is shown in Job 1:6–20. Satan's systemic attack on believers through governing bodies is exposed in Daniel 10:10–21. And, Jesus was tempted by Satan in Matthew 4:1–11.

Spirituality

The word spirituality is often misconstrued with religion. While spirituality is necessary for religion, religion is not necessary for spirituality. The French philosopher, Pierre Teilhard de Chardin stated, "We are not human beings having a spiritual experience. We are spiritual beings having a human experience." The concept of workplace spirituality focuses on nourishing the soul at work. For some employees, this includes religious practices and for others, it may include things like going to the gym, journaling, singing, or walking in nature. There are plenty of empirical articles defining spirituality in regard to the difference between spirituality and religion. For the purpose of this chapter, the focus is on religion and the spiritual practices that nourish the Christian soul at work.

Christian prayer in the workplace

Billy Graham once said, "I believe that one of the next great moves of God is going to be through the believers in the workplace" (Hillman, n.d.). Offices around the world have incorporated prayer into their daily routine. Some airports, hospitals, and universities have reserved a room for prayer. Prayer rooms are also in some public schools in Maine and Texas. They have been added to businesses such as Bak USA, a mobile computer manufacturer in Buffalo, NY, and Maple Holistics, a beauty product provider in Farmingdale, NJ. Another option for companies to integrate faith at work is with silence. Companies such as Amazon, LinkedIn, and Square provide silent starts to business meetings. Some last for a minute or two and others for 30 minutes. It provides an opportunity for employees to think, clear their mind, organize their thoughts, and/or pray. Corporate chaplains are another option for faith in the workplace. The following companies have a corporate chaplain that provides employee care: American Lube Fast, Baillie, Bandwidth, Barnart, Bickford Senior Living, Coca-Cola Bottling, David Weekley Homes, Fast Change Lube & Oil, General Motors, McLane, Pace Industries, Pilgrims, Pioneer Natural Resources, Regal Boats, Southeastern Freight Lines, Tyson Foods, and Ward Black Law.

Mindfulness research

The overarching desire with mindfulness from a practitioner viewpoint seems to be a pursuit of helping people to cope with stress and reduce burnout. It is also aimed at helping people improve their health and focus. Eby et al. (2019) conducted a review of 67 published articles and found the main purpose for mindfulness-based training of employees was to reduce stress or strain. Research has shown that mindfulness concepts reduce anxiety, chronic pain, stress, and substance abuse (Kopel & Habermas, 2019, p. 308). Frederick, Dunbar and Thai (2018) note that "Mindfulness and Christian spirituality are useful tools in preventing and coping with burnout and compassion fatigue" (p. 267). Knabb and Grigorian-Routon (2014) found that performing Christian spiritual practices reduced anxiety, depression, and stress among Christians.

In 2014, Charoensukmongkol conducted a study with 317 participants in Thailand. He found a positive relationship between mindfulness meditation and emotional intelligence. He also found a negative correlation between mindfulness meditation and general perceived stress. Birnie, Speca and Carlson (2010) found that mindfulness reduced stress and increased self-compassion. Hofmann, Sawyer, Fang and Asnaani (2012) found that mindfulness decreased anxiety and increased mood when participants faced a difficult situation such as cancer, depression, or an anxiety disorder. In 2009, Chandler found that personal renewal strategies of Bible reading, personal devotion time, and prayer helped pastors prevent and cope with emotional exhaustion as well as burnout, stress, and worry.

As with any new field of research, it takes time to define terms, study the effects, build theory, and develop useful tools. Table 28.3 provides a list of questionnaires used to examine mindfulness. This list is not exhaustive but provides a small inventory of surveys that can be used to measure this topic for future research. Notice that these are not Christian-specific and a recommendation for future research is to develop more tools specifically pertaining to Christian spiritual practices.

Based on the research to date, the conflict between Christianity, spirituality, and mindfulness could stem from the fear of pagan practices or non-Christian practices. This chapter will continue with certain exercises that some fear or worry may interfere with their Christianity as well as those that appear to be safe.

Christian prayer research

McCullough and Larson (1999) recommended additional research on different types of prayer rather than a one-item categorization. Shearer (2015) examined prayer in detail with 36 individual participants to determine different uses of prayer, as shown in Table 28.4. He found the four most frequent uses of prayer were (a) asking God to help through difficult times, (b) praying for strength to handle difficulties, (c) praying for God to lead the person in the right direction, and (d) giving thanks.

Black, Pössel, Jeppsen, Tariq and Rosmarin (2015) examined the following four types of prayer: colloquial, meditative, petitionary, and ritual. Colloquial is the method of talking to God in your own words. Meditative is the process of asking God to speak and then waiting for Him to answer. Petitionary is the method of asking God for material things. And ritual is the process of reciting memorized prayers.

Table 28.3 Inventory of mindfulness tools

Questionnaire	*Author(s)*	*Subscales*
Cognitive and Affective Mindfulness Scale-Revised (CAMS-R)	Feldman, Hayes, Kumar, Greeson and Laurenceau (2007)	Attention, Present-Focus, Awareness, Acceptance/non-judgment
Experiences Questionnaire (EQ)	Fresco et al. (2007)	Decentering, Rumination
Five Facet Mindfulness Questionnaire (FFMQ)	Baer, Smith, Hopkins, Krietemeyer and Toney (2006)	Observing, Describing, Acting with Awareness, Non-judging of experience, Non-reactivity to experience
Freiburg Mindfulness Inventory (FMI)	Buchheld, Grossman and Walach (2001)	Self-awareness, Dissociation, Global Severity Index, Meditation Experience in Years
Kentucky Inventory of Mindfulness Scale (KIMS)	Baer et al. (2006)	Observe, Describe, Act with Awareness, Accept without Judgment
Mindful Attention Awareness Scale (MAAS)	Brown and Ryan (2003)	
Mindfulness/Mindlessness Scale (MMS)	Bodner and Langer (2001)	Novelty Seeking, Novelty Producing, Engagement, Flexibility
Philadelphia Mindfulness Scale (PHLMS)	Cardaciotto, Herbert, Forman, Moitra and Farrow (2008)	Awareness, Acceptance
Self-Awareness Questionnaire (SAQ)	Hughes, Betka and Longarzo (2019)	Body Self-Awareness
Southampton Mindfulness Questionnaire (SMQ)	Chadwick et al. (2008)	Mindful Awareness of Distressing Thoughts and Images
Toronto Mindfulness Scale (TMS)	Bishop, et al. (2006)	Curiosity, Decentering

Table 28.4 Concept map of prayer functions (Shearer, 2015)

Concept map of prayer functions
Seeking God's Help to Handle Difficulties
Seeking Direction
Focusing on Others
Focusing on the Situation
Asking for (Seeking) Resources
Gaining a Sense of Calm and Focus
Meditating and Reflecting
Giving Control to God
Putting Faith and Trust in God
Acknowledge Lack of Control to God

Practical options for Christians

Christians have many options to commune with God throughout their day. They can pray, memorize and meditate on scripture, read the Bible, sing worship songs, and much more.

In the book *The Practice of the Presence of God* by Brother Lawrence, he describes a pure and uncomplicated way to continually walk with God. In the book *Experiencing God* by Henry and Richard Blackaby, they describe observations of how God is working in life and how believers can adjust their life to the Will of God, thus intimately and personally becoming more acquainted with the Father. Throughout the following examples, the important affirmation for Christians to know if they are using an option pleasing to God is to trace it back to scripture. Simply stated, if it's not in the Bible, don't do it.

Christians' avoidance of certain spiritual practices

It is important to note up front that some Christians find much distress with various pagan spiritual practices such as affirmation, meditation, and yoga and many believe such practices should be avoided entirely, even though they may seem harmless and popular (Revelation, 2015). A debate is ongoing about yoga and whether Christians should practice yoga. Candy (2018) explains that "some evangelicals and Pentecostals view yoga as idolatry or an opening to demonic spirits" (p. 659). Yogānanda (2007) wrote *The Yoga of Jesus*. Although the author passed away in 1952, he left his society, the Self-Realization Fellowship (SRF), with an extensive body of unpublished work. In the text, Yogānanda discusses the "hidden yoga of the Gospels" and proclaims that Jesus not only knew about yoga but taught it to his disciples. Considering your view of such things as affirmation, meditation, and yoga, it is important to guard against unwanted spirits. Albert Magnus, the "father of Christian mysticism" said,

> When thou prayest, shut thy door; that is, the door of the senses. Keep them barred and bolted against all phantasms and images. Nothing pleases God more than a mind free from all occupations and distractions. Such a mind is in a manner transformed into God, for it can think of and understand nothing, and love nothing except God. He who penetrates into himself and so transcends himself, ascends truly to God.
>
> *(Moses, 1906, p. 84)*

For those concerned with their particular Christian spiritual practice, the Philokalia offers five volumes of text that may offer guidance of guarding one's intellect and heart. Additionally, beginning the Christian spiritual time with a command from Matt 16:23 is a way to remain vigilant throughout the practice and ensure the believer is filled with the Holy Spirit.

Christian practical application

There are many different denominations of Christianity. Some will share prayer methods and others will not. A list of Catholic prayers is provided in Table 28.5. Each of these has specific words that are spoken or rituals that are performed throughout the prayer. Other types of Christians may not have as much structure with their prayers but view them as open conversations with God that can be had at any time throughout the day and for any length of time. Some compare such prayer to a phone call you would have with your loved one. Simply start talking to God. If a more formal structure is desired, there is a format available to follow with the Moms in Prayer website. They typically start prayer with praise, then there is a time for confession, followed with thanksgiving, and ending with time for intercession.

Table 28.5 List of common Catholic prayers

Act of Contrition	Divine Praises	Miraculous Medal Prayer	Prayer in Honor of St. Peter Julian Eymard	Salve Regina (Hail, Holy Queen)
Act of Faith	Doxology	Morning Offering	Prayer of St. Benedict	Sign of the Cross
Act of Hope	Evening Prayer	Nicene Creed	Prayer of St. Dominic	The Angelus
Act of Love	From the "Breast-plate of St. Patrick"	Our Father or The Lord's Prayer	Prayer of St. Francis of Assisi	The Fragrance of Christ
Anima Christi	Glory Be	Pope Benedict XVI's Prayer for Vocations	Prayer of St. Thomas Aquinas	The Hail Mary
Apostles Creed	Guardian Angel Prayer	Prayer [Grace] After Meals	Prayer to Our Guard-ian Angel	The Holy Rosary
Chaplet of Divine Mercy	Hail Joseph	Prayer [Grace] Before Meals	Prayer to St. Christopher	The Magnificat
Come, Holy Spirit	Hail Mary	Prayer at Night	Prayer to St. Joseph	The Memorare
Dear God	Litany of Mary	Prayer for the Year of Faith	Prayer to St. Michael the Archangel	Way of the Cross

Devotionals and Bible reading plans

Reading the Bible is an obvious place to connect with God. However, many people struggle with reading the Bible. It can be challenging to understand, and it can be difficult to even know where to start. Devotionals help by giving the person a specific scripture to read on a certain day and they often have relevant commentaries written on the same page to make it easy for the person to read and comprehend the text. Some popular devotionals include *Jesus Calling* by Sarah Young, *Morning and Evening* by Charles Spurgeon, *My Utmost for His Highest* by Oswald Chambers, and *Our Daily Bread.* Additionally, email devotionals can be sent by Chuck Swindoll, John Piper, Rick Warren, and Tony Evans. And, Bible reading plans are available on the Bible app as well as through The Bible Kick Start and You Version.

Specific times of day

As shown in the research by Dean (2017), several of the participants prayed more than once a day. Psalm 55:17 and Daniel 6:10 provide guidance on praying three times a day. Canonical hours refer to the specific time of day a person prays. This is also referred to as fixed-hour prayer. *Matins* is the nighttime prayer. *Lauds* is for early morning. *Prime* is the first hour of daylight. *Terce* is the third hour of the day. *Sext* is at noon. *Nones* is the ninth hour of the day. *Vespers* is at sunset or evening. And, *Compline* is at the end of the day. Pope Paul VI focused on the following three canonical hours: morning was a time for praise, evening prayer was a time for thanksgiving, and night prayer was a time of reflection and preparing the soul for eternal life. Matt 26:40 provides an example of the Holy Hour. This is where Jesus went into the Garden of Gethsemane to pray. In 1673, St. Margaret Mary Alacoque said she saw a vision instructing her to pray each Thursday night for one hour. Mother Teresa prayed using a similar practice of the Holy Hour; however, she did it daily.

Fasting

Fasting is another option to grow closer to God. It is common for Christians to fast during Lent—the time between Ash Wednesday and Easter—although fasting can be done at any time. Paul stated that fasting and prayer is a regular part of the Christian life (1 Cor 7:5). When Esther had a pivotal moment in life, she fasted for three days along with her attendants, Mordecai, and all the Jews in Susa (Esther 4:15–16). David fasted while pleading with God for the life of his son (2 Samuel 12:14–16). And, Jesus fasted for 40 days (Luke 4:1–13, Matt 4:1–11). There are different types of fasting, but the most common is food. Most people will continue to drink liquids but will not have any food for a period of time. A partial fast is the removal or avoidance of a particular food item for a period of time. Daniel provides an example of a partial fast in Daniel 1:12. A full fast is where food and drink are avoided; Paul did this in Acts 9:9. Other types of fasting can include avoiding electronics, sex, sleep, television, or something else that would represent a sacrifice.

Praying Psalms

Bonhoeffer (1996, 1974) wrote of the importance of memorizing and meditating on the Psalms. He stated, "I read the Psalms every day, as I have done for years; I know them and love them more than any other book." In his two books, *Life Together* and *Prayerbook of the Bible*, Bonhoeffer points out three vital points of the Christian prayer life. First, Psalms teach us to pray Christ's prayer. Second, Psalms teach us what to pray. And, third, Psalms teach us to pray in community. Merton (1981) stated:

> I am sorry that it has taken me so long to begin to discover the Psalms. I am sorry that I have not lived in them. Their words are full of the living waters of those true tears with which You taught the Samaritan your mercy.
>
> *(p. 290)*

Worship music

The Latin phrase *lex orandi, lex credenda* means what is to be prayed is what is to be believed. Roby further explained, "the things we see, do, say, hear, and sing in worship shape our theological understands and thus are formative of our faith" (p. 60). *Amazing Grace*, the 1779 song by John Newton, is one of the most popular Christian hymns. Other famous hymns include *How Great Thou Art* written by Carl Gustav Boberg in 1885 and *Holy, Holy, Holy* by Reginald Heiber in 1826. In 2019, the African song, *Waymaker,* went viral. It was written by Sinach. Such contemporary music has grown in popularity and provides a spiritual experience as one can visually see the singer's body move, their hands raise, tears stream down their face, and they personally connect with God through music on a deeper level.

Christian devotion meditation

Unlike meditation practices from the East which call for the practitioner to empty their mind with mental passivity and detach from the world, Paul states in Phil 4:8 to think about things that are commendable, excellent, honorable, lovely, pure, true, and worthy of praise.

Christian meditation requires one to fill their mind with God and His truth; thus, attaching to God and detaching from the distractions and temptations of the world. The Old Testament refers to meditation as *Haga* and *Siach*. The Hebrew word *Haga* means to roar, growl, groan, utter, speak, meditate, devise, muse, or imagine. The Hebrew word *Siach* also means to muse, complain, or talk. Christians are instructed to meditate on scripture (Joshua 1:8) and pray without ceasing (Ps. 1:1–2, 1 Thess 5:16–18). Frederick and White (2015) explain that Christian Devotion Meditation (CDM) is "a broad term referring to many strategies, often derived from spiritual formation exercises, designed to foster awareness and attention on God" (p. 850). The scholars note that centering prayer has been the main focus of incorporating CDM and mindfulness meditation. Frederick et al. (2018) explained that practices of "the Jesus Prayer, the Daily Examen, and the Prayer of Consideration" help to stave off burnout by "reconnecting with the empowering, living spirit of God" (p. 267). Each of the three spiritual practices are "intended to rekindle one's spiritual connection to the divine" (p. 273.)

Centering prayer

According to Knabb (2012), "centering prayer was developed in the 1970s by Meninger, Pennington, and Keating, three Trappist monks at St. Joseph's Abbey in Spencer, Massachusetts" (p. 913). This type of prayer consists of several characteristics, including (a) allowing the person to get in touch with their center of being, (b) offering the person an easy and effortless form of prayer, and (c) helping the person to think differently. Pennington (1982) provides the three following rules for centering prayer: (a) at the start of prayer, quietly invite God into the conversation; and at the end of praying close with the Our Father or some other memorized prayer; (b) while resting in God's unconditional loving presence, choose a word from scripture and allow it to hover in the mind; and (c) if anything distracts during prayer, gently return to the Presence of God using the chosen word. Frederick and White (2015) note that surrender is a key ingredient to centering prayer.

Lectio Divina

This scripture engagement technique is slow, contemplative praying of scriptures and is referred to as *Lectio Divina*. *Lectio Divina* means sacred reading and is a way to become immersed in scripture in a very personal way. The process is broken down into the following four parts: *lectio* (reading) is comparable to taking a bite of food, *meditatio* (discursive meditation) is similar to chewing the food, *oratio* (affective prayer) is analogous to savoring the food, and *contemplatio* (contemplation) is equivalent to digesting the food so it nourishes and becomes part of the body. This technique was introduced by St. Gregory of Nyssa (330–395) and was originally practiced by Benedictine monks and offers the chance for a two-way conversation with God by ruminating on His word and listening to what He says. This technique could take 15–60 minutes at each setting depending on the spiritual maturity of the Christian.

The Daily Examen

The Daily Examen Prayer (sometimes called the prayer that changes everything) is more of an attitude than a method. It is a time set aside each day for a "thankful reflection on where God is in your everyday life" (Ignatian, n.d.). This prayer generally takes 15–20 minutes per day and has five steps, including (a) asking God for light, (b) giving thanks, (c) reviewing the day, (d) facing shortcomings, and (e) looking towards the day to come.

The Jesus Prayer

The Jesus Prayer, also known as *Hesychasm*, originated with St. Diadochos of Photiki (400–486). The classical form of the Jesus Prayer is, "Lord Jesus Christ, Son of God, have mercy on me, a sinner." The prayer can be said with a prayer rope or *chotki*. Paul said to pray at all times, and the Jesus Prayer is a way to continually desire God. Some say this prayer can be dangerous if not practiced correctly as there is a risk of delusion, such as satanic or demonic imagery, when the imagination is used or when the breathing is done; however, the repetition of the prayer is fine, if one keeps their mind focused on God.

The Prayer of Consideration

The 19th Annotation of the Spiritual Exercises by St. Ignatius Loyola provides descriptions of exercises and prayer retreats that usually take days, weeks, months, or more to perform. Father Joseph Tetlow, S.J. wrote that the Prayer of Consideration makes the most sense for people with busy lives. It requires the person to conduct daily prayer, meditation, and reading for a minimum of 45 minutes each day. Throughout this practice, believers consider creation, people, work, and children from the perspective of finding God in all things.

Conclusion

This chapter on mindfulness at work focused on Christian spiritual practices and divulged the concern and confusion many have with the phrases meditation, mindfulness, and spirituality. Research shows a gaping hole needs to be filled to show qualitative and quantitative examination of Christian spiritual practices in the workplace. This chapter sheds light on some of the research that has been done in addition to the comparison of mindfulness techniques with Christian spiritual practices. Additionally, this chapter provides a plethora of Christian spiritual techniques that can be used anywhere, including the workplace. While many Christians feel a sense of revival among Christianity in the workplace and beyond, much more work is needed to show how allowing and embracing such spiritual practices at work can help employees on a deep, personal level, ultimately giving rise to high performance and world-class products and services. It is believed that making space and time for such practices will help nourish the souls of employees.

Chapter takeaways

This chapter offers five takeaways. The first is encouraging as we see proof that Christians are practicing their faith at work. The second is comfort for Christians that have felt a little awkward or uncomfortable with topics of mindfulness or spirituality; those feelings are God-inspired and give a healthy boundary to ward off the enemy. The third takeaway is prompting for Christians to take action and begin a Christian spiritual practice at work. It can be private such as praying at your desk or in a conference room all alone, it can be with a group of other Christians that pray together at lunch, or it can be advocating for a prayer room or moment of silence before meetings. The fourth takeaway is hopefully a realization that paganism, secularism, and spiritual warfare are real efforts of the enemy in a battle for your soul. The good news is that Jesus wins, and our job is to pray without ceasing and continually be in communion with God. And, the final takeaway from this chapter is to see that much work is left to be done with regard to advocating practically for Christian spiritual practices to be allowed in the workplace and theoretically for more studies to show the impact of such practices on employee health and well-being.

Reflection questions

As this chapter comes to a close, the following five reflection questions are geared at moving you beyond the text and implementing a spiritual routine in your daily life.

1. Of all of the examples provided in this chapter, did one or more resonate with you as a viable option to begin a Christian spiritual practice in your workplace?
2. If yes, what next steps will you take to schedule time and actively pursue a daily faith-based routine at work?
3. If no, what research is left for you to do in order to find a Christian spiritual practice that will work for you?
4. Community is important for Christianity. The first three reflection questions focused on you personally. In this fourth question, how can you reach out to another Christian to meet as a group on a routine basis (daily, weekly) and practice some agreed-upon form of Christian spiritual practice?
5. Beyond the routine of praying, memorizing and meditating on scripture, reading the Bible, singing worship songs, etc., how will you know you are maturing in your faith?

References

Baer, R. A., Smith, G. T., Hopkins, J., Krietemeyer, J., & Toney, L. (2006). Using self-report assessment methods to explore facets of mindfulness. *Assessment, 13*, 27–45.

Bester, A. & Muller, J. (2017). Religion, an obstacle to workplace spirituality and employee wellness? *Verbum Et Ecclesia, 38*(1). doi:10.4102/ve.v38i1.1779

Birnie, K., Speca, M., & Carlson, L. E. (2010). Exploring self-compassion and empathy in the context of mindfulness-based stress reduction (MBSR). *Stress and Health, 26*(5), 359–371. doi:10.1002/smi.1305

Black, S. W., Pössel, P., Jeppsen, B. D., Tariq, A., & Rosmarin, D. H. (2015). Poloma and Pendleton's (1989) prayer types scale in christian, jewish, and muslim praying adults: One scale or a family of scales? *Psychology of Religion and Spirituality*, 7(3), 205–216. doi:10.1037/rel0000018

Bodner, T. & Langer, E. (2001, June). Individual differences in mindfulness: The Mindfulness/Mindlessness Scale. Poster presented at the 13th annual American Psychological Society Conference, Toronto, Ontario, Canada.

Boin, D. (2014). Hellenistic "judaism" and the social origins of the "pagan-christian" debate. *Journal of Early Christian Studies, 22*(2), 167.

Bonhoeffer, D. (1996). *Life together.* New York: Harper San Francisco.

Bonhoeffer, D. & Bethge, E. (1974). *Psalms: The prayer book of the Bible.* Minneapolis, MN: Augsburg Pub. House.

Brown, K. W., & Ryan, R. M. (2003). The benefits of being present: Mindfulness and its role in psychological well-being. *Journal of Personality and Social Psychology, 84*, 822–848. https://doi-org.ezproxy.regent.edu/10.1037/0022-3514.84.4.822

Buchheld, N., Grossman, P., & Walach, G. (2001). Measuring mindfulness in insight meditation (vipassana) and meditation-based psychotherapy: The development of the Freiburg Mindfulness Inventory (FMI). *Journal for Meditation and Meditation Research, 1*(2001), 11–34.

Burk, D. (2014). *Mindfulness* NY, NY, USA: Alpha, a member of Penguin Group (USA) Inc..

Candy, G. (2018). Christian yoga: Something new under the Sun/Son? *Church History, 87*(3), 659–683. Retrieved from http://dx.doi.org.ezproxy.regent.edu:2048/10.1017/S0009640718001555

Cardaciotto, L., Herbert, J., Forman, E., Moitra, E., & Farrow, V. (2008). The assessment of present-moment awareness and acceptance: The philadelphia mindfulness scale. *Assessment, 15*(2), 204–223. doi:10.1177/1073191107311467

Chadwick, P., Hember, M., Symes, J., Peters, E., Kuipers, E., & Dagnan, D. (2008). Responding mindfully to unpleasant thoughts and images: Reliability and validity of the southampton mindfulness questionnaire (SMQ). *The British Journal of Clinical Psychology, 47(Pt*(4)), 451–455. doi:10.1348/014466508X314891

Charoensukmongkol, P. (2014). Benefits of mindfulness meditation on emotional intelligence, general self-efficacy, and perceived stress: Evidence from thailand. *Journal of Spirituality in Mental Health, 16*(3), 171–192. doi:10.1080/19349637.2014.925364

Dean, D. (2017). *Religion and spirituality in the workplace: A quantitative evaluation of job satisfaction and organizational commitment.* Regent University, School of Business & Leadership.

Eby, L. T., Allen, T. D., Conley, K. M., Williamson, R. L., Henderson, T. G., & Mancini, V. S. (2019). Mindfulness-based training interventions for employees: A qualitative review of the literature. *Human Resource Management Review, 29*(2), 156–178. doi:10.1016/j.hrmr.2017.03.004

Feldman, G., Hayes, A., Kumar, S., Greeson, J., & Laurenceau, J. (2007). Mindfulness and emotion regulation: The development and initial validation of the cognitive and affective mindfulness scale-revised (CAMS-R). *Journal of Psychopathology and Behavioral Assessment, 29*(3), 177–190. Retrieved from http://dx.doi.org.ezproxy.regent.edu:2048/10.1007/s10862-006-9035-8

Fernandez, S. R. (2015). *Equipping a small group on spiritual warfare dynamics through an educational seminar* (Order No. 3732808). Available from Dissertations & Theses @ Regent University; ProQuest Dissertations & Theses Global. (1735788817). Retrieved from http://eres.regent.edu:2048/login?url=https://search-proquest-com.ezproxy.regent.edu/docview/1735788817?accountid=13479.

Frederick, T. & White, K. M. (2015). Mindfulness, christian devotion meditation, surrender, and worry. *Mental Health, Religion & Culture, 18*(10), 850–858. doi:10.1080/13674676.2015.1107892

Frederick, T. V., Dunbar, S., & Thai, Y. (2018). Burnout in christian perspective. *Pastoral Psychology, 67*(3), 267–276. Retrieved from http://dx.doi.org.ezproxy.regent.edu:2048/10.1007/s11089-017-0799-4

Fresco, D. M., Moore, M. T., van Dulmen, M. H. M., Segal, Z. V., Ma, S. H., Teasdale, J. D., & Williams, J. M. G. (2007). Initial psychometric properties of the experiences questionnaire: Validation of a self-report measure of decentering. *Behavior Therapy, 38*(3), 234–246. doi:10.1016/j.beth.2006.08.003

Fry, L. (2003). Toward a theory of spiritual leadership. *Leadership Quarterly, 14*(6), 693. doi:10.1016/j.leaqua.2003.09.001

Gäbler, G., Lycett, D., & Hefti, R. (2017). Association between health behaviours and religion in austrian high school Pupils—A cross-sectional survey. *Religions, 8*(10), 210. doi:10.3390/rel8100210

Giacalone, R. (2010). JMSR: Where are we now—Where are we going? *Journal of Management, Spirituality, and Religion*, 7(1), 3–6. doi:10.1080/14766080903497276

Giacalone, R., Jurkiewicz, C., & Fry, L. (2005). From advocacy to science: The next steps in workplace spirituality research. In R. Paloutzian (Ed.), *Handbook of the psychology of religion and spirituality* (pp. 515–528). Newbury Park, CA: Sage.

Glomb, T. M., Duffy, M. K., Bono, J. E., & Yang, T. (2011). *Mindfulness at work* (pp. 115–157). Emerald Group Publishing Limited. doi:10.1108/S0742-7301(2011)0000030005

Hackett, C. & McClendon, D. (2017). World's largest religion by population is still Christianity. Retrieved from www.pewresearch.org/fact-tank/2017/04/05/christians-remain-worlds-largest-religious-group-but-they-are-declining-in-europe/.

Hicks, D. (2003). *Religion and the workplace: Pluralism, spirituality, leadership.* Cambridge, UK: Cambridge University Press.

Hillman, O. (n.d.). Are we on the verge of another reformation? Retrieved from www.intheworkplace.com/apps/articles/default.asp?articleid=68281&columnid=1935.

Hofmann, S. G., Sawyer, A. T., Fang, A., & Asnaani, A. (2012). Emotion dysregulation model of mood and anxiety disorders. *Depression and Anxiety, 29*(5), 409–416. doi:10.1002/da.21888

Hughes, L., Betka, S., & Longarzo, M. (2019). Validation of an electronic version of the Self-Awareness questionnaire in english and italian healthy samples. *International Journal of Methods in Psychiatric Research, 28*(1), e1758-n/a. doi:10.1002/mpr.17

Ignatian. (n.d.). Examen Prayer Card. (n.d.). Retrieved from www.ignatianspirituality.com/wp-content/uploads/2019/06/Examen-Prayer-Card.pdf.

Knabb, J. (2012). Centering prayer as an alternative to mindfulness-based cognitive therapy for depression relapse prevention. *Journal of Religion and Health, 51*(3), 908–924. doi:10.1007/s10943-010-9404-1

Knabb, J. J. & Grigorian-Routon, A. (2014). The role of experiential avoidance in the relationship between faith maturity, religious coping, and psychological adjustment among christian university students. *Mental Health, Religion & Culture, 17*(5), 458–469. doi:10.1080/13674676.2013.846310

Kopel, J. & Habermas, G. (2019). Neural buddhism and christian mindfulness in medicine. *Baylor University Medical Center.Proceedings, 32*(2), 308–310. Retrieved from http://dx.doi.org.ezproxy.regent.edu:2048/10.1080/08998280.2019.1581525

Land, G. (2019). The 12 gods and goddesses of Pagan Rome. Retrieved from www.historyhit.com/the-gods-and-goddesses-of-pagan-rome/.

Lau, M. A., Bishop, S. R., Segal, Z. V., Buis, T., Anderson, N. D., Carlson, L., . . . Devins, G. (2006). The toronto mindfulness scale: Development and validation. *Journal of Clinical Psychology, 62*(12), 1445–1467. doi:10.1002/jclp.20326

McCullough, M. & Larson, D. (1999). Prayer. In W. R. Miller (Ed.), *Integrating spirituality into treatment: Resources for practitioners* (pp. 85–110). Washington, DC: American Psychological Association.

Merton, T. (1981). *The sign of Jonas*. San Diego, CA: Harcourt Brace Jovanovich.

Moses, H. (1906). Pathological aspects of religions. Clark University Press. *American Journal of Religious Psychology and Education*, 1. Clark Univ. Press.

Pennington, M. B. (1982). *Centering prayer: Renewing an ancient Christian prayer form*. Garden City, NY: Image Books.

Pew. (2015). Religion in America: U.S. religious data, demographics and statistics. Retrieved from www.pewforum.org/religious-landscape-study/.

Revelation. (2015). Should Christians practice yoga, meditation, or affirmation? Retrieved from www.revelation.co/2015/02/04/christians-yoga-meditation-affirmation/.

Shearer, T. M. (2015). Invoking crisis: Performative christian prayer and the civil rights movement. *Journal of the American Academy of Religion, 83*(2), 490–512. doi:10.1093/jaarel/lfv005

Stambach, A. (2009). Spiritual warfare 101: Preparing the student for christian battle. *Journal of Religion in Africa, 39*(2), 137–157. doi:10.1163/157006609X433358

Stansfield, R., O'Connor, T., & Duncan, J. (2019). Religious identity and the long-term effects of religious involvement, orientation, and coping in prison. *Criminal Justice and Behavior, 46*(2), 337–354. doi:10.1177/0093854818801410

Trammel, R. (2015). Mindfulness as enhancing ethical decision-making and the christian integration of mindful practice. *Social Work and Christianity, 42*(2), 165–177. Retrieved from http://eres.regent.edu:2048/login?url=https://search-proquest-com.ezproxy.regent.edu/docview/1736913746?accountid=13479

Yogānanda. (2007). *The yoga of Jesus: Understanding the hidden teachings of the gospels: Selections from the writings*. Los Angeles, CA: Self-Realization Fellowship.

29

BOOSTING CREATIVITY THROUGH THE REDUCTION POWER OF MINDFULNESS ON EMOTIONAL EXHAUSTION

Ayça Kübra Hizarci-Payne and Alev Katrinli

Introduction

For decades, scholars put increasingly great emphasis on revealing the benefits of mindfulness (Good et al., 2016). Mindfulness as a psychological state indicates the extent of the given attention on events happening in the current moment (Brown & Ryan, 2003; Dane, 2011). Mindfulness is widely related with philosophical traditions; however, in recent years, there is an increasing interest that surrounds mindfulness from various fields, including social psychology, clinical psychology and neuroscience, industrial and organizational psychology (e.g., Creswell, Way, Eisenberger & Lieberman, 2007; Grossman, Niemann, Schmidt & Walach, 2004; Hülsheger, Alberts, Feinholdt & Lang, 2013; Reb, Narayanan & Ho, 2015). Some scholars took the initial step to highlight the power of mindfulness in the workplace and asserted that mindfulness plays an important role in employees' psychological health, generating positive attitudes and outcomes (Dane, 2011; Glomb, Duffy, Bono & Yang, 2011). The majority of the studies that address the role of mindfulness are conducted by using clinical samples, which may not be applied to the work context (Glomb et al., 2011).

A rich body of research points out the association between mindfulness and mental health, and psychological wellbeing (Brown, Ryan & Creswell, 2007; Gu, Strauss, Bond & Cavanagh, 2015). Accounting for the benefits of mindfulness, studies showed constructive effects of mindfulness on emotion regulation (Feldman, Hayes, Kumar, Greeson & Laurenceau, 2007), job performance (Reb, Narayanan, Chaturvedi & Ekkirala, 2017), emotional intelligence (Schutte & Malouff, 2011), emotional exhaustion and burnout (Hülsheger et al., 2013; Taylor & Millear, 2016), satisfaction (Karing & Beelmann, 2018), turnover intention (Dane & Brummel, 2014), innovative working behavior (Afsar & Rehman, 2015), engagement (Roof, 2015), creativity (Lebuda, Zabelina & Karwowski,

2016), insight problem-solving (Ostafin & Kassman, 2012), overall wellbeing, and social relationships (Hyland, Lee & Mills, 2015).

Mindfulness helps individuals to cope with their negative emotions and garner their positive states, as well as foster positive organizational behaviors; therefore, organizations and scholars show a growing attention to the role of mindfulness in the workplace (Good et al., 2016; Reb & Atkins, 2015). However, the present understanding of the interrelationship between mindfulness, emotional exhaustion, and creativity still needs to be investigated where emotional exhaustion mediates the relationship between mindfulness and creativity. Thus, the current study seeks to contribute to the existing literature on mindfulness by investigating the explanatory power of emotional exhaustion on the relationship between mindfulness and creativity. In doing so, this study suggests that mindfulness has a reductive effect on emotional exhaustion that results in higher creativity. To the best of the authors' knowledge, this is the first study that uncovers the mediation effect of emotional exhaustion on the relationship between mindfulness and creativity. Although prior research has provided valuable insights on the contributions of mindfulness on creativity, limited attention has been directed to examine how mindfulness can contribute to creativity by reducing emotional exhaustion. In addition, studies that focus on mindfulness at the workplace with an empirical approach are still limited (Dane & Brummel, 2014; Hülsheger et al., 2013).

Having these objectives in mind, the chapter is structured as follows. After providing a brief view of the constructs, the hypotheses are developed in the light of the literature. Later, the research design and findings of the study are presented. In the discussion section, findings and the theoretical and practical implications of the current study are addressed. The limitations of the study provide insights for future studies.

Mindfulness and its reductive power on emotional exhaustion

Mindfulness reflects a consciousness state in which individuals can focus on their experiences happening in the current moment with an accepting attitude (Brown & Ryan, 2003). Mindfulness is originated from Buddhist traditions, which suggest that mindfulness can be improved by practice of meditation (Agnoli, Vanucci, Pelagatti & Corazza, 2018). Since the concept of mindfulness has its origins from Buddhist philosophy and is an internal state hard to observe, its definitions can be complicated. Mindfulness is considered as an ability of an individual to focus on internal and external stimuli in a nonjudgmental manner (Glomb et al., 2011). Therefore, a mindful individual is one who can be fully in the present moment with full attention (Reb et al., 2015). Mindful individuals' receptive awareness helps them to record their inner experiences and what is happening around at the current moment. This observing stance of mindfulness stops individuals from making judgments (Weick & Putnam, 2006). As mindful individuals have present-oriented consciousness, they do not go back to what has happened in the past or dream and/or concern themselves about their future; instead, they focus on their experiences happening at the current moment. Practitioners assert that "mindfulness is a nonconceptual awareness" that prevents people from getting stuck in ideas or memories and drives them to interpret things as they are happening for the first time (Gunaratana, 2002, p. 140). Therefore, mindfulness helps individuals to inactivate the autopilot that gives reactions to situations based on past experiences. Previous research suggests that mindfulness and mindfulness training can reduce the effect of past experience on current-moment interpretation. The level of mindfulness can differ in individuals and situations, and individuals can be trained to develop their abilities to reach mindful states (Allen et al., 2015; Eby et al., 2019). Scholars argue that mindfulness can be experienced by every individual, including untrained ones (Brown et al., 2011; Glomb et al., 2011). Therefore, mindfulness is considered to also have trait-like characteristics that can be measured by self-report scales (Brown & Ryan, 2003; Brown et al., 2007; 2011). An increasing number of studies using these self-report measures indicate that mindfulness is associated with behavior outcomes and psychological wellbeing (Montani, Dagenais-Desmarais, Giorgi & Grégoire, 2018; Reb et al., 2015; Schultz, Ryan, Niemiec, Legate & Williams, 2015). The ability to observe things in a nonjudgmental manner is considered to play an important role in emotion regulation (Papies, Barsalou & Custers, 2012). Having this ability is considered to be related with the level of sensitivity to changes in an individual's emotional state and help to regulate the emerged emotions with a potential to detriment the evaluation of the event (Chambers, Gullone & Allen, 2009). Flexibility in experiencing emotions can allow individuals to keep themselves in more positive states and give less automatic reactions (Malinowski & Lim, 2015). In the same vein, research confirms that mindfulness is associated with garnering better attentional skills in order to use emotion regulation skills (Chiesa, Serretti & Jakobsen, 2013; Malinowski, 2013). Accordingly, mindfulness has the power to impact the reaction of individuals towards an emotional stimulus (Good et al., 2016). Mindful individuals can reduce their negative emotions (Arch & Craske, 2010). Therefore, mindful employees experience negative emotional states less as they are able to regulate their emotions. Those self-regulatory capabilities can decrease emotional frustration and the generation of negative affection (Reb et al., 2017).

Emotional exhaustion research was initiated with the studies by Maslach, Jackson, Leiter, Schaufeli and Schwab (1986), according to which burnout was conceptualized under three components: emotional exhaustion, depersonalization, and personal accomplishment. Emotional exhaustion as the core part of job burnout is defined as the emergence of fatigue feelings due to depletion of emotional resources. Emotional exhaustion reflects the state of an emotionally overextended employee or individual who experiences physical fatigue and is psychologically drained, which can decrease employees' motivation or willingness to work.

Employees can be confronted with stressful or challenging situations at the workplace every day. Mindfulness has the power to prevent individuals from generating negative thoughts and emotions that can cause emotional exhaustion (Hülsheger et al., 2013). Mindful employees can use adaptive evaluation manners towards stressful events. The more mindful the employees, the less negative the emotions they generate, and the more positive their perceptions of events, which in turn generates more positive reactions at the workplace. Mindfulness triggers intentions to experience the present moment without judgments and evaluation of stressful events; therefore, it can prevent individuals from getting stuck in negative emotional states and facilitate moving on with the present moment. Accordingly, the lifecycle of emotional reactions is shorter in mindful individuals, which in turn provides a faster recovery from negative emotional states (Keng, Smoski & Robins, 2011) and the ability to avoid experiencing emotional exhaustion (Goodman & Schorling, 2012; Li, Wong & Kim, 2017; Reb et al., 2017). In this vein, mindfulness has a buffering role that helps individuals to remain in a positive emotional state (Grandey, Foo, Groth & Goodwin, 2012), and has the potential to stimulate individuals' self-regulatory skills by suppressing impediments and reducing the negative reactions towards stressful events; therefore, individuals high in mindfulness display higher self-determination and less defensive reactions (Jimenez,

Niles & Park, 2010). Hülsheger et al. (2013) analyzed whether mindfulness trainings have an effect on the emotional exhaustion of employees who directly deal with customers. The results of their study showed that mindfulness trainings can enhance the mindfulness of employees, decrease their emotional exhaustion, and improve job satisfaction.

Mindfulness and creativity

Mindfulness plays an important role in work-related behaviors and outcomes as it can foster individuals' cognitive and emotional functioning, and stress regulation (Lebuda et al., 2016). Prior studies showed that mindfulness is associated with the ability to reduce judgmental evaluations and fear of being judged (Brown et al., 2007), and helps to cope with thoughts and feelings, which increases the ability to concentrate (Sedlmeier et al., 2012; Shapiro, Carlson, Astin & Freedman, 2006). Moreover, mindfulness is related to a number of skills and abilities that are also linked to creativity. For example, mindfulness is related to the flexible cognition that enables adaptation by generating new ideas and perspectives, improving the ability to switch perspectives (Feldman et al., 2007), enhancing working memory (Chiesa, Calati & Serretti, 2011), and the ability to enhance divergent thinking (Moore & Malinowski, 2009; Penman, 2015), which also lead to the generation of creative ideas (Baas, De Dreu & Nijstad, 2008). Consequently, mindfulness and mindfulness trainings are considered to boost creativity (Colzato, Szapora & Hommel, 2012; Ding, Tang, Deng, Tang & Posner, 2015; Langer, 2014; Ostafin & Kassman, 2012). However, studies focusing on the relationship between mindfulness and creativity generated mixed results (Agnoli et al., 2018; Lebuda et al., 2016). Despite those inconsistencies in the literature, a meta-analysis by Lebuda et al. (2016) revealed a positive association between mindfulness and creativity. Creativity is defined as the ability to generate new and innovative ideas that can be useful for related outcomes (Amabile, 1996). Creativity reflects the extent of an employee's ability to produce suggestions for product creation, product or process improvements, and finding solutions through divergent thinking or thinking out of the box (Baer, 2012; Zhou & George, 2001). Given the highly volatile global marketplace, fierce competition, and unpredictable and fast technological changes, employee creativity became a significant resource for organizations as companies are subject to adapt to the rapid changes through their innovation capabilities for which creative human resources are crucial (Amabile, Schatzel, Moneta & Kramer, 2004). Employee creativity can be influenced by internal factors (e.g., personality; Chiang, Hsu & Shih, 2017) and external factors (e.g., organizational climate; Khalili, 2016). According to Amabile (1996), employees' creativity can significantly be affected by their work environment.

Employee creativity can be useful in making improvements in product or process innovations, generating technological breakthroughs or developing solutions for problems (Baer, 2012; Zhou & George, 2001). Mindfulness is considered more influential for employees working in dynamic environments (Vogus, 2011). Mindfulness can reduce habitual reactions by changing the way individuals interpret and react in everyday life; therefore, it can enhance creative thinking through those non-habitual reactions (Ostafin & Kassman, 2012). In a related vein, mindfulness has the unique potential to ignite creativity by decreasing the tendency to count on habitual reactions while looking for a new solution. Prior research showed that mindfulness and mindfulness trainings can improve creativity (Colzato et al., 2012; Ding et al., 2015; Ding, Tang, Tang & Posner, 2014; Grant, Langer, Falk & Capodilupo, 2004).

Mindfulness enhances the improvement of attention to generate and realize novel ideas and resilience towards barriers or failures (Penman, 2015). Mindfulness and mindfulness trainings help individuals to improve their cognitive ability to pay full attention to things happening at the present time without any thoughts related to the past or future. This cognitive ability of focusing on the present moment facilitates different or unconventional thinking and the generation of new perspectives (Langer, Russel & Eisenkraft, 2009). Langer (2014) asserts that mindless individuals who can respond to situations without fully understanding are usually triggered by their environment. In addition, mindless individuals, compared with mindful ones, can limit themselves due to their past assumptions and experiences. Those individuals can get stuck in past experiences and set themselves barriers; therefore, they are not open to new ideas, perspectives, or products (Byrne & Thatchenkery, 2019). Mindful individuals can observe and view things with a fresh mind and are not blinded by the cognitive barriers built by past experiences (Fabrizio, 2009; Greenberg, Reiner & Meiran, 2012).

The interplay between emotional exhaustion, creativity, and mindfulness

Emotional exhaustion can cause physical and psychological harm to individuals (Chang & Chiu, 2009). Especially since emotional exhaustion can deplete the emotional resources of individuals (Hobfoll, 2002), it can result in lower self-esteem, depression, feelings of helplessness, hopelessness, etc. (Pines & Aronson, 1988). Those negative feelings or moods can inhibit the creative behavior of an individual as they decrease the positive energy (Golparvar, Kamkar & Javadian, 2012).

Emotionally exhausted individuals can feel emotionally overextended (Cordes & Dougherty, 1993; Maslach & Jackson, 1981). Employees who lack emotional resources can be reluctant to carry out any actions that go beyond what they are required to do. In this related domain, it is considered that emotional exhaustion inhibits creativity (Shin, Hur & Oh, 2015). A rich body of research emphasized the role of energy in creative behavior (Atwater & Carmeli, 2009; Mumford, Scott, Gaddis & Strange, 2002; Tierney, Farmer & Graen, 1999). Emotional exhaustion causes lack of energy and negative affect in employees (Cordes & Dougherty, 1993). In this vein, emotional exhaustion can decrease creative behavior. Additionally, emotionally exhausted employees can show less willingness to put effort into their work, which leads to less creative behavior (Hur, Moon & Jun, 2016).

Creative behavior inherently requires a certain level of motivation in order to pursue and implement new approaches to solve problems or generate diversified thinking (Mumford, 2003; Van Dyne, Jehn & Cummings, 2002). Therefore, employees need to have enough energy to put towards developing new ideas. When individuals experience emotional frustration, their motivational energy decreases; therefore, they ignore evaluating situations from different perspectives and challenging things (Van Dyne et al., 2002). Accordingly, emotional exhaustion acts as an inhibitor that impedes the creativity of individuals. Mindful individuals can improve their creativity by decreasing the negative effects of emotional exhaustion since mindful individuals do not evaluate stressful moments and can focus on what they are already doing. Therefore, mindfulness can help improve creativity by decreasing the level of emotional frustration.

In the light of the literature, the following hypotheses are developed:

H1: Mindfulness has a negative effect on emotional exhaustion.
H2: Mindfulness has a positive effect on creativity.
H3: Emotional exhaustion has a negative effect on creativity.
H4: Emotional exhaustion mediates the relationship between mindfulness and creativity.

Research design

Participants

A total of 120 (67 female, 53 male) full-time employees were recruited online through Amazon's Mechanical Turk (MTurk); however, due to missing values, two participants' responses were excluded from the analysis (67 female, 51 male). MTurk has become the dominant crowdsourcing tool in social sciences by providing large samples at low cost (Shapiro, Chandler & Mueller, 2013). Previous research has shown that data gathered through crowdsourcing methods are reliable (Buhrmester, Kwang & Gosling, 2011; Casler, Bickel & Hackett, 2013), and data quality is not affected by the amount of compensation or the survey duration (Buhrmester et al., 2011; Shapiro et al., 2013). The study materials were administered online by Google Survey, through which participants are provided a link in MTurk. At the end of the survey, participants were given a code to use in MTurk to indicate that they have done the survey. In addition, an attention control question was asked to check whether the participants paid attention to the survey. Participants were compensated $0.50 upon their completion of the survey, which took approximately 5 minutes. Participants ranged in age from 19 to 60 years (mean=36.19, SD=8.802).

Measurements

All of the instruments used in this study indicated accepted levels of reliability and validity as the reliability values are higher than 0.70, average extracted values are higher than 0.50, composite reliability values are higher than 0.70, and the values of the square root of average extracted values are higher than the correlations (Fornell & Larcker, 1981; Nunnally, 1982). The item loadings of the constructs were statistically significant and higher than 0.50 (Hair, Hult, Ringle & Sarstedt, 2016). The variance inflation factor values are lower than 5 (Henseler, Ringle & Sinkovics, 2009); therefore, constructs do not show high correlation. In order to evaluate the measurement model, a confirmatory factor analysis was carried out by AMOS. A three-factor model involving creativity, mindfulness, and emotional exhaustion showed better fit results than one- and two-factor models ($\chi2$=301.7, df=206, $\chi2$/df=1.464, NFI=0.78, CFI=0.916, RMSEA=0.063), which confirms the discriminant validity of the study. The results aforementioned show that reliability and validity issues are not a concern for this study.

Mindfulness

Mindfulness was measured by the unidimensional version of the Freiburg Mindfulness Inventory (FMI), which includes 14 items for which participants do not need any previous knowledge of mindfulness (Walach, Buchheld, Buttenmüller, Kleinknecht & Schmidt, 2006). FMI is among the most used instruments to measure mindfulness. Responses range from 1 (rarely) to 4 (almost always). A sample item is as follows: "I accept unpleasant experiences" (Cronbach's α=0.89).

Creativity

Creativity was measured through the four-item scale by Farmer, Tierney and Kung-Mcintyre (2003). Participants were asked to rate themselves based on a five-point Likert scale ranging from 1=completely disagree to 5=completely agree. A sample item is: "I generate ground-breaking ideas related to my field" (Cronbach's α=0.78).

Emotional exhaustion

Emotional exhaustion was measured with the four-item scale adapted by Wilk and Moynihan (2005) based on the study of Maslach and Jackson (1981). Participants evaluated the frequency of their experiences based on a five-point Likert scale ranging from 1 (once a month or less) to 5 (several times a day). A sample item is: "I feel burned out from my work" (Cronbach's α=0.92).

Results

Table 29.1 shows the means, standard deviations, and correlation coefficients of all variables. In order to test the developed hypotheses, the analytical method of Preacher and Hayes (2008) was followed. The bootstrapping method was used to analyze the significance level of the indirect effect of mindfulness on creativity (Preacher & Hayes, 2008). Some researchers point out that bootstrapping is a better technique than the Sobels' test (Preacher & Hayes, 2008). In bootstrapping, the indirect effects are analyzed based on the confidence intervals. To test the hypotheses, the SPSS macro, Process (Preacher & Hayes, 2008), was used. According to the results, mindfulness was negatively related to emotional exhaustion ($\beta = -0.63$, $t = -3.56$, $p<0.001$), supporting Hypothesis 1. Mindfulness was positively related to creativity ($\beta = 0.51$, $t = 4.80$, $p<0.001$), while emotional exhaustion was negatively related to creativity ($\beta = -0.112$, $t = -2.18$, $p<0.05$), supporting Hypotheses 2 and 3. To test the significance level of indirect effect, 5,000 samples were bootstrapped to construct a confidence interval (Preacher & Hayes, 2008). Bootstrapping showed that bootstrapped confidence intervals of the indirect effect do not involve zero, which supports the mediation effect of emotional exhaustion on the relationship between mindfulness and creativity, therefore supporting Hypothesis 4. The indirect effect of mindfulness on creativity was 0.07 (0.043–0.1730). In addition, as both indirect and direct effect are significant, there is a partial mediation. Bootstrapping results are shown in Table 29.2.

Discussion

The extant literature emphasizes the benefits of mindfulness, particularly on psychological wellbeing and mental health. Mindful individuals can avoid getting stuck in memories or past situations and give reactions to the situations as they are happening for the first time,

Table 29.1 Descriptive statistics

Construct	*Mean*	*SD*	*1*	*2*	*3*
1. Mindfulness	2.86	0.544	–		
2. Emotional Exhaustion	2.12	1.11	–0.302**	–	–
3. Creativity	3.76	6.87	0.449**	–0.301**	–

N=118, ** Correlation is significant at the 0.01 level

Table 29.2 Direct and indirect effects

	Relationships	*β*	*p*	*LLCI*	*ULCI*
H1	**Mindfulness → Emotional Exhaustion (Model 1)**	–0.63	.0005	–0.989	–0.281
H2	**Mindfulness → Creativity (Model 2)**	0.51	.0000	0.301	0.724
H3	**Emotional Exhaustion → Creativity (Model 2)**	–0.112	0.031	–0.217	–0.010
Bootstrapping Results for Indirect Effect		0.073	——	0.043	0.1730
H4Indirect effects of mindfulness on creativity					

which in turn drives them to stay in more positive states and pay full attention to what is happening at that current moment. By virtue of mindfulness, individuals can engage in a nonjudgmental state with full awareness that promotes concentration, and cognitive and emotional abilities. In addition, mindful individuals in their nonjudgmental state can decrease their concern of being judged by others and deal with negative thoughts and feelings. Correspondingly, the level of stress and emotional frustration residing within that individual can be regulated. Recent research attempted to investigate the role of mindfulness in emotion regulation.

The present study contributes to the existing literature by providing a better understanding of how mindfulness can contribute to creativity by reducing the negative effect of emotional exhaustion, which can be a detriment to the creative behavior of employees. As the results show, mindfulness can help employees to deal with their negative emotional states, improve their positive states, and foster positive organizational behaviors. As in this study, prior research supported the buffering role of mindfulness on emotional exhaustion. Mindfulness can help individuals to improve their creativity by decreasing the level of emotional exhaustion they experience. In addition, mindful employees have a tendency to prevent any negative appraisal or evaluation of a situation and garner negative emotion generation; therefore, they can engage in broadened attention with cognitive flexibility. Mindful employees can become resilient to emotional exhaustion as they have the ability to manage stressful situations with a nonjudgmental manner. The findings of this study attempted to enrich the present understanding of the role of mindfulness on creativity by its reductive role on employees' emotional frustration or depletion. It is paramount to note that this study fulfils a gap in the literature by unveiling the interrelations between mindfulness, emotional exhaustion, and creativity. While a rich body of research investigated the relationship between mindfulness and creativity, and mindfulness and emotional exhaustion, studies that address those constructs in an integrative approach are scarce. Based on the results, it can be asserted that mindful employees can boost their creativity by reducing their emotional exhaustion. Therefore, organizations that prioritize employee creativity can focus on improving their employees' mindfulness. In addition, employees who work in stressful working environments and to whom creativity is important can improve their mindfulness in order to cope with emotional frustration.

In terms of theoretical standpoint, the results of the interrelationships between emotional exhaustion, creativity, and mindfulness are in line with the existing literature. From a practical standpoint, as mindfulness can be enhanced through practicing meditation, organizations that prioritize creativity can encourage their employees to engage in meditation practices in order to enhance mindfulness. The association between mindfulness and creativity can be a fruitful result for the educational psychology in terms of the promotion of creative thinking and practicing creative education. There are some limitations of this current research that need to be mentioned. First, although the hypotheses were developed based on literature, the findings may not be appropriate for generalizability. Future studies can replicate the current study for certain industries or job positions. Another limitation worth mentioning is the common method variance. Despite utilizing several procedures to decrease common method variance, recommended by Podsakoff, MacKenzie and Podsakoff (2012), the instruments were based on self-reports of the participants, which can overstate the revealed relationships between the constructs. For example, different scale formats were used, and participants were informed about the guaranteed privacy of their responses.

Chapter takeaways

1. All efforts given to investigate mindfulness have shown that there are a number of benefits of mindfulness for all individuals, regardless of job position, age, or gender.
2. Mindfulness has been under the spotlight of scholars because of its potential to provide individuals with a psychologically and physically healthy life.
3. From the psychological standpoint, mindfulness has a boosting effect on cognitive and emotional abilities. By virtue of those effects, mindful individuals can focus, regulate emotions in a moment of emotional frustration, and garner positive emotions, which reflects on their daily lives, especially on interpersonal interactions. In this sense, reduction of emotional exhaustion is one of the benefits that mindfulness enables.
4. Among the countless benefits of mindfulness is its boosting effect on creativity. Individuals whose jobs demand high levels of creativity can utilize the benefits of mindfulness.
5. Mindful individuals can become resilient to emotional exhaustion as they can manage stressful situations in a nonjudgmental manner, through which they can foster their creativity.

Reflection questions

1. What kinds of benefits does mindfulness provide? What are the major characteristics of mindful individuals?
2. Suppose that you are a manager in a quite stressful environment and you consistently observe tension among your workers. You also observe that they sometimes have problems controlling their emotions, to the extent that it decreases their creativity and performance. What are some recommendations you can make in order to resolve these issues? What kinds of practical actions would you take to fix this problem?
3. What are some other potential future directions for research on mindfulness? What kind of work behaviors do you think mindfulness can influence?
4. In the present study, the interrelationships between mindfulness, creativity, and emotional exhaustion are addressed. Explain why and how these constructs are associated with each other.
5. Suppose that you are a manager and you know about the potential of mindfulness. How would you apply the results of this study to your working environment?

References

Afsar, B. & Rehman, M. (2015). The relationship between workplace spirituality and innovative work behavior: The mediating role of perceived person–Organization fit. *Journal of Management, Spirituality & Religion, 12*(4), 329–353.

Agnoli, S., Vanucci, M., Pelagatti, C., & Corazza, G. E. (2018). Exploring the link between mind wandering, mindfulness, and creativity: A multidimensional approach. *Creativity Research Journal, 30* (1), 41–53.

Allen, T. D., Eby, L. T., Conley, K. M., Williamson, R. L., Mancini, V. S., & Mitchell, M. E. (2015). What do we really know about the effects of mindfulness-based training in the workplace? *Industrial and Organizational Psychology, 8*(4), 652–661.

Amabile, T. M. (1996). *Creativity and innovation in organizations.* Boston: Harvard Business School Press.

Amabile, T. M., Schatzel, E. A., Moneta, G. B., & Kramer, S. J. (2004). Leader behaviors and the work environment for creativity: Perceived leader support. *The Leadership Quarterly, 15*(1), 5–32.

Arch, J. J. & Craske, M. G. (2010). Laboratory stressors in clinically anxious and non-anxious individuals: The moderating role of mindfulness. *Behavior Research and Therapy, 48*(6), 495–505.

Atwater, L. & Carmeli, A. (2009). Leader–member exchange, feelings of energy, and involvement in creative work. *The Leadership Quarterly, 20*(3), 264–275.

Baas, M., De Dreu, C. K., & Nijstad, B. A. (2008). A meta-analysis of 25 years of mood-creativity research: Hedonic tone, activation, or regulatory focus? *Psychological Bulletin, 134*(6), 779–806.

Baer, M. (2012). Putting creativity to work: The implementation of creative ideas in organizations. *Academy of Management Journal, 55*(5), 1102–1119.

Brown, K. W. & Ryan, R. M. (2003). The benefits of being present: Mindfulness and its role in psychological well-being. *Journal of Personality and Social Psychology, 84*(4), 822–848.

Brown, K. W., Ryan, R. M., & Creswell, J. D. (2007). Mindfulness: Theoretical foundations and evidence for its salutary effects. *Psychological Inquiry, 18*(4), 211–237.

Brown, K. W., Ryan, R. M., Loverich, T. M., Biegel, G. M., & West, A. M. (2011). Out of the armchair and into the streets: Measuring mindfulness advances knowledge and improves interventions: Reply to Grossman (2011). *Psychological Assessment, 23,* 1041–1046. doi:10.1037/a0025781

Buhrmester, M., Kwang, T., & Gosling, S. (2011). Amazon's mechanical Turk: A new source of inexpensive, yet high quality, data? *Perspectives on Psychological Science, 6*(1), 3–5.

Byrne, E. K. & Thatchenkery, T. (2019). Cultivating creative workplaces through mindfulness. *Journal of Organizational Change Management, 32*(1), 15–31.

Casler, K., Bickel, L., & Hackett, E. (2013). Separate but equal? A comparison of participants and data gathered via Amazon's MTurk, social media, and face-to-face behavioral testing. *Computers in Human Behavior, 29*(6), 2156–2160.

Chambers, R., Gullone, E., & Allen, N. B. (2009). Mindful emotion regulation: An integrative review. *Clinical Psychology Review, 29*(6), 560–572.

Chang, C. P. & Chiu, J. M. (2009). Flight attendants' emotional labor and exhaustion in the Taiwanese airline industry. *Journal of Service Science & Management, 2*(4), 305–311.

Chiang, Y. H., Hsu, C. C., & Shih, H. A. (2017). Extroversion personality, domain knowledge, and the creativity of new product development engineers. *Creativity Research Journal, 29*(4), 387–396.

Chiesa, A., Calati, R., & Serretti, A. (2011). Does mindfulness training improve cognitive abilities? A systematic review of neuropsychological findings. *Clinical Psychology Review, 31*(3), 449–464.

Chiesa, A., Serretti, A., & Jakobsen, J. C. (2013). Mindfulness: Top-down or bottom-up emotion regulation strategy? *Clinical Psychology Review, 33*(1), 82–96.

Colzato, L. S., Szapora, A., & Hommel, B. (2012). Meditate to create: The impact of focused-attention and open-monitoring training on convergent and divergent thinking. *Frontiers in Psychology, 3,* 116–128.

Cordes, C. L. & Dougherty, T. W. (1993). A review and an integration of research on job burnout. *Academy of Management Review, 18*(4), 621–656.

Creswell, J. D., Way, B. M., Eisenberger, N. I., & Lieberman, M. D. (2007). Neural correlates of dispositional mindfulness during affect labeling. *Psychosomatic Medicine, 69*(6), 560–565.

Dane, E. (2011). Paying attention to mindfulness and its effects on task performance in the workplace. *Journal of Management, 37*(4), 997–1018.

Dane, E. & Brummel, B. J. (2014). Examining workplace mindfulness and its relations to job performance and turnover intention. *Human Relations, 67*(1), 105–128.

Ding, X., Tang, Y. Y., Deng, Y., Tang, R., & Posner, M. I. (2015). Mood and personality predict improvement in creativity due to meditation training. *Learning and Individual Differences, 37*, 217–221.

Ding, X., Tang, Y. Y., Tang, R., & Posner, M. I. (2014). Improving creativity performance by short-term meditation. *Behavioral and Brain Functions, 10*(1), 1–8.

Eby, L. T., Allen, T. D., Conley, K. M., Williamson, R. L., Henderson, T. G., & Mancini, V. S. (2019). Mindfulness-based training interventions for employees: A qualitative review of the literature. *Human Resource Management Review, 29*(2), 156–178.

Fabrizio, D. (2009). *Clinical Handbook of Mindfulness.* New York, NY: Springer Science + Business Media.

Farmer, S. M., Tierney, P., & Kung-Mcintyre, K. (2003). Employee creativity in Taiwan: An application of role identity theory. *Academy of Management Journal, 46*(5), 618–630.

Feldman, G., Hayes, A., Kumar, S., Greeson, J., & Laurenceau, J. P. (2007). Mindfulness and emotion regulation: The development and initial validation of the Cognitive and Affective Mindfulness Scale-Revised (CAMS-R). *Journal of Psychopathology and Behavioral Assessment, 29*(3), 177–190.

Fornell, C. & Larcker, D. F. (1981). Structural equation models with unobservable variables and measurement error: Algebra and statistics. *Journal of Marketing Research, 18*(3), 382–388.

Glomb, T. M., Duffy, M. K., Bono, J. E., & Yang, T. (2011). Mindfulness at work. In A. Joshi, H. Liao, and J.J. Martocchio (Eds.), *Research in personnel and human resources management* (Vol. 30, pp. 115–157). Bingley: Emerald Group Publishing Limited.

Golparvar, M., Kamkar, M., & Javadian, Z. (2012). Moderating effects of job stress in emotional exhaustion and feeling of energy relationships with positive and negative behaviors: Job stress multiple functions approach. *International Journal of Psychological Studies, 4*(4), 99–112.

Good, D. J., Lyddy, C. J., Glomb, T. M., Bono, J. E., Brown, K. W., Duffy, M. K., . . . Lazar, S. W. (2016). Contemplating mindfulness at work: An integrative review. *Journal of Management, 42*(1), 114–142.

Goodman, M. J. & Schorling, J. B. (2012). A mindfulness course decreases burnout and improves well-being among healthcare providers. *The International Journal of Psychiatry in Medicine, 43*(2), 119–128.

Grandey, A., Foo, S. C., Groth, M., & Goodwin, R. E. (2012). Free to be you and me: A climate of authenticity alleviates burnout from emotional labor. *Journal of Occupational Health Psychology, 17*(1), 1–14.

Grant, A. M., Langer, E. J., Falk, E., & Capodilupo, C. (2004). Mindful creativity: Drawing to draw distinctions. *Creativity Research Journal, 16*(2–3), 261–265.

Greenberg, J., Reiner, K., & Meiran, N. (2012). Mind the trap': Mindfulness practice reduces cognitive rigidity. *PLoS One*, 7(5), 1–8.

Grossman, P., Niemann, L., Schmidt, S., & Walach, H. (2004). Mindfulness-based stress reduction and health benefits: A meta-analysis. *Journal of Psychosomatic Research, 57*(1), 35–43.

Gu, J., Strauss, C., Bond, R., & Cavanagh, K. (2015). How do mindfulness-based cognitive therapy and mindfulness-based stress reduction improve mental health and wellbeing? A systematic review and meta-analysis of mediation studies. *Clinical Psychology Review, 37*, 1–12.

Gunaratana, H. (2002). *Mindfulness in plain English.* Boston: Widom.

Hair, J. F., Jr, Hult, G. T. M., Ringle, C., & Sarstedt, M. (2016). *A primer on partial least squares structural equation modeling (PLS-SEM).* Thousand Oaks, CA: Sage publications.

Henseler, J., Ringle, C. M., & Sinkovics, R. R. (2009). The use of partial least squares path modeling in international marketing. In R. Sinkovics & P. Ghauri (Eds.), *New challenges to international marketing* (pp. 277–319). Bingley: Emerald Group Publishing Limited.

Hobfoll, S. E. (2002). Social and psychological resources and adaptation. *Review of General Psychology, 6* (4), 307–324.

Hülsheger, U. R., Alberts, H. J., Feinholdt, A., & Lang, J. W. (2013). Benefits of mindfulness at work: The role of mindfulness in emotion regulation, emotional exhaustion, and job satisfaction. *Journal of Applied Psychology, 98*(2), 1–16.

Hur, W. M., Moon, T., & Jun, J. K. (2016). The effect of workplace incivility on service employee creativity: The mediating role of emotional exhaustion and intrinsic motivation. *Journal of Services Marketing, 30*(3), 302–315.

Hyland, P. K., Lee, R. A., & Mills, M. J. (2015). Mindfulness at work: A new approach to improving individual and organizational performance. *Industrial and Organizational Psychology*, *8*(4), 576–602.

Jimenez, S. S., Niles, B. L., & Park, C. L. (2010). A mindfulness model of affect regulation and depressive symptoms: Positive emotions, mood regulation expectancies, and self-acceptance as regulatory mechanisms. *Personality and Individual Differences*, *49*(6), 645–650.

Karing, C. & Beelmann, A. (2018). Cognitive emotional regulation strategies: Potential mediators in the relationship between mindfulness, emotional exhaustion, and satisfaction? *Mindfulness*, *10*(3), 459–468.

Keng, S. L., Smoski, M. J., & Robins, C. J. (2011). Effects of mindfulness on psychological health: A review of empirical studies. *Clinical Psychology Review*, *31*(6), 1041–1056.

Khalili, A. (2016). Linking transformational leadership, creativity, innovation, and innovation-supportive climate. *Management Decision*, *54*(9), 2277–2293.

Langer, E. (2014). *Mindfulness*. Philadelphia, PA: Second Da Capo Press.

Langer, E., Russel, T., & Eisenkraft, N. (2009). Orchestral performance and the footprint of mindfulness. *Psychology of Music*, *37*(2), 125–136.

Lebuda, I., Zabelina, D. L., & Karwowski, M. (2016). Mind full of ideas: A meta-analysis of the mindfulness–creativity link. *Personality and Individual Differences*, *93*, 22–26.

Li, J. J., Wong, I. A., & Kim, W. G. (2017). Does mindfulness reduce emotional exhaustion? A multilevel analysis of emotional labor among casino employees. *International Journal of Hospitality Management*, *64*, 21–30.

Malinowski, P. (2013). Neural mechanisms of attentional control in mindfulness meditation. *Frontiers in Neuroscience*, 7, 1–11.

Malinowski, P. & Lim, H. J. (2015). Mindfulness at work: Positive affect, hope, and optimism mediate the relationship between dispositional mindfulness, work engagement, and well-being. *Mindfulness*, *6* (6), 1250–1262.

Maslach, C. & Jackson, S. E. (1981). The measurement of experienced burnout. *Journal of Occupational Behavior*, *2*(2), 99–113.

Maslach, C., Jackson, S. E., Leiter, M. P., Schaufeli, W. B., & Schwab, R. L. (1986). *Maslach Burnout Inventory*. Palo Alto, CA. *Consulting Psychologists Press*, *21*, p: 3463–3464.

Montani, F., Dagenais-Desmarais, V., Giorgi, G., & Grégoire, S. (2018). A conservation of resources perspective on negative affect and innovative work behavior: The role of affect activation and mindfulness. *Journal of Business and Psychology*, *33*(1), 123–139.

Moore, A. & Malinowski, P. (2009). Meditation, mindfulness and cognitive flexibility. *Consciousness and Cognition*, *18*(1), 176–186.

Mumford, M. D. (2003). Where have we been, where are we going? Taking stock in creativity research. *Creativity Research Journal*, *15*(2–3), 107–120.

Mumford, M. D., Scott, G. M., Gaddis, B., & Strange, J. M. (2002). Leading creative people: Orchestrating expertise and relationships. *Leadership Quarterly*, *13*, 705–750.

Nunnally, J. C. (1982). *Reliability of measurement*. *Encyclopedia of educational research* (Vol. 4). New York: Free Press.

Ostafin, B. D. & Kassman, K. T. (2012). Stepping out of history: Mindfulness improves insight problem solving. *Consciousness and Cognition*, *21*(2), 1031–1036.

Papies, E. K., Barsalou, L. W., & Custers, R. (2012). Mindful attention prevents mindless impulses. *Social Psychological and Personality Science*, *3*(3), 291–299.

Penman, D. (2015). *Mindfulness for creativity: Adapt, create and thrive in a frantic world*. London: Piatkus.

Pines, A. & Aronson, E. (1988). *Career burnout: Causes and cures*. New York, NY: Free press.

Podsakoff, P. M., MacKenzie, S. B., & Podsakoff, N. P. (2012). Sources of method bias in social science research and recommendations on how to control it. *Annual Review of Psychology*, *63*, 539–569.

Preacher, K. J. & Hayes, A. F. (2008). Asymptotic and resampling strategies for assessing and comparing indirect effects in multiple mediator models. *Behavior Research Methods*, *40*(3), 879–891.

Reb, J. & Atkins, P. W. (Eds.). (2015). *Mindfulness in organizations: Foundations, research, and applications*. Cambridge, UK: Cambridge University Press.

Reb, J., Narayanan, J., Chaturvedi, S., & Ekkirala, S. (2017). The mediating role of emotional exhaustion in the relationship of mindfulness with turnover intentions and job performance. *Mindfulness*, *8*(3), 707–716.

Reb, J., Narayanan, J., & Ho, Z. W. (2015). Mindfulness at work: Antecedents and consequences of employee awareness and absent-mindedness. *Mindfulness*, *6*(1), 111–122.

Roof, R. A. (2015). The association of individual spirituality on employee engagement: The spirit at work. *Journal of Business Ethics, 130*(3), 585–599.

Schultz, P. P., Ryan, R. M., Niemiec, C. P., Legate, N., & Williams, G. C. (2015). Mindfulness, work climate, and psychological need satisfaction in employee well-being. *Mindfulness, 6*(5), 971–985.

Schutte, N. S. & Malouff, J. M. (2011). Emotional intelligence mediates the relationship between mindfulness and subjective well-being. *Personality and Individual Differences, 50*(7), 1116–1119.

Sedlmeier, P., Eberth, J., Schwarz, M., Zimmermann, D., Haarig, F., Jaeger, S., & Kunze, S. (2012). The psychological effects of meditation: A meta-analysis. *Psychological Bulletin, 138*(6), 1139–1171.

Shapiro, D. N., Chandler, J., & Mueller, P. A. (2013). Using Mechanical Turk to study clinical populations. *Clinical Psychological Science, 1*(2), 213–220.

Shapiro, S. L., Carlson, L. E., Astin, J. A., & Freedman, B. (2006). Mechanisms of mindfulness. *Journal of Clinical Psychology, 62*(3), 373–386.

Shin, I., Hur, W. M., & Oh, H. (2015). Essential precursors and effects of employee creativity in a service context: Emotional labor strategies and official job performance. *Career Development International, 20*(7), 733–752.

Taylor, N. Z. & Millear, P. M. R. (2016). The contribution of mindfulness to predicting burnout in the workplace. *Personality and Individual Differences, 89*, 123–128.

Tierney, P., Farmer, S. M., & Graen, G. B. (1999). An examination of leadership and employee creativity: The relevance of traits and relationship. *Personnel Psychology, 52*(3), 591–620.

Van Dyne, L., Jehn, K. A., & Cummings, A. (2002). Differential effects of strain on two forms of work performance: Individual employee sales and creativity. *Journal of Organizational Behavior, 23*(1), 57–74.

Vogus, T. J. (2011). Mindful organizing: Establishing and extending the foundations of highly reliable performance. In K. Cameron & G. Spreitzer (Eds.), *Handbook of Positive Organizational Scholarship* (pp. 664–676). New York: Oxford University Press.

Walach, H., Buchheld, N., Buttenmüller, V., Kleinknecht, N., & Schmidt, S. (2006). Measuring mindfulness-the Freiburg mindfulness inventory (FMI). *Personality and Individual Differences, 40*(8), 1543–1555.

Weick, K. E. & Putnam, T. (2006). Organizing for mindfulness: Eastern wisdom and Western knowledge. *Journal of Management Inquiry, 15*(3), 275–287.

Wilk, S. L. & Moynihan, L. M. (2005). Display rule "regulators": The relationship between supervisors and worker emotional exhaustion. *Journal of Applied Psychology, 90*(5), 917–927.

Zhou, J. & George, J. M. (2001). When job dissatisfaction leads to creativity: Encouraging the expression of voice. *Academy of Management Journal, 44*(4), 682–696.

30

LOVE, CREATIVITY, AND MINDFULNESS IN INTERNATIONAL LEADERS

Qualities for a successful future world of work

Claude-Hélène Mayer and Rudolf Oosthuizen

1. Introduction

Mindfulness is a spiritual concept that has been discussed increasingly in recent decades, specifically in the leadership context. It is uncontested that leadership in the Fourth Industrial Revolution (4IR) and future work needs to change, since new skills, perspectives, and processes are needed to compete with global changes and manage 4IR-related challenges effectively, such as information and operational technology, engagement, predictive maintenance, and machine–machine and machine–human interactions (Bloem et al., 2014; Stubbings, 2018; WEF, 2016). It has been argued before that "mindfulness" is an important concept for leaders to act in a state of consciousness within the future-related work context (Leonhardt & Wiedemann, 2015; Mayer & Geldenhuys, 2019). It has further been reported that holistic leadership needs to be practiced to deal with insecurities due to rapid changes and to ensure competitiveness and the ability to work with the complexities of future-related workplaces (Leonhardt & Wiedemann, 2015).

Parallel to the relatively scarce literature on processes, skills, and changes of the 4IR and future workplaces and their impact on employees and leaders, it would appear that there is a gap in the literature on the qualities future work leaders need to drive and navigate the 4IR successfully. A very few papers indicate that future leaders need to be mindful (Caring-Lobel, 2016), loving (Larson & Murtadha, 2005; Mayer, 2020a), and creative (Rojanapanich & Pimpa, 2011). However, there is no in-depth exploration in the literature about what it *means* to be mindful, loving, and creative as a leader while dealing with new work challenges. In this chapter it is basically assumed that mindfulness, love (in terms of a compassionate love for humankind and humanness), and creativity can build a constructive and powerful foundation for leaders to respond to 4IR and future work challenges. It is further argued that these concepts, highlighted as qualities of leaders and expected skills of leaders in the 4IR, need to be filled with content and life. Therefore, the voices of these leaders need to be heard to understand how mindfulness, love, and creativity can impact positively in future-related leadership.

The objective of this chapter is therefore to present insights into leaders' concepts of mindful, loving, and creative leadership for the future world of work, and to explore what leaders mean by addressing these concepts and their interrelationships. The chapter presents qualitative findings from a study including 22 international leaders and their views on mindfulness, love, and creativity in leadership in the 4IR. To reach this objective, the following research questions are responded to in this chapter:

- What do the concepts of "mindfulness," "love," and "creativity" entail for leaders?
- How are mindfulness and love connected in the eyes of leaders?
- How do love and creativity impact on leaders?
- What is love's contribution to becoming a creative and mindful leader?

In the following section the concepts will be explored with regard to previous research; the research methodology will be explained and findings will be presented and discussed; a conclusion will be drawn; and recommendations will be made.

2. The world of work during the Fourth Industrial Revolution

By referring to Bag, Telukdarie, Pretorius, and Gupta (2018), Spath et al. (2013), and Stubbings (2018), it is assumed that with growing internationalization, digitalization, new technologies, upgraded SMART applications, and increasingly decentralized work and organizational frameworks, the leadership and skills required to lead will also change rapidly as will organizational and work cultures. Leadership will require different knowledge, skills, and communication processes, and will have to integrate new applications, technologization, and human interaction, as described previously (Caring-Lobel, 2016; Stubbings, 2018).

Research on 4IR during the past few years (WEF, 2016) further pointed out that emotional intelligence, creativity, and complex problem-solving as skills would be high in demand to cater for the rapid changes, challenges, and new work processes. Therefore, leading leadership institutes (SIYLI, 2017) argued that emotional intelligence and competences would be the key to successful and effective collaboration. It was previously argued that leaders would need compassionate love to manage their surroundings in a meaningful, successful, human, and sustainable way, primarily within the 4IR context (Larson & Murtadha, 2005; Mayer, 2020a); and that mindfulness, love, and creativity in leadership could act as foundations for dealing with the emerging challenges in a smart, sustainable, and healthy way to find SMART solutions to be implemented for sustainable development, environmental protection, and the betterment of the global human society. Therefore, the concepts of mindfulness, love, and creativity will be explored regarding their potential impact on the 4IR and findings based on interviews with contemporary, international leaders will be presented.

3. Mindfulness in leadership

Mindfulness is associated with a spiritual practice and with certain attitudes towards the world, which include self-awareness, non-judgmental attitudes, focused attention, and open monitoring (Mayer & Geldenhuys, 2019). Germer (2005) has pointed out that mindfulness is not only associated with non-judgmental acceptance but with enthusiasm for life and curiosity.

Other researchers specifically agree that mindfulness is regarded as being connected to non-judgmental acceptance and with a kind or mindful presence and insight Mayer and Geldenhuys (2019). Walach, Buchheld, Buttenmüller, Kleinknecht, and Schmidt (2006) define mindful presence as an ongoing awareness and consciousness, while they think of insights as an ability of self-understanding and understanding of the world and the environment. Well-known mindfulness researchers, such as Brown and Ryan (2003) and Kabat-Zinn (2006), have highlighted that mindfulness is strongly connected with living in the present moment, but also with an in-depth connection to self and others. Mindfulness is, furthermore, associated with mental health and well-being, specifically with comprehensibility, manageability, and meaningfulness (Mayer, Surtee, & Visser, 2016). Also, it has been pointed out that the need for pleasure maximization is similar to the concept of flow and can be reached through mindfulness, which is a spiritual concept in the workplace (Mayer & Geldenhuys, 2014, 2019).

Mindfulness can be viewed as an applied intervention to support leadership in order to ask for alternatives before decisions can be taken (Brann, 2014; Henson & Rossouw, 2013); and, according to a rather critical view by Caring-Lobel (2016), mindfulness interventions promise to deal with the discontent of employees without challenging the social and economic causes of discontent, and therefore is happily adopted by the managerial and leadership elite. Other researchers (Mayer, 2014; Mayer & Walach, 2018) emphasize that economic approaches have been redefined through mindfulness interventions not only as being orientated via the *homo economicus* alone and thus via egotistical maximizing of profits, but also beyond the ad hoc need of the organization while striving for sustainability and "a more transcendent reality," strengthening human connection through the transcendental (Mayer & Walach, 2018, p. 5).

4. Love and leadership

Love has been defined in many different ways, in relation to socio-cultural contexts and specific timeframes (Beall & Sternberg, 1995; Jahoda & Lewis, 2015; Javaid, 2018), and as gender-related meaning-making (Carter, 2013; Mayer, 2020b). According to Gratzke (2017), love is connected to taking pleasure in doing something and as a humanistic concept, with compassion, caring, and tenderness (Barsade & O'Neill, 2014). Mayer (2020b) emphasizes that love is connected to trust and intimacy, responsibility, respect, belonging, and attachment, and with a trans-human experience, such as a deep connection, eternal commitment, and personal freedom and growth.

Research in the context of love and leadership often refers to love as "compassionate love" (Patterson, 2010), which further includes caring, serving, tenderness and generosity (Eldor, 2017; O'Neill, 2018), and empowerment and authenticity (Van Dierendonck & Patterson, 2014). According to Rynes et al. (2012), love seems to have a positive effect on work and work relationships; and other researchers, such as Winston (2002), have pointed out that love in leaders would contribute to a positive attitude and positive actions towards employees. Love in leaders further adds to a spiritual leadership perspective (Fry & Matherly, 2006) and increased well-being (Cooper, 2013).

Compassionate love in times of the 4IR can help to increase human relations and cooperation (Chandsoda & Salsing, 2018) and might further impact on meaningfulness with regard to individuals working in digitalized work places (Schwab, 2017). Compassionate love can further support a deeper connection to the self in leaders and to overcome negative emotions, such as fears and depression (Van der Hoven, 2017). It can therefore be used as guidance to tackle new challenges.

5. Creativity in leaders

In recent years, it has been emphasized that creativity is one of the major skills needed within work and leadership settings in 4IR workplaces (WEF, 2016), since creativity supports the effective resolution of complex problems. Rojanapanich and Pimpa (2011) and Csikszentmihalyi (2014) described creativity as an important and extraordinary mental process which creates original output and new and impactful ideas to manage challenges effectively (Csikszentmihalyi & Wolfe, 2014).

Leaders are specifically in need of creativity to manage challenges such as innovation, competition, or motivation at work, particularly in rapidly changing workplaces, such as the 4IR. Creativity is a major skill to overcome challenges and manage work meaningfully (Mayer & van Niekerk, 2019, in press; Stubbings, 2018; Mayer, 2019). At the same time it can help to apply multiple perspectives (Sternberg, 2005) because creativity is an attitude and a skill which is divided into process creativity and application creativity (Sternberg, 2003). "Leadership" and "creativity" are interconnected concepts which influence each other and because creativity impacts on leadership success, leadership can also impact positively on creativity (Sternberg & Grigorenko, 2007; Vessey, Barrett, Mumford, Johnson, & Litwiller, 2014).

6. The interrelationship of mindfulness, love, and creativity

Mindfulness is strongly connected with love through the idea that both the concepts can foster a deep trans-human, transcultural, and spiritual connection (as in Mayer, 2020a, 2020b; Mayer & Walach, 2018) and both can contribute strongly to individual growth, positive self-esteem, self-worth, strength, and enrichment. Mindfulness, love, and creativity are viewed as increasing in energy and passion. Nandram and Borden (2011) have emphasized that an increased mindfulness in business and at work not only contributes to developing love but also to forgiveness, gratitude, and equanimity. It further helps leaders to develop their communication skills, relationships with others, and their personal development (Nandram & Borden, 2011). Uusiautti, Määttä, and Määttä (2013) have also described that love-based leadership can be intensified through training and activities that increase mindfulness. Fatemi (2016) has further pointed out that mindfulness results in increased creativity and improved leadership; and Langer and Ngnoumen (2017) emphasized that mindfulness fosters the expansion of "the cognitive and physical limitations towards greater creativity and more optimal functioning." In their meta-analysis, Lebuda, Zabelina, and Karwowski (2016) have pointed out that there is a significant link between the two concepts "mindfulness" and "creativity," depending on the type of mindfulness referred to.

The results from the study of Yang and Hung (2015) demonstrated that positive emotions can constrain negative emotions and foster creative performance. More specifically, they have found that companionate love constrains creativity, whereas anger facilitates it. Furthermore, their qualitative analyses of interviews with employees justify the implications of the experimental results in an organizational context. Their findings suggest that nurturing a moderate degree of hostility towards the ideas of others in an idea-generation process while concurrently encouraging thoughtfulness in an idea-implementation process can facilitate the management of organizational innovation processes. They assert that companionate love elicited by team cohesion is beneficial for team member cooperation and exchanging ideas, but detrimental to team member idea generation.

Mohsen, Rasoul, and Ali (2015) have indicated that there is a significant and positive association between dispositional positive emotion dimensions and positive affect and creativity. The results of hierarchical regression analysis also indicated that a positive affect moderates the association between contentment, pride, love, and creativity. The results of the research further showed that a positive affect could have discriminating effects on the relationship between some aspects of dispositional positive emotions and creativity.

7. Research methodology

The study is anchored in the tradition of qualitative studies within the hermeneutic phenomenology paradigm (Creswell, 2013; Yin, 2009). Thereby, hermeneutic phenomenology is viewed as the study of the subjective experience of individuals of a specific topic (Kaffle, 2011): mindfulness, love, and creativity in leadership, in this instance. In this study we focus on the shared meaning and interpretation of mindfulness, love, and creativity in the context of leadership to understand the concepts, their interplay, and their meaning for the leaders interviewed. This study forms part of a larger study on love and culture, and other parts of this study were previously published (Mayer, 2020a, 2020b). Data was collected through interviews to investigate the concepts described. Thereby, the interviews were conducted through an online questionnaire. Altogether 21 questions were asked and the participants used on average 90 minutes to complete the questionnaire.

The researchers used the five-step process of content analysis (Terre Blanche, 2006, pp. 322–326) to analyze the data: Step 1 involved familiarization and immersion; step 2 inducing themes; step 3, coding; step 4, elaboration; and step 5 involved interpretation and checking to ensure the quality of the data. In this chapter, the authors present the findings on mindfulness, love, and creativity in a qualitative reporting style. As in other parts of this study, quality criteria were used to guarantee the rigorous scientific approach (Fleck, 2018). The study took Tracey's eight big qualitative research criteria into account, referring to the idea that high-quality research is marked by the following eight criteria: (1) worthy topic, (2) rich rigor, (3) sincerity, (4) credibility, (5) resonance, (6) significant contribution, (7) ethics, and (8) meaningful coherence (Tracy & Hinrichs, 2017). With regard to this study, which is based on Tracy's model (Tracy, 2010), the researchers derived from the literature the importance of the topic (1) and explained the theoretical background and the methodology to discuss the findings in light of previous research transparency (2). Transparency about the research was provided through detailed descriptions and the reflexivity of the interpretation of the data (3), through triangulation of theories and methods (4), and the creation of transferable findings (5). The researchers described the significant contribution in their conclusions and recommendations (6), presented the ethical context of the research (7), and through the coherent presentation of the research, its process; the aims and findings; and a coherent interconnection of literature, research questions, responses, and interpretations created a meaningful coherence (8).

The sample comprised purposeful sampling and snowball sampling (Naderifar, Goli, & Ghaljaie, 2017) and included 22 participants. The participants comprised 9 female and 13 male participants with the following nationalities: eight Germans, five US-Americans, two Japanese, two South Africans and one participant each from German-Iranian, Israeli, Romanian and Bavarian[1] origin[2] (as described in Mayer, 2020a). The participants were between 33 and 80 years old at the time of the interview; and with reference to their religious affiliation, there were Christians, four Roman Catholics, two Protestants, one atheist, agnostic, atheist/agnostic, Buddhist, Muslim, Jew, Jesuit, and one without religious affiliation. Twenty of the participants had university degrees, while one had a national diploma and another one had a high school certificate. In terms of ethical conduct, the participants were afforded informed consent, confidentiality, anonymity, and transparency (Roth & Unger, 2018). Ethical approval for this research study was given by the participants as well as the German university. The limitations of the study were taken into account, only 22 participants were interviewed through an online questionnaire, and selected theories and methods were applied with regard to the specifically presented topic.

8. Findings

In the following section we present the findings on defining mindfulness, love, and creativity and their impact on leadership, by referring to the research questions mentioned above.

8.1 Mindfulness and love in leadership

Mindfulness and love are strongly related concepts, according to the leaders interviewed. There are several concepts which are important in leadership and which are also connected to mindfulness and love. They build a strong base for leadership. Table 30.1 presents an overview of the frequency of statements, the categories developed, and the participants who referred to this concept.

Leadership needs a deep connection for 12 out of the 22 leaders interviewed in terms of the love and mindfulness they experienced. For them, the deep connection of the self to others is the foundation of leading and working with others. A 58-year-old Catholic, German director of a large adult education institution, emphasized the following:

> I would say, it is the deep, unique connection, deep between individuals…

Love and mindfulness foster the connection with others through the inner attitude. People can experience an unconditional self-acceptance and acceptance of others through love and mindfulness. This supports an attitude of servant leadership and

Table 30.1 Mindfulness and love

Frequency	*Category*	*Participants*
12	Deep connection	P1, P4, P5, P6, P7, P8, P9. P11, P16, P17, P19, P21
10	Unconditional acceptance	P2, P4, P6, P7, P9, P11, P13, P16, P20, P22
6	Trust	P1, P2, P4, P7, P17, P18
6	Caring and responsibility	P4, P5, P8, P15, P16, P19
6	Meaning	P5, P7, P10, P14, P21, P22
5	Compassion	P2, P4, P9, P12, P13, P17
5	Growth	P4, P7, P10, P15, P18
4	Respect	P2, P4, P15, P22

leadership based on love and not on power. Ten participants highlighted unconditional love as a basis for leadership which is anchored in love and a mindful attitude; six participants emphasized that trust is a key to leadership as well as caring, responsibility, and meaningfulness.

According to the leaders, trust is built through love and mindfulness and contributes to successful cooperation and private and work relationships.

Caring, responsibility, and meaningfulness are also key to successful leadership for the leaders interviewed. Compassion was mentioned six times as well as growth and aspects of mindfulness and love in leadership. A male Muslim German CEO (P13), aged 46, emphasized the following:

> Love is work in respect and compassion. It creatives meaning which is a core to being a successful leader. With a loving attitude we act mindfully, we focus on our inner strengths, are compassionate, and ... the employees will go an extra mile.

Finally, four of the leaders stated that respect is part of mindfulness and love and is strongly needed in 4IR workplaces. Respect is viewed as an expression of a mindful attitude towards other individuals, such as colleagues or employees. Respecting oneself and others is also part of servant leadership, according to the interviewees

8.2 Love and creativity in leadership

The leaders also explained how love and creativity are interrelated for them within their respective leadership practices. Table 30.2 presents an overview of the frequency of statements, the categories developed, and the participants who refer to this concept. Thirteen out of 22 leaders highlighted that love makes them creative. P8, a German-Iranian male Christian, aged 45, stated the following:

> Without the support of love, it is very difficult for me to find the courage to be creative. Creativity means to think about alternative ways of running the business and this can only be done by some support within that business.

Table 30.2 Love and creativity in leadership

Frequency	*Category*	*Participants*
13	Love makes me creative	P1, P4, P6, P7, P8, P9, P11, P12, P13, P14, P15, P21, P22
12	Love and creativity combined make me happy	P4, P6, P7, P9, P11, P12, P13, P14, P15, P18, P21, P22
10	Love and creativity combined increase possibilities of actions	P5, P7, P8, P9, P10, P12, P14, P15, P16, P21
6	The more creative you are, the more you love	P3, P4, P6, P11, P15, P22
5	Love and creativity combined show my entire potential and talents	P1, P7, P9, P11, P22
4	Love and creativity combined help to change for the better	P10, P11, P12, P14

Furthermore, 12 leaders stated that it makes them happy in their life and work contexts to experience love and creativity. Both concepts are therefore strongly positively correlated and positively impact on the participants' mental health and well-being. P18, a 33-year-old Americana Christian woman highlighted the following with regard to love, creativity, well-being, and happiness:

> The experience of the love of other people is something that is connected to well-being and mental health. If one's mental health suffers, one may be unable to feel the love of other people, thus adding to one's own struggles. Properly loving others and being loved in return are incredibly important for well-being. So many struggles in life come from the improper love of the other....
>
> For some people love and creativity go hand in hand. Love is a grounding of all human emotion and feeling, it is that which is desire and happiness. Insofar as creativity is an expression of desire it is connected to love.

The leaders also explained that love and creativity not only impact on their emotional strengths, but also impact positively on their possibilities to increase their actions in a positive and applied manner, leading them to have impact and success at work. One 63-year-old German Catholic male stated the following:

> Love and creativity, both together, can release lots of energy and inspire each other. Accordingly, creativity and love impact on our actions, can increase the ability to act, but also influence how to act ... creativity fosters love and love can massively influence and foster creativity.

Six leaders highlighted that the more creative people are, the more they love. P15, a 54-year-old Israeli, Hebrew-speaking, Jewish woman, emphasized that the interconnectedness of love, creativity, and connection of humans is important in life:

> Through love, the layers of connection are becoming deeper and deeper. Thus, when you love, you have to become creative in order not to enter a routine. Easily and frequently we are falling into the routine of life ... When you are not creative and when you do not feed love, then you can become disconnected. If one is acting out of personal resilience, when one feels that she is worth to love and to be loved, then love is a strength, growth, peace, and blessing.

Five leaders are of the opinion that both concepts help to express the potential and talents of the self and others in a mindful way, based on a deep human connection. A 61-year-old German, Catholic male leader referred to love and creativity, potential and leadership:

> Leadership means for me to awake creativity and energy in others and explore their talents and potentials and to guide them in a kind manner. For doing this, I need a loving and creative attitude. Love will foster the potentials of creativity in me and the other, but one has to be careful that the leadership is not neglected when we focus on love and creativity. We still have to lead and guide and not forget about that.

Finally, love and creativity support leaders to "change towards the better," according to four statements. Both concepts help individuals to grow personally towards a positive development and towards wanting to contribute positively to their own development and the development of others in a mindful and caring way. P6, an 80-year-old multicultural, Eastern European Jewish senior leader based in the US, who had been in many different leadership positions throughout his life, stated the following:

> When I have been a leader in the academic setting, I certainly have invested in seeing to it that things go well for students, staff, and colleagues who I love, but I work hard to be the same for everyone else. I always have tried to be fair and do my best for everyone, even people who I definitely did not love. And being in a leadership position has required me to have a certain amount of emotional and decisional distance from people I love. I have to be objective, fair, an agent of the system, and responsive to the demands of my bosses, creative, mindful, and if I can't be all of that, I don't belong in the leadership position. I also have had leadership roles in community and professional organizations. Probably in all leadership positions but particularly in community and professional organization leadership positions my love has typically been more abstract, not so connected to specific individuals, but connected to making things good or better for a community, an institution, or even the planet.

This statement includes several aspects with regard to love, leadership, and mindful leadership and concludes that the higher meaning of a loving and mindful leadership is to make things good or better.

8.3 Love's contribution to become a creative and mindful leader

In the following section, the leaders responded to the question of what love's contribution is for leaders to become creative and mindful. Table 30.3 presents an overview on the frequency of statements; the categories developed; and the participants who referred to this concept. Altogether, 12 leaders emphasized that love helps them to come up with new and original ideas needed in 4IR workplaces in a kind and mindful way. P14, a 65-year-old Christian, South African white male leader, pointed out the following:

> If there is love for what you do, a happy heart and mental wellbeing, creativity would be stimulated on various levels and could trigger new and creative ideas, responses and acts in various ways and settings . . . in mindful ways.

Ten leaders each highlighted that love impacts positively on their well-being and that love brings life and energy into their work. P19, a 44-year-old female, Romanian Christian leader, related to love:

> Humans were made to function optimally in an environment saturated with love. Just as plants need soil, sunshine, and water in order to survive, humans need love for their mental and emotional wellbeing, Love maintains a healthy life in all aspects which can be reached through mindfulness and acting in a mindful manner.

Furthermore, nine individuals said that love is like a "moral compass" that provides direction for leadership. It guides them, as shown in the statement above by P6, and makes them to be perceived as leaders. P5, a 34-year-old American male atheist, commented on love as a moral compass in leadership.

Table 30.3 Love's contribution to creative and mindful leadership

Frequency	*Category*	*Participants*
12	Love creates new and original ideas	P1, P5, P7, P8, P9, P10, P11, P14, P15, P16, P21, P22
10	Love impacts positively on my well-being as a leader	P1, P3, P5, P7, P8, P9, P14, P15, P16, P17
10	Love brings life and work energy	P1, P4, P5, P7, P8, P9, P14, P15, P21, P22
9	Love is the moral compass of leadership	P5, P6, P7, P10, P12, P14, P15, P19, P22
8	Love helps to lead by empowerment, enablement	P2, P4, P5, P8, P9, P11, P14, P15
8	Love increases commitment	P3, P5, P6, P7, P15, P16, P19, P21
8	Love fosters collaboration	P6, P7, P10, P14, P15, P16, P19, P21
8	Love is a humane and positive (servant) leadership approach	P6, P7, P10, P14, P15, P16, P19, P21
7	Through love I feel recognized and acknowledged	P3, P5, P12, P15, P16, P19, P21
6	Love helps problem-solving	P1, P5, P7, P8, P14, P21
5	Love facilitates trust and respect in collaboration	P2, P6, P7, P16, P21
2	Love increases success	P6, P10

> Love should be the moral compass of leadership that keeps leaders from simply becoming selfish tyrants. Love for people or for a cause might direct a leader to come up with a creative solution since if one loves what they are trying to work for then they may be inclined to try harder to come up with an acceptable solution which may lead to more creative solutions. But I think creativity can come from lots of other places than love.

Eight individuals stated that love increases empowerment and enablement, commitment, collaboration, and servant leadership, which is viewed as a humane and positive leadership. Seven individuals pointed out that, through love, they feel recognized and acknowledged and that love boosts their self-esteem and thereby contributes to creativity and mindful leadership, centered and balanced within themselves (P7) and, according to P2, in the "centeredness of the in-between (I & Thou, Martin Buber)."

Love was furthermore also viewed by six leaders as a support in solving problems. P5 related to the importance of love, creativity, and mindfulness in terms of finding new solutions to problems and expanding worldviews:

> Love makes us willing to do things we wouldn't normally do for our loved one's sake, which could lead to coming up with creative solutions to problems and a generally expanded repertoire of actions.

Five leaders were of the opinion that love facilitates trust and respect in collaboration and also highlighted that love in leadership increases success. P2, for example, mentioned positive collaboration and success as two aspects of leadership. He is a 78-year-old American male leader with a Christian background who lives in Japan:

> By facilitating love, trust, and respect among teams and organizational members, a leader can engage, empower, and enable a caring and loving workplace in multiple small places ... hence, the role of leadership includes such expressions to others or simply by delegating, supporting, and trusting in others' work. I tried very hard with lots of little successes and failures to create love cultures in organizations. I am dedicated to spending the rest of my life writing about those many opportunities and leading with love in my own personal relationships hereon.

A loving leadership is an important topic for all the interviewees which develops within the person and beyond across the life span. To implement it within organizations it needs a sustainable and continuous approach and mindful development across the lifetime.

9. Discussion

This study focused primarily on love, creativity, and mindfulness in international leaders. It responded to four major research questions. The findings showed that the international leaders interviewed are highly aware of the qualities needed in future-oriented, sustainable global and local leadership to effectively manage the rapid changes of the 4IR. This study therefore contributes to previous research (Bloem et al., 2014; Stubbings, 2018; WEF, 2016), in that it emphasizes the importance of new leadership qualities and skills needed. "Consciousness" was cited as a concept of mindful leadership (Leonhardt & Wiedemann, 2015; Mayer & Geldenhuys, 2019); and this research corresponds with the idea that particularly in times of rapid changes, mindful thought and action in leaders are needed to deal with the complexities of future workplaces, as mentioned by Leonhardt and Wiedemann (2015).

However, this study also wanted to contribute to expanding the literature stating that mindful leadership is needed in 4IR workplaces (as indicated by Caring-Lobel, 2016) as well as loving leadership and creativity (see also Larson & Murtadha, 2005; Mayer, 2020a; Rojanapanich & Pimpa, 2011). International leaders highlighted that love, creativity, and mindfulness contribute to leading for humankind and humanness, through the voices presented. As stated by previous 4IR research (SIYLI Search Inside Yourself Leadership Institute, 2017; WEF, 2016), creativity and complex problem-solving through a loving and mindful leadership are regarded as key to effective, human, sustainable, peaceful leadership and creating meaning in organizations.

Mindfulness is viewed as non-judgmental focused energy and attention (Mayer & Geldenhuys, 2019); and the findings support that leadership should not only be based on unconditional, loving acceptance, but also on a deep connection. Love and mindfulness are intertwined concepts for leaders as they contribute to loving kindness in leadership and a base that is non-judgmental and accepting, derived from a deep acceptance of self and others in the sense of "servant leadership." Love and mindfulness are viewed as contributing positively to mental health and well-being; and this study supports previous findings from Mayer et al. (2016) that mindfulness contributes to meaningfulness. This seems to be of major importance in the context of the 4IR, which is often experienced as an uncertain context. The international leaders further highlighted that mindfulness and love mainly contribute to informed decision-making (as in Brann, 2014; Henson & Rossouw, 2013); and is not viewed critically. As indicated by Mayer and Walach (2018), future-oriented leadership needs to strive for sustainability and transcendence with human connections rather than further profit maximizing. "Love" and "mindfulness" can therefore be viewed as concepts balancing the previous economical concepts of egoistical maximizing of profits.

As in the literature, love is associated with compassion (Barsade & O'Neill, 2014; Patterson, 2010) in this study, and with responsibility, respect, a deep connection, and growth (as in Mayer, 2020b). Leaders feel empowered through love and creativity (as in Van Dierendonck & Patterson, 2014). As presented in previous research, love and leadership are associated with a positive attitude (Winston, 2002), expressed in the findings for example in terms of happiness, mental health, and increased well-being (as in Cooper, 2013). The leaders also highlighted that love in leadership supports positive relationships and cooperation (as in Chandsoda & Salsing, 2018) and a deep connection to self and others (Van der Hoven, 2017). Love as a "moral compass" is also described in the literature as a leadership orientation including positive attitude and emotions (Van der Hoven, 2017).

10. Conclusions and recommendations

Love, creativity, and mindfulness are increasingly gaining importance in leading people and organizations in the Fourth Industrial Revolution. They can contribute to building emotional strengths, human connections, and complex problem-solving processes that support leaders in gaining new ideas, being innovative and moving into the direction of creating human and healthy organizations. Creativity, in combination with love, leads to empowerment and enablement, commitment, collaboration, and a balanced leadership, and expands world views and mindfulness. In the time of the Fourth Industrial Revolution, many leaders are working in remote workplaces; leading digitalization processes and smart solutions; and navigating future-oriented workplaces and organizations.

The voices of the leaders show across cultures that they endeavor to build creativity, love, and mindfulness in their respective organizations and work lives to connect with colleagues, employees, clients, and customers on a deep level, thereby building a foundation for cooperation, trust, and meaningfulness in their lives and workplaces. Creative, mindful, and loving leadership are part of managing the Fourth Industrial Revolution constructively and sustainably and with care for the self, others, and the broader environment.

Finally, it can be recommended that international leaders and organizations focus on fostering creativity, love, and mindfulness in leadership and organizations to empower a healthy workforce and organization. This practical recommendation should be accompanied through scientific research and mixed-method studies that evaluate the concepts of creativity, love, and mindfulness and their impact on leaders, employees, and organizations from qualitative and quantitative perspectives to increase their impacts globally and drive the Fourth Industrial Revolution with sustainable and meaningful depths that consider humanness, mental health, well-being as well as positivity and constructiveness.

Chapter takeaways

1. The Fourth Industrial Revolution requires new skills, flexibility, new mindsets, and attitudes owing to changing work and organizational environments.
2. "Mindfulness," "love," and "creativity" are concepts which increasingly gain importance in leading people and organizations in the Fourth Industrial Revolution.
3. To gear up for transnational and global success, the three concepts need to be internalized in leadership and contribute to stimulating improved and applied forms of

leadership that are contemporary and support the concepts of sustainability, connectedness, and the creative solution-orientation for man-made problems and challenges.
4. Transforming negative emotions and creating positive emotions is a key to successful work and leadership in the new digitalized and technologized workplaces.
5. To recognize that leadership and success need to be redefined for the survival of the planet, mindfulness, love, and creativity are a valuable mindset triangle that will foster leadership for the improvement of humankind and sustainable solutions.

Reflective questions

1. How are the concepts of "mindfulness," "love," and "creativity" in leadership interconnected?
2. What is the Fourth Industrial Revolution?
3. What do international leaders say with regard to the importance of mindfulness, love, and creativity in leadership?
4. What are the three concepts increasingly important for in leadership during the Fourth Industrial Revolution?
5. When you think about yourself, how does mindfulness, love, and creativity come to play within yourself and your organizational environment?
6. What do you think you could improve in your own leadership in the context of the Fourth Industrial Revolution?

Acknowledgments

We would like to thank our interviewees across the world for their highly interesting and in-depth information on love, creativity, and mindfulness. Special thanks to Professor Satinder K. Dhiman, for advancing the field of leadership regarding mindfulness and creativity, and Professor Freddie Crous, for his mindful, compassionate, and creative leadership and his continuous support of our research projects.

Notes

1 *Bundesland* (provincial state) in Germany.
2 All information is based on participants' self-descriptions.

References

Bag, S., Telukdarie, A., Pretorius, J. H. C., & Gupta, S. (2018). Industry 4.0 and supply chain sustainability: Framework and future research directions. *Benchmarking: An International Journal*. https://www.researchgate.net/publication/324911795_Industry_40_and_Supply_Chain_Sustainability_Framework_and_Future_Research_Directions (asccessed 23.5.2020).

Barsade, S. G. & O'Neill, O. A. (2014). What's love got to do with it? A longitudinal study of the culture of companionate love and employee and client outcomes in a long-term care setting. *Administrative Science Quarterly*, 1–48. http://dx.doi.org/10.1177/0001839214538636

Beall, A. E. & Sternberg, R. J. (1995). The social construction of love. *Journal of Social and Personal Relationships*, *12*(3), 417–438.

Bloem, J., van Doom, M., Duivenstein, S., Excoffier, D., Mass, R., & van Ommeren, E. (2014). *The fourth industrial revolution*. VINT research report 3 of 4. Groningen: Sogeti. www.sogeti.com/globalassets/global/special/sogeti-things3en.pdf

Brann, A. (2014). *Neuroscience for Coaches: How to use the latest insights for the benefit of your clients*. London: Kogan Page.

Brown, K. & Ryan, R. (2003). The benefits of being present: Mindfulness and its role in psychological well-being. *Journal of Personality and Social Psychology, 84*, 822–848. http://dx.doi.org/10.1037/0022-3514.84.4.822

Caring-Lobel, A. (2016). Corporate mindfulness and the pathologization of workplace stress. In R. Purser, D. Forbes, & A. Burke (Eds.), *Handbook of mindfulness. Mindfulness in behavioral health* (pp. 195–214). Cham: Springer.

Carter, J. (2013). The curious absence of love stories in women's talk. *The Sociological Review, 61*(4), 728–744.

Chandsoda, S. & Salsing, P. S. (2018). Compassion and cooperation: The two challenging ethical perspectives in the Fourth Industrial Revolution. *Journal of International Business Studies, 9*, 1.

Cooper, M. (2013). *The compassionate mind approach to reducing stress*. London: Constable & Robinson.

Creswell, J. W. (2013). *Qualitative inquiry and research design: Choosing among five approaches* (4th ed.). Thousand Oaks, CA: Sage.

Csikszentmihalyi, M. (2014). Society, culture, and person: A systems view of creativity. In M. Csikszentmihalyi (Ed.), *The systems model of creativity* (pp. 47–61). Dordrecht: Springer.

Csikszentmihalyi, M. & Wolfe, R. (2014). New conceptions and research approaches to creativity: Implications of a systems perspective for creativity in education. In M. Csikszentmihalyi (Ed.), *The systems model of creativity* (pp. 161–184). Dordrecht: Springer.

Eldor, L. (2017). Public Service Sector: The compassionate workplace – the effect of compassion and stress on employee engagement, burnout, and performance. *Journal of Public Administration Research and Theory, 28*(1), 86–103.

Fatemi, S. M. (2016). *Critical mindfulness. Exploring langerian models*. Cham, Switzerland: Springer.

Fleck, U. (2018). *Designing qualitative research* (2nd ed.). Thousand Oaks, CA: Sage.

Fry, L.W., & Matherly, L.L. (2006). Spiritual leadership and organizational performance: an explorative study. Presentation at the Academy of Management meeting, Atlanta, Georgia. https://www.iispiritualleadership.com/wp-content/uploads/docs/SLTOrgPerfAOM2006.pdf

Germer, C. K. (2005). Mindfulness: What is it? What does it matter? In C. K. Germer, R. D. Diegel, & P. R. Fulton (Eds.), *Mindfulness and psychotherapy* (pp. 3–27). New York: Guilford Press.

Gratzke, M. (2017). Love is what people say it is: Performativity and narrativity in critical love stories. *Journal of Popular Romance Studies, 6*. http://jprstudies.org/wp-content/uploads/2017/04/LIWPSII.4.2017.pdf

Henson, C. & Rossouw, P. (2013). *Brainwise leadership: Practical neuroscience to survive and thrive at work*. Sydney: Learning Quest.

Jahoda, G. & Lewis, I. M. (2015). *Acquiring culture: Cross cultural studies in child development* (3rd ed.). New York: Psychology Press.

Javaid, A. (2018). *Masculinities, sexualities and love*. London: Routledge.

Kabat-Zinn, J. (2006). Mindfulness MI-based interventions in context: Past, present and future. *Clinical Psychology: Science and Practice, 10*(2), 144–156. http://dx.doi.org/10.1093/clipsy.bpg016

Kaffle, N. P. (2011). Hermeneutic phenomenological research method simplified. *Bodhi: An Interdisciplinary Journal, 5*, 181–200.

Langer, E. J. & Ngnoumen, C. T. (2018). Mindfulness. In D. S. Dunn (Ed.), *Frontiers of social psychology. Positive psychology: Established and emerging issues* (pp. 97–111). New York: Routledge/Taylor & Francis Group..

Larson, C. L. & Murtadha, K. (2005). Leadership for social justice. *Yearbook of the National Society for the Study of Education, 101*(1), 134–161.

Lebuda, I., Zabelina, D. L., & Karwowski, M. (2016). Mind full of ideas: A meta-analysis of the mindfulness-creativity link. *Personality and Individual Differences, 93*, 22–26.

Leonhardt, F. & Wiedemann, A. (2015). Realigning risk management in the light of industry 4.0 (October 23, 2015). Available at SSRN: https://ssrn.com/abstract=2678947 or http://dx.doi.org/10.2139/ssrn.2678947

Mayer, C.-H. (2014). Spiritualität in organisationen: Orientierung an Werten. *Wirtschaftspsychologie aktuell, 21*(4), 57–59.

Mayer, C.-H. (2019). Key factors of creativity and the art of collaboration in twenty-first-century workpaces. In M. Coetzee (Ed.), *Thriving in digital workplaces: Innovations in theory, research and practice* (pp. 147–166). Cham, Switzerland: Springer Nature.

Mayer, C.-H. (2020a in press). Love in leaders. Leadership solutions in the Fourth Industrial Revolution? In C.-H. Mayer & E. Vanderheiden (Eds.), *Handbook of love in cultural and transcultural contexts* (pp. xxx–xxx). Cham, Switzerland: Springer International.

Mayer, C.-H. (2020b in press). Stories of love in cultural perspectives. Meaning-making through expressions, rituals and symbols. In C.-H. Mayer & E. Vanderheiden (Eds.), *Handbook of love in cultural and transcultural contexts* (pp. xxx–xxx). Cham, Switzerland: Springer International.

Mayer, C.-H. & Geldenhuys, D. (2014). Editorial. Spirituality, culture and health in management. *International Review of Psychiatry*, *26*(3), 263–264.

Mayer, C.-H. & Geldenhuys, D. (2019). Workplace spirituality and wellness. An organizational neuroscientific perspective. In J. Marquis (Ed.), *The Routledge companion to management and workplace spirituality* (pp. 140–153). New York: Routledge.

Mayer, C.-H., Surtee, S., & Visser, D. (2016). Exploring personality traits, mindfulness and sense of coherence of women working in higher education. *SA Journal of Human Resource Management/SA Tydskrif Vir Menslikehulpbronbestuur*, *14*(1), a674. http://dx.doi.org/10.4102/sajhrm.v14i1.674

Mayer, C.-H. & van Niekerk, R. (2019 in press). Creative minds of leaders in psychobiographical perspectives: Exploring the life and work of Christian Barnard and Angela Merkel. In S. Dhiman & J. Marquis (Ed.), *New Horizons in Positive leadership and change* (pp. 189–205). Cham, Switzerland: Springer.

Mayer, C.-H. & Walach, H. (2018). Workplace spirituality in contemporary South Africa. In S. K. Dhiman, G. E. Roberts, & J. Crossman (Eds.), *The Palgrave handbook of workplace spirituality and fulfillment* (pp. 1–18). New York: Palgrave Macmillian.

Mohsen, G., Rasoul, R. E., & Ali, M. (2015). Relationship between dispositional positive emotions and creativity: Synergistic role of trait positive affect. *Research Journal of Recent Sciences*, ISSN, 2277, 2502.

Naderifar, M., Goli, H., & Ghaljaie, F. (2017). Snowball sampling: A purposeful method of sampling in qualitative research. *Strides in Development of Medical Education*, *14*(3), e67670.

Nandram S. S. & Borden M. E. (Eds.), (2011). *Spirituality and business*. Heidelberg: Springer.

Nandram, S. & Borden, M. E. (2019). Mindfulness in business. In L. Bouckaert & L. Zsolnai (Eds.), *Handbook of Spirituality and Business* (pp. 315–323). London: Palgrave MacMillain.

O'Neill, O.M. (2018). The FACCTs of (work) life: How relationships (and returns) are linked to the emotional culture of companionate love. *American Journal for Health Promotion*, *32*(5), 1312–1315.

Patterson, K. (2010). Servant leadership and love. In D. van Dierendonck & K. Patterson (Eds.), *Servant leadership* (pp. 67–76). London: Palgrave Macmillan.

Rojanapanich, P. and Pimpa, N. (2011). Creative education, globalization and social imaginary. *Creative Education*, *2*(4), 77–89.

Roth, W. M. & Unger, H. V. (2018). Current perspectives on research ethics in qualitative research. In *Forum qualitative sozialforschung/forum: Qualitative social research* (Vol. 19, No. 3, p. 12). DEU. http://www.qualitative-research.net/index.php/fqs/article/view/3155/4305 accessed 23.5.2020

Rynes, S.I., Bartunek, J.M., Dutton, J.E., & Margolis, J.D. (2012). Care and compassion through an organizational lens: Opening up new possibilities. *Academy of Management Review*, *37*, 503–523.

SIYLI Search Inside Yourself Leadership Institute (2017). *The emotional intelligence revolution*. April 15, 2017. https://siyli.org/resources/the-emotional-intelligence-revolution

Schwab, K. (2017). *The fourth industrial revolution*. Crown Business.

Spath, D., Ganschar, O., Gerlach, S., Hämmerle, M., Krause, T., & Schlund, S. (2013). *Produktionsarbeit der Zukunft - Industrie 4.0*. Stuttgart: Fraunhofer Verlag.

Sternberg, R. J. (2003). Creative thinking in the classroom. *Scandinavian Journal of Educational Research*, *47*, 325–338. doi:10.1080/00313830308595

Sternberg, R. J. (2005). The WICS model of organizational leadership. https://dspace.mit.edu/bitstream/handle/1721.1/55937/CPL_WP_05_06_Sternberg.pdf

Sternberg, R. J., & Grigorenko, E. L. (2007). *Teaching for successful intelligence* (2nd ed.). Thousand Oaks, CA: Corwin.

Stubbings, C. (2018). Workforce of the future: The competing forces shaping 2030. *PwC*. Retrieved from www.pwc.com/gx/en/services/people-organisation/publications/workforce-of-the-future.html

Terre Blanche, M. (2006). Two nations: Race and poverty in post-apartheid South Africa. In *A race against time: Psychology and challenges to deracialisation in South Africa* (pp. 73–90). Pretoria: UNISA Press.

Tracy, S. J. (2010). Qualitative quality: Eight "big-tent" criteria for excellent qualitative research. *Qualitative Inquiry, 16*, 837–851.

Tracy, S. J. & Hinrichs, M. M. (2017). Big tent criteria for qualitative quality. *The International Encyclopedia of Communication Research Methods*. Retrieved from https://onlinelibrary.wiley.com/doi/pdf/10.1002/9781118901731.iecrm0016

Uusiautti, S., Määttä, M., & Määttä, K. (2013). Loved-based practice in education. *International Journal about Parents in Education*, 7(2), 134–144.

Van Dierendonck, D., & Patterson, K. (2014). Compassionate love as a cornerstone in servant leadership: An integration of previous theorizing and research. *Journal of Business Ethics, 128*(1), 119–131.

Van der Hoven, J. (2017). Using flow to create meaningful work in the Fourth Industrial Revolution. Retrieved October 22, 2017, from. https://leaderless.co/blog/2017/10/22/the-flow-of-the-fourth-industrial-revolution/

Vessey, W. B., Barrett, J. D., Mumford, M. D., Johnson, G., & Litwiller, B. (2014). Leadership of highly creative people in highly creative fields: A historiometric study of scientific leaders. *The Leadership Quarterly, 25*(4), 672–691. doi:10.1016/j.leaqua.2014.03.001

Walach, H., Buchheld, N., Buttenmüller, V., Kleinknecht, N., & Schmidt, S. (2006). Measuring mindfulness – The Freidburger Mindfulness Inventory (FMI). *Personality and Individual Differences, 40*, 1543–1555. http://dx.doi.org/10.1016/j.paid.2005.11.025

WEF (2016). *The future of jobs. Employment, skills and workforce strategy for the Fourth Industrial Revolution.* Global Challenge Insight Report. Retrieved from www3.weforum.org/docs/WEF_Future_of_Jobs.pdf

Winston, B. E. (2002). *Be a leader for god's sake.* Virginia Beach, VA: Regent University School of Leadership Studies.

Yang, J. S. & Hung, H. V. (2015). Emotions as constraining and facilitating factors for creativity: Companionate love and anger. *Creativity and Innovation Management, 24*(2), 217–230.

Yin, R. K. (2009). *Case study research: Design and methods* (4th ed.). London: Sage.

31

THE GENESIS OF MINDFULNESS IN THE EAST AND WORKPLACE APPROPRIATION IN THE WEST

R. Ray Gehani and Sunita Gehani

Introduction

The practice of mindfulness develops an un-fogged mind that senses dynamic reality truthfully. It helps us see the changes in real time taking place in the present moment "now." The genesis of mindfulness took place 2,500 years ago in the agrarian East. It is, however, appropriated most extensively in the corporate workplaces of the industrialized West in a wide variety of sectors, from healthcare to business, military, schools, and the U.S. Congress (Dhiman, 2009; Gehani, 2011, 2014; Ryan, 2012).

This epic 15,000-mile journey over 100 generations started with Gautam Buddha (c. 563 BC–c. 483 BC), who offered a lotus flower to a common man, Maha-kashyap, because he was able to grasp the truth without the use of any words. This chapter is based on a qualitative historic research study and is grounded in Ken Wilber's integral theory of inward–outward integration. We start our exploration from the genesis of *Dhyan* mindfulness in Northern India by the Shakyamuni prince. Then we will investigate how monk Bodhi-Dharma from South India took *Dhyan* mindfulness in the 6th century AD to China, where it evolved into *Chan* mindfulness. Japanese Prince Shotoku (576–662 AD) then imported mindfulness, via *Son* mindfulness in the Korean peninsula, to inspire and civilize native Japanese fishermen (King, 2019). The Japanese culture gave birth to multiple streams of *Zen* mindfulness. A version of *Zen* mindfulness was brought in the 1960s to the West in the United States by pioneers Roshi Daisuke Teitaro Suzuki (1870–1966), Zen master Roshi Philip Kapleau (1912–2004), Maharishi Mahesh Yogi (1918–2008) of Beatles fame, and others. Mindfulness was appropriated in the Western marketplace by lay professionals with a focus on extracting outward material benefits, including advantages in violent military warfare.

Need for a new mindful lens in the age of mindlessness

The surreal (super-real) mindful mind is not limited by time, space, or mass (Dreyfus, 2011; Gehani, 2014; Hanh, 1992; Langer, 1989, 1998). Mindfulness can help us learn to "live" in the present moment. It is not fogged by our delusional inflated or intimidated ego, our debilitating fears about an uncertain and unfathomable future, or the regrets from our past, which are set in stone (Bodhi, 2011; Gethin, 2011). The Western appropriation of mindfulness is rooted in psychology, whereas it is rooted in spirituality in the East (Badiner, 2002; Williams, 2011). The West leverages the mindful practice of paying non-judgmental attention to the changes in the live present moment to enhance workplace productivity, concentration, effectiveness, and creativity (Essig, 2013; Gehani, 2014; Pickert, 2014; Schumpeter, 2013).

Our cultural contexts determine our mindsets (Langer & Moldoveanu, 2000). Traditional agrarian societies of Ancient India were localized into the nature-sphere. Industrialized societies like the US become more globalized and dispersed into the techno-sphere (Norberg-Hodge, 2002). Information technology, the Internet, and social media have fractured Westerners' attention with micro multi-tasking (Epstein, 1995; Wallace, 2006). Millions of young and old Americans are purchasing online goods while driving on highways or waiting at a red light in heavy traffic. By the mid-2010s, American teens were exchanging more than 100 text messages a day (more than ten per hour). Every day they were spending three to five hours on social media (Pickert, 2014). Such distraction will get worse with smart watches and Google glasses, lowering overall productivity (Wallace, 2006).

Western workplace appropriation

Interest in mindfulness in the US has been booming with the launch of multiple magazines and dozens of books (Williams & Kabat-Zinn, 2013). More than a decade ago, the National Institutes of Health (NIHs) estimated that Americans were spending more than $4 billion on alternative medicine based on mindfulness in 2007, estimated to be close to $10 billion by 2020 (Pickert, 2014; Wilson, 2014).

In the industrial and post-industrial knowledge-driven capitalist societies of the West, innovative global enterprises, such as Apple, Facebook, and Google, have integrated their use of mindfulness training. They improve their organizational effectiveness by enhancing the mental and physical well-being of their valued human talent (Schumpeter, 2013).

Roadmap of this research study

In this qualitative research study, we historically investigate the genesis, global diffusion, and appropriation of mindfulness with a phenomenological qualitative research approach. This is grounded in Ken Wilber's (1974, 2000) integral leadership theory. He integrated the inward and outward orientations of our mindsets and coupled these with the individual and community focus of our actions (Gehani (2018, 2019). The trajectory of appropriation of mindfulness in Western workplaces can be tied back to its genesis in the Ancient Indian civilization, more than 2,500 years ago, in the innovative sermons of Gautam Buddha (c. 563 BCE–c. 483 BCE).

The roadmap of this research study is as follows. We examine how the socio-cultural context of a society influences the mindfulness practice and mindsets of that society's people. We begin by examining how Gautam Buddha framed and formulated *Dhyan* mindfulness in Ancient India. We do the same for *Chan* mindfulness in China, and *Zen* mindfulness in Japan. We explore how the industrialization of the West significantly altered the way mindfulness plays its pivotal role in US society. In the East, mindfulness was primarily targeted to explore the inner world of human beings (*Purusha*, or Individual). In the industrialized West, on the other hand, mindfulness is appropriated for material gains, and for extracting benefits from the external world (*Prakriti*, Nature). We delve deep into the genesis and roots of mindfulness in Ancient Indian civilization, and briefly examine the branches at the end: how the West appropriated mindfulness in commercial organizations for actionable knowledge, faster, more resilient decision-making, and maximization of the profit potential of a workplace.

Genesis of *Dhyan* mindfulness in agrarian ancient India

During the age of Gautam Buddha (c. 563 BCE–c. 483 BCE), the ancient Great Indian civilization was deeply rooted in the natural world. The economy was dependent locally. Most human beings were directly dependent on other fellow beings and their local resources. Intermediation in their economic and social exchanges was limited. They traded with each other via a short supply chain (like eBay's seller–buyer transactions). Their survival, as well as their ethical decisions, relied heavily on their direct observations of Mother Nature (Dunne, 2011; King, 2019).

When mindfulness was developed in India, it was deeply rooted in people's close observations of the cycles of life, joy and suffering, their growth and decline, and birth and death (Kuan, 2008). They saw the blooming of a flower they offered to their lover and their deity, and they grew fruits like mangos and bananas which they ate for breakfast. The grains they ate for lunch and dinner were not bought from a shop with money, but were harvested by them in farms not far from their homes. They often bartered for what they needed.

The start of the 2,500-year-long epic journey in the Indus River Valley civilization

Mindfulness is generally recognized as *Dhyan* mindfulness that was first proposed by the Indian prince Siddhartha Gautam (c. 563 BC–c. 483 BC) from the clan of Shakya (Dunne, 2011; Gehani, 2014). He saw this as an enlightened quantum holistic way of living harmoniously in peace. The realities caused suffering from a constantly changing life (Bodhi, 2005).

But, the images of a person sitting in a lotus yoga posture meditating mindfully (wearing a ceremonious headdress) have been archeologically traced about 20 centuries further back to c. 2,500 BC in the excavations of Harappa and Moen-Jo-Daro in the Indus River Valley plains of the northwestern province of Sindh in Greater India (Gehani, 2014). Suddenly and somewhat mysteriously (perhaps due to climate change), in c. 1,200 BCE, the prosperous people of Sindhu River were forced to migrate to the West to the Plains of the Ganges River in Northern India. The language of their baked seals has yet to be decoded.

Dhyan mindfulness?

Dhyan is an ancient Sanskrit word from Vedic scriptures with no exact English translation. *Dhyan* means deep self-awareness and heightened outer consciousness so that no unwanted thought can enter or interfere with one's mind (Dunne, 2011; Gehani, 2014). The English word meditation seems close, but it usually implies use of an object on which one meditates. Christians meditate on Jesus, Mary, or the Cross. Muslims meditate on the Quran. And Indians meditate on *The Bhagavad Gita*. Contemplation usually implies thinking and reflection. *Dhyan*, or mindfulness, means pure consciousness, with a clear blue sky and no clouds of undesirable distracting thoughts (Dhiman, 2008).

Innovative birthing of mindfulness

How was mindfulness born? One day, Prince Gautam Buddha, late in his years, sat under a tree surrounded by hundreds of his disciples and lay followers (Gehani, 2014). He was offered a lotus flower by a disciple or a devotee. All flowers in general, and lotus flowers in particular, are highly receptive to consciousness around them. Gautam Buddha raised the lotus flower to his audience, smiled, and said nothing for a long time. The crowd waited and looked at him in anticipation. Gautam Buddha kept smiling at the flower. People became more and more restless waiting. Gradually, Gautam Buddha seemed to become one with the lotus flower (Bodhi, 2005).

One disciple started explaining the beautiful shape and color of the lotus flower. Another devotee explained its fragrance and its utility for decoration and offering in prayer. Then another disciple explained the symbolic significance of the lotus flower for humankind. That the lotus flower grows in muddy waters, but it is always clean and above the surrounding dirt. This spontaneous discourse went on with detailed descriptions of the visible and invisible physical attributes of the lotus flower (Dunne, 2011).

Suddenly, a common man named Maha-kashyap, sitting at the back in a corner, laughed out hilariously. Instead of getting upset by the distraction, Gautam Buddha called him to the front, and gave him the lotus flower with a smile. Gautam Buddha then addressed the audience (Bodhi, 2005, p. 221):

> All that can be shared verbally with words, I have already given to you. But with this flower, I give to Maha-kashyap what cannot be said with words. The final most important key cannot be communicated verbally. It is my message beyond words. I hand over this essential key to Maha-kashyap.

Maha-kashyap realized that truth is simple and transparent, and that it cannot be fully verbalized. It must be realized by each individual through personal practice. Maha-kashyap was a common man, not highly well versed in ancient religious scriptures. Yet he understood the truth within that Gautam Buddha referred.

Gautam Buddha elaborated details of *The Right Mindfulness* in his discourse in *Sati-patthaana* (Nayana-ponika, 1962). He gave this discourse while he was staying with his disciples in a park in the capital of Koshala kingdom. The word *Sati* means our memory, and remembering of our past events. The word *Pattana* means bringing the buried stuff to the surface, or paying attention to it (King, 2019; Shulman, 2010). He summarized the progress that his community of learning disciples had made in developing mindfulness via engaging in daily duties, engaging in relationships, working, and spiritual search. This discourse liberates our monkey mind from doubts, delusion, and greed. Gautama Buddha (Bodhi, 2005, p. 281; Nanamoli, 1972, 1992, p. 207) underscored that:

> We have a great and rare Sangha community with no useless and conceited task, and worthy of many people visiting us from far off distances.

> Many of our practitioners [of mindfulness] have achieved Arahatship (a state of developing Right Understanding, and transforming most of their worldly afflictions and sufferings).
>
> ...There are many among us who regularly practice the Four Foundations of Mindfulness, and others who practice the Four Efforts.
>
> Many practice the Four Basic Truth Bases of Success, which are: (1) diligence, (2) energizing, (3) total awareness, and (4) penetrative insights.
>
> There are those who practice the Eightfold Path ... and those who practice the Four Immeasurable Meditations of (1) loving-kindness, (2) compassion, (3) joy, and (4) equanimity.
>
> There are those who practice the Full Awareness of Breathing.

This is the most comprehensive yet simplest summary, and the most effective way to train and develop mindfulness. This is done by engaging mindfully in daily duties, relationships, work, and spiritual search. As noted before, this mindfulness liberates our monkey mind from its doubts, delusion, and greed.

Gautam Buddha from the Great Ancient Indian Civilization discovered, organized, and taught his disciples the *Four Founding Pillars of (Dhyan) Mindfulness* (Bodhi, 2005). This is the genesis of the priceless wisdom of mindfulness training that very few Westerners mention or recall. Gautam Buddha explained everything in clear, crisp, and concise ways. As a result, his teachings on mindfulness have lasted and grown for the past 2,500 years through wars, famines, and devastations that humans and nature unleashed from time to time. Given below is what Gautam Buddha gifted us with compassion to help us alleviate our worldly sufferings mindfully (Nanamoli, 1972, 1992, p. 240; Bodhi, 2005, p. 290).

A. Become Mindful of Your Breathing

Sit cross-legged in a calm empty space.
Preferably in the Nature,
with body erect and mind alert.
Then become aware of each breath going in and out.

When inhaling become aware that you are inhaling.
When exhaling become aware that you are exhaling.
When inhaling a long breath
become aware that you are inhaling a long breath.
When inhaling a short breath
become aware that you are inhaling a short breath.

When turning from inhaling to exhaling,
become aware that you are turning.
Become aware how each breath originates
and how it dissolves.

Contemplate internally on your breathing,
as well as externally on others' breathing.

B. Become Mindful of Postures of Your Body

Become aware that you are standing
when you are standing,
and become aware that you are sitting
when you are sitting.

Thus contemplate on your bodies—
internally as well as externally.

C. Become Mindful of All Elements of Your Bodies

Be mindful of what your bodies are made up of—
from the sole of your feet to nails,
through hairy skin on your legs,
from genitals in the pelvis,
to feces in your bowels,

from intestines in the stomach,
to fat on your belly,
from bones in your lungs,
to muscles of the neck,

from tendons in the shoulders,
to sweat on your arms,
from nails on the hands,
to phlegm and buggers in your noses,

from tears in your eyes,
to wax in your ears,
and hair on your head.

Like a butcher become aware
that your bodies are nothing but bags of skins
with all kinds of disgusting materials
and impurities mixed in.

Also contemplate your body as composed of
[five] elements earth, water, air, fire,
[and space] elements.

D. Become Mindful of How Your Bodies Decay

Visit a cemetery,
and see how the bodies of a dead animal
or a human being
decay over time.

Become aware how a body swells
and turns blue within two or three days,

how it feels heavier after four or five days,
how it starts swelling after a week.

Contemplate and be aware
how a body turns into a skeleton of bones
after a few months,
and becomes [just] a heap of dust
after a year or more.

Contemplate and become aware of
your body internally and externally.
Contemplate how our bodies
originate and grow,

And how they dissolve and decay.
Be mindfully aware of
the transient nature of your bodies,
And stop clinging to it.

What is born is likely to decay and die.
It is [merely] a matter of time.

2. Contemplate on your [Emotional] Feelings

Mindfully contemplate on
the variety of feelings you experience.
When you feel sad,
you should mindfully contemplate
how you experience sadness.

When you experience a painful feeling,
mindfully contemplate how the pain hurts you.
When experiencing a joyful feeling with pleasure,
mindfully contemplate why and
how you feel the worldly pleasure.

Become aware that some of your feelings
seem to come primarily from within you.
Other feelings seem to originate
more from outside you.

Be mindfully aware of
How you experience these
inwardly and outwardly feelings.

With this mindfulness,
We should try not to cling
To any particular feelings.

3. Contemplate on Your Mind (*Chitta*)

Contemplate and be mindful of
how your monkey mind drives you around.

When your mind is filled with lust,
contemplate on the lustful mind.
When the mind is free of lust,
Contemplate on the lust-less mind.

When your mind is filled with hate or pettiness,
Contemplate on the hateful and petty mind, respectfully.
When your mind is delusional,
Contemplate on your delusional mind.

Contemplate mindfully on
when your mind originates a state,
And when it departs that state.

Contemplate your mind internally
from within the mind,
as well as externally,
as seen from outside the mind.

4. Contemplate on Your Mind Objects (*Dhamma*)

Contemplate mindfully on
How different desires arise in our minds,
And when these sense-desires
Are missing.

Gautam Buddha goes on to refer to the various mind objects such as anger, sloth and laziness, agitation and worries, doubts (Bodhi, 2005; Gehani, 2014). The Buddha continues:

Be more mindful of
How your different mind objects
Arise internally in you(r memory),
And externally in others.

How these arise,
And how these subside.

Mindfulness is
You becoming aware
Of the life cycles.

When you become vividly aware of
The starts and finishes of the five hindrances,

And the different stages of
Growth and maturation in between,
You become free,
of clinging to nothing in the world.

Gautam Buddha generously shared the priceless wisdom of *Dhyan* mindfulness he had discovered, and that he felt he could simplify and share with others around him to help us alleviate our suffering (Bodhi, 2005; Gehani, 2014).

After Gautam Buddha's Nirvana

After Gautam Buddha's Nirvana in c. 483 BCE, some of his monk followers started rejoicing because they could practice as they pleased, without following Gautam Buddha's disciplined prescriptions for mindfulness (Gehani, 2014, p. 61). When Maha-kashyap heard this, he felt a strong urge to gather and compile Gautam Buddha's teachings and practice for mindful living. Maha-kashyap gathered approximately 500 disciples of Gautam Buddha, and organized the first Buddhist Council meeting on *Dhyan* mindfulness (Nayana-ponika, 1962, 1975). In 480 BCE, the first sutras about *Dhyan* mindfulness were organized in India into three baskets or *Tri.pitaka*:

Sutra Pitaka was for discourses,
Abhi.dharma Pitaka was for special teachings, and
VinayaPitaka for disciples.

During the rule of Maurian Emperor Ashoka (c. 276 BCE–232 BCE), a Third Council of Buddha's followers of *Dhyan* mindfulness was called at Pataliputra in c. 248 BCE. Emperor Ashoka embraced teachings of mindfulness for the governance of his immense Indian empire. Compassion, non-violence, and peace became the national law of the land (Bodhi, 2011). Ashoka's and his government officials' primary concern was the welfare of the common people. Hospitals, hotels, and animal shelters were built for people throughout the country. This was Ashoka's Golden Age of a Mindful Nation, and Ashoka was one of the all-time greatest mindful leaders.

After emperor Ashoka passed, the principles and practices of mindfulness persisted even after the Mauriyan Empire started fragmenting (Skilton, 1994). In the 2nd century AD, Nagarjuna, the head of Nalanda University, established in Bihar a few miles from Gautam Buddha's favorite place Rajagriha. He compiled *Prajna.Paramita Sutras* of Mahayanists. For the next 1,000 years, the Nalanda University was the primary center for learning Gautam Buddha's teachings on mindfulness. *Dhyan* mindfulness persisted in India through multiple invasions by the Huns from the North in the 6th century, and the Turks and Persians from the West in 10th to 12th centuries.

From *Dhyan* mindfulness in India to *Chan* in China: Boddhi Dharma's global mindful transfer

The first key holder of *Dhyan* mindfulness, Maha-kashyap, was followed by five more key holders. The sixth key holder, Bodhi-Dharma, who lived in the 5th and 6th century AD, was another highly enlightened monk (Broughton, 1999; Pine, 1987). He took the practice of *Dhyan* mindfulness invented in India to China, where it became *Chan* mindfulness. He also physically trained monks of the Shaolin Monastery, which led to the creation of Shaolin Kungfu, the weapon-less self-protection against state violence.

Bodhi-Dharma was the third son of a king of the large Pallava Empire in the southern part of the Indian peninsula, around modern-day Chennai (Gehani, 2014). He was extremely intelligent, and he observed things with great clarity (Broughton, 1999; Pine, 1987). His father Pallava king saw great potential in his son, and chose him to be the best successor for his great kingdom. Bodhi-Dharma, however, chose to renounce the Pallava kingdom. He told his king father, "I am seeking for something that is beyond death. If you cannot help me, then let me go" (Gehani, 2014, p. 57). The Pallava king replied, "I cannot help you with your search, so I will not stop you. I will be sad because I am attached, and because I wanted you to be my successor and make the Pallava Empire the greatest" (Bodhi-Dharma by Hakuin Eikaku, 7th century AD).

Migration of mindfulness to China

China has often claimed to be Chu-Goku, or the "central country," or the middle of the universe. Chinese also like "the middle path," and not think too much of this world, or too little of it. The Chinese rely on the morality of Confucius (551–479 BC), or The Way (Tao) of life—without extremes. There were other mystics contemporary to Confucius, such as Lao Tzu, Chuang Tzu, and Lieh Tzu.

The Chinese term *Chan* is an abbreviated transliteration of the Sanskrit term *Dhyan*, which is closest to the English word mindfulness (Sharf, 1998). Some researchers date the emergence of *Chan* mindfulness to the Tang dynasty (608–907 AD), with institutional maturity in the early Song era (960–1279) (Sharf, 2014). Chinese *Chan* mindfulness subsequently spread to Vietnam as *Thien* mindfulness, to Korea as *Son* mindfulness, and to Japan as *Zen* mindfulness.

Dhyan mindfulness perhaps traveled from India to China, more than 600 years before the arrival of Bodhi-Dharma in China in the 6th century AD (Gehani, 2014; Sharf, 2014). By then, there were more than 2 million Buddhist monks in China in over 30,000 Buddhist temples. More than 40 million native Chinese people visited these temples regularly. It took Bodhi-Dharma more than three years to travel from Southern India to Eastern China in c. 520 AD. His fame preceded him. Chinese rulers and common people knew that enlightened Bodhi-Dharma was coming to China with the teachings of Gautam Buddha's *Dhyan* mindfulness.

When Bodhi-Dharma entered China, he was greeted by the Chinese emperor Wu Ti, perhaps somewhere near the modern city of Nanking in Eastern China (Broughton, 1999; Pine, 1987). To the Chinese emperor and common Chinese people, bearded Bodhi-Dharma from the southern part of India (modern-day Tamil Nadu and Kerala) looked ferocious. He had sharp big eyes, thick eyebrows, and a soft voice (Gehani, 2014, p. 74).

The Chinese Emperor Wu Ti was a great supporter of Buddhist philosophy and *Dhyan* mindfulness (Gehani, 2014, p. 74; Sharf, 2014). The Emperor Ti met and shared with Bodhi-Dharma that he had built thousands of Buddhist monasteries and temples. Therein, Emperor Wu Ti fed thousands of monks. The emperor sponsored the translation of hundreds of Buddhist scriptures from the Pali language into native Chinese at a Buddhist university (Broughton, 1999; Pine, 1987).

Emperor Wu Ti asked the visiting Indian monk Bodhi-Dharma, "What is going to be my reward for doing all this good to promote Buddhist philosophy in the name of Gautam Buddha?" (Gehani, 2014, p. 75).

Bodhi-Dharma candidly and fearlessly replied to the great Chinese Emperor Wu Ti, "No rewards. Emperor, please be ready to fall into the seventh hell."

Emperor Wu Ti was shocked by Bodhi-Dharma's candid harsh reply. The emperor became very angry. Nobody had ever spoken to him so bluntly before in the whole land of China, the Central State. Emperor Wu Ti inquired, "Why am I going to the seventh hell when I have done nothing wrong according to the morality of Confucius, Loa Tzu, and other mystics?"

Bodhi-Dharma replied calmly (Gehani, 2014, p. 75):

> Nobody can help you unless you start hearing your own voice (from within). It seems that you have not been hearing your inner voice, otherwise you would not have asked me such a stupid question. There is no reward on the path of Gautam Buddha. The very desire for reward comes from a greedy mind.
>
> The key teaching of Gautam Buddha is desire-less-ness. If you are doing all these virtuous acts with a desire, then you are preparing your path to hell. Do these virtuous things out of the joy of sharing your prosperity with your (common) people, without any desire. Then that joy is your reward.
>
> Listen to your inner voice otherwise you are missing the whole point.

Emperor Wu apologized. He shared that his mind was always filled with thoughts, worries, and anxieties about running his empire (Broughton, 1999; Pine, 1987). He was unable to have any peace of mind because of all these noises in his constantly chattering mind. He did not hear any inner voice that Bodhi-Dharma was talking about (Gehani, 2014).

Bodhi-Dharma fearlessly instructed the emperor to come alone the next morning at 4am to his temple in the Tai mountains. Bodhi-Dharma was then going to put the emperor's chattering mind forever at ease.

Emperor Wu's enlightenment

Bodhi-Dharma greeted Emperor Wu at the temple steps, and asked the emperor to sit in the courtyard in front of him (Broughton, 1999; Pine, 1987). Bodhi-Dhrama then said:

> Close your eyes, look inside, and try to catch your mind. The minute you catch your mind, tell me where it is, and I will do the rest with my strong wooden staff.

Emperor Wu closed his eyes (Broughton, 1999; Pine, 1987). He looked inside, here and there, and everywhere to search for his wandering mind for a long time. Hours passed, the sun rose, but he could not find his worrying, chattering mind. He realized that his mind seemed to exist when he was not aware of it. When he was aware of the mind, the awareness calmed and killed his chattering mind. Emperor Wu became calm, still, and peaceful.

Bodhi-Dharma did not disturb Emperor Wu for many hours. Then he asked Emperor Wu, "Did you find your worrying mind?"

Emperor Wu respectfully bowed to Bodhi-Dharma and said:

> You have calmed my mind. With silence I could go deep beyond my mind and hear my inner voice. I heard that my each act has to be a reward by itself, with no desire attached and desired from the act.

Bodhi-Dharma smiled and replied:

> You are an exceptional disciple. I love you and admire you as a disciple, and not as an emperor. In one sitting you have acquired so much self-awareness, and achieved so much enlightenment that all the darkness in your mind disappeared.

Emperor Wu tried to woo Bodhi-Dharma to come and live with him in his luxurious palace. Bodhi-dharma gently refused, sharing that he had left behind a large kingdom of his father in South India (Broughton, 1999; Pine, 1987). Now he preferred to live with nature in the Tai mountains.

Sitting meditation

After sending emperor Wu back to his palace, Bodhi-Dharma decided to sit for meditation while staring at a blank wall. He trained his mind to go blank just like the blank wall, and either not think, or let the thoughts come and go. He started to look like a big soccer ball or a bean-bag (Gehani, 2014).

Some early *Chan* mindfulness patriarchs, such as fourth patriarch Daoxin (580–651) from the East Mountain (Dong Shan) tradition, urged his disciples in his *Record of the Transmission of the Dharma Treasure* (*Chuan Fabio ji*) to do sitting mindful meditation diligently for three to five years (Sharf, 1995). Daoxin recommended them to take:

> a mouthful of food to stave off starvation and illness, and then just close your doors and sit. Do not read the scriptures or talk with anyone. One who is able to do this, after some time, will find it effective.
>
> *(Sharf, 2014)*

Daoxin reasserted silent seated *Dhyan* mindful meditation in his subsequent work *Fundamental Expedient Teaching for Calming the Mind to Enter the Way* (*Rudao Anxin Yao Fang-bian Famen*).

As more Chinese kings adopted *Chan* mindfulness, it traveled for centuries with the trading caravans along the Silk Road: Westwards to Taxila in Afghanistan, and Eastwards to the South Korean peninsula (Sharf, 2014). From South Korea, *Chan* mindfulness spread to Japan a few centuries later, primarily to civilize the island-dwelling fishermen of Japan. To the rustic fishermen of Japan, everything related to *Dhyan* and *Chan* mindfulness and Buddhism seemed like a highly civilized culture from a blissful perfect paradise in the West, referring to Ancient India.

Mindfulness imported into Japan

Dhyan mindfulness of Ancient India transformed into *Chan* mindfulness in China when coupled with Confucius and *The Dao Way*, and then into *Zen* mindfulness in Japan when coupled with some influences of native Shinto worship (via *Son* mindfulness in South Korea) (Sharf, 1993).

Prince Shotoku (576–662) introduced *Chan* mindfulness to the island nation of Japan. He wrote a commentary on three major Mahayana Sutras, including *Saddharma Pundarika*, also known as *Lotus Sutra* (Collcut, 1981; Gehani, 2014). At first Buddhist mindfulness in Japan was monastic, with monks studying the scriptures brought from India and China. The royal state built temples in different provinces to spread Buddhist culture among common Japanese. In 607 AD, the Horyuji set of temples were built near Osaka, and in 694 AD a massive bronze statue of Vairocana Buddha was installed in nearby Nara (Skilton, 1994). Six different splinter sects of *Chan* mindfulness were imported from the Chinese capital of Chiang-an (Collcut, 1981; Sharf, 1993).

For more than a millennium, from 794 AD to 1868 AD, Heian (modern-day Kyoto, north of Osaka) became the seat of the Japanese emperors, and the capital of Japan. It was the center for spreading Gautam Buddha's teachings and mindfulness practice (Miura & Sasaki, 1966). In the Mount Hiei hills around Kyoto, monk Saicho (767–822 CE), also known as Dengyo̲ Daishi, developed a new Tendai center away from Nara with a focus on *Lotus Sutra* from the Indian Mahayana scriptures (King, 2019). By 800 AD, Japan's political and cultural contacts with China were completely disconnected.

Rin Zai *Zen* mindfulness

In 1191, a Tendai monk, Eisai (1141–1215), introduced *Rin Zai way* (*Lin-chi* in Chinese) seeking spontaneous *Zen* mindfulness (King, 2019). This had no connection with China, and it was an indigenous Japanese form primarily developed for the common Japanese people. This drew the attention of the powerful samurai leader shoguns based in Kamakura, south of Tokyo and far removed from Japan's imperial capital at Kyoto. The samurai shoguns essentially ruled Japan from 1192 to 1868, while the emperor of Japan was exiled to live in Kyoto (Skilton, 1994, p. 179; Gehani, 2014, p. 88).

The samurai warrior leaders preferred the intense sudden approach of Rin-zai "warrior" *Zen* mindfulness over the gradual gentler approach of So-to *Zen* mindfulness, referred to as "farmer or civilian *Zen*" (Gehani, 2014). The Japanese samurai leaders also believed that enlightenment could be achieved with *jiriki* persistent personal practice, rather than *tariki* external help, as in the case of the *Pure Land Buddhists*. The Samurai leaders use hundreds of short paradoxical and intriguing questions known as Koans (Hori, 2003; Merton, 1966). These riddles are to stimulate the enlightenment of the mind spontaneously. Some famous Koans are:

> What is the sound of one hand clapping?
> When you meet Buddha, will you kill him?
> Who is dragging this dead corpse?

The progress of a disciple's mindfulness is guided by a close personal relationship between the Zen master and the disciple (Chit, 1963). It involves tough love, and a judicious use of physical and mental punishment. Archery and swordsmanship were integrated into mindfulness training. Mindful archers strive to make their minds, bodies, bow, arrow, and their distant target into one integrated universal cosmic reality. The archer's arrow hitting the central bull's eye is of secondary significance.

A personal Zen mindfulness experience

In the northern part of Kyoto, there is a small Rin-Zai temple, Ryo-anji. In the early 1980s, one of the authors (RG) visited this place multiple times to meditate mindfully while he was working in the Pioneering Research and Development Center of Japan's leading polymer company Toray Industries in Kyoto's northern suburbs. Ryo.anji temple has remained unchanged in the past 30 years. It is surrounded on three sides by earthen walls, and the fourth side opens into a clearing verandah. In the middle of this verandah is a rectangle of white gravel, raked with great mindfulness. It has 15 rocks, organized in five groups, spread all around. From any angle, one can see only 14 rocks. The symbolism is that the 15th rock is the viewer. This is the most profound expression of *Zen* mindfulness. It is a great serene place for meditation in the middle of a crowded city, Kyoto. The only changes meditators observe are the changes within the mind of the mindful meditator (King, 2009).

Distinctive characteristics of Zen mindfulness

Whereas *Zen (Rinzai)* mindfulness in Japan shares a common approach of self-realization with meditation with the Theravada tradition of mindfulness in India, it evolved with some distinctly different characteristics compared with its genesis as *Dhyan* mindfulness in India (King, 2019). In *Zen* mindfulness, the self-realization (*Satori*) is available and possible to all. Some people achieve this internally by their self-awareness, and others are certified externally by their coercive Roshi (teacher) with some authoritarian touches commonly accepted in the Japanese culture and society.

Theravada mindfulness from India refers to human suffering, no-self impersonality, and constant change in somewhat negative terms (King, 2009). Our sensory physical body is considered under a constant attack by worldly *Samsaric* infections. *Zen* mindfulness, on the other hand, highlights oneness positively with "I," "hear," "bell" transforming into a unitary "bell-sounding" experience. This is well illustrated by the following *Zen* passage (Suzuki, 1956, p. 240):

> When the mountains are seen as not standing against me, when they are dissolved into the oneness of things, they are not mountains; they cease to exist as objects of Nature. But when they are seen as standing against me, they are separate from me. The mountains are really mountains (of obstacles) when they are assimilated into my being, and I am absorbed by them (as obstacles).

These "mountain in me" and "I in mountain" concepts are deeply influenced by Shinto's naturalistic mysticism and Chinese Daoism, modified by tolerance and gradualism in the Indian Theravada tradition. Both the Indian Theravada *Dhyan* mindfulness tradition and Japanese *Zen* mindfulness share the awareness of the illusion of self as a separate individuality in empty reality *Anatta* and *Shunyata* (King, 2019).

A Burmese mindfulness meditator Khin Myo Chit (1963) describes his mindful experience and progress as follows:

> One day while I was practicing (mindfulness) at home, I felt my body was dashing away at a terrific speed toward something, but I did know what. It was like a runaway car crashing against a rocky hill. I thought I would be smashed to pieces. A great fear seized me and I jerked myself away from the sensation. Once I was free from the clutches of the terrible sensation, I realized that I had missed a great experience. I should have faced that terrible sensation without fear, with mindfulness as my way...
>
> Why had I turned back? The reason was quite simple. I did not want to be free from what is suffering; for the end of suffering means the end of life. Life and suffering cannot be separated ... I realized that my clinging desire for life had made me turn back from the bound of freedom.

The Meiji revolution and return to Shinto

In 1868, the Kamakura shogun samurais were dethroned and Emperor Meiji was reinstated in the new capital Edo (modern-day Tokyo) (King, 2009). The national religion of Japan switched to native Shinto, and formally Buddhism and Buddhist practices were discouraged. But, most of the Japanese people continued to believe in the teachings and the mindfulness practices of Gautam Buddha to alleviate their day-to-day sufferings.

Appropriation of *Zen* mindfulness in the West

Whereas *Dhyan* mindfulness was innovated insightfully with an epiphany by Gautam Buddha 2,500 years ago in Ancient India, and it evolved into small *chan* and big *Chan* mindfulness groups in China, *Son* mindfulness in Korea, and *Soto Zen* and *Rinzai Zen* mindfulness in Japan for human enlightenment, it was primarily appropriated for health-related, educational, financial, and military gains in the West, particularly in the United States (Gehani, 2014; King, 2019).

In the 1950s and 1960s, Daisuke Teitaro Suzuki (1870–1966), a *Zen* meditation practitioner in California, joined hands with American psychologist Erich Fromm (1950) and the propositions of Carl Jung and William James. They shared mindfulness with the American clinical community of psychoanalysts struggling with returning military personnel and the general public's anxieties of the nuclear Cold War (Harrington, 2008; Iwamura, 2010).

Suzuki (1962, 1969) and his associates proposed to followers such as Apple founder Steve Jobs, Beat poet Allen Ginsberg, and others that experiencing the real world by mindfulness by transcending dichotomies and preconceived notions of right and wrong can be transformative for the human mind (Faure, 1994, 1996; McMahan, 2008; Sharf, 1993, 1995; Suzuki, 1962, 1969; Williams, 2011). Suzuki also noted that mindfulness practice did not require any ethical preferences (Harrington, 2008; Jackson, 2010).

Fromm (1997) and Fromm, Suzuki, and Merino (1960) proposed that *Zen* mindfulness can help enrich the present moment, and liberate the Western capitalist mindset from illusive greed. The *Zen* mindfulness that came to the West coast of the USA is closer to *Soto* civilian *Zen* mindfulness than the *Samurai* style *Rinzai Zen* mindfulness. Since it did not favor a monastic lifestyle, therefore, the teaching of mindfulness in the United States fell more on the shoulders of scholars and lay practitioners than on the monks (as in Japan and elsewhere in India and China in the East).

East Coast Zen mindfulness

In 1965, while the Vietnam War was raging, Rochester, New York based *Zen* master Roshi Philip Kapleau (1912–2004) wrote *The Three Pillars of Zen*, a seminal introductory book on *Zen* mindfulness. Roshi Philip was a court reporter and a businessman, and he integrated these talents in his talks and teachings. He interacted closely with the business community, including Chester Carlson, the Rochester-based inventor of xerography and founder of Xerox Corporation, as well as his wife Doris Carlson. In 1968, the Carlsons helped establish the Rochester Zen Center, headed by a Westerner. The San Francisco Zen Center was always led by a Japanese monk (Goldstein, 2002).

In Japan, Honda and Toyota automakers and many other *Kaisha* corporations use flexible, holistic, and intuitive management ideology, highlighted in business best-sellers such as *Theory Z*, and the *Art of Japanese Management*. Unfortunately, this connection dwindled somewhat during the early 1980s, and did not re-emerge strongly until the late 1990s (Epstein, 1995; Molino, 2001).

Early advent of mindfulness in the US: in healthcare therapies

In the late 1970s, Herbert Benson was one of the early clinical adopters of "relaxation response" of mindfulness in the West (Benson, 2001; Benson & Klipper, 1975). He followed in the footsteps of extensive scientific investigation of *Dhyan* mindfulness of Maharishi Mahesh Yogi (of the Beatles Harrison fame) (Harrington, 2008).

Relaxation response, meditation, and Maharishi Mahesh Yogi

In the late 1960s, a large number of Americans were disenchanted by the nuclear Cold War and the Vietnam War. They were busy experimenting with psychedelic drugs and the somewhat self-destructing but peace-loving flower culture. In the late 1960s, one of the authors (Dr. Gehani), as a college student at the Indian Institute of Technology, Kanpur (IITK), met personally with Maharishi Mahesh Yogi when Maharishi visited his American engineering school, started by an American institutional consortium of the Massachusetts Institute of Technology (MIT), the California Institute of Technology (Cat-Tech), the University of California at Berkeley, Purdue University, and others. Maharishi Mahesh challenged the select young IITK students, "Where was your thought before you thoughted [*sic*]?" And then Maharishi elaborated on consciousness, sub-consciousness, and Omega waves for creativity. In 1967 Maharishi had become world famous when Beatle George Harrison and others, including Mick Jagger, adopted Maharishi Yogi as their spiritual teacher and advisor. They followed him to his training center in Bangor, Wales, and then his ashram in Rishikesh, in the Himalayan Mountains in Northern India. The Beatles admitted that with a regular and periodic practice of mindful transcendental meditation (TM) they were able to create and perform music with their peak potential, while discontinuing the use of drugs.

Meditation and research

Maharishi Mahesh supported extensive scientific clinical research and developed a new scientific connection between a convenient 20-minute-long meditation practice twice a day and a sustained drug-free relaxation response that resulted in a higher state of trans-ego consciousness, peace, and creativity (e.g., Domash, 1977). The Beatles have admitted that Maharishi's mindful meditation helped them become musically more creative. The *New York Times* declared the Maharishi as the Chief Guru of the West (Lefferts, 1967).

At the University of California in Los Angeles, M. Robert Keith Wallace (1970) did an independent scientific PhD research dissertation on the physiological benefits of transcendental meditation (TM). The TM practitioners improved their skin resistance, and reduced their resting heart rate coupled with a transformational shift to a highly coherent brain wave measured by electro-encephalogram. Wallace's (1970, p. 1734) rediscovery was published in the prestigious scientific journal *Science*:

> Physiologically, the (fourth major) state (of consciousness) produced by transcendental meditation seems to be distinct from commonly encountered states of

consciousness, such as wakefulness, sleep, and dreaming, and from altered states of consciousness, such as hypnosis and auto-suggestion.

Clinical appropriation of mindfulness

In the 1960s, cardiologist Herbert Benson of Harvard Medical School was conducting pioneering research on the relationships between stress-related risks of heart diseases such as high blood pressure and the influence of biofeedback in monkeys (Benson, 2001; Harrington, 2008; Harrington & Dunne, 2015). Benson worked with a group of meditation practitioners, and empirically discovered that, with the TM practice of meditating with a chant to concentrate the mind, they could regulate their blood pressure, heart rates, and coherent brain wave frequencies, at will without the use of a cumbersome biofeedback machine. Benson invited Wallace to join him at Harvard University. Together they collaborated their research studies with Archie F. Wilson, and reported "astounding" results (Benson, 2001). They called the reversal of stress-induced "fight or flight" reaction, the "relaxation response" (Benson & Klipper, 1975). Benson published this in his 1975 best-selling book, *The Relaxation Response*.

Since the 1970s, applications of mindfulness in clinical and recuperative therapies have evolved from its marginal esoteric interests to an integration with the mainstream clinical practices (Wilson, 2014). According to a professional research association, the number of research studies in mindfulness in a year increased geometrically from a small single-digit number in 1980, to 773 in 2014. One of the key players in this exponential growth was Dr. Jon Kabat-Zinn.

Jon Kabat-Zinn's mindfulness-based stress relaxation (MBSR)

In 1979, a young Jon Kabat-Zinn, soon after he obtained a PhD in molecular biology from MIT, approached the leaders of the University of Massachusetts Medical Center in Worcester, Massachusetts, to help his patients suffering with chronic pain by teaching them mindfulness at an onsite self-care training center to complement their medical treatment (Graham, 1991). They were falling through the cracks of the US healthcare–medical–big pharma complex (Kabat-Zinn, Lipworth, & Burney, 1985).

Jon Kabat-Zinn invested substantial effort and most of his life to bring mindfulness into the mainstream of modern medicine. Kabat-Zinn (2005) noted that the ancient Buddhist view of the natural laws of the mind and mindfulness offer "a coherent phenomenological description of the mind, emotions, suffering, and its potential release." The operational working definition of mindfulness by Kabat-Zinn (2005, pp. 145–146) is:

> the awareness that emerges through paying attention on purpose, in the present moment, and non-judgmentally to the unfolding experience moment by moment.

Kabat-Zinn (1990, 1994) defined mindfulness as a non-judgmental meditative practice on the present moment to alleviate stress, pain, anxiety, and suffering in a healthcare service provider setting. He prescribed the right meditative postures, and non-judgmental awareness of breath, emotions, and thoughts (Williams & Kabat-Zinn, 2013). This resembles what Gautam Buddha taught 2,500 years earlier. These practices helped lift mindfulness to a universal secular experience of practical worldly benefit.

The non-judgmental aspect of a mindful mind, unlike a mindless mind, does not routinely evaluate and assess to rush to make judgments. The Asian languages often use the same word for mind and heart. Thus, mindfulness includes an affectionate interest and openhearted compassionate quality within its attention. Being mindful is also inherently universal inward and outward (Wilber, 1977, 2000).

Grounding mindfulness in science

Some early critics in the West claimed that mindfulness is New Age mumbo jumbo, rooted in alien Eastern religions (Pickert, 2014).

Kabat-Zinn promoted mindfulness not as a spiritual practice but as common sense: it is nothing but muscle building of our attentive and focusing mind muscle. It was also scientifically related to building neuro-plasticity of the human brain (Pickert, 2014).

In an interview, Kabat-Zinn (2011) noted that above all, mindfulness was about love. He shared in "Mindfulness in the Modern World" that:

> Mindfulness is about love and loving life. When you cultivate this love, it gives you clarity and compassion for life, and your actions happen in accordance with that. All ethics and morality, and a sense of interconnectedness, come out of the act of paying attention.

Since 2007, the National Institutes of Health (NIH) have been funding dozens of rigorous research studies relating human health to effectiveness of mindfulness for alcoholism, heart disease, and more. Since then, the number of research publications related to mindfulness has grown almost ten-fold, from 52 in 2003, to 477 in 2012 (Pickert, 2014).

Society-wide appropriation of mindfulness organizational workplace appropriation

The corporate workplace in America has been increasingly interested in mindfulness (Langer, 1989, 1998; Williams & Kabat-Zinn, 2013). Since 2006, former vice president Janice Marturano of General Mills has trained close to 1,000 employees, and established the Institute for Mindful Leadership in 2011 to facilitate and expand the same (Pickert, 2014). In the company's Minneapolis facility, every building has a meditation room. In 2013, she introduced mindfulness to the World Economic Forum at Davos, and wrote *Finding the Space to Lead: A practical guide to mindful leadership*.

Since 2009, an annual mindfulness gathering, *Wisdom 2.0*, in California's Silicon Valley has been attracting thousands of attendees sharing experiences of mindfulness at Google, Facebook, Twitter, Instagram, and many more high-tech enterprises (Wilson, 2014). Google offers a seven-week course four times a year at its campus in Mountain View, California. This has helped thousands of Googlers enhance their attentive capability and boost their creative thinking. Steve Jobs, co-founder of Apple and a regular meditator, attributed mindfulness and meditation to his ability to ignore distractions and concentrate deeper. It is, therefore, not surprising that Apple's iTunes offers hundreds of meditation and mindfulness apps.

Mindfulness can help one become more aware and be present in the "now" moment. Thus, one is less distracted and frazzled by what happened before, or the fear of the uncertainty of what is likely to happen next. These fears and anxieties often result in depression, chronic anxiety, and heightened stress (Ryan, 2012). Chase Bank even advises its customers to spend money more mindfully (Pickert, 2014).

Mindfulness in military

The practice of mindfulness has been found very effective even in the US military sector (Fraher, Branicki & Grint, 2017; Weick, 2017). The US Navy Sea Air Land (SEAL) commandos form a high reliability organization (HRO), where mindfulness has been playing a significant role in building the soldiers' capabilities to face high unpredictability in their highly dangerous operating environment. Their empirical research discovered new links between individual mindfulness and collective mindfulness of their workplace. Gautam Buddha, grounded in non-violence 2,500 years ago, would have never imagined that the practice of *Dhyan* mindfulness he was proposing for peace could be appropriated for violent military actions in war hundreds of generations later in the West.

In the early 1990s, Elizabeth Stanley was an army intelligence officer deployed in Eastern Europe (Pickert, 2014). When she left active duty, she enrolled in an MBA program at MIT, and a doctoral program at Harvard University researching national security affairs. She became overwhelmed, and started practicing mindful meditation and yoga. She collaborated with neuroscientist Amrishi Jha at the University of Miami, who was clinically researching human attention. With the help of some private resources and funding, they launched a new mindfulness program to help Marines in stressful combat become more resilient.

Their successful findings led to two $1 million grants from the Department of Defense to develop Mindfulness-Based Mind Fitness (MBMF) training (Pickert, 2014). Jha subsequently received a $3.4 million federal grant to investigate the benefits of mindfulness practice to accountants in their peak tax season, and undergraduate students taking their exams.

From corporate corridors to US Congress

With a successful appropriation of mindfulness in the corporate sector and military organizations in the West, mindfulness has also been appropriated by other sectors in the industrialized US society, such as in public sector administration, public schools in our neighborhoods, correction facilities, military, and even in the congressional corridors of legislators (Ryan, 2012; Wilson, 2014).

Ohio Congressman Tim Ryan, a 2020 Democratic presidential candidate, attended a Kabat-Zinn mindfulness training session in 2008 when he was stressed and exhausted after his successful congressional election. After a 36-hour silence retreat, he discovered that as his mind quietened, it synchronized better with his body. Ryan (2012) wrote about his experience and the future potential of mindfulness in *A Mindful Nation*. In 2013, Ryan received a $1 million federal grant to teach mindfulness in public schools in his Youngstown home district. He even hosted mindfulness sessions for House members and congressional staff on Capitol Hill.

Hundreds of teachers have been offered online mindfulness training by Mindful Schools, a San Francisco Bay area-based program started in 2010. They help school children cope with stress and concentrate better in class (Langer, 1998; Pickert, 2014). Within five years, 300,000 teachers were trained in 48 US states and 43 countries.

In summary, what does all this research and qualitative phenomenological investigation add up to? What are the major takeaways we can learn from this qualitative research study based chapter?

Key contributions and takeaways of this research study

The key contributions and main chapter takeaways of this qualitative historic research study are in the following areas:

1. This chapter fills the gap in perception in the minds of some researchers who rush to note that the genesis of mindfulness originated in the 1970s in the West, with the pioneering appropriations of mindfulness by Jon Kabat-Zinn in healthcare, Ellen Langer in learning, and others. The origins of mindfulness actually go back more than 100 generations to Gautam Buddha (c. 563–c. 483) in Kapilvastu in the Ancient Indian civilization (see Table 31.1).
2. The key characteristics of the constructs of mindfulness differ significantly in the East, and its appropriations in the West. In the Eastern genesis, the primary interest and orientation in mindfulness was, and still is, inward, in the spiritual well-being and effectiveness of the individual and the surrounding community. In the workplace appropriation of mindfulness in the industrialized West in the US, the primary interest became external in the organizational effectiveness and maximization of profits and productivity.
3. In the East, the interest is per se in clearer understanding of mindfulness, in relation to human consciousness, sensory perceptions, and attachments that lead to much of human suffering. In the appropriation of mindfulness in the West, more effort is put in contrasting mindfulness with mindlessness. And then in relating these to their material outcomes and organizational suffering, which is quite different from the original tenets of mindfulness.
4. The mindfulness practice in the East, whether in *Dhyan* mindfulness in India, or *Chan* mindfulness in China, or *Zen* mindfulness in Japan, is always based on the foundation of an extended and regular practice of quiet and spiritual sitting meditation. In the case of workplace appropriation of mindfulness in the US, practitioners are sometimes assured that they need not meditate to use mindfulness to improve their resilience, decision-making, or productivity. Instead, they are encouraged to compare and contrast their utilitarian mindfulness with their mindlessness.
5. The original intent of the genesis of mindfulness was in non-labeling of our perceptions of the external world so that we are more in tune with our internal world. In the appropriation of mindfulness in the West, it is primarily leveraged for faster information processing and more profitable decision-making.

Table 31.1 Five takeaways of mindfulness: from genesis in India to appropriation in the US

	Genesis in the East (India)	*Appropriations in the West (US)*
1. Origins	c. 500 BCE Gautam Buddha	1970s Kabat-Zinn, Langer, others
2. Orientation	Inward; spiritual Individual suffering	Outward; material Organizational suffering
3. Process	Mindfulness per se	Mindfulness contrasted with mindlessness
4. Practice	Sitting meditation	Meditation not required
5. Outcome	Non-labeling of perceptions; calmness	Faster processing of information and decisions

Source: this Author, this study.

In conclusion, mindfulness as it has evolved from its genesis in Ancient India 2,500 years ago, to more than 100 generations later with its appropriation in the United States, has a broad bandwidth of benefits for our internal world, calming our chattering minds, as well as enhancing our external world by appropriating mindfulness in our workplaces.

Five key questions

1. What is the genesis of mindfulness? When did this genesis take place, and where?
2. Who is the primary innovator of mindfulness? What did he preach, and why?
3. What are the characteristics of *Chan* mindfulness in China and who introduced it to the Chinese?
4. How did the contextual socio-cultural setting influence and mold *Zen* mindfulness in Japan?
5. What are the key attributes and applications of workplace appropriation of mindfulness in the West in general, and the US in particular?

References

Badiner, A. H.. Ed (Hon). (2002). *Mindfulness in the Marketplace.* Berkeley, CA: Parallex Press.

Benson, H. (2001). Mind-body pioneer. *Psychology Today.* Available at https://www.psychologytoday.com/us/articles/200105/mind-body-pioneer. Accessed April 1, 2019.

Benson, H. & Klipper, M. (1975). *The Relaxation Response.* New York: Harper Collins.

Bodhi, B. (2005). *In the Buddha's Words: An Anthology of Discourses from the Pali Canon* (Edited & Introduced). Boston: Wisdom.

Bodhi, B. (2011). What does mindfulness really mean? A canonical perspective. *Contemporary Buddhism,* 12(1): 19–39.

Broughton, J. L. (1999). *The Bodhidharma Anthology: The Earliest Records of Zen.* Berkeley, CA: University of California Press.

Chit, K. M. (1963). Buddhist pilgrim's progress. *Guardian Magazine (Rangoon),* February: 17.

Collcut, M. (1981). *Five Mountains: The Rinzai Zen Monastic Institution in Medieval Japan.* Cambridge, MA: Harvard University Press.

Dhiman, S. (2008). Cultivating mindfulness: The Buddhist art of paying attention to attention. *Interbeing,* 2(2): 35–52.

Dhiman, S. (2009). Mindfulness in life and leadership: An exploratory survey. *Interbeing,* 3(1, Spring/Summer): 55–80.

Domash, I. (1977). The Transcendental Meditation technique and quantum physics. In D. Orne-Johnson & J. Farrow *Scientific Research on Maharishi's Transcendental Meditation and TM-Sidhi Program: Collected Papers,* 2nd Ed., Vol. 1. Weggis, Switzerland: Maharishi European University Press. Pp. 652–670.

Dreyfus, G. (2011). Is mindfulness present-centered and non-judgmental? A discussion of the cognitive dimensions of mindfulness. *Contemporary Buddhism,* 12(1): 41–54.

Dunne, J. (2011). Toward an understanding of non-dual mindfulness. *Contemporary Buddhism,* 12: 71–88. Available at http://dx.doi.org/10.1080/14639947.2011.564820

Epstein, M. (1995). Thoughts without a thinker: Buddhism and psychoanalysis. *Psychoanalytic Review,* 82: 391–406.

Essig, T. (2013). Mindfulness is a useful business skill, new research suggests. *Forbes,* Nov. 27.

Faure, B. (1994). *The Rhetoric of Immediacy: A Culture Critique of Chan Zen Buddhism.* Princeton, NJ: Princeton University Press.

Faure, B. (1996). *Chan Insights and Oversights.* Princeton, NJ: Princeton University Press.

Fraher, A. L., Branicki, L. J., & Grint, K. (2017). Mindfulness in action: Discovering how U.S. Navy Seals build capacity for mindfulness in high-reliability organizations (HROs). *Academy of Management Discoveries,* 3(3): 239–261.

Fromm, E. (1950). *Escape from Freedom*. New York: Rinehardt.

Fromm, E. (1997). *The Art of Being*. London: Constable.

Fromm, E., Suzuki, D. T., & Merino, R. (1960). *Zen Mindfulness and Psychoanalysis*. New York: Harper.

Gehani, R. R. (2011). Individual creativity and the role of mindful leaders. *Journal of Technology Management and Innovation*, 8(2): 144–155.

Gehani, R. R. (2014). *Innovation of Mindfulness in India and Its Global Diffusion to the West*. Hudson: Jaishri Krishna Foundation.

Gehani, R. R. (2018). Gandhi's dialectic struggle with interior – Exterior integration: 6S lessons from the paradoxical success of an integral leader. *Integral Leadership Review*, Nov.: 15–33.

Gehani, R. R. (2019). Gandhi's integral leadership to Greatness for All (*Survodaya*) with Truth (*Satya)*, Nonviolence (*Ahimsa)*, and Self-Rule (*Swaraj*). *Integral Leadership Review*, 19(1): 39–46.

Gethin, R. (2011). On some definitions of mindfulness. *Contemporary Buddhism*, 12(1): 263–279.

Goldstein, J. (2002). *One Dharma: The Emergence of Western Buddhism*. San Francisco, CA: Harper.

Graham, B. (1991). In the Dukkha magnet zone: An interview with Jon Kabat-Zinn. *Tricycle*. Available at https://tricycle.org/magazine/dukkha-magnet-zone/. Accessed April 1, 2019.

Hanh, T. N. (1992). *The Miracle of Mindfulness: A Manual on Mindfulness*. Boston: Boston Press.

Harrington, A. (2008). *The Cure Within: A History of Mind Body Medicine*. Cambridge, MA: Harvard University Press.

Harrington, A. & Dunne, J. D. (2015). When mindfulness is therapy. Ethical qualms, historical perspectives. *American Psychologist*, Oct. 70(7): 621–631.

Hori, V. S. (2003). Zen Sand: The book of capping phrases for Koan practice. In V. S., Hori (Ed.) *Nanzan Library of Asian Religion and Culture*. Honolulu, HI: University of Hawaii Press.

Iwamura, R. (2010). *Virtual Orientalism: Asian Regions and American Popular Culture*. New York: Oxford University Press.

Jackson, C. T. (2010). D.T. Suzuki, 'Suzuki's Zen' and the American reception of Zen Buddhism. In G. Storhoff & J. Whalen-Bridge (Eds.), *American Buddhism as a Way of Life*. Albany, NY: SUNY Press. Pp. 39–56.

Kabat-Zinn, J. (1990). *Full Catastrophe Living: Using the Wisdom of Your Body and Mind to Face Stress, Pain, and Illness*. New York: Bantam Books. 2013 Edition.

Kabat-Zinn, J. (1994). *Wherever You Go, There You Are: Mindfulness Meditation in Everyday Life*. New York: Hyperion.

Kabat-Zinn, J. (2005). *Coming to Our Senses: Healing Ourselves and the World Through Mindfulness*. New York: Hyperion.

Kabat-Zinn, J. (2011). Some reflections on the origins of of MBSR, skillful means, and the trouble with maps. *Contemporary Buddhism*, 12: 281–306.

Kabat-Zinn, J., Lipworth, L., & Burney, R. (1985). The clinical use of mindfulness meditation for the self-regulation of chronic pain. *Journal of Behavioral Medicine*, 8: 163–190.

King, S. B. (2009). *Socially Engaged Buddhism*. Honolulu, HI: University of Hawaii Press.

King, W. L. (2019). A comparison of Theravada and Zen Buddhist meditational methods and goals. *History of Religion*, 9(4, May): 304–325.

Kuan, T. (2008). *Mindfulness in Early Buddhism: New Approaches Through Psychology and Textual Analysis of Pali, Chinese, and Sanskrit Sources*. Routledge Critical Studies in Buddhism. London and New York: Routledge.

Langer, E. (1989). *Mindfulness*. Reading, MA: Addison-Wesley.

Langer, E. (1998). *Power of Mindful Learning*. Reading, MA: Addison/Wesley: Longman.

Langer, E. J. & Moldoveanu, M. (2000). The construct of mindfulness. *Journal of Social Issues*, 56(1): 1–9.

Lefferts, B. (1967). Chief Guru of the Western World. *New York Times*. Dec. 17.

McMahan, D. L. (2008). *The Making of Buddhist Modernism*. Oxford: Oxford University Press.

Merton, T. (1966). The Zen Koan. *Lugano Review*, 1: 126.

Miura, I. & Sasaki, R. F. (1966). *Zen Dust*. Kyoto: First Zen Institute of America in Japan. Pp. 58–59.

Molino, A. (2001). *The Couch and the Tree: Dialogues in Psychoanalysis and Buddhism*. London: Open Press.

Nanamoli, B. (1972,1992). *The Life of the Buddha: According to the Pali Canon*. Seattle, WA: Buddhist Publication Society Pariyatti Editions.

Nayana-ponika, T. (1962, 1975). *The Heart of Buddhist Meditation*. New York: Samuel Weiser.

Norberg-Hodge, H. (2002). Buddhism in the global economy. In A. H. Badiner (Ed.), *Mindfulness in the Marketplace*. Berkeley, CA: Parallex Press. Pp. 15–27.

Pickert, K. (2014). The art of being mindful. *Time: International (South Pacific Edition)*, 183(4): 40, Feb. 3.

Pine, R. (1987). *The Zen Teaching of Bodhidharma*. New York: North Point Press.
Ryan, T. (2012). *A Mindful Nation: How a Simple Practice Can Help Us Reduce Stress*. Carlsbad, CA: Hay House.
Schumpeter, R. R. (2013). The mindfulness business. *The Economist*, Nov. 16. Available at www.economist.com/news/business..
Sharf, R. H. (1993). The Zen of Japanese nationalism. *History of Religion*, 33: 1–43.
Sharf, R. H. (1995). Buddhist modernism and the rhetoric of meditative experience. *Numen*, 42(3): 228–283.
Sharf, R. H. (1998). Experience. In M. Taylor (Ed.), *Critical Terms for Religious Studies*. Chicago, IL: University of Chicago Press. Pp. 94–116.
Sharf, R. H. (2014). Mindfulness and mindlessness in early Chan. *Philosophy of East and West*, 64(4): 933–964.
Shulman, E. (2010). Mindful wisdom: The Sat-patthaana-suttanon mindfulness, memory, and liberation. *History of Religions*, 49(4): 393–420.
Skilton, R. R. (1994). *Concise History of Buddhism. From Gehani, R. R. 2014. Innovation and Diffusion of Mindfulness*. Hudson: Jai Krishan Foundation.
Suzuki, D. T. (Ed.). (1956). *Zen Buddhism* (p. 240). New York: Doubleday.
Suzuki, D. T. (1962). *The Essentials of Zen Buddhism*. New York: E.P. Dutton & Co.
Suzuki, D. T. (1969). *The Field of Zen*. London: The Buddhist Society.
Wallace, B. (2006). *The Attention Revolution: Unlocking the Power of the Focused Mind*. Boston, MA: Wisdom Publications.
Wallace, R. K. (1970). Psychological effects of transcendental meditation. *Science*, 167: 1751–1754.
Weick, K. E. (2017). Commentary on mindfulness in action. *Academy of Management Discoveries*, 3(3): 322–323.
Wilber, K. (1974), The spectrum of consciousness. *Main Currents in Modern Thought*, 31 (3): 15–21.
Wilber, K. (1977). *The Spectrum of Consciousness*. New York: Quantum Books.
Wilber, K. (2000). *Integral Psychology: Consciousness, Spirit, Psychology, Therapy, and Postmodern Worlds*. Boston, MA: Shambhala Publications.
Williams, J. & Kabat-Zinn, J. (2013). Mindfulness: Diverse perspectives on its meaning, origins, and multiple applications of the intersection of science and Dharma. In M. Williams & J. Kabat-Zinn (Eds.), *Mindfulness: Diverse Perspectives on its Meaning, Origins, and Applications*. London: Routeledge. Pp 1–18.
Williams, R. J. (2011). Techne-Zen and the spiritual quality of global capitalism. *Critical Inquiry*, 38(1): 17–70.
Wilson, J. (2014). *Mindful America: The Mutual Transformation of Buddhist Meditation and American Culture*. New York: Oxford University Press.

32

THE ROLE OF MINDFULNESS IN LEADERSHIP, FOLLOWERSHIP, AND ORGANIZATIONS

Kerri Cissna and H. Eric Schockman

Introduction

Constant distraction has become the default setting for many humans, as access and connection to digital devices is now commonplace in most parts of the world. Therefore, a growing trend for mindfulness to enter the modern workplace is being further explored by global leaders who want to thrive in the 21st century. The concept of "mindfulness" has been around for centuries, yet it has traditionally been associated with religion, which may have created resistance for its integration into secular workplace settings. Much of its conceptualization can be derived from Hindu spiritualism, where the value of the individual and collective path to self-realization (contrast: Maslow, 1972) leads to the light of *Dhamma*—righteousness of conduct. Knowledge and learning are reached in this state of bliss (contrast: Csikszentmihalyi, 1996) through the study of *Jnana*, which leads to *Vijnana*, or the realization and consciousness of the self (Rupčić, 2017). According to Passmore (2019, p. 105), it comes from the translation of *sati*, which combines the elements of awareness, remembering, focus in a nonjudgmental way, acceptance, and kindness to oneself and others. Eastern traditions focus on the transcendence of self-consciousness, while Western focus has been placed on the seeking and fulfilling of the self. Mindfulness in the workplace can resolve the dichotomy of selflessness and selfishness by introducing a new way to achieve the ultimate expression of real self that transcends ego and embraces singularity (Maslow, 1972).

Also associated with Buddhism, mindfulness has been practiced for centuries as an open, receptive, nonjudgmental awareness of one's current state (Brown & Ryan, 2003). It includes the concentrated observation of one's present-moment perceptions, thoughts, and emotions, with an attitude of equanimity, curiosity, openness, and acceptance (Bishop et al., 2004; Brown & Ryan, 2003). More recently, mindfulness has been capturing the attention of wide audiences through social media and mainstream news outlets, as a means of enhancing wellbeing (Widdicombe, 2015). It has also begun to interest anyone who cares about workplace stress; interpersonal relations at work; managerial competence; or spirituality at work (Hunter & McCormick, 2008).

Kabat-Zinn (1991) advances the notion that mindfulness comes with paying deep attention in the present moment to yourself and the more existential world around us in a nonjudgmental way. More explicitly, "mindfulness is simply a practical way to be more in touch with the fullness of your being through a systematic process of self-observation, self-inquiry and mindful action" (Kabat-Zinn, 1991, p. 13). Recent research has demonstrated that mindfulness provides long-term benefits to organizations by enhanced employee engagement and job satisfaction (Davidson et al., 2003; Pratt & Ashforth, 2003; Reb & Choi, 2014; Williams & Pennman, 2013). In scanning the literature, Dane (2011) identifies three reoccurring themes regarding the attempt to define mindfulness: first, mindfulness is a state of consciousness (i.e., an inherent human capacity) that can also be assessed at the trait level (i.e., because of dispositional tendencies, some people may be in a mindful state of consciousness more often than others); second, attention that is focused on present-moment phenomena; and third, simultaneous awareness of both external (the environment) and internal (intrapsychic).

Just as mindfully selecting a companion for a partnership based on values alignment and compatibility factors can contribute to a higher quality of life, it is equally important to mindfully select an organization to invest time, energy, and creative capacity. From the mindful union of the follower–leader–organization, mindfulness can then contribute to higher qualities of life through the lifespan/expansion of the employee. Bringing practices of mindfulness into every practical interaction at work can dramatically increase the daily experience of employees, which can presumably impress the organization's measurable aspirations as well. This book chapter seeks to serve as a mindfulness companion for those who want to better understand the role of mindfulness in leadership, followership, and organizational practices for the modern world.

Attention for this topic has grown as studies have shown that more mindful employees will experience better health, lower healthcare costs, and higher levels of productivity (Carleton, Barling, & Trivisonno, 2018). Research has shown that mindfulness can improve stress management, which is an important leadership skill (Whetten & Cameron, 2007). Mindfulness also helps build relationships and increases empathy, which are both important managerial competencies (Goleman, 1998; Whetten & Cameron, 2007). Mindfulness practices have been shown to reduce depression and anxiety (Chiesa & Serretti, 2011) and substance abuse (Bowen et al., 2009). Studies on the use of mindfulness in pain management show a similar effectiveness as traditional pain interventions or cognitive behavioral therapy approaches (Ehde, Dillworth, & Turner, 2014). Qualitative studies have shown that persons who:

> practice mindfulness may have more external awareness at work; be more accepting of their work situation; have more modest, realistic work goals; be more selfless; be less concerned with material acquisition and wealth; have a more internal locus of evaluation; be more likely to derive meaning in life from more sources than just work; be better able to cope and remain calm in difficult work situations; be more likely to experience work difficulties as challenges than threats; enjoy their work more; be more adaptable at work; and have more positive interpersonal relations at work.
>
> *(Hunter & McCormick, 2008)*

Traditional view

Although mindfulness is used as a tool in most faith traditions, such as Hindu, Sufi, and Christian Orthodox, it has played a key role, most notably in the Buddhist spiritual path. Mindfulness has its roots in Buddhist meditation, which dates back as early as the 1st century BC (Purser & Milillo, 2015). The concept of mindfulness within Buddhism is subject to a variety of understandings, and mindfulness training represents a small fraction of Buddhist meditation methods (Lopez, 2012). As Dunne (2011) stated, "the Buddhist tradition is not monolithic" (p. 71). However, in its original Buddhist form, the practice of mindfulness refers to the cultivation of awareness in the body and the mind in each present moment.

Despite the variety of applications of Buddhist traditions, there is common ground for the purpose that mindfulness meditation plays in psycho-spiritual development (Purser & Milillo, 2015). It is widely accepted that a goal of the Buddhist practice is the elimination of the root causes of suffering. Traditional Buddhist meditative training can also eliminate suffering by inducing changes in one's cognitive and emotional states, which leads to changes in behavioral and psychological traits (Purser & Milillo, 2015). This process transforms the root causes of suffering, "a set of correctable defects that affect all the mental states of an untrained person" (Lutz, Dunne, & Davidson, 2007, p. 503; Purser & Milillo, 2015). Mindful leaders utilize these practices to address and eliminate the workplace suffering, which typically goes unnoticed.

Modern view

As the field of research on positive effects of mindfulness expands, it is important to recognize that there are two schools of thought about mindfulness that have emerged for the modern world. The first one began when Jon Kabat-Zinn (1991) developed a mindfulness-based stress reduction program (Hunter & McCormick, 2008). Though it is rooted in Buddhist meditation, this secular practice, called Mindfulness-Based Stress Reduction (MBSR), was launched at the University of Massachusetts Medical School in 1979. As a result, thousands of research studies have documented the physical and mental health benefits of mindfulness (Purser & Milillo, 2015). This research has inspired countless programs to adapt this MBSR model to schools, prisons, hospitals, and veterans' centers (Purser & Milillo, 2015). His program took the traditional techniques of mindfulness meditation from Buddhism and removed its religious aspects. His patients then learned sitting and walking mindfulness meditation, and how to spread this mindfulness throughout the rest of their lives (Hunter & McCormick, 2008). This project became the catalyst for hundreds of mindfulness studies in medicine, psychology, education, and law. The results were profound and showed that mindfulness has positive effects on the psychological, educational, and medical aspects of human life.

Many scholars have made contributions towards bringing mindfulness to the mainstream consciousness in Western cultures, including Nyanaponika Thera (1962), Thich Nhat Hanh (1975), Joseph Goldstein (2013), and Jack Kornfield (2001). Yet, the second most widely recognized vein of mindfulness research in management scholarship comes from the work of psychologist Ellen Langer (1989, 2005, 2010). Langer distinguishes her work on mindfulness from the way it is used in Buddhism.

Ellen Langer, psychology professor from Harvard University, explains the difference between mindlessness (inattentive behavior) and mindfulness (intentionally reflective cognition) (Fox Lee, 2019). Mindlessness is a state of being that is determined by past behaviors, similar to automation (Langer, 2010). Mindfulness, on the other hand, is a flexible state that is governed by being actively present in each moment, noticing new things and being sensitive to context (Langer, 2010). According to Professor Langer, mindless leaders will govern with rules and regulations, while mindful leaders are guided by rules but not determined by them (Langer, 2010).

According to Langer (1989), mindless people act like robots or "programmed automatons," evaluating everything in a rigid way. Being mindful allows people to be oriented in the present moment, open to surprise, sensitive to context, and liberated from the tyranny of old mindsets (Langer, 1989). Professor Langer shows the tragic and far-reaching consequences of mindlessness and the benefits of mindfulness: in health, productivity, overcoming addictions, avoiding burnout, and increasing our control and potential as we grow older (Langer, 1989).

Langer's work, stretching over four decades, provides empirical evidence that attests to the beneficial effects of mindfulness (Carson & Langer, 2006). The mindful perspective increases cognitive and behavioral flexibility as a way for humans to adapt to change in a meaningful way (Carson & Langer, 2006). Exploring mindfulness can lead to important advantages in self-acceptance that include: authenticity, evaluation, the benefits of making mistakes, the trap of rigidity, and the acceptance of self as a mindful habit (Carson & Langer, 2006). Langer's work on mindfulness is expansive and will be touched upon further in other ways throughout this chapter.

Problem statement

Constant access to digital devices has led to a perpetual state of distraction amongst human beings in the modern world. For example, 95% of US teens have access to a smartphone, and 45% are online "almost constantly" (Anderson & Jiang, 2018). Technology increases our ability to connect with others virtually, but digital devices cannot replace the human interactions and importance of emotional connection. Therefore, as the use of technology increases, so has the necessity for mindful leaders who are sensitive to the role of emotions in the workplace. Technology is removing the demand for face-to-face human interaction and the result can be any range of consequences, from distraction to isolation to toxic work environments. In order to counteract these negative implications of accelerated digital contexts, mindfulness needs to be integrated into leadership, followership, and organizations.

Technological advances have also led to an acceleration of material obsessions, creating an imbalance between the material and spiritual life (Bhunia & Mukhuti, 2011). This has left people facing spiritual emptiness, moral abnormalities, twisted values, lack of trust, greed, and all kinds of crimes. Cynicism and mistrust can contribute to organizational culture that stagnates growth. CEOs who were forced out of their positions for ethical lapses in 2018 outweighed the number who were fired for financial performance or board issues (PricewaterhouseCoopers, 2018). This is central for recognizing the need for psychological, spiritual, and emotional expectations at work (Cartwright & Holmes, 2006).

A void in leaders who are mindful has led researchers to examine the fundamental reasons that leaders are needed in the first place. This means that several important questions are being asked as leadership is examined for the 21st century. Do leaders have more knowledge and abilities than others that make them exceptional? Are leaders needed to ensure that people are able to reach their goals? The basic assumption that leaders are needed for their judgment, expertise, and direction is being challenged for the modern age, as humans seem to have a capacity to operate at higher levels (led by access to technological advances). Mindfulness is needed to help leaders unleash the full potential of their diverse workforce. Unfortunately, mindfulness is not a priority in school systems, which then leads to a void of mindfulness at work and leadership competency.

Mindfulness in leadership

Mindful leadership is a bit more complex and muddled in the literature with topics like "meaningfulness," which share the outcome of mindfulness. For example, Bailey and Madden (2016) found meaningful work something very essential to employees in their limited study (N=135). Meaningfulness tended to be very personal and individual. Furthermore, their research showed: "that the quality of leadership received virtually no mention when people described meaningful moments at work, but poor management was the top destroyer of meaningfulness" (p. 54). We shall return to Bailey and Madden shortly, but suffice to say here they recommend five qualities of meaningful work that mindful leaders should adopt: (1) self-transcendent (a lá Maslow), (2) poignant, (3) episodic, (4) reflective, and (5) personal (2016).

Other researchers have placed a more positive spin regarding mindful leadership as a pathway for developing more mindful organizations. Joshua Ehrlich (2015), for example, views "tantalizing prospects" for leaders to create high-performance, self-aware mindful organizations. Schaufenbuel (2014) reviewed over a dozen Fortune 500 companies, the United States Army, and a multitude of top MBA programs around the country who teach mindfulness to produce better decision-making, productivity, and overall organizational engagement. Brown and Ryan (2003) argue that "mindfulness is inherently a state of consciousness" (p. 824). Mindful leaders are thought to possess a certain characteristic or "trait mindfulness" that sets them apart from the herd and are better equipped to bring followers along (Dane & Brummel, 2013; Giluk, 2009; Hülscheger, Alberts, Feinholdt & Lang, 2013).

The popular press has shown a growing interest in the topic of mindfulness in the workplace, with books like *The Power of Now* (Tolle, 2004), *The Mindful Leader* (Carroll, 2007), *Awake at Work* (Carroll, 2004), and *Resonant Leadership: Renewing yourself and connecting with others through mindfulness, hope, and compassion* (Boyatzis & McKee, 2005), *10% Happier* (Harris, 2014a), *Waking Up* (Harris, 2014b), and many more. Popular phone apps such as *Calm* and *Headspace* teach mindfulness and meditation techniques. This demonstrates a demand for leaders to understand and embrace mindfulness for leadership in the 21st century.

Mindfulness is a gift that allows people to be fully engaged in the present circumstances, rather than concerned about the past or worried about the future. When leaders practice mindfulness, they are able to remain calm and focused during the ups and downs of life, which is a critical managerial competency. Mindfulness refers to awareness and presence of mind (Dhiman, 2012). This extends beyond what typically happens when humans are barely paying attention to what is happening in the present moment by detached observations. Langer said that "it is only when we've awakened that we realize how much of our lives we've actually slept through" (2005, p. 16). Until that point, humans rarely go beyond a surface level of awareness to reach deeper layers of the mind (Gunaratana, 2002). Bodhi (1994) explained that mindfulness trains the mind to remain present, open, quiet, and alert. Mindfulness involves paying attention in the present moment without judging or being critical (Dhiman, 2012). It is a practice of undoing: not thinking, not judging, not associating, not planning, not imagining, not wishing (Bodhi, 1994, p. 7). Mindfulness can teach emotional regulation, social and coping skills, and can improve self-awareness, self-esteem, and resilience (Coholic, 2011). It can also teach cognitive flexibility, which has become an asset for leaders in the 21st century.

Cognitive flexibility

An important factor in understanding the theory of mindfulness is that it places an emphasis on the importance of *cognitive flexibility* (Langer, 1989). Cognitive flexibility is the human ability to adapt cognitive processing strategies to face new and unexpected conditions and is intrinsically linked to the attention processes (Cañas, Quesada, Antolí, & Fajardo, 2003; Moore & Malinowski, 2009). As mindfulness meditation depends on attention being focused in a moment-by-moment basis, mindfulness training can increase cognitive flexibility and the ability to respond to things in a non-habitual way (Moore & Malinowski, 2009).

The mindful approach to cognitive flexibility differs from intelligence theory in the relationship between individuals and their environments (Brown & Langer, 1990). Intelligence theory assumes that there is an optimal fit between individuals and their environment. Mindfulness theory recognizes that individuals define their relation to their environment in different ways. Intelligence has been embedded in a theory of correspondence which was inherited from the 19th century, and current intelligence theories continue to focus on thought as adaptively corresponding to external reality (Brown & Langer, 1990). There are detrimental effects of intelligence theories that place an external evaluative standard of "optimal fit" which impacts self-perception, perception of others, and the educational process (Brown & Langer, 1990). Alternatively, mindfulness theory enhances personal control and places emphasis on the educational process.

Mindful leaders understand the holistic needs of the human experience. When humans are seen as having spiritual dimensions, they are given the opportunity to lead from their highest version of self (Maslow, 1943). Self-actualization exists when people are encouraged to grow and develop, to create new ideas and innovate across positional borders. Mindful leadership gives people the ability to bring one's whole self to work without fear of rejection (sense of belonging) and by confidence (self-esteem), which is built on trust, physiological and psychological safety (Maslow, 1943).

Antiquated forms of leadership rely on the figurehead to give direction, create vision, and make decisions. However, leadership for the 21st century relies heavily on innovation and agility, which stem from cognitive flexibility. Mindful leaders are needed for the modern age, as agility becomes a more valued contribution. "A leader of innovation creates a place—a context, an environment—where people are willing and able to do the hard work that innovative problem solving requires" (Hill, Brandeau, Truelove, & Lineback, 2014). This new type of leadership can leverage the creative capacity of each member of the group so that the sum becomes greater than its parts. The leader's role is to create a space where individual capacity can be combined and converted into a new form of collective genius. The shift in power moves from an individual at the top towards a distributed leadership model which empowers and leverages mindfulness amongst followers. The practicality of this type of leadership can be understood by mindfully identifying the strengths and passions of each team member and sharing an evolving type of responsibility, rather than pigeon-holing employees into a stagnant position. Aligning the employee's strengths with the organizational needs is important, but is an evolving process as humans (and organizations) are in a constant state of change.

Mindfulness in followership

Mindful leadership consists of intentional practices that include and empower followers. Mindful followers generate teams that are considered "high-performing" and emerge from inclusive environments that nourish the human spirit. They represent distributed power amongst a group of people that are regularly included in the leadership process. Wiese and Ricci share that "high performing teams report that it's fun and satisfying to work on collaborative teams because they are asked to contribute at their highest potential and they learn a lot along the way" (2010). Wiese and Ricci give ten characteristics of high-performing teams:

1. People have solid and deep trust in each other and in the team's purpose—they feel free to express feelings and ideas.
2. Everybody is working toward the same goals.
3. Team members are clear on how to work together and how to accomplish tasks.
4. Everyone understands both team and individual performance goals and knows what is expected.
5. Team members actively diffuse tension and friction in a relaxed and informal atmosphere.
6. The team engages in extensive discussion, and everyone gets a chance to contribute—even the introverts.
7. Disagreement is viewed as a good thing and conflicts are managed. Criticism is constructive and is oriented toward problem-solving and removing obstacles.
8. The team makes decisions when there is natural agreement—in the cases where agreement is elusive, a decision is made by the team lead or executive sponsor, after which little second-guessing occurs.
9. Each team member carries their own weight and respects the team processes and other members.
10. The leadership of the team shifts from time to time, as appropriate, to drive results. No individual members are more important than the team (2010, p. 1).

Mindful leaders know how to build teams of mindful followers. Google mindfully studied teams for over two years and found the ingredients for a successful team (Rozovsky, 2015). This study introduced five key dynamics that set successful teams apart from other teams (Rozovsky, 2015):

1. Psychological safety: Can we take risks on this team without feeling insecure or embarrassed?
2. Dependability: Can we count on each other to do high-quality work on time?
3. Structure and clarity: Are goals, roles, and execution plans on our team clear?
4. Meaning of work: Are we working on something that is personally important for each of us?
5. Impact of work: Do we fundamentally believe that the work we're doing matters?

Mindful leaders know how to create inclusive environments where each follower feels valued and accepted. The result is a healthy organizational culture that capitalizes on diverse individual strengths and demolishes homogeneity. Followers want connection with others and to be invested in the mission of an organization.

Mindful leaders find ways to create this type of environment for high performance among followers. Therefore, mindful followers are able to contribute at higher levels because of the psychological safety that has been created for them. Delizonna (2017) gives six mindful ways to create psychological safety in the workplace as: approach conflict as a collaborator (not adversary), speak human to human, anticipate reactions and countermoves, replace blame with curiosity, ask for feedback on delivery, and measure psychological safety by asking your team how safe they feel. The workforce is moving into an era where human capacity towards leadership is widespread. Organizations will thrive under mindful leaders who embrace new concepts, inclusive environments, and mindful teams that lead to higher levels of innovation.

Mindfulness in organizations (creativity/flow)

Mindful leaders and followers create organizations that cultivate creative flow. When people are included in the decision-making and creative processes of organizational systems, great things can happen. "Inclusion increases the total human energy available to organizations" (Miller, 1994, p. 151). This creativity that is available through each individual person establishes the credibility for followers to add as much value to organizations as leaders. Since creativity is a hot commodity in today's marketplace, mindful leaders should make it a high priority to cultivate the innovation that is available to them by leveraging the talents of each team member. Langer (2005) expressed that "creativity is not a blessing some special few are born with or receive from above. Our creative nature is an integral part of our daily lives, expressed through our culture, our language, and even our most mundane activities." (p. 4).

As modern leaders continue to focus on innovation as a critical task for the foreseeable future, mindfulness will play an essential role. Mindful leaders are able to see the asset that each person can bring to a team through innovation and creativity. Dhiman (2012) explores the relationship between mindfulness and the creative process and suggests that the Buddhist meditative practice called mindfulness contributes to creativity and "flow." As a researcher, he utilizes the Buddhist mindfulness framework of attentiveness or awareness of the present to build on the works of Langer, a Harvard psychologist, and Csikszentmihalyi, the celebrated author who popularized the concept of *flow* (Dhiman, 2012).

After interviewing both Csikszentmihalyi and Langer, Dhiman (2012) states that mindfulness is a cognitive state of "flow," characterized by energized engagement with all of one's mind and attention to the activity at hand. He compares this with how Theravada Buddhism employs a more traditional view of mindfulness, while Langer and Csikszentmihalyi create more modern views of mindfulness (Dhiman, 2012). Langer (2005) describes mindful creativity by total engagement and immersion in everything done. Csikszentmihalyi's (1996) concept of "flow" is a state of effortless concentration towards an activity in which one transcends any sense of time, space, and self-absorption. These concepts are similar to the Buddhist doctrine of mindfulness, a knowledge of reality that is based in awareness beyond bare attention. True mindfulness will not emanate from the three unwholesome tendencies of mind—greed, hatred, and ignorance—which blocks right mindfulness and forms the seventh factor of the Noble Eightfold Path (Dhiman, 2012; Nyanaponika, 1962).

Creativity is one of the greatest contributions of mindful leadership, which enhances the meaning and happiness of employees.

> Of all human activities, creativity comes closest to providing the fulfillment we all hope to get in our lives. Call it full-blast living. Creativity is a central source of meaning in our lives. Most of the things that are interesting, important, and human are the result of creativity. What makes us different from apes—our language, values, artistic expression, scientific understanding, and technology—is the result of individual ingenuity that was recognized, rewarded, and transmitted through learning.
>
> *(Csikszentmihalyi, 1996, pp. 1–2)*

Langer (2005) shares this conviction for each person "to learn to act and engage with ourselves mindfully, creatively, actively, and happily" (p. 21). But what type of leaders are capable of unleashing the creative capacity in each team member?

Leading innovation takes a distinct kind of leader who harnesses the "collective genius" of all people in the organization (Hill et al., 2014). As creativity becomes essential for followers to find meaning, virtue, and happiness, this becomes a priority for mindful leaders. Mindfulness holds leaders accountable to draw out the unique genius in every follower and to assemble teams according to what is known as a collective genius (Hill et al., 2014). Collective genius is created by the sum of each organization's parts (individual creative capacity). This creates a mutually beneficial relationship amongst leaders and followers and plays a critical role in creating environments where employees thrive. Collective genius relies on mindful leaders to introduce new ways of innovation for such agile contexts. Collective genius is cultivated by mindful leaders who understand that the direction of the organization should be created with the people who will be responsible for executing the organizational mission. "Direction-setting" leadership can work well when the solution to a problem is known and straightforward, but if a problem calls for a truly innovative response, teams are needed to decide what that response should be. Mindful leaders understand that creative solutions and decisions cannot be made in isolation. By definition, then, leading innovation cannot be about creating and selling a vision to people and then somehow inspiring them to execute it (Hill et al., 2014).

Benefits of mindfulness in the workplace

Approximately 15% of the US workforce engaged in some form of mindfulness activity in 2007, according to estimates from a large sample of surveys (Kachan et al., 2017). To live mindfully is to be aware of what is happening in the present moment. It is the process of actively noticing new things, which puts you there and makes you more sensitive to context and perspective (Langer, 2014). When people practice mindfulness in the workplace, they can avoid the fear and worry that is associated with concerns about the past/future and having control.

Humans seek stability and control, especially in workplace situations. It is natural for people to think that there is a certain way to do things, regimented by rules and regulations. However, there are many ways to do things depending on context and perspective. Change is constant, and environments need to be agile in order to create new solutions to problems that arise. Langer (2014) says that rules and routines should be guides, but not governance. Mindfulness in the workplace allows for flexibility in understanding that there are always multiple ways of approaching any situation. Mindful leadership can assist in the creation of mindful workplaces. They also help followers in the pursuit of meaning and happiness.

Search for meaning

Victor Frankl wrote *Man's Search for Meaning*, which describes the universal human craving for hope, purpose, and connection. He describes these elements as key for getting people through the toughest circumstances in life. Frankl shares that humans need to find meaning each day, regardless of social class. Pauchant (2002) states that spirituality (mindfulness) in the workplace meets this fundamental human need for meaning, integration, establishing roots, and transcendence. This research provides defensive strategies for the search for meaning as amplification and escape; however, the more functional response is a learning process that can lead to transformation (Pauchant, 2002). The final strategy requires courage to recognize crisis and trauma in a way that transcends it to create "new values, behaviors, and a new level of consciousness" (Pauchant, 2002, p. 5). All of these measures can be made through mindful leadership.

Man's search for meaning has led humans to seek fulfillment through work (Gotsis & Kortezi, 2008). Man's pursuit of purpose in life can be a healthy response to the existential crisis or collapse of meaning humans seem to grapple with (Frankl, 2014). Mindful leaders should find confidence in attending to the spiritual needs of employees through mindfulness, which can greatly enhance the experience of all involved. It is (generally) accepted that workplace spirituality positively impacts the outcomes of an organization, quantitatively and qualitatively (Heaton, Schmidt-Wilk, & Travis, 2004; King & Crowther, 2004).

Benefits of workplace spirituality

In the literature, mindfulness in organizations falls under the umbrella of workplace spirituality. The benefits of workplace spirituality can be discerned both organizationally and individually. To begin, the literature suggests that there is a link between spirit in the workplace and an increased commitment to organizational goals (Delbecq, 1999; Fry, 2003; Kinjierski & Skrypnek, 2004; Leigh, 1997). Mindful leadership can positively influence the quality of work life, and result in the increase of commitment, well-being, greater productivity, and life satisfaction (Sweeney & Fry, 2012). Workplace spirituality leads to an increase in honesty and trust within the organization (Brown, 2003; Krishnakumar & Neck, 2002; Wagner-Marsh & Conely, 1999). Greater kindness and fairness is found when there is workplace spirituality (Biberman & Whitty, 1997), and increased creativity (Kinjierski & Skrypnek, 2004). Additional evidence points to an increase in profits and improved morale (Benefiel, 2003). There are higher levels of productivity and enhanced performance, as well as reduced absenteeism and turnover (Eisler & Montouori, 2003; Fry, 2003; Giacalone & Jurkiewicz, 2003a; Sass, 2000).

Sheep (2006) examined organizations and found that the influences of spirituality will transcend individuals, organizations, and societies. Garcia-Zamor (2003) suggests that people can enhance work freedom when they pursue spirituality in the workplace. Organizations can link spirituality and ethics, which mirrors an organizational culture to improve productivity (Garcia-Zamor, 2003). There are two levels for analyzing workplace spirituality: spiritual awakening of individuals and organizational spirituality (Garcia-Zamor, 2003). This is helpful for the design of organizations who want to implement spirituality in the workplace culture. Practices that help individual awakening are mindfulness, yoga, lifelong learning, professional development, coaching, mentoring, experiential learning, etc.

Other research studies show a positive correlation between workplace spirituality and outcomes such as job involvement (Milliman, Czaplewski, & Ferguson, 2003; Van der Walt & Swanepoel, 2015), job satisfaction (Van der Walt & De Klerk, 2014), commitment to the organization (Rego & Cunha, 2008), and employee performance and effectiveness (Karakas, 2010). Spiritual leadership was studied in various environments and the outcomes were positive (Latham, 2013; Sweeney & Fry, 2012). Spiritual leaders advocate for employee needs as being vital to the success of the individual and the company. This creates authentic work environments where people experience a community, purpose, appreciation, and integration of spirituality with business (Sweeney & Fry, 2012). Modern leadership requires a holistic perspective that can integrate financial and non-economic factors (Latham, 2013). Spiritual leadership leads to personal fulfillment and development, and an ultimate competitive advantage in the marketplace (Matthews, 2010; Rozuel & Kakabadse, 2010; Fry, 2003).

Individual benefits of spirituality in the workplace include creativity, enhanced sense of personal fulfillment, greater work success, authenticity, increased joy, and satisfaction (Burack, 1999; Driver, 2005; Freshman, 1999; Giacalone & Jurkiewicz, 2003a; Krishnakumar & Neck, 2002; Tischler, 1999). Marques (2006) suggests that spirituality leads to feelings of connectedness with colleagues, which enhances mutuality and reciprocity. Spiritual employees will increase trust and intrinsic motivation, which can increase team and organizational performance. Spirituality in the workplace is used to create greater awareness, mindfulness, and trusted workplace environments.

Milliman et al. (2003) provide empirical evidence of this by exploring a positive association between employee job outcomes and workplace spirituality. This study found a positive relationship between spirituality at work and organizational commitment. Markow and Klenke (2005) demonstrate relationships between personal meaning, calling, and organizational commitment in the context of spiritual leadership. "There is a relationship between the spiritual climate of a work unit and its overall performance" (Duchon & Plowman, 2005, p. 822). The implications for this are real opportunities for faith-based institutions who are already primed and ready for integrating the work of faith and purpose into every work life. And this means that organizations who open their doors for spirituality will see improvements in the performance of all constituents.

Meaningful work allows employees to see meaning in their lives through their work (Gupta, 2017). This can ignite the personal spirit and engage the soul of each person. The benefits of this are countless. What makes work "feel" meaningful to employees? When they understand the mission and can align personal values with that of the institution? When an organization is not clear on the cultural values, chaos ensues. An organization that does not provide a cause to fight for will eventually see the fighting turn inwards (peer to peer and departmental competition). Any time the members of one team are fighting amongst themselves, there is ground to be lost in the greater arena of organizational transformation.

Employees that work holistically are aligned with the organizational goals. A culture is then established that is grounded in collaboration instead of competition. This is the recipe for increased job performance and can result in more profitability for the company (Neck, 2002). There is less stress and tension in these environments, which leads to fewer consequences in bodily ailments that are stress-related (Gupta, 2017). It also leads to increased levels of happiness and creativity. Creativity flows from a relaxed state of psychological safety and sense of belonging.

When work is meaningful, it can become a source of healing and employees will want to work despite slight discomforts when no further injury to their body and mind at work will occur (Marques, Dhiman, & King, 2007). This creates a safe context for employees to thrive, regardless of what home life might be. Employees that feel a sense of purpose in life through their work will go above and beyond the call of duty in order to help the organization fulfill its mission and goals (Gupta, 2017). They will find reasons to convert failures into successes on behalf of the organization (Pawar, 2009). The job of mindfulness and workplace spirituality is to bring culture-shaping to the conscious level in a way that truly develops people and quenches their thirst for lifelong growth.

An increase in workplace spirituality leads to extrinsic job satisfaction and reward satisfaction also increases (Kolodinsky, Giacalone, & Jurkiewicz, 2008). When people align their personal values with the organizational values, they have a sense of purpose at work. They find themselves happier and satisfied in life. They are able to enjoy the present moment and practice mindfulness in interactions they have with each other. They feel that they have a network of mentors and colleagues that value their individual voice(s). These are just a few examples of how workplace spirituality can start to shape a corporate culture through mindful leadership.

Conclusion

Mindful leaders are needed now more than ever. Access to technology has led to more distractions than ever before, despite the opportunities that tech affords. More CEOs have been forced out of their positions for ethical lapses than ever before, requiring solutions that bring virtue and mindfulness to the forefront (PricewaterhouseCoopers, 2018). Mindful leaders who value people over profits are needed in this modern context. As mentioned, mindfulness is a means for keeping leaders accountable and followers pursuing a life of meaning, virtue, and happiness. Therefore, this chapter will conclude with a new conceptual model for creating organizations that thrive due to their commitment to mindfulness and meaning.

Building a conceptual model

The authors of this chapter have taken the results from the literature review and have created a conceptual model for the role of mindfulness in leadership, followership, and organizations. Returning to Bailey and Madden's (2016) conceptualization of an "ecosystem of meaningfulness," we introduce a better juxtaposition to further build upon this model as the inter-changeability of the following:

mindful leadership ← → spiritual leadership ← → mindflow integration ← → inclusive leadership

The elements of a meaningfulness ecosystem has at its core what these two scholars call "holistic meaningfulness." Perhaps the pursuit of the holy grail of meaningfulness theory is not just a single focus. It is best conceptualized as various compartments within a holistic ecosystem, each bringing something unique to a learning organization seeking to integrate meaningfulness into their structure with mindful leaders. Bailey and Madden (2016) constructed a model around this holistic core with other essential elements of meaningfulness: organizational meaningfulness, job meaningfulness, task meaningfulness, and interactional meaningfulness (see Figure 32.1).

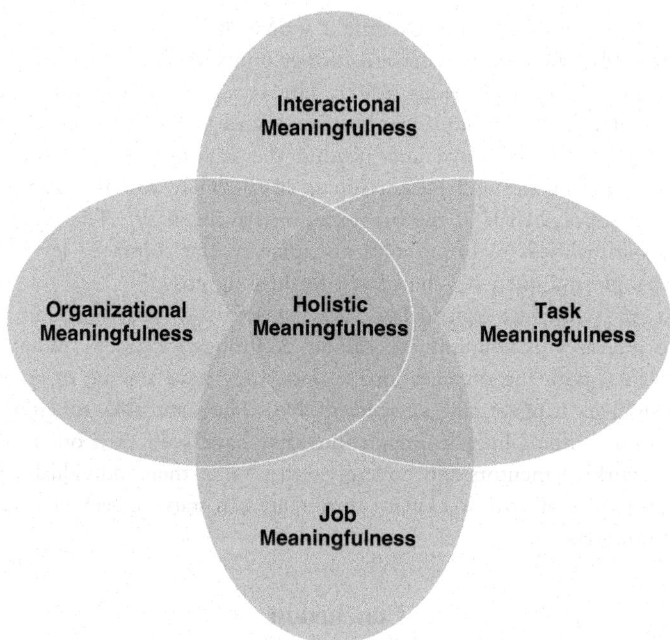

Figure 32.1 Elements of a meaningfulness ecosystem (Bailey & Madden, 2016)

The authors have slightly adjusted this model by condensing three of the compartments (task, job, and interactional) into organizational meaningfulness and add three additional compartments: spiritual meaningfulness, inclusive meaningfulness, and mindflow meaningfulness (see Figure 32.2).

For the sake of unpacking each of these compartments, we advance the following for dissection. *Holistic meaningfulness* situates mindful leaders at the center of this advanced ecosystem. Gethin (1998), in his seminal work on the *Foundations of Buddhism*, reminds us that the Buddha advised his followers to be mindful and follow their own deontological moral compass. The Buddha said: "do good, refrain from evil, purify the mind" (Fronsdal, 2005). By doing good, mindful leaders set the internal mechanisms of both the organization and the individual employee towards purity, awareness, and *Dhamma*.

Organizational meaningfulness places organizational mission and vision as critical to success. Meaningful organizations encompass purpose and uniqueness. They bring a philosophy of concern for their employees, the general public, and growth as well as survival. Regarding "task," Grant (2007) discusses how certain organizational tasks constitute greater sources of meaningfulness than others. One of Bailey and Madden's (2016) research interviewees stated: "I'm pretty good with tedious work, as long as it's got a larger meaning" (p. 59). In terms of "job meaningfulness," various studies have shown a direct correlation between greater worker productivity (and flow) if their employment status permits challenging growth (Chalofsky, 2003; Wrzesnieski & Dutton, 2001; Wrzesnieski, Dutton, & Debebe, 2003). These intentionally lead to "interactional meaningfulness," where leaders and managers must ethically ignite the intrapsychic consciousness of their workers (followers), connecting them to the external environment and bridging the personal/work divide.

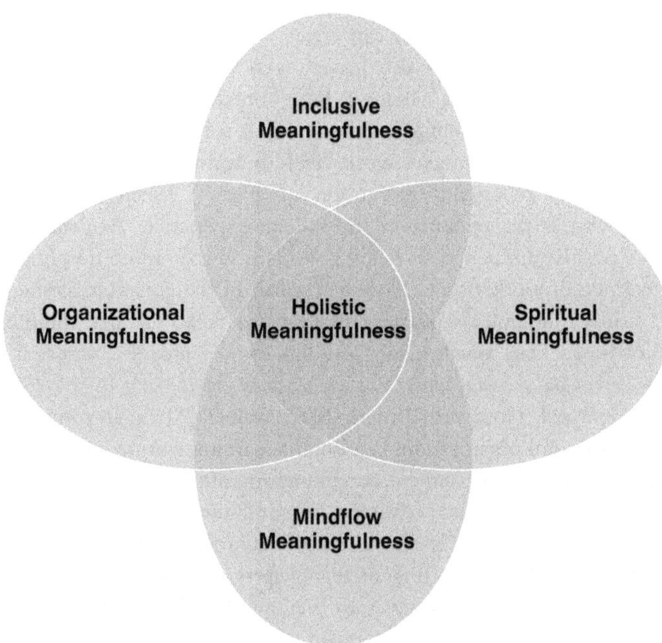

Figure 32.2 Mindful meaningfulness ecosystem (adapted from Bailey & Madden, 2016)

Inclusive meaningfulness is based on the seminal work of Edwin Hollander's (2009) "inclusive leadership theory," where the *inclusion* and *belonging* of all diverse constituencies in an organization brings about more holistic integration and meaningfulness. This requires engaged humility on the part of leaders. A humble leader accepts their own strengths (and weaknesses) and, in turn, empowers others to develop their own unique strengths. Humble leaders understand the value of promoting inclusiveness by suspending judgments and allowing the free flow of ideas from employees. The more an employee feels that their uniqueness is valued, the more a sense of meaningfulness will occur. The prime job of the inclusive leader is to prevent the decay of the human spirit into meaninglessness. According to Hollander (1958), leaders receive "idiosyncrasy credits" from followers when they bond over a shared vision. This gives the leader credibility when trying to experiment and innovate new ideas. However, if the leader is not creating these bonds over a shared purpose, the credibility of the leader will be diminished. Hollander re-emphasized the role of "followership" as he focused on the leader–follower relationship as a two-way influence process. Inclusive leadership seeks to create results, which is the true essence of *belonging* and *meaningfulness* (Hollander, 2009). His model does not rely on one person's leadership capabilities in decision-making and achieving goals, but relies on the group to make decisions together. It promotes an environment that allows for input to come from everyone. It also respects competition and cooperation as part of a participative process (Hollander, 2009). The word is "hungry" for inclusive leaders who design organizations where every member can thrive and experience inclusive meaningfulness.

Spiritual mindfulness or spirituality in the workplace, according to the preponderance of literature cited earlier in this study, produces greater job satisfaction and retention, higher degrees of employee performance and effectiveness, and an increase in trust and honesty within the organization. Spiritual leaders can create a vital authentic workplace for spiritual meaningfulness. Spiritual mindfulness also leaves open a more profound elevation of self-actualization and transcendence (a lá Maslow). Re-contextualizing human motivational need also fulfills a "higher vocational calling" as the research study later in this chapter validates. Spirituality might be the key that makes work "feel" meaningful.

Mindflow meaningfulness represents the notion of "flow," which has been described by Csikszentmihalyi (1996) as the epitome of the human experience. As detailed earlier in this chapter, flow has a positive influence on helping workers engage more deeply in creativity and play in lifestyle balance of work/home. Flow is just half of the equation, as suggested by Ron Cacioppe (2017), since mindfulness is a precondition for flow, but that mindfulness can also occur in a state of flow. Thus *mindfulness-in-flow* hits some "integral absorption point" where they conjoin into *mindflow meaningfulness*, which actually dates back to the 1930s mind flow process taught by George I. Gurdjieff (Brown, 2002; Wilber, 2016). In some form or fashion, all this leads to how mindful organizations can build a learning culture set forth by leaders who adopt a conducive workplace environment combining mindfulness, meditation, and flow.

This new conceptual model for creating a mindful meaningfulness ecosystem (adapted from Bailey & Madden, 2016) builds on the traditional and popular versions of mindfulness that were mentioned in the introduction of this chapter. This model creates a roadmap for leaders who want to integrate mindfulness into their work rather than continue to sleepwalk their way through leadership. Mindful leaders are more capable of creating a meaningfulness ecosystem that will generate positive experiences that reverberate throughout the organization. This mindfulness companion summarizes the role of mindfulness in leadership, followership, and organizations. For leaders, mindfulness involves the art of paying attention in the present moment without judgment or criticism. For followers, mindfulness teaches one to be more accepting and less concerned about the future. Organizations will become calmer, creative, and more focused through the art of mindfulness. As evidenced throughout this chapter, mindfulness can produce meaningful experiences, greater productivity, and healthier forms of work–life integration. Mindfulness can also improve job satisfaction, rational thinking, emotional resilience, stress management, and long-term mental and physical health. The benefits and opportunities for mindful leaders are increasing, therefore research in this field needs to expand to better prepare leaders who want to thrive for the modern age.

Chapter takeaways

1. Mindfulness is not just a religious practice. "Mindfulness is simply a practical way to be more in touch with the fullness of your being through a systematic process of self-observation, self-inquiry and mindful action" (Kabat-Zinn, 1991, p. 13).
2. Research studies demonstrate that mindfulness can improve employee health, lower healthcare costs, increase productivity, improve stress management, build relationships, increase empathy, reduce depression, anxiety and substance abuse, and assist with pain management.
3. Mindfulness helps employees to be more accepting of their work situations; have more modest, realistic work goals; be more selfless; be less concerned with material acquisition and wealth; have a more internal locus of evaluation; be more likely to derive meaning in life from more sources than just work; be better able to cope and remain calm in difficult work situations; be more likely to experience work difficulties as

challenges than threats; enjoy their work more; be more adaptable at work; and have more positive interpersonal relations at work (Hunter & McCormick, 2008).

4. Mindful leaders can create intentional environments for followers to thrive, based on psychological safety and inclusion.
5. A meaningful mindfulness ecosystem supplies a roadmap that can help leaders lay a foundation for mindfulness in the workplace.

Reflection questions

1. You spend a lot of time at your workspace and your home. What are ways that you can be more mindful with the space that you create? What furniture/décor inspires you and helps you to be more productive and at peace?
2. How can you be more mindful in the way that you treat your body? Can you be more mindful of the way your body feels when you ingest different foods/drinks? How do you feel when you engage in physical activity?
3. How can you be more mindful in your relationships at work and in your community? Can you be more selective with people you spend time with by engaging more frequently with people who inspire you and challenge you, and less time with people who drain your energy and leave you feeling exhausted?
4. Do you have a daily spiritual practice of quieting the mind and finding rest?
5. Can you be more mindful in how you spend money, making sure that each purchase is aligned with your values? Focus on supporting causes, organizations, and people that you feel are making an impact in the world for good.

References

Anderson & Jiang. (2018). Teens, social media & technology. *Pew Research Center*, May 31, 2018.

Bailey, C. & Madden, A. (Summer 2016). What makes work meaningful—Or meaningless. *MIT Sloan Management Review*, *57*(4), 53–61 (Cambridge).

Benefiel, M. (2003). Irreconcilable foes? The discourse of spirituality and the discourse of organizational science. *Organization*, *10*(2), 383–391.

Bhunia, A. & Mukhuti, S. (2011). Workplace spirituality on motivations for earnings management. An empirical analysis. *Business Management Dynamics*, *1*(4), 73–78.

Biberman, J. & Whitty, M. (1997). A postmodern spiritual future for work. *Journal of Organizational Change Management*, *10*(2), 130–138.

Bishop, S. R., Lau, M., Shapiro, S., Carlson, L., Anderson, N. D., Carmody, J., & Devins, G. (2004). Mindfulness: A proposed operational definition. *Clinical Psychology: Science and Practice*, *11*(3), 230–241.

Bodhi, B. (1994). Dhamma and non-duality. *Buddhist Publication Society Newsletter*. Retrieved from http://enlight.lib.ntu.edu.tw/FULLTEXT/JR-AN/an140804.pdf.

Bowen, S., Chawla, N., Collins, S. E., Witkiewitz, K., Hsu, S., Grow, J., & Marlatt, A. (2009). Mindfulness-based relapse prevention for substance use disorders: A pilot efficacy trial. *Substance Abuse*, *30*, 295305. http://dx.doi.org/10.1080/08897070903250084

Boyatzis, R. & McKee, A. (2005). *Resonant leadership: Renewing yourself and connecting with others through mindfulness, hope, and compassion*. Boston, MA: Harvard Business Press.

Brown, C. (2002). *How to start a Gurdjieff Group and other essays about the practical Christianity of G.I. Gurdjieff*. Lincoln, NE: Writers Clube Press, iUniverse, Inc..

Brown, F. & Ryan, R. (2003). The benefits of being present: Mindfulness and its role in psychological well-being. *Journal of Personality and Social Psychology*, *84*(4), 822–830. http://dx.doi.org/10.1037/0022-3514.84.4.822

Brown, J. & Langer, E. (1990). Mindfulness and intelligence: A comparison. *Educational Psychologist*, *25* (3–4), 305–335.

Brown, R. B. (2003). Organizational spirituality: The sceptics version. *Organization, 12*(2), 393–400.
Burack, E. (1999). Spirituality in the workplace. *Journal of Organizational Change Management, 12*(4), 280–292. https://doi.org/10.1108/09534819910282126
Cacioppe, R. (2017). Integral mindflow. *The Learning Organization, 24*(6), 408–417.
Cañas, J. J., Quesada, J. F., Antolí, A., & Fajardo, I. (2003). Cognitive flexibility and adaptability to environmental changes in dynamic complex problem-solving tasks. *Ergonomics, 46*(5), 482–501.
Carleton, E. L., Barling, J., & Trivisonno, M. (2018). Leaders' trait mindfulness and transformational leadership: The mediating roles of leaders' positive affect and leadership self-efficacy. *Canadian Journal of Behavioural Science/Revue canadienne des sciences du comportement, 50*(3), 185.
Carroll, M. (2004). *Awake at work: Facing the challenges of life on the job.* Berkeley, CA: Shambhala Publications.
Carroll, M. (2007). *The mindful leader: Ten principles for bringing out the best in ourselves and others.* Berkeley, CA: Shambhala Publications.
Carson, S. H. & Langer, E. J. (2006). Mindfulness and self-acceptance. *Journal of Rational- Emotive and Cognitive-behavior Therapy, 24*(1), 29–43.
Cartwright, S. & Holmes, N. (2006). The meaning of work. The challenge of regaining employee engagement and reducing cynicism. *Human Resource Management Review, 16*(2), 199–208.
Chalofsky, N. (2003). An emerging construct for meaningful work. *Human Resource Development International, 6*(1), 69–83.
Chiesa, A. & Serretti, A. (2011). Mindfulness based cognitive therapy for psychiatric disorders: A systematic review and meta-analysis. *Psychiatry Research, 187*, 441–453. http://dx.doi.org/10.1016/j.psychres.2010.08.011
Coholic, D. A. (2011). Exploring the feasibility and benefits of arts-based mindfulness-based practices with young people in need: Aiming to improve aspects of self-awareness and resilience. In *Child & Youth Care Forum* (Vol. 40, No. 4, pp. 303-317). Springer US.
Csikszentmihalyi, M. (1996). *Creativity: Flow and the psychology of discovery and invention.* New York, NY: HarperCollins.
Dane, E. (2011). Paying attention to mindfulness and its effects on task performance in the workplace. *Journal of Management, 37*(4), 670–685.
Dane, E. & Brummel, B. (2013). Examining workplace mindfulness and its relations to job performance and turnover intention. *Human Relations, 67*(1), 105–128.
Davidson, R., Kabat-Zinn, J., Schumacher, J., Rosenkranz, M., Muller, D., Santorelli, S., … Sheridan, J. (2003). Alterations in brain and immune function produced by mindfulness meditation. *Psychosomatic Medicine, 65*(4), 564–570.
Delbecq, L. A. (1999). Christian spirituality and contemporary business leadership. *Journal of Organizational Business Management, 12*(4), 345–349.
Delizonna, L. (2017). High-performing teams need psychological safety. Here's how to create it. *Harvard Business Review, 24.* https://hbr.org/2017/08/high-performing-teams-need-psychological-safety-heres-how-to-create-it.
Dhiman, S. (2012). Mindfulness and the art of living creatively: Cultivating a creative life by minding our mind. *Journal of Social Change, 4*(1), 1.
Driver, M. (2005). From empty speech to full speech? Reconceptualizing spirituality in organizations based on a psychoanalytically grounded understanding of the self. *Human Relations, 58*(9), 1091–1110. https://doi.org/10.1177/0018726705059038
Duchon, D. & Plowman, D. A. (2005). Nurturing the spirit at work: Impact on work unit performance. *The Leadership Quarterly, 16*(5), 807–833.
Dunne, J. (2011). Toward an understanding of non-dual mindfulness. *Contemporary Buddhism, 12*, 71–88.
Ehde, D. M., Dillworth, T. M., & Turner, J. A. (2014). Cognitive behavioral therapy for individuals with chronic pain: Efficacy, innovations, and directions for research. *American Psychologist, 69*, 153–166. http://dx.doi.org/10.1037/a0035747
Ehrlich, J. (2015). Creating mindful leaders and organizations. *People + Strategy, 38*(3), 22–25.
Eisler, R. & Montouori, A. (2003). The human side of spirituality. In R. A. Giacalone & C. L. Jurkiewicz (Eds.), *Handbook of workplace spirituality and organizational performance* (pp. 46–56). Armonk, NY: M. E. Sharpe.
Freshman, B. (1999). An exploratory analysis of definitions and applications of spirituality in the workplace. *Journal of Organizational Change Management, 12*(4), 318–329. https://doi.org/10.1108/09534819910282153

Fox Lee, S. (2019). Psychology's own mindfulness: Ellen Langer and the social politics of scientific interest in "active noticing". *Journal of the History of the Behavioral Sciences*. 02 Jun 2019, 55(3), 216–229. doi: 10.1002/jhbs.21975

Frankl, V. (2014). *The will to meaning: Foundations and applications of logotherapy*. Penguin Publishing Group. Retrieved from https://books.google.com/books?id=fMxbBAAAQBAJ

Fronsdal, G. (2005). *The Dhammapada: A new translation of the Buddhist classic with annotations*. Boston: Shambhala.

Fry, L. W. (2003). Towards a theory of spiritual leadership. *The Leadership Quarterly*, *14*(6), 693–727.

Garcia-Zamor, J. C. (2003). Workplace spirituality and organizational performance. *Public Administration Review*, *63*(3), 355–363.

Gethin, R. (1998). *The foundations of Buddhism*. Oxford, England: Oxford University Press.

Giacalone, R. A. & Jurkiewicz, C. L. (2003a). Toward a science of workplace spirituality. In R. A. Giacalone & C. L. Jurkiewicz (Eds.), *Handbook of workplace spirituality and organizational performance* (pp. 3–28). Armonk, NY: M. E. Sharpe.

Giluk, T. (2009). Mindfulness, big five personality, and affect: A meta-analysis. *Personality and Individual Differences*, *47*(8), 805–811.

Goldstein, J. (2013). *Mindfulness: A practical guide to awakening*. Louisville, CO: Sounds True.

Goleman, D. (1998). *Working with emotional intelligence*. New York, NY: Bantam Books.

Gotsis, G. & Kortezi, Z. (2008). Philosophical foundations of workplace spirituality: A critical approach. *Journal of Business Ethics*, *78*(4), 575–600.

Grant, A. (2007). Relational job design and the motivation to make a prosocial difference. *Academy of Management Review*, *32*(2), 393–417.

Gunaratana, H. (2002). *Mindfulness in plain English* (Rev. ed.). Boston, MA: Wisdom.

Gupta, A. A. K. (2017). Workplace spirituality-A new paradigm in management. *Ushus-Journal of Business Management*, *16*(2), 45–52.

Harris, D. (2014a). *10% happier: How I tamed the voice in my head, reduced stress without losing my edge and found self-help that actually works-a true story*. London: Hachette, UK.

Harris, S. (2014b). *Waking up: A guide to spirituality without religion*. New York: Simon and Schuster.

Heaton, D. P., Schmidt-Wilk, J., & Travis, F. (2004). Constructs, methods and measures for researching spirituality in organizations. *Journal of Organizational Change Management*, *17*(1), 62–82.

Hill, L. A., Brandeau, G., Truelove, E., & Lineback, K. (2014). Collective genius. *Harvard Business Review*, *92*(6), 94–102.

Hollander, E. (1958). Conformity, status and idiosyncrasy credit. *Psychological Review*, *65*(2), 117–127.

Hollander, E. (2009). *Inclusive leadership: The essential leader-follower relationship*. New York, NY: Routledge.

Hülscheger, U., Alberts, H., Feinholdt, A., & Lang, J. (2013). Benefits of mindfulness at work: The role of mindfulness in emotion regulation, emotion exhaustion, and job satisfaction. *Journal of Applied Psychology*, *98*(2), 310–327.

Hunter, J. & McCormick, D. W. (2008). Mindfulness in the workplace: An exploratory study. In *SE Newell (Facilitator), Weickian Ideas. Symposium conducted at the annual meeting of the Academy of Management*, Anaheim, CA.

Kabat-Zinn, J. (1991). *Full catastrophe living: Using wisdom of your body and mind to face stress, pain and illness*. New York, NY: Delta Trade Paperbacks.

Kachan, D., Olano, H., Tannenbaum, S. L., Annane, D. W., Mehta, A., Arheart, K. L., & Lee, D. J. (2017). Peer reviewed: prevalence of mindfulness practices in the US workforce: National health interview survey. *Preventing Chronic Disease*, 2017 Jan, *14*, E01. doi: 10.5888/pcd14.160034.

Karakas, F. (2010). Spirituality and performance in organizations: A literature review. *Journal of Business Ethics*, *94*(1), 89–106. https://doi.org/10.1007/s10551-009-0251-5

King, J. E. & Crowther, M. R. (2004). The measurement of religiosity and spirituality examples and issues from psychology. *Journal of Organizational Change Management*, *17*(1), 83–101.

Kinjierski, V. M. & Skrypnek, B. J. (2004). Defining spirit at work. *Finding Common Ground, Journal of Organizational Change Management*, *17*(3), 165–182.

Kolodinsky, R. W., Giacalone, R. A., & Jurkiewicz, C. L. (2008). Workplace values and outcomes: Exploring personal, organizational, and interactive workplace spirituality. *Journal of Business Ethics*, *81* (2), 465–480. https://doi.org/10.1007/s10551-007-9507-0

Kornfield, J. (2001). *After the ecstasy, the laundry: How the heart grows wise on the spiritual path*. New York: Bantam.

Krishnakumar, S. & Neck, C. P. (2002). The what, why, and how of spirituality in the workplace. *Journal of Managerial Psychology, 17*(3), 153–164.

Langer, E. (1989). *Mindfulness*. New York, NY: Addison-Wesley.

Langer, E. (2005). *On becoming an artist: Reinventing yourself through mindful creativity*. New York, NY: Ballantine Books.

Langer, E. (2010). A call for mindful leadership. *Harvard Business Review, 28*. Retrieved from https://hbr.org/2010/04/leaders-time-to-wake-up

Langer, E. J. (2014). Mindfulness forward and back. *The Wiley Blackwell Handbook of Mindfulness, 1*, 7–20.

Latham, J. R. (2013). A framework for leading the transformation to performance excellence, part I: CEO perspectives on forces, facilitators, and strategic leadership systems. *The Quality Management Journal, 20*(2), 12–33. https://doi.org/10.1080/10686967.2013.11918095

Leigh, P. (1997). The new spirit at work. *Training & Development, 51*(3), 26–41.

Lopez, D. S., Jr. (2012). *The scientific Buddha: His short and happy life*. New Haven, CT: Yale University Press.

Lutz, A., Dunne, J. D., & Davidson, R. J. (2007). Meditation and the neuroscience of consciousness: An introduction. In P. D. Zelazo, M. Moscovitch, & E. Thompson (Eds.), *The Cambridge handbook of consciousness* (pp. 497–549). New York, NY: Cambridge University Press.

Markow, F. & Klenke, K. (2005). The effects of personal meaning and calling on organisational commitment: An empirical investigation of spiritual leadership. *International Journal of Organisational Analysis, 13*(1), 8–27.

Marques, J. F. (2006). The spiritual worker: An examination of the ripple effect that enhances quality of life in and outside the work environment. *Journal of Management Development, 25*(9), 884–895. http://dx.doi.org/10.1108/02621710610692089.

Marques, J., Dhiman, D. S., & King, D. R. (2007). *Spirituality in the workplace*. USA: Personhood Press.

Maslow, A. H. (1943). A theory of human motivation. *Psychological Review, 50*(4), 370–396. https://doi.org/10.1037/h0054346

Maslow, A. (1972). *The farther reaches of human nature*. New York, NY: Viking Press.

Matthews, D. (2010). Trust me: Credible leadership delivers results. *Chief Learning Officer: Solutions for Enterprise Productivity*. Retrieved from http://www.clomedia.com

Miller, F. A. (1994). Forks in the road: Critical issues on the path to diversity. In E.Y. Cross, J.H. Katz, F. A. Miller, & E. W. Seashore (Eds.), *The promise of diversity: Over 40 voices discuss strategies for eliminating discrimination in organizations* (pp. 38–45). Burr Ridge, IL: Irwin.

Milliman, J., Czaplewski, A. J., & Ferguson, J. (2003). Workplace spirituality and employee work attitudes: An exploratory empirical assessment. *Journal of Organizational Change Management, 16*(4), 426–447.

Moore, A. & Malinowski, P. (2009). Meditation, mindfulness and cognitive flexibility. *Consciousness and Cognition, 18*(1), 176–186.

Neck, C. P. (2002). The "what", "why" and "how" of spirituality in the workplace. *Journal of Managerial Psychology, 17*(3), 153–164.

Nhat Hanh, T. (1975). *The miracle of mindfulness*. Boston: Boston Beacon.

Nyanaponika, T. (1962). *The heart of Buddhist meditation: A handbook of mental training based on Buddha's way of mindfulness*. London: Ryder.

Passmore, J. (2019). Mindfulness in organizations (part 1): A critical literature review". *Industrial and Commercial Training, 51*(2), 104–113.

Pauchant, T. (2002). *Ethics and spirituality at work: Hopes and pitfalls of the search for meaning in organizations*. Westport, CT: Quorum Books.

Pawar, B. S. (2009). Some of the recent organizational behavior concepts as precursor to workplace spirituality. *Journal of Business Ethics, 88*(2), 245–261.

Pratt, M. & Ashforth, B. (2003). Fostering meaningfulness in working and work. In K. Cameron, J. Dutton, & R. Quinn (Eds.), *Positive organizational scholarship* (pp. 309–327). San Francisco, CA: Berrett-Koehler.

PricewaterhouseCoopers. (2018). CEO success story: PricewaterhouseCoopers 20th CEO Survey Strategy and part of the PWC network. Retrieved from: www.strategyand.pwc.com/ceosuccess.

Purser, R. E. & Milillo, J. (2015). Mindfulness revisited: A Buddhist-based conceptualization. *Journal of Management Inquiry, 24*(1), 3–24.

Reb, Jochen & Choi, Ellen. Chapter 13 Mindfulness in organizations. (2014). *The psychology of meditation* (pp. 1–31). Research Collection Lee Kong Chian School Of Business. Available at: https://ink.library.smu.edu.sg/lkcsb_research/4719

Rego, A. & Cunha, M.P. (2008). Workplace spirituality and organizational commitment: An empirical study. *Journal of Organizational Change Management, 21*(1), 53–75. https://doi.org/10.1108/09534810810847039

Rozovsky, J. (2015). The five keys to a successful Google team. Retrieved from https://rework.withgoogle.com/blog/five-keys-to-a-successful-google-team/

Rozuel, C. & Kakabadse, N. (2010). Ethics, spirituality and self: Managerial perspective and leadership implications. *Business Ethics: A European Review, 19*(4), 423–436. doi: 10.1111/j.1467-8608.2010.01603.x

Rupčić, N. (2017). Spiritual development–a missing and powerful leverage when building learning organizations. *The Learning Organization, 24*(6), 418–426.

Sass, J. S. (2000). Characterizing organizational spirituality: An organizational communication culture approach. *Communication Studies, 51*(3), 195–207.

Schaufenbuel, K. (2014). Bringing mindfulness into the workplace. UNC Kenan-Flagler School of Business, white paper.

Sheep, M. L. (2006). Nurturing the whole person: The ethics of workplace spirituality in a society of organizations. *Journal of Business Ethics, 66*(4), 357–369.

Sweeney, P. J. & Fry, L. W. (2012). Character development through spiritual leadership. *Consulting Psychology Journal: Practice and Research, 64*(2), 89–107. 10.1037/a0028966

Tischler, L. (1999). The growing interest in spirituality in business: A long term socio-economic explanation. *Journal of Organizational Change Management, 12*(4), 273–279. https://doi.org/10.1108/09534819910282117

Tolle, E. (2004). *The power of now: A guide to spiritual enlightenment.* Novato, CA: New World Library.

Van der Walt, F. & De Klerk, J. J. (2014). Workplace spirituality and job satisfaction. *International Review of Psychiatry, 26*(3), 379–389.

Van der Walt, F. & Swanepoel, H. (2015). The relationship between workplace spirituality and job involvement: A South African study. *African Journal of Business and Economic Research, 10*(1), 95–116. https://hdl.handle.net

Wagner-Marsh, F. & Conely, J. (1999). The fourth wave: The spiritually based firm. *Journal of Organizational Change Management, 12*(4), 292–301.

Whetten, D. A. & Cameron, K. S. (2007). *Developing management skills* (7th ed.). Upper Saddle River, NJ: Prentice Hall.

Widdicombe, L. (2015). The higher life. *The New Yorker.* Retrieved from https://www.newyorker.com/magazine/2015/07/06/the-higher-life

Wiese, C. & Ricci, R. (2010). 10 characteristics of high-performing teams. Retrieved from: www.huffingtonpost.com/carl-wiese/10-characteristics-of-hig_b_1536155.html#

Wilber, K. (2016). *Integral meditation, mindfulness as a path to grow up, wake up, and show up in your life.* Boulder, CO: Shambala.

Williams, M. & Pennman, D. (2013). *Mindfulness: A practical guide to finding peace in a frantic world.* Great Britain: Piakus.

Wrzesnieski, A. & Dutton, J. (2001). Crafting a job: Revisioning employees as active crafters of their work. *Academy of Management Review, 26*(2), 179–201.

Wrzesnieski, A., Dutton, J., & Debebe, G. (2003). Interpersonal sensemaking and the meaning of work. *Research in Organizational Behavior, 25*, 93–135.

33

THE ROLE OF MINDFULNESS IN CLOSING THE INTENTION–BEHAVIOR GAP IN EMPLOYEE PRO-ENVIRONMENTAL BEHAVIOR

Julia Hufnagel and Katharina Spraul

Employee pro-environmental behaviors may make a significant contribution to organizational environmental performance by playing a vital role in the greening process of organizations (Boiral, Talbot, & Paillé, 2015; Temminck, Mearns, & Fruhen, 2015; Unsworth, Dmitrieva, & Adriasola, 2013). On the one hand, employees engage in specific actions to protect the environment (e.g., avoid waste, save energy, use resources efficiently) and thereby reduce the negative environmental impact of the whole organization (Norton, Zacher, Parker, & Ashkanasy, 2017; Ones, Wiernik, Dilchert, & Klein, 2018). On the other hand, employees' individual initiative for the environment can serve as the critical spark for sustainability-oriented innovation: new products, services, processes, or business models that create social and environmental value in addition to economic returns (Adams, Jeanrenaud, Bessant, Denyer, & Overy, 2016; Helling, 2015; Wagner & Llerena, 2011; Weng, Chen, & Chen, 2015).

In recent years, research on employee pro-environmental behaviors has been growing, especially in the field of organizational behavior and sustainability management (e.g., Bissing-Olson, Iyer, Fielding, & Zacher, 2013; Ciocirlan, 2016; Kim, Kim, Han, Jackson, & Ployhart, 2013; Manika, Wells, Gregory-Smith, & Gentry, 2015), mainly in order to answer the call for research on the micro-foundations of business sustainability (Aguinis & Glavas, 2012; Strauss, Lepoutre, & Wood, 2017).

According to the theory of planned behavior (Ajzen, 1985, 1991), the theory of reasoned action (Fishbein, 1980; Madden, Scholder Ellen, & Ajzen, 1992), and the model of interpersonal behavior (Triandis, 1977), the intention toward the behavior is the main antecedent of an individual's behavior. However, the intention to do something does not necessarily explain the respective actual behavior. Meta-analyses have revealed that intentions account for a weighted average of only about 30% of the variance in social behavior (Armitage & Conner, 2001; Sheeran, 2002), and that a medium-to-large change in intention leads to a small-to-medium change in behavior (Webb & Sheeran, 2006).

As Chatzisarantis and Hagger (2007) show in their study on binge-drinking and physical exercise, mindfulness can generally serve as a moderator of the intention–behavior relationship, meaning that greater awareness of and attention to present experiences can alleviate the translation of intentions into behavior. Additionally, mindfulness is associated with empathy and compassion (Kernochan, McCormick, & White, 2007), ethical living, a consideration of future consequences and a reduction of hedonism, which are all aspects that lead to more environmental-friendly actions (Brown, Ryan, & Creswell, 2007; Ericson, Kjønstad, & Barstad, 2014).

In our quantitative study, we want to investigate whether mindfulness affects the enactment of employees' environmental workplace behavioral intentions. The following sections explain employee pro-environmental behaviors, the concept of mindfulness, its effects on employees, and green behavior in more detail. We also provide specific justifications based on which theories mindfulness can be seen as a moderator for the gap between intention and behavior. This way, we substantiate our hypothesis.

Theoretical background and hypothesis development

Employee pro-environmental behavior (EPEB)

In general, employee pro-environmental behaviors cover the five different categories of conserving, avoiding harm, influencing others, taking initiative, and transforming (see Table 33.1 for an overview of different behaviors in each category) and can be defined as "scalable actions and behaviors that employees engage in that are linked with and contribute to [...] environmental sustainability" (adapted from Ones & Dilchert, 2012, p. 87). Ones et al. (2018) highlight some important features of this definition. First, it focuses explicitly on individuals, who highly differ in their environmental behavior and lay the ground for bigger units' (group, department, or organizational) environmental performance. Second, the definition focuses on actual pro-environmental behavior, not on its outcomes. Third, employee pro-environmental behaviors are scalable and measurable, which is necessary when researching them.

Employee pro-environmental behaviors differ from general pro-environmental behaviors in several ways. Generally speaking, people have more control over their behavior in non-work contexts, which makes it easier to act environmentally friendly in non-work contexts. In offices, behaviors are also influenced by the physical, social, and organizational context (Littleford, Ryley, & Firth, 2014).

Mindfulness as a concept

The concept of mindfulness has its roots in the Buddhist philosophy (Brown et al., 2007; Glomb, Duffy, Bono, & Yang, 2015) and describes "the process of paying attention to what is happening in the moment—both internal (thoughts, bodily sensations,) and external stimuli (physical and social environment)—and observing those stimuli without judgement or evaluation, and without assigning meaning to them" (Glomb et al., 2015, p. 118). "Attention" and "awareness" are at the heart of mindfulness. Put into

Table 33.1 Categories of employee pro-environmental behaviors with examples (adapted from Ones et al., 2018)

Meta-category	*Subcategories*	*Examples*
Conserving	Reducing use; Reusing; Repurposing; Recycling and composting	Printing double sided; Washing plastic lab equipment rather than discarding; Collecting rainwater for industrial use; Recycling cans, bottles, paper
Avoiding harm	Preventing pollution; Strengthening ecosystems; Monitoring environmental impact	Scrubbing emissions before release; Cleaning up litter around local area; Calculating the lifecycle carbon cost of a product
Influencing others	Leading, encouraging, and supporting; Managing, facilitating, and coordinating; Educating and training	Providing incentives for biking or using public transit commute; Making recycle bins accessible to all employees; Training employees in proper chemical handling
Taking initiative	Initiating programs and policies; Lobbying and activism; Putting environmental interests first	Creating a new sustainable purchasing policy; Forming a green team to plan sustainability programs; Advocating for environmental issues to supervisor; Not using an air conditioner on hot days
Transforming	Choosing responsible alternatives; Changing how work is done; Embracing sustainable innovations; Creating sustainable products and services	Purchasing energy-efficient equipment; Using public transit to commute; Removing toxic chemicals from a manufacturing process; Using virtual rather than in-person meetings

a simplified definition, mindfulness is the "receptive attention to and awareness of present events and experience" (Brown et al., 2007, p. 212). Some clarifications to these simple definitions may prove to be helpful. First, mindfulness is not about "not thinking." Rather, thoughts and their accompanying emotions are—just like sounds and other sensory impressions—seen as objects of attention and awareness. This stance helps to not get caught up in thoughts and emotions about past experiences or anticipated futures (Brown et al., 2007). Second, non-judgmental attention is not to be confused with "disinterested spectatorship" (Brown et al., 2007, p. 214). Rather than a passive dissociating from the observed present experience, a mindful state is an active engaging (Baer, Smith, Hopkins, Krietemeyer, & Toney, 2006). For example, while noticing a physical sensation or feeling, one feels it at the same time.

In order to measure mindfulness, two basic approaches are used in the literature: self-report questionnaires and engagement in mindfulness practices. Self-report questionnaires include state (Mindful Attention Awareness Scale (MAAS): Brown & Ryan, 2003; Toronto Mindfulness Scale: Lau et al., 2006), and trait measures (e.g., Five Facets of Mindfulness Questionnaire: Baer et al., 2006). It has been shown that mindfulness has trait-like qualities and that these can be reliably assessed with a number of self-report measures explicitly designed for untrained respondents (Baer et al., 2008; Brown & Ryan, 2003). However, researchers have also argued that mindfulness inherently is a psychological state that varies from moment to moment within individuals (Bishop, 2004; Hülsheger, Alberts, Feinholdt, & Lang, 2013).

Regardless of the classification of mindfulness as trait or state, it could be shown that people who meditate report higher values, both for trait (de Bruin, Topper, Muskens, Bögels, & Kamphuis, 2012) and for state mindfulness (MacKillop & Anderson, 2007) measures. This shows that mindfulness can be cultivated or strengthened through training, such as mindfulness meditation (Bishop, 2004; Brown & Ryan, 2003) or mindfulness-based stress reduction (Kabat-Zinn, 2003). When mindfulness practices are used as measures for mindfulness, programs (e.g., Mindfulness-Based Stress Reduction) that train in mindfulness practices (e.g., mindful eating, movement, mindfulness meditation) are used as proxies for mindfulness (Good et al., 2016).

Mindfulness has—according to a wealth of research—many positive effects on health issues (see for example Brown & Ryan, 2003; Chiesa & Serretti, 2009; Grossman, Niemann, Schmidt, & Walach, 2004; Keng, Smoski, & Robins, 2011; Shapiro, Brown, & Biegel, 2007), and despite its roots, mindfulness practices rarely have a religious connotation today and are becoming increasingly popular in Western countries (Glomb et al., 2015).

Organizations such as Google, the US Navy, Apple, McKinsey, Nike, Procter & Gamble, and many others use mindfulness training in order to improve workplace performance (Fraher, Branicki, & Grint, 2017; Jha et al., 2015; Wang & Adams, 2016; West et al., 2014; Wolever et al., 2012). Therefore, in recent years, mindfulness research activity has been growing also within organizational science (Glomb et al., 2015; Good et al., 2016; Reb, Narayanan, & Ho, 2015). Good et al. (2016) systematically review the mindfulness literature in multiple fields in order to draw a framework for business researchers. The authors conclude that—as mindfulness increases the stability, control, and efficiency of one's attention and therefore has a direct impact on cognitive performance, emotion regulation, behavior, and physiology—it draws its circles into workplace performance, workplace relationships, and workplace well-being (Good et al., 2016).

Mindfulness and pro-environmental behavior

Research on mindfulness and pro-environmental behavior is limited, but first studies do exist (Wamsler et al., 2018). Based on a literature review on mindfulness and sustainability, Wamsler et al. (2018) conclude that mindfulness can be understood as a link between the individual and global dimensions in the sustainability discussion. The authors argue that mindfulness, although so far empirically hardly associated with sustainability, can promote sustainability by impacting (1) subjective well-being; (2) the activation of (intrinsic/non-materialistic) core values; (3) consumption and sustainable behavior; (4) the human–nature connection; (5) equity issues; (6) social activism; and (7) deliberate, flexible, and adaptive responses to climate change.

Amel, Manning, and Scott (2009) claim that mindful people are more inclined to be attentive and to consciously process information about the impact of their behavior on the environment. In the area of consumer choices, mindful shoppers are more likely to gather detailed information on ingredients and effects on the environment (Amel et al., 2009). In 2011, Sheth, Sethia, and Srinivas (2011) introduced the concept of the mindful consumer whose mindful mindset reflects a conscious sense of caring toward the self, the community, and nature. Ericson et al. (2014) argue conceptually that—as mindfulness contributes to well-being by strengthening the focus on the here and now, empathy and compassion—it allows people to avoid the "hedonic" treadmill and can thus inhibit overconsumption and environmental pollution (Ericson et al., 2014).

Brown and Kasser (2005) could show empirically that state mindfulness (self-reported) supports environmental-friendly consumer choices (diet, transportation, and housing). Also, Amel et al. (2009) showed a significant correlation between "acting with awareness," a facet of trait mindfulness (self-reported), and sustainable behavior. The authors therefore postulate that until sustainable decisions become the societal default, their enactment may depend on focused reflection of options and mindful behavior. However, Amel et al.'s (2009) finding may not be that sound, as sustainable behavior was measured with a single self-assessing item, where participants rate how often they make "sustainable" choices. Only recently, Dhandra (2019) could demonstrate empirically that trait mindfulness (self-reported) positively impacts green purchase intentions, social conscious purchasing, frugal purchasing, and reduces materialism. Additionally, these four variables positively impact life satisfaction and significantly mediate the relationship between mindfulness and life satisfaction. In her model, rather than proposing life satisfaction as the mediator between mindfulness and pro-environmental consumer behaviors, she shows that it is the dependent variable and mindfulness the mediator.

Barbaro and Pickett (2016) could show that trait mindfulness (self-reported) is significantly associated with pro-environmental behavior. The authors were also able to reveal that connectedness to nature (Howell, Dopko, Passmore, & Buro, 2011) indirectly affects the relationship between mindfulness and pro-environmental behavior, arguing that mindfulness widens one's self-world connection (Amel et al., 2009) and helps orient one's focus toward the natural environment (Bishop, 2004), resulting in a greater connectedness to nature.

Panno et al. (2017) found that state mindfulness (self-reported) is related to pro-environmental behavior through low social dominance orientation, the view that interpersonal and intergroup relationships are, or should be, highly hierarchical (Pratto, Sidanius, & Levin, 2006).

In organizational scholarship, Patel and Holm (2018) concentrate conceptually on the impact of mindfulness on workplace pro-environmental behaviors among managers. As already equally described for consumers in the literature, they argue that connectedness with nature and non-materialism are appropriate mediators between mindfulness and pro-environmental behaviors in the workplace. However, they introduce openness to change as a third possible mediator between managerial mindfulness and managerial pro-environmental behavior. As compared with mindlessness, which boosts getting caught in self-fulfilling prophecies and commitment to previous cognitive activities, mindfulness helps overcome the cognitive distortions, thereby giving space to new ways of thinking and doing, lessening the reliance on old habitual patterns and encouraging openness to change.

As show in Figure 33.1, our literature overview shows the following aspects:

1. In former research models, mindfulness served as the independent variable, which explains pro-environmental behavior through a mediator relationship.
2. Up to now, all empirical studies aim at relating mindfulness to pro-environmental choices that individuals make in their private life and as consumers instead of at the workplace.
3. Those studies all use self-reported standardized questionnaires. As to our knowledge, researchers have not yet investigated the field of pro-environmental behavior and mindfulness with qualitative, mixed methods, or experimental approaches.

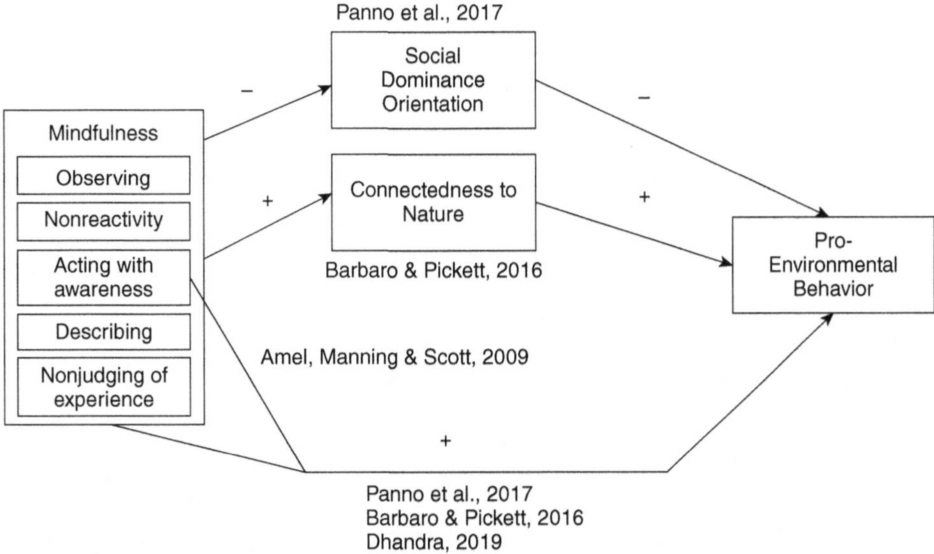

Figure 33.1 Mindfulness and pro-environmental behavior—previous empirical research

We address the outlined gaps by introducing mindfulness as a moderator for the intention–behavior gap in the field of employee pro-environmental behavior. We will test the following hypothesis.

H1: Mindfulness moderates the relationship between employee pro-environmental behavioral intentions and employee pro-environmental behaviors.

In the next section, we provide specific justification for our hypothesis by introducing two theories that allow us to consider mindfulness as a moderator of the intention–behavior relationship.

Mindfulness as a moderator of the intention–behavior relationship

Mindfulness and self-control theory

Enhanced attention to present inner and outer experiences and events, characterizing mindful individuals (Brown et al., 2007), may influence the intention–behavior relationship (Chatzisarantis & Hagger, 2007) by strengthening their ability for self-control (Fetterman, Robinson, Ode, & Gordon, 2010; Bowlin & Baer, 2012; Figure 33.2). Self-control can be

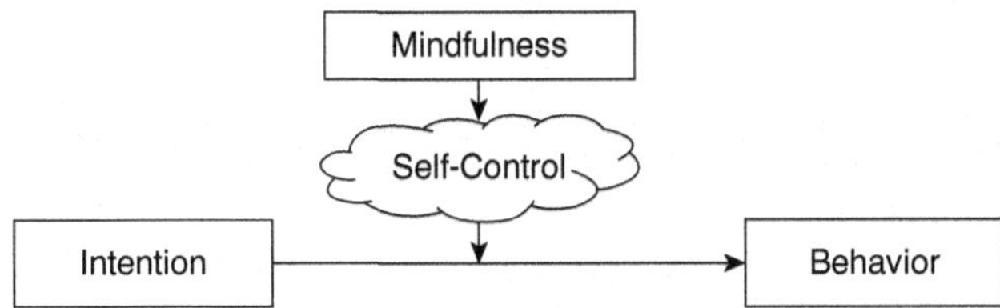

Figure 33.2 Mindfulness, self-control, and the intention–behavior gap

defined as "the ability to override or change one's inner responses, as well as to interrupt undesired behavioral tendencies (such as impulses) and refrain from acting on them" (Tangney, Baumeister, & Boone, 2004, p. 274), and consists of four main domains, namely controlling thoughts, emotions, impulses, and performance (Tangney et al., 2004). Generally speaking, self-control helps people to delay immediate gratification of desires and resist short-term temptations (reaching the workplace fast by car instead of using public transport) in order to alternatively achieve long-term goals (use public transport and save money, protect the environment; Buker, 2011; Gino, Schweitzer, Mead, & Ariely, 2011). People with a high level of trait mindfulness tend to observe their thoughts, emotions, and impulses, which allows a disengagement from automatic counter-intentional thought patterns and perceptual filtering driven by emotions and schemas from the past, and does not necessarily lead to acting on them (Bowlin & Baer, 2012; Jacob, Jovic, & Brinkerhoff, 2009; Shapiro, Carlson, Astin, & Freedman, 2006). Recent studies could show that trait mindfulness and self-control are strongly correlated with each other (Bowlin & Baer, 2012; Fetterman et al., 2010). Friese, Messner, and Schaffner (2012) explicitly showed that a short sequence of mindfulness meditation has a negative, immediate, short-term effect on self-control depletion and can therefore serve as a quick and efficient strategy to foster self-control under conditions of low psychological resources.

Mindfulness and self-determination theory

Self-determination theory distinguishes between consciously chosen "self-determined" and automated, "mindless" behavior (Deci & Ryan, 1980). Awareness, which is at the heart of mindfulness, facilitates the choice of behaviors that are consistent with one's needs, values, and interests (Deci & Ryan, 1980), while, in contrast, automatic or controlled processing often prevents considerations of options that would be more congruent with needs and values (Brown & Ryan, 2003). According to self-determination theory, human beings have three innate psychological needs: competence, autonomy, and relatedness (Ryan & Deci, 2000). Brown and Ryan (2003) showed that state mindfulness correlates positively with competence, autonomy, and relatedness and therefore supports self-determined behavior. The authors could also explicitly show that people with a high level of state mindfulness tend to act in a manner that is more congruent with their actual needs, values, and interests (Brown & Ryan, 2003; Shapiro et al., 2006). As mindful individuals better understand their goals and values and generally act more self-determined and more congruently with these goals and values, their intentions might be better predictors of their behaviors (Glomb et al., 2015; Figure 33.3).

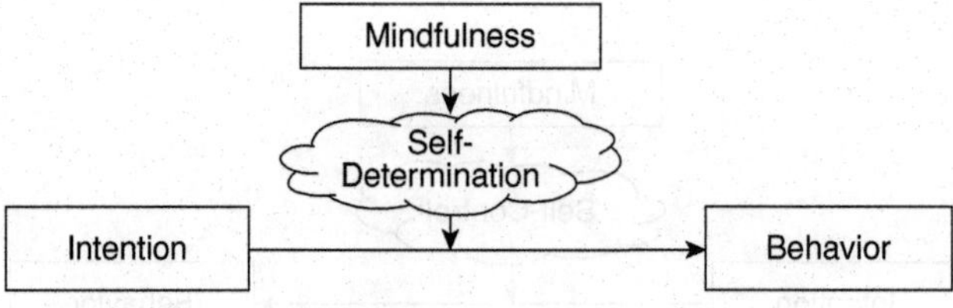

Figure 33.3 Mindfulness, self-determination and the intention–behavior gap

Method

Participants and procedure

In order to test our hypothesis, we employed the method of a prospective design (Chatzisarantis & Hagger, 2007), assessing variables in two points of time (see Figure 33.4 for the research model).

To familiarize ourselves with the scales and the prospective design procedure, we decided to conduct a pre-study with a student sample. To ensure that students would participate at two points of time and in order to fully care for privacy concerns, we used a platform for teaching administration, where students of the University of Kaiserslautern log into our courses with their name and email address. Using this, we contacted them directly via email. In this manner, we contacted 492 potential participants, while we gave the possibility of winning one of three vouchers of 20 euros for our university bookshop as an incentive in case they participate in both studies. We first (Time 1) provided the potential participants with a link to a survey which included scales that measure the intention towards the employee pro-environmental behavior, mindfulness, perceived organizational environmental strategy, perceived top management commitment, perceived impact of participants' own employee pro-environmental behavior on the environmental performance of the organization, and demographic questions. 127 students took part in this study (Time 1), but we had to exclude data from 29 students who provided incomplete data. For the second part of the survey (Time 2), we emailed a link to the remaining 98 participants exactly 21 days after each participant had completed the first part of the survey (Time 1). The relatively small three-week time lag was chosen to reflect optimal predictive accuracy (Rhodes, Courneya, & Jones, 2003). Still, other authors state that even a time lag of one week might introduce a retrospective reporting bias according to which people do not remember what they actually did (Bissing-Olson, Fielding, & Iyer, 2015). From the data of 46 students who took part in the second part of the study, we had to exclude 5 so that the final sample consisted of 41 students. The participants were 43.9% female, 53,7% male, no answer 2.4% (SD = 15.23). They studied industrial engineering, 43.9%; business studies, 12.2%; business studies with technical qualifications, 4.9%; and other courses of study, 34.1%. 57.5% had a car available, while 42.5% had no car available (SD =.50). 65% had less than 400 euros available per month (SD = 1.12). 58.5% were bachelor's students, 39% were master's students, 2.4% already had a master's degree.

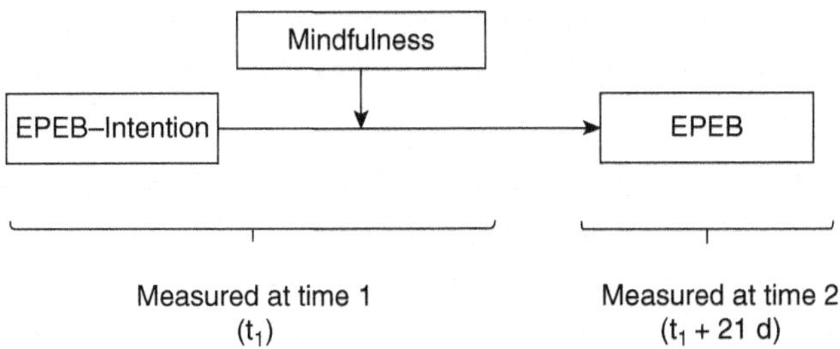

Figure 33.4 Research model: Mindfulness as a moderator for the intention–behavior relationship in employee pro-environmental behavior (EPEB)

We anticipated that students of business administration and engineering could have a lower general tendency to be mindful (Mean(n = 109) = 25.87) than students of other subjects such as psychology, where mindfulness trainings are often part of the curriculum and students are more open to inner development as it is part of their study interest. However, Baer et al. (2008) recruited undergraduate psychology students to test construct validity of the five facets and for them, the mean of mindfulness was even lower (Mean(n = 259) = 24.87).

Measures

Behavioral intentions

Employee pro-environmental behavioral intention was assessed with a published German translation of the 13 items of the Organizational Citizenship Behavior for the Environment (OCBE) scale. The scale covers the five organizational citizenship behavior (OCB) dimensions regarding environmental behavior: individual initiative, sportsmanship, helping, organizational loyalty, and self-development (Boiral & Paillé, 2012). In a review of existing measures for employee pro-environmental behavior, Ones et al. (2018) show that the Organizational Citizenship Behavior for the Environment (OCBE) scale addresses three dimensions of the *green five dimensions* "avoiding harm," "influencing others," "taking initiative." The statement "in the next three weeks I intend to..." preceded each item. Examples were "to protect the environment voluntarily and with my own initiative in my everyday life at the university," or "to assess the possible consequences and environmental effects of my everyday life at the university before I act." Participants were asked to rate the answers on a five-point scale ranging from 1 (completely disagree) to 5 (completely agree). Cronbach's alpha was .93 (n = 103). In order to cover "conserving" and "transforming," we included one specific action, which everyone does and is able to influence: mobility. We assessed green mobility intention as a formative construct, introducing the items/the construct as follows: "In the next three weeks I will cover the main part of my journey to the university..." Participants were then asked to rate the options "by car," "by public transport," "by bicycle," or "on foot" on a five-point scale ranging from never, less than once per week, up to five times and more per week. The item "by car" was reverse-scaled.

Behavior

Employee pro-environmental behavior was assessed similarly to employee pro-environmental behavioral intention and was introduced with the prompt: "For the past three weeks I...." The answers ranged from 1 (completely disagree) to 5 (completely agree) and were designed as follows: "protected the environment voluntarily and with my own initiative in my everyday life at the university," and "assessed the possible consequences and environmental effects of my everyday life at the university before I acted." Cronbach's alpha was 0.911 (n = 41). We proceeded similarly for green mobility behavior.

Mindfulness

Mindfulness was measured as a trait using the 39 items of the German version of the Five Facets of Mindfulness Questionnaire (FFMQ; Baer et al., 2006; Michalak et al., 2016). The trait mindfulness scale measures the general tendency to be mindful in daily life and was derived from an exploratory factor analysis of several previously developed mindfulness questionnaires (Baer et al., 2006). The authors distinguish between five facets, which are observing, describing, acting with awareness, non-judging of inner experience, and nonreactivity to inner experience. The five facets are internally consistent and show construct validity in a number of samples (Baer et al., 2006, 2008)

Following Michalak, Heidenreich, Ströhle, and Nachtigall (2008), we provided participants with the following prompt: "Please answer as you really experience these things right now, not as you think you should experience them. Please treat each statement independently of the other statements." Exemplary items were: "When I walk, I consciously perceive how the movements of my body feel," or "I find it difficult to remain focused on what is happening at the present moment." Respondents could choose answers on a five-point scale ranging from on 1 (not applicable at all) to 5 (completely applicable). Cronbach's alpha for this scale (n = 103) was .85. We also calculated Cronbach's alpha for each facet of mindfulness: observing (α = .60; e.g., "When I walk, I consciously perceive how the movements of my body feel"); acting with awareness (α = .81; e.g., "I find it difficult to remain focused on what is happening at the present moment"); nonreactivity to inner experience (α = .75; e.g., "In difficult situations, I can pause without immediately reacting"); describing (α = .87; e.g., "Even when I'm terribly upset, I can put it into words"); and nonjudging of experience (α = .88; e.g., "I make judgments about whether my thoughts are good or bad").

Control variables

We included several control variables such as gender, course of study, money available per month, and general availability of a car. We additionally included top management commitment, measured with a translated scale consisting of three items from Banerjee, Iyer, and Kashyap (2003; five -point Likert scale; Cronbach's alpha = .80; n = 61) as well as corporate environmental strategy with a translated 13-item scale from Banerjee et al. (2003; five-point Likert scale; Cronbach's alpha = .94; n = 95). We included the perceived impact of participants' own pro-environmental behavior on the environmental performance of the organization with three items, such as: "I am convinced that my mobility behavior towards the university has an influence on the environmental performance of my university" (similar approach of asking in a different context: Sharma & Morwitz, 2016). Participants were asked to rate on a five-point Likert scale, Cronbach's alpha was .74. Since these variables are not related to our central constructs, we excluded them from the analysis.

Results

Preliminary analysis

We present descriptive statistics, internal consistency information, and Pearson's correlations in Table 33.2. All variables show satisfactory levels of internal consistency reliability. We could neither find any significant correlations between intention and behavior, nor could we find significant correlations between mindfulness and intention or behavior. Nevertheless, it is evident from Table 33.2 that there is a significantly positive relationship between organizational citizenship behavior for the environment and green mobility behavior.

Table 33.2 Descriptive statistics and correlations

Variable	*M*	*SD*	*α*	*1*	*2*	*3*	*4*	*5*
Time 1 Variables								
1. Mindfulness	25.87⁺	3.24	.85	1	−.18	.12	.00	.11
2. Green mobility intention	2.44	.87	–	−.18	1	.27	.04	.17
3. Organizational citizenship intention	3.05	1.15	.93	.12	.27	1	−.79	.05
Time 2 Variables								
4. Green mobility behavior	1.94	.78	.52	.00	.04	−.79	1	.37*
5. Organizational citizenship behavior	1.96	.77	.91	.11	.17	.05	.37*	1

Note. α = Cronbach's alpha; *p < .05. **p < .01.
⁺For the nonreact facet, possible range of scores is 7–35. For all other facets, possible range is 8–40 (Baer et al., 2008).
*p < .05.

Hypothesis tests

According to our hypothesis, mindfulness moderates the relationship between employee pro-environmental intentions and employee pro-environmental behaviors, such that the relationship between intentions and behaviors is stronger for those employees who are more mindful. In order to test this hypothesis, we conducted a linear regression analysis with organizational citizenship behavior and green mobility behavior as dependent variables. Organizational citizenship intentions, green mobility intentions, mindfulness as well as the mindfulness × intention product terms were the independent variables. We z-standardized all variables. Table 33.3 shows that the interaction of green mobility intention and mindfulness is not significantly associated with green mobility behavior. Table 33.4 shows

Table 33.3 Regression analysis examining the effect of mindfulness on green mobility behavior

Variables	R^2	*ß*	$SE_ß$	*t*	*p*
Green mobility intention	.01	.03	.14	.23	.82
Mindfulness		.01	.15	.04	.97
Green mobility intention × Mindfulness		−.07	.15	−.46	.65

Note. ß = unstandardized regression coefficient; $SE_ß$ = standard error of ß

Table 33.4 Regression analysis examining the effect of mindfulness on organizational citizenship behavior for the environment

Variables	R^2	*ß*	$SE_ß$	*t*	*p*
Organizational citizenship intention for the environment	.015	.02	.15	.14	.89
Mindfulness		.09	.15	.59	.56
Organizational citizenship intention for the environment × mindfulness		.04	.15	.25	.80

Note. ß = unstandardized regression coefficient; $SE_ß$ = standard error of ß something similar with regard to organizational citizenship behavior for the environment: the interaction of mindfulness and organizational citizenship intention for the environment were not significantly related to organizational citizenship behavior for the environment.

To examine further the relationship between intentions and mindfulness, we used cross-level simple slope tests (Preacher, Curran, & Bauer, 2016). We conducted a regression analysis, assessing the relationship between organizational citizenship intention for the environment and organizational citizenship behavior for the environment on high (one standard deviation greater than the mean score of mindfulness) and low (one standard deviation less than the mean score of mindfulness) levels of mindfulness. The simple slope tests did not reveal more insights: For both (low mindfulness and high mindfulness), no significant effect could be found. This means that we could not find a significant relationship between organizational citizenship intention for the environment and actual behavior, neither for low trait mindful nor for high trait mindful students.

Further analysis

Since we could not support our main hypothesis, we calculated Pearson's correlations for the data of Time 1 (see Table 33.5) as the sample was larger than at Time 2 ($n = 103$) and integrated control variables. The correlations revealed that there are significant correlations between the perceived impact of participants' own pro-environmental behavior on the environmental performance of the organization and organizational citizenship intention for the environment. Regression analysis showed that the perceived impact of participants' own pro-environmental behavior has a positive ($B = .56$; $SE = .10$; $\beta = .51$; $t = 5.74$) and significant ($p = .00$) relationship with organizational citizenship intention for the environment.

As anticipated from the literature (Erdogan, Bauer, & Taylor, 2015), top management commitment and the intention to take initiative (which is a sub-scale of organizational citizenship intention for the environment) are significantly correlated. Here, regression analysis showed that top management commitment has a positive ($B = 4.16$; $SE = 1.94$; $\beta = .27$; $t = 2.15$) and significant ($p = .04$) relationship with the intention to take initiative. However, moderator analysis with the variables mindfulness (as well as sub-scales of mindfulness), top management commitment, and perceived impact of the own pro-environmental behavior did not reveal further insights.

We further wanted to find out whether students who took part in study 2 (put their intention to participate in study 2 into action) differ significantly from those who did not participate in study 2 (failed to put their intention to participate in study 2 into action) in their level of mindfulness. Therefore, we used an ANOVA and chose the two groups (no participation in study 2, participation in study 2) as independent variables with mindfulness as the dependent variable. Since the average mindfulness is higher ($M = 26.5$ vs. $M = 25.5$), we assume that people who are more mindful tend to put their intention into action. However, this was not significant ($p = .12$; $F = 2.43$).

Discussion

The data of our described pre-study reveals that our hypothesis on mindfulness as a moderator of the intention–behavior relationship in employee pro-environmental behavior cannot be supported.

Table 33.5 Additional analysis—correlations of Time 1 variables

Time 1 Variables	*M*	*SD*	*α*	*1*	*2*	*3*	*4*	*5*	*6*	*7*	*8*	*9*	*10*	*11*	*12*
1. Mindfulness (5 facets)	25.87	3.24	.85	1	.65**	.57**	.69**	.32**	.68**	.05	−.06	−.11	−.22*	−.13	−.15
2. Nonjudge (facet of mindfulness)	26.98	6.65	.88	.65**	1	.24*	.20*	−.10	.37**	−.06	−.15	−.17	−.19	−.19	−.24
3. Nonreactivity (facet of mindfulness)	21.31	4.15	.75	.57**	.24*	1	.21*	.19*	.20*	.00	.07	−.15	−.10	.05	.10
4. Describe (facet of mindfulness)	27.40	6.03	.87	.69**	.20*	.21*	1	.17	.36**	.08	.03	.00	−.07	−.07	−.18
5. Observing (facet of mindfulness)	27.40	4.48	.60	.32**	−.10	.19*	.17	1	−.06	.20*	−.03	−.11	.07	.05	.26*
6. Acting with awareness (facet of mindfulness)	26.50	5.39	.81	.68**	.37**	.20*	.36**	−.06	1	−.01	−.05	.06	−.30**	−.14	−.26*
7. Organizational citizenship intention for the environment (OCIE)	2.72	1.09	.93	.05	−.06	.00	.08	.20*	−.01	1	.83**	.13	.51**	−.08	.15
8. Individual initiative (facet of OCIE)	9.08	23.69	.73	−.06	−.15	.07	.06	−.03	−.05	.83**	1	.04	.13	−.05	.27*
9. Green mobility intention	2.59	.81	–	−.11	−.17	−.14	.00	−.11	.06	.13	.04	1	.19	−.18	−.18
10. Perceived impact	3.28	.99	.73	−.22*	−.19	−.10	−.07	.07	−.29**	.51**	.12	.19	1	.03	.27*
11. Environmental strategy	3.46	1.24	.94	−.13	−.19	.05	−.07	.05	−.14	−.08	−.05	−.18	.03	1	.37**
12. Top management commitment	3.47	.80	.80	−.15	−.24	.10	−.18	.26*	−.26*	.15	.27*	−.18	.27*	.37**	1

Note. α = Cronbach's alpha; *$p < .05$. **$p < .01$.

Regardless of the rejection of our hypothesis, our additional analyses helped us to gain some interesting insights for higher education institutions: In our pre-study with a student sample, we found out that top management commitment has a positive and significant relationship with the intention to take initiative, which reveals that if the management of higher education institutions wants students to show environmental-friendly initiative, they should make their commitment visible. This result is rather surprising, since top management is generally not seen as the major reference group for students, in contrast to companies (Johnson & Deem, 2003). The perceived impact of participants' own pro-environmental behavior has a positive and significant relationship with organizational citizenship intention for the environment. This means that students who believe that their own behavior impacts the environmental performance of their institution are more likely to develop environmental-friendly citizenship behaviors. However, students do not necessarily know that the environmental performance of their higher education institution is influenced by them. On-campus activities of environmentally friendly groups could help raise awareness for this fact among students.

Potential reasons for the rejection of our hypothesis are, first, that the pre-study suffers from a small sample especially due to the low response rate at the second data collection. We plan to increase the incentives to participate in Time 2 in the larger study. Second, the time of the survey was during the semester break. On the one hand, this means that some students were not on campus, on the other hand, there were no offers at the university to participate in environmental events or to show initiatives (both items of the OCBE scale). To overcome this problem in our main study, we will discuss those external factors such as holiday periods, opportunities for initiative, or upcoming environmental events with corporate executives beforehand. Furthermore, knowledge about the potential effects of mindfulness on behavior might lead to endogeneity. Another limitation is the fact that the applied measure for mindfulness and all the other variables were self-report measures as social desirability bias affects the measurement of personality variables and behaviors (Fisher & Katz, 2000). We therefore intend to control for social desirability bias. Since the overall time to respond to the survey was not too long (mean time: 7.49 minutes), we will follow the suggestion by Good et al. (2016) to control for common individual differences (intelligence, attitudes, personality), which allow alternative explanations for mindfulness effects. In our case, we will at least control for self-control and self-determination as we use them to describe the moderator effect.

In our pre-study, we are not able to enhance the theory on the intention–behavior gap by finding evidence for the moderator effect of the variable mindfulness in the specific context of environmental-workplace behavior. We are also not able to draw conclusions on how organizations can support individuals to translate their environmental workplace behavioral intentions into actual employee pro-environmental behaviors: Might organizations enhance their greening by introducing mindfulness practices?

Chapter takeaways

1. Thus far, the empirical literature on mindfulness and pro-environmental behavior focuses on private and consumer decisions rather than employee behavior. This is an important research gap since employee pro-environmental behaviors play a vital role in the greening process of organizations.
2. We hypothesize that mindfulness moderates the relationship between employee pro-environmental intentions and employee pro-environmental behaviors, such that the

relationship between intentions and behaviors is stronger for those employees who are more mindful.

3. The moderator relationship of mindfulness can be supported by self-control and self-determination theory.
4. Our hypothesis cannot be supported through our quantitative, prospective design pre-study with a student sample. We assume this is mainly due to the small sample size at Time 2.
5. For collecting data from employees at two points in time, researchers should clarify vacation times (sample size) as well as upcoming initiative opportunities or environmental events (parts of the employee pro-environmental behavior scale) with corporate executives beforehand.

Reflection questions

1. How can mindfulness impact individuals' pro-environmental behaviors?
2. Which theories could be used to describe the relationship between mindfulness and pro-environmental behaviors?
3. How far do employee pro-environmental behaviors differ from private pro-environmental behaviors?
4. How far can student pro-environmental behavior be seen as similar to or different from employee pro-environmental workplace behavior?
5. Are more mindful employees better able to translate their intentions into their behaviors?

References

Adams, R., Jeanrenaud, S., Bessant, J., Denyer, D., & Overy, P. (2016). Sustainability-oriented innovation: A systematic review. *International Journal of Management Reviews, 18*(2), 180–205. https://doi.org/10.1111/ijmr.12068

Aguinis, H. & Glavas, A. (2012). What we know and don't know about corporate social responsibility: A review and research agenda. *Journal of Management, 38*(4), 932–968. https://doi.org/10.1177/0149206311436079

Ajzen, I. (1985). From intentions to actions: A theory of planned behavior. In J. Kuhl & J. Beckmann (Eds.), *Springer series in social psychology. action control: From cognition to behavior* (pp. 11–39). Berlin: Springer.

Ajzen, I. (1991). The theory of planned behavior. *Organizational Behavior and Human Decision Processes, 50* (2), 179–211. https://doi.org/10.1016/0749-5978(91)90020-T

Amel, E. L., Manning, C. M., & Scott, B. A. (2009). Mindfulness and sustainable behavior: Pondering attention and awareness as means for increasing green behavior. *Ecopsychology, 1*(1), 14–25. https://doi.org/10.1089/eco.2008.0005

Armitage, C. J. & Conner, M. (2001). Efficacy of the theory of planned behaviour: A meta-analytic review. *British Journal of Social Psychology., 40*(4), 471–499. https://doi.org/10.1348/014466601164939

Baer, R. A., Smith, G. T., Hopkins, J., Krietemeyer, J., & Toney, L. (2006). Using self-report assessment methods to explore facets of mindfulness. *Assessment, 13*(1), 27–45. https://doi.org/10.1177/1073191105283504

Baer, R. A., Smith, G. T., Lykins, E., Button, D., Krietemeyer, J., Sauer, S., … Williams, J. M. G. (2008). Construct validity of the five facet mindfulness questionnaire in meditating and nonmeditating samples. *Assessment, 15*(3), 329–342. https://doi.org/10.1177/1073191107313003

Banerjee, S. B., Iyer, E. S., & Kashyap, R. K. (2003). Corporate environmentalism: Antecedents and influence of industry type. *Journal of Marketing, 67*(2), 106–122. Retrieved from www.jstor.org/stable/30040526

Barbaro, N. & Pickett, S. M. (2016). Mindfully green: Examining the effect of connectedness to nature on the relationship between mindfulness and engagement in pro-environmental behavior. *Personality and Individual Differences, 93*, 137–142. https://doi.org/10.1016/j.paid.2015.05.026

Bishop, S. R. (2004). Mindfulness: A proposed operational definition. *Clinical Psychology: Science and Practice, 11*(3), 230–241. https://doi.org/10.1093/clipsy/bph077

Bissing-Olson, M. J., Fielding, K. S., & Iyer, A. (2015). Diary methods and workplace pro-environmental behaviours. In J. L. Robertson & J. Barling (Eds.), *The psychology of green organizations* (pp. 95–116). Oxford, New York: Oxford University Press.

Bissing-Olson, M. J., Iyer, A., Fielding, K. S., & Zacher, H. (2013). Relationships between daily affect and pro-environmental behavior at work: The moderating role of pro-environmental attitude. *Journal of Organizational Behavior, 34*(2), 156–175. https://doi.org/10.1002/job.1788

Boiral, O. & Paillé, P. (2012). Organizational citizenship behaviour for the environment: Measurement and validation. *Journal of Business Ethics, 109*(4), 431–445. https://doi.org/10.1007/s10551-011-1138-9

Boiral, O., Talbot, D., & Paillé, P. (2015). Leading by example: A model of organizational citizenship behavior for the environment. *Business Strategy and the Environment, 24*(6), 532–550. https://doi.org/10.1002/bse.1835

Bowlin, S. L. & Baer, R. A. (2012). Relationships between mindfulness, self-control, and psychological functioning. *Personality and Individual Differences, 52*(3), 411–415. https://doi.org/10.1016/j.paid.2011.10.050

Brown, K. W. & Kasser, T. (2005). Are psychological and ecological well-being compatible? The role of values, mindfulness, and lifestyle. *Social Indicators Research, 74*(2), 349–368. https://doi.org/10.1007/s11205-004-8207-8

Brown, K. W. & Ryan, R. M. (2003). The benefits of being present: Mindfulness and its role in psychological well-being. *Journal of Personality and Social Psychology, 84*(4), 822–848. https://doi.org/10.1037/0022-3514.84.4.822

Brown, K. W., Ryan, R. M., & Creswell, J. D. (2007). Mindfulness: Theoretical foundations and evidence for its salutary effects. *Psychological Inquiry, 18*(4), 211–237. https://doi.org/10.1080/10478400701598298

Buker, H. (2011). Formation of self-control: Gottfredson and Hirschi's general theory of crime and beyond. *Aggression and Violent Behavior, 16*(3), 265–276. https://doi.org/10.1016/j.avb.2011.03.005

Chatzisarantis, N. L. D. & Hagger, M. S. (2007). Mindfulness and the intention–behavior relationship within the theory of planned behavior. *Personality & Social Psychology Bulletin, 33*(5), 663–676. https://doi.org/10.1177/0146167206297401

Chiesa, A. & Serretti, A. (2009). Mindfulness-based stress reduction for stress management in healthy people: A review and meta-analysis. *The Journal of Alternative and Complementary Medicine, 15*(5), 593–600. https://doi.org/10.1089/acm.2008.0495

Ciocirlan, C. E. (2016). Environmental workplace behaviors. *Organization & Environment, 30*(1), 51–70. https://doi.org/10.1177/1086026615628036

de Bruin, E. I., Topper, M., Muskens, J. G. A. M., Bögels, S. M., & Kamphuis, J. H. (2012). Psychometric properties of the five facets mindfulness questionnaire (FFMQ) in a meditating and a non-meditating sample. *Assessment, 19*(2), 187–197. https://doi.org/10.1177/1073191112446654

Deci, E. L. & Ryan, R. M. (1980). Self-determination theory: When mind mediates behavior. *The Journal of Mind and Behavior, 1*(1), 33–43. Retrieved from www.jstor.org/stable/43852807

Dhandra, T. K. (2019). Achieving triple dividend through mindfulness: More sustainable consumption, less unsustainable consumption and more life satisfaction. *Ecological Economics, 161*, 83–90. https://doi.org/10.1016/j.ecolecon.2019.03.021

Erdogan, B., Bauer, T. N., & Taylor, S. (2015). Management commitment to the ecological environment and employees: Implications for employee attitudes and citizenship behaviors. *Human Relations, 68*(11), 1669–1691. https://doi.org/10.1177/0018726714565723

Ericson, T., Kjønstad, B. G., & Barstad, A. (2014). Mindfulness and sustainability. *Ecological Economics, 104*, 73–79. https://doi.org/10.1016/j.ecolecon.2014.04.007

Fetterman, A. K., Robinson, M. D., Ode, S., & Gordon, K. H. (2010). Neuroticism as a risk factor for behavioral dysregulation: A mindfulness-mediation perspective. *Journal of Social and Clinical Psychology, 29*(3), 301–321. https://doi.org/10.1521/jscp.2010.29.3.301

Fishbein, M. (1980). The theory of reasoned action: Some applications and implications. In H. E. Howe & M. M. Page (Eds.), *Nebraska Symposium on Motivation* (Vol. 27, pp. 65–116). Lincoln: University of Nebraska Press.

Fisher, R. J. & Katz, J. E. (2000). Social-desirability bias and the validity of self-reported values. *Psychology and Marketing, 17*(2), 105–120. https://doi.org/10.1002/(SICI)1520-6793(200002)17:2105::AID-MAR33.0.CO;2-9

Fraher, A. L., Branicki, L. J., & Grint, K. (2017). Mindfulness in action: Discovering how U.S. navy seals build capacity for mindfulness in High-Reliability Organizations (HROs). *Academy of Management Discoveries, 3*(3), 239–261. https://doi.org/10.5465/amd.2014.0146

Friese, M., Messner, C., & Schaffner, Y. (2012). Mindfulness meditation counteracts self-control depletion. *Consciousness and Cognition, 21*(2), 1016–1022. https://doi.org/10.1016/j.concog.2012.01.008

Gino, F., Schweitzer, M. E., Mead, N. L., & Ariely, D. (2011). Unable to resist temptation: How self-control depletion promotes unethical behavior. *Organizational Behavior and Human Decision Processes, 115*(2), 191–203. https://doi.org/10.1016/j.obhdp.2011.03.001

Glomb, T. M., Duffy, M. K., Bono, J. E., & Yang, T. (2015). Mindfulness at work. *Research in Human Resources Management., 30*, 115–157.

Good, D. J., Lyddy, C. J., Glomb, T. M., Bono, J. E., Brown, K. W., Duffy, M. K., ... Lazar, S. W. (2016). Contemplating mindfulness at work. *Journal of Management, 42*(1), 114–142. https://doi.org/10.1177/0149206315617003

Grossman, P., Niemann, L., Schmidt, S., & Walach, H. (2004). Mindfulness-based stress reduction and health benefits. *Journal of Psychosomatic Research, 57*(1), 35–43. https://doi.org/10.1016/S0022-3999(03)00573-7

Helling, R. (2015). Driving innovation through life-cycle thinking. *Clean Technologies and Environmental Policy, 17*(7), 1769–1779. https://doi.org/10.1007/s10098-015-0928-7

Howell, A. J., Dopko, R. L., Passmore, H.-A., & Buro, K. (2011). Nature connectedness: Associations with well-being and mindfulness. *Personality and Individual Differences, 51*(2), 166–171. https://doi.org/10.1016/j.paid.2011.03.037

Hülsheger, U. R., Alberts, H. J., Feinholdt, A., & Lang, J. W. B. (2013). Benefits of mindfulness at work: The role of mindfulness in emotion regulation, emotional exhaustion, and job satisfaction. *Journal of Applied Psychology, 98*(2), 310. Retrieved from http://psycnet.apa.org/record/2012-34922-001

Jacob, J., Jovic, E., & Brinkerhoff, M. B. (2009). Personal and planetary well-being: Mindfulness meditation, pro-environmental behavior and personal quality of life in a survey from the social justice and ecological sustainability movement. *Social Indicators Research, 93*(2), 275–294. https://doi.org/10.1007/s11205-008-9308-6

Jha, A. P., Morrison, A. B., Dainer-Best, J., Parker, S., Rostrup, N., & Stanley, E. A. (2015). Minds "at attention": Mindfulness training curbs attentional lapses in military cohorts. *PloS One, 10*(2), e0116889. https://doi.org/10.1371/journal.pone.0116889

Johnson, R. N. & Deem, R. (2003). Talking of students: Tensions and contradictions for the manager-academic and the university in contemporary higher education. *Higher Education, 46*(3), 289–314. Retrieved from https://link.springer.com/article/10.1023%2FA%3A1025377826704

Kabat-Zinn, J. (2003). Mindfulness-based interventions in context: Past, present, and future. *Clinical Psychology: Science and Practice, 10*(2), 144–156. https://doi.org/10.1093/clipsy/bpg016

Keng, S.-L., Smoski, M. J., & Robins, C. J. (2011). Effects of mindfulness on psychological health: A review of empirical studies. *Clinical Psychology Review, 31*(6), 1041–1056. https://doi.org/10.1016/j.cpr.2011.04.006

Kernochan, R. A., McCormick, D. W., & White, J. A. (2007). Spirituality and the management teacher: Reflections of three buddhists on compassion, mindfulness, and selflessness in the classroom. *Journal of Management Inquiry, 16*(1), 61–75. https://doi.org/10.1177/1056492606297545

Kim, A., Kim, Y., Han, K., Jackson, S. E., & Ployhart, R. E. (2013). Multilevel influences on voluntary workplace green behavior: Individual differences, leader behavior, and coworker advocacy. *Journal of Management, 43*(5), 1335–1358. https://doi.org/10.1177/0149206314547386

Lau, M. A., Bishop, S. R., Segal, Z. V., Buis, T., Anderson, N. D., Carlson, L., ... Devins, G. (2006). The Toronto mindfulness scale: Development and validation. *Journal of Clinical Psychology, 62*(12), 1445–1467. https://doi.org/10.1002/jclp.20326

Littleford, C., Ryley, T. J., & Firth, S. K. (2014). Context, control and the spillover of energy use behaviours between office and home settings. *Journal of Environmental Psychology, 40*, 157–166. https://doi.org/10.1016/j.jenvp.2014.06.002

MacKillop, J. & Anderson, E. J. (2007). Further psychometric validation of the mindful attention awareness scale (MAAS). *Journal of Psychopathology and Behavioral Assessment, 29*(4), 289–293. https://doi.org/10.1007/s10862-007-9045-1

Madden, T. J., Scholder Ellen, P., & Ajzen, I. (1992). A comparison of the theory of planned behavior and the theory of reasoned action. *Personality and Social Psychology Bulletin, 18*(1). https://doi.org/10.1177/0146167292181001

Manika, D., Wells, V. K., Gregory-Smith, D., & Gentry, M. (2015). The impact of individual attitudinal and organisational variables on workplace environmentally friendly behaviours. *Journal of Business Ethics, 126*(4), 663–684. https://doi.org/10.1007/s10551-013-1978-6

Michalak, J., Heidenreich, T., Ströhle, G., & Nachtigall, C. (2008). Die Deutsche Version der Mindful Attention and Awareness Scale (MAAS): Psychometrische Befunde zu einem Achtsamkeitsfragebogen. *Zeitschrift Für Klinische Psychologie Und Psychotherapie, 37*(3), 200–208. https://doi.org/10.1026/1616-3443.37.3.200

Michalak, J., Zarbock, G., Drews, M., Otto, D., Mertens, D., Ströhle, G., . . . Heidenreich, T. (2016). Erfassung von Achtsamkeit mit der deutschen Version des Five Facet Mindfulness Questionnaires (FFMQ-D). *Zeitschrift Für Gesundheitspsychologie, 24*(1), 1–12. https://doi.org/10.1026/0943-8149/a000149

Norton, T. A., Zacher, H., Parker, S. L., & Ashkanasy, N. M. (2017). Bridging the gap between green behavioral intentions and employee green behavior: The role of green psychological climate. *Journal of Organizational Behavior, 38*(7), 996–1015. https://doi.org/10.1002/job.2178

Ones, D. S. & Dilchert, S. (2012). Employee green behaviors. In S. E. Jackson, D. S. Ones, & S. Dilchert (Eds.), *Managing human resources for environmental sustainability* (pp. 85–116). San Francisco, CA: John Wiley & Sons.

Ones, D. S., Wiernik, B. M., Dilchert, S., & Klein, R. M. (2018). Multiple domains and categories of employee green behaviors: More than conservation. In V. K. Well, D. Gregory-Smith, & D. Manika (Eds.), *Research handbook on employee pro-environmental behavior* (pp. 13–38). Cheltenham, UK, Northhampton, MA: Edward Elgar Publishing.

Panno, A., Giacomantonio, M., Carrus, G., Maricchiolo, F., Pirchio, S., & Mannetti, L. (2017). Mindfulness, pro-environmental behavior, and belief in climate change: The mediating role of social dominance. *Environment and Behavior, 22*, 1–25. https://doi.org/10.1177/0013916517718887

Patel, T. & Holm, M. (2018). Practicing mindfulness as a means for enhancing workplace pro-environmental behaviors among managers. *Journal of Environmental Planning and Management, 61* (13), 2231–2256. https://doi.org/10.1080/09640568.2017.1394819

Pratto, F., Sidanius, J., & Levin, S. (2006). Social dominance theory and the dynamics of intergroup relations: Taking stock and looking forward. *European Review of Social Psychology, 17*(1), 271–320. https://doi.org/10.1080/10463280601055772

Preacher, K. J., Curran, P. J., & Bauer, D. J. (2016). Computational tools for probing interactions in multiple linear regression, multilevel modeling, and latent curve analysis. *Journal of Educational and Behavioral Statistics, 31*(4), 437–448. https://doi.org/10.3102/10769986031004437

Reb, J., Narayanan, J., & Ho, Z. W. (2015). Mindfulness at work: Antecedents and consequences of employee awareness and absent-mindedness. *Mindfulness, 6*(1), 111–122. https://doi.org/10.1007/s12671-013-0236-4

Rhodes, R. E., Courneya, K. S., & Jones, L. W. (2003). Translating exercise intentions into behavior: Personality and social cognitive correlates. *Journal of Health Psychology, 8*(4), 447–458. https://doi.org/10.1177/13591053030084004

Ryan, R. M. & Deci, E. L. (2000). Self-determination theory and the facilitation of intrinsic motivation, social development, and well-being. *American Psychologist, 55*(1), 68–78. https://doi.org/10.1037//0003-066X.55.1.68

Shapiro, S. L., Brown, K. W., & Biegel, G. M. (2007). Teaching self-care to caregivers: Effects of mindfulness-based stress reduction on the mental health of therapists in training. *Training and Education in Professional Psychology, 1*(2), 105–115. https://doi.org/10.1037/1931-3918.1.2.105

Shapiro, S. L., Carlson, L. E., Astin, J. A., & Freedman, B. (2006). Mechanisms of mindfulness. *Journal of Clinical Psychology, 62*(3), 373–386. https://doi.org/10.1002/jclp.20237

Sharma, E. & Morwitz, V. G. (2016). Saving the masses: The impact of perceived efficacy on charitable giving to single vs. multiple beneficiaries. *Organizational Behavior and Human Decision Processes, 135*, 45–54. https://doi.org/10.1016/j.obhdp.2016.06.001

Sheeran, P. (2002). Intention—Behavior relations: A conceptual and empirical review. *European Review of Social Psychology, 12*(1), 1–36. https://doi.org/10.1080/14792772143000003

Sheth, J. N., Sethia, N. K., & Srinivas, S. (2011). Mindful consumption: A customer-centric approach to sustainability. *Journal of the Academy of Marketing Science, 39*(1), 21–39. https://doi.org/10.1007/s11747-010-0216-3

Strauss, K., Lepoutre, J., & Wood, G. (2017). Fifty shades of green: How microfoundations of sustainability dynamic capabilities vary across organizational contexts. *Journal of Organizational Behavior, 38*(9), 1338–1355. https://doi.org/10.1002/job.2186

Tangney, J. P., Baumeister, R. F., & Boone, A. L. (2004). High self-control predicts good adjustment, less pathology, better grades, and interpersonal success. *Journal of Personality, 72*(2), 271–324. https://doi.org/10.1111/j.0022-3506.2004.00263.x

Temminck, E., Mearns, K., & Fruhen, L. (2015). Motivating employees towards sustainable behaviour. *Business Strategy and the Environment, 24*(6), 402–412. https://doi.org/10.1002/bse.1827

Triandis, H. C. (1977). *Interpersonal behaviour.* Monterey, CA: Brooks/Cole.

Unsworth, K. L., Dmitrieva, A., & Adriasola, E. (2013). Changing behaviour: Increasing the effectiveness of workplace interventions in creating pro-environmental behaviour change. *Journal of Organizational Behavior, 34*(2), 211–229. https://doi.org/10.1002/job.1837

Wagner, M. & Llerena, P. (2011). Eco-innovation through integration, regulation and cooperation: Comparative insights from case studies in three manufacturing sectors. *Industry and Innovation, 18*(8), 747–764. https://doi.org/10.1080/13662716.2011.621744

Wamsler, C., Brossmann, J., Hendersson, H., Kristjansdottir, R., McDonald, C., & Scarampi, P. (2018). Mindfulness in sustainability science, practice, and teaching. *Sustainability Science, 13*(1), 143–162. https://doi.org/10.1007/s11625-017-0428-2

Wang, Z. & Adams, J. (2016). *Bringing mindfulness to your workplace.* Alexandria, VA: Association for Talent Development.

Webb, T. L. & Sheeran, P. (2006). Does changing behavioral intentions engender behavior change? A meta-analysis of the experimental evidence. *Psychological Bulletin, 132*(2), 249–268. https://doi.org/10.1037/0033-2909.132.2.249

Weng, -H.-H., Chen, J.-S., & Chen, P.-C. (2015). Effects of green innovation on environmental and corporate performance: A stakeholder perspective. *Sustainability*, 7(5), 4997–5026. https://doi.org/10.3390/su7054997

West, C. P., Dyrbye, L. N., Rabatin, J. T., Call, T. G., Davidson, J. H., Multari, A., … Shanafelt, T. D. (2014). Intervention to promote physician well-being, job satisfaction, and professionalism: A randomized clinical trial. *JAMA Internal Medicine, 174*(4), 527–533. https://doi.org/10.1001/jamainternmed.2013.14387

Wolever, R. Q., Bobinet, K. J., McCabe, K., Mackenzie, E. R., Fekete, E., Kusnick, C. A., & Baime, M. (2012). Effective and viable mind-body stress reduction in the workplace: A randomized controlled trial. *Journal of Occupational Health Psychology, 17*(2), 246–258. https://doi.org/10.1037/a0027278

34

DOING VIPASSANA THE BUDDHA'S WAY

A seeker's immersion in mindfulness in life and leadership

Satinder K. Dhiman

Introduction

This chapter presents an overview of the essential elements of Buddhist psychology as a mental discipline. Right mindfulness, right concentration, and right effort constitute the entire terrain of the Buddhist mental landscape. The mind is trained, disciplined, and developed through these three practices, which aim at cleansing the mind of impurities and disturbances such as lustful desires, hatred, ill-will, indolence, worries and restlessness, skeptical doubts. The goal is to cultivate such positive qualities as concentration, awareness, intelligence, will, energy, the analytical faculty, confidence, joy, and tranquility, leading finally to the attainment of the highest wisdom which sees things as they are. These qualities have a direct bearing on how we live our lives and how we conduct ourselves toward others in any relationship, including the leader–follower relationship. This chapter briefly discusses two basic forms of meditative practices—Samatha and Vipassana—and the concomitant practices of mindfulness of breathing and insight meditation. As a case in point, this overview is followed by a detailed description of the author's recent experience with a form of Buddhist meditation called Vipassana as taught by S.N. Goenka in the tradition of Sayagyi U Ba Khin.

This chapter also illustrates how we unconsciously carry our daily activities, as if on autopilot, mostly oblivious to what is happening right in front of us. Jayankar (1996) provides a vivid example of this in the following anecdote:

> We were speaking of awareness, and splitting hairs as to its nature, when suddenly we felt a jolt. We paid no attention to it and continued our conversation. A few seconds later, Krishnaji turned around and asked us what we were discussing. "Awareness," we said and immediately started asking him questions about it. He listened, looked at us quizzically, and then asked, "Did you notice what happened just now?" "No." "We knocked down a goat; did you not see it?"
>
> "No." Then with great gravity he said, "And you were discussing awareness." No more words were necessary. It was devastating.
>
> *(pp. 195–196)*

This story about mindless driving splendidly illustrates the importance, and the resulting challenge, of cultivating mindfulness in our life. By making us aware of our unconscious reactions, it points out in a telling manner how pervasive mindlessness is.

The law of elsewhere: taming the monkey-mind

Mindfulness is essentially a way of taming our wayward mind. If we observe our mind, we discover that it hops from past to future and from future to past, endlessly. It rarely, if ever, dwells in the present. This phenomenon can be called, half-jokingly, the Law of Elsewhere: our mind always likes to be elsewhere! Interestingly, "now" is rightly called "present"—it truly is a "gift" from gods. We must make a habit of this one by learning to be alertly present in the present moment—to be keenly attuned to the current reality. It is a strange realization that even past and future can only be experienced in the now, the eternal present moment. The ability to be in the present moment, from moment to moment, is the master key to enjoy small pleasures that life accords us unexpectedly.

An impartial observation of our moment-to-moment state of mind will reveal that most of the time our mind is roaming elsewhere when we outwardly seem engaged in an activity. For example, when taking a shower or eating our breakfast, our mind may be worrying about a meeting that is not going to happen until later during the day. So if we are thinking about our meeting while eating our breakfast, we are actually eating our meeting and not our breakfast! This waywardness plays havoc with the essential quality of every activity of our life, and we seem to go through the motions, sleepwalking or at best half-awake. Whether living or leading, we are actually half-alive. "To be awake," said Henry David Thoreau, "is to be alive. I have never yet met a man who was quite awake." Perhaps that is why we have modern-day reminders such as "Live the moment!" or "Carpe Diem"—"Seize the day!"

A sign in Las Vegas says, "In order to win, you have to be present." Likewise, in order to be successful at the game of life, we have to be alertly present in everything we do. Being present requires the development of a special faculty called self-awareness. Intrinsically, our being is of the nature of pure awareness—of the nature of "wisdom-seeking wisdom"—always available to all of us right here and right now, whenever and wherever we need it, if only we open ourselves to it unconditionally. Mindfulness is a special form of self-awareness where the attention is kept effortlessly focused in the present moment.

Paying attention to attention

A modern Zen story talks about a novice approaching a Zen master, inquiring about the most important thing in life. "Attention," said the master. The student persisted: "What is the second most important thing in life?" "Attention," replied the master. "And the third thing?" asked the student. "Attention," the master added firmly. "Anything else?" continued the student. "You do not seem to be paying attention!" roared the master. Paying attention is the hardest of all tasks because we tend to forget it. As a modern Theravada teacher, Thanissaro Bhikkhu, told this author, "It is easy to be mindful. What is difficult is to remember to be mindful." This then is the entire challenge of mindfulness practice—remembering to be mindful. And, paradoxically, we have to cultivate mindfulness to remember mindfulness.

The term *mindfulness* has come to be used in a variety of ways and contexts in the modern times. Starting as a meditation technique more than 2,500 years ago, mindfulness has found its way in recent times into health clinics, prison houses, wellness centers, government offices, law firms, and corporate boardrooms. In its original Buddhist form, the practice of mindfulness refers to the technique of developing alert awareness of the body and the mind in the present moment.

Two forms of meditation: Samatha and Vipassana

As we have seen throughout our presentation in this volume, there are two main types of Buddhist meditation: *Samatha* meditation, which facilitates the development of serenity or calm, and *Vipassana* meditation, which facilitates the development of insight. Calm meditation aims to provide the mind an essential clarity to make it serene, stable, and strong. By preparing the mind to see the things as they really are, it serves as a necessary foundation for insight meditation. Together, calm meditation and insight meditation form the Buddhist path that leads to the realization of final awakening or enlightenment. Explaining the role and relationship of calm and insight meditation, Harvey (2008, pp. 253, 255) observed:

> Calm meditation alone cannot lead to *Nibbana* [Sanskrit: *Nirvana*], for while it can temporarily suspend, and thus weaken, attachment, hatred, and delusion, it cannot destroy them; only Insight combined with Calm can do this.... Calm "tunes" the mind, making it a more adequate instrument for knowledge and insight.... Insight meditation is more analytical and probing than Calm meditation, as it aims to investigate the nature of reality, rather than remaining fixed on one apparently stable object.

Buddhism believes the mind as such to be intrinsically pure, but sometimes it is sullied or defiled by extrinsic impurities, such as greed, hatred, and delusion. The purpose of meditative practice is to expunge these adventitious impurities and to help restore the pristine purity of our natural mind so that it can see things as they truly are. The practice of meditation, therefore, starts with stilling or calming the mind to enable it to attain a measure of serenity, and then turns it toward insight into reality.

The practice of mindfulness

Mindfulness refers to a special form of awareness or presence of mind. Although we are always aware to some degree in a general way, this awareness rarely goes beyond the familiarity level to reach the mind's deeper layers. However, with the practice of mindfulness, normal awareness or attentiveness is applied with greater intensity and at a special pitch.

Renowned Buddhist scholar-monk Bhikkhu Bodhi (2006, p. 76) explains the practice of right mindfulness in the following clear terms:

> The mind is deliberately kept at the level of *bare attention*, a detached observation of what is happening within us and around us in the present moment. In the practice of right mindfulness the mind is trained to remain in the present, open, quiet, and alert, contemplating the present event. All judgments and interpretations have to be suspended, or if they occur, just registered and dropped.... To practice mindfulness is thus a matter not so much of doing but of undoing:

not thinking, not judging, not associating, not planning, not imagining, not wishing. All these "doings" of ours are modes of interference, ways the mind manipulates experience and tries to establish its dominance.

The Satipatthana Sutta

The most important and original discourse on the subject of meditation delivered by the Buddha is called *Satipatthana Sutta,* as it occurs in the collection of Long Discourses (Digya Nikaya No. 22) and in the collection of Middle Length Discourses (Majjhima Nikaya No. 10). Right mindfulness also constitutes the sixth step in the Noble Eightfold Path, the Buddhist path to awakening, so much so that the Buddha regarded *satipatthana* ("presence of mindfulness" or "attending with mindfulness") to be "the direct path to realization" (Analayo, 2006, pp. 27–28).

The *Satipatthana Sutta* (Sanskrit: *Sutra*) is divided into four sections that list "four foundations of mindfulness," the four spheres in which to develop mindfulness:

1. Contemplation of the body through observing breathing
2. Contemplation of the feelings through mindfulness
3. Contemplation of the states of mind through observing different emotions
4. Contemplation of the mental objects, especially the Four Noble Truths (Analayo, 2006, pp. 3–7).

As is clear from the above classification, we start with the contemplation of the body, the first sphere of mindfulness, and move through contemplations of the next three spheres of the mind. We begin with the body because it is our most immediate experience and is most accessible to us. From the body, we proceed to the contemplation of feelings and note their emotive and ethical qualities. Then we observe the mental states and objects, reflecting upon the Four Noble Truths—the truth regarding the reality of suffering, the cause of suffering, the cessation of suffering, and the path leading to the cessation of suffering.

It is important to keep in mind that, although the Pali word *sati* originally meant *memory* or *remembrance,* in its general Buddhist usage it mostly connotes a certain quality of attentiveness to or awareness of the present that the Buddhist doctrine specifies as good, wholesome, skillful, or right. It is not just bare attention referred to here; rather, it is appropriate or wholesome attention, connoted by the Pali word *yonisomaniskara.* In Buddhism, the term *mindfulness* always implies *right mindfulness*—the adjective *right* connoting a state emanating from wholesome roots of mind such as kindness, compassion, joy, and equanimity.

Buddhist psychology also identifies three unwholesome roots of mind: greed, hatred, and ignorance. If our attention emanates from any of these three unwholesome roots, it is not appropriate and will not give us the knowledge of reality as it truly is. A sniper's concentration, for example, will not qualify as right state of mindfulness since it is does not spring from wholesome intention. It is only in this sense that right mindfulness *(samma-sati)* forms the seventh factor of the Noble Eightfold Path (see: Nyanaponika, 1962, pp. 9–10).

Mindfulness of breathing *(Anapanasati)*

All forms of *Samatha* meditation start with an object or phrase to gain one-pointedness of mind. In most meditation traditions, breath is used as a choice object for concentration of the mind because it is closely linked to mind and "it is always available to us" (Bodhi, 2006, p. 80). For example, in the Sufi and Greek Orthodox Church traditions, breath is employed as a primary vehicle to immerse the mind into the heart through a special prayer called "Prayer of the Heart." Similarly, Patanjali, the famous author of *Yoga-Sutras*, realized like Buddha that the "breath had close connection with the mind and that was the reason why excitement, anger, agitation, *et cetera* led to short and irregular breathing" (Tandon, 2007, p. 76).

The meditation practice most respected by Buddhists is called "mindfulness of breathing" *(Anapanasati)*. Referring to its great importance, Bodhi (2006, p. 80) observed, "By itself mindfulness of breathing can lead to all the stages of the path culminating in full awakening. In fact, it was this meditation subject that the Buddha used on the night of his own enlightenment." Accordingly, the practice of mindfulness of breathing is considered to be the supreme meditation in Buddhism to awaken the mind to its full potential. It is believed that it was through the practice of mindfulness of breathing that the Buddha attained his breakthrough that led to his enlightenment.

The basic Buddhist practice here is being mindful of our breathing. It is said that proper breathing is more important than food. Proper breathing holds a special place in the practice of *Yoga*, as breathing provides the conscious connection between our body and our mind. It is common knowledge that when we are agitated, we breathe differently than when we are calm and relaxed. Our breath has a wonderful capacity to help us awaken to complete awareness.

Getting the knack of mindfulness

Here is the basic practice of mindfulness of breathing, in the words of Rahula (1974):

> Breathe in and out as usual, without any effort or strain. Now, bring your mind on your breathing in and breathing out; let your mind be aware and observe your breathing in and breathing out.... Your mind should be so concentrated on your breathing that you are aware of its movements and changes. Forget all other things, your surroundings, your environment; do not raise your eyes or look at anything. Try to do this for five or ten minutes.
>
> *(p. 70)*

After some practice, we are assured, we develop a knack for being mindful so that we can extend this awareness to all spheres of our life. Whatever we happen to be doing at the moment—eating, washing dishes, walking, etc.—we should try to become fully aware and mindful of the act we are performing at the moment. This is called living in the present moment or the present activity.

The idea is to be fully present to one activity since our mind can only competently handle one function at a time. When informed about the English expression of "killing two birds with one stone," Suzuki Roshi (cited in Murphy, 2013, p. vi) said: "our way is to kill just one Bird with one stone."

Nhat Hanh, the modern Zen Master, uses the term *mindfulness* to refer to "keeping one's consciousness alive to the present reality.... We must be conscious of each breath, each movement, every thought and feeling, everything which has any relation to ourselves" (1987, pp. 11, 8; see also Hanh, 1988, 1998; Hart, 2009; Nanamoli, 1992, 2000). Nhat Hanh further clarifies the miracle of mindfulness by providing these practical guidelines:

> Keep your attention focused on the work, be alert and ready to handle ably and intelligently any situation which may arise—this is mindfulness: Mindfulness is the miracle by which we master and restore ourselves . . . it is the miracle which can call back in a flash our dispersed mind and restore it to wholeness so that we can live each minute of life.
>
> *(pp. 20–21)*

How can we practice mindfulness, we may object, when modern life seems to be maddeningly hectic and when so many activities clamor to claim our precious little time? Ajahn Chah, a renowned Thai meditation master, provides the perfect answer: "If you have time to breathe, you have time to meditate."

Insight meditation

As noted above, mindfulness of breathing occupies a prominent place in the practice of calm and insight meditation. Although each religious tradition has some form of serenity meditation as a part of its spiritual repertoire, the practice of insight meditation is the distinctive contribution of Buddhism to the spiritual heritage of humanity. Mindfulness of breathing is employed in both calm meditation and insight meditation with a different purpose and emphasis. In calm meditation, the purpose of employing mindfulness is to gain a certain measure of clarity and serenity of mind through the power of concentration. However, in insight meditation, concentration achieved through mindfulness of breathing is employed in a more analytical manner to gain insight into the very nature of the phenomenon, that is, seeing reality in the light of its three signs of existence, namely: impermanence, unsatisfactoriness, and not-self. In sum, insight meditation is practiced to gain direct insight into the very nature of ultimate reality.

What is the benefit of gaining this insight into the real nature of things? What does a person gain through this hard-won understanding? In two words: spiritual freedom, that is, freedom from dependence and clinging. In the words of the recurring refrain of *Satipatthana Sutta*, the Buddha states it like this: "He lives independent, clinging to nothing in the world" (Analayo, 2006, p. 3).

Two broad divisions of mindfulness: Eastern and Western

Mindfulness, as it is currently used, seems to draw its meaning from two fields: Buddhist philosophy and cognitive psychology. First, when it is used within the Buddhist context or at least when its Buddhist roots are explicitly or implicitly acknowledged. Second, when mindfulness is used in its traditional English language meaning or as Western scientific research paradigm, without any reference to Buddhist meditative practices. Most modern-day healthcare-related adaptations of mindfulness belong to the first category. Ellen Langer (1989, 2000a, 2000b, 2005, 2009), a Harvard psychologist, uses the term mindfulness exclusively in the cognitive sense. Langer uses the term mindfulness in its traditional English meaning, as the opposite of mindlessness. Weick and Putnam (2006) categorize these divisions as the "Eastern" and "Western" usage of the term mindfulness respectively.

Approaching mindfulness as a metacognitive skill, Bishop et al. (2004, p. 232) have proposed a two-component operational model of mindfulness that involves: (1) "self-regulation of attention so that it is maintained on immediate experience, thereby allowing for increased recognition of mental events in the present moment;" and (2) "adopting a particular orientation toward one's experiences in the present moment, an orientation that is characterized by curiosity, openness, and acceptance." Bishop et al. (2004, p. 234) further see mindfulness as:

> a process of gaining insight into the nature of one's mind and the adoption of a de-centered perspective on thoughts and feelings so that they can be experienced in terms of their subjectivity (versus their necessary validity) and transient nature (versus their permanence).

Vipassana meditation: author's experience

This author had the blessed opportunity to participate twice in a ten-day *Vipassana* meditation course at North Fork, California, and at the Northern California Vipassana Center. It was a life-transforming experience in the most complete sense of the word, as if the Buddha's teachings became vividly alive after 2,600 years! I am deeply grateful to Shri S. N. Goenkaji for this gift of *Dhamma*—the *Dhamma*, which is beautiful in the beginning, beautiful in the middle, and beautiful in the end.

The text given in italics represents the actual (or near actual) instructions that were given during the two ten-day *Vipassana* courses that the author attended.

The daily schedule of *Vipassana* meditation course (Goenka, 2008, p. 4) was as follows:

4:00 a.m.	Morning wake-up bell
4:30–6:30 a.m.	Meditation in the hall or in your room
6:30–8:00 a.m.	Breakfast break
8:00–9:00 a.m.	Group meditation in the hall
9:00–11:00 a.m.	Meditation in hall or in your room
11:00–12 noon	Lunch break
12:00–1:00 p.m.	Rest, and interviews with the teacher
1:00–2:30 p.m.	Meditation in hall or in your room
2:30–3:30 p.m.	Group meditation in the hall
3:30–5:00 p.m.	Meditation in the hall or your room
5:00–6:00 p.m.	Tea break
6:00–7:00 p.m.	Group meditation in the hall
7:00–8:15 p.m.	Discourse
8:15–9:00 p.m.	Group meditation in the hall
9:00–9:30 p.m.	Question time in the hall
9:30 p.m.	Retire to your room; lights out

The following pages present a synopsis of the recollection of this wonderful experience. I have made a sincere attempt to convey the essence of meditation instructions imparted during the course as clearly and as faithfully as possible (see italicized portions below). The description that follows is offered only with a view to share what the reader could expect during such a course. Ideally, interested spiritual aspirants would attend the course themselves, as there is really no substitute for learning the *Vipassana* meditative practice firsthand.

Day one

Develop awareness of the process of respiration: Focusing only on the spot where the breath enters and leaves the nostrils (that is, the nostrils and upper lip area), *concentrate on the triangular area starting from the base of the nostrils and covering air passages of the nostrils. Observe incoming and outgoing breath, naturally and purely.*

Why use breath as an object? Breath is neutral and non-sectarian: Everybody breathes and breathes all the time, whether awake, sleeping, sitting, walking, standing, and so on. Most importantly, breathing takes place only in the present, in the now. So to bring our mind back to the present, focusing on breathing is the most natural and effective way.

Watch the breath entering the nostrils; feel the "touch" and be aware of it within the triangular area. Breathe normally and naturally. The Buddha's instructions are: The meditator should breathe naturally, without attempting to change the length or depth of the breath. If the breath is short, the meditator should simply observe that the breath is short. If the breath is long, the meditator should simply observe that the breath is long. (Note that it is not about controlling or regulating the breath, as in the case of *Pranayama. Pranayama* is a *yogic* practice in which breath is regulated to control the mind.) Just be aware of the bare breath in its most natural, pure state. Observe, notice, and be aware of it is passing through the left nostril or the right nostril or at times passing through both nostrils. That's all. Feel distinctively at what point the breath touches the area above the upper lip or the outer rings of the nostrils or inside the air passages (inner walls) of the nostrils.

Day two

Continue with the awareness of breath entering the triangular area. Additionally, try to feel the touch—the point where the incoming or outgoing breath touches anywhere within the triangular area. Try harder to feel it: *The touch is always there, we are just not aware of it yet.* (If you still cannot feel the touch, try breathing a little harder than normal; you are bound to feel it.)

Day three

Continue with the awareness of the touch of the breath. Additionally, be aware of any sensations that you may experience within this triangular area. Some examples of sensations are tingling, pulsating, vibrating, heat, cold, perspiration, heaviness, lightness, contraction, expansion, prickling, numbness, pain, pressure, itching, hardness, softness, and so on. Do not try to look for any specific sensations. Just be naturally aware of any sensations if and when they crop up in this area.

Day four

Reduce the triangular area of your focus to the moustache line (the area below the nostrils and above the upper lip). First, try to feel, to be aware of the touch of air, and then feel and be aware of any sensations in this small area. The smaller area will sharpen your focus: the smaller the area, the sharper the focus. The idea is to improve the concentration and to make it the sharpest. *You need the sharpest concentration to dissect and scan the subtle, deeper layers of your mind. This and the prior exercises will prepare the mind for* Samadhi*—the state of meditative absorption.*

Days five through ten: Vipassana meditation

Day Five

Vipassana *means seeing things as they really are. It is a process of self-purification by self-observation. One begins by observing the natural breath to concentrate the mind. With sharpened awareness one proceeds to observing the changing nature of body and mind, and experiences the universal truths of impermanence, suffering, and egolessness. This truth realization by direct experience is the process of self-purification.* (See Goenka, 2008, p. 1.)

***Vipassana* technique:** With sharpened focus and concentration, *Vipassana* technique is pursued after practicing *anapana* (mindfulness of breathing) meditation. *Vipassana* means insight into reality. It is a technique whereby one scans the entire body—from head to toe and from toe to head—with razor-sharp awareness, looking for any and every sensation experienced anywhere on the body.

Start with scanning (moving your attention through) the scalp; move down to the face, part by part, piece by piece. Then move your attention through the right shoulder, upper arm, elbow, forearm, wrist, palm, fingers, and finger tips. Likewise, move your attention through the left shoulder down to the finger tips. Then scan the throat area, upper chest, and abdomen area; then the neck, upper back to lower back; then the right thigh, knee, leg, foot, and toes; then, likewise the left thigh, knee, leg, foot, and toes.

Every part of our body has changing sensations at all times; we are just not aware of them yet. If you cannot feel any sensations in any part of the body, spend a minute or two on that part by concentrating on your natural sensations. Observe and just be aware of your sensations. Do not choose for the pleasant sensations and do not try to avoid the unpleasant sensations. This is the habitual pattern of mind that we are trying to change at the deepest level.

While moving through the entire body like this, be aware of *anicca*—the law of impermanence. Every sensation is arising and passing away, changing, and changing again. Nothing is constant even for a few seconds. Observe with a balanced and equanimous mind, an objective mind—a mind that is balanced and observes reality as it is. Become aware at the deepest level of this universal law of change working with your body and mind. This is what the Enlightened One found out. And *when you would have experienced and know it through the experience of your own body and mind, you would have experienced the truth of the first turning of the wheel of* Dharma. *This is what Buddha called* bhavana-maya pannya—*wisdom borne of experience of insight meditation or wisdom based on direct personal experience.*

According to S.N. Goenka, "*Vipassana* is about two things: awareness and equanimity. It is about changing from *Vedana-paccaya tanha* to *Vedana-paccaya pannya*—from sensations leading to craving to sensations leading to wisdom." Our habit pattern at the very deepest level is the automatic generation of *sankharas* by reacting through craving and clinging if the sensations are pleasant, and through aversion and anger if the sensations are unpleasant. *Sankharas* (Sanskrit: *Sanskaras*) are accumulated mental tendencies formed over many lifetimes due to repeated patterns of reactive behavior. An awakened, equanimous mind understands that every formation is impermanent *(sabbe sankharas anicca)*. In other words, it understands the universal law of impermanence. Hence, it does not react as usual to sensations by developing craving or aversion. By helping us become constantly aware and equanimous about our sensations, moment to moment, *Vipassana* cuts at the very root, that is, at the sensation (*vedana*) level.

The evening discourse on the fifth day by Goenkaji was wonderful. I felt that this man's every word is worth its weight in gold! While explaining 12 links of dependent co-arising, Goenkaji commented that from this point—the point of *vedana* sensations—onward, there are basically two paths, one path leading to *Samsara* (*Bhava Sansaar*) and the other leading to *Nirvana*, the path of liberation borne of wisdom generated by insight meditation.

If we keep on reacting to sensations with craving and aversion, we will keep on adding to our cyclic misery. However, through *Vipassana* we develop a faculty of constant awareness and understanding of the universal law of impermanence—that sensations are not eternal but arise and pass away. This awareness and understanding allows us to respond to sensations with equanimity. By not reacting to craving and aversion, we cut at the very root of the problem. This is what Buddha was referring to:

> The house builder (that is, craving) has been recognized... At the sensations level, no more new *Sankharas* are created by reacting with craving and aversion to pleasant and unpleasant sensations respectively, and the old *Sankharas* have been purified, so no more rebirth—the *Nirvanic* peace of being liberated from craving and clinging has been achieved.

There are three basic attachments to be aware of: the attachment to "I," the attachment to "mine," and the attachment to "my" beliefs or "my" views. *The greater the attachment, the greater the misery at the time of separation.*

Days six and seven: continuing with Vipassana meditation

The sixth day continued with moving our awareness throughout our body from the top of the head to the tip of the toes and from the tip of the toes to the top of the head, with a calm, equanimous mind noticing any and every sensation on any part of the body; always remembering the nature of every sensation—it arises, it passes away; not reacting to pleasant sensations with craving and to unpleasant sensations with aversion, and thus not generating any new *sankharas*. When we do this, no new *sankharas* are made. *It is the law of nature that the old* sankharas *that lie very deep in our mind get eradicated through this mind-purifying process.* Through the practice of *Vipassana*, sensations do not generate craving or aversion but generate the *pannya*, that is, the wisdom borne of insight into the nature of reality—reality that is changing all the time and whose very nature is impermanence. *The whole idea of* Vipassana *is to change the habit pattern of mind that automatically reacts with craving to pleasant sensations and with aversion to unpleasant sensations.* By experiencing the truth of impermanence within one's body through *Vipassana*, one sees through the madness and is able to stop this automatic response mechanism at the deepest level of the mind.

> Learn to work with a calm and quiet mind, alert and attentive mind, equanimous and balanced mind. Learn to work objectively with your sensations without identifying with the pleasant ones with craving and unpleasant ones with aversion. Remember the nature of all sensations—whether solidified, gross, or subtle—they arise and pass away. So, observe them objectively without the feeling of I, my, and mine.
>
> *Remember* anicca*—impermanence—the changing nature of phenomenon and work diligently to experience this truth within your body-mind complex. If you do not identify with pleasant sensations with craving and unpleasant sensation with aversion, you do not generate any new* sankharas. *And working objectively without a sense of I, my, and mine, the old ones get eradicated automatically. This is a law.*

Move your attention from head to toe and from toe to head:

- Top of the head to abdomen area, back of the head to the lower back
- Both shoulders down to the fingertips of both hands
- Hips/thighs to the toes of both feet and back up.

Instructions: For areas that are blank—that is, areas where no sensation is felt—move your attention slowly, part by part, piece by piece. If you experience vibration-like subtle sensations through entire portions of the body, you will be able to sweep *en masse* through areas that are experiencing subtle sensations. After two or three such sweeps, go back to blind areas or blank areas where sensations were hazy. If you continue like this, you will soon experience subtle sensations throughout the body. But do not crave for subtle sensations. Work patiently but persistently. You are bound to succeed. You are bound to succeed. Remember:

> *In this essenceless, substanceless, ephemeral mind-matter phenomenon, there is nothing that is permanent; there is nothing that is not changing. This sensation or that sensation does not make any difference. All sensations have the same characteristic—of arising and passing away—of* anicca. *So, what's the use of reacting with craving to something that is temporarily pleasant and with aversion to something that is temporarily unpleasant? With this understanding, always maintain equanimity. This way you will not generate new* sankharas. *No* sankharas *means no misery! This is liberation! And this is the purpose of insight meditation.*
>
> *The equanimity is the wisdom (*pannya*) of not reacting through craving and aversion to pleasant and unpleasant sensations but remaining equanimous. It is the insight that is developed through* Vipassana *by being aware of one's breath and sensations all the time. By remaining equanimous, one does not generate new* sankharas. *And when one does not generate new* sankharas, *then the old* sankharas *start coming to the surface. Through observation and remaining aware, one eradicates them slowly and slowly until they are fully wiped out. This is the* Nirvana *Buddha talked about—*Nirvana *of total extinction!*
>
> *Always be aware of your breath or your sensations: either breath or sensations. In whatever you are doing—sitting, standing, walking, working or sleeping—always be aware of your breath or sensations. This is Buddha's unique contribution to help sentient beings to come out of* dukkha, *to come out of deep misery. Everything else he taught was already present in the then-prevalent teachings of India. By developing awareness of our breath and sensations, we start living in the present because breath and sensations can only happen in the present. This is the* Dhamma *he taught for 45 years, the* Dhamma *that is good in the beginning, good in the middle, and good in the end.*
>
> *(aadi kalyankaari, madhaya kalyaankari,* and *anntah kalyaankaari)*

Day eight: the wonderful teaching of Dhamma continues

Recorded instructions by Shri S.N. Goenka and *Vipassana* teachers:

> *Your progress on the path of* Vipassana *is measured by only one yardstick: the degree of equanimity you have developed, the mental equilibrium, the equipoise. Always remember that every experience—however pleasant or unpleasant at the moment—is impermanent. So by not reacting blindly to sensations, one does not generate new* sankharas. *Fewer* sankharas, *less misery. No* sankharas, *no misery.*

An Important Note: The whole purpose of moving attention throughout the body and observing different sensations is to develop one's awareness and to train one's mind to always remain equanimous toward our experience by remembering the law of impermanence. With the mind deeply established in equanimity, whenever deep-seated old *sankharas* come to the surface during meditations, they are eradicated: thus, pleasant *sankharas* do not result in craving, and unpleasant *sankharas* do not result in aversion.

The alchemy of purification of mind through Vipassana meditation

This is the alchemy of purifying the mind: No new sankharas *are generated, and accumulated old* sankharas *get eradicated through* Vipassana. Although it is clear that when we respond with equanimity to our pleasant as well as unpleasant sensations, we do not develop any craving or aversion toward them. Hence, no new *sankharas*; no new misery!

But how does *Vipassana* help to eradicate old *sankharas*? This requires some further explanation. When we are equanimously observing our sensations in *Vipassana* meditation—especially when we get to the point where we can sweep our attention with a free flow up and down throughout our body—we come across areas where we may have coarse or solidified sensations. Generally speaking, one is able to do a quick sweep when one is experiencing subtle sensations. And for the areas that are blank/blind where one is feeling coarse sensations, one has to go back and work on them, part by part, piece by piece. Now it is the old, habitual pattern of mind to react with aversion to gross or coarse (unpleasant) sensations and to react with craving to subtle (pleasant) sensations.

If we keep an equanimous mind, we counter the mind's habitual pattern and thereby disempower its habit of reacting blindly. Our old *sankharas* sit as latent psychological tendencies at the deepest level of our mind. During *Vipassana* meditation, the latent mental tendencies borne out of accumulated past *sankharas* come to the surface. *By observing them with equanimous mind and not reacting to them, we do not give them the opportunity to reestablish themselves.* Hence, they are eradicated at the root level.

It is not uncommon during *Vipassana* meditation for some past experiences buried deep into our subconscious mind to resurface. If the experience had been pleasant and resurfaces again as a pleasant sensation, generating a craving for reliving it, then the grooves of *sankharas* deepen. *Vipassana* meditation teaches us to remain equanimous in the wake of such sensations in order to eradicate these old, deep-seated *sankharas.* Success on the path of *Vipassana* meditation does not depend upon experiencing this sensation or that sensation. *Vipassana* teaches us that all sensations—pleasant or unpleasant—are of the nature of arising and passing away; hence, they are impermanent. What is important is to keep an equanimous mind, a balanced mind.

During his *Dhamma* discourse on the eighth day, Shri Goenkaji summed up the *Vipassana* technique with a bird analogy: Just as a bird has two wings, likewise the two wings of the bird of *Vipassana* are awareness and equanimity. To explain how deep-seated, old *sankharas* come to the surface when you stop making new *sankharas,* Goenkaji gave the example of burning a pile of firewood. *On a pile of burning firewood, if we add new pieces of wood on the top, the new ones will start burning first. But if we stop adding the new pieces of wood to the fire, then the old ones have to burn themselves up.*

Another example Goenkaji gave was of fasting: if you fast one day and then fast the second day and still another day—that is, when you stop putting new food in the body —the body starts using what it has stored in the past. Goenkaji also made a categorical statement: *Sensations are always in contact with the deepest level of the mind. By not reacting with craving or aversion, we purify our mind at the deepest level.*

Day nine: the most detailed instructions on the path of Vipassana meditation

The morning meditation instructions on the ninth day were most detailed and profound. The instructions mentioned three types of experiences pertaining to sensations. On the path of *Vipassana* meditation, the meditator experiences:

1. coarse, gross, solidified sensations denoted by hazy or blind areas;
2. some areas with gross sensations and some with subtle sensations;
3. subtle sensations.

- If you are feeling subtle sensations, then sweep your attention *en masse* two to three times with a free-flow sweep from head to toe and from toe to head.
- Go back and survey, part by part, the areas that were left out during the free-flow sweep. Make sure that you do not leave out any areas, even a tiny part of the body, without scanning for sensations.
- If you feel solidified, gross, blank, hazy, or misty areas, do not feel discouraged. Use them as tools to uncover your hidden *sankharas* of craving and aversion accumulated over countless lifetimes. With practice observing these areas patiently and objectively, you will find them becoming full of subtle sensations.

Bhanga Nyana: *Collapse of the entire physical structure as we know it!*

From time to time, now or in future, you may experience a flow of very subtle sensations throughout your body. You will feel that the entire structure of physical body is nothing but a field of subtle vibrations—wavelets of ripples of energy vibrating, like electric current, at the speed of light. There is nothing solid, so to speak, in the entire physical structure of your body, only a whirling dance of the subatomic particles (tiny *kalapas*). At that time, you may experience that the entire physical structure collapses into a field of vibrations; there is nothing solid in this constantly changing field of vibrations, nothing substantial or permanent. This is *bhanga nyana*—the wisdom (*nyana*) of dissolution (*bhanga*). This is when you experience two important aspects of reality according to Buddhism: *anicca* and *anatta*—impermanence and no-self.

Basically, *Vipassana* mediation has four progressive steps. The first three steps basically involve scanning the external part of the body, the skin area, moving the attention during these three steps vertically, up and down. The fourth step is an internal scan.

1. Slow scan: Moving attention slowly from the top of the head to the tip of the toes and back, part by part, piece by piece.
2. Free-flow sweep: Sweeping attention freely *en masse* upward and downward where subtle sensations are experienced, then going back to observe those areas that have solidified coarse sensations or the areas that were initially left blank.
3. Spot check: Being able to quickly take your attention to any fingertip-sized spot and move back and forth. Try only four or five spot checks and then go back to normal scan and sweep.

4. Penetrate and pierce: Scanning internally, moving attention inside the body areas, left to right, right to left, front to back, back to front. This is a highly advanced technique, reserved for advance-level practitioners who work under the close guidance of an experienced teacher during 20- to 90-day meditation retreats.

In the practice of all of these techniques, the meditator is reminded of the universal law of impermanence, to always maintain perfect equanimity, and not to generate new *sankharas* by reacting with craving or aversion to pleasant or unpleasant sensations. It is the old habit of our unconscious mind to react with craving to pleasant sensations or with aversion to unpleasant sensations; after all, *sankhara* is reacting mind! If we react to unpleasant sensations as we sweep or scan, we not only create new *sankharas* but also multiply the effects of the old *sankharas* of aversion, which means multiplying our misery!

However, when we remain equanimous, understanding the wisdom of impermanence, not only do we not create any new *sankharas* of aversion, we also dissolve or help eradicate the accumulated old *sankharas*. The same applies to responding with equanimity to pleasant sensations. Remember, sensations are in contact with the deepest level of our mind, always. This is the insight into wisdom that the Buddha taught: the wisdom of *upekha*, the wisdom of equanimity. And this is the culmination of the path of insight meditation.

Day 10: Metta (loving-kindness) meditation

Metta is a Pali word that means loving-kindness. The last day of the *Vipassana* meditation course is devoted to practicing *metta* meditation, which involves filling the mind and body with thoughts and feelings of goodwill for all beings. The practice begins with cultivating a deep sense of loving-kindness toward oneself and then extending it toward one's loved ones, friends, teachers, strangers, enemies, and finally toward all beings. *Metta* meditation serves as a great antidote to the feeling of anger and contention. The whole atmosphere is filled with sharing the feeling of joy and goodwill with the whole of creation—a befitting grand finale to nine days of intense meditation!

Application of mindfulness in life, leadership, and change management: a brief guide to teaching/learning resources

This author knows no better resource regarding the power of mindfulness meditation in life and leadership than a documentary film titled *Doing Time Doing Vipassana*, by Eilona Ariel and Ayelet Menahemi, available free to view on YouTube: www.youtube.com/watch?v=WkxSyv5R1sg

This life-changing and deeply moving film begins with a powerful message: "We are all prisoners, undergoing a life sentence, imprisoned by our own minds, we are all seeking parole, being hostages of our anger, fear, desire, etc." As the video description succinctly put it:

> It is the story of a strong woman named Kiran Bedi, the former Inspector General of Prisons in New Delhi, who strove to transform the notorious Tihar Prison and turn it into an oasis of peace. But most of all it is the story of prison inmates who underwent profound change, and who realized that incarceration is not the end but possibly a fresh start toward an improved and more positive life.

Doing Time, Doing Vipassana: Winner of the Golden Spire Award at the 1998 San Francisco International Film Festival, this extraordinary documentary takes viewers into India's largest prison—known as one of the toughest in the world—and shows the dramatic change brought about by the introduction of *Vipassana* meditation. In 1993, Kiran Bedi, a reformist Inspector General of India's prisons, learned of the success of using *Vipassana* in a jail in Jaipur, Rajasthan. This ten-day course involved officials and inmates alike. In India's largest prison, Tihar Jail, near New Delhi, another attempt was made. This program was said to have dramatically changed the behavior of inmates and jailers alike. It was actually found that inmates who completed the ten-day course were less violent and had a lower recidivism rate than other inmates. This project was documented in the television documentary, *Doing Time, Doing Vipassana*. So successful was this program that it was adopted by correctional facilities in the United States and other countries as well. (See: http://psychology.wikia.com/wiki/Vipassana#Vipassan.C4.81_in_prisons)

The leadership portrayed by the charismatic Ms. Kiran Bedi[1] is nothing short of miraculous. She was given the assignment to police one of the largest and toughest jails in Asia, Tihar Jail (10,000 criminals, 9,600 men and 400 women). She exhibits great leadership qualities of managing change in the most extreme circumstances. By dint of her perseverance and panache, she was able to change the culture of one of the toughest jails in all of Asia. Above all, she was able to bring personal transformation to the lives of inmates, which shows that if the leader is mindful and compassionate, the transformation is inevitable. In teaching various leadership and change management courses over last two decades, this author has found nothing so gripping and transformational as this video. Semester after semester, students find renewed strength and a message of hope and courage by watching and critiquing this video.

Ms. Bedi narrates her experiences of how she transformed India's toughest jail in this widely watched TED Talk: "Kiran Bedi: How I remade one of India's toughest prisons" (www.youtube.com/watch?v=g_CSsL3it9Y). In this video, Ms. Kiran Bedi says that through education, she helped to convert "a prison into an ashram." Imagine 1,000 hard-core prisoners sitting quietly in deep *Vipassana* meditation in the jail. When asked why she brought mindfulness to the prison, Ms. Bedi replied, "Crime is the product of distorted mind. So, I wanted to address that through meditation. Not through telling, not through preaching or force, but through meditation." What an enlightened view of change and what a great testimony to the transformative power of mindfulness.

Since the successful implementation of mindfulness in Indian jails, *Vipassana* meditation has been tried in jails around the world, including in the US. Another documentary of note is *The Dhamma Brothers Vipassana Meditation* (www.youtube.com/watch?v=phHib5VaCeE). When the prison administration tried to introduce the mindfulness program, there were widespread misgivings about the intention behind it. As one inmate put it: "I am all for meditation as long as it is not about Buddhism against Christianity." Another dissenting voice said, "I do not understand all this push for meditation." The officer on duty responded in an insightful manner: "What's not to understand about focusing your mind and about compassion, love, and caring?" Although in 2002, due to commissioners' orders, the *Vipassana* program was shut down officially as some prisoners felt uncomfortable about the Buddhist origins of the mindfulness practice, some prisoners still contribute their sitting practice for the obvious psychological benefits. The *Dhamma Brothers* chronicles what happens when two Buddhist teachers enter Alabama's tough William E. Donaldson Correctional Facility to teach prisoners an ancient meditation technique called *Vipassana*. In one of the short video clips, Dhamma Brother John Johnson describes how *Vipassana* helped him overcome tobacco and question his other addictions. *Vipassana* helps deal with the root of addiction (see: www.youtube.com/watch?v=9JVrzc_dxK4).

The Prison Mindfulness Institute provides a searchable directory of the network of organizations, associates, and groups providing meditation, mindfulness, or contemplative programs in prisons around the world. The institute offers several programs, including the Path of Freedom (PoF) program. It is a mindfulness-based, emotional intelligence (MBEI), and integral approach to self-transformation, personal development, and leadership capacity for at-risk and incarcerated youth and adult prisoners. The program has received very positive reviews from experts in the corrections field (see: www.prisonmindfulness.org/projects/network-directory/).

Another related resource is Max Strom's "Breathe to Heal" TEDxCapeMay talk (www.youtube.com/watch?v=4Lb5L-VEm34&t=410s). In this important short video, Max Storm tells us that the:

> Defense Department is advocating Breathing and Yoga for veterans! Navy SEALs use breath-work to help them focus and calm before they go into battle. And Navy SEALs are not New Age cuddly people. Navy SEALs only use technologies that work; they will not use anything else ... Benefits of intentional breath-work are: focus, calmness, non-reactiveness which we can all use.

Linking the intentional breath-work to mindfulness, Max Strom observes:

> I think 25% of corporations have mindfulness programs ... Meditation is an advanced technique ... We teach people first to breathe. If you teach people to breathe [intentionally] first, it calms their nervous system, this triggers fight-or-flight to switch off, and rest-and-digest to switch on, then people can sit and meditate without a problem.

It is important to note that the traditional practice of mindfulness of breathing accomplishes exactly the same goal as Max Strom is describing above.

Perhaps the best single-volume introduction in English to the Buddha's life and teachings based on authentic sources is *The Life of the Buddha: According to the Pali Canon* by the British Theravada monk, Bhikkhu Nanamoli. Before becoming a monk, he worked in British intelligence. Reading a biography of the Buddha while posted in Italy, he had a religious conversion and went to Sri Lanka in 1949 to become a Buddhist monk and spent almost his entire monk life of 11 years at the Island Hermitage. He trained under Nyanatiloka Mahathera, the great German monk. Nanamoli's translations (*The Path of Purification (Visuddhimagga)* by Bhadantācariya Buddhaghosa) and books are marked by a certain precocious fidelity and sincerity rarely encountered these days. His book, *Mindfulness of Breathing (Ānāpānasati): Buddhist Texts from the Pali Canon and Extracts from the Pali Commentaries* (2000), is a classic text for both scholars and practitioners on this topic.

Perhaps the single best book on the Buddha's Eightfold Path is Bhikkhu Bodhi's *The Noble Eightfold Path: Way to the End of Suffering*. A major part of the concluding portion of the book is devoted to the practice of mindfulness. Bhikkhu Bodhi is an American Buddhist monk in the tradition of Nyanatiloka, Nyanaponika, and Nanamoli. He studied with Nyanaponika and edited some of the writings of Nanamoli. He is perhaps the most prolific translator of the Buddhist Pali Canon in the world today. This author has had the good fortune of interviewing Bhikkhu Bodhi for his doctoral work on mindfulness. Walpola

Rahula's *What the Buddha Taught*, originally published in the 1950s, remains the best overall book on Buddhist theory and practice and gets better with age.

Two more books of note on the topic of mindfulness are: Analayo, *Satipatthana: Direct Path to Realization*, and Thera Nyanaponika, *The Heart of Buddhist Meditation: A Handbook of Mental Training Based on Buddha's Way of Mindfulness*. Both books provide an authentic guide to the practice of mindfulness. Vietnamese monk Thich Nhat Hahn's *The Miracle of Mindfulness* remains an all-time classic for its practical advice and resourcefulness. Perhaps the best book on the theory and practice of *Vipassana* is William Hart's 2009 book *The Art of Living: Vipassana Meditation as Taught by S.N. Goenka*. S.N. Goenka's *Discourse Summaries* contains 11 discourses that provide an overview of the teachings of Buddha to help meditators achieve the proper results.

Concluding remarks

Underscoring the universal importance of mindfulness, the Buddha observed, "Mindfulness, I declare, is helpful everywhere" (Khantipalo, 2006, p. 8). Carrying out our daily activities mindfully has a direct bearing on our daily lives. Thich Nhat Hanh (cited in Murphy, 2013, p. 164) once told a student: "There are two ways to wash the dishes. The first is to wash the dishes in order to have clean dishes. The second is to wash the dishes in order to wash the dishes." Living mindfully from moment to moment is what Thich Nhat Hanh (1987, pp. 20–21) called the "miracle of mindfulness": "Mindfulness is the miracle by which we master and restore ourselves . . . it is the miracle which can call back in a flash our dispersed mind and restore it to wholeness so that we can live each minute of life." But the real challenge is to remember to remember oneself. As Bhikkhu Thanissaro (2009) pointed out to this author, "It is easy to be mindful. What is difficult is to remember to be mindful."

Dr. Ellen Langer of Harvard University once told this author in an interview: "It is only when we've awakened that we realize how much of our lives we've actually slept through." *Vipassana* is about *really* waking up, *after* we wake up in the morning! When we carry out all activities in our usual daily life with mindfulness, with conscious presence, then every task becomes special, every act becomes a rite and a ceremony. And our whole life becomes a wondrous celebration! "If we practice the art of mindful living," says Thich Nhat Hanh (1998, p. 124), "when things change, we won't have any regrets. We can smile because we have done our best to enjoy every moment of our life and to make others happy." And in making others happy, moment to moment, we discover the true secret to our happiness!

Just as in the middle and deep down, the ocean remains calm and unperturbed by the raging waves at the surface, even so is the mind of one who has cultivated mindfulness. It remains unruffled amidst the turmoil of raging emotions and sensations. They are seen as they truly are: impermanent, chimerical, and passing—subject to arising and subsiding. How does one know this? Because one has seen it so during insight meditation. It has provided the practitioner with the true insight into the reality. Now they can go about their business in life and leadership calmly and placidly, armed with compassion and wisdom.

Chapter takeaways

1. Right mindfulness, right concentration, and right effort constitute the entire terrain of Buddhist mental landscape. The mind is trained, disciplined, and developed through these three practices, which aim at cleansing the mind of impurities and disturbances such as lustful desires, hatred, ill-will, indolence, worries and restlessness, skeptical doubts.

2. The goal of mindfulness meditation is to cultivate such positive qualities as concentration, awareness, intelligence, will, energy, the analytical faculty, confidence, joy, and tranquility, leading finally to the attainment of the highest wisdom which sees things as they are. These qualities have a direct bearing on how we live our lives and how we conduct ourselves toward others in any relationship, including the leader–follower relationship.
3. In its original Buddhist form, the practice of mindfulness refers to the technique of developing awareness of the body and the mind in the present moment. In modern terms, mindfulness refers to the practice of intentionally bringing one's attention to experiences occurring in the present moment in a non-judgmental way.
4. Buddhism believes the mind as such to be intrinsically pure, but sometimes it is sullied or defiled by extrinsic impurities, such as greed, hatred, and delusion. The purpose of meditative practice is to expunge these adventitious impurities and to help restore the pristine purity of our natural mind so that it can see things as they truly are. The practice of meditation, therefore, starts with stilling or calming the mind to enable it to attain a measure of serenity, and then turns it toward insight into reality.
5. The meditation practice most respected by Buddhists is called "mindfulness of breathing" (*Anapanasati*). The practice of mindfulness of breathing is considered to be the supreme meditation in Buddhism to awaken the mind to its full potential. It is believed that it was through this practice that the Buddha attained his final psychological breakthrough that led to his enlightenment.

Reflection questions

1. Briefly explain the basics of mindfulness practice. Why it is necessary to calm the mind?
2. Describe some of the applications of mindfulness in life and leadership.
3. How does mindfulness meditative practice differ from other meditation and contemplative practices? Where does its uniqueness lie?
4. The meditative practice of mindfulness of breathing has been described as the summit of mindfulness practices. Why do almost all meditative traditions work with breath to quieten the mind?
5. What are the differences between the Buddhist version of mindfulness and its secular form?

Note

1 Ms. Kiran Bedi, the first woman to join the Indian Police Service (IPS), was truly a daring police officer. It is well known that when she was a police inspector, she got issued a ticket to and towed away the car of the then prime minister of India! This is very rare and unprecedented—the first time (and perhaps also the last time) in Indian history to issue a parking violation ticket to the most powerful person in the Indian democracy! See: http://timesofindia.indiatimes.com/articleshow/69003837.cms?utm_source=contentofinterest&utm_medium=text&utm_campaign=cppst

References

Analayo, V. (2006). *Satipatthana: Direct Path to Realization*. Birmingham: Windhorse.

Bishop, S., Lau, M., Shapiro, S., Carlson, L., Anderson, N. D., Carmody, J. et al. (2004). Mindfulness: A Proposed Operational Definition. *Clinical Psychology: Science and Practice*, *11*, 230–241.

Bodhi, B. (2006). *The Noble Eightfold Path: Way to the End of Suffering, BPS Pariyatti Editions*, 3rd edition. WA: Onalaska, USA.

Goenka, S. N. (2008). *Vipassana Meditation: As Taught by S.N. Goenka in the Tradition of Sayagyi U Ba Khin*. North Fork, CA: California Vipassana Center. (A Pamphlet. Hampton Roads Publishing).
Hanh, T. N. (1987). *The Miracle of Mindfulness: A Manual on Meditation*. Boston, MA: Beacon Press.
Hanh, T. N. (1988). *The Heart of Understanding: Commentaries on the Prajnaparamita Heart Sutra*. Berkeley, CA: Parallax Press.
Hanh, T. N. (1998). *The Heart of the Buddha's Teaching: Transforming Suffering into Peace, Joy, and Liberation*. Berkeley, CA: Parallax Press.
Hart, W. (2009). *The Art of Living: Vipassana Meditation*. New York: Harper One.
Harvey, P. (2008). *An Introduction to Buddhism*. Cambridge: Cambridge University Press.
Jayankar, P. (1996). *Krishnamurti: A Biography*. New York: Penguin.
Khantipalo, B. (2006). *Practical Advice for Meditators*. Kandy, Sri Lanka: Buddhist Publication Society.
Langer, E. (1989). *Mindfulness*. New York: Addison-Wesley.
Langer, E. (2000a). Mindrulness Research and the Future. *Journal of Soical Issues*, *56*(1), 129–139.
Langer, E. (2000b). The Construct of Mindfulness. *Journal of Social Issues*, *56*(1), 1–9.
Langer, E. (2005). *On Becoming an Artist: Reinventing Yourself Through Mindful Creativity*. New York: Ballantine Books.
Langer, E. (2009, April 5). Personal Interview with the Author. Unpublished Transcripts.
Murphy, S. (2013). *One Bird, One Stone: 108 Contemporary Zen Stories*. Charlottesville, VA: Hampton Roads Publishing Company, Inc.
Nanamoli, B. (1992). *The Life of the Buddha: According to the Pali Canon*. Onalaska, WA: BPS Pariyatti Editions.
Nanamoli, B. (2000). *Mindfulness of Breathing: Buddhist Texts from the Pali Canon and Commentaries*, 6th edition. Sri Lanka: Buddhist Publication Society.
Nyanaponika, T. (1962). *The Heart of Buddhist Meditation: A Handbook of Mental Training Based on Buddha's Way of Mindfulness*. London: Ryder.
Rahula, W. (1974). *What the Buddha Taught: Revised and Expanded Edition with Texts from Suttas and Dhammapada*, Revised edition. New York: Grove Press.
Tandon, S. N. (2007). *A Reappraisal of Patanjali's Yoga-Sutras In the Light of the Buddha's Teaching*. Igatpuri: Vipassana Research Institute.
Thanissaro, B. (July 15, 2009). Personal Interview with the Author. Unpublished Transcripts.
Weick, K. E., & Putnam, T. (2006). Organizing for Mindfulness: Eastern Wisdom and Western Knowledge. *Journal of Management Inquiry*, *15*(3), 275–288.

INDEX

Printed in the United States
By Bookmasters